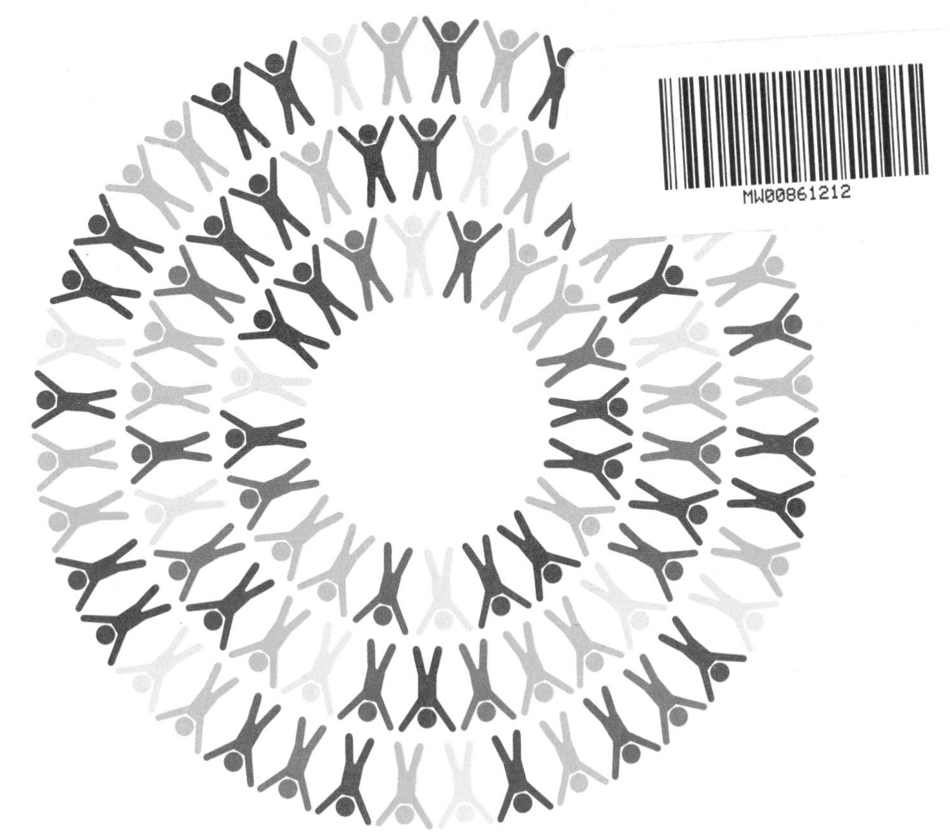

fundamentals of Human Resource MANAGEMENT

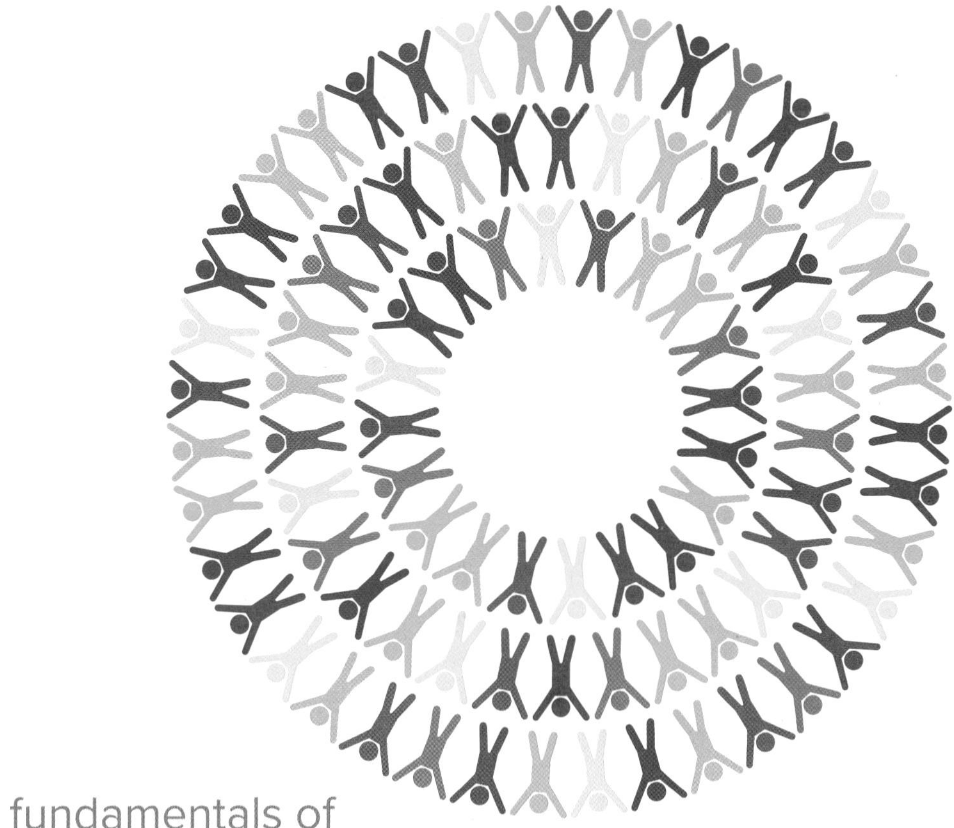

fundamentals of Human Resource Management

NINTH EDITION

Raymond A. Noe
The Ohio State University

John R. Hollenbeck
Michigan State University

Barry Gerhart
University of Wisconsin–Madison

Patrick M. Wright
University of South Carolina

FUNDAMENTALS OF HUMAN RESOURCE MANAGEMENT

Published by McGraw Hill LLC, 1325 Avenue of the Americas, New York, NY 10121.

Some ancillaries, including electronic and print components, may not be available to customers outside the United States.

This book is printed on acid-free paper.

1 2 3 4 5 6 7 8 9 LWI 24 23 22 21

ISBN 978-1-266-10793-1
MHID 1-266-10793-2

Cover Image: *freesoulproduction/Shutterstock*

All credits appearing on page or at the end of the book are considered to be an extension of the copyright page.

mheducation.com/highered

To my independent yet loving kids, Ray, Tim, and Melissa, and cats, Lucky, Chester, and Milo

—R.A.N.

To my beloved Plus-ones, Jonathon, Kelsey, Mariano, and Sabrina

—J.R.H.

To my parents, Robert and Shirley, my wife, Heather, and my children, Chris and Annie

—B.G.

To my late parents, Patricia and Paul, my wife, Mary, and my sons, Michael and Matthew

—P.M.W.

About the Authors

Raymond A. Noe is the Robert and Anne Hoyt Designated Professor of Management at The Ohio State University. Before joining the faculty at Ohio State, he was a professor in the Department of Management at Michigan State University and the Industrial Relations Center of the Carlson School of Management, University of Minnesota. He received his BS in psychology from The Ohio State University and his MA and PhD in psychology from Michigan State University. Professor Noe conducts research and teaches all levels of students—from undergraduates to executives—in human resource management, training and development, performance management, and talent management. He has published articles in the *Academy of Management Annals, Academy of Management Journal, Academy of Management Review, Journal of Applied Psychology, Journal of Vocational Behavior,* and *Personnel Psychology.* Professor Noe is currently on the editorial boards of several journals including *Academy of Management Learning & Education, Personnel Psychology, Journal of Applied Psychology, Journal of Management,* and *Human Resources Management Review.* Professor Noe has received awards for his teaching and research excellence, including the Ernest J. McCormick Award for Distinguished Early Career Contribution from the Society for Industrial and Organizational Psychology. He is also a fellow of the Society of Industrial and Organizational Psychology.

John R. Hollenbeck holds the positions of University Distinguished Professor at Michigan State University and Eli Broad Professor of Management at the Eli Broad Graduate School of Business Administration. Dr. Hollenbeck received his PhD in Management from New York University in 1984. He served as the acting editor at *Organizational Behavior and Human Decision Processes* in 1995, the associate editor of *Decision Sciences* from 1999 to 2004, and the editor of *Personnel Psychology* from 1996 to 2002. He has published over 90 articles and book chapters on the topics of team decision making and work motivation. According to the Institute for Scientific Information, this body of work has been cited over 4,000 times by other researchers. Dr. Hollenbeck has been awarded fellowship status in both the Academy of Management and the American Psychological Association, and was recognized with the Career Achievement Award by the HR Division of the Academy of Management (2011), The Distinguished Service Contributions Award (2014), and the Early Career Award by the Society of Industrial and Organizational Psychology (1992). At Michigan State, Dr. Hollenbeck has won several teaching awards including the Michigan State Distinguished Faculty Award, the Michigan State Teacher-Scholar Award, and the Broad MBA Most Outstanding Faculty Member.

Barry Gerhart is Professor of Management and Human Resources and the Bruce R. Ellig Distinguished Chair in Pay and Organizational Effectiveness, School of Business, University of Wisconsin-Madison. He has also served as department chair or area coordinator at Cornell, Vanderbilt, and Wisconsin. His research interests include compensation, human resource strategy, international human resources, and employee retention. Professor Gerhart received his BS in psychology from Bowling Green State University and his PhD in industrial relations from the University of Wisconsin-Madison. His research has been published in a variety of outlets, including the *Academy of Management Annals, Academy of Management Journal, Annual Review of Psychology, International Journal of Human Resource Management, Journal of Applied Psychology, Management and Organization Review,* and *Personnel Psychology.* He has co-authored two books in the area of compensation. He serves on the editorial boards of journals such as the *Academy of Management Journal, Industrial and Labor Relations Review, International Journal of Human Resource Management, Journal of Applied Psychology, Journal of World Business, Management & Organization Review,* and *Personnel Psychology.* Professor Gerhart is a past recipient of the Heneman Career Achievement Award, the Scholarly Achievement Award, and (twice) the International Human Resource Management Scholarly Research Award, all from the Human Resources Division, Academy of Management. He is a Fellow of the Academy of Management, the American Psychological Association, and the Society for Industrial and Organizational Psychology.

Patrick M. Wright is the Thomas C. Vandiver Bicentennial Chair and the Director of the Center for Executive Succession in the Darla Moore School of Business at the University of South Carolina. Prior to joining USC, he served on the faculties at Cornell University, Texas A&M University, and the University of Notre Dame. Professor Wright teaches, conducts research, and consults in the area of strategic human resource management (SHRM), particularly focusing on how firms use people as a source of competitive advantage and the changing nature of the chief HR officer (CHRO) role. He is the faculty leader for the Cornell ILR Executive Education/NAHR program, "The Chief HR Officer: Strategies for Success," aimed at developing potential successors to the CHRO role. He served as the lead editor on the recently released book, *The Chief HR Officer: Defining the New Role of Human Resource Leaders,* published by John Wiley and Sons. He has published more than 60 research articles in journals as well as more than 20 chapters in books and edited volumes. He is the Editor at the *Journal of Management.* He has coedited a special issue of *Research in Personnel and Human Resources Management* titled "Strategic Human Resource Management in the 21st Century" and guest edited a special issue of *Human Resource Management Review* titled "Research in Strategic HRM for the 21st Century." He currently serves as a member on the Board of Directors for the National Academy of Human Resources (NAHR). He is a former board member of HRPS, SHRM Foundation, and World at Work (formerly American Compensation Association). From 2011 to 2015 he was named by *HRM Magazine* as one of the 20 "Most Influential Thought Leaders in HR."

Preface

Managing human resources is a critical component of any company's overall mission to provide value to customers, shareholders, employees, and the community in which it does business. Value includes profits as well as employee growth and satisfaction, creation of new jobs, contributions to community programs, protection of the environment, and innovative use of new technologies.

Our Approach: Engage, Focus, and Apply

Following graduation, most students will find themselves working in businesses or not-for-profit organizations. Regardless of position or career aspirations, their role in directly managing other employees or understanding human resource management (HRM) practices is critical for ensuring both company and personal success. Therefore, *Fundamentals of Human Resource Management,* Ninth Edition, focuses on human resource issues and how HR is a key component of any company's overall corporate strategy. *Fundamentals* is applicable to both HR majors and students from other majors or colleges who are taking an HR course as an elective or a requirement.

Our approach to teaching human resource management involves *engaging* students in learning through the use of real-world examples and best practices; *focusing* them on important HR issues and concepts; and *applying* what they have learned through chapter features and end-of-chapter exercises and cases. Students not only learn about best practices but are actively engaged through the use of cases and decision making. As a result, students will be able to take what they have learned in the course and apply it to solving HRM problems they will encounter on the job.

Each chapter includes several different pedagogical features. "Best Practices" provides examples of companies whose HR activities work well. "HR Oops!" highlights HRM issues that have been handled poorly. "Did You Know?" offers interesting statistics about chapter topics and how they play out in real-world companies. "HRM Social" demonstrates how social media and the Internet can be useful in managing HR activities in any organization. "Thinking Ethically" confronts students with issues that occur in managing human resources. Each feature includes questions to assist students with critical thinking and to spark classroom discussions.

Fundamentals also assists students with learning "How To" perform HR activities, such as applying HR data to solve business problems, devising plans for workplace flexibility, and making incentive pay part of a total-rewards package. These are all work situations students are likely to encounter as part of their professional careers. The end-of-chapter cases focus on corporate sustainability ("Taking Responsibility"), managing the workforce ("Managing Talent"), and HR activities in small organizations ("HR in Small Business").

Organization of the Ninth Edition

Part 1 (Chapters 1-4) discusses the environmental forces that companies face in trying to manage human resources effectively. These forces include economic, technological, and social trends; employment laws; and work design. Employers typically have more control over work design than over trends and equal employment laws, but all of these factors influence how companies attract, retain, and motivate human resources. Chapter 1 discusses why HRM is a critical component to an organization's overall success. The chapter introduces HRM practices and the roles and responsibilities of HR professionals and other managers in managing human resources. Chapter 2 looks at current trends that impact human resources in the workplace, including automation, robots, artificial intelligence, alternative work arrangements, and diversity and inclusion. Chapter 3 provides an overview of the major laws affecting employees and the ways organizations can develop HR practices that comply with the laws. Chapter 4 highlights how jobs and work systems determine the knowledge, skills, and abilities employees need to perform their jobs and influence workers' motivation, satisfaction, and safety at work.

Part 2 (Chapters 5-8) deals with acquiring, training, and developing human resources. Chapter 5 discusses how to develop an HR plan. It emphasizes the strengths and weaknesses of different options for dealing with shortages and excesses of human resources. Chapter 6 emphasizes that employee selection is a process that starts with screening applications and résumés and concludes with a job offer. Chapter 7 covers the features of effective training systems. Chapter 8 demonstrates how assessment, job experiences, formal courses, and mentoring relationships can be used to develop employees for future success.

Part 3 (Chapters 9-11) focuses on assessing and improving performance. Chapter 9 sets the tone for this section by discussing the important role of HRM in creating and maintaining an organization that achieves a high level of performance for employees, managers, customers, shareholders, and the community. Chapter 10 examines the strengths and weaknesses of different performance management systems. Chapter 11 discusses how to maximize employee engagement and productivity and retain valuable employees as well as how to fairly and humanely separate employees when the need arises.

Part 4 (Chapters 12-14) covers rewarding and compensating human resources, including how to design pay structures, recognize good performers, and provide benefits. Chapter 12 discusses how managers weigh the importance and costs of pay to develop a compensation structure and levels of pay for each job given the worth of the jobs, legal requirements, and employee judgments about the fairness of pay levels. Chapter 13 covers the advantages and disadvantages of different types of incentive pay, including merit pay, gainsharing, and stock ownership. Chapter 14 highlights the contents of employee benefits packages, the ways organizations administer benefits, and what companies can do to help employees understand the value of benefits and control benefits costs.

Part 5 (Chapters 15-16) covers other HR topics including collective bargaining and labor relations and managing human resources in a global organization. Chapter 15 explores HR activities as they pertain to employees who belong to unions or who are seeking to join unions. Concluding Part 5, Chapter 16 focuses on HR activities in international settings, including planning, selecting, training, and compensating employees who work overseas. The chapter also explores how cultural differences among countries and workers affect decisions about human resources.

Content Changes in the New Edition

While preparing this new edition, we could not overlook the COVID-19 pandemic and its profound and possibly long-lasting effects on the way the world conducts business. As companies were forced to temporarily (and in some cases permanently) close their doors, and more than 40 million U.S. workers filed for unemployment, professionals across organizations large and small continued to look for ways to keep their employees safe while still conducting business. Throughout the chapters, we have included examples of how companies and HR professionals have implemented strategies to keep operations moving forward during these uncertain times.

In addition, as we finalized the manuscript for this edition, the call for racial equality, social justice, and equal opportunity in the form of massive protests and demonstrations around the country found organizations large and small taking a deeper look into how they can become agents for positive change both in terms of their own workforce and within their communities. We have included two new cases in Chapters 1 and 2 describing how PwC and Adidas have taken steps to address racism and other related issues.

We have also added questions to the *HR Analytics & Decision Making* features to help students use their critical-thinking skills to understand the importance of data analytics. Also, we have included additional *Video Conversations with Chief HR Officers* (CHROs), created by the Center for Executive Succession at the Darla Moore School of Business, University of South Carolina, to pertinent chapters. These videos are featured in Connect, along with questions related to chapter content. Finally, we have written all-new *HR in Small Business* cases for each chapter.

In addition to new or updated chapter pedagogy and real-world examples, the text contains the following content changes to help students and instructors keep current on important HR trends and topics.

- **Chapter 1** opens with a discussion about how technology continues to change the way work gets done and its impact on HRM. The chapter also includes updated information on the top qualities employers are looking for when recruiting recent graduates (Table 1.2) and new data to reflect current median salaries for various HRM positions (Figure 1.6).
- **Chapter 2** provides recent workforce statistics, as well as a discussion about various age, gender, and ethnic groups within the U.S. labor force. Illustrations have been updated to reflect current labor force data. Other recent trends discussed include the impact of COVID-19 on business operations; the restrictive immigration policies that have caused a shortage of workers to perform critical, low-paying jobs; the increased prevalence of gig workers and other alternative work arrangements; the importance of offering employees opportunities to learn new skills; and the push to address the importance of diversity and inclusion for all in today's workforce.
- **Chapter 3** covers updates and features on the topic of sexual harassment; the effects of neurodiversity in the workforce; and employers' ethical obligations to workers during a pandemic. In addition, illustrations have been updated to reflect current statistics on age discrimination, types of charges filed with the EEOC, and the rates of occupational injuries and illnesses.
- **Chapter 4** includes new discussions on the increasing use of robots and other types of automation to free up workers to perform tasks that require new and higher-level skills; the importance of workplace flexibility and the careful planning this new arrangement requires from HR and other managers; and employers' responsibilities when it comes to ergonomics in workers' remote workspaces.

- **Chapter 5** covers the process of HR planning and addresses how some companies are taking steps to build a bigger talent pool from within the organization by developing skills in existing employees, training workers in hard-to-fill skills, and broadening their search criteria when seeking new employees from outside the organization—especially in a tight labor market. In addition, the discussion on campus recruiting describes how recruiters are scheduling individual sessions with prospective hires via Skype, Face Time, and Zoom due to the COVID-19 pandemic and how an AI start-up has launched a virtual event recruiting system to help companies match candidates with open positions.
- **Chapter 6** discusses how companies are using video games in the selection process, which tests different traits associated with emotional intelligence and risk taking. The chapter also discusses how organizations can measure cultural fit when it comes to the selection process; the pros and cons of using artificial intelligence in the hiring process; and the experience of an Ohio manufacturing company that hires employees who are in need of a second chance when it comes to life and work.
- **Chapter 7** looks at the increasing use of simulations and other tools in the employee training process; how Domino's uses an interactive software program with an animated trainer to assist managers in training new hires; updated statistics on the different instruction methods used in the training process; and how strategies to deepen trainees' involvement in the learning process can pay big dividends.
- **Chapter 8** discusses strategies to make employee development more inclusive for workers of color, persons with disabilities, and LGBTQ employees; how employees can use LinkedIn and its learning portal to help steer their career trajectory; statistics on the dearth of female executives at the top of major organizations; and the importance of a strong succession plan for top management positions.
- **Chapter 9** opens with a feature on how ADP helps its client companies achieve high performance. In addition, the chapter discusses the importance of empathy in the workplace and how it can lead to increased productivity and employee retention, and how U.S. employee engagement rates have hit a record high in recent years. In addition, a new discussion focuses on how employers can enable high performance from employees working remotely—even during a pandemic.
- **Chapter 10** discusses recent trends in managing employees' performance and how such reviews are becoming more frequent and less formal. In addition, the chapter describes how companies are using data analytics to modify their performance management systems with input from employees and why "sugarcoating" employee feedback during reviews won't help workers improve their performance.
- **Chapter 11** open with the story of insurance giant Aflac's approach to establishing and maintaining strong relationships with its workers. In addition, the ethics of laying off employees via videoconferencing are discussed. The end-of-chapter Taking Responsibility case on manufacturing Lysol during COVID-19 underscores the importance of corporate values and workers' untiring commitment to help in this time of need.
- **Chapter 12** provides updated pay data for women, men, and minorities and describes strategies companies are using to close the earnings gap. In addition, recent research suggests that many workers have begun to negotiate pay levels with their employers, possibly due to the stronger economy and lower national unemployment rate (prior to the pandemic). The end-of-chapter Managing Talent case focuses on how the TSA is working to improve its pay structure in an effort to retain employees.

- **Chapter 13** focuses on recognizing employee contributions with pay, including new examples of how businesses are changing their approach to employee bonuses in an effort to retain and motivate their workforce. In addition, recent research points out that a majority of companies use variable pay as part of their total compensation to employees, as annual merit raises continue to be stagnant. The ethics of paying hazard pay are discussed in light of the impact of COVID-19 on front-line workers such as grocery employees, medical professionals, and police officers.
- **Chapter 14** updates information on employee benefits, Social Security, and taxes paid by both employers and employees.
- **Chapter 15** provides information on current trends and statistics in union membership. In addition, the chapter points out how unions are working together with companies to reduce benefit costs.
- **Chapter 16** includes a new discussion about companies being "born global" and the addition of material on the sixth dimension of Hofstede's cultural dimensions, indulgence/restraint. New material has also been added to update the discussion on Brexit and the UK's new points-based immigration plan that will reduce the free movement of workers from other European countries to the UK, which could have a negative impact on certain business sectors.

The author team believes that the focused, engaging, and applied approach of *Fundamentals* distinguishes it from other books that have similar coverage of HR topics. The new Ninth Edition has timely coverage of important HR issues, is easy to read, has many features that grab the students' attention, and gets students actively involved in learning.

We would like to thank those of you who have adopted previous editions of *Fundamentals,* and we hope that you will continue to use upcoming editions. For those of you considering *Fundamentals* for adoption, we believe that our approach makes *Fundamentals* your text of choice for human resource management.

Acknowledgments

The Ninth Edition of *Fundamentals of Human Resource Management* would not have been possible without the staff of McGraw-Hill Education. Mike Ablassmeier deserves kudos for ensuring that we continue to improve the book based on the ideas of both adopters and students. John Weimeister, our former editor, helped us develop the vision for the book and gave us the resources we needed to develop a top-of-the-line HRM teaching package. We would also like to thank Cate Rzasa who worked diligently to make sure that the book was interesting, practical, and readable and remained true to the findings of human resource management research. We also thank Kelly Pekelder and Mary Powers for their efforts on behalf of this new edition.

We would like to extend our sincere appreciation to all of the reviewers whose thoughtful input helped make this text one of the market's leading textbooks.

Dr. Roger Blair
Palm Beach State College

Marian Extejt
Bridgewater State University

Qing Gong
Georgia Institute of Technology

Todd Harris
Bridgewater State University

Heidi Helgren
Delta College

William Knapp
University of South Carolina

Dr. Shamira Malekar
City University of New York-Borough of Manhattan Community College

Colleen McLaughlin
Liberty University

Dan Morrell
Middle Tennessee State University

Sharon Palmitier
Grand Rapids Community College

Eivis Qenani
California Polytechnic State University, San Luis Obispo

Sarah Shepler
Ivy Tech Community College-Terre Haute

Amy Simon
Carlson School of Management, University of Minnesota

Raymond A. Noe
John R. Hollenbeck
Barry Gerhart
Patrick M. Wright

Instructors: Student Success Starts with You

Tools to enhance your unique voice

Want to build your own course? No problem. Prefer to use our turnkey, prebuilt course? Easy. Want to make changes throughout the semester? Sure. And you'll save time with Connect's auto-grading too.

65%
Less Time Grading

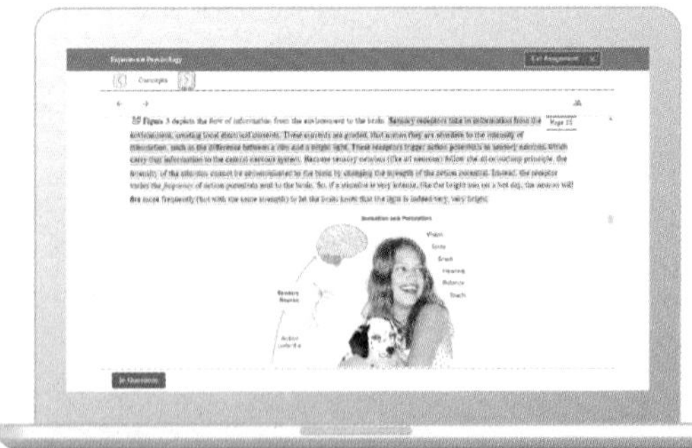

Laptop: McGraw Hill; Woman/dog: George Doyle/Getty Images

Study made personal

Incorporate adaptive study resources like SmartBook® 2.0 into your course and help your students be better prepared in less time. Learn more about the powerful personalized learning experience available in SmartBook 2.0 at **www.mheducation.com/highered/connect/smartbook**

Affordable solutions, added value

Make technology work for you with LMS integration for single sign-on access, mobile access to the digital textbook, and reports to quickly show you how each of your students is doing. And with our Inclusive Access program you can provide all these tools at a discount to your students. Ask your McGraw Hill representative for more information.

Padlock: Jobalou/Getty Images

Solutions for your challenges

A product isn't a solution. Real solutions are affordable, reliable, and come with training and ongoing support when you need it and how you want it. Visit **www.supportateverystep.com** for videos and resources both you and your students can use throughout the semester.

Checkmark: Jobalou/Getty Images

Students: Get Learning That Fits You

Effective tools for efficient studying

Connect is designed to make you more productive with simple, flexible, intuitive tools that maximize your study time and meet your individual learning needs. Get learning that works for you with Connect.

Study anytime, anywhere

Download the free ReadAnywhere app and access your online eBook or SmartBook 2.0 assignments when it's convenient, even if you're offline. And since the app automatically syncs with your eBook and SmartBook 2.0 assignments in Connect, all of your work is available every time you open it. Find out more at **www.mheducation.com/readanywhere**

"I really liked this app—it made it easy to study when you don't have your text-book in front of you."

- Jordan Cunningham, Eastern Washington University

Calendar: owattaphotos/Getty Images

Everything you need in one place

Your Connect course has everything you need—whether reading on your digital eBook or completing assignments for class, Connect makes it easy to get your work done.

Learning for everyone

McGraw Hill works directly with Accessibility Services Departments and faculty to meet the learning needs of all students. Please contact your Accessibility Services Office and ask them to email accessibility@mheducation.com, or visit **www.mheducation.com/about/accessibility** for more information.

Top: Jenner Images/Getty Images, Left: Hero Images/Getty Images, Right: Hero Images/Getty Images

Brief Contents

Contents

The Human Resource Environment

freesoulproduction/Shutterstock

1 Managing Human Resources

Introduction

According to David Windley, the CEO of IQTalent Partners, this is an excellent time to be working in human resource management. Internet-based technology is changing the way work gets done, automating many tasks once carried out by humans. As Windley sees it, this will result in organizations needing people for their creativity and good judgment, not their ability to carry out routine, repetitive tasks. When machines are doing routine work, what differentiates companies will be having the best—the most creative, the most insightful—people and setting up an environment in which they can and will contribute. Doing this requires professionals with high ethical standards and strong skills in applying data to complex situations.

For those who specialize in HR, these changes put them in the key role of providing talent, keeping talent, and bringing out the best in talent. Windley sees this because his own career was in human resources. At the age of 27, he took his first job heading an HR department, at a company called Mediagenic (now Activision). He later held executive roles at Intuit, Microsoft, Yahoo, and others. Windley says one of his greatest challenges was implementing a cultural shift in a company—taking managers who had viewed their individual units as separate kingdoms and persuading them to unite in a common purpose.

Windley, who holds bachelor's and master's degrees in business, says he chose human resource management as a career because the "people side of business" was what interested him the most. At an early age, he could see that doing a good job at acquiring and managing people would have more impact on a business's success than working on just about any other kind of business resource. Now that he runs his own company, he is delivering HR expertise to clients by helping them find talent. Windley remains active in the field, serving as chair of the board for the Society for Human Resource Management.[1]

As technology changes the way work gets done, human resource management has become an important partner in developing and implementing corporate strategies.

Fizkes/Getty Images

What Do I Need to Know?

After reading this chapter, you should be able to:

- **LO 1-1** Define human resource management, and explain how HRM contributes to an organization's performance.
- **LO 1-2** Identify the responsibilities of human resource departments.
- **LO 1-3** Summarize the types of competencies needed for human resource management.
- **LO 1-4** Explain the role of supervisors in human resource management.
- **LO 1-5** Discuss ethical issues in human resource management.
- **LO 1-6** Describe typical careers in human resource management.

As business leaders like David Windley know from experience, a company's success requires skillful **human resource management (HRM),** the policies, practices, and systems that influence employees' behavior, attitudes, and performance. Many companies refer to HRM as involving "people practices." Figure 1.1 emphasizes that there are several important HRM practices that should support the organization's business strategy: analyzing work and designing jobs, determining how many employees with specific knowledge and skills are needed (human resource planning), attracting potential employees (recruiting), choosing employees (selection), teaching employees how to perform their jobs and preparing them for the future (training and development), evaluating their performance (performance management), rewarding employees (compensation), and creating a positive work environment (employee relations). An organization performs best when all of these practices are managed well. At businesses and other organizations with effective HRM, employees and customers tend to be more satisfied, and the companies tend to be more innovative, have greater productivity, and develop a more favorable reputation in the community.[2]

Human Resource Management (HRM)
The policies, practices, and systems that influence employees' behavior, attitudes, and performance.

In this chapter, we introduce the scope of human resource management. We begin by discussing why human resource management is an essential element of an organization's success. We then turn to the elements of managing human resources: the roles and skills needed for effective human resource management. Next, the chapter describes how all managers, not just human resource professionals, participate in the activities related to human resource management. The following section of the chapter addresses some of the ethical issues that arise with regard to human resource management. We then provide an overview of careers in human resource management. The chapter concludes by highlighting the HRM practices covered in the remainder of this book.

Human Resources and Company Performance

LO 1-1 Define human resource management, and explain how HRM contributes to an organization's performance.

Managers and economists traditionally have seen human resource management as a necessary expense, rather than as a source of value to their organizations. Economic value is usually associated with *capital*—cash, equipment, technology, and facilities. However, research has demonstrated that HRM practices can be valuable.[3] Decisions such as whom to hire, what to pay, what training to offer, and how to evaluate employee performance directly affect employees' motivation and ability to provide goods and services that customers value. Companies that attempt to increase their competitiveness by investing in new technology

FIGURE 1.1
Human Resource Management Practices

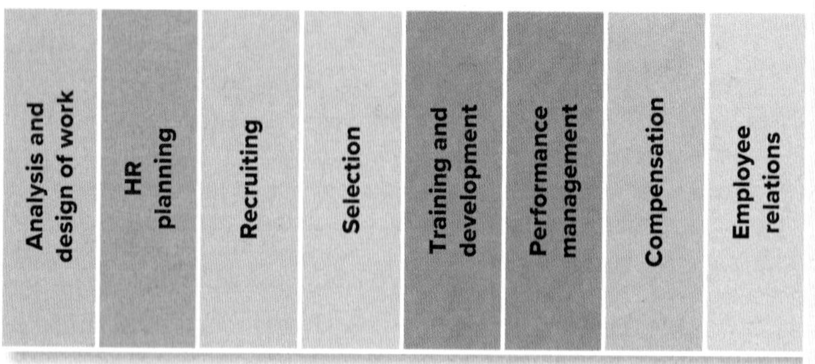

FIGURE 1.2
Impact of Human Resource Management

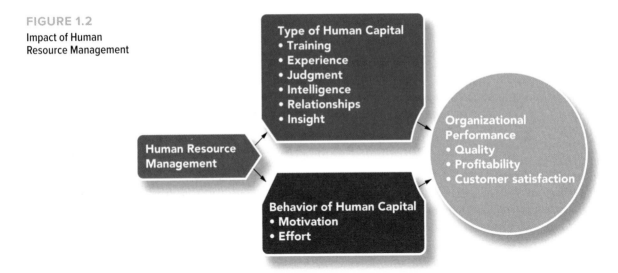

Type of Human Capital
- Training
- Experience
- Judgment
- Intelligence
- Relationships
- Insight

Human Resource Management

Behavior of Human Capital
- Motivation
- Effort

Organizational Performance
- Quality
- Profitability
- Customer satisfaction

and promoting quality throughout the organization also invest in state-of-the-art staffing, training, and compensation practices.[4]

Human Capital
An organization's employees, described in terms of their training, experience, judgment, intelligence, relationships, and insight.

The concept of "human resource management" implies that employees are *resources* of the employer. As a type of resource, **human capital** means the organization's employees, described in terms of their training, experience, judgment, intelligence, relationships, and insight—employee characteristics that add economic value to the organization. In other words, whether it manufactures automobiles or forecasts the weather, for an organization to succeed at what it does, it needs employees with certain qualities, such as particular kinds of training and experience. Employees in today's organizations are not interchangeable, easily replaced parts of a system but a source of the company's success or failure. By influencing *who* works for the organization and *how* those people work, human resource management therefore contributes to basic measures of an organization's performance, such as quality, profitability, and customer satisfaction. Figure 1.2 shows this relationship.

In the United States, low-price retailers are notorious for the ways they keep labor costs down. They pay low wages, limit employees to part-time status (providing few or no employee benefits), and alter schedules at the last minute in order to minimize staffing when store traffic is light. But as the demand for workers has risen over the past few years, these companies tend to lose employees—often their best performers—to competitors. Some retailers are trying to up their game by becoming more desirable employers. For example, in March 2020, discount retailer Dollar General announced it would distribute $35 million in bonuses to all store, distribution center, and private freight fleet employees who worked for the company during a six-week period that coincided with the peak of the COVID-19 pandemic in some states.[5]

At Google, the company's focus is on making employees feel valued, trained, and well compensated. In turn, there is a low turnover rate and a high degree of satisfaction.
maglara/Shutterstock

Human resource management is critical to the success of organizations because human capital has certain qualities that make it valuable. In terms of business strategy, an organization can succeed if it has a *sustainable competitive advantage* (is better than competitors at something and can hold that advantage over a sustained period of time). Therefore, we can conclude that organizations need the kind of resources that will give them such an advantage. Human resources have these necessary qualities:

HR Oops!

Business Execs Doubt HR's Message on Employee Experience

A recent survey of executives by the Mercer consulting firm found that the top priority for HR managers was "employee experience"—employees' perceptions of how well their work life matches their expectations. This experience begins when the new employee arrives at work for the first time and learns about procedures, colleagues, company values, and how people are treated. It includes the work load and the process of enrolling in and receiving pay and benefits. Feedback from managers, opportunities for training, and the general health and safety of the workplace are other components of the employee experience. However, these factors may shift in relevance depending on other concerns. For example, during the COVID-19 pandemic, personal health became a top priority, whereas before that, in a competitive job market, employees were more tuned in to other factors, such as meaningful work.

HR professionals have seen that employees perform better and are likelier to stay with the organization if they have positive employee experiences. However, business leaders—the managers responsible for product lines, production, and so on—seem to doubt that the employee experience is significant. Barely one-fourth of them believe there is a return on investment from improving the employee experience. The difference in perceptions implies that HR professionals have a long way to go in making a case for why their work matters.

To step up their game, HR professionals should consider how to make the business case for employee experience. They might start by improving experiences that have a measurable payoff, such as making it easier for employees to manage their benefits such as retirement savings and health insurance. An easy-to-use self-service system fits with this strategy, so employees don't tie up HR staff to resolve questions and problems. With a change such as this, HR departments can set measurable goals, gather data, and demonstrate results. Similarly, for improvements in training programs or performance feedback, the organization can gather data on business performance before and after the programs are launched. Business managers get interested when HR programs deliver results they can see.

Questions

1. What kinds of experiences in your current or recent job (or a job you would like to have) are positive? Consider, for example, company policies, procedures you must follow, relationships with your supervisor and others, nature of the work, and the pay you earn.
2. Why is it important to be able to measure the impact of an HR initiative?

Sources: Mercer, *Win with Empathy: Global Talent Trends 2020,* https://www.mercer.com, accessed April 7, 2020; Chris Voce, "Why Employee Experience Matters Now More than Ever," *Employee Benefit News,* March 25, 2020, https://www.benefitnews.com; Mary Ann Sardone and Lauren Mason, "Building a Better Employee Experience," September 20, 2019, https://www.mercer.com.

- Human resources are *valuable.* High-quality employees provide a needed service as they perform many critical functions.
- Human resources are *rare* in the sense that a person with high levels of the needed skills and knowledge is not common. An organization may spend months looking for a talented and experienced manager or technician.
- Human resources *cannot be imitated.* To imitate human resources at a high-performing competitor, you would have to figure out which employees are providing the advantage and how. Then you would have to recruit people who can do precisely the same thing and set up the systems that enable those people to imitate your competitor.
- Human resources have *no good substitutes.* When people are well trained and highly motivated, they learn, develop their abilities, and care about customers. It is difficult to imagine another resource that can match committed and talented employees.

These qualities imply that human resources have enormous potential. An organization realizes this potential through the ways it practices human resource management. Conversely, a missed opportunity to provide HR expertise is a missed opportunity to realize the potential of human resources (see "HR Oops!").

Effective management of human resources can form the foundation of a *high-performance work system*—an organization in which technology, organizational structure, people, and processes work together seamlessly to give an organization an advantage in the competitive environment. As technology changes the ways organizations manufacture, transport, communicate, and keep track of information, human resource management must ensure that the organization has the right kinds of people to meet the new challenges. High-performance work systems also have been essential in making organizations strong enough to weather the storm of the recent recession and remain profitable as the economy slowly begins to expand again. Maintaining a high-performance work system may include development of training programs, recruitment of people with new skill sets, and establishment of rewards for such behaviors as teamwork, flexibility, and learning. In Chapter 2, we will see some of the changes that human resource managers are planning for, and Chapter 9 examines high-performance work systems in greater detail.

LO 1-2 Identify the responsibilities of human resource departments.

Responsibilities of Human Resource Departments

In all but the smallest organizations, a human resource department is responsible for the functions of human resource management. On average, an organization has almost one-and-a-half full-time HR staff persons for every hundred employees on the payroll.[6] One way to define the responsibilities of HR departments is to think of HR as a business within the company with three product lines:[7]

1. *Administrative services and transactions*—Handling administrative tasks (for example, hiring employees and answering questions about benefits) efficiently and with a commitment to quality. This requires expertise in the particular tasks.
2. *Business partner services*—Developing effective HR systems that help the organization meet its goals for attracting, keeping, and developing people with the skills it needs. For the systems to be effective, HR people must understand the business so they can understand what the business needs.
3. *Strategic partner*—Contributing to the company's strategy through an understanding of its existing and needed human resources and ways HR practices can give the company a competitive advantage. For strategic ideas to be effective, HR people must understand the business, its industry, and its competitors.

Another way to think of HR responsibilities is in terms of specific activities. Table 1.1 details the responsibilities of human resource departments. These responsibilities include the practices introduced in Figure 1.1 plus two areas of responsibility that support those practices: (1) establishing and administering personnel policies and (2) ensuring compliance with labor laws.

HR responsibilities include administrative tasks, business services, and working as a strategic corporate partner within the organization.
Rido/Shutterstock

Although the human resource department has responsibility for these areas, many of the tasks may be performed by supervisors or others inside or outside the organization. No two human resource departments have precisely the same roles, because there are differences in organization sizes and characteristics of the workforce, the industry, and management's values. In some companies the HR department handles all the activities listed in Table 1.1. In others it may share the roles and duties with managers of other departments, such as finance, operations, or information technology. In some companies the HR department actively advises top management. In others the department responds to top-level management decisions and implements staffing, training, and compensation activities in light of company strategy and policies.

Let's take an overview of the HR functions and some of the options available for carrying them out. Human resource management

TABLE 1.1
Responsibilities of HR Departments

FUNCTION	RESPONSIBILITIES
Analysis and design of work	Work analysis; job design; job descriptions
Recruitment and selection	Recruiting; job postings; interviewing; testing; coordinating use of temporary labor
Training and development	Orientation; skills training; career development programs
Performance management	Performance measures; preparation and administration of performance appraisals; feedback and coaching; discipline
Compensation and benefits	Wage and salary administration; incentive pay; insurance; vacation leave administration; retirement plans; profit sharing; health and wellness; stock plans
Employee relations	Attitude surveys; labor relations; employee handbooks; company publications; labor law compliance; relocation and outplacement services
Personnel policies	Policy creation; policy communication
Employee data and information systems	Record keeping; HR information systems; workforce analytics
Compliance with laws	Policies to ensure lawful behavior; reporting; posting information; safety inspections; accessibility accommodations
Support for strategy	Human resource planning and forecasting; talent management; change management

Sources: "Human Resources Managers," *O*NET OnLine,* https://www.onetonline.org, updated April 7, 2020; Society for Human Resource Management, "SHRM Essentials of Human Resources," https://www.shrm.org, accessed April 7, 2020; SHRM-BNA Survey No. 66, "Policy and Practice Forum: Human Resource Activities, Budgets, and Staffs, 2000–2001," *Bulletin to Management,* Bureau of National Affairs Policy and Practice Series (Washington, DC: Bureau of National Affairs, June 28, 2001).

involves both the selection of which options to use and the activities involved with using those options. Later chapters of this book will explore each function in greater detail.

Job Analysis
The process of getting detailed information about jobs.

Analyzing and Designing Jobs

Job Design
The process of defining how work will be performed and what tasks will be required in a given job.

To produce their given product or service (or set of products or services), companies require that a number of tasks be performed. The tasks are grouped together in various combinations to form jobs. Ideally, the tasks should be grouped in ways that help the organization operate efficiently and obtain people with the right qualifications to do the jobs well. This function involves the activities of job analysis and job design. **Job analysis** is the process of getting detailed information about jobs. **Job design** is the process of defining the way work will be performed and the tasks that a given job requires.

In general, jobs can vary from having a narrow range of simple tasks to having a broad array of complex tasks requiring multiple skills. At one extreme is a worker on an assembly line at a poultry-processing facility; at the other extreme is a doctor in an emergency room. In the past, many companies have emphasized the use of narrowly defined jobs to increase efficiency. With many simple jobs, a company can easily find workers who can quickly be trained to perform the jobs at relatively low pay. However, greater concern for innovation and quality has shifted the trend to using more broadly defined jobs. Also, as we will see in Chapters 2 and 4, some organizations assign work even more broadly, to teams instead of individuals.

REI is one of only five companies to make *Fortune's* list of "100 Best Companies to Work For" every year since the rankings began in 1998. The retailer of outdoor gear and apparel provides health care benefits to all employees working at least 10 hours per week, plus extra time off with pay for getting outside to enjoy nature. How do you think this boosts morale?
Matt Peyton/REI/AP Images

Recruiting and Hiring Employees

Based on job analysis and design, an organization can determine the kinds of employees it needs. With this knowledge, it carries out the function of recruiting and hiring employees. **Recruitment** is the process through which the organization seeks applicants for potential employment. **Selection** refers to the process by which the organization attempts to identify applicants with the necessary knowledge, skills, abilities, and other characteristics that will help the organization achieve its goals. An organization makes selection decisions in order to add employees to its workforce, as well as to transfer existing employees to new positions.

Recruitment
The process through which the organization seeks applicants for potential employment.

Selection
The process by which the organization attempts to identify applicants with the necessary knowledge, skills, abilities, and other characteristics that will help the organization achieve its goals.

Approaches to recruiting and selection involve a variety of alternatives. Some organizations may actively recruit from many external sources, such as Internet job postings, online social networks, and college recruiting events. Other organizations may rely heavily on promotions from within, applicants referred by current employees, and the availability of in-house people with the necessary skills.

At some organizations the selection process may focus on specific skills, such as experience with a particular programming language or type of equipment. At other organizations, selection may focus on general abilities, such as the ability to work as part of a team or find creative solutions. The focus an organization favors will affect many choices, from the way the organization measures ability, to the questions it asks in interviews, to the places where it recruits. Table 1.2 lists the top five qualities that employers say they are looking for in job candidates.

Training and Developing Employees

Although organizations base hiring decisions on candidates' existing qualifications, most organizations provide ways for their employees to broaden or deepen their knowledge, skills, and abilities. To do this, organizations provide for employee training and development. **Training** is a planned effort to enable employees to learn job-related knowledge, skills, and behavior. For example, many organizations offer safety training to teach employees safe work habits. **Development** involves acquiring knowledge, skills, and behaviors that improve employees' ability to meet the challenges of a variety of new or existing jobs, including the client and customer demands of those jobs. Development programs often focus on preparing employees for management responsibility. Likewise, if a company plans to set up teams to manufacture products, it might offer a development program to help employees learn the ins and outs of effective teamwork.

Training
An organization's planned efforts to help employees acquire job-related knowledge, skills, abilities, and behaviors, with the goal of applying these on the job.

Development
The acquisition of knowledge, skills, and behaviors that improve an employee's ability to meet changes in job requirements and in customer demands.

Decisions related to training and development include whether the organization will emphasize enabling employees to perform their current jobs, preparing them for future jobs, or both. An organization may offer programs to a few employees in whom the organization wants to invest, or it may have a philosophy of investing in the training of all its workers. Some organizations, especially large ones, may have extensive formal training programs, including classroom sessions and training programs online. Other organizations may prefer a simpler, more flexible approach of encouraging employees to participate in outside training and development programs as needs are identified.

TABLE 1.2

Top Qualities Employers Look For in Employees

1. Problem-solving skills
2. Teamwork skills
3. Strong work ethic
4. Analytical/quantitative skills
5. Written communication skills

Source: Based on National Association of Colleges and Employers, "Key Attributes Employers Want to See on Students' Resumes," January 13, 2020, https://www.naceweb.org.

Managing Performance

Managing human resources includes keeping track of how well employees are performing relative to objectives such as job descriptions and goals for a particular position. The process of ensuring that employees' activities and outputs match the organization's goals is called **performance management.** The activities of performance management include specifying the tasks and outcomes of a job that contribute to the organization's success. Then various measures are used to compare the employee's performance over some time period with the desired performance. Often, rewards—the topic of the next section—are offered to encourage good performance.

Performance Management
The process through which managers ensure that employees' activities and outputs contribute to the organization's goals.

The human resource department may be responsible for developing or obtaining questionnaires and other devices for measuring performance. The performance measures may emphasize observable behaviors (for example, answering the phone by the second ring), outcomes (number of customer complaints and compliments), or both. When the person evaluating performance is not familiar with the details of the job, outcomes tend to be easier to evaluate than specific behaviors.[8] The evaluation may focus on the short term or the long term and on individual employees or groups. Typically the person who completes the evaluation is the employee's supervisor. Often employees also evaluate their own performance, and in some organizations, peers and subordinates participate, too.

Planning and Administering Pay and Benefits

The pay and benefits that employees earn play an important role in motivating them. This is especially true when rewards such as bonuses are linked to the individual's or group's achievements. Decisions about pay and benefits can also support other aspects of an organization's strategy. For example, a company that wants to provide an exceptional level of service or be exceptionally innovative might pay significantly more than competitors in order to attract and keep the best employees. At other companies, a low-cost strategy requires knowledge of industry norms, so that the company does not spend more than it must.

Planning pay and benefits involves many decisions, often complex and based on knowledge of a multitude of legal requirements. An important decision is how much to offer in salary or wages, as opposed to bonuses, commissions, and other performance-related pay. Other decisions involve which benefits to offer, from retirement plans to various kinds of insurance to time off with pay. All such decisions have implications for the organization's bottom line, as well as for employee motivation.

Administering pay and benefits is another big responsibility. Organizations need systems for keeping track of each employee's earnings and benefits. Employees need information about their health plan, retirement plan, and other benefits. Keeping track of this involves extensive record keeping and reporting to management, employees, the government, and others.

Maintaining Positive Employee Relations

Organizations often depend on human resource professionals to help them maintain positive relations with employees. This function includes preparing and distributing employee handbooks that detail company policies and, in large organizations, company publications such as a monthly newsletter or a website on the organization's intranet. Preparing these communications may be a regular task for the human resource department.

The human resource department can also expect to handle certain kinds of communications from individual employees. Employees turn to the HR department for answers to questions about benefits and company policy. If employees feel they have been discriminated against, see safety hazards, or have other problems and are dissatisfied with their supervisor's response, they may turn to the HR department for help. Members of the department

HRM Social

Social-Media Tools for HR Professionals

When people think of social media, they tend to think first of social-networking sites, like Facebook, Instagram, or Twitter. The user creates a profile, builds connections to a network of others, and then posts and views content within that network. The definition of social media is, in fact, broader: online applications that help users share content and collaborate with one another, whether on a game, a work assignment, or a collaborative document like Wikipedia. For HR professionals, those purposes are relevant for networks within the profession, within their organization, and beyond.

For professional networking, HR professionals can participate in social-networking sites like LinkedIn, where there are groups devoted to the profession. The Society for Human Resource Management (SHRM) also has a social-networking group for its members. Some professionals have set up open-source collaborations on sites like HR Open Source and Google's re:Work. Participants can share creations such as sample documents and stories of successful projects, and others can use these to create plans at their own organization. Users must be careful not to post confidential information on an open-source site.

Within organizations, social-media tools are a practical way to communicate with employees. The company may provide a social-networking application or project management system for employees to collaborate on projects and share ideas. Users can search for inside experts to join a team, serve as a mentor, or answer a question. The HR department can post or text announcements and reminders, such as the enrollment period for employee benefits or a link to a new training program.

Beyond the organization, HR departments want to present a favorable image of the company to possible future employees. One way to do this is with a blog that features stories about the organization's values, projects, and employees. Many organizations participate in industry- or career-related social-networking sites. They also use content-sharing sites like YouTube and SlideShare to post rich media such as videos.

Questions

1. Of the social-media applications described here, which, if any, have you already used? On which, if any, have you observed messages from employers or co-workers?
2. Based on the descriptions here and your experiences with social media, briefly describe one way the use of social media might help you start or advance your career.

Sources: Carol Patton, "Does Social Media Hurt or Help Your Recruitment Efforts," *Human Resource Executive,* February 14, 2020, https://hrexecutive.com; Nathan Resnick, "Why Social Media Is Key to Keeping Employees Engaged at Work," *The Next Web,* July 11, 2019, https://thenextweb.com; "The Importance of Social Media in HR," *Society for Human Resource Management* (South Asia blog), May 2, 2018, https://blog.shrm.org; Stephen Baer, "Social Media Proves to Boost Employee Engagement," *Forbes,* February 13, 2018, https://www.forbes.com; Tamara Lytle, "The New Sharing Community," *HR Magazine,* June/July 2017, pp. 100–106.

should be prepared to address such problems. For some of these communications, HR professionals are increasingly using social-media tools, as described in the "HRM Social" box.

In organizations where employees belong to a union, employee relations entail additional responsibilities. The organization periodically conducts collective bargaining to negotiate an employment contract with union members. The HR department maintains communication with union representatives to ensure that problems are resolved as they arise.

Establishing and Administering Personnel Policies

All the human resource activities described so far require fair and consistent decisions, and most require substantial record keeping. Organizations depend on their HR department to help establish policies related to hiring, discipline, promotions, and benefits. For example, with a policy in place that an intoxicated worker will be immediately terminated, the company can handle such a situation more fairly and objectively than if it addressed such incidents on a case-by-case basis. The company depends on its HR professionals to help develop and then communicate the policy to every employee, so that everyone knows its importance. If anyone violates the rule, a supervisor can quickly intervene—confident that the employee knew the consequences and that any other employee would be treated the same way. Not only do such policies promote fair decision making, but they also promote other objectives, such as workplace safety and customer service.

Developing fair and effective policies requires strong decision-making skills, the ability to think ethically, and a broad understanding of business activities that will be covered by the policies. In addition, for employees to comply with policies, they have to know and understand the policies. Therefore, human resource management requires the ability to communicate through a variety of channels. Human resource personnel may teach policies by giving presentations at meetings, posting documents online, writing e-mail messages, setting up social-media pages for employees, and in many other ways.

Managing and Using Human Resource Data

All aspects of human resource management require careful and discreet record keeping, from processing job applications, to performance appraisals, benefits enrollment, and government-mandated reports. Handling records about employees requires accuracy as well as sensitivity to employee privacy. Whether the organization keeps records in file cabinets or on a sophisticated computer information system, it must have methods for ensuring accuracy and for balancing privacy concerns with easy access for those who need information and are authorized to see it.

Thanks to computer tools, employee-related information is not just an administrative responsibility; it also can be the basis for knowledge that gives organizations an edge over their competitors. Data about employees can show, for example, which of the company's talent has the most promise for future leadership, what kinds of employees tend to perform best in particular positions, and in which departments the need for hiring will be most pressing. To use the data for answering questions such as these, many organizations have set up human resource information systems. They may engage in **workforce analytics,** which is the use of quantitative tools and scientific methods to analyze data from human resource databases and other sources to make evidence-based decisions that support business goals. For ideas on how to make analytics relevant to business goals, see the "HR How To" box. Chapter 2 will take a closer look at how developments in technology are enabling more sophisticated analysis of employee data to support decision making.

Workforce Analytics
The use of quantitative tools and scientific methods to analyze data from human resource databases and other sources to make evidence-based decisions that support business goals.

Ensuring Compliance with Labor Laws

As we will discuss in later chapters, especially Chapter 3, the government has many laws and regulations concerning the treatment of employees. These laws govern such matters as equal employment opportunity, employee safety and health, employee pay and benefits, employee privacy, and job security. Government requirements include filing reports and displaying posters, as well as avoiding unlawful behavior. Most managers depend on human resource professionals to help them keep track of these requirements.

Ensuring compliance with laws requires that human resource personnel keep watch over a rapidly changing legal landscape. For example, the increased use of and access to electronic databases by employees and employers suggest that in the near future legislation will be needed to protect employee privacy rights. Currently no federal laws outline how to use employee databases in a way that protects employees' privacy while also meeting employers' and society's concern for security.

Lawsuits that will continue to influence HRM practices concern job security. Because economic or competitive conditions can force companies to close facilities and lay off employees, cases dealing with the illegal discharge of employees have increased. The issue of "employment at will"–that is, the principle that an employer may terminate employment at any time without notice–will be debated. As the age of the overall workforce increases, as described in Chapter 2, the number of cases dealing with age discrimination in layoffs, promotions,

HR How To

Using HR Data to Solve Business Problems

Companies are increasingly valuing HR professionals who can analyze data to provide support for business decisions. An understanding of statistics and knowledge about information systems are important technical competencies. But these are relevant only if applied well to the needs of the business. Here are some guidelines for making the connection:

- Communicate formally and informally with people in the organization. Ask open-ended questions, and actively listen to the answers. Identify areas of concern and goals that will deliver important wins.
- Become a student of the organization. Understand its strategic goals, including the main sources of revenues and expenses. Learn to read financial reports, and read them regularly. Keep up with news about the organization and its industry. Pay attention to how decisions get made and who wields influence.
- Stay familiar with research in the HR field. When a question or problem arises, be able to call to mind relevant research that suggests a way to address the problem. Research these initial ideas to build on existing knowledge and avoid chasing after methods that have been demonstrated to be ineffective.
- Use employee data appropriately. Protect employees' private information, and ensure that employees are aware of what data the company collects about them and how it uses the data. Indicate how the data will benefit employees as well as the organization—for example, by pinpointing knowledge or skills that, if acquired, will help them succeed on the job.

Questions

1. Review the categories of HR responsibilities (see Table 1.1). For any of the categories, write a question that analytics might be able to answer.
2. In light of the tips listed here, how should an HR professional use data to address the business issue you identified in question 1?

Sources: Dave Weisbeck, "How to Transform HR Data into Business Results," *HR Technologist,* March 9, 2020, https://www.hrtechnologist.com; Adam Rogers, "How HR Can Use Data to Drive C-Suite Buy-In," *HCM Technology Report,* March 14, 2019, https://www.hcmtechnologyreport.com; Bernard Marr, "5 Inspiring Ways Organizations Are Using HR Data," *Forbes,* May 11, 2018, https://www.forbes.com; Julie Winkle Giulioni, "Earn a Seat without Missing a Beat," *TD,* January 2018, pp. 64–66.

Mc Graw Hill connect

Visit your instructor's Connect® course and access your eBook to view this video.

"HR touches every aspect of the business and we're a critical driver of success to the business."

—Tracy Keogh
Chief HR Officer, HP, Inc.

Video Produced for the Center for Executive Succession in the Darla Moore School of Business at the University of South Carolina by Coal Powered Filmworks

and benefits will likely rise. Employers will need to review work rules, recruitment practices, and performance evaluation systems, and if necessary revise them to ensure that they do not falsely communicate employment agreements the company does not intend to honor (such as lifetime employment) or discriminate on the basis of age.

Supporting the Organization's Strategy

At one time, human resource management was primarily an administrative function. The HR department focused on filling out forms and processing paperwork. As more organizations have come to appreciate the significance of highly skilled human resources, however, many HR departments have taken on a more active role in supporting the organization's strategy. As a result, today's HR professionals need to understand the organization's business operations, project how business trends might affect the business, reinforce positive aspects of the organization's culture, develop talent for present and future needs, craft effective HR strategies, and make a case for them to top management. Amtrak hired Barry Melnkovic to promote this skill set within the human resources function. After spending hours learning about employees' and customers' experiences, Melnkovic crafted a plan to support Amtrak's strategy. He set up systems in which his employees evaluate the processes they carry out, continually looking for ways to carry out work more efficiently and accurately. He set up a team to develop training aimed at improving passengers' customer experiences. He added bonuses for high performance and replaced task-oriented HR managers with people focused on business performance.[9]

An important element of this responsibility is **human resource planning,** identifying the numbers and types of employees the organization will require in order to meet its objectives. Using these estimates, the human resource department helps the organization forecast its needs for hiring, training, and reassigning employees. Planning also may show that the organization will need fewer employees to meet anticipated needs. In that situation, human resource planning includes how to handle or avoid layoffs. Human resource planning provides important information for **talent management**—a systematic, planned effort to attract, retain, develop, and motivate highly skilled employees and managers. When managers are clear about the kinds of people they will need to achieve the organization's goals, talent management combines recruiting, selection, training, and motivational practices to meet those needs. Approaching these tasks in terms of talent management is one way HR managers are making the link to organizational strategy. At Ochsner Health System in Louisiana, Missy Sparks applied talent management to the challenge of finding and keeping medical assistants at the company's hospitals and health clinics. The demand for qualified workers—especially those with the necessary people skills—was outstripping the supply. Sparks, the company's assistant vice president for talent management and workforce development, partnered with a community college to develop a training program targeting community members who are unemployed and underemployed. The program equips students with technical and people skills, so they can join the workforce and succeed. Ochsner also provides support services to employees when they run into problems that could interfere with staying on the job. Employees recruited through the program are highly committed to their work.[10]

Human Resource Planning
Identifying the numbers and types of employees the organization will require in order to meet its objectives.

Talent Management
A systematic, planned effort to attract, retain, develop, and motivate highly skilled employees and managers.

As part of its strategic role, one of the key contributions HR can make is to engage in **evidence-based HR,** the collection and use of data to demonstrate that human resource practices have a positive influence on the company's profits or key stakeholders (employees, customers, community, shareholders). This practice helps show that the money invested in HR programs is justified and that HRM is contributing to the company's goals and objectives. For example, data collected on the relationship between HR practices and productivity, turnover, accidents, employee attitudes, and medical costs may show that the HR function is as important to the business as finance, accounting, and marketing.

Evidence-Based HR
Collecting and using data to show that human resource practices have a positive influence on the company's bottom line or key stakeholders.

Often an organization's strategy requires some type of change—for example, adding, moving, or closing facilities; applying new technology; or entering markets in other regions or countries. Common reactions to change include fear, anger, and confusion. The organization may turn to its HR department for help in managing the change process. Skilled human resource professionals can apply knowledge of human behavior, along with performance management tools, to help the organization manage change constructively.

Another strategic challenge tackled by a growing number of companies is how to seek profits in ways that communities, customers, and suppliers will support over the long run. This concern is called **sustainability**—broadly defined as an organization's ability to profit without depleting its resources, including employees, natural resources, and the support of the surrounding community. Success at sustainability comes from meeting the needs of the organization's **stakeholders,** all the parties who have an interest in the organization's success. Typically an organization's stakeholders include shareholders, the community, customers, and employees. Sustainable organizations meet their needs by minimizing their environmental impact, providing high-quality products and services, ensuring workplace safety, offering fair compensation, and delivering an adequate return to investors. Sustainability delivers a strategic advantage when it boosts the organization's image with customers, opens access to new

Sustainability
An organization's ability to profit without depleting its resources, including employees, natural resources, and the support of the surrounding community.

Stakeholders
The parties with an interest in the company's success (typically, shareholders, the community, customers, and employees).

HR Analytics & Decision Making

At Sanfoli, a global health care company with more than 100,000 employees, women were well represented, except in top management. A team investigated the underrepresentation of women at the top and found that when decision makers identified candidates for advancement through management ranks, no process encouraged the selection of women for the roles. They established a six-month program, called ELEVATE, to develop skills in leadership and problem solving. Managers use the results of performance appraisals to nominate female employees to participate in ELEVATE.

In ELEVATE's initial years, 80 women completed the program. Of them, 60% received promotions or other new roles in the company. Participants rate themselves as better leaders, and the participants have been coaching and supporting one another. Based on the early positive reactions, Sanfoli committed to making ELEVATE available to other segments of its employees that also are underrepresented in top jobs.

Questions

1. What potential problem(s) did the data gathered by Sanfoli point to?
2. What additional data would you look for in determining whether HR activities had solved the problem(s)?

Sources: Chandni Patel, "Sanfoli's ELEVATE Program Supports Women Leaders," *MassBio* (Massachusetts Biotechnology Council), January 8, 2018, https://www.massbio.org; Jennifer London, "ELEVATE: Sanfoli's Leadership Development Program," *Diversity Best Practices,* May 9, 2017, https://www.diversitybestpractices.com.

markets, and helps attract and retain talented employees. In an organization with a sustainable strategy, HR departments focus on employee development and empowerment rather than short-term costs, on long-term planning rather than smooth turnover and outsourcing, and on justice and fairness over short-term profits.[11] For example, in the midst of the COVID-19 pandemic, many businesses around the world stepped up and repurposed some of their manufacturing facilities to make personal protection equipment (PPE) for health care professionals, including masks, face shields, isolation gowns, hand sanitizer, and parts for ventilators.[12]

LO 1-3 Summarize the types of competencies needed for human resource management.

Skills of HRM Professionals

With such varied responsibilities, the human resource department needs to bring together a large pool of skills. The Society for Human Resource Management (SHRM) has defined sets of knowledge and skills associated with success, grouping these into nine categories it calls *HR success competencies:* HR expertise, relationship management, consultation, leadership and navigation, communication, global and cultural effectiveness, ethical practice, critical evaluation, and business acumen.[13] As Figure 1.3 shows, these fall into four clusters of competencies: technical, interpersonal, business, and leadership. In other words, it is not enough to know how to perform tasks specific to human resource management. HR professionals also must be able to work effectively with others, contribute to business success, and lead others ethically.

For each competency, the SHRM model provides definitions, specifics, and standards for the behavior necessary for success at every level in an organization. Here are some examples for each:[14]

- *Human resource expertise* essentially involves understanding and carrying out the functions of human resource management. These behaviors include using HR technology, applying policies and procedures, and keeping up-to-date on HR laws.

FIGURE 1.3
Competencies for HR Professionals

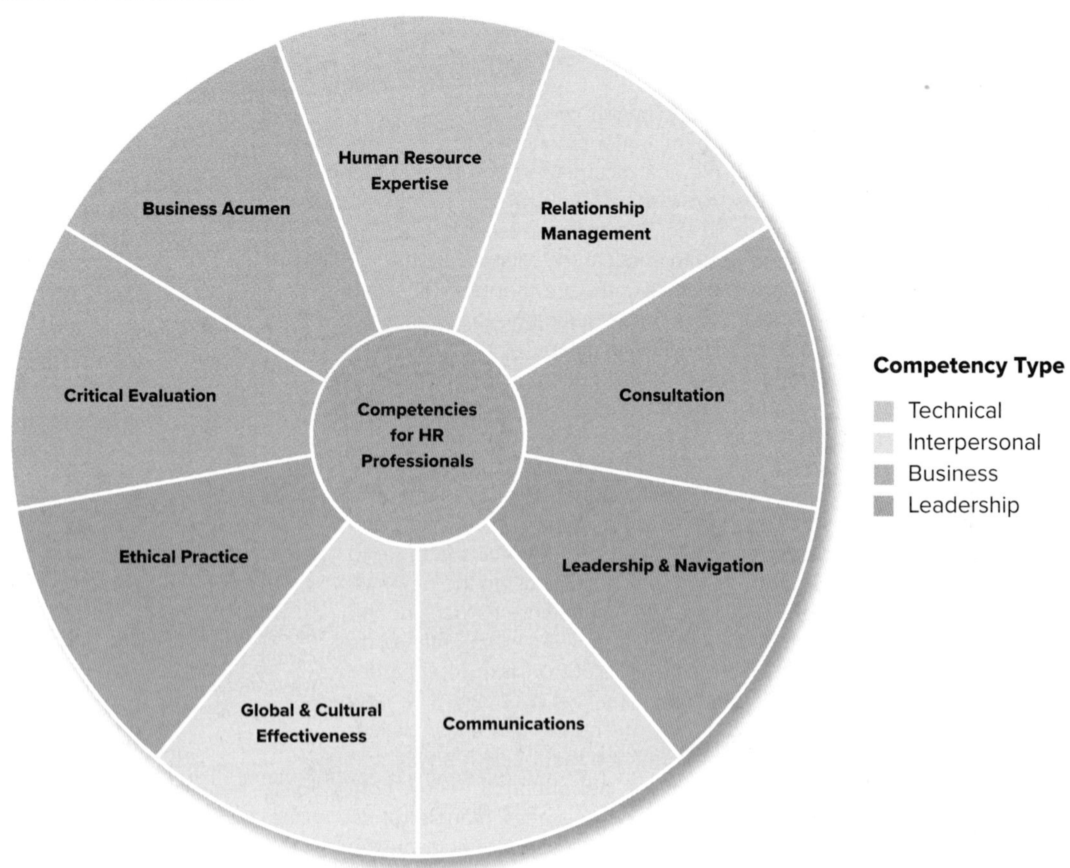

Source: Based on Society for Human Resource Management, *SHRM Competency Model,* www.shrm.org, accessed April 7, 2020.

- *Relationship management* involves handling the personal interactions necessary for providing services and supporting the organization's goals. Behaviors include treating employees respectfully, building trust, and providing great customer service to those served by HR functions.
- *Consultation* refers to the ways HR employees guide others in the organization. They do this through behaviors such as coaching, gathering data to support business decisions, and especially at a senior level, designing solutions in support of business strategy.
- *Leadership and navigation* refer to directing the organization's processes and programs. Depending on one's level in the organization, the necessary behaviors would include behaving consistently with the organization's culture, encouraging people to collaborate, or setting a vision for the HR function or entire organization.
- *Communication* involves the skills needed to exchange information with others inside and outside the organization. Behavior examples include expressing information clearly, providing constructive feedback, and listening effectively.
- *Global and cultural effectiveness* means valuing and considering various people's perspectives. Behaviors include acquiring knowledge of other cultures, resolving conflicts, and supporting inclusiveness so that all can contribute to their fullest.

Best Practices

At Merck, Analytic Skills Have a Measurable Impact

Merck is a global science and technology company based in Germany that makes pharmaceuticals and other product lines. While employees on the business side were used to working with data, the approach to HR management was too often informal and uninformed by analysis. Further, decision makers at facilities around the world applied their own systems and data to arrive at decisions, making it difficult to apply lessons learned in one location to problems experienced in another.

The company decided to improve the analytics capabilities so that they could better serve the company's strategic needs. The People Analytics and Strategic Workforce Planning Group brought together all Merck's employee- and job-related data into a single analytics platform that includes software for modeling future scenarios and conducting statistical analyses. Decision makers around the world now use the same sets of data to answer their own questions. The software interprets natural language, and users are taught to approach analytics from the perspective of the problems they want to solve, not merely report generation or tabulation of annual opinion surveys.

Implementation of Merck's people analytics platform requires much more than technical competencies. In fact, the software takes care of the mathematical calculations. The HR professionals are therefore charged with understanding the business issues that managers can benefit from investigating. They play a role in helping users frame questions and interpret the recommendations.

Even before this, the company's HR professionals needed significant relationship management and communication competencies in order to make the case for using the new system. They made sure to focus not on the idea they were giving managers a new tool, but on the potential for solving practical problems like how to allocate bonus money or deliver performance feedback in a way that improves performance. They consulted with business managers, so models in the system would be relevant and trusted. Managers saw the value of all this effort, and today Merck views the analytics platform as one of its core strengths.

Questions

1. What categories of competencies can you find described in this story?
2. Suppose the HR division had brought in people analytics experts whose other competencies (i.e., outside of critical evaluation) were just average. How would that staffing approach have affected the introduction and use of the data analytics platform at Merck?

Sources: "Merck KGaA Achieved Strategic Value through Self-Serve Analytics," https://www.visier.com, accessed April 7, 2020; Shweta Modgil, "People Analytics Should Be a Part of Company's DNA: Alexis Saussinan, Merck Group," *People Matters,* December 10, 2019, https://www.peoplemattersglobal.com; Aditi Sharma Kalra, "'Data Is Great, But So What?' How Merck Overcame Barriers to Adopting a People Analytics Mindset," *Human Resources,* August 29, 2019, https://www.humanresourcesonline.net; "Leaders in People Analytics: Merck & Co. on the Research-Practice Divide," *re: Work,* March 21, 2018, https://rework.withgoogle.com.

- *Ethical practice* involves applying integrity, accountability, and other core values. Examples include maintaining confidentiality, rewarding ethical behavior, and responding to reports of unethical conduct.
- *Critical evaluation* refers to the interpretation of information needed for making business decisions. Behaviors include gathering relevant data, applying statistical knowledge to understand the data, and finding root causes of problems. (see "Best Practices" for an example).
- *Business acumen* involves understanding how information can be used to support the organization's strategy. Behaviors include gaining and applying knowledge of business principles and how HR functions relate to business success.

An HR organization that doesn't fully identify and acquire these necessary competencies can wind up with shortcomings in knowledge or skills. Given the strategic importance of human resources, a shortcoming in ethics, business relevance, or any of the other competencies can pose significant problems.

HR Responsibilities of Supervisors

LO 1-4 Explain the role of supervisors in human resource management.

Although many organizations have human resource departments, HR activities are by no means limited to the specialists who staff those departments. In large organizations, HR departments advise and support the activities of the other departments. In small organizations, there may be an HR specialist, but many HR activities are carried out by line supervisors. Either way, non-HR managers need to be familiar with the basics of HRM and their role in managing human resources.

At a start-up company, the supervisors are typically the company's founders. Unfortunately, not all founders recognize their HR responsibilities, but those that do have a powerful advantage. For example, Becky Robinson handled hiring, payroll, and other HR needs when she started Weaving Influence, a marketing company. When she was concentrating her efforts on HR activities for the small business, company revenues dropped. Robinson quickly recognized she needed to keep her focus on building the business and turned the HR tasks over to an outside consultant.[15]

As we will see in later chapters, supervisors typically have responsibilities related to all the HR functions. Figure 1.4 shows some HR responsibilities that supervisors are likely to be involved in. Organizations depend on supervisors to help them determine what kinds of work need to be done (job analysis and design) and how many employees are needed (HR planning). Supervisors typically interview job candidates and participate in the decisions about which candidates to hire. Many organizations expect supervisors to train employees in some or all aspects of the employees' jobs. Supervisors conduct performance appraisals and may recommend pay increases. And, of course, supervisors play a key role in employee relations because they are most often the voice of management for their employees, representing the company on a day-to-day basis. In all these activities, supervisors can participate in HRM by taking into consideration the ways that decisions and policies will affect their employees. Understanding the principles of communication, motivation, and other elements of human behavior can help supervisors inspire the best from the organization's human resources.

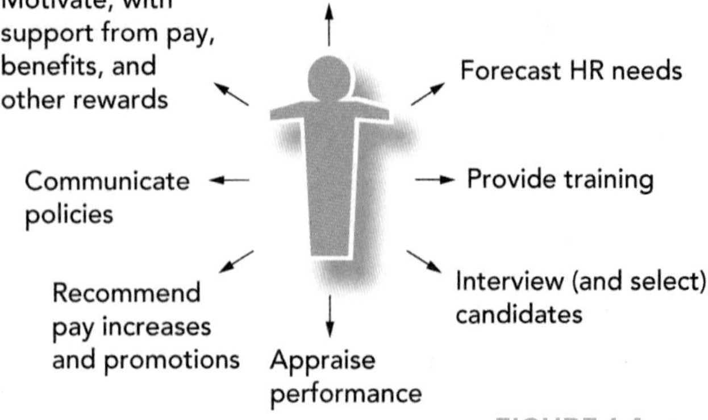

FIGURE 1.4
Supervisors' Involvement in HRM: Common Areas of Involvement

Ethics in Human Resource Management

LO 1-5 Discuss ethical issues in human resource management.

Ethics
The fundamental principles of right and wrong.

Whenever people's actions affect one another, ethical issues arise, and business decisions are no exception. **Ethics** refers to fundamental principles of right and wrong; ethical behavior is behavior that is consistent with those principles. Business decisions, including HRM decisions, should be ethical, and many executives see treatment of employees as a top concern (see "Did You Know?"). Nevertheless, surveys indicate that the general public and managers do not have positive perceptions of the ethical conduct of U.S. businesses. For example, in a Gallup poll on honesty and ethics in 23 occupations, only 20% of Americans rated business executives high or very high, while 30% rated them low or very low. And within organizations, a recent survey of workers found that nearly 30% of U.S. workers had witnessed some form of unethical conduct at their workplace.[16]

Many ethical issues in the workplace involve human resource management. An issue that has recently received attention is the treatment of women in the workplace. While

Did You Know?

HR Is Focused on Employee Well-Being

According to Mercer's recent survey of business and HR executives, their most widespread concern is supporting employees' health and well-being. Number two on the list is employees' expectations for a positive digital experience at work.

The concern for employee well-being is especially impressive, given that the survey data were being analyzed as the COVID-19 pandemic was gaining momentum in many parts of the world. For their part, employees surveyed months earlier, before the pandemic dominated the news, were particularly concerned about help with long-term financial planning and keeping up with expenses. The financial shock associated with the pandemic is likely to have intensified those concerns, increasing the stress of being a worker in today's tumultuous economy.

Concern for the well-being of others is a basic ethical value. Some ways employers can put into practice their concern for employees include open and honest communication about changes, giving employees control over working conditions when that is feasible, and creating conditions in which employees can build positive relationships, such as teamwork and mentoring.

Question

To what extent do you think employers are responsible for the well-being of their employees?

Sources: Win with Empathy: Global Talent Trends 2020, Mercer, https://www.mercer.com, accessed March 31, 2020; "Employee Well-Being Is Critical to Business Success, Say CEOs," LifeWorks, October 31, 2019, https://www.lifeworks.com; Jeffrey Pfeffer, "The Overlooked Essentials of Employee Well-Being," *McKinsey Quarterly,* September 2018, https://www.mckinsey.com.

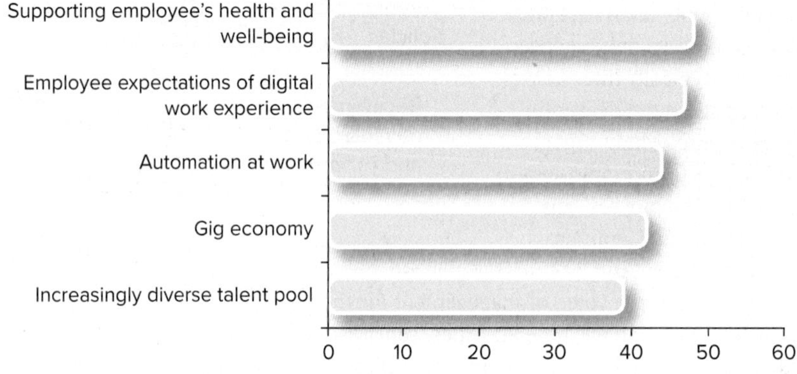

basic principles of dignity and respect would indicate that harassing employees is out of bounds, the recent #MeToo social movement highlighting the widespread sexual harassment of women may be to thank for the decrease in reports of harassment of women and men in the workplace. As we will see in Chapter 3, this kind of conduct is illegal. Providing training about sexual harassment and establishing processes for handling complaints fall under the umbrella of HR responsibilities.[17] In addition to addressing ethics-related embarrassments, HR professionals should consider that a reputation for being ethical may help companies attract employees.

Employee Rights

In the context of ethical human resource management, HR managers must view employees as having basic rights. Such a view reflects ethical principles embodied in the U.S. Constitution and Bill of Rights. A widely adopted understanding of human rights, based on the work of the philosopher Immanuel Kant, as well as the tradition of the Enlightenment, assumes that in a moral universe, every person has certain basic rights:

- *Right of free consent*—People have the right to be treated only as they knowingly and willingly consent to be treated. An example that applies to employees would be that employees should know the nature of the job they are being hired to do; the employer should not deceive them.
- *Right of privacy*—People have the right to do as they wish in their private lives, and they have the right to control what they reveal about private activities. One way an employer respects this right is by keeping employees' personal records confidential.
- *Right of freedom of conscience*—People have the right to refuse to do what violates their moral beliefs, as long as these beliefs reflect commonly accepted norms. A supervisor who demands that an employee do something that is unsafe or environmentally damaging may be violating this right if the task conflicts with the employee's values. (Such behavior could be illegal as well as unethical.)
- *Right of freedom of speech*—People have the right to criticize an organization's ethics if they do so in good conscience and their criticism does not violate the rights of individuals in the organization. Many organizations address this right by offering hot lines or policies and procedures designed to handle complaints from employees.
- *Right to due process*—If people believe their rights are being violated, they have the right to a fair and impartial hearing. As we will see in Chapter 3, Congress has addressed this right in some circumstances by establishing agencies to hear complaints when employees believe their employer has not provided a fair hearing. For example, the Equal Employment Opportunity Commission may prosecute complaints of discrimination if it believes the employer did not fairly handle the problem.

One way to think about ethics in business is that the morally correct action is the one that minimizes encroachments on and avoids violations of these rights.

Organizations often face situations in which the rights of employees are affected. In particular, the right of privacy of health information has received much attention in recent years. Computerized record keeping and computer networks have greatly increased the ways people can gain (authorized or unauthorized) access to records about individuals. Health-related records can be particularly sensitive. HRM responsibilities include the ever-growing challenge of maintaining confidentiality and security of employees' health information as required by the Health Insurance Portability and Accountability Act (HIPAA).

Standards for Ethical Behavior

Ethical, successful companies act according to four principles.[18] First, in their relationships with customers, vendors, and clients, ethical and successful companies emphasize mutual benefits. Second, employees assume responsibility for the actions of the company. Third, such companies have a sense of purpose or vision that employees value and use in their day-to-day work. Finally, they emphasize fairness; that is, another person's interests count as much as their own.

Consider how these principles might apply to Xplane, a consulting firm based in Portland, Oregon. The company brings together highly creative people to solve complex problems. The commitment to helping clients craft visionary solutions provides a sense of purpose. Ensuring that employees take time to rest and recharge, so they can do their best thinking, generates mutual benefits for the company and its clients, as well as for the employees personally. HR supports the need for time off with a very flexible benefits package. Employees may take as much paid time off as they want, whenever they want. They also have the ability to choose from up to $200 in reimbursements for expenses related to work/life

FIGURE 1.5
Standards for Identifying Ethical Practices

balance–say, gym fees, baby-sitting, or dog walking.[19] If all of this helps people work harder on projects, that result is another mutual benefit.

For human resource practices to be considered ethical, they must satisfy the three basic standards summarized in Figure 1.5.[20] First, HRM practices must result in the greatest good for the largest number of people. Second, employment practices must respect basic human rights of privacy, due process, consent, and free speech. Third, managers must treat employees and customers equitably and fairly. The issue of equity and fairness arises at Xplane with regard to the $200 monthly allotment for work/life benefits. In one sense, it is fairer than the more common approach of the HR department selecting particular benefits, in that everyone has a chance to get benefits of equal value. If, for example, the company offered child care, this benefit would only have value to employees with young children; at Xplane, a childless employee has other benefits to choose from. Not every employee spends the full $200, but the choice is left to the employee. Similarly, with no defined limit for paid time off, some employees will take more than others, but the employees have control over their own choices. Katie Augsburger, Xplane's manager of employee experience, says the issue she needs to address is that some employees take less time away than the company believes is necessary for recharging, so the company is considering communications to encourage employees to take time off at least three weeks a year.[21]

Careers in Human Resource Management

LO 1-6 Describe typical careers in human resource management.

There are many different types of jobs in the HRM profession. Figure 1.6 shows selected HRM positions and their salaries. The salaries vary depending on education and experience, as well as the type of industry in which the person works. As you can see from Figure 1.6, some positions involve work in specialized areas of HRM such as recruiting, compensation, or employee benefits. Most HR generalists make $40,000 to $115,000, depending on their experience and education level. Generalists usually perform the full range of HRM activities, including recruiting, training, compensation, and employee relations.

The vast majority of HRM professionals have a college degree, and many also have completed postgraduate work. The typical field of study is business (especially human resources or industrial relations), but some HRM professionals have degrees in the social sciences (economics or psychology), the humanities, and law programs. Those who have completed

FIGURE 1.6
Median Salaries for HRM Positions

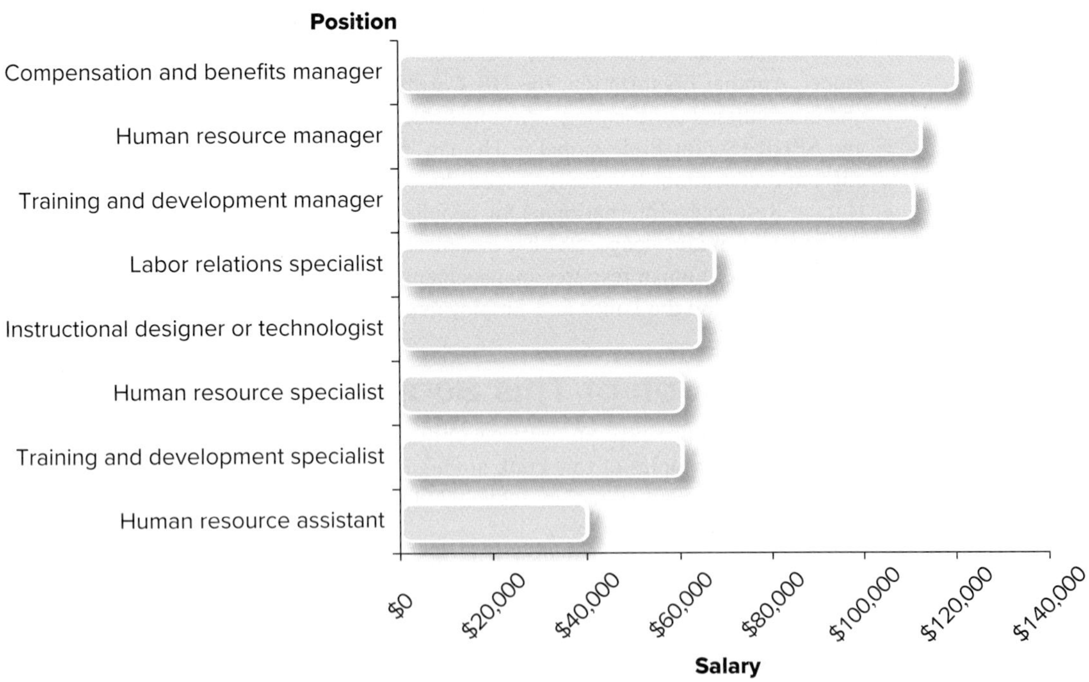

Source: Data from *O*NET OnLine*, https://www.onetonline.org, accessed April 8, 2020.

graduate work have master's degrees in HR management, business management, or a similar field. This is important because to be successful in HR, you need to speak the same language as people in the other business functions. You have to have credibility as a business leader, so you must be able to understand finance and to build a business case for HR activities.

HR professionals can increase their career opportunities by taking advantage of training and development programs. These may include taking courses toward a master's degree, studying to pass an exam for a professional certification, accepting assignments to spend time observing, or "shadowing," a manager in another department, or taking a position in another department to learn more about the business. An HR leader who has benefited from this approach is Chuck Edward, Microsoft's head of global talent acquisition. Edward, who told an interviewer he has "always craved learning," became interested in organizational psychology while in college. After he earned his psychology degree, he went to graduate school to study for a master's degree in human resources. Realizing that his fellow students had business experience and he did not, he spent his first summer of graduate school at an unpaid internship, supplemented with helping out at area staffing agencies. This gave him enough experience to land a job as an HR manager with 3M, which rotated him through different roles, moving him to a new job every 18 months. The challenge of mastering a broad range of HR positions prepared Edward to move to a regional HR leadership role at Pepsi, where management urged him to learn about the business. That meant learning took the form of watching and listening to be sure he understood business needs and constraints before moving forward with his ideas. Edward's drive for learning makes him an excellent fit for Microsoft's culture of smart people with a desire to constantly improve.[22]

Some HRM professionals have a professional certification in HRM, but many more are members of professional associations. The primary professional organization for HRM is the Society for Human Resource Management (SHRM). SHRM, the world's largest human resource management association, provides education and information services, conferences and seminars, government and media representation, and online services and publications (such as *HR Magazine*). SHRM has developed two levels of certification (SHRM-Certified Professional and SHRM-Senior Certified Professional) related to its nine-competency model. Another organization, the HR Certification Institute (HRCI), also offers national and international certifications. Among these are PHR (Professional in Human Resources) and SPHR (Senior Professional in Human Resources), based on work experience, knowledge, and education. It recently added the certification aPHRi (Associate Professional in Human Resources-International) for people who are new to the field and want to acquire a foundation of knowledge.[23] Other organizations support professional development in particular areas of human resource management; two examples are the Association for Talent Development and the Labor and Employment Relations Association.

Organization of This Book

This chapter has provided an overview of human resource management to give you a sense of its scope. The topics of this book are organized according to the broad areas of human resource management shown in Table 1.3. The numbers in the table refer to the part and chapter numbers.

The remaining chapters in Part 1 discuss aspects of the human resource environment: trends shaping the field (Chapter 2), legal requirements (Chapter 3), and the work to be done by the organization, which is the basis for designing jobs (Chapter 4). Part 2 explores the responsibilities involved in acquiring and equipping human resources for current and future positions: HR planning and recruiting (Chapter 5), selection and placement of employees (Chapter 6), training (Chapter 7), and developing (Chapter 8). Part 3 turns to the assessment and improvement of performance through creation of high-performance

TABLE 1.3

Topics Covered in This Book

I. The Human Resource Environment
   1. Managing Human Resources
   2. Trends in Human Resource Management
   3. Providing Equal Employment Opportunity and a Safe Workplace
   4. Analyzing Work and Designing Jobs

II. Acquiring, Training, and Developing Human Resources
   5. Planning for and Recruiting Human Resources
   6. Selecting Employees and Placing Them in Jobs
   7. Training Employees
   8. Developing Employees for Future Success

III. Assessing and Improving Performance
   9. Creating and Maintaining High-Performance Organizations
   10. Managing Employees' Performance
   11. Separating and Retaining Employees

IV. Compensating Human Resources
   12. Establishing a Pay Structure
   13. Recognizing Employee Contributions with Pay
   14. Providing Employee Benefits

V. Meeting Other HR Goals
   15. Collective Bargaining and Labor Relations
   16. Managing Human Resources Globally

organizations (Chapter 9), performance management (Chapter 10), and appropriate handling of employee separation when the organization determines it no longer wants or needs certain employees (Chapter 11). Part 4 addresses topics related to compensation: pay structure (Chapter 12), pay to recognize performance (Chapter 13), and benefits (Chapter 14). Part 5 explores special topics faced by HR managers today: human resource management in organizations where employees have or are seeking union representation (Chapter 15) and international human resource management (Chapter 16).

Along with examples highlighting how HRM helps a company maintain high performance, the chapters offer various other features to help you connect the principles to real-world situations. "Best Practices" boxes tell success stories related to the chapter's topic. "HR Oops!" boxes identify situations gone wrong and invite you to find better alternatives. "HR How To" boxes provide details about how to carry out a practice in each HR area. "Did You Know?" boxes are snapshots of interesting statistics related to chapter topics. Many chapters also include an "HRM Social" box identifying ways that human resource professionals are applying social media to help their organizations excel in the fast-changing modern world. In addition, "HR Analytics & Decision Making" features throughout the book highlight an evidence-based approach to management, which focuses on people, employees, and human capital.

THINKING ETHICALLY

WHOSE SIDE ARE YOU ON?

The roles of HR professionals can be complex. The HR goal of equipping the organization with a well-qualified, highly motivated workforce should be consistent with managers' and the organization's goals for business performance. But at the level of particular decisions, employees and managers may not see much alignment between their positions. Decisions about pay, for example, affect the employee's wallet and the company's bottom line in opposite ways. HR professionals develop skills in navigating these differences with clear expectations and accurate data, so both parties feel they have been treated fairly.

Experienced HR professionals advise that most of these conflicting sets of expectations can be resolved by putting the company's long-term value ahead of any quick wins for a particular employee or manager. Managers generally understand that treating employees fairly and honestly is in the company's long-term interest, and employees generally understand that the company has to set spending limits in order to survive.

Ethical challenges arise for HR practitioners in the less common situations where managers fail to align their interests with the company's. This problem arises when an employee complains that a highly valued manager or employee has been engaging in harassment. If the HR professional conducts an investigation and finds evidence of misconduct, executives may hesitate to take action against the valuable harasser. They may pressure the HR department to let it go or simply move one of the parties to another department. They may press to keep the story quiet, which means other victims will miss a chance to come forward and future victims will have no warning. In these situations, HR professionals are caught between doing what serves the executives who want to maintain the status quo and doing what serves the employee who spoke up. Victims have complained that the usual choice is to serve the executives, so some do not bother to speak up about misconduct–thus contributing to a climate in which misdeeds continue.

Questions

1. Consider a situation where a new sales associate complains that a top-earning sales manager has been harassing her. Who would be affected by (a) a decision to fire the sales manager; and (b) a decision to tell the employee the manager is valuable, and she should figure out how to handle the situation herself?
2. What duties does the HR department receiving this complaint have to (a) the sales associate; (b) the sales manager; and (c) the company that employs them?

Sources: Laurie Ruettimann, "Why HR Is Powerless to Effectively Handle Sexual Harassment Claims," *Vox,* October 3, 2019, https://www.vox.com; Anne Sanders, "HR's Delicate Balancing Act," *Business NH,* January 2018, pp. 46–48; Jennifer Arnold, "Whose Side Are You On, Anyway?" *HR Magazine,* June/July 2017, pp. 109–112; Desda Moss, "Career Lessons from Coretta Rushing: Always Re-Create Yourself," *HR Magazine,* February 2017, pp. 61–63.

SUMMARY

LO 1-1 Define human resource management, and explain how HRM contributes to an organization's performance.

- Human resource management consists of an organization's policies, practices, and systems that influence employees' behavior, attitudes, and performance.
- HRM influences who works for an organization and how.
- Well-managed human resources can be a source of sustainable competitive advantage by contributing to quality, profits, and customer satisfaction.

LO 1-2 Identify the responsibilities of human resource departments.

- Analyze and design jobs.
- Recruit and select employees.
- Equip employees by training and developing them.
- Through performance management, ensure that employees' activities and outputs match the organization's goals.
- Plan and administer pay and employee benefits.
- Engage in employee relations–for example, communications and collective bargaining.
- Establish and administer personnel policies and keep records.
- Help ensure compliance with labor laws.
- Support the development and execution of corporate strategy.

LO 1-3 Summarize the types of competencies needed for human resource management.

- Technical competencies involve HR expertise.
- Interpersonal competencies are relationship management, communication, and global and cultural effectiveness.
- Business competencies are business acumen, critical evaluation, and consultation.
- Leadership competencies are leadership and navigation, as well as ethical practice.
- For each competency, the SHRM model provides definitions, specifics, and standards for the behavior necessary for success at every level in an organization.

LO 1-4 Explain the role of supervisors in human resource management.

- Help analyze work.
- Interview job candidates and participate in selection decisions.
- Provide employee training.
- Conduct performance appraisals.
- Recommend pay increases.
- Represent the company to their employees.

LO 1-5 Discuss ethical issues in human resource management.

- Should make decisions that result in the greatest good for the largest number of people.
- Should respect basic rights of privacy, due process, consent, and free speech.
- Should treat others equitably and fairly.
- Should recognize ethical issues that arise in areas such as employee privacy, protection of employee safety, and fairness in employment practices.

LO 1-6 Describe typical careers in human resource management.

- Careers may involve specialized work (e.g., recruiting, training, or labor relations).
- Others may be generalists, performing a range of activities.
- A college degree in business or social sciences usually is required.
- People skills must be balanced with attention to details of law and knowledge of business.

KEY TERMS

human resource management (HRM), 3
human capital, 4
job analysis, 7
job design, 7
recruitment, 8
selection, 8
training, 8
development, 8
performance management, 9
workforce analytics, 11
human resource planning, 13
talent management, 13
evidence-based HR, 13
sustainability, 13
stakeholders, 13
ethics, 17

REVIEW AND DISCUSSION QUESTIONS

1. How can human resource management contribute to a company's success? *(LO 1-1)*
2. Imagine that a small manufacturing company decides to invest in a materials resource planning (MRP) system. This is a computerized information system that improves efficiency by automating such work as planning needs for resources, ordering materials, and scheduling work on the shop floor. The company hopes that with the new MRP system, it can grow by quickly and efficiently processing small orders for a variety of products. Which of the human resource functions are likely to be affected by this change? How can human resource management help the organization carry out this change successfully? *(LO 1-2)*
3. What competencies are important for success in human resource management? Which of these competencies are already strengths of yours? Which would you like to develop? *(LO 1-3)*
4. Traditionally, human resource management practices were developed and administered by the company's human resource department. Line managers are now playing a major role in developing and implementing HRM practices. Why do you think non-HR managers are becoming more involved? *(LO 1-4)*
5. If you were to start a business, which aspects of human resource management would you want to entrust to specialists? Why? *(LO 1-3)*
6. Why do all managers and supervisors need knowledge and skills related to human resource management? *(LO 1-4)*
7. Federal law requires that employers not discriminate on the basis of a person's race, sex, national origin, or age over 40. Is this also an ethical requirement? A competitive requirement? Explain. *(LO 1-5)*
8. When a restaurant employee slipped on spilled soup and fell, requiring the evening off to recover, the owner realized that workplace safety was an issue to which she had not devoted much time. A friend warned the owner that if she started creating a lot of safety rules and procedures, she would lose her focus on customers and might jeopardize the future of the restaurant. The safety problem is beginning to feel like an ethical dilemma. Suggest some ways the restaurant owner might address this dilemma. What aspects of human resource management are involved? *(LO 1-5)*
9. A friend hears you are taking this course and mentions an interest in an HRM career. Based on this chapter's description, what advice would you give your friend? *(LO 1-6)*

SELF-ASSESSMENT EXERCISE

Do You Have What It Takes to Work in HR?

Instructions: Read each statement and circle *yes* or *no.*

Yes No 1. I have leadership and management skills I have developed through prior job experiences, extracurricular activities, community service, or other noncourse activities.

Yes No 2. I have excellent communications, dispute resolution, and interpersonal skills.

Yes No 3. I can demonstrate an understanding of the fundamentals of running a business and making a profit.

Yes No 4. I can use spreadsheets and the Internet, and I am familiar with information systems technology.

Yes No 5. I can work effectively with people of different cultural backgrounds.

Yes No 6. I have expertise in more than one area of human resource management.

Yes No 7. I have a willingness to learn.

Yes No 8. I listen to issues before reacting with solutions.

Yes No 9. I can collect and analyze data for business solutions.

Yes No 10. I am a good team member.

Yes No 11. I have knowledge of local and global economic trends.

Yes No 12. I demonstrate accountability for my actions.

Scoring: The greater the number of yes answers, the better prepared you are to work as an HR professional. For questions you answered no, you should seek courses and experiences to change your answers to *yes*–and better prepare yourself for a career in HR!

Sources: Based on J. Trammell, "4 Things CEOs Want from HR Leadership," *Entrepreneur,* January 19, 2016, https://www.entrepreneur.com; SHRM, "Elements for Success Competency Model, 2012," www.shrm.org, March 21, 2012; B.E. Kaufman, "What Companies Want from HR Graduates," *HR Magazine,* September 1994.

TAKING RESPONSIBILITY

PwC's Anti-Racism Strategy Starts at the Top

PwC (formerly PricewaterhouseCoopers) is a global firm providing businesses with auditing, tax preparation, and management consulting services. Given that its clientele has diverse employees and customers, PwC has long appreciated the strategic importance of talented employees representing many different perspectives. So when the death of George Floyd under the knee of a Minneapolis police officer once again brought issues of racial justice into the limelight in the United States in the spring of 2020, PwC managers had already been engaged with the topic.

Sadly, another police killing of a Black man had stimulated the conversation at PwC two years before this. A senior PwC associate, Botham Jean, had been shot to death by an off-duty police officer while watching football in his Dallas apartment. At trial, the officer said she had entered the apartment by mistake, thinking it was her own and that Jean was an intruder, but the officer was convicted of murder. PwC's U.S. chairman, Tim Ryan, joined the mourning and sent employees an e-mail saying, "It is important that we all take time to understand the experiences our underrepresented minorities–and especially, in this situation, our Black colleagues–experience in everyday life so that we can all be better coworkers, friends and allies." Ryan (who is white) had already been encouraging employees to engage in constructive conversations about race, but the shooting of one of the firm's own brought a new intensity to the concern.

According to Ryan, the motive for encouraging these conversations is a fundamental belief that people contribute the most to the organization when they can openly share their views and experiences. Further, employees are likelier to commit to staying with the organization when they feel heard and able to contribute. So for Ryan, the effort to communicate is part of the culture, not a short-term program. He talked with the rest of the leadership team to ensure they were in agreement with these principles.

One of those leaders is Shannon Schuyler, PwC's chief purpose and inclusion officer. When Ryan opened up racial issues for conversation, she was impressed with the openness and the lessons about how racial justice affects employees. For example, participants learned that at times, when Black employees were tardy, it was because they had been delayed by police stopping them during their drive to work.

In 2020, following the shooting of George Floyd, Ryan again wrote to all his employees, this time listing six actions PwC would be taking "to support our Black colleagues, to improve diversity and inclusion efforts within our firm, and to contribute to the efforts of those who are fighting for racial justice and equality on the front lines." The first action was creation of a staff advisory council composed of employees at all levels to consider how to advance progress on diversity and inclusion. The company's leadership also committed to transparency in communicating its goals and progress on diversity, as well as support for outside organizations working on justice and inclusion. Employees interested in working at nonprofits or on policy issues can do so on company time. In public comments, Ryan noted that employees were upset, exhausted, and looking for action, not just statements, from employers.

Despite all the good intentions at the top, PwC has work to do if it wants to excel at diversity and inclusion. While Ryan notes that efforts at planning for future leadership have led to two of three heads of major business lines being Black men, only one member of the board of directors was Black at the time of the 2020 promises. PwC's leadership hopes that their goals and transparency about progress will help the firm continue to improve.

Questions

1. A major responsibility of HR departments is to support the organization's strategy. Pick one of the other HR responsibilities (such as recruiting, hiring, or training), and briefly say how it could support PwC's strategy of enabling full participation by diverse employees.
2. PwC's CEO aims to communicate fully the firm's progress in achieving diversity and inclusion. Suggest two measures PwC could use to track its progress.

Sources: PwC corporate website, "Careers" and "About Us," https://www.pwc.com, accessed June 21, 2020; Jeanne Sahadi, "PwC Chairman: How Corporate America Can Stop Failing Black Workers and Diversify Its Ranks," *CNN*, June 10, 2020, https://www.cnn.com; Timothy F. Ryan, "What PwC Is Doing to Stand Up against Racism," *LinkedIn*, June 4, 2020, https://www.linkedin.com; Kevin Stankiewicz, "Executive at Top U.S. Accounting Firm Details Plan to Combat Racism, Says Workers 'Want Action,'" *CNBC*, June 4, 2020, https://www.cnbc.com; Kathryn Dill, "CEOs and Big Businesses Speak Out on Racism, Police Violence," *The Wall Street Journal*, June 2, 2020, https://www.wsj.com; Mareesa Nicosia, "20 Minutes With: Shannon Schuyler, U.S. Chief Purpose and Inclusion Officer at PwC," *Barrons*, October 28, 2019, https://www.barrons.com; Vanessa Fuhrmans, "This Boss Is Making Race Relations a Business Matter," *The Wall Street Journal*, March 13, 2019, https://www.wsj.com.

MANAGING TALENT

Old Navy's Talent Strategy Fills Some Gaps

Retailing is a difficult business, involving stiff competition both online and off, along with fast-changing consumer preferences. So far, Old Navy is one of the winners. A division of The Gap, Old Navy has an attractive position in the market, offering what it calls "democracy of style": low prices on "American essentials," so that almost anyone can afford them. As Gap closes hundreds of its Banana Republic and Gap locations, it is opening Old Navy and Athleta stores.

This strategy for Old Navy requires low costs, even as a strong economy with falling unemployment rates is making jobs harder to fill. Retail jobs tend to be low-paying, and job applicants are not always well qualified. Worse, those who do take jobs often quit. Therefore, a key business challenge for Old Navy is to keep entry-level positions filled with qualified, motivated workers.

One solution to the need for talent started out as an effort by Gap to address a social problem–the struggle of teens, especially in poor neighborhoods, to land a job. Teens who have never worked tend to lag behind the overall workforce for years afterward. To combat the problem, Gap created an internship program called This Way Ahead (TWA). The program partners with local nonprofits that provide training in basic job skills such as customer service, time management, and communication. Participants get part-time jobs at Old Navy and other stores under the Gap umbrella, where they can practice the skills they are learning. Most of them go on to get an offer of a permanent job.

According to Old Navy HR director Andrea Shimer, the retailer discovered that these employees are particularly well equipped for work in the stores. They tend to be enthusiastic about their jobs, and they stay with the company twice as long as employees hired through other channels. Some of them go on to college but continue to work part-time; some move up to management positions. An additional benefit is that store managers who serve in the TWA program increase their skills in developing the employees who report to them.

Based on the success of This Way Ahead, Gap has made it part of the company's strategy for talent acquisition. It uses the program to provide interns to 172 Old Navy and other Gap-owned stores. Looking ahead, the company has set a goal to make TWA the source of 5% of its entry-level employees by 2025. TWA's creation and rollout are also consistent with Old Navy's HR goal of creating "a workplace culture that embraces diversity and inclusion and treats every individual with dignity and respect," in the words of Kisha Modica, Gap's senior director of diversity and inclusion.

Questions

1. In your own words, briefly summarize the business problem facing The Gap and the effectiveness of This Way Ahead as a solution to the problem.
2. Suggest one or two ways Old Navy's HR department could use data to measure the success of This Way Ahead in providing a source of talent. That is, what measures would indicate success?

Sources: Gap Inc., "This Way Ahead," https://www.gapincsustainability.com, accessed April 8, 2020; Pamela N. Danziger, "What Gap Needs to Do Next after Canceling Old Navy Spin-Off," *Forbes,* January 19, 2020, https://www.forbes.com; "Old Navy Named One of the 2019 Best Places in Retail by Great Place to Work® and Fortune," November 7, 2019, https://corporate.gapinc.com; "Gap Inc. Expands Its Job Program for Opportunity Youth to 53 Cities, Introduces Year-Round Hiring Strategy," *BusinessWire,* August 15, 2018, https://www.businesswire.com; Brian Sodoma, "A Running Start: How Gap, Old Navy, and Banana Republic Help Teens and Young Adults Land That All-Important First Job," *Forbes,* September 12, 2016, https://www.forbes.com.

HR IN SMALL BUSINESS

Impossible Foods' Business Mission

If ever there was a mission-driven company, Impossible Foods is it. Pat Brown, the founder and CEO, is a biochemist who decided in his mid-fifties to shift from corporate research to helping the planet. Brown observed that one of the biggest contributors to climate change is beef production. In the United States, more than one-fourth of the land is devoted to cattle, which emit methane, a particularly damaging greenhouse gas. Recognizing that people love hamburgers, Brown set up a laboratory to identify the components of beef and bring together the same chemistry from plant sources. As Brown sees it, if the world's beef lovers would switch to his Impossible Burger, humans would eat delicious food without destroying the planet as we know it. This requires a product that is widely available and affordable.

Brown and his team of scientists pinned down a recipe that has received favorable reviews, but building a company to make it available is at least as challenging. For the first few years, most Impossible Foods employees were research scientists. Brown hired Dana Worth to run a sales operation, which won orders from grocery stores, Burger King, Qdoba, and White Castle. This put a strain on the company's single assembly line, which was running just one shift. Still, for Brown, the mission has remained central. He says a key part of his job is "reminding people of the importance of what we are doing."

The company hired Dennis Woodside from Google to serve as president, applying his experience in managing operations. Woodside, who expected to focus on the sales team, quickly became aware that production workers were overstressed and exhausted. Woodside sought volunteers from the sales force to work on a second assembly line while the company arranged a deal with a food processor in Chicago to make the plant-based meat product.

Despite the stress induced by the fast ramp-up of activity, Brown cares about doing the right thing for his people as well as the planet. He aims to pay what he calls a "thriving wage," that is, more than a living wage. And during the COVID-19 epidemic, he put safety ahead of production targets, sending workers home with full pay. Because the company produces food, it could have continued operating, but Brown determined that enough products were in inventory already to fill its existing orders.

Impossible Foods recently hired Brian Miller to be its chief people officer, reporting to Woodside. Miller's prior position was vice president for talent, development, and inclusion at another biotech start-up, Gilead Sciences, so he has experienced the rapid expansion of a business. He previously ran a consulting firm that specialized in helping HR departments apply technology.

Questions

1. Brian Miller is taking over the top HR job at a company that has been moving fast without a strategic HR vision. Which of the HR functions would you recommend that Miller prioritize? Why?
2. Based on the information provided, what ethical standards is Impossible Foods demonstrating with regard to its employees? Where do you see areas for improvement?

Sources: Impossible Foods company page, https://impossiblefoods.com/company, accessed April 8, 2020; John D. Stoll, "Impossible Foods CEO on Running a $4 Billion Startup from Children's Bedroom," *The Wall Street Journal,* March 19, 2020, https://www.wsj.com; John D. Stoll, "The Anti-CEO's Mission Impossible: Use Capitalism to Kill Meat," *The Wall Street Journal,* February 15, 2020, https://www.wsj.com; "Impossible Foods Hires Biotech Executive and Startup Founder Brian Miller as Chief People Officer," news release, February 4, 2020, https://impossiblefoods.com; Burt Helm, "Company of the Year: Impossible Foods," *Inc.,* Winter 2019-2020, pp. 28-40, 118.

NOTES

1. "Leadership at IQTalent Partners," https://www.iqtalentpartners.com, accessed April 7, 2020; J. McHenry, "The Changing World of Work: A Conversation with David Windley and Jeff McHenry," *The Changing World of Work* (blog of the University of Southern California Bovard College), https://bovardcollege.usc.edu, accessed April 7, 2020; N. Parsi, "Elevating the Profession," *HR Magazine,* Summer 2019, p. 26.
2. C. Boon, D. N. Den Hartog, D. P. Lepak, "A Systematic Review of Human Resource Management Systems and Their Measurement," *Journal of Management* 45 (2019), pp. 2498-2537; E. K. Melton and K. J. Meier, "For the Want of a Nail: The Interaction of Managerial Capacity and Human Resource Management on Organizational Performance," *Public Administration Review* 77 (1) (January/February 2017), pp. 118-130.
3. J. Molis, "Attracting and Retaining Top Talent: 5 Ways to Make Them Come to You," *Triangle Business Journal,* August 29, 2019, https://www.bizjournals.com; S. Keller and M. Meaney, "Attracting and Retaining the Right Talent," *McKinsey & Company,* November 2017, https://mckinsey.com.
4. J. Boitnott, "5 Steps to Investing Wisely in Human Capital Development," *Entrepreneur,* https://www.entrepreneur.com, accessed April 7, 2020; A. A. Fink, "The Case for Competencies," *HR Magazine,* May 2017, pp. 22-23; S. A. Snell and J. W. Dean, "Integrated Manufacturing and Human Resource Management," *Academy of Management Journal* 35 (1992), pp. 467-504.
5. Business Wire, "Dollar General Announces Approximately $35 Million Investment in Employees," *Yahoo Finance,* March 24, 2020, https://finance.yahoo.com.
6. V. Bolden-Barrett, "Report: HR Staffing Is at 1.4 per 100 Employees, an All-Time High," *HR Dive,* July 20, 2017, https://www.hrdive.com.
7. E. E. Lawler, "From Human Resource Management to Organizational Effectiveness," *Human Resource Management* 44 (2005), pp. 165-169.
8. S. Snell, "Control Theory in Strategic Human Resource Management: The Mediating Effect of Administrative Information," *Academy of Management Journal* 35 (1992), pp. 292-327.
9. "All Aboard at Amtrak," https://careers.amtrak.com, accessed April 7, 2020; Mark McGraw, "Back on Track," *Human Resource Executive,* October 2016, pp. 14-16.
10. K. Foster, "Tuition-Free Program for Aspiring Medical Assistants, Phlebotomist Offered by Ochsner Health System," *WAFB,* March 29, 2019, https://www.wafb.com; D. Meinert, "Is Your Workforce Ready?" *HR Magazine,* June/July 2017, pp. 42-48.
11. G. Shaughnessy, "9 Ways That HR and People Teams Can Drive Sustainability," *Sage People,* November 25, 2019, https://www.sagepeople.com; "15 Effective Ways HR Can Help Create a Sustainable Company Culture," *Forbes,* September 25, 2018, https://www.forbes.com.
12. G. Tognini, "Coronavirus Business Tracker: How the Private Sector Is Fighting the COVID-19 Pandemic," *Forbes,* April 8, 2020, https://www.forbes.com.
13. Society for Human Resource Management (SHRM), "SHRM Competency Model," https://www.shrm.org, accessed April 7, 2020.
14. "SHRM Competency Model."
15. J. M. Rosenberg, "Don't DIY: Business Owners Delegate Human Resources Tasks," *USA Today,* August 6, 2017, https://www.usatoday.com.
16. Z. Ivcevic, J. I. Menges, and A. Miller, "How Common Is Unethical Behavior in U.S. Organizations?" *Harvard Business Review,* March 20, 2020, https://hbr.org; R. J. Reinhart, "Nurses Continue to Rate Highest in Honesty, Ethics," *Gallup,* January 6, 2020, https://news.gallup.com.
17. K. Sullivan, "Reports of Sexual Harassment Wane at Work, Possibly Thanks to #MeToo," *NBC News,* July 17, 2019, https://www.nbcnews.com.
18. M. Pastin, *The Hard Problems of Management: Gaining the Ethics Edge* (San Francisco: Jossey-Bass, 1986); T. Thomas, J. Schermerhorn Jr., and J. Dienhart, "Strategic Leadership of Ethical Behavior in Business," *Academy of Management Executive* 18 (2004), pp. 56-66.
19. "Careers at XPLANE," http://xplane.com/careers, accessed April 9, 2020; Kathy Gurchiek, "Winning with Workflex," *HR Magazine,* November 2017, pp. 34-39.
20. G. F. Cavanaugh, D. Moberg, and M. Velasquez, "The Ethics of Organizational Politics," *Academy of Management Review* 6 (1981), pp. 363-374.
21. "Careers at XPLANE"; Gurchiek, "Winning with Workflex," p. 38.
22. M. Williamson, "Interview with Chuck Edward, Head of Global Talent Acquisition at Microsoft," *Business Today* (online journal), May 28, 2019, https://journal.businesstoday.org; D. Moss, "Chuck Edward Embraces a Growth Mindset," *HR Magazine,* October 2017, pp. 43-45.
23. "About HRCI," https://www.hrci.org, accessed April 8, 2020; "HRCI Practice Analysis for PHR and SPHR Certification Reveals Greater HR Emphasis on Employee Experience, Data-Drive Decisions and Business Results," news release, January 16, 2018, https://www.hrci.org.

Trends in Human Resource Management

2

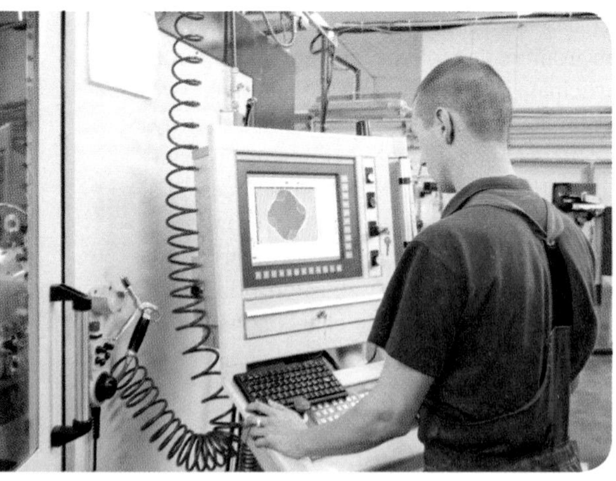

Some manufacturers are charging their HR departments with identifying current workers who have the intellect and process knowledge necessary to learn and utilize advanced work technologies.

Dmitry Kalinovsky/Shutterstock

What Do I Need to Know?

After reading this chapter, you should be able to:

LO 2-1 Describe trends in the labor force composition and how they affect human resource management.

LO 2-2 Summarize areas in which human resource management can support the goal of creating a high-performance work system.

LO 2-3 Define employee empowerment, and explain its role in the modern organization.

LO 2-4 Identify ways HR professionals can support organizational strategies for growth, quality, and efficiency.

LO 2-5 Summarize ways in which human resource management can support organizations expanding internationally.

LO 2-6 Discuss how technological developments are affecting human resource management.

LO 2-7 Explain how the nature of the employment relationship is changing.

LO 2-8 Discuss how the need for flexibility affects human resource management.

Introduction

Vision, salesmanship, and technology kept Pioneer Service in business when its customers started looking overseas for lower prices. The machine shop, based in the Chicago suburb of Addison, used to make parts for heating and cooling systems. When sales plummeted, Pioneer's president, Aneesa Muthana, hired salespeople to find out what kinds of machining were in demand; they discovered a market in making parts for luxury cars. To meet the demand, they would have to speed up production, using modern automated equipment. Pioneer gave employees the opportunity to learn the new skills required. However, only one-quarter of the company's workers were able to make the transition from manual labor to working with computers and data.

For those who can make the switch to high-tech work, the opportunities are great. Today's manufacturers are constantly searching for people who can do the coding that tells computer-controlled machinery how to make precision parts. Much of these workers' days is spent analyzing data produced by manufacturing systems and addressing maintenance and other problems identified. Whereas manufacturing jobs used to go to people who could apply physical strength and stamina to their work, today's employers tend to be looking for an associate's degree or certification that shows mastery of technical and analytic skills.

Some companies are charging their HR departments with identifying which of their current workers have the intellect and understanding of processes necessary for learning to work with computers. These companies commit to training because it gives them a more reliable supply of talent for the new era of manufacturing. This type of HR expertise gives an advantage not only to manufacturers but also to companies in any industry where technology is transforming the way work gets done.[1]

Aneesa Muthana and other forward-thinking managers are succeeding in a fast-changing business environment because they are creative in addressing the trends shaping human resources today. In Muthana's case, she has responded creatively to the shift of making basic parts in low-wage countries, as well as to the potential of using technology to make processes faster and more accurate. These trends have transformed the kinds of talent needed and forced companies to meet their talent needs with training as well as hiring decisions.

Viewing the trends more broadly, this chapter describes major trends that are affecting human resource management. It begins with an examination of the modern labor force, including trends that are determining who will participate in the workforce of the future. Next is an exploration of the ways HRM can support a number of trends in organizational strategy, from efforts to maintain high-performance work systems to an increased emphasis on teamwork and employee empowerment. Often, growth includes the use of human resources on a global scale, as more and more organizations hire immigrants or open operations overseas. The chapter then turns to major changes in technology, especially the role of the Internet. As we will explain, the Internet is changing organizations themselves, as well as providing new ways to carry out human resource management. Finally, we explore the changing nature of the employment relationship, in which careers and jobs are becoming more flexible.

LO 2-1 Describe trends in labor force composition and how they affect human resource management.

Change in the Labor Force

The term *labor force* is a general way to refer to all the people willing and able to work. For an organization, the **internal labor force** consists of the organization's workers–its employees and the people who have contracts to work at the organization. This internal labor force has been drawn from the organization's **external labor market,** that is, individuals who are actively seeking employment. The number and kinds of people in the external labor market determine the kinds of human resources available to an organization (and their cost). Human resource professionals need to be aware of trends in the composition of the external labor market because these trends affect the organization's options for creating a well-skilled, motivated internal labor force.

Internal Labor Force
An organization's workers (its employees and the people who have contracts to work at the organization).

External Labor Market
Individuals who are actively seeking employment.

An Aging Workforce

In the United States, the Bureau of Labor Statistics (BLS), an agency of the Department of Labor, tracks changes in the composition of the U.S. labor force and forecasts employment trends. The BLS has projected that from 2018 to 2028, the total U.S. civilian labor force will grow from 162 million to 171 million workers. This represents growth of 5.5% over the 10-year span, an improvement over the 5.0% growth of 2008–2018 (a period that included a severe recession) but noticeably behind the growth of the preceding decade (12.1% for 1998–2008).[2]

Some of the expected changes involve the distribution of workers by age. From 2018 to 2028, the fastest-growing age group continues to be workers 55 and older, although the growth has slowed from the previous decade. Participation by the 25- to 44-year-old age group continues to increase. And young workers between the ages of 16 and 24 will actually be fewer in number. This combination of trends will cause the overall workforce to continue to age. Figure 2.1 shows the change in age distribution from 2018 to 2028, as forecast by the Bureau of Labor Statistics.[3]

As more and more of the workforce reaches retirement age, some companies have set up mentoring programs between older and younger workers so that knowledge is not lost but passed on. How does the company benefit from these mentoring programs?
Hero Images/Getty Images

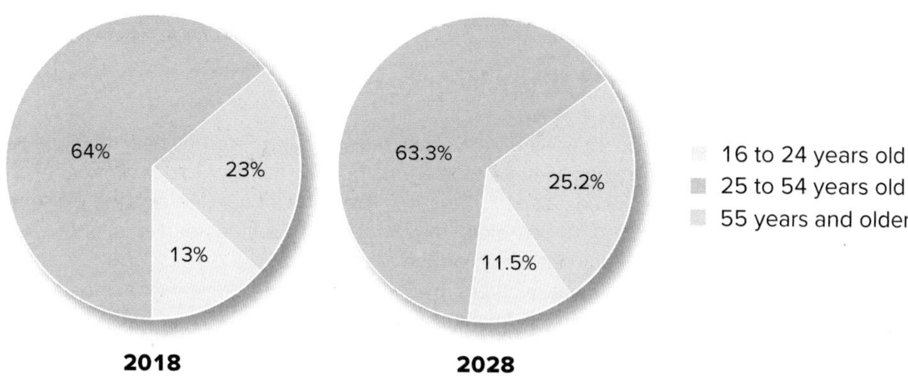

FIGURE 2.1
Age Distribution of U.S. Labor Force, 2018 and 2028

Source: Bureau of Labor Statistics, "Employment Projections, Table 3.1," September 4, 2019, https://www.bls.gov.

With a growing share of the workforce nearing retirement age, human resource professionals will need to spend much of their time on concerns related to planning retirement, retraining older workers, and motivating workers whose careers have plateaued. Organizations will struggle with ways to control the rising costs of health care and other benefits, and many of tomorrow's managers will supervise employees much older than themselves. At the same time, organizations will have to find ways to compete in attracting and preparing young workers from a labor force that is growing more slowly.

Today's older generation includes many people who are in no hurry to retire. They may enjoy making a contribution at work, have ambitious plans for which they want to earn money, or simply be among the many who have inadequate savings for full retirement. Therefore, many older workers want to be allowed to gradually move toward retirement by working part-time or taking temporary assignments. Accommodating such preferences of older workers may become an essential HR practice, given recent Census Bureau projections that by 2035, adults older than 65 will outnumber children in the United States.[4] Unless a significant share of these older workers stay in the workforce, it could be difficult for some companies to fill all their open positions. To address this issue, however, employers will need to overcome stereotypes about older workers (see "HR Oops!").

With older workers continuing to hold jobs at least part-time, today's workplaces often bring together employees representing four, or even five, generations. This creates a need for understanding the values and work habits that tend to characterize each generation.[5] For example, members of the silent generation (born between 1925 and 1945) tend to value income and employment security and avoid challenging authority. Baby boomers (born between 1946 and 1964) tend to value unexpected rewards, opportunities for learning, and time with management. Members of Generation X (1965–1980) tend to be pragmatic and cynical, and they have well-developed self-management skills. Those born from 1981 to 1995, often called millennials, are comfortable with the latest technology, and they want to be noticed, respected, and involved. And Generation Z, who are fresh out of college, value individual expression and ongoing dialogue to solve conflicts and improve the world. Some generational differences can be addressed through effective human resource management. For example, organizations train managers to provide frequent feedback to millennials, and they show respect for older generations' hard work and respect for authority by asking them to mentor younger workers.

A Diverse Workforce

Another kind of change affecting the U.S. labor force is that it is growing more diverse in racial, ethnic, and gender terms. As Figure 2.2 shows, the 2028 workforce is expected to be

HR Oops!

Employers Overlook the Potential of Older Workers

Financial-services companies, such as banks and insurers, have struggled for years with a talent shortage. A recent research effort found that the industry needs about 3 million more professionals than it has. Financial-services work involves a lot of data and analysis, so the companies are seeking their idea of who can use analytics tools: "digital natives," the generations who grew up in the era of the Internet. This assumption that youth equates to technology skills is common enough that highly skilled, greatly experienced workers 50 and older report going to great lengths to hide their age from their co-workers.

Age-related stereotyping creates a new set of difficulties. Research into the career preferences of the millennial generation finds that younger workers are less likely than average to desire work in financial services. And among the tech workers who had taken jobs in financial services, most said they preferred to work for technology companies. Even as financial companies chase after workers statistically less likely to be interested, they may be overlooking a highly motivated segment: workers 55 and older.

An employee in an older age bracket may or may not be up on the latest technology, but workers over 50 have had years to develop an understanding of the industry and their customers, including how to solve problems and manage relationships. They may be eager to continue learning and committed to staying with the company. In fact, a survey of financial-services employees found that employees in the oldest age group expressed the most expectation that they should continually update their skills. However, these workers were the least likely to say they got support from their organization to do so.

Employment discrimination, including unequal access to training, is illegal in the United States, but it can be difficult for an older employee to prove it is occurring. Some members of Congress have supported making age discrimination claims easier to prove. But for employers experiencing a skills gap, addressing stereotypes that cause them to overlook older workers might be less a legal matter and more a smart way to meet the need for talent.

Questions

1. How important do you think age is for identifying which persons would be good at using a computer system to analyze data?
2. What other kinds of information besides age would you want to use to identify people who would be good at using a computer system to analyze data?

Sources: Allen Smith, "House Passes Protecting Older Workers Against Discrimination Act," *Society for Human Resource Management,* January 16, 2020, https://www.shrm.org; Carol Hymowitz, "Older Workers Have a Big Secret: Their Age," *The Wall Street Journal,* November 17, 2019, https://www.wsj.com; Steve Hatfield and Surabhi Kejriwal, "Tapping into the Aging Workforce in Financial Services," Deloitte, June 11, 2019, https://www2.deloitte.com.

FIGURE 2.2
Projected Racial/Ethnic Makeup of the U.S. Workforce, 2028

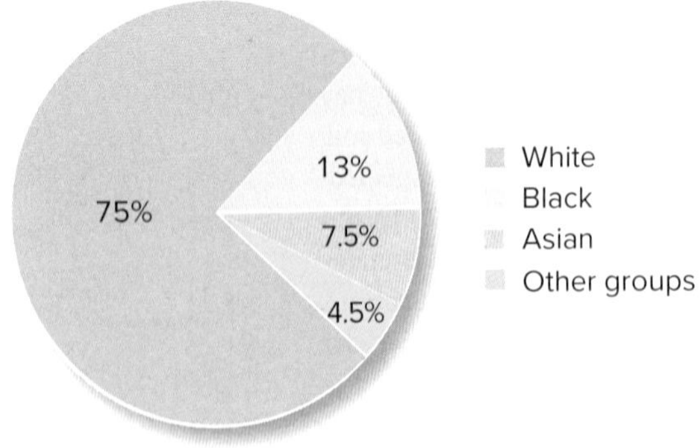

Source: Bureau of Labor Statistics, "Employment Projections, Table 3.1," September 4, 2019, https://www.bls.gov.

75% white, 13% African American, and 12% Asian and other minorities. The fastest growing of these categories is "other groups" because of their multiracial origin. In addition to these racial categories, the ethnic category of Hispanics is growing even faster, and the Hispanic share of the U.S. labor force is expected to top 21% of the total by 2028.[6] Along with greater racial and ethnic diversity, there is also greater gender diversity. More women today than in the past are in the paid labor force. Between 2018 and 2028, women's share of the labor force is expected to increase slightly, at around 48%.[7]

One important source of racial and ethnic diversity is immigration. The U.S. government establishes procedures for foreign nationals to follow if they wish to live and work permanently in the United States, and it sets limits on the number of immigrants who are admitted through these channels. Of the more than 1 million immigrants who come to the United States legally each year, more than 7 out of 10 are relatives of U.S. citizens. Another 14% come on work-related visas, some of which are set aside for workers with exceptional qualifications in science, business, or the arts, and another 8% are refugees from other countries, including Ukraine, Syria, Congo, and Afghanistan.[8] The U.S. government also grants temporary work visas to a limited number of highly educated workers, permitting them to work in the United States for a set period of time but not to remain as immigrants. U.S. law requires employers to verify that any job candidate who is not a U.S. citizen has received permission to work in the United States as an immigrant or with a temporary work permit. (This requirement is discussed in Chapter 6.)

Other foreign-born workers in the United States arrived in this country without meeting the legal requirements for immigration or asylum. These individuals, known as undocumented or illegal immigrants, likely number more than 10 million. While government policy toward immigrants has become more restrictive during the Trump administration, the human resource implications have two practical parts. The first involves the supply of and demand for labor (see the "Best Practices" box for an example). Many U.S. industries, including meatpacking, construction, farming, and services, rely on immigrants to perform demanding work that may be low paid. In other industries, such as computer software development, employers say they have difficulty finding enough qualified U.S. workers to fill technical jobs. These employers are pressing for immigration laws to allow a greater supply of foreign-born workers.

The other HR concern is the need to comply with laws. In recent years, Immigration and Customs and Enforcement has intensified its enforcement of immigration laws, including more audits of employers to ensure that they are following proper procedures to avoid employing undocumented immigrants and more unannounced raids on worksites suspected of being out of compliance.[9] Even as some companies are lobbying for changes to immigration laws, the constraints on labor supply force companies to consider a variety of ways to meet their demand for labor, including job redesign (Chapter 4), higher pay (Chapter 12), and foreign operations (Chapter 16).

The greater diversity of the U.S. labor force challenges employers to create HRM practices that ensure that they fully utilize the talents, skills, and values of all employees. As a result, organizations cannot afford to ignore or discount the potential contributions of women and minorities. Employers will have to ensure that employees and HRM systems are free of bias and value the perspectives and experience that women and minorities can contribute to organizational goals such as product quality and customer service. As we will discuss further in Chapter 3, managing cultural diversity involves many different activities. These include creating an organizational culture that values diversity, ensuring that HRM systems are bias-free, encouraging career development for women and minorities, promoting knowledge and acceptance of cultural differences, ensuring involvement in education both within and outside the organization, and dealing with employees' resistance to diversity.[10]

Although many U.S. companies have committed themselves to recognizing the diversity of their internal labor force and using it to gain competitive advantage, some workers believe there is more work to be done, particularly those in underrepresented groups such as women, racial and ethnic minorities, and LGBTQ employees. In a recent global survey conducted by Boston Consulting Group, nearly 75% of individuals in these underrepresented groups said they do not believe they have personally benefited from their companies' diversity and inclusion programs. In another diversity and inclusion study conducted for Glassdoor, 60% of employees surveyed said they had witnessed or experienced discrimination based on age, race, gender, or LGBTQ identity in the workplace. Diversity and inclusion will continue to be important topics that need to be discussed and addressed at all organizational levels. Recent statistics suggest that companies continue to take diversity and

Helping Panda Express Workers Communicate

Panda Express is as diverse as America: the restaurant chain's majority-Hispanic workforce, led by a Chinese-American management team, sells American-style Chinese food in more than 2,000 restaurants. And management wants everyone to speak English, the language of most of the restaurants' customers. The company's founders, Andrew and Peggy Cherng, were immigrants who (despite Mrs. Cherng's advanced engineering degree) had difficulty landing professional jobs but identified great financial potential in launching a restaurant business. Today they see their role as enabling a brighter future for their employees. Therefore, they see the language differences as an opportunity for their people to develop.

To provide that opportunity, Panda turned to Rosetta Stone, a pioneer in online language instruction. Rosetta Stone recently released a product called Rosetta Stone Catalyst to provide instruction in business communication in 24 languages. Unlike most language-teaching software, Catalyst provides lessons customized for particular companies and employees. If an employee needs to learn to speak about an industry or about a function such as sales, it teaches the way the language is spoken about those topics in a business context. Also, the user starts out with a test of his or her existing skills, and the instruction begins at the level of knowledge the learner already possesses. Finally, Catalyst delivers progress reports to training managers, so they can see how well each employee is acquiring the necessary skills.

At Panda, the company pays for the language course, and employees sign up through their personal e-mail accounts, using their own computer or mobile device. They learn the lessons on their time off work, whenever and wherever it is convenient. Alvin Tang, Panda's learning and development coordinator, says employees have responded favorably, viewing the program as an opportunity to gain valuable skills.

Kevin Kwan, Panda's technology manager, learning and development, sees Catalyst achieving the company's goal to foster the personal development of its employees. Kwan says offering Catalyst shows employees that the company "care[s] about their growth." It removes language differences as an obstacle to success at work and enables employees to achieve "greater things at our store and also in their lives."

Questions

1. What business reasons might support Panda Express's practice of hiring many workers whose first language is not English?
2. What advantages do you think Panda Express gains from offering English-language instruction as an employee benefit?

Sources: "Our Family Story," https://www.pandaexpress.com, accessed April 10, 2020; Phil Albinus, "Language Training Benefits Speak Volumes for Panda Restaurants," *Employee Benefit News,* https://www.benefitnews.com, accessed April 10, 2020; Mark Abadi and Taylor Nicole Rogers, "Meet the Billionaire Couple Behind Panda Express, Who Built a $3 Billion Fortune Selling 90 Million Pounds of Orange Chicken Each Year and Run 2,000 Restaurants across the Globe," *Business Insider,* December 12, 2019, https://www.businessinsider.com; Tricia Contreras, "Breaking Down Language Barriers in Foodservice," *SmartBrief,* September 26, 2018, https://www.smartbrief.com; Kerry Hannon, "For Panda Express Owners, It's About Family," *The New York Times,* March 22, 2018, https://www.nytimes.com; Juan Martinez, "Rosetta Stone Catalyst Reimagines Language Learning for Business," *PC Magazine,* September 13, 2016, https://www.pcmag.com.

inclusion issues seriously: hiring for diversity and inclusion jobs is up 30% over the past few years.[11] Figure 2.3 highlights some ways in which HRM can support the management of diversity and inclusion for organizational success.

An organization doesn't have to be a huge global enterprise to benefit from valuing diversity. The Spice Center store in Manchester, New Hampshire, widened its customer base along with the diversity of its employees. Previous owners had recruited employees mainly by word of mouth; as a result, all of their employees were of Middle Eastern heritage. When new owners, Jawed Ali Shaikh and Ali Faraz, purchased the business, they advertised openings to the community at large. Soon the ethnic origins of their employees began to be more reflective of the entire community. The owners also developed training to help store

FIGURE 2.3

HRM Practices That Support Diversity Management

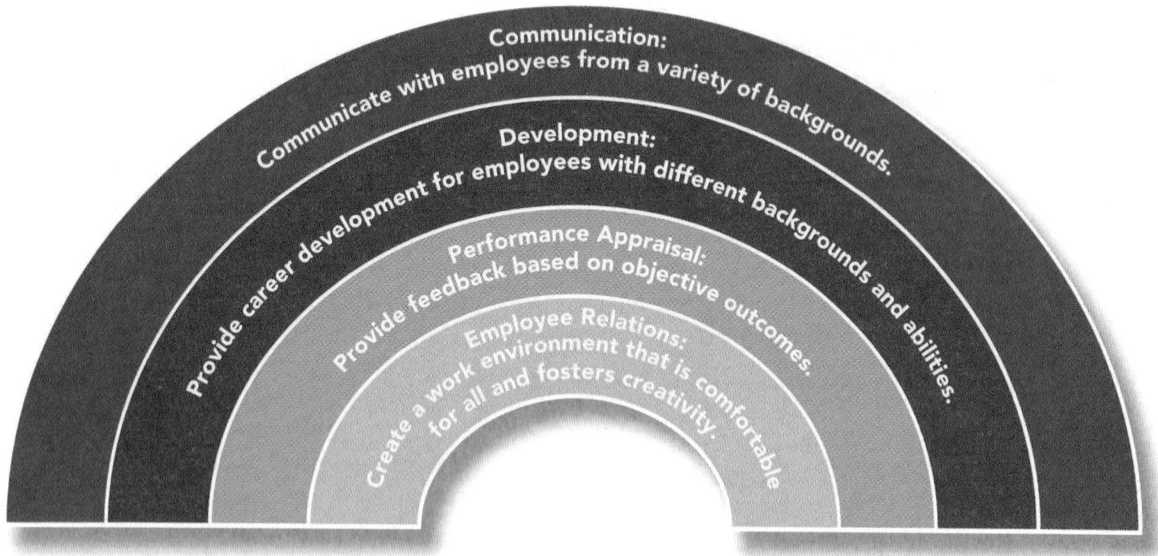

Source: Based on M. Loden and J. B. Rosener, *Workforce America!* (Homewood, IL: Business One Irwin, 1991).

managers understand religious and cultural differences. The effort pays off as shoppers from more ethnic groups can satisfy their tastes at the Spice Center.[12]

Throughout this book we will show how diversity affects HRM practices. For example, from a staffing perspective, it is important to ensure that tests used to select employees are not unfairly biased against minority groups. From the perspective of work design, employees need flexible schedules that allow them to meet nonwork needs. In terms of training, it is clear that employees must be made aware of the damage that stereotypes can do. With regard to compensation, organizations are providing benefits such as elder care and day care as a way to accommodate the needs of a diverse workforce. As we will see later in the chapter, successfully managing diversity is also critical for companies that compete in international markets.

Skill Deficiencies of the Workforce

The increasing use of computers to do routine tasks has shifted the kinds of skills needed for employees in the U.S. economy. Such qualities as physical strength and mastery of a particular piece of machinery are no longer important for many jobs. More employers are looking for mathematical, verbal, and interpersonal skills, such as the ability to solve math or other problems or reach decisions as part of a team. Often, when organizations are looking for technical skills, they are looking for skills related to computers and using the Internet. Today's employees must be able to handle a variety of responsibilities, interact with customers, and think creatively.

To find such employees, most organizations are looking for educational achievements. A college degree is a basic requirement for many jobs today. Competition for qualified college graduates in many fields is intense. More employers are rewriting job requirements to accept candidates without a degree or even without particular technical skills required for the job; then they offer training to correct any skills gaps.[13] Other companies team up with universities, community colleges, and high schools to design and teach courses ranging from basic reading to design blueprint reading, as we describe in Chapter 7.

HR Analytics & Decision Making

Dollar General is known for low prices in its thousands of retail stores and a company mission of serving others to deliver value to customers, employees, and communities in which they operate. In 2017, the retailer planned to open two distribution centers and more than 1,300 new stores (three stores every day), which would require attracting many new talented employees to get these new ventures up and running.

To support current and future planned growth, Dollar General invested in a new recruiting management system. The training and development team created a computer-based learning course and reference guides for the various groups who use the new recruiting system. These include HR team members, store managers, district managers, and job candidates who landed on the careers page of Dollar General's corporate website. Providing training support for the new system also helped ensure its effectiveness. After the new recruiting system was implemented, the number of job candidate applications doubled, and the time for job seekers to complete an online application dropped by 60%.

Questions

1. Why do you think the number of applications increased after Dollar General put the new system on its careers page?
2. A recruiting management system would give managers updates about applications, including which applicants in the system best meet the hiring standards. How would this help store managers address skills shortages?

Sources: "Mission and Profile" and "Serving Others," www.dollargeneral.com, accessed April 10, 2020; Margery Weinstein, "Dollar General Registers Growth and Development," *Training*, January/February 2018, pp. 42–44.

LO 2-2 Summarize areas in which human resource management can support the goal of creating a high-performance work system.

Not all the skills employers want require a college education. The National Association of Manufacturers year after year has reported that the manufacturing companies in the United States have difficulty finding enough people who can operate sophisticated computer-controlled machinery. These jobs rely at least as much on intelligence and teamwork as on physical strength. In some areas, companies and communities have set up apprenticeship and training programs to fix the worker shortage. High schools, too, are getting the message that today's students are worried about college debt and sometimes attracted to opportunities to do technical work like welding and software coding. One teenager interested in career and technical education is Raelee Nicholson, who has her sights set on a two-year program in diesel mechanics. She excels in academics, but after a summer spent rebuilding a car, Nicholson realized she loves to work with her hands.[14]

High-Performance Work System
An organization in which technology, organizational structure, people, and processes work together seamlessly to give an organization an advantage in the competitive environment.

High-Performance Work Systems

Human resource management is playing an important role in helping organizations gain and keep an advantage over competitors by becoming **high-performance work systems.** These are organizations that have the best possible fit between their social system (people and how they interact) and technical system (equipment and processes).[15] As the nature of the workforce and the technology available to organizations have changed, so have the requirements for creating a high-performance work system. Customers are demanding high quality and customized products, employees are seeking flexible work arrangements, and employers are looking for ways to tap people's creativity and interpersonal skills. Such demands require that organizations make full use of their people's knowledge and skills, and skilled human resource management can help organizations do this.

Among the trends that are occurring in today's high-performance work systems are reliance on knowledge workers, empowerment of employees to make decisions, and use of teamwork. The following sections describe those three trends, and Chapter 9 will explore the ways HRM can support the creation and maintenance of a high-performance work system. HR professionals who keep up with change are well positioned to help create high-performance work systems.

Knowledge Workers

Because of the growth in e-commerce, plus the shift from a manufacturing to a service and information economy, the qualities that are in most demand in employees have changed. The Bureau of Labor Statistics forecasts that between 2018 and 2028, most new jobs will be in service occupations, especially health care.

The number of service jobs has important implications for human resource management. Research shows that if employees have a favorable view of HRM practices—career opportunities, training, pay, and feedback on performance—they are more likely to provide good service to customers. Therefore, quality HRM for service employees can translate into customer satisfaction.

Besides differences among industries, job growth varies according to the type of job. Table 2.1 lists the 10 occupations expected to gain the most jobs between 2018 and 2028 and the 10 expected to grow at the fastest rate. Occupations with the most jobs are expected to be mainly in the service sector, especially positions providing health care and food service.[16] Occupations expected to see the fastest growth are in health care and technical jobs. Although nearly two-thirds of the fastest-growing occupations require education beyond high school, many of the occupations with the most jobs require only on-the-job training (with registered nurses, in third place, being a notable exception). This means that many companies' HRM departments will need to provide excellent training as well as hiring.

TABLE 2.1

Top 10 Occupations for Job Growth

MOST NEW JOBS	FASTEST RATE OF GROWTH
Personal care aides	Solar voltaic installers
Combined food preparation and serving workers [a]	Wind turbine service technicians
Registered nurses	Home health aides
Home health aides	Personal care aides
Cooks, restaurant	Occupational therapy assistants
Software developers, applications	Information security analysts
Waiters and waitresses	Physician assistants
General and operations managers	Statisticians
Janitors and cleaners [b]	Nurse practitioners
Medical assistants	Speech-language pathologists

[a]Includes fast food

[b]Excludes maids and housekeeping cleaners

Sources: U.S. Bureau of Labor Statistics, "Fastest Growing Occupations, 2018–2028" and "Most New Jobs," *Occupational Outlook Handbook,* last modified September 4, 2019, https://www.bls.gov.

These high-growth jobs are evidence of another trend: The future U.S. labor market will be both a knowledge economy and a service economy.[17] Along with low-education jobs in services like health care and food preparation, there will be many high-education professional and managerial jobs. To meet these human capital needs, companies are increasingly trying to attract, develop, and retain knowledge workers. **Knowledge workers** are employees whose main contribution to the organization is specialized knowledge, such as knowledge of customers, a process, or a profession. Further complicating that challenge, many of these knowledge workers will have to be "technoservice" workers who not only know a specialized field such as computer programming or engineering, but also must be able to work directly with customers.

Knowledge Workers
Employees whose main contribution to the organization is specialized knowledge, such as knowledge of customers, a process, or a profession.

Knowledge workers are in a position of power because they own the knowledge that the company needs in order to produce its products and services, and they must share their knowledge and collaborate with others in order for their employer to succeed. An employer cannot simply order these employees to perform tasks. Managers depend on the employees' willingness to share information. Furthermore, skilled knowledge workers have many job opportunities, even in a slow economy. If they choose, they can leave a company and take their knowledge to another employer. Replacing them may be difficult and time consuming.

The idea that only some of an organization's workers are knowledge workers has come under criticism.[18] To the critics, this definition is no longer realistic in a day of computerized information systems and computer-controlled production processes. For the company to excel, everyone must know how their work contributes to the organization's success. At the same time, employees—especially younger ones who grew up with the Internet—will expect to have wide access to information. From this perspective, successful organizations treat *all* their workers as knowledge workers. They let employees know how well the organization is performing, and they invite ideas about how the organization can do better. For an example of a company doing this, see the "HRM Social" box.

Can the "knowledge worker" label really fit everywhere? Think of the expectations organizations have for the typical computer programmer. These high-in-demand employees expect to be valued for their skills, not the hours they put in or the way they dress. Organizations that successfully recruit and retain computer programmers give them plenty of freedom to set up their work space and their own schedule. They motivate by assigning tasks that are interesting and challenging and by encouraging friendly collaboration. To some degree these kinds of measures apply to many employees and many work situations. For example, EJ Ajax Metalforming Solutions posts a skills matrix on a bulletin board where all employees can see it. On the matrix, each employee can find his or her skills levels relative to all the machines and tasks required within the department. Employees can use the information to identify the available training opportunities, which they can request from their supervisor.[19]

LO 2-3 Define employee empowerment, and explain its role in the modern organization.

Employee Empowerment

To completely benefit from employees' knowledge, organizations need a management style that focuses on developing and empowering employees. **Employee empowerment** means giving employees responsibility and authority to make decisions regarding all aspects of product development or customer service.[20] Employees are then held accountable for products and services. In return, they share the resulting losses and rewards. Employee empowerment can also extend to innovation. Employees at all levels are encouraged to share their ideas for satisfying customers better and operating more efficiently and safely. This is empowering if management actually listens to the ideas, implements valuable ones, and rewards employees for their innovations.

Employee Empowerment
Giving employees responsibility and authority to make decisions regarding all aspects of product development or customer service.

HRM practices such as performance management, training, work design, and compensation are important for ensuring the success of employee empowerment. Jobs must

HRM Social

Employee Reviews Foster Better Communication

Anonymous employee reviews about what it's like to work for the company—does that sound like a recruiting advantage or a public relations nightmare? Employee reviews are one of the information services of Glassdoor, a jobs website featuring employee-provided reviews and salary information along with employer-provided job listings. Employers might see a loss of control over information sharing, but Glassdoor, the second most popular jobs website after Indeed, also lets employers respond to reviews and gather data about what people are saying and doing on the site. Some employers make changes in response to complaints. Some with a track record of good employee relations even encourage employees to post reviews.

Nestlé Purina PetCare, based in St. Louis, treats Glassdoor as a means to foster better communication with employees. Purina has a reputation for treating its employees well, with benefits including a policy that allows for bringing pets to work. But management understands that perks alone do not create a favorable work environment. The company also makes a practice of listening to employees and responding to their concerns.

Purina's human resources department monitors employee comments on Glassdoor and prepares a summary to include in its monthly report to executives. Also, the company investigates and responds to any complaints it sees. At one point the department noticed a pattern of employees complaining that it was difficult to balance the demands of work and their personal lives. The department responded by creating a video in which top managers acknowledged the problem and suggested ways to address it, such as being more careful to consider the timing and length of meetings. A survey after the video was distributed showed that 40% of employees immediately saw "a definite change."

Questions

1. In what ways is knowledge a source of power for workers in this example? In what ways does the knowledge sharing on Glassdoor empower Purina?
2. Besides opinions about their company, what other kinds of knowledge could employees constructively share on social media (Glassdoor and other tools)?

Sources: Rolfe Winkler and Andrea Fuller, "How Companies Secretly Boost Their Glassdoor Ratings," *The Wall Street Journal*, January 22, 2019, https://www.wsj.com; "2018 Best Places to Work," *Glassdoor*, https://www.glassdoor.com; Lizzie Widdicombe, "Improving Workplace Culture, One Review at a Time," *The New Yorker*, January 22, 2018, https://www.newyorker.com; "Why Employees Love Working for Nestlé Purina," *Flagstaff Business News*, January 3, 2018, https://www.flagstaffbusinessnews; Caryn Freeman, "Value Placed on Feedback Boosts Nestlé Purina to Top of Glassdoor List," *HR Focus*, February 2015, pp. 3–4.

be designed to give employees the necessary latitude for making a variety of decisions. Employees must be properly trained to exert their wider authority and use information resources such as the Internet as well as tools for communicating information. Employees also need feedback to help them evaluate their success. Pay and other rewards should reflect employees' authority and be related to successful handling of their responsibility. In addition, for empowerment to succeed, managers must be trained to link employees to resources within and outside the organization, such as customers, co-workers in other departments, and websites with needed information. Managers must also encourage employees to interact with staff throughout the organization, must ensure that employees receive the information they need, and must reward cooperation. Finally, empowered employees deliver the best results if they are fully engaged in their work. *Employee engagement*–full involvement in one's work and commitment to one's job and company–is associated with higher productivity, better customer service, and lower turnover.[21]

As with the need for knowledge workers, use of employee empowerment shifts the recruiting focus away from technical skills and toward general cognitive and interpersonal skills. Employees who have responsibility for a final product or service must be able to listen to customers, adapt to changing needs, and creatively solve a variety of problems.

One way companies can increase employee responsibility and control is to assign work to teams. Pixtal/age fotostock

Teamwork

Modern technology places the information that employees need for improving quality and providing customer service right at the point of sale or production. As a result, the employees who engage in selling and producing must also be able to make decisions about how to do their work. Organizations need to set up work in a way that gives employees the authority and ability to make those decisions. One of the most popular ways to increase employee responsibility and control is to assign work to teams. **Teamwork** is the assignment of work to groups of employees with various skills who interact to assemble a product or provide a service. Work teams often assume many activities traditionally reserved for managers, such as selecting new team members, scheduling work, and coordinating work with customers and other units of the organization. Work teams also contribute to total quality by performing inspection and quality-control activities while the product or service is being completed.

Teamwork
The assignment of work to groups of employees with various skills who interact to assemble a product or provide a service.

In some organizations, technology is enabling teamwork even when workers are at different locations or work at different times. These organizations use *virtual teams*—teams that rely on communications technology such as videoconferences, e-mail, and cell phones to keep in touch and coordinate activities.

Teamwork can motivate employees by making work more interesting and significant. At organizations that rely on teamwork, labor costs may be lower as well. Spurred by such advantages, a number of companies are reorganizing assembly operations—abandoning the assembly line in favor of operations that combine mass production with jobs in which employees perform multiple tasks, use many skills, control the pace of work, and assemble the entire final product.

Witnessing the resulting improvements, companies in the service sector also have moved toward greater use of teamwork. Companies that develop software pioneered an approach they call *agile,* which involves weaving the development process more tightly into the organization's activities and strategies. A self-directed team of developers and programmers, which works directly with those who will use the software, delivers components and seeks feedback. The process is "agile" because the team changes specifications and code as a result of the feedback throughout the development process. Today, other service providers are applying the model of agile teamwork to their services. For example, ING, a global banking organization, wanted to improve how it delivers customer service. The HR department started by assigning customer service staff to large teams called "tribes," each with a leader who allocates tribe members to smaller "squads" to handle particular projects and needs as they arise. Tribes also include "chapters" of technical specialists who can be quickly deployed to a squad when their area of expertise is needed.[22]

LO 2-4 Identify ways HR professionals can support organizational strategies for growth, quality, and efficiency.

Focus on Strategy

As we saw in Chapter 1, traditional management thinking treated human resource management primarily as an administrative function, but managers today are beginning to see a more central role for HRM. They are looking at HRM as a means to support a company's *strategy*—its plan for meeting broad goals such as profitability, quality, and market share. This strategic role for HRM has evolved gradually. At many organizations, managers still treat HR professionals primarily as experts in designing and delivering HR systems. But at a growing number of organizations, HR professionals are strategic partners with other managers.

This means they use their knowledge of the business and of human resources to help the organization develop strategies and to align HRM policies and practices with those strategies. To do this, human resource managers must focus on the future as well as the present, and on company goals as well as human resource activities. They may, for example, become experts at analyzing the business impact of HR decisions or at developing and keeping the best talent to support business strategy. Organizations do this, for example, when they integrate all the activities involved in talent management with each other and with the organization's other processes in order to provide the skills the organization needs to pursue its strategy. An integrated approach to talent management includes acquiring talent (recruiting and selection), providing the right opportunities for training and development, measuring performance, and creating compensation plans that reward the needed behaviors. To choose the right talent, provide the right training, and so on, HR professionals need to be in ongoing close contact with the members of the organization who need the talent. And when the organization modifies its strategy, HR professionals are part of the planning process so they can modify talent management efforts to support the revised strategy. HR professionals can support such efforts even in small companies, which often have a human resource department of one. In these situations, the company depends on that one person to understand both HRM principles and the ways they can help the business perform better. Cheryl Stargratt, chief people and operations officer at the Canadian bank Tangerine, describes this strategic focus as both essential and highly rewarding. She encourages her colleagues in HRM to "focus on the organization as a whole" and "see themselves as business leaders that happen to have an expertise in HR."[23]

The specific ways in which human resource professionals support the organization's strategy vary according to their level of involvement and the nature of the strategy. Strategic issues include emphasis on quality and decisions about growth and efficiency. Human resource management can support these strategies, including efforts such as quality improvement programs, mergers and acquisitions, and restructuring. Decisions to use reengineering and outsourcing can make an organization more efficient and also give rise to many human resource challenges. International expansion presents a wide variety of HRM challenges and opportunities. Figure 2.4 summarizes these strategic issues facing human resource management.

Mergers and Acquisitions

Often organizations join forces through mergers (two companies becoming one) and acquisitions (one company buying another). Some mergers and acquisitions result in consolidation within an industry, meaning that two firms in one industry join to hold a greater share of the industry. For example, Royal Dutch Shell's acquisition of British energy supplier BG represented a consolidation, or a reduction of the number of companies in the oil industry. Other mergers and acquisitions cross industry lines. In a merger to form Citigroup, Citicorp combined its banking business with Traveler's Group's insurance business. Furthermore, these deals more frequently take the form of global megamergers, or mergers of big companies based in different countries (as in the case of Shell–BG).

HRM should have a significant role in carrying out a merger or acquisition. Differences between the businesses involved in the deal make conflict inevitable. Training efforts should therefore include development of skills in conflict resolution. Also, HR professionals have to sort out differences in the two companies' practices with regard to compensation, performance appraisal, and other HR systems. Settling on a consistent structure to meet the combined organization's goals may help bring employees together.[24]

High-Quality Standards

To compete in today's economy, companies need to provide high-quality products and services. If companies do not adhere to quality standards, they will have difficulty selling their

FIGURE 2.4
Business Strategy: Issues Affecting HRM

product or service to vendors, suppliers, or customers. Therefore, many organizations have adopted some form of **total quality management (TQM)**—a companywide effort to continually improve the ways people, machines, and systems accomplish work.[25] TQM has several core values:[26]

Total Quality Management (TQM)
A companywide effort to continuously improve the ways people, machines, and systems accomplish work.

- Methods and processes are designed to meet the needs of internal and external customers (that is, whomever the process is intended to serve).
- Every employee in the organization receives training in quality.
- Quality is designed into a product or service so that errors are prevented from occurring, rather than being detected and corrected in an error-prone product or service.
- The organization promotes cooperation with vendors, suppliers, and customers to improve quality and hold down costs.
- Managers measure progress with feedback based on data.

Based on these values, the TQM approach provides guidelines for all the organization's activities, including human resource management. To promote quality, organizations need an environment that supports innovation, creativity, and risk taking to meet customer demands. Problem solving should bring together managers, employees, and customers. Employees should communicate with managers about customer needs.

Quality improvement can focus on the HRM function itself. One area where managers are increasingly pressing for improvement is in applying data to improve business processes. For example, the HR department of a transportation company determined that its high employee turnover rate was costing the company $68 million a year. Further analysis showed that the company had not been selecting employees based on the criteria associated with employee satisfaction and retention. Changing the selection process improved performance on all of these measures. At the Coca-Cola Company, the HR department looked beyond performance appraisals to find and correct performance problems. An analysis of work by call-center employees found there were certain kinds of questions that the employees had difficulty answering. The department revamped training to focus on the difficult questions, and customer service became more efficient as well as more helpful to customers.[27]

Cost Control

Some organizations have a low-cost, low-price strategy. These organizations particularly depend on human resource management to identify ways for limiting costs related to maintaining a qualified, motivated workforce. However, this challenge is relevant in any organization. HR managers contribute to success whenever they help lower costs without compromising quality.

Human resource management supports cost control both by helping the organization use human resources more efficiently and by making HRM processes as efficient as possible. This has become particularly relevant to employee benefits, specifically health insurance.[28] As we will discuss in Chapter 14, the cost of this benefit has grown rapidly, while the Affordable Care Act has introduced a set of employer requirements that can be expensive. How to manage the costs while meeting the requirements is complicated. Employers need to weigh factors such as legal requirements, the costs and types of plans available, the impact on departments' budgets, and the effect on employee morale and retention, as well as on the ability to recruit new employees. Management relies on well-informed HR managers to identify alternatives and recommend which ones will best support the company's strategy.

Beyond specific issues such as health insurance and the Affordable Care Act, human resource management can support strategic efforts to control costs through downsizing, reengineering, and outsourcing.

Downsizing As measured by the number of job cuts announced by employers, downsizing in the United States surged above 1.2 million per year in 2009, the height of the Great Recession (Figure 2.5). Since then, downsizing activity fell to roughly half that level and

FIGURE 2.5
Number of Job Cuts Announced by Employers during the Past Decade

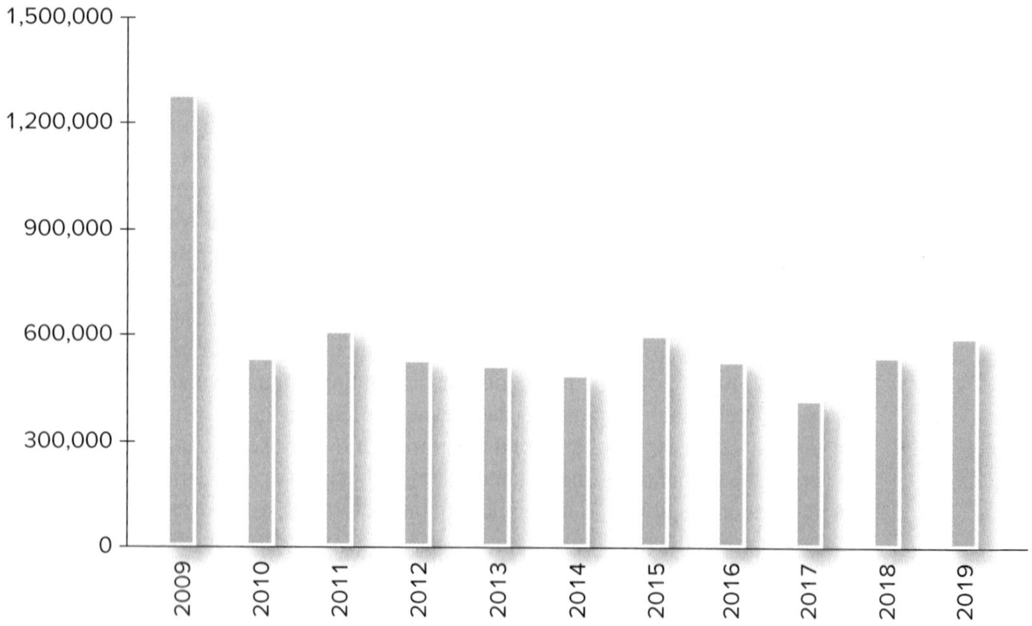

Source: Gina Heeb, "2019 Was One of the Decade's Worst Years for Job Cuts in the US," *Markets Insider*, January 2, 2020, https://markets.businessinsider.com.

then declined somewhat more till the end of 2018, when companies, particularly those in the financial services sector, started to announce upcoming layoffs for 2019. Surprisingly, even with a 10% increase in job cuts from 2018 to 2019, the United States hit an historic low in the unemployment rate in October 2019 before the coronavirus started to spread in China in late 2019—a significant event we discuss in the next section.[29]

Downsizing presents a number of challenges and opportunities for HRM. In terms of challenges, the HRM function must "surgically" reduce the workforce by cutting only the workers who are less valuable in their performance. Achieving this is difficult because the best workers are most able (and often willing) to find alternative employment and may leave voluntarily before the organization lays off anyone. Early-retirement programs are humane, but they essentially reduce the workforce with a "grenade" approach—not distinguishing good from poor performers but instead eliminating an entire group of employees. In fact, contrary to popular belief, research has found that downsizing is associated with negative stock returns and lower profitability following the layoffs. One reason may be that although labor costs fall after a downsizing, sales per employee also tend to fall. Circuit City, for example, tried to save money by laying off its highest-paid salespeople. Customers soon found that they preferred other electronics retailers, and Circuit City went out of business. In contrast, Intuitive Research & Technology, based in Huntsville, Alabama, has never laid off any employees. Unlike many other defense contractors, which hire employees to fulfill particular contracts and then let them go when the contracts end, Intuitive hires employees according to whether they will bring exceptional talent. The company then supports continued learning and rewards high performance—policies that together focus on having great people bring in projects, rather than staffing up and down as projects come and go.[30]

Another HRM challenge is to boost the morale of employees who remain after the reduction; this is discussed in greater detail in Chapter 5. HR professionals should maintain open communication with remaining employees to build their trust and commitment, rather than withhold information.[31] All employees should be informed why the downsizing is necessary, what costs are to be cut, how long the downsizing will last, and what strategies the organization intends to pursue. Finally, HRM can provide downsized employees with outplacement services to help them find new jobs. Such services are ways an organization can show that it cares about its employees, even though it cannot afford to keep all of them on the payroll.

COVID-19 The COVID-19 pandemic caused major layoffs and furloughs in businesses throughout the United States in 2020 and will undoubtedly influence business operations including HRM for the foreseeable future. By early April 2020, more than 17 million workers in the U.S. labor force were forced out of their jobs, particularly in the hospitality, retail, auto, and travel industries.[32] The unemployment numbers from this pandemic are staggering and will continue to impact business and life in general over the coming year or possibly longer. In an unprecedented move, Congress passed several pieces of emergency legislation to lessen the blow from this catastrophic event, including help to workers who were laid off (increasing unemployment payments and extending unemployment benefits for an additional 13 weeks); aid to small business owners forced to shut down (providing $350 billion for loans to cover expenses and loan forgiveness if owners keep employees on payroll during the crisis); tax relief to businesses and individual taxpayers; and for the first time expanding unemployment eligibility to independent contractors, gig workers, and the self-employed.[33]

Dealing with the pandemic effectively provided many challenges to both businesses and their HR staffs.[34] In a survey of more than 300 HR executives in Asia, nearly 70% of the respondents cited crisis management and business continuity planning as their top challenge during the COVID-19 outbreak, along with managing flexible work arrangements and employee communications to increase awareness. Among their communication strategies: provide continuous updates to employees regarding measures adopted by the company; issue guidance to employees regarding travel; share updates from business leaders via e-mail or video; provide ongoing information on HR policies related to the outbreak; and offer education through health talks.[35]

Reengineering Rapidly changing customer needs and technology have caused many organizations to rethink the way they get work done. For example, when an organization adopts new technology, its existing processes may no longer result in acceptable quality levels, meet customer expectations for speed, or keep costs to profitable levels. Therefore, many organizations have undertaken **reengineering**—a complete review of the organization's critical work processes to make them more efficient and able to deliver higher quality.

Reengineering
A complete review of the organization's critical work processes to make them more efficient and able to deliver higher quality.

Ideally, reengineering involves reviewing all the processes performed by all the organization's major functions, including production, sales, accounting, and human resources. Therefore, reengineering affects human resource management in two ways. First, the way the HR department itself accomplishes its goals may change dramatically. Second, the fundamental change throughout the organization requires the HR department to help design and implement change so that all employees will be committed to the success of the reengineered organization. Employees may need training for their reengineered jobs. The organization may need to redesign the structure of its pay and benefits to make them more appropriate for its new way of operating. It also may need to recruit employees with a new set of skills. Reengineering often results in employees being laid off or reassigned to new jobs, as the organization's needs change. HR professionals should also help with this transition, as they do for downsizing.

Outsourcing Many organizations are increasingly outsourcing some of their business activities. **Outsourcing** refers to the practice of having another company (a vendor, third-party provider, or consultant) provide services. For instance, a manufacturing company might outsource its accounting and transportation functions to businesses that specialize in these activities. Outsourcing gives the company access to in-depth expertise and is often more economical as well. The "Did You Know?" box provides some insight into the economics of outsourcing.

Outsourcing
Contracting with another organization (vendor, third-party provider, or consultant) to provide services.

Not only do HR departments help with a transition to outsourcing, but many HR functions are being outsourced. Outsourcing initially focused on routine transactions such as payroll processing and on complex technical specialties such as managing retirement accounts and, more recently, health care coverage. Today's outsourcing is moving more into areas that automate processes and support decision making. For example, recruitment process outsourcing helps employers use data to figure out how to build a pipeline for the right kinds of talent. Providers of benefits administration help companies set up enrollment and training via online platforms that employees—especially younger ones—have come to expect. Small organizations sometimes outsource most of their HR work. For example, Bryan Read, administrator for the City of Brandon, South Dakota, oversees 36 full-time employees and brings in about 90 more for summertime work. That summertime surge could overwhelm his small staff, so he finds it practical to outsource the processes of hiring seasonal employees and delivering safety training.[36]

LO 2-5 Summarize ways in which human resource management can support organizations expanding internationally.

Expanding into Global Markets

Companies are finding that to survive they must compete in international markets as well as fend off foreign competitors' attempts to gain ground in the United States. To meet these challenges, U.S. businesses must develop global markets, keep up with competition from

Did You Know?

Outsourcing Is on the Rise

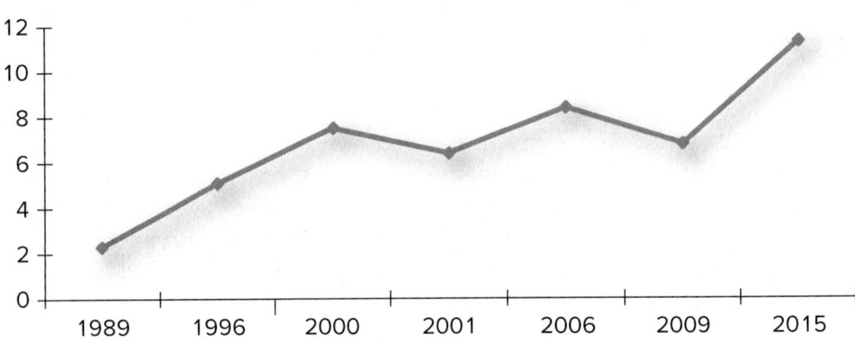

[1]Staffing workers are manufacturing workers employed not by the manufacturer but by a temporary-help agency, professional employer organization, or employment agency.

Companies are increasingly acquiring talent through outsourcing. In manufacturing, for example, the share of workers employed by outside agencies has risen from just 2% in the 1980s to more than one in 10. This trend toward using agencies has lowered costs, because the workers typically earn less—in one study, 29% lower for team assemblers. The change shows up in the wages of manufacturing jobs relative to all jobs for comparable education levels. In the 1980s, manufacturing jobs used to pay almost 15% more overall than comparable jobs in other industries; in the 2010s, that fell to a 10% premium. However, benefits packages for manufacturing have improved.

Similar patterns are affecting employers and workers in other industries. Many companies use service agencies to provide them with noncore workers such as security guards and call-center operators. Some use agencies for core work, too. Estimates of the share of outsourced workers have been in the range of 20 to 50% of a company's workforce. Alphabet, the parent of Google, has had more outsourced workers than full-time employees.

Recently, this trend has raised challenges particularly for outsourced work in other parts of the world. As the coronavirus pandemic spread, companies found that workers in India, the Philippines, and other locations had difficulty working remotely, because housing conditions, Internet services, and other infrastructure did not adequately support working from home.

Question

Would you say that the trend toward outsourcing has been beneficial overall? Why or why not?

Sources: Rajesh Roy and Jon Emont, "Coronavirus Sends Outsource Workers Home, Causing a Ripple Effect," *The Wall Street Journal,* April 1, 2020, https://www.wsj.com; Lauren Weber, "Outsourcing Has Upended the Labor Market—but Not Exactly as Expected," *The Wall Street Journal,* December 17, 2019, https://www.wsj.com; Lawrence Mishel, "Yes, Manufacturing Still Provides a Pay Advantage, but Staffing Firm Outsourcing Is Eroding It," Economic Policy Institute, March 12, 2018, https://www.epi.org.

overseas, hire from an international labor pool, and prepare employees for global assignments. This global expansion can pose some challenges for human resource management as HR employees learn about the cultural differences that shape the conduct of employees in other parts of the world.

Companies that are successful and widely admired not only operate on a multinational scale, but also have workforces and corporate cultures that reflect their global markets. Starbucks entered China in 1999, and today the country is Starbucks' second largest and fastest-growing market, with more than 4,200 stores in 177 cities in mainland China, employing more than 57,000 employees. Despite the economic fallout from COVID-19 in China, Starbucks continued to pay its employees there during the crisis, as well as offered mental health and sick day benefits, child care support, and more.[37]

The Global Workforce For today's and tomorrow's employers, talent comes from a global workforce. Organizations with international operations hire at least some of their employees in the foreign countries where they operate. In fact, regardless of where their customers are located, organizations are looking overseas to hire talented people willing to work for less pay than the U.S. labor market requires. The efforts to hire workers in other countries are common enough that they have spurred the creation of a popular name for the practice: **offshoring.** Just a few years ago, most offshoring involved big manufacturers building factories in countries with lower labor costs. But it has become so easy to send information and software around the world that even start-ups joined the offshoring movement. During the 2000s, large U.S.-based multinational companies were shrinking their domestic employment while hiring overseas. More recently, greater reliance on automation (which reduces the importance of labor costs), even in the services sector, and concern for quality and flexibility have driven a trend toward **reshoring,** or reestablishing operations in North America. Although offshoring continues, the number of manufacturing jobs returning to the United States in 2018 exceeded the number moving overseas. The majority returned from China, where labor costs have risen. According to Deloitte's 2020 Manufacturing Industry Outlook report, however, optimism on the part of U.S. manufacturers is mixed as hiring has slowed due to tariffs and difficulty filling jobs because of applicants' lack of critical skills.[38]

Offshoring
Moving operations from the country where a company is headquartered to a country where pay rates are lower but the necessary skills are available.

Reshoring
Reestablishing operations back in the country where a company is headquartered due to quality and flexibility concerns.

Hiring in developing nations such as India, Mexico, and Brazil gives employers access to people with potential who are eager to work yet who will accept lower wages than elsewhere in the world. Challenges, however, may include employees' lack of familiarity with technology and corporate practices, as well as political and economic instability in the areas. Important issues that HR experts can help companies weigh include whether workers in the offshore locations can provide the same or better skills, how offshoring will affect motivation and recruitment of employees needed in the United States, and whether managers are well prepared to manage and lead offshore employees. At the same time, as companies based in these parts of the world are developing experienced employees and managers, they are becoming competitors for global talent.

Expatriates
Employees assigned to work in another country.

Even hiring at home may involve selection of employees from other countries. The beginning of the 21st century, like the beginning of the last century, has been a time of significant immigration, with more than a million people obtaining permanent resident status in 2018 alone.[39] Figure 2.6 shows the distribution of immigration by continent of origin. The impact of immigration is especially large in some regions of the United States, with the largest immigrant populations being in the states of California, New York, Florida, and Texas. About three-fourths of foreign-born workers are Hispanics and Asians.[40] Employers in tight labor markets—such as those seeking experts in computer science, engineering, and information systems—have been especially likely to recruit international students.

FIGURE 2.6
Where Immigrants to the United States Came from in 2018

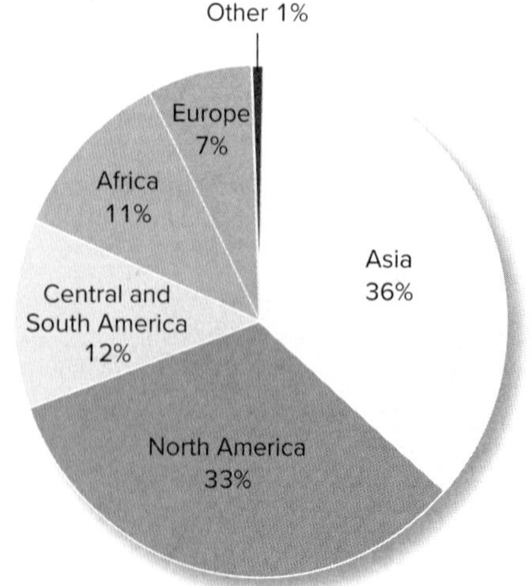

Source: Ryan Baugh, "U.S. Lawful Permanent Residents: 2018," Annual Flow Report (Department of Homeland Security, Office of Immigration Statistics, October 2019), http://www.dhs.gov.

International Assignments Besides hiring an international workforce, organizations must be prepared to send employees to other countries. This requires HR expertise in selecting employees for international assignments and preparing them for those assignments. Employees who take assignments in other countries are called **expatriates.**

U.S. companies must better prepare employees to work in other countries. The failure rate for U.S. expatriates is greater than that for European and Japanese expatriates.[41] To improve in this area, U.S. companies must carefully select employees to work abroad based on their ability to understand and respect the cultural and business norms of the host country. Qualified candidates also need language skills and technical ability. In Chapter 16, we discuss practices for training employees to understand other cultures.

LO 2-6 Discuss how technological developments are affecting human resource management.

Technological Change in HRM

Advances in computer-related technology have had a major impact on the use of information for managing human resources. Decision makers can easily obtain large quantities of data and manipulate it with spreadsheets and statistical software. Furthermore, much of the data can be processed automatically, as illustrated in Table 2.2. Two areas of development have recently been transforming the work of HR departments: advances in information systems and tools for analyzing data about human resources.

HR Information Systems

Human Resource Information System (HRIS)
A computer system used to acquire, store, manipulate, analyze, retrieve, and distribute information related to an organization's human resources.

Cloud Computing
The practice of using a network of remote servers hosted on the Internet to store, manage, and process data.

Many organizations have a **human resource information system (HRIS),** a computer system used to acquire, store, manipulate, analyze, retrieve, and distribute information related to an organization's human resources.[42] Automating these processes can improve accuracy and efficiency, leading some companies to replace routine HR clerical positions with specialists in developing and maintaining information systems. An HRIS can support strategic decision making, help the organization avoid lawsuits, provide data for evaluating programs or policies, and support day-to-day HR decisions. Reflecting this strategic role, some companies call their HRIS a *human capital management system.* This type of system both provides information and automates HR tasks.[43]

The use of an HRIS is more widespread today, largely thanks to the Internet. For example, companies that cannot afford powerful computers can still use sophisticated software and large databases. They can opt for **cloud computing** services, arrangements in which remote server computers do the user's computing tasks. The Internet also expands the use of an HRIS by enabling managers in different locations to share data in real time. And the Internet makes it practical to collect greater amounts of data, including social-media commentary and communications among employees.

TABLE 2.2
Automating HR Tasks

APPLICATION	EXAMPLE
Employee selection	Developers are working on software that can analyze videos of interviews to provide data about candidates' behavior associated with particular characteristics.
Workforce planning	Software can analyze hourly pay to identify and predict situations in which companies are paying for overtime, pointing to opportunities for better workforce management to reduce this expense.
Compensation	A payroll system maintains information about salaries, bonuses, and other pay and automatically computes taxes and benefits costs to be withheld. It keeps pay records up-to-date and shares information with banks receiving direct deposits.
Orientation of new employees	New hires at Royal Bank of Canada use a "preboarding" system to get information about the job, their team, and the company culture.
Training	Training modules are available online for employees to download as they identify relevant skills they want to learn. A training system may also include information about career paths and the necessary skills for each.

Sources: Erica Volini, Pascal Ocean, Michael Stephan, and Brett Walsh, "Digital HR: Platforms, People, and Work," *Rewriting the Rules for the Digital Age* (Deloitte, 2017), pp. 87–94; Mary E. Shacklett, "What Is HCM Software, and What Are the HR Software Benefits?" *TechTarget,* February 2018, http://searchhrsoftware.techtarget.com.

The key advantage of investing in an HRIS is that it helps HR professionals think strategically. As organizations plan, implement, and change strategies, decision makers must be constantly prepared to have the right talent in place at all levels. This requires keeping track of an enormous amount of information related to employees' skills, experience, and training needs, as well as the organization's shifting needs for the future. An HRIS can support talent management by integrating data on recruiting, performance management, and training. Integrating the data means, for example, that the HRIS user can see how specific kinds of recruiting, hiring, and training decisions relate to high performance. Of course, the value of the guidance is only as good as the value of the data and the relevance to actual business situations.[44] Ideally, the company collects accurate, timely data associated with performance outcomes. For example, suppose the level of customer service deteriorates when employees are stressed out and unclear about their goals. The company can conduct frequent one- or two-question surveys about stress levels and goal clarity to identify periods when management needs to intervene.

Organizations need to protect the data in their HRIS databases—a particular concern when data are stored in the cloud or accessed online. A great deal of information is confidential and not suitable for posting on a website for everyone to see. One solution is to set up an *intranet,* which is a network that uses Internet tools but limits access to authorized users in the organization. With any online application, however, the organization must ensure that it has sufficient security measures in place to protect employees' privacy.

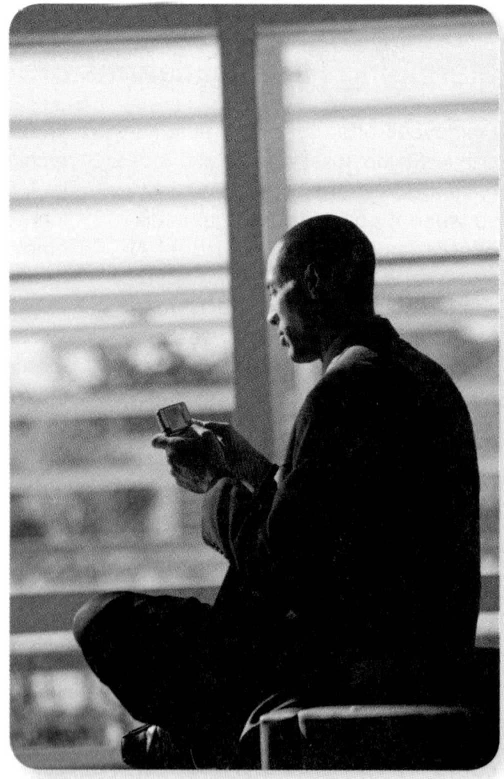

Access to an HRIS from mobile devices is helpful for employees who work outside the office because they can receive and share information online easily. The benefits of products such as smartphones are enormous, but is it possible to be too accessible?
Comstock/PunchStock

People Analytics

Applied to human resource management, the use of computers to analyze large amounts of data and offer information to guide decisions is often called *people analytics.* So far, many businesses are investigating how people analytics can improve HR decisions, but only a few are fully using the capabilities.[45] However, the potential is great, and so is the demand for strategic thinking in HRM. So people analytics may be the future of the field.

Some of the most powerful applications of people analytics apply **artificial intelligence (AI),** a technology that simulates human thinking. It is programmed to conduct queries that enable the software to learn from data, identifying trends and patterns that enable it to deliver better results over time.[46] Systems that include AI can adapt to change and can be set up to make decisions automatically. Another promising technology is the use of *chatbots,* a voice interface that, like Alexa or Siri, answers employees' questions about their insurance, vacation time, and so on.

Artificial Intelligence (AI)
Technology that simulates human thinking, applying experience to deliver better results over time.

AI applications can improve decision making or smooth processes in many areas of human resource management. Here are just a few examples:[47]

- **Job analysis.** Software by Unitive can take data from meetings, create job descriptions, and review them for unintended bias.
- **Recruiting and selection.** Firstjob has a chatbot that fields questions from job candidates; early results show it handling three-fourths of their questions.

HR How To

Managing HR Implications of AI

Employees often associate automation with job loss (historically, jobs have been both gained and lost), so when it comes to artificial intelligence, employees worry whether AI software will replace them. Experts see a more complex picture. HR professionals can help employees and their companies navigate the complexity. Here are some suggestions:

- Instead of thinking about work primarily in terms of jobs and tasks, consider the processes and desired outcomes. Identify the skills needed for the process to proceed smoothly and deliver the desired outcome. Most likely, some skills will be well suited to AI, while others—for example, creativity and ethical reasoning—are still best handled by humans.
- Identify the skills that will be needed for success at the work to be retained by humans. Make employees aware of those skills, and if possible, give them an opportunity to develop skills the organization will need in the future. This respects employees and protects the company's reputation as an ethical employer.
- When bringing in AI and other technology to automate work, look for systems that are easy to learn to use correctly, so more employees can qualify to use the new systems.
- Avoid automating poor decisions. AI models are based on existing information, but new information might provide a better model. If, for example, an organization uses its best performers as a model for the kinds of employees it wants to hire in the future, the organization is ruling out the possibility that a new kind of employee could outperform the current best performers. Even worse, if the current practice rules out candidates in such a way that the company discriminates, the AI model could make such decisions its standard.
- Use the AI system as a source of information to back up creative decision making. Automated tasks can be a rich source of data. Imagine, for instance, a new system for scheduling vacation time; if reports show that hardly any vacation time has been scheduled, it could be a signal that employees are having trouble using the system.

Questions

1. Based on the information given here, suggest a problem that could cause an AI system to give poor results.
2. What should an HR department consider besides cost savings when evaluating the use of artificial intelligence?

Sources: Maria Aspan, "A.I. Is Transforming the Job Interview and Everything After," *Fortune,* January 20, 2020, https://fortune.com; Khalid Durrani, "The Impact of AI in Human Resource Decision-Making Processes," *HR Technologist,* January 6, 2020, https://www.hrtechnologist.com; Peter Cappelli and Prasanna Tambe, "Can Artificial Intelligence Help Answer HR's Toughest Questions?" *Knowledge@Wharton,* August 30, 2019, https://knowledge.wharton.upenn.edu; Jeff Schwartz, Laurence Collins, Heather Stockton, Darryl Wagner, and Brett Walsh, "The Future of Work: The Augmented Workforce," in *Rewriting the Rules for the Digital Age: 2017 Deloitte Global Human Capital Trends* (Deloitte University Press, 2017), pp. 119–129.

- **Performance management.** At a consumer products company, the HR and sales departments teamed up to create a model that predicts and corrects problems in sales performance, including poor hiring decisions.
- **Employee relations.** IBM has a chatbot that answers employees' HR-related questions, submitted by text, data entry, or voice.

The "HR How To" box offers guidance on the HR implications of introducing AI to handle tasks inside and outside the HR department.

Sharing of Human Resource Information

Information technology is changing the way HR departments handle record keeping and information sharing. Today HR employees use technology to automate much of their work in managing employee records and giving employees access to information and enrollment forms for training, benefits, and other programs. As a result, HR employees play a smaller role in maintaining records, and employees now get information through **self-service.** This means employees have online access to information about HR issues such as training, benefits, compensation, and contracts; go online to enroll themselves in programs and services; and provide feedback through online surveys. Today employees routinely look up workplace policies and information about their benefits online, and they may receive electronic notification when deposits are made directly to their bank accounts.

Self-service is especially convenient when combined with the use of mobile computing devices such as smartphones and tablet computers. Self-service offers obvious benefits in terms of privacy and efficiency for tasks such as updating personal information in payroll accounts and scheduling vacation time. It is particularly appealing to millennials and younger workers, who have grown up expecting the flexibility and ease of sharing and retrieving information on the Internet.[48] Reflecting this attitude, today's efforts at self-service are increasingly focused on "employee enablement"—that is, empowering employees to get the information or services they need—rather than mere cost savings.

A growing number of companies are combining employee self-service with management self-service, such as the ability to go online to authorize pay increases, approve expenses, and transfer employees to new positions. More sophisticated systems extend management applications to decision making in areas such as compensation and performance management. To further support management decisions, the company may create an *HR dashboard,* or a display of how the company is performing on specific HR metrics, such as productivity and absenteeism. Advanced users of HRIS are getting the metrics in real time along with guidance on how to respond. At IBM, for example, managers get regular updates on team performance. The system flags patterns that suggest a need to intervene with coaching, recognition of successes, and other measures.[49]

Mc Graw Hill connect

Visit your instructor's Connect® course and access your eBook to view this video.

"In the digital age, an organization's most important source of competitive strength is their people. We have a strongly held belief that technology is going to elevate humans, not eliminate them."

—Ellyn J. Shook
Chief Leadership & Chief HR Officer, Accenture

Video Produced for the Center for Executive Succession in the Darla Moore School of Business at the University of South Carolina by Coal Powered Filmworks

Self-Service
System in which employees have online access to information about HR issues and go online to enroll themselves in programs and provide feedback through surveys.

Change in the Employment Relationship

LO 2-7 Explain how the nature of the employment relationship is changing.

Technology and the other trends we have described in this chapter require managers at all levels to make rapid changes in response to new opportunities, competitive challenges, and customer demands. These changes are most likely to succeed in flexible, forward-thinking organizations, and the employees who will thrive in such organizations need to be flexible and open to change as well. In this environment, employers and employees have begun to reshape the employment relationship.[50]

A Psychological Contract

We can think of that relationship in terms of a **psychological contract,** a description of what an employee expects to contribute in an employment relationship and what the employer will provide the employee in exchange for those contributions.[51] Unlike a written sales contract, the psychological contract is not formally put into words. Instead it describes unspoken expectations that are widely held by employers and employees. In the traditional version of this psychological contract, organizations expected their employees to contribute time, effort, skills, abilities, and loyalty. In return, the organizations would provide job security and opportunities for promotion.

Psychological Contract
A description of what an employee expects to contribute in an employment relationship and what the employer will provide the employee in exchange for those contributions.

However, this arrangement is being replaced with a new type of psychological contract. Companies expect employees to take more responsibility for their own careers, from seeking training to balancing work and family. These expectations result in less job security for employees, who can count on working for several companies over the course of a career. In exchange for top performance and working longer hours without job security, employees want companies to provide flexible work schedules, comfortable working conditions, more control over how they accomplish work, training and development opportunities, and financial incentives based on how the organization performs. Employees realize that companies cannot provide employment security, so they want *employability*. This means they want their company to provide training and job experiences to help ensure that they can find other employment opportunities.

In the federal government's most recent survey of employee tenure in 2018, workers age 25 and older report they had been working with their present employer for a median of just 4.2 years.[52] Workers 55 and older tend to have a much longer tenure, and so do workers in government jobs. Still, if less than five years with a company is typical, this amounts to many employers in the course of one's career. In fact, some employees engage in *job hopping,* the intentional practice of changing jobs frequently—say, every year or two—especially in recent years, when the national unemployment rate had dropped to historic lows with employers offering attractive salaries and benefits to fill open positions.[53] Job hopping can be appealing to an employee as a way to stave off boredom and win some rapid increases in pay and responsibility. Some employees even are able to pick short-term jobs that give them valuable, carefully targeted experiences. However, there are some significant disadvantages. Every time the employee starts with a new employer, the employee needs to learn a new network of contacts and a new set of policies and procedures. This can slow down the employee's ability to learn a career in depth and reduce the employee's value to each employer. Therefore, employers tend to be wary of a job candidate who seems to have a history of job hopping. They may interpret job hopping as evidence of a character flaw such as inability to make a commitment or lack of conscientiousness. Often, employees can enjoy variety, develop skills, and build an interesting career without job hopping by asking for challenging assignments and cultivating a network of professional contacts within their present company.

Declining Union Membership

Another trend affecting the employment relationship has been ongoing for several decades. As we will explore in Chapter 15, the percentage of employees who belong to unions has been declining since the 1980s. Outside of government agencies, fewer U.S. workers today are union members. This trend is consistent with the idea of individual workers taking responsibility for their own careers. Whereas once many workers saw strength in numbers from joining a union, perhaps workers of the Internet era will prefer using numbers a different way: finding salary data and employer reviews online to negotiate their own career paths.

LO 2-8 Discuss how the need for flexibility affects human resource management.

Flexibility

The psychological contract largely results from the HRM challenge of building a committed, productive workforce in turbulent economic conditions—conditions that offer opportunity for financial success but can also quickly turn sour, making every employee expendable. From the organization's perspective, the key to survival in a fast-changing environment is flexibility. Organizations want to be able to change as fast as customer needs and economic conditions change. Flexibility in human resource management includes flexible staffing levels and flexible work schedules.

Flexible Staffing Levels A flexible workforce is one the organization can quickly reshape and resize to meet its changing needs. To be able to do this without massive hiring and firing campaigns, organizations are using more alternative work arrangements. **Alternative work arrangements** are methods of staffing other than the traditional hiring of full-time employees. There are a variety of methods, with the following being most common:

Alternative Work Arrangements
Methods of staffing other than the traditional hiring of full-time employees (for example, use of independent contractors, on-call workers, temporary workers, and contract workers).

- *Independent contractors* are self-employed individuals with multiple clients.
- *On-call workers* are persons who work for an organization only when they are needed.
- *Temporary workers* are employed by a temporary agency; client organizations pay the agency for the services of these workers.
- *Contract workers* are employed directly by a company for a specific time or on a specific project as stipulated in a written contract.

However, employers need to use these options with care. In general, if employers direct workers in the details of how and when they do their jobs, these workers are legally defined as employees, not contractors. In that case, employers must meet the legal requirements for paying the employer's share of Social Security, Medicare, and unemployment insurance.

Recent research estimates that more than one-third of the U.S. workforce consists of contingent workers of one kind or another. Most of them are on the payrolls of the companies they serve, with self-employed workers representing around 11% of workers.[54] Employers once mainly relied on contingent workers to fill administrative jobs, but now turn to contingent work arrangements for production workers, technical support, and even some professional tasks, such as graphic design, engineering, and finance. A major reason for the popularity of contingent work arrangements is that paying contractors enables an organization to pay only for completion of specific tasks and therefore to control costs.

Companies that rely primarily on alternative work arrangements to meet service and product demand are competing in the **gig economy.** Gig workers are typically independent contractors who control when and where they work and often are assigned work through a website or mobile app (for example, a ride-sharing driver). The model for the gig economy focuses more on using a contingent workforce and more project-based assignments and has now been adopted in part by more and more U.S. businesses. This approach to project-based employment will require a different set of management skills for line managers who might need to manage virtual teams, remote workers, and constantly changing work terms. According to the ADP Research Institute, the share of gig workers at U.S. businesses has increased by more than 15% over the last decade with no end in sight.[55]

Gig Economy
Situation in which companies rely primarily on alternative work arrangements to meet service and product demands.

More workers in alternative employment relationships are choosing these arrangements, but preferences vary. Most independent contractors and contract workers have this type of arrangement by choice. In contrast, temporary agency workers and on-call workers are likely to prefer traditional full-time employment. There is some debate about whether nontraditional employment relationships are good or bad. Some labor analysts argue that alternative work arrangements are substandard jobs featuring low pay, fear of unemployment, poor health insurance and retirement benefits, and dissatisfying work. Sometimes it is difficult or impossible for organizations to know whether these contract workers, located anywhere in the world, have safe working conditions and are not children. Others claim that these jobs provide flexibility for companies and employees alike. With alternative work arrangements, organizations can more easily modify the number of their employees. Continually adjusting staffing levels is especially cost effective for an organization that has fluctuating demand for its products and services. And when an organization downsizes by laying off temporary and part-time employees, the damage to morale among permanent full-time workers is likely to be less severe.

Flexible Work Schedules The globalization of the world economy and the development of e-commerce have made the notion of a 40-hour workweek obsolete. As a result, companies need to be staffed 24 hours a day, seven days a week. Employees in manufacturing environments and service call centers are being asked to work 12-hour days or to work afternoon or

Multitasking has become a way of life for many employees who need to make the most of every minute. This trend is affecting human resource management and the employees it supports. Fuse/Getty Images

midnight shifts. Similarly, professional employees face long hours and work demands that spill over into their personal lives. E-mail, texts, and tweets bombard employees with information and work demands. In the car, on vacation, on planes, and even in the bathroom, employees can be interrupted by work demands. More demanding work results in greater employee stress, less satisfied employees, loss of productivity, and higher turnover–all of which are costly for companies.

Many organizations are taking steps to provide more flexible work schedules, to protect employees' free time, and to more productively use employees' work time. Workers consider flexible schedules a valuable way to ease the pressures and conflicts of trying to balance work and nonwork activities. Employers are using flexible schedules to recruit and retain employees and to increase satisfaction and productivity. In a recent survey by FlexJobs, 69% of respondents said that flexible work options were one of the most important factors they consider when evaluating a job prospect.[56]

THINKING ETHICALLY

HOW SOLID IS YOUR DIGITAL FOOTPRINT?

Survey results suggest that today people consider it appropriate to make connections on social media sites like Instagram and Facebook. Younger employees are likelier than older ones to feel comfortable with counting co-workers among their friends.

Blurring the lines between professional and personal communications has become especially perilous in today's political climate, where politically oriented comments often have a tone that is angry or mistrustful of those with different views. Some employees have been fired for critical posts that employers believe cross a line into offensiveness. The response is especially likely when the employee has a prominent position in the organization or includes the employer's name in his or her profile. Some employers try to prevent trouble by establishing a social-media policy that may express legally supported boundaries, such as not using the organization's hardware, time, or accounts to make posts on personal social-media accounts.

Personal social-media posts are more a matter of values than the law. Some widely shared standards include try to be honest, avoid slurs and insults, and listen if an inner voice is making you feel uncomfortable about a message or photo you're about to post. Some social-media users set strict standards for themselves–for example, taking care to comment respectfully and to present a professional image.

Questions

1. Which of the following would you include in your social-media networks? Current co-workers? Past co-workers? Current supervisor? Competitors?
2. What standards do you apply to your own social-media conduct? Which of these, if any, would you consider ethical standards?

Sources: Ema Linaker, "How to Develop a Digital Presence for Professional Success," *Entrepreneur,* www.entrepreneur.com, accessed April 11, 2020; Josh Ochs, "How Can Your Online Footprint Impact Your Career?" *Media Leaders,* October 11, 2019, https://medialeaders.com; Debby Carreau, "Never, Ever Friend These 5 Types of Co-workers on Facebook, Instagram–or Any Social Media Sites," *CNBC,* March 29, 2019, https://www.cnbc.com; Purdue Global University, "3 Tips to Protect Your Online Reputation and Keep Your Digital Footprint under Control," November 30, 2018, https://www.purdueglobal.edu; Aliah D. Wright, "Social Postings Still Land Employees in Hot Water," *Society for Human Resource Management,* March 6, 2017, https://www.shrm.org.

SUMMARY

LO 2-1 Describe trends in labor force composition and how they affect human resource management.

- An organization's internal labor force comes from its external labor market–individuals actively seeking employment.
- In the United States, the labor market is aging and becoming more racially and ethnically diverse, with women constituting roughly half of the total.
- To compete for talent, organizations must be flexible enough to meet the needs of older workers and must recruit from a diverse population; establish bias-free HR systems; and help employees understand and appreciate cultural differences.
- Organizations need employees with skills that may be hard to find: decision making, customer service, and teamwork, as well as technical skills.

- To meet this challenge, organizations may hire employees who lack certain skills, then train them for their jobs.

LO 2-2 Summarize areas in which human resource management can support the goal of creating a high-performance work system.

- To find and keep the best possible fit between their social system and technical system, HRM recruits and selects employees with broad skills and strong motivation, especially in organizations that rely on knowledge workers.
- Job design and appropriate systems for assessment and rewards have a central role in supporting employee empowerment and teamwork.

LO 2-3 Define employee empowerment, and explain its role in the modern organization.

- Employee empowerment means giving employees responsibility and authority to make decisions regarding all aspects of product development or customer service. The organization holds employees accountable for products and services, and in exchange, the employees share in the rewards (or losses) that result.
- Selection decisions should provide employees who have the necessary decision-making and interpersonal skills.
- Job design should give employees latitude for decision making.
- Employees should be trained to handle their broad responsibilities.
- Feedback and rewards must be appropriate for the work of empowered employees.
- HRM can also play a role in giving employees access to the information they need.

LO 2-4 Identify ways HR professionals can support organizational strategies for growth, quality, and efficiency.

- HR professionals should be familiar with the organization's strategy and may even play a role in developing the strategy.
- In a merger or acquisition, HRM must lead efforts to manage change with skillful employee relations and meaningful rewards. HR professionals can bring "people issues" to the attention of the managers leading change, provide training in conflict-resolution skills, and apply knowledge of the other organization's culture. HR professionals also must resolve differences between the companies' HR systems, such as benefits packages and performance appraisals.
- For empowering employees to practice total quality management, job design is essential.
- Cost control may focus on a specific issue, such as managing health benefits, or on support for a strategic move such as downsizing, reengineering, or outsourcing.
- To support cost control through downsizing, the HR department can develop voluntary programs to reduce the workforce or can help identify the least valuable employees to lay off. Employee relations can help maintain the morale of employees who remain after a downsizing.
- In reengineering, the HR department can lead in communicating with employees and providing training. It will also have to prepare new approaches for recruiting and appraising employees that are better suited to the reengineered jobs.
- Outsourcing presents similar issues related to job design and employee selection.

LO 2-5 Summarize ways in which human resource management can support organizations expanding internationally.

- Organizations with international operations hire employees in foreign countries where they operate, so they need knowledge of differences in culture and business practices.
- At home, qualified candidates include immigrants, so HRM needs to understand and train employees to deal with differences in cultures, as well as to ensure laws are followed.
- HRM helps organizations select and prepare employees for overseas assignments.
- To support efficiency and growth, HR staff can prepare companies for offshoring, in which operations are moved to countries where wages are lower or demand is growing. HR experts can help organizations determine whether workers in offshore locations can provide the same or better skills, how offshoring will affect motivation and recruitment of employees needed in the United States, and whether managers are prepared to manage offshore employees.

LO 2-6 Discuss how technological developments are affecting human resource management.

- Information systems for HRM are widely used and often are provided through the Internet.
- Internet applications include searching for talent globally, using online job postings, screening candidates online, providing career-related information on the organization's website, and delivering training online.
- Online information sharing enables employee self-service for many HR needs, from application forms to training modules to information about the details of company policies and benefits.
- Using computers to analyze large amounts of data is often called people analytics. Some of the most powerful applications of people analytics apply artificial intelligence (AI), which simulates human thinking. AI applications can improve decision making or smooth processes in many areas of HRM.

LO 2-7 Explain how the nature of the employment relationship is changing.

- The employment relationship takes the form of a "psychological contract" that describes what employees and employers expect from the employment relationship, including unspoken expectations that are widely held.
- In the traditional version, organizations expected their employees to contribute time, effort, skills, abilities, and loyalty in exchange for job security and opportunities for promotion.
- Modern organizations' needs are constantly changing, so organizations require top performance and longer work hours but cannot provide job security. Instead, employees seek flexible work schedules, comfortable working conditions, greater autonomy, opportunities for training and development, and performance-related financial incentives.
- For HRM, the changes require planning for flexible staffing levels.
- For employees, the changes may make job hopping look attractive, but this career strategy often backfires.
- Union membership has been declining, which is consistent with the idea of taking personal responsibility for one's career.

LO 2-8 Discuss how the need for flexibility affects human resource management.

- Organizations seek flexibility in staffing levels through alternatives to the traditional employment relationship–outsourcing and temporary and contract workers who might be hired on a project basis as part of the new "gig economy." The use of such workers can affect job design and also the motivation of the organization's permanent employees.
- Organizations also may seek flexible work schedules, including shortened workweeks, which can be a way for employees to adjust work hours to meet personal and family needs.
- Organizations also may move employees to different jobs to meet changes in demand.

KEY TERMS

internal labor force, 30
external labor market, 30
high-performance work systems, 36
knowledge workers, 38
employee empowerment, 38
teamwork, 40
total quality management (TQM), 42
reengineering, 45
outsourcing, 45
offshoring, 47
reshoring, 47
expatriates, 47
human resource information system (HRIS), 48
cloud computing, 48
artificial intelligence (AI), 49
self-service, 51
psychological contract, 51
alternative work arrangements, 53
gig economy, 53

REVIEW AND DISCUSSION QUESTIONS

1. How does each of the following labor force trends affect HRM? *(LO 2-1)*
   a. Aging of the labor force.
   b. Diversity of the labor force.
   c. Skill deficiencies of the labor force.
2. At many organizations, goals include improving people's performance by relying on knowledge workers, empowering employees, and assigning work to teams. How can HRM support these efforts? *(LO 2-2)*
3. How do HRM practices such as performance management and work design encourage employee empowerment? *(LO 2-3)*
4. Merging, downsizing, and reengineering all can radically change the structure of an organization. Choose one of these changes, and describe HRM's role in making the change succeed. If possible, apply your discussion to an actual merger, downsizing, or reengineering effort that has recently occurred. *(LO 2-4)*
5. When an organization decides to operate facilities in other countries, how can HRM practices support this change? *(LO 2-5)*
6. Why do organizations outsource HRM functions? How does outsourcing affect the role of human resource professionals? Would you be more attracted to the role of the HR professional in an organization that outsources many HR activities or in the outside firm that has the contract to provide the HR services? Why? *(LO 2-6)*
7. What HRM functions could an organization provide through self-service? What are some advantages and disadvantages of using self-service for these functions? *(LO 2-6)*
8. How is the employment relationship that is typical of modern organizations different from the relationship of a generation ago? *(LO 2-7)*
9. Discuss several advantages of flexible work schedules. What are some disadvantages? *(LO 2-8)*

SELF-ASSESSMENT EXERCISE

How Do HR Trends Affect a Company That You Like?

Think of a company you have worked for, or find an annual report for a company you are interested in working for. (Many companies post their annual reports on their website.) Then answer the following questions.

Questions

1. How has the company been affected by the trends discussed in this chapter?
2. Does the company use the HR practices recommended in this chapter?
3. What else should the company do to deal with the challenges posed by the trends discussed in this chapter?

TAKING RESPONSIBILITY

New on Restaurant Menus: Predictive Scheduling

Restaurants and other businesses have improved their efficiency by adjusting workers' schedules day by day and even hour by hour. If the weather turns bad, some waiters and kitchen staff might get a call not to come in for hours they expected to work. A surge in traffic after a local event might lead managers to call in extra workers. With this approach to scheduling, the business is paying only for the workers it needs.

This practice poses difficulties for the workers, however. Many restaurant jobs are part-time, and many employees say they want to work more hours. One option would be to take a second part-time job, but being on call at the first job makes it impossible. Other challenges with a schedule that changes from week to week are that these employees have difficulty attending school and arranging child care. When variable schedules combine working through closing one night and starting at the next day's opening, it may also be impossible to get enough sleep. Despite these challenges, workers typically say they are available anytime, because they have found that employers otherwise do not hire them.

In New Hampshire, Oregon, and some U.S. cities (including Chicago, New York, Philadelphia, and Seattle), workers' complaints about these conditions have led governments to pass laws requiring "predictive scheduling." These laws specify the amount of notice (say, seven days) that restaurants must give employees before they have to compensate them. Employees called with less notice must be paid extra. Employers may also have to pay a few hours' wages to employees who are on call but not called in. Some of the laws set a minimum amount of rest time between the end of one shift and start of the next.

Where predictive-scheduling laws apply, restaurant managers are scrambling to meet the challenge of predicting work far enough ahead, often with scheduling software such as Homebase, 7shifts, and HotSchedules, which estimate demand and provide a way for employees to opt in or out of working certain blocks of time. Even where these laws are not in place, some managers consider predictable schedules as the right way to treat employees. Mary Cho, co-owner of Dak & Bop in Houston, says scheduling is a constant challenge but also "an essential part of being a good employer," because it recognizes that workers are human beings with a variety of obligations, not just being available to work. She asks employees to tell her when they're available, and then she uses Homebase to assign workers to hours they have not blocked off.

Questions

1. Would you describe the way restaurants schedule workers as an example of a "flexible" work schedule? Why or why not?
2. What would you say are a restaurant manager's ethical responsibilities in scheduling workers? How would a policy of ethical scheduling practices affect a restaurant's business outcomes?

Sources: Chris Marr and Andrew Wallender, "Philadelphia Worker Scheduling Law Takes Effect During Pandemic," *Bloomberg Law*, March 31, 2020, https://news.bloomberglaw.com; Gloria Dawson, "It's about Time: Making Restaurant Schedules More Predictable and Why It Matters," *Restaurant Hospitality*, January 2020, pp. 28–31; Lisa Jennings, "Preparing for Predictive Scheduling," *Restaurant Hospitality*, September 2019, pp. 20–21.

MANAGING TALENT

Adidas Races to Address Racial Injustice

While some employers have treated the growing racial and ethnic diversity of the U.S. workforce as a strategic opportunity, other companies have maintained practices that result in employees being mostly white, especially at the top. Makers of athletic shoes have come under pointed criticism for relying on marketing strategies that highlight exceptional Black athletes and performers while placing few people of color in leadership positions. One of those companies is the

U.S. unit of Germany-based Adidas, which has an all-white team of top executives and an all-white board of directors. Adidas has responded with plans to change.

Seeds for change were sown in late 2018, when Zion Armstrong became president of Adidas North America. An employee publicly requested more diverse leadership, a request backed up by other employees in statements to the industry publication *Footwear News*. These employees objected to what they saw as a culture that rewards white employees with opportunities that employees of color struggle to obtain. The following summer, a group of Asian and LGBTQ Adidas employees issued statements to say that they, too, were cut off from opportunities for development and advancement.

The issue came to a head in 2020. Deaths of unarmed Black persons, including George Floyd and Breonna Taylor, at the hands of police inspired demonstrations across the country. Discussions about racism in policing spilled over into discussions of racism in society as a whole, including the treatment of workers. At Adidas, a group of 13 Black employees formed a coalition to achieve greater support for Black employees, including change at the company's highest ranks in Germany. The coalition sent top management a document called "Our State of Emergency," in which they requested investment in Black employees, investment in the Black community, support for racial justice, and a demonstration of accountability. Even as U.S. and German managers were engaged in meetings and educating themselves about the situation, hundreds of employees of color agreed to set their status to "out of office" until they received a favorable response.

Within days, Adidas issued a response. The company acknowledged that its success rests on Black employees, Black consumers, and the Black stars who promote the brand. It promised that 30% of future hires in its U.S. office would be Black and Hispanic individuals and that it would enforce its existing zero-tolerance policy on discrimination. Adidas promised to bring in a third-party investigator to ensure the policy would be enforced without any retaliation against employees who complain. It also promised to invest in Black communities with scholarships and support for community programs.

Employees kept up the pressure. Some drew attention to a 2019 meeting of U.S. employees in which the company's HR chief, Karen Parkin, had referred to racism as "noise" that was not an issue for Adidas. That same month, an Adidas designer later said, she received a package of "design inspiration" materials from corporate headquarters in which one image was an Asian man wearing a T-shirt displaying the Confederate battle flag. A group of more than 80 employees asked the company to investigate whether Parkin was adequately addressing racism. She apologized for her word choice, and the company said it had no plans to investigate her. Parkin recently announced her retirement, saying she had become a distraction that "inhibits the company from moving forward."

Questions

1. Why is the growing diversity of the U.S. population a significant trend for Adidas? What grade would you give the company for its response to this trend?
2. Adidas is a global company based in Europe. What HR challenges might that pose for addressing employees' concerns about racial discrimination?

Sources: Khadeeja Safdar, "Adidas HR Chief to Retire after Criticism from Black Employees," *The Wall Street Journal*, June 30, 2020, https://www.wsj.com; Reuters, "Adidas Rejects Investigating HR Chief in Race Row," *The New York Times*, June 17, 2020; Khadeeja Safdar, "Some Adidas Staff Ask Board to Investigate HR Chief," *The Wall Street Journal*, June 16, 2020, https://www.wsj.com; Sheena Butler-Young," How Adidas Became the Shoe Industry's Unwitting Racial Equality Case Study," *Footwear News*, accessed at *Yahoo News*, June 15, 2020, https://www.yahoo.com; Rachel Ranosa, "Adidas: 'It's Time to Own Up to Our Silence,'" *Human Resources Director*, June 15, 2020, https://www.hcamag.com; Khadeeja Safdar, "Adidas Promises to Hire Black, Latino People for 30% of New U.S. Jobs," *The Wall Street Journal*, June 9, 2020, https://www.wsj.com; Jacob Gallagher, Khadeeja Safdar, and Sharon Terlep, "Adidas Tweeted against Racism; Its Black Workers Say That Isn't Enough," *The Wall Street Journal*, June 9, 2020, https://www.wsj.com.

HR IN SMALL BUSINESS

Lob Aims High in Employee Retention

The software company called Lob is cofounder and CEO Leore Avidar's attempt to create a workplace that is the opposite of what he experienced in his first job. Avidar started his career at a Wall Street firm trading mortgage-backed securities. He felt that he and his co-workers were going through the motions each day without any meaningful collaboration. He had expected to feel a sense of mutual loyalty between himself and his organization, but instead he felt insignificant. So Avidar decided to start his own company, which he could run consistently with his values. That company, Lob, provides the systems and software to automate the creation and delivery of direct mail, bringing that form of marketing into the Internet age.

Most important to Avidar are Lob's values, beginning with the idea that people are the company's foundation. In particular, the company values diversity; it recently won Tech in Motion's Timmy Award for the Best Tech Workplace for Diversity. The criteria were that it hires for diversity, promotes collaboration and diverse thinking in support of innovation, and gives employees the resources they need to value diversity.

Avidar's key HR goal for Lob is that employees will want to stay for 30 years. This is a startling goal for the high-tech industry, where employee turnover is over 13%, and the giant companies typically keep an employee for an average of just one year. To achieve this, Lob emphasizes career growth. Employees have access to offsite development programs, industry conferences, and regular feedback from their managers, with the expectation that the work of pursuing a career path is the employee's personal responsibility. For Avidar, this focus is personal. He says coaching employees and seeing their development are what make him the most excited and proud as a business owner. Lob also offers attractive benefits, including an open policy for time off. When the COVID-19 pandemic shifted work to employees' homes, Avidar himself communicated directly with employees, citing his company's core value of "drawing the blueprint," to lay out the details of how employees, suppliers, and customers would be protected as they continued to enable customers' ability to stay in touch with *their* customers.

Avidar's values seem to be working well for Lob, which before the 2020 economic downturn caused by COVID-19 was aiming to pass the 100-employee mark. Lob's revenues grew more than sevenfold between 2015 and 2018, placing it on some lists of the fastest-growing companies. As the company has grown, it has been able to keep recruiting and hiring focused on filling new jobs, not replacing workers who cycle out after a couple of years. It even helps Avidar attract the best investors, the ones focused on long-term value.

Questions

1. Describe Avidar's experience of his psychological contract with his first employer. How does it compare with the psychological contract he seeks with employees at Lob?
2. How do Avidar's values and approach to human resource management support Lob's business success?

Sources: Company website, "Careers," https://lob.com, accessed April 11, 2020; Leore Avidar, "Our Commitment to Employee Health and Business Community," *Lob Blog,* https://lob.com, accessed April 9, 2020; Timmy Awards, "About Us," *Tech in Motion,* https://timmyawards.techinmotionevents.com, accessed April 3, 2020; Rob Dube, "In a High Turnover Industry, He Built a Startup Where Team Members Want to Stay for Life," *Forbes,* April 2, 2020, https://www.forbes.com.

NOTES

1. L. Weber, "A Counterintuitive Fix for Robot-Driven Unemployment," *The Wall Street Journal,* January 6, 2020, https://www.wsj.com; A. Hufford, "American Factories Demand White-Collar Education for Blue-Collar Work," *The Wall Street Journal,* December 9, 2019, https://www.wsj.com; A. Shah, "Factory Workers Become Coders as Companies Automate," *The Wall Street Journal,* May 17, 2019, https://www.wsj.com.
2. Bureau of Labor Statistics, "Employment Projections: 2018-2028," news release, September 4, 2019, and "Employment Projections, Table 3.1," https://www.bls.gov, accessed April 10, 2020.
3. Bureau of Labor Statistics, Employment Projections, Table 3.1.
4. P. Overberg and J. Adamy, "Elderly in U.S. Are Projected to Outnumber Children for First Time," *The Wall Street Journal,* March 13, 2018, https://www.wsj.com.
5. T. Francis and F. Hoefel, 'True Gen': Generation Z and Its Implications for Companies," *McKinsey & Company,* https://www.mckinsey.com, accessed April 10, 2020; G. Pryor, "Generational Differences and the Shifting Workplace," *Forbes,* September 12, 2019, https://www.forbes.com.
6. Bureau of Labor Statistics, Employment Projections, Table 3.1.
7. Ibid.
8. U.S. Department of Homeland Security, "Legal Immigration and Adjustment of Status Report Fiscal Year 2019, Quarter 4," https://www.dhs.gov, accessed April 10, 2020.
9. R. Sanchez, "Indictments of Workers Mount after the Mississippi Immigration Raids, But No Employers Have Been Charged," *CNN,* August 21, 2019, https://www.cnn.com; R. Merie, "As Workplace Raids Multiply, Trump Administration Charges Few Companies," *The Washington Post,* August 9, 2019, https://www.washingtonpost.com.
10. T. H. Cox and S. Blake, "Managing Cultural Diversity: Implications for Organizational Competitiveness," *The Executive* 5 (1991), pp. 45–56.
11. "Glassdoor Survey Finds Three in Five U.S. Employees Have Experienced or Witnessed Discrimination Based on Age, Race, Gender or LGBTQ Identity at Work," October 23, 2019, https://www.glassdoor.com; M. Krentz, "Survey: What Diversity and Inclusion Policies Do Employees Actually Want?" *Harvard Business Review,* February 5, 2019, https://hbr.org.
12. L. L. C. Brady and E. Ratinoff, "Do Your 'Now Hiring' Signs Point toward Inclusion?" *New Hampshire Business Review,* April 17, 2015, www.nhbr.com.
13. D. Belkin, "More Companies Teach Workers What College Can't," *The Wall Street Journal,* http://www.wsj.com, March 22, 2018; Geoff Colvin, "Ready, Set, Jump!" *Fortune,* February 1, 2018, pp. 44–52.
14. National Association of Manufacturers, "Top 20 Facts about Manufacturing," http://www.nam.org, accessed April 10, 2020; Douglas Belkin, "Why an Honors Student Wants to Skip College and Go to Trade School," *The Wall Street Journal,* March 5, 2018, https://www.wsj.com; Edwin Koc, "Is There Really a Skills Gap?" *NACE Journal,* February 2018, http://www.naceweb.org.
15. J. A. Neal and C. L. Trombley, "From Incremental Change to Retrofit: Creating High-Performance Work Systems," *Academy of Management Executive* 9 (1995), pp. 42–54.
16. U.S. Bureau of Labor Statistics, "Fastest Growing Occupations, 2018–2028" and "Most New Jobs," *Occupational Outlook Handbook,* last modified September 4, 2019, https://www.bls.gov.
17. McKinsey Global Institute, *The Future of Work in America: People and Places, Today and Tomorrow,* July 2019, https://www.mckinsey.com.
18. M. Vickers, "Struggling to Manage Knowledge Workers," *American Management Association,* January 24, 2019, https://www.amanet.org; E. Eyl, "You're More than Just a 'Knowledge Worker,'" *Huffington Post,* May 11, 2015, http://www.huffingtonpost.com; R. Wartzman, "What Peter Drucker Knew about 2020," *Harvard Business Review,* October 16, 2014, https://hbr.org.
19. P. Cappelli, "Your Approach to Hiring Is All Wrong," *Harvard Business Review,* May–June 2019, https://hbr.org; D. Meinert, "HR Gets Creative to Hire Manufacturing Workers," *HR Magazine,* November 2015, http://www.shrm.org.
20. A. Lee, S. Willis, and A. W. Tan, "When Empowering Employees Works, and When It Doesn't," *Harvard Business Review,* March 2, 2018, https://hbr.org; T. J. Atchison, "The Employment Relationship," *Academy of Management Executive* 5 (1991), pp. 52–62.

21. University of Oxford, "Happy Workers Are 13% More Productive," October 25, 2019, https://phys.org; R. Vance, *Employee Engagement and Commitment* (Alexandria, VA: Society for Human Resource Management, 2006); M. Huselid, "The Impact of Human Resource Management Practices on Turnover, Productivity, and Corporate Financial Performance," *Academy of Management Journal* 38 (1995), pp. 635–672; S. Payne and S. Webber, "Effects of Service Provider Attitudes and Employment Status on Citizenship Behaviors and Customers" Attitudes and Loyalty Behavior," *Journal of Applied Psychology* 91 (2006), pp. 365–368.
22. Dominic Barton, Dennis Carey, and Ram Charan, "One Bank's Agile Team Experiment," *Harvard Business Review,* March/April 2018, https://hbr.org.
23. "HR in the Hot Seat: Cheryl Stargratt, Tangerine," *Human Resources Director,* September 11, 2017, https://www.hrmonline.ca.
24. G. Brooks, "How HR Is Key to Successful Mergers and Acquisitions," *Forbes*, March 15, 2019, https://www.forbes.com.
25. J. R. Jablonski, *Implementing Total Quality Management: An Overview* (San Diego: Pfeiffer, 1991).
26. R. Hodgetts, F. Luthans, and S. Lee, "New Paradigm Organizations: From Total Quality to Learning to World-Class," *Organizational Dynamics,* Winter 1994, pp. 5–19.
27. Karl-Heinz Oehler and Salvatore Falletta, "Should Companies Have Free Rein to Use Predictive Analytics?" *HR Magazine,* June 2015, https://www.shrm.org; Mark Feffer, "Processing People," *HR Magazine,* October 2015, https://www.shrm.org.
28. S. Miller, "15 Ways Employers Can Reduce Health Care Spending That Aren't Cost-Sharing," *Society for Human Resource Management,* February 27, 2019, https://www.shrm.org.
29. G. Heeb, "2019 Was One of the Decade's Worst Years for Job Cuts in the US," *Markets Insider,* January 2, 2020, https://markets.businessinsider.com.
30. Claire Zillman, "A Company with No Job Openings," *Fortune,* November 1, 2015, p. 44.
31. A. Church, "Organizational Downsizing: What Is the Role of the Practitioner?," *Industrial–Organizational Psychologist* 33, no. 1 (1995), pp. 63–74.
32. S. Chaney and D. Harrison, "U.S. Jobless Claims Soar for Third Straight Week," *The Wall Street Journal,* April 9, 2020, https://www.wsj.com.
33. R. Maurer, "Gig Workers, Self-Employed Covered under the CARES Act," *Society for Human Resource Management,* April 3, 2020, https://www.shrm.org; G. Watson, T. LaJoie, H. Li, and D. Bunn, "Congress Approves Economic Relief Plan for Individuals and Businesses," *Tax Foundation,* April 1, 2020, https://taxfoundation.org.
34. "Collection: Strategies to Manage Coronavirus in the Workplace," *Human Resource Executive,* April 13, 2020, https://hrexecutive.com.
35. N. Syed, "COVID-19: HR's Main Challenges Revealed," *Human Resources Director,* April 1, 2020, https://www.hcamag.com.
36. Rebecca Baldridge, "Best HR Outsourcing for Small Business in 2018," *Inc.*, February 2, 2018, https://www.inc.com; Lisa Peterson, "Time to Outsource Human Resources?" *Argus Leader (Sioux Falls, SD),* May 8, 2017, https://www.argus.leader.com; Amanda McGrory-Dixon, "The Outsourcing Experience," *Employee Benefit News,* April 1, 2015, http://www.benefitnews.com.
37. P. Bajpai, "How Starbucks (SBUX) Is Getting Itself Back on Track in China in Wake of COVID-19," *NASDAQ,* March 25, 2020, https://www.nasdaq.com.
38. P. Wellener, "2020 Outlook Mixed for U.S. Manufacturing," *The Wall Street Journal,* February 13, 2020, https://deloitte.wsj.com; K. Trafecante, "The Myth of the Manufacturing Jobs Renaissance," *CNN Business,* February 9, 2020, https://www.cnn.com.
39. R. Baugh, "U.S. Lawful Permanent Resident: 2018," *Annual Flow Report* (Department of Homeland Security, Office of Immigration Statistics), October 2019, http://www.dhs.gov.
40. Ibid.; Bureau of Labor Statistics, "Foreign-Born Workers: Labor Force Characteristics, 2018," news release, May 16, 2019, https://bls.gov.
41. R. L. Tung, "Expatriate Assignments: Enhancing Success and Minimizing Failure," *Academy of Management Executive* 12, no. 4 (1988), pp. 93–106.
42. P. Cappelli and A. Tavis, "HR Goes Agile," *Harvard Business Review,* https://hbr.org, accessed April 11, 2020; M. V. Rafter, "Plugging In," *Workforce,* January 1, 2018, http://www.workforce.com.
43. P. Ghosh, "What Is Human Capital Management (HCM)?" *HR Technologist,* June 19, 2019, https://www.hrtechnologist.com.
44. P. Cappelli, "There Is No Such Thing as Big Data in HR," *Harvard Business Review,* June 2, 2017, https://hbr.org.
45. D. Zielinski, "People Analytics Software Is Changing the HR Game," *HR Magazine,* December 4, 2019, https://www.shrm.org; V. Ratanjee, "How HR Can Optimize People Analytics," *Gallup,* July 5, 2019, https://www.gallup.com.
46. J. Meister, "Ten HR Trends in the Age of Artificial Intelligence," *Forbes,* January 8, 2019, https://www.forbes.com; S. Gale, "Ready or Not, the Future Is Now," *Chief Learning Officer,* March 2017, pp. 20–21.
47. E. Volini, P. Ocean, M. Stephan, and B. Walsh, "Digital HR: Platforms, People, and Work," in *Rewriting the Rules for the Digital Age: 2017 Deloitte Global Human Capital Trends* (Deloitte University Press, 2017), pp. 87–94.
48. L. Collins, D. Fineman, and A. Tsuchida, "People Analytics: Recalculating the Route," in *Rewriting the Rules for the Digital Age,* pp. 97–105.
49. Volini et al., "Digital HR," p. 89
50. R. Baldwin, "How Technology Changed Work, the Workplace, and Contracts," *VoxEU,* April 24, 2019, https://voxeu.org; D. Shimkus, "Time for a New Employer-Employee Contract," *Forbes,* May 10, 2018, https://www.forbes.com.
51. D. M. Rousseau, "Psychological and Implied Contracts in Organizations," *Employee Rights and Responsibilities Journal* 2 (1989), pp. 121–129.
52. Bureau of Labor Statistics, "Employee Tenure in 2018," news release, September 20, 2018, http://www.bls.gov.
53. Indeed, "Why 2020 Will Be the Year of Job Switching (and What It Means for You)," January 28, 2020, https://www.indeed.com.
54. D. Desilver, "10 Facts About American Workers," *Pew Research Center,* August 29, 2019, https://www.pewresearch.org; McKinsey Global Institute, "Independent Work: Choice, Necessity, and the Gig Economy," October 2016, http://www.mckinsey.com.
55. G. Iacurci, "The Gig Economy Has Ballooned by 6 Million People since 2010. Financial Worries May Follow," *CNBC,* February 4, 2020, https://www.cnbc.com.
56. "Workers Value Flexibility Perhaps Even More than Employers Realize," *Payscale,* October 4, 2019, https://www.payscale.com; B. W. Reynolds, "FlexJobs 2019 Annual Survey: Flexible Work Plays Big Role in Job Choices," August 13, 2019, https://www.flexjobs.com.

Providing Equal Employment Opportunity and a Safe Workplace

3

The employee resource groups at Stanley Black & Decker help the company ensure that diverse employees are fully included in decision making and equipped for success.

Rawpixel.com/Shutterstock

What Do I Need to Know?

After reading this chapter, you should be able to:

LO 3-1 Explain how the three branches of government regulate human resource management.

LO 3-2 Summarize the major federal laws requiring equal employment opportunity.

LO 3-3 Identify the federal agencies that enforce equal employment opportunity, and describe the role of each.

LO 3-4 Describe ways employers can avoid illegal discrimination and provide reasonable accommodation.

LO 3-5 Define sexual harassment, and tell how employers can eliminate or minimize it.

LO 3-6 Explain employers' duties under the Occupational Safety and Health Act.

LO 3-7 Describe the role of the Occupational Safety and Health Administration.

LO 3-8 Discuss ways employers promote worker safety and health.

Introduction

Stanley Black & Decker defines itself not merely as a leading producer of tools but as a developer of products that enable "those who make the world." The company has a 10-year strategy for customer empowerment, purposeful innovation, and environmental sustainability. To reach goals in these areas, it has charged Joseph Voelker, the chief human resources officer, with equipping employees to contribute fully. Under Voelker, Stanley Black & Decker aims to make inclusion of diverse people's contributions a daily routine.

According to Voelker, HR plays a key role because a company that "gets the people right" will be able to succeed at its strategy. He identifies tapping into diversity as an important tactic. When diverse employees are fully included in decision making and equipped for success, they can keep the company learning and moving forward. One of the mechanisms by which Stanley Black & Decker does this is to encourage participation in the 75-plus chapters of its employee resource groups, located at its facilities around the world. Groups have been formed for those of African, Asian, and Hispanic heritage, as well as for women, veterans, working parents, developing professionals, LGBTQ employees and their allies, and persons with disabilities. The company also hosts activities aimed at building awareness of diversity-related issues.

Voelker, who started as a production worker and then a benefits specialist, describes himself as a lifelong learner, including on the topic of diversity. He notes that all individuals, including himself, operate with biases. For Voelker, his curiosity and value placed on learning prompt him to react to diversity as a chance to learn more. He notes, "We can't afford to stifle even one voice."[1]

Joseph Voelker's view that diversity adds value helps Stanley Black & Decker comply with the letter and spirit of the law as well as meet strategic objectives. As we saw in Chapter 1, human resource management takes place in the context of the company's goals and society's expectations for how a company should operate. In the United States, the federal government has set some limits on how an organization can practice human resource management. Among these limits are requirements intended to prevent discrimination in hiring and employment practices and to protect the health and safety of workers while they are on the job. Questions about a company's compliance with these requirements can result in lawsuits and negative publicity, which often cause serious problems for a company's success and survival. Conversely, a company that skillfully navigates the maze of regulations can gain an advantage over its competitors. A further advantage may go to companies that go beyond mere legal compliance to make fair employment and worker safety important components of the company's business strategy. So, for example, if Stanley Black & Decker outdoes its competitors in finding the best talent from underused sources, the company not only can develop a highly motivated workforce but also might benefit from insights into customer groups or new perspectives on challenging problems. Similarly, an employer that requires employees to treat one another with respect or emphasizes workers' safety and well-being fosters a climate that attracts and keeps talented workers.

This chapter provides an overview of the ways government bodies regulate equal employment opportunity and workplace safety and health. It introduces you to major laws affecting employers in these areas, as well as the agencies charged with enforcing those laws. The chapter also discusses ways organizations can develop practices that ensure they are in compliance with the laws.

One point to make at the outset is that managers often want a list of dos and don'ts that will keep them out of legal trouble. Some managers rely on strict rules such as "Don't ever ask a female applicant if she is married," rather than learning the reasons behind those rules. Clearly, certain practices are illegal or at least inadvisable, and this chapter will provide guidance on avoiding such practices. However, managers who merely focus on how to avoid breaking the law are not thinking about how to be ethical or how to acquire and use human resources in the best way to carry out the company's mission. This chapter introduces ways to think more creatively and constructively about fair employment and workplace safety.

LO 3-1 Explain how the three branches of government regulate human resource management.

Regulation of Human Resource Management

All three branches of the U.S. government–legislative, executive, and judicial–play an important role in creating the legal environment for human resource management. The legislative branch, which consists of the two houses of Congress, has enacted a number of laws governing human resource activities. U.S. senators and representatives generally develop these laws in response to perceived societal needs. For example, during the civil rights movement of the early 1960s, Congress enacted Title VII of the Civil Rights Act to ensure that various minority groups received equal opportunities in many areas of life.

The executive branch, including the many regulatory agencies that the president oversees, is responsible for enforcing the laws passed by Congress. Agencies do this through a variety of actions, from drawing up regulations detailing how to abide by the laws to filing suit against alleged violators. Some federal agencies involved in regulating human resource management include the Equal Employment Opportunity Commission and the Occupational Safety and Health Administration. In addition, the president may issue executive orders, which are directives issued solely by the president, without requiring congressional approval. Some executive orders regulate the activities of organizations that have contracts with the federal government. For example, President Lyndon Johnson signed Executive Order 11246, which requires all federal contractors and subcontractors to engage in affirmative-action programs designed to hire and promote women and minorities. (We will explore the topic of affirmative action later in this chapter.)

The judicial branch, the federal court system, influences employment law by interpreting the law and holding trials concerning violations of the law. Recently, federal appeals courts have considered the question of whether discriminating against a gay person is an instance of discrimination based on sex, which is illegal. Courts in Chicago and New York determined that discrimination based on sexual orientation is a kind of sex discrimination; a court in Atlanta came to the opposite conclusion. Differing opinions by appeals courts led the U.S. Supreme Court to take up the question in its most recent term. In a 6 to 3 decision, the Supreme Court ruled that discrimination based on sexual orientation or gender identity is considered discrimination based on sex (*Bostock v. Clayton County*). In this case, a government employee had been fired for conduct "unbecoming of a county official" shortly after he began participating in a gay recreational softball league.[2]

One way the executive branch communicates information about laws is through websites like Youth Rules! This site is designed to provide young workers with a safe workplace by making them aware of laws that, for example, restrict the amount of work they can do and the machinery they can operate.
U. S. Department of Labor

The Supreme Court, at the head of the judicial branch, is the court of final appeal. Decisions made by the Supreme Court are binding; they can be overturned only through laws passed by Congress. The Civil Rights Act of 1991 was partly designed to overturn Supreme Court decisions.

Equal Employment Opportunity

LO 3-2 Summarize the major federal laws requiring equal employment opportunity.

Equal Employment Opportunity (EEO) The condition in which all individuals have an equal chance for employment, regardless of their race, color, religion, sex, age, disability, or national origin.

Among the most significant efforts to regulate human resource management are those aimed at achieving **equal employment opportunity (EEO)**—the condition in which all individuals have an equal chance for employment, regardless of their race, color, religion, sex, age, disability, or national origin. The federal government's efforts to create equal employment opportunity include constitutional amendments, legislation, and executive orders, as well as court decisions that interpret the laws. Table 3.1 summarizes major EEO laws discussed in this chapter. These are U.S. laws; equal employment laws in other countries may differ.

Constitutional Amendments

Two amendments to the U.S. Constitution—the Thirteenth and Fourteenth—have implications for human resource management. The Thirteenth Amendment abolished slavery in the United States. Though you might be hard-pressed to cite an example of

TABLE 3.1

Summary of Major EEO Laws and Regulations

ACT	REQUIREMENTS	COVERS	ENFORCEMENT AGENCY
Thirteenth Amendment	Abolished slavery	All individuals	Court system
Fourteenth Amendment	Provides equal protection for all citizens and requires due process in state action	State actions (e.g., decisions of government organizations)	Court system
Civil Rights Acts (CRAs) of 1866 and 1871 (as amended)	Grant all citizens the right to make, perform, modify, and terminate contracts and enjoy all benefits, terms, and conditions of the contractual relationship	All individuals	Court system
Equal Pay Act of 1963	Requires that men and women performing equal jobs receive equal pay	Employers engaged in interstate commerce	EEOC
Title VII of CRA	Forbids discrimination based on race, color, religion, sex, or national origin	Employers with 15 or more employees working 20 or more weeks per year; labor unions; and employment agencies	EEOC
Age Discrimination in Employment Act of 1967	Prohibits discrimination in employment against individuals 40 years of age and older	Employers with 15 or more employees working 20 or more weeks per year; labor unions; employment agencies; federal government	EEOC
Rehabilitation Act of 1973	Requires affirmative action in the employment of individuals with disabilities	Government agencies; federal contractors and subcontractors with contracts greater than $2,500	OFCCP
Pregnancy Discrimination Act of 1978	Treats discrimination based on pregnancy-related conditions as illegal sex discrimination	All employees covered by Title VII	EEOC
Americans with Disabilities Act of 1990	Prohibits discrimination against individuals with disabilities	Employers with more than 15 employees	EEOC
Executive Order 11246	Requires affirmative action in hiring women and minorities	Federal contractors and subcontractors with contracts greater than $10,000	OFCCP
Civil Rights Act of 1991	Prohibits discrimination (same as Title VII)	Same as Title VII, plus applies Section 1981 to employment discrimination cases	EEOC
Uniformed Services Employment and Reemployment Rights Act of 1994	Requires rehiring of employees who are absent for military service, with training and accommodations as needed	Veterans and members of reserve components	Veterans' Employment and Training Service
Genetic Information Nondiscrimination Act of 2008	Prohibits discrimination because of genetic information	Employers with 15 or more employees	EEOC
Lilly Ledbetter Fair Pay Act of 2009	Allows employees to claim discriminatory compensation within a set time after receiving a discriminatory paycheck	Employees covered by Title VII of CRA, Age Discrimination in Employment Act, and Americans with Disabilities Act	EEOC

race-based slavery in the United States today, the Thirteenth Amendment has been applied in cases where discrimination involved the "badges" (symbols) and "incidents" of slavery.

The Fourteenth Amendment forbids the states from taking life, liberty, or property without due process of law and prevents the states from denying equal protection of the laws. Recently it has been applied to the protection of whites in charges of reverse discrimination. In a case that marked the early stages of a move away from race-based quotas, Alan Bakke alleged that as a white man he had been discriminated against in the selection of entrants to the University of California at Davis medical school.[3] The university had set aside 16 of the available 100 places for "disadvantaged" applicants who were members of racial minority groups. Under this quota system, Bakke was able to compete for only 84 positions, whereas a minority applicant was able to compete for all 100. The federal court ruled in favor of Bakke, noting that this quota system had violated white individuals' right to equal protection under the law.

An important point regarding the Fourteenth Amendment is that it applies only to the decisions or actions of the government or of private groups whose activities are deemed government actions. Thus, a person could file a claim under the Fourteenth Amendment if he or she had been fired from a state university (a government organization) but not if the person had been fired by a private employer.

Legislation

The periods following the Civil War and during the civil rights movement of the 1960s were times when many voices in society pressed for equal rights for all without regard to a person's race or sex. In response, Congress passed laws designed to provide for equal opportunity. In later years Congress has passed additional laws that have extended EEO protection more broadly.

Civil Rights Acts of 1866 and 1871 During Reconstruction, Congress passed two Civil Rights Acts to further the Thirteenth Amendment's goal of abolishing slavery. The Civil Rights Act of 1866 granted all persons the same property rights as white citizens, as well as the right to enter into and enforce contracts. Courts have interpreted the latter right as including employment contracts. The Civil Rights Act of 1871 granted all citizens the right to sue in federal court if they feel they have been deprived of some civil right. Although these laws might seem outdated, they are still used because they allow the plaintiff to recover both compensatory and punitive damages (that is, payment to compensate them for their loss plus additional damages to punish the offender).

Equal Pay Act of 1963 Under the Equal Pay Act of 1963, if men and women in an organization are doing equal work, the employer must pay them equally. The act defines *equal* in terms of skill, effort, responsibility, and working conditions. However, the act allows for reasons why men and women performing the same job might be paid differently. If the pay differences result from differences in seniority, merit, quantity or quality of production, or any factor other than sex (such as participating in a training program or working the night shift), then the differences are legal.

Title VII of the Civil Rights Act of 1964 The major law regulating equal employment opportunity in the United States is Title VII of the Civil Rights Act of 1964. Title VII directly resulted from the civil rights movement of the early 1960s, led by such individuals as Dr. Martin Luther King Jr. To ensure that employment opportunities would be based on character or ability rather than on race, Congress wrote and passed Title VII, and President Lyndon Johnson signed it into law in 1964. The law is enforced by the **Equal Employment Opportunity Commission (EEOC),** an agency of the Department of Justice.

Equal Employment Opportunity Commission (EEOC)
Agency of the Department of Justice charged with enforcing Title VII of the Civil Rights Act of 1964 and other antidiscrimination laws.

Title VII prohibits employers from discriminating against individuals because of their race, color, religion, sex, or national origin. An employer may not use these characteristics as the basis for not hiring someone, for firing someone, or for discriminating against them in the terms of their pay, conditions of employment, or privileges of employment. In addition, an employer may not use these characteristics to limit, segregate, or classify employees or job applicants in any way that would deprive any individual of employment opportunities or otherwise adversely affect his or her status as an employee. The act applies to organizations that employ 15 or more persons working 20 or more weeks a year and that are involved in interstate commerce, as well as state and local governments, employment agencies, and labor organizations.

Title VII also states that employers may not retaliate against employees for either "opposing" a perceived illegal employment practice or "participating in a proceeding" related to an alleged illegal employment practice. *Opposition* refers to expressing to someone through proper channels that you believe an illegal employment act has taken place or is taking place. *Participation in a proceeding* refers to testifying in an investigation, hearing, or court proceeding regarding an illegal employment act. The purpose of this provision is to protect employees from employers' threats and other forms of intimidation aimed at discouraging employees from bringing to light acts they believe to be illegal. Companies that violate this prohibition may be liable for punitive damages.

Age Discrimination in Employment Act (ADEA) One category of employees not covered by Title VII is older workers. Older workers sometimes are concerned that they will be the targets of discrimination, especially when a company is downsizing. Older workers tend to be paid more, so a company that wants to cut labor costs may save by laying off its oldest workers. To counter such discrimination, Congress in 1967 passed the Age Discrimination in Employment Act (ADEA), which prohibits discrimination against workers who are over the age of 40. Similar to Title VII, the ADEA outlaws hiring, firing, setting compensation rates, or other employment decisions based on a person's age being over 40.

Many firms have offered early-retirement incentives as an alternative or supplement to involuntary layoffs. Because this approach to workforce reduction focuses on older employees, who would be eligible for early retirement, it may be in violation of the ADEA. Early-retirement incentives require that participating employees sign an agreement waiving their rights to sue under the ADEA. Courts have tended to uphold the use of early-retirement incentives and waivers as long as the individuals were not coerced into signing the agreements, the agreements were presented in a way the employees could understand (including technical legal requirements such as the ages of discharged and retained employees in the employee's work unit), and the employees had been given enough time to make a decision.[4] Also, these waivers must meet the basic requirements of a contract, so the employer must offer something of value—for example, payment of a percentage of the employee's salary—in exchange for the employee giving up rights under the waiver.

One practical way to defend against claims of discrimination is to establish performance-related criteria for layoffs, rather than age- or salary-related criteria. Of course, those criteria must be genuinely related to performance. The EEOC recently settled a case in which a Colorado hospital had dismissed 29 employees aged 40 and older. The hospital attributed the firings and forced resignations to performance problems, but employees who were younger had not experienced the same consequences for the same

FIGURE 3.1
Age Discrimination Complaints, 2006–2019

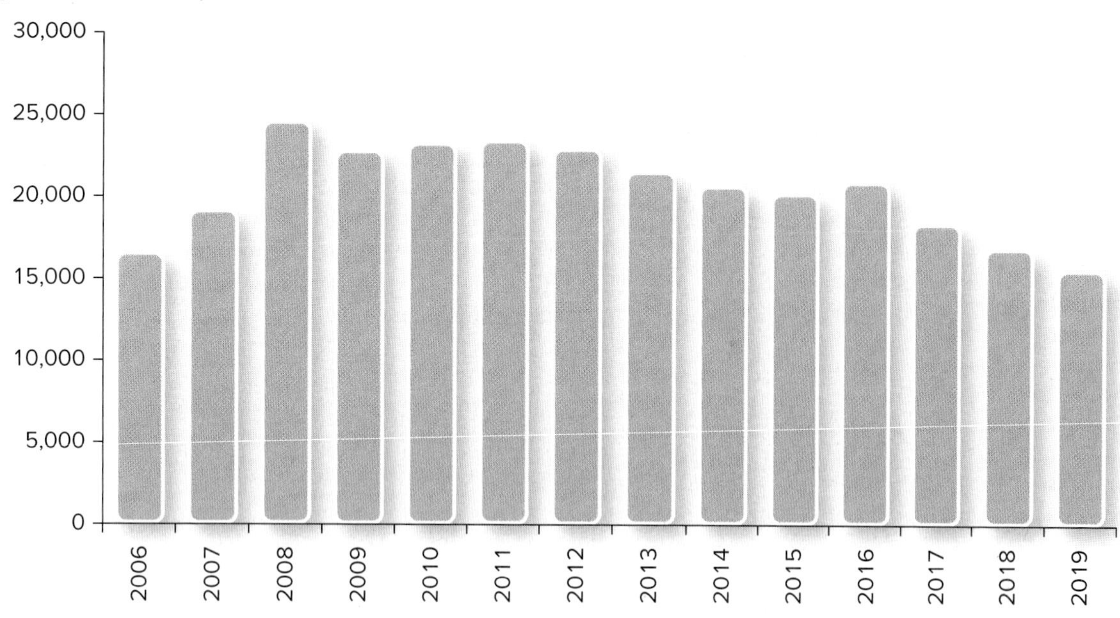

Source: Equal Employment Opportunity Commission, "Charge Statistics," https://www.eeoc.gov, accessed March 26, 2020.

performance issues. Furthermore, the dismissed workers presented evidence that managers had made remarks about younger workers being preferable. After the hospital and EEOC could not reach a settlement during a conciliation process, the EEOC filed a lawsuit, and the hospital settled the suit by agreeing to pay a $400,000 fine and provide training to prevent future discrimination.[5]

Age discrimination complaints make up a large percentage of the complaints filed with the Equal Employment Opportunity Commission, and whenever the economy is slow, the number of complaints grows. For example, as shown in Figure 3.1, the number of age discrimination cases jumped in 2008, when many firms were downsizing, and has been gradually falling during the long economic recovery. As of this writing, however, it is unclear whether age discrimination cases will rise in the near future as companies try to rebound from the effects of COVID-19 in 2020 and take additional steps to recover by shedding jobs.

In today's environment, in which firms are seeking talented individuals to achieve the company's goals, older employees can be a tremendous pool of potential resources. Researchers have found that although muscle power tends to decline with age, older workers tend to offer other important strengths, including conscientiousness and interpersonal skills. Older workers also may have acquired deep knowledge of their work, industry, and employer. Successful companies are finding ways to keep these valuable older workers on the job and contributing. The strategic advantages of this approach are becoming ever more important because of the trend toward older persons making up more of the U.S. population, as described in Chapter 2.

Vocational Rehabilitation Act of 1973 In 1973, Congress passed the Vocational Rehabilitation Act to enhance employment opportunity for individuals with disabilities. This act covers executive agencies and contractors and subcontractors that receive more than $2,500 annually from the federal government. These organizations must engage in affirmative action for individuals with disabilities. **Affirmative action** is an organization's active effort to find opportunities to hire or promote people in a particular group. Thus, Congress intended this act to encourage employers to recruit qualified individuals with disabilities and to make reasonable accommodations to all those people to become active members of the labor market. The Department of Labor's Employment Standards Administration enforces this act.

Affirmative Action
An organization's active effort to find opportunities to hire or promote people in a particular group.

Vietnam Era Veterans' Readjustment Act of 1974 Similar to the Rehabilitation Act, the Vietnam Era Veterans' Readjustment Act of 1974 requires federal contractors and subcontractors to take affirmative action toward employing veterans of the Vietnam War (those serving between August 5, 1964, and May 7, 1975). The Office of Federal Contract Compliance Procedures, discussed later in this chapter, has authority to enforce this act.

Pregnancy Discrimination Act of 1978 An amendment to Title VII of the Civil Rights Act of 1964, the Pregnancy Discrimination Act of 1978 defines discrimination on the basis of pregnancy, childbirth, or related medical conditions to be a form of illegal sex discrimination. According to the EEOC, this means that employers may not treat a female applicant or employee "unfavorably because of pregnancy, childbirth, or a medical condition related to pregnancy or childbirth."[6] For example, an employer may not refuse to hire a woman because she is pregnant. Decisions about work absences or accommodations must be based on the same policies as the organization uses for other disabilities. Benefits, including health insurance, should cover pregnancy and related medical conditions in the same way that it covers other medical conditions.

Americans with Disabilities Act (ADA) of 1990 One of the farthest-reaching acts concerning the management of human resources is the Americans with Disabilities Act. This 1990 law protects individuals with disabilities from being discriminated against in the workplace. It prohibits discrimination based on disability in all employment practices, such as job application procedures, hiring, firing, promotions, compensation, and training. Other employment activities covered by the ADA are employment advertising, recruitment, tenure, layoff, leave, and fringe benefits.

The ADA defines **disability** as a physical or mental impairment that substantially limits one or more major life activities, a record of having such an impairment, or being regarded as having such an impairment. The first part of the definition refers to individuals who have serious disabilities–such as epilepsy, blindness, deafness, or paralysis–that affect their ability to perform major bodily functions and major life activities such as walking, learning (for example, functions of the brain and immune system), caring for oneself, and working. The second part refers to individuals who have a history of disability, such as someone who has had cancer but is currently in remission, someone with a history of mental illness, and someone with a history of heart disease. The third part of the definition, "being regarded as having a disability," refers to people's subjective reactions, as in the case of someone who is severely disfigured; an employer might hesitate to hire such a person on the grounds that people will react negatively to such an employee.[7]

Disability
Under the Americans with Disabilities Act, a physical or mental impairment that substantially limits one or more major life activities, a record of having such an impairment, or being regarded as having such an impairment.

The ADA covers specific physiological disabilities such as cosmetic disfigurement and anatomical loss affecting the body's systems. In addition, it covers mental and psychological disorders such as autism, bipolar disorder, and intellectual disabilities. Conditions not covered include compulsive gambling, personality traits, homosexuality and transsexualism, physical characteristics (such as eye or hair color or left-handedness), and other conditions not considered impairments. Also, if a person needs ordinary eyeglasses or contact lenses to perform each major life activity with little or no difficulty, the person is not considered

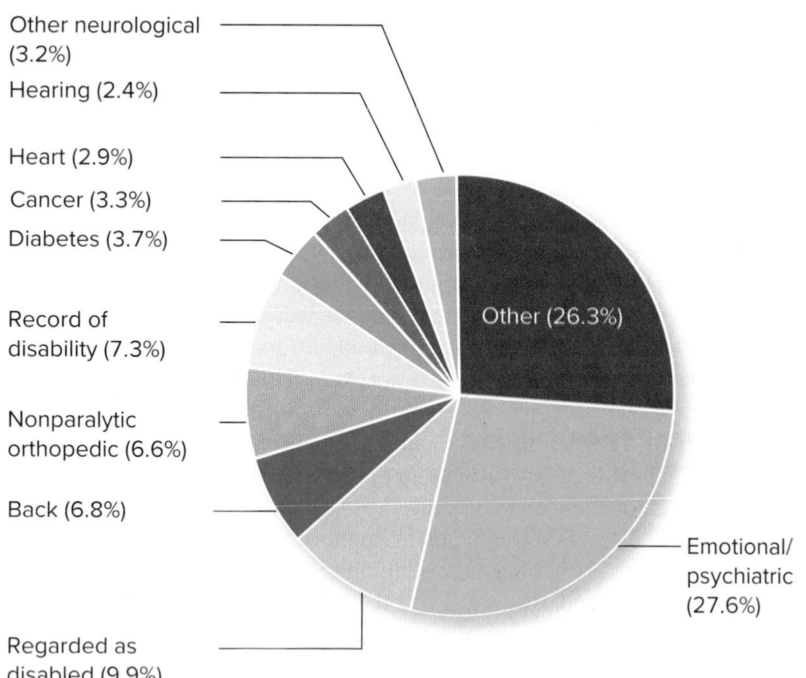

FIGURE 3.2
Disabilities Associated with Complaints Filed under ADA for 2019

Source: Equal Employment Opportunity Commission, "ADA Charge Data by Impairments/Bases: Receipts, FY1997–FY2019," http://www1.eeoc.gov, accessed March 26, 2020.

disabled under the ADA. The EEOC has treated morbid obesity as a covered disability, but in a recent case that went to trial, the court held that the employee did not meet the requirement of proving that the condition was caused by a physiological disorder.[8] Figure 3.2 shows the types of disabilities associated with complaints filed under the ADA in 2019.

HR Analytics & Decision Making

Weight discrimination, that is, making decisions based on negative stereotypes about people who are perceived as overweight, is not illegal and has been described as the last acceptable form of discrimination. A recent study used experts to rate male and female CEOs regarding their weight. These ratings suggested that 5-22% of top female CEOs in the United States are overweight and approximately 5% are obese, and that 45-61% of male CEOs are overweight and approximately 5% are obese. Compared to the general U.S. population, overweight and obese women are significantly underrepresented among top female CEOs. Compared to the population, these results show that overweight and obese female CEOs are underrepresented, overweight male CEOs are overrepresented, and obese male CEOs are underrepresented. In other words, weight discrimination occurs at the highest levels in organizations, and it impacts women more negatively than men.

Questions

1. Would you expect weight to be related to ability to perform the job of corporate CEO? Why or why not?
2. What additional data could help you test your answer to question 1?

Source: Patricia V. Roehling, Mark V. Roehling, Jeffrey D. Vandlen. Justin Blazek, William C. Guy. (2009) "Weight discrimination and the glass ceiling effect among top US CEOs," *Equal Opportunities International,* Vol. 28 Iss: 2, pp. 179–196.

In contrast to other EEO laws, the ADA goes beyond prohibiting discrimination to require that employers take steps to accommodate individuals covered under the act. If a disabled person is selected to perform a job, the employer (perhaps in consultation with the disabled employee) determines what accommodations are necessary for the employee to perform the job. Examples include using ramps and lifts to make facilities accessible, redesigning job procedures, and providing technology such as screen readers for visually impaired employees. Some employers have feared that accommodations under the ADA would be expensive. However, the Department of Labor has found that more than half of accommodations cost nothing, with the rest costing just a few hundred dollars.[9] As technology advances, the cost of many technologies has been falling. In addition, the federal government has created a tax credit, the Work Opportunity Tax Credit, which applies to certain disabled workers. This means that accommodating qualified disabled workers can lower an employer's income taxes.

Civil Rights Act of 1991 In 1991 Congress broadened the relief available to victims of discrimination by passing a Civil Rights Act (CRA 1991). CRA 1991 amends Title VII of the Civil Rights Act of 1964, as well as the Civil Rights Act of 1866, the Americans with Disabilities Act, and the Age Discrimination in Employment Act of 1967. One major change in EEO law under CRA 1991 has been the addition of compensatory and punitive damages in cases of discrimination under Title VII and the Americans with Disabilities Act. Before CRA 1991, Title VII limited damage claims to *equitable relief,* which courts have defined to include back pay, lost benefits, front pay in some cases, and attorney's fees and costs. CRA 1991 allows judges to award compensatory and punitive damages when the plaintiff proves the discrimination was intentional or reckless. Compensatory damages include such things as future monetary loss, emotional pain, suffering, and loss of enjoyment of life. Punitive damages are a punishment; by requiring violators to pay the plaintiff an amount beyond the actual losses suffered, the courts try to discourage employers from discriminating.

Recognizing that one or a few discrimination cases could put an organization out of business, and so harm many innocent employees, Congress has limited the amount of punitive damages. As shown in Table 3.2, the amount of damages depends on the size of the organization charged with discrimination. The limits range from $50,000 per violation at a small company (14 to 100 employees) to $300,000 at a company with more than 500 employees. A company has to pay punitive damages only if it discriminated intentionally or with malice or reckless indifference to the employee's federally protected rights.

Uniformed Services Employment and Reemployment Rights Act of 1994 When members of the armed services were called up following the terrorist attacks of September 2001, a 1994 employment law–the Uniformed Services Employment and Reemployment Rights Act (USERRA)–assumed new significance. Under this law, employers must reemploy workers who left jobs to fulfill military duties for up to five years. When service members return from active duty, the employer must reemploy them in the job they would have held if they had not left to serve in the military, providing them with the same seniority, status, and pay rate they would have earned if their employment had not been interrupted. Disabled veterans also have up to two years to recover from injuries received during their

TABLE 3.2

Maximum Punitive Damages Allowed under the Civil Rights Act of 1991

EMPLOYER SIZE	DAMAGE LIMIT
14 to 100 employees	$ 50,000
101 to 200 employees	$100,000
201 to 500 employees	$200,000
More than 500 employees	$300,000

service or training, and employers must make reasonable accommodations for a remaining disability.

Service members also have duties under USERRA. Before leaving for duty, they are to give their employers notice, if possible. After their service, the law sets time limits for applying to be reemployed. Depending on the length of service, these limits range from approximately 2 to 90 days. Veterans with complaints under USERRA can obtain assistance from the Veterans' Employment and Training Service of the Department of Labor.

Aric Miller, an Army reservist sergeant, was deployed for service with the 363rd military police unit in Iraq for over a year. When he returned to the states, he was able to resume his job as an elementary school teacher thanks to the 1994 Uniformed Services Employment and Reemployment Rights Act. The act requires employers to reemploy service members in the job they would have held if they had not left to serve in the military. Why is this act important? The Free Lance-Star, Mike Morones/AP Images

Genetic Information Nondiscrimination Act of 2008 Thanks to the decoding of the human genome and developments in the fields of genetics and medicine, researchers can now identify more and more genes associated with risks for developing particular diseases or disorders. Although learning that you are at risk of, say, colon cancer may be a useful motivator to take precautions, the information opens up some risks as well. For example, what if companies began using genetic screening to identify and avoid hiring job candidates who are at risk of developing costly diseases? Concerns such as this prompted Congress to pass the Genetic Information Nondiscrimination Act (GINA) of 2008.

Under GINA's requirements, companies with 15 or more employees may not use genetic information in making decisions related to the terms, conditions, or privileges of employment—for example, decisions to hire, promote, or lay off a worker. This genetic information includes information about a person's genetic tests, genetic tests of the person's family members, and family medical histories. Furthermore, employers may not intentionally obtain this information, except in certain limited situations (such as an employee voluntarily participating in a wellness program or requesting time off to care for a sick relative). If companies do acquire such information, they must keep the information confidential. The law also forbids harassment of any employee because of that person's genetic information.

Lilly Ledbetter Fair Pay Act of 2009 In reaction to a Supreme Court decision overturning an EEOC policy that defined the time frame when employees may file a complaint, Congress passed the Lilly Ledbetter Fair Pay Act. The act covers discrimination in pay—that is, not being paid the same as one's co-workers, where the difference is due to race, color, religion, sex, national origin, age, or disability. Named after the worker whose pay discrimination complaint did not withstand the Supreme Court's ruling, the act made the EEOC's policy a federal law. It provides three ways to determine the time period within which an employee may file a complaint: counting from (1) when the employer's decision or other discriminatory practice happened; (2) when the person became subject to the decision or practice; or (3) when the compensation was affected by the decision or practice, including each time the employee received a discriminatory level of compensation from the employer.

Executive Orders

Two executive orders that directly affect human resource management are Executive Order 11246, issued by Lyndon Johnson, and Executive Order 11478, issued by Richard Nixon. Executive Order 11246 prohibits federal contractors and subcontractors from discriminating based on race, color, religion, sex, or national origin. In addition, employers whose contracts meet minimum size requirements must engage in affirmative action to ensure against discrimination. Those receiving more than $10,000 from the federal government must take affirmative action, and those with contracts exceeding $50,000 must develop a written affirmative-action plan for each of their establishments. This plan must be in place within 120 days of the beginning of the contract. This executive order is enforced by the Office of Federal Contract Compliance Procedures.

Executive Order 11478 requires the federal government to base all its employment policies on merit and fitness. It specifies that race, color, sex, religion, and national origin may not be considered. Along with the government, the act covers all contractors and subcontractors doing at least $10,000 worth of business with the federal government. The U.S. Office of Personnel Management is in charge of ensuring that the government is in compliance, and the relevant government agencies are responsible for ensuring the compliance of contractors and subcontractors.

LO 3-3 Identify the federal agencies that enforce equal employment opportunity, and describe the role of each.

The Government's Role in Providing for Equal Employment Opportunity

At a minimum, equal employment opportunity requires that employers comply with EEO laws. To enforce those laws, the executive branch of the federal government uses the Equal Employment Opportunity Commission and the Office of Federal Contract Compliance Programs.

Equal Employment Opportunity Commission (EEOC)

The Equal Employment Opportunity Commission (EEOC) is responsible for enforcing most of the EEO laws, including Title VII, the Equal Pay Act, and the Americans with Disabilities Act. To do this, the EEOC investigates and resolves complaints about discrimination, gathers information, and issues guidelines. The EEOC has tried to increase its effectiveness by setting priorities where it believes its enforcement will have the most impact.

When individuals believe they have been discriminated against, they may file a complaint with the EEOC or a similar state agency. They must file the complaint within 180 days of the incident. The meaning of an "incident" for this purpose is defined by law. For example, the Lilly Ledbetter Fair Pay Act establishes that for determining pay discrimination, an incident can be receiving a paycheck. Figure 3.3 illustrates the number of charges filed with the EEOC for different types of discrimination in 2019. Many individuals file more than one type of charge (for instance, both race discrimination and retaliation), so the total number of complaints filed with the EEOC is less than the total of the amounts in each category.

After the EEOC receives a charge of discrimination, it has 60 days to investigate the complaint. If the EEOC either does not believe the complaint to be valid or fails to complete the investigation within 60 days, the individual has the right to sue in federal court. If the EEOC determines that discrimination has taken place, its representatives will attempt to work with the individual and the employer to try to achieve a reconciliation without a lawsuit. Sometimes the EEOC enters into a consent decree with the discriminating organization. This decree is an agreement between the agency and the organization that the organization will cease certain discriminatory practices and possibly institute additional affirmative-action practices to rectify its history of discrimination. A settlement with the EEOC can be costly, including such remedies as back pay, reinstatement of the employee, and promotions.

If the attempt at a settlement fails, the EEOC has two options. It may issue a "right to sue" letter to the alleged victim. This letter certifies that the agency has investigated the victim's allegations and found them to be valid. The EEOC's other option, which it uses less often, is to aid the alleged victim in bringing suit in federal court.

EEO-1 Report
The EEOC's Employer Information Report, which details the number of women and minorities employed in nine different job categories.

The EEOC also monitors organizations' hiring practices. Each year organizations that are government contractors or subcontractors or have 100 or more employees must file an Employer Information Report (EEO-1) with the EEOC. The **EEO-1 report** is an online

FIGURE 3.3
Types of Charges Filed with the EEOC: 2019

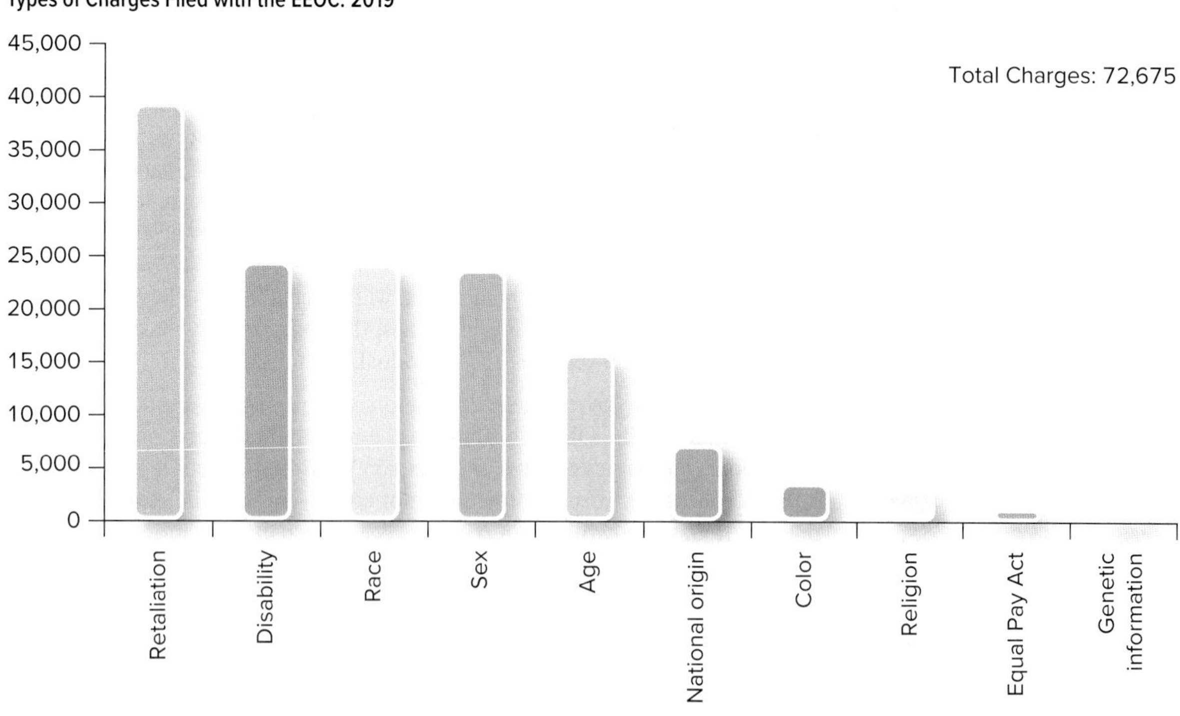

Source: Equal Employment Opportunity Commission, "Charge Statistics," http://www.eeoc.gov, accessed March 26, 2020.

questionnaire requesting the number of employees in each job category (such as managers, professionals, and laborers), broken down by their status as male or female, Hispanic or non-Hispanic, and members of various racial groups. The EEOC analyzes those reports to identify patterns of discrimination, which the agency can then attack through class-action lawsuits. Employers must display EEOC posters detailing employment rights. These posters must be in prominent and accessible locations–for example, in a company's cafeteria or near its time clock. Also, employers should retain copies of documents related to employment decisions–recruitment letters, announcements of jobs, completed job applications, selections for training, and so on. Employers must keep these records for at least six months or until a complaint is resolved, whichever is later.

Uniform Guidelines on Employee Selection Procedures
Guidelines issued by the EEOC and other agencies to identify how an organization should develop and administer its system for selecting employees so as not to violate anti-discrimination laws.

Besides resolving complaints and suing alleged violators, the EEOC issues guidelines designed to help employers determine when their decisions violate the laws enforced by the EEOC. These guidelines are not laws themselves. However, the courts give great consideration to them when hearing employment discrimination cases. For example, the **Uniform Guidelines on Employee Selection Procedures** is a set of guidelines issued by the EEOC and other government agencies. The guidelines identify ways an organization should develop and administer its system for selecting employees so as not to violate Title VII. The courts often refer to the *Uniform Guidelines* to determine whether a company has engaged in discriminatory conduct. Similarly, in the *Federal Register,* the EEOC has published guidelines providing details about what the agency will consider illegal and legal in the treatment of disabled individuals under the Americans with Disabilities Act.

Office of Federal Contract Compliance Programs (OFCCP)
The agency responsible for enforcing the executive orders that cover companies doing business with the federal government.

Office of Federal Contract Compliance Programs (OFCCP)

The **Office of Federal Contract Compliance Programs (OFCCP)** is the agency responsible for enforcing the executive orders that cover companies doing business with the federal government. As we stated earlier in this chapter, businesses with contracts for more than $50,000 may not discriminate in employment based on race, color, religion, national origin, or sex, and they must have a written affirmative-action plan on file. This plan must include three basic components:

1. *Utilization analysis*–A comparison of the race, sex, and ethnic composition of the employer's workforce with that of the available labor supply. The percentages in the employer's workforce should not be greatly lower than the percentages in the labor supply.
2. *Goals and timetables*–The percentages of women and minorities the organization seeks to employ in each job group, and the dates by which the percentages are to be attained. These are meant to be more flexible than quotas, requiring only that the employer have goals and be seeking to achieve the goals.
3. *Action steps*–A plan for how the organization will meet its goals. Besides working toward its goals for hiring women and minorities, the company must take affirmative steps toward hiring Vietnam veterans and individuals with disabilities.

Each year, the OFCCP audits government contractors to ensure they are actively pursuing the goals in their plans. The OFCCP examines the plan and conducts on-site visits to examine how individual employees perceive the company's affirmative-action policies. If the agency finds that a contractor or subcontractor is not complying with the requirements, it has several options. It may notify the EEOC (if there is evidence of a violation of Title VII), advise the Department of Justice to begin criminal proceedings, request that the Secretary of Labor cancel or suspend any current contracts with the company, and forbid the firm from bidding on future contracts. For a company that depends on the federal government for a sizable share of its business, that last penalty is severe.

LO 3-4 Describe ways employers can avoid illegal discrimination and provide reasonable accommodation.

Businesses' Role in Providing for Equal Employment Opportunity

Rare is the business owner or manager who wants to wait for the government to discover that the business has failed to provide for equal employment opportunity. Instead, out of motives ranging from concern for fairness to the desire to avoid costly lawsuits and settlements, most companies recognize the importance of complying with these laws. Often management depends on the expertise of human resource professionals to help in identifying how to comply. These professionals can help organizations take steps to avoid discrimination and provide reasonable accommodation.

Avoiding Discrimination

How would you know if you had been discriminated against? Decisions about human resources are so complex that discrimination is often difficult to identify and prove. However, legal scholars and court rulings have arrived at some ways to show evidence of discrimination.

Disparate Treatment
Differing treatment of individuals, where the differences are based on the individuals' race, color, religion, sex, national origin, age, or disability status.

Disparate Treatment One potential sign of discrimination is **disparate treatment**–differing treatment of individuals, where the differences are based on the individuals' race, color, religion, sex, national origin, age, or disability status. For example, disparate treatment would include hiring or promoting one person over an equally qualified person because of the individual's race. Or suppose a company fails to hire women with school-age children (claiming the women will be frequently absent) but hires men with school-age children. In that situation, the women are victims of disparate treatment, because they are being treated differently based on their sex. To sustain a claim of discrimination based on disparate treatment, the women would have to prove that the employer intended to discriminate.

For an example, consider the first major federal court case dealing with disparate treatment, *McDonnell Douglas Corporation v. Green.*[10] In 1964, McDonnell Douglas laid off employees, including the plaintiff in this case, a Black mechanic. During the period of the workforce reduction, Green and other employees participated in demonstrations at the company's site. A few weeks after the layoffs, McDonnell Douglas advertised for mechanics, and Green was among those who applied. After the company did not hire him, Green sued on the grounds that the company had discriminated against him because of his race and involvement in the civil rights movement. Green demonstrated to the court that he was qualified for the job and that the company continued to advertise the opening after it turned him down. The company said it had rejected his application because he had participated in the demonstrations, but Green was able to show that white employees who had done so were rehired. The court agreed that this was evidence of disparate treatment.

To avoid disparate treatment, companies can evaluate the questions and investigations they use in making employment decisions. These should be applied equally. For example, if the company investigates conviction records of job applicants, it should investigate them for all applicants, not just for applicants from certain racial groups. Companies may want to avoid some types of questions altogether. For example, questions about marital status can cause problems, because interviewers may unfairly make different assumptions about men and women. (Common stereotypes about women have been that a married woman is less flexible or more likely to get pregnant than a single woman, in contrast to the assumption that a married man is more stable and committed to his work.)

Evaluating interview questions and decision criteria to make sure they are job related is especially important given that bias is not always intentional or even conscious. Researchers have conducted studies finding differences between what people *say* about how they evaluate others and how people actually *act* on their attitudes. Duke University business professor Ashleigh Shelby Rosette has found various ways to uncover how individuals evaluate the performance of others.[11] In a recent study, she and colleagues compared the way sports reporters interpreted the performance of college quarterbacks–the leaders of football teams. The researchers found that when teams with a white quarterback performed well, the commentators more often gave credit to the intelligence of the quarterback. When the winning teams had a Black quarterback, the announcers were more likely to praise the athletic strengths of the quarterback. When teams with a Black quarterback lost, the announcers blamed the quarterback's decision making. In prior research, Rosette has found similar patterns in commentary about the leadership of corporations. In describing successful companies led by Black managers, analysts more often credit the managers for their good sense of humor or speaking ability or even point to a favorable market rather than crediting the leaders for their intelligence. Notice that the pattern is not to say people consciously think the Black leaders lack intelligence; rather, the association between the leader and intelligence simply is not made. These results suggest that even when we doubt that we have biases, it may be helpful to use decision-making tools that keep the focus on the most important criteria.

Is disparate treatment ever legal? The courts have held that in some situations, a factor such as sex or religion may be a **bona fide occupational qualification (BFOQ),** that is, a necessary (not merely preferred) qualification for performing a job. A typical example is a job that includes handing out towels in a locker room. Requiring that employees who perform this job in the women's locker room be female is a BFOQ. However, it is very difficult to think of many jobs where criteria such as sex and religion are BFOQs. In a widely publicized case from the 1990s, Johnson Controls, a manufacturer of car batteries, instituted a "fetal protection" policy that excluded women of childbearing age from jobs that would expose them to lead, which can cause birth defects. Johnson Controls argued that the policy was intended to provide a safe work place and that sex was a BFOQ for jobs that involved exposure to lead. However, the Supreme Court disagreed, ruling that BFOQs are limited to policies directly related to a worker's ability to do the job.[12]

Bona Fide Occupational Qualification (BFOQ)
A necessary (not merely preferred) qualification for performing a job.

Hiring via Social Media Poses Discrimination Risk

At many organizations, the people who make hiring decisions conduct an online search of social media to learn more about candidates. The objective is to gain greater insight into people's character and spot red flags that a person might behave unprofessionally. However, some recent research at Carnegie Mellon University suggests that screening candidates with social media contributes to discriminatory hiring decisions.

The study was an experiment in which the researchers created fictional résumés and social-media profiles and sent the résumés to U.S. businesses that had advertised job openings. All the résumés listed the same qualifications under different names, but the social media hinted that applicants were either Christian or Muslim or that they were either gay or straight. The companies were more likely to call the applicants with the Christian-sounding profiles than the ones who seemed to be Muslim. Broken down geographically, the difference was statistically significant in some states. The researchers did not find a difference in response rates related to sexual orientation.

In practice, the ability to target job-related advertising on social media has made it easy to cross lines that recruiters avoided with ads in mass media such as newspapers and jobs websites. A recent investigation by *ProPublica* and *The New York Times* found ads on Facebook targeting users in particular age groups who lived in or visited particular locations and expressed particular categories of interests. Selecting for an interest in finance or marketing is fine, but targeting ads to an age group that excludes older workers is a possible violation of the Age Discrimination in Employment Act. The investigators also succeeded in a test of purchasing ads on Google and LinkedIn targeting workers 40 and under.

Questions

1. Explain how the findings of the Carnegie Mellon study provide an example of disparate impact.
2. For the employee characteristics protected by EEO laws, which could you avoid revealing on a social-media career site such as LinkedIn? Which would be difficult or impossible to avoid disclosing?

Sources: "The Pros and Cons of Using Social Media in the Hiring Process," https://blog.newtontalent.com, accessed March 27, 2020; Kathy Gurchiek, "Is It Discriminatory to Show Job Ads to Only Young Social Media Users?" *Society for Human Resources Management,* www.shrm.org, accessed March 27, 2020; Matthew T. Anderson, "Potential Discrimination through Social Media Ads," *Lexology,* January 2, 2018, https://www.lexology.com; Julia Angwin, Noam Scheiber, and Ariana Tobin, "Dozens of Companies Are Using Facebook to Exclude Older Workers from Job Ads," *ProPublica,* December 20, 2017, https://www.propublica.org; Michael Bologna, "Social Media Strategies in Recruiting, Hiring Post Legal Risks for Employers," *Bloomberg BNA,* April 21, 2014, http://www.bna.com.

Disparate Impact
A condition in which employment practices are seemingly neutral yet disproportionately exclude a protected group from employment opportunities.

Disparate Impact Another way to assess potential discrimination is by identifying **disparate impact**—a condition in which employment practices are seemingly neutral yet disproportionately exclude a protected group from employment opportunities. In other words, the company's employment practices lack obvious discriminatory content, but they affect one group differently than others. Examples of employment practices that might result in disparate impact include pay, hiring, promotions, or training. In the area of hiring, for example, many companies encourage their employees to refer friends and family members for open positions. These referrals can produce a pool of well-qualified candidates who would be a good fit with the organization's culture and highly motivated to work with people they already know. However, given people's tendency to associate with others like themselves, this practice also can have an unintentional disparate impact. A pattern of bias can also arise from overreliance on information systems that use algorithms—sets of rules for software to follow—to identify qualified candidates. Suppose a company uses characteristics of its most successful salespeople as measures for selecting future salespeople. Depending on who currently excels at the organization, an algorithm might unintentionally reinforce the hiring of, say, young males or white females. Because of this risk, the EEOC has cautioned employers to exercise caution in using algorithms to automate decision making.[13] (Caution also is important as a strategic matter: using existing employees as the measure of future success limits the organization's potential to exceed past performance with fresh perspectives.) For another example of disparate impact, see "HRM Social."

FIGURE 3.4
Applying the Four-Fifths Rule

Example: A new hotel has to hire employees to fill 100 positions. Out of 300 total applicants, 200 are black and the remaining 100 are white. The hotel hires 40 of the black applicants and 60 of the white applicants.

Step 1: Find the Rates

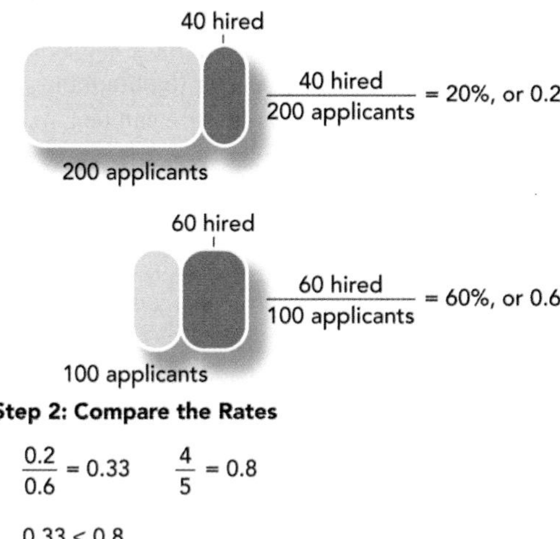

Step 2: Compare the Rates

$\frac{0.2}{0.6} = 0.33 \quad \frac{4}{5} = 0.8$

$0.33 < 0.8$

The four-fifths requirement is not satisfied, providing evidence of potential discrimination.

A commonly used test of disparate impact is the **four-fifths rule,** which finds evidence of potential discrimination if the hiring rate for a minority group is less than four-fifths the hiring rate for the majority group. Keep in mind that this rule of thumb compares *rates* of hiring, not numbers of employees hired. Figure 3.4 illustrates how to apply the four-fifths rule.

Four-Fifths Rule
Rule of thumb that provides (or shows) evidence of potential discrimination if an organization's hiring rate for a minority group is less than four-fifths the hiring rate for the majority group.

If the four-fifths rule is not satisfied, it provides evidence of potential discrimination. To avoid declarations of practicing illegally, an organization must show that the disparate impact caused by the practice is based on a "business necessity." This is accomplished by showing that the employment practice is related to a legitimate business need or goal. Of course, it is ultimately up to the court to decide if the evidence provided by the organization shows a real business necessity or is illegal. The court will also consider if other practices could have been used that would have met the business need or goal but not resulted in discrimination.

An important distinction between disparate treatment and disparate impact is the role of the employer's intent. Proving disparate treatment in court requires showing that the employer intended the disparate treatment, but a plaintiff need not show intent in the case of disparate impact. It is enough to show that the result of the treatment was unequal. For example, the requirements for some jobs, such as firefighters or pilots, have sometimes included a minimum height. Although the intent may be to identify people who can perform the jobs, an unintended result may be disparate impact on groups that are shorter than average. Women tend to be shorter than men, and people of Asian ancestry tend to be shorter than people of European ancestry.

To see how this works, consider the federal court case that created disparate-impact theory, *Griggs v. Duke Power.*[14] Duke Power had decided to base hiring and promotion decisions on whether applicants had a high school diploma or scored at the national median for high school graduates on two professionally developed tests. The individuals filing the lawsuit demonstrated that these requirements had an adverse impact on Black workers, because Black males at that time had a lower rate of high school graduation and a lower rate of passing the tests. Duke could not demonstrate that it had studied the relationship of the selection criteria to job performance, and it admitted the company already had competent workers who hadn't met those requirements. Therefore, while the court recognized that Duke had not shown intent to discriminate, it found that Duke's policy had a discriminatory adverse impact.

One way employers can avoid disparate impact is to be sure that employment decisions are really based on relevant, valid measurements. If a job requires a certain amount of strength and stamina, the employer would want measures of strength and stamina, not simply individuals' height and weight. The latter numbers are easier to obtain but more likely to result in charges of discrimination. Assessing validity of a measure can be a highly technical exercise requiring the use of statistics. The essence of such an assessment is to show that test scores or other measurements are significantly related to job performance. Some employers are also distancing themselves from information that could be seen as producing a disparate impact. For example, many employers are investigating candidates by looking up their social-media profiles. This raises the possibility that candidates for hiring or promotion could say the company passes them over because of information revealed about, say, their religion or ethnic background. Therefore, some companies hire an outside researcher to check profiles and report only information related to the person's job-related qualifications.[15]

Many employers also address the challenge of disparate impact by analyzing their pay data to look for patterns that could signal unintended discrimination. If they find such patterns, they face difficult decisions about how to correct any inequities. An obvious but possibly expensive option is to increase the lower-paid employees' pay so it is comparable to pay for the higher-paid group. If these pay increases are difficult to afford, the employer could phase in the change gradually. Another way to handle the issue is to keep detailed performance records, because they may explain any pay differences. Finally, to make a pay gap less likely in the future, employers can ensure that lower-paid employees are getting enough training, experience, and support to reach their full potential and earn raises.[16]

EEO Policy Employers can also avoid discrimination and defend against claims of discrimination by establishing and enforcing an EEO policy. The policy should define and prohibit unlawful behaviors, as well as provide procedures for making and investigating complaints. The policy also should require that employees at all levels engage in fair conduct and respectful language. Derogatory language can support a court claim of discrimination.

Affirmative Action and Reverse Discrimination In the search for ways to avoid discrimination, some organizations have used affirmative-action programs, usually to increase the representation of minorities. In its original form, affirmative action was meant as taking extra effort to attract and retain minority employees. These efforts have included extensively recruiting minority candidates on college campuses, advertising in minority-oriented publications, and providing educational and training opportunities to minorities. Such efforts have helped to increase diversity among entry-level employees. Over the years, however, many organizations have resorted to quotas, or numerical goals for the proportion of certain minority groups, to ensure that their workforce mirrors the proportions of the labor market. Sometimes these organizations act voluntarily; in other cases the quotas are imposed by the courts or the EEOC.

Whatever the reasons for these hiring programs, by increasing the proportion of minority or female candidates hired or promoted, they necessarily reduce the proportion of white or male candidates hired or promoted. In many cases, white and/or male individuals have fought against affirmative action and quotas, alleging what is called *reverse discrimination*. In other words, the organizations are allegedly discriminating against white males by preferring women and minorities. Affirmative action remains controversial in the United States. Surveys have found that Americans are least likely to favor affirmative action when programs use quotas.[17]

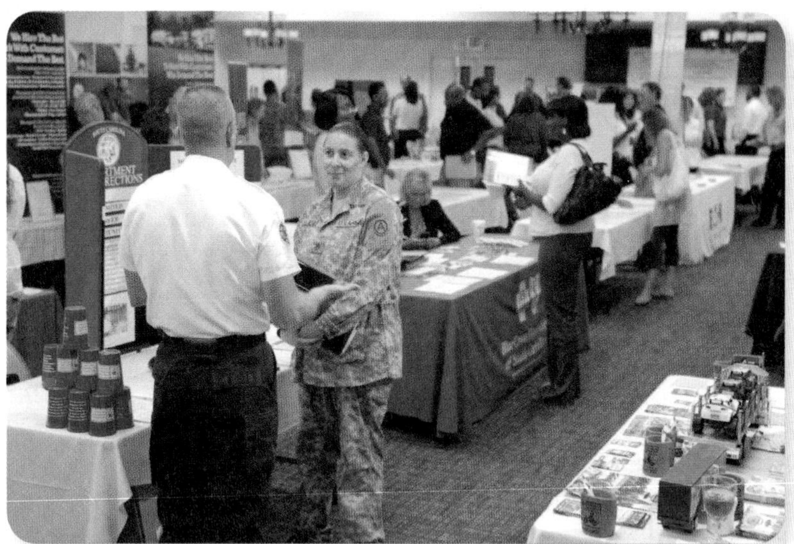

Military veterans continue to be a sought-after group of motivated workers in today's labor force.
PJF Military Collection/Alamy Stock Photo

Besides going beyond EEO laws to actively recruit women and minorities, some companies go beyond the USERRA's requirement to reemploy workers returning from military service. These companies actively seek returning veterans to hire. In doing so, they have tapped into what the numbers suggest is a highly motivated group of workers. Among Gulf War-era II veterans (those on active duty any time since September 2001), about 4 in 10 have a service-connected disability. Even so, their rate of participation in the labor force–working or actively looking for work–is comparable to that of nonveterans. The unemployment rate of Gulf War-era II veterans in 2019 was 3.5%.[18]

Providing Reasonable Accommodation

Especially in situations involving religion and individuals with disabilities, equal employment opportunity may require that an employer make **reasonable accommodation.** In employment law, this term refers to an employer's obligation to do something to enable an otherwise qualified person to perform a job. Accommodations for an employee's religion often involve decisions about what kinds of clothing to permit or require or when the employee must be at work. A Colorado meat-processing company called JBS USA had Muslim workers who requested time for prayer breaks called for by their religion. The company objected on the grounds that losing 12 minutes per day of production work was an undue hardship. But when the EEOC sued for religious discrimination, the company was unable to provide records documenting this hardship, so it lost the case.[19]

Reasonable Accommodation
An employer's obligation to do something to enable an otherwise qualified person to perform a job.

In the context of religion, this principle recognizes that for some individuals, religious observations and practices may present a conflict with work duties, dress codes, or company practices. For example, some religions require head coverings, or individuals might need time off to observe the sabbath or other holy days, when the company might have them scheduled to work. When the employee has a legitimate religious belief requiring accommodation, the employee should demonstrate this need to the employer. Assuming that it would not present an undue hardship, employers are required to accommodate such religious practices. They may have to adjust schedules so that employees do not have to work on days when their religion forbids it, or they may have to alter dress or grooming requirements.

FIGURE 3.5
Examples of Reasonable Accommodations under the ADA

Note: Reasonable accommodations do *not* include hiring an unqualified person, lowering quality standards, or compromising co-workers' safety.

Source: Based on Equal Employment Opportunity Commission, "The ADA: Your Responsibilities as an Employer," modified August 1, 2008, www.eeoc.gov.

For employees with disabilities, reasonable accommodations also vary according to the individuals' needs. As shown in Figure 3.5, employers may restructure jobs, make facilities in the workplace more accessible, modify equipment, or reassign an employee to a job that the person can perform. In some situations, a disabled individual may provide his or her own accommodation, which the employer allows, as in the case of a blind worker who brings a guide dog to work.

If accommodating a disability would require significant expense or difficulty, however, the employer may be exempt from the reasonable accommodation requirement (although the employer may have to defend this position in court). An accommodation is considered "reasonable" if it does not impose an undue hardship on the employer, such as an expense that is large in relation to a company's resources. Some employers may believe there is more of a hardship than actually exists. It is important to investigate the possibilities rather than assume that they will be difficult or expensive.

Sexual Harassment
Unwelcome sexual advances as defined by the EEOC.

LO 3-5 Define sexual harassment, and tell how employers can eliminate or minimize it

Preventing Sexual Harassment

Based on Title VII's prohibition of sex discrimination, the EEOC defines sexual harassment of employees as unlawful employment discrimination. **Sexual harassment** refers to workplace conduct of a sexual nature, including sexual advances, requests for sexual favors, and other contact of a sexual nature, whether verbal (such as jokes) or physical (such as grabbing or kissing). The EEOC defines this conduct as harassment when it is unwelcome and meets at least one of the following conditions:

1. Submitting to the sexual conduct is explicitly or implicitly a term or condition of employment—that is, necessary for getting or keeping a job.
2. Whether the person submits to or rejects the conduct becomes a basis for employment decisions, such as a raise or a desirable assignment.
3. The unwanted sexual conduct unreasonably interferes with an employee's work performance or creates a work environment that is intimidating, hostile, or offensive.

Under these guidelines, preventing sexual discrimination includes managing the workplace in a way that does not permit anybody to threaten or intimidate employees through sexual behavior.

In general, the most obvious examples of sexual harassment involve *quid pro quo harassment,* meaning that a person makes a benefit (or punishment) contingent on an employee's submitting to (or rejecting) sexual advances. For example, a manager who promises a raise to an employee who will participate in sexual activities is engaging in quid pro quo harassment. Likewise, it would be sexual harassment to threaten to reassign someone to a less-desirable job if that person refuses sexual favors.

A more subtle, and possibly more pervasive, form of sexual harassment is to create or permit a hostile working environment. This occurs when someone's behavior in the workplace creates an environment in which it is difficult for someone of a particular sex to work. Common complaints in sexual harassment lawsuits include claims that harassers ran their fingers through the plaintiffs' hair, made suggestive remarks, touched intimate body parts, posted pictures with sexual content in the workplace, and used sexually explicit language or told sex-related jokes. The reason that these behaviors are considered discrimination is that they treat individuals differently based on their sex.

Although a large majority of sexual harassment complaints received by the EEOC involve women being harassed by men, more than 15% of sexual harassment claims have been filed by men in recent years. Some of the men claimed that they were harassed by women, but same-sex harassment also occurs and is illegal.

To ensure a workplace free from sexual harassment, organizations can follow some important steps. First, the organization can develop a policy statement making it very clear that sexual harassment will not be tolerated in the workplace. Second, all employees, new and old, can be trained to identify inappropriate workplace behavior. In addition, the organization can develop a mechanism for reporting sexual harassment in a way that encourages people to speak out. Finally, management can prepare to act promptly to discipline those who engage in sexual harassment, as well as to protect the victims of sexual harassment.

Unfortunately, a wave of news reports about sexual harassment has shown that this conduct affects many workers in every industry, at every pay grade. Those who have spoken up often kept the situation secret for years, out of awkwardness or fear, and all too many say they appealed to their HR department but considered the response inadequate. Some observers say HR departments may focus on protecting the company from lawsuits, which conflicts with a commitment to uncovering wrongdoing. Others say the act of speaking up has made the problem even more difficult for women in the workplace (see "HR Oops!" box). However, properly investigating complaints is one way to *protect* the company, although it may result in consequences for individuals, even high-level executives. In addition, HR departments should help their organization define the kinds of behavior it expects from employees—for example, professionalism, integrity, and respect. Violations of these standards should have consequences, which sets the tone for proper behavior before misdeeds risk crossing the line into illegal harassment.[20]

#MeToo Is Hurting Women, Some Say

A few years ago, a surge of public statements about having been sexually harassed became tied together with hashtags into a #MeToo movement. Encouraged by the boldness of some to speak up about an awkward topic, more and more women and men shared experiences, and hope grew that sexual harassment would fade away in the light of day. In fact, some research found that reports of harassment went up, but that can be interpreted as a sign that women are more confident about reporting such behavior.

While some predicted the end of sexual harassment, others feared a backlash. Researchers led by the University of Houston's Leanne Atwater investigated responses to the #MeToo movement. In their first survey, a majority of women said they would be more likely to speak up about harassment in the future, and a majority of men said they intended to be more careful to avoid harassing. However, a follow-up study a year later uncovered negative consequences for women. Roughly one in five men said they were hesitant to hire attractive women, and one-quarter said they avoided one-on-one meetings with female colleagues. In another study, fully 60% of male managers said being alone with a female colleague felt uncomfortable. Given the importance of mentoring relationships, such reactions seem destined to short-circuit the career goals of even the women who pass the "attractiveness" hurdle.

Korn Ferry vice president Evelyn Orr notes that businesses face enormous, fast-moving challenges that "require all hands on deck." She points out that 30% of the #MeToo posts came from males, suggesting that workers who can't refrain from harassment are a potential risk to colleagues of both sexes.

Questions

1. Imagine you are an employee in your chosen field, and a more experienced manager has offered to give you career guidance. How would you hope that person would behave during one-on-one meetings?
2. Imagine you are an experienced manager with a high-potential employee. How could you arrange meetings and behave during them so as to make the employee comfortable and able to receive coaching from you?

Sources: Evelyn Orr, "A #MeToo Backlash That Shouldn't Be Ignored," Korn Ferry Institute, https://www.kornferry.com, accessed March 17, 2020; "The #MeToo Backlash," *Harvard Business Review,* September–October 2019, pp. 19–22; James Wellemeyer, "Sexual Harassment at Work Is Finally on the Decline—Now for the Bad News," *MarketWatch,* July 27, 2019, https://www.marketwatch.com.

Valuing Diversity

As we mentioned in Chapter 2, the United States is a diverse nation, and becoming more so. In addition, many U.S. companies have customers and operations in more than one country. Managers differ in how they approach the challenges related to this diversity. Some define a diverse workforce as a competitive advantage that brings them a wider pool of talent and greater insight into the needs and behaviors of their diverse customers. This view may reflect corporate values, and it is consistent with research showing greater profitability at companies with more diverse executive teams.[21] These organizations say they have a policy of *valuing diversity.* To ensure they are reaping the benefits of diversity, organizations that value diversity plan not just for numbers but for actual inclusion in leadership and decision making.

The practice of valuing diversity has no single form; it is not written into law or business theory. Organizations that value diversity may practice some form of affirmative action, discussed earlier. They may have policies stating their value of understanding and respecting differences. Organizations may try to hire, reward, and promote employees who demonstrate respect for others. They may sponsor training programs designed to teach employees about differences among groups. Whatever their form, these efforts are intended to make each individual feel respected. Also, these actions can support equal employment opportunity by cultivating an environment in which individuals feel welcome and able to do their best.

Valuing diversity, especially in support of an organization's mission and strategy, need not be limited to the categories protected by law. For example, many organizations see workers

Accenture's Inclusion and Diversity Policies Welcome All Workers

While many companies today value diversity, Accenture is not content to be like the rest. The global accounting and consulting firm has defined its goal to be "the most inclusive and diverse company in the world." This commitment to diversity is a way to recruit from the largest possible talent pool to find the best people and then create an environment where they can contribute fully.

Diversity and inclusion initiatives at Accenture explicitly recognize lesbian, gay, bisexual, transgender, and intersex (LGBTI) employees. The company's website extends equal protection and value not only by age, ethnicity, and gender, but also "gender identity and expression . . . [and] sexual orientation." The HR department has incorporated performance on diversity goals into its performance management system, and it analyzes employee satisfaction by diversity categories to ensure that no groups are being left out of feeling fully engaged with the firm. It also has launched a training program addressing how employees feel about their experience at the firm, aiming to ensure everyone feels empowered to contribute.

Some of the ways Accenture expresses its commitment to LGBTI employees include equal opportunity, mentoring, and employee networks such as Global Pride at Accenture. Community involvement such as support for Pride parades gives the effort a public face. The firm has taken its use of networks to a new level of inclusiveness by redefining them more broadly. For example, the former women's network now looks at gender issues, and the family network takes into account that a "parent" is not necessarily a mother (or vice versa). Such efforts create a culture where employees are seen more as unique individuals, rather than occupants of rigid categories. A UK employee noted to a reporter that not feeling pressured to hide one's sexual orientation frees up an enormous amount of energy otherwise devoted to keeping personal matters secret. In a global firm, such efforts are especially appreciated by employees from cultures where LGBTI status can hinder a career.

Questions

1. How would you summarize the business rationale for Accenture's policy of diversity and inclusion?
2. Do Accenture's measures to promote diversity and inclusion also place less value on heterosexual employees? Why or why not?

Sources: Accenture, "Our Commitment to Inclusion & Diversity," https://www.accenture.com, accessed March 27, 2020; Amy Elisa Jackson, "Amazing Companies That Champion LGBTQ Equality Hiring Now," *Glassdoor,* June 5, 2019, https://www.glassdoor.com; World Economic Forum, "Global Businesses Launch Partnership for Global LGBTI Equality," January 22, 2019, https://www.weforum.org; David Artavia and Jacob Anderson-Minshall, "10 Companies Leading the Way on Global LGBTI Rights," *Advocate,* November 6, 2017, https://www.advocate.com; Sheryl Estrada, "Accenture Says 'Inclusion Starts with I,'" *DiversityInc,* June 26, 2017, http://www.diveresityinc.com; Robert Jeffery, "We Want to Be the Most Diverse Organisation on the Planet," *People Management,* April 2017, pp. 20–21.

struggling to meet the demands of family and career, so they provide family-friendly benefits and policies, as described in Chapter 14. Managers and human resource professionals also are concerned about learning how to treat lesbian, gay, bisexual, transgender, and intersex (LGBTI) employees respectfully and appropriately (for an example, see the "Best Practices" feature). Transgender individuals who are transitioning to the opposite sex typically change their names. This change involves administrative decisions for a human resource department. Some of these–for example, changing e-mail addresses and business cards–are a simple matter of calling employees by the names they wish to use. Typically, organizations already do this when, for example, Rebecca Jones wants to be known as Becky or Paul John Smith wants to be known as P. J. If company policies are too rigid to allow this kind of personal decision, the needs of the transgender employee may prompt a review of the policies. Other aspects of the change must meet legal requirements; for example, the name on tax documents must match the name on the employee's Social Security card, so changing those documents must wait for a legal name change. Even so, employers can respect diversity by demanding no more documentation for name changes in this situation than in other types of name changes (for example, for a woman who wishes to change her name after getting married).[22]

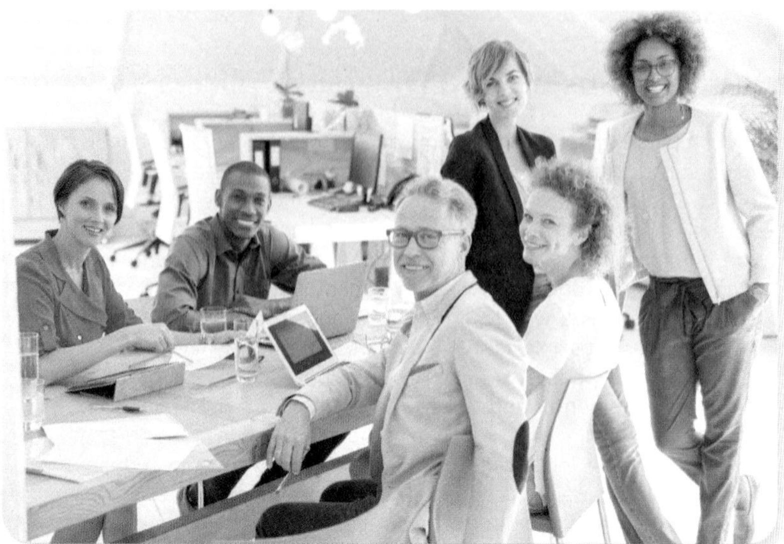

Organizations that value diversity may try to hire, reward, and promote employees who demonstrate respect for others.
Caiaimage/Sam Edwards/Getty Images

LO 3-6 Explain employers' duties under the Occupational Safety and Health Act

Occupational Safety and Health Act
U.S. law authorizing the federal government to establish and enforce occupational safety and health standards for all places of employment engaging in interstate commerce.

Occupational Safety and Health Administration (OSHA)
Labor Department agency responsible for inspecting employers, applying safety and health standards, and levying fines for violation.

Occupational Safety and Health Act

Like equal employment opportunity, the protection of employee safety and health is regulated by the government. Through the 1960s, workplace safety was primarily an issue between workers and employers. By 1970, however, roughly 15,000 work-related fatalities occurred every year. That year, Congress enacted the **Occupational Safety and Health Act,** the most comprehensive U.S. law regarding worker safety. The OSH Act authorized the federal government to establish and enforce occupational safety and health standards for all places of employment engaging in interstate commerce.

The Occupational Safety and Health Act divided enforcement responsibilities between the Department of Labor and the Department of Health. Under the Department of Labor, the **Occupational Safety and Health Administration (OSHA)** is responsible for inspecting employers, applying safety and health standards, and levying fines for violation. The Department of Health is responsible for conducting research to determine the criteria for specific operations or occupations and for training employers to comply with the act. Much of the research is conducted by the National Institute for Occupational Safety and Health (NIOSH).

General and Specific Duties

The main provision of the Occupational Safety and Health Act states that each employer has a general duty to furnish each employee a place of employment free from recognized hazards that cause or are likely to cause death or serious physical harm. This is called the act's *general-duty clause.* Employers also must keep records of work-related injuries and illnesses and post an annual summary of these records from February 1 to April 30 in the following year. Figure 3.6 shows a sample of OSHA's Form 300A, the annual summary that must be posted, even if no injuries or illnesses occurred.

The act also grants specific rights; for example, employees have the right to:

- Request an inspection
- Have a representative present at an inspection

FIGURE 3.6

OSHA Form 300A: Summary of Work-Related Injuries and Illnesses

OSHA's Form 300A (Rev. 01/2004)

Summary of Work-Related Injuries and Illnesses

Year 20__ __

U.S. Department of Labor
Occupational Safety and Health Administration

Form approved OMB no. 1218-0176

All establishments covered by Part 1904 must complete this Summary page, even if no work-related injuries or illnesses occurred during the year. Remember to review the Log to verify that the entries are complete and accurate before completing this summary.

Using the Log, count the individual entries you made for each category. Then write the totals below, making sure you've added the entries from every page of the Log. If you had no cases, write "0."

Employees, former employees, and their representatives have the right to review the OSHA Form 300 in its entirety. They also have limited access to the OSHA Form 301 or its equivalent. See 29 CFR Part 1904.35, in OSHA's recordkeeping rule, for further details on the access provisions for these forms.

Number of Cases

Total number of deaths	Total number of cases with days away from work	Total number of cases with job transfer or restriction	Total number of other recordable cases
______	______	______	______
(G)	(H)	(I)	(J)

Number of Days

Total number of days away from work	Total number of days of job transfer or restriction
______	______
(K)	(L)

Injury and Illness Types

Total number of . . .
(M)

(1) Injuries	______	(4) Poisonings	______
(2) Skin disorders	______	(5) Hearing loss	______
(3) Respiratory conditions	______	(6) All other illnesses	______

Post this Summary page from February 1 to April 30 of the year following the year covered by the form.

Public reporting burden for this collection of information is estimated to average 58 minutes per response, including time to review the instructions, search and gather the data needed, and complete and review the collection of information. Persons are not required to respond to the collection of information unless it displays a currently valid OMB control number. If you have any comments about these estimates or any other aspects of this data collection, contact: US Department of Labor, OSHA Office of Statistical Analysis, Room N-3644, 200 Constitution Avenue, NW, Washington, DC 20210. Do not send the completed forms to this office.

Establishment information

Your establishment name ______

Street ______

City ______ State ____ ZIP ______

Industry description (*e.g., Manufacture of motor truck trailers*) ______

Standard Industrial Classification (SIC), if known (*e.g., 3715*) __ __ __ __

OR

North American Industrial Classification (NAICS), if known (e.g., 336212) __ __ __ __ __ __

Employment information (*If you don't have these figures, see the Worksheet on the back of this page to estimate.*)

Annual average number of employees ______

Total hours worked by all employees last year ______

Sign here

Knowingly falsifying this document may result in a fine.

I certify that I have examined this document and that to the best of my knowledge the entries are true, accurate, and complete.

______ Company executive ______ Title

( ) ______ Phone / / Date

Source: Occupational Safety and Health Administration, "Injury & Illness Recordkeeping Forms," accessed at https://www.osha.gov.

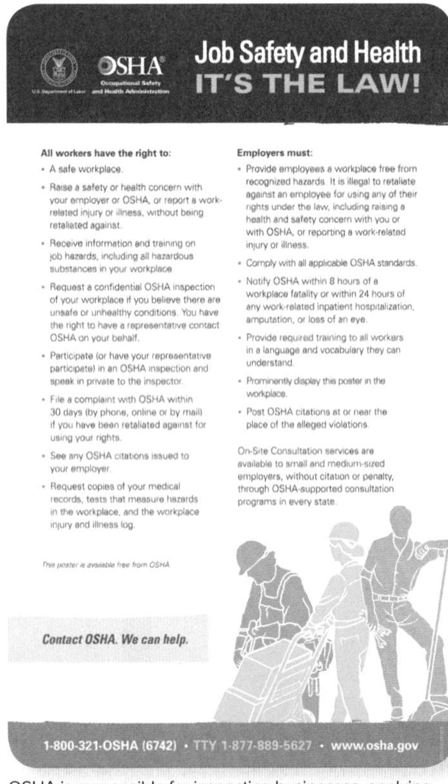

OSHA is responsible for inspecting businesses, applying safety and health standards, and levying fines for violations. OSHA regulations prohibit notifying employers of inspections in advance. U. S. Department of Labor/OSHA

- Have dangerous substances identified
- Be promptly informed about exposure to hazards and be given access to accurate records regarding exposure
- Have employer violations posted at the work site

Although OSHA regulations have a (sometimes justifiable) reputation for being complex, a company can get started in meeting these requirements by visiting OSHA's website (www.osha.gov) and looking up resources such as the agency's *Small Business Handbook* and its step-by-step guide called "Compliance Assistance Quick Start."

The Department of Labor recognizes many specific types of hazards, and employers must comply with all the occupational safety and health standards published by NIOSH. One area of concern is associated with the opioid epidemic: exposure to fentanyl, a powerful synthetic drug. As people who are addicted to morphine, heroin, and other opioids look for drugs, demand is increasing for fentanyl, which has a similar effect but 50 to 100 times more powerful than morphine. Those whose work brings them into contact with these people–for example, ambulance crews, police officers, and emergency room personnel–are at risk of absorbing fentanyl through their skin, eyes, nose, or mouth. Even a small amount can cause serious health effects, even death.

As NIOSH continues to investigate the problem and determine effective safety measures, it is recommending at a minimum facemasks, gloves, and eye protection. In an environment with likely contamination, drug enforcement personnel are encouraged to wear chemical-resistant suits. Of course, in an emergency, a first responder might not always have a chance to pull on gloves before discovering fentanyl in the area, so the risks remain great, and safety training can literally be life-saving.[23]

Although NIOSH publishes numerous standards, it is impossible for regulators to anticipate all possible hazards that could occur in the workplace. Thus, the general-duty clause requires employers to be constantly alert for potential sources of harm in the workplace (as defined by the standard of what a reasonably prudent person would do) and to correct them. Information about hazards can come from employees or from outside researchers. The union-backed Center for Construction Research and Training sponsored research into the safety problems related to constructing energy-efficient buildings. The study found that workers in "green" construction faced greater risks of falling and were exposed to new risks from building innovations such as rooftop gardens and facilities for treating wastewater. Employers need to make these construction sites safer through measures such as better fall protection and more use of prefabrication.[24] Read the "HR How To" box for another example: the challenge of protecting workers from gun violence.

LO 3-7 Describe the role of the Occupational Safety and Health Administration.

Enforcement of the Occupational Safety and Health Act

To enforce the act, the Occupational Safety and Health Administration conducts inspections. OSHA compliance officers typically arrive at a workplace unannounced; for obvious reasons, OSHA regulations prohibit notifying employers of inspections in advance. After presenting credentials, the compliance officer tells the employer the reasons for the inspection and describes, in a general way, the procedures necessary to conduct the investigation.

Providing a Workplace Safe from Gun Violence

Headline-grabbing stories about shootings in schools, entertainment venues, and other workplaces cause employees to worry about their safety. OSHA imposes on employers a duty to maintain a safe workplace. Protection from gun violence is difficult, partly because individuals disagree about whether allowing employees to bring guns to work would make them safer or increase their risks. Further, employers must recognize the constitutional amendment providing a right to bear arms, as well as a host of state laws restricting and/or expanding gun rights. Despite this complexity, experts agree on some steps that employers should take:

- *Develop a no-violence policy for all employees.* Forbid all violent and disruptive conduct, including intimidation, threats, harassment, and intoxication. Enforce the consequences for such behavior. A policy cannot stop bullets, but it provides a way to eliminate problem behavior before it rises to the level of bringing weapons to work.
- *Establish a reporting system.* Create a way for employees to report—and management to respond to—threats of violence in the workplace.
- *Conduct background checks.* Hire employees with the right temperament for the job.
- *Provide for security.* Some options include cameras, locks, security guards, and safety drills.
- *Know applicable state laws.* Many states require that employees be allowed to store weapons in their cars in company parking lots, as long as the guns are concealed and locked. States generally let employers ban guns inside the workplace, but some require posting a public notice of this restriction. A company with facilities in more than one state must apply the laws based on where each facility is located.
- *Consider whether guns belong in your workplace.* If state law allows prohibiting guns, doing so might minimize one kind of injury, including gun-related accidents. However, some employees and employers will conclude that in a high-risk situation with well-trained employees who meet all requirements to possess a weapon, carrying a gun is an effective defense against harm from outsiders who enter the premises.

Questions

1. Describe a situation where an employee with a gun could make a workplace safer. Then describe a situation where allowing an employee to have a gun could pose a safety risk.
2. Suppose you run the HR department of an advertising agency in a town that has recently experienced gun violence. Employees are worried about their safety at work. Which of the listed ideas would you implement first? Why?

Sources: Rachel Feintzeig, "The Gun Issue Comes to the Office," *The Wall Street Journal,* https://www.wsj.com, accessed March 27, 2020; J. Kasperkevic, "Is Your Office Prepared for a Workplace Shooting?" *Marketplace,* June 26, 2019, www.marketplace.org; N. Spector, "How Companies Should Deal with the Threat of Gun Violence," *NBC,* April 4, 2018, https://www.nbc.news.com; Lisa Nagele-Piazza, "Sticking to Their Guns," *HR Magazine,* November 2017, pp. 62–63; Lisa Nagele-Piazza, "How to Respond to Employees Who Want to Bring Guns to Work," Society for Human Resource Management, October 19, 2017, https://www.shrm.org.

An OSHA inspection has four major components. First, the compliance officer reviews the company's records of deaths, injuries, and illnesses. OSHA requires this kind of record keeping at all firms with 11 or more full- or part-time employees. Next, the officer–typically accompanied by a representative of the employer (and perhaps by a representative of the employees)–conducts a "walkaround" tour of the employer's premises. On this tour, the officer notes any conditions that may violate specific published standards or the less specific general-duty clause. The third component of the inspection, employee interviews, may take place during the tour. At this time, anyone who is aware of a violation can bring it to the officer's attention. Finally, in a closing conference, the compliance officer discusses the findings with the employer, noting any violations.

Following an inspection, OSHA gives the employer a reasonable time frame within which to correct the violations identified. If a violation could cause serious injury or death, the officer may seek a restraining order from a U.S. District Court. The restraining order compels the employer to correct the problem immediately. In addition, if an OSHA violation results in citations, the employer must post each citation in a prominent place near the location of the violation.

Besides correcting violations identified during the inspection, employers may have to pay fines. Civil fines, which increase annually with inflation, were $13,494 per violation in 2020, up to $134,937 for a violation determined to be willful or repeated. OSHA also may impose criminal penalties for willful violations causing loss of human life. These crimes are classified as misdemeanors but may involve prison terms as well as fines of up to $500,000 for organizations. In practice, most OSHA penalties are civil, not criminal.[25]

Employee Rights and Responsibilities

Although the Occupational Safety and Health Act makes employers responsible for protecting workers from safety and health hazards, employees have responsibilities as well. They have to follow OSHA's safety rules and regulations governing employee behavior. Employees also have a duty to report hazardous conditions.

Along with those responsibilities go certain rights. Employees may file a complaint and request an OSHA inspection of the workplace, and their employers may not retaliate against them for complaining. Employees also have a right to receive information about any hazardous chemicals they handle in the course of their jobs.

Impact of the Occupational Safety and Health Act

The Occupational Safety and Health Act has unquestionably succeeded in raising the level of awareness of occupational safety. Yet legislation alone cannot solve all the problems of work site safety. Indeed, the rate of occupational illnesses more than doubled between 1985 and 1990, according to the Bureau of Labor Statistics, while the rate of injuries rose by about 8%. However, as depicted in Figure 3.7, the combined rate of injuries and illnesses has shown a steady downward trend since then, and illnesses remain a small share of the total.[26] A more troubling trend is an increase in the number of claims of retaliation against employees who report injuries. However, OSHA has been educating workers about their rights and making it easier to lodge complaints online. Therefore, it is reasonable to conclude that the increase in complaints has more to do with greater ability to file than with an increase in retaliation by employers.[27]

Many industrial accidents are a product of unsafe behaviors, not unsafe working conditions. Because the act does not directly regulate employee behavior, little behavior change can be expected unless employees are convinced of the standards' importance.[28]

Conforming to the law alone does not necessarily guarantee their employees will be safe, so many employers go beyond the letter of the law. The legal implications and ethical obligations of employers and the influence of OSHA in the workplace during the COVID-19 pandemic are discussed in the "Thinking Ethically" case at the end of the chapter.

LO 3-8 Discuss ways employers promote worker safety and health.

Employer-Sponsored Safety and Health Programs

Many employers establish safety awareness programs to go beyond mere compliance with the law and attempt to instill an emphasis on safety. A safety awareness program has three primary components: identifying and communicating hazards, reinforcing safe practices,

FIGURE 3.7
Rates of Occupational Injuries and Illnesses

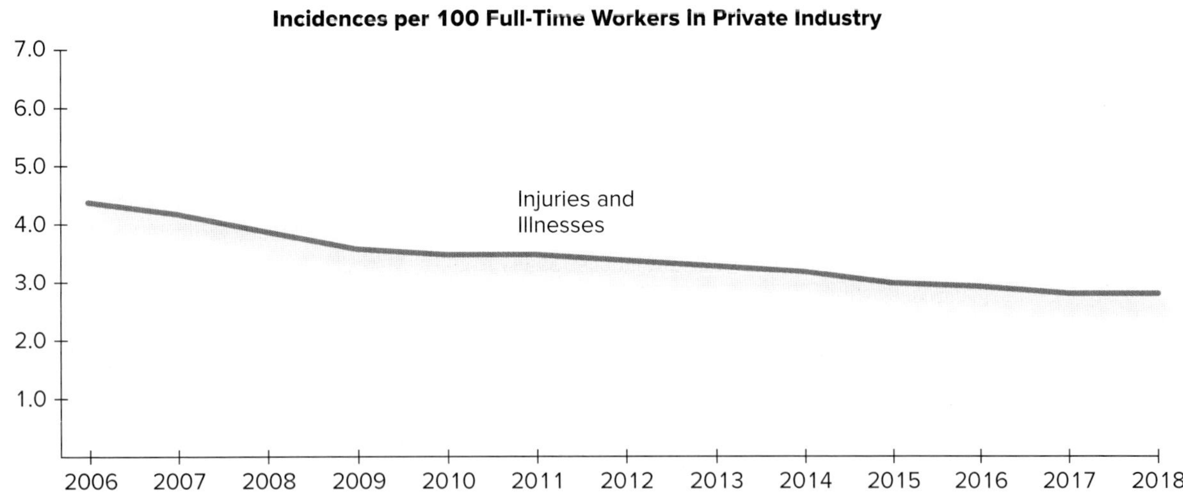

Note: Data does not include fatal work-related injuries and illnesses.

Source: Bureau of Labor Statistics, "Employer-Reported Workplace Injuries and Illnesses, 2018," news release, November 7, 2019, http://www.bls.gov.

and promoting safety internationally. All three components can be more effective when supported with today's methods of collecting and analyzing data. In the health care industry, for example, organizations can participate in NIOSH's Occupational Health Safety Network, a web-based system for using OSHA data. Participating organizations can learn what kinds of injuries are most common in their facilities and see whether safety programs have reduced their injury rates.[29]

Identifying and Communicating Job Hazards

Employees, supervisors, and other knowledgeable sources need to sit down and discuss potential problems related to safety. One method for doing this is the **job hazard analysis technique.**[30] With this technique, each job is broken down into basic elements, and each of these is rated for its potential for harm or injury. If there is agreement that some job element has high hazard potential, the group isolates the element and considers possible technological or behavior changes to reduce or eliminate the hazard. This method poses some special challenges for high-tech companies, where workers may be exposed to materials and conditions that are not yet well understood. An example is nanotechnology, which involves applications of extremely tiny products. Masks and other traditional protective equipment do not necessarily prevent nanoparticles from entering the body, and their impact on health is not known. Some exposures may be harmless, but researchers are only beginning to learn their impact.[31]

Job Hazard Analysis Technique
Safety promotion technique that involves breaking down a job into basic elements, then rating each element for its potential for harm or injury.

Job analysis may be entering a new level of sophistication, thanks to the development of wearable devices that connect to the Internet. For example, Honeywell and Intel together have been developing a wearable device that contains sensors and monitors for gathering and communicating data related to the wearer's safety. The device provides immediate feedback to the wearer and his or her supervisor. Workers in high-risk environments could transmit data about their whereabouts, movements, and conditions in their environment, allowing supervisors to monitor their well-being. The data collected in particular incidents also could prove useful for future safety training.[32]

To communicate with employees about job hazards, managers should talk directly with their employees about safety. Memos also are important because the written communication helps establish a "paper trail" that can later document a history of the employer's concern regarding the job hazard. Posters, especially if placed near the hazard, serve as a constant reminder, reinforcing other messages. Modern technology, such as mobile devices, also can provide convenient, effective channels for communicating safety messages.

In communicating risk, managers should recognize that different groups of individuals may constitute different audiences. Safety trainer Michael Topf often encounters workplaces where employees speak more than one language. In those situations, Topf says, it is important to provide bilingual training and signs. But English skills alone do not guarantee that safety messages will be understood. Supervisors and trainers need to use vocabulary and examples that employees will understand, and they need to ask for feedback in a culturally appropriate way. For example, in some cultures, employees will think it is improper to speak up if they see a problem. It is therefore important for managers to promote many opportunities for communication.[33] Human resource managers can support this effort by providing opportunities for supervisors to learn about the values and communication styles of the cultures represented at work.

Safety concerns and safety training needs also vary by age group. According to the Bureau of Labor Statistics, injuries and illnesses requiring time off from work occurred at the highest rate among workers between the ages of 45 and 54; workers aged 55 to 64 were the next highest group. However, patterns vary according to type of injury. Consider the safety risks associated with the time changes related to daylight savings time. When clocks are set ahead, people can have trouble falling asleep on time and can become sleep deprived, making injuries more likely. The adjustment is particularly difficult for those who naturally tend to stay up late–a pattern that is most common among younger workers. Safety training in ways to prepare one's body for the time change might be particularly relevant for a young workforce. As people age, they tend to move toward becoming "morning" people. For people with a strong pattern of getting up early, setting the clocks back in the fall, with the drive home suddenly in the dark, might provide more of a safety risk. The need for training on this issue in the fall might be especially great among older workers.[34]

Reinforcing Safe Practices

To ensure safe behaviors, employers should not only define how to work safely but reinforce the desired behavior. One common technique for reinforcing safe practices is implementing a safety incentive program to reward workers for their support of and commitment to safety goals. Such programs start by focusing on monthly or quarterly goals or by encouraging suggestions for improving safety. Possible goals might include good housekeeping practices, adherence to safety rules, and proper use of protective equipment. Later, the program expands to include more wide-ranging, long-term goals. Typically, the employer distributes prizes in highly public forums, such as company or department meetings. Surprisingly, one of the most obvious ways to reinforce behavior often does not occur: when employees report unsafe conditions or behavior, the employer should take action to correct the problem. This response signals that the organization is serious when it says it values safety. In a recent survey of employees, most said their organization had a policy that encouraged reporting safety concerns, but many said they did not bother because they had come to expect a negative reaction or no response at all.[35]

A practical way to get started with reinforcement is to target jobs or hazards that are most likely to be associated with injuries in the company's workplace. The "Did You Know?" box identifies the top safety violations cited by OSHA; some of these might be more likely in a particular business, depending on the jobs involved. Besides focusing on specific jobs, organizations can target particular types of injuries or disabilities, especially those for which employees may be at risk. For example, Prevent Blindness America estimates that more than 2,000 eye injuries occur every day in occupational settings.[36] Organizations can prevent such injuries through a combination of job analysis, written policies, safety training, protective eyewear, rewards and sanctions for safe and unsafe behavior, and management support for the safety effort. Similar practices for preventing other types of injuries are available in trade publications, through the National Safety Council, and on the website of the Occupational Safety and Health Administration (www.osha.gov).

Promoting Safety Internationally

Given the increasing focus on international management, organizations also need to consider how to ensure the safety of their employees regardless of the nation in which they operate. Cultural differences may make this more difficult than it seems. For example, cultures may shape different ideas about who is responsible for safety (the supervisor or the employee) or about the appropriate boundaries for what an employee may do in a situation that appears unsafe. A study examined the impact of one standardized corporation-wide safety policy on employees in three different countries: the United States, France, and Argentina. The results of this study indicate that employees in the three countries interpreted the policy differently because of cultural differences. The individualistic, control-oriented culture of the United States stressed the role of top management in ensuring safety in a top-down fashion. However, this policy failed to work in Argentina, where the culture is more "collectivist" (emphasizing the group). Argentine employees tend to feel that safety is everyone's joint concern, so the safety programs needed to be defined from the bottom of the organization up. As in this study, training and supervision must apply cultural knowledge so that efforts to ensure safety are effective.[37]

Another challenge in promoting safety internationally is that laws, enforcement practices, and political climates vary from country to country. With the extensive use of offshoring, described in Chapter 2, many companies have operations in countries where labor standards are far less strict than U.S. standards. Managers and employees in these countries may not think the company is serious about protecting workers' health and safety. In that case, strong communication and oversight will be necessary if the company intends to adhere to the ethical principle of valuing its foreign workers' safety as much as the safety of its U.S. workers.

Overseas experience also can provide insights for improving safety at home as well as abroad. Liberty Mutual's Center for Injury Epidemiology (CIE) noticed that during harvest season in Vietnam, people who worked in both agricultural and industrial jobs were injured at far higher rates than those who worked only in one position. The CIE applied that insight to the U.S. workforce and investigated accident rates among employees holding two jobs at the same time. The researchers found much higher accident rates for these workers, both on and off the job. Possible reasons include that they may be less experienced, under more stress, or more poorly trained than employees holding one job.[38] Given that many employers today are hiring people to work part-time, they should consider that these workers may try to hold two jobs and be at greater risk of injury. Training programs and incentives should take that risk into account—for example, with more flexible schedules for safety training.

Did You Know?

Top 10 OSHA Violations in 2019

Falls are a serious risk to workers, especially in the construction industry. Failure to meet requirements for fall protection was the safety violation most often cited by OSHA in 2019. Failure to provide proper training in fall prevention also made the list of the top 10 violations. OSHA uses information such as this to raise awareness and prepare informational materials for industries where workers are particularly at risk. OSHA official Patrick Kapust notes that the key to preventing many of these violations is effective training.

Question

How can an organization's HR department support the organization in preventing safety violations such as the ones shown?

Sources: Kevin Druley, "OSHA's Top 10 Most Cited Violations for 2019," *Safety and Health,* November 24, 2019, https://www.safetyandhealthmagazine.com; "OSHA Launches Regional Campaign on 'Focus Four' Construction Hazards," *Safety and Health,* March 21, 2018, http://www.safetyandhealth.com; Kevin Druley, "Q&A with OSHA's Patrick Kapust," *Safety and Health,* November 25, 2017, http://www.safetyandhealthmagazine.com.

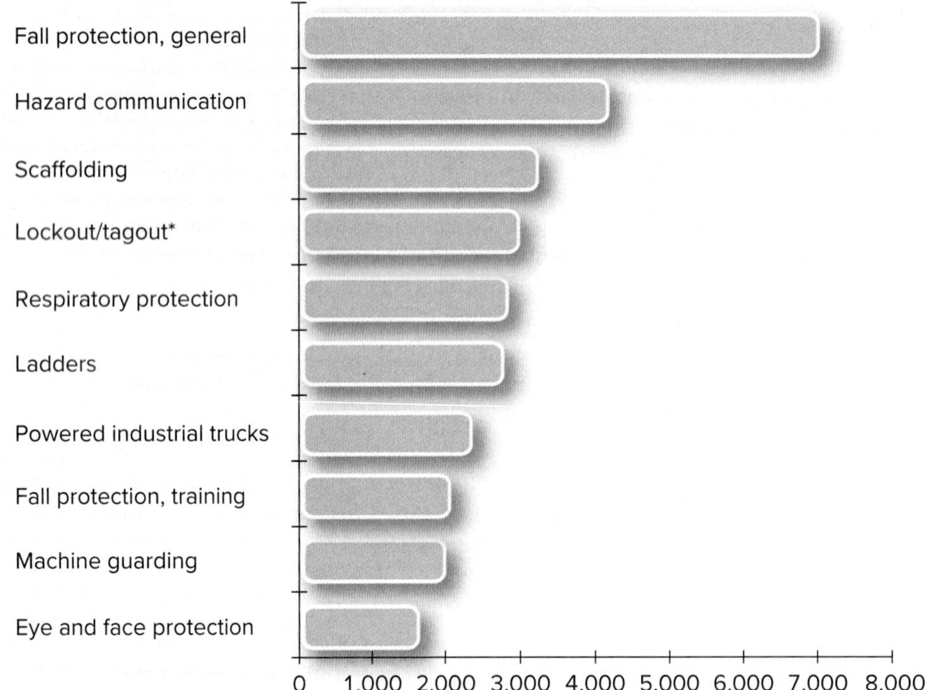

*Lockout/tagout procedures protect workers from electric shocks and injuries caused by machinery unexpectedly starting up. Basically, they include unplugging machines, using devices that keep them from being switched on, and affixing tags with warnings.

THINKING ETHICALLY

WHAT ARE EMPLOYERS' LEGAL AND ETHICAL OBLIGATIONS IN A PANDEMIC?

When the coronavirus named COVID-19 spread throughout the United States during the global pandemic, concerns escalated for how to protect public health. Even as advice and orders from all levels of government were in flux, employers had to decide what to require of their workers. One law they had to apply was the general-duty clause of the Occupational Safety and Health Act, which requires that employers provide a place of employment free from recognized hazards likely to cause death or serious physical harm. They had to do this while avoiding discrimination, accommodating disabilities, and protecting employees' private medical information.

The general-duty clause seems simple but remember that COVID-19 was not well understood. At one point, it was considered sufficient to practice good hygiene to battle the illness; later evidence began showing that the virus was highly contagious. Also, an employee might not experience serious harm from catching the virus but might transmit it to others with compromised immune systems. Over time, questions shifted from whether workers could stay healthy to whether they should avoid situations in which they could spread the virus.

Privacy becomes an issue with regard to the rights of disabled persons. This could be taken to include people whose health conditions make them more vulnerable to serious illness. Another sensitive issue related to discrimination is that historically, there has been a tendency to associate a disease with the country where it originated and with people who came from there or appear to have come from there. COVID-19 surfaced in China, and persons from Asia or of Asian descent reported being singled out as objects of fear. It would be legal to ask whether a person had traveled from a high-risk area but not to make assumptions based on their ethnicity—race and national origin were unrelated to the transmission of COVID-19.

With regard to both discrimination and privacy, employers typically may not subject employees to medical tests (including temperature checks) or ask about their health conditions. During the COVID-19 pandemic, however, the EEOC issued guidance giving employers the right to take employees' temperatures. It is acceptable for employers to have a policy of sending home employees with obvious signs of illness, as long as they do it in a nondiscriminatory way. They can provide information about health and safety, and they can require employees to follow safe practices.

Beyond legal considerations such as these, along with any emergency orders to close, employers should weigh the ethical criteria for how to treat people during a time of heightened health risks.

Questions

1. Imagine you were managing a supermarket during the COVID-19 outbreak. What would be the impact on employees, customers, and the community of keeping the store open? What would be the impact of closing or reducing hours? Outside of following any emergency directives, what would you decide to do?
2. In that same supermarket during the pandemic, what would be the ethical way to handle an employee who comes to work with a persistent cough? What would be the ethical way to handle an employee who calls in saying she is scared to work because her elderly mother lives with her?

Sources: "EEOC Issues Guidance on Taking Employee Temperatures," *National Law Review*, March 21, 2020, https://www.natlawreview.org; Steven Alvarado, "Coronavirus: Workplace Safety and Discrimination Concerns," *Occupational Health and Safety*, March 17, 2020, https://ohsonline.com; M. Scott LeBlanc, Christine McLaughlin, and Katheryn A. Mills, "FAQ: Employee Safety during Coronavirus," *National Law Review*, March 17, 2020, https://www.natlawreview.com; Aldo Svaldi, "Coronavirus Outbreak Raises Tricky Workplace Legal Questions," *Colorado Daily*, March 17, 2020, https://www.coloradodaily.com.

SUMMARY

LO 3-1 Explain how the three branches of government regulate human resource management.

- The legislative branch develops laws such as those governing equal employment opportunity and worker safety and health.
- The executive branch establishes agencies such as the Equal Employment Opportunity Commission and Occupational Safety and Health Administration to enforce the laws by publishing regulations, filing lawsuits, and performing other activities. The president may also issue executive orders, such as requirements for federal contractors.
- The judicial branch hears cases related to employment law and interprets the law.

LO 3-2 Summarize the major federal laws requiring equal employment opportunity.

- The Civil Rights Acts of 1866 and 1871 grant all persons equal property rights, contract rights, and the right to sue in federal court if they have been deprived of civil rights.
- The Equal Pay Act of 1963 requires equal pay for men and women who are doing work that is equal in terms of skill, effort, responsibility, and working conditions.
- Title VII of the Civil Rights Act of 1964 prohibits employment discrimination on the basis of race, color, religion, sex, or national origin.
- The Age Discrimination in Employment Act prohibits employment discrimination against persons older than 40.
- The Vocational Rehabilitation Act of 1973 requires that federal contractors engage in affirmative action in the employment of persons with disabilities.
- The Vietnam Era Veterans' Readjustment Act of 1974 requires affirmative action in employment of veterans who served during the Vietnam War.
- The Pregnancy Discrimination Act of 1978 treats discrimination based on pregnancy-related conditions as illegal sex discrimination.
- The Americans with Disabilities Act of 1990 requires reasonable accommodations for qualified workers with disabilities.
- The Civil Rights Act of 1991 provides for compensatory and punitive damages in cases of discrimination.
- The Uniformed Services Employment and Reemployment Rights Act of 1994 requires that employers reemploy service members who left jobs to fulfill military duties.
- The Genetic Information Nondiscrimination Act (GINA) of 2008 forbids employers from using genetic information in making decisions related to the terms, conditions, or privileges of employment.
- Lilly Ledbetter Fair Pay Act of 2009 allows employees to claim discriminatory compensation within a set time after receiving a discriminatory paycheck.

LO 3-3 Identify the federal agencies that enforce equal employment opportunity, and describe the role of each.

- The Equal Employment Opportunity Commission is responsible for enforcing most of the EEO laws, including Title VII and the Americans with Disabilities Act. It investigates and resolves complaints, gathers information, and issues guidelines.
- The Office of Federal Contract Compliance Procedures is responsible for enforcing executive orders that call for affirmative action by companies that do business with the federal government. It monitors affirmative-action plans and takes action against companies that fail to comply.

LO 3-4 Describe ways employers can avoid illegal discrimination and provide reasonable accommodation.

- Employers can avoid discrimination by avoiding disparate treatment of job applicants and employees, as well as policies that result in disparate impact.
- Companies can develop and enforce an EEO policy coupled with policies and practices that demonstrate a high value placed on diversity.
- Affirmative action may correct past discrimination, but quota-based activities can result in charges of reverse discrimination.
- To provide reasonable accommodation, companies should recognize needs based on individuals' religion or disabilities. Accommodations could include adjusting schedules or dress codes, making the workplace more accessible, or restructuring jobs.

LO 3-5 Define sexual harassment, and tell how employers can eliminate or minimize it.

- Sexual harassment is unwelcome sexual advances and related behavior that makes submitting to the conduct a term of employment or the basis for employment decisions or that interferes with an individual's work performance or creates a work environment that is intimidating, hostile, or offensive.
- Organizations can prevent sexual harassment by developing a policy that defines and forbids it, training employees to recognize and avoid this behavior, and providing a means for employees to complain and be protected.

LO 3-6 Explain employers' duties under the Occupational Safety and Health Act.

- Under the Occupational Safety and Health Act, employers have a general duty to provide employees a place of employment free from recognized safety and health hazards.
- They must inform employees about hazardous substances.
- They must maintain and post records of accidents and illnesses.
- They must comply with NIOSH standards about specific occupational hazards.

LO 3-7 Describe the role of the Occupational Safety and Health Administration.

- The Occupational Safety and Health Administration publishes regulations and conducts inspections.
- If OSHA finds violations, it discusses them with the employer and monitors the employer's response in correcting the violation.

LO 3-8 Discuss ways employers promote worker safety and health.

- Besides complying with OSHA regulations, employers often establish safety awareness programs designed to instill an emphasis on safety.
- They may identify and communicate hazards through the job hazard analysis technique.
- They may adapt communications and training to the needs of different employees, such as differences in experience levels or cultural differences from one country to another.
- Employers may also establish incentive programs to reward safe behavior.

KEY TERMS

equal employment opportunity (EEO), 63
Equal Employment Opportunity Commission (EEOC), 66
affirmative action, 68
disability, 68
EEO-1 report, 72
Uniform Guidelines on Employee Selection Procedures, 73
Office of Federal Contract Compliance Programs (OFCCP), 73
disparate treatment, 74
bona fide occupational qualification (BFOQ), 75
disparate impact, 76
four-fifths rule, 77
reasonable accommodation, 79
sexual harassment, 80
Occupational Safety and Health Act, 84
Occupational Safety and Health Administration (OSHA), 84
job hazard analysis technique, 89

REVIEW AND DISCUSSION QUESTIONS

1. What is the role of each branch of the federal government with regard to equal employment opportunity? *(LO 3-1)*
2. For each of the following situations, identify one or more constitutional amendments, laws, or executive orders that might apply. *(LO 3-2)*
   a. A veteran of the Iraqi conflict experiences lower-back pain after sitting for extended periods of time. He has applied for promotion to a supervisory position that has traditionally involved spending most of the workday behind a desk.
   b. One of two female workers on a road construction crew complains to her supervisor that she feels uncomfortable during breaks, because the other employees routinely tell off-color jokes.
   c. A manager at an architectural firm receives a call from the local newspaper. The reporter wonders how the firm wishes to respond to calls from two of its employees alleging racial discrimination. About half of the firm's employees (including all of its partners and most of its architects) are white. One of the firm's clients is the federal government.
3. For each situation in Question 2, what actions, if any, should the organization take? *(LO 3-4)*
4. The Americans with Disabilities Act requires that employers make reasonable accommodations for individuals with disabilities. How might this requirement affect law enforcement officers and firefighters? *(LO 3-4)*
5. To identify instances of sexual harassment, the courts may use a "reasonable woman" standard of what constitutes offensive behavior. This standard is based on the idea that women and men have different ideas of what behavior is appropriate. What are the implications of this distinction? Do you think this distinction is helpful or harmful? Why? *(LO 3-5)*
6. Given that the "reasonable woman" standard referred to in Question 5 is based on women's ideas of what is appropriate, how might an organization with mostly male employees identify and avoid behavior that could be found to be sexual harassment? *(LO 3-5)*
7. What are an organization's basic duties under the Occupational Safety and Health Act? *(LO 3-6)*
8. OSHA penalties are aimed at employers, rather than employees. How does this affect employee safety? *(LO 3-7)*
9. How can organizations motivate employees to promote safety and health in the workplace? *(LO 3-8)*
10. For each of the following occupations, identify at least one possible hazard and at least one action employers could take to minimize the risk of an injury or illness related to that hazard. *(LO 3-8)*
    a. Worker in a fast-food restaurant
    b. IT specialist
    c. Truck driver
    d. House painter

SELF-ASSESSMENT EXERCISE

Take the following self-assessment quiz. For each statement, circle T if the statement is true or F if the statement is false.

What Do You Know about Sexual Harassment?

1. A man cannot be the victim of sexual harassment. T F
2. The harasser can only be the victim's manager or a manager in another work area. T F
3. Sexual harassment charges can be filed only by the person who directly experiences the harassment. T F
4. The best way to discourage sexual harassment is to have a policy that discourages employees from dating each other. T F
5. Sexual harassment is not a form of sex discrimination. T F
6. After receiving a sexual harassment complaint, the employer should let the situation cool off before investigating the complaint. T F
7. Sexual harassment is illegal only if it results in the victim being laid off or receiving lower pay. T F

TAKING RESPONSIBILITY

Neurodiversity at Work: SAP Takes the Lead

The software company SAP has a program called Autism at Work, which places individuals with autism into positions at its facilities in 13 countries. This is not a feel-good project to help the needy; rather, it is a dedicated effort to place talent in hard-to-fill positions in the tech industry. SAP has found that a focus on skills leads the company to identify particular people on the autism spectrum who can do the challenging work required. Some persons with autism excel in memory and identification of patterns in data. One SAP employee with autism contributed to two patents in his first year on the job.

Even the challenges associated with autism in the workplace can generate benefits. Employees with autism often require that communication be extremely clear. Managers at SAP who have these employees on staff therefore develop their communication skills to meet the needs of their employees. One manager noted that many IT projects fail due to ambiguous communication, so the extra effort probably benefits the company in terms of more completed projects.

As more companies are learning to appreciate the contributions of qualified employees with autism, a new term is being used to describe them: neurodiverse. Neurodiversity typically refers to individuals on the autism spectrum. Referring to their brain function as "diverse" points up the fact that the differences are not necessarily a defect, especially in a setting where they can reach their full potential.

Mike Civello, founder and vice president of the Neurodiversity Inclusion Center, acknowledges that hiring a neurodiverse staff is not necessarily simple. Co-workers are not always comfortable with this kind of diversity and may have difficulty knowing how to engage with an employee on the spectrum. Civello advises that HR staffers and managers learn about the potential of neurodiverse employees first, so they can shape the organization's culture and management. Then the broader workforce can undergo training. In addition, the organization may need to make accommodations for certain employees, such as providing noise-cancelling headphones so that the work environment is not overstimulating. Paul Shattuck of the A. J. Drexel Autism Institute has a similar perspective. He notes that co-workers can learn that repetitive behaviors, such as rocking, that are associated with autism are just a way of calming oneself and that coping with anxiety is a common human situation.

Shattuck, like the managers at SAP, has found that hiring neurodiverse employees is a way to build a diverse and inclusive workforce and help managers develop excellent supervisory skills. It may involve recognizing that a lack of eye contact is not a problem when it means someone is working hard to pay attention. It may involve hiring someone who doesn't care to socialize but can analyze data with care or treat customers with kindness. It certainly involves building a work culture where people can accept one another's diversity.

Questions

1. For a company such as SAP that is recruiting neurodiverse workers in the United States, how would the Americans with Disabilities Act apply to the process?
2. What challenges do you see to building a neurodiverse workforce? What advantages?

Sources: Ronnie Polaneczky, "A 'Rich Ecosystem of Support' for Adults with Autism Led to One Young Employee Filing Two Patents for SAP," *Philadelphia Inquirer,* November 13, 2019, https://www.inquirer.com; Aiyana Bailin, "Clearing Up Some Misconceptions about Neurodiversity," *Scientific American,* June 6, 2019, https://blogs.scientificamerican.com; "How Companies Are Increasing Neurodiversity in the Workplace," *Knowledge@Wharton,* March 28, 2019, https://knowledge.wharton.upenn.edu; Maura C. Ciccarelli, "Tapping into the Neurodiverse Talent Pool," *Human Resource Executive,* March 19, 2019, https://hrexecutive.com.

MANAGING TALENT

Google Continues Its Search for Diverse Talent

Google dominates Internet search, a position that has made it one of the largest U.S. businesses, with $75 billion in revenues. In a matter of seconds, with its powerful software, the Google search engine can give you the quickest route to your destination, the history of Peru, or the funny video your friend was telling you about. But despite all that search prowess, Google has been struggling to find diverse talent.

Given a growing body of evidence that associates diversity with success in innovation and superior financial performance, Google's management has made diversity a goal. Like most tech giants in Silicon Valley, the company has far to go. In 2014 Google published its first report on employee diversity, which showed a workforce of mainly white and Asian males. Three years later, a follow-up report showed only slight improvements–to 69% male (75% of leadership positions and 80% of technical jobs), 56% white, most of the rest Asian. Representation by Hispanic and Black workers was in the single digits.

The drive toward diversity is mainly built on going public with the numbers and directing resources to hiring, education, inclusion efforts, and support for employee affinity groups such as Women at Google and the Greyglers (older employees). Although the company hired a vice president of diversity, there is neither broad leadership from the top nor a reward structure for high performance on diversity and inclusion. Rather, individuals with an interest in making progress are taking up various initiatives. The company has offered training in identifying and addressing biases. Recruiters are encouraged to consider candidates from other than the few top universities the company has targeted in the past. A program called Google in Residence sets up Google engineers at historically Black colleges and universities, with the hope they will connect with top Black talent there.

Various managers encourage their peers to mentor employees of color or consider diversity issues. Among them, Michael Gardner, who works in Ann Arbor as an account manager, started an Inclusion Week at which the Michigan employees participated in presentations and conversations on the topic. Jack Chen, in the New York office, leads an employee group focused on making the company a great employer for persons with disabilities.

As Google struggles to get results from its campaign for greater diversity, a new hurdle has arisen. Two former employees sued the company for setting race- and gender-based quotas that discriminate against white males. They described a desperate effort by recruiters to raise numbers of unrepresented groups, overlooking qualified white men in the process. The lawsuits present the risk that the public-relations problem of discrimination will be replaced by the legal problem of reverse discrimination.

Questions

1. Which problem do you think is more serious at Google: possible racial discrimination or possible reverse discrimination? Why?
2. Suggest two ways Google could improve how it provides equal employment opportunity and manages its talent objectives.

Sources: "Google Diversity Annual Report 2019," https://diversity.google, accessed March 27, 2020; Nick Kolakowski, "Diversity Struggles Still Real at Google, Other Tech Giants," *Dice*, October 4, 2019, https://insights.dice.com; Janice Gassam, "Google's 2019 Diversity Report Reveals More Progress Must Be Made," *Forbes*, April 7, 2019, https://www.forbes.com; Lauren Weber, "White Men Challenge Workplace Diversity Efforts," *The Wall Street Journal*, March 14, 2018, https://www.wsj.com; Nitasha Tiku, "New Lawsuit Exposes Google's Desperation to Improve Diversity," *Wired*, March 2, 2018, https://www.wired.com; Ellen Huet and Mark Bergen, "Google Sued by Ex-recruiter Alleging Anti-white, Asian Bias," *Bloomberg News*, March 1, 2018, https://www.bloomberg.com.

HR IN SMALL BUSINESS

Buffer Isn't Bashful about Mental Health

Buffer doesn't even try to operate like a traditional business. The company, which makes products for businesses to use in managing their brands on social media, says it has focused on "building one of the most unique and fulfilling workplaces by rethinking a lot of traditional practices." The company's 85 employees work in 15 different countries, without any central headquarters. Guiding them are six values: transparency, positivity, gratitude, reflection, ongoing improvement, and consideration of the larger picture, beyond oneself.

The first value, transparency, is intended to be Buffer's default mode of operation. It assumes that geographically dispersed employees will trust one another better if they are open and honest. Buffer makes known its pay structure and all salaries, as well as information about product development and employee diversity. Anyone can visit the website to see the share of employees who have a disability, consider themselves LGBTQIA, or have served in the military, as well as demographic data on employee age, ethnicity, and country of location. Recent data show the company as 55% male, 73% white, and 64% in households with no children.

Perhaps the clearest marker of the commitment to diversity is Buffer's Open Blog, which speaks frankly about the work experience at and aims of Buffer and is available to the public. Buffer's founder and CEO Joel Gascoigne contributes to the blog and does not hold back when it comes to the topic of his own mental-health care. As the leader, Gascoigne sets the tone, and employees also feel free to mention their own experiences with issues like anxiety or depression.

This would be extraordinary at many, probably most, companies. It may seem natural to Buffer's employees, because they are of a generation where the stigma of mental illness is less than it has been in the past. Almost seven in ten Buffer employees, including Gascoigne, are between the ages of 25 and 34, and most of the remainder are 35 to 44. Millennial and Generation Z employees typically are used to sharing personal information online, and they grew up at a time when it was relatively common for children to get help with anxiety, depression, or attention-deficit disorder. Further, many have experienced seeking accommodations for these conditions in high school or college, suggesting that they may want the same at work.

Questions

1. How likely do you think it is that Buffer could experience challenges related to age discrimination? Explain.
2. Imagine that Buffer brought you in to advise on its HR policies. Suggest how the company can maintain its openness while maintaining privacy of health information.

Sources: Company website, "About Us," https://buffer.com, accessed March 27, 2020; Lauren Weber, "Young Workers Seek Mental Health Accommodations, Employers Try to Keep Up," *The Wall Street Journal,* February 12, 2020, https://www.wsj.com; Theresa Agovino, "Out of the Darkness," *HR Magazine,* Fall 2019, pp. 69–74; Buffer, "Buffer's Six Values, Version 2.0," SlideShare, August 20, 2018, http://www.slideshare.net.

NOTES

1. Company website, "Who We Are" and "Careers," https://www.stanleyblackanddecker.com, accessed March 17, 2020; L. Connell, "CHRO Connection: Joseph Voelker," *People + Strategy,* Fall 2019, pp. 78–80.
2. "Bostock v. Clayton County, Georgia," *Legal Information Institute,* https://www.law.cornell.edu, accessed August 9, 2020; D. G. Savage, "Major Rulings from Supreme Court in 2020 Term on Abortion, Religion and Trump Taxes," *Los Angeles Times,* https://www.latimes.com, accessed August 9, 2020.
3. *Bakke v. Regents of the University of California,* 17 F.E.P.C. 1000 (1978).
4. Equal Employment Opportunity Commission, "Understanding Waivers of Discrimination Claims in Employee Severance Agreements," http://www.eeoc.gov; Equal Employment Opportunity Commission, "Age Discrimination," http://www1.eeoc.gov.
5. Equal Employment Opportunity Commission, "Montrose Memorial Hospital to Pay $400,000 to Settle EEOC Age Discrimination Lawsuit," news release, January 4, 2018, https://www1.eeoc.gov.
6. Equal Employment Opportunity Commission, "Pregnancy Discrimination," http://www.eeoc.gov, accessed March 27, 2020.
7. Equal Employment Opportunity Commission, "Facts about the Americans with Disabilities Act," http://www.eeoc.gov//eeoc/publications/; Equal Employment Opportunity Commission, "Notice Concerning the Americans with Disabilities Act (ADA) Amendments Act of 2008 (ADAAA)," https://www.eeoc.gov.
8. Society for Human Resource Management, "Disability Accommodations: Conditions; Does the Americans with Disabilities Act (ADA) Provide a List of the Conditions That Are Covered under the Act?" November 6, 2017, https://www.shrm.org; Marjory D. Robertson, "Is Morbid Obesity a Disability under the ADA? Courts Say No," *Lexology,* February 7, 2017, https://www.lexology.com; Equal Employment Opportunity Commission, "Questions and Answers on the Final Rule Implementing the ADA Amendment Act for 2008," https://www.eeoc.gov.
9. U.S. Department of Labor, Office of Disability Policy (ODEP), "Accommodations," https://www.dol.gov/odep, accessed March 27, 2020; ODEP, "Employers and the ADA: Myths and Facts," https://www.dol.gov/odep, accessed March 27, 2020.
10. *McDonnell Douglas v. Green,* 411 U.S. 972 (1973).
11. Melissa Korn, "Race Influences How Leaders Are Assessed," *The Wall Street Journal,* January 3, 2012, http://online.wsj.com; Katherine W. Phillips, "Transparent Barriers," *Kellogg Insight* (Kellogg School of Management), November 2008, http://insight.kellogg.northwestern.edu.
12. *UAW v. Johnson Controls, Inc.,* 499 U.S. 187 (1991).
13. Lisa Milam-Perez, "The Promise and Peril of 'Big Data,'" *HR Magazine,* March 2017, pp. 72–73; Equal Employment Opportunity Commission, "Use of Big Data Has Implications for Equal Employment Opportunity, Panel Tells EEOC," news release, October 13, 2016, https://www1.eeoc.gov.
14. *Griggs v. Duke Power Company,* 401 U.S. 424 (1971).
15. Anne Fisher, "Checking Out Job Applicants on Facebook? Better Ask a Lawyer," *Fortune,* March 2, 2011, http://management.fortune.cnn.com.
16. Lauren Weber, "What Women—and Men—Say about the Gender Wage Gap," *The Wall Street Journal,* February 25, 2016, http://blogs.wsj.com; Bureau of National Affairs, "HR Pros Believe Gender Pay Gaps Exist—but What to Do about It?" *Report on Salary Surveys,* April 2011, pp. 1–8; Joann S. Lublin, "Coaching Urged for Women," *The Wall Street Journal,* April 4, 2011, http://online.wsj.com.
17. D. Kravitz and J. Platania, "Attitudes and Beliefs about Affirmative Action: Effects of Target and of Respondent Sex and Ethnicity," *Journal of Applied Psychology* 78 (1993), pp. 928–938.
18. Bureau of Labor Statistics, "Employment Situation of Veterans—2019," March 27, 2020, www.bls.gov.

19. Kate Tornone, "Telecommuting Becomes a More Reasonable ADA Accommodation Every Year," *HR Dive,* March 14, 2018, https://www.hrdive.com; Jon Hyman, "When Does Telecommuting Qualify as a Reasonable Accommodation?" *Workforce,* February 22, 2018, http://www.workforce.com; Lisa Nagele-Piazza, "EEOC Religious Accommodation Lawsuit Holds Lessons for Employers," Society for Human Resource Management, August 21, 2017, https://www.shrm.org.
20. EEOC, "Charges Alleging Sex-Based Harassment FY 2010-FY2019," https://www.eeoc.gov, accessed March 28, 2020; Catalyst, "Sex Discrimination and Sexual Harassment: Quick Take," December 5, 2019, https://www.catalyst.org; E. N. Bass, "Reexamine Your Company's Harassment Investigation Protocol in Light of #MeToo," *Lexology,* February 2, 2018, https://www.lexology.com.
21. Vivian Hunt, Sara Prince, Sundiatu Dixon-Fyle, and Lareina Yee, *Delivering through Diversity,* McKinsey & Company, January 2018, http://www.mckinsey.com.
22. D. Stahl, "Making a Name for Yourself: For Trans People, It's 'Life-Changing,'" *NBC News,* September 6, 2019, https://www.nbcnews.com.
23. Jennifer Hornsby-Myers, G. Scott Dotson, and Deborah Hornback, "Fentanyl Exposure Risks for Law Enforcement and Emergency Response Workers," *NIOSH Science Blog,* June 22, 2017, https://blogs.cdc.gov; U.S. Department of Justice, Drug Enforcement Administration, *Fentanyl: A Briefing Guide for First Responders,* 2017, http://www.dea.gov.
24. J. Staver, "Safety Hazards of Green Construction," *Green Building Insider,* April 4, 2018, https://greenbuildinginsider.com.
25. U.S. Department of Labor, "OSHA Penalties," https://www.osha.gov, accessed March 27, 2020; K. W. Morrison, "Facing Time: Will Criminal Prosecutions under the OSH Act Become More Common?" *Safety and Health,* April 24, 2016, http://www.safetyandhealthmagazine.com.
26. U.S. Bureau of Labor Statistics, "Employer-Reported Workplace Injuries and Illnesses–2018," https://www.bls.gov, accessed March 27, 2020.
27. Joseph Dreesen, "OSHA Releases New Online Whistleblower Complaint Form for Workers," Jackson Lewis, August 7, 2017, https://www.jacksonlewis.com; Nickole Winnett, "Responding to OSHA Whistleblower Complaints," *Construction Executive,* December 1, 2014, http://enewsletters.constructionexec.com.
28. L. Gizzi, "How to Address Unsafe Behaviors Through Safety Training," *Assurance Agency,* March 8, 2019, https://www.assuranceagency.com.
29. Centers for Disease Control and Prevention, "Occupational Health Safety Network (OHSN)," updated February 22, 2018, https://www.cdc.gov/niosh.
30. "The Basics of Job Hazard Analysis," *Safety Compliance Letter,* September 2013, Business Insights: Global, http://bi.galegroup.com.
31. Duncan Graham-Rowe, "Is Nanotechnology Safe in the Workplace?" *Guardian,* February 13, 2012, http://www.guardian.co.uk; Jennifer L. Topmiller and Kevin H. Dunn, "Controlling Exposures to Workers Who Make or Use Nanomaterials," *NIOSH Science Blog,* December 9, 2013, http://blogs.cdc.gov.
32. Sandy Smith, "Worker Safety: Intelligence at the Edge," *EHS Today,* December 8, 2015, http://ehstoday.com.
33. Jill Jusko, "Meeting the Safety Challenge of a Diverse Workforce," *Industry Week,* December 2011, p. 14.
34. Claire Caruso, "Daylight Saving: Suggestions to Help Workers Adapt to the Time Change," *NIOSH Science Blog,* March 9, 2016, http://blogs.cdc.gov; Bureau of Labor Statistics, "Nonfatal Occupational Injuries and Illnesses Requiring Days Away from Work, 2014," news release, November 19, 2015, http://www.bls.gov.
35. Ray Ruiz, "Four Reasons Why Employees Should Speak Up about Safety Concerns," American Equity Underwriters, February 4, 2019, https://www.amequity.com; Phillip Ragain, Ron Ragain, Michael Allen, and Mike Allen, "A Study of Safety Intervention: The Causes and Consequences of Employees' Silence," *EHS Today,* July 2011, pp. 36–38.
36. Prevent Blindness America, "Eye Safety at Work," http://www.preventblindness.org, accessed March 27, 2020; American Optometric Association, "Protecting Your Eyes at Work," https://www.aoa.org, accessed March 27, 2020
37. Michael Flynn, "Safety Across Cultures," *NIOSH Science Blog,* March 13, 2018, https://blogs.cdc.gov; M. Janssens, J. M. Brett, and F. J. Smith, "Confirmatory Cross-Cultural Research: Testing the Viability of a Corporation-Wide Safety Policy," *Academy of Management Journal* 38 (1995), pp. 364–382.
38. Liberty Mutual Research Institute for Safety (RIS), "Multiple Job Holding: Present-Day Reality Raises New Questions," *From Research to Reality* (Winter 2013–14), p. 3; RIS, "Research Focus: Does Multiple Job Holding Increase Risk of Injury?" *From Research to Reality* (Winter 2013–14), pp. 4–5.

4 Analyzing Work and Designing Jobs

Introduction

Some of the most exciting innovations in supermarkets are happening away from the view of shoppers. In micro-fulfillment centers built into the back of stores, employees have begun interacting with robots to fill orders streaming in from online shoppers. Walmart, for example, has a system called Alphabot. Robots on wheels move among 24-foot-high, floor-to-ceiling shelves, gathering items for each order. These items are delivered to an employee standing on a platform and observing a screen showing the order they will pack from the robot-delivered products. Albertsons, Kroger, and other supermarkets are testing and installing similar systems.

Alphabot is much more efficient than human workers. It can bring together about 800 products per hour, 10 times faster than a human worker picking products from store shelves. Back-of-store robots also avoid the problem of employees who fill online orders getting in the way of store shoppers. Systems like Alphabot can keep more accurate count of inventory, because store shelves are hard to monitor, and customers tend to move products around as they shop. Given all these benefits, store retailers hope robotics will help them stay competitive as Amazon moves further into the grocery business. Online shopping has been a sliver of total grocery sales, but the share has been rising fast.

However, this type of automation has not yet replaced human jobs, but merely introduced a new kind of work. Workers need to be able to use the computer interface to interact with the robot. They also pick fresh produce to be included in orders, and some systems require employees to pick frozen foods. Employees may also be needed to run orders to cars or deliver to customers. In its initial use of Alphabot, Walmart said it added about 10 employees to stock the robotic system and had no net change in the total number of employees as a result.[1]

Walmart's Alphabot automated fulfillment system has helped the company stay competitive and introduced a new kind of work for Walmart employees.

Suzanne Kreiter/The Boston Globe/Getty Images

What Do I Need to Know?

After reading this chapter, you should be able to:

LO 4-1 Summarize the elements of work flow analysis.

LO 4-2 Describe how work flow is related to an organization's structure.

LO 4-3 Define the elements of a job analysis, and discuss their significance for human resource management.

LO 4-4 Tell how to obtain information for a job analysis.

LO 4-5 Summarize recent trends in job analysis.

LO 4-6 Describe methods for designing a job so that it can be done efficiently.

LO 4-7 Identify approaches to designing a job to make it motivating.

LO 4-8 Explain how organizations apply ergonomics to design safe jobs.

LO 4-9 Discuss how organizations can plan for the mental demands of a job.

Before Walmart introduced Alphabot in its retail stores, many employees needed focus and patience to carry out repetitive tasks under time constraints. With the new robotic process in place, some employee jobs now depend on higher-level skills, including how to use the computer interface that organizes and tracks various customer orders. Consideration of such elements is at the heart of analyzing work, whether in a start-up business, a multinational corporation, or a government agency.

This chapter discusses the analysis and design of work and, in doing so, lays out some considerations that go into making informed decisions about how to create and link jobs. The chapter begins with a look at the big-picture issues related to analyzing work flow and organizational structure. The discussion then turns to the more specific issues of analyzing and designing jobs. Traditionally, job analysis has emphasized the study of existing jobs in order to make decisions such as employee selection, training, and compensation. In contrast, job design has emphasized making jobs more efficient or more motivating. However, as this chapter shows, the two activities are interrelated.

Work Flow in Organizations

LO 4-1 Summarize the elements of work flow analysis.

Informed decisions about jobs take place in the context of the organization's overall work flow. Through the process of **work flow design,** managers analyze the tasks needed to produce a product or service. With this information, they assign these tasks to specific jobs and positions. (A **job** is a set of related duties. A **position** is the set of duties performed by one person. A school has many teaching *positions;* the person filling each of those positions is performing the *job* of teacher.) Basing these decisions on work flow design can lead to better results than the more traditional practice of looking at jobs individually.

Work Flow Design
The process of analyzing the tasks necessary for the production of a product or service.

Job
A set of related duties.

Position
The set of duties (job) performed by a particular person.

Work Flow Analysis

Before designing its work flow, the organization's planners need to analyze what work needs to be done. Figure 4.1 shows the elements of a work flow analysis. For each type of work, such as producing a product line or providing a support service (accounting, legal support, and so on), the analysis identifies the output of the process, the activities involved, and the three categories of inputs (materials and information, equipment, and human resources).

Outputs are the products of any work unit, say, a department or team. Outputs may be tangible, as in the case of a restaurant meal or finished part. They may be intangible, such as building security or an answered question about employee benefits. In identifying the outputs of particular work units, work flow analysis considers both quantity and quality. Thinking in terms of these outputs gives HRM professionals a clearer view of how to increase each work unit's effectiveness.

Work flow analysis next considers the *work processes* used to generate the outputs identified. Work processes are the activities that a work unit's members engage in to produce a given output. They are described in terms of operating procedures for every task performed by each employee at each stage of the process. Specifying the processes helps HRM professionals design efficient work systems by clarifying which tasks are necessary. Knowledge of work processes also can guide staffing changes when work is automated, outsourced, or restructured.

Finally, work flow analysis identifies the *inputs* required to carry out the work processes. As shown in Figure 4.1, inputs fall into three categories: raw inputs (materials and information), equipment, and human resources (knowledge, skills, and abilities). In an Amazon warehouse, for example, inputs include the items held in inventory to fill orders, a variety of automated equipment to move and track items, and workers to fill boxes, dispatch robots,

FIGURE 4.1
Developing a Work Flow Analysis

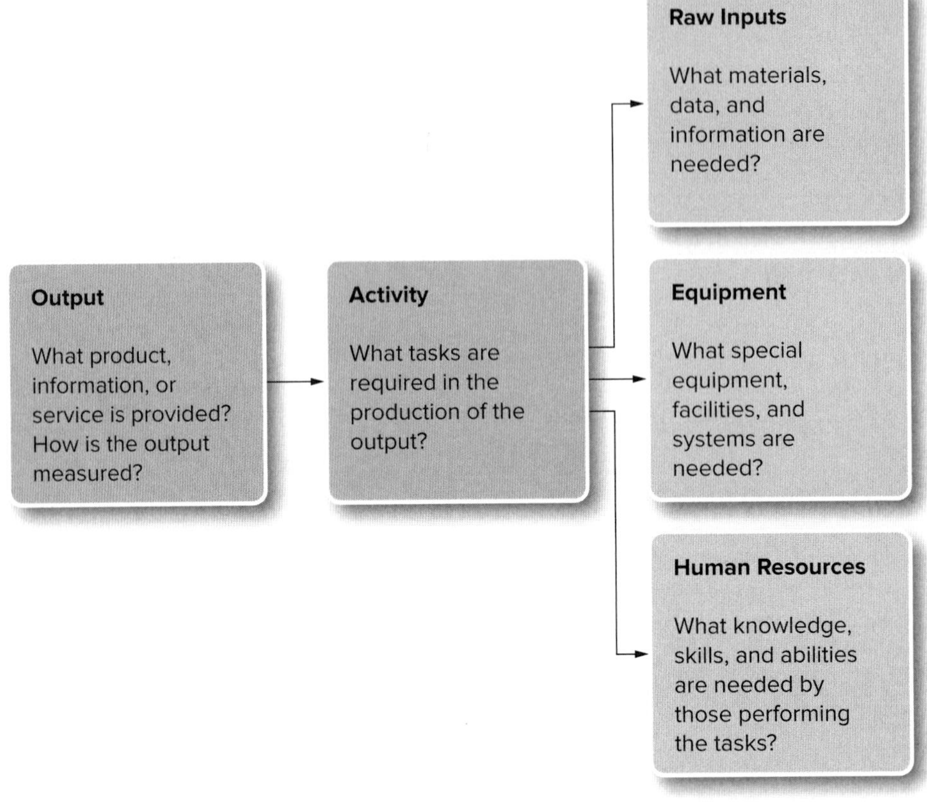

and ensure orders are filled accurately. Automation has taken over tasks such as heavy lifting, memorization of warehouse locations, and even efficient use of packaging tape, but it has not reduced the quantity of human resources needed in the warehouses. Rather, the ability to move more products efficiently through each warehouse has contributed to growing demand for Amazon's services.[2] Another way to understand the importance of identifying inputs is to consider what can go wrong. The "HR Oops!" feature discusses the problem of evaluating inputs apart from processes.

LO 4-2 Describe how work flow is related to an organization's structure.

Work Flow Design and an Organization's Structure

Work flow takes place in the context of an organization's structure. It requires the cooperation of individuals and groups. Ideally, the organization's structure brings together the people who must collaborate to create the desired outputs efficiently. The structure may do this in a way that is highly centralized (that is, with authority concentrated in a few people at the top of the organization) or decentralized (with authority spread among many people). The organization may group jobs according to functions (for example, welding, painting, packaging), or it may set up divisions to focus on products or customer groups.

Although there are an infinite number of ways to combine the elements of an organization's structure, we can make some general observations about structure and work design. If the structure is strongly based on function, workers tend to have low authority and to work alone at highly specialized jobs. Jobs that involve teamwork or broad responsibility tend to require a structure based on divisions other than functions. When the goal is to empower employees, companies need to set up structures and jobs that enable broad responsibility,

HR Oops!

Poor Planning for Robotic Automation

Factory robots have been around for a while, but using robotics to automate office work is still a fairly new development. Managers are seeing the potential for robotic process automation, including claims of process costs being cut by more than half. Furthermore, robots don't get distracted or tired, so they can work faster and more accurately at tasks like entering or formatting data.

Despite the advantages, organizations struggle to achieve the full benefits of automating business processes. One problem is the temptation to skip steps in planning: looking at existing tasks and picking out a few to automate, without considering how the tasks fit into the whole process. If the current process is inefficient, robots speed up efficiency, but if the current process is unfriendly to customers, robots just do unfriendliness more efficiently.

Furthermore, planners do not always fully assess their current inputs. Data must be accurate, whether processed by humans or computers. And shifting routine tasks from humans to bots will change the human resource requirements. Organizations need to redefine what skills will be needed, including the potential for employees to contribute more in the realm of analyzing information and using people skills to build stronger relationships with customers and suppliers.

Questions

1. Suppose a company receives orders by e-mail and has employees read the orders and enter data about each one into a spreadsheet for the billing department and a planning system for the production department. Then the employees generate e-mail messages to each customer to acknowledge each order. Would you describe this process as efficient? Why or why not?
2. Suppose the same company wants to use bots to automate these tasks. How should the company go about planning for this change in inputs?

Sources: Tom Taulli, "Aisera: The Next Generation for RPA (Robotic Process Automation)," *Forbes,* March 26, 2020, https://www.forbes.com; Samantha Dalrymple, "You've Probably Never Heard of Robotic Process Automation, but . . . ," *Scientific American,* January 27, 2020, https://blogs.scientificamerican.com; Naveen Joshi, "Leverage RPA, But Plan for Its Inherent Risks, Too!" *Forbes,* June 28, 2019, https://www.forbes.com; Sara Castellanos and Steven Norton, "Robotic Process Automation Efforts Suffer from Poor Planning: Study," *The Wall Street Journal,* March 22, 2018, https://blogs.wsj.com.

such as jobs that involve employees in serving a particular group of customers or producing a particular product, rather than performing a narrowly defined function. The organization's structure also affects managers' jobs. Managing a division responsible for a product or customer group tends to require more experience and cognitive (thinking) ability than managing a department that handles a particular function. In contrast, managing a functional department requires skill in managing conflicts and aligning employees' efforts with higher-level goals, because these employees tend to identify heavily with their department or profession.[3]

Work design often emphasizes the analysis and design of jobs, as described in the remainder of this chapter. Although all of these approaches can succeed, each focuses on one isolated job at a time. These approaches do not necessarily consider how that single job fits into the overall work flow or structure of the organization. To use these techniques effectively, human resource personnel should also understand their organization as a whole. Ronald Capelle, an organization design consultant, has identified commonly overlooked issues. An example is for an organization to set up several levels of employees without clearly distinguishing the results to be delivered at each level. In a sales organization, the first-level employees might handle individual sales, the manager at the second level focuses on developing customer relationships, and the third level strategizes the growth of entire territories over a one- or two-year time span. But often, Capelle says, the top sales managers don't understand how to take the strategic approach and therefore focus on what the second level is doing. Similarly, he cites the situation of an organization where executives want employees from different departments to collaborate more effectively, but they fail to define which positions in the organization are responsible for resolving issues that cause conflicts.[4]

LO 4-3 Define the elements of a job analysis, and discuss their significance for human resource management.

Job Analysis

Job Analysis
The process of getting detailed information about jobs.

To achieve high-quality performance, organizations have to understand and match job requirements and people. This understanding requires **job analysis,** the process of getting detailed information about jobs. Analyzing jobs and understanding what is required to carry out a job provide essential knowledge for staffing, training, performance appraisal, and many other HR activities. For instance, a supervisor's evaluation of an employee's work should be based on performance relative to job requirements. In very small organizations, line managers may perform a job analysis, but usually the work is done by a human resource professional. A large company may have a compensation management department that includes job analysts (also called personnel analysts). Organizations may also contract with firms that provide this service.

Job Descriptions

Job Description
A list of the tasks, duties, and responsibilities (TDRs) that a particular job entails.

An essential part of job analysis is the creation of job descriptions. A **job description** is a list of the tasks, duties, and responsibilities (TDRs) that a job entails. TDRs are observable actions. For example, a news photographer's job requires the jobholder to use a camera to take photographs. If you were to observe someone in that position for a day, you would almost certainly see some pictures being taken. When a manager attempts to evaluate job performance, it is most important to have detailed information about the work performed in the job (that is, the TDRs). This information makes it possible to determine how well an individual is meeting each job requirement.

A job description typically has the format shown in Figure 4.2. It includes the job title, a brief description of the TDRs, and a list of the essential duties with detailed specifications of the tasks involved in carrying out each duty. Although organizations may modify this format according to their particular needs, all job descriptions within an organization should follow the same format. This helps the organization make consistent decisions about such matters as pay and promotions. It also helps the organization show that it makes human resource decisions fairly.

Whenever the organization creates a new job, it needs a new job description. Preparation of a job description begins with gathering information about the job from people already performing the task, the position's supervisor, or the managers creating the position. Based on that information, the writer of the job description identifies the essential duties of the job, including mental and physical tasks and any methods and resources required. Job descriptions should then be reviewed periodically (say, once a year) and updated if necessary. Performance appraisals can provide a good opportunity for updating job descriptions, as the employee and supervisor compare what the employee has been doing against the details of the job description.

Careful job analysis makes it possible to define what a person in a certain position does and what qualifications are needed for the job. Firefighters use specific equipment to extinguish fires, require physical strength to do their jobs, and must possess the ability to make decisions under pressure. Stockbyte/Getty Images

Organizations should give each newly hired employee a copy of his or her job description. This helps the employee to understand what is expected, but it shouldn't be presented as limiting the employee's commitment to quality and customer satisfaction. Ideally, employees will want to go above and beyond the listed duties when the situation

TRAIN CREW/SERVICE AT UNION PACIFIC

OVERVIEW

When you work on a Union Pacific train crew, you're working at the very heart of our railroad. Train crew employees are responsible for serving our customers by providing the safe, on-time, and on-plan movement of freight trains.

JOB DESCRIPTION

In this entry-level position, you'll start as a Switchperson or Brakeperson, working as on-the-ground traffic control. You don't need any previous railroad experience; we provide all training. These jobs directly lead to becoming a Conductor and a Locomotive Engineer, where you will have a rare opportunity to work on board a moving locomotive. The Conductor is responsible for the train, the freight and the crew. The Locomotive Engineer actually operates the locomotive.

DUTIES

You will work outdoors in all weather conditions and frequently at elevations more than 12 feet above the ground. You must wear personal protective equipment, such as safety glasses and safety boots. You will frequently carry loads and regularly step on and off equipment and work from ladders. You will use and interpret hand signals and sounds, use computers, count train cars, and follow posted regulations.

MAJOR TASKS AND RESPONSIBILITIES

You won't work a standard 40-hour workweek. Train crews are always on call, even on weekends and holidays. You'll travel with our trains, sometimes spending a day or more away from your home terminal.

FIGURE 4.2
Sample Job Description

Source: Union Pacific, "Union Pacific Careers: Train Crew," https://up.jobs/careers/railroad/train-crew/index.htm, accessed March 29, 2020.

and their abilities call for that. Many job descriptions include the phrase *and other duties as requested* as a way to remind employees not to tell their supervisor, "But that's not part of my job." Organizations using this language in job descriptions should ensure that supervisors understand how to assign the additional work fairly, without violating antidiscrimination laws. For example, a supervisor who assigns only the female employees the job of stocking the coffee station or who comes up with physically taxing assignments as a pretext for firing a disabled worker is on shaky legal ground.[5]

Job Specifications

Whereas the job description focuses on the activities involved in carrying out a job, a **job specification** looks at the qualities or requirements the person performing the job must possess. It is a list of the knowledge, skills, abilities, and other characteristics (KSAOs) that an individual must have to perform the job. *Knowledge* refers to factual or procedural information that is necessary for successfully performing a task. For example, this course is providing you with knowledge in how to manage human resources. A *skill* is an individual's level of proficiency at performing a particular task—that is, the capability to perform it well.

Job Specification
A list of the knowledge, skills, abilities, and other characteristics (KSAOs) that an individual must have to perform a particular job.

With knowledge and experience, you could acquire skill in the task of preparing job specifications. *Ability,* in contrast to skill, refers to a more general enduring capability that an individual possesses. A person might have the ability to cooperate with others or to write clearly and precisely. Finally, *other characteristics* might be personality traits such as someone's persistence or motivation to achieve. Some jobs also have legal requirements, such as licensing or certification. Figure 4.3 is a set of sample job specifications for the job description in Figure 4.2.

In developing job specifications, it is important to consider all of the elements of KSAOs. As with writing a job description, the information can come from a combination of people performing the job, people supervising or planning for the job, and trained job analysts. A study by ACT's Workforce Development Division interviewed manufacturing supervisors to learn what they do each day and what skills they rely on. The researchers learned that the supervisors spend much of their day monitoring their employees to make sure the workplace is safe, product quality is maintained, and work processes are optimal. Also, they rely heavily on their technical knowledge of the work processes they supervise.[6] Based on this information, job specifications for a manufacturing supervisor would include skill in observing how people work, as well as in-depth knowledge of manufacturing processes and tools.

In contrast to tasks, duties, and responsibilities, KSAOs are characteristics of people and are not directly observable. They are observable only when individuals are carrying out the TDRs of the job—and afterward, if they can show the product of their labor. Thus, if someone applied for a job as a news photographer, you could not simply look at the individual to determine whether he or she can spot and take effective photographs. However, you could draw

FIGURE 4.3
Sample Job Specifications

Source: Union Pacific, "Union Pacific Careers: Train Crew," https://up.jobs/careers/railroad/train-crew/index.htm, accessed March 29, 2020.

TRAIN CREW/SERVICE AT UNION PACIFIC

REQUIREMENTS

You must be at least 18 years old. You must speak and read English because you'll be asked to follow posted bulletins, regulations, rule books, timetables, switch lists, etc. You must pass a reading comprehension test (see sample) to be considered for an interview.

JOB REQUIREMENTS

You must be able to use a computer keyboard, and you must be able to count and compare numbers. (You might, for example, be asked to count the cars on a train during switching.)

You must be able to solve problems quickly and react to changing conditions on the job.

You must have strong vision and hearing, including the ability to: see and read hand signals from near and far; distinguish between colors; visually judge the speed and distance of moving objects; see at night; and recognize changes in sounds.

You must also be physically strong: able to push, pull, lift, and carry up to 25 pounds frequently; up to 50 pounds occasionally; and up to 83 pounds infrequently. You'll need good balance to regularly step on and off equipment and work from ladders to perform various tasks. And you must be able to walk, sit, stand, and stoop comfortably.

conclusions later about the person's skills by looking at examples of his or her photographs. Similarly, many employers specify educational requirements. Meeting these requirements is treated as an indication that a person has some desired level of knowledge and skills.

Accurate information about KSAOs is especially important for making decisions about who will fill a job. A manager attempting to fill a position needs information about the characteristics required and about the characteristics of each applicant. Interviews and selection decisions should therefore focus on KSAOs.

Sources of Job Information

LO 4-4 Tell how to obtain information for a job analysis.

Information for analyzing an existing job often comes from incumbents, that is, people who currently hold that position in the organization. They are a logical source of information because they are most acquainted with the details of the job. Incumbents should be able to provide very accurate information.

A drawback of relying solely on incumbents' information is that they may have an incentive to exaggerate what they do in order to appear more valuable to the organization. Information from incumbents should therefore be supplemented with information from observers, such as supervisors, who look for a match between what incumbents are doing and what they are supposed to do. Research suggests that supervisors may provide the most accurate estimates of the importance of job duties, whereas incumbents may be more accurate in reporting information about the actual time spent performing job tasks and safety-related risk factors.[7] Some employers and researchers are seeking more objective measures of employees' activities by capturing keystrokes or other digital information. With wearable Bluetooth devices, they can even measure physical activities, including the number of times employees come into contact with other members of the organization. Patterns of interaction coupled with performance outcomes can suggest the kinds of activity associated with high performance.[8] For analyzing skill levels, the best source may be external job analysts who have more experience rating a wide range of jobs.[9]

The U.S. Department of Labor also provides background information for analyzing jobs. The effort began with the *Dictionary of Occupational Titles,* first published in the 1930s, and has since been upgraded to an online database called the Occupational Information Network (O*NET). The O*NET uses a common language that generalizes across jobs to describe the abilities, work styles, work activities, and work context required for 1,000 broadly defined occupations. Users can visit the O*NET Resource Center (https://www.onetcenter.org) to review jobs' tasks, work styles and context, and requirements including skills, training, and experience. Piedmont Natural Gas has used O*NET to conduct job analyses and match candidates to entry-level jobs, thereby improving employee retention. Trustmark Insurance Company used O*NET

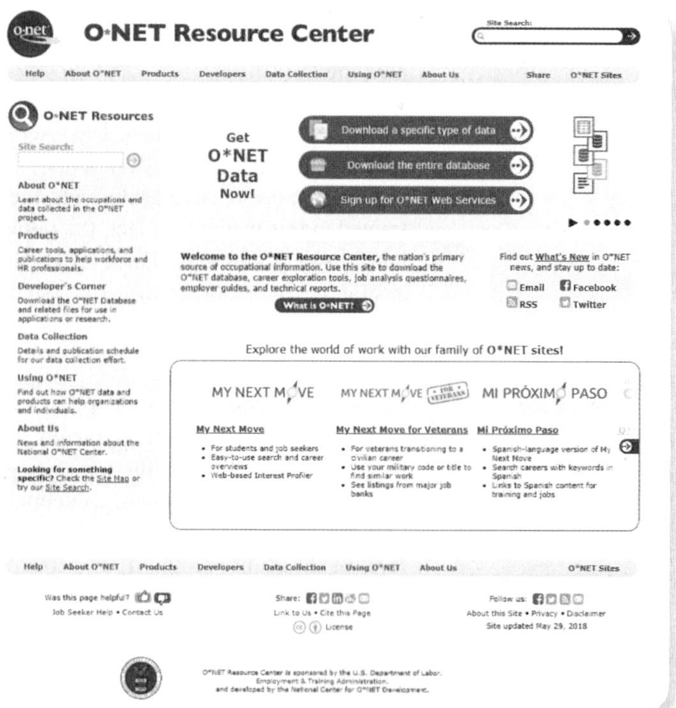

O*NET OnLine provides job seekers with detailed descriptions of many broadly defined occupations. O*NET OnLine/U.S. Department of Labor

to improve descriptions of sales support positions.[10] Furthermore, although the O*NET was developed to analyze jobs in the U.S. economy, research suggests that its ratings tend to be the same for jobs located in other countries.[11]

Position Analysis Questionnaire

Position Analysis Questionnaire (PAQ)
A standardized job analysis questionnaire containing 194 questions about work behaviors, work conditions, and job characteristics that apply to a wide variety of jobs.

After gathering information, the job analyst uses the information to analyze the job. One of the broadest and best-researched instruments for analyzing jobs is the **Position Analysis Questionnaire (PAQ).** This is a standardized job analysis questionnaire containing 194 items that represent work behaviors, work conditions, and job characteristics that apply to a wide variety of jobs. The questionnaire organizes these items into six sections concerning different aspects of the job:

1. *Information input*–Where and how a worker gets information needed to perform the job.
2. *Mental processes*–The reasoning, decision making, planning, and information-processing activities involved in performing the job.
3. *Work output*–The physical activities, tools, and devices used by the worker to perform the job.
4. *Relationships with other persons*–The relationships with other people required in performing the job.
5. *Job context*–The physical and social contexts where the work is performed.
6. *Other characteristics*–The activities, conditions, and characteristics other than those previously described that are relevant to the job.

For each item on the questionnaire, the person analyzing a job determines whether that item applies to the job being analyzed. The analyst rates each item on six scales: extent of use, amount of time, importance to the job, possibility of occurrence, applicability, and special code (special rating scales used with a particular item). The PAQ headquarters use a computer to score the questionnaire and generate a report that describes the scores on the job dimensions.

Using the PAQ provides an organization with information that helps in comparing jobs, even when they are dissimilar. The PAQ also has the advantage that it considers the whole work process, from inputs through outputs. However, the person who fills out the questionnaire must have college-level reading skills, and the PAQ is meant to be completed only by job analysts trained in this method. In fact, the ratings of job incumbents tend to be less reliable than ratings by supervisors and trained analysts.[12] Also, the descriptions in the PAQ reports are rather abstract, so the reports may not be useful for writing job descriptions or redesigning jobs.

Fleishman Job Analysis System

Fleishman Job Analysis System
Job analysis technique that asks subject-matter experts to evaluate a job in terms of the abilities required to perform the job.

To gather information about worker requirements, the **Fleishman Job Analysis System** asks subject-matter experts (typically job incumbents) to evaluate a job in terms of the abilities required to perform the job. The survey is based on 52 categories of abilities, ranging from written comprehension to deductive reasoning, manual dexterity, stamina, and originality. The person completing the survey indicates which point on the scale represents the level of the ability required for performing the job being analyzed. For example, consider the ability, "written comprehension." Written comprehension includes understanding written English words, sentences, and paragraphs. It is different from oral comprehension (listen to and understand spoken English words and sentences) and oral expression (speak English words and sentences so others can understand). The phrase for the highest point on the seven-point scale is "requires understanding of complex or detailed information in writing containing unusual words and phrases and involves fine distinctions in meaning among words." The phrase for the lowest point on the scale is "requires written understanding of short, simple written information containing common words and phrases."[13]

When the survey has been completed in all 52 categories, the results provide a picture of the ability requirements of a job. Such information is especially useful for employee selection, training, and career development.

Analyzing Teamwork

Work design increasingly relies on teams to accomplish an organization's objectives, so HR managers often must identify the best ways to handle jobs that are highly interdependent. Just as there are standardized instruments for assessing the nature of a job, there are standard ways to measure the nature of teams. Three dimensions are most critical:[14]

1. *Skill differentiation*–The degree to which team members have specialized knowledge or functional capacities.
2. *Authority differentiation*–The allocation of decision-making authority among individuals, subgroups, and the team as a whole.
3. *Temporal (time) stability*–The length of time over which team members must work together.

Importance of Job Analysis

Job analysis is so important to HR managers that it has been called the building block of everything that personnel does.[15] The fact is that almost every human resource management program requires some type of information that is gleaned from job analysis:[16]

- *Work redesign*–Often an organization seeks to redesign work to make it more efficient or to improve quality. The redesign requires detailed information about the existing job(s). In addition, preparing the redesign is similar to analyzing a job that does not yet exist.
- *Human resource planning*–As planners analyze human resource needs and how to meet those needs, they must have accurate information about the levels of skill required in various jobs, so that they can tell what kinds of human resources will be needed.
- *Selection*–To identify the most qualified applicants for various positions, decision makers need to know what tasks the individuals must perform, as well as the necessary knowledge, skills, and abilities.
- *Training*–Almost every employee hired by an organization will require training. Any training program requires knowledge of the tasks performed in a job so that the training is related to the necessary knowledge and skills.
- *Performance appraisal*–An accurate performance appraisal requires information about how well each employee is performing in order to reward employees who perform well and to improve their performance if it is below standard. Job analysis helps in identifying the behaviors and the results associated with effective performance.
- *Career planning*–Matching an individual's skills and aspirations with career opportunities requires that those in charge of career planning know the skill requirements of the various jobs. This allows them to guide individuals into jobs in which they will succeed and be satisfied.
- *Job evaluation*–The process of job evaluation involves assessing the relative dollar value of each job to the organization in order to set up fair pay structures. If employees do not believe pay structures are fair, they will become dissatisfied and may quit, or they will not see much benefit in striving for promotions. To put dollar values on jobs, it is necessary to get information about different jobs and compare them.

Required Skills for a Social-Media Specialist

The idea of hiring someone to engage with customers, potential buyers, and the community via social media is still new enough that O*NET's Occupation Reports do not include the categories of social-media specialists and managers. However, many companies are hiring people to represent the company in social media. They are defining job requirements in light of the basic needs: someone who communicates well, uses information technology, and responds constructively to the kinds of problems people raise on social media. Posts on job websites provide some insights into the details.

Communication skills include writing clear and engaging content for several formats, including blog posts, microblogging (notably, posting tweets on Twitter), and posting comments on a variety of sites. A social-media specialist might also identify appropriate content to share and even create visuals or videos for sites like Instagram, YouTube, and Pinterest. To apply these skills, the employee must have knowledge about what kinds of content are most effective in which media, as well as the technology used to create the content. The person also must understand the desired image of each of the organization's brands. To find this set of skills, organizations often look for a person with a college degree in marketing or communications.

To solve problems, the social-media specialist must be able to interpret customers' and community members' comments accurately. Then the employee needs to craft responses that demonstrate the company's values while also demonstrating concern for those affected by the company. Experience in the field of public relations can provide practice with these skills as well as communication skills.

Some organizations give the social-media specialist managerial responsibilities. These include planning what to post as part of a marketing strategy. Another area of responsibility is to measure the success of the media presence, using metrics such as number of followers, number of people who view and share content, and customer attitudes toward the company. The employee would also gather performance data and prepare regular reports.

Questions

1. Suppose an organization wants to add a social-media specialist to its marketing team. How can the information provided here help with HR planning and selection?
2. Suppose a small business has a salesperson who enjoys written communication and has been handling social-media posts. The company considers whether she could expand this role into a more strategic approach to the company's social-media presence. How can it use the information here to help the salesperson with the necessary career planning?

Sources: "O*NET Occupation Reports," O*NET Resource Center, https://www.onetcenter.org, accessed March 29, 2020; "Social Media Manager Responsibilities and Duties," *Indeed,* https://www.indeed.com, accessed March 29, 2020; R. Samuels, "9 Skills Every Social Media Manager Must Have," *Sprout Social,* August 1, 2019, https://sproutsocial.com; Alfred Lua, "10 Important Skills and Traits Your Social Media Manager Will Need," *Buffer,* May 21, 2019, htps://buffer.com/resources/social-media-manager-job-description.

Consider, for example, how you would apply the information about job requirements for a social-media specialist, described in the "HRM Social" box.

Job analysis is also important from a legal standpoint. As we saw in Chapter 3, the government imposes requirements related to equal employment opportunity. Detailed, accurate, objective job specifications help decision makers comply with these regulations by keeping the focus on tasks and abilities. These documents also provide evidence of efforts made to engage in fair employment practices. For example, to enforce the Americans with Disabilities Act, the Equal Employment Opportunity Commission may look at job descriptions to identify the essential functions of a job and determine whether a disabled person could have performed those functions with reasonable accommodations. Likewise, lists of duties in different jobs could be compared to evaluate claims under the Equal Pay Act. However, job descriptions and job specifications are not a substitute for fair employment practices.

Besides helping human resource professionals, job analysis helps supervisors and other managers carry out their duties. Data from job analysis can help managers identify the types of work in their units, as well as provide information about the work flow process, so that managers can evaluate whether work is done in the most efficient way. Job analysis information also supports managers as they make hiring decisions, review performance, and recommend rewards.

Competency Models

LO 4-5 Summarize recent trends in job analysis.

These traditional approaches to job analysis are too limited for some HRM needs, however. When human resource management is actively engaged in talent management as a way to support strategy, organizations need to think beyond skills for particular jobs. They must identify the capabilities they need to acquire and develop in order to promote the organization's success. For this purpose, organizations develop competency models.

Competency An area of personal capability that enables employees to perform their work successfully.

A **competency** is an area of personal capability that enables employees to perform their work successfully.[17] For example, success in a job or career path might require leadership strength, skill in coaching others, and the ability to bring out the best in each member of a diverse team of employees. A competency model identifies and describes all the competencies required for success in a particular occupation or set of jobs. Organizations may create competency models for occupational groups, levels of the organization, or even the entire organization. A competency model might require that all middle managers or all members of the organization be able to act with integrity, value diversity, and commit themselves to delighting customers. Table 4.1 shows an example of a competency model for a project manager. The left side of the table lists competencies required for a project manager (organizational and planning skills; communications; and financial and quantitative skills). The right side of the table shows behaviors that might be used to determine a project manager's level of proficiency for each competency. As in these examples, competency models focus more on how people work, whereas job analysis focuses more on work tasks and outcomes.

Competency models help HR professionals ensure that all aspects of talent management are aligned with the organization's strategy. Hiring based on competencies

TABLE 4.1

Example of Competencies and a Competency Model

PROJECT MANAGER COMPETENCIES	PROFICIENCY RATINGS
Organizational & Planning Skills Ability to establish priorities on projects and schedule activities to achieve results.	1—**Below Expectations:** Unable to perform basic tasks. 2—**Meets Expectations:** Understands basic principles and performs routine tasks with reliable results; works with minimal supervision or assistance. 3—**Exceeds Expectations:** Performs complex and multiple tasks; can coach, teach, or lead others.
Communications Ability to build credibility and trust through open and direct communications with internal and external customers.	1—**Below Expectations:** Unable to perform basic tasks. 2—**Meets Expectations:** Understands basic principles and performs routine tasks with reliable results; works with minimal supervision or assistance. 3—**Exceeds Expectations:** Performs complex and multiple tasks; can coach, teach, or lead others.
Financial & Quantitative Skills Ability to analyze financial information accurately and set financial goals that have a positive impact on company's bottom line and fiscal objectives.	1—**Below Expectations:** Unable to perform basic tasks. 2—**Meets Expectations:** Understands basic principles and performs routine tasks with reliable results; works with minimal supervision or assistance. 3—**Exceeds Expectations:** Performs complex and multiple tasks; can coach, teach, or lead others.

Source: Based on R. J. Mirabile, "Everything You Wanted to Know about Competency Modeling," *Training and Development* (August 1997), pp. 73–77.

associated with job success promotes diversity and lowers the risk of selecting people who will be unhappy in a particular job. Information about employees' competencies can guide training and development, and competency models can serve as a fair basis for defining performance measures. A-dec, a maker of dental equipment, identified competencies for production workers, including teamwork and a customer service orientation. When A-dec began hiring based on competencies, the quality of hired workers improved, employees were less likely to quit, and claims for job-related injuries fell. Colliers International, a real estate firm, also hires for competencies. The firm's chief people officer advises identifying a few main competencies and asking candidates to provide examples of how they demonstrated each–for example, how they motivated themselves to get started on a tough assignment.[18]

Trends in Job Analysis

As we noted in the earlier discussion of work flow analysis, organizations have been appreciating the need to analyze jobs in the context of the organization's structure and strategy. In addition, organizations are recognizing that today's workplace must be adaptable and is constantly subject to change. Thus, although we tend to think of "jobs" as something stable, they actually tend to change and evolve over time. Those who occupy or manage jobs often make minor adjustments to match personal preferences or changing conditions.[19] Indeed, although errors in job analysis can have many sources, most inaccuracy is likely to result from job descriptions being outdated. For this reason, job analysis must not only define jobs when they are created, but also detect changes in jobs as time passes.

The pace of change is accelerating because of the widening availability of robotics, artificial intelligence, voice recognition, and new applications of information technology. These developments let organizations automate processes once assumed to be the domain of humans. These changes lower costs and improve the quality of output. Analysts disagree about the impact on the number of jobs but agree that jobs are changing. One expectation is more jobs where robots and computers *augment,* rather than replace, workers (see "Did You Know?" feature). The technology provides information and assistance so employees can do more than they previously could. Job analysis will therefore need to consider which tasks are best assigned to humans, and which to technology. A case in point for the HR function is the help desk, which used to involve HR professionals taking phone calls from employees who had questions to ask or clerical tasks to carry out. In a growing number of organizations, employees now are talking (or typing) to a chatbot, which can suggest answers or carry out routine tasks like updating insurance information. HR employees who aren't busy answering the phone now have time to analyze data and plan for future talent needs. Clearly, this changes the KSAOs the organization needs for tomorrow's HR staff.[20]

These changes in the nature of work and the expanded use of "project-based" organizational structures require the type of broader understanding that comes from an analysis of work flows. Because the work can change rapidly and it is impossible to rewrite job descriptions every week, job descriptions and specifications need to be flexible. At the same time, legal

Visit your instructor's Connect® course and access your eBook to view this video.

"We are looking at those work systems in the back of the restaurant in terms of where to use potential automation that actually elevates the experience of the employee and makes it a better place to work."

—Scott A. Weisberg
Former Chief People Officer, The Wendy's Company

Video Produced for the Center for Executive Succession in the Darla Moore School of Business at the University of South Carolina by Coal Powered Filmworks

Did You Know?

Automation Potential Affects Most Jobs

Automation and artificial intelligence have already changed the way work gets done, and in the future, most jobs will be affected to some degree. The difference will vary considerably by type of job, with the greatest change affecting jobs that are routine and repetitive.

Almost 4 in 10 jobs have low automation potential, with automation of up to 30% of tasks. These jobs are a mix of highly complex or creative positions and those involving frequent interpersonal activity. Examples include market research analysts, software developers, home health aides, and housekeepers.

About one-fourth of jobs have high automation potential, with more than 70% of their tasks—and as much as all tasks—possibly being automated. These jobs include food preparers, packaging-machine operators, and payroll clerks.

About 36% of jobs have medium automation potential. Examples are computer programmers, salespeople, and medical assistants.

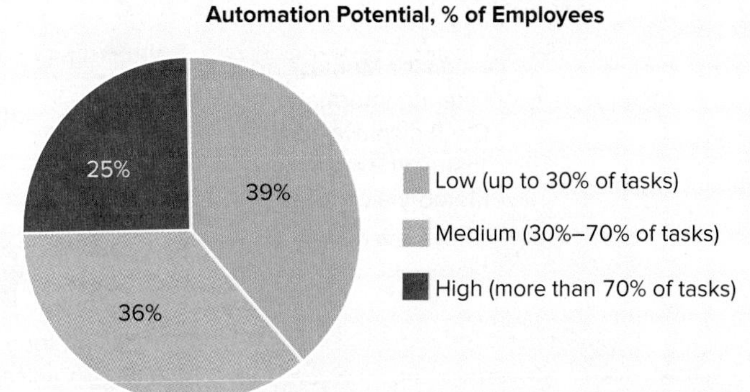

Question

Do you see changes in the nature of jobs resulting from AI and automation as having mostly positive consequences (e.g., more interesting work), mostly negative consequences (e.g., fewer job opportunities), or both? Explain.

Sources: Eric Morath, "AI Is the Next Workplace Disrupter—and It's Coming for High-Skilled Jobs," *The Wall Street Journal,* February 23, 2020, https://www.wsj.com; Mark Muro, Robert Maxim, and Jacob Whiton, *Automation and Artificial Intelligence: How Machines Are Affecting People and Places,* Metropolitan Policy Program at Brookings, January 2019, https://www.brookings.edu; "Over 30 Million U.S. Workers Will Lose Their Jobs Because of AI," *MarketWatch,* January 24, 2019, https://www.marketwatch.com.

requirements (as discussed in Chapter 3) may discourage organizations from writing flexible job descriptions. Consequently, organizations must balance the need for flexibility with the need for legal documentation. This presents one of the major challenges to be faced by HRM departments in the next decade. Many professionals are meeting the challenge with a greater emphasis on careful job design.

Job Design

LO 4-6 Describe methods for designing a job so that it can be done efficiently.

Although job analysis, as just described, is important for an understanding of existing jobs, organizations also must plan for new jobs and periodically consider whether they should revise existing jobs. When an organization is expanding, supervisors and human resource professionals must help plan for new or growing work units. When an organization is trying to improve quality or efficiency, a review of work units and processes may require a fresh look at how jobs are designed.

Job Design
The process of defining how work will be performed and what tasks will be required in a given job.

These situations call for **job design,** the process of defining how work will be performed and what tasks will be required in a given job, or *job redesign,* a similar process that involves changing an existing job design. To design jobs effectively, a person must thoroughly

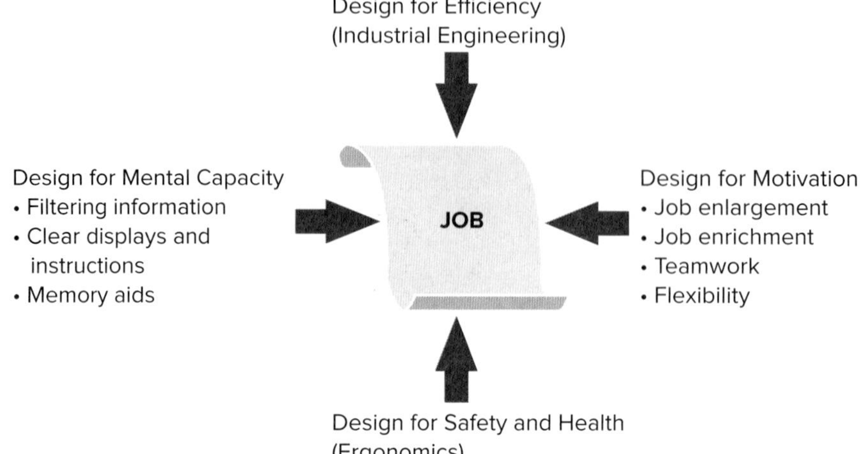

FIGURE 4.4
Approaches to Job Design

understand the job itself (through job analysis) and its place in the larger work unit's work flow process (through work flow analysis). Having a detailed knowledge of the tasks performed in the work unit and in the job, a manager then has many alternative ways to design a job. As shown in Figure 4.4, the available approaches emphasize different aspects of the job: the mechanics of doing a job efficiently, the job's impact on motivation, the use of safe work practices, and the mental demands of the job.

Designing Efficient Jobs

If workers perform tasks as efficiently as possible, not only does the organization benefit from lower costs and greater output per worker, but workers should be less fatigued.

Industrial Engineering
The study of jobs to find the simplest way to structure work in order to maximize efficiency.

This point of view has for years formed the basis of classical **industrial engineering,** which looks for the simplest way to structure work in order to maximize efficiency. Typically, applying industrial engineering to a job reduces the complexity of the work, making it so simple that almost anyone can be trained quickly and easily to perform the job. Such jobs tend to be highly specialized and repetitive.

In practice, the scientific method traditionally seeks the "one best way" to perform a job by performing time-and-motion studies to identify the most efficient movements for workers to make. Once the engineers have identified the most efficient sequence of motions, the organization should select workers based on their ability to do the job, then train them in the details of the "one best way" to perform that job. The company also should offer pay structured to motivate workers to do their best. (Chapters 12 and 13 discuss pay and pay structures.) For an example of an organization analyzing work to improve efficiency, see "Best Practices."

Industrial engineering provides measurable and practical benefits. However, a focus on efficiency alone can create jobs that are so simple and repetitive that workers get bored. Workers performing these jobs may feel their work is meaningless. Hence, most organizations combine industrial engineering with other approaches to job design.

LO 4-7 Identify approaches to designing a job to make it motivating.

Designing Jobs That Motivate

Especially when organizations must compete for employees, depend on skilled knowledge workers, or need a workforce that cares about customer satisfaction, a pure focus on efficiency will not achieve human resource objectives. Employers also need to ensure that workers have a positive attitude toward their jobs so that they show up at work with enthusiasm,

Navicent Health Gets Lean for the Sake of Its Patients

Navicent Health, part of the not-for-profit Central Georgia Health System, operates a teaching hospital, provides home health and hospice care, and operates an emergency medical service (EMS). Its stated vision is to be "a national leader in providing the safest, highest quality, community-centered healthcare and wellness services." Its efforts at quality improvement have brought better outcomes for patients, along with several awards.

Navicent pursues its vision by applying lean Six Sigma techniques for improvement of quality and efficiency. Its Six Sigma projects review work processes to identify and correct the sources of service defects. These efforts often yield changes in job design.

Consider for example, an evaluation of emergency medical services, which were inefficient and led to unacceptable wait times. The Navicent review found shortcomings in the way jobs and pay were structured. In terms of jobs, a key problem was the division of locations into urban and rural areas. Urban areas were overwhelmed by calls, and rural staff were idle much of the time. Compounding the problem, workers were assigned to 24-hour shifts, so urban workers were especially exhausted and dissatisfied. Navicent redesigned the urban jobs into 12-hour shifts and gave employees a chance to submit preferences for where and when they wanted to work. (Pay is higher for the urban locations, to reflect the heavier work load.) More ambulances were allocated to the urban areas during periods of peak demand. These and other changes have reduced response times and made the EMS group more efficient.

Another example of job redesign involved the collection of samples for blood cultures in the hospital's emergency department. Infection rates associated with the blood draws were unacceptably high, and the department's response was to assume employee turnover meant employees lacked sufficient training. Attempts to correct the problem with training repeatedly failed to deliver long-term improvement. A Six Sigma team investigated the problem and found shortcomings in work design. Necessary supplies were often out of stock in the emergency department's storage areas, and employees were unfamiliar with some steps for disinfection. The hospital assigned microbiology staff to spend some off-peak time assembling kits of supplies and instruction sheets. The department also tried assigning a phlebotomist (technician specializing in blood draws) to the emergency department. Infection rates (and costs of treating infection) dropped off to the point of demonstrating that a phlebotomist on staff was a worthwhile investment. This change removed the task of blood draws from the jobs of the department nurses and technicians, freeing them to focus on direct patient care. In the first few years of improving the blood draw process, Navicent saved more than $1.5 million and—at least as important—improved patients' health and well-being.

Questions

1. What inefficiencies did the emergency medical service identify? How did the response change employees' jobs?
2. What inefficiencies did the emergency department identify? How did the response change employees' jobs?

Sources: Navicent Health, "About Us," https://www.navicenthealth.org, accessed March 28, 2020; Navicent Health, "Navicent Health Black Belt Improves Blood Draw Procedures, Reduces Costs," https://www.navicenthealth.org, accessed March 28, 2020; Paul Barkley, "Six Sigma Sticks Patients Less," *ISE Magazine*, February 2018, pp. 28–33; NEJM Catalyst, "What Is Lean Healthcare?" April 27, 2018, https://catalyst.nejm.org.

commitment, and creativity. To improve job satisfaction, organizations need to design jobs that take into account factors that make jobs motivating and satisfying for employees.

A model that shows how to make jobs more motivating is the Job Characteristics Model, developed by Richard Hackman and Greg Oldham. This model describes jobs in terms of five characteristics:[21]

1. *Skill variety*—The extent to which a job requires a variety of skills to carry out the tasks involved.
2. *Task identity*—The degree to which a job requires completing a "whole" piece of work from beginning to end (for example, building an entire component or resolving a customer's complaint).

FIGURE 4.5
Characteristics of a Motivating Job

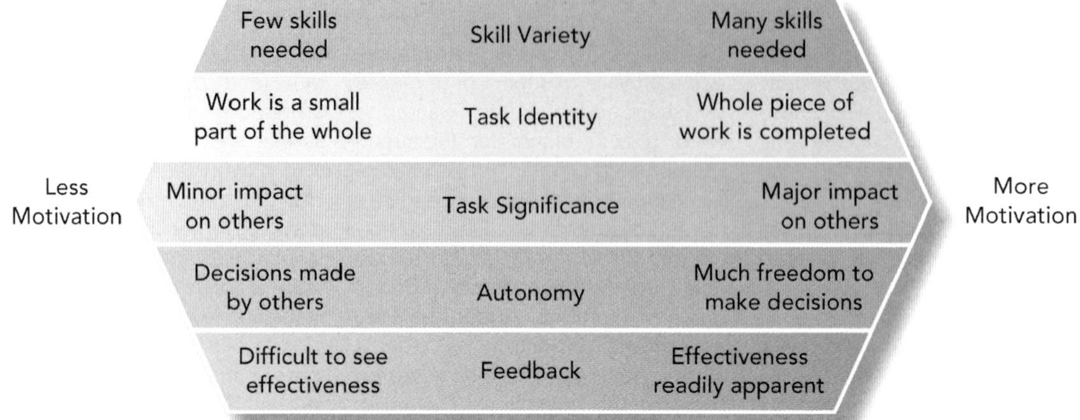

3. *Task significance*–The extent to which the job has an important impact on the lives of other people.
4. *Autonomy*–The degree to which the job allows an individual to make decisions about the way the work will be carried out.
5. *Feedback*–The extent to which a person receives clear information about performance effectiveness from the work itself.

As shown in Figure 4.5, the more of each of these characteristics a job has, the more motivating the job will be, according to the Job Characteristics Model. The model predicts that a person with such a job will be more satisfied and will produce more and better work. For an example of such a job, consider the skill variety and task significance of some of the positions companies are filling in order to have a stronger presence on the Internet. Front-end developers apply knowledge of software, design, and user behavior to create a user interface that is clear and simple to use. Data scientists translate business problems into mathematical models they can test and then translate their statistical test results into business solutions. Now imagine employees in jobs like these working in an environment such as Square Root, a tech company that analyzes data to help retailers improve their performance. Square Root's policies are based on a belief that employees do their best work when they have autonomy concerning their schedule and other working conditions. Its employees say the company provides great challenges and a great atmosphere–and that their co-workers go the extra mile to meet goals.[22]

Applications of the job characteristics approach to job design include job enlargement, job enrichment, self-managing work teams, flexible work schedules, and telework. In applying these methods, HR managers should keep in mind that individual differences among workers will affect how much they are motivated by job characteristics and able to do their best work.[23] For example, someone who thrives in a highly structured environment might not actually be motivated by autonomy and would be a better fit for a job where a supervisor makes most decisions.

Job Enlargement
Broadening the types of tasks performed in a job.

Job Enlargement In a job design, **job enlargement** refers to broadening the types of tasks performed. The objective of job enlargement is to make jobs less repetitive and more interesting. Jobs also become enlarged when organizations add new goals or ask fewer workers to accomplish work that had been spread among more people. In those situations, the challenge is to avoid crossing the line from interesting jobs into jobs that burn out employees. The hospital industry is facing this challenge in positions as basic as patient access staff, the employees who check in patients when they arrive. In the past, these were entry-level positions requiring pleasant communication and accurate entry of basic data such as name, address, and insurance policy number. Today, hospitals face greater accountability for patient satisfaction and more likelihood that patients will have insurance but often in high-deductible plans. If patients don't understand how to use their insurance, they may be upset with their hospital experience and less prepared to pay their share of the bill. Therefore, hospitals are enlarging patient access jobs to include financial counseling. Michael Scriarabba, director of patient access for University of California San Francisco Medical Center, says, "Our whole front-end team must have the level of competency to answer patients' questions about costs." He adds, "It's more than a job–it's a service." Hospitals like UCSF Medical Center therefore are hiring, training for, and paying for competency in helping patients understand their financial responsibility and the available options for assistance. The result of equipping employees for these enlarged jobs, says Scriarabba, is that patients are more satisfied with how they have been treated and also more likely to pay their share of the bill.[24]

Hospitals have begun to enlarge patient access jobs such as admissions to include financial counseling, in an effort to increase patient satisfaction levels.
Mic Pics/Alamy Stock Photo

Organizations that use job enlargement to make jobs more motivational employ techniques such as job extension and job rotation. **Job extension** is enlarging jobs by combining several relatively simple jobs to form a job with a wider range of tasks. An example might be combining the jobs of receptionist, typist, and file clerk into jobs containing all three kinds of work. This approach to job enlargement is relatively simple, but if all the tasks are dull, workers will not necessarily be more motivated by the redesigned job.

Job Extension
Enlarging jobs by combining several relatively simple jobs to form a job with a wider range of tasks.

Job rotation does not actually redesign the jobs themselves, but moves employees among several different jobs. This approach to job enlargement is common among production teams. During the course of a week, a team member may carry out each of the jobs handled by the team. Team members might assemble components one day and pack products into cases another day. As with job extension, the enlarged jobs may still consist of repetitious activities, but with greater variation among those activities.

Job Rotation
Enlarging jobs by moving employees among several different jobs.

Job Enrichment The idea of **job enrichment,** or empowering workers by adding more decision-making authority to their jobs, comes from the work of Frederick Herzberg. According to Herzberg's two-factor theory, individuals are motivated more by the intrinsic aspects of work (for example, the meaningfulness of a job) than by extrinsic rewards, such as pay. Herzberg identified five factors he associated with motivating jobs: achievement, recognition, growth, responsibility, and performance of the entire job. Thus, ways to enrich a manufacturing job might include giving employees authority to stop production when quality standards are not being met and having each employee perform several tasks to complete a particular stage of the process, rather than dividing up the tasks among the employees. For a salesperson in a store, job enrichment might involve the authority to resolve customer problems, including the authority to decide whether to issue refunds or replace merchandise.

Job Enrichment
Empowering workers by adding more decision-making authority to jobs.

In practice, however, it is important to note that not every worker responds positively to enriched jobs. These jobs are best suited to workers who are flexible and responsive to others; for these workers, enriched jobs can dramatically improve motivation.[25]

Self-Managing Work Teams Instead of merely enriching individual jobs, some organizations empower employees by designing work to be done by self-managing work teams.

As described in Chapter 2, these teams have authority for an entire work process or segment. Team members typically have authority to schedule work, hire team members, resolve problems related to the team's performance, and perform other duties traditionally handled by management. Teamwork can give a job such motivating characteristics as autonomy, skill variety, and task identity.

Because team members' responsibilities are great, their jobs usually are defined broadly and include sharing of work assignments. Team members may, at one time or another, perform every duty of the team. The challenge for the organization is to provide enough training so that the team members can learn the necessary skills. Another approach, when teams are responsible for particular work processes or customers, is to assign the team responsibility for the process or customer, then let the team decide which members will carry out which tasks.

A study of work teams at a large financial services company found that the right job design was associated with effective teamwork.[26] In particular, when teams are self-managed and team members are highly involved in decision making, teams are more productive, employees more satisfied, and managers are more pleased with performance. Teams also tend to do better when each team member performs a variety of tasks and when team members view their effort as significant.

Flexible Work Schedules One way in which an organization can give employees some say in how their work is structured is to offer flexible work schedules. Depending on the requirements of the organization and the individual jobs, organizations may be able to be flexible about when employees work. As introduced in Chapter 2, types of flexibility include flextime and job sharing. Figure 4.6 illustrates alternatives to the traditional 40-hour workweek.

FIGURE 4.6
Alternatives to the 8-to-5 Job

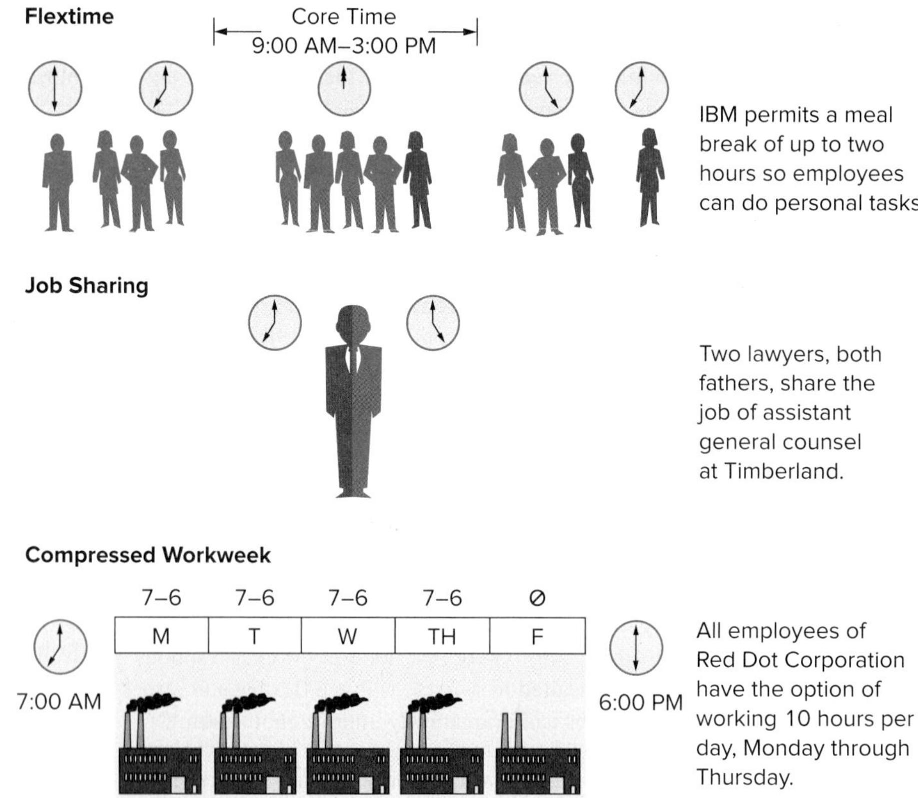
Flextime
Core Time
9:00 AM–3:00 PM
IBM permits a meal break of up to two hours so employees can do personal tasks.
Job Sharing
Two lawyers, both fathers, share the job of assistant general counsel at Timberland.
Compressed Workweek
7–6
7–6
7–6
7–6
Ø
M
T
W
TH
F
7:00 AM
6:00 PM
All employees of Red Dot Corporation have the option of working 10 hours per day, Monday through Thursday.

Flextime is a scheduling policy in which full-time employees may choose starting and ending times within guidelines specified by the organization. The flextime policy may require that employees be at work between certain hours, say, 10:00 am and 3:00 pm. Employees work additional hours before or after this period in order to work the full day. One employee might arrive early in the morning in order to leave at 3:00 pm to pick up children after school. Another employee might be a night owl who prefers to arrive at 10:00 am and work until 6:00, 7:00, or even later in the evening. A flextime policy also may enable workers to adjust a particular day's hours in order to make time for doctor's appointments, children's activities, hobbies, or volunteer work. A work schedule that allows time for community and family interests can be extremely motivating for some employees.

Flextime
A scheduling policy in which full-time employees may choose starting and ending times within guidelines specified by the organization.

Job sharing is a work option in which two part-time employees carry out the tasks associated with a single job. Such arrangements can enable an organization to attract or retain valued employees who want more time to attend school or to care for family members. The job requirements in such an arrangement include the ability to work cooperatively and coordinate the details of one's job with another person.

Job Sharing
A work option in which two part-time employees carry out the tasks associated with a single job.

Although not strictly a form of flexibility for all individual employees, another scheduling alternative is the *compressed workweek.* A compressed workweek is a schedule in which full-time workers complete their weekly hours in fewer than five days. For example, instead of working eight hours a day for five days, the employees could complete 40 hours of work in four 10-hour days. This alternative is most common, but some companies use other alternatives, such as scheduling 80 hours over nine days (with a three-day weekend every other week) or reducing the workweek from 40 to 38 or 36 hours. Employees may appreciate the extra days available for leisure, family, or volunteer activities. An organization might even use this schedule to offer a kind of flexibility—for example, letting workers vote whether they want a compressed workweek during the summer months. This type of schedule has a couple of drawbacks, however. One is that employees may become exhausted on the longer workdays. Another is that if the arrangement involves working more than 40 hours during a week, the Fair Labor Standards Act requires the payment of overtime wages to nonsupervisory employees. For ideas on how to set up flexible scheduling, see the "HR How To" box.

Telework Flexibility can extend to work locations as well as work schedules. Before the Industrial Revolution, most people worked either close to or inside their own homes. Mass production technologies changed all this, separating work life from home life, as people began to travel to centrally located factories and offices. Today, however, skyrocketing prices for office space, combined with drastically reduced prices for mobile computing devices, have made alternatives possible.

The broad term for doing one's work away from a centrally located office is *telework,* or telecommuting, and even essential, as many organizations struggled to survive during the COVID-19 pandemic.

For employers, advantages of telework include less need for office space and the ability to offer greater flexibility to employees who are disabled or need to be available for children or elderly relatives. The employees using telework arrangements may have fewer absences from work than employees with similar demands who must commute to work. Telecommuting can also support a strategy of corporate social responsibility because these employees do not produce the greenhouse gas emissions that result from commuting by car. Telework is easiest to implement for people in managerial, professional, or sales jobs, especially those that involve working and communicating on a computer. A telework arrangement is generally difficult to set up for manufacturing workers. Some observers see an especially strong desire for telecommuting among younger workers, who have grown up expecting to communicate remotely from a mobile device.[27]

HR How To

Planning for Workplace Flexibility

In recent years, employers have increasingly had to consider workers' preference for flexible workplaces. First came the tumble in unemployment rates, which made competition for workers a major driving force for employers to think about flexible work hours. Then more recently the coronavirus pandemic forced employers to look at how they could keep employees on the job when schools and customer-facing businesses shut their doors. They had to move beyond common assumptions that flexible work was just for a handful of highly educated office workers seeking part-time hours or work-from-home arrangements.

Organizations seeking to increase workplace flexibility can benefit from careful planning. The following strategies can contribute to their success:

- Define the organization's requirements. Rather than merely assuming that office hours should be 8:30 to 5:00, ask what work needs to be done during which hours. And instead of assuming that one job needs to encompass 40 hours' worth of activities, consider whether some work could be shared or reallocated for greater flexibility.
- Identify specific kinds of employee needs. A provider of hospital services observed that it operated in school districts where children were in school nine weeks and off for three weeks on schedules that rotated throughout the year. So it offered this type of schedule to its employees and found that the option reduced employee turnover.
- Plan for supervision. Working from a remote location requires self-direction and access to needed resources such as data and web conferencing software (eg, Zoom), which give employees the capability to hold virtual meetings. Managers need training in how to keep up with what employees are doing in other locations.
- Prepare for legal requirements. For example, if workers are eligible for overtime pay (see Chapter 12), the plans need to include a way of tracking hours actually worked each week.
- Keep an open mind about flexibility. Employers with modern scheduling software can let employees request the kind of flexibility they need, whether that means Fridays off, early start and finish times, all the overtime they can get, or assignments within a certain distance from home.

Questions

1. In this list of strategies, identify where HR expertise can help managers implement flexible work arrangements.
2. Imagine you are an HR manager in a small manufacturing company, and the production manager comes to you with concerns that some employees have been expressing a wish for more flexible work arrangements. The production manager doubts that this could apply to manufacturing. How would you begin discussing this topic with the production manager?

Sources: "Managing Flexible Work Arrangements," *Society for Human Resource Management,* https://www.shrm.org, accessed March 29, 2020; Dennis Martino, "Meeting the Challenge of Flexible Scheduling in the Public Sector," *PA Times,* Fall 2019, pp. 32–33; "The Pros and Cons of Flexible Work Arrangements," *Paycor,* July 8, 2019, https://www.paycor.com; Jo Faragher, "Does Flexible Working Work for Everyone?" *People Management,* March 2019, pp. 24–30.

The degree to which companies permit or even encourage telework is subject to debate, because it is difficult to measure. According to research by Global Workplace Analytics, regular work-at-home days have grown more than 170% since 2005, with 43% of U.S. employees working remotely with some frequency. In addition, more than 5 million employees (3.6% of U.S. workforce) currently work at home half-time or more. (These data do not reflect any temporary remote work caused by the coronavirus pandemic in 2020.) In contrast, some companies, including IBM, Aetna, and Best Buy, have ended or drastically reduced employees' telecommuting programs. In some cases, these companies have indicated a desire to bring people together as a way to spark innovation and increase collaboration.[28] Organizations that want to offer telework because employees value this work arrangement will have to ensure that they measure outcomes and have appropriate performance controls.

Designing Ergonomic Jobs

LO 4-8 Explain how organizations apply ergonomics to design safe jobs.

The way people use their bodies when they work—whether toting heavy furniture onto a moving van or sitting quietly before a computer screen—affects their physical well-being and may affect how well and how long they can work. The study of the interface between individuals' physiology and the characteristics of the physical work environment is called **ergonomics.** The goal of ergonomics is to minimize physical strain on the worker by structuring the physical work environment around the way the human body works. Ergonomics therefore focuses on outcomes such as reducing physical fatigue, aches and pains, and health complaints. Ergonomic research includes the context in which work takes place, such as the lighting, space, and hours worked.[29]

Ergonomics
The study of the interface between individuals' physiology and the characteristics of the physical work environment.

Ergonomic job design has been applied in redesigning equipment used in jobs that are physically demanding. Such redesign is often aimed at reducing the physical demands of certain jobs so that anyone can perform them. In addition, many interventions focus on redesigning machines and technology to minimize occupational illnesses—for instance, adjusting the height of a computer keyboard to minimize carpal tunnel syndrome. The design of chairs and desks to fit posture requirements is very important in many office jobs. Researchers studying ergonomic redesign of factory workstations found improvements in injury rates, productivity, quality of output, and employee engagement and retention. Ford makes ergonomics part of the initial design of each facility and production line. To gather data, the automaker uses motion-capture technology collected from sensors on workers' bodies to identify potential problems such as imbalance and muscle strain. Workers simulate the planned movements, and engineers study the movement data to improve their design of each workstation.[30]

A recent ergonomic challenge comes from the popularity of mobile devices. As workers find more and more uses for these devices, they are at risk for repetitive-stress injuries (RSIs). Typing with one's thumbs to send frequent text messages on a smartphone can result in inflammation of the tendons that move the thumbs. Laptop and notebook computers are handy to carry, but because the screen and keyboard are attached in a single device, the computer can't be positioned to the ergonomically correct standards of screen at eye level and keyboard low enough to type with arms bent at a 90-degree angle. Heavy users of these devices must therefore trade off eyestrain against physical strain to wrists, unless they can hook up their device to an extra, properly positioned keyboard or monitor. Touchscreens pose their own risks. Although touchscreens are typically part of a mobile device, making them easy to move around for comfortable use, the employer can't ensure an ergonomic setup. If the screen is part of a laptop or desktop computer, so that a user has to frequently tap on a screen set up at a distance, shoulder pain can result. Workers can protect themselves by taking frequent breaks, paying attention to their posture, and using a variety of input devices, such as a mouse, keyboard, and stylus, in addition to tapping a screen. Furthermore, researchers are developing software to adapt touchscreens for use by people with disabilities such as tremors. The software applies artificial intelligence to measure the user's movements and correct for input errors.[31]

The Occupational Safety and Health Administration has a "four-pronged" strategy for encouraging ergonomic job design. The first prong is to issue guidelines (rather than regulations) for specific industries. To date, these guidelines have been issued for poultry-processing and meatpacking plants, foundries, nursing homes, shipyards, and grocery stores. Second, OSHA enforces violations of its requirement that employers have a general duty to protect workers from hazards, including ergonomic hazards. Third, OSHA works with industry groups to advise employers in those industries. And finally, OSHA established a National Advisory Committee on Ergonomics to define needs for further research. You can learn more about OSHA's guidelines at the agency's website, www.osha.gov.

HR Analytics & Decision Making

A potential contributor to workplace illnesses is pollution, which can occur indoors as well as outdoors. Volatile organic compounds (VOCs) are an example of workplace pollution. These carbon compounds are emitted from materials or processes, including carpets, furniture, cleaning products, markers, and printing or photocopying.

Besides looking at the potential impact of VOCs on health, researchers have investigated their impact on workers' mental capacity on the job. The Syracuse Center for Excellence, which focuses on "green" technologies, gathered data on VOC levels and cognitive ability. The study divided workers into three groups, which worked under different conditions. The control group experienced the average level of VOCs in an office (considered to be an acceptable level). The experimental groups had a 50% increase in ventilation and a 100% increase. Over the course of six days, workers completed cognitive tests under their assigned condition.

According to the data, workers whose environments had 50% more ventilation outscored the control group by 61% The workers with the greatest level of ventilation outscored the control group by 100%. In other words, cleaner indoor air was associated with clearer thinking.

Questions

1. How could an organization benefit from its people functioning at peak mental capacity rather than half that level?
2. If you were a manager, what additional information would you want to have before you invested in better ventilation or switched to lower-polluting materials and processes?

Source: Tori DeAngelis, "Healthy Buildings, Productive People," *Monitor on Psychology,* May 2017, pp. 40–45.

LO 4-9 Discuss how organizations can plan for the mental demands of a job.

Designing Jobs That Meet Mental Capabilities and Limitations

Just as the human body has capabilities and limitations, addressed by ergonomics, the mind, too, has capabilities and limitations. Besides hiring people with certain mental skills, organizations can design jobs so that they can be accurately and safely performed given the way the brain processes information. Generally, this means reducing the information-processing requirements of a job. In these simpler jobs, workers may be less likely to make mistakes or have accidents. Of course, the simpler jobs also may be less motivating. Research has found that challenging jobs tend to fatigue and dissatisfy workers when they feel little control over their situation, lack social support, and feel motivated mainly to avoid errors. In contrast, they may enjoy the challenges of a difficult job where they have some control and social support, especially if they enjoy learning and are unafraid of making mistakes.[32] Because of this drawback, it can be most beneficial to simplify jobs where employees will most appreciate having the mental demands reduced (as in a job that is extremely challenging) or where the costs of errors are severe (as in the job of a surgeon or air-traffic controller).

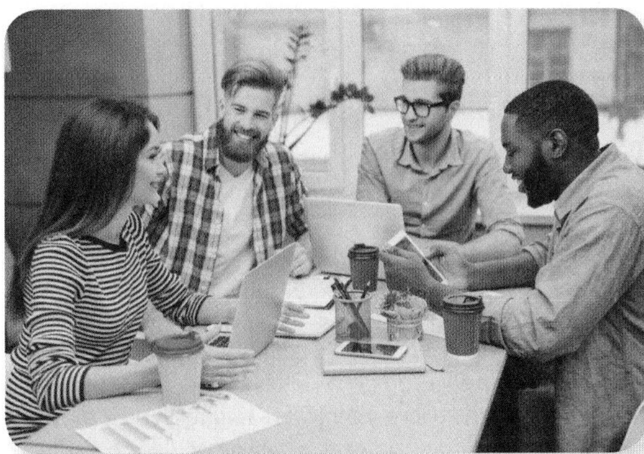

Technological advances can sometimes increase job demands. Some employees may be required to juggle information from several sources at once, which may distract them from their primary job task.
Roman Samborskyi/Shutterstock

There are several ways to simplify a job's mental demands. One is to limit the amount of information and memorization that the job requires. Organizations can also provide adequate lighting, easy-to-understand gauges and displays, simple-to-operate equipment, and clear instructions. For project management, teamwork, and work done by employees in different locations, organizations may provide software that helps with tracking progress. Often, employees try to simplify some of the mental demands of their own jobs by creating checklists, charts, or other aids. Finally, every job requires some degree of thinking, remembering, and paying attention, so for every job, organizations need to evaluate whether their employees can handle the job's mental demands.

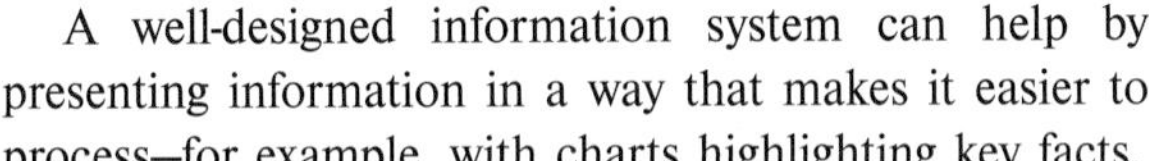

A well-designed information system can help by presenting information in a way that makes it easier to process—for example, with charts highlighting key facts. This has become important in the medical field, where the move to electronic health records has placed an enormous amount of patient data at doctors' fingertips. There is so much data that finding the relevant information has become time consuming. To help doctors treating patients with diabetes, the University of Missouri School of Medicine developed a "diabetes dashboard" that presents key test results and other measures on one screen. Doctors shortened the time they need to absorb this information from an average of five minutes down to just one, which frees up more time for talking to patients. The simpler process also reduces the risk of errors.[33]

Changes in technology sometimes reduce job demands and errors, but in some cases, technology has made the problem worse. Some employees try to juggle information from several sources at once—say, talking on a cell phone while typing, surfing the web for information during a team member's business presentation, or repeatedly stopping work on a project to check e-mail or Twitter feeds. In these cases, the cell phone, handheld computer, and e-mail or tweets are distracting the employees from their primary task. They may convey important information, but they also break the employee's train of thought, reducing performance and increasing the likelihood of errors. Research by a firm called Basex, which specializes in the knowledge economy, found that a big part of the information overload problem is recovery time, that is, the time it takes a person's thinking to switch back from an interruption to the task at hand. The Basex researchers found that recovery time is from 10 to 20 times the length of the interruption. For example, after a 30-second pause to check a Twitter feed, the recovery time could be five minutes or longer.[34]

Organizations probably can't design interruption-free jobs, and few employees would want to isolate themselves entirely from the information and relationships available online. But employers can design jobs that empower workers to manage their time—for example, allowing them to schedule blocks of time when they concentrate on work and do not answer phone calls, e-mails, or text messages. Some employees set aside one or two periods during the day when they will open their e-mail programs, read messages, and respond to the messages immediately. As head of brand and co-founder of DigitalOcean, a cloud infrastructure provider based in New York City, Mitch Wainer blocks off several one- to three-hour time slots in his weekly calendar and labels them as "busy," to give himself some "head-down time" to review goals and initiatives to make sure they are on track.[35]

THINKING ETHICALLY

ARE EMPLOYERS RESPONSIBLE FOR ERGONOMICS IN WORKERS' HOMES?

For years, ergonomics has been a staple of designing physically taxing jobs. Starting around the 1980s, ergonomics specialists addressed office work, with guidelines for good posture and even for breaking up hours spent seated at a desk. It's normal today for office workers to be given adjustable chairs, big computer screens, and desks of the proper height. But what happens when employees work from remote locations? Employers tend not to get involved in home-based workspaces. Employees might spend a morning on the couch, curled up over a tablet, or devote hours to peering into a tiny phone screen and tapping out messages with their thumbs.

Employees and employers are used to the idea of home being a private space. But if workers get backaches and repetitive-strain injuries from working in less-than-optimal positions without sufficient breaks to move around, it hurts the workers. And if the workers need time off to recover or file claims for workers' compensation, it becomes a problem for the employer as well. Companies concerned about these possibilities are exploring ways to discuss remote-work setups with their employees, and they might provide employees with the necessary technology and furniture to set up an ergonomic work station.

Even with equipment or an equipment allowance, remote workers might not think about how they can work safely—for example, how to remove hazards, use good posture, or take breaks to move around. Technology might play a role here. Researchers have used motion-sensing technology to map the motions involved in proper lifting. Workers can use wearable technology to alert them when they are moving in patterns associated with injuries. In theory, similar technology could measure workers' behavior behind desks. This approach requires consideration of the value of privacy relative to the value of injury prevention.

Questions

1. What are the benefits and costs when employers leave it up to workers to set up work areas at home? What are the benefits and costs when employers set standards for home office space? Which approach has the ethically superior balance of benefits and costs?
2. How could an employer address privacy concerns when working with an employee to ensure that home-based work will meet ergonomic standards?

Sources: Mark Benden, "The Future of Office Ergonomics: Standardize or Optimize?" *ISE Magazine,* March 2020, pp. 28–32; Alicja Grzadkowska, "The Workers' Comp Risks When Employees Work from Home," *Insurance Business,* February 28, 2020, https://www.insurancebusinessmag.com; "How Ergonomic Is Your Warehouse Job?" *ISE Magazine,* November 2019, p. 14.

SUMMARY

LO 4-1 Summarize the elements of work flow analysis.

- First, the analysis identifies the amount and quality of a work unit's outputs (products, parts of products, or services).
- Next, the analyst determines the work processes required to produce the outputs, breaking down tasks into those performed by each person.
- Finally, the work flow analysis identifies the inputs used to carry out the processes.

LO 4-2 Describe how work flow is related to an organization's structure.

- Within an organization, units and individuals must cooperate to create outputs, and the organization's structure brings people together for this purpose.
- The structure may be centralized or decentralized.
- People may be grouped according to function or into divisions focusing on particular products or customer groups.
- A functional structure is most appropriate for people who perform highly specialized jobs and hold relatively little authority.
- Employee empowerment and teamwork succeed best in a divisional structure.

LO 4-3 Define the elements of a job analysis, and discuss their significance for human resource management.

- Job analysis is the process of getting detailed information about jobs. It includes preparation of job descriptions and job specifications.
- A job description lists the tasks, duties, and responsibilities of a job.

- Job specifications look at the qualities needed in a person performing the job. They list the knowledge, skills, abilities, and other characteristics that are required for successful performance of a job.
- Job analysis provides a foundation for carrying out many HRM responsibilities, including work redesign, human resource planning, employee selection and training, performance appraisal, career planning, and job evaluation to determine pay scales.

LO 4-4 Tell how to obtain information for a job analysis.

- Information for analyzing an existing job often comes from incumbents and their supervisors.
- The Labor Department publishes general background information about jobs in the *Dictionary of Occupational Titles* and Occupational Information Network (O*NET).
- Job analysts, employees, and managers may complete a Position Analysis Questionnaire or fill out a survey for the Fleishman Job Analysis System.
- In the case of teamwork, there are standard ways to measure the nature of teams, such as looking at three critical dimensions: skill differentiation, authority differentiation, and temporal (time) stability.

LO 4-5 Summarize recent trends in job analysis.

- To broaden traditional approaches to job analysis in support of talent management, organizations develop competency models. A competency model identifies and describes all the competencies, or personal capabilities, required for success in a particular occupation or set of jobs.
- Because today's workplace requires a high degree of adaptability, job tasks and requirements are subject to constant change. For example, as some organizations downsize, they are defining jobs more broadly, with less supervision of those positions.
- Organizations are also adopting project-based structures and teamwork, which also require flexibility and the ability to handle broad responsibilities.
- The pace of change in job design continues to accelerate due to the widening availability of robotics, artificial intelligence, voice recognition, and new applications of information technology. These developments let organizations automate processes once assumed to be the domain of humans. However, more research is needed to determine how these advances will affect the number of jobs in the workplace, although analysts agree that jobs will continue to evolve.

LO 4-6 Describe methods for designing a job so that it can be done efficiently.

- The basic technique for designing efficient jobs is industrial engineering, which looks for the simplest way to structure work to maximize efficiency.
- Through methods such as time-and-motion studies, the industrial engineer creates jobs that are relatively simple and typically repetitive.
- These jobs may bore workers because they are so simple.

LO 4-7 Identify approaches to designing a job to make it motivating.

- According to the Job Characteristics Model, jobs are more motivating if they have greater skill variety, task identity, task significance, autonomy, and feedback about performance effectiveness.
- Ways to create such jobs include job enlargement (through job extension or job rotation) and job enrichment.
- Self-managing work teams also offer greater skill variety and task identity.
- Flexible work schedules and telework offer greater autonomy.

LO 4-8 Explain how organizations apply ergonomics to design safe jobs.

- The goal of ergonomics is to minimize physical strain on the worker by structuring the physical work environment around the way the human body works.
- Ergonomic design may involve (1) modifying equipment to reduce the physical demands of performing certain jobs or (2) redesigning the jobs themselves to reduce strain.
- Ergonomic design may target work practices associated with injuries.

LO 4-9 Discuss how organizations can plan for the mental demands of a job.

- Employers may seek to reduce mental as well as physical strain.
- The job design may limit the amount of information and memorization involved.
- Adequate lighting, easy-to-read gauges and displays, simple-to-operate equipment, and clear instructions also can minimize mental strain.
- Computer software can simplify jobs—for example, by performing calculations or filtering out spam from important e-mails.
- Organizations can select employees with the necessary abilities to handle a job's mental demands.

KEY TERMS

work flow design, 101
job, 101
position, 101
job analysis, 104
job description, 104
job specification, 105
Position Analysis Questionnaire (PAQ), 108
Fleishman Job Analysis System, 108
competency, 111
job design, 113
industrial engineering, 114
job enlargement, 116
job extension, 117
job rotation, 117
job enrichment, 117
flextime, 119
job sharing, 119
ergonomics, 121

REVIEW AND DISCUSSION QUESTIONS

1. Assume you are the manager of a fast-food restaurant. What are the outputs of your work unit? What are the activities required to produce those outputs? What are the inputs? *(LO 4-1)*
2. Based on Question 1, consider the cashier's job in the restaurant. What are the outputs, activities, and inputs for that job? *(LO 4-1)*
3. Consider the "job" of college student. Perform a job analysis on this job. What tasks are required in the job? What knowledge, skills, and abilities are necessary to perform those tasks? Prepare a job description based on your analysis. *(LO 4-3)*
4. Discuss how the following trends are changing the skill requirements for managerial jobs in the United States. *(LO 4-5)*
   a. Increasing use of social media
   b. Increasing international competition
   c. Increasing work-family conflicts
5. Suppose you have taken a job as a trainer in a large bank that has created competency models for all its positions. How could the competency models help you succeed in your career at the bank? How could the competency models help you develop the bank's employees? *(LO 4-5)*
6. Consider the job of a customer service representative who fields telephone calls from customers of a retailer that sells online and through catalogs. What measures can an employer take to design this job to make it efficient? What might be some drawbacks or challenges of designing this job for efficiency? *(LO 4-6)*
7. How might the job in Question 6 be designed to make it more motivating? How well would these considerations apply to the cashier's job in Question 2? *(LO 4-7)*
8. What ergonomic considerations might apply to each of the following jobs? For each job, what kinds of costs would result from addressing ergonomics? What costs might result from failing to address ergonomics? *(LO 4-8)*
   a. A computer programmer
   b. A UPS delivery person
   c. A child care worker
9. Modern electronics have eliminated the need for a store's cashiers to calculate change due on a purchase. How does this development modify the job description for a cashier? If you were a store manager, how would it affect the skills and qualities of job candidates you would want to hire? Does this change in mental processing requirements affect what you would expect from a cashier? How? *(LO 4-9)*
10. Consider a job you hold now or have held recently. Would you want this job to be redesigned to place more emphasis on efficiency, motivation, ergonomics, or mental processing? What changes would you want, and why? (Or why do you not want the job to be redesigned?) *(LO 4-9)*

SELF-ASSESSMENT EXERCISE

Do You Have the Necessary Skills for Your Dream Job?

The chapter described how the Department of Labor's Occupational Information Network (O*NET) can help employers. The system was also designed to help job seekers. To see if you think this new system meets the goal of promoting "the effective education, training, counseling, and employment needs of the American workforce," visit O*NET's website at https://www.onetonline.org/.

Look up the listing for your current job or dream job. List the skills identified for that job. For each skill, evaluate how well your own experiences and abilities enable you to match the job requirements.

TAKING RESPONSIBILITY

Mayo Clinic Redesigns Work to Improve Care

The Mayo Clinic might seem like a strange candidate for work redesign. The organization is known for setting the gold standard for patient care. Each year, more than a million patients, many with complex health conditions, travel to the main campus in Rochester, Minnesota, or to facilities in Arizona and Florida. There they receive "patient-centered care," in which a team of doctors collaborates on treatment, consulting one shared medical record for each patient. Providing these services brings in annual revenues of nearly $14 billion.

Changes in the U.S. health care system are making past practices unsustainable, however. Mayo's CEO, Dr. John Noseworthy, observed that as health care costs continue to rise faster than inflation, payers–Medicare, Medicaid, and private insurance companies–are all putting caps on what they will pay, even as an aging population needs more care. Payers are insisting that doctors and hospitals start thinking more like businesses and figure out ways to deliver consistent patient care more efficiently. Dr. Noseworthy determined that protecting Mayo Clinic's future would require him to lead a rethinking of how work is done in every part of the organization, a project he named the Mayo Clinic 2020 Initiative.

For the hundreds of projects in this initiative, the changes include some restructuring of jobs. For example, a review of the care given to patients with epilepsy found that some services doctors were providing could be delivered just as well by nurses. Expanding nurses' jobs in this way not only lowered the cost of a visit, it also freed up a quarter hour of time per patient for doctors to visit new patients. Similarly, a review of care following heart surgery led to a decision that nurses should have more control over that process.

The very act of launching the 2020 Initiative changed the jobs of Mayo's physicians. Previously their role was all about health care, with the doctors assuming the clinic would provide whatever resources they requested. Now their role has expanded to include decision making aimed at eliminating wasted time and money. For example, heart surgery teams competed to see which team could best shrink the time to set up operating rooms between surgeries. No prizes were awarded, but the friendly competition cut the average time in half.

Efforts to improve work processes have also addressed the problem of information overload. Mayo Clinic observed that doctors had available as many as 50,000 data points about any given patient–too much to process quickly and accurately. To improve care in the clinic's intensive-care units, a team of researchers and IT experts interviewed doctors to identify which pieces of data are most important to their work. They identified several dozen and designed a system to display this data set, highlight relevant measures with color coding, and deliver alarms when certain measures do not conform to the requirements for providing quality care in a situation. Using the system, the ICUs have improved their efficiency, patient outcomes, and operating costs.

Questions

1. What responsibilities were added to the jobs of doctors and nurses at Mayo Clinic? What impact do you think those changes had on the motivational aspect of the work?
2. What would you expect are the potential consequences of information overload in an intensive-care unit? Why is it important for ICUs to help doctors meet this kind of mental demand?

Sources: Mayo Clinic, "About Us," https://www.mayoclinic.com, accessed March 29, 2020; "Clinic Redesign Increases Efficiency and Teamwork, Shortens Patient Wait Time," December 21, 2019 https://www.mayoclinic.com; Vitaly Herasevich, Brian Pickering, and Ognjen Gajic, "How Mayo Clinic Is Combating Information Overload in Critical Care Units," *Harvard Business Review*, March 22, 2018, https://hbr.org; Ron Winslow, "Mayo Clinic's Unusual Challenge: Overhaul a Business That's Working," *The Wall Street Journal*, June 2, 2017, https://www.wsj.com.

MANAGING TALENT

Flexibility Drives Uber's Growth

The fastest-growing start-up on record operates in hundreds of cities around the world but has just a few thousand full-time employees. That company is Uber, the ride-sharing service. Most of its transportation work is carried out not by employees on the payroll but by more than a million individuals who have signed up to give Uber rides as independent contractors.

The decision to use this type of flexible work arrangement means Uber has chosen to limit the degree to which it controls the way work is done. Uber drivers use their own cars and decide when they want to work. They pay about 20% of each fare to Uber and control how they use the rest to pay the cost of maintaining and operating their vehicles, as well as the taxes due on their driving income. Anything above those expenses is theirs to keep for fun money–or if they work long hours, as their main source of income.

Still, Uber does retain control over many aspects of these jobs and the services provided. Uber uses a computer system to set the price of a ride, which varies according to demand. Drivers can choose to work more during high-demand periods, when prices are higher, but if they want to work when demand is low, they have to accept the lower prices. Drivers also must pass a background check, keep passenger ratings above a set level, and use Uber's smartphone app. If they violate these and other terms–for example, engaging in risky driving behavior or driving a vehicle they didn't register with Uber–the company can deactivate their driver status.

To maintain long-term success with this work design, Uber will have to overcome some challenges of the independent-contractor model. Employees receive certain protections and benefits, such as extra pay for overtime, insurance benefits, and reimbursement for their mileage. Some drivers have sued to be classified as employees and receive these benefits. The courts have so far been divided on the status of Uber's drivers, meaning that how to stay on the right side of the law remains an open question. In addition, even if the courts come to accept these work arrangements with independent contractors, the fact remains that drivers who are full-time employees generally would receive a benefits package, including paid holidays and health insurance. Other companies could compete for the best drivers this way, so Uber has to ensure that its jobs continue to be motivating enough to attract and keep good drivers.

Questions

1. Applying the Job Characteristics Model, how motivating are Uber's jobs for drivers?
2. List the competencies you think would be important for success as an Uber driver.

Sources: Uber Blog, "To California Drivers: Keeping You in the Driver's Seat," https://www.uber.com, accessed March 29, 2020; M. Keith Chen, Peter E. Rossi, Judith A. Chevalier, and E. Oehlsen, "The Value of Flexible Work: Evidence from Uber Drivers," *Journal of Political Economy,* October 31, 2019, https://www.journals.uchicago.edu; Daniel Wiessner, "Uber Drivers Are Contractors, Not Employees, U.S. Labor Agency Says," *Reuters,* May 14, 2019, https://www.reuters.com; Andrew Khouri, "Uber Drivers, Freelancers and Other Independent Contractors Are Getting a Tax Cut," *Los Angeles Times,* January 16, 2018, http://www.latimes.com; Omri Ben-Shahar, "Are Uber Drivers Employees? The Answer Will Shape the Sharing Economy," *Forbes,* November 15, 2017, https://www.forbes.com.

HR IN SMALL BUSINESS

Johnson County Library Checks Out Job Rotation

A few years ago, some branch managers in the Johnson County Library (JCL) system in Kansas met with the director of branch services to discuss a problem: after years on the job, they were feeling burned out. The director invited them to talk to the other branch managers and propose a solution. The full group of managers considered their strengths and desires for future career opportunities, as well as the culture of the library's 14 branches (it has since grown to 16). They saw fresh opportunities within their organization and developed a proposal to try job rotations. The proposal included plans for communicating the changes to those who would be affected.

After a year of planning, the job rotation began with assistant managers spending one week as assistant manager in a different branch. Even this short job rotation was considered a success. The assistant librarians found that they were building networks with more of their colleagues and strengthening relationships with more staff and library patrons. Building on this success, JCL then did two-week job rotations of clerks and then information specialists. Again, the employees completing the rotations built work relationships. They also reported developing greater flexibility and appreciation of the JCL system beyond the particular branch where they had been working. Being in a different place with different people caused them to look at the library's work with greater attentiveness. Following the series of job rotation, some staff members permanently moved to new positions where they could contribute more or had better working relationships with their colleagues.

Some examples illustrate the impact of the job rotations. A developer of web content had been wanting to work more with patrons. Rotating jobs led him to a position as an information specialist, which involves working with the public. A clerk who rotated to another branch was promoted there to assistant branch manager. Because of her experience as a clerk, she was quickly able to size up opportunities for improving efficiency in her new branch. A branch manager who got experience with several locations helped JCL identify a more effective way to pair small branches with shared leadership.

The turnover in librarians in the JCL system is small, and there are only 16 locations serving the 20 cities of Johnson County, Kansas. This means that the career path for any given librarian is limited within the organization. With job rotation, the employees found a way to inject variety into their work. This refreshed their thinking, sparked some improvements in operations, and launched an approach to work design that seems likely to endure.

Questions

1. Job rotation is a method of designing jobs that motivate. How did its use at Johnson County Library also help the organization improve efficiency?
2. According to Hackman and Oldham's Job Characteristics Model, what other aspects of jobs contribute to making work more motivating? Which of these do you think could apply to the librarians at JCL?

Sources: Monica Duffield and Terry Velasquez, "A Fresh Approach to Job Rotation," *Public Libraries,* May/June 2019, pp. 44–49; Johnson County Library, "About Us," https://www.jocolibrary.org, accessed March 24, 2020; Johnson County, Kansas, "About Us," https://www.jocogov.org, accessed March 24, 2020.

NOTES

1. A. Rosen, "This Automated Supermarket Can Bag 60 Items in 5 Minutes," *Boston Globe,* February 7, 2020, https://www.bostonglobe.com; S. Nassauer, "Welcome to Walmart: The Robot Will Grab Your Groceries," *The Wall Street Journal,* January 8, 2020, https://www.wsj.com; M. Boyle, "Robots in Aisle Two: Supermarket Survival Means Matching Amazon," *Bloomberg,* December 3, 2019, https://www.bloomberg.com.
2. J. Del Rey, "How Robots Are Transforming Amazon Warehouse Jobs—for Better and Worse," *Vox,* December 11, 2019, https://www.vox.com; J. Dastin, "Exclusive: Amazon Rolls Out Machines That Pack Orders and Replace Jobs," *Reuters,* May 13, 2019, https://www.reuters.com.
3. J. R. Hollenbeck, H. Moon, A. Ellis, et al., "Structural Contingency Theory and Individual Differences: Examination of External and Internal Person-Team Fit," *Journal of Applied Psychology* 87 (2002), pp. 599–606; Sam Grobart, "Hooray for Hierarchy," *Bloomberg Businessweek,* January 14, 2013, p. 74.
4. Ronald G. Capelle, "Improving Organization Performance by Optimizing Organization Design," *People & Strategy* 40(2) (Spring 2017), pp. 26–31.
5. Ann Potratz, "Avoiding Headaches with the 'Other Duties as Assigned' Provision," *Business Journals,* March 7, 2018, https://www.bizjournals.com.
6. Oliver W. Cummings, "What Do Manufacturing Supervisors Really Do on the Job?" *Industry Week,* February 2010, p. 53.
7. A. O'Reilly, "Skill Requirements: Supervisor-Subordinate Conflict," *Personnel Psychology* 26 (1973), pp. 75–80; J. Hazel, J. Madden, and R. Christal, "Agreement between Worker-Supervisor Descriptions of the Worker's Job," *Journal of Industrial Psychology* 2 (1964), pp. 71–79; A. K. Weyman, "Investigating the Influence of Organizational Role on Perceptions of Risk in Deep Coal Mines," *Journal of Applied Psychology* 88 (2003), pp. 404–412.
8. T. D. Chaffin, R. Heidl, J. R. Hollenbeck, R. Calantone, M. Howe, C. Voorhees, and A. Yu, "The Promise and Perils of Wearable Sensors in Organizational Research," *Organizational Research Methods* 20 (2017), pp. 3–31; J. R. Hollenbeck and B. Jamieson, "Human Capital, Social Capital, and Social Network Analysis: Implications for Strategic Human Resource Management," *Academy of Management Perspectives* 29 (2015), pp. 370–385.
9. L. E. Baranowski and L. E. Anderson, "Examining Rater Source Variation in Work Behavior to KSA Linkages," *Personnel Psychology* 58 (2005), pp. 1041–1054.
10. "O*NET® Products at Work," O*NET Resource Center, https://www.onetcenter.org, accessed March 29, 2020.
11. P. J. Taylor, W. D. Li, K. Shi, and W. C. Borman, "The Transportability of Job Information across Countries," *Personnel Psychology* 61 (2008), pp. 69–111.
12. *PAQ Newsletter,* August 1989; E. C. Dierdorff and M. A. Wilson, "A Meta-Analysis of Job Analysis Reliability," *Journal of Applied Psychology* 88 (2003), pp. 635–646.
13. E. Fleishman and M. Reilly, *Handbook of Human Abilities* (Palo Alto, CA: Consulting Psychologists Press, 1992); E. Fleishman and M. Mumford, "Evaluating Classifications of Job Behavior: A Construct Validation of the Ability Requirements Scales," *Personnel Psychology* 44 (1991), pp. 523–575.
14. J. R. Hollenbeck, B. Beersma, and M. E. Schouten, "Beyond Team Types and Taxonomies: A Dimensional Scaling Approach for Team Description," *Academy of Management Review* 37 (2012), pp. 82–108; Capelle, "Improving Organization Performance."
15. M. Markovska, "The 3 Job Analysis Methods Every HR Professional Needs to Know," *Career Minds,* https://blog.careerminds.com, accessed March 29, 2020.
16. P. Wright and K. Wexley, "How to Choose the Kind of Job Analysis You Really Need," *Personnel,* May 1985, pp. 51–55; Capelle, "Improving Organization Performance."
17. R. A. Noe, *Employee Training & Development,* 8e (New York: McGraw-Hill, 2020); M. Campion, A. Fink, B. Ruggeberg, L. Carr, G. Phillips, and R. Odman, "Doing Competencies Well: Best Practices in Competency Modeling," *Personal Psychology* 64 (2011), pp. 225–262.
18. Lee Michael Katz, "Cool and Competent," *HR Magazine,* March 2015, https://www.shrm.org.
19. M. K. Lindell, C. S. Clause, C. J. Brandt, and R. S. Landis, "Relationship between Organizational Context and Job Analysis Ratings," *Journal of Applied Psychology* 83 (1998), pp. 769–776.
20. A. Dalal, "5 Reasons How AI Will Change Careers and Working Set-Ups," *Entrepreneur,* November 15, 2019; S. Mike, "How Is Human Resources Evolving with Technology?" *HR Technologist,* August 23, 2019, https://www.hrtechnologist.com; A. Loten, "AI-Powered Tools Cutting Tasks, Not Jobs: Survey," *The Wall Street Journal,* January 23, 2018, https://blogs.wsj.com.
21. R. Hackman and G. Oldham, *Work Redesign* (Boston: Addison-Wesley, 1980).
22. "Happy Thriving from Square Root," https://square-root.com, accessed March 29, 2020; J. McKendrick, "13 Jobs That Now Matter the Most, from a Digital Perspective," *Forbes,* January 30, 2016, http://www.forbes.com.
23. O. Shkoler and T. Kimura, "How Does Work Motivation Impact Employees' Investment at Work and Their Job Engagement? A Moderated-Moderation Perspective Through an International Lens," *Frontiers in Psychology,* February 21, 2020, https://www.frontiersin.org.
24. "Improve Upfront Collections by Improving Basics," *Receivables Report,* January 2016, pp. 1, 10–11; Glenn Gross, "We're All

Financial Counselors Here!" *LinkedIn,* July 20, 2015, https://www.linkedin.com.

25. F. W. Bond, P. E. Flaxman, and D. Bunce, "The Influence of Psychological Flexibility on Work Redesign: Mediated Moderation of a Work Reorganization Intervention," *Journal of Applied Psychology* 93 (2008), pp. 645-654.
26. M. A. Campion, G. J. Medsker, and A. C. Higgs, "Relations between Work Group Characteristics and Effectiveness: Implications for Designing Effective Work Groups," *Personnel Psychology* 46 (1993), pp. 823-850.
27 B. Bond, "Millennials Want to Work Remotely–Should We Let Them?" *Medium,* https://medium.com, accessed March 28, 2020.
28. "Telecommuting Trend Data," March 13, 2020, https://globalworkplaceanalytics.com; D. Wilkie, "Why Are Companies Ending Remote Work?" *Society for Human Resource Management,* May 7, 2019, https://www.shrm.org.
29. "New Workplace Ergonomics Research: Emerging Risks and Solutions," https://www.knoll.com, accessed March 29, 2020.
30. John Sprovieri, "Do Ergonomics Investments Pay Off?," *Assembly,* June 2015, pp. 36-39; Laura Putre, "A Stand-Up Job: Great Moments in Assembly Line Ergonomics," *Industry Week,* August 27, 2015, http://www.industryweek.com.
31. Ryan Black, "AI Can Tailor Touchscreens for Those with Disabilities," *Healthcare Analytics News,* March 27, 2018, http://www.hcanews.com; Brad Kelechava, "Ergonomic Hazards of Touch Screens," *American National Standards Institute blog,* January 29, 2016, https://blog.ansi.org.
32. N. W. Van Yperen and M. Hagerdoorn, "Do High Job Demands Increase Intrinsic Motivation or Fatigue or Both? The Role of Job Support and Social Control," *Academy of Management Journal* 46 (2003), pp. 339-348; N. W. Van Yperen and O. Janssen, "Fatigued and Dissatisfied or Fatigued but Satisfied? Goal Orientations and Responses to High Job Demands," *Academy of Management Journal* 45 (2002), pp. 1161-1171.
33. Robert Joiner, "Software Creates 'Dashboard' for Diabetes Docs," St. Louis Public Radio, March 18, 2018, http://news.stlpublicradio.org.
34. D. Lavenda, "Information Overload Comes in 3 Flavors: Here's How to Combat It," *CMS Wire,* July 5, 2017, https://www.cmswire.com; J. Spira, "Information Overload: None Are Immune," *Information Management,* September/October 2011, p. 32.
35. C. DesMarais, "17 Simple Things These Successful Executives Do Every Day No Matter What," *Inc.,* https://www.inc.com, accessed March 29, 2020.

Acquiring, Training, and Developing Human Resources

freesoulproduction/Shutterstock

PART TWO

5 Planning for and Recruiting Human Resources

Introduction

Amazon's senior vice president of human resources, Beth Galetti, didn't enter the field in the usual way. She studied electrical engineering, earned an MBA, and worked for FedEx, helping to run logistics. When a hiring manager interviewed her about bringing that experience to Amazon, it quickly became apparent that Galetti's passion was bringing out the best in her people. The company convinced her to use her analytics skills to help with the dramatic expansion of hiring at Amazon. The second-largest employer after Walmart, Amazon has close to 650,000 employees and is still growing.

No surprise, given her background, Galetti uses technology and data to empower employees, enabling them to work more effectively. When she moved into the top HR position at Amazon, the development of HR software was shifted from the IT group to her division. Hundreds of software development personnel are working on systems for data analysis and decision making related to HRM.

The data-driven approach supports a shift in Amazon's recruitment. Until a few years ago, Amazon mimicked many high-tech firms in the way it recruited management trainees. It would send recruiters to about 25 elite business schools to interview students working on master's degrees in business administration. That meant cost-conscious Amazon was competing for the most sought-after sliver of the market for management talent. And it was missing candidates who might have rich experiences in the business world. So now the company recruits MBA candidates at 80 schools and conducts more interviews online. Some elite-school students are put off by online interviewing, but they also tend to be the ones who are less impressed with an offer from Amazon. Now Amazon is finding a thousand new hires a year who are excited to be tapped to work at a well-known high-tech company.[1]

Amazon's data-driven approach to HRM has caused a shift in how the company recruits managerial talent.

George Frey/Getty Image

What Do I Need to Know?

After reading this chapter, you should be able to:

LO 5-1 Discuss how to plan for human resources needed to carry out the organization's strategy.

LO 5-2 Determine the labor demand for workers in various job categories.

LO 5-3 Summarize the advantages and disadvantages of ways to eliminate a labor surplus and avoid a labor shortage.

LO 5-4 Describe recruitment policies organizations use to make job vacancies more attractive.

LO 5-5 List and compare sources of job applicants.

LO 5-6 Describe the recruiter's role in the recruitment process, including limits and opportunities.

Amazon illustrates how, when the demand for a segment of the labor market is intense, employers need to strategize how they can afford to meet their needs for talent. Furthermore, when the labor market changes—say, when more people go to college or when a sizable share of the population retires—the supply of qualified workers may grow, shrink, or change in nature. To prepare for and respond to these challenges, organizations engage in *human resource planning*—defined in Chapter 1 as identifying the numbers and types of employees the organization will require to meet its objectives.

This chapter describes how organizations carry out human resource planning. In the first part of the chapter, we lay out the steps that go into developing and implementing a human resource plan. Throughout each section, we focus especially on recent trends and practices, including downsizing, employing temporary workers, and outsourcing. The remainder of the chapter explores the process of recruiting. We describe the process by which organizations look for people to fill job vacancies and the usual sources of job candidates. Finally, we discuss the role of recruiters.

The Process of Human Resource Planning

LO 5-1 Discuss how to plan for human resources needed to carry out the organization's strategy.

In order to meet business objectives and gain an advantage over competitors, organizations should carry out human resource planning. To do this, organizations need a clear idea of the strengths and weaknesses of their existing internal labor force. They also must know what they want to be doing in the future—what size they want the organization to be, what products and services it should be producing, and so on. This knowledge helps them define the number and kinds of employees they will need. Human resource planning compares the present state of the organization with its goals for the future, then identifies what changes it must make in its human resources to meet those goals. The changes may include downsizing, training existing employees in new skills, or hiring new employees.

These activities give a general view of HR planning. They take place in the human resource planning process shown in Figure 5.1. The process consists of three stages: forecasting, goal setting and strategic planning, and program implementation and evaluation.

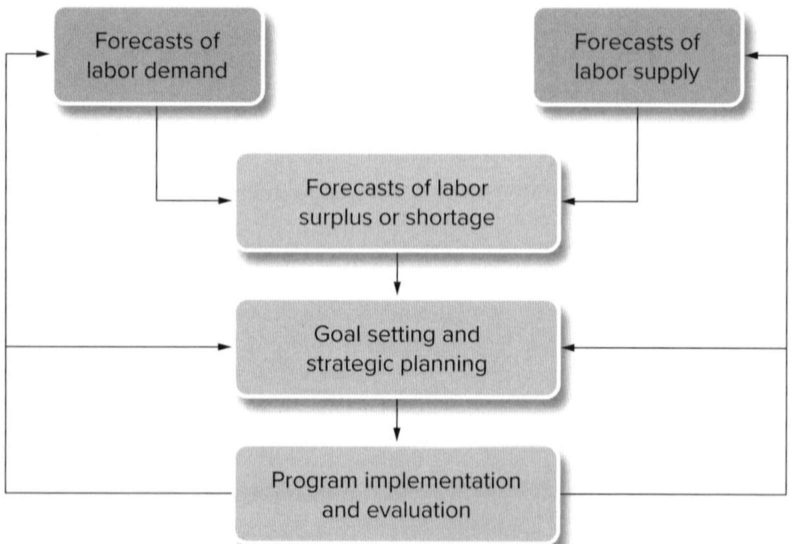

FIGURE 5.1
Overview of the Human Resource Planning Process

Forecasting
The attempts to determine the supply of and demand for various types of human resources to predict areas within the organization where there will be labor shortages or surpluses.

Forecasting

The first step in human resource planning is **forecasting,** as shown in the top portion of Figure 5.1. In personnel forecasting, the HR professional tries to determine the supply of and demand for various types of human resources. The primary goal is to predict which areas of the organization will experience labor shortages or surpluses.

Forecasting supply and demand can use statistical methods or judgment. Statistical methods capture historical trends in a company's demand for labor. Under the right conditions, these methods predict demand and supply more precisely than a human forecaster can using subjective judgment. But many important events in the labor market have no precedent, the most disruptive recent example being the worldwide 2020 coronavirus pandemic. When such events occur, statistical methods are of little use. To prepare for these situations, the organization must rely on the subjective judgments of experts. Pooling their experiences and "best guesses" is an important source of ideas about the future, as has been the case after the pandemic.

LO 5-2 Determine the labor demand for workers in various job categories.

Trend Analysis
Constructing and applying statistical models that predict labor demand for the next year, given relatively objective statistics from the previous year.

Leading Indicators
Objective measures that accurately predict future labor demand.

Forecasting the Demand for Labor

Usually an organization forecasts demand for specific job categories or skill areas. After identifying the relevant job categories or skills, the planner investigates the likely demand for each. The planner must forecast whether the need for people with the necessary skills and experience will increase or decrease. There are several ways of making such forecasts.

At the most sophisticated level, an organization might use **trend analysis,** constructing and applying statistical models that predict labor demand for the next year, given relatively objective statistics from the previous year. These statistics are called **leading indicators**—objective measures that accurately predict future labor demand. They might include measures of the economy (such as sales or inventory levels), actions of competitors, changes in technology, and trends in the composition of the workforce and overall population. Trends affecting labor demand today include years of economic growth, causing businesses and consumers to have more money to spend on machinery, vehicles, houses, and other purchases. The demand to buy means that companies need to produce more. At the same time, advances in technology such as robots, 3D printing, and artificial intelligence are making it possible for businesses to produce more per worker. So in the manufacturing sector of the economy, the trend is for production output to grow faster than employment. In new industries, such as sustainable consumer goods and next-wave logistics, however, demand for goods is growing so fast that the demand for labor is increasing.[2]

Statistical planning models are useful when there is a long, stable history that can be used to reliably detect relationships among variables. However, these models almost always have to be complemented with subjective judgments of experts. There are simply too many "once-in-a-lifetime" changes to consider, and statistical models cannot capture them.

Mc Graw Hill connect®
Visit your instructor's Connect® course and access your eBook to view this video.

"How do we think about making sure this company has access to the right skills and capabilities to grow a company for the future?"

—Heidi B. Capozzi
Senior Vice President, Human Resources
The Boeing Company

Video Produced for the Center for Executive Succession in the Darla Moore School of Business at the University of South Carolina by Coal Powered Filmworks

Determining Labor Supply

Once a company has forecast the demand for labor, it needs an indication of the firm's labor supply. Determining the internal labor supply calls for a detailed analysis of how many people are currently in various job categories or have specific skills within the organization. The planner then modifies this analysis to reflect changes

TABLE 5.1

Transitional Matrix: Example for an Auto Parts Manufacturer

	2020							
2017	**(1)**	**(2)**	**(3)**	**(4)**	**(5)**	**(6)**	**(7)**	**(8)**
(1) Sales manager	.95							.05
(2) Sales representative	.05	.60						.35
(3) Sales apprentice		.20	.50					.30
(4) Assistant plant manager				.90	.05			.05
(5) Production manager				.10	.75			.15
(6) Production assembler					.10	.80		.10
(7) Clerical							.70	.30
(8) Not in organization	.00	.20	.50	.00	.10	.20	.30	

expected in the near future as a result of retirements, promotions, transfers, voluntary turnover, and terminations.

One type of statistical procedure that can be used for this purpose is the analysis of a **transitional matrix.** This is a chart that lists job categories held in one period and shows the proportion of employees in each of those job categories in a future period. It answers two questions: "Where did people who were in each job category go?" and "Where did people now in each job category come from?" Table 5.1 is an example of a transitional matrix.

Transitional Matrix
A chart that lists job categories held in one period and shows the proportion of employees in each of those job categories in a future period.

This example lists job categories for an auto parts manufacturer. The jobs listed at the left were held in 2017, the numbers at the right show what happened to the people in 2020. The numbers represent proportions. For example, .95 means 95% of the people represented by a row in the matrix. The column headings under 2020 refer to the row numbers. The first row is sales managers, so the numbers under column (1) represent people who became sales managers. Reading across the first row, we see that 95 of the people who were sales managers in 2017 are still sales managers in 2020. The other 5% correspond to position (8), "Not in organization," meaning the 5% of employees who are not still sales managers have left the organization. In the second row are sales representatives. Of those who were sales reps in 2017, 5% were promoted to sales manager, 60% are still sales reps, and 35% have left the organization. In row (3), half (50%) of sales apprentices are still in that job, but 20% are now sales reps and 30% have left the organization. This pattern of jobs shows a career path from sales apprentice to sales representative to sales manager. Of course, not everyone is promoted, and some of the people leave instead.

Reading down the columns provides another kind of information: the sources of employees holding the positions in 2020. In the first column, we see that most sales managers (95%) held that same job three years earlier. The other 5% were promoted from sales representative positions. Skipping over to column (3), half the sales apprentices on the payroll in 2020 held the same job three years before, and the other half were hired from outside the organization. This suggests that the organization fills sales manager positions primarily through promotions, so planning for this job would focus on preparing sales representatives. In contrast, planning to meet the organization's needs for sales apprentices would emphasize recruitment and selection of new employees.

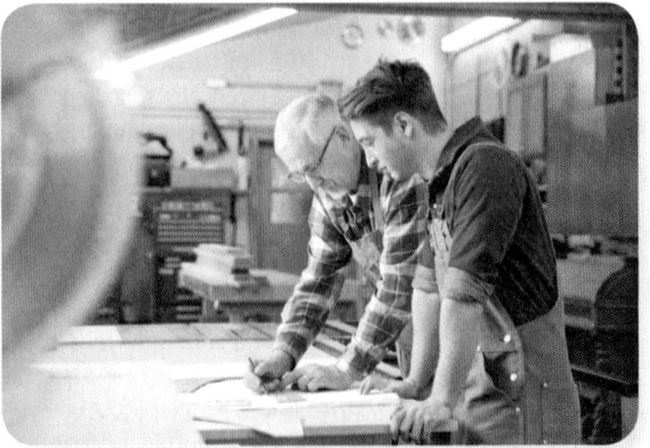

As the average age of many workers in skilled trades grows, the coming demand for workers in many trades is expected to outstrip supply. How can HR managers prepare for this reality?
Hero Images/Getty Images

Matrices such as this one are extremely useful for charting historical trends in the company's supply of labor. More important, if conditions remain somewhat constant, they can also be used to plan for the future. For example, if we believe that we are going to have a surplus of labor in the production assembler job category in the next three years, we can plan to avoid layoffs. Still, historical data may not always reliably indicate future trends because demand for products and services tends to fluctuate based on a variety of reasons. Planners need to combine statistical forecasts of labor supply with expert judgments. For example, managers in the organization may see that a new training program will likely increase the number of employees qualified for new openings. Forecasts of labor supply also should take into account the organization's pool of skills. Many organizations include inventories of employees' skills in an HR database. When the organization forecasts that it will need new skills in the future, planners can consult the database to see how many existing employees have those skills.

Besides looking at the labor supply within the organization, the planner should examine trends in the external labor market. The planner should keep abreast of labor market forecasts, including the size of the labor market, the unemployment rate, and the kinds of people who will be in the labor market. For example, the popularity of online shopping, along with overall growth in the economy, has increased the demand for trucking companies to deliver packages. At the same time, many truck drivers are nearing retirement, while new workers aren't eligible to drive until they are 21 years old, when they often have already found another line of work. Thus, finding enough drivers has been difficult, even when companies increase wages. Another example is Elkhart, Indiana, where companies that build recreational vehicles are clustered. RVs are a luxury item that consumers buy in good times. RV sales have been strong over the past several years as a result of a strong economy and low unemployment rates. However, sales started to slip as U.S. tariffs on aluminum and steel from China increased prices. But in 2020, as travel restrictions went into effect due to COVID-19, demand for RVs increased and manufacturers had trouble keeping up.[3] To monitor these and other kinds of trends, important sources of data on the external labor market include the *Occupational Outlook Quarterly* and the *Monthly Labor Review,* published by the Labor Department's Bureau of Labor Statistics. Details and news releases are available at the website of the Bureau of Labor Statistics (www.bls.gov).

LO 5-3 Summarize the advantages and disadvantages of ways to eliminate a labor surplus and avoid a labor shortage.

Determining Labor Surplus or Shortage Based on the forecasts for labor demand and supply, the planner can compare the figures to determine whether there will be a shortage or surplus of labor for each job category. Determining expected shortages and surpluses allows the organization to plan how to address these challenges. Liberty Mutual Insurance Company determined that continued demand for software developers would make those positions difficult to fill. So the company's chief information officer set up an opportunity for its employees to learn coding online and in classes held at the workplace. Hundreds of employees have signed up to learn new skills that open more favorable career paths. In Vermont, GW Plastics is preparing to address shortages in manufacturing workers by setting up programs for on-the-job training of students from the local high schools.[4]

Goal Setting and Strategic Planning

The second step in human resource planning is goal setting and strategic planning, as shown in the middle of Figure 5.1. The purpose of setting specific numerical goals is to focus attention on the problem and provide a basis for measuring the organization's success in addressing labor shortages and surpluses. The goals should come directly from the analysis of labor supply and demand. They should include a specific figure indicating what should happen with the job category or skill area and a specific timetable for when the results should be achieved.

For each goal, the organization must choose one or more human resource strategies. A variety of strategies is available for handling expected shortages and surpluses of labor.

TABLE 5.2

HR Strategies for Addressing a Labor Shortage or Surplus

OPTIONS FOR REDUCING A SURPLUS		
OPTION	**SPEED OF RESULTS**	**AMOUNT OF SUFFERING CAUSED**
Downsizing	Fast	High
Pay reductions	Fast	High
Demotions	Fast	High
Transfers	Fast	Moderate
Work sharing	Fast	Moderate
Hiring freeze	Slow	Low
Natural attrition	Slow	Low
Early retirement	Slow	Low
Retraining	Slow	Low
OPTIONS FOR AVOIDING A SHORTAGE		
OPTION	**SPEED OF RESULTS**	**ABILITY TO CHANGE LATER**
Overtime	Fast	High
Temporary employees	Fast	High
Outsourcing	Fast	High
Retrained transfers	Slow	High
Turnover reductions	Slow	Moderate
New external hires	Slow	Low
Technological innovation	Slow	Low

Core Competency
A set of knowledges and skills that make the organization superior to competitors and create value for customers.

The top of Table 5.2 shows major options for reducing an expected labor surplus, and the bottom of the table lists options for avoiding an expected labor shortage.

This planning stage is critical. The options differ widely in their expense, speed, and effectiveness. Options for reducing a labor surplus cause differing amounts of human suffering. The options for avoiding a labor shortage differ in terms of how easily the organization can undo the change if it no longer faces a labor shortage. For example, an organization probably would not want to handle every expected labor shortage by hiring new employees. The process is relatively slow and involves expenses to find and train new employees. Also, if the shortage becomes a surplus, the organization will have to consider laying off some of the employees—which, as just noted, has consequences. The "HR How To" box addresses an alternative, which is to develop in the company's current workforce the skills that the organization lacks. This approach is most likely to be beneficial when the company has a shortage of employees with some skills and a surplus of employees with other skills.

Cold Stone Creamery employees give their company the competitive advantage with their "entertainment factor." The company is known to seek out employees who like to perform and then "audition" rather than interview potential employees.
Courtesy of Cold Stone Creamery

Another consideration in choosing an HR strategy is whether the employees needed will contribute directly to the organization's success. Organizations are most likely to benefit from hiring and retaining employees who provide a **core competency**—that is, a set of knowledge and skills that make the organization superior to competitors and create value for customers. At a store, for example, core competencies include choosing merchandise that shoppers want and providing shoppers with excellent service. For other work that is not a core competency—say, cleaning the store and providing security—the organization may benefit from using HR strategies other than hiring full-time employees.

Organizations try to anticipate labor surpluses far enough ahead that they can freeze hiring and let natural attrition (people leaving on their own) reduce the

HR How To

Building a Bigger Talent Pool

Employees are not just numbers; they bring to the organization a variety of skills. When the skills an organization needs are in high demand, hiring new people can be difficult and expensive. An approach that may deliver results more efficiently is to find needed skills in new places. Here are some ideas for doing so:

- Develop skills in existing employees. Some employers struggling to find tech workers avoid hiring older workers, on the assumption their skills haven't kept up with technology. Sometimes that assumption is accurate, but those workers still may have other strengths. Companies that invest in training them in the latest programming language can end up with highly qualified employees who can help out with older technologies as well as the new ones.
- Train workers in hard-to-find skills. IBM, for example, has an apprenticeship program that teaches coding to interested workers. It has hired 90% of the people it trains. The e-commerce business Shopify has a program leading to a degree in computer science; it combines education and on-the-job experience, and students earn a salary while they learn.
- Broaden your search area and search criteria. IBM expanded its search for computer programmers beyond universities to find motivated people at community colleges and coding "boot camps." This effort has the side benefit of helping the company meet diversity objectives.
- Locate where the talent is. High-tech companies may assume they have to locate in Silicon Valley or Boston to be near enough talent. But this view fails to take into account the stiff competition for tech workers in those locations. Turnover may be high, as tech workers hop from one opportunity to another. At the same time, schools around the country (and world) are teaching technical skills. Virginia's Crossroads, a region in the south central part of the state near the intersection of Interstates 81 and 77, is an example of an area that is less expensive than Silicon Valley and has a pool of talent. Some companies, including Zapier, founded in Missouri, are able to let most employees work remotely, from the location of their choice. Co-founder Wade Foster notes that this gives the company a "worldwide talent pool."

Questions

1. What do you think are the risks of the options described here?
2. What do you think are some advantages of increasing the talent pool with each option?

Sources: Alex Lazarow, "Beyond Silicon Valley: How Start-Ups Succeed in Unlikely Places," *Harvard Business Review,* March–April 2020, pp. 126–133; Zachery Eanes, "Struggling to Find Tech Workers? You Might Need to Train Them Yourself," *News & Observer (Raleigh, NC),* February 14, 2020, https://www.greensboro.com; Angus Loten, "Older IT Workers Left Out Despite Tech Talent Shortage," *The Wall Street Journal,* November 25, 2019, https://www.wsj.com; "Why Companies Keep Growing in the Crossroads Region," *Site Selection,* November 2019, pp. 133–140.

labor force. Unfortunately for many workers, organizations often stay competitive in a fast-changing environment by responding to a labor surplus with downsizing, which delivers fast results. The impact is painful for those who lose jobs, as well as those left behind to carry on without them. To handle a labor shortage, organizations typically hire temporary employees or use outsourcing. Because downsizing, using temporary employees, and outsourcing are most common, we will look at each of these in greater detail in the following sections.

Downsizing
The planned elimination of large numbers of personnel with the goal of enhancing the organization's competitiveness.

Downsizing As we discussed in Chapter 2, **downsizing** is the planned elimination of large numbers of personnel with the goal of enhancing the organization's competitiveness. The primary reason organizations engage in downsizing is to promote future competitiveness. According to surveys, they do this by meeting four objectives:

1. *Reducing costs*–Labor is a large part of a company's total costs, so downsizing is an attractive place to start cutting costs.

2. *Replacing labor with technology*—Closing outdated factories, automating, or introducing other technological changes reduces the need for labor. Often, the labor savings outweigh the cost of the new technology.
3. *Mergers and acquisitions*—When organizations combine, they often need less bureaucratic overhead, so they lay off managers and some professional staff members.
4. *Moving to more economical locations*—Some organizations move from one area of the United States to another, especially from the Northeast and Midwest to the South and the mountain regions of the West. Other moves have shifted jobs to other countries, including Mexico, India, and Malaysia, where wages are lower.

Although downsizing has an immediate effect on costs, much of the evidence suggests that it hurts long-term organizational effectiveness. This is especially true for certain kinds of companies, such as those that emphasize research and development and where employees have extensive contact with customers.[5] The negative effect of downsizing was especially high among firms that engaged in high-involvement work practices, such as the use of teams and performance-related pay incentives. As a result, the more a company tries to compete through its human resources, the more layoffs hurt productivity.[6]

Why do so many downsizing efforts fail to meet expectations? It appears there are several reasons. First, although the initial cost savings give a temporary boost to profits, the long-term effects of an improperly managed downsizing effort can be negative. Downsizing leads to a loss of talent, and it often disrupts the social networks through which people are creative and flexible.[7] Unless the downsizing is managed well, employees feel confused, demoralized, and even less willing to stay with the organization. Organizations may not take (or even know) the steps that can counter these reactions—for example, demonstrating how they are treating employees fairly, building confidence in the company's plans for a stronger future, and showing the organization's commitment to behaving responsibly with regard to all its stakeholders, including employees, customers, and the community.[8]

Also, many companies wind up rehiring. Downsizing campaigns often eliminate people who turn out to be irreplaceable. In one survey, 80% of the firms that had downsized later replaced some of the very people they had laid off. However, if companies automated and restructured to get more work done with fewer people, they might not replace all or even some of the positions eliminated. Demand for workers in electric power plants has been declining because of the switch from coal and nuclear power plants, which require more employees, to newer natural gas, wind, and solar facilities that produce power using a smaller workforce. Other trends suggest a declining demand for a company's product line. Kimberly-Clark, for example, closed 10 factories, in part because shoppers are moving away from brand-name goods such as its Huggies diapers and Kleenex tissues. Furthermore, the U.S. birth rate has fallen, further suppressing product demand.[9] In these situations, the problem of rehiring may exist only in the distant future, if at all.

Finally, downsizing efforts often fail because employees who survive the purge become self-absorbed and afraid to take risks. Motivation drops because any hope of future promotions—or any future—with the company dies. Many employees start looking for other employment opportunities. The negative publicity associated with a downsizing campaign can also hurt the company's image in the labor market, making it harder to recruit employees later.

Many problems with downsizing can be reduced with better planning. Instead of slashing jobs across the board, successful downsizing makes surgical strategic cuts that improve the company's competitive position, and management addresses the problem of employees becoming demoralized. Retaining only the top-quality, dedicated workers may actually improve morale among those who remain.

Reducing Hours Given the limitations of downsizing, many organizations are more carefully considering other avenues for eliminating a labor surplus. Among the alternatives listed in Table 5.2, one that is seen as a way to spread the burden more fairly is cutting work hours, generally with a corresponding reduction in pay. Companies will choose a reduction in work hours not only because this is considered a more equitable way to weather a slump in demand, but also because it is less costly than layoffs requiring severance pay and it is easier to restore the work hours than to hire new employees after a downsizing effort. When plastics manufacturer Saint-Gobain in Bristol, Rhode Island, experienced a business slowdown, it did not lay off any workers but cut many workers' hours by 40%. The state stepped in and contributed 70% of the lost wages in exchange for the workers' continued employment–less than it would have paid in unemployment compensation. This kind of "work share" program, which helps employers keep experienced employees, has been popular in Europe but is fairly new to the United States.[10]

Early-Retirement Programs Another popular way to reduce a labor surplus is with an early-retirement program. As we discussed in Chapter 2, the average age of the U.S. workforce is increasing. But even though many baby boomers are reaching traditional retirement age, indications are that this group (especially women) has no intention of leaving the workforce soon.[11] Reasons include improved health of older people, jobs becoming less physically demanding, insufficient savings, high levels of debt, lack of pensions, enjoyment of work (especially in the higher-paying occupations), and laws against age discrimination. Under the pressures associated with an aging labor force, many employers try to encourage older workers to leave voluntarily by offering a variety of early-retirement incentives. The more lucrative of these programs succeed by some measures. Research suggests that these programs encourage lower-performing older workers to retire.[12] Sometimes they work so well that too many workers retire.

Many organizations are moving from early-retirement programs to phased-retirement programs. In a *phased-retirement program,* the organization can continue to benefit from the experience of older workers while reducing the number of hours these employees work, as well as the cost of those employees. This option also can give older employees the economic and psychological benefits of easing into retirement, rather than being thrust entirely into a new way of life.

Employing Temporary and Contract Workers While downsizing has been a popular way to reduce a labor surplus, the most widespread method for eliminating a labor shortage is hiring temporary and contract workers. Employers may arrange to hire a temporary worker through an agency that specializes in linking employers with people who have the necessary skills. The employer pays the agency, which in turn pays the temporary worker. Employers also may contract directly with individuals, often professionals, to provide a particular service.

To use this source of labor effectively, employers need to overcome some disadvantages. In particular, temporary and contract workers may not be as committed to the organization, so if they work directly with customers, that attitude may spill over and affect customer loyalty. Some companies have found that the workers they contracted with aren't even reliable about showing up to work. Therefore, many organizations try to use permanent employees in key jobs and use temporary and contract workers in ways that clearly supplement–and do not potentially replace–the permanent employees.[13] Procter & Gamble encourages managers to think about whether they need talent for the long term or for specific short-term projects. For the latter needs, it has built relationships with online services such as Upwork that match needed skills with a database of freelance workers, including software coders, graphic designers, lawyers, and more. P&G hires these contract workers to fill needs quickly where it doesn't need a long-term employment relationship.

Temporary Workers Staffing agencies are providing companies with a growing number of workers, exceeding 3.2 million per week in 2018. Temporary employment is popular with employers because it gives them flexibility they need to operate efficiently when demand for their products changes rapidly. If an employer believes a higher level of demand will persist, it often can hire the temps as permanent workers. Thus, employment levels for temporary employees tend to fall ahead of a recession and rise ahead of a recovery as companies make these quick adjustments to falling and rising demand.[14]

In addition to flexibility, temporary employment offers lower costs. Using temporary workers frees the employer from many administrative tasks and financial burdens associated with being the "employer of record." The cost of employee benefits, including health care, pension, life insurance, workers' compensation, and unemployment insurance, can account for 40% of payroll expenses for permanent employees. Assuming the agency pays for these benefits, a company using temporary workers may save money even if it pays the agency a higher rate for that worker than the usual wage paid to a permanent employee.

Agencies that provide temporary employees also may handle some of the tasks associated with hiring. Small companies that cannot afford their own testing programs often get employees who have been tested by a temporary agency. Many temporary agencies also train employees before sending them to employers. This reduces employers' training costs and eases the transition for the temporary worker and employer.

Finally, temporary workers may offer value not available from permanent employees. Because the temporary worker has little experience at the employer's organization, this person brings an objective point of view to the organization's problems and procedures. Also, a temporary worker may have a great deal of experience in other organizations that can be applied to the current assignment.

To obtain these benefits, organizations need to overcome the disadvantages associated with temporary workers. For example, tension can develop between temporary and permanent employees. Employers can minimize resentment and ensure that all workers feel valued by not bringing in temporary or contract workers immediately after downsizing and by hiring temporary workers from agencies that provide benefits.

Employee or Contractor? Besides using a temporary employment agency, a company can obtain workers for limited assignments by entering into contracts with them. If the person providing the services is an independent contractor, rather than an employee, the company does not pay employee benefits, such as health insurance and vacations. As with using temporary employees, the savings can be significant, even if the contractor works at a higher rate of pay.

This strategy carries risks, however. If the person providing the service is a contractor and not an employee, the company is not supposed to directly supervise the worker. The company can tell the contractor what criteria the finished assignment should meet but not, for example, where or what hours to work. This distinction is significant, because under federal law, if the company treats the contractor as an employee, the company has certain legal obligations, described in Part 4, related to matters such as overtime pay and withholding taxes. Furthermore, the pool of talented contractors may be much smaller than stories about the "gig economy" have suggested. As the "Did You Know?" box explains, an analysis of the earnings of contract workers shows most are employees earning a little money on the side.

When an organization wants to consider using independent contractors as a way to expand its labor force temporarily, human resource professionals can help by alerting the company to the need to verify that the arrangement will meet the legal requirements. A good place to start is with the advice to small businesses at the Internal Revenue Service website (www.irs.gov); search for "independent contractor" to find links to information and guidance. In addition, the organization may need to obtain professional legal advice.

Did You Know?

Contracting Is Not Most Workers' Normal Work

Of the almost 11% of U.S. workers who reported income from self-employment, a majority get most of their income from wages and are doing contracting work for extra income. Of the contractors who earn mostly self-employment income (rather than wages), only half reported earnings of more than $15,000. Those who earned self-employment income from online platforms (for example, Uber or DoorDash) most often earned less than $2,500.

Given that most work, measured by the amount of earnings, is still being done by employees, employers looking to meet talent needs through contracting need to consider where to find the workers who prefer this type of work. The 5% of the workforce earning more than $15,000 mainly from self-employment income could be concentrated in certain kinds of work or certain segments of the labor force. In addition, contract work might be an attractive option for companies interested in having tasks performed on a part-time basis.

Share of Tax-Filing Workers, %

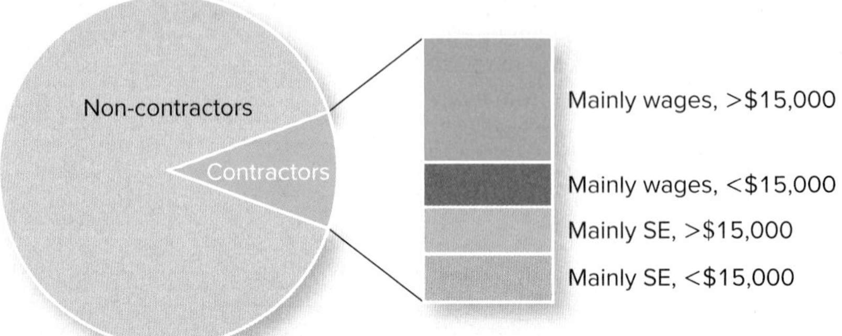

Note: "Contractors" are all workers whose tax returns included self-employment (SE) income. Earnings are described as being mainly (majority) from wages or self-employment. Greater or less than $15,000 refers to the amount of earnings reported.

For those seeking full-time workers on a contract basis, an option is to work with a firm that uses its own employees to provide services to other companies.

Question

If a company needed to add employees to answer customer service calls on Monday mornings, would you recommend contractors as a source of labor? Why or why not?

Sources: Sarah Zimmerman, "Another Take on Gigs," *Crain's Chicago Business,* December 23, 2019, p. 20; Lauren Weber, "Outsourcing Has Upended the Labor Market—but Not Exactly as Expected," *The Wall Street Journal,* December 17, 2019, https://www.wsj.com; Brett Collins, Andrew Garin, Emilie Jackson, et al., "Is Gig Work Replacing Traditional Employment? Evidence from Two Decades of Tax Returns," IRS Statistics of Income Joint Statistical Research Program, March 25, 2019, https://www.irs.gov.

Outsourcing
Contracting with another organization (vendor, third-party provider, or consultant) to provide services.

Outsourcing Instead of using a temporary or contract employee to fill a single job, an organization might want a broader set of services. Contracting with another organization to perform a broad set of services is called **outsourcing.** Organizations use outsourcing as a way to operate more efficiently and save money. They choose outsourcing firms that promise to deliver the same or better quality at a lower cost. One reason they can do this is that the outside company specializes in the service and can benefit from economies of scale (the economic principle that producing something in large volume tends to cost less for each additional unit than producing in small volume). This efficiency is often the attraction for outsourcing human resource functions such as payroll. Costs also are lower when the outsourcing firm is located in a part of the world where wages are relatively low. The labor forces of countries such as China, India, Jamaica, and those in Eastern Europe have been creating an abundant supply of labor for unskilled and low-skilled work.

The first uses of outsourcing emphasized manufacturing and routine tasks. However, technological advances in cloud computing, computer networks, and transmission have speeded up the outsourcing process and have helped it spread beyond manufacturing areas and low-skilled jobs. Recent reports suggest that more than half of all U.S. companies use third-party support teams to connect with customers, including AT&T.[15] Southwest Airlines contracts with about 10,000 workers to supplement the work of its 60,000 employees. Using contractors to handle IT work and push travelers in wheelchairs helps Southwest stay lean so that when travel demand slows, it doesn't have to lay off employees.

Using outsourcing may be a necessary way to operate as efficiently as competitors, but it does pose challenges. Quality-control problems, security violations, and poor customer service have sometimes wiped out the cost savings attributed to lower wages. To ensure success with an outsourcing strategy, companies should follow these guidelines:

- Learn about what the provider can do for the company, not just the costs. Make sure the company has the necessary skills, including an environment that can meet standards for clear communication, on-time shipping, contract enforcement, fair labor practices, and environmental protection. To focus on its strengths as a maker of jet engines, Pratt & Whitney outsourced the work of coordinating deliveries of parts to its factories. UPS specializes in moving packages swiftly, accurately, and efficiently, and it has the latest automation to excel. UPS even built a customized facility to handle the process for Pratt & Whitney.[16]
- Do not offshore any work that is proprietary or requires tight security.[17]
- Start small and monitor the work closely, especially in the beginning, when problems are most likely. This was an issue for Pratt & Whitney. The UPS employees were unfamiliar with the jet engine business, and they initially made many shipping mistakes resulting in parts missing or damaged. The two companies' computer systems also had problems sharing data. In the first quarter of the new arrangement, Pratt & Whitney's product deliveries fell behind schedule. However, the two companies worked out the issues by the following quarter, and the UPS workers are now more productive than Pratt & Whitney's logistics used to be.[18]
- Look for opportunities to outsource work in areas that promote growth, for example, by partnering with experts who can help the organization tap new markets. Mansfield Sales Partners offers this type of advantage to companies that have a limited sales force or want to test a new market. Such companies can use Mansfield's team of experienced salespeople to introduce their products in markets around the world.[19]

Overtime and Expanded Hours Organizations facing a labor shortage may be reluctant to hire employees, even temporary workers, or to commit to an outsourcing arrangement. Especially if the organization expects the shortage to be temporary, it may prefer an arrangement that is simpler and less costly. Under some conditions, these organizations may try to garner more hours from the existing labor force, asking them to go from part-time to full-time status or to work overtime.

A major downside of overtime is that the employer must pay nonmanagement employees one-and-a-half times their normal wages for work done overtime. Even so, employers see overtime pay as preferable to the costs of hiring and training new employees. The preference is especially strong if the organization doubts that the current higher level of demand for its products will last long.

For a short time at least, many workers appreciate the added compensation for working overtime. Over extended periods, however, employees feel stress and frustration from working long hours. Overtime therefore is best suited for short-term labor shortages.

Implementing and Evaluating the HR Plan

For whatever HR strategies are selected, the final stage of human resource planning involves implementing the strategies and evaluating the outcomes. This stage is represented by the

Bayer Harvests Leadership from Strategic HR Planning

Buddy Benge, the HR digital and analytics leader for Bayer, crafted a strategic approach to HR planning when he led the same function for Monsanto, later acquired by Bayer's Crop Science division. The division's more than 100,000 employees meet the growing worldwide demand for food by developing seeds and chemicals for protecting crops from pests. Benge is adamant that HR plans be the responsibility of business leaders, not HR staffers. This forces all managers, not just HR, to think about talent needs and how they relate to business success. Therefore, leaders of Bayer's business lines present their needs to the HR leadership, not the other way around.

In this context, Benge provides the businesses with analysis that steers plans in directions relevant to business success. Rather than merely looking at numbers of positions and numbers of employees, Benge's team crunches historical performance data to identify what competencies are associated with success, and focuses on the existing talent—that is, where those competencies exist within the company.

For example, in looking at leadership roles, Benge and his team found that out of 200 variables about which the company had data, three factors were associated with leadership success: acumen (insight into complex matters), inclusion, and employee and team development. Looking at managers' performance according to employee assessments, business results, and bonuses paid, Benge's analysis found that managers overall scored lowest on developing people and teams. In other words, one of the most important competencies of a leader at Bayer is development, but it was also an area of weakness in the leadership ranks. This information enabled the HR department to advise on priorities for action, not just priorities for hiring.

Following this assessment, the HR team could help managers set goals such as learning to give employees development opportunities and making development an area on which their own performance would be measured. During the implementation of the resulting business strategies, Monsanto's leaders guided their teams through the acquisition by Bayer, raising employee engagement and lowering turnover along the way.

Questions

1. How does Bayer's focus on competencies and talent differ from the typical focus on numbers of positions and employees?
2. Why does Buddy Benge want company business leaders, rather than HR personnel, to be accountable for achieving HR goals? Do you agree? Why or why not?

Sources: Bayer, "Profile and Organization," https://www.bayer.com, accessed March 30, 2020; Lisa Henderson, "Paving Bayer's Future Path," *Pharmaceutical Executive,* January 2020, pp. 32–35; Buddy Benge, "Analytics and Strategic Workforce Planning Increase Leadership Success at Bayer," *People + Strategy,* Fall 2019, pp. 40–45.

bottom part of Figure 5.1. When implementing the HR strategy, the organization must hold some individual accountable for achieving the goals, as Bayer does, as described in the "Best Practices" box. That person also must have the authority and resources needed to accomplish those goals. It is also important that this person issue regular progress reports, so the organization can be sure that all activities occur on schedule and that the early results are as expected.

Implementation that ties planning and recruiting to the organization's strategy and to its efforts to develop employees becomes a complete program of talent management. Today's computer systems have made talent management more practical. Companies can tap into databases and use analytic tools to keep track of which skills and knowledge they need, which needs have already been filled, which employees are developing experiences to help them meet future needs, and which sources of talent have met talent needs most efficiently. Artificial intelligence and predictive analytics can help organizations identify the qualities they need in their workforce and the workers likely to be interested in a position with the company. However, these tools will only bring about what Dan Shapero, chief business officer at LinkedIn, calls "intelligent recruiting" when HR departments invest in the technology and ensure they are collecting valid data about jobs, candidates, and employees.[20]

In evaluating the results of HR planning, the most obvious step is checking whether the organization has succeeded in avoiding labor shortages or surpluses. Along with measuring these numbers, the evaluation should identify which parts of the planning process contributed to success or failure. For example, consider a company where meeting human resource needs requires that employees continually learn new skills. If there is a gap between needed skills and current skill levels, the evaluation should consider whether the problem lies with failure to forecast the needed skills or with implementation. Are employees signing up for training, and is the right kind of training available?

HR managers should also measure the efficiency of the processes. Sometimes the best way to improve results is to cut costs or shorten time lines. For example, Hilton Hotels recognized it needed to speed up the hiring process (average of 42 days to hire) if it wanted to compete for top talent. Hilton turned to an on-demand, digital interview platform called HireVue, which allowed the company to interview multiple candidates at once without a recruiter being present. Candidates sign into the platform at their convenience and work through a list of built-in questions. Then company recruiters watch the videos and quickly determine whether a candidate could be suited for a particular job. After implementing the video interviews, Hilton's time to hire dropped from 42 days to just 5 days.[21]

HR Analytics & Decision Making

Several years ago, AT&T reacted to the rapid change in the telecommunications industry by assessing what skills would be needed in the future and what skills already existed in the company. They determined that only half of AT&T's 250,000 employees had skills matching the company's future needs. In fact, around 100,000 of them were experts at working on hardware likely to not be used in the future.

Bill Blase, AT&T's senior executive vice president of human resources, had to make a tough choice: Would the company lay off half its workforce and try to compete with other high-tech companies to replace them? Or would it prepare its existing workforce to meet future needs? Blase decided that even if filling so many positions would be possible, it would be too expensive, especially given the intense demand for workers skilled in computers and data analytics.

Bringing in contractors would cost more than $100 million, so Blase's team set up an internal program. They offered online courses and collaborated with universities and makers of Internet-based training. They created a web portal where workers select career paths and identify the training they need. About half of employees have participated, and they are already twice as likely as outsiders to be selected to fill new positions. The company also is saving money on contractors, as more employees qualify for projects. Blase has declared the initiative a success.

Questions

1. How has AT&T's planning shrunk its expected labor shortage?
2. What additional data could support Blase's opinion that the reskilling initiative succeeded?

Source: Susan Caminiti, "AT&T's $1 Billion Gambit: Retraining Nearly Half Its Workforce for Jobs of the Future," CNBC, March 13, 2018, https://www.cnbc.com.

Applying HR Planning to Affirmative Action

As we discussed in Chapter 3, many organizations have a human resource strategy that includes affirmative action to manage diversity or meet government requirements. Meeting affirmative-action goals requires that employers carry out an additional level of human resource planning aimed at those goals. In other words, besides looking at its overall workforce and needs, the organization looks at the representation of subgroups in its labor force—for example, the proportion of women and minorities.

Affirmative-action plans forecast and monitor the proportion of employees who are members of various protected groups (typically, women and racial or ethnic minorities). The planning looks at the representation of these employees in the organization's job categories and career tracks. The planner can compare the proportion of employees who are in each group with the proportion each group represents in the labor market. For example, the organization might note that in a labor market that is 25% Hispanic, 60% of its customer service personnel are Hispanic. This type of comparison is called a **workforce utilization review.** The organization can use this process to determine whether there is any subgroup whose proportion in the relevant labor market differs substantially from the proportion in the job category.

Workforce Utilization Review
A comparison of the proportion of employees in protected groups with the proportion that each group represents in the relevant labor market.

If the workforce utilization review indicates that some group—for example, African Americans—makes up 35% of the relevant labor market for a job category but that this same group constitutes only 5% of the employees actually in the job category at the organization, this is evidence of underutilization. That situation could result from problems in selection or from problems in internal movement (promotions or other movement along a career path). One way to diagnose the situation would be to use transitional matrices, such as the matrix shown in Table 5.1 earlier in this chapter.

The steps in a workforce utilization review are identical to the steps in the HR planning process that were shown in Figure 5.1. The organization must assess current utilization patterns, then forecast how they are likely to change in the near future. If these analyses suggest the organization is underutilizing certain groups and if forecasts suggest this pattern is likely to continue, the organization may need to set goals and timetables for changing. The planning process may identify new strategies for recruitment or selection. The organization carries out these HR strategies and evaluates their success.

Recruiting Human Resources

LO 5-4 Describe recruitment policies organizations use to make job vacancies more attractive.

As the first part of this chapter shows, it is difficult to always predict exactly how many (if any) new employees the organization will have to hire in a given year in a given job category. The role of human resource recruitment is to build a supply of potential new hires that the organization can draw on if the need arises. In human resource management, **recruiting** consists of any practice or activity carried on by the organization with the primary purpose of identifying and attracting potential employees.[22] It thus creates a buffer between planning and the actual selection of new employees (the topic of the next chapter). The goals of recruiting (encouraging qualified people to apply for jobs) and selection (deciding which candidates would be the best fit) are different enough that they are most effective when performed separately, rather than combined as in a job interview that also involves selling candidates on the company.[23]

Recruiting
Any activity carried on by the organization with the primary purpose of identifying and attracting potential employees.

Because companies differ in their strategies, they may assign different degrees of importance to recruiting.[24] In general, however, all companies have to make decisions in three areas of recruiting: personnel policies, recruitment sources, and the characteristics and behavior of the recruiter. As shown in Figure 5.2, these aspects of recruiting have different effects on whom the organization ultimately hires. Personnel policies influence the characteristics of the positions to be filled. Recruitment sources influence the kinds of job applicants an organization reaches. And the nature and behavior of the recruiter affect the

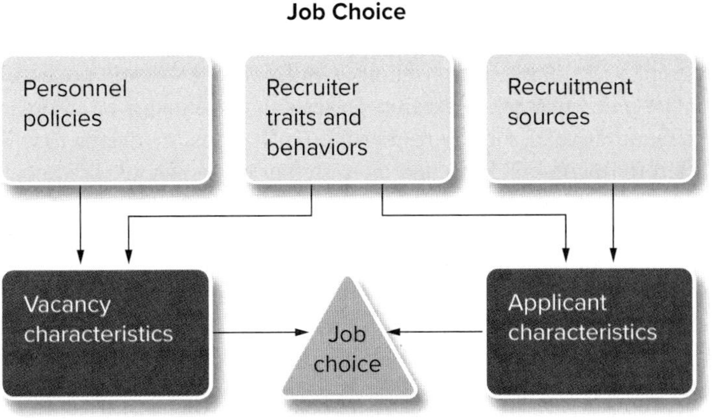

FIGURE 5.2
Three Aspects of Recruiting

characteristics of both the vacancies and the applicants. Ultimately, an applicant's decision to accept a job offer–and the organization's decision to make the offer–depend on the match between vacancy characteristics and applicant characteristics.

The remainder of this chapter explores these three aspects of recruiting: personnel policies, recruitment sources, and recruiter traits and behaviors.

Personnel Policies

An organization's *personnel policies* are its decisions about how it will carry out human resource management, including how it will fill job vacancies. These policies influence the nature of the positions that are vacant. According to the research on recruitment, it is clear that characteristics of the vacancy are more important than recruiters or recruiting sources for predicting job choice. Several personnel policies are especially relevant to recruitment:

- *Internal versus external recruiting*–Organizations with policies to "promote from within" try to fill upper-level vacancies by recruiting candidates internally–that is, finding candidates who already work for the organization. Opportunities for advancement make a job more attractive to applicants and employees. Decisions about internal versus external recruiting affect the nature of jobs, recruitment sources, and the nature of applicants, as we will describe later in the next section.
- *Lead-the-market pay strategies*–Pay is an important job characteristic for almost all applicants. Organizations have a recruiting advantage if their policy is to take a "lead-the-market" approach to pay–that is, pay more than the current market wages for a job. Higher pay can also make up for a job's less desirable features, such as working on a night shift or in dangerous conditions. Organizations that compete for applicants based on pay may use bonuses, stock options, and other forms of pay besides wages and salaries. Chapters 12 and 13 will take a closer look at these and other decisions about pay.
- *Employment-at-will policies*–Within the laws of the state where they are operating, employers have latitude to set polices about their rights in an employment relationship. A widespread policy follows the principle of **employment at will,** which holds that if there is no specific employment contract saying otherwise, the employer or employee may end an employment relationship at any time. An alternative is to establish extensive **due-process policies,** which formally lay out the steps an employee may take to appeal an employer's decision to terminate that employee. An organization's lawyers may advise the company to ensure that all recruitment documents say the employment is "at will" to protect the company from lawsuits about wrongful charge. Management must decide how to weigh any

Employment at Will
Employment principle that if there is no specific employment contract saying otherwise, the employer or employee may end an employment relationship at any time, regardless of cause.

Due-Process Policies
Policies that formally lay out the steps an employee may take to appeal the employer's decision to terminate that employee.

legal advantages against the impact on recruitment. Job applicants are more attracted to organizations with due-process policies, which imply greater job security and concern for protecting employees, than to organizations with employment-at-will policies.[25]

- *Social presence and reputation*–Research suggests that the image of an organization (as, for example, innovative or socially responsible) influences the degree to which a person feels attracted to the organization and interested in being part of it.[26] Surveyed workers have expressed that they value working for a company whose values align with their own.[27] Building a positive image in workers' minds requires cultivating both awareness and attractiveness.[28] Of course, the image needs to be aligned with the actual experience of working for the company. The Internet provides a variety of opportunities for achieving these goals with photos, videos, and stories on the company's website and direct engagement with workers in social media. The software company SAP developed a series of cartoons and video games to demonstrate what being an SAP employee is like. The interactive nature of this approach and social media in general has the potential to shape attitudes more than a one-way message such as an advertisement.

LO 5-5 List and compare sources of job applicants.

Recruitment Sources

Another critical element of an organization's recruitment strategy is its decisions about where to look for applicants. The total labor market is enormous and spread over the entire globe. As a practical matter, an organization will draw from a small fraction of that total market. The methods the organization chooses for communicating its labor needs and the audiences it targets will determine the size and nature of the labor market the organization taps to fill its vacant positions.[29] A person who responds to a help-wanted sign in a store window is likely to be different from a person who responds to an employer seeking his or her high-demand skills named in a LinkedIn profile. Each of the major sources from which organizations draw recruits has advantages and disadvantages.

Internal Sources

As we discussed with regard to personnel policies, an organization may emphasize internal or external sources of job applicants. Internal sources are employees who currently hold other positions in the organization. Organizations recruit existing employees through **job posting,** or communicating information about the vacancy on company bulletin boards, in employee publications, on corporate intranets, and anywhere else the organization communicates with employees. Managers also may identify candidates to recommend for vacancies. Policies that emphasize promotions and even lateral moves to achieve broader career experience can give applicants a favorable impression of the organization's jobs. The use of internal sources also affects what kinds of people the organization recruits.

Job Posting
The process of communicating information about a job vacancy on company bulletin boards, in employee publications, on corporate intranets, and anywhere else the organization communicates with employees.

For the employer, relying on internal sources offers several advantages.[30] First, it generates applicants who are well known to the organization. In addition, these applicants are relatively knowledgeable about the organization's vacancies, which minimizes the possibility they will have unrealistic expectations about the job. Finally, filling vacancies through internal recruiting is generally cheaper and faster than looking outside the organization.

Chad Rabello, director of people operations at NakedWines.com, recognized these benefits and set up processes that would help the company fill more positions internally. One process helps employees build a career at the company, not just carry out a job. Rabello meets with each of the company's employees (there are fewer than a hundred) to create a career development plan, which may involve learning skills needed for the same or a different position. Another program invites employees to present new business ideas to top management; the executives pick one idea to fund. This process develops creative thinking and helps

Rabello and the other executives identify employees with leadership potential. These programs encourage employees to stay, and they prepare management to fill openings with insiders who have already shared their career goals and practiced solving problems creatively.[31]

External Sources

Despite the advantages of internal recruitment, organizations often have good reasons to recruit externally.[32] For entry-level positions and perhaps for specialized upper-level positions, the organization has no internal recruits from which to draw. Also, bringing in outsiders may expose the organization to new ideas or new ways of doing business. An organization that uses only internal recruitment can wind up with a workforce whose members all think alike and therefore may be poorly suited to innovation.[33] And finally, companies that are able to grow during a slow economy can gain a competitive edge by hiring the best talent when other organizations are forced to avoid hiring, freeze pay increases, or even lay off talented people. For example, during the COVID-19 crisis, hundreds of thousands of workers in the hospitality and retail industries were furloughed, laid off, or let go because of many states' stay-at-home orders for residents. At the same time, companies such as Amazon, Walmart, and other companies were taking steps to hire huge numbers of new workers for delivery, security, warehousing, manufacturing, and distribution jobs.[34]

Organizations often recruit through direct applicants and referrals, websites, advertisements, employment agencies, and schools. Figure 5.3 shows which of these sources are used most among large companies surveyed. Keep in mind that several sources may work

FIGURE 5.3

Top Recruiting Sources Reported by Employers

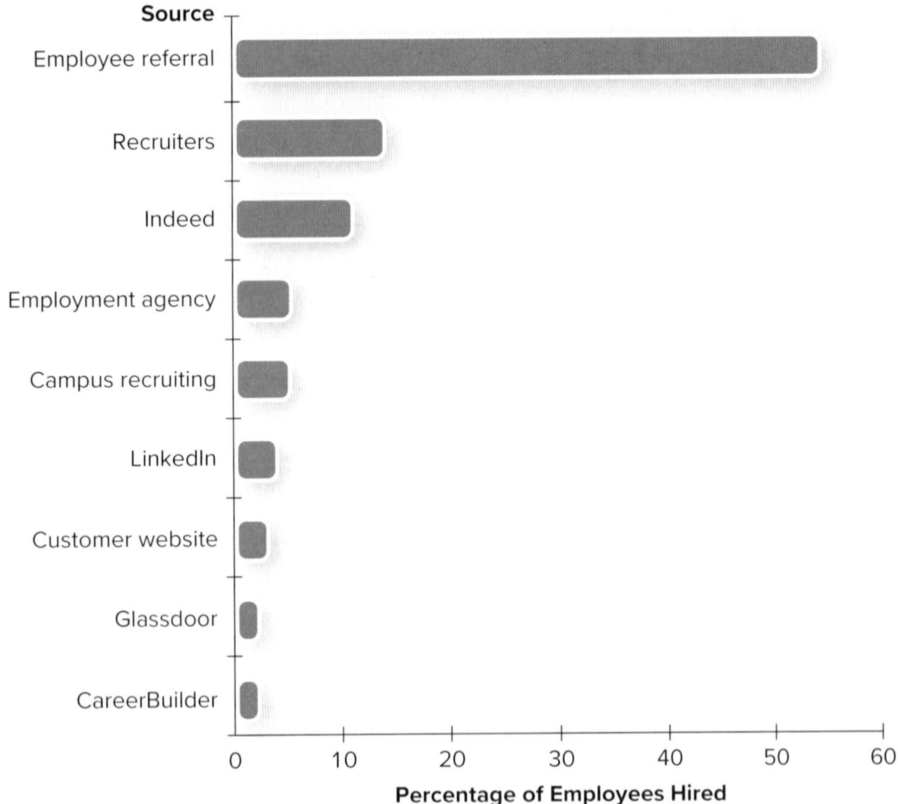

Source: Based on SilkRoad, *Sources of Hire 2018: Where the Candidate Journey Begins*, May 2018, https://www.silkroadtechnology.com.

together to attract a given candidate. The most effective recruiters don't just opt for the most profitable methods but choose the methods that best work together to attract the right candidates for a particular kind of job in a particular kind of company.

Direct Applicants
People who apply for a vacancy without prompting from the organization.

Referrals
People who apply for a vacancy because someone in the organization prompted them to do so.

Direct Applicants and Referrals Even without a formal effort to reach job applicants, an organization may hear from candidates through direct applicants and referrals. **Direct applicants** are people who apply for a vacancy without prompting from the organization. **Referrals** are people who apply because someone in the organization prompted them to do so. Direct applicants are likeliest to result when an employer has created such a positive image that workers seek out the company to apply. But given the convenience and power of online job searching, even those candidates may wind up connecting with the company through job-related Internet services. This impact of the Internet shows up in surveys that ask employers to identify their top sources of candidates. The results place referrals as the top source.[35] In Figure 5.3, company websites were ranked by the top five sources of hires; these employees may have included many direct applicants.

These two sources of recruits share some characteristics that make them excellent pools from which to draw. One advantage is that many direct applicants are to some extent already "sold" on the organization. Most have done some research and concluded there is enough fit between themselves and the vacant position to warrant submitting an application, a process called *self-selection,* which, when it works, eases the pressure on the organization's recruiting and selection systems. A form of aided self-selection occurs with referrals. Many job seekers look to friends, relatives, and acquaintances to help find employment. Using these social networks not only helps the job seeker but also simplifies recruitment for employers.[36] Current employees (who are familiar with the vacancy as well as the person they are referring) decide that there is a fit between the person and the vacancy, so they convince the person to apply for the job. Extending this self-selection advantage, some companies, including Procter & Gamble, Citi, and Nestle, are even setting up social networks of former employees, or "alumni." High-performing employees who left to pursue other opportunities and perhaps add to their skills may be well prepared to contribute when they return. Similarly, UPS has an alumni network of retirees it calls on to fill the demand for seasonal workers with already-trained people.[37]

Nepotism
The practice of hiring relatives.

An additional benefit of using such sources is that it costs much less than formal recruiting efforts. Considering these combined benefits, referrals and direct applications are among the best sources of new hires. Some employers offer current employees financial incentives for referring applicants who are hired and perform acceptably on the job (for example, if they stay 180 days). Flynn Restaurant Group pays a bonus for referrals–if they are hired–because the company identified a practical benefit. Based on an analysis of hiring and performance data, Flynn determined that employees who had been recommended by people working for the company went on to outperform employees who had been recruited through other channels.[38]

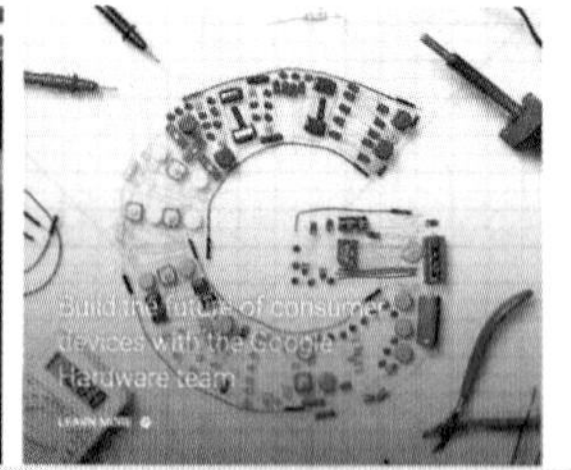

Career pages on corporate websites can build a positive image of the employer and provide a convenient way for direct applicants to try for a job.
Google LLC

The major downside of referrals is that they limit the likelihood of exposing the organization to fresh viewpoints. People tend to refer others who are like themselves. Furthermore, sometimes referrals contribute to hiring practices that are or that appear unfair, an example being **nepotism,** or the hiring of relatives. Employees may resent the hiring and rapid promotion of "the boss's son" or "the boss's daughter," or even the boss's friend.

Job Search and Networking Platforms Few employers can fill all their vacant positions through direct applications and referrals, and even if they could, many want to cast a wider net. This means that external recruiting must seek out people who don't know about the job openings and might not even be actively looking for work. The ways they do this used to be based on the tools and methods of advertising, but today's efforts are increasingly looking like information systems and social networks. As the methods shift, the lines between recruiting categories are blurred. But the most popular methods now tend to involve some combination of job search and networking.

The number-two source of hiring in Figure 5.3 is Indeed, an example of a job search platform. Another provider of similar services is ZipRecruiter. These services search the résumés that workers have posted on their site and other websites. Employers can specify the criteria they are looking for and have the system filter results and deliver résumés of qualified candidates. Other features of a site such as this include dashboards for employers and job seekers to view matches and keep track of the progress of job applications. The site may offer the capability to ask the candidate additional screening questions. This recruiting method increases the likelihood of finding candidates who closely match the company's specifications, at least among candidates with the skill of preparing a résumé with relevant key terms. In addition, the service may send e-mail alerts to workers who are a close match, encouraging them to apply with a tap on their mobile device. This enables employers to reach out to workers who aren't actively seeking a new job—potentially a high-quality pool of workers.[39]

By far the majority of companies today use social media as a tool for recruiting, although it is rarely the main tool used.[40] A familiar example of a job-related networking site is LinkedIn. Members of LinkedIn post their experience, educational background, and interests, along with their interest in considering job offers. Employers can find employees who match their criteria. They also can host web pages and participate in the news feeds and other interactions offered by the site. This makes the site a place to develop a positive image of the company as well as to invite people to apply for jobs. For more on ways to recruit with social media, see the "HRM Social" box.

Help-Wanted Advertising Although recruiters are reporting more use of other methods, many still place advertisements in online and offline media. Until recently, job boards such as CareerBuilder and Monster were top ways to recruit, and they still play a role in recruiting. These services are evolving to offer more than an online space for advertisements. Workers who are actively interested in a new job can set up a profile to send them notifications when a job matching their criteria is posted. Just as job search sites will generate résumés from candidates who create profiles with the right key terms, online job advertisements will reach the right eyes if they contain terms that job seekers will be searching for. Some employers that have a goal to improve diversity are using the services of Textio. This company's software searches a client's job postings and analyzes each to estimate the likelihood that its language will appeal to diverse candidates.[41]

A variety of media accept advertisements, including help-wanted ads. These include local newspapers, professional and trade publications (online and off), Craigslist, results pages of search engines, and even signs on transit and at workplaces. The goal of choosing advertising media is to place messages where qualified job seekers are most likely to see them. The ad should be easy to scan for information and easy to act on. Today's job hunters increasingly want to be able to apply via smartphone by texting a response or using an app.

Public Employment Agencies The Social Security Act of 1935 requires that everyone receiving unemployment compensation be registered with a local state employment office. These state employment offices work with the U.S. Employment Service (USES) to

Recruiting Success via Social Networks

Most employers today are opting for recruiting that reaches workers anytime, anywhere on their mobile devices. That often means using social media. According to research by the Society for Human Resource Management, 84% of employers use social media as a recruiting method. McDonald's, for example, connects with young workers by inviting them to submit an easy "snaplication" using Snapchat.

The social-media site most often used for recruiting is LinkedIn. On this career-related networking site, employers can run searches to identify individuals whose profiles mention particular skills, interests, or areas of experience. They also can advertise openings in special-interest groups (taking care to follow each group's rules for this type of posting). Employers also can benefit from participating on social-media sites that serve groups for professions or trades. And they can tap into their LinkedIn networks to seek referrals of qualified employees. This can lead employers to workers who are not actively seeking a new job but might be open to a change.

To use social media effectively, HR departments need a two-pronged approach. The first prong is to develop a favorable online "brand" as an employer. This requires not only posting helpful, informative messages from the company regularly, but also monitoring conversations in order to identify concerns and problems—and address them with solutions. When an employer's brand is favorable, workers who admire a company on Facebook might apply for a job or share a story about job openings, even if they didn't go on Facebook to look for work.

The second prong is to gather and analyze useful data about talented people who are or might become job candidates. Social-media data can tell employers where people are talking about the brand, the company, or the industry. Searches can point recruiters to discussions on particular topics, where they can see who is making a valuable contribution. The most sophisticated users of social media use analytic tools to help them find desirable candidates for key positions, so they can reach out with an offer to talk. In doing so, recruiters must take care not to limit searches to finding candidates with a limited set of technical skills; they also should consider how to identify other important qualifications, such as teamwork or leadership skills.

Questions

1. Based on this description, what are some advantages of finding a candidate via social media compared with posting openings on the company's website?
2. Based on this description, would you want to post a profile for yourself on LinkedIn and make posts on LinkedIn? Why or why not?

Sources: Carol Patton, "Does Social Media Hurt or Help Your Recruitment Efforts?" *Human Resource Executive,* February 14, 2020, https://hrexecutive.com; Amy Elisa Jackson, "The Key to Hiring Gen Z Candidates? Thinking Like Them," *Fast Company,* June 27, 2019, https://www.fastcompany.com; Payal Sondhi, "Are You Capitalizing LinkedIn for Recruitment?" *Entrepreneur,* December 18, 2018, https://www.entrepreneur.com; Nadav Olmert, "The Use of Digital Recruitment Tools Is on the Rise. Here's What You Need to Know," *Entrepreneur,* June 19, 2018, https://www.entrepreneur.com; "Using Social Media for Talent Acquisition," *Society for Human Resource Management,* https://www.shrm.org.

try to ensure that unemployed individuals eventually get off state aid and back on employer payrolls. To accomplish this, agencies collect information from the unemployed people about their skills and experience.

Employers can register their job vacancies with their local state employment office, and the agency will try to find someone suitable, using its computerized inventory of local unemployed individuals. The agency refers candidates to the employer at no charge. The organization can interview or test them to see if they are suitable for its vacancies. Besides offering access to job candidates at low cost, public employment agencies can be a useful resource for meeting certain diversity objectives. Laws often mandate that the agencies maintain specialized "desks" for minorities, disabled individuals, and war veterans. Employers that feel they currently are underutilizing any of these subgroups of the labor force may find the agencies to be an excellent source.

Government-run employment agencies also may partner with nonprofit groups to meet the needs of a community. In California's Alameda and Contra Costa Counties, several agencies have cooperated to form EastBay Works. This organization is dedicated to bringing together employers and workers in the two counties. EastBay Works offer a variety of recruiting tools at its website. Employers can post job openings, research the local labor market, and set up a search tool to identify candidates who have skills the employer is looking for. Job seekers can visit the site to hunt for jobs, set up a search tool that finds jobs related to the skills in their profile, assess their existing skills, and arrange for training in skills that employers want.[42]

Private Employment Agencies In contrast to public employment agencies, which primarily serve the blue-collar labor market, private employment agencies provide much the same service for the white-collar labor market. Workers interested in finding a job can sign up with a private employment agency whether or not they are currently unemployed. Another difference between the two types of agencies is that private agencies charge the employers for providing referrals. Therefore, using a private employment agency is more expensive than using a public agency, but the private agency is a more suitable source for certain kinds of applicants.

For managers or professionals, an employer may use the services of a type of private agency called an *executive search firm (ESF).* People often call these agencies "headhunters" because, unlike other employment agencies, they find new jobs for people almost exclusively already employed. For job candidates, dealing with executive search firms can be sensitive. Typically, executives do not want to advertise their availability, because it could trigger a negative reaction from their current employer. ESFs serve as a buffer, providing confidentiality between the employer and the recruit. That benefit may give an employer access to candidates it cannot recruit in other, more direct ways. Executive recruiters also may specialize in particular industries or business functions, so they can guide their clients toward candidates the clients might not otherwise consider. Catherine Lepard, for example, heads the global Retail Practice for the search firm Heidrick & Struggles. In this role, she helps retailers find people prepared to lead a business through the dramatic changes the industry is undergoing. Often, that means choosing someone who has *not* spent a career in retail but has learned to navigate different cultures, apply technology, and build agile organizations.[43]

Colleges and Universities Most colleges and universities have placement services that seek to help their graduates obtain employment. On-campus interviewing is the most important source of recruits for entry-level professional and managerial vacancies. Organizations tend to focus especially on colleges that have strong reputations in areas for which they have critical needs—say, chemical engineering or public accounting. They also may contribute to the development of skills they will need. Ford Motor Company recruits at a set of universities including the University of Michigan, Ann Arbor, and University of California, Berkeley. It also partners with these schools in research projects, funds scholarships, and sponsors student teams that are building vehicles for competitions.[44]

One of the best ways for a company to establish a stronger presence on campus is with a college internship program. How does this benefit the company and the students at the same time? Hill Street Studios/Blend Images LLC

Many employers have found that successfully competing for the best students requires more than just signing up prospective graduates for interview slots. One of the best ways to establish a stronger presence on a campus is with a college internship program. Internship programs give an organization early access to potential applicants and let the organization assess their capabilities directly. Internships also give applicants firsthand experience with the employer, so both parties can make well-informed choices about fit when it comes time to consider long-term commitment.[45] Ariel Lopez, a consultant who helps companies recruit diverse talent, worked with Spotify to launch a program called The Opening Act: HBCU Conference. The event brings together students at historically Black colleges and universities (HBCUs) with employers in the media and music technology industries. Spotify and the other participating employers have found talented employees through this event.[46]

Another way of increasing the employer's presence on campus is to participate in university job fairs. In general, a job fair is an event where many employers gather for a short time to meet large numbers of potential job applicants. Although job fairs can be held anywhere (such as at a hotel or convention center), campuses are ideal locations because of the many well-educated, yet unemployed, individuals who are there. Job fairs are an inexpensive means of generating an on-campus presence. Unfortunately, the COVID-19 pandemic quickly changed the way companies recruit at on-campus events and job fairs. With most college campuses closed for the Spring 2020 semester and possibly beyond, college recruiters resorted to individual sessions with prospective hires via Skype, Face Time, or Zoom. Seeing an opportunity to help organizations find and recruit using online events, Eightfold.ai has created and launched a virtual event recruiting system that can quickly and efficiently help companies match potential candidates with open positions.[47]

Evaluating the Quality of a Source

In general, there are few rules that say what recruitment source is best for a given job vacancy. Therefore, it is wise for employers to monitor the quality of all their recruitment sources. One way to do this is to develop and compare **yield ratios** for each source.[48] A yield ratio expresses the percentage of applicants who successfully move from one stage of the recruitment and selection process to the next. For example, the organization could find the number of candidates interviewed as a percentage of the total number of résumés generated by a given source (that is, number of interviews divided by number of résumés). A high yield ratio (large percentage) means that the source is an effective way to find candidates to interview. By comparing the yield ratios of different recruitment sources, HR professionals can determine which source is the best or most efficient for the type of vacancy.

Yield Ratio
A ratio that expresses the percentage of applicants who successfully move from one stage of the recruitment and selection process to the next.

Another measure of recruitment success is the **cost per hire.** To compute this amount, find the cost of using a particular recruitment source for a particular type of vacancy. Then divide that cost by the number of people hired to fill that type of vacancy. A low cost per hire means that the recruitment source is efficient; it delivers qualified candidates at minimal cost.

Cost per Hire
The total amount of money spent to fill a vacancy. The number is computed by finding the cost of using a particular recruitment source and dividing that cost by the number of people hired to fill that type of vacancy.

To see how HR professionals use these measures, look at the examples in Table 5.3. This table shows the results for a hypothetical organization that used five kinds of recruitment sources to fill a number of vacancies. For each recruitment source, the table shows four yield ratios and the cost per hire. To fill these jobs, the best two sources of recruits were local universities and employee referral programs. Recruiting at renowned universities generated highly qualified applicants, but relatively few of them ultimately accepted positions with the organization. Executive search firms produced the highest cumulative yield ratio. These generated only 20 applicants, but all of them accepted interview offers, most were judged acceptable, and 79% of these acceptable candidates took jobs with the organization. However, notice the cost per hire. The executive search firms charged $90,000 for finding these 15 employees, resulting in the largest cost per hire. In contrast, local universities

TABLE 5.3

Results of a Hypothetical Recruiting Effort

	RECRUITING SOURCE				
	LOCAL UNIVERSITY	**RENOWNED UNIVERSITY**	**EMPLOYEE REFERRALS**	**ADVERTISING**	**EXECUTIVE SEARCH FIRMS**
Résumés generated	200	400	50	500	20
Interview offers accepted	175	100	45	400	20
Yield ratio	**87%**	**25%**	**90%**	**80%**	**100%**
Applicants judged acceptable	100	95	40	50	19
Yield ratio	**57%**	**95%**	**89%**	**12%**	**95%**
Accept employment offers	90	10	35	25	15
Yield ratio	**90%**	**11%**	**88%**	**50%**	**79%**
Cumulative yield ratio	**90/200**	**10/400**	**35/50**	**25/500**	**15/20**
	45%	**3%**	**70%**	**5%**	**75%**
Cost	$30,000	$50,000	$15,000	$20,000	$90,000
Cost per hire	**$333**	**$5,000**	**$428**	**$800**	**$6,000**

provided modest yield ratios at the lowest cost per hire. Employee referrals provided excellent yield ratios at a slightly higher cost.

The cost per hire is not simply related to the type of recruiting method. These costs also tend to vary by industry and organization size. While the median cost per hire is about $4,500 per person,[49] large companies may benefit from having in-house experts, and companies needing hard-to-find skills may spend a lot to find them. Gathering accurate data can be difficult, as the "HR Oops!" box describes. But companies that make the effort to track employee sources and successes have an edge–if they analyze the data so they can target future efforts more specifically to the sources that deliver the best results. At any employer, recruiters' challenge is to identify the particular methods that will yield the best candidates as efficiently as possible.

Costs and yield ratios are not, of course, the end point to measure in acquiring talent. Companies also need to know whether they are hiring people who deliver high-quality work and contribute to the organization's success. As we will discuss in the next chapter, leading companies are addressing this need with applicant-tracking systems, some of which are using artificial intelligence to improve hiring decisions.[50]

Recruiter Traits and Behaviors

LO 5-6 Describe the recruiter's role in the recruitment process, including limits and opportunities.

As we saw in Figure 5.2, the third influence on recruitment outcomes is the recruiter, including this person's characteristics and the way he or she behaves. The recruiter affects the nature of both the job vacancy and the applicants generated. However, the recruiter often becomes involved late in the recruitment process. In many cases, by the time a recruiter meets some applicants, they have already made up their minds about what they desire in a job, what the vacant job has to offer, and their likelihood of receiving a job offer.[51]

Many applicants approach the recruiter with some skepticism. Knowing it is the recruiter's job to sell them on a vacancy, some applicants discount what the recruiter says in light of what they have heard from other sources, such as friends, magazine articles,

Source-of-Hire Data Is Not So Clear

Getting source-of-hire data sounds straightforward, right? Count up who applied on the company website, who an existing employee referred, and whose résumé recruiters found through Indeed. Compute the percentages, and you can see a distribution of sources of hire. But job hunting is rarely a one-step process. Suppose an employee mentions to her friend Pat that the company is hiring. Pat looks up reviews of the company on Indeed, thinks about it for a few days, then goes to the website to apply. What was the source of hire? It was three sources, in combination.

Ideally, an employer's data would collect information about all the sources used and offer the ability to analyze sources individually and in combinations. In practice, many organizations are not that sophisticated. They may ask about "the" source of information (ignoring that there may be several), the initial source, the most recent website, or the source of the application or résumé. Sometimes one analysis compares answers to differing questions. And, in fact, recruiters admit that they are dissatisfied with their analysis.

There are some basic ways to improve the data. One is for an employer gathering data to ask each new hire the same question, such as "How did you first learn about this position?" or "List all the sources of information you used [from a list of possibilities]." Related to this is a need to decide what exactly the company wants to measure. For example, if the measurement is to be what the source of an application is—say, company website, LinkedIn, Indeed, or a job board—then a computer can gather this information automatically. If the measurement is where the candidate heard about the job, then the source of data needs to be the employee answering a question.

Questions

1. Which piece of information do you think would be most important for measuring the value of recruitment sources: where candidates discover job openings, where they gather information about positions and employers, or where they submit applications and résumés? Why?
2. Based on the information here, review the graph in Figure 5.3, and write down three questions you would want to answer about the source data before applying the data in an HR department.

Sources: Nikoletta Bika, "Source of Hire: What It Is, How to Measure It and How to Use It," *Workable tutorial,* https://resources.workable.com, accessed April 2, 2020; Sam Holzman, "Source of Hire: Why Understanding Recruiting Sources Is Key to Successful Recruiting," *Zoominfo,* December 11, 2018, https://blog.zoominfo.com; WorkPlace Group, "Source-of-Hire Metrics," February 2017, http://www.workplacegroup.com.

and professors. When candidates are already familiar with the company through knowing about its products, the recruiter's impact is especially weak.[52] For these and other reasons, recruiters' characteristics and behaviors seem to have limited impact on applicants' job choices.

Characteristics of the Recruiter

Most organizations must choose whether their recruiters are specialists in human resources or are experts at particular jobs (that is, those who currently hold the same kinds of jobs or supervise people who hold the jobs). According to some studies, applicants perceive HR specialists as less credible and are less attracted to jobs when recruiters are HR specialists.[53] The evidence does not completely discount a positive role for personnel specialists in recruiting. It does indicate, however, that these specialists need to take extra steps to ensure that applicants perceive them as knowledgeable and credible.

In general, applicants respond positively to recruiters whom they perceive as warm and informative. "Warm" means the recruiter seems to care about the applicant and to be enthusiastic about the applicant's potential to contribute to the organization. "Informative" means the recruiter provides the kind of information the applicant is seeking. The evidence of impact of other characteristics of recruiters–including their age, sex, and race–is complex and inconsistent.[54]

Behavior of the Recruiter

Recruiters affect results not only by providing plenty of information, but by providing the right kind of information. Perhaps the most-researched aspect of recruiting is the level of realism in the recruiter's message. Because the recruiter's job is to attract candidates, recruiters may feel pressure to exaggerate the positive qualities of the vacancy and to downplay its negative qualities. Applicants are highly sensitive to negative information. The highest-quality applicants may be less willing to pursue jobs when this type of information comes out.[55] But if the recruiter goes too far in a positive direction, the candidate can be misled and lured into taking a job that has been misrepresented. Then unmet expectations can contribute to a high turnover rate. When recruiters describe jobs unrealistically, people who take those jobs may come to believe that the employer is deceitful.[56]

Many studies have looked at how well **realistic job previews**–background information about jobs' positive and negative qualities–can get around this problem and help organizations minimize turnover among new employees. On the whole, the research suggests that realistic job previews have a weak and inconsistent effect on turnover.[57] Although realistic job previews have only a weak association with reduced turnover, the cost of the effort is low, and they are relatively easy to implement. Consequently, employers should consider using them as a way to reduce turnover among new hires.[58]

Realistic Job Preview
Background information about a job's positive and negative qualities.

Finally, for affecting whether people choose to take a job, but even more so, whether they stick with a job, the recruiter seems less important than an organization's personnel policies that directly affect the job's features (pay, security, advancement opportunities, and so on).

Enhancing the Recruiter's Impact

Nevertheless, although recruiters are probably not the most important influence on people's job choices, this does not mean recruiters cannot have an impact. Most recruiters receive little training.[59] If we were to determine what does matter to job candidates, perhaps recruiters could be trained in those areas.

Researchers have tried to find the conditions in which recruiters do make a difference. Such research suggests that an organization can take several steps to increase the positive impact that recruiters have on job candidates:

- Recruiters should provide timely feedback. Applicants dislike delays in feedback. They may draw negative conclusions about the organization (for starters, that the organization doesn't care about their application).
- Recruiters should avoid offensive behavior. They should avoid behaving in ways that might convey the wrong impression about the organization.[60] Figure 5.4 quotes applicants who felt they had extremely bad experiences with recruiters. Their statements provide examples of behaviors to avoid.
- The organization can recruit with teams rather than individual recruiters. Applicants view job experts as more credible than HR specialists, and a team can include both kinds of recruiters. HR specialists on the team provide knowledge about company policies and procedures.

Through such positive behavior, recruiters can give organizations a better chance of competing for talented human resources. In Chapter 6 we will describe how an organization selects the candidates who best meet its needs.

FIGURE 5.4
Recruits Who Were Offended by Recruiters

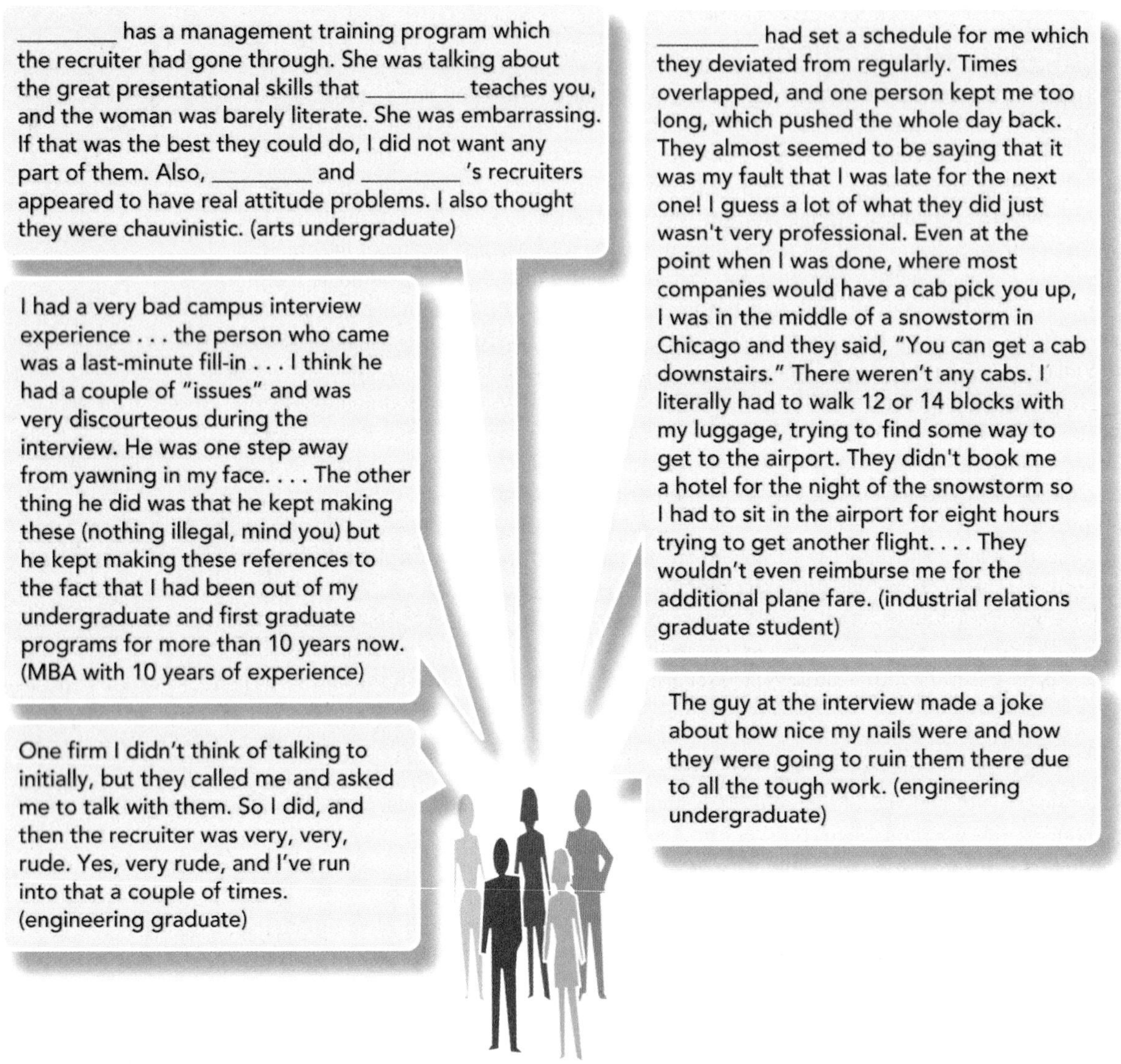

________ has a management training program which the recruiter had gone through. She was talking about the great presentational skills that ________ teaches you, and the woman was barely literate. She was embarrassing. If that was the best they could do, I did not want any part of them. Also, ________ and ________'s recruiters appeared to have real attitude problems. I also thought they were chauvinistic. (arts undergraduate)

I had a very bad campus interview experience . . . the person who came was a last-minute fill-in . . . I think he had a couple of "issues" and was very discourteous during the interview. He was one step away from yawning in my face. . . . The other thing he did was that he kept making these (nothing illegal, mind you) but he kept making these references to the fact that I had been out of my undergraduate and first graduate programs for more than 10 years now. (MBA with 10 years of experience)

One firm I didn't think of talking to initially, but they called me and asked me to talk with them. So I did, and then the recruiter was very, very, rude. Yes, very rude, and I've run into that a couple of times. (engineering graduate)

________ had set a schedule for me which they deviated from regularly. Times overlapped, and one person kept me too long, which pushed the whole day back. They almost seemed to be saying that it was my fault that I was late for the next one! I guess a lot of what they did just wasn't very professional. Even at the point when I was done, where most companies would have a cab pick you up, I was in the middle of a snowstorm in Chicago and they said, "You can get a cab downstairs." There weren't any cabs. I literally had to walk 12 or 14 blocks with my luggage, trying to find some way to get to the airport. They didn't book me a hotel for the night of the snowstorm so I had to sit in the airport for eight hours trying to get another flight. . . . They wouldn't even reimburse me for the additional plane fare. (industrial relations graduate student)

The guy at the interview made a joke about how nice my nails were and how they were going to ruin them there due to all the tough work. (engineering undergraduate)

THINKING ETHICALLY

HOW FAIR IS TEMP AND CONTRACT WORK TO WORKERS?

As the chapter has explained, contracting for temporary workers, freelancers, and other independent contractors is a flexible way to meet the demand for labor. Companies can bring in people to complete projects during busy times and not have to lay off employees when projects are finished. And they can let the contracting firms handle the paperwork for jobs that aren't critical to the organization's main mission. But what about the impact on the contingent workers? Is this approach to HR planning fair to them?

A variety of concerns have been raised. The most common criticisms are that contractors seldom get employee benefits such as paid time off and health insurance, and many laws in place to protect employees do not apply to contract workers. Evidence suggests that the people taking temporary assignments through contractors tend to earn less than their counterparts on the payroll of the companies where they work. Safety training may fall through the cracks as contractors assume their clients are handling it while clients assume the contractor has already taken care of it.

Also, a contingent worker's income is more uncertain than that of a typical full-time employee. When the demand for the contractors' labor drops, they earn nothing until a client needs their services. This might happen every few months–or every few days. Even when they are working, their earnings can fluctuate unpredictably from day to day. Some contract arrangements require that the workers cover operating costs, such as a driver paying for gas and vehicle maintenance.

Still, many workers like the arrangement. It might be better than widely available part-time employment that also lacks benefits and predictable hours. Some people are happier with contract work that lets them set their own hours, choose how to get the job done, and get involved with a variety of projects. Some have skills that command good pay, which makes up for the lack of employer-provided benefits.

Questions

1. One ethical standard is the "greatest good for the greatest number." When an employer decides to meet its demand for labor with contract workers, who benefits? Think about the impact on the individual workers, the employer, and the other stakeholders affected.
2. If you were evaluating the fairness of a contract arrangement, what conditions would you look for to decide if the arrangement was fair to the workers?

Sources: Jacob Passy, "Google Has More Temp and Contract Workers Than Actual Employees," *Market Watch,* May 30, 2019, https://www.marketwatch.com; Alan Ferguson, "Protecting Temp Workers," *Safety + Health,* February 24, 2019, https://www.safetyandhealthmagazine.com; Yuki Noguchi, "Unequal Rights: Contract Workers Have Few Workplace Protections," *NPR,* March 26, 2018, https://www.npr.org; Yuki Noguchi, "Freelanced: The Rise of the Contract Workforce," *All Things Considered,* January 22, 2018, https://www.npr.org.

SUMMARY

LO 5-1 Discuss how to plan for human resources needed to carry out the organization's strategy.

- The first step in human resource planning is personnel forecasting. Through trend analysis and good judgment, the planner tries to determine the supply of and demand for various human resources.
- Based on whether a surplus or a shortage is expected, the planner sets goals and creates a strategy for achieving those goals.
- The organization then implements its HR strategy and evaluates the results.

LO 5-2 Determine the labor demand for workers in various job categories.

- The planner can look at leading indicators, assuming trends will continue in the future.
- Multiple regression can convert several leading indicators into a single prediction of labor needs.
- Analysis of a transitional matrix can help the planner identify which job categories can be filled internally and where high turnover is likely.

LO 5-3 Summarize the advantages and disadvantages of ways to eliminate a labor surplus and avoid a labor shortage.

- To reduce a surplus, downsizing, pay reductions, and demotions deliver fast results but at a high cost in human suffering that may hurt surviving employees' motivation and future recruiting. Also, the organization may lose some of its best employees.
- Transferring employees and requiring them to share work are also fast methods, and the consequences in human suffering are less severe.
- A hiring freeze or natural attrition is slow to take effect but avoids the pain of layoffs.
- Early-retirement packages may unfortunately induce the best employees to leave and may be slow to implement; however, they, too, are less painful than layoffs.
- Retraining can improve the organization's overall pool of human resources and maintain high morale, but it is relatively slow and costly.
- To avoid a labor shortage, requiring overtime is the easiest and fastest strategy, which can easily be changed if conditions change. However, overtime may exhaust workers and can hurt morale.
- Using temporary employees and outsourcing do not build an in-house pool of talent, but they quickly and easily modify staffing levels.
- Transferring and retraining employees require investment of time and money, but can enhance the quality of the organization's human resources; however, this may backfire if a labor surplus develops.
- Hiring new employees is slow and expensive, but strengthens the organization if labor needs are

expected to expand for the long term. Hiring is difficult to reverse if conditions change.

- Using technology as a substitute for labor can be slow to implement and costly, but it may improve the organization's long-term performance. New technology also is difficult to reverse.

LO 5-4 Describe recruitment policies organizations use to make job vacancies more attractive.

- Internal recruiting (promotions from within) generally makes job vacancies more attractive because candidates see opportunities for growth and advancement.
- Lead-the-market pay strategies make jobs economically desirable.
- Due-process policies signal that employers are concerned about employee rights.
- The Internet provides opportunities for an organization to align its image with the actual experience of working for the company with photos, videos, and stories on the company's website, as well as direct engagement with workers via social media.

LO 5-5 List and compare sources of job applicants.

- Internal sources, promoted through job postings, generate applicants who are familiar to the organization and motivate other employees by demonstrating opportunities for advancement. However, internal sources are usually insufficient for all of an organization's labor needs.
- Direct applicants and referrals tend to be inexpensive and to generate applicants who have self-selected; this source risks charges of unfairness, especially in cases of nepotism.
- External recruiting, such as job search and networking platforms, gives organizations access to both people looking for jobs and those who may not be actively looking for work.
- Although they still play a role in recruiting, job boards have evolved to offer more than online space for advertisements. They now allow job seekers to set up profiles and alert them when job openings are posted that match their search criteria.
- Public employment agencies are inexpensive and typically have screened applicants.
- Private employment agencies charge fees but may provide many services.
- Another inexpensive channel is schools and colleges, which may give the employer access to top-notch entrants to the labor market.

LO 5-6 Describe the recruiter's role in the recruitment process, including limits and opportunities.

- Through their behavior and other characteristics, recruiters influence the nature of the job vacancy and the kinds of applicants generated.
- Applicants tend to perceive job experts as more credible than recruiters who are HR specialists.
- Applicants tend to react more favorably to recruiters who are warm and informative.
- Recruiters should not mislead candidates. Realistic job previews have only a weak association with reduced turnover, but given their low cost and ease of implementation, employers should consider using them.
- Recruiters can improve their impact by providing timely feedback, avoiding behavior that contributes to a negative impression of the organization, and teaming up with job experts.

KEY TERMS

forecasting, 134
trend analysis, 134
leading indicators, 134
transitional matrix, 135
core competency, 137
downsizing, 138
outsourcing, 142
workforce utilization review, 146
recruiting, 146
employment at will, 147
due-process policies, 147
job posting, 148
direct applicants, 150
referrals, 150
nepotism, 150
yield ratio, 154
cost per hire, 154
realistic job preview, 157

REVIEW AND DISCUSSION QUESTIONS

1. Suppose an organization expects a labor shortage to develop in key job areas over the next few years. Recommend general responses the organization could make in each of the following areas: *(LO 5-1)*
   a. Recruitment
   b. Training
   c. Compensation (pay and employee benefits)

2. Some organizations have detailed affirmative-action plans, complete with goals and timetables, for women and minorities, yet have no formal human resource plan for the organization as a whole. Why might this be the case? What does this practice suggest about the role of human resource management in these organizations? *(LO 5-1)*
3. Review the sample transitional matrix shown in Table 5.1. What jobs experience the greatest turnover (employees leaving the organization)? How might an organization with this combination of jobs reduce the turnover? *(LO 5-2)*
4. In the same transitional matrix, which jobs seem to rely the most on internal recruitment? Which seem to rely most on external recruitment? Why? *(LO 5-2)*
5. Why do organizations combine statistical and judgmental forecasts of labor demand, rather than relying on statistics or judgment alone? Give an example of a situation in which each type of forecast would be inaccurate. *(LO 5-3)*
6. Give an example of a personnel policy that would help attract a larger pool of job candidates. Give an example of a personnel policy that would likely reduce the pool of candidates. Would you expect these policies to influence the quality as well as the number of applicants? Why or why not? *(LO 5-4)*
7. Discuss the relative merits of internal versus external recruitment. Give an example of a situation in which each of these approaches might be particularly effective. *(LO 5-4)*
8. List the jobs you have held. How were you recruited for each of these? From the organization's perspective, what were some pros and cons of recruiting you through these methods? *(LO 5-4)*
9. Recruiting people for jobs that require international assignments is increasingly important for many organizations. Where might an organization go to recruit people interested in such assignments? *(LO 5-5)*
10. A large share of HR professionals have rated online recruiting platforms as their best source of new talent. What qualities of online recruiting do you think contribute to this opinion? *(LO 5-5)*
11. How can organizations improve the effectiveness of their recruiters? *(LO 5-6)*

SELF-ASSESSMENT EXERCISE

Does Your Résumé Attract Employers?

Most employers have to evaluate hundreds of résumés each week. If you want your résumé to have a good chance of being read by prospective employers, you must invest time and energy not only in its content but also in its appearance. Review your résumé and answer yes or no to each of the following questions.

1. Does it avoid typos and grammatical errors?
2. Does it avoid using personal pronouns (such as I and me)?
3. Does it clearly identify what you have done and accomplished?
4. Does it highlight your accomplishments rather than your duties?
5. Does it exceed two pages in length?
6. Does it have correct contact information?
7. Does it have an employment objective that is specific and focuses on the employer's needs as well as your own?
8. Does it have at least one-inch margins?
9. Does it use a maximum of two typefaces or fonts?
10. Does it use bullet points to emphasize your skills and accomplishments?
11. Does it avoid use of underlining?
12. Is the presentation consistent? (Example: If you use all caps for the name of your most recent workplace, do you do that for previous workplaces as well?)

The more "yes" answers you gave, the more likely your résumé will attract an employer's attention and get you a job interview!

TAKING RESPONSIBILITY

Facebook Struggles to Rebuild Employee Trust

Treating employees well can be part of a recruiting strategy. This approach assumes that if you want the best people, it's easiest to get them if they would love to work for you. Evidence that Facebook pursues such a policy comes from its recurring position on the Glassdoor job-review site's list of the best places to work.

When people compile and read about such lists, they often are thinking of fancy perks, like on-site gyms and free meals. Indeed, these are part of the experience of working at Facebook's facility in Menlo Park, California. But more important, according Janelle Gale, the vice president of human resources, is that people do "meaningful work in areas that matter to Facebook, and areas that matter to them." The company's mission, "connecting the world," appeals to employees and gives them a sense of purpose. Another consideration is relationships between employees and their managers. The company conducts an employee satisfaction survey, which asks employees to rate their managers, so it can determine the qualities associated with effective managers. (Answer: They support, rather than dictate orders to, employees.)

The company seeks to maintain a culture in which talented, hardworking people thrive. The layout of the offices provides opportunities for employees to connect and work on ideas. Employees describe this situation as an opportunity to learn and to see interesting projects. (Due to COVID-19, Facebook is allowing employees to work at home until July 2021.) Consistent with the company's mission, CEO Mark Zuckerberg communicates openly about the company with its employees, including in question-and-answer sessions once a week. Lori Goler, vice president of people, says this kind of behavior is intentional, to align with the mission: as Facebook users build communities, so employees build community within the company.

All of this has been challenged recently, following revelations of an organization called Cambridge Analytica using quizzes on Facebook to get data about millions of users and their networks, then improperly making the data available for other purposes. This news comes on top of reports that others who misrepresented themselves published misinformation related to the 2016 presidential election. These stories have damaged Facebook's reputation, caused many users to avoid the site, and reportedly hurt employee morale. Until this occurred, Facebook had become an essential means of staying connected. Now the company must figure out how to resell its vision to its users and its current and future employees.

Questions

1. What socially responsible practices can you identify at Facebook, as described here? Where are some areas in which improvement could help its reputation with employees?
2. What are two recruiting methods that Facebook could use that would be consistent with its mission and its efforts to be a great place to work?

Sources: Reuters, "Facebook Employees to Work from Home until July 2021," *U.S. News*, http://money.usnews.com, accessed August 9, 2020; Salvador Rodriquez, "Facebook Has Moved Fast During Coronavirus Outbreak, and It Could Restore the Company's Reputation," *CNBC*, March 21, 2020, https://www.cnbc.com; Joshua Brustein, "Facebook Grappling with Employee Anger over Moderator Conditions," *Bloomberg*, February 25, 2019, https://www.bloomberg.com; Michael Schneider, "The Problems Aren't Over. Facebook Now Has to Deal with Its Declining Employee Morale," *Inc.*, April 16, 2018, https://www.inc.com; Aarti Shahani, "Facebook Says Cambridge Analytica May Have Obtained Data on as Many as 87M Users," *All Things Considered*, April 4, 2018, https://npr.org.

MANAGING TALENT

Techtonic Group Builds Its Own Labor Supply

Techtonic Group, a software development company based in Boulder, Colorado, originally met its demand for app developers by offshoring the work. Founder and CEO Heather Terenzio said they arranged to have the work done in Armenia, and she flew there often to oversee the work. Originally, the setup seemed like a practical way to keep costs down, but eventually, salaries in the region began to rise, and the distance made the work hard to control.

After several years of increasing difficulty, Terenzio decided Techtonic needed a different way to meet its talent needs. The solution came to her when she was visiting a Boulder vocational school to talk about technology careers. A young man from the catering team approached her and described how, in spite of having no education beyond a GED, he had taught himself coding. She realized that for the same amount of training and supervision as she was devoting to the workforce in Armenia, she could hire average coders in the United States and develop them into excellent employees.

Terenzio took the young man's pitch seriously and hired him. He learned quickly and got along with his co-workers. Soon Techtronic was wondering if they could plan a system to recruit nontraditional job candidates.

The solution they introduced was a six-week training program called Techtonic Academy. Through social media and Craigslist, the program recruits a diverse group of would-be software developers to learn the basics. The program emphasizes hiring at-risk youth, minorities, women, and military veterans–groups that traditional recruiting channels often overlook. Graduates can apply for an eight-month paid apprenticeship at Techtonic or for other jobs in the area. Techtonic hires most of them. The program is free, and the number of applicants far exceeds the space. Trainers can observe which trainees excel in problem-solving skills, which helps Techtonic bring onboard those with the most potential. Now employees who had been apprentices in the early years of the program are mentoring the newer apprentices, creating a career path they value.

Terenzio was so pleased with the results of Techtonic Academy that she applied for and received a state government grant to expand the program to more cities. More recently, the Markle Foundation funded the Skillful State Network, which is using Techtonic Academy as a model to expand to other states.

Questions

1. Briefly describe the labor supply and demand facing Techtonic Group.
2. What basic options did Techtonic have for addressing a labor shortage? What is your evaluation of the approach Techtonic established?

Sources: Company website, "Techtonic Apprenticeship," https://www.techtonic.com, accessed April 2, 2020; Jeff Haden, "How This Company Created the First Software Development Apprenticeship Program Approved by the Department of Labor," *Inc.*, January 28, 2019, https://www.inc.com; "Boulder's Techtonic Group Raises $2M to Expand Training, Apprenticeship Program," *Daily Camera*, April 25, 2018, https://www.dailycamera.com; Lauren Weber and Rachel Feintzeig, "To Fill Jobs in a Tight Labor Market, Employers May Need to Get Creative," *The Wall Street Journal*, February 15, 2018; Tony Bingham and Pat Galagan, "Offshore No More," *TD*, December 2017, pp. 27–31.

HR IN SMALL BUSINESS

Horizon Therapeutics Plans for Strong Future

With roughly 1,200 employees on its payroll and 11 medicines in its product mix, Horizon Therapeutics goes up against stiff competition to meet its talent needs. Irina Konstantinovsky, the company's chief human resources officer, aims to meet the challenge by emphasizing the advantages of a small employer and by stressing Horizon's core values, including transparency, accountability, and growth, as well as empathy for the patients served by its products. The company was founded in 2008 to sell primary-care drugs, but it has recently transitioned to a more focused approach that targets rare and rheumatic conditions.

Horizon is based in Dublin, with a headquarters in Chicago. It has facilities in Illinois, California, the District of Columbia, and Mannheim, Germany. The most recently opened facility, in South San Francisco, puts the company near a center of biotech talent. This makes the location attractive to these workers, who can maintain connections to colleagues in their professions, but it also places Horizon squarely in the middle of stiff competition for these workers.

This is more than a matter of hiring scientists. Konstantinovsky cites marketing as a particularly difficult skill area to recruit. For example, it recently launched a new drug for treating eye inflammation associated with thyroid disease, and this required hiring for more than 40 positions at once. Most people who go into marketing are interested in consumer goods. Selling pharmaceuticals requires scientific knowledge and the ability to discuss products with medical professionals. In the example of the drug for eye inflammation, salespeople need to call on thousands of physicians, including specialists in eye surgery. Horizon therefore combines recruiting with ongoing development, so employees can grow in their profession.

Konstantinovsky's recruiting message is that Horizon moves fast and grows fast, making it an exciting place to work. She notes that in a small company, employees can take on wider responsibility and move up faster in the organization. She also notes that many of the people at Horizon actually know some of the patients who benefit from the company's products, so the impact of treating conditions takes on a personal and significant meaning.

It's a stiff challenge, but Konstantinovsky brings to the job years of experience at pharmaceutical firm Baxter International, where she oversaw talent acquisition and other HR functions for more than 50,000 employees. As she now promises others, Horizon has provided her a fast-paced environment in which to make a difference.

Questions

1. Would you say this case describes a situation of a labor surplus or a labor shortage? Why?
2. Horizon has grown rapidly since its founding, but what if the environment changes so that the company has to scale back some products? How would you recommend the company handle a drop in the need for marketing professionals? Explain your reasoning.

Sources: Horizon Therapeutics, "About Us," https://www.horizontherapeutics.com, accessed April 2, 2020; Kyle Blankenship, "Horizon Looks to the Future with Massive San Francisco Manufacturing, R&D Facility," *FiercePharma*, December 4, 2019, https://www.fiercepharma.com; Angus Liu, "Horizon Bulks Up Sales Force Ahead of $750M Inflammatory Eye Drug Launch," *FiercePharma*, June 25, 2019, https://www.fiercepharma.com; Julian Upton, "True Grit: Talent Management from the Ground Up," *Pharmaceutical Executive*, April 2019, pp. 20–21.

NOTES

1. Harry McCracken, "Amazon's People Person," *Fast Company*, May 2019, pp. 50–92; Patrick Thomas, "Amazon Changes the Way It Recruits M.B.A.s," *The Wall Street Journal*, February 18, 2020, https://www.wsj.com; Emma Goldberg, "'Techlash' Hits College Campuses," *The New York Times*, January 11, 2020, https://www.nytimes.com.
2. S. Downes and G. Winfrey, "8 Best Industries for Starting a Business in 2020," *Inc.*, February 4, 2020, https://www.inc.com; P. Kushmaro, "5 Ways Industrial AI Is Revolutionizing Manufacturing," *CIO*, September 27, 2018, https://www.cio.com.
3. B. Chang, "RV Makers Are Seeing Surging Demand as Stay-at-Home Orders Lift and Some Companies are Struggling to Keep

Up," *Business Insider*, https://www.businessinsider.com, accessed August 9, 2020.

4. Steven Norton, "Seeking Developers, Liberty Mutual Sends Employees to Coding Bootcamps," *The Wall Street Journal*, March 26, 2018, https://blogs.wsj.com; Ruth Simon, "Small Business Thinks Big about Recruiting," *The Wall Street Journal*, February 21, 2018, https://www.wsj.com.
5. J. P. Guthrie, "Dumb and Dumber: The Impact of Downsizing on Firm Performance as Moderated by Industry Conditions," *Organization Science* 19 (2008), pp. 108–123.
6. C. D. Zatzick and R. D. Iverson, "High-Involvement Management and Workforce Reduction: Competitive Advantage or Disadvantage?" *Academy of Management Journal* 49 (2006), pp. 999–1015.
7. P. P. Shaw, "Network Destruction: The Structural Implications of Downsizing," *Academy of Management Journal* 43 (2000), pp. 101–112.
8. Brenda Kowske, Kyle Lundby, and Rena Rasch, "Turning 'Survive' into 'Thrive': Managing Survivor Engagement in a Downsized Organization," *People & Strategy* 32, no. 4 (2009), pp. 48–56.
9. W. F. Cascio, "Downsizing: What Do We Know? What Have We Learned?" *Academy of Management Executive* 7 (1993), pp. 95–104; Sharon Terlep, "Kimberly-Clark to Cut 5,000 Jobs, Close 10 Factories," *The Wall Street Journal*, January 23, 2018, https://www.wsj.com; Russell Gold, "Utility Jobs Lost as New Power Plants Need Fewer Workers," *The Wall Street Journal*, January 15, 2018, https://www.wsj.com.
10. Derek Thomas, "Work Sharing Calms Economic Waves," *Indianapolis Business Journal*, March 2-8, 2015, p. 11; L. Woellert, "Half the Hours, Most of the Pay," *Bloomberg Businessweek*, January 31, 2013, pp. 23–24.
11. Nick Timiraos, "How Older Women Are Reshaping U.S. Job Market," *The Wall Street Journal*, February 22, 2016, http://www.wsj.com.
12. S. Kim and D. Feldman, "Healthy, Wealthy, or Wise: Predicting Actual Acceptances of Early Retirement Incentives at Three Points in Time," *Personnel Psychology* 51 (1998), pp. 623–642.
13. Richard Stolz, "How P&G Uses Gig Worker Matching Platforms to Fuel Talent Strategy," *Employee Benefit News*, January 29, 2018, https://www.benefitnews.com; Tamara Lytle, "Temp Tales," *HR Magazine*, December 2017-January 2018, pp. 51–55; S. A. Johnson and B. E. Ashforth, "Externalization of Employment in a Service Environment: The Role of Organizational and Customer Identification," *Journal of Organizational Behavior* 29 (2008), pp. 287–309; M. Vidal and L. M. Tigges, "Temporary Employment and Strategic Staffing in the Manufacturing Sector," *Industrial Relations* 48 (2009), pp. 55–72.
14. L. Padin, "Lasting Solutions for America's Temporary Workers," *National Employment Law Project*, August 26, 2019, https://www.nelp.org; Lytle, "Temp Tales"; J. R. Nicholson, "Temporary Help Workers in the U.S. Labor Market," ESA Issue Brief 03-15, U.S. Department of Commerce, Economics and Statistics Administration, July 1, 2015, http://www.esa.doc.gov.
15. G. Dautovic, "15 Must-Know Outsourcing Statistics (2020 Update)," *Fortunly*, https://fortunly.com, accessed March 31, 2020; L. DePillis, "To Stay Competitive, US Call Centers Are Training Workers to Be Super Agents," *CNN Business*, May 18, 2018, https://money.cnn.com.
16. L. Weber, "The End of Employees," *The Wall Street Journal*, February 2, 2017, https://www.wsj.com.
17. A. Jordan, "The Danger in Outsourcing Cybersecurity to Foreign-Based Firms," *Security Boulevard*, April 25, 2018, https://securityboulevard.com.
18. Weber, "The End of Employees."
19. Mansfield Sales Partners, "Our Story," https://www.mansfieldsp.com, accessed March 31, 2020.
20. V. Bolden-Barrett, "HR and IT May Need to Reconnect to Modernize Recruiting," *HR Dive*, January 31, 2020, https://www.hrdive.com; S. F. Gale, "Recruiting Tech Is Expanding–Unlike Recruiters' Willingness to Use It," *Workforce*, January 2018, https://www.workforce.com.
21. H. L. Kurter, "How Hilton Reduced Their Time to Hire from 43 Days Down to Five," *Forbes*, September 19, 2019, https://www.forbes.com; S. McLaren, "How Hilton, Google, and More Have Dramatically Reduced Their Time to Hire," *LinkedIn*, May 24, 2018, https://business.linkedin.com.
22. A. E. Barber, *Recruiting Employees* (Thousand Oaks, CA: Sage, 1998).
23. C. K. Stevens, "Antecedents of Interview Interactions, Interviewers' Ratings, and Applicants' Reactions," *Personnel Psychology* 51 (1998), pp. 55–85; A. E. Barber, J. R. Hollenbeck, S. L. Tower, and J. M. Phillips, "The Effects of Interview Focus on Recruitment Effectiveness: A Field Experiment," *Journal of Applied Psychology* 79 (1994), pp. 886–896; D. S. Chapman and D. I. Zweig, "Developing a Nomological Network for Interview Structure: Antecedents and Consequences of the Structured Selection Interview," *Personnel Psychology* 58 (2005), pp. 673–702.
24. J. D. Olian and S. L. Rynes, "Organizational Staffing: Integrating Practice with Strategy," *Industrial Relations* 23 (1984), pp. 170–183.
25. M. Leonard, "Challenges to the Termination-at-Will Doctrine," *Personnel Administrator* 28 (1983), pp. 49–56; C. Schowerer and B. Rosen, "Effects of Employment-at-Will Policies and Compensation Policies on Corporate Image and Job Pursuit Intentions," *Journal of Applied Psychology* 74 (1989), pp. 653–656.
26. S. L. Rynes and A. E. Barber, "Applicant Attraction Strategies: An Organizational Perspective," *Academy of Management Review* 15 (1990), pp. 286–310; J. A. Breaugh, *Recruitment: Science and Practice* (Boston: PWS-Kent, 1992), p. 34; D. S. Chapman, K. L. Uggerslev, S. A. Carroll, K. A. Piasentin, and D. A. Jones, "Applicant Attraction to Organizations and Job Choice: A Meta-analytic Review of the Correlates of Recruiting Outcomes," *Journal of Applied Psychology* 90 (2005), pp. 928–944.
27. A. Robertson and B. Wigert, "Why You Need to Compete for Employees Like You Do for Customers," *Gallup*, https://www.gallup.com, accessed March 31, 2020.
28. B. Weinreb, "How to Develop a Brand Story That Attracts Great Talent," *Glassdoor*, January 27, 2020, https://www.glassdoor.com; M. Stephan, D. Brown, and R. Erickson, "Talent Acquisition: Enter the Cognitive Recruiter," in *Rewriting the Rules for the Digital Age: 2017 Deloitte Global Human Capital Trends* (Deloitte University Press, 2017), pp. 39–48.
29. M. A. Conrad and S. D. Ashworth, "Recruiting Source Effectiveness: A Meta-Analysis and Re-examination of Two Rival Hypotheses," paper presented at the annual meeting of the Society of Industrial/Organizational Psychology, Chicago, 1986.
30. P. Capelli, "Your Approach to Hiring Is All Wrong," *Harvard Business Review*, https://hbr.org, accessed March 31, 2020; T. Fica,

"The Benefits of Internal Recruiting," *BambooHR*, https://www.bamboohr.com/blog, accessed March 31, 2020.

31. C. Rabello, "How I've Learned to Cut Back on New Hires and Make More Promotions," *Fast Company*, March 25, 2016, http://www.fastcompany.com.
32. E. Krell, "Weighing Internal vs. External Hires," *HR Magazine*, January/February 2015, https://www.shrm.org.
33. R. S. Schuler and S. E. Jackson, "Linking Competitive Strategies with Human Resource Management Practices," *Academy of Management Executive* 1 (1987), pp. 207–219.
34. R. O'Donnell, "Employers Still Hiring During Coronavirus Pandemic," *Society for Human Resource Management*, March 29, 2020, https://shrm.org; R. Burns, "More than 2,000 Michigan Companies Are Hiring Amid COVID-19 Pandemic," *WMMT*, March 31, 2020, https://wwmt.com.
35. Stephan et al., "Talent Acquisition"; SilkRoad, *Sources of Hire 2018: Where the Candidate Journey Begins*, May 2018, https://www.silkroadtechnology.com.
36. C. R. Wanberg, R. Kanfer, and J. T. Banas, "Predictors and Outcomes of Networking Intensity among Job Seekers," *Journal of Applied Psychology* 85 (2000), pp. 491–503.
37. "Top 10 Best Corporate Alumni Networks," *Enterprise Alumni*, March 25, 2020, https://enterprisealumni; C. Farrell, "Hiring Older Workers Is Suddenly in Season," *Forbes*, November 17, 2017, https://www.forbes.com.
38. S. Lucas, "Greg Flynn Owns 1,245 Restaurants and Makes $2 Billion a Year. Here's How He Did It," *Entrepreneur*, May 28, 2019, https://www.entrepreneur.com; T. Lytle, "Managing Employees by the Hour," *HR Magazine*, April 2016, https://www.shrm.org.
39. Council Post (by Emily Nhaissi), "Using Social Media for Recruitment and Retention," *Forbes*, https://www.forbes.com, accessed March 31, 2020.
40. Robert Half, "The Benefits of Using Social Media for Recruiting Employees," https://www.roberthalf.com, accessed March 31, 2020.
41. N. Parsi, "Diversity and Innovation," *HR Magazine*, February 2017, pp. 39–45.
42. EastBay Works, "What Is EastBay Works?" http://www.eastbayworks.com, accessed March 31, 2020.
43. "Our People: Catherine A. Lepard," https://www.heidrick.com, accessed March 31, 2020; L. Zumbach, "Executive Recruiter Helps Retailers Keep Up with Industry Changes," *Chicago Tribune*, March 25, 2016, http://www.chicagotribune.com.
44. Frank Kalman, "Connect the Skills," *Chief Learning Officer*, March 2015, pp. 26–29, 51.
45. Hao Zhao and Robert C. Liden, "Internship: A Recruitment and Selection Perspective," *Journal of Applied Psychology* 96 (2011), pp. 221–229.
46. Brittney Oliver, "Top Companies Are Missing Talent from Historically Black Colleges," *Fast Company*, February 27, 2018, https://www.fastcompany.com.
47. "About Us," https://eightfold.ai/about, accessed April 2, 2020; L. Columbus, "Remote Recruiting in a Post COVID-19 World," *Forbes*, March 30, 2020, https://www.forbes.com; N. Scheiber, "A.I. as Talent Scout: Unorthodox Hires, and Maybe Lower Pay," *The New York Times*, December 6, 2018, https://www.nytimes.com.
48. R. Hawk, *The Recruitment Function* (New York: American Management Association, 1967).
49. Society for Human Resource Management, *Customized Talent Acquisition Benchmarking Report*, https://www.shrm.org, accessed April 2, 2020.
50. Stephan et al., "Talent Acquisition."
51. C. K. Stevens, "Effects of Preinterview Beliefs on Applicants' Reactions to Campus Interviews," *Academy of Management Journal* 40 (1997), pp. 947–966.
52. C. Collins, "The Interactive Effects of Recruitment Practices and Product Awareness on Job Seekers' Employer Knowledge and Application Behaviors," *Journal of Applied Psychology* 92 (2007), pp. 180–190.
53. M. S. Taylor and T. J. Bergman, "Organizational Recruitment Activities and Applicants' Reactions at Different Stages of the Recruitment Process," *Personnel Psychology* 40 (1984), pp. 261–285; C. D. Fisher, D. R. Ilgen, and W. D. Hoyer, "Source Credibility, Information Favorability, and Job Offer Acceptance," *Academy of Management Journal* 22 (1979), pp. 94–103.
54. L. M. Graves and G. N. Powell, "The Effect of Sex Similarity on Recruiters' Evaluation of Actual Applicants: A Test of the Similarity-Attraction Paradigm," *Personnel Psychology* 48 (1995), pp. 85–98.
55. R. D. Tretz and T. A. Judge, "Realistic Job Previews: A Test of the Adverse Self-Selection Hypothesis," *Journal of Applied Psychology* 83 (1998), pp. 330–337.
56. P. Hom, R. W. Griffeth, L. E. Palich, and J. S. Bracker, "An Exploratory Investigation into Theoretical Mechanisms Underlying Realistic Job Previews," *Personnel Psychology* 51 (1998), pp. 421–451.
57. G. M. McEvoy and W. F. Cascio, "Strategies for Reducing Employee Turnover: A Meta-Analysis," *Journal of Applied Psychology* 70 (1985), pp. 342–353; S. L. Premack and J. P. Wanous, "A Meta-Analysis of Realistic Job Preview Experiments," *Journal of Applied Psychology* 70 (1985), pp. 706–719.
58. D. R. Earnest, D. G. Allen, and R. S. Landis, "Mechanisms Linking Realistic Job Previews with Turnover: A Meta-Analytic Path Analysis," *Personnel Psychology* 64 (2011), pp. 865–897.
59. Capelli, "Your Approach to Hiring Is All Wrong."
60. S. L. Rynes, R. D. Bretz, and B. Gerhart, "The Importance of Recruitment in Job Choice: A Different Way of Looking," *Personnel Psychology* 44 (1991), pp. 487–522.

6 Selecting Employees and Placing Them in Jobs

Introduction

At Kraft Heinz's Amsterdam offices, Pieter Schalkwijk, the head of talent acquisition for Europe, the Middle East, and Africa, is responsible for hiring new employees. Each year, the need includes as many as 50 recent university graduates filling trainee positions. Thousands of applications pour in for these slots, and Schalkwijk needs a way to fill them efficiently with the people most likely to succeed at Kraft.

Recently, Schalkwijk brought video games into the trainee selection process. The games, developed by a company called Pymetrics, test several different traits thought to be associated with emotional intelligence and an appropriate level of risk taking. One game measures risk tolerance by having players tap to inflate balloons, accumulating points until they cash in or burst the balloon, losing everything. Another game measures concentration and memory by posting strings of numbers for players to memorize. Still others test players' levels of trust and generosity with team members. Scores are measured against previously measured scores of 250 top-performing Kraft employees, to identify candidates possessing similar traits.

Schalkwijk hopes that these criteria will be more relevant than some of the simpler measures used in the past, such as business degrees from a limited set of top-tier schools. However, he does not use the same method to fill all positions. For positions requiring more experience, Schalkwijk is concerned that video games would be awkward for older generations, and he doesn't want to discriminate against these workers.

The new approach to employee selection has already diversified the hiring to bring in people from more varied backgrounds, including engineering as well as business majors. But the real test of the selection method will come after the new hires have been onboard for a few years. Data from performance reviews will help Kraft determine whether these employees outperform previous hires.[1]

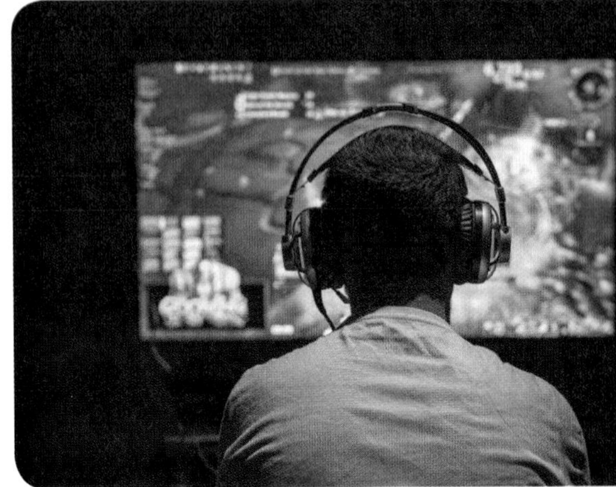

Kraft Heinz recently brought video games into the trainee selection process, which test different traits associated with emotional intelligence and an appropriate level of risk taking.

sezer66/Shutterstock

What Do I Need to Know?

After reading this chapter, you should be able to:

LO 6-1 Identify the elements of the selection process.

LO 6-2 Define ways to measure the success of a selection method.

LO 6-3 Summarize the government's requirements for employee selection.

LO 6-4 Compare the common methods used for selecting human resources.

LO 6-5 Describe major types of employment tests.

LO 6-6 Discuss how to conduct effective interviews.

LO 6-7 Explain how employers carry out the process of making a selection decision.

Hiring decisions are about finding the people who will be a good fit with the job and the organization. Any organization that appreciates the competitive edge provided by good people must take the utmost care in choosing its members. The organization's decisions about selecting personnel are central to its ability to survive, adapt, and grow. Selection decisions become especially critical when organizations face tight labor markets or must compete for talent with other organizations in the same industry. If a competitor keeps getting the best applicants, the remaining companies must make do with who is left.

This chapter will familiarize you with ways to minimize errors in employee selection and placement. The chapter starts by describing the selection process and how to evaluate possible methods for carrying out that process. It then takes an in-depth look at the most widely used methods: applications and résumés, employment tests, and interviews. The chapter ends by describing the process by which organizations arrive at a final selection decision.

Selection Process

LO 6-1 Identify the elements of the selection process.

Through **personnel selection,** organizations make decisions about who will or will not be invited to join the organization. Selection begins with the candidates identified through recruitment and with attempts to reduce their number to the individuals best qualified to perform the available jobs. At the end of the process, the selected individuals are placed in jobs with the organization.

Personnel Selection
The process through which organizations make decisions about who will or will not be invited to join the organization.

The process of selecting employees varies considerably from organization to organization and from job to job. At most organizations, however, selection includes the steps illustrated in Figure 6.1. First, a human resource professional reviews the applications received to see which meet the basic requirements of the job. For candidates who meet the basic requirements, the organization administers tests and reviews work samples to rate the candidates' abilities. Those with the best abilities are invited to the organization for one or more interviews. Supervisors and team members often are involved in this stage of the process. By this point, the decision makers are beginning to form opinions about which candidates are most desirable. For the top few candidates, the organization should check references and conduct background checks to verify that the organization's information is correct. Then supervisors, teams, and other decision makers select a person to receive a job offer. In some cases, the candidate may negotiate with the organization regarding salary, benefits, and the like. If the candidate accepts the job, the organization places him or her in that job.

Nowadays, the ease of applying online has made this process overwhelming for many recruiters. A simple job posting online could generate hundreds of résumés in one day. Many employers are coping by automating much of the selection process with an **applicant-tracking system.** Typically, the system starts by receiving the data provided in electronically submitted résumés and matching it against the company's selection criteria.

Applicant-Tracking System
Automated approach to selection process that reviews electronically submitted résumés, matches them against company selection criteria, and allows hiring managers to track job candidate information and hiring outcomes.

FIGURE 6.1 Steps in the Selection Process

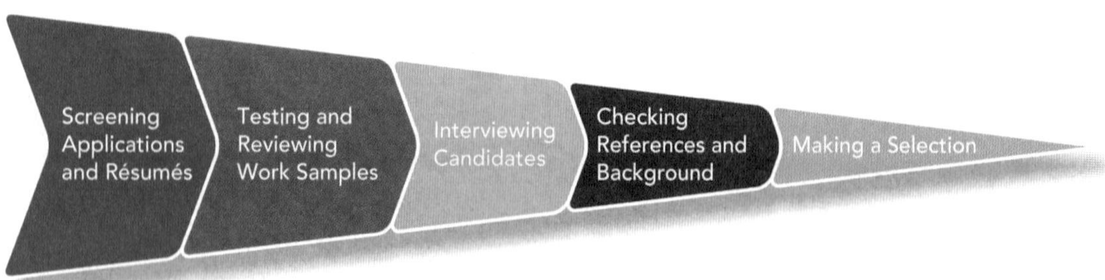

For employees who work directly with customers, companies should create a selection process that measures employees' interest in customers and their ability to interact in a positive way. © Image Source/age fotostock

The system might find that half the résumés lack necessary keywords, so it sends those applicants a polite "no thank you" e-mail. The applications that survive the automated screening go to a hiring manager, often ranked by how well they meet preset criteria. The manager reviews these applications and selects candidates to contact for a telephone or face-to-face interview and/or testing. For an example of a company that is pleased with a high-tech selection approach, see the "Best Practices" box.

As with any automation, an applicant-tracking system is only as good as the process it automates. A system that just matches a few keywords between résumés and job descriptions might screen out high-potential employees who didn't use exactly the same term. The problem is even worse if the employer didn't bother to carefully analyze which keywords are really associated with success on the job. However, a well-designed system has many attractive features that provide the ability to initiate background checks; store past applicants in the system who might be a good fit for a future position; maintain all job candidate documents in one place (e.g., résumés, cover letters, and additional information); allow the hiring manager, HR, and the job candidate to coordinate interview schedules; and allow hiring managers to review and store their comments about each candidate. The system may also support decision making by measuring the performance of the hiring process—for example, time to hire and steps in the process where bottlenecks most often occur. CVS Health's applicant-tracking system includes a screening assessment in which applicants try out a job simulation that demonstrates their skills and gives them a preview of the job. Comparing assessment data with performance data enables the company to see that it is hiring better-performing employees.[2]

How does an organization decide which of these steps to use and in what order? Some organizations simply repeat a selection process that is familiar. If members of the organization underwent job interviews, *they* conduct job interviews, asking familiar questions. However, what organizations *should* do is to create a selection process in support of its job descriptions. In Chapter 3 we explained that a job description identifies the knowledge, skills, abilities, and other characteristics (KSAOs) required for successfully performing a job. The selection process should be set up in such a way that it lets the organization identify people who have the necessary KSAOs. This not only helps the company choose the right people, it offers a basis to build positive experiences for job hunters. According to surveys, job candidates want to understand what is happening during the selection process, but few organizations are responsive to that desire.[3] Those who have a great process and communicate about it should gain an edge in the market for talent.

A strategic approach to selection requires ways to measure the effectiveness of selection tools. From science, we have basic standards for this:

- The method provides *reliable* information.
- The method provides *valid* information.
- The information can be *generalized* to apply to the candidates.
- The method offers *high utility* (practical value).
- The selection criteria are *legal.*

LO 6-2 Define ways to measure the success of a selection method.

Reliability

Reliability
The extent to which a measurement is free from random error.

The **reliability** of a type of measurement indicates how free that measurement is from random error.[4] A reliable measurement therefore generates consistent results. Assuming that a person's intelligence is fairly stable over time, a reliable test of intelligence should generate consistent

Best Practices

Unilever Uses AI to Improve Selection Results

Unilever, with 155,000 employees worldwide, needed a way to compete for talent, find a more diverse group of qualified people, and do so more efficiently. The consumer products company (its brands include Axe and Dove) achieved all of those goals by delegating more of the day-to-day work to computer software. It brought in two digital-HR companies, Pymetrics and HireVue, to help it automate the initial steps, so that job candidates coming to visit the company would already be very likely to succeed.

The company connects with candidates on major jobs sites and social media, inviting them to apply online. Those who are interested reply by submitting a link to their LinkedIn profile. Then they generate a skills profile by playing a dozen online games for about 20 minutes. AI software analyzes their scores to arrive at a profile of several traits, including memory, tolerance for risk, and ability to focus. The software looks for a link between those traits and types of jobs available at Unilever. The relationship is based on scores in a database of the results of high-performing Unilever employees, who had been asked to take the test. Candidates learn their results immediately after taking the test, and recruiters see the results along with the benchmarks established for the company.

When the system finds a match between a candidate's profile and a job category, it invites them to participate in an online interview, at their convenience, using the camera on their computer or mobile device. The interview involves recording the answers to a set of prepared questions, rather than speaking live to another person. The system uses AI to analyze their words, tone, and body language. Based on the results, the system delivers to the hiring manager a list of the candidates who scored highest. These candidates receive invitations to visit a Unilever office for a preview of what the job is like. By the end of the day, they know whether they have a job offer.

Unilever has rated the new system a win by several measures. One is the increase in the pool of applicants. The number of job applications has soared, and most applicants complete the initial screening games. In some cases, candidates who aren't a good fit for the job they had in mind turn out to be a good fit for another job they had not considered. Another advantage is efficiency. The average time from application to hire fell from four months to four weeks. Recruiters are spending far less time reviewing applications and can focus on people who already are known to have potential. The diversity of applicants is greater, both ethnically and in terms of colleges attended. The percentage of candidates who make it to the interview stage and the percentage of offers accepted both increased as well.

Questions

1. What aspects of Unilever's selection process do you think would contribute to cost savings?
2. How did the introduction of artificial intelligence add to the utility of this process?

Sources: "About Unilever," https://www.unilever.com, accessed April 3, 2020; "Unilever Finds Top Talent Faster with HireVue Assessments," https://www.hirevue.com, accessed April 3, 2020; Rebecca Heilweil, "Artificial Intelligence Will Help Determine If You Get Your Next Job," *Vox,* December 12, 2019, https://www.vox.com; Richard Feloni, "Consumer-Goods Giant Unilever Has Been Hiring Employees Using Brain Games and Artificial Intelligence—and It's a Huge Success," *Business Insider,* June 28, 2017, http://www.businessinsider.com.

results if the same person takes the test several times. Organizations that construct intelligence tests should be able to provide (and explain) information about the reliability of their tests.

Usually this information involves statistics such as *correlation coefficients.* These statistics measure the degree to which two sets of numbers are related. A higher correlation coefficient signifies a stronger relationship. At one extreme, a correlation coefficient of 1.0 means a perfect positive relationship—as one set of numbers goes up, so does the other. If you took the same vision test three days in a row, those scores would probably have nearly a perfect correlation. At the other extreme, a correlation of −1.0 means a perfect negative correlation—when one set of numbers goes up, the other goes down. In the middle, a correlation of 0 means there is no correlation at all. For example, the correlation (or relationship) between weather and intelligence would be at or near 0. A reliable test would be one for which scores by the same person (or people with similar attributes) have a correlation close to 1.0.

Reliability answers one important question—whether you are measuring something accurately—but ignores another question that is as important: Are you measuring something that matters? Think about how this applies at companies that try to identify workers who will fit in well with the company's culture. Often these companies depend on teamwork, social networking, and creativity, and they expect those behaviors to prevail when workers get along well and share similar values. However, efforts to seek cultural fit often translate into favoring the most likable candidates—for example, those who make eye contact, display an interest in others, and tell engaging stories.[5] This approach not only raises questions of reliability—for example, whether making eye contact in a job interview is a reliable measure of a person's behavior on the job over time—it also raises questions about the extent to which being likable really translates into effective teamwork and creative problem solving. Perhaps the prickly member of the team will be the one who opens up a new and valuable line of thinking. As in this example, employers need to consider both the reliability of their selection methods and their validity, defined next.

Validity

Validity
The extent to which performance on a measure (such as a test score) is related to what the measure is designed to assess (such as job performance).

For a selection measure, **validity** describes the extent to which performance on the measure (such as a test score) is related to what the measure is designed to assess (such as job performance). Although we can reliably measure such characteristics as weight and height, these measurements do not provide much information about how a person will perform most kinds of jobs. Thus, for most jobs height and weight provide little validity as selection criteria. One way to determine whether a measure is valid is to compare many people's scores on that measure with their job performance. For example, suppose people who score above 60 words per minute on a keyboarding test consistently get high marks for their performance in data-entry jobs. This observation suggests the keyboarding test is valid for predicting success in that job.

As with reliability, information about the validity of selection methods often uses correlation coefficients. A strong positive (or negative) correlation between a measure and job performance means the measure should be a valid basis for selecting (or rejecting) a candidate. This information is important not only because it helps organizations identify the best employees, but also because organizations can demonstrate fair employment practices by showing that their selection process is valid. The federal government's *Uniform Guidelines on Employee Selection Procedures* accept three ways of measuring validity: criterion-related, content, and construct validity.

Criterion-Related Validity
A measure of validity based on showing a substantial correlation between test scores and job performance scores.

Criterion-Related Validity The first category, **criterion-related validity,** is a measure of validity based on showing a substantial correlation between test scores and job performance scores. In the example in Figure 6.2, a company compares two measures—an intelligence test and college grade point average—with performance as sales representative. In the left graph, which shows the relationship between the intelligence test scores and job performance, the points for the 20 sales reps fall near the 45-degree line. The correlation coefficient is near .90 (for a perfect 1.0, all the points would be on the 45-degree line). In the graph at the right, the points are scattered more widely. The correlation between college GPA and sales reps' performance is much lower. In this hypothetical example, the intelligence test is more valid than GPA for predicting success at this job.

Predictive Validation
Research that uses the test scores of all applicants and looks for a relationship between the scores and the future performance of the applicants who were hired.

Two kinds of research are possible for arriving at criterion-related validity:

1. **Predictive validation**—This research uses the test scores of all applicants and looks for a relationship between the scores and the future performance of those who were hired. The researcher administers the tests, waits a set period of time, and then measures the performance of the applicants who were hired.

FIGURE 6.2 Criterion-Related Measurements of a Student's Aptitude

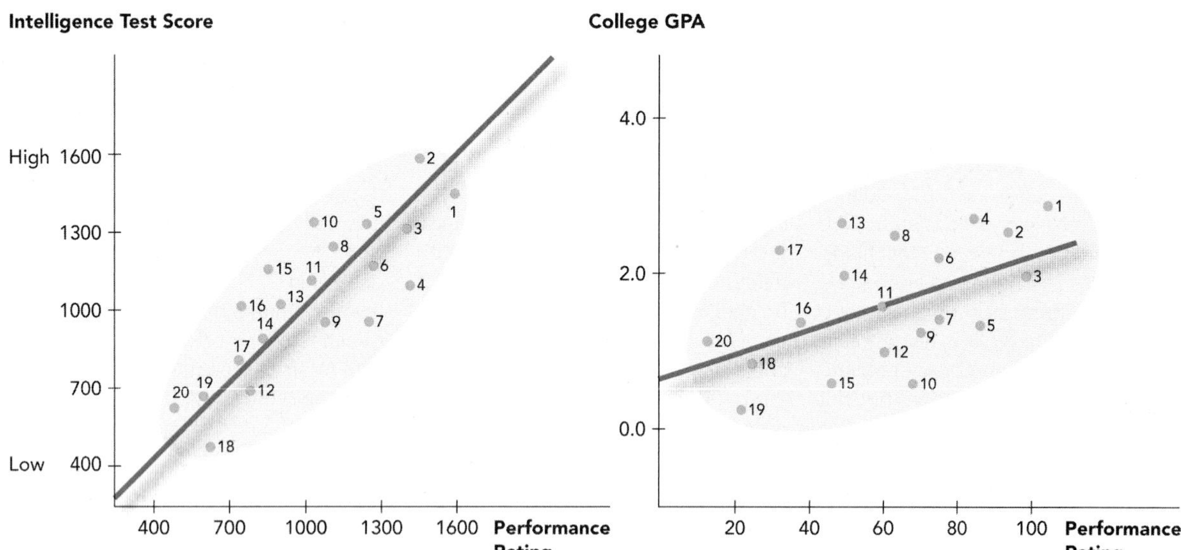

2. **Concurrent validation**–This type of research administers a test to people who currently hold a job, then compares their scores to existing measures of job performance. If the people who score highest on the test also do better on the job, the test is assumed to be valid.

Concurrent Validation
Research that consists of administering a test to people who currently hold a job, then comparing their scores to existing measures of job performance.

Predictive validation is more time consuming and difficult, but it is the best measure of validity. Job applicants tend to be more motivated to do well on the tests, and their performance on the tests is not influenced by their firsthand experience with the job. Also, the group studied is more likely to include people who perform poorly on the test–a necessary ingredient to accurately validate a test.[6]

Content and Construct Validity Another way to show validity is to establish **content validity**–that is, consistency between the test items or problems and the kinds of situations or problems that occur on the job. A test that is "content valid" exposes the job applicant to situations that are likely to occur on the job. It tests whether the applicant has the knowledge, skills, or ability to handle such situations. In the case of a company using tests for selecting a construction superintendent, tests with content validity included organizing a random list of subcontractors into the order they would appear at a construction site and entering a shed to identify construction errors that had intentionally been made for testing purposes.[7] More commonly today, employers use computer role-playing games in which software is created to include situations that occur on the job. Such games measure relevant skills by giving candidates tasks like the ones that would be part of the job.[8]

Content Validity
Consistency between the test items or problems and the kinds of situations or problems that occur on the job.

The usual basis for deciding that a test has content validity is through expert judgment. Experts can rate the test items according to whether they mirror essential functions of the job. Because establishing validity is based on the experts' subjective judgments, content validity is most suitable for measuring behavior that is concrete and observable.

For tests that measure abstract qualities such as intelligence or leadership ability, establishment of validity may have to rely on **construct validity.** This involves establishing that tests really do measure intelligence, leadership ability, or other such "constructs," as well as

Construct Validity
Consistency between a high score on a test and high level of a construct such as intelligence or leadership ability, as well as between mastery of this construct and successful performance of the job.

HR How To

Measuring Cultural Fit

An organization's culture can play a valuable role in directing and motivating employees, so it makes sense that managers would want to hire people who embrace that culture and behave in ways consistent with it. Until recently, however, most hiring for "cultural fit" involved managers having an impression or gut feeling that a candidate fits in. This tends to result in the selection of people who are similar to the manager—but not necessarily similar in ways that avoid discrimination and are associated with job performance.

An important first step is to identify measurable ways of defining the important features of the culture—typically, core values such as agility and integrity. The usual approach has been to conduct surveys asking employees about their values. Then the selection process uses the same tools to measure candidates' values. When this works, the company hires those who share the same core values as the organization espouses. However, individuals may not be self-reflective enough to know, or they may give the answers they think they are supposed to give, whether or not these are accurate.

Today's ability to analyze large quantities of data is helping organizations measure cultural fit in more meaningful ways. One approach uses an element of artificial intelligence known as natural-language processing, which looks at written evidence such as internal e-mails or chat messages, identifying word choices and other patterns that characterize various teams and team members. Natural-language processing can look for particular words, as well as synonyms and antonyms, to see what values are being advocated and observed in the context being studied. In addition to internal communications, the analysis can include anonymous employee reviews of the company on websites like Glassdoor, again to find patterns. Software can find correlations between patterns of communication and business performance to identify which patterns or values are associated with success. Then the selection process can seek these values in candidates.

Experience with this type of analysis is helping managers fine-tune the ways they seek cultural fit. For example, one lesson is that "fit" may not be a static measure. Some employees are culturally *adaptable*, meaning they adjust their language and behavior according to the team they are part of. A candidate who is culturally adaptable may become a good fit, even if a test shows some differences. Finding alignment on a few key values but diversity on other qualities may bring in employees with fresh perspectives without compromising the organization's culture.

Questions

1. Why is cultural fit important to employers?
2. Briefly, how can a company with a culture of collaboration and integrity go about finding employees who fit this type of culture?

Sources: Matthew Corritore, Amir Goldberg, and Sameer B. Srivastava, "The New Analytics of Culture," *Harvard Business Review*, January–February 2020, pp. 77–83; Joeri Hofmans and Timothy A. Judge, "Hiring for Culture Fit Doesn't Have to Undermine Diversity," *Harvard Business Review*, September 18, 2019, https://hbr.org; Donald Sull, Charles Sull, and Andrew Chamberlain, "Measuring Culture in Leading Companies," *MIT Sloan Management Review*, June 24, 2019, https://sloanreview.mit.edu.

showing that mastery of this construct is associated with successful performance of the job. For example, if you could show that a test measures something called "mechanical ability," and that people with superior mechanical ability perform well as assemblers, then the test has construct validity for the assembler job. Tests that measure a construct usually measure a combination of behaviors thought to be associated with the construct. The "HR How To" box provides guidance on measuring one construct, "cultural fit."

Ability to Generalize

Generalizable
Valid in other contexts beyond the context in which the selection method was developed.

Along with validity in general, we need to know whether a selection method is valid in the context in which the organization wants to use it. A **generalizable** method applies not only to the conditions in which the method was originally developed–job, organization, people, time period, and so on. It also applies to other organizations, jobs, applicants, and so on. In other words, is a selection method that was valid in one context also valid in other contexts?

Researchers have studied whether tests of intelligence and thinking skills (called *cognitive ability*) can be generalized. The research has supported the idea that these tests are generalizable across many jobs. However, as jobs become more complex, the validity of many of these tests increases. In other words, they are most valid for complex jobs.[9]

Practical Value

Not only should selection methods such as tests and interview responses accurately predict how well individuals will perform, but they should also produce information that actually benefits the organization. Being valid, reliable, and generalizable adds value to a method. Another consideration is the cost of using the selection method. Selection procedures such as testing and interviewing cost money. They should cost significantly less than the benefits of hiring the new employees. Methods that provide economic value greater than the cost of using them are said to have **utility.**

Utility
The extent to which something provides economic value greater than its cost.

The choice of a selection method may differ according to the job being filled. If the job involves providing a product or service of high value to the organization, it is worthwhile to spend more to find a top performer. At a company where salespeople are responsible for closing million-dollar deals, the company will be willing to invest more in selection decisions. At a fast-food restaurant, such an investment will not be worthwhile; the employer will prefer faster, simpler ways to select workers who ring up orders, prepare food, and keep the facility clean.

Legal Standards for Selection

LO 6-3 Summarize the government's requirements for employee selection.

As we discussed in Chapter 3, the U.S. government imposes legal limits on selection decisions. The government requires that the selection process be conducted in a way that avoids discrimination and provides access to employees with disabilities. The laws described in Chapter 3 have many applications to the selection process:

- The Civil Rights Act of 1991 and the Age Discrimination in Employment Act of 1967 place requirements on the choice of selection methods. An employer that uses a neutral-appearing selection method that damages a protected group is obligated to show that there is a business necessity for using that method. For example, if an organization uses a test that eliminates many candidates from minority groups, the organization must show that the test is valid for predicting performance of that job. In this context, good performance does not include "customer preference" or "brand image" as a justification for adverse impact. As we saw in Chapter 3, the courts may view a discriminatory pattern of hiring as evidence that the company is engaged in illegal discrimination. This can be a risk with using social media to screen candidates, as described in the "HRM Social" box.
- The Civil Rights Act of 1991 also prohibits preferential treatment in favor of minority groups. In the case of an organization using a test that tends to reject members of minority groups, the organization may not simply adjust minority applicants' scores upward. Such practices can create an environment that is demotivating to all employees and can lead to government sanctions. In Buffalo, New York, minority firefighters scored poorly on civil service exams, so the city let its list of candidates for promotion expire rather than promote only white firefighters. White firefighters who had been on the list filed a lawsuit claiming they were discriminated against, and they won back pay, benefits, and damages for emotional distress. Their attorney said the situation had created morale problems among firefighters who saw the discriminatory treatment as unfair.[10]

Applicant Screening with Social Media Poses Risks

Many employers use social media as a way to get information about job candidates, but the nature of these sites raises some concerns about discrimination. Social media use typically starts with the creation of a user profile, and this may contain information about categories that are protected under antidiscrimination laws. For example, users might tell about their families, religious practices, pregnancy status, or disabilities. They might indirectly suggest these by identifying interests or describing vacations. Profile pictures, too, may suggest that the person is a particular race or age.

Ideally, decision makers would ignore information unrelated to job performance, but this ideal overlooks the human tendency to have preferences and biases. Even well-meaning employers who use social media as a screening tool may unconsciously prefer applicants from certain groups. One way to address this is to try to make the social media research more valid by establishing job-related criteria to search for. If searching a social-media site is unlikely to provide information about those criteria, then perhaps it is not a valid enough way to check a candidate's qualifications.

Another concern is that even if information is valid, it still may not be accurate. Information about a user comes from the user and his or her network. Users tend to want to present a certain image of themselves. Members of a network may have a very wide variety of motives, from encouragement and praise to disparagement and misguided attempts at humor. Therefore, to the extent the employer thinks information is relevant, it is important to confirm its accuracy with another source. This is necessary for accuracy and fair treatment of the applicant; it also could guard against discrimination resulting from, say, different groups' norms about what is appropriate to post.

Some companies minimize the risk of discrimination by hiring third parties to check social media—for example, as part of a background check. Some vendors will review public information from social media and provide a report that specifically excludes information an employer may not legally consider. In these situations, employers should ensure that the information they request and review is truly related to job requirements, and they should monitor hiring to avoid any resulting pattern of discrimination.

Questions

1. Think about your own use of social media. What kinds of information, if any, in your profile or posts would be relevant to your job qualifications?
2. Knowing that many potential employers use social media and Internet searches as part of their recruiting and background checks, what might you like them to find about you online?

Sources: Tylar Suckau, "Social Media Screening by Employers," *Smith & Carson*, https://www.smithcarson.com, accessed April 3, 2020; Saige Driver, "Keep It Clean: Social Media Screenings Gain in Popularity," *Business News Daily*, March 23, 2020, https://www.businessnewsdaily.com; "To Stalk or Not to Stalk . . . That Is the Question—Using Social Media for Applicant Review," *National Law Review*, October 21, 2019, https://www.natlawreview.com; Jennifer Spencer, "3 Ways Companies Are Analyzing Social Media to Make Hiring Decisions," *Entrepreneur*, November 14, 2018, https://www.entrepreneur.com; Mile Zivkovic, "The Dos and Don'ts of Social Media Screening in the Hiring Process," *Toggl Hire*, November 13, 2018, https://toggl.com.

- Equal employment opportunity laws affect the kinds of information an organization may gather on application forms and in interviews. As summarized in Table 6.1, the organization may not ask questions that gather information about a person's protected status, even indirectly. For example, requesting the dates a person attended high school and college could indirectly gather information about an applicant's age.
- The Americans with Disabilities Act (ADA) of 1991 requires employers to make "reasonable accommodation" to disabled individuals and restricts many kinds of questions during the selection process. Under the ADA, preemployment questions may not investigate disabilities, but must focus on job performance. An interviewer may ask, "Can you meet the attendance requirements for this job?" but may not ask, "How many days did you miss work last year because you were sick?" Also, the employer may not, in making hiring decisions, use employment physical exams or other tests that could reveal a psychological or physical disability.

TABLE 6.1

Permissible and Impermissible Questions for Applications and Interviews

PERMISSIBLE QUESTIONS	IMPERMISSIBLE QUESTIONS
What is your full name? Have you ever worked under a different name? [Ask all candidates.]	What was your maiden name? What's the nationality of your name?
If you are hired, can you show proof of age (to meet a legal age requirement)?	How old are you? How would you feel about working for someone younger than you?
Will you need any reasonable accommodation for this hiring process? Are you able to perform this job, with or without reasonable accommodation?	What is your height? Your weight? Do you have any disabilities? Have you been seriously ill? Please provide a photograph of yourself.
Are you fluent in [language needed for job]? [Statement that employment is subject to verification of applicant's identity and employment eligibility under immigration laws]	What is your ancestry? Are you a citizen of the United States? Where were you born? How did you learn to speak that language?
What schools have you attended? What degrees have you earned? What was your major?	Is that school affiliated with [religious group]? When did you attend high school? [to learn applicant's age]
Can you meet the requirements of the work schedule? [Ask all candidates.]	What is your religion? What religious holidays do you observe?
Can you meet the job requirement to travel overnight several times a month?	What is your marital status? Would you like to be addressed as Mrs., Ms., or Miss? Do you have any children?
Have you ever been convicted of a crime?	Have you ever been arrested?
What organizations or groups do you belong to that you consider relevant to being able to perform this job?	What organizations or groups do you belong to?

Note: This table provides examples and is not intended as a complete listing of permissible and impermissible questions. The examples are based on federal requirements; state laws vary and may affect these examples.

Sources: Equal Employment Opportunity Commission, "Prohibited Employment Policies/Practices, http://www.eeoc.gov, accessed April 3, 2020; "Appendix E: Guide to Legally Permissible Interview Questions and Discussions," http://hr.fas.harvard.edu, accessed April 3, 2020; Nikoletta Bika, "6 Illegal Interview Questions Not to Ask—and Legal Alternatives," *Workable,* https://resources.workable.com, accessed April 3, 2020; "Guidelines on Interview and Employment Application Questions," *Society for Human Resource Management,* May 2, 2018, https://www.shrm.org.

Along with equal employment opportunity, organizations must be concerned about candidates' privacy rights. The information gathered during the selection process may include information that employees consider confidential. Confidentiality is a particular concern when job applicants provide information online. Employers should collect data only at secure websites, and they may have to be understanding if online applicants are reluctant to provide data such as Social Security numbers, which hackers could use for identity theft. For some jobs, background checks look at candidates' credit history. The Fair Credit Reporting Act requires employers to obtain a candidate's consent before using a third party to check the candidate's credit history or references. If the employer then decides to take an adverse action (such as not hiring) based on the report, the employer must give the applicant a copy of the report and summary of the applicant's rights *before* taking the action.

Immigration Reform and Control Act of 1986
Federal law requiring employers to verify and maintain records on applicants' legal rights to work in the United States.

Another legal requirement is that employers hiring people to work in the United States must ensure that anyone they hire is eligible for employment in this country. Under the **Immigration Reform and Control Act of 1986,** employers must verify and maintain records on the legal rights of applicants to work in the United States. They do this by having applicants fill out the U.S. Citizenship and Immigration Services' Form I-9 and present documents showing their identity and eligibility to work. Employers must complete their portion of each Form I-9, check the applicant's documents, and retain the Form I-9. Immigration and Customs Enforcement (ICE) is authorized to check compliance by examining records, and companies may be fined for violations, so it is important to check each form for accuracy and completeness, including proper signatures.[11] Employers may (and in some cases must) also use the federal government's electronic system for verifying eligibility to work. To use the system, called E-Verify, employers go online (www.uscis.gov/e-verify) to submit information on the applicant's I-9. The system compares it against information in databases of the Social Security Administration and Department of Homeland Security. It then notifies the employer of the candidate's eligibility, usually within 24 hours. At the same time, assuming a person is eligible to work under the Immigration Reform and Control Act, the law prohibits the employer from discriminating against the person on the basis of national origin or citizenship status.

Finally, state laws also may affect employee selection. Many states (about half, as of this writing) have passed laws that forbid employers from asking applicants about their pay history. These *pay inquiry bans* arose out of concern that asking about pay was locking in the pattern of pay disparity that already exists between equally qualified men and women. Employers use pay history to gauge what level of pay a candidate would value. One possibly legal alternative is to ask candidates about their expectations for the position being considered. As this area of the law has been changing, HR departments should seek legal guidance about the current requirements in each state where the company hires employees.[12] Similarly, about half the states have laws forbidding employers from asking employees about their arrest and conviction records on job applications. The assumption is that such laws will prevent employers from disregarding otherwise-qualified workers before they have a chance to make a case for their worth as an employee. The evidence on the effectiveness of the laws is mixed[13] but regardless, HR professionals need to comply with this requirement—for example, postponing background checks until late in the hiring process.

An important principle of selection is to combine several sources of information about candidates, rather than relying solely on interviews or a single type of testing. The sources should be chosen carefully to relate to the characteristics identified in the job description. When organizations do this, they are increasing the validity of the decision criteria. They are more likely to make hiring decisions that are fair and unbiased. They also are more likely to choose the best candidates.

LO 6-4 Compare the common methods used for selecting human resources.

Job Applications and Résumés

Nearly all employers gather background information on applicants at the beginning of the selection process. The usual ways of gathering background information are by asking applicants to fill out application forms and provide résumés. Organizations also verify the information by checking references and conducting background checks.

Asking job candidates to provide background information is inexpensive. The organization can get reasonably accurate information by combining applications and résumés with background checks and well-designed interviews.[14] A major challenge with applications and résumés has been the sheer volume of work they generate for the organization. Human resource departments often are swamped with far more résumés than they can carefully review. However, employers are alleviating this problem by using software to analyze the contents and identify applicants who meet basic criteria for the position. They may set up their own analytics to screen applications they receive or use online job search tools such as Indeed, ZipRecruiter, and LinkedIn to identify applicants to invite.

Application Forms

Asking each applicant to fill out an employment application is a low-cost way to gather basic data from many applicants. It also ensures that the organization has certain standard categories of information, such as mailing address and employment history, from each. Figure 6.3 illustrates the format of an online application form.

Employers can buy general-purpose application templates or create their own forms to meet unique needs. Either way, employment applications include areas for applicants to provide several types of information:

- *Contact information*–The applicant's name, address, phone number, and e-mail address.
- *Work experience*–Companies the applicant worked for, job titles, and dates of employment.
- *Educational background*–High school, college, and universities attended and degree(s) awarded.
- *Applicant's signature*–Signature following a statement that the applicant has provided true and complete information.

The application form may include other areas for the applicant to provide additional information, such as specific work experiences, technical skills, or memberships in professional or trade groups. Online application forms often allow the applicant to provide details by uploading a résumé. The application form should not request information that could violate equal opportunity standards. In fact, some companies are hiring services that will submit applications and résumés that enable "blind auditions" by removing details such as names, which may unconsciously be used to consider candidates' gender, race, and so on. Typically, such efforts would be combined with matching applications to open positions based on skills, rather than, say, college attended.[15]

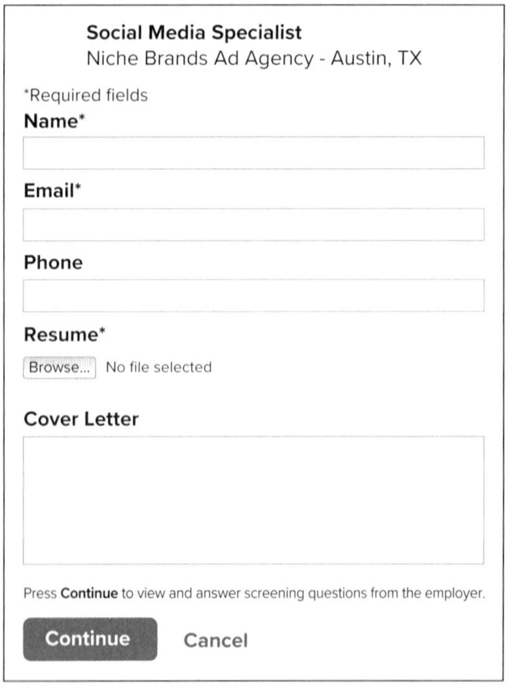

Social Media Specialist
Niche Brands Ad Agency - Austin, TX

*Required fields

Name*

Email*

Phone

Resume*

Browse... No file selected

Cover Letter

Press **Continue** to view and answer screening questions from the employer.

Continue Cancel

FIGURE 6.3
Sample Format for an Online Application Form

By reviewing application forms, HR personnel can identify which candidates meet minimum requirements for education and experience. They may be able to rank applicants—for example, giving applicants with 10 years of experience a higher ranking than applicants with 2 years of experience. In this way, the applications enable the organization to narrow the pool of candidates to a number it can afford to test and interview.

Résumés

The usual way that applicants introduce themselves to a potential employer is to submit a résumé. An obvious drawback of this information source is that applicants control the content of the information as well as the way it is presented. This type of information is therefore biased in favor of the applicant and (although this is unethical) may not even be accurate. However, résumés are an inexpensive way to gather information and provide employers with a starting point. Organizations typically use résumés as a basis for deciding which candidates to investigate further.

As with employment applications, an HR staff member or automated system reviews the résumés to identify candidates reporting essential skills and/or credentials. Because résumés are created by the job applicants (or the applicants have at least approved résumés created by someone else), they also may provide some insight into how candidates communicate and present themselves. Employers tend to decide against applicants whose résumés are unclear, sloppy, or full of mistakes. On the positive side, résumés may enable applicants to highlight accomplishments that might not show up in the format of an employment application. Review of résumés is most valid when the content of the résumés is evaluated in terms of the elements of a job description.

References

Application forms often ask that applicants provide the names of several references. Applicants provide the names and phone numbers of former employers or others who can vouch for their abilities and past job performance. In some situations, the applicant may provide letters of reference written by those people. It is then up to the organization to have someone contact the references to gather information or verify the accuracy of the information provided by the applicant.

As you might expect, references are not an unbiased source of information. Most applicants are careful to choose references who will say something positive. In addition, former employers and others may be afraid that if they express negative opinions, they will be sued. Equally problematic from the standpoint of getting useful information is that some candidates fail to list people who can speak about their work history. On occasion, references barely know the candidate or know him or her only in a social context.

An HR staff member typically reviews résumés from job applicants to identify candidates who meet basic job requirements, such as education and skills.
©Brand X Pictures/PunchStock

Usually the organization checks references after it has determined that the applicant is a finalist for the job. Contacting references for all applicants would be time consuming, and it does pose some burden on the people contacted. Part of that burden is the risk of giving information that is seen as too negative or too positive. If the person who is a reference gives negative information, there is a chance the candidate will claim *defamation,* meaning the person damaged the applicant's reputation by making statements that cannot be proved truthful.[16] At the other extreme, if the person gives a glowing statement about a candidate, and the new employer later learns of misdeeds such as sexual misconduct or workplace violence, the new employer might sue the former employer for misrepresentation.[17]

Because such situations occasionally arise, often with much publicity, people who give references tend to give as little information as possible. Most organizations have policies that the human resource department will handle all requests for references and that they will only verify employment dates and sometimes the employee's final salary. In organizations without such a policy, HR professionals should be careful–and train managers to be careful–to stick to observable, job-related behaviors and to avoid broad opinions that may be misinterpreted. In spite of these drawbacks of references, the risks of not learning about significant problems in a candidate's past outweigh the possibility of getting only a little information. Potential employers should check references. In general, the results of this effort will be most valid if the employer contacts many references (if possible, going beyond the list of names provided by the applicant), speaks with them directly by phone, and is as specific as possible about job-related skills and behaviors. In addition, telling the candidate about reference checks ahead of interviews may prompt greater honesty and some insightful disclosures about past work.[18]

Background Checks

A background check is a way to verify that applicants are as they represent themselves to be. Unfortunately, not all candidates are open and honest. In recent survey of HR professionals, more than half said they had caught at least one piece of false information on a résumé.[19] Note that this is *not* the same as saying half of résumés contain lies. However, it's also possible that some professionals saw but didn't recognize misinformation. With the problem arising at so many organizations, it's no wonder that hiring managers are interested in using social media to check employees' backgrounds (see "Did You Know?"). Along with establishing such practices, HR departments need to set standards for what to do if information from different sources is inconsistent. For example, the policy might be to disqualify the candidate immediately; other companies might give candidates a chance to explain the discrepancy.

Besides checking employment references, many employers also conduct criminal background checks. Some positions are so sensitive that the law may even limit hiring a person with certain kinds of convictions: for example, a person convicted of domestic violence may not hold positions that involve shipping firearms. The use of criminal background checks is a sensitive issue in the United States, however, especially since crackdowns on crime have resulted in many arrests. An additional concern is the disparate impact of considering criminal history. Men are far more likely to have a criminal record than women, and arrests and convictions are far more common among African Americans than whites. The Equal Employment Opportunity Commission has published guidelines that employers who check criminal histories do so consistently; that is, they should conduct the same type of background check for all candidates and apply the same standards for acting on the information. However, the EEOC also recommends that employers review the particular details of each situation, including the seriousness of each offense, the amount of time that has passed since conviction or completion of sentence, and the crime's relevance to the job the candidate is applying for. Target, for example, recently settled a complaint that it had policies for criminal background checks that were too broad and had the effect of discriminating against African Americans and Latinos.[20]

Another type of background check that has recently drawn greater scrutiny is the use of credit checks. Employers in certain situations, such as processes that involve handling money, are concerned that employees with credit problems will behave less honestly. To avoid hiring such employees, these employers conduct a background check. Also, some employers see good credit as an indicator that a person is responsible. But especially in times of high unemployment and many home foreclosures, people may see this type of investigation as unfair to

Did You Know?

Most Employers Use Social Media in Employee Selection

The use of social media by employers has been escalating, according to a recent survey by CareerBuilder, an online recruiting service. Seven in 10 respondents say they use social media to screen candidates.

What they are looking for varies. The most respondents (58%) said they are looking for information that supports their job qualifications. Fewer said they are checking whether applicants have an online professional persona (50%), want to see what others are saying about the candidate (34%), and want to see if they find a reason *not* to hire a candidate (22%).

Job candidates wanting to make a good impression should especially avoid posting any public images of themselves looking provocative or using alcohol or drugs. Comments that are demeaning to a race, religion, or gender also raise a red flag with potential employers.

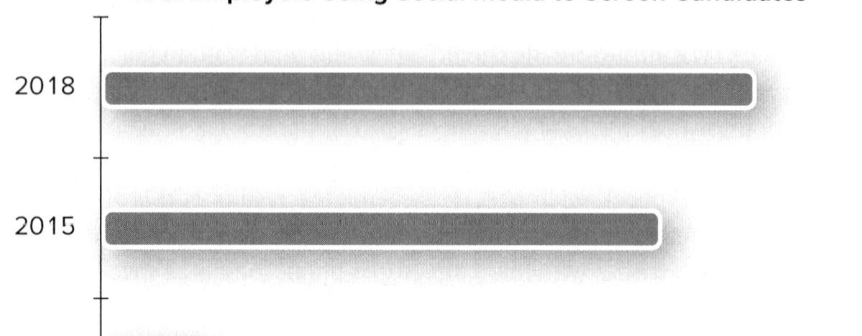

Question

In general, do you think the use of social media to screen job applicants will be an advantage or a disadvantage to members of your generation (age group)? Explain.

Sources: Saige Driver, "Keep It Clean: Social Media Screenings Gain in Popularity," *Business News Daily,* March 23, 2020, https://www.businessnewsdaily.com; Eileen Brown, "US Job Seekers Scrub Their Social Media Accounts to Get Success," *ZDNet,* October 9, 2019, https://www.zdnet.com; "More Than Half of Employers Have Found Content on Social Media That Caused Them NOT to Hire a Candidate, According to Recent CareerBuilder Survey," *PR Newswire,* August 9, 2018, https://www.prnewswire.com; Thomas Ahearn, "Millennials Expanding in Workforce Will Make Background Checks More Applicant Friendly in 2018," *ESR News Blog,* December 27, 2017, http://www.esrcheck.com.

people who are desperately trying to find work: the worse their financial situation, the harder the job search becomes. Under federal law, conducting a credit check is legal if the person consents, but some states ban or are considering bans on the practice.

LO 6-5 Describe major types of employment tests.

Employment Tests and Work Samples

When the organization has identified candidates whose applications or résumés indicate they meet basic requirements, the organization continues the selection process with this narrower pool of candidates. Often the next step is to gather objective data through one or more employment tests. These tests fall into two broad categories:

Aptitude Tests
Tests that assess how well a person can learn or acquire skills and abilities.

Achievement Tests
Tests that measure a person's existing knowledge and skills.

1. **Aptitude tests** assess how well a person can learn or acquire skills and abilities. In the realm of employment testing, the best-known aptitude test is the General Aptitude Test Battery (GATB), used by the U.S. Employment Service.
2. **Achievement tests** measure a person's existing knowledge and skills. For example, government agencies conduct civil service examinations to see whether applicants are qualified to perform certain jobs.

Before using any test, organizations should investigate the test's validity and reliability. Besides asking the testing service to provide this information, it is wise to consult more impartial sources of information, such as the ones identified in Table 6.2.

Physical Ability Tests

Physical strength and endurance play less of a role in the modern workplace than in the past, thanks to the use of automation and modern technology. Even so, many jobs still require certain physical abilities or psychomotor abilities (those connecting brain and body, as in the case of eye-hand coordination). When these abilities are essential to job performance or avoidance of injury, the organization may use physical ability tests. These evaluate one or more of the following areas of physical ability: muscular tension, muscular power, muscular endurance, cardiovascular endurance, flexibility, balance, and coordination.[21]

Although these tests can accurately predict success at certain kinds of jobs, they also tend to exclude women and people with disabilities. As a result, use of physical ability tests can make the organization vulnerable to charges of discrimination. It is therefore important to be certain that the abilities tested for really are essential to job performance or that the absence of these abilities really does create a safety hazard.

Cognitive Ability Tests

Although fewer jobs require muscle power today, brainpower is essential for most jobs. Organizations therefore benefit from people who have strong mental abilities. **Cognitive ability tests**–sometimes called "intelligence tests"–are designed to measure such mental abilities as verbal skills (skill in using written and spoken language), quantitative skills (skill in working with numbers), and reasoning ability (skill in thinking through the answer to a problem). Many jobs require all of these cognitive skills, so employers often get valid information from general tests. Many reliable tests are commercially available. The tests are especially valid for complex jobs and for those requiring adaptability in changing circumstances.[22] Employers should, however, be sure tests are administered with security measures to prevent cheating.

Cognitive Ability Tests
Tests designed to measure such mental abilities as verbal skills, quantitative skills, and reasoning ability.

The evidence of validity, coupled with the relatively low cost of these tests, makes them appealing, except for one problem: concern about legal issues. These concerns arise from a historical pattern in which use of the tests has had an adverse impact on African Americans. Some organizations responded with *race norming,* establishing different norms for hiring members of different racial groups. Race norming poses its own problems, not the least of which is the negative reputation it bestows on the minority employees selected using a lower standard. In addition, the Civil Rights Act of 1991 forbids the use of race or sex norming. As a result, organizations that want to base selection decisions on cognitive

TABLE 6.2
Sources of Information about Employment Tests

Source	Description
Mental Measurements Yearbook	Descriptions and reviews of tests that are commercially available
Principles for the Validation and Use of Personnel Selection Procedures (Society for Industrial and Organizational Psychology)	Guide to help organizations evaluate tests
Standards for Educational and Psychological Tests (American Psychological Association)	Description of standards for testing programs
Tests: A Comprehensive Reference for Assessments in Psychology, Education, and Business	Descriptions of thousands of tests
Test Critiques	Reviews of tests, written by professionals in the field

ability must make difficult decisions about how to measure this ability while avoiding legal problems. One possibility is a concept called *banding*. This concept treats a range of scores as being similar, as when an instructor gives the grade of A to any student whose average test score is at least 90. All applicants within a range of scores, or band, are treated as having the same score. Then within the set of "tied" scores, employers give preference to underrepresented groups. This is a controversial practice, and some have questioned its legality.[23]

Job Performance Tests and Work Samples

Many kinds of jobs require candidates who excel at performing specialized tasks, such as operating a certain machine, handling phone calls from customers, or designing advertising materials. To evaluate candidates for such jobs, the organization may administer tests of the necessary skills. Sometimes the candidates take tests that involve a sample of work, or they may show existing samples of their work. Testing may involve a difficult team project, a complex computer programming puzzle, or a game simulating the work environment. Examples of job performance tests include tests of keyboarding speed and *in-basket tests*. An in-basket test measures the ability to juggle a variety of demands, as in a manager's job. The candidate is presented with simulated memos and phone messages describing the kinds of problems that confront a person in the job. The candidate has to decide how to respond to these messages and in what order. Examples of jobs for which candidates provide work samples include graphic designers and writers.

Assessment Center
A wide variety of specific selection programs that use multiple selection methods to rate applicants or job incumbents on their management potential.

Tests for selecting managers may take the form of an **assessment center**—a wide variety of specific selection programs that use multiple selection methods to rate applicants or job incumbents on their management potential. An assessment center typically includes in-basket tests, tests of more general abilities, and personality tests. Combining several assessment methods increases the validity of this approach. Research suggests that the two most important skill types identified by an assessment center are problem-solving ability and interpersonal skills, but it may be that what makes the assessments valid is that they provide work samples.[24]

Job performance tests have the advantage of giving applicants a chance to show what they can do, which leads them to feel that the evaluation was fair.[25] Games and other kinds of tests also may be a way to avoid discrimination, since they focus on skills rather than credentials. The tests also are job specific—that is, tailored to the kind of work done in a specific job. So they have a high level of validity, especially when combined with cognitive ability tests and a highly structured interview.[26] This advantage can become a disadvantage, however, if the organization wants to generalize the results of a test for one job to candidates for other jobs. The tests are more appropriate for identifying candidates who are generally able to solve the problems associated with a job, rather than for identifying which particular skills or traits the individual possesses.[27] Developing different tests for different jobs can become expensive. One way to save money is to prepare computerized tests that can be delivered online to various locations.

HR Analytics & Decision Making

The evidence is crystal clear that hiring practices in high tech can have an adverse impact on female job applicants. In contrast to the 1980s, when tech jobs were evenly split between men and women, only 15% of software engineers working in Silicon Valley in 2017 were women. The numbers give rise to questions about whether employers are engaged in discrimination against women.

Some evidence comes from the way experts interpret work samples. A group of computer scientists reviewed assessments of computer code on GitHub, a site where open-source code is posted. When the developers reviewed the code developed by women but did not know their gender, they accepted over 70% of it. When they knew that women had written the code, the acceptance rate fell by 10 percentage points. The results suggest that something about knowing the gender of the coder led them to evaluate the work differently.

Questions

1. If a company's use of employment tests followed the pattern found in this experiment, would that indicate sex discrimination? Why or why not?
2. Suppose a company needs to fill computer programming jobs and wants to use job performance tests. How can it do so in a way that avoids discrimination?

Sources: Katharine Zalesky, "Job Interviews without Gender," *The New York Times*, January 6, 2018; Claire Suddath, "Girl Code," *Bloomberg Businessweeek*, May 14, 2015.

Personality Inventories

In some situations, employers may also want to know about candidates' personalities. For example, one way that psychologists think about personality is in terms of the "Big Five" traits: extroversion, adjustment, agreeableness, conscientiousness, and inquisitiveness (explained in Table 6.3). There is evidence that people who score high on conscientiousness tend to excel at work, because they use self-control to pursue goals and excel at overcoming obstacles.[28] The relevance of personality dimensions may also be job specific. For example, extroverts tend to excel in sales jobs, because these jobs call upon traits associated with extroversion—notably, being gregarious and assertive.[29] Companies also are crunching their data to see which traits are associated with success at their particular organization. At JetBlue, for example, the director of talent acquisition and assessment says his company can measure specific traits to determine who will deliver the best job performance.[30]

The usual way to identify a candidate's personality traits is to administer one of the personality tests that are commercially available. The employer pays for the use of the test, and the organization that owns the test then scores the responses and provides a report about the test taker's personality. An organization that provides such tests should be able to discuss the test's validity and reliability. It is possible to find reliable, commercially available measures of each trait, but the evidence of their validity and generalizability is mixed at best.[31] Some people don't have enough insight about themselves to answer accurately, or their personalities vary on and off the job. Also, compared with intelligence tests, people are better at "faking" their answers to a personality test to score higher on desirable traits.[32] Evidence includes higher scores for conscientiousness when people take job-related tests than when they take research-related tests. Also, candidates who don't get hired have scored much higher when they retry the test. Ways to address this problem include using trained

TABLE 6.3

Five Major Personality Dimensions Measured by Personality Inventories

1. Extroversion	Sociable, gregarious, assertive, talkative, expressive
2. Adjustment	Emotionally stable, nondepressed, secure, content
3. Agreeableness	Courteous, trusting, good-natured, tolerant, cooperative, forgiving
4. Conscientiousness	Dependable, organized, persevering, thorough, achievement-oriented
5. Inquisitiveness	Curious, imaginative, artistically sensitive, broad-minded, playful

Administering tests to job candidates helps employers assess qualifications. Why are problem-solving skills important for an electrical technician? ©themorningglory/123RF

interviewers rather than surveys, collecting information about the applicant from several sources, and letting applicants know that several sources will be used.[33]

Employers also must ensure that their use of these tests meets legal standards. Some test measures related to personality dimensions, especially those related to emotional stability, come close to categories of mental illness. People with an illness who can perform job requirements are protected under the Americans with Disabilities Act. Job candidates with mental-health-related disabilities have challenged the use of such tests for employment decisions.[34] Also, it is important to ensure that the tests are measuring job-related criteria.

One trend in favor of personality tests is organizations' greater use of teamwork. Because team members must work together closely, the selection of one member can affect the personality requirements for other team members.[35] An organization might try to select team members with similar traits and values in order to promote a strong culture where people work together harmoniously, or they instead might look for a diversity of personalities and values as a way to promote debate and creativity. Pinterest, for example, assembles teams one person at a time, selecting each new team member based on the person having some unique trait or perspective not already present on the team.

Honesty Tests and Drug Tests

No matter what employees' personalities may be like, organizations want employees to be honest and to behave safely. Some organizations are satisfied to assess these qualities based on judgments from reference checks and interviews. Others investigate these characteristics more directly through the use of honesty tests and drug tests.

The most famous kind of honesty test is the polygraph, the so-called lie detector test. However, in 1988 the passage of the Polygraph Act banned the use of polygraphs for screening job candidates. As a result, testing services have developed paper-and-pencil honesty (or integrity) tests. Generally these tests ask applicants directly about their attitudes toward theft and their own experiences with theft. Much of the research into the validity of these tests has been conducted by the testing companies, which tend to find stronger correlations. However, evidence suggests that honesty tests do have some ability to predict such behavior as theft of the employer's property.[36]

As concerns about substance abuse have grown, especially in the context of the opioid epidemic and the spread of marijuana legalization, so has the use of drug testing.[37] As a measure of a person's exposure to drugs, chemical testing has high reliability and validity. However, these tests are controversial for several reasons. Some people are concerned that they invade individuals' privacy. Others object from a legal perspective. When all applicants or employees are subject to testing, whether or not they have shown evidence of drug use, the tests might be an unreasonable search and seizure or a violation of due process. Taking urine and blood samples involves invasive procedures, and accusing someone of drug use is a serious matter. On the positive side, a recent analysis of hiring data suggests that drug tests may provide a correction for discriminatory employment decisions. In states that adopted laws encouraging drug testing, hiring trends for white males were unchanged, but the hiring of Black men increased. That change did not occur in states where laws were unfavorable to drug testing. Although the study did not prove (or disprove) discrimination, it does show an influence that is helpful to Black males.[38]

Employers considering the use of drug tests should ensure that their drug-testing programs conform to some general rules:[39]

- Administer the tests systematically to all applicants for the same job.
- Use drug testing for jobs that involve safety hazards.
- Have a report of the results sent to the applicant, along with information about how to appeal the results and be retested if appropriate.
- Respect applicants' privacy by conducting tests in an environment that is not intrusive and keeping results confidential.

Even at an organization with these best practices, employers have to keep in mind that drug testing will not uncover all problems with impairment. One recent concern is that much drug abuse today involves legal prescription painkillers rather than substances traditionally tested for. Routine testing for prescription drugs (or possibly even marijuana in states that have legalized medical marijuana) is difficult because the employer has to be careful not to discriminate on the basis of disabilities.

Medical Examinations

Especially for physically demanding jobs, organizations may wish to conduct medical examinations to see that the applicant can meet the job's requirements. Employers may also wish to establish an employee's physical condition at the beginning of employment, so that there is a basis for measuring whether the employee has suffered a work-related disability later on. At the same time, as described in Chapter 3, organizations may not discriminate against individuals with disabilities who could perform a job with reasonable accommodations. Likewise, they may not use a measure of size or strength that discriminates against women, unless those requirements are valid in predicting the ability to perform a job. Furthermore, to protect candidates' privacy, medical exams must be related to job requirements and may not be given until the candidate has received a job offer. Therefore, organizations must be careful in how they use medical examinations. Many organizations make selection decisions first and then conduct the exams to confirm that the employee can handle the job with any reasonable accommodations required. Limiting the use of medical exams in this way also holds down the cost of what tends to be an expensive process.

LO 6-6 Discuss how to conduct effective interviews.

Interviews

Supervisors and team members most often get involved in the selection process at the stage of employment interviews. These interviews bring together job applicants and representatives of the employer to obtain information and evaluate the applicant's qualifications. While the applicant is providing information, he or she is also forming opinions about what it is like to work for the organization. Most organizations use interviewing as part of the selection process. In fact, this method is used more than any other.

Interviewing Techniques

Interview techniques include choices about the type of questions to ask and the number of people who conduct the interview. Several question types are possible:

Nondirective Interview
A selection interview in which the interviewer has great discretion in choosing questions to ask each candidate.

Structured Interview
A selection interview that consists of a predetermined set of questions for the interviewer to ask.

Situational Interview
A structured interview in which the interviewer describes a situation likely to arise on the job, then asks the candidate what he or she would do in that situation.

Behavior Description Interview (BDI)
A structured interview in which the interviewer asks the candidate to describe how he or she handled a type of situation in the past.

Panel Interview
Selection interview in which several members of the organization meet to interview each candidate.

- In a **nondirective interview,** the interviewer has great discretion in choosing questions. The candidate's reply to one question may suggest other questions to ask. Nondirective interviews typically include open-ended questions about the candidate's strengths, weaknesses, career goals, and work experience. Because these interviews give the interviewer wide latitude, their reliability is not great, and some interviewers ask questions that are not valid or even legal.
- A **structured interview** establishes a set of questions for the interviewer to ask. Ideally, the questions are related to job requirements and cover relevant knowledge, skills, and experiences. The interviewer is supposed to avoid asking questions that are not on the list. Although interviewers may object to being restricted, the results may be more valid and reliable than with a nondirective interview.
- A **situational interview** is a structured interview in which the interviewer describes a situation likely to arise on the job and asks the candidate what he or she would do in that situation. This type of interview may have high validity in predicting job performance.[40]
- A **behavior description interview (BDI)** is a structured interview in which the interviewer asks the candidate to describe how he or she handled a type of situation in the past. Questions about candidates' actual experiences tend to have the highest validity.[41]

For examples of the kinds of questions appropriate for a situational interview and a BDI, see Table 6.4. The common setup for either a nondirected or structured interview is for an individual (an HR professional or the supervisor for the vacant position) to interview each candidate face to face. However, variations on this approach are possible. In a **panel interview,** several members of the organization meet to interview each candidate. A panel interview gives the candidate a chance to meet more people and see how people interact in that organization. It provides the organization with the judgments of more than one person, to reduce the effect of personal biases in selection decisions. Panel interviews can be especially appropriate in organizations that use teamwork. At the other extreme, some organizations conduct interviews without any interviewers; they use a computerized interviewing process. The candidate sits at a computer and enters replies to the questions presented by the computer. Such a format eliminates a lot of personal bias—along with the opportunity to see how people interact. Therefore, computer interviews are useful for gathering objective data, rather than assessing people skills.

Advantages and Disadvantages of Interviewing

The wide use of interviewing is not surprising. People naturally want to see prospective employees firsthand. As we noted in Chapter 1, the top qualities that employers seek in new hires include communication skills and interpersonal skills. Talking face to face can

TABLE 6.4
Sample Interview Questions

SKILL TO BE MEASURED	SITUATIONAL INTERVIEW	BEHAVIOR DESCRIPTION INTERVIEW
Motivating employees	Suppose you were working with an employee who you knew greatly disliked performing a particular task. You needed to get this task completed, however, and this person was the only one available to do it. What would you do to motivate that person?	Think about an instance when you had to motivate an employee to perform a task that he or she disliked but that you needed to have done. How did you handle that situation?
Resolving conflict	Imagine that you and a co-worker disagree about the best way to handle an absenteeism problem with another member of your team. How would you resolve that situation?	What was the biggest difference of opinion you ever had with a co-worker? How did you resolve that situation?
Overcoming resistance to change	Suppose you had an idea for a change in work procedures that would enhance quality, but some members of your work group were hesitant to make the change. What would you do in that situation?	What was the hardest change you ever had to bring about in a past job, and what did you do to get the people around you to change their thoughts or behaviors?

provide evidence of these skills. Interviews can give insights into candidates' personalities and interpersonal styles. They are more valid, however, when they focus on job knowledge and skill. Interviews also provide a means to check the accuracy of information on the applicant's résumé or job application. Asking applicants to elaborate about their experiences and offer details reduces the likelihood of a candidate being able to invent a work history.[42]

Despite these benefits, interviewing is not necessarily the most accurate basis for making a selection decision. Research has shown that interviews can be unreliable, low in validity,[43] and biased against a number of different groups.[44] Interviews are also costly. They require that at least one person devote time to interviewing each candidate, and the applicants typically have to be brought to one geographic location. Interviews are also subjective, so they place the organization at greater risk of discrimination complaints by applicants who were not hired, especially if those individuals were asked questions not entirely related to the job. The Supreme Court has held that subjective selection methods like interviews must be validated, using methods that provide criterion-related or content validation.[45]

Organizations can avoid some of these pitfalls.[46] Human resource staff should keep the interviews narrow, structured, and standardized. The interview should focus on accomplishing a few goals, so that at the end of the interview, the organization has ratings on several observable measures, such as ability to express ideas that are relevant to the position. As noted earlier, situational interviews are especially effective for doing this. Organizations can prevent problems related to subjectivity by training interviewers and using more than one person to conduct interviews. Training typically includes focusing on the recording of observable facts, rather than on making subjective judgments, as well as developing interviewers' awareness of their biases.[47] Using a

Visit your instructor's Connect® course and access your eBook to view this video.

"It's really about understanding whether or not they'll fit into an organization. Things like behavioral interviews are really important."

—Jim Duffy, Executive Vice President and Chief Human Resources Officer, CIT Group, Inc.

Source: Video produced for the Center for Executive Succession in the Darla Moore School of Business at the University of South Carolina by Coal Powered Filmworks

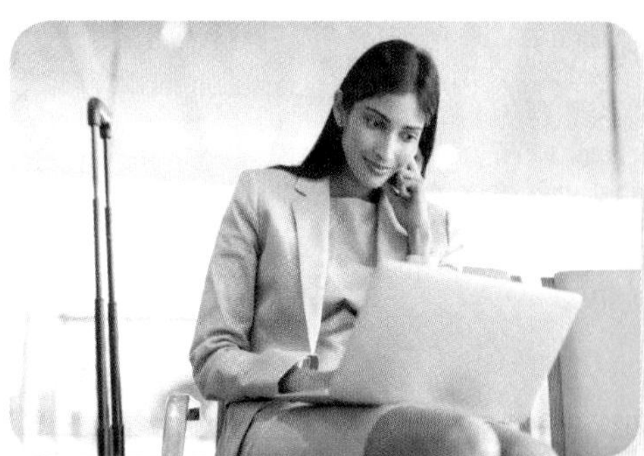

When interviewing candidates, it's valid to ask about willingness to travel if that is part of the job. Interviewers might ask questions about previous business travel experiences and/or how interviewees handled situations requiring flexibility and self-motivation (qualities that would be an asset in someone who is traveling alone and solving business problems on the road).
michaeljung/iStock/Getty Images

structured system for taking notes or scoring responses may help limit subjectivity and help the interviewer remember and justify an evaluation later.[48] In addition, such methods enable the interviewers to gather data the organization can later compare with hired employees' performance to see which measures are the best predictors of success.

As artificial intelligence advances, organizations are finding ways to make interview data more objective and useful for such predictions. Some companies are recording video interviews and using AI software to analyze the responses. Besides the potential to increase structure and reduce biases, this approach also may significantly shorten the time required to carry out the hiring process, especially to the degree that analysis enables companies to narrow the interview questions to the ones shown to be most relevant.[49]

Preparing to Interview

Organizations can reap the greatest benefits from interviewing if they prepare carefully. A well-planned interview should be standardized, comfortable for the participants, and focused on the job and the organization. The interviewer should have a quiet place in which to conduct interviews without interruption. This person should be trained in how to ask objective questions, what subject matter to avoid, and how to detect and handle his or her own personal biases or other distractions in order to fairly evaluate candidates.

The interviewer should have enough documents to conduct a complete interview. These should include a list of the questions to be asked in a structured interview, with plenty of space for recording the responses. When the questions are prepared, it is also helpful to determine how the answers will be scored. For example, if questions ask how interviewees would handle certain situations, consider what responses are best in terms of meeting job requirements. If the job requires someone who motivates others, then a response that shows motivating behavior would receive a higher score. The interviewer also should have a copy of the interviewee's employment application and résumé to review before the interview and refer to during the interview. If possible, the interviewer should also have printed information about the organization and the job. Near the beginning of the interview, it is a good idea to go over the job specifications, organizational policies, and so on, so that the interviewee has a clearer understanding of the organization's needs.

The interviewer should schedule enough time to review the job requirements, discuss the interview questions, and give the interviewee a chance to ask questions. To close, the interviewer should thank the candidate for coming and provide information about what to expect—for example, that the organization will contact a few finalists within the next two weeks or that a decision will be made by the end of the week.

The "HR Oops!" box identifies some common mistakes that managers tend to make during this process, along with ideas for better interviews.

Selection Decisions

LO 6-7 Explain how employers carry out the process of making a selection decision.

After reviewing applications, scoring tests, conducting interviews, and checking references, the organization needs to make decisions about which candidates to place in which jobs. In practice, most organizations find more than one qualified candidate to fill an open position. The selection decision typically combines ranking based on objective criteria along with subjective judgments about which candidate will make the greatest contribution.

Interview Failures—and How to Avoid Them

A widespread failure of interviewers is not planning a set of structured, relevant questions. Especially when interviews are not conducted by expert recruiters, the untrained interviewer often assumes the time should be a friendly conversation in which people get a gut feeling about whether there is a "fit." As noted in the text, this approach tends to lack reliability. A better tactic is to plan what qualities to identify in candidates and then devise questions that uncover those qualities.

For years, Google was legendary for using puzzles and brain teasers to select intelligent candidates. Other high-tech firms adopted similar practices. This is not an ideal interview method, however, because these puzzles measure a particular kind of mental agility under stress but rarely represent the kind of thinking a person does on the job. Work-related questions are more relevant.

When describing the position, many interviewers are tempted to see themselves in the role of seller, convincing the candidate that their organization would be a great employer. While a positive outlook is great, overselling the company to an ambivalent candidate could turn out to be a mistake. It could lead the company to hire someone with low commitment, in which case another, more engaged person would have been more successful in the position.

Of course, job candidates often make mistakes in interviews, too. So it merits saying that a job candidate should avoid mistakes like arriving late and being unprepared. Candidates can make a good impression by being able to say why they are qualified to succeed in the particular job they are interviewing for. They can improve their interview performance by practicing ahead of time how to explain their strengths and experiences in an engaging tone and easily understandable language.

Questions

1. Imagine you have been hired as the first HR manager at a small start-up business. You learn that the owner, who interviews all job candidates, believes that structured, skills-focused interview questions are "boring" and "not cool." How would you advise this person about the selection process?
2. Suppose you are interviewing for a position, but the interviewer has failed to prepare a set of structured questions and is instead asking broad questions like "Why do you want this job?" How could you as the candidate help the interview be successful?

Sources: Anisa Purbasari Horton, "The Problems with These Five Dumb (but Common) Hiring Practices," *Fast Company,* May 29, 2019, https://www.fastcompany.com; Caroline Ceniza-Levine, "Seven Job Interview Mistakes You Probably Don't Realize You're Making," *Forbes,* November 17, 2019, https://www.forbes.com; Lindsay Tigar, "Seven Ways to Streamline Your Hiring Process in 2019," *Fast Company,* January 2, 2019, https://www.fastcompany.com.

How Organizations Select Employees

The selection decision should not be a simple matter of whom the supervisor likes best or which candidate will take the lowest offer. Also, observing confidence in job candidates does not necessarily mean they are competent. Rather, the people making the selection should look for the best fit between candidate and position. In general, the person's performance will result from a combination of ability and motivation. Often, the selection is a choice among a few people who possess the basic qualifications. The decision makers therefore have to decide which of those people have the best combination of ability and motivation to fit in the position and in the organization as a whole.

The usual process for arriving at a selection decision is to gradually narrow the pool of candidates for each job. This approach, called the **multiple-hurdle model,** is based on a process such as the one shown earlier in Figure 6.1. Each stage of the process is a hurdle, and candidates who overcome a hurdle continue to the next stage of the process. For example, the organization reviews applications and/or résumés of all candidates, conducts some tests on those who meet minimum requirements, conducts initial interviews with those who had the highest test scores, follows up with additional interviews or testing, and then selects

Multiple-Hurdle Model
Process of arriving at a selection decision by eliminating some candidates at each stage of the selection process.

a candidate from the few who survived this process. Another, more expensive alternative is to take most applicants through all steps of the process and then to review all the scores to find the most desirable candidates. With this alternative, decision makers may use a **compensatory model,** in which a very high score on one type of assessment can make up for a low score on another. For example, Prudential is among the major insurance companies that have shifted away from focusing on college degrees in risk management and insurance when hiring entry-level employees. Prudential has defined competencies for each position and is increasing the use of games as a test of important skills. Chrisoula Toskos, vice president of campus recruiting, is particularly interested in candidates' level of "intelligent risk taking."[50]

Compensatory Model
Process of arriving at a selection decision in which a very high score on one type of assessment can make up for a low score on another.

Whether the organization uses a multiple-hurdle model or conducts the same assessments on all candidates, the decision maker or makers need criteria for choosing among qualified candidates. An obvious strategy is to select the candidates who score highest on tests and interviews. However, employee performance depends on motivation as well as ability. It is possible that a candidate who scores very high on an ability test might be "overqualified"–that is, the employee might be bored by the job the organization needs to fill, and a less-able employee might actually be a better fit. Similarly, a highly motivated person might learn some kinds of jobs very quickly, potentially outperforming someone who has the necessary skills. Furthermore, some organizations have policies of developing employees for career paths in the organization. Such organizations might place less emphasis on the skills needed for a particular job and more emphasis on hiring candidates who share the organization's values, show that they have the people skills to work with others in the organization, and are able to learn the skills needed for advancement. This type of reasoning may help to explain why experienced workers report difficulty finding new jobs. HR departments ask them about pay requirements early in the selection process, presumably as a way to ensure they can fill positions with people who will feel highly motivated by the company's desired salary level and policies related to career development.[51]

Finally, organizations have choices about who will make the decision. Usually a supervisor makes the final decision, often alone. This person may couple knowledge of the job with a judgment about who will fit in best with others in the department. The decision could also be made by a human resource professional using standardized, objective criteria. Especially in organizations that use teamwork, selection decisions may be made by a work team or other panel of decision makers.

Communicating the Decision

The human resource department is often responsible for notifying applicants about the results of the selection process. When a candidate has been selected, the organization should communicate the offer to the candidate. The offer should include the job responsibilities, work schedule, rate of pay, starting date, and other relevant details. If placement in a job requires that the applicant pass a physical examination, the offer should state that contingency. The person communicating the offer should also indicate a date by which the candidate should reply with an acceptance or rejection of the offer. For some jobs, such as management and professional positions, the candidate and organization may negotiate pay, benefits, and work arrangements before they arrive at a final employment agreement.

The person who communicates this decision should keep accurate records of who was contacted, when, and for which position, as well as of the candidate's reply. The HR department and the supervisor also should be in close communication about the job offer. When an applicant accepts a job offer, the HR department must notify the supervisor so that he or she can be prepared for the new employee's arrival.

THINKING ETHICALLY

HOW FAIR IS AI IN HIRING?

Many companies have automated parts of the selection process by using systems that scan résumés for keywords in order to reduce a pool of applicants to the ones who meet job-related criteria. Artificial intelligence takes this a couple of steps further. First, it uses the company's data about existing employees' job performance to identify traits associated with success in the job. Second, it uses machine learning to draw conclusions about which candidates will succeed and then uses newly gathered data to assess the accuracy of its decisions in order to improve future decisions.

Companies that sell AI systems for selecting employees have developed these systems as a way to improve hiring decisions by making them less biased and more accurate. However, even the system providers note that artificial intelligence is only as "intelligent" as the data the company gathers. A company that has only rudimentary information about its employees will not be able to provide a satisfactory model for the system to apply. Candidates could be screened out for random criteria that happened to correlate with a handful of successful employees.

Another concern is that candidates may not understand how companies are using data about them. An employer using AI in hiring might analyze all of a candidate's public posts online, whether or not they are job related. It could interview online and then analyze the facial expressions to look for empathy or irritability. Some people consider this to be invasive. Illinois recently became the first state to pass a law requiring employers to notify applicants when the screening process will use AI. However, the law does not say the company has to consider hiring a candidate who declines to participate in that type of screening.

Companies that want to use AI in the screening process generally do not disclose the criteria they are screening for. And the systems generally apply criteria that are specific to particular positions at particular companies, so it can be difficult to guess how to prepare for an interview or employment test. This can help companies protect themselves against candidates trying to game the system. If employers are not careful, it can also create a process that excellent job candidates come to distrust and avoid.

Questions

1. What benefits to employers does AI screening provide? What are the potential benefits to job seekers? What possible harm does AI screening do to employers and to job seekers?
2. Applying the basic human rights listed in Chapter 1's discussion of ethics, how can employers respect those rights in their use of AI to select job candidates?

Sources: Abdel Jimenez, "Illinois Leading AI Hire Rules," *Chicago Tribune,* January 26, 2020, sec. 2, pp. 1, 4; Hilke Schellmann, "How Job Interviews Will Transform in the Next Decade," *The Wall Street Journal,* January 7, 2020, https://www.wsj.com; Sue Shellenbarger, "Make Your Job Application Robot-Proof," *The Wall Street Journal,* December 16, 2019, https://www.wsj.com.

SUMMARY

LO 6-1 Identify the elements of the selection process.

- Selection typically begins with a review of candidates' employment applications and résumés.
- The organization administers tests to candidates who meet basic requirements.
- Qualified candidates undergo one or more interviews.
- Organizations check references and conduct background checks to verify the accuracy of information provided by candidates.
- A candidate is selected to fill each vacant position.
- Candidates who accept offers are placed in the positions for which they were selected.

LO 6-2 Define ways to measure the success of a selection method.

- One criterion is reliability, meaning free from random error, so that measurements are consistent.
- A selection method should also be valid, meaning that performance on the measure (such as a test score) is related to what the measure is designed to assess (such as job performance).
- Criterion-related validity shows a correlation between test scores and job performance scores.
- Content validity shows consistency between the test items or problems and the kinds of situations or problems that occur on the job.
- Construct validity establishes that the test actually measures a specified construct, such as intelligence or leadership ability, which is presumed to be associated with success on the job.
- A selection method also should be generalizable, or applicable to more than one specific situation.
- Each selection method should have utility, meaning it provides economic value greater than its cost.
- Selection methods should meet the legal requirements for employment decisions.

LO 6-3 Summarize the government's requirements for employee selection.

- The selection process must be conducted in a way that avoids discrimination and provides access to persons with disabilities.
- Selection methods must be valid for job performance, and scores may not be adjusted to discriminate against or give preference to any group.
- Questions may not gather information about a person's membership in a protected class, such as race, sex, or religion, nor may the employer investigate a person's disability status.
- Employers must respect candidates' privacy rights and ensure that they keep personal information confidential.
- Employers must obtain consent before conducting background checks and notify candidates about adverse decisions made as a result of background checks.

LO 6-4 Compare the common methods used for selecting human resources.

- Nearly all organizations gather information through employment applications and résumés. Today, most applications can be found online, either on a company website or a job search engine platform like Indeed or ZipRecruiter. These methods are inexpensive, and an application form standardizes basic information received from all applicants. The information is not necessarily reliable, because each applicant provides the information. These methods are most valid when evaluated in terms of the criteria in a job description.
- References and background checks help verify the accuracy of applicant-provided information.
- Employment tests and work samples are more objective. To be legal, any test must measure abilities that actually are associated with successful job performance. Employment tests range from general to specific. General-purpose tests are relatively inexpensive and simple to administer. Tests should be selected to be related to successful job performance and avoid charges of discrimination.
- Interviews are widely used to obtain information about a candidate's interpersonal and communication skills and to gather more detailed information about a candidate's background. Structured interviews are more valid than unstructured ones. Situational interviews provide greater validity than general questions. Interviews are costly and may introduce bias into the selection process. Organizations can minimize the drawbacks through preparation and training.

LO 6-5 Describe major types of employment tests.

- Physical ability tests measure strength, endurance, psychomotor abilities, and other physical abilities. They can be accurate but can discriminate and are not always job related.
- Cognitive ability tests, or intelligence tests, tend to be valid, especially for complex jobs and those requiring adaptability. They are a relatively low-cost way to predict job performance but have been challenged as discriminatory.
- Job performance tests tend to be valid but are not always generalizable. Using a wide variety of job performance tests can be expensive.
- Personality tests measure personality traits such as extroversion and adjustment. Research supports their validity for appropriate job situations, especially for individuals who score high on conscientiousness, extroversion, and agreeableness. These tests are relatively simple to administer and generally meet legal requirements.
- Organizations may use paper-and-pencil honesty or integrity tests, which can predict certain behaviors, including employee theft. Organizations may not use polygraphs to screen job candidates.
- Organizations may also administer drug tests (if all candidates are tested and drug use can be an on-the-job safety hazard).
- Passing a medical examination may be a condition of employment, but to avoid discrimination against persons with disabilities, organizations usually administer a medical exam only after making a job offer.

LO 6-6 Discuss how to conduct effective interviews.

- Interviews should be narrow, structured, and standardized.
- Interviewers should identify job requirements and create a list of questions related to the requirements.
- Interviewers should be trained to recognize their own personal biases and conduct objective interviews.
- Panel interviews can reduce problems related to interviewer bias.
- Interviewers should put candidates at ease in a comfortable place that is free of distractions. Questions should ask for descriptions of relevant experiences and job-related behaviors.
- The interviewers also should be prepared to provide information about the job and the organization.

LO 6-7 Explain how employers carry out the process of making a selection decision.

- The organization should focus on the objective of finding the person who will be the best fit with the job and organization. This includes an assessment of ability and motivation.

- Decision makers may use a multiple-hurdle model in which each stage of the selection process eliminates some of the candidates from consideration at the following stages. At the final stage, only a few candidates remain, and the selection decision determines which candidate is the best fit.
- An alternative is a compensatory model, in which all candidates are evaluated with all methods. A candidate who scores poorly with one method may be selected if he or she scores very high on another measure.

KEY TERMS

personnel selection, 167
applicant-tracking system, 167
reliability, 168
validity, 170
criterion-related validity, 170
predictive validation, 170
concurrent validation, 171
content validity, 171
construct validity, 171
generalizable, 172
utility, 173
Immigration Reform and Control Act of 1986, 175
aptitude tests, 180
achievement tests, 180
cognitive ability tests, 181
assessment center, 182
nondirective interview, 186
structured interview, 186
situational interview, 186
behavior description interview (BDI), 186
panel interview, 186
multiple-hurdle model, 189
compensatory model, 190

REVIEW AND DISCUSSION QUESTIONS

1. What activities are involved in the selection process? Think of the last time you were hired for a job. Which of those activities were used in selecting you? Should the organization that hired you have used other methods as well? *(LO 6-1)*
2. Why should the selection process be adapted to fit the organization's job descriptions? *(LO 6-1)*
3. Choose two of the selection methods identified in this chapter. Describe how you can compare them in terms of reliability, validity, ability to generalize, utility, and compliance with the law. *(LO 6-2)*
4. Why does predictive validation provide better information than concurrent validation? Why is this type of validation more difficult? *(LO 6-2)*
5. How do U.S. laws affect organizations' use of each of the employment tests? Interviews? *(LO 6-3)*
6. Suppose your organization needs to hire several computer programmers, and you are reviewing résumés you obtained from an online service. What kinds of information will you want to gather from the "work experience" portion of these résumés? What kinds of information will you want to gather from the "education" portion of these résumés? What methods would you use for verifying or exploring this information? Why would you use those methods? *(LO 6-4)*
7. For each of the following jobs, select the two kinds of tests you think would be most important to include in the selection process. Explain why you chose those tests. *(LO 6-5)*
   a. City bus driver
   b. Insurance salesperson
   c. Member of a team that sells complex high-tech equipment to manufacturers
   d. Member of a team that makes a component of the equipment in (c)
8. Suppose you are a human resource professional at a large retail chain. You want to improve the company's hiring process by creating standard designs for interviews, so that every time someone is interviewed for a particular job category, that person answers the same questions. You also want to make sure the questions asked are relevant to the job and maintain equal employment opportunity. Think of three questions to include in interviews for each of the following jobs. For each question, state why you think it should be included. *(LO 6-6)*
   a. Cashier at one of the company's stores
   b. Buyer of the stores' teen clothing line
   c. Accounts payable clerk at company headquarters
9. How can organizations improve the quality of their interviewing so that interviews provide valid information? *(LO 6-6)*
10. Some organizations set up a selection process that is long and complex. In some people's opinion, this kind of selection process not only is more valid but also has symbolic value. What can the use of a long, complex selection process symbolize to job seekers? How do you think this would affect the organization's ability to attract the best employees? *(LO 6-7)*

SELF-ASSESSMENT EXERCISE

What Are Your Prominent Big Five Personality Traits?

Reviews of research about personality have identified five common aspects of personality, referred to as the Big Five personality traits. Find out which are your most prominent traits. Read each of the following statements, marking "Yes" if it describes you and "No" if it does not.

1. In conversations, I tend to do most of the talking.
2. Often people look to me to make decisions.
3. I am a very active person.
4. I usually seem to be in a hurry.
5. I am dominant, forceful, and assertive.
6. I have a very active imagination.
7. I have an active fantasy life.
8. How I feel about things is important to me.
9. I find it easy to feel myself what others are feeling.
10. I think it's interesting to learn and develop new hobbies.
11. My first reaction is to trust people.
12. I believe that most persons are basically well intentioned.
13. I'm not crafty or shy.
14. I'd rather not talk about myself and my accomplishments.
15. I'd rather praise others than be praised myself.
16. I come into situations being fully prepared.
17. I pride myself on my sound judgment.
18. I have a lot of self-discipline.
19. I try to do jobs carefully so that they don't have to be done again.
20. I like to keep everything in place so that I know where it is.
21. I enjoy performing under pressure.
22. I am seldom sad or depressed.
23. I'm an even-tempered person.
24. I am levelheaded in emergencies.
25. I feel I am capable of coping with most of my problems.

The statements are grouped into categories. Statements 1-5 describe extroversion; 6-10, openness to experience; 11-15, agreeableness; 16-20, conscientiousness; and 21-25, emotional stability. The more times you wrote "Yes" for the statements in a category, the more likely you are to have the associated trait.

TAKING RESPONSIBILITY

At PepsiCo, Workers with Disabilities Are Encouraged, Not Disqualified

When one in five workers in the United States has some disability, selection processes that include these people are not only socially responsible, but also meet practical needs in a tight labor market. The practicality of this attitude is even more relevant in light of the aging population (assuming that age brings more health conditions) and the ongoing wars that increase the share of workers who are veterans with disabilities.

One company that has appreciated the opportunities that come with openness to hiring disabled workers is PepsiCo. The company partnered with an organization called Disability Solutions to create a program called Pepsi ACT (for Achieving Change Together). The staff of Disability Solutions worked with PepsiCo's HR department to identify job requirements, and it reached out to community groups such as veterans' organizations and public employment agencies to identify job seekers who might have the necessary qualifications.

In the first few years of Pepsi ACT, about 300 employees with disabilities were hired for jobs in nine U.S. cities. The company tracked the performance of employees hired through the program. The results included practical benefits, most notably a higher retention rate for employees with disabilities, relative to nondisabled workers in comparable jobs. Also, at some of the company's locations, hiring has become more efficient: the ratio of the number of interviews per hire is lower with the Pepsi ACT applicants. One successful hire is Juan Olivo, who was wounded during his almost dozen years of military service. He struggled to find a job that would fully use his talents until he had a chance to apply to PepsiCo through the Pepsi ACT program. Three years later, he remains a loyal employee, envisioning a long-term future with the company.

Pepsi ACT started as a test case with a socially responsible goal of inclusiveness. Based on its utility to the company, it has become a part of PepsiCo's overall strategy for meeting its talent needs. The results have been impressive enough to convince other companies, including American Express and Aon, to follow PepsiCo's lead and partner with Disability Solutions to meet their own talent needs. PepsiCo and Disability Solutions were recently given top honors by the U.S. Department of Labor for their hiring efforts on behalf of individuals with disabilities.

Questions

1. U.S. law requires that employers make reasonable accommodations for qualified employees with disabilities. But although discrimination is illegal, some employers are reluctant to consider disabled workers or at least to actively recruit them. What advantages and disadvantages could arise from actively seeking out disabled workers?

2. Do you think the Pepsi ACT program gives PepsiCo a competitive advantage? Why or why not? How could the company determine this?

Sources: "U.S. Department of Labor Announces Recipients of Excellence in Disability Inclusion Awards," U.S. Department of Labor, March 11, 2020, https://www.dol.gov/newsroom; Kristine Foss, "From Pepsi to Polaris, Talent with Disabilities Gets Results," *Industry Week,* March 5, 2019, https://www.industryweek.com; Alisa Picerno, "Disability Solutions Contributes Expertise to National Organizations," *Hartford Courant,* February 8, 2018, http://www.courant.com; "Veteran Rolls the Dice: Pepsi ACT Las Vegas," *Ability Beyond,* December 4, 2017, http://abilitybeyond.org; Kris Foss, "Changing Minds and Changing Lives," *TD,* November 2017, pp. 20–22.

MANAGING TALENT

Office of Professional Management Upgrades U.S. Government Hiring

In a survey conducted several years ago, supervisors in federal government agencies identified what they considered to be the most difficult tasks related to workforce management. The task rated most difficult was getting a pool of qualified candidates. Other evidence supports the difficulty government managers have had with employee selection. When managers get a list of candidates who passed the screening process, only half the time do the managers find someone on the list to hire. And a survey of federal government employees found that only 42% think their work unit is able to recruit people with the necessary skills.

The process typical of hiring civil servants would surprise many HR professionals in the private sector. Jobs are posted to the USA Jobs database, each specifying minimum requirements for qualifying. These requirements tend to be broad, vague, and sometimes outdated, written solely by HR staffers without input from experts in the type of occupation or field of work. Writers lacking intimate knowledge of the work to be performed generally express requirements in terms of years of experience in the job level one step down plus a list of duties that might be expected. Candidates for a job listed on USA Jobs submit an often lengthy "federal résumé" in which they list their career accomplishments and a questionnaire on which they use a 1-to-5 scale to rate their competencies. Employees with federal government experience know that to be considered, they should rate themselves 5 for Expert on each competency. Candidates who give themselves high ratings and indicate they have the necessary experience get placed on a list of qualifying candidates submitted to the hiring manager. Often that manager finds the self-ratings misleading and the list populated with candidates lacking relevant competencies.

These practices are in place because they are inexpensive for agencies to administer and easy for applicants to complete. In 1981, the federal government replaced a civil service examination with a policy of leaving the selection process up to individual agencies. Few could find money in their budgets to create a more complex selection process. In the meantime, the usual process is so widespread that many government employees have come to believe it is required.

A recent pilot study tried improving selection practices. For IT specialists at the Department of Health and Human Services (HHS) and the National Park Service (NPS), HR specialists worked with subject-matter experts to define competencies for open positions. Candidates were asked to provide a standard two-page résumé, and the HR and subject-matter partners conducted structured interviews to select applicants having the predefined competencies. At the end of six months, 22% of candidates for HHS jobs qualified, and seven were hired. At the NPS, 11% qualified, and seven were hired. Another six people were placed in other Interior Department positions. The time to hire dropped from 47 days with the usual methods to just 11 days in HHS and 17 days for the NPS jobs. The process of having subject-matter experts evaluate résumés and develop structured interviews took 50 to 60 hours, but much of that work would not have to be repeated for future hires.

In light of these results, the Office of Professional Management recommended that agencies adopt this approach to employee selection, including the use of subject-matter experts to develop a variety of assessments related to the needed skills. The OPM notes that agencies already are allowed to make these changes without any amendment to federal laws. A related federal agency, the Merit Systems Protection Board, notes that supervisors are more satisfied with hiring decisions when subject-matter experts are involved in defining requirements and screening candidates.

Questions

1. How well would you say the standard government hiring process was meeting the criteria for successful selection methods? Explain.
2. How would the proposed changes improve the hiring process in terms of the criteria for successful selection methods?

Sources: Erich Wagner, "Efforts to Reform Federal Hiring Already Showing Results," *Government Executive,* October 22, 2019, https://www.govexec.com; "Building on OPM's Hiring Improvement Memo," U.S. Merit Systems Protection Board, October 2019, https://www.mspb.gov; Erich Wagner, "Weichert: Agencies Should Include Experts in Hiring Process," *Government Executive,* September 13, 2019, https://www.govexec.com; Margaret M. Weichert, "Improving Federal Hiring through the Use of Effective Assessment Strategies to Advance Mission Outcomes," memo, September 13, 2019, Chief Human Capital Officers Council, https://www.chcoc.gov.

HR IN SMALL BUSINESS

Nehemiah Manufacturing Provides a Second Chance

Richard Palmer already had a successful track record in the consumer products industry when he decided to start his own company. With another experienced manager, Dan Meyer, he wanted to bring jobs back to their city, Cincinnati, Ohio. They opened Nehemiah Manufacturing Company to make consumer products for Palmer's former employer, Procter & Gamble. Inspired by their Christian faith, they named the company after the prophet Nehemiah, who inspired the Israelites to rebuild the walls of Jerusalem after years in exile.

The goal was to hire inner-city workers who had lost jobs when businesses moved out of the city into the suburbs. Before long, a local nonprofit approached the company about hiring workers who had been incarcerated. They brought in a few, but the experience was rocky. For many people, prison is just one of many hurdles, accompanied by mental health issues, substance abuse, and homelessness. People in these conditions do not always manage to be reliable or work effectively with others.

Rather than give up on what Palmer now calls the "second-chance population," he doubled down to make it work. He hired a social-service worker, Dana Merida, to help employees navigate their life challenges. With Merida, who now heads a three-person team, they crafted a careful hiring process that takes into account the need for a transition into stable employment. Early on, candidates work with a member of the social-service team to evaluate candidates' histories and social support; applicants must allow the team to contact any agencies involved in helping them with housing, drug treatment, or other needs. Half of the candidates pass this initial screening and are hired as temporary workers, assigned to a job coach to help them navigate the norms of the business world. After about six months, about 60% of them are hired full time. Wages are set at about the national average for employees doing the same kinds of work, and compensation includes health insurance, tuition reimbursement, and more. Employees are subject to random drug tests, and the company sometimes pays for treatment for those who fail a test, if the circumstances make it appropriate.

Today about 80% of the company's 180 employees have criminal records, and the company's founders could not be more pleased. Although a few have relapsed into addiction, the founders count the second-chance population as their hardest-working, most stable employees. The turnover rate is about 15%, less than half the 38.5% average for the industry. Palmer notes that Nehemiah is careful about who it hires, and he is pleased with the qualities he finds in the second-chance population. They may have troubled pasts, but they include people with passion, leadership ability, and a drive to help their co-workers. With the contributions of these people, Nehemiah has expanded its product line, which includes laundry products and baby wipes, and its number of customers while remaining profitable. And they are indeed bringing jobs back to Cincinnati.

Questions

1. How has Nehemiah Manufacturing adapted the steps of the basic selection process to meet the needs of recruiting workers with a history of incarceration?
2. Would you describe Nehemiah's selection methods as valid and practical? Why or why not?

Sources: Company website, "Our Mission," https://www.nehemiahmfg.com, accessed April 3, 2020; Katie Ellington, "How a Cincinnati Manufacturer Is Changing Lives and Slashing Turnover," *Richland Source,* January 29, 2020, https://www.richlandsource.com; Ruth Simon, "The Company of Second Chances," *The Wall Street Journal,* January 25, 2020, https://www.wsj.com; Adrienne M. Selko, "A Manufacturer's Secret to High Productivity, Low Turnover," *Industry Week,* March 27, 2019, https://www.industryweek.com.

NOTES

1. M. Aspan, "Siri, Did I Ace the Interview?" *Fortune,* February 2020, pp. 86–91.
2. "CVS Health Recognized for Evidence-Based HR," *Society for Human Resource Management,* https://www.shrm.org, accessed April 3, 2020; M-B Gorvine, "Analytics Said to Help Refine Recruiting Methods," *Bloomberg,* March 28, 2016, http://www.bloomberg.com.
3. S. Driver, "The Modern Hiring Process: What Job Seekers and Employers Should Know," *Business News Daily,* December 4, 2018, https://www.businessnewsdaily.com.
4. J. C. Nunnally, *Psychometric Theory* (New York: McGraw-Hill, 1978).
5. J. Kelly, "In an Interview, Being Likable Is Sometimes Better Than Having All of the Right Skills," *Forbes,* March 12, 2020, https://www.forbes.com; P. Di Michiel, "How Important Is 'Likeability' in Job Interviews?" *LinkedIn,* June 3, 2018, https://www.linkedin.com.
6. N. Schmitt, R. Z. Gooding, R. A. Noe, and M. Kirsch, "Meta-Analysis of Validity Studies Published between 1964 and 1982 and the Investigation of Study Characteristics," *Personnel Psychology* 37 (1984), pp. 407–422.
7. D. D. Robinson, "Content-Oriented Personnel Selection in a Small Business Setting," *Personnel Psychology* 34 (1981), pp. 77–87.
8. HR Council Post, "Seven Benefits of Gamification in the Hiring Process," *Forbes,* March 9, 2020, https://www.forbes.com.
9. F. L. Schmidt and J. E. Hunter, "The Future of Criterion-Related Validity," *Personnel Psychology* 33 (1980), pp. 41–60; F. L. Schmidt, J. E. Hunter, and K. Pearlman, "Task Differences as Moderators of Aptitude Test Validity: A Red Herring," *Journal of Applied Psychology* 66 (1982), pp. 166–185; R. L. Gutenberg,

R. D. Arvey, H. G. Osburn, and R. P. Jeanneret, "Moderating Effects of Decision-Making/Information Processing Dimensions on Test Validities," *Journal of Applied Psychology* 68 (1983), pp. 600–608.

10. Buffalo News, "Buffalo Firefighters Awarded $2.7 Million in Bias Case," *Firehouse,* https://www.firehouse.com, accessed April 3, 2020.
11. U.S. Immigration and Customs Enforcement, "Guidance for Employers Conducting Internal Employment Eligibility Verification Form I-9 Audits," https://www.ice.gov, accessed April 3, 2020; R. Ford, "Are You Prepared for an I-9 Compliance Audit?" *Society for Human Resource Management,* September 15, 2017, https://www.shrm.org.
12. G. Douglas, "Pay Inquiry Banks Give Some Employers Compliance Headaches," *HR Blog (Bloomberg),* March 5, 2018, https://www.bna.com; "Legislative Trends: Pay Equity and Inquiries," *Labor and Employment (Winston & Strawn),* September 2017, http://www.winston.com.
13. M. Barthel, "Employers Are Still Avoiding Former Inmates," *The Atlantic,* November 5, 2019, https://www.theatlantic.com.
14. T. W. Dougherty, D. B. Turban, and J. C. Callender, "Confirming First Impressions in the Employment Interview: A Field Study of Interviewer Behavior," *Journal of Applied Psychology* 79 (1994), pp. 659–665.
15. E. L. Thomas, "Your Blind Hiring Process Is (Probably) Still Biased. Here's How to Change That," *Fast Company,* June 27, 2019, https://www.fastcompany.com; J. Feldmann, "The Benefits and Shortcomings of Blind Hiring in the Recruitment Process," *Forbes,* April 3, 2018, https://www.forbes.com.
16. A. Ryan and M. Lasek, "Negligent Hiring and Defamation: Areas of Liability Related to Preemployment Inquiries," *Personnel Psychology* 44 (1991), pp. 293–319.
17. A. Long, "Addressing the Cloud over Employee References: A Survey of Recently Enacted State Legislation," *William and Mary Law Review* 39 (October 1997), pp. 177–228.
18. J. Hyman, "Are You Wasting Your Time Checking Candidate References?" *Forbes,* March 20, 2019, https://www.forbes.com; "Here's How to Check References the Right Way," *Robert Half,* March 19, 2019, https://www.roberthalf.com.
19. H. R. Huhman, "What to Do When Good Talent Has Suspicious Social Media," *Entrepreneur,* March 21, 2016, http://www.entrepreneur.com.
20. Equal Employment Opportunity Commission, "Background Checks: What Employers Need to Know," EEOC and Federal Trade Commission, http://www1.eeoc.gov; Maria Armental, "Target to Pay $3.7 Million in Settlement over Job-Screening Policies," *The Wall Street Journal,* April 5, 2018, https://www.wsj.com; Bureau of National Affairs, "Gray Areas Remain on Background Checks under EEOC Guidance," *HR Focus,* January 2014, pp. 14–15.
21. L. C. Buffardi, E. A. Fleishman, R. A. Morath, and P. M. McCarthy, "Relationships between Ability Requirements and Human Errors in Job Tasks," *Journal of Applied Psychology* 85 (2000), pp. 551–564; J. Hogan, "Structure of Physical Performance in Occupational Tasks," *Journal of Applied Psychology* 76 (1991), pp. 495–507.
22. J. F. Salagado, N. Anderson, S. Moscoso, C. Bertuas, and F. De Fruyt, "International Validity Generalization of GMA and Cognitive Abilities: A European Community Meta-analysis," *Personnel Psychology* 56 (2003), pp. 573–605; M. J. Ree, J. A. Earles, and M. S. Teachout, "Predicting Job Performance: Not Much More than *g*," *Journal of Applied Psychology* 79 (1994), pp. 518–524; L. S. Gottfredson, "The *g* Factor in Employment," *Journal of Vocational Behavior* 29 (1986), pp. 293–296; J. E. Hunter and R. H. Hunter, "Validity and Utility of Alternative Predictors of Job Performance," *Psychological Bulletin* 96 (1984), pp. 72–98; Gutenberg et al., "Moderating Effects of Decision-Making/Information Processing Dimensions on Test Validities"; F. L. Schmidt, J. G. Berner, and J. E. Hunter, "Racial Differences in Validity of Employment Tests: Reality or Illusion," *Journal of Applied Psychology* 58 (1974), pp. 5–6; J. A. LePine, J. A. Colquitt, and A. Erez, "Adaptability to Changing Task Contexts: Effects of General Cognitive Ability, Conscientiousness, and Openness to Experience," *Personnel Psychology* 53 (2000), pp. 563–593.
23. D. A. Kravitz and S. L. Klineberg, "Reactions to Versions of Affirmative Action among Whites, Blacks, and Hispanics," *Journal of Applied Psychology* (2000), pp. 597–611.
24. T. Oliver, P. Hausdorf, F. Lievens, and P. Conlon, "Interpersonal Dynamics in Assessment Center Exercises: Effects of Role Player Portrayed Disposition," *Journal of Management* 42 (2016), pp. 1992–2017; D. J. Jackson, G. Michaelides, C. Dewberry, and Y. J. Kim, "Everything That You Have Ever Been Told about Assessment Center Ratings Is Confounded," *Journal of Applied Psychology* 101 (2016), pp. 976–994.
25. D. Savage and R. Bales, "Video Games in Job Interviews: Using Algorithms to Minimize Discrimination and Unconscious Bias," *ABA Journal of Labor & Employment Law* 32(2) (Winter 2017), pp. 211–223; D. J. Schleiger, V. Venkataramani, F. P. Morgeson, and M. A. Campion, "So You Didn't Get the Job . . . Now What Do You Think? Examining Opportunity to Perform Fairness Perceptions," *Personnel Psychology* 59 (2006), pp. 559–590.
26. F. L. Schmidt and J. E. Hunter, "The Validity and Utility of Selection Methods in Personnel Psychology: Practical and Theoretical Implications of 85 Years of Research Findings," *Psychological Bulletin* 124 (1998), pp. 262–274.
27. W. Arthur, E. A. Day, T. L. McNelly, and P. S. Edens, "Meta-Analysis of the Criterion-Related Validity of Assessment Center Dimensions," *Personnel Psychology* 56 (2003), pp. 125–54; C. E. Lance, T. A. Lambert, A. G. Gewin, F. Lievens, and J. M. Conway, "Revised Estimates of Dimension and Exercise Variance Components in Assessment Center Postexercise Dimension Ratings," *Journal of Applied Psychology* 89 (2004), pp. 377–385.
28. L. Daskal, "7 Valuable Skills That Top Leaders and High Achievers Have Mastered," *Inc.,* https://www.inc.com, accessed April 3, 2020.
29. R. Nauert, "Extroverts May Enjoy Workplace Advantages," *PsychCentral,* May 31, 2019, https://psychcentral.com; M. Mount, M. R. Barrick, and J. P. Strauss, "Validity of Observer Ratings of the Big Five Personality Factors," *Journal of Applied Psychology* 79 (1993), pp. 272–280.
30. E. Gray, "Do You Understand Why Stars Twinkle? Would You Rather Read than Watch TV? Do You Trust Data More than Your Instincts," *Time,* June 2015, pp. 41–46.
31. P. Galahan, "Tester Beware," *TD,* September 2015, EBSCO host, http://web.a.ebscohost.com; J. A. Shaffer and J. E. Postlewaite," A Matter of Context: A Meta-analytic Investigation of the Relative Validity of Contextualized and Non-contextualized Personality Measures," *Personnel Psychology* 63 (2010), pp. 299–324; F. P. Morgeson, M. A. Campion, R. L. Dipboye, J. R. Hollenbeck, K. R. Murphy, and N. Schmitt, "Reconsidering the Use of

Personality Tests in Personnel Selection Contexts," *Personnel Psychology* 60 (2007), pp. 683-729.

32. J. P. Hausknecht, "Candidate Persistence and Personality Test Practice Effects: Implications for Staffing System Management," *Personnel Psychology* 63 (2010), pp. 299-324; S. A. Birkland, T. M. Manson, J. L. Kisamore, M. T. Brannick, and M. A. Smith, "Faking on Personality Measures," *International Journal of Selection and Assessment* 14 (December 2006), pp. 317-355.
33. C. H. Van Iddekinge, P. H. Raymark, and P. L. Roth, "Assessing Personality with a Structured Employment Interview: Construct-Related Validity and Susceptibility to Response Inflation," *Journal of Applied Psychology* 90 (2005), pp. 536-552; R. Mueller-Hanson, E. D. Heggestad, and G. C. Thornton, "Faking and Selection: Considering the Use of Personality from Select-In and Select-Out Perspectives," *Journal of Applied Psychology* 88 (2003), pp. 348-355; N. L. Vasilopoulos, J. M. Cucina, and J. M. McElreath, "Do Warnings of Response Verification Moderate the Relationship between Personality and Cognitive Ability?" *Journal of Applied Psychology* 90 (2005), pp. 306-322.
34. A. P. Horton, "The Downsides of Using Personality Tests for Hiring," *Fast Company,* February 23, 2018.
35. E. Huet, "In the Land of the Blind Hire," *Bloomberg Businessweek,* January 23, 2017, pp. 27-28; J. Welch and S. Welch, "Team Building: Right and Wrong," *BusinessWeek,* November 24, 2008, p. 130; S. E. Humphrey, J. R. Hollenbeck, C. J. Meyer, and D. R. Ilgen, "Trait Configurations in Self-Managed Teams: A Conceptual Examination of the Use of Seeding for Maximizing and Minimizing Trait Variance in Teams," *Journal of Applied Psychology* 92 (2007), pp. 885-892.
36. D. S. Ones, C. Viswesvaran, and F. L. Schmidt, "Comprehensive Meta-analysis of Integrity Test Validities: Findings and Implications for Personnel Selection and Theories of Job Performance," *Journal of Applied Psychology,* 78 (1993), pp. 679-703; C. H. Van Iddekinge, P. L. Roth, P. H. Raymark, and H. N. Odle-Dusseau, "The Criterion-Related Validity of Integrity Tests," *Journal of Applied Psychology* 97 (2012), pp. 499-530.
37. L. Nagele-Piazza, "Workplace Drug Testing: Can Employers Still Screen for Marijuana?" *Society for Human Resource Management,* January 21, 2020, https://www.shrm.org.
38. A. K. Wosniak, "Discrimination and the Effects of Drug Testing on Black Employment," NBER Working Paper 20095, May 2014, National Bureau of Economic Research, http://www.nber.org. For discussion of the research, see R. J. Rosen, "Racism, Again: Why Drug Tests Are Helping Black Americans Get Jobs," *The Atlantic,* May 8, 2014, http://finance.yahoo.com; B. Steverman, "How to Fight Racism with a Drug Test," *Bloomberg News,* May 5, 2014, http://www.bloomberg.com.
39. K. R. Murphy, G. C. Thornton, and D. H. Reynolds, "College Students' Attitudes toward Drug Test Programs," *Personnel Psychology* 43 (1990), pp. 615-631; M. E. Paronto, D. M. Truxillo, T. N. Bauer, and M. C. Leo, "Drug Testing, Drug Treatment, and Marijuana Use: A Fairness Perspective," *Journal of Applied Psychology* 87 (2002), pp. 1159-1166.
40. M. A. McDaniel, F. P. Morgeson, E. G. Finnegan, M. A. Campion, and E. P. Braverman, "Use of Situational Judgment Tests to Predict Job Performance: A Clarification of the Literature," *Journal of Applied Psychology* 86 (2001), pp. 730-740; J. Clavenger, G. M. Perreira, D. Weichmann, N. Schmitt, and V. S. Harvey, "Incremental Validity of Situational Judgment Tests," *Journal of Applied Psychology* 86 (2001), pp. 410-417.
41. M. A. Campion, J. E. Campion, and J. P. Hudson, "Structured Interviewing: A Note of Incremental Validity and Alternative Question Types," *Journal of Applied Psychology* 79 (1994), pp. 998-1002; E. D. Pulakos and N. Schmitt, "Experience-Based and Situational Interview Questions: Studies of Validity," *Personnel Psychology* 48 (1995), pp. 289-308; A. P. J. Ellis, B. J. West, A. M. Ryan, and R. P. DeShon, "The Use of Impression Management Tactics in Structured Interviews: A Function of Question Type?" *Journal of Applied Psychology* 87 (2002), pp. 1200-1208.
42. N. Schmitt, F. L. Oswald, B. H. Kim, M. A. Gillespie, L. J. Ramsey, and T. Y Yoo, "The Impact of Elaboration on Socially Desirable Responding and the Validity of Biodata Measures," *Journal of Applied Psychology* 88 (2003), pp. 979-988; N. Schmitt and C. Kunce, "The Effects of Required Elaboration of Answers to Biodata Questions," *Personnel Psychology* 55 (2002), pp. 569-587.
43. Hunter and Hunter, "Validity and Utility of Alternative Predictors of Job Performance."
44. R. Pingitore, B. L. Dugoni, R. S. Tindale, and B. Spring, "Bias against Overweight Job Applicants in a Simulated Interview," *Journal of Applied Psychology* 79 (1994), pp. 184-190.
45. *Watson v. Fort Worth Bank and Trust,* 108 Supreme Court 2791 (1988).
46. A. Wilhelmy, M. Kleinmann, C. J. Konig, K. G. Melchers, and D. M. Truxillo, "How and Why Do Interviewers Try to Make Impressions on Applicants? A Qualitative Study," *Journal of Applied Psychology* 101 (2016), pp. 313-332; M. A. McDaniel, D. L. Whetzel, F. L. Schmidt, and S. D. Maurer, "The Validity of Employment Interviews: A Comprehensive Review and Meta-Analysis," *Journal of Applied Psychology* 79 (1994), pp. 599-616.
47. Y. Ganzach, A. N. Kluger, and N. Klayman, "Making Decisions from an Interview: Expert Measurement and Mechanical Combination," *Personnel Psychology* 53 (2000), pp. 1-21; G. Stasser and W. Titus, "Effects of Information Load and Percentage of Shared Information on the Dissemination of Unshared Information during Group Discussion," *Journal of Personality and Social Psychology* 53 (1987), pp. 81-93.
48. C. J. Hartwell and M. A. Campion, "Getting on the Same Page: The Effect of Normative Feedback Interventions on Structured Interview Ratings," *Journal of Applied Psychology* 101 (2016), pp. 757-778; C. H. Middendorf and T. H. Macan, "Note-Taking in the Interview: Effects on Recall and Judgments," *Journal of Applied Psychology* 87 (2002), pp. 293-303; K. G. Melchers, N. Lienhardt, M. Von Aartburg, and M. Kleinmann, "Is More Structure Really Better? A Comparison of Frame of Reference Training and Descriptively Anchored Rating Scales to Improve Interviewers' Rating Quality," *Personnel Psychology* 64 (2011), pp. 53-87.
49. M. Aspan, "A.I. Is Transforming the Job Interview—and Everything After," *Fortune,* January 20, 2020, https://fortune.com.
50. J. Roberts, "The Quest for Talent," *Best's Review,* February 2018, pp. 68-73.
51. J. Boitnott, "7 Reasons You Should Pay Your Employees Above-Average Salaries," *Inc.,* June 18, 2018, https://www.inc.com; L. Weber, "High Salaries Haunt Some Job Hunters," *The Wall Street Journal,* February 4, 2016, https://www.wsj.com.

Training Employees

7

Domino's emphasis on training helps store managers and new employees work together to ensure a successful approach to learning.

Rogan Thomson/Jmp/Shutterstock

What Do I Need to Know?

After reading this chapter, you should be able to:

LO 7-1 Discuss how to link training programs to organizational needs.

LO 7-2 Explain how to assess the need for training.

LO 7-3 Explain how to assess employees' readiness for training.

LO 7-4 Describe how to plan an effective training program.

LO 7-5 Compare widely used training methods.

LO 7-6 Summarize how to implement a successful training program.

LO 7-7 Evaluate the success of a training program.

LO 7-8 Describe training methods for employee orientation and onboarding and for diversity management.

Introduction

The HR professionals at Domino's recognized how crucial training is for newly hired employees, and they were dissatisfied with the orientation process that had existed for years. New hires would travel to a location with a conference room, where they would sit with others hired to work at various locations and listen to a presentation about the pizza company's rules, culture, and expectations. The class was dull and disconnected from the actual work experience. Because the presenter needed a broad experience of the company, Domino's assigned a manager of multiple locations, not the new employees' supervisors, to conduct the training session.

Domino's training and development team wanted an orientation experience that gets employees immediately into the relevant environment: the stores where they will work, with their supervisor and co-workers. But store supervisors lack the experience and knowledge to present the necessary corporate material. The training team decided to bridge the gap with technology: interactive software running on a tablet computer and featuring an animated trainer. They hired a contractor to create Natalie, an animated character dressed in a Domino's uniform, and they gathered information from company experts to write scripts for Natalie to use to present information, evaluate input, and answer questions.

Now on new employees' first day at Domino's, they go straight to the store where they have been assigned to work, and they meet with their own supervisor. Natalie presents short segments of information and prompts the supervisor to provide a tour and demonstrations. Natalie calls on the trainee to engage in interactive tasks, such as quizzing the supervisor about company culture. The supervisor and trainee pause and restart Natalie as they work through the activities. This back-and-forth process with direct attention from the supervisor keeps participants engaged and builds the personal connections necessary for working successfully in a food service operation. It also is much more efficient for the company than pulling managers away from other key functions to a remote location to lead orientation classes.[1]

Training
An organization's planned efforts to help employees acquire job-related knowledge, skills, abilities, and behaviors, with the goal of applying these on the job.

LO 7-1 Discuss how to link training programs to organizational needs.

Instructional Design
A process of systematically developing training to meet specified needs.

Employers use simulations like the ones just described because they consider them an investment in talent—spending that will deliver valuable results through better employee performance. Human resource professionals help their organization make these investments by establishing a training program. **Training** consists of an organization's planned efforts to help employees acquire job-related knowledge, skills, abilities, and behaviors, with the goal of applying these on the job. A training program may range from formal classes to one-on-one mentoring, and it may take place on the job or at remote locations. No matter what its form, training can benefit the organization when it is linked to organizational needs and when it motivates employees.

This chapter describes how to plan and carry out an effective training program. We begin by discussing how to develop effective training in the context of the organization's strategy. Next, we discuss how organizations assess employees' training needs. We then review training methods and the process of evaluating a training program. The chapter concludes by discussing some special applications of training: orientation and onboarding of new employees and the management of diversity.

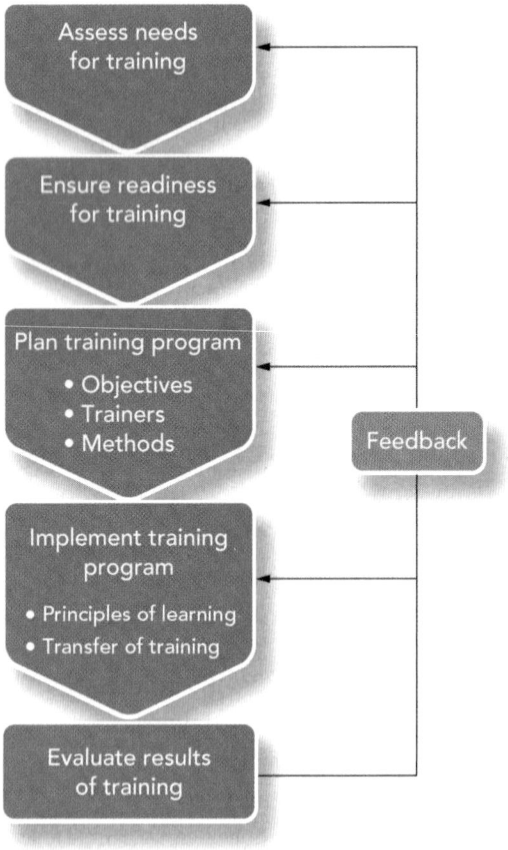

FIGURE 7.1
Stages of Instructional Design

Training Linked to Organizational Needs

The nature of the modern business environment makes training more important today than it ever has been. Rapid change, especially in the area of technology, requires that employees continually learn new skills. The new psychological contract, described in Chapter 2, has created the expectation that employees invest in their own career development, which requires learning opportunities.[2] Growing reliance on teamwork creates a demand for the ability to solve problems in teams, an ability that often requires formal training. Finally, the diversity of the U.S. population, coupled with the globalization of business, requires that employees be able to work well with people who are different from them. Successful organizations often take the lead in developing this ability.

With training so essential in modern organizations, it is important to provide training that is effective. An effective training program actually teaches what it is designed to teach, and it teaches skills and behaviors that will help the organization achieve its goals. To achieve those goals, HR professionals approach training through **instructional design**—a process of systematically developing training to meet specified needs.[3]

A complete instructional design process includes the steps shown in Figure 7.1. It begins with an assessment of the needs for training—what the organization requires that its people learn. Next, the organization ensures that employees are ready for training in terms of their attitudes, motivation, basic skills, and work environment. The third step is to plan the training program, including the program's objectives, instructors, and methods. The organization then implements the program. Finally, evaluating the results of the training provides feedback for planning future training programs.

To carry out this process more efficiently and effectively, a growing number of organizations are using a **learning management system (LMS),** a computer application that automates the administration, development, and delivery of a company's training programs.[4] Managers and employees can use the LMS to identify training needs and enroll in or download courses. LMSs can make training programs more widely available and help companies reduce travel and other costs by providing online training. Administrative tools let managers track course enrollments and program completion. The system can be linked to the organization's performance management system to plan for and manage training needs, training outcomes, and associated rewards.

Learning Management System (LMS)
A computer application that automates the administration, development, and delivery of training programs.

Needs Assessment

LO 7-2 Explain how to assess the need for training.

Instructional design logically should begin with a **needs assessment,** the process of evaluating the organization, individual employees, and employees' tasks to determine what kinds of training, if any, are necessary. As this definition indicates, the needs assessment answers questions in three broad areas:[5]

1. *Organization*—What is the context in which training will occur?
2. *Person*—Who needs training?
3. *Task*—What subjects should the training cover?

Needs Assessment
The process of evaluating the organization, individual employees, and employees' tasks to determine what kinds of training, if any, are necessary.

The answers to these questions provide the basis for planning an effective training program.

A variety of conditions may prompt an organization to conduct a needs assessment. Management may observe that some employees lack basic skills or are performing poorly. Unfortunately, this is a common situation in many service businesses, as described in the "Did You Know?" feature. Decisions to produce new products, apply new technology, or design new jobs should prompt a needs assessment because these changes tend to require new skills. The decision to conduct a needs assessment also may be prompted by outside forces, such as customer requests or legal requirements.

The outcome of the needs assessment is a set of decisions about how to address the issues that prompted the needs assessment. These decisions do not necessarily include a training program, because some issues should be resolved through methods other than training. For example, suppose a company uses delivery trucks to transport anesthetic gases to medical facilities, and a driver of one of these trucks mistakenly hooks up the supply line of a mild anesthetic from the truck to the hospital's oxygen system, contaminating the hospital's oxygen supply. This performance problem prompts a needs assessment. Whether or not the hospital decides to provide more training will depend partly on the reasons the driver erred. The driver may have hooked up the supply lines incorrectly because of a lack of knowledge about the appropriate line hookup, anger over a request for a pay raise being denied, or mislabeled valves for connecting the supply lines. Out of these three possibilities, only the lack of knowledge can be corrected through training. Other outcomes of a needs assessment might include plans for better rewards to improve motivation, better hiring decisions, and better safety precautions.

The remainder of this chapter discusses needs assessment and then what the organization should do when assessment indicates a need for training. The possibilities for action include offering existing training programs to more employees; buying or developing new training programs; and improving existing training programs. Before we consider the available training options, let's examine the elements of the needs assessment in more detail.

Did You Know?

Many Service Workers Lack Basic Skills

Roughly 6 in 10 service-sector workers in high-demand industries have only limited literacy skills. Limited skill levels are even more common in the areas of numeracy (understanding and working with numbers) and digital problem solving. These findings are from research by the National Skills Coalition, which looked at three service industries that together employ almost one-third of all U.S. workers: retail; health and social assistance; and leisure and hospitality.

Despite the workers' limited skills, jobs in these industries call upon the workers to use skills in these categories. In fact, the demand for low-skill jobs is low; about half of the jobs being filled require moderate skills—equivalent to education beyond high school but not a college degree. Many are expected to read directions and write e-mail, for example. Some of them are enrolling in adult education and pursuing certificates or other work credentials, but many say it is difficult to find the time and money to do so.

This lack of basic skills is a serious problem because the abilities to read, write, use numbers, and use computers to solve problems are "foundational," that is, essential across jobs and also necessary for learning more advanced skills. Many employers are concerned about the need for foundational skills, and some are addressing the problem by providing or paying for training.

Percentage of service-sector workers with limited skills	
Numeracy	74%
Digital problem solving	73%
Literacy	62%

Question

Suppose you are a store manager. Would it be important for your company to offer training in foundational skills? Why or why not?

Sources: Amanda Bergson-Shilcock, *Foundational Skills in the Service Sector,* National Skills Coalition, https://www.nationalskillscoalition.org, accessed April 15, 2020; National Skills Coalition, "United States' Forgotten Middle," infographic, https://www.nationalskillscoalition.org, accessed April 15, 2020; American Institutes for Research, "Do U.S. Adults Have the Skills Needed to Thrive in the 21st Century? Four PIACC Studies by AIR," February 28, 2019, https://www.air.org.

Organization Analysis

Organization Analysis
A process for determining the appropriateness of training by evaluating the characteristics of the organization.

Usually the needs assessment begins with the **organization analysis.** This is a process for determining the appropriateness of training by evaluating the characteristics of the organization. The organization analysis looks at training needs in light of the organization's strategy, resources available for training, and management's support for training activities.

Training needs will vary depending on whether the organization's strategy is based on growing or shrinking its personnel, whether it is seeking to serve a broad customer base or focusing on the specific needs of a narrow market segment, and various other strategic scenarios. An organization that concentrates on serving a niche market may need to continually update its workforce on a specialized skills set. A company that is cutting costs with a downsizing strategy may need to provide training in job search skills for employees who will be laid off. The employees who remain following the downsizing may need cross-training so that they can handle a wider variety of responsibilities.

Employee training must fit with the organization's strategy and budget. Such training can only be successful if managers are willing to help trainees use their newly learned knowledge and skills on the job.
Rawpixel.com/Shutterstock

Anyone planning a training program must consider whether the organization has the budget, time, and expertise for training. For example, if the company is installing computer-based manufacturing equipment in one of its plants, there are three ways it can ensure that it has the necessary computer-literate employees. If it has the technical experts on its staff, they can train the employees affected by the change. Or the company may use testing to determine which of its employees are already computer literate and then replace or reassign employees who lack the necessary skills. The third choice is to purchase training from an outside individual or organization.

Even if training fits the organization's strategy and budget, it can be viable only if the organization is willing to support the investment in training. Managers increase the success of training when they support it through such actions as helping trainees see how they can use their newly learned knowledge, skills, and behaviors on the job.[6] First, though, training professionals need to win that support by showing it will solve a significant problem or result in a significant improvement, relative to cost. Managers appreciate training proposals with specific goals, timetables, budgets, and methods for measuring success. Even more important, managers want to hear how the training will help them achieve business goals such as increasing sales and efficiency or lowering risks and costs.

Person Analysis

Following the organizational assessment, needs assessment turns to the remaining areas of analysis: person and task. The **person analysis** is a process for determining individuals' needs and readiness for training. It involves answering several questions:

Person Analysis
A process for determining individuals' needs and readiness for training.

- Do performance deficiencies result from a lack of knowledge, skill, or ability? (If so, training is appropriate; if not, other solutions are more relevant.)
- Who needs training?
- Are these employees ready for training?

The answers to these questions help the manager identify whether training is appropriate and which employees need training. In certain situations, such as the introduction of a new technology or service, all employees may need training. However, when needs assessment is conducted in response to a performance problem, training is not always the best solution.

The person analysis is therefore critical when training is considered in response to a performance problem. In assessing the need for training, the manager should identify all the variables that can influence performance. The primary variables are the person's ability and skills, his or her attitudes and motivation, the organization's input (including clear directions, necessary resources, and freedom from interference and distractions), performance feedback (including praise and performance standards), and positive consequences to motivate good performance. Of these variables, only ability and skills can be affected by training. Therefore, before planning a training program, it is important to be sure that any performance problem results from a deficiency in knowledge and skills. Otherwise, training dollars will be wasted, because the training is unlikely to have much effect on performance.

The person analysis also should determine whether employees are ready to undergo training. In other words, the employees to receive training not only should require additional knowledge and skill, but must be willing and able to learn. (After our discussion of the needs assessment, we will explore the topic of employee readiness in greater detail.)

Task Analysis

Task Analysis
The process of identifying the tasks, knowledge, skills, and behaviors that training should emphasize.

The third area of needs assessment is **task analysis,** the process of identifying the tasks, knowledge, skills, and behaviors that training should emphasize. Usually task analysis is conducted along with person analysis. Understanding shortcomings in performance usually requires knowledge about the tasks and work environment as well as the employee.

To carry out the task analysis, the HR professional looks at the conditions in which tasks are performed. These conditions include the equipment and environment of the job, time constraints (for example, deadlines), safety considerations, and performance standards. These observations form the basis for a description of work activities, or the tasks required by the person's job. For a selected job, the analyst interviews employees and their supervisors to prepare a list of tasks performed in that job. Then the analyst validates the list by showing it to employees, supervisors, and other subject-matter experts and asking them to complete a questionnaire about the importance, frequency, and difficulty of the tasks. For each task listed, the subject-matter expert uses a sliding scale (for example, 0 = task never performed, to 5 = task often performed) to rate the task's importance, frequency, and difficulty.[7]

The information from these questionnaires is the basis for determining which tasks will be the focus of the training. The person or committee conducting the needs assessment must decide what levels of importance, frequency, and difficulty signal a need for training. Logically, training is most needed for tasks that are important, frequent, and at least moderately difficult. For each of these tasks, the analysts must identify the knowledge, skills, and abilities required to perform the task. This information usually comes from interviews with subject-matter experts, such as employees who currently hold the job.

Readiness for Training
A combination of employee characteristics and positive work environment that permit training.

Readiness for Training

LO 7-3 Explain how to assess employees' readiness for training.

Effective training requires not only a program that addresses real needs but also a condition of employee readiness. **Readiness for training** is a combination of employee characteristics and positive work environment that permit training. It exists when employees are able and eager to learn and when their organizations encourage learning.

Employee Readiness Characteristics

To be ready to learn, employees need basic learning skills, especially *cognitive ability,* which includes being able to use written and spoken language, solve math problems, and use logic to solve problems. Ideally, the selection process identified job candidates with enough cognitive ability to handle not only the requirements for doing a job but also the training associated with that job. However, since forecasts of the skill levels of the U.S. workforce indicate that many companies will have to work with employees who lack basic skills, they may have to provide literacy training or access to classes teaching math skills before some employees can participate in job-related training.[8]

Employees learn more from training programs when they are highly motivated to learn—that is, when they really want to learn the content of the training program.[9] Employees tend to feel this way if they believe they are able to learn, see potential benefits from the training program, are aware of their need to learn, see a fit between the training and their career goals, and have the basic skills needed for participating in the program. Managers can influence a ready attitude in a variety of ways—for example, by providing feedback that encourages employees, establishing rewards for learning, and communicating with employees about the organization's career paths and future needs.

Managers encourage readiness to learn at Schweitzer Engineering Laboratories, located in Pullman, Washington. The company has a library and offers classes in math, science, and writing. The company hires for problem-solving skills, rather than educational credentials, so workers without a college degree can learn skills as needed to pursue a career path. One such worker is Roy Edwards, who was not motivated by the academic environment he experienced in college but quickly became fascinated by the activities and problems he encountered on the job. He began enrolling in the company-sponsored classes and reading about robotics and now supervises the workers who code them. His story is not uncommon at Schweitzer, where other entry-level employees also have worked their way up to positions as technicians.[10]

In today's work environment, employees' attitudes toward learning are also shaped by their experiences with technology. The "HRM Social" box describes the appeal of learning small bites of knowledge.

Work Environment

Readiness for training also depends on two broad characteristics of the work environment: situational constraints and social support.[11] *Situational constraints* are the limits on training's effectiveness that arise from the situation or the conditions within the organization. Constraints can include a lack of money for training, lack of time for training or practicing, and failure to provide proper tools and materials for learning or applying the lessons of training. Conversely, trainees are likely to apply what they learn if the organization gives them opportunities to use their new skills and if it rewards them for doing so.[12]

Social support refers to the ways the organization's people encourage training, including giving trainees praise and encouraging words, sharing information about participating in training programs, and expressing positive attitudes toward the organization's training programs. Table 7.1 summarizes some ways in which managers can support training.

Support can also come from employees' peers. Readiness for training is greater in an organization where employees share knowledge, encourage one another to learn, and have a positive attitude about carrying the extra load when co-workers are attending classes. Employers foster such attitudes and behavior when they reward learning.

LinkedIn Learning: Today's Corporate Training Center

As more and more employees communicate on social media and mobile devices, they grow used to sharing a quick sentence, headline, photo, or funny picture. They read small screens in short bursts of attention. They expect to find answers quickly and conveniently. And the sources they trust the most may not be professionals in institutions, but their friends and networks with shared values and concerns.

This pattern of behavior is affecting the way employees want to learn. They aren't patient enough to study a book or take notes in an all-day seminar. They would rather ask a question and find the answer in a video or even check out a bit of advice from a speaker with a well-known persona.

Companies are responding with short learning modules that individuals can locate online when they are interested and feel they have a few minutes for learning. Some large businesses have built libraries of lessons for their own people. And recently, the business-oriented social-media site LinkedIn has built its own version, which it hopes will appeal to workers in many organizations.

LinkedIn's venture, called LinkedIn Learning, contains thousands of video-based courses in several languages. The topics include technical skills such as marketing with social media and using various kinds of software, as well as soft skills such as communication and time management. In addition to making these courses available, LinkedIn will use data gathered from its members to recommend courses on skills relevant to members' careers. For more general recommendations, LinkedIn has also compiled playlists of courses on career themes such as starting a small business or retaining employees. Jeff Weiner, LinkedIn's CEO, describes the videos as high-quality content that will help the company fulfill its vision of "connecting people to opportunity" by giving them the knowledge they need for career success.

Questions

1. Why might an employer encourage its people to take advantage of learning on a social-media site like LinkedIn?
2. Why might an employer prefer that its people rely more on learning from resources provided by the employer?

Sources: Michael Horn, "The Future of LinkedIn Learning and the Link between Education and Work," *Forbes,* March 13, 2019, https://www.forbes.com; Frank Catalano, "LinkedIn Learning Embraces Content from Education Companies, Integrating It in One Platform," *Geek Wire,* November 9, 2018, https://www.geekwire.com; Robyn Shulman, "This Is How Entrepreneurs, Students and Teachers Can Benefit from LinkedIn Learning," *Forbes,* September 11, 2017; Ingrid Lunden, "LinkedIn Doubles Down on Education with LinkedIn Learning, Updates Desktop Site," *Tech Crunch,* September 22, 2016, https://techcrunch.com.

TABLE 7.1

What Managers Should Do to Support Training

What Managers Should Do to Support Training
Understand the content of the training.
Know how training relates to what you need employees to do.
In performance appraisals, evaluate employees on how they apply training to their jobs.
Support employees' use of training when they return to work.
Ensure that employees have the equipment and technology needed to use training.
Prior to training, discuss with employees how they plan to use training.
Recognize newly trained employees who use training content.
Give employees release time from their work to attend training.
Explain to employees why they have been asked to attend training.
Give employees feedback related to skills or behavior they are trying to develop.
If possible, be a trainer.

Sources: J. Kirsch and S. Wzientek, "The Manager's Role in Reinforcing Learning," *Training Industry Magazine,* March–April 2018, pp. 38–41; D. W. Ballard, "Managers Aren't Doing Enough to Train Employees for the Future," *Harvard Business Review,* November 14, 2017, https://hbr.org; S. Bailey, "The Answer to Transfer," *Chief Learning Officer,* November 2014, pp. 33–41; R. Hewes, "Step by Step," *TD,* February 2014, pp. 56–61.

Planning the Training Program

LO 7-4 Describe how to plan an effective training program.

Decisions about training are often the responsibility of a specialist in the organization's training or human resources department. When the needs assessment indicates a need for training and employees are ready to learn, the person responsible for training should plan a training program that directly relates to the needs identified. Planning begins with establishing objectives for the training program. Based on those objectives, the planner decides who will provide the training, what topics the training will cover, what training methods to use, and how to evaluate the training.

Objectives of the Program

Formally establishing objectives for the training program has several benefits. First, a training program based on clear objectives will be more focused and more likely to succeed. In addition, when trainers know the objectives, they can communicate them to the employees participating in the program. Employees learn best when they know what the training is supposed to accomplish. Finally, down the road, establishing objectives provides a basis for measuring whether the program succeeded, as we will discuss later in this chapter.

Effective training objectives have several characteristics:

- They include a statement of what the employee is expected to do, the quality or level of performance that is acceptable, and the conditions under which the employee is to apply what he or she learned (for instance, physical conditions, mental stresses, or equipment failure).[13]
- They include performance standards that are measurable.
- They identify the resources needed to carry out the desired performance or outcome. Successful training requires employees to learn but also employers to provide the necessary resources.

A related issue at the outset is who will participate in the training program. Some training programs are developed for all employees of the organization or all members of a team. Other training programs identify individuals who lack desirable skills or have potential to be promoted, then provide training in the areas of need that are identified for the particular employees. When deciding who to include in training, the organization has to avoid illegal discrimination. The organization should not–intentionally or unintentionally–exclude members of protected groups, such as women, minorities, and older employees. During the training, all participants should receive equal treatment, such as equal opportunities for practice. In addition, the training program should provide reasonable accommodation for trainees with disabilities. The kinds of accommodations that are appropriate will vary according to the type of training and type of disability. One employee might need an interpreter, whereas another might need to have classroom instruction provided in a location accessible to wheelchairs.

In-House or Contracted Out?

An organization can provide an effective training program, even if it lacks expertise in training. Often, many organizations use outside experts to develop and present training courses. Many companies and consultants provide training services to organizations. Community colleges also work with employers to train employees in a variety of skills.

To select a training service, an organization can mail several vendors a *request for proposal (RFP),* which is a document outlining the type of service needed, the type and number of references needed, the number of employees to be trained, the date by which the training is to be completed, and the date by which proposals should be received. A complete RFP also indicates funding for the project and the process by which the organization will determine its level of satisfaction. Putting together a request for proposal is time consuming but worthwhile because it helps the organization clarify its objectives, compare vendors, and measure results.

Vendors that believe they are able to provide the services outlined in the RFP submit proposals that provide the types of information requested. The organization reviews the proposals to eliminate any vendors that do not meet requirements and to compare the vendors that do qualify. They check references and select a candidate, based on the proposal and the vendor's answers to questions about its experience, work samples, and evidence that its training programs meet objectives.

The cost of purchasing training from a contractor can vary substantially. In general, it is much costlier to purchase specialized training that is tailored to the organization's unique requirements than to participate in a seminar or training course that teaches general skills or knowledge. Preparing a specialized training program can require a significant investment of time for material the consultant won't be able to sell to other clients. Not surprisingly, then, spending for outside training services has decreased, along with total training expenditures, despite an increase in training payroll among companies of all sizes.[14]

Even in organizations that send employees to outside training programs, someone in the organization may be responsible for coordinating the overall training program. Called *training administration,* this is typically the responsibility of a human resources professional. Training administration includes activities before, during, and after training sessions.

Choice of Training Methods

Whether the organization prepares its own training programs or buys training from other organizations, it is important to verify that the content of the training relates directly to the training objectives. Relevance to the organization's needs and objectives ensures that training money is well spent. Tying training content closely to objectives also improves trainees' learning, because it increases the likelihood that the training will be meaningful and helpful.

After deciding on the goals and content of the training program, planners must decide how the training will be conducted. As we will describe in the next section, a wide variety of methods is available. Training methods fall into the broad categories described in Table 7.2: presentation, hands-on, and group-building methods.

TABLE 7.2
Categories of Training Methods

METHOD	TECHNIQUES	APPLICATIONS
Presentation methods: trainees receive information provided by others	Lectures, workbooks, video clips, podcasts, websites	Conveying facts or comparing alternatives
Hands-on methods: trainees are actively involved in trying out skills	On-the-job training, simulations, role-plays, computer games	Teaching specific skills; showing how skills are related to job or how to handle interpersonal issues
Group-building methods: trainees share ideas and experiences, build group identities, learn about interpersonal relationships and the group	Group discussions, experiential programs, team training	Establishing teams or work groups; managing performance of teams or work groups

Training programs may use these methods alone or in combination. In general, the methods used should be suitable for the course content and the learning abilities of the participants. The following section explores the options in greater detail.

Training Methods

LO 7-5 Compare widely used training methods.

A wide variety of methods is available for conducting training. Figure 7.2 shows the percentage of training hours delivered to employees by each of several methods: instructor-led classrooms, computer-based instruction, virtual classrooms, mobile devices, and combinations of these methods. Although the share of instruction provided online has grown over the past few years, classroom training remains the most widely used of these methods.[15]

Classroom Instruction

At school, we tend to associate learning with classroom instruction, and that type of training is most widely used in the workplace, too. Classroom instruction typically involves a trainer lecturing a group. Trainers often supplement lectures with slides, discussions, case studies, question-and-answer sessions, and role playing. Actively involving trainees enhances learning.

When the course objectives call for presenting information on a specific topic to many trainees, classroom instruction is one of the least expensive and least time-consuming ways to accomplish that goal. Learning will be more effective if trainers enhance lectures with job-related examples and opportunities for hands-on learning. Trainers can increase the clarity and impact of their message by using audiovisual techniques such as slides (for example, PowerPoint), video clips, interactive links to the Internet, and other sounds and images. Videos can show situations and equipment that would be difficult to demonstrate in a classroom. And when training objectives require that several trainers provide the same message, recording a video can deliver that consistency.

Communications technology has expanded the notion of the classroom to classes of trainees scattered in various locations. With *distance learning,* trainees at different locations attend programs online, using their computers to view lectures, participate in discussions, and share documents. Technology applications in distance learning may include videoconferencing, e-mail, instant messaging, document-sharing software, and web cameras. When Steelcase was ready to begin selling its Node chair, a flexible classroom chair with a

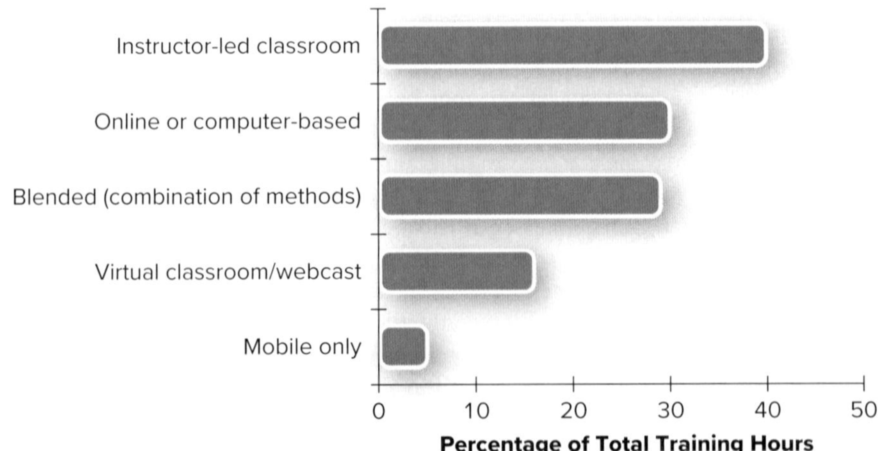

FIGURE 7.2
Use of Instructional Methods

Source: "2019 Training Industry Report," *Training,* https://trainingmag.com, accessed April 16, 2020.

swivel seat, storage for backpacks, and a customizable work surface, it needed to show its global sales force how adaptable it was to today's classrooms and teaching methods. Steelcase also had to deliver the training fast, so that the sales reps would be prepared before schools were making their annual purchases for the next academic year. The solution was a virtual classroom, which allowed trainees to see the chair as well as hear the training.[16]

Distance learning provides many of the benefits of classroom training without the cost and time of travel to a shared classroom. In fact, distance learning has become an essential tool during the COVID-19 pandemic, as many organizations continue to offer workplace learning while employees work remotely from their homes in order to stay safe.[17] The major disadvantage of distance learning is that interaction between the trainer and audience may be limited. To overcome this hurdle, distance learning usually provides a communications link between trainees and trainer. Also, on-site instructors or facilitators should be available to answer questions and moderate question-and-answer sessions.

Computer-Based Training

Although almost all organizations use classroom training, new technologies are gaining in popularity as technology improves and becomes cheaper. With computer-based training, participants receive course materials and instruction on a computer or mobile device. This method also allows for inclusion of audiovisual content, with the added benefit that users often can control aspects of the presentation–for example, by slowing down or speeding up the pace of the presentation or rewinding to review material. Many of these materials are interactive, so participants can answer questions and try out techniques, with course materials adjusted according to participants' responses. Online training programs may allow trainees to submit questions via e-mail and to participate in online discussions. Multimedia capabilities enable computers to provide sounds, images, and video presentations, along with text.

Computer-based training is generally less expensive than putting an instructor in a classroom of trainees. The low cost to deliver information gives the company flexibility in scheduling training so that it can fit around work requirements. Training can be delivered in smaller doses so material is easier to remember. Trainees today generally have experience interacting with computers, both in work and in gaming; trainers can learn what makes these experiences successful (see "HR How To"). For example, trainees may appreciate the multimedia capabilities, which appeal to several senses, and the chance to learn from experts anywhere in the world. Finally, it is easier to customize computer-based training for individual learners.

Current applications of computer-based training can extend its benefits:

E-Learning
Receiving training via the Internet or the organization's intranet.

- **E-learning** involves receiving training via the Internet or the organization's intranet, typically through some combination of web-based training modules, distance learning, and virtual classrooms. E-learning uses electronic networks for delivering and sharing information, and it offers tools and information for helping trainees improve performance. Training programs may include links to other online information resources and to trainees and experts for collaboration on problem solving. The e-learning system may also process enrollments, test and evaluate participants, and monitor progress. Quicken Loans uses e-learning to motivate employees to learn from their peers' best practices in customer service. It created an online contest called "Quicken's Got Talent." Employees who serve customers over the phone can submit recordings of calls they handled well. Trainers pick one submission per day to post on the game. Employees listen to the recordings and rate their co-worker's performance on a scale of 1 to 5. Each month the employee who submitted the top-scoring call receives a prize worth up to $200; winners of the monthly round are eligible for a competition with a $1,000 prize. The e-learning program tracks participation and creates a library of best-practices clips that are available for future learning.[18]

HR How To

Deepening Trainees' Involvement

More and more employees today have experience playing video games. And like any skill, the ability to get a high score on a video game requires learning. The best games have elements that apply to learning online and often to learning when computer-based training is coupled with other methods. Here are some game-related training ideas for deepening trainees' involvement with the lessons, which should boost their understanding and retention:

- Keep rules simple. While complex, immersive games can be appealing, people can get quickly involved with a simple game of tapping and swiping. Divide up complicated topics into small chunks that trainees can move into and out of as time becomes available for learning. This also lets them build on small successes.
- Don't use words as a crutch. Remember, there are more ways to convey information on a screen. Visual and sound cues can direct learners to needed information, such as icons and animations indicating how a tap or swipe will advance them through a task. Sounds also can be associated with successes, cautions, or other topics.
- Plan for different learning styles. With e-learning, trainees typically have (and probably want) some control over their progress. These controls should take into account that some trainees will want to be led through a demonstration while others prefer to try out different paths and learn from what happens. For the latter group, training that just keeps delivering information will be holding back trainees from their real learning.
- Tell stories. One reason video games are so appealing is that most involve at least a rudimentary story. A compelling story that is relevant, personal, and enriched with details is even more effective. In training, stories could present a problem to solve or allow time for participants and trainees to share personal experiences relevant to the topic. Today's training and conferencing software often has features that let participants break into small groups to share experiences. Even individual trainees can pause a training presentation to hear audio or view video clips.

Questions

1. Which of the ideas in this list apply only to computer-based training, and which could also be used in a classroom setting?
2. Do you prefer to learn from someone telling you what to do or from experimenting yourself? How hard is it to imagine a preference for the other style of learning?

Sources: Galen Midford, "Video Game Tutorials Exhibit Good Design Techniques," *TD,* April 2019, pp. 444–449; Martha Bird, "The Art of Storytelling," *Training,* March/April 2019, pp. 108, 110; Jonathan Halls, "Move Beyond Words to Experience," *TD,* February 2019, pp. 69–72.

- **Electronic performance support systems (EPSSs)** are computer applications that provide access to skills training, information, and expert advice when a problem occurs on the job.[19] Employees needing guidance can use the EPSS to look up the particular information they need, such as detailed instructions on how to perform an unfamiliar task. Using an EPSS is faster and more relevant than attending classes, even classes offered online, and can make training available to a global workforce. Cathay Life Insurance provides its sales agents with iPads loaded with apps designed to support what they have learned and give them access to additional training. One app helps agents arrange schedules and assess their performance. A learning-related app offers access to multimedia courses and short videos. Data generated by the agents' use of the apps guides managers in coaching the agents and guiding them to additional training.[20]

Electronic Performance Support System (EPSS) Computer application that provides access to skills training, information, and expert advice as needed.

The best e-learning combines the advantages of the Internet with the principles of a good learning environment. It takes advantage of the web's dynamic nature and ability to use many positive learning features, including hyperlinks to other training sites and content, control by the trainee, and ability for trainees to collaborate.

On-the-Job Training

On-the-Job Training (OJT)
Training methods in which a person with job experience and skill guides trainees in practicing job skills at the workplace.

Apprenticeship
A work-study training method that teaches job skills through a combination of on-the-job training and classroom training.

Internship
On-the-job learning sponsored by an educational institution as a component of an academic program.

Although people often associate training with classrooms, much learning occurs while employees are performing their jobs. **On-the-job training (OJT)** refers to training methods in which a person with job experience and skill guides trainees in practicing job skills at the workplace. This type of training takes various forms, including apprenticeships and internships.

An **apprenticeship** is a work-study training method that teaches job skills through a combination of structured on-the-job training and classroom training. The OJT component of an apprenticeship involves the apprentice assisting a certified tradesperson (a journeyman) at the work site. Typically, the classroom training is provided by local trade schools, high schools, and community colleges. Government requirements for an apprenticeship program vary by occupation, but programs generally range from one to six years. Requirements may be based on a minimum amount of time (often at least 2,000 hours of on-the-job learning), mastery of specified skills following classroom or online instruction plus on-the-job learning, or some combination of the two measures.[21] Some apprenticeship programs are sponsored by individual companies, others by employee unions. As shown in the left column of Table 7.3, most apprenticeship programs are in the skilled trades, such as plumbing, carpentry, and electrical work.

For trainees, a major advantage of apprenticeship is the ability to earn an income while learning a trade. In addition, training through an apprenticeship is usually effective because it involves hands-on learning and extensive practice. Some employers are concerned that an apprenticeship program will require working with a union or that employees who receive such training will leave for a better job. However, unionization is not strongly associated with employer-paid training in most industries, and when an employer provides apprenticeships, employees may in fact feel greater loyalty.[22] Furthermore, companies need not avoid the apprenticeship approach for work outside the construction trades. Zurich North America set up a two-year apprenticeship program in which the apprentices work in the office three days a week, rotating between the insurance company's claims and underwriting departments. They take courses at nearby Harper College on the other two days of the workweek. The company pays the apprentices $14 an hour as well as the cost of their tuition. Apprentices also have support from managers, mentors, and tutors.[23]

An **internship** is on-the-job learning sponsored by an educational institution as a component of an academic program. The sponsoring school works with local employers to place students in positions where they can gain experience related to their area of study. As described in more detail in the ethics case at the end of the chapter, the federal government regulates the use of internships in order to protect students from being exploited by employers using them as a form of low-cost or free labor rather than training them. Recent rules provide guidance on how employers can meet the requirements and have loosened previous regulations. The new rules offer tests for showing that the internship primarily benefits the intern rather than the company. For example, the company should provide training "similar to that which would be given in an educational environment."[24] Many internships prepare students for professions such as those listed in the right column of Table 7.3.

TABLE 7.3
Typical Jobs for Apprentices and Interns

APPRENTICESHIP	INTERNSHIP
Bricklayer	Accountant
Carpenter	Doctor
Electrician	Journalist
Plumber	Lawyer
Nursing assistant	Nurse
Welder	

To be effective, OJT programs should include several characteristics:

- The organization should issue a policy statement describing the purpose of OJT and emphasizing the organization's support for it.
- The organization should specify who is accountable for conducting OJT. This accountability should be included in the relevant job descriptions.
- The organization should review OJT practices at companies in similar industries.
- Managers and peers should be trained in OJT principles.
- Employees who conduct OJT should have access to lesson plans, checklists, procedure manuals, training manuals, learning contracts, and progress report forms.
- Before conducting OJT with an employee, the organization should assess the employee's level of basic skills.[25]

Simulations

A **simulation** is a training method that represents a real-life situation, with trainees making decisions resulting in outcomes that mirror what would happen on the job. Simulations enable trainees to see the impact of their decisions in an artificial, risk-free environment. They are used for teaching production and process skills as well as management and interpersonal skills. Simulations used in training include call centers stocked with phones and reference materials, as well as mock-ups of houses used for training cable installers. OhioHealth's three hospitals have simulation centers where doctors, nurses, and first responders can get training in how to handle various kinds of emergencies. The centers feature patient simulators, which are a kind of mannequin that can simulate human functions such as breathing, coughing, blinking, and displaying vital signs—and even deliver simulated babies. Trainers can make the simulators realistic for particular situations by applying makeup, adding props, and arranging the scene. A paramedic who has received training through simulation praises this method for providing a chance to practice and make mistakes in a low-pressure environment, so the paramedic is ready to perform similar activities under pressure in real emergencies.[26]

Simulation
A training method that represents a real-life situation, with trainees making decisions resulting in outcomes that mirror what would happen on the job.

Simulators must have elements identical to those found in the work environment. The simulator needs to respond exactly as equipment would under the conditions and response given by the trainee. For this reason, simulators are expensive to develop and need constant updating as new information about the work environment becomes available. Still, they are an excellent training method when the risks of a mistake on the job are great. Trainees do not have to be afraid of the impact of wrong decisions when using the simulator, as they would be with on-the-job training. Also, trainees tend to be enthusiastic about this type of learning and to learn quickly, and the lessons are generally related very closely to job performance. Given these benefits, this training method is likely to become more widespread as its development costs fall into a range more companies can afford.[27]

When simulations are conducted online, trainees often participate by creating **avatars,** or computer depictions of themselves, which they manipulate onscreen to play roles as workers or other participants in a job-related situation. Another way to enhance the simulation experience is to use **virtual reality,** a computer-based technology that provides an interactive, three-dimensional learning experience. Using specialized equipment or viewing the virtual model on a computer screen, trainees move through the simulated environment and interact with its components. Devices relay information from the environment to the trainees' senses. For example, audio interfaces, gloves that provide a sense of touch, treadmills, or motion platforms create a realistic but artificial environment. Devices also communicate information about the trainee's movements to a computer. The "Best Practices" box describes how Verizon successfully uses virtual reality as part of its employee training.

Avatars
Computer depictions of trainees, which the trainees manipulate in an online role-play.

Virtual Reality
A computer-based technology that provides an interactive, three-dimensional learning experience.

Best Practices

Virtual Reality at Verizon Generates Real Learning

Verizon's learning and development team actively pursues innovation in support of its strategy. One recent result is the use of virtual reality to train its retail store managers how to handle an all-too-common security risk: robberies. Verizon worked with its security and HR business practices groups to identify the most common robbery scenarios, using the information to create scripts. They chose a store, hired actors, and filmed various ways the scenarios could play out, depending on choices made by the trainees. To participate in the training, managers wear Oculus Go headsets during a 10-minute session in which they see the scenario play out as if they are in the store. The training generates an emotional response, which enables the trainees to practice being calm under stress. The trainers explain the purpose beforehand and debrief the trainees afterward so they can understand how well they performed relative to the company's standards. In an assessment of the training, the store managers gave high ratings for their engagement in the training and preparedness to handle similar situations. The feedback is enabling Verizon to identify stores where managers may need additional training.

Verizon also is using a similar technology, called augmented reality. With AR, the trainee can see the real-world situation but is also wearing glasses equipped with a computer that can record videos and display information overlaid on the real world. The company is using this technology to train technicians to handle unfamiliar situations they encounter in their work. The technicians can call a coach for live technical assistance; the coach can view what the technician is seeing and provide instructions. In a test of AR for this purpose, Verizon found that using it reduced errors by 77% and cut the time to complete tasks almost in half. In addition, managers didn't have to spend time fielding questions from technicians. Verizon estimated that rolling out the program to all its technicians could save millions of dollars.

These are just two of the creative approaches Verizon has taken to make training more effective. For teaching leadership to management trainees, the company's training and development team has also built fully functioning models of retail stores for simulating a variety of situations. In addition, it constructed 15 inventory rooms in which management trainees played an escape-room game involving completion of inventory management tasks. Learning apps help trainees keep track of training sessions and offer a social-media option for interacting with other trainees. After the management training initiative, most participants said they acquired valuable knowledge and improved their performance of key behaviors; further, they posted better store performance on several efficiency and financial indicators.

Questions

1. What benefits can you identify from Verizon's use of technology in training?
2. Suggest one other possible application of virtual reality to employees' jobs in Verizon stores. That is, what could trainees practice doing?

Sources: Yuki Noguchi, "Virtual Reality Goes to Work, Helping Train Employees," *Morning Edition,* October 8, 2019, https://www.npr.org; "Training Top 10 Hall of Fame: Outstanding Training Initiatives," *Training,* March/April 2019, pp. 90–93; "BEST Award: Verizon," *TD,* October 2018, https://www.td.org.

BNSF Railway uses virtual reality for training employees on how to conduct a brake safety inspection. Employees take the role of avatars in a 3D simulation in which they perform brake inspections on rail cars. The simulation includes all the important parts that have to be examined, including air hoses, angle cocks, and hand brakes. It represents all defects that can occur but cannot be incorporated into on-the-job training because doing so would be unsafe or difficult to demonstrate. The program improves employees' ability to identify problems and correct malfunctions.[28]

Business Games and Case Studies

Training programs use business games and case studies to develop employees' management skills. A case study is a detailed description of a situation that trainees study and discuss. Cases are designed to develop higher-order thinking skills, such as the ability to analyze and evaluate information. They also can be a safe way to encourage trainees to take appropriate risks, by giving them practice in weighing and acting on uncertain outcomes. There are many sources of case studies, including Harvard Business School, the Darden Business School at the University of Virginia, and McGraw-Hill publishing company.

Here an individual works within a virtual reality training lab during a recent coal mine rescue simulation. Virtual reality is one way to provide an interactive learning experience for workers.
The Columbus Dispatch, Adam Cairns/AP Images

With business games, trainees gather information, analyze it, and make decisions that influence the outcome of the game. To train salespeople in its Winning Major program, Humana assembles teams of five trainees and has each team imagine it is a salesperson for a robotics company. Each team plays three rounds of simulations in which it handles issues from three imaginary clients. The team that generates the most revenue is declared the winner.[29] Games stimulate learning because they actively involve participants and mimic the competitive nature of business. A realistic game may be more meaningful to trainees than presentation techniques such as classroom instruction.

Training with case studies and games requires that participants come together to discuss the cases or the progress of the game. This requires face-to-face or electronic meetings. Also, participants must be willing to be actively involved in analyzing the situation and defending their decisions.

Behavior Modeling

Research suggests that one of the most effective ways to teach interpersonal skills is through behavior modeling.[30] This involves training sessions in which participants observe other people demonstrating the desired behavior, then have opportunities to practice the behavior themselves. For example, a training program could involve several days of four-hour sessions, each focusing on one interpersonal skill, such as communicating or coaching. At the beginning of each session, participants hear the reasons for using the key behaviors; then they watch a video of a model performing the key behaviors. They practice through role-playing and receive feedback about their performance. In addition, they evaluate the performance of the model in the video and discuss how they can apply the behavior on the job.

Experiential Programs

To develop teamwork and leadership skills, some organizations enroll their employees in a form of training called **experiential programs.** In experiential programs, participants learn concepts and then apply them by simulating the behaviors involved and analyzing the activity, connecting it with real-life situations.[31] Grant Thornton, a firm that provides auditing and tax services, uses an experiential program called CLEAR Engagement for training employees in problem solving and teamwork. Groups of about five people each meet for a day and a half to work through several dozen business decisions that could arise in work

Experiential Programs
Training programs in which participants learn concepts and apply them by simulating behaviors involved and analyzing the activity, connecting it with real-life situations.

with a client. As participants work through the problems together, they see how people from other departments bring helpful perspectives, and they build relationships they can use when they return to work.[32]

Experiential training programs should follow several guidelines. A program should be related to a specific business problem. Participants should feel challenged and move outside their comfort zones but within limits that keep their motivation strong and help them understand the purpose of the program.

Adventure Learning
A teamwork and leadership training program based on the use of challenging, structured outdoor activities.

One form of experiential program, called **adventure learning,** uses challenging, structured outdoor activities, which may include difficult sports such as rafting or mountain climbing. Other activities may be structured tasks like climbing walls, completing rope courses, climbing ladders, or making "trust falls" (in which each trainee stands on a table and falls backward into the arms of other group members).

The impact of adventure learning programs has not been rigorously tested, but participants report they gained a greater understanding of themselves and the ways they interact with their co-workers. One key to the success of such programs may be that the organization needs to insist that entire work groups participate together. This encourages people to see, discuss, and correct the kinds of behavior that keep the group from performing well.

Before requiring employees to participate in experiential programs, the organization should consider the possible drawbacks. Because these programs are usually physically demanding and often require participants to touch each other, companies face certain risks. Some employees may be injured or may feel that they were sexually harassed or that their privacy was invaded. Also, the Americans with Disabilities Act (discussed in Chapter 3) raises questions about requiring employees with disabilities to participate in physically demanding training experiences.

One of the most important features of organizations today is teamwork. Experiential programs include team-building exercises like wall climbing and rafting to help build trust and cooperation among employees.
David Pu'u/Getty Images

Team Training

A possible alternative to experiential programs is team training, which coordinates the performance of individuals who work together to achieve a common goal. An organization may benefit from providing such training to groups when group members must share information and group performance depends on the performance of the individual group members. Examples include the military, nuclear power plants, and commercial airlines. In those work settings, much work is performed by crews, groups, or teams. Success depends on individuals' coordinating their activities to make decisions, perhaps in dangerous situations.

Ways to conduct team training include cross-training and coordination training.[33] In **cross-training,** team members understand and practice each other's skills so that they are prepared to step in and take another member's place. In a factory, for example, production workers could be cross-trained to handle all phases of assembly. This enables the company to move them to the positions where they are most needed to complete an order on time.

Cross-Training
Team training in which team members understand and practice each other's skills so that they are prepared to step in and take another member's place.

Coordination training trains the team in how to share information and decisions to obtain the best team performance. This type of training is especially important for commercial aviation and surgical teams. Both of these kinds of teams must monitor different aspects of equipment and the environment, at the same time sharing information to make the most effective decisions regarding patient care or aircraft safety and performance. One way to focus on teamwork behaviors is to have team members participate in an unfamiliar type of project. For example, a group of managers from Thermo Fisher Scientific divided into five teams, each assigned to make one course for the night's dinner. Each team was given the ingredients for a particular dish but not a recipe, and the group members had to figure out how they would solve the problem together. A similar type of learning occurs in a team training program called Dig This, which assigns teams to complete a mission using heavy construction equipment.[34]

Coordination Training
Team training that teaches the team how to share information and make decisions to obtain the best team performance.

Training may also target the skills needed by the teams' leaders. **Team leader training** refers to training people in the skills necessary for team leadership. For example, the training may be aimed at helping team leaders learn to resolve conflicts or coordinate activities.

Team Leader Training
Training in the skills necessary for effectively leading the organization's teams.

Action Learning

Another form of group building is **action learning.** In this type of training, teams or work groups get an actual problem, work on solving it and commit to an action plan, and are accountable for carrying out the plan. Ideally, the project is one for which the efforts and results will be visible not only to participants but also to others in the organization. The visibility and impact of the task are intended to make participation exciting, relevant, and engaging. Keller William Realty incorporates action learning into its training program for real estate agents. New agents participate in a 12-session program that includes cold-calling prospective customers. Getting used to making those calls is essential to winning the contracts that are the source of a real estate agent's income. Later, they participate in another training program aimed at learning how to keep generating a steady flow of leads. In that seven-week program, participants are supposed to make 20 new contacts every day. On average, this results in participants signing 14 contracts during the training period, so they are seeing practical benefits even while training.[35]

Action Learning
Training in which teams get an actual problem, work on solving it and commit to an action plan, and are accountable for carrying it out.

The effectiveness of action learning has not been formally evaluated. This type of training seems to result in a great deal of learning, however, and employees are able to apply what they learn because action learning involves actual problems the organization is facing. The group approach also helps teams identify behaviors that interfere with problem solving.

LO 7-6 Summarize how to implement a successful training program.

Implementing the Training Program

Learning permanently changes behavior. For employees to acquire knowledge and skills in the training program, the training program must be implemented in a way that applies what is known about how people learn. Equally important, implementation of a training program should enable employees to transfer what they have learned to the workplace—in other words, employees should behave differently as a result of the training.

Principles of Learning

Researchers have identified a number of ways employees learn best.[36] Table 7.4 summarizes ways that training can best encourage learning. In general, effective training communicates learning objectives clearly, presents information in distinctive and memorable ways, and helps trainees link the subject matter to their jobs.

Employees are most likely to learn when training is linked to their current job experiences and tasks.[37] There are a number of ways trainers can make this link. Training sessions should present material using familiar concepts, terms, and examples. As far as possible, the training context—such as the physical setting or the images presented on a computer—should mirror the work environment. Along with physical elements, the context should include emotional elements. Training expert Alan Landers takes into account the variety of

TABLE 7.4

Ways That Training Helps Employees Learn

TRAINING ACTIVITY	WAYS TO PROVIDE TRAINING ACTIVITY
Communicate the learning objective.	Demonstrate the performance to be expected. Give examples of questions to be answered.
Use distinctive, attention-getting messages.	Emphasize key points. Use pictures, not just words.
Limit the content of training.	Group lengthy material into chunks. Provide a visual image of the course material. Provide opportunities to repeat and practice material.
Guide trainees as they learn.	Use words as reminders about sequence of activities. Use words and pictures to relate concepts to one another and to their context. Prompt trainees to evaluate whether they understand and are using effective tactics to learn the material.
Elaborate on the subject.	Present the material in different contexts and settings. Relate new ideas to previously learned concepts. Practice in a variety of contexts and settings.
Provide memory cues.	Suggest memory aids. Use familiar sounds or rhymes as memory cues.
Transfer course content to the workplace.	Design the learning environment so that it has elements in common with the workplace. Require learners to develop action plans that apply training content to their jobs. Use words that link the course to the workplace.
Provide feedback about performance.	Tell trainees how accurately and quickly they are performing their new skill. Show how trainees have met the objectives of the training.

Sources: Adapted from R. M. Gagne, "Learning Processes and Instruction," *Training Research Journal* 1 (1995/96), pp. 17–28; and Traci Sitzmann, "Self-Regulating Online Course Engagement," *T&D,* March 2010, https://www.td.org.

experience levels that trainees may bring to the sessions. In classroom training, he advises identifying which participants have been working with the subject matter for less than a year, one to two years, and three or more years. Then he assigns a different role to each group. The most experienced participants become the group's "reality checkers," making sure the content is relevant. The middle group becomes the "progress experts," who are encouraged to share their experiences in learning the subject. And those new to the subject are urged to ask questions. In this way, all participants have a valued, engaging role.[38]

To fully understand and remember the content of the training, employees need a chance to demonstrate and practice what they have learned. Trainers should provide ways to actively involve the trainees, have them practice repeatedly, and have them complete tasks within a time that is appropriate in light of the learning objectives. Practice requires physically carrying out the desired behaviors, not just describing them. Practice sessions could include role-playing interactions, filling out relevant forms, or operating machinery or equipment to be used on the job. The more the trainee practices these activities, the more comfortable he or she will be in applying the skills on the job. People tend to benefit most from practice that occurs over several sessions, rather than one long practice session.[39] For complex tasks, it may be most effective to practice a few skills or behaviors at a time, then combine them in later practice sessions.

Trainees need to understand whether or not they are succeeding. Therefore, training sessions should offer feedback. Effective feedback focuses on specific behaviors and is delivered as soon as possible after the trainees practice or demonstrate what they have learned.[40] One way to do this is to videotape trainees, then show the video while indicating specific behaviors that do or do not match the desired outcomes of the training. Feedback should include praise when trainees show they have learned material, as well as guidance on how to improve.

Well-designed training helps people remember the content. Training programs need to break information into chunks that people can remember. Research suggests that people can attend to no more than four to five items at a time. If a concept or procedure involves more than five items, the training program should deliver information in shorter sessions or chunks.[41] Other ways to make information more memorable include presenting it with visual images and practicing some tasks enough that they become automatic.

Written materials should have an appropriate reading level. A simple way to assess **readability**—the difficulty level of written materials—is to look at the words being used and at the length of sentences. In general, it is easiest to read short sentences and simple, standard words. If training materials are too difficult to understand, several adjustments can help. The basic approach is to rewrite the material looking for ways to simplify it.

Readability
The difficulty level of written materials.

- Substitute simple, concrete words for unfamiliar or abstract words.
- Divide long sentences into two or more short sentences.
- Divide long paragraphs into two or more short paragraphs.
- Add checklists (like this one) and illustrations to clarify the text.

Another approach is to substitute video, hands-on learning, or other nonwritten methods for some of the written material. A longer-term solution is to use tests to identify employees who need training to improve their reading levels and to provide that training first.

Transfer of Training

Ultimately, the goal of implementation is **transfer of training,** or on-the-job use of knowledge, skills, and behaviors learned in training. As described in the "HR Oops!" box, transfer of training has been particularly difficult to achieve in training aimed at preventing sexual harassment. Transfer of training requires that employees actually learn the content of the

Transfer of Training
On-the-job use of knowledge, skills, and behaviors learned in training.

So Far, Anti-Harassment Training Has Not Ended Harassment

Despite laws on the books for several decades and training programs in place at many, if not most, employers, sexual harassment has continued to plague the workplace. According to a recent report from the Equal Employment Opportunity Commission, 85% of women said they had experienced sexual harassment in some form. HR professionals are trying to help employers understand what is going wrong and plan for improved transfer of training.

Criticisms of anti-harassment training point to a lack of management commitment and a lack of practical content. When organizations require employees to watch a 20-minute video featuring bad acting in implausible scenarios and then check a box to indicate they underwent training, this cursory approach signals a lack of interest in the training objectives. Employees may conclude that the employer just wants to avoid legal trouble. They might even learn to disrespect the whole issue themselves. Furthermore, if training merely displays blatantly bad behavior for viewers to criticize, it does not help employees prepare to respond appropriately to situations they are more likely to encounter.

In contrast, transfer of training is likelier when a trainer with in-depth knowledge leads discussions in person. This gets participants engaged and helps them identify ways to apply principles to their situation. Trainers should understand the employees' situation well enough to come up with scenarios that are relevant. The course content should include practical actions to take, such as body language to avoid, ways to keep the situation respectful, and questions to ask oneself about whether a type of behavior might be harassment or not. The training should highlight ways that witnesses of harassment can respond to short-circuit the behavior.

Furthermore, successful training needs to be just one piece of a culture that does not tolerate harassment. Leaders need to believe in the message and be rewarded for promoting tolerance and civility. The organization needs to establish—and employ—ways of reporting problems as well as consequences for harassing others.

Questions

1. What are two ways an organization can ensure that social support is in place to promote transfer of anti-harassment training?
2. What goal might an employee set to apply skills from anti-harassment training on the job?

Sources: Rebecca Grant, "Why Do Employers Keep Providing the Same Ineffective Sexual Harassment Training? *Quartz at Work,* June 19, 2019, https://qz.com; Kathy Gurchiek, "Sexual Harassment Prevention Training Should Involve Real Conversations," *Society for Human Resource Management,* May 30, 2018, https://www.shrm.org; Ken Cooper, "Lessons from the Sexual Harassment Scandals," *Leadership Excellence,* February 2018, pp. 12–14; Neal Goodman, "Sexual Harassment Training: Myths and Reality," *Training,* January/February 2018, pp. 114, 116.

training program. Then, for employees to apply what they learned, certain conditions must be in place: social support, technical support, and self-management.

Social support, as we saw in the discussion of readiness for training, includes support from the organization and from trainees' peers. Before, during, and after implementation, the organization's managers need to emphasize the importance of training, encourage their employees to attend training programs, and point out connections between training content and employees' job requirements. The organization can formally provide peer support by establishing **communities of practice**–groups of employees who work together, learn from each other, and develop a common understanding of how to get work accomplished. It also may assign experienced employees to act as mentors, who provide advice and support to the trainees. Social support was a key to the success of safety training at Honda of America's East Liberty, Ohio, assembly plant. Managers identified workers with a concern for quality and safety, willingness to learn, and a desire to help others by sharing their knowledge. After seven days of training in ergonomic work processes, these employees became "ergo coaches,"

Communities of Practice
Groups of employees who work together, learn from each other, and develop a common understanding of how to get work accomplished.

who teach new employees proper techniques and share tips with their co-workers. Employees are positive about learning from their peers, and the facility's injury rate has fallen.[42]

Transfer of training is greater when organizations also provide technical resources that help people acquire and share information. Technical support may come from electronic performance support systems (EPSS), described earlier as a type of computer-based training. Knowledge management systems including online and database tools also make it easy for employees to look up information they want to review or consult later.

Finally, to ensure transfer of training, an organization's training programs should prepare employees to self-manage their use of new skills and behaviors on the job.[43] To that end, the trainer should have trainees set goals for using skills or behaviors on the job, identify conditions under which they might fail to use the skills and behaviors, and identify the consequences (positive and negative) of using them. Employees should practice monitoring their use of the new skills and behaviors. The trainer should stress that learning to use new skills on the job is naturally difficult and will not necessarily proceed perfectly, but that employees should keep trying. Trainers also should support managers and peers in finding ways to reward employees for applying what they learned. After trainees at Sonic Automotive, an automobile retailer, complete a training program, they are asked to identify an opportunity to use their new skills in their showroom. They are supposed to develop their action plan within 7 days and implement it within 45 days.[44]

Measuring the Results of Training

LO 7-7 Evaluate the success of a training program.

After a training program ends, or at intervals during an ongoing training program, organizations should ensure that the training is meeting objectives. The stage to prepare for evaluating a training program is when the program is being developed. Along with designing course objectives and content, the planner should identify how to measure achievement of objectives. Depending on the objectives, the evaluation can use one or more of the measures shown in Figure 7.3: trainee satisfaction with the program, knowledge or abilities gained, use of new skills and behavior on the job (transfer of training), and improvements in individual and organizational performance. The usual way to measure whether participants have acquired information is to administer tests on paper or electronically. Trainers or supervisors can observe whether participants demonstrate the desired skills and behaviors. Surveys measure changes in attitude. Changes in company performance have a variety of measures, many of which organizations keep track of for preparing performance appraisals, annual reports, and other routine documents in order to demonstrate the final measure of success shown in Figure 7.3: return on investment.

FIGURE 7.3
Measures of Training Success

Evaluation Methods

To measure whether the conditions are in place for transfer of training, the organization can ask employees three questions about specific training-related tasks:

1. Do you perform the task?
2. How many times do you perform the task?
3. To what extent do you perform difficult and challenging learned tasks?

Frequent performance of difficult training-related tasks would signal great opportunity to perform. If there is low opportunity to perform, the organization should conduct further needs assessment and reevaluate readiness to learn. Perhaps the organization does not fully support the training activities in general or the employee's supervisor does not provide opportunities to apply new skills. Lack of transfer can also mean that employees have not learned the course material. The organization might offer a refresher course to give trainees more practice. Another reason for poor transfer of training is that the content of the training may not be important for the employee's job.

Assessment of training also should evaluate training *outcomes,* that is, what (if anything) has changed as a result of the training. The relevant training outcomes are the ones related to the organization's goals for the training and its overall performance. Possible outcomes include the following:

- Information such as facts, techniques, and procedures that trainees can recall after the training.
- Skills that trainees can demonstrate in tests or on the job.
- Trainee and supervisor satisfaction with the training program.
- Changes in attitude related to the content of the training (for example, concern for safety or tolerance of diversity).
- Improvements in individual, group, or company performance (for example, greater customer satisfaction, more sales, fewer defects).

HR Analytics & Decision Making

The financial-services firm Edward Jones needed to train employees to participate in its Insurance Partnership program. This program brings together a financial adviser, an office administrator, and an insurance consultant to serve clients who might need insurance. To prepare the teams, the training teaches how to identify prospective insurance clients and how to design and present information to help these clients understand how a proposed policy can help them.

Edward Jones measured business results before the training program launched and again 15 months later, after teams in 500 branches had been trained. This evaluation found improvements in branch performance. The trained branches increased the average number of policies placed, the average number of permanent policies, and gross revenue from insurance sales. The increased earnings represented a training return on investment of more than 600%.

Questions

1. To assess the value of the training, what could Edward Jones measure besides the changes in branch performance?
2. Would you describe this training project as successful? Why or why not?

Source: Based on "Training Top 125: Best Practices and Outstanding Training Initiatives," *Training,* January/February 2018, pp. 86–93.

Training is a significant part of many organizations' budgets. Therefore, economic measures are an important way to evaluate the success of a training program. Businesses that invest in training want to achieve a high *return on investment*—the monetary benefits of the investment compared to the amount invested, expressed as a percentage. For example, the Sacramento Municipal Utility District (SMUD) measured return on investment when it rolled out a program to train its strategic account advisers. The California electric utility was concerned that as more choices of energy providers became available to the state's businesses, its large commercial customers weren't turning to the SMUD's account advisers for guidance. So it set up an action-learning program to teach the account advisers to understand business strategies and help match products and services to customer needs. Following the training, which cost about $50,000 to develop and deliver, the advisers completed two deals with corporate customers, bringing in additional revenues of about $800,000. Dividing the revenues by the cost, SMUD measured a return of 1,500%.[45]

For any of these methods, the most accurate but most costly way to evaluate the training program is to measure performance, knowledge, or attitudes among all employees before the training and then train only part of the employees. After the training is complete, the performance, knowledge, or attitudes are again measured, and the trained group is compared with the untrained group. A simpler but less accurate way to assess the training is to conduct the pretest and posttest on all trainees, comparing their performance, knowledge, or attitudes before and after the training. This form of measurement does not rule out the possibility that change resulted from something other than training (for example, a change in the compensation system). The simplest approach is to use only a posttest. Use of only a posttest can show if trainees have reached a specified level of competency, knowledge, or skill. Of course, this type of measurement does not enable accurate comparisons, but it may be sufficient, depending on the cost and purpose of the training.

Applying the Evaluation

The purpose of evaluating training is to help with future decisions about the organization's training programs. Using the evaluation, the organization may identify a need to modify the training and gain information about the kinds of changes needed. The organization may decide to expand on successful areas of training and cut back on training that has not delivered significant benefits.

Clearlink, which operates call centers, conducted and applied an evaluation after overhauling its training for new employees. The company had observed a spike in the percentage of employees who quit within their first 90 days on the job. So it brought together a team of employees, managers, and coaches to review the training it was using to get new employees acquainted with their jobs and then develop a new program. After implementing the program, Clearlink measured turnover and production levels. Not only did employee turnover rates fall, but employees were getting up to speed on their jobs faster than ever before. The company determined that the new program had been the right change to make.[46]

Applications of Training

Training applications that have become widespread among U.S. companies include orientation and onboarding of new employees and training in how to manage workforce diversity.

LO 7-8 Describe training methods for employee orientation and onboarding and for diversity management.

Orientation and Onboarding of New Employees

Many employees receive their first training during their first days on the job. This training is the organization's **orientation** program–its training designed to prepare employees to perform their job effectively, learn about the organization, and establish work relationships. Organizations provide orientation because employees need to become familiar with job tasks and learn the details of the organization's practices, policies, and procedures.

Orientation
Training designed to prepare employees to perform their jobs effectively, learn about their organization, and establish work relationships.

Increasingly, employers understand that success in today's work environment requires more than employees being able to complete an orientation program, follow rules, and navigate around the workplace. These employers have taken orientation to the next level, with

Onboarding
Ongoing process that aims to prepare new employees for full participation in the organization.

the process of **onboarding,** which aims to prepare new employees for full participation in the organization. Onboarding is a conscious attempt to get new employees to connect and identify with their employer by encouraging them to gather more information about the company, its history and culture, and its products or services. In so doing, onboarding also helps new employees adjust to both the social and the performance aspects of their jobs so they can quickly become productive contributors to the organization.[47] As Figure 7.4 shows, a comprehensive onboarding process prepares employees in four areas: complying with policies and rules, clarifying job requirements, understanding the organization's culture, and connecting with co-workers. To achieve these objectives, onboarding activities address social as well as task-related aspects of work. Onboarding is an ongoing process with follow-up to ensure the new employees are making a successful transition.

Orientation programs may combine various training methods, such as documents to read, classroom instruction, on-the-job training, and e-learning. Decisions about how to conduct the orientation depend on the type of material to be covered and the number of new employees, among other factors. University Health System, located in San Antonio, Texas, wanted an onboarding program that would address the challenges of keeping health care professionals with the organization, given that health care operates in a highly competitive labor market. To achieve this goal, University Health System created a two-day program that combines classroom training with e-learning. Most importantly, the program builds connections with people who can help the new employees navigate their departments and jobs. New hires involved in direct patient care are assigned to a "preceptor" in the department; during the first 90 days, this person shares information about the organization's procedures and values.[48]

Diversity
The characteristics of individuals that make them unique.

Inclusion
Creating a work environment in which individuals are treated fairly and with mutual respect and have equal access to opportunities and resources so that they can contribute fully to the organization's success.

Diversity Training

In response to Equal Employment Opportunity laws and market forces, many organizations today are concerned about managing diversity and inclusion. **Diversity** refers to the characteristics of individuals that make them unique, such as gender, age, race, sexual orientation, and so forth. **Inclusion** refers to creating a work environment in which all individuals are treated fairly and with mutual respect, have equal access to opportunities and resources, and can contribute fully to the organization's success.[49] This kind of environment includes access to jobs as well as fair and positive treatment of all employees. Chapter 3 described how organizations manage diversity by complying with the law. Besides these efforts, many organizations provide training designed to teach employees attitudes and behaviors that

FIGURE 7.4
Goals for a Four-Stage Onboarding Process

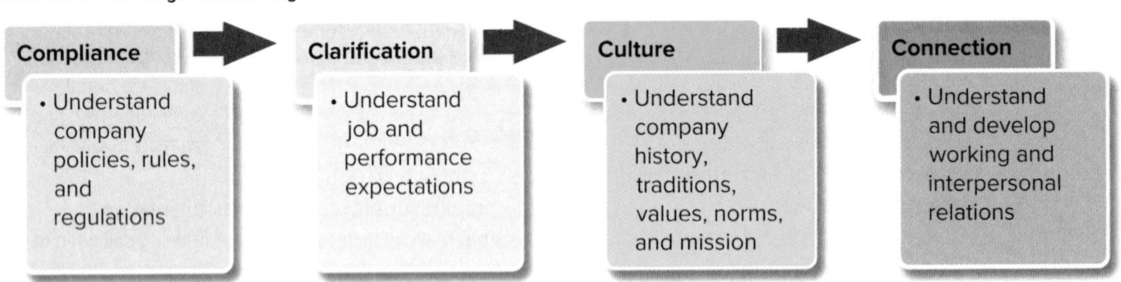

Sources: Based on Tayla N. Bauer, *Onboarding New Employees: Maximizing Success, Effective Practice Guidelines* (Alexandria, VA: SHRM Foundation, 2010); G. Chao, A. O'Leary-Kelly, S. Wolf, H. Klein, and P. Gardner, "Organizational Socialization: Its Content and Consequences," *Journal of Applied Psychology* 79 (1994), pp. 730–43.

support the management of diversity, such as appreciation of cultural differences and avoidance of behaviors that isolate or intimidate others.

Training designed to change employee attitudes about diversity and/or develop skills needed to work with a diverse workforce is called **diversity training.** These programs generally emphasize either attitude awareness and change or behavior change.

Diversity Training
Training designed to change employee attitudes about diversity and/or develop skills needed to work with a diverse workforce.

Programs that focus on attitudes have objectives to increase participants' awareness of cultural and ethnic differences, as well as differences in personal characteristics and physical characteristics (such as disabilities). These programs are based on the assumption that people who become aware of differences and their stereotypes about those differences will be able to avoid letting stereotypes influence their interactions with people. Many of these programs use video and experiential exercises to increase employees' awareness of the negative emotional and performance effects of stereotypes and resulting behaviors on members of minority groups. A risk of these programs—especially when they define diversity mainly in terms of race, ethnicity, and sex—is that they may alienate white male employees, who conclude that if the company values diversity more, it values them less.[50] Diversity training is more likely to get everyone onboard if it emphasizes respecting and valuing all the organization's employees in order to bring out the best work from everyone to open up the best opportunities for everyone.

After an incident in a Philadelphia Starbucks store in which two Black men were arrested for loitering while waiting for a friend, the coffee giant announced it would shut down 8,000 company-owned stores for an afternoon of diversity training for more than 175,000 employees. Starbucks CEO Kevin Johnson, who met with the two men, apologized for the incident and said the training program will address potential unconscious racial bias among employees and help ensure that all customers feel welcome in any Starbucks store. (Charges against the two men were dropped.)[51]

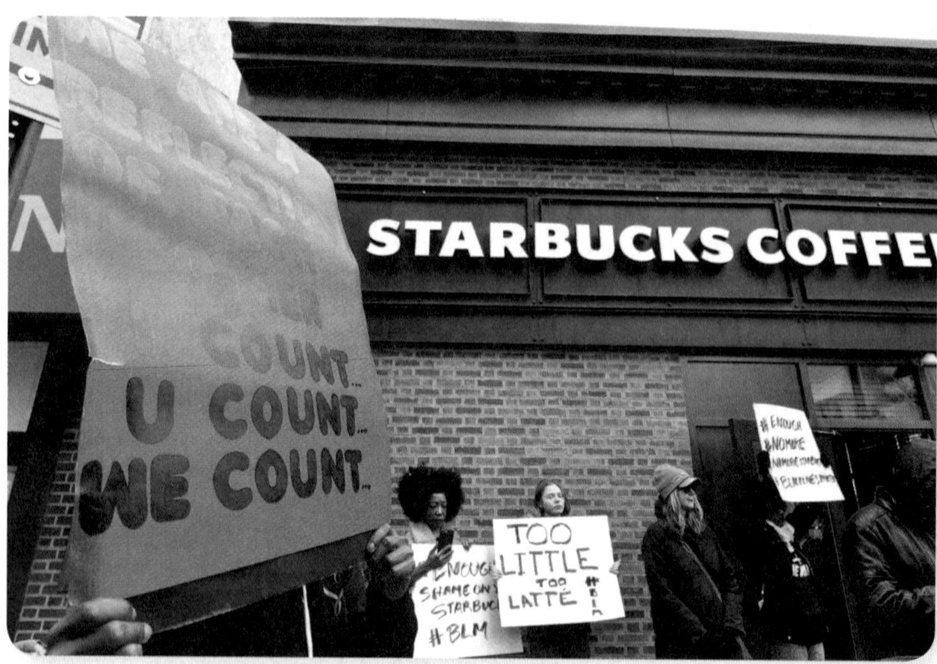

After two Black men were arrested for loitering in a Philadelphia Starbucks store, the company closed 8,000 stores for an afternoon of diversity training for employees.
NurPhoto/Getty Images

McGraw Hill connect®

Visit your instructor's Connect® course and access your eBook to view this video.

"Diversity is when you're invited to the party. Inclusion is when someone actually asks you to dance."

—Mirian M. Graddick-Weir
Executive Vice President, Human Resources, Merck

Source: Video produced for the Center for Executive Succession in the Darla Moore School of Business at the University of South Carolina by Coal Powered Filmworks

Programs that focus on behavior aim at changing the organizational policies and individual behaviors that inhibit employees' personal growth and productivity. Sometimes these programs identify incidents that discourage employees from working up to their potential. Employees work in groups to discuss specific promotion opportunities or management practices that they believe were handled unfairly. Another approach starts with the assumption that all individuals differ in various ways and teaches skills for constructively handling the communication barriers, conflicts, and misunderstandings that necessarily arise when different people try to work together.[52] Trainees may be more positive about receiving this type of training than other kinds of diversity training. Finally, some organizations provide diversity training in the form of *cultural immersion,* sending employees directly into communities where they have to interact with persons from different cultures, races, and nationalities. Participants might talk with community members, work in community organizations, or learn about events that are significant to the community they visit. Sometimes cultural immersion comes with the job. A U.S.-based consulting firm with a global clientele used the skills-based focus in its cross-culture training of consultants. The focus was on learning how to understand cultural differences within teams and among clients. The program involved case studies related to the challenges consultants face in their assignments. Small-group discussions provided a chance for participants to know one another and share insights. At the end of the program, participants used a 40-foot roll of paper to write down the main lessons they learned, and then they had time to view the list and take note of one another's ideas.[53]

Does diversity training yield improvements in business performance? So far, research has not demonstrated a direct relationship.[54] Training may, however, contribute to the kind of environment in which diversity can enhance performance because people learn from one another's differences. This is most likely when diversity training is part of management's long-term commitment to managing diversity because the company's leaders consider diversity to be an opportunity for employees to learn from one another, work in a supportive environment, and acquire teamwork skills. In other words, successful diversity programs are not merely a training topic but part of an organizational culture that expresses its appreciation for diversity also through other actions, including recruiting, hiring, and developing diverse employees.[55]

One organization that is getting diversity training right is the University Corporation for Atmospheric Research, an institute that supports research and has had difficulty attracting and including women and people of color. Part of its effort to promote diversity and inclusion is a four-part training program offered on a voluntary basis. Given the voluntary nature of the program and the difficulties associated with teaching bias reduction, this program focuses on ways to ensure all employees feel valued and included. Discussions and hands-on activities address how to intervene when observing harassment or bias, as well as how to talk to others about diversity in the organization. Participants especially value knowing how to intervene, and more than three-quarters report actually intervening at some point after the training.[56]

THINKING ETHICALLY

INTERNSHIPS: OPPORTUNITY OR EXPLOITATION?

For many college students, an important summer experience is completing an internship and seeing firsthand the career they hope to pursue. The pay might be somewhat below the entry-level rate for a full-time employee, but the interns get practice they hope will aid in their job search after graduation. Some employers, however, do not even pay a low wage; they expect their interns to work for free.

The idea of working for little or no pay has been justified on the grounds that the internship experience is valuable training. Schools that agree may provide course credit for an internship. However, some students and schools are questioning that argument. Not every internship has students doing activities that are relevant to their chosen field, and some students feel they are merely unpaid labor.

Employers that want to offer unpaid internships need to meet legal requirements. Under the Fair Labor Standards Act, an unpaid internship must be educational, and the primary beneficiary must be the employee, not the employer. In addition, the company may not hire unpaid interns as replacements for paid employees. State laws may impose further requirements. In New York, for example, employers must sacrifice some productivity for the sake of providing training to the interns, and the training should cover skills that apply beyond the particular job at the particular company. For-profit companies that do not meet the requirements for an unpaid internship must pay at least minimum wage plus a higher rate for overtime. In some publicized cases, interns have filed lawsuits against companies they say did not meet those requirements.

At least until recently, unpaid internships were common in some industries, such as fashion, entertainment, and publishing. However, with the negative attention and heightened competition for talent, some employers have pulled back from the practice–either ending their internships or beginning to pay for positions that had been unpaid. Nevertheless, especially in the case of employers that pay interns at least minimum wage, advocates of internship continue to say these programs provide valuable preparation for careers. One way to check whether internships can withstand legal scrutiny is to consider the organization's purpose for creating these programs–whether it is to deliver training or to fill positions inexpensively.

Questions

1. Suppose a publishing company wants to hire an intern to help the company catch up with its paperwork over the summer. Who would be affected by this decision? What would be the benefits or harm to each person?
2. How could a well-designed training program help make this idea meet ethical as well as legal standards?

Sources: National Association of Colleges and Employers, "15 Best Practices for Internship Programs," https://www.naceweb.org, accessed April 16, 2020; Kat Tretina, "Why Unpaid Internships May Not Be Worth It," *Student Loan Hero,* February 14, 2020, https://studentloanhero.com; Anisa Purbasari Horton, "4 Former Interns Look Back at Exploitation, Power Dynamics, and Ultimate Career Payoff," *Fast Company,* August 20, 2019, https://www.fastcompany.com; David Z. Morris, "Are Unpaid Internships Exploitation or Opportunity? Twitter Has Some Opinions," *Fortune,* July 8, 2018, https://fortune.com; Frank Witsil, "Are Unpaid Internships Good for Students, Companies?" *Detroit Free Press,* March 24, 2018, https://www.freep.com.

SUMMARY

LO 7-1 Discuss how to link training programs to organizational needs.

- Organizations need to establish training programs that are effective–in other words, programs that (1) teach what they are designed to teach and (2) teach skills and behaviors that will help the organization achieve its goals.
- Organizations create such programs through instructional design.
- The steps in this process are to conduct a needs assessment, ensure readiness for training (including employee characteristics and organizational support), plan a training program, implement the program, and evaluate the results.

LO 7-2 Explain how to assess the need for training.

- Needs assessment consists of an organization analysis, person analysis, and task analysis.
- The organization analysis determines the appropriateness of training by evaluating the characteristics of the organization, including its strategy, resources, and management support.
- The person analysis determines individuals' needs and readiness for training.
- The task analysis identifies the tasks, knowledge, skills, and behaviors that training should emphasize. It is based on examination of the conditions in which tasks are performed, including equipment and environment of the job, time constraints, safety considerations, and performance standards.

LO 7-3 Explain how to assess employees' readiness for training.

- Readiness for training is a combination of employee characteristics and positive work environment that permit training.
- The necessary employee characteristics include ability to learn the subject matter, favorable attitudes toward the training, and motivation to learn.
- A positive work environment avoids situational constraints such as lack of money and time. In a positive environment, both peers and management support training.

LO 7-4 Describe how to plan an effective training program.

- Planning begins with establishing training objectives, which should define an expected performance or outcome, the desired level of performance, and the conditions under which the performance should occur.
- Based on the objectives, the planner decides who will provide the training, what topics the training will cover, what training methods to use, and how to evaluate the training.
- Even when organizations purchase outside training, someone in the organization, usually a member of the HR department, often is responsible for training administration.
- The training methods selected should be related to the objectives and content of the training program.
- Training methods may include presentation methods, hands-on methods, or group-building methods.

LO 7-5 Compare widely used training methods.

- Classroom instruction is most widely used and is one of the least expensive and least time-consuming ways to present information on a specific topic to many trainees. It also allows for group interaction and may include hands-on practice.
- Audiovisual techniques and computer-based training (often called e-learning) need not require that trainees attend a class, so organizations can reduce time and money spent on training. Computer-based training may be interactive and may provide for group interaction.
- On-the-job training methods such as apprenticeships and internships give trainees firsthand experiences.
- A simulation represents a real-life situation, enabling trainees to see the effects of their decisions without dangerous or expensive consequences.
- Business games and case studies are other methods for practicing decision-making skills. Participants need to come together in one location or collaborate online.
- Behavior modeling gives trainees a chance to observe desired behaviors, so this technique can be effective for teaching interpersonal skills.
- Experiential and adventure learning programs provide an opportunity for group members to interact in challenging circumstances but may exclude members with disabilities.
- Team training focuses a team on achievement of a common goal.
- Action learning offers relevance, because the training focuses on an actual work-related problem.

LO7-6 Summarize how to implement a successful training program.

- Implementation should apply principles of learning and seek transfer of training.
- In general, effective training communicates learning objectives, presents information in distinctive and memorable ways, and helps trainees link the subject matter to their jobs.
- Employees are most likely to learn when training is linked to job experiences and tasks. Employees learn best when they demonstrate or practice what they have learned and when they receive feedback that helps them improve.
- Trainees remember information better when it is broken into small chunks, presented with visual images, and practiced many times. Written materials should be easily readable by trainees.
- Transfer of training is most likely when there is social support (from managers and peers), technical support, and self-management.

LO 7-7 Evaluate the success of a training program.

- Evaluation of training should look for transfer of training by measuring whether employees are performing the tasks taught in the training program.
- Assessment of training also should evaluate training outcomes, such as change in attitude, ability to perform a new skill, and recall of facts or behaviors taught in the training program.
- Training should result in improvement in the group's or organization's outcomes, such as customer satisfaction or sales. An economic measure of training success is return on investment.

LO 7-8 Describe training methods for employee orientation and onboarding and for diversity management.

- Employee orientation is training designed to prepare employees to perform their job effectively, learn about the organization, and establish work relationships.
- Because success in today's work environment requires more than following rules, employers have begun supplementing basic orientation programs with an onboarding process, aimed at preparing new employees for full participation in the organization.

- Onboarding is an ongoing process that addresses social as well as task-related aspects of work in order to prepare employees for complying with policies and rules, clarifying job requirements, understanding the organization's culture, and connecting with co-workers.
- Orientation programs may combine several training methods, from printed materials to on-the-job training to e-learning.
- Diversity training is designed to change employee attitudes about diversity and/or develop skills needed to work with a diverse workforce.
- Evidence regarding these programs suggests that diversity training is most effective if it is part of management's long-term commitment to managing diversity as an opportunity for people to learn from one another and acquire teamwork skills.

KEY TERMS

training, 200
instructional design, 200
learning management system (LMS), 201
needs assessment, 201
organization analysis, 202
person analysis, 203
task analysis, 204
readiness for training, 204
e-learning, 210
electronic performance support system (EPSS), 211
on-the-job training (OJT), 212
apprenticeship, 212
internship, 212
simulation, 213
avatars, 213
virtual reality, 213
experiential programs, 215
adventure learning, 216
cross-training, 217
coordination training, 217
team leader training, 217
action learning, 217
readability, 219
transfer of training, 219
communities of practice, 220
orientation, 223
onboarding, 224
diversity, 224
inclusion, 224
diversity training, 225

REVIEW AND DISCUSSION QUESTIONS

1. "Alicia!" bellowed David to the company's HR specialist, "I've got a problem, and you've got to solve it. I can't get people in this plant to work together as a team. As if I don't have enough trouble with our competitors and our past-due accounts, now I have to put up with running a zoo. You're responsible for seeing that the staff gets along. I want a training proposal on my desk by Monday." Assume you are Alicia. *(LO 7-1)*
   a. Is training the solution to this problem? How can you determine the need for training?
   b. Summarize how you would conduct a needs assessment.
2. How should an organization assess readiness for learning? In Question 1, how do David's comments suggest readiness (or lack of readiness) for learning? *(LO 7-2)*
3. Assume you are the human resource manager of a small seafood company. The general manager has told you that customers have begun complaining about the quality of your company's fresh fish. Currently, training consists of senior fish cleaners showing new employees how to perform the job. Assuming your needs assessment indicates a need for training, how would you plan a training program? What steps should you take in planning the program? *(LO 7-4)*
4. Many organizations turn to e-learning as a less-expensive alternative to classroom training. What are some other advantages of substituting e-learning for classroom training? What are some disadvantages? *(LO 7-5)*
5. Suppose the managers in your organization tend to avoid delegating projects to the people in their groups. As a result, they rarely meet their goals. A training needs analysis indicates that an appropriate solution is training in management skills. You have identified two outside training programs that are consistent with your goals. One program involves experiential programs, and the other is an interactive computer program. What are the strengths and weaknesses of each technique? Which would you choose? Why? *(LO 7-5)*
6. Consider your current job or a job you recently held. What types of training did you receive for the job? What types of training would you like to receive? Why? *(LO 7-5)*

7. A manufacturing company employs several maintenance employees. When a problem occurs with the equipment, a maintenance employee receives a description of the symptoms and is supposed to locate and fix the source of the problem. The company recently installed a new, complex electronics system. To prepare its maintenance workers, the company provided classroom training. The trainer displayed electrical drawings of system components and posed problems about the system. The trainer would point to a component in a drawing and ask, "What would happen if this component were faulty?" Trainees would study the diagrams, describe the likely symptoms, and discuss how to repair the problem. If you were responsible for this company's training, how would you evaluate the success of this training program? *(LO 7-6)*
8. In Question 7, suppose the maintenance supervisor has complained that trainees are having difficulty trouble shooting problems with the new electronics system. They are spending a great deal of time on problems with the system and coming to the supervisor with frequent questions that show a lack of understanding. The supervisor is convinced that the employees are motivated to learn the system, and they are well qualified. What do you think might be the problems with the current training program? What recommendations can you make for improving the program? *(LO 7-7)*
9. Who should be involved in onboarding of new employees? Why would it not be appropriate to provide orientation programs purely online? *(LO 7-8)*
10. Why do organizations provide diversity training? What kinds of goals are most suitable for such training? *(LO 7-8)*

SELF-ASSESSMENT EXERCISE

What Is Your Motivation to Learn?

In this chapter, we discussed the need for learners to be motivated so that training will be effective. What is your motivation to learn? Find out by answering the following questions. Read each statement and indicate how much you agree with it, using the following scale:

1. I try to learn as much as I can from the courses I take.	5	4	3	2	1
2. I believe I tend to learn more from my courses than other students do.	5	4	3	2	1
3. When I'm involved in courses and can't understand something, I consider it a challenge and try harder to learn.	5	4	3	2	1

5 = Strongly agree
4 = Somewhat agree
3 = Neutral
2 = Somewhat disagree
1 = Strongly disagree

Add up your points across the three statements. Your points could range from 3 to 15. What's your score? The higher your score the greater your motivation to learn.

TAKING RESPONSIBILITY

Dollar General Trains Employees to Serve Others

Training is a massive undertaking for Dollar General, which has about 143,000 employees and has been opening new stores at a steady clip. The company's strategy couples low prices with customer service, so it needs to get everyone aligned with its mission, Serving Others. It also aims to serve its employees by opening up opportunities for learning and advancement; a recent evaluation found that more than half of the company's job openings were filled by internal candidates, and 12,000 store managers were promoted into those positions from within. These priorities require training that is widely available. Dollar General meets the challenge by employing a variety of training methods developed with the assistance of consultants who have technology expertise.

For example, Dollar General launched a Customer First initiative to get all employees focused on creating a great customer experience. Based on the results of customer feedback and observations of employee interactions with customers, the planners identified learning objectives in how to develop and maintain customer loyalty. In the first phase of the training, company managers participated in a four-hour simulation aimed at understanding the importance of what the customer experienced. Following this, participants accessed training on the company's learning management system to focus on a different aspect of customer experience each quarter. They also received activities for their store teams to engage in, putting into practice the lessons their managers were learning.

Dollar General's learning and development team determined that employees wanted training that would fit into their schedules. The team responded with the Core Curriculum, a set of learning programs categorized according to level of responsibility in the organization: leading self, leading others, and leading leaders. Each level includes on-demand computer courses plus experiential exercises and instructor-led training. Every new store employee also is expected to complete a computer-based training series on customer service.

Store managers participate in a 12-month training program that begins with a computer-based simulation of a store environment, practicing the store manager's job. They also spend time in a high-performing store to learn on the job. After three months, they attend classroom learning about leadership. During that time, they and their peers share stories about their on-the-job experiences and learn from one another, the trainers, and other experienced managers. The learning and development team empowers store managers to play an active role in training the employees they are responsible for. To support these efforts, it delivers a Certified Store Training Manager (CSTM) program to prepare its top-performing managers for filling that role. Store managers who successfully complete the training modules receive a CSTM certification and may be eligible for nine semester hours of college credit. They go on to be a valuable source of on-the-job training for Dollar General workers.

Dollar General credits these and other training initiatives with making training widely available and making the company an attractive place to work. The highly trained workforce has supported years of sales growth and provided a wealth of talent to fill management positions.

Questions

1. What training methods are included in Dollar General's training programs?
2. How did the training and development team assess training needs? What other criteria should the team consider in its needs assessments?

Sources: Corporate website, "Careers," https://careers.dollargeneral.com, accessed April 16, 2020; Launch Consulting, "Case Study: Dollar General," https://launchconsulting.com, accessed April 16, 2020; Lorri Freifeld, "Dollar General Does It Again!" *Training,* March/April 2020, pp. 22–25; "Dollar General Earns Top Spot on Training Magazine's Top 125 List for Second Consecutive Year," *Businesswire,* February 25, 2020, https://www.businesswire.com; Lorri Freifeld, "What's in Store for Dollar General?" *Training,* March/April 2019, pp. 24–28.

MANAGING TALENT

Huntington Ingalls Builds a Workforce to Do "Hard Stuff"

Huntington Ingalls Industries (HII) is the largest U.S. shipbuilding company serving the military; its products include aircraft carriers, submarines, Coast Guard cutters, and more. A military ship is a hugely complex product, and the sailors' lives depend on it being precisely made to specifications. To meet its motto of "Hard stuff done right" in the hands-on work of shipbuilding, HII combines careful hiring with a commitment to training. Building military ships is highly specialized, possibly requiring a military clearance as well as technical skills and physical strength, so positions are hard to fill. HII finds educated, strong people and then trains them to do the job.

One aspect of training is a set of apprenticeship programs. These run for four to eight years and combine classroom learning with on-the-job training. The latter may include training in crafts like welding and pipe fitting or in specialized areas such as rigging or nuclear testing. The program at the Newport News, Virginia, shipbuilding facility covers 19 trades, along with the choice to participate in eight advanced programs. Another facility, in Mississippi, offers apprenticeships in 13 trades. The two programs together have 130 instructors, many of whom themselves attended one of the schools. Employees are paid for a 40-hour week, including their time on the job and in classes. A first-year apprentice can earn $35,000 a year, with raises bringing the salary up to $58,000 after completion of the program–and because the program is paid for, they graduate without student loans to repay.

The training culminates in an apprentice degree that comes close to meeting the standards for an associate's degree, so employees with a desire to continue on toward a college degree are well on their way. Employees who stay with HII for 40 years also can apply that experience to becoming designated a master shipbuilder. HII's 1,400 master shipbuilders are another source of instructors for its apprenticeship program.

Another way in which HII seeks excellence through training is in its use of technology. Several years ago, it began researching ways to employ "augmented reality" in business applications including training. Augmented reality refers to displaying an overlay of digital information over a view of the physical world, the way football broadcasts on television draw lines on the field to illustrate plays. In HII's training, it is used for showing the steps required to operate equipment while the trainee is at the equipment, viewing it on a tablet computer. HII's success with this method has drawn the interest of the U.S. Navy, which may begin using HII's augmented-reality technology to help sailors learn how to conduct maintenance.

Questions

1. What training methods does Huntington Ingalls use, according to the information given? How do these support its business needs?
2. How might HII evaluate the success of its training?

Sources: Huntington Ingalls Industries, "Who We Are," https://www.huntingtoningalls.com, accessed April 16, 2020; Apprentice School, "About Us," http://www.as.edu, accessed April 16, 2020; "Huntington Ingalls Industries' Digital Shipbuilding Transformation Earns 2019 CIO 100 Award," May 2, 2019, https://newsroom.huntingtoningalls.com; Tony Bingham and Pat Galagan, "Hard Stuff Done Right," *TD,* December 2015, pp. 31–34; Bill Ermatinger, "Craftsmanship, Scholarship and Leadership," *TD,* December 2015, pp. 37–40; Allyson Versprille, "Augmented Reality Could Help Solve Ford-Class Carrier Cost Woes," *National Defense,* December 2015, pp. 38–40.

HR IN SMALL BUSINESS

PM Mold Company Draws In Talent by Training

Finding, equipping, and keeping talent has been difficult for manufacturers, in part because many people making career decisions are unfamiliar with the kinds of work involved. They might think of production jobs as dirty and dangerous, or they might think the only exciting work involves engineering robots. They might overlook a business like Schaumburg, Illinois-based PM Mold Company. In fact, mold making has been and still is a highly creative type of work that is essential to producing an enormous variety of products we depend on. PM Mold and similar companies assess a particular product to be made, and then they design and produce finely detailed molds out of steel, which their customers use to make parts of all sizes out of plastic or rubber. A good mold delivers precise, accurate, and consistent results.

Carrying out this work requires a combination of problem solving, creative thinking, and careful craftsmanship. PM Mold looks for people with thinking skills and then uses an apprenticeship program to train them to apply those skills to mold making. In response to the challenge of recruiting for these jobs, the company has become creative in making the apprenticeship program motivational as well as informational.

Apprentices at PM Mold attend classes and engage in on-the-job learning as they earn a starting wage. In addition to these basics, the apprentices are asked to work together on a creative mold-making project. One year, for example, the company had decided to produce a specialty golf tee for a trade show. Tom White, the company's vice president of operations and business development, asked the apprentices to go out and look at golf tees on the market to see what features and functions caught their eye. They discussed their findings and brainstormed how to incorporate the most beneficial ideas into the giveaway tees. The apprentices agreed on a design and built the mold to make the tees. At the trade show, a golf company executive happened to see the giveaway tees and expressed interest in working with PM Mold to make something similar for sale. After some discussion of his needs, the golf executive wound up placing an order for a mold to use in making a modified version of what the apprentices had developed.

Although the group project amounts to less than 10% of the training time, White considers it a key part of apprentices' training. Making something valuable gets them excited about what they are learning, and that makes them think harder and learn more. It helps them envision not just their first job but also a career path they can follow at PM Mold as they gain experience.

Questions

1. Based on the information given, what is your assessment of apprentices' readiness for training at PM Mold? How does the company enable readiness for training?
2. Recommend two measures for PM Mold to use in determining the success of its apprenticeship training.

Sources: Company website, "About Us" and "PM Mold Apprenticeship," https://www.pmmold.com, accessed April 16, 2020; Schaumburg Business Association member list, https://members.schaumburgbusiness.com, accessed April 16, 2020; Cynthia Kustush, "Workforce Development with a Twist," *Mold-Making Technology,* March 2019, pp. 32–37.

NOTES

1. E. Kammerer, "Virtually Terrific Employee Orientation," *TD,* April 2019, pp. 22–23.
2. S. Lauby, "Help Employees Take Charge of Their Learning Needs," *Saba Blog,* https://www.saba.com, accessed April 15, 2020.
3. R. A. Noe, *Employee Training and Development,* 8th ed. (New York: McGraw-Hill, 2020).
4. E. Volini, J. Schwartz, I. Roy et al., "Learning in the Flow of Life," in *2019 Global Human Capital Trends,* Deloitte Insights, https://www.2.deloitte.com, accessed April 15, 2020; R. K. Ellis, *A Field Guide to Learning Management Systems,* Learning Circuits (American Society for Training & Development, 2009), http://www.astd.org.
5. Noe, *Employee Training and Development;* E. A. Surface, "Training Needs Assessment: Aligning Learning and Capability with Performance Requirements and Organizational Objectives," in *The Handbook of Work Analysis: Methods, Systems, Applications and Science of Work Measurement in Organizations,* eds. M. A. Wilson, W. Bennett, S. G. Gibson, and G. M. Alliger (New York: Routledge Academic, 2012), pp. 437–462.
6. C. Hall and J. R. Mattox II, "Communicate L&D's Value So the C-Suite Listens," *TD,* February 2018, pp. 61ME–64ME; D. Robinson, "Transitioning from Order-Taker to Impact-Maker," *TD,* January 2018, pp. 43–46.
7. E. F. Holton III and C. Bailey, "Top-to-Bottom Curriculum Redesign," *Training and Development,* March 1995, pp. 40–44.
8. C. Gewertz, "What Literacy Skills Do Students Really Need for Work?" *Education Week,* October 4, 2018, https://www.edweek.org; K. Everson, "Can Your Employees Read This?" *Chief Learning Officer,* September 2015, pp. 22–24.
9. R. A. Noe, "Trainees' Attributes and Attitudes: Neglected Influences on Training Effectiveness," *Academy of Management Review* 11 (1986), pp. 736–749; T. T. Baldwin, R. T. Magjuka, and B. T. Loher, "The Perils of Participation: Effects of Choice on Trainee Motivation and Learning," *Personnel Psychology* 44 (1991), pp. 51–66; S. I. Tannenbaum, J. E. Mathieu, E. Salas, and J. A. Cannon-Bowers, "Meeting Trainees' Expectations: The Influence of Training Fulfillment on the Development of Commitment, Self-Efficacy, and Motivation," *Journal of Applied Psychology* 76 (1991), pp. 759–769.
10. D. Belkin, "More Companies Teach Workers What Colleges Don't," *The Wall Street Journal,* March 22, 2018, https://www.wsj.com.
11. L. H. Peters, E. J. O'Connor, and J. R. Eulberg, "Situational Constraints: Sources, Consequences, and Future Considerations," in *Research in Personnel and Human Resource Management,* eds. K. M. Rowland and G. R. Ferris (Greenwich, CT: JAI Press, 1985), vol. 3, pp. 79–114; E. J. O'Connor, L. H. Peters, A. Pooyan, J. Weekley, B. Frank, and B. Erenkranz, "Situational Constraints' Effects on Performance, Affective Reactions, and Turnover: A Field Replication and Extension," *Journal of Applied Psychology* 69 (1984), pp. 663–672; D. J. Cohen, "What Motivates Trainees?" *Training and Development Journal,* November 1990, pp. 91–93; J. S. Russell, J. R. Terborg, and M. L. Powers, "Organizational Performance and Organizational Level Training and Support," *Personnel Psychology* 38 (1985), pp. 849–863.
12. J. B. Tracey, S. I. Trannenbaum, and M. J. Kavanaugh, "Applying Trade Skills on the Job: The Importance of the Work Environment," *Journal of Applied Psychology* 80 (1995), pp. 239–252; P. E. Tesluk, J. L. Farr, J. E. Mathieu, and R. J. Vance, "Generalization of Employee Involvement Training to the Job Setting: Individuals and Situational Effects," *Personnel Psychology* 48 (1995), pp. 607–632; J. K. Ford, M. A. Quinones, D. J. Sego, and J. S. Sorra, "Factors Affecting the Opportunity to Perform Trained Tasks on the Job," *Personnel Psychology* 45 (1992), pp. 511–527.
13. B. Mager, *Preparing Instructional Objectives,* 2nd ed. (Belmont, CA: Lake, 1984); B. J. Smith and B. L. Delahaye, *How to Be an Effective Trainer,* 2nd ed. (New York: Wiley, 1987).
14. "2019 Training Industry Report," *Training,* https://trainingmag.com, accessed April 16, 2020.
15. Ibid.
16. J. J. Salopek, "Learning Has a Seat at the Table," *T+D,* October 2011, pp. 49–50.
17. A. Kshirsagar, T. Mansour, L. McNally, and M. Metakis, "Adapting Workplace Learning in the Time of Coronavirus," *McKinsey Insights,* March 2020, https://www.mckinsey.com.
18. "Best Practices and Outstanding Initiatives," *Training,* January/February 2011, EBSCOhost, http://web.ebscohost.com.
19. J. Ford and T. Meyer, "Advances in Talent Development, Deep Specialization, and Collaborative Learning," in *The Psychology of Workplace Technology,* eds. M. Coovert and L. Thompson (New York: Routledge, 2014), pp. 43–76.
20. J. Salopek, "Mobile and Social Learning Attracts, Equips Young Insurance Agents," *TD,* October 2016, pp. 42–44.
21. U.S. Department of Labor, "Apprenticeship," https://www.dol.gov/apprenticeship, accessed April 16, 2020.
22. M. Lauer, "The Future of Work Requires a Return to Apprenticeships," *World Economic Forum,* December 16, 2019, https://www.weforum.org.
23. Alexia Elejalde-Ruiz, "Apprentice Idea Expands," *Chicago Tribune,* March 8, 2016, sec. 2, pp. 1, 4.
24. R. Greenfield, "New Rules Spell Out Unpaid Internships," *Chicago Tribune,* January 21, 2018, sec. 2, p. 3.
25. W. J. Rothwell and H. C. Kanzanas, "Planned OJT Is Productive OJT," *Training and Development Journal,* October 1990, pp. 53–56.
26. "Revolutionizing Medical Education Training," https://www.ohiohealth.com, accessed April 16, 2020; "OhioHealth Simulation Program Prepares First Responders," news release, March 14, 2016, http://newsroom.ohiohealth.com.
27. T. Sitzmann, "A Meta-analytic Examination of the Instructional Effectiveness of Computer-Based Simulation Games," *Personnel Psychology* 64 (2011), pp. 489–528; C. Cornell, "Better Than the Real Thing?" *Human Resource Executive,* August 2005, pp. 34–37; S. Boehle, "Simulations: The Next Generation of E-Learning," *Training,* January 2005, pp. 22–31.
28. "BNSF Railway: Virtual Power Brake Law (VPBL)," *Training,* January/February 2017, p. 102.

29. L. Nikravan, "More than Fun and Games," *Chief Learning Officer,* January 2012, pp. 20–21.
30. G. P. Latham and L. M. Saari, "Application of Social Learning Theory to Training Supervisors through Behavior Modeling," *Journal of Applied Psychology* 64 (1979), pp. 239–246.
31. D. Brown and D. Harvey, *An Experiential Approach to Organizational Development* (Englewood Cliffs, NJ: Prentice Hall, 2000); Larissa Jõgi, review of *The Handbook of Experiential Learning and Management Education,* eds. Michael Reynolds and Russ Vince, *Studies in the Education of Adults* 40, no. 2 (Autumn 2008), pp. 232–234, accessed at OCLC FirstSearch, http://newfirstsearch.oclc.org.
32. G. Dutton, "Get in the Game!" *Training,* September/October 2017, pp. 40–42.
33. J. Cannon-Bowers and C. Bowers, "Team Development and Functioning," in *Handbook of Industrial and Organizational Psychology,* ed. S. Zedeck, volume 1 (Washington, DC: American Psychological Association, 2011) pp. 597–650; L. Delise, C. Gorman, A. Brooks, J. Rentsch, and D. Steele-Johnson, "The Effects of Team Training on Team Outcomes: A Meta-analysis," *Performance Improvement Quarterly* 22 (2010), pp. 53–80.
34. T. Gutner, "For Team-Building Events, a New Ingredient: Fun," *The Wall Street Journal,* April 27, 2014, http://online.wsj.com.
35. S. Thompson, "Leveraging Action-Based Learning," *Training,* November/December 2017, pp. 10–11.
36. K. Palmer and D. Blake, "How to Help Your Employees Learn from Each Other," *Harvard Business Review,* November 8, 2018, https://hbr.org; M. Knowles, "Adult Learning," in *Training and Development Handbook,* 3rd ed., ed. R. L. Craig (New York: McGraw-Hill, 1987), pp. 168–179; C. E. Schneier, "Training and Development Programs: What Learning Theory and Research Have to Offer," *Personnel Journal,* April 1974, pp. 288–293.
37. K. A. Smith-Jentsch, F. G. Jentsch, S. C. Payne, and E. Salas, "Can Pretraining Experiences Explain Individual Differences in Learning?" *Journal of Applied Psychology* 81 (1996), pp. 110–116.
38. A. Landers, "Conduct an Audience Analysis," *Training,* November/December 2017, p. 16.
39. W. McGehee and P. W. Thayer, *Training in Business and Industry* (New York: Wiley, 1961).
40. "Microlearning Is the New Black," *iSpring,* July 2, 2018, https://www.ispringsolutions.com; R. M. Gagne and K. L. Medsker, *The Condition of Learning* (Fort Worth, TX: Harcourt, 1996).
41. J. C. Naylor and G. D. Briggs, "The Effects of Task Complexity and Task Organization on the Relative Efficiency of Part and Whole Training Methods," *Journal of Experimental Psychology* 65 (1963), pp. 217–224.
42. David Brandt, "Learning to Play It Safe," *Industrial Engineer,* May 2015, pp. 50–51.
43. R. D. Marx, "Relapse Prevention for Managerial Training: A Model for Maintenance of Behavior Change," *Academy of Management Review* 7 (1982): 433–441; G. P. Latham and C. A. Frayne, "Self-Management Training for Increasing Job Attendance: A Follow-Up and Replication," *Journal of Applied Psychology* 74 (1989): 411–416.
44. M. Weinstein, "Sonic Automotive Revs Its Leadership Engine," *Training,* January/February 2017, pp. 46–50.
45. "Best Practices and Outstanding Training Initiatives," *Training,* January/February 2016, pp. 102–107.
46. "Q&A: Human Resources," *Utah Business,* October 2015, http://dev.utahbusiness.com.
47. R. Maurer, "New Employee Onboarding Guide," *Society for Human Resource Management,* https://www.shrm.org, accessed April 16, 2020; K. Ferrazzi and T. Davis, "The Employee Integration Equation," *TD,* October 2015, pp. 57–60; T. Bauer and B. Erdogan, "Delineating and Reviewing the Role of Newcomer Capital in Organizational Socialization," *Annual Review of Organizational Psychology and Organizational Behavior* 1 (2014), pp. 439–457.
48. P. Gaul, "Onboarding Is Critical," *TD,* August 2017, pp. 28–32.
49. "Understanding Diversity and Inclusion," *Builtin,* https://builtin.com, accessed April 16, 2020; K. Gurchiek, "6 Steps for Building an Inclusive Workplace," *Society for Human Resource Management,* March 19, 2018, https://www.shrm.org.
50. J. Baron, "Traditional Diversity Training Doesn't Work. Why Not? And What Does?" *Diversity Jobs,* December 11, 2019, https://www.diversityjobs.com.
51. Corporate website, "Starbucks Equity, Inclusion and Diversity Timeline," July 17, 2019, https://stories.starbucks.com; Associated Press, "Black Men Arrested at Philadelphia Starbucks Feared for Their Lives," *The Guardian,* April 19, 2018, https://www.theguardian.com; E. Sacks, "Starbucks Goes Big on Racial-Bias Training, But Will It Work?" *NBC News,* April 18, 2018, https://www.nbc.com; J. Jargon and L. Webber, "Starbucks to Shut Stores for Antibias Training," *The Wall Street Journal,* April 17, 2018, https://www.wsj.com.
52. J. Gassam, "5 Reasons Why Diversity Programs Fail," *Forbes,* March 31, 2019, https://www.forbes.com; F. Dobbins and A. Kalev, "Why Diversity Programs Fail," *Harvard Business Review,* July/August 2016, pp. 52–60.
53. N. Goodman, "Going Global with Training and Development," *Training,* November/December 2017, pp. 62–63.
54. E. H. Chang, K. L. Milkman, L. J. Zarrow, K. Brabaw, D. M. Gromet, R. Rebele, C. Massey, A. L. Duckworth, and A. Grant, "Does Diversity Training Work the Way It's Supposed To?" *Harvard Business Review,* July 9, 2019, https://hbr.org; R. Anand and M. Winters, "A Retrospective View of Corporate Diversity Training from 1964 to the Present," *Academy of Management Learning and Education* 7 (2008), pp. 356–372; T. Kochan, K. Bezrukova, R. Ely, S. Jackson, A. Joshi, K. Jehn, J. Leonard, D. Levine, and D. Thomas, "The Effects of Diversity on Business Performance: Report of the Diversity Research Network," *Human Resource Management* 42 (2003), pp. 8–21.
55. D. Dunbar, "Are Diversity and Inclusion Part of Your Organization's Culture?" *BioSpace,* November 4, 2019, https://www.biospace.com; K. Bezrukova, C. Spell, J. Perry, and K. Jehn, "A Meta-analytical Integration of Over 40 Years of Research on Diversity Training Evaluation," *Psychological Bulletin* 142 (2016), pp. 1227–1274.
56. A. Pruitt, C. Brinkworth, J. Young, and K. L. Aponte, "Five Things We Learned about Creating a Successful Workplace Diversity Program," *Harvard Business Review,* March 30, 2018, https://hbr.org.

Developing Employees for Future Success

8

Recognizing potential in employees and helping them develop new skills allows Anthem to attract and retain top talent.

suedhang/Getty Images

What Do I Need to Know?

After reading this chapter, you should be able to:

LO 8-1 Discuss how development is related to training and careers.

LO 8-2 Identify the methods organizations use for employee development.

LO 8-3 Describe how organizations use assessment of personality type, work behaviors, and job performance to plan employee development.

LO 8-4 Explain how job experiences can be used for developing skills.

LO 8-5 Summarize principles of successful mentoring programs.

LO 8-6 Tell how managers and peers develop employees through coaching.

LO 8-7 Identify the steps in the process of career management.

LO 8-8 Discuss how organizations are meeting the challenges of the "glass ceiling," succession planning, and dysfunctional managers.

Introduction

Holly Prince's impressive career path from teaching in the Peace Corps to a regional vice president of the 40-million-member Anthem insurance company demonstrates the potential for those who work at organizations committed to developing their employees' talents. Prince joined the Peace Corps and headed to the South Pacific for two years of teaching in the Solomon Islands after she finished college and then stayed in that location to work for an accounting firm. When she returned to the United States, she continued her work in accounting and made professional connections in her community that led to a job at Anthem.

Anthem saw leadership potential in Prince and brought her into its program for high-potential employees. She received training in how to manage financial performance, build a stronger career network, and understand the health insurance business. Anthem also assigned a senior employee to be her mentor. The mentor helped Prince navigate the complex environment of a large corporation, including ways to speak clearly and assertively with managers from a variety of functions. She also learned how to draw out the contributions of her team. As she gained insight into the leadership role, Prince moved into her job as vice president, overseeing Anthem's Medicaid operations, including 180 employees, for states on the East Coast. Prince credits the leadership development program with teaching her "how to be successful," but it is clear that her willingness to grow and explore new career options also has played a role.[1]

Holly Prince is an outstanding example of how employees today take responsibility for their careers. Employers know that people with this kind of drive and talent do not stick around unless they have opportunities to make a difference and achieve success. Therefore, to fully benefit from their employees' strengths and skills, managers must be able to identify high-potential employees, make sure the organization uses the talents of these people, and reassure them of their value so that they do not become dissatisfied and leave the organization. Managers also must be able to listen. Although new employees need strong direction, they expect to be able to think independently and be treated with respect. In all these ways, managers provide for **employee development**—the combination of formal education, job experiences, relationships, and assessment of personality and abilities to help employees prepare for the future of their careers. Human resource management establishes a process for employee development that prepares employees to help the organization meet its goals.

Employee Development
The combination of formal education, job experiences, relationships, and assessment of personality and abilities to help employees prepare for the future of their careers.

This chapter explores the purpose and activities of employee development. We begin by discussing the relationships among development, training, and career management. Next we look at development approaches, including formal education, assessment, job experiences, and interpersonal relationships. The chapter emphasizes the types of skills, knowledge, and behaviors that are strengthened by each development method, so employees and their managers can choose appropriate methods when planning for development. The third section of the chapter describes the steps of the career management process, emphasizing the responsibilities of employee and employer at each step of the process. The chapter concludes with a discussion of special challenges related to employee development—the so-called glass ceiling, succession planning, and dysfunctional managers.

LO 8-1 Discuss how development is related to training and careers.

Training, Development, and Career Management

Organizations and their employees must constantly expand their knowledge, skills, and behavior to meet customer needs and compete in today's demanding and rapidly changing business environment. More and more companies operate internationally, requiring that employees understand different cultures and customs. More companies organize work in terms of projects or customers, rather than specialized functions, so employees need to acquire a broad range of technical and interpersonal skills. Many companies expect employees at all levels to perform roles once reserved for management. Modern organizations are expected to provide development opportunities to employees without regard to their sex, race, ethnic background, or age so that they have equal opportunity for advancement. In this climate, organizations are placing greater emphasis on training and development. To do this, organizations must understand development's relationship to training and career management.

Development and Training

The definition of development indicates that it is future oriented. Development implies learning that is not necessarily related to the employee's current job.[2] Instead, it prepares employees for other jobs or positions in the organization and increases their ability to move into jobs that may not yet exist.[3] Development also may help employees prepare for changes in responsibilities and requirements in their current jobs, such as changes resulting from new technology, work designs, or customers.

In contrast, training traditionally focuses on helping employees improve performance of their current jobs. Many organizations have focused on linking training programs to

TABLE 8.1

Training versus Development

	TRAINING	DEVELOPMENT
Focus	Current	Future
Use of work experiences	Low	High
Goal	Preparation for current job	Preparation for changes
Participation	Required	Voluntary

business goals. In these organizations, the distinction between training and development is more blurred. Table 8.1 summarizes the traditional differences.

For an example of a company that links training and development to future-oriented business goals, see the "Best Practices" box.

Development for Careers

In the past, workers and employees might think of a career as something a person pursues at one company, rising through the ranks. Today, however, the more common model is that of a **protean career,** one that a person frequently changes based on changes in the person's interests, abilities, and values and in the work environment.[4] In the story at the beginning of this chapter, Holly Prince chose to move from teaching students in the Solomon Islands to administering insurance policies in the United States. Her willingness to move from accounting to insurance to management also exemplifies a protean career. As in this example, employees in protean careers take responsibility for managing their careers. This practice is consistent with the modern psychological contract described in Chapter 2. Employees look for organizations to provide not job security and a career ladder to climb, but instead development opportunities and flexible work arrangements.

Protean Career
A career that frequently changes based on changes in the person's interests, abilities, and values and in the work environment.

For the employee, success in a protean career requires continuous learning, coupled with a willingness to embrace change, even moving across the boundaries that separate functions and industries. A career path that once would have been criticized as "job hopping" may now be praised as increasing one's value in the labor force. For the employer, this means either adding value to the employee's career experience or watching that employee leave to pursue a better opportunity elsewhere. It may even mean investing in employees despite the knowledge that many of them will follow a career path to another organization—but perhaps come back again later, with an even more valuable set of skills.[5] In this context, employers and employees alike must find matches between (1) employees' interests, skills, and weaknesses and (2) development experiences involving jobs, relationships, and formal courses. As discussed later in the chapter, organizations can meet these needs through a system for *career management* or *development planning.* Career management helps employees select development activities that prepare them to meet their career goals. It helps employers select development activities in line with their human resource needs.

Approaches to Employee Development

LO 8-2 Identify the methods organizations use for employee development.

The many approaches to employee development fall into four broad categories: formal education, assessment, job experiences, and interpersonal relationships.[6] Figure 8.1 summarizes these four methods. Many organizations combine these approaches.

Formal Education

Organizations may support employee development through a variety of formal educational programs, either at the workplace or off-site. These may include workshops designed

Best Practices

Valvoline's Development Program Ensures Internal Advancement

Like other quick-service oil change businesses, Valvoline hires multitudes of entry-level workers. That means it is competing with many other retail businesses to sort through a flood of applicants who need work but do not necessarily hope to stay in this type of job for very long. Valvoline's strategy for meeting this challenge is to select candidates with leadership potential and give them opportunities to participate in its voluntary employee development program. This results in a workforce that is above-average in employee retention and provides a supply of qualified candidates to promote to management positions.

The development program, called Super-Pro 10, is structured around certificates. The talent development team identified the knowledge and skills necessary to succeed in jobs at various levels, and prepared a training process to meet those requirements. Training sessions focus on hands-on learning, supplemented with readings and online interactive lessons. Every time an employee completes a level of training by demonstrating all the skills on the checklist for that level, the employee receives a certificate that identifies him or her as qualified for a promotion (and an increase in pay). This sets up employees to begin practicing supervisory skills within their first year on the job, even as they continue to add to their technical skills.

Employees also receive performance feedback at least every four months, with performance measures including how well employees develop whomever they supervise. The automated review system asks managers to indicate whether the employee is ready for promotion. The company's performance management system uses the data to indicate to management where the level of talent indicates opportunities to expand the business.

This approach is creating increasing numbers of management talent to meet Valvoline's present needs and future growth. Over the past few years, all of Valvoline's service center managers have been promoted to that position from hourly jobs with the company. In addition, 100% of its area manager positions and more than 90% of its market manager positions (responsible for 25 or more stores) have been filled through promotions. Many headquarters managers also started out in Valvoline's shops.

Questions

1. Describe how the activities summarized here fit the definition of employee development.
2. How would it affect the business for Valvoline to hire its managers externally, rather than developing entry-level employees to fill the positions?

Sources: "Training Top 125 Best Practice: Leadership Development at Valvoline Instant Oil Change," *Training,* August 20, 2019, https://trainingmag.com; Kelsey Gee, "Who Deserves a Promotion? One Company Has It Figured Out," *The Wall Street Journal,* January 31, 2018, https://www.wsj.com; Stephanie Castellano, "A Well-Oiled Machine," *TD,* October 2017, pp. 32–34; Lorri Freifeld, "Training Top 125 Best Practice: Super-Pro 10 Certification at Valvoline Instant Oil Change," *Training,* May 31, 2016, https://www.trainingmag.com.

specifically for the organization's employees, short courses offered by consultants or universities, university programs offered to employees who live on campus during the program, and executive MBA programs (which enroll managers to meet on weekends or evenings to earn a master's degree in business administration). These programs may involve lectures by business experts, business games and simulations, experiential programs, and meetings with customers. Chapter 7 described most of these training methods, including their pros and cons.

Many companies operate training and development centers that offer seminars and longer-term programs. Among the most famous are General Electric's John F. Welch Leadership Center in Crotonville, New York, and McDonald's Hamburger University in Chicago, Illinois. At Northwell Health, the teaching is often done by the organization's leaders, which brings them into contact with the employees, so they can build relationships and convey the organization's culture along with particular skills. Another way the training center is beneficial is that it provides practice in teamwork, which is necessary in health care to ensure the safety of employees and patients.[7]

FIGURE 8.1
Four Approaches to Employee Development

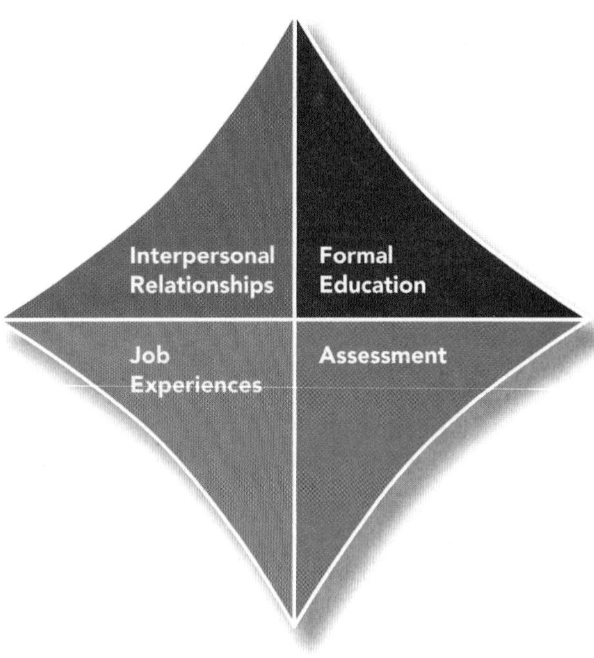

Independent institutions offering executive education include Harvard, the Wharton School of Business, the University of Michigan, and the Center for Creative Leadership. At the University of Virginia, the Darden School of Business offers an executive MBA program in which students meet at its Charlottesville campus or in Washington, DC, for a long weekend once a month. This face-to-face time provides opportunities for students to attend classes and collaborate on presentations, simulations, and case studies. The school also brings executive MBA students to campus for leadership residencies at the beginning and end of the program. During each of the week-long residencies, the students use workshops, coaching, and reflection to get better at handling their everyday management challenges. Between the times on campus, the students continue their education with independent study, online classes, and tools for virtual meetings and online exams.[8]

Whether provided through universities or the employer's own learning and development program, formal education is increasingly moving away from classrooms to the Internet. This enables the organization to use data about employees to pinpoint each employee's developmental needs and then direct the employee to the most relevant resources for meeting those needs. At IBM, the learning and development system applies artificial intelligence to review employee profiles and direct employees to the learning that is most important for their current and desired roles.[9]

Assessment

LO 8-3 Describe how organizations use assessment of personality type, work behaviors, and job performance to plan employee development.

Another way to provide for employee development is **assessment**—collecting information and providing feedback to employees about their behavior, communication style, or skills.[10] Information for assessment may come from the employees, their peers, managers, and customers. The most frequent uses of assessment are to identify employees with managerial potential to measure current managers' strengths and weaknesses. Organizations also use assessment to identify managers with potential to move into higher-level executive positions. Organizations that assign work to teams may use assessment to identify the strengths and weaknesses of individual team members and the effects of the team members' decision-making and communication styles on the team's productivity. The "HR Oops!" feature discusses an example of the challenges that underlie the important decisions of what to assess and how.

Assessment
Collecting information and providing feedback to employees about their behavior, communication style, or skills.

For assessment to support development, the information must be shared with the employee being assessed. Along with that assessment information, the employee needs suggestions for correcting skill weaknesses and for using skills already learned. The suggestions might be to participate in training courses or develop skills through new job experiences. Based on the assessment information and available development opportunities, employees should develop action plans to guide their efforts at self-improvement.

Organizations vary in the methods and sources of information they use in developmental assessment. Many organizations appraise performance. Organizations with sophisticated development systems use psychological tests to measure employees' skills, personality types,

Simplistic Views of Leadership

Cal State management professor Ryan Gottfredson notes that all too often efforts at leadership development fall short of their goals. Furthermore, he has found that efforts to improve the development programs don't dig deep enough. Too often, the planners find themselves having to reconsider the combination of methods used or the specific leadership traits that programs select for with their assessment tools. The usual ways of thinking about leadership do not fully take into account the latest understandings of the psychology of leadership. It is simplistic to think that it is possible to obtain leadership by just choosing someone more extroverted or teaching someone to behave a certain way across the wide variety of situations facing managers.

The alternative Gottfredson proposes is to consider more broadly how personalities and situations interact, particularly the ways that leaders interpret situations, the mind-sets that leaders adopt toward problems and challenges. Leaders can learn to apply certain mind-sets that are more productive and helpful. For example, a *growth* mind-set leads managers to approach a challenge with curiosity, seeking information and testing ideas. An *open* mind-set enables a leader to listen to ideas from others and use disagreements as a chance to think through a situation more completely. A *promotion* mind-set is purposeful and goal oriented. And an *outward* mind-set values other people as well as oneself.

Standard Chartered, a multinational financial-services company, incorporated elements of the growth and open mind-sets into its leadership development. The company wanted to prepare leaders to thrive in the present and future world of information technology. Businesses that excel will be those that maximize their ability to make data-driven decisions, rather than operating on hunches and decision makers' recall of past experiences. So where leadership development had in the past focused on personal qualities, it shifted toward preparing leaders to analyze, experiment, and back up their decisions. The mind-set that Standard Chartered is teaching is that when leaders make decisions, they should develop a hypothesis to test, experiment with ideas, and see what works and what doesn't. They are expected to listen to others and in turn to share what they learn. Instead of being rewarded for being right, they are being encouraged to explore and increase their knowledge.

Questions

1. What do you think makes "leadership" difficult to measure and teach?
2. Assuming that a person leads more effectively if he or she learns to adopt the right mind-sets, what would you measure when assessing employees to determine if they have potential to be leaders?

Sources: Ryan Gottfredson, "Get in a Leadership State of Mind," *TD*, March 2020, pp. 34–39; Ryan Gottfredson, "Why Leaders Are Often Villain-Like and How They Can Become More Hero-Like," *CEO World*, February 27, 2020, https://ceoworld.biz; Abbie Lundberg and George Westerman, "The Transformer CIO," *Harvard Business Review*, January–February 2020, pp. 84–93.

and communication styles. They may collect self, peer, and manager ratings of employees' behavior and style of working with others. In a survey by the Institute for Corporate Productivity, business professionals said the tool used most widely in their organization was a type of performance appraisal known as 360-degree assessments, followed by two popular psychological tests (the Myers-Briggs Type Indicator and the DiSC assessment).[11] A less-used but potentially beneficial approach is to send employees to an assessment center for in-depth evaluation of their skills, strengths, and weaknesses. Whether or not they use an assessment center, employers often combine assessment tools for a fuller picture of employees.

Psychological Profiles When organizations choose assessment tools, they often include some type of questionnaire in which employees answer questions about themselves or select words or statements they agree describe themselves. From the answers, a testing service creates an inventory or profile describing the person's traits or the way the person tends to behave. Two of the most widely used assessments are the ones mentioned in the previous paragraph: the Myers-Briggs Type Indicator and the DiSC assessment.

Myers-Briggs Type Indicator (MBTI) identifies individuals' preferences for source of energy, means of information gathering, way of decision making, and lifestyle. The assessment consists of more than 100 questions about how the person feels or prefers to behave in different situations (such as "Are you usually a good 'mixer' or rather quiet and reserved?"). The results describe these individuals' preferences in the four areas:

Myers-Briggs Type Indicator (MBTI)
Psychological inventory that identifies individuals' preferences for source of energy, means of information gathering, way of decision making, and lifestyle, providing information for team building and leadership development.

1. The *energy* dichotomy indicates where individuals gain interpersonal strength and vitality, measured as their degree of introversion or extroversion. Extroverted types (E) gain energy through interpersonal relationships. Introverted types (I) gain energy by focusing on inner thoughts and feelings.
2. The *information-gathering* dichotomy relates to the preparations individuals make before making decisions. Individuals with a Sensing (S) preference tend to gather the facts and details to prepare for a decision. Intuitive types (N) tend to focus less on the facts and more on possibilities and relationships among them.
3. In *decision making,* individuals differ in the amount of consideration they give to their own and others' values and feelings, as opposed to the hard facts of a situation. Individuals with a Thinking (T) preference try always to be objective in making decisions. Individuals with a Feeling (F) preference tend to evaluate the impact of the alternatives on others, as well as their own feelings; they are more subjective.
4. The *lifestyle* dichotomy describes an individual's tendency to be either flexible or structured. Individuals with a Judging (J) preference focus on goals, establish deadlines, and prefer to be conclusive. Individuals with a Perceiving (P) preference enjoy surprises, are comfortable with changing a decision, and dislike deadlines.

The alternatives for each of the four dichotomies result in 16 possible combinations. Of course people are likely to be mixtures of these types, but the point of the assessment is that certain types predominate in individuals.

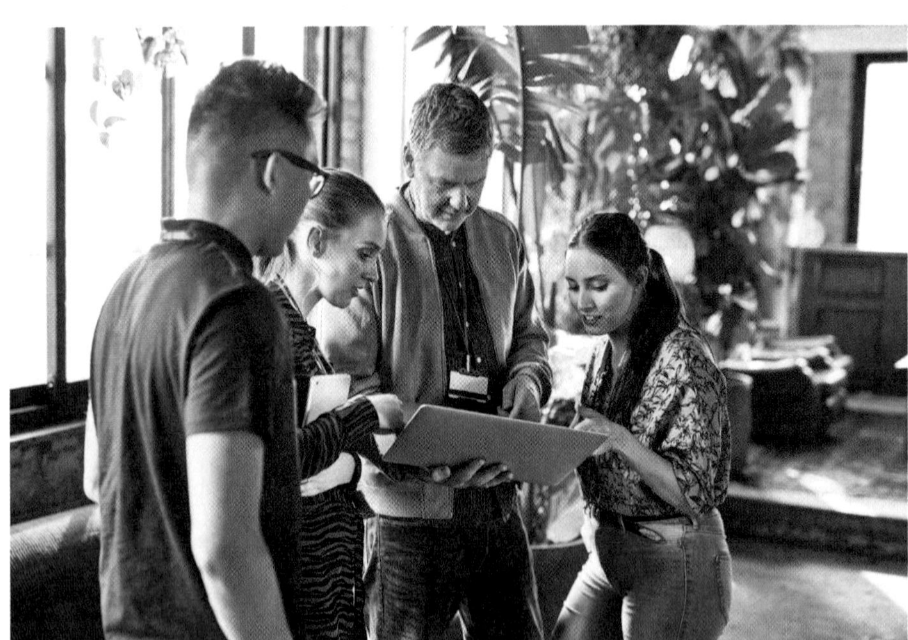

Learning about employees' preferences for communicating and getting work done may help them contribute to teams and choose career paths in which they are likely to thrive.
10'000 Hours/DigitalVision/Getty Images

As a result of their psychological types, people have developed strengths and weaknesses. For example, individuals who are Introverted, Sensing, Thinking, and Judging (known as ISTJs) tend to be serious, quiet, practical, orderly, and logical. They can organize tasks, be decisive, and follow through on plans and goals. But because they do not have the opposite preferences (Extroversion, Intuition, Feeling, and Perceiving), ISTJs have several weaknesses. They may have difficulty responding to unexpected opportunities, appear to their colleagues to be too task-oriented or impersonal, and make decisions too fast. The same goes for other combinations and types.

Applying this kind of information about employees' preferences or tendencies helps organizations understand the communication, motivation, teamwork, work styles, and leadership of the people in their groups. For example, salespeople or executives who want to communicate better can apply what they learn about their own personality styles and the way other people perceive them. For team development, the MBTI can help teams match team members with assignments based on their preferences and thus improve problem solving.[12] The team could assign brainstorming (idea-generating) tasks to employees with an Intuitive preference and evaluation of the ideas to employees with a Sensing preference.

Research on the validity, reliability, and effectiveness of the MBTI is inconclusive.[13] People who take the MBTI find it a positive experience and say it helps them change their behavior. However, MBTI scores are not necessarily stable over time. Studies in which the MBTI was administered at two different times found that as few as one-fourth of those who took the assessment were classified as exactly the same type the second time. Still, the MBTI is a valuable tool for understanding communication styles and the ways people prefer to interact with others. It is not appropriate for measuring job performance, however, or as the only means of evaluating promotion potential.

DiSC
Brand of assessment tool that identifies individuals' behavioral patterns in terms of dominance, influence, steadiness, and conscientiousness.

The **DiSC** assessment tool is an inventory of behavioral styles based on the work of William Marston, a psychologist who attempted to categorize normal behavior patterns.[14] Over the years, different people have used Marston's model to construct tests to measure versions of Marston's categories; the most widely used instrument, published by Wiley under the name of Everything DiSC®, distinguishes itself with the lowercase *i* in its name. Because there are variations in these inventories, employers should be careful to use a version that has been tested and shown to be valid and reliable.

An employee taking this DiSC inventory receives a profile report describing his or her behavioral style, preferred environment, and strategies for effectiveness. The style is described in terms of the following categories (which provide the letters for the DiSC acronym):

- *Dominance* means the person emphasizes results and displays confidence. This type of person takes on challenges, sees the big picture, and can be blunt and to the point.
- *Influence* means the person emphasizes relationships and persuasion. This type of person likes to collaborate, dislikes being ignored, and displays optimism and enthusiasm.
- *Steadiness* means the person emphasizes cooperation, sincerity, and dependability. This type of person behaves calmly and with humility, dislikes rushing, and is supportive of others.
- *Conscientiousness* means the person emphasizes quality and accuracy, displaying competency. This type of person worries about mistakes and wants to get the details. He or she favors objective thinking and enjoys working independently.

Assessment Center
A wide variety of specific selection programs that use multiple selection methods to rate applicants or job incumbents on their management potential.

Assessment Centers At an **assessment center,** multiple raters or evaluators (assessors) evaluate employees' performance on a number of exercises.[15] An assessment center is usually an off-site location such as a conference center. Usually 6 to 12 employees participate at one time. The primary use of assessment centers is to identify whether employees have the personality characteristics, administrative skills, and interpersonal skills needed for managerial jobs. Organizations also use them to determine whether employees have the skills needed for working in teams. A complete half-day or full-day assessment at an assessment center can cost as much as $20,000, so employers tend to use this method mainly for employees in the highest levels of management.

The types of exercises used in assessment centers include leaderless group discussions, interviews, in-baskets, and role-plays.[16] In a **leaderless group discussion** a team of five to seven employees is assigned a problem and must work together to solve it within a certain time period. The problem may involve buying and selling supplies, nominating a subordinate for an award, or assembling a product. Interview questions typically cover each employee's work and personal experiences, skill strengths and weaknesses, and career plans. In-basket exercises, discussed as a selection method in Chapter 6, simulate the administrative tasks of a manager's job, using a pile of documents for the employee to handle. In role-plays, the participant takes the part of a manager or employee in a situation involving the skills to be assessed. For example, a participant might be given the role of a manager who must discuss performance problems with an employee, played by someone who works for the assessment center. Other exercises in assessment centers might include interest and aptitude tests to evaluate an employee's vocabulary, general mental ability, and reasoning skills. Personality tests may be used to determine employees' ability to get along with others, tolerance for uncertainty, and other traits related to success as a manager or team member.

One way to develop employees is to begin with an assessment that may consist of assigning an activity to a team and seeing who brings what skills and strengths to the team. How can this assessment help employees? Karen Moskowitz/Getty Images

Leaderless Group Discussion
An assessment center exercise in which a team of five to seven employees is assigned a problem and must work together to solve it within a certain time period.

The assessors are usually managers who have been trained to look for employee behaviors that are related to the skills being assessed. Typically, each assessor observes and records one or two employees' behaviors in each exercise. The assessors review their notes and rate each employee's level of skills (for example, 5 = high level of leadership skills, 1 = low level of leadership skills). After all the employees have completed the exercises, the assessors discuss their observations of each employee. They compare their ratings and try to agree on each employee's rating for each of the skills.

As we mentioned in Chapter 6, research suggests that assessment center ratings are valid for predicting performance, salary level, and career advancement.[17] Assessment centers may also be useful for development because of the feedback that participants receive about their attitudes, skill strengths, and weaknesses.[18]

Performance Appraisals and 360-Degree Feedback A *performance appraisal,* or formal process for measuring employee performance, is a major component of performance management, which will be described in Chapter 10. This information also can be useful for employee development under certain conditions.[19] The appraisal system must tell employees specifically about their performance problems and ways to improve their performance. Employees must gain a clear understanding of the differences between current performance and expected performance. The appraisal process must identify causes of the performance discrepancy and develop plans for improving performance. Managers must be trained to deliver frequent performance feedback and must monitor employees' progress in carrying out their action plans.

A recent trend in performance appraisals, also discussed in Chapter 10, is *360-degree feedback*—performance measurement by the employee's supervisor, peers, employees, and customers. Often the feedback involves rating the individual in terms of work-related behaviors. For development purposes, the rater would identify an area of behavior as a strength of that employee or an area requiring further development. The results presented to the employee show how he or she was rated on each item and how self-evaluations differ from other raters' evaluations. The individual reviews the results, seeks clarification from the raters, and sets specific development goals based on the strengths and weaknesses identified.[20] Luck Companies, a Virginia miner and supplier of crushed stone, uses 360-degree assessments for all its managers to measure their performance in terms of criteria such as company values and competencies associated with good leadership.[21]

There are several benefits of 360-degree feedback. Organizations collect multiple perspectives of managers' performance, allowing employees to compare their own personal evaluations with the views of others. This method also establishes formal communications about behaviors and skill ratings between employees and their internal and external customers. Several studies have shown that performance improves and behavior changes as a result of participating in upward feedback and 360-degree feedback systems.[22] The change is greatest in people who received lower ratings from others than what they gave themselves. The 360-degree feedback system is most likely to be effective if the rating instrument enables reliable or consistent ratings, assesses behaviors related to the organization's success, focuses on developing strengths, not just correcting weaknesses, and is easy to use. Other ways the organization can make it more likely that 360-degree feedback will yield benefits are to have the assessment results delivered by a trained person and to hold the employees accountable in follow-up meetings with their manager or a coach.[23]

There are potential limitations of 360-degree feedback. This method demands a significant amount of time for raters to complete the evaluations. If raters, especially subordinates or peers, provide negative feedback, some managers might try to identify and punish them. A facilitator is needed to help interpret results. Finally, simply delivering ratings to a manager does not provide ways for the manager to act on the feedback (for example, development planning, meeting with raters, or taking courses). As noted earlier, any form of assessment should be accompanied by suggestions for improvement and development of an action plan.

Job Experiences

LO 8-4 Explain how job experiences can be used for developing skills.

Job Experiences
The combination of relationships, problems, demands, tasks, and other features of an employee's job.

Most employee development occurs through **job experiences**[24]—the combination of relationships, problems, demands, tasks, and other features of an employee's jobs. Using job experiences for employee development assumes that development is most likely to occur when the employee's skills and experiences do not entirely match the skills required for the employee's current job. To succeed, employees must stretch their skills. In other words, they must learn new skills, apply their skills and knowledge in new ways, and master new experiences.[25] For example, companies that want to prepare employees to expand overseas markets are assigning them to a variety of international jobs. The "HR How To" feature discusses some of the challenges of being more inclusive in selecting employees for stretch assignments.

Most of what we know about development through job experiences comes from a series of studies conducted by the Center for Creative Leadership.[26] These studies asked executives to identify key career events that made a difference in their managerial styles and the lessons they learned from these experiences. The key events included job assignments (such as fixing a failed operation), interpersonal relationships (getting along with supervisors), and types of transitions (situations in which the manager at first lacked the necessary background). Through job experiences like these, managers learn how to handle common challenges, prove themselves, lead change, handle pressure, and influence others.

HR How To

Making Development More Inclusive

Researchers who investigate diversity and inclusion find that although companies are placing more women into top positions, the overall representation of women in management continues to be relatively low. The data point to a low rate of moving women into management assignments in the first place. Similar patterns are leaving behind workers of color, persons with disabilities, and LGBTQ employees. Workers who fall into more than one of these categories are at even greater disadvantage.

In this context, selecting diverse candidates for important stretch or developmental job experiences, including promotions, is a key part of developing a diverse group of decision makers in organizations. Here are a few ideas for achieving more inclusive access to development opportunities:

- Set measurable targets for hiring women and minorities for first-line management jobs. Having a goal to reach motivates decision makers to give more consideration to how they might change any practices or unconscious bias that gets in the way of identifying a diverse array of candidates for promotion. For example, business managers might require that HR departments provide at least two women and two persons of color in each list of candidates for developmental job experiences.
- Ensure that selection criteria are objectively related to job performance. For example, selection practices might favor people who work in a certain department or who know the business manager already. If so, the criteria are likely missing individuals with exceptional decision-making or leadership capabilities. In this case, the organization needs better assessment methods.
- Create an organizational role of sponsor. A sponsor is someone who goes beyond offering advice to recommending an employee when opportunities arise for developmental assignments. Managers who are skilled leaders often identify employees to sponsor, but explicitly making sponsorship a role means that processes are in place to connect high-potential employees with higher-level managers who commit to this kind of development. These efforts can include employees who might be overlooked by managers and uncertain how to make their interests known.

Questions

1. What is the downside of a company making stretch or developmental job experiences available only to employees selected based on asking supervisors who on their team would be a good manager?
2. Suppose a company's customer service team fills dozens of supervisory positions every year. The company's HR department analyzes its workforce and discovers that almost all the supervisors are white males, even though customer service employees are diverse. How could the company increase diversity while selecting qualified candidates?

Sources: Martin Lanik, "Why Women and Minorities Are Being Left Behind in the Leadership Pipeline," *CEO World,* March 29, 2020, https://ceoworld.biz; Pooja Jain-Link, Julia Taylor Kennedy, and Trudy Bourgeois, "Five Strategies for Creating an Inclusive Workplace," *Harvard Business Review,* January 13, 2020, https://hbr.org; Jess Huang, Alexis Krivkovich, Irina Starikova, et al., *Women in the Workplace 2019,* McKinsey & Company, October 2019, https://www.mckinsey.com.

The usefulness of job experiences for employee development varies depending on whether the employee views the experiences as positive or negative sources of stress. When employees view job experiences as positive stressors, the experiences challenge them and stimulate learning. When they view job experiences as negative stressors, employees may suffer from high levels of harmful stress. Of the job demands studied, managers were most likely to experience negative stress from creating change and overcoming obstacles (adverse business conditions, lack of management support, lack of personal support, or a difficult boss). Research suggests that all of the job demands except obstacles are related to learning.[27] Organizations should offer job experiences that are most likely to increase learning, and they should consider the consequences of situations that involve negative stress.

Visit your instructor's Connect® course and access your eBook to view this video.

"We believe everybody, in HR or in any other function, should be in a situation or a job in which they are stretched—I would almost use the word 'uncomfortable'—because learning happens when people are outside of their comfort zones."

—Susan P. Peters
Senior Vice President, Human Resources, GE

Source: Video Produced for the Center for Executive Succession in the Darla Moore School of Business at the University of South Carolina by Coal Powered Filmworks

Although the research on development through job experiences has focused on managers, line employees also can learn through job experiences. Organizations may, for example, use job experiences to develop skills needed for teamwork, including conflict resolution, data analysis, and customer service. These experiences may occur when forming a team and when employees switch roles within a team.

Various job assignments can provide for employee development. The organization may enlarge the employee's current job or move the employee to different jobs. Lateral moves include job rotation, transfer, or temporary assignment to another organization. The organization may also use downward moves or promotions as a source of job experience. Figure 8.2 summarizes these alternatives.

Job Enlargement As Chapter 4 stated in the context of job design, *job enlargement* involves adding challenges or new responsibilities to employees' current jobs. Examples include completing a special project, switching roles within a work team, or researching new ways to serve customers. An engineering employee might join a task force developing new career paths for technical employees. The work on the project could give the engineer a leadership role through which the engineer learns about the company's career development system while also practicing leadership skills to help the task force reach its goals. In this way, job enlargement not only makes a job more interesting but also creates an opportunity for employees to develop new skills.

Job Rotation Another job design technique that can be applied to employee development is *job rotation,* moving employees through a series of job assignments in one or more functional areas. Clothing retailer H&M makes job rotation part of the employee development process for all its office and warehouse employees,

FIGURE 8.2
How Job Experiences Are Used for Employee Development

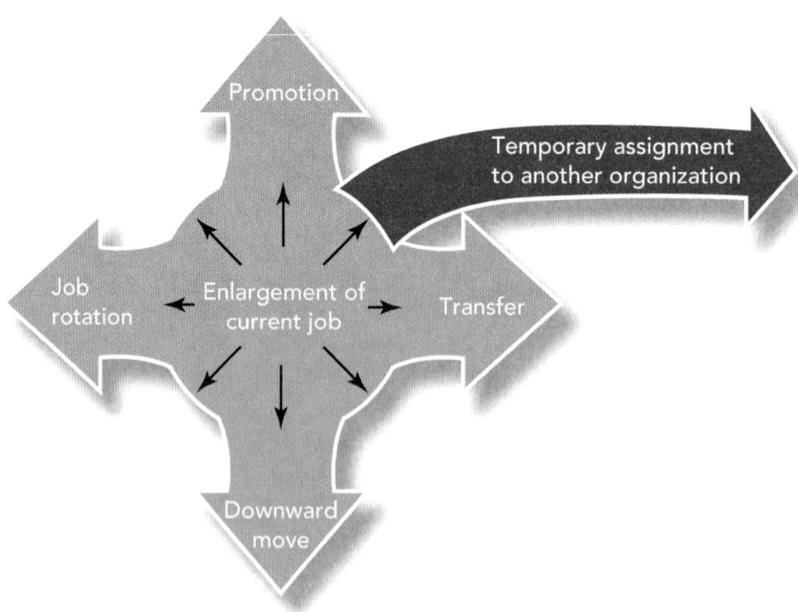

even executives. When the company hires a new employee, that person begins by spending up to 13 weeks working in a store. The employee first staffs the fitting rooms, then tries sales positions, and for management jobs, works on store and cash management. That way, employees who work behind the scenes understand the challenges of the store workers, as well as how customer service, store environment, and other factors contribute to the company's performance.[28]

Job rotation helps employees gain an appreciation for the company's goals, increases their understanding of different company functions, develops a network of contacts, and improves problem-solving and decision-making skills.[29] Job rotation also helps employees increase their salary and earn promotions faster. However, job rotation poses some problems for employees and the organization. Knowing they will be rotated to another job may give the employees a short-term perspective on problems and their solutions. Employees may feel less satisfied and motivated because they have difficulty developing specialized skills and leave the position too soon to fulfill any challenging assignments. The rotation of employees through a department may hurt productivity and increase the workload of those who remain after employees are rotated out. Job rotation is most likely to succeed when it meets certain conditions:[30]

- The organization establishes and communicates clear policies about which positions are eligible for job rotation. Job rotation for nonmanagement employees as well as managers can be beneficial, depending on the program's objectives.
- Employees and their managers understand and agree on the expectations for the job rotation, including which skills are to be developed.
- Goals for the program support business goals. These might include exposing high-potential employees to a variety of business units, customers, or geographic areas in preparation for management positions or rotating an experienced, talented employee through several business units to mentor or coach employees.
- The rotation schedule is realistic, taking into account how long employees will need to become familiar with their new position, as well as how much time is needed for employees to complete the assignments.
- Top management is committed to the program's success.
- Someone is responsible for measuring whether the program is meeting its goals.

Transfer
Assignment of an employee to a position in a different area of the company, usually in a lateral move.

Transfers, Promotions, and Downward Moves Most companies use upward, downward, and lateral moves as an option for employee development. In a **transfer,** the organization assigns an employee to a position in a different area of the company. Transfers do not necessarily increase job responsibilities or compensation. They are usually lateral moves, that is, moves to a job with a similar level of responsibility. They may involve relocation to another part of the country or even to another country.

Relocation can be stressful because of the demands of moving, especially when family members are affected. People have to find new housing, shopping, health care, and leisure facilities, and they often lack the support of nearby friends and family. These stresses come at the same time the employee must learn the expectations and responsibilities associated with the new position. Because transfers can provoke anxiety, many companies have difficulty getting employees to accept them. Employees most willing to accept transfers tend to be those with high career ambitions and beliefs that the organization offers a promising future and that accepting the transfer will help the company succeed.[31]

Downward Move
Assignment of an employee to a position with less responsibility and authority.

A **downward move** occurs when an employee is given less responsibility and authority. The organization may demote an employee because of poor performance or move the employee to a lower-level position in another function so that the employee can develop different skills. The temporary cross-functional move is the most common way to use

Working outside one's home country is the most important job experience that can develop an employee for a career in the global economy.
Radius Images/Alamy Stock Photo

downward moves for employee development. For example, engineers who want to move into management often take lower-level positions, such as shift supervisor, to develop their management skills.

Many employees have difficulty associating transfers and downward moves with development; these changes may feel more like forms of punishment. Employees often decide to leave an organization rather than accept such a change, and then the organization must bear the costs of replacing those employees. Employees will be more likely to accept transfers and downward moves as development opportunities if the organization provides information about the change and its possible benefits and involves the employee in planning the change. Employees are also more likely to be positive about such a recommendation if the organization provides clear performance objectives and frequent feedback. Employers can encourage an employee to relocate by providing financial assistance with the move, information about the new location and job, and help for family members, such as identifying schools, child care and elder care options, and job search assistance for the employee's spouse.[32]

Promotion
Assignment of an employee to a position with greater challenges, more responsibility, and more authority than in the previous job, usually accompanied by a pay increase.

A **promotion** involves moving an employee into a position with greater challenges, more responsibility, and more authority than in the previous job. Usually promotions include pay increases. Because promotions improve the person's pay, status, and feelings of accomplishment, employees are more willing to accept promotions than lateral or downward moves. Even so, employers can increase the likelihood that employees will accept promotions by providing the same kind of information and assistance that are used to support transfers and downward moves. Organizations can more easily offer promotions if they are profitable and growing. In other conditions, opportunities for promoting employees may be limited.

Temporary Assignments with Other Organizations In some cases, an employer may benefit from the skills an employee can learn at another organization. The employer may encourage the employee to participate in an **externship**—a full-time temporary position at another organization. Externships are an attractive option for employees in analytical positions, who otherwise might solve the same kinds of problems over and over, becoming bored as they miss out on exposure to challenging new ideas and techniques. A variation on this approach that may not require a full-time commitment of employees is to encourage skills-based volunteering, in which employees apply and increase their skills by engaging in community service projects. The company pays the employees for the time they spend on the projects, and the employees apply their developing talents to a good cause. For example, 3M's Visiting Wizards program encourages company employees to share the magic of science with students through demonstrations and hands-on experiments in an effort to increase student interest in STEM (science, technology, engineering, and math) careers and help build a diverse pipeline of future business leaders.[33]

Externship
Employee development through a full-time temporary position at another organization.

Sabbatical
A leave of absence from an organization to renew or develop skills.

Temporary assignments can include a **sabbatical**—a leave of absence from an organization to renew or develop skills. Employees on sabbatical often receive full pay and benefits. Sabbaticals let employees get away from the day-to-day stresses of their jobs and acquire new skills and perspectives. Sabbaticals also allow employees more time for personal pursuits such as writing a book or spending more time with family members. Universities often give sabbaticals to faculty members; some offer these development opportunities to staff members as well. How employees spend their sabbaticals varies from company to company. Some employees may work for a nonprofit service agency; others may study at a college or university or travel and work on special projects in non-U.S. subsidiaries of the company. At Edelman Financial Services, located in Fairfax, Virginia, employees are eligible for four weeks of paid sabbatical after five years with the company. As a motivation to use the time well, the company requires that employees submit a syllabus outlining their plans for the time away from work. Adviser Rey Roy took a cross-country bike ride, raising money for charity. The time he spent pedaling cleared his mind and gave him a fresh perspective, so that when he returned to work, he had renewed enthusiasm. In addition, Roy saw that other employees were inspired by his experience.[34]

HR Analytics & Decision Making

BB&T Corporation, now Truist Financial, wanted to ensure that its efforts to develop leaders would equip them to deliver better results, so it rolled out the program gradually and measured their career progress. Employees participating in BB&T's Leadership Excellence Program received coaching by a leadership consultant, attended workshops focused on different aspects of leadership, and worked on a project designed to benefit their area of business.

The outcomes of those who participated in the program were superior to those who had not yet participated. Program participants were promoted two times faster than the others. Further, their 31% retention rate translated into saving $13 million not spent to hire and train replacements for their positions.

Questions

1. What benefits would you expect from including special work projects in leadership development, along with the workshops and coaching?
2. How could Truist Financial benefit from analyzing results of the leadership development program before it was rolled out to all the eligible employees?

Sources: "Training Top 125 Best Practices and Outstanding Training Initiatives," *Training*, January/February 2017, p. 97; Joanna Castaneda, "Bench Strength," *TD*, June 2015, pp. 30–35.

Mentor
An experienced, productive senior employee who helps develop a less experienced employee (a protégé).

Interpersonal Relationships

Employees can also develop skills and increase their knowledge about the organization and its customers by interacting with a more experienced organization member. Typically, the two types of relationships used for employee development are mentoring and coaching.

LO 8-5 Summarize principles of successful mentoring programs.

Mentors A **mentor** is an experienced, productive senior employee who helps develop a less-experienced employee, called the *protégé*. Most mentoring relationships develop informally as a result of interests or values shared by the mentor and protégé. According to research, the employees most likely to seek and attract a mentor have certain personality characteristics: emotional stability, ability to adapt their behavior to the situation, and high needs for power and achievement. These traits seem to have been present in the HR employee mentored by Vanessa Alvarado Guevara of Stryker Global Supply. The employee wanted to move from a role emphasizing administration to one that was more advisory. Alvarado Guevara reviewed with her the HR competencies related to consultation; the employee was able to identify the behaviors she needed to develop, and then she set goals for doing so.[35]

Mentoring relationships also can develop as part of the organization's planned effort to bring together successful senior employees with less-experienced employees. One major advantage of formal mentoring programs is that they ensure access to mentors for all employees, regardless of gender or race. A mentoring program also can ensure that high-potential employees are matched with wise, experienced mentors in key areas–and that mentors are hearing the challenges facing employees who have less authority, work directly with customers, or hold positions in other parts of the organization.[36] However, in an artificially created relationship, mentors may have difficulty providing counseling and coaching.[37] One practical way employees can address this shortcoming is to look for more than one mentor, including informal relationships with interested people outside the organization. For their part, mentors should accept mentees who exhibit responsibility and a desire to learn. Some employees might expect the mentor to take charge of the mentee's career, and ultimately this is not beneficial for either person. To ensure the relationship is likely to succeed, the mentor can guide the mentee in agreeing on expectations for the relationship, including the frequency and type of communication.[38]

Mentoring programs tend to be most successful when they are voluntary and participants understand the details of the program. Rewarding managers for employee development is also important because it signals that mentoring and other development activities are worthwhile. In addition, the organization should carefully select mentors based on their interpersonal and technical skills, train them for the role, and evaluate whether the program has met its objectives.[39]

Mentors and protégés can both benefit from a mentoring relationship. Protégés receive career support, including coaching, protection, sponsorship, challenging assignments, and visibility among the organization's managers. They also receive benefits of a positive relationship–a friend and role model who accepts them, has a positive opinion toward them, and gives them a chance to talk about their worries. Employees with mentors are also more likely to be promoted, earn higher salaries, and have more influence within their organization.[40] Acting as a mentor gives managers a chance to develop their interpersonal skills and increase their feelings that they are contributing something important to the organization. Working with a technically trained protégé on matters such as new research in the field may also increase the mentor's technical knowledge.

So that more employees can benefit from mentoring, some organizations use *group mentoring programs,* which assign four to six protégés to a successful senior employee. A potential advantage of group mentoring is that protégés can learn from each other as well as from the mentor. The leader helps protégés understand the organization, guides them in analyzing their experiences, and helps them clarify career directions. Each member of the group may complete specific assignments, or the group may work together on a problem or issue.

Coach
A peer or manager who works with an employee to motivate the employee, help him or her develop skills, and provide reinforcement and feedback.

LO 8-6 Tell how managers and peers develop employees through coaching.

Coaching A **coach** is a peer or manager who works with an employee to motivate the employee, help him or her develop skills, and provide reinforcement and feedback. Coaches may play one or more of three roles:[41]

1. Working one-on-one with an employee, as when giving feedback.

2. Helping employees learn for themselves—for example, helping them find experts and teaching them to obtain feedback from others
3. Providing resources such as mentors, courses, or job experiences

The role of coaches at PwC includes at least the first and third roles listed. The consulting firm prepares new employees by combining classroom training with one-on-one coaching by trained coaches. The employees receive suggested readings and practice exercises, and they receive practice and feedback in meetings with their coach. When they complete the program, PwC offers online support through a "Mobile Coach," which delivers reminders and links to development-related content.[42]

Coaching is an expected part of managers' role at Procter & Gamble. The company has trained its managers to give employees positive feedback and to match career goals with business needs, among other coaching skills. P&G's aim is to develop managers who can in turn develop their people, resulting in a highly engaged workforce that thinks creatively.[43]

Research suggests that coaching helps managers improve by identifying areas for improvement and setting goals. Getting results from a coaching relationship can take at least six months of weekly or monthly meetings. To be effective, a coach generally conducts an assessment, asks questions that challenge the employee to think deeply about his or her goals and motives, helps the employee create an action plan, and follows up regularly to help the employee stay on track. Management professor Sydney Finkelstein describes exceptional leaders he has studied as "great teachers," who through their words and actions convey lessons in professionalism, business knowledge, and human relations. These lessons delivered quietly and tactfully become a memorable form of coaching.[44]

Systems for Career Management

LO 8-7 Identify the steps in the process of career management.

Employee development is most likely to meet the organization's needs if it is part of a human resource system of career management. In practice, organizations' career management systems vary. Some rely heavily on informal relationships, while others are sophisticated programs. As shown in Figure 8.3, a basic career management system involves four steps: data gathering, feedback, goal setting, and action planning and follow-up. Human resource professionals can contribute to the system's success by ensuring that it is linked to other HR practices such as performance management, training, and recruiting. AT&T's approach to career management seeks to address the protean nature of today's careers and the rapid pace of change in its business environment. The company assumes that its workers must learn new skills continually in order to keep up with change and achieve their career objectives. It has placed many of its learning options online, so employees can dip into them as needed, from any location. AT&T also encourages employees to seek mentors and to apply for work assignments that are challenging and relevant to them. Thus, much of the goal setting, action planning, and follow-up are tailored to individual interests and can be quickly changed when conditions change.[45]

Data Gathering

Self-Assessment
The use of information by employees to determine their career interests, values, aptitudes, and behavioral tendencies.

Organizations gather data to identify and fill gaps in their development practices. In addition, data gathering for career management is often aimed at providing individual employees with information about themselves. For the latter purpose, data gathering often involves the kinds of assessment tools previously described in the discussion of employee development methods. Applied to career management, these become tools for **self-assessment,** or the use of information by employees to determine their career interests, values, aptitudes, and behavioral tendencies. The employee's responsibility is to identify opportunities and personal areas

FIGURE 8.3
Steps in the Career Management Process

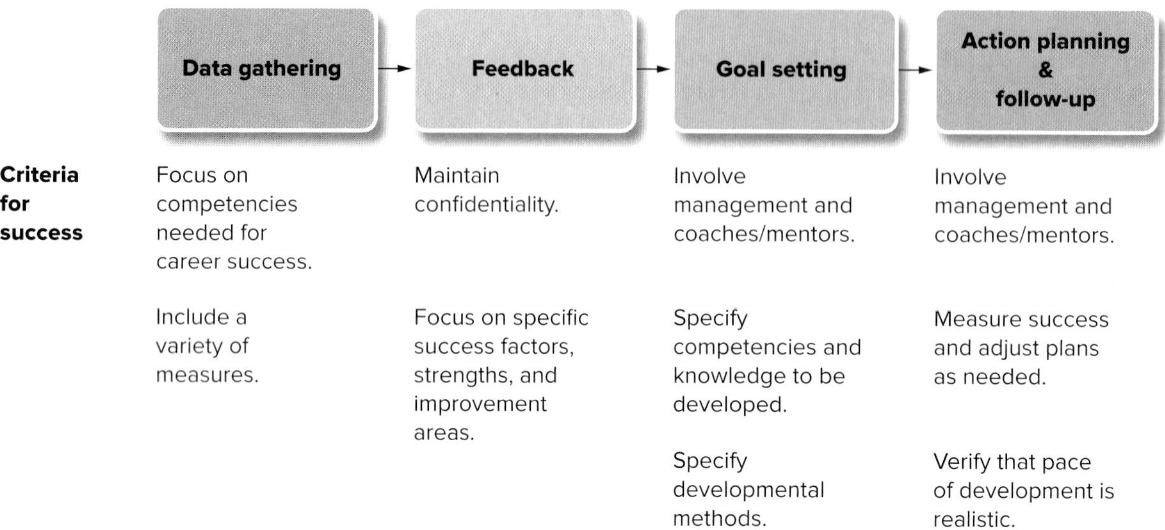

needing improvement. The organization's responsibility is to provide assessment information for identifying strengths, weaknesses, interests, and values.

Data gathering
Feedback
Goal setting
Action planning & follow-up
Criteria for success
Focus on competencies needed for career success.
Include a variety of measures.
Maintain confidentiality.
Focus on specific success factors, strengths, and improvement areas.
Involve management and coaches/mentors.
Specify competencies and knowledge to be developed.
Specify developmental methods.
Involve management and coaches/mentors.
Measure success and adjust plans as needed.
Verify that pace of development is realistic.

Self-assessment tools often include psychological tests such as the Myers-Briggs Type Indicator (described earlier in the chapter), the Strong-Campbell Interest Inventory, and the Self-Directed Search. The Strong-Campbell inventory helps employees identify their occupational and job interests. The Self-Directed Search identifies employees' preferences for working in different kinds of environments—sales, counseling, and so on. Tests may also help employees identify the relative values they place on work and leisure activities. Self-assessment tools can include exercises such as the one in Figure 8.4. This type of exercise helps an employee consider his or her current career status, future plans, and the fit between the career and the employee's current situation and resources. Some organizations provide counselors to help employees in the self-assessment process and to interpret the results of psychological tests. Completing the self-assessment can help employees identify a development need. Such a need can result from gaps between current skills or interests and the type of work or position the employee has or wants.

The self-assessment early in Nicole Ortiz's career started with input from her high school chemistry teacher, who observed Ortiz's skill in math and science and encouraged her to become a chemical engineer. Ortiz enrolled in engineering school but continued to evaluate the requirements of various branches of engineering. She learned that industrial engineers combine technical work with a great deal of human interaction and leadership, and she saw a better fit with her full skill set and interests than she expected from chemical engineering. She majored in industrial engineering and took a position with Hewlett Packard. She continues to engage in data gathering for her next move: learning more about business, so she can take on a management role, because she is fascinated by the entire organization, not just the department where she works.[46]

Feedback
Information employers give employees about their skills and knowledge and where these assets fit into the organization's plans.

Feedback

In the next step of career management, **feedback,** employees receive information about their skills and knowledge and where these assets fit into the organization's plans. The

FIGURE 8.4
Sample Self-Assessment Exercise

Step 1: Where am I?
Examine current position of life and career.
Think about your life from past and present to the future. Draw a time line to represent important events.

Step 2: Who am I?
Examine different roles.
Using 3" × 5" cards, write down one answer per card to the question "Who am I?"

Step 3: Where would I like to be, and what would I like to happen?
Begin setting goals.
Consider your life from present to future. Write an autobiography answering these questions:
- What do you want to have accomplished?
- What milestones do you want to achieve?
- What do you want to be remembered for?

Step 4: An ideal year in the future
Identify resources needed.
Consider a one-year period in the future.
Answer these questions:
- If you had unlimited resources, what would you do?
- What would the ideal environment look like?
- Does the ideal environment match Step 3?

Step 5: An ideal job
Create current goal.
In the present, think about an ideal job for you with your available resources. Describe your role, resources, and type of training or education needed.

Step 6: Career by objective inventory
Summarize current situation.
- What gets you excited each day?
- What do you do well? What are you known for?
- What do you need to achieve your goals?
- What could interfere with reaching your goals?
- What should you do now to move toward reaching your goals?
- What is your long-term career objective?

Source: Based on J. E. McMahon and S. K. Merman, "Career Development," in *The ASTD Training and Development Handbook*, 4e, ed. R. L. Craig (New York: McGraw-Hill, 1996), pp. 679–97.

employee's responsibility is to identify what skills she or he could realistically develop in light of the opportunities available. The organization's responsibility is to communicate the performance evaluation and the opportunities available to the employee, given the organization's long-range plans. Opportunities might include promotions and transfers.

Usually the employer conducts the reality check as part of a performance appraisal or as the feedback stage of performance management. In well-developed career management systems, the manager may hold separate discussions for performance feedback and career development.

Management consulting firm Booz Allen has shifted its feedback away from its performance appraisal system by introducing a program called SnapShot. With SnapShot, managers conduct 10- to 15-minute meetings with each of their employees every month to discuss performance and career development. The firm trained its managers in the kinds of questions that develop insights and suggested topics for discussion. Although some managers had been concerned that the monthly meetings would be too time consuming, the initial results of using SnapShot showed that employees were using their time more efficiently, managers felt they were more effective leaders, and employees were more satisfied with their role in the firm.[47]

Goal Setting

Based on the information from the self-assessment and reality check, the employee sets short- and long-term career objectives. These goals usually involve one or more of the following categories:

- Desired positions, such as becoming sales manager within three years.
- Level of skill to apply—for example, to use one's budgeting skills to improve the unit's cash flow problems.
- Work setting—for example, to move to corporate marketing within two years.
- Skill acquisition, such as learning how to use the company's human resource information system.

As in these examples, the goals should be specific, and they should include a date by which the goal is to be achieved. It is the employee's responsibility to identify the goal and the method of determining her or his progress toward that goal.

Usually the employee discusses the goals with his or her manager. The organization's responsibilities are to ensure that the goal is specific, challenging, and attainable and to help the employee reach the goal. The leadership development program at CA Technologies, a software company, includes setting goals based on assessments of existing leadership skills. Besides working on areas that need strengthening, the participants align their goals with skills the HR department has identified as necessary to support business objectives. To develop the goals, participants in CA's leadership program meet with their manager. The company supports the effort by equipping its managers with descriptions of the necessary leadership skills and recommendations for reinforcing development of the skills.[48]

Action Planning and Follow-Up

During the final step, employees prepare an action plan for how they will achieve their short- and long-term career goals. The employee is responsible for identifying the steps and timetable to reach the goals. The employer should identify resources needed, including courses, work experiences, and relationships. The employee and the manager should meet in the future to discuss progress toward career goals.

Action plans may involve any one or a combination of the development methods discussed earlier in the chapter—training, assessment, job experiences, or the help of a mentor or coach. (See "HRM Social" for examples of using social media to achieve some goals.) The approach used depends on the particular developmental needs and career objectives. For example, suppose the program manager in an information systems department uses feedback from performance appraisals to determine that he needs greater knowledge of project management software. The manager plans to increase that knowledge by reading articles (formal education), meeting with software vendors, and contacting the vendors' customers to ask them about the software they have used (job experiences). The manager and his supervisor agree that six months will be the target date for achieving the higher level of knowledge through these activities.

The outcome of action planning often takes the form of a career development plan. Figure 8.5 is an example of a development plan for a product manager. Development plans usually include descriptions of strengths and weaknesses, career goals, and development activities for reaching each goal.

HRM Social

Action Plan Ideas Using LinkedIn

The career-oriented social-networking platform LinkedIn provides a major online resource for those taking the reins of their career. To achieve learning goals, its LinkedIn Learning portal offers a variety of career- and industry-related videos. The main attraction, of course, is the chance to build professional relationships with the site's hundreds of millions of accounts and 30 million participating companies. Some of them have the potential to offer informal mentoring or coaching; sometimes the connections lead to a new job or other development opportunity.

Your LinkedIn network should consist of people who somehow share an interest in your field of work or your career path. However, you don't need to limit it to colleagues, because sometimes one connection can lead you to another, more relevant one. It's fine to start building a network with family, friends, and co-workers. Also, look up former colleagues to continue positive relationships online. Sign up for LinkedIn's interest groups, such as industry or alumni groups, and follow companies that interest you. Read, comment on, and share their posts. As you start to interact online, look for openings to invite a connection. When you send an invitation to connect, refer to your common interests; don't just ask to connect because you need a job or, worse, with no explanation. You wouldn't go up to random people on the street and ask to be friends; it's also awkward online.

Less than 1% of the LinkedIn accounts post content, so if you do, you will quickly stand out as a contributor. Keeping in mind that LinkedIn is a career-focused site, present your best professional self—positive, goal oriented, helpful, and informed. To comment, look for posts you can respond to constructively. (Save sarcasm and criticism for your private journal.) Add factual information or ask relevant, open-ended questions. Asking questions is a powerful way to get a conversation started, and the back-and-forth is what leads to more in-depth discussions and relationships down the road.

Besides commenting, consider creating your own posts. Share information that is likely to interest the people in your network. Also, ask questions related to your career. Open-ended questions that relate to topics you hope to pursue in your career can build connections with people involved in the same areas. If you do initial research on your own or write about experiences you've had, you can begin to showcase your strengths and interests even as you are seeking information. As you begin dialogues with others, ask them about their career experiences, and respond thoughtfully to what they share. Remember that online conversations, like offline ones, flow in two directions.

Questions

1. What methods of career development are mentioned in this description of LinkedIn?
2. What are some advantages of including social media in a career action plan, rather than relying only on in-person activities?

Sources: Seb Murray, "The Chance to Craft a Large and Varied Professional Network Is a Big Draw for Would-Be MBA Students Looking to Advance Their Career," *Find-MBA,* April 7, 2020, https://find-mba.com; Sheila Callaham, "Five Ways to Advance Your Career While Social Distancing," *Forbes,* March 18, 2020, https://www.forbes.com; Ashley Stahl, "How to Use LinkedIn to Your Advantage: Tips to Build Career Success," *Forbes,* January 29, 2020, https://www.forbes.com.

LO 8-8 Discuss how organizations are meeting the challenges of the "glass ceiling," succession planning, and dysfunctional managers.

Development-Related Challenges

A well-designed system for employee development can help organizations face three widespread challenges: the glass ceiling, succession planning, and dysfunctional behavior by managers.

The Glass Ceiling

Glass Ceiling Circumstances resembling an invisible barrier that keep most women and minorities from attaining the top jobs in organizations.

As we mentioned in Chapter 1, women and minorities are rare in the top level of U.S. corporations. Observers of this situation have noted that it looks as if an invisible barrier is keeping women and minorities from reaching the top jobs, a barrier that has come to be known as the **glass ceiling.** Although women represent 47% of the U.S. labor force and hold nearly 52% of management, professional, and related positions, their presence falls as

FIGURE 8.5
Career Development Plan

Name: [ ] **Title:** Product Manager **Immediate Manager:** [ ]

Competencies
Please identify your three greatest strengths and areas for improvement.

Strengths
- Strategic thinking and execution (confidence, command skills, action orientation)
- Results orientation (competence, motivating others, perseverance)
- Spirit for winning (building team spirit, customer focus, respect colleagues)

Areas for Improvement
- Patience (tolerance of people or processes and sensitivity to pacing)
- Written communications (ability to write clearly and succinctly)
- Overly ambitious (too much focus on successful completion of projects rather than developing relationships with individuals involved in the projects)

Career Goals
Please describe your overall career goals.

Long-term: Accept positions of increased responsibility to a level of general manager (or beyond).
The areas of specific interest include, but are not limited to, product and brand management, technology and development, strategic planning, and marketing.

Short-term: Continue to improve my skills in marketing and brand management.
Utilize my skills in product management, strategic planning, and global relations.

Next Assignments
Identify potential next assignments (including timing) that would help you develop toward your career goals.
- Manager or director level in planning, development, product, or brand management. Timing estimated to be Spring 2022.

Training and Development Needs
List both training and development activities that will either help you develop in your current assignment or provide overall career development.
- Master's degree classes will allow me to practice and improve my written communications skills. The dynamics of my current position, teamwork, and reliance on other individuals allow me to practice patience and to focus on individual team members' needs along with the success of the projects.

position in the organization rises. At the large companies of the S&P 500, just over one-quarter of executive positions are held by women, and 6% of CEOs are female.[49] Interestingly, the share of female chief operating officers, considered the number-two position in an organization, has been growing, so observers are curious whether more women will start to move to the CEO spot—or whether the COO job will come to be seen as a new glass ceiling. For more evidence of the glass ceiling, see "Did You Know?"

The glass ceiling is likely caused by a lack of access to training programs, to appropriate developmental job experiences, and to developmental relationships such as mentoring.[50] With regard to developmental relationships, women and minorities often have trouble finding mentors. They may not participate in the organization's, profession's, or community's "old boys' network." Also, recent evidence finds differences in how women and men pursue

Did You Know?

Men Named John Outnumber Female CEOs

For a fresh look at the glass ceiling, researchers compared the representation of women against the representation of males with names common in the United States. They found that men named John are as likely to be the CEO of a major corporation as women are.

According to the data used, females make up roughly half (50.8%) of the U.S. population. Males named John make up 3.3% of the *male* population, or just 1.6% of the total population. Yet each group represents about 5% of the CEOs of Fortune 500 companies.

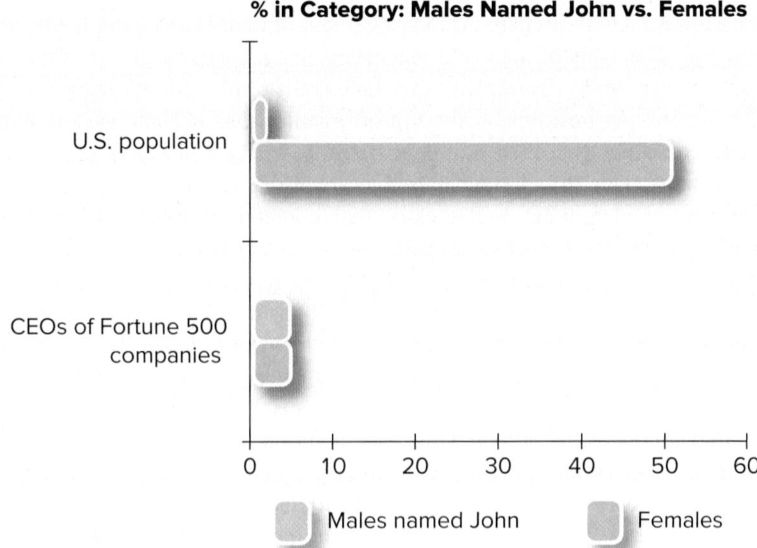

The researchers found similar patterns (with various names) when analyzing other positions of power, such as governors, members of Congress, editors of large-circulation newspapers, and presidents of private colleges.

Question

What issues do the data presented here suggest that organizations could (or should) address with employee development?

Sources: "#ChangePays: There Were More Male CEOs Named John than Female CEOs," *S&P Global,* October 16, 2019, https://www.spglobal.com; Brandon A. Weber, "Glass Ceiling Study: Women Have Less Power than Men Named 'John,'" *Big Think,* April 25, 2018, http://bigthink.com; Claire Cain Miller, Kevin Quealy, and Margot Sanger-Katz, "The Top Jobs Where Women Are Outnumbered by Men Named John," *The New York Times,* April 24, 2018, https://www.nytimes.com; "300 Most Common Male Names in the U.S.," *Mongabay,* https://names.mongabay.com, accessed May 2, 2018.

advancement and in how executives perceive women's and men's qualifications and ambitions. Female managers tend to find more mentors, but primarily mentors who give advice; their male counterparts find, on average, mentors who are more senior and will sponsor them for key positions. Patterns of promotion suggest that companies are more willing to select men from outside the organization based on their potential, while women do better when they stay with the same company where they can demonstrate a track record of achievements. Consistent with this difference, women who actively promote their achievements tend to advance further in an organization, whereas broadcasting their achievements does not make much difference in their male colleagues' advancement.[51]

Organizations can use development systems to help break through the glass ceiling. Managers making developmental assignments need to carefully consider whether stereotypes are influencing the types of assignments men and women receive. A formal process for regularly identifying development needs and creating action plans can make these decisions more objective.

A growing number of managers and organizations are coming to recognize that unequal opportunities are not just a problem for women to cope with, but a problem for men and women to solve together. In their quest for diversity and inclusion, organizations are engaging men to consider their role in maintaining a workplace that draws fully upon the contributions of female as well as male employees. This can involve teaching how to speak up when a situation involves harassment or bullying, as well as identifying the kinds of behavior that may be well intentioned but create awkwardness on teams and in mentoring relationships. Going further to draw out women's talents more fully, some managers are learning tactics like imposing a rule against interruptions in meetings and making a conscious practice of ensuring that every person in the room has had a chance to speak and be heard. Of course, this kind of management practice not only draws out the ideas of women, who on average are interrupted more often than men; it also gathers ideas from any employees who tend to be quieter than others.[52]

Succession Planning

Organizations have always had to prepare for the retirement of their leaders, but the need is more intense than ever. The aging of the workforce means that a greater share of employees are reaching retirement age. Many organizations are fueling the trend by downsizing through early-retirement programs. As positions at the top of organizations become vacant, many organizations have determined that their middle managers are fewer and often unprepared for top-level responsibility. This situation has raised awareness of the need for **succession planning**—the process of identifying and tracking high-potential employees who will be able to fill key positions when they become vacant.

Succession Planning
The process of identifying and tracking high-potential employees who will be able to fill top management positions when they become vacant.

Succession planning offers several benefits.[53] It forces senior management to regularly and thoughtfully review the company's leadership talent. It ensures that critical, sometimes hard-to-find talent is available. It provides a set of development experiences that managers must complete to be considered for key positions, so the organization does not promote managers before they are ready. Succession planning systems also help attract and retain ambitious managerial employees by providing development opportunities.

Succession planning focuses on *high-potential employees,* that is, employees the organization believes can succeed in higher-level business positions such as general manager of a business unit, director of a function (such as marketing or finance), or chief executive officer.[54] A typical approach to development of high-potential employees is to have them complete an individual development program including education, executive mentoring and coaching, and rotation through job assignments. Job assignments are based on the successful career paths of the managers whom the high-potential employees are preparing to replace. High-potential employees may also receive special assignments, such as making presentations and serving on committees and task forces.

Research shows that an effective program for developing high-potential employees has three stages:[55]

1. *Selection of high-potential employees*—Organizations may select outstanding performers and employees who have completed elite academic programs, such as earning a master's degree in business administration from a prestigious university. They may also use the results of psychological tests such as assessment centers. Ideally, organizations would use such assessments to find candidates scoring high in intellect, social skills, and drive to achieve, which together would be associated with getting exceptional results as a manager.
2. *Developmental experiences*—As employees participate in developmental experiences, the organization identifies those who succeed in the experiences. The organization looks for employees who continue to show qualities associated with success in top jobs, such as communication skills, leadership talent, and willingness to make sacrifices for the organization. In today's high-performance business environment, these assessments

should measure whether participants in the program are demonstrating an ability to lead and delivering results that contribute to the company's success. Employees who display these qualities continue to be considered high-potential employees.

3. *Active involvement with the CEO*—High-potential employees seen by top management as fitting into the organization's culture and having personality characteristics necessary for representing the company become actively involved with the chief executive officer. The CEO exposes these employees to the organization's key people and gives them a greater understanding of the organization's culture. The development of high-potential employees is a slow process. Reaching stage 3 may take 15 to 20 years.

Figure 8.6 breaks this process into eight steps. It begins with identifying the positions to be planned for and the employees to be included in the plan. Planning should also include establishing position requirements and deciding how to measure employees' potential for being able to fill those requirements. The organization also needs to develop a process for reviewing the existing talent. The next step is to link succession planning with other human resource systems. Then the organization needs a way to provide employees with feedback about career paths available to them and how well they are progressing toward their goals. Finally, measuring the plan's effectiveness provides information for continuing or adjusting future succession plans.

In practice, organizations encounter some difficulties in following this process.[56] One challenge is that today's business environment is changing so fast that succession plans go out of date or unforeseen events, like the COVID-19 pandemic, can alter an organization's approach to changing leadership. For example, during the COVID-19 outbreak, some organizations rethought their succession plans and requested senior leaders to stay in place rather than retire to provide a steady hand in guiding business operations during such uncertain times.[57]

Another issue involves the selection of candidates to label as having high potential. People have sometimes-unconscious ideas of what a "high-potential" person is like, and those ideas might look like a certain age or race or physical size. Or a manager might select or reject an employee for reasons other than potential—say, to avoid hurt feelings or to keep a valued staffer on the team, rather than in a development assignment elsewhere. To address the selection issue, organizations should define measurable criteria, rather than leaving it up to managers' intuition.

FIGURE 8.6
Process for Developing a Succession Plan

Sources: Based on B. Dowell, "Succession Planning," in *Implementing Organizational Interventions*, eds. J. Hedge and E. Pulakos (San Francisco: Jossey-Bass, 2002), pp. 78–109; R. Barnett and S. Davis, "Creating Greater Success in Succession Planning," *Advances in Developing Human Resources* 10 (2008), pp. 721–739.

Dysfunctional Managers

A manager who is otherwise competent may engage in some behaviors that make him or her ineffective or even "toxic"—someone who stifles good ideas and drives away employees. These dysfunctional behaviors include insensitivity to others, inability to be a team player, arrogance, poor conflict-management skills, inability to meet business objectives, and inability to adapt to change.[58] For example, a manager who has strong technical knowledge but is abrasive and discourages employees from contributing their ideas is likely to have difficulty motivating employees and may alienate people inside and outside the organization.

When a manager is an otherwise valuable employee and is willing to improve, the organization may try to help him or her change the dysfunctional behavior. The usual ways to provide this type of development include assessment, training, and counseling. Development programs for managers with dysfunctional behavior may also include specialized programs such as one called Individual Coaching for Effectiveness (ICE). The ICE program includes diagnosis, coaching, and support activities tailored to each manager's needs.[59] Psychologists conduct the diagnosis, coach and counsel the manager, and develop action plans for implementing new skills on the job. Research suggests that managers who participate in programs like ICE improve their skills and are less likely to be terminated.[60] One possible conclusion is that organizations can benefit from offering development opportunities to valuable employees with performance problems, not just to star performers.

THINKING ETHICALLY

SHOULD COMPANIES TELL EMPLOYEES THEY HAVE "HIGH POTENTIAL"?

Employee development programs aimed at meeting future leadership needs typically start by identifying high-potential employees and offering them an opportunity to participate in the program. In so doing, a company is setting apart certain employees for special treatment. What are the consequences of this practice?

For the employees identified as having high potential, the immediate impact of being called high-potential is that they feel valued. They may increase their commitment to the company and want to stick around to contribute more. Their enthusiasm to build on their strengths may translate into fast development of skills in leadership, time management, and decision making. Furthermore, these employees are likely already contributing at a high level, and holding back the information might cause them to think they have a better future elsewhere. Despite these advantages, some managers worry about telling employees they have such high potential, on the grounds that these employees might take the label as permission to coast, feeling secure in their favored status. In addition, the employees might hear more of a promise in that label than the organization can actually deliver on. Then, when someone else gets promoted or a new manager is recruited externally, the high-potential employees actually lose motivation.

Other negatives involve the employees who are left out. When they see that the organization does not consider them to have high potential, they may feel devalued. They may give up on their own development or start looking for a job at a company that will value them more.

Organizations that want to continue leadership development programs can take some steps to minimize the downside of the "high-potential" label. With regard to the high-potential employees, they should emphasize that the designation is more than a signal of high status; it is a challenge to take on greater responsibility and contribute more. The label shouldn't come with any implied promises about promotions or special status. For the other employees, the company should provide other avenues for development, with the message that employees can increase their potential as they gain skills and experience. For all employees, it is beneficial to have clear, objective standards for how the company measures their potential.

Questions

1. Can a leadership development program for high-potential employees be fair and equitable? If so, how? If not, why not?
2. If the company has identified high-potential employees, should managers tell these employees that they have high potential? Why or why not?

Sources: Jess Fuhl, "How to Successfully Identify and Develop High Potential Employees," *Sage People,* November 27, 2019, https://www.sagepeople.com; Gwen Moran, "4 Signs Your Company Views You as a High-Potential Employee," *Fast Company,* September 27, 2019, https://www.fastcompany.com; R. J. Morris, "Telling High Potential Employees That They're High Potential," *Fistful of Talent,* June 13, 2017, http://fistfuloftalent.com; Institute for Corporate Productivity, "Stop Using the Term 'High-Potential Employee,'" *i4cp Productivity Blog,* May 24, 2017, https://www.i4cp.com; Gail Dutton, "High Potentials: Tell Them or Not?" *Training,* July/August 2015, https://trainingmag.com.

SUMMARY

LO 8-1 Discuss how development is related to training and careers.

- Employee development is the combination of formal education, job experiences, relationships, and assessment of personality and abilities to help employees prepare for the future of their careers.
- Training is more focused on improving performance in the current job, but training programs may support employee development.
- In modern organizations, the concept of a career is fluid—a protean career that changes along with changes in a person's interests, abilities, and values and changes in the work environment. To plan and prepare for a protean career requires active career management, which includes planning for employee development.

LO 8-2 Identify the methods organizations use for employee development.

- Organizations may use formal educational programs at the workplace or off-site, such as workshops, university courses and degree programs, company-sponsored training, or programs offered by independent institutions.
- An assessment process can help employees identify strengths and areas requiring further development. Assessment can help the organization identify employees with managerial potential or identify areas in which teams need to develop.
- Job experiences help employees develop by stretching their skills as they meet new challenges.
- Interpersonal relationships with a more experienced member of the organization—often in the role of mentor or coach—can help employees develop their understanding of the organization and its customers.

LO 8-3 Describe how organizations use assessment of personality type, work behaviors, and job performance to plan employee development.

- Organizations collect information and provide feedback to employees about their behavior, communication style, and skills.
- The information may come from the employees, their peers, managers, and customers.
- Many organizations use performance appraisals as a source of assessment information. Appraisals may take the form of 360-degree feedback.
- Some organizations use psychological tests designed for this purpose, including the Myers-Briggs Type Indicator and the DiSC assessment.
- Assessment centers combine a variety of methods to provide assessment information.
- Managers must share the assessments, along with suggestions for improvement.

LO 8-4 Explain how job experiences can be used for developing skills.

- Job experiences contribute to development through a combination of relationships, problems, demands, tasks, and other features of an employee's jobs.
- The assumption is that development is most likely to occur when the employee's skills and experiences do not entirely match the skills required for the employee's current job, so employees must stretch to meet the demands of the new assignment.
- The impact varies according to whether the employee views the experience as a positive or negative source of stress.
- Job experiences that support employee development may include job enlargement, job rotations, transfers, promotions, downward moves, and temporary assignments with other organizations.

LO 8-5 Summarize principles of successful mentoring programs.

- A mentor is an experienced, productive senior employee who helps develop a less-experienced employee.
- Although most mentoring relationships develop informally, organizations can link mentoring to development goals by establishing a formal mentoring program. A formal program provides a basis for ensuring that all eligible employees are included.
- Mentoring programs tend to be most successful when they are voluntary and participants understand the details of the program.
- The organization should reward managers for employee development, carefully select mentors based on interpersonal and technical skills, train them for the role, and evaluate whether the program has met its objectives.

LO 8-6 Tell how managers and peers develop employees through coaching.

- A coach is a peer or manager who works with an employee to motivate the employee, help him or her develop skills, and provide reinforcement and feedback.
- Coaches should be prepared to take on one or more of three roles: working one-on-one with an employee, helping employees learn for themselves, and providing resources, such as mentors, courses, or job experiences.

LO 8-7 Identify the steps in the process of career management.

- The process begins with data gathering. Employees use information to determine their career interests, values, aptitudes, and behavioral tendencies, looking for opportunities and areas needing improvement. Data-gathering tools often include psychological tests or exercises that ask about career status and plans.
- The organization then provides feedback by communicating information about the employee's skills and knowledge and how these fit into the organization's plan.
- The employee sets goals and discusses them with his or her manager, who ensures that the goals are specific, challenging, and attainable.
- Finally, the employee works with his or her manager to create an action plan and follow-up for development activities that will help the employee achieve the goals.

LO 8-8 Discuss how organizations are meeting the challenges of the "glass ceiling," succession planning, and dysfunctional managers.

- The glass ceiling is a barrier that has been observed preventing women and other minorities from achieving top jobs in an organization. Development programs can ensure that these employees receive access to development resources, such as coaches, mentors, and developmental job assignments.
- Succession planning ensures that the organization prepares qualified employees to fill management jobs as managers retire. It focuses on applying employee development to high-potential employees. Effective succession planning includes methods for selecting these employees, providing them with developmental experiences, and getting the CEO actively involved with employees who display qualities associated with success as they participate in the developmental activities.
- For dysfunctional managers who have the potential to contribute to the organization, the organization may offer development targeted at correcting the areas of dysfunction. Typically, the process includes collecting information about the manager's personality, skills, and interests; providing feedback, training, and counseling; and ensuring that the manager can apply new, functional behaviors on the job.

KEY TERMS

employee development, 236
protean career, 237
assessment, 239
Myers-Briggs Type Indicator (MBTI), 241
DiSC, 242
assessment center, 242
leaderless group discussion, 243
job experiences, 244
transfer, 247
downward move, 247
promotion, 248
externship, 248
sabbatical, 248
mentor, 249
coach, 250
self-assessment, 251
feedback, 252
glass ceiling, 255
succession planning, 258

REVIEW AND DISCUSSION QUESTIONS

1. How does development differ from training? How does development support career management in modern organizations? *(LO 8-1)*
2. What are the four broad categories of development methods? Why might it be beneficial to combine all of these methods into a formal development program? *(LO 8-2)*
3. Recommend a development method for each of the following situations, and explain why you chose that method. *(LO 8-2)*
   a. An employee recently promoted to the job of plant supervisor is having difficulty motivating employees to meet quality standards.
   b. A sales manager annoys salespeople by dictating every detail of their work.
   c. An employee has excellent leadership skills but lacks knowledge of the financial side of business.
   d. An organization is planning to organize its production workers into teams for the first time.
4. A company that markets sophisticated business management software systems uses sales teams to help customers define needs and to create systems that meet those needs. The teams include programmers, salespeople who specialize in client industries, and software designers. Occasionally sales are lost as a result of conflict or communication problems among

team members. The company wants to improve the effectiveness of these teams, and it wants to begin with assessment. How can the teams use 360-degree feedback and psychological tests to develop? *(LO 8-3)*

5. In an organization that wants to use work experiences as a method of employee development, what basic options are available? Which of these options would be most attractive to you as an employee? Why? *(LO 8-4)*
6. Many employees are unwilling to relocate because they like their current community and family members prefer not to move. Yet preparation for management requires that employees develop new skills, strengthen areas of weakness, and be exposed to new aspects of the organization's business. How can an organization change an employee's current job to develop management skills? *(LO 8-4)*
7. Many people feel that mentoring relationships should occur naturally, in situations where senior managers feel inclined to play that role. What are some advantages of setting up a formal mentoring program, rather than letting senior managers decide how and whom to help? *(LO 8-5)*
8. What are the three roles of a coach? How is a coach different from a mentor? What are some advantages of using someone outside the organization as a coach? Some disadvantages? *(LO 8-6)*
9. Why should organizations be interested in helping employees plan their careers? What benefits can companies gain? What are the risks? *(LO 8-7)*
10. What are the manager's roles in a career management system? Which role do you think is most difficult for the typical manager? Which is the easiest role? List reasons why managers might resist becoming involved in career management. *(LO 8-7)*
11. What is the glass ceiling? What are the possible consequences to an organization that has a glass ceiling? How can employee development break the glass ceiling? Can succession planning help? Explain. *(LO 8-8)*
12. Why might an organization benefit from giving employee development opportunities to a dysfunctional manager, rather than simply dismissing the manager? Do these reasons apply to nonmanagement employees as well? *(LO 8-8)*

SELF-ASSESSMENT EXERCISE

What Is Your Keirsey Temperament?

Go to www.keirsey.com. Complete the Keirsey Temperament Sorter. What did you learn about yourself? How could the instrument you completed be useful for employee development? What might be some disadvantages of using this instrument?

TAKING RESPONSIBILITY

Employee Ambitions Drive Development at West Monroe Partners

A key stakeholder group for any organization is its employees, and technology consulting firm West Monroe Partners is highly committed to that area of social responsibility. The organization was founded on the four partners' vision for an ideal consulting firm, with values such as diversity of thought, quality over growth, and practical innovation. Treating employees well is also practical. Technology strategy is a valuable skill set; furthermore, the employees in West Monroe's 10 offices share in the ownership of the firm. Therefore, says Chief People Officer Susan Stelter, the company is committed to the idea that employees "have to be engaged in work, cultivate meaningful relationships here, and believe that we are an organization that will challenge them to learn and grow."

Maintaining such a culture requires a strong program for employee development. The foundation of development at West Monroe is what the firm calls the Three Year Letter, and it starts with the employee. Each West Monroe employee writes a description of what he or she hopes to accomplish over the three years ahead. Then the employee and his or her manager meet to discuss the employee's goals and how the manager can support the employee in realizing them—even if they include leaving the firm in the long run.

Job experiences also play a role in employee development at West Monroe Partners and demonstrate social responsibility to community stakeholders. West Monroe's 1 + 1 + 1 program budgets for giving 1% of employees' time in volunteer hours, 1% of its employees to work for nonprofits at no charge, and 1% of its profits in charitable contributions. The firm has established the Fischer Fellowship, which pays several employees a year to do volunteer work for three to six months anywhere in the world. Employees selected for the fellowship tackle difficult problems and may collaborate with their colleagues in the firm. For example, an employee who taught computer and technology skills in Ghana worked with experts in the company to get the dilapidated equipment up and running and got ideas for sustainable energy from consultants in the energy and utilities practice. Another consultant, Tricia Anklan, worked on improving water quality in rural Nicaragua. She credits the program with making her a more inspirational leader, and motivating people in the community to act, because it was obvious she would not be able to solve the problem on her own.

Another job experience program focuses more specifically on leadership skills. The so-called "chiefs program" invites employees to submit proposals for what they want to be "chief" of for up to two years. They must prepare a budget and a charter (statement of goals and principles), and recruiting members for the team is the applicant's responsibility as well. The chiefs programs must support the organization's culture and bring employees together. For example, the chief adventure officer in the Chicago office has planned a variety of fun and challenging outings for employees, the chief hot sauce officer provides a variety of options to make lunchtime a spicier occasion, and the chief green officer has introduced eco-friendly measures that other offices of the firm have picked up. While some chiefs are already in the management ranks, the program also provides junior employees with their first experiences in budgeting, planning, and cost control.

Questions

1. For employees pursuing protean careers, how appropriate is West Monroe Partners' development approach? Explain.
2. What development methods not mentioned in this case could also help prepare consultants for a larger leadership role in the organization?

Sources: West Monroe Partners, "About Us," https://westmonroepartners.com, accessed April 17, 2020; "New Research: Employers and Employees Agree There Is an Upskilling Crisis, Both Want Managers to Be More Effective," September 30, 2019, https://www.westmonroepartners.com; Kathy Gurchiek, "'Chief of Anything' Program Develops Skills, Workplace Community," Society for Human Resource Management, April 12, 2018, https://www.shrm.org; Andreas Rekdal, "Courses, Coaching, Career Guidance: How 5 Chicago Tech Companies Help New Leaders Grow," *Built in Chicago,* February 7, 2018, https://www.builtinchicago.org.

MANAGING TALENT

Mondelēz Bakes Development into Its Talent Strategy

Mondelēz International is one of the largest snack companies in the world. Its corporate name might be unfamiliar, but some of its brands will ring a bell: Oreo cookies, Ritz crackers, Toblerone chocolate bars, Trident gum, and Halls cough drops, to name a few. With famous brands and customers in 160 countries, the company needs a continuing supply of management talent to keep the business growing. The leaders' recognition of this is evident in the company's strategy statement, which includes the objective to "grow our people" through efforts including training and "world-class career experiences."

One of its notable talent initiatives, called F1, is aimed at developing greater business insight among its finance professionals. The program begins with 12 weeks of formal education in the Financial Acumen Skills Training (FAST) program. FAST participants work in teams to complete a computerized business simulation. Team membership intentionally brings together participants from different locations, so they can build a wider professional network. The teams compete to see which will do the best job of restoring performance at a fictional company facing multiple difficulties. Because they are geographically spread out, they have to deal with the realities of a global economy, arranging meetings very early and late in the day to accommodate different time zones. The winning team is the one with the highest overall score on revenues, income, and cash flow, plus the smallest variance from plan.

Bruce Gladden, chief financial officer of Mondelēz, emphasizes the importance of professional relationships. He insists that the senior managers in his group coach the employees participating in the FAST program, and he evaluates the managers' performance. The coaching content is important to Gladden, and so is the way that the act of coaching demonstrates to employees at all levels that Mondelēz values them.

In addition, for employees across functions, Mondelēz International offers challenging job experiences to those who participate in the company's social-impact program. The program, building on the company's purpose statement to "create more moments of joy," sends Joy Ambassadors–teams of about 15 employees–to cocoa-farming communities in Ghana. These "ambassadors" work alongside farmers and visit processing plants and schools to learn about the challenges and opportunities facing the communities. Applying their own knowledge and skills to what they observe, the teams develop and teach ideas for building a more successful farming economy. The experience develops teamwork and problem-solving skills and inspires employees by giving them a meaningful way to contribute. At the same time, it strengthens the supply chain that Mondelēz depends on for a key ingredient and brings sustainable agriculture to a part of the world where the need is great.

Questions

1. What kinds of value could Mondelēz International reasonably expect to get from the development programs described in this case?
2. How might a career management process increase the value of these development programs?

Sources: Mondelēz International, "Growth & Strategy," https://www.mondelezinternational.com, accessed April 17, 2020; Mondelēz International, "2019 Fact Sheet," https://www.mondelezinternational.com, accessed April 17, 2020; Sean Czarnecki, "Five Steps from Mondelez You Can Take to Mobilize Purpose," *PR Week,* October 16, 2019, https://www.prweek.com; Kelly C. France, "How a 'Skills-Exchange' Program Can Improve Your Workplace," *Daily Herald (Arlington Heights, IL),* March 16, 2018, http://www.dailyherald.com; Greg Trotter, "More Companies Find Spending on Corporate Responsibility Increases the Bottom Line," *Chicago Tribune,* December 8, 2017, http://www.chicagotribune.com.

HR IN SMALL BUSINESS

At Conductix-Wampfler, Anyone Can Have a Mentor

Like other manufacturers today, Conductix-Wampfler struggles to find and keep qualified workers. The maker of systems for transmitting energy and data to mobile machinery and equipment has three manufacturing facilities—two in Nebraska and one in Iowa. Across these facilities, the rate of employee turnover is 7%, below the industry average, thanks in part to the work of Jessica Jones, Conductix's learning management coordinator. Her programs include leadership development for middle managers and a mentorship program that spreads career development opportunities to the entire workforce.

At Conductix-Wampfler, every new hire is assigned to a mentor. Furthermore, existing employees can request a mentor when they have moved to a new position, taken on additional responsibilities, or simply want to explore additional career growth. For example, an employee might want to better interact with new technology or better understand the business side of operations. These opportunities are available to management and nonmanagement employees. Jones and her team select mentors based on identifying the employee who can best help the protégé achieve his or her goals. The mentor may come from the same department or another department. In Jones's experience, sometimes a mentor from another group is particularly helpful for enabling a protégé to understand a situation from a fresh perspective.

Conductix does not merely assign mentors; it also develops their capabilities for filling this role. The company provides one-on-one coaching in how to start a mentoring relationship. They participate in online training about how to set goals, give feedback, and handle confidential information. Protégés, too, receive training in how to get the most out of the program by participating effectively in meetings and setting goals. The company expects protégés to take responsibility for their role in these developmental relationships.

Conductix rewards mentors for participating in its mentorship program. Mentors who fulfill the requirements of the role earn a $500 bonus after 90 days and are eligible for additional bonuses at their twice-yearly performance reviews. They also may receive recognition in spotlight stories in the company newsletter. But bonuses and recognition may not be the most significant reward. Mentors often have told Jones that because of the preparation necessary to guide another person, they learned as much as they taught their protégés. Mentoring becomes a development experience for the mentors themselves, giving them leadership experience and opportunities to interact with management and co-workers in other functions. It may become a stepping stone to a promotion for the mentors.

Benefits also flow to the protégés, who quickly gain a better understanding of their job and the company as a whole. They can more readily increase their skills and identify opportunities to move ahead. Conductix, in turn, benefits from loyal employees, a safer work environment, and a pool of talent to fill open positions from within.

Questions

1. Suggest some ways that effective assessment could contribute to the success of Conductix-Wampfler's mentorship program.
2. How does Conductix-Wampfler's mentorship program support career management?

Sources: Company website, "Company & Career," https://www.conductix.us, accessed April 17, 2020; Jessica Jones, "Manufacturing Meets Mentoring," *TD,* September 2019, pp. 34–39; "Honing Management and Leadership Skills," interview of Jessica Jones, *Leadership Excellence,* October 2018, pp. 12–13.

NOTES

1. Barbara Frankel, "Cracking the Code," *Working Mother,* April/May 2020, pp. 42–45.
2. M. London, *Managing the Training Enterprise* (San Francisco: Jossey-Bass, 1989); D. Day, *Developing Leadership Talent* (Alexandria, VA: SHRM Foundation, 2007).
3. R. W. Pace, P. C. Smith, and G. E. Mills, *Human Resource Development* (Englewood Cliffs, NJ: Prentice Hall, 1991); W. Fitzgerald, "Training versus Development," *Training and Development Journal,* May 1992, pp. 81–84; R. A. Noe, S. L. Wilk, E. J. Mullen, and J. E. Wanek, "Employee Development: Issues in Construct Definition and Investigation of Antecedents," in *Improving Training Effectiveness in Work Organizations,* ed. J. K. Ford (Mahwah, NJ: Lawrence Erlbaum, 1997), pp. 153–189.
4. M. Gubler, J. Arnold, and C. Coombs, "Reassessing the Protean Career Concept: Empirical Findings, Conceptual Components, and Measurement," *Journal of Organizational Behavior* 35 (2014), pp. 23–40; D. Hall, *Careers In and Out of Organizations* (Thousand Oaks, CA: Sage, 2002); D. T. Hall, "Protean Careers of the 21st Century," *Academy of Management Executive* 11 (1996), pp. 8–16.
5. M. Wang and C. Wanberg, "100 Years of Applied Psychology Research on Individual Careers: From Career Management to Retirement," *Journal of Applied Psychology* 102 (2017), pp. 546–563; C. Yeh, "Tours of Duty: The New Employer-Employee Compact," *Harvard Business Review,* June 2013, pp. 48–58; M. Lazarova and S. Taylor, "Boundaryless Careers, Social Capital, and Knowledge Management: Implications for Organizational Performance," *Journal of Organizational Behavior* 30 (2009), pp. 119–139; K. R. Brousseau, M. J. Driver, K. Eneroth, and R. Larsson, "Career Pandemonium: Realigning Organizations and Individuals," *Academy of Management Executive* 11 (1996), pp. 52–66.
6. R. A. Noe, *Employee Training and Development,* 8th ed. (New York: McGraw-Hill, 2020); K. O'Leonard and L. Loew, "Investing in the Future," *Human Resource Executive,* July/August 2012, pp. 30–34.
7. Ave Rio, "The Future of the Corporate University," *Chief Learning Officer,* May 3, 2018, http://www.clomedia.com.
8. University of Virginia Darden School of Business, "Executive MBA Formats," http://www.darden.virginia.edu, accessed April 17, 2020.
9. Rio, "The Future of the Corporate University"; P. Cappelli and A. Tavis, "HR Goes Agile," *Harvard Business Review,* March-April 2018, https://hbr.org.
10. J. R. Hinrichs and G. P. Hollenbeck, "Leadership Development," in K. N. Wexley, ed., *BNA Handbook Series on Human Resource Management* 5 (Washington, DC: BNA Books, 1991), pp. 221–237; A. Howard and D. W. Bray, *Managerial Lives in Transition: Advancing Age and Changing Times* (New York: Guilford, 1988); J. Bolt, *Executive Development* (New York: Harper Business, 1989).
11. A. Fox, "Organizational and Employee Development Special Report: Upon Further Assessment . . .," *HR Magazine,* August 2013, http://www.shrm.org.
12. S. Florentine, "How Myers-Briggs Can Create a Stronger IT Team," *CIO,* April 25, 2017, https://www.cio.com; A. Thorne and H. Gough, *Portraits of Type* (Palo Alto, CA: Consulting Psychologists Press, 1993).
13. D. Druckman and R. A. Bjork, eds., *In the Mind's Eye: Enhancing Human Performance* (Washington, DC: National Academy Press, 1991); M. H. McCaulley, "The Myers-Briggs Type Indicator and Leadership," in *Measures of Leadership,* eds. K. E. Clark and M. B. Clark (West Orange, NJ: Leadership Library of America, 1990), pp. 381–418.
14. "The Everything DiSC Difference," https://www.everythingdisc.com, accessed April 17, 2020; Fox, "Organizational and Employee Development Special Report."
15. G. C. Thornton III and W. C. Byham, *Assessment Centers and Managerial Performance* (New York: Academic Press, 1982); L. F. Schoenfeldt and J. A. Steger, "Identification and Development of Management Talent," in *Research in Personnel and Human Resource Management,* eds. K. N. Rowland and G. Ferris (Greenwich, CT: JAI Press, 1989), vol. 7, pp. 151–181; Fox, "Organizational and Employee Development Special Report."
16. Thornton and Byham, *Assessment Centers and Managerial Performance.*
17. P. G. W. Jansen and B. A. M. Stoop, "The Dynamics of Assessment Center Validity: Results of a Seven-Year Study," *Journal of Applied Psychology* 86 (2001), pp. 741–753; D. Chan, "Criterion and Construct Validation of an Assessment Centre," *Journal of Occupational and Organizational Psychology* 69 (1996), pp. 167–181.
18. R. G. Jones and M. D. Whitmore, "Evaluating Developmental Assessment Centers as Interventions," *Personnel Psychology* 48 (1995), pp. 377–388.
19. S. B. Silverman, "Individual Development through Performance Appraisal," *Developing Human Resources* 5 (1991), pp. 120–151.
20. J. F. Brett and L. E. Atwater, "360-Degree Feedback: Accuracy, Reactions, and Perceptions of Usefulness," *Journal of Applied Psychology* 86 (2001), pp. 930–942.
21. Fox, "Organizational and Employee Development Special Report."
22. L. Atwater, P. Roush, and A. Fischthal, "The Influence of Upward Feedback on Self- and Follower Ratings of Leadership," *Personnel Psychology* 48 (1995), pp. 35–59; J. F. Hazucha, S. A. Hezlett, and R. J. Schneider, "The Impact of 360-Degree Feedback on Management Skill Development," *Human Resource Management* 32 (1993), pp. 325–351; J. W. Smither, M. London, N. Vasilopoulos, R. R. Reilly, R. E. Millsap, and N. Salvemini, "An Examination of the Effects of an Upward Feedback Program over Time," *Personnel Psychology* 48 (1995), pp. 1–34; J. Smither and A. Walker, "Are the Characteristics of Narrative Comments Related to Improvements in Multirater Feedback Ratings over Time?" *Journal of Applied Psychology* 89 (2004), pp. 575–581; J. Smither, M. London, and R. Reilly, "Does Performance Improve Following Multisource Feedback? A Theoretical Model, Meta-analysis, and Review of Empirical Findings," *Personnel Psychology* 58 (2005), pp. 33–66.
23. J. Porter, "How to Give Feedback People Can Actually Use," *Harvard Business Review,* October 27, 2017, https://hbr.org; Center for Creative Leadership, "360-Degree Feedback: Best Practices to Ensure Impact," http://www.ccl.org, accessed April 26, 2016; Harriet Edleson, "Do 360 Evaluations Work?" *Monitor on Psychology* 43 (November 2012), accessed at http://www.apa.org.
24. J. Bersin, J. Flynn, A. Mazor, and V. Melian, "The Employee Experience: Culture, Engagement, and Beyond," in *2017 Global*

Human Capital Trends, Deloitte Insights, https://www2.deloitte.com, accessed April 17, 2020; M. W. McCall Jr., *High Flyers* (Boston: Harvard Business School Press, 1998).

25. R. S. Snell, "Congenial Ways of Learning: So Near yet So Far," *Journal of Management Development* 9 (1990), pp. 17–23.
26. M. McCall, M. Lombardo, and A. Morrison, *Lessons of Experience* (Lexington, MA: Lexington Books, 1988); M. W. McCall, "Developing Executives through Work Experiences," *Human Resource Planning* 11 (1988), pp. 1–11; M. N. Ruderman, P. J. Ohlott, and C. D. McCauley, "Assessing Opportunities for Leadership Development," in *Measures of Leadership,* pp. 547–562; C. D. McCauley, L. J. Estman, and P. J. Ohlott, "Linking Management Selection and Development through Stretch Assignments," *Human Resource Management* 34 (1995), pp. 93–115.
27. C. D. McCauley, M. N. Ruderman, P. J. Ohlott, and J. E. Morrow, "Assessing the Developmental Components of Managerial Jobs," *Journal of Applied Psychology* 79 (1994), pp. 544–560.
28. Martha Porado, "Try This Job on for Size," *Benefits Canada,* January/February 2018, pp. 8–9.
29. M. London, *Developing Managers* (San Francisco: Jossey-Bass, 1985); M. A. Camion, L. Cheraskin, and M. J. Stevens, "Career-Related Antecedents and Outcomes of Job Rotation," *Academy of Management Journal* 37 (1994), pp. 1518–1542; London, *Managing the Training Enterprise.*
30. C. Leddy, "The Benefits and Challenges of Job Rotation," *Forbes,* December 5, 2017, https://www.forbes.com; M. Fiester, A. Collis, and N. Cossack, "Job Rotation, Total Rewards, Measuring Value," *HR Magazine,* August 1, 2008, https://www.shrm.org.
31. R. A. Noe, B. D. Steffy, and A. E. Barber, "An Investigation of the Factors Influencing Employees' Willingness to Accept Mobility Opportunities," *Personnel Psychology* 41 (1988), pp. 559–580; S. Gould and L. E. Penley, "A Study of the Correlates of Willingness to Relocate," *Academy of Management Journal* 28 (1984), pp. 472–478; J. Landau and T. H. Hammer, "Clerical Employees' Perceptions of Intraorganizational Career Opportunities," *Academy of Management Journal* 29 (1986), pp. 385–405; M. Brett and A. H. Reilly, "On the Road Again: Predicting the Job Transfer Decision," *Journal of Applied Psychology* 73 (1988), pp. 614–620.
32. J. M. Brett, "Job Transfer and Well-Being," *Journal of Applied Psychology* 67 (1992), pp. 450–463; F. J. Minor, L. A. Slade, and R. A. Myers, "Career Transitions in Changing Times," in *Contemporary Career Development Issues,* eds. R. F. Morrison and J. Adams (Hillsdale, NJ: Lawrence Erlbaum, 1991), pp. 109–120; C. C. Pinder and K. G. Schroeder, "Time to Proficiency Following Job Transfers," *Academy of Management Journal* 30 (1987), pp. 336–353; Beverly Kaye, "Up Is Not the Only Way . . . Really!" *T + D,* September 2011, pp. 40–45.
33. Glassdoor, "10 Companies with Unique Volunteer Opportunities," February 18, 2019, https://www.glassdoor.com.
34. S. Sataline, "Breaking Away," *Washingtonian,* August 2016, pp. 105–108.
35. L. Nagele-Piazza, "Putting Competencies to Work," *HR Magazine,* May 2017, pp. 26–34; D. B. Turban and T. W. Dougherty, "Role of Protégé Personality in Receipt of Monitoring and Career Success," *Academy of Management Journal* 37 (1994), pp. 688–702; E. A. Fagenson, "Mentoring: Who Needs It? A Comparison of Protégés' and Nonprotégés' Needs for Power, Achievement, Affiliation, and Autonomy," *Journal of Vocational Behavior* 41 (1992), pp. 48–60.
36. B. Hassell, "Create Mentorships, Not Minions," *Chief Learning Officer,* May 2016, pp. 30–33; L. Martin and T. Robinson, "Why You Should Get on Board the Mentor Ship," *Public Manager,* Winter 2011, pp. 42–45; A. H. Geiger, "Measures for Mentors," *Training and Development Journal,* February 1992, pp. 65–67.
37. K. E. Kram, *Mentoring at Work: Developmental Relationships in Organizational Life* (Glenview, IL: Scott-Foresman, 1985); L. L. Phillips-Jones, "Establishing a Formalized Mentoring Program," *Training and Development Journal* 2 (1983), pp. 38–42; K. Kram, "Phases of the Mentoring Relationship," *Academy of Management Journal* 26 (1983), pp. 608–625; G. T. Chao, P. M. Walz, and P. D. Gardner, "Formal and Informal Mentorships: A Comparison of Mentoring Functions and Contrasts with Nonmentored Counterparts," *Personnel Psychology* 45 (1992), pp. 619–636; C. Wanberg, E. Welsh, and S. Hezlett, "Mentoring Research: A Review and Dynamic Process Model," in *Research in Personnel and Human Resources Management,* eds. J. Martocchio and G. Ferris (New York: Elsevier Science, 2003), pp. 39–124.
38. C. Ceniza-Levine, "Ten Tips for a Successful Mentorship," *Forbes,* January 10, 2019, https://www.forbes.com; V. Chopra and S. Saint, "Six Things Every Mentor Should Do," *Harvard Business Review,* March 29, 2017, https://hbr.org.
39. L. Eby, M. Butts, A. Lockwood, and A. Simon, "'Protégés' Negative Mentoring Experiences: Construct Development and Nomological Validation," *Personnel Psychology* 57 (2004), pp. 411–447; R. Emelo, "Conversations with Mentoring Leaders," *T + D,* June 2011, pp. 32–37; M. Weinstein, "Please Don't Go," *Training,* May/June 2011, pp. 38–34; "Training Top 125," *Training,* January/February 2011, pp. 54–93.
40. R. A. Noe, D. B. Greenberger, and S. Wang, "Mentoring: What We Know and Where We Might Go," in *Research in Personnel and Human Resources Management,* eds. G. Ferris and J. Martocchio (New York: Elsevier Science, 2002), vol. 21, pp. 129–174; T. D. Allen, L. T. Eby, M. L. Poteet, E. Lentz, and L. Lima, "Career Benefits Associated with Mentoring for Protégés: A Meta-Analysis," *Journal of Applied Psychology* 89 (2004), pp. 127–136.
41. J. Milner and T. Milner, "Most Managers Don't Know How to Coach People. But They Can Learn," *Harvard Business Review,* August 16, 2018, https://hbr.org; D. B. Peterson and M. D. Hicks, *Leader as Coach* (Minneapolis: Personnel Decisions, 1996).
42. "Outstanding Training Initiatives," *Training,* May/June 2017, pp. 50–52.
43. Cappelli and Tavis, "HR Goes Agile."
44. S. Finkelstein, "The Best Leaders Are Great Teachers," *Harvard Business Review,* January–February 2018, pp. 142–145; J. Smither, M. London, R. Flautt, Y. Vargas, and L. Kucine, "Can Working with an Executive Coach Improve Multisource Ratings over Time? A Quasi-experimental Field Study," *Personnel Psychology* 56 (2003), pp. 23–44.
45. S. Caminiti, "AT&T's $1 Billion Gambit: Retraining Nearly Half Its Workforce for Jobs of the Future," *CNBC,* March 13, 2018, https://www.cnbc.com; B. Pelster, D. Johnson, J. Stempel, and B. van der Vyver, "Careers and Learning: Real Time, All the Time," in *Rewriting the Rules for the Digital Age: 2017 Deloitte Global Human Resource Capital Trends* (Deloitte University, 2017), pp. 29–37.
46. "Chemically Suited for Working with People," *ISE Magazine,* June 2017, p. 58.

47. Institute for Corporate Productivity, "How Booz Allen Created an Inclusive Culture of Performance Feedback," case study, February 28, 2018, https://www.i4cp.com.
48. Joanna Castaneda, "Bench Strength," *TD*, June 2015, pp. 31–35.
49. Catalyst, "Women CEOs of the S&P 500," August 3, 2020, and "Pyramid: Women in S&P 500 Companies, January 15, 2020" https://www.catalyst.org; R. Morad, "Are Women COOs Facing a New Kind of Glass Ceiling?" *NBC News*, March 29, 2018, http://www.nbcnews.com.
50. W. T. Wallace, "The Journey for Women in the Transition to Senior Leadership," *People + Strategy*, Winter 2017, pp. 34–38; P. J. Ohlott, M. N. Ruderman, and C. D. McCauley, "Gender Differences in Managers' Developmental Job Experiences," *Academy of Management Journal* 37 (1994), pp. 46–67; L. A. Mainiero, "Getting Anointed for Advancement: The Case of Executive Women," *Academy of Management Executive* 8 (1994), pp. 53–67; P. Tharenov, S. Latimer, and D. Conroy, "How Do You Make It to the Top? An Examination of Influences on Women's and Men's Managerial Advancements," *Academy of Management Journal* 37 (1994), pp. 899–931.
51. V. Fuhrmans, "Where Are All the Women CEOs?" *The Wall Street Journal*, February 6, 2020, https://www.wsj.com; T. Allen, "Six Hard Truths for Women Regarding the Glass Ceiling," *Forbes*, August 25, 2018, https://www.forbes.com; R. A. Noe, "Women and Mentoring: A Review and Research Agenda," *Academy of Management Review* 13 (1988), pp. 65–78.
52. R. H. Anderson, "Challenging Our Gendered Idea of Mentorship," *Harvard Business Review*, January 6, 2020, https://hbr.org; "Chevron Partners with Catalyst to Advance Gender Equality," February 26, 2019, https://www.chevron.com; J. Simons, "Men Learn How to Be 'Allies' without Fear, to Female Colleagues," *The Wall Street Journal*, April 4, 2018; R. G. McGrath, "Eight Simple Ways to Keep More Women in the Executive Pipeline," *The Wall Street Journal*, February 22, 2018.
53. D. Ciampa, "Should a Crisis Change Your CEO Succession Plan?" *Harvard Business Review*, April 17, 2020, https://hbr.org; J. Rosenthal, K. Routch, K. Monahan, and M. Doherty, "The Holy Grail of Effective Leadership Succession Planning," *Deloitte Insights*, https://www2.deloitte.com, accessed April 17, 2020; "Succession Planning Problems: 6 Pitfalls to Avoid," *Insperity*, https://www.insperity.com, accessed April 17, 2020.
54. B. E. Dowell, "Succession Planning," in *Implementing Organizational Interventions*, eds. J. Hedge and E. D. Pulakos (San Francisco: Jossey-Bass, 2002), pp. 78–109.
55. T. Chamorro-Premuzic, S. Adler, and R. B. Kaiser, "What Science Says about Identifying High-Potential Employees," *Harvard Business Review*, October 3, 2017, https://hbr.org; C. B. Derr, C. Jones, and E. L. Toomey, "Managing High-Potential Employees: Current Practices in Thirty-Three U.S. Corporations," *Human Resource Management* 27 (1988), pp. 273–290; K. M. Nowack, "The Secrets of Succession," *Training and Development* 48 (1994), pp. 49–54; W. J. Rothwell, *Effective Succession Planning*, 4th ed. (New York: AMACOM, 2010).
56. Cappelli and Tavis, "HR Goes Agile"; T. Chamorro-Premuzic and A. Bhaduri, "How Office Politics Corrupts the Search for High-Potential Employees," Society for Human Resource Management, October 25, 2017, https://www.shrm.org.
57. Ciampa, "Should a Crisis Change Your CEO Succession Plan?"
58. "5 Signs You Have a Toxic Boss," *Ladders*, November 15, 2019, https://theladders.com; M. Abbajay, "What to Do When You Have a Bad Boss," *Harvard Business Review*, September 7, 2018, https://hbr.org; J. McLaughlin, "Four Types of Dysfunctional Manager," *Training Journal*, September 16, 2014, https://www.trainingjournal.com.
59. L. W. Hellervik, J. F. Hazucha, and R. J. Schneider, "Behavior Change: Models, Methods, and a Review of Evidence," in *Handbook of Industrial and Organizational Psychology*, 2nd ed., ed. M. D. Dunnette and L. M. Hough (Palo Alto, CA: Consulting Psychologists Press, 1992), vol. 3, pp. 823–899.
60. D. B. Peterson, "Measuring and Evaluating Change in Executive and Managerial Development," paper presented at the annual conference of the Society for Industrial and Organizational Psychology, Miami, 1990.

Assessing and Improving Performance

PART THREE

freesoulproduction/Shutterstock

9 Creating and Maintaining High-Performance Organizations

Introduction

ADP says, "What we do is about people"—an apt description of a company that uses the talents of its own human resources to enable other companies to manage *their* human resources. The company sells software for HR processes including payroll, time sheets, and benefits administration, as well as analytics and decision support. The profitable company rose into the middle ranks of the Fortune 500 during the 1990s and now operates in more than 140 countries with 57,000 employees.

ADP systems help its clients achieve high performance. Automating payroll and time records makes employers more efficient and helps them avoid mistakes. Even more powerfully, ADP's software and services can help managers make sense of the enormous amount of data they have related to employees and their work. For example, analysis of payroll records can show a company where meeting goals requires a lot of overtime hours or where employees quit after a short time. A product called Compass analyzes the contents of internal communications to find patterns that indicate management issues such as morale problems in a department. It also can alert managers with tips on how to improve employee relations, based on the patterns of praise, development opportunities, and other behaviors associated with employee satisfaction.

ADP applies its skill in HR management to create its own high-performance culture. Accolades from the *Wall Street Journal*'s Best-Managed Companies list and employer-branding service Comparably's list of Best Places to Work point to ADP's success in creating an atmosphere where employees are loyal and fully engaged. In Comparably's recent survey, ADP employees expressed great satisfaction with their employer. Almost nine in 10 said they are proud to be part of the

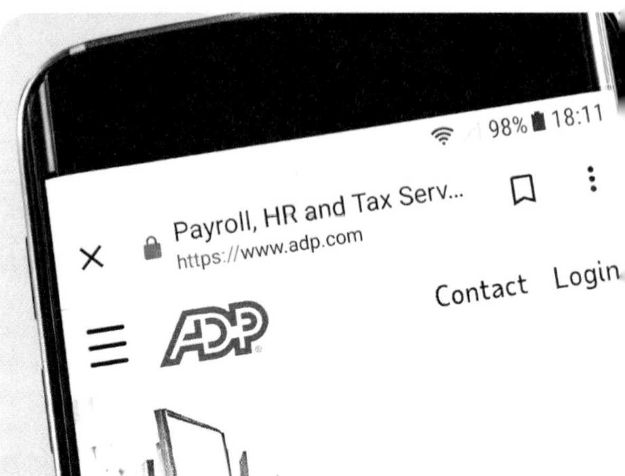

ADP, an HR services company, helps its clients achieve high performance while creating its own high-performance organizational culture.

madamF/Shutterstock

What Do I Need to Know?

After reading this chapter, you should be able to:

LO 9-1 Define high-performance work systems, and identify the elements of such a system.

LO 9-2 Summarize the outcomes of a high-performance work system.

LO 9-3 Describe the conditions that create a high-performance work system.

LO 9-4 Explain how human resource management can contribute to high performance.

LO 9-5 Discuss the role of HRM technology in high-performance work systems.

LO 9-6 Summarize ways to measure the effectiveness of human resource management.

company, 84% described their work environment as positive, and 74% said they typically are "excited about going to work each day."[1]

ADP's products help its clients and the company itself evaluate how to get employees fully engaged. The commitment of employees plus the efficiency of automated HR systems enable companies to innovate, achieve high quality, and operate more profitably. The gears of these systems run smoothly when, at every level of the organization, human resource management is contributing to high performance–creating work systems associated with high performance, managing the performance of individual employees (discussed in Chapter 10), and maintaining a high-performing workforce through decisions to separate and retain employees (discussed in Chapter 11).

This chapter begins with the basic goal for performance: the creation of *high-performance work systems.* The chapter defines these systems and describes their elements and outcomes. We explain how human resource management can contribute to high performance. Finally, we introduce ways to measure the effectiveness of human resource management.

High-Performance Work Systems

LO 9-1 Define high-performance work systems, and identify the elements of such a system.

The challenge facing managers today is how to make their organizations into **high-performance work systems,** with the right combination of people, technology, and organizational structure to make full use of resources and opportunities in achieving their organizations' goals. Put more simply, these organizations have what it takes to perform well on such measures as profitability, reputation, and achievement of their mission. To function as a high-performance work system, each of these elements must fit well with the others in a smoothly functioning whole. Many manufacturers use the latest in processes, including flexible manufacturing technology, total quality management, and just-in-time inventory control (meaning parts and supplies are automatically restocked as needed), but of course these processes do not work on their own; they must be run by qualified people. Organizations need to determine what kinds of people fit their needs, and then locate, train, and motivate those special people.[2] According to research, organizations that introduce integrated high-performance work practices usually experience increases in productivity and long-term financial success.[3]

High-Performance Work System
An organization in which technology, organizational structure, people, and processes work together seamlessly to give an organization an advantage in the competitive environment.

Creating a high-performance work system contrasts with traditional management practices. In the past, decisions about technology, organizational structure, and human resources were treated as if they were unrelated. An organization might acquire a new information system, restructure jobs, or add an office in another country without considering the impact on its people. More recently, managers have realized that success depends on how well all the elements work together. This has become evident to some observers of manufacturing in Japan, where managers in the 1980s became role models for their focus on quality. More recently, at several Japanese manufacturers, problems have emerged in quality control, with the most notorious being the defective airbags Takata sold to car manufacturers and later had to replace in a massive recall, an ongoing problem that continues even today.[4] The problems have coincided with changes in elements of the work system. In the past, continuous improvement was the responsibility of highly skilled factory workers, who had decision-making authority and were rewarded with lifetime careers. Competition from lower-wage countries led companies to cut many of those positions, relying more on automation and part-time workers, who are less invested in their company's success. Yet management continued to delegate the responsibility for quality, a practice that has been less effective in the revised organizational structure and with the new workers.[5] Returning to high quality will therefore require a new approach to all elements of the companies' work systems.

FIGURE 9.1
Elements of a High-Performance Work System

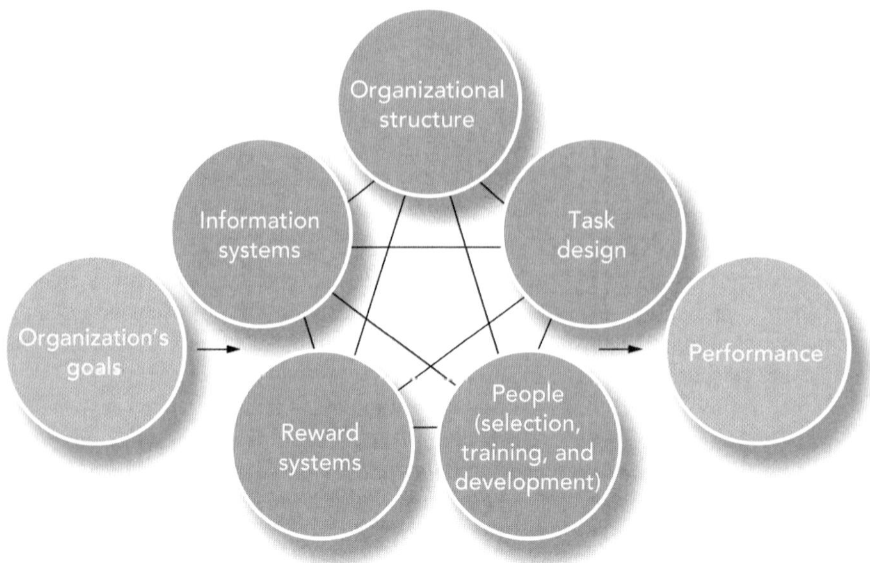

Elements of a High-Performance Work System

As shown in Figure 9.1, in a high-performance work system, the elements that must work together include organizational structure, task design, people (the selection, training, and development of employees), reward systems, and information systems, and human resource management plays an important role in establishing all these.

Organizational structure is the way the organization's people are grouped into useful divisions, departments, and reporting relationships. The organization's top management makes most decisions about structure, such as how many employees report to each supervisor and whether employees are grouped according to the functions they carry out or the customers they serve. Such decisions affect how well employees coordinate their activities and respond to change. In a high-performance work system, organizational structure promotes cooperation, learning, and continuous improvement.

Task design determines how the details of the organization's necessary activities will be grouped, whether into jobs or team responsibilities. In a high-performance work system, task design makes jobs efficient while encouraging high quality. In Chapter 4, we discussed how to carry out this HRM function through job analysis and job design.

The right *people* are a key element of high-performance work systems. HRM has a significant role in providing people who are well suited to and well prepared for their jobs. Human resource personnel help the organization recruit and select people with the needed qualifications. Training, development, and career management ensure that these people are able to perform their current and future jobs with the organization. The "Did You Know?" box describes one quality of an organization's people that can contribute to high performance: empathy.

Reward systems contribute to high performance by encouraging people to strive for objectives that support the organization's overall goals. Reward systems include the performance measures by which employees are judged, the methods of measuring performance, and the incentive pay and other rewards linked to success. Human resource management plays an important role in developing and administering reward systems, as we will explore in Chapters 12 to 14.

The final element of high-performance work systems is the organization's *information systems*. Managers make decisions about the types of information to gather and the sources of information. They also must decide who in the organization should have access to the information and how they will make the information available. Modern information systems, including

Did You Know?

Empathy Is Associated with High Performance

Noticing, understanding, and experiencing another person's feelings—the behavior known as empathy—can help us build trusting relationships. It's not surprising then that employees appreciate working in organizations where empathy is practiced. In a survey of U.S. workplaces, more than three-quarters of employees said they would work longer hours for a more empathetic employer, and most employees said they would stick with an empathetic employer. Employee commitment and low employee turnover are factors that contribute to high performance.

Employees described empathy as being expressed in managers' behavior and company policies. Examples include respect for employees' needs to take time off, expressions of interest in employees' lives ("How was your weekend?"), and the availability of benefits that help with life challenges, including financial emergencies and mental health. Employees expect empathy to be more likely when the company has a diverse workforce—another area in which HR decisions play a role.

Employer efforts to develop a healthy level of empathy in managers can identify particular competencies associated with empathetic leadership. For example, coaching and HR systems can nudge managers to set aside time for checking in on employees' well-being as well as their work progress, especially while employees work remotely due to the COVID-19 pandemic. Attentive listening is another skill that individuals can learn. An operations executive at an automotive-parts supplier learned this when he joined a new company and asked each of his employees what they wanted from him. He was surprised at their answers, gained new respect for his people, and realized that hearing what is on employees' minds is illuminating—and makes him a better manager.

Question

How can HR managers contribute to creating an empathetic organization? Suggest two or three ways.

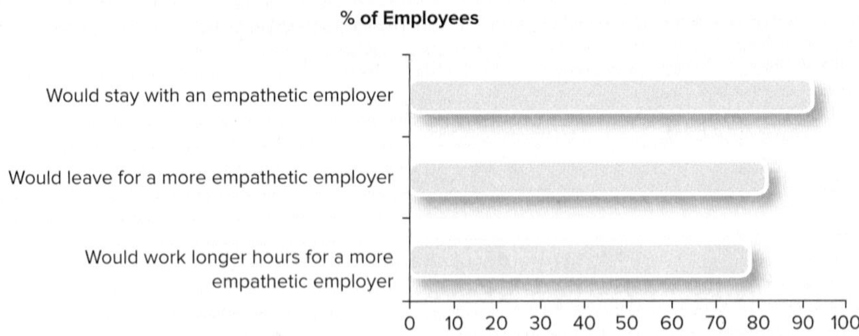

Sources: *2019 State of Workplace Empathy,* executive summary, https://info.businessolver.com, accessed April 22, 2020; Jennifer Thomas, "Empathy Amplified," *PM Network,* January 2020, pp. 42–45; Mark Whitten, "The Importance of Listening to Employees," *Industry Week,* September/October 2019, pp. 29–31; Carol Fitzgerald Tyler, "The Rise of Empathic Leadership," *Leadership Excellence,* May 2019, pp. 8–9.

the Internet, have enabled organizations to gather and share information widely. HR departments take advantage of this technology to give employees access to information about benefits, training opportunities, job openings, and more, as we will describe later in this chapter.

Outcomes of a High-Performance Work System

LO 9-2 Summarize the outcomes of a high-performance work system.

Calling a work system "high-performance" means that the way it operates leads to successful outcomes. To see what this looks like, consider Starwood Hotels, now part of Marriott. The hotel chain wanted to be profitable, and loyal customers contribute to profitability by returning again and again, not needing a lot of advertising to win them over for every trip they take. To obtain loyal customers, Starwood needs employees to create an environment and level of service that guests want to return to. Management had found that employees who are very positive about working for Starwood tend to deliver the desired customer experiences. Furthermore, Starwood recognized that these connections are fundamental to its business success, so it committed to better measuring these performance factors. The company developed an employee survey about factors related to the guest experience–for

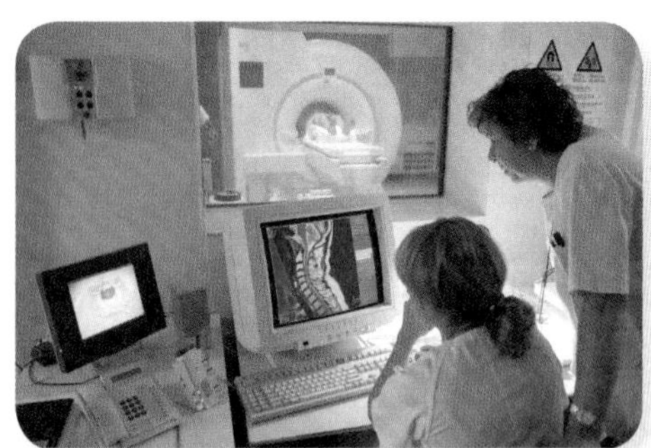

In a high-performance work system, all the elements—people, technology, and organizational structure—work together for success. Pixtal/age fotostock

example, housekeepers having ready access to enough towels and front-desk personnel feeling pride in their work. The company analyzed work processes, customer interactions, and customer satisfaction measures to identify jobs and work processes with the most impact on customer satisfaction. Based on information gained in the analysis, Starwood began using data from employee and guest surveys to generate reports to hotel managers on actions that will have the most impact on their hotel's performance.[6]

In general, outcomes of a high-performance work system include higher productivity and efficiency. These outcomes contribute to higher profits. A high-performance work system may have other outcomes, including high product quality, great customer satisfaction, and low employee turnover. Some of these outcomes meet intermediate goals that lead to higher profits (see Figure 9.2). For example, high quality contributes to customer satisfaction, and customer satisfaction contributes to growth of the business. Likewise, improving productivity lets the organization do more with less, which satisfies price-conscious customers and may help the organization win over customers from its competitors. Other ways to lower cost and improve quality are to reduce absenteeism and turnover, providing the organization with a steady supply of experienced workers.

In a high-performance work system, the outcomes of each employee and work group contribute to the system's overall high performance. The organization's individuals and groups work efficiently, provide high-quality goods and services, and so on, and in this way, they contribute to meeting the organization's goals. When the organization adds or changes goals, people are flexible and make changes as needed to meet the new goals.

FIGURE 9.2
Outcomes of a High-Performance Work System

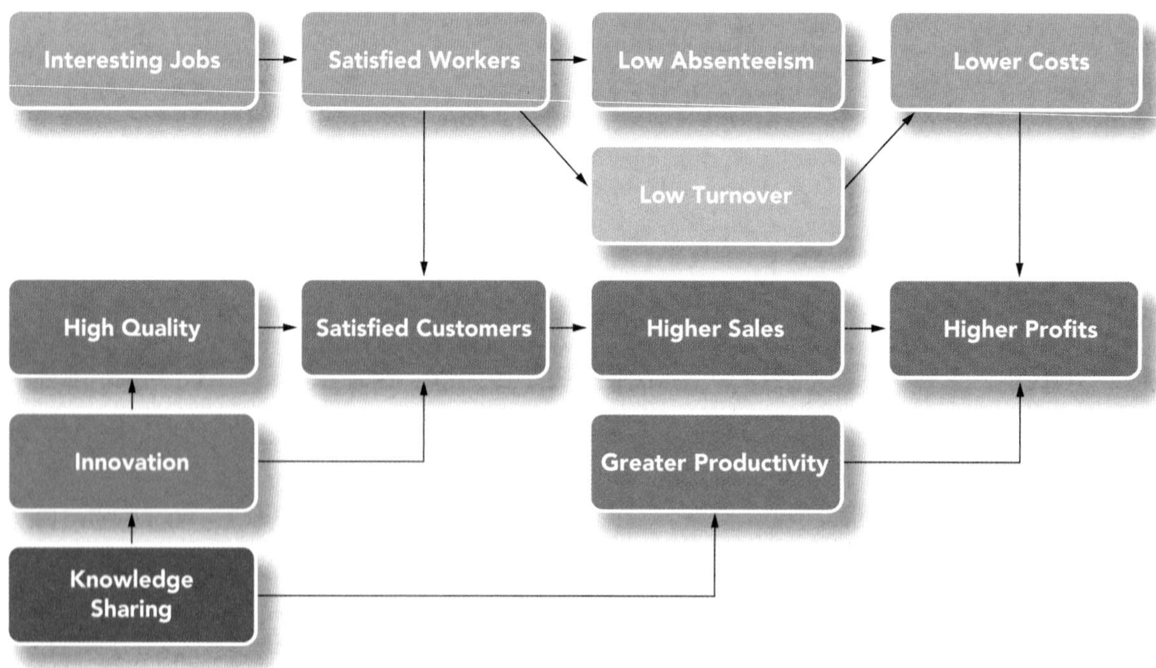

Conditions That Contribute to High Performance

LO 9-3 Describe the conditions that create a high-performance work system.

Certain conditions have been found in organizations with high performance. Managers consider these when seeking to create a high-performance work system:[7]

- Teams perform work.
- Employees participate in selection—presumably, with the necessary guidance to ensure they comply with employment laws and focus on relevant criteria.
- Employees receive formal performance feedback and are actively involved in the performance improvement process.
- Ongoing training is emphasized and rewarded.
- Employees' rewards and compensation relate to the company's financial performance.
- Equipment and work processes are structured, and technology is used to encourage maximum flexibility and interaction among employees.
- Employees participate in planning changes in equipment, layout, and work methods.
- Work design allows employees to use a variety of skills.
- Employees understand how their jobs contribute to the finished product or service.
- Ethical behavior is encouraged.

Practices involving rewards, employee empowerment, and jobs with variety contribute to high performance by giving employees skills, incentives, knowledge, autonomy—and satisfaction, another condition associated with high performance. Ethical behavior is a necessary condition of high performance because it contributes to good long-term relationships with employees, customers, and the public.

Teamwork and Empowerment

As we discussed in Chapter 2, today's organizations empower employees. They expect employees to make more decisions about how they perform their jobs. One of the most popular ways to empower employees is to design work so that it is performed by teams. On a work team, employees bring together various skills and experiences to produce goods or provide services. The organization may charge the team with making decisions traditionally made by managers, such as hiring team members and planning work schedules. Teamwork and empowerment contribute to high performance when they improve job satisfaction and give the organization fuller use of employees' ideas and expertise.

For CPS Energy, the country's largest public natural gas and electric company, teamwork and empowerment are key drivers of high performance. The San Antonio, TX-based utility focuses on "people first," both within the community it serves and for the employees who work for the organization. CPS's customer response unit consists of a dedicated group of workers who regularly visit customers during power outages, not only to restore power but to check in and make sure everyone is doing okay. The team also delivers meals to those in need during the holidays. Within the organization, the people-first mentality is evident in the company's mentorship and learning programs, which include an executive-in-residence program, in which employees spend up to two years working in a business area vastly different from their own and learning about different facets of the energy business. According to the company's CEO, giving employees the flexibility to seek different work experiences helps the entire organization operate at a higher level of performance.[8]

For empowerment to succeed, managers must serve in linking and coordinating roles and provide the team with the resources it needs to carry out its work.[9] The manager should help the team and its members interact with employees from other departments or teams and should make sure communication flows in both directions—the manager keeps the team updated on important issues and ensures that the team shares information and resources

HR Oops!

How Starbucks Recovered from a Decision Gone Wrong

In 2018, Starbucks received a dose of negative publicity when two young Black men in a Philadelphia store were arrested. The manager observed that the two sat at a table but did not place an order while they waited for a business associate to arrive. The manager asked them to leave, and when they did not, the manager called the police, who arrested the men. The incident was seen as an example of racial profiling, with the manager assuming the men were loiterers, not potential customers. The men later reached a settlement with Starbucks that included free online-college tuition through a program the company offers its employees.

Besides settling with the men, Starbucks identified a resource problem within the organization. Store employees needed better skills in running an operation that serves diverse customers. If they were to be empowered to make decisions about customer service, they could not allow their perceptions to be clouded by stereotypes.

Therefore, Starbucks announced soon after the incident that it would hold a half-day training event for all U.S. employees that would launch more extensive diversity training throughout the company. The day of a companywide shutdown for training was selected even before the training program was developed, but the company defined the content as focusing on how to recognize one's often-unconscious biases. For example, reports of the Philadelphia incident describe the men at the center of events as behaving calmly and politely, yet the manager seems to have defined them as a threat. Someone who is aware of biases might consider whether the defensive response was objective or based on commonly held biases about young Black men.

To date, the most effective kinds of training treat such awareness as a habit that people can learn to employ in order to treat customers and colleagues fairly. But critics of anti-bias training point out that it can be exhausting to look for biases in every encounter and say it is better to develop policies for how to behave in particular situations. However, an organization cannot craft a policy for every situation, especially if it values employee empowerment.

Questions

1. In this situation, what is the resource that Starbucks is providing to its employees in order to prevent future incidents like the one in Philadelphia?
2. Starbucks empowers store managers to make decisions about how to handle the people in each store. It also defines certain values such as respect for diversity. Do you expect that this combination leads to higher performance than if the company had a checklist for every situation (no empowerment) or let managers set their own values (no controls)? Explain.

Sources: Covington, "An Examination of Starbucks' Commitment to Civil Rights, Equity, Diversity, and Inclusion," January 23, 2019, https://stories.starbucks.com; Scott Neuman, "Men Arrested in Philadelphia Starbucks Reach Settlements," *The Two-Way* (NPR), May 3, 2018, https://www.npr.org; Jessica Nordell, "Does Starbucks Understand the Science of Racial Bias?" *The Atlantic,* May 2, 2018, https://www.theatlantic.com; Starbucks, "Starbucks Shares Further Details on Multi-phase Anti-bias Training Efforts," April 24, 2018, https://news.starbucks.com.

with others who need them. For an example of managers providing the necessary resources, see the "HR Oops!" box.

Knowledge Sharing

Learning Organization
An organization that supports lifelong learning by enabling all employees to acquire and share knowledge.

For more than a decade, managers have been interested in creating a **learning organization,** that is, an organization in which the culture values and supports lifelong learning by enabling all employees to continually acquire and share knowledge. The people in a learning organization have resources for training, and they are encouraged to share their knowledge with colleagues. Managers take an active role in identifying training needs and encouraging the sharing of ideas.[10] An organization's information systems, discussed later in this chapter, have an important role in making this learning activity possible. Information systems capture knowledge and make it available even after individual employees who provided the knowledge have left the organization. Ultimately, people are the essential ingredients in a learning organization. They must be committed to learning and willing to share what they have learned.

A learning organization has several key features:[11]

It's important for companies to capture and share the knowledge of workers who have had years to learn their specialty. Marcel Weber/Getty Images

- It engages in **continuous learning,** each employee's and each group's ongoing efforts to gather information and apply the information to their decisions. In many organizations, the process of continuous learning is aimed at improving quality. To engage in continuous learning, employees must understand the entire work system they participate in, the relationships among jobs, their work units, and the organization as a whole. Employees who continuously learn about their work system are adding to their ability to improve performance.
- Knowledge is *shared.* Therefore, to create a learning organization, one challenge is to shift the focus of training away from merely teaching skills and toward a broader focus on generating and sharing knowledge.[12] In this view, training is an investment in the organization's human resources; it increases employees' value to the organization. Also, training content should be related to the organization's goals. Human resource departments can support the creation of a learning organization by planning training programs that meet these criteria, and they can help create both face-to-face and electronic systems for employee collaboration to create, capture, and share knowledge.
- *Critical, systematic thinking* is widespread. This occurs when organizations encourage employees to see relationships among ideas and to test assumptions and observe the results of their actions. Reward systems can be set up to encourage employees and teams to think in new ways. Managers should be role models when it comes to measuring outcomes and analyzing data. Another way to contribute to better thinking about decisions is to ensure that software for gathering and analyzing data is widely available.
- The organization has a *learning culture*—a culture in which learning is rewarded, promoted, and supported by managers and organizational objectives. This culture may be reflected in performance management systems and pay structures that reward employees for gathering and sharing more knowledge. A learning culture creates the conditions in which managers encourage *flexibility* and *experimentation.* The organization should encourage employees to take risks and innovate, which means it cannot be quick to punish ideas that do not work out as intended.
- *Employees are valued.* The organization recognizes that employees are the source of its knowledge. It therefore focuses on ensuring the development and well-being of each employee.

Continuous Learning
Each employee's and each group's ongoing efforts to gather information and apply the information to their decisions in a learning organization.

The significance of critical thinking and knowledge sharing is greater than ever as more routine tasks become automated. Software using artificial intelligence, introduced in Chapter 2, is handling work once done by humans. The employees who will be most valuable in the AI-enabled workplace are those skilled in the kinds of thinking that are harder to automate. Joseph Aoun, president of Northeastern University, has explored what is important for college students to learn in preparation for this kind of business environment. He advocates learning that incorporates teamwork and crosses the boundaries still separating academic disciplines. Relevant learning goals include developing an understanding of technology and the ability to gather and interpret data.[13]

Job Satisfaction and Employee Engagement

A condition underpinning any high-performance organization is that employees be fully engaged with their work. **Employee engagement** is the degree to which employees are fully

Employee Engagement
The degree to which employees are fully involved in their work and the strength of their job and company commitment.

involved in their work and the strength of their commitment to their job and company. Being fully engaged tends to require that employees experience their jobs as fulfilling or allowing them to fulfill important values. Research supports the idea that employees' job satisfaction and job performance are related.[14] Higher performance at the individual level should contribute to higher performance for the organization as a whole. According to research conducted by Gallup, employee engagement in the United States reached a record high in 2019—35% of workers said they were highly involved in and committed to their work and workplace. In the same study, the percentage of workers who were "actively disengaged" in their work tied the lowest level Gallup had recorded (13%) since the organization began tracking employment engagement back in 2000. According to the Gallup researchers, team members with high levels of engagement produce substantially better outcomes; treat customers better and attract new ones; and are more likely to remain with their organization than those who are less engaged. In addition, engaged employees are also healthier and are less likely to experience burnout.[15]

As we will explore further in Chapter 11, organizations can promote job satisfaction and employee engagement in several ways. They include making jobs more interesting, setting clear and challenging goals, and providing valued rewards that are linked to performance in a performance management system that employees consider fair. Globally, management and HR consulting firms, such as Kincentric, have found that the practices that do the most to promote employee engagement include brand alignment.[16]

Brand Alignment
The process of ensuring that HR policies, practices, and programs support or are congruent with an organization's overall culture (or brand), products, and services.

Brand alignment is the process of ensuring that HR policies, practices, and programs support or are congruent with an organization's overall culture or brand, including its products and services. For example, if a retailer wants to be known for making customers happy, it will hire people with strong people skills, and it will reward exceptional service. If, however, its reward systems and job design are focused on keeping costs as low as possible, it will develop a workforce driven by cost containment, and it will have much more difficulty carrying out its customer-friendly strategy. Furthermore, employees who believed they took jobs with a customer-friendly company, only to be told to stop chatting with customers, are likely to feel confused and then alienated and will not stay with the company for long. Thus, organizations should know their brand and cultivate brand alignment in their recruiting, selection, training, and other HR practices. This includes being honest with job candidates about the brand, so it can maintain credibility in the labor market and hire people who will support the culture. Amazon, for example, is straightforward about the fact that its employees have challenging jobs, and it therefore attracts job applicants who are inspired by a culture that works hard in order to achieve excellence.[17]

Some organizations are moving beyond concern with mere job satisfaction and are trying to foster employees' *passion* for their work. Passionate people are fully engaged with something so that it becomes part of their sense of who they are. Feeling this way about one's work has been called *occupational intimacy.*[18] People experience occupational intimacy when they love their work, when they and their co-workers care about one another, and when they find their work meaningful. Human resource managers have a significant role in creating these conditions. For example, they can select people who care about their work and customers, provide methods for sharing knowledge, design work to make jobs interesting, and establish policies and programs that show concern for employees' needs. Such efforts may become increasingly important as the business world increasingly uses employee empowerment, teamwork, and knowledge sharing to build flexible organizations.[19]

Ethics

In the long run, a high-performance organization meets high ethical standards. Ethics, defined in Chapter 1, establishes fundamental principles for behavior, such as honesty and fairness.

Organizations and their employees must meet these standards if they are to maintain positive long-term relationships with their customers and their community. In contrast, experiments suggest that working in a climate where dishonesty is tolerated creates stress that can lead to employee burnout.[20] Those who do not leave the organization are likelier to be disengaged.

Ethical behavior is most likely to result from values held by the organization's leaders combined with systems that promote ethical behavior. Costco has a simple values statement, "Do the right thing," as well as a code of ethics that includes taking care of members (customers) and employees. The company expresses those values in above-average pay, avoidance of job cuts, and practices for ensuring that managers treat their employees with respect. This culture supports trust in management. The payoff is that employee turnover is very low and customer retention is high.[21]

A number of organizational systems can promote ethical behavior.[22] These include a written code of ethics that the organization distributes to employees and expects them to use in decision making. This type of guidance can be especially effective if developed with input from employees about situations they encounter. However, standards alone are not enough—the organization should reinforce ethical behavior. For example, performance measures should include ethical standards, and misdeeds should receive swift discipline. The organization should provide channels employees can use to ask questions about ethical behavior or to seek help if they are expected to do something they believe is wrong. Organizations also can provide training in ethical decision making, including training for supervisors in how to handle employees' concerns about ethical matters and how to provide ethical leadership.

As these examples suggest, ethical behavior is a human resource management concern. The systems that promote ethical behavior include such HRM functions as training, performance management, and discipline policies. A reputation for high ethical standards can also help a company attract and engage workers who share those high standards. Conversely, breakdowns in ethics can generate performance problems, so HR data analytics can help companies spot and correct these problems. Consider a situation identified by Matthew Quade and colleagues researching ethical behavior: employees who rate themselves as more ethical than their co-workers tend to look down on co-workers or feel stressed around them.[23] Furthermore, according to these co-workers, the supposedly ethically superior employees are likelier than others to undermine or ignore co-workers. HR practices should include some ways to minimize this potentially toxic situation. In particular, performance standards and rewards for all employees should include measures of ethical conduct, so that ethical behavior is a clear norm for all.

HRM's Contribution to High Performance

LO 9-4 Explain how human resource management can contribute to high performance.

Management of human resources plays a critical role in determining companies' success in meeting the challenges of a rapidly changing, highly competitive environment.[24] The HR practices introduced in Chapter 1 are investments that directly affect employees' motivation and ability to provide products and services that are valued by customers. Table 9.1 lists examples of HRM practices that contribute to high performance.

Research suggests that it is more effective to improve HRM practices as a whole than to focus on one or two isolated practices, such as the organization's pay structure or selection system.[25] Also, to have the intended influence on performance, the HRM practices must fit well with one another and the organization as a whole.[26]

HRM Practices

Let's take a closer look at how the HRM practices can contribute to high performance. Some of these are practices we have introduced already; others will be the subject of later chapters.

TABLE 9.1

HRM Practices That Can Help Organizations Achieve High Performance

HRM practices match organization's goals.	Performance management system measures customer satisfaction and quality.
Individuals and groups share knowledge.	Organization monitors employees' satisfaction.
Work is performed by teams.	Discipline system is progressive.
Organization encourages continuous learning.	Pay systems reward skills and accomplishments.
Work design permits flexibility in where and when tasks are performed.	Skills and values of a diverse workforce are valued and used.
Selection system is job related and legal.	Technology reduces time and costs of tasks while preserving quality.

Mc Graw Hill connect

Visit your instructor's Connect® course and access your eBook to view this video.

"You want a leader who understands the value the HR process brings to driving strategy. Every strategic decision, issue, or initiative a business leader faces comes down to people."

—Benjamin Gilman
Senior Vice President & Human Resources Executive, Bank of America/Merrill Lynch, US Wealth Management

Source: Video Produced for the Center for Executive Succession in the Darla Moore School of Business at the University of South Carolina by Coal Powered Filmworks

Job design can enable the organization to benefit from teamwork and employee empowerment, two of the work conditions associated with high performance. Job design aimed at empowerment includes access to resources such as information technology. For companies delivering electric power to homes and businesses, usage data used to be available only at headquarters, where decisions were made about service problems and maintenance. Now service providers are using mobile devices to make the data available to technicians in the field. A technician out in a neighborhood can be equipped with a rugged tablet computer to view reports of data from voltage sensors, customer comments on social media, and other sources to make more informed judgments about the source of an outage. Empowering well-trained technicians to decide how to respond can speed up response times. Also, since the technicians are near the customers, empowering them to make decisions and answer questions can improve customer satisfaction.[27] Technology and job design that enable flexible work arrangements are often associated with empowerment. In the recent COVID-19 pandemic, this flexibility also became necessary for enabling work to move forward (see "HR How To").

Recruitment and selection aim at obtaining employees who are enthusiastic about and able to contribute to teamwork, empowerment, and knowledge sharing. Qualities such as creativity and the ability to cooperate as part of a team may play a large role in selection decisions. High-performance organizations need selection methods that identify more than technical skills like ability to perform accounting or engineering tasks. Employers may use group interviews, open-ended questions, and psychological tests to find employees who innovate, share ideas, and take initiative.

When organizations base hiring decisions on qualities like decision-making and teamwork skills, *training* may be required to teach employees the specific skills they need to perform the duties of their job. Extensive training and development also are part of a learning organization, described earlier in this chapter. And when organizations delegate many decisions to work teams, the members of those teams likely will benefit from participating in team development activities that prepare them for their roles as team members. In addition, high-performance organizations are developing their talent to move into positions with greater responsibility.

Performance management, introduced in Chapter 1 and explored in Chapter 10, ensures that employees' work contributes to achieving the organization's goals. In a high-performance

HR How To

Enabling High-Performance Remote Work

Advancing technology and the desire to offer flexibility in a competitive job market had already made work-from-home arrangements part of the business landscape when the COVID-19 pandemic swept the globe. Then the need to protect employees while keeping businesses afloat caused a major surge in remote work. Even at companies that had not devoted much effort to planning for it, HR departments suddenly had to support an expansion of remote working. Here are some principles applied by organizations doing it well:

- Assess employees' resources. When employees go to the workplace, the employer provides the space, equipment, and supplies. Employers cannot assume that employees are well prepared with these at home, and ill-equipped employees cannot deliver the same high performance. HR departments should prepare managers to discuss work-at-home arrangements one-on-one with each employee on the manager's team. Employees may need mentoring programs even more when they work remotely, so HR departments can consider establishing such programs or ensuring that existing mentors are set up to connect online.
- Establish and support remote communication. Knowledge sharing and coordination are essential for high performance. HR departments can use skills in work analysis and job design to help managers identify the kinds of communication that are important and the information technology that will support such communication. For example, videoconferencing and video chats recreate the facial expressions and other nonverbal cues that help people assess the emotional content of messages. Instant messaging and phone calls are helpful for getting quick answers. Teams working in different time zones or juggling work and other responsibilities benefit from tools that let them post work or messages for others to review at their convenience.
- Recognize the needed skill sets for remote workers and their managers. People may need training to use communication tools and other technology provided for working remotely. Skills such as written communication and telephone etiquette may become more central to effective work. Managers may need training in how to support workers from a distance—for example, not shifting to a pure focus on task completion but also checking in to see that employees have what they need, including encouragement that they are still part of a team.
- Restructure jobs and performance measurement as needed. Some employees who work remotely report that their productivity rises in this environment. Companies have an opportunity to gather performance data and identify the job requirements and work habits of the more productive employees. Patterns in the data can suggest training needs, behaviors to reward, and ways to redesign jobs so more of the work involves independent activities.

Questions

1. What HRM practices from Table 9.1 are described here?
2. Find an additional practice from Table 9.1, and suggest how it could help a company shifting to remote work. How can this practice help to achieve high performance when work is done from home?

Sources: "Managing the Suddenly Distributed Workforce," *Silicon Valley Business Journal,* April 14, 2020, https://www.bizjournals.com/sanjose; Tammy Perkins, "How to Activate Mentoring and Career Development When You Work from Home," *Fast Company,* April 10, 2020, https://www.fastcompany.com; Josh Lowy, "Overcoming Remote Work Challenges," *MIT Sloan Management Review,* April 9, 2020, https://sloanreview.mit.edu; Phanish Puranam and Marco Minervini, "What Newly Remote Teams Need, Right Now," INSEAD blog, April 2, 2020, https://knowledge.insead.edu.

organization, this requires making sure that employees know the organization's goals and what they must do to contribute to goal achievement. A performance management system that meets those requirements applies the process of employee performance, diagrammed in Figure 9.3. Individuals bring a set of skills and abilities to the job, and by applying a set of behaviors to the skills and abilities, they achieve results. The organization's goals should influence each step of that process. The situation also has an influence on every step. For example, an organization's culture might influence how hard individuals try to

FIGURE 9.3
Employee Performance as a Process

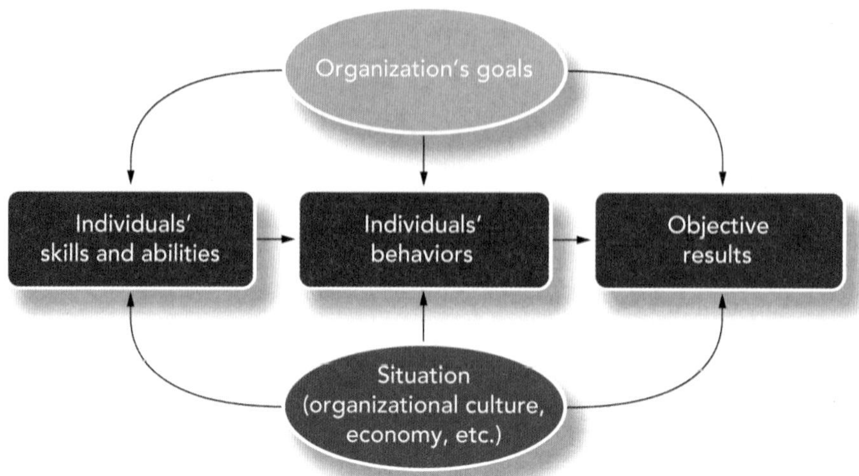

please customers, and economic conditions might influence how much a salesperson sells, no matter how hard she tries.

This model suggests some guidelines for performance management. First, each aspect of performance management should be related to the organization's goals. Business goals should influence the kinds of employees selected and their training, the requirements of each job, and the measures used for evaluating results. Generally, this means the organization identifies what each department must do to achieve the desired results, then defines how individual employees should contribute to their department's goals. More specifically, the following guidelines describe how to make the performance management system support organizational goals:[28]

- *Define and measure performance in precise terms*—Focus on outcomes that can be defined in terms of how frequently certain behaviors occur. Include criteria that describe ways employees can add value to a product or service (such as through quantity, quality, or timeliness). Include behaviors that go beyond the minimum required to perform a job (such as helping co-workers).
- *Link performance measures to meeting customer needs*—"Customers" may be the organization's external customers, or they may be internal customers (employees receiving services from a co-worker). Service goals for internal customers should be related to satisfying external customers.
- *Measure and correct for the effect of situational constraints*—Monitor economic conditions, the organization's culture, and other influences on performance. Measures of employees' performance should take these influences into account.

Compensation supports high-performance organizations when it is linked in part to performance measures. Chapter 13 will describe methods for doing this. An example is paying bonuses to reward innovation and knowledge sharing. Compensation also can be tied to performance-related conditions such as successful teamwork or—for a manager—job satisfaction among employees in the manager's department. Furthermore, organizations can increase empowerment and job satisfaction by including employees in decisions about compensation and communicating the basis for pay decisions.[29] Some organizations share financial information with employees or have them participate in setting group goals used as the basis for paying bonuses.

HRM Technology

LO 9-5 Discuss the role of HRM technology in high-performance work systems.

Human resource departments can improve their own and their organization's performance by appropriately using new technology. New technology usually involves *automation and collaboration*–that is, using equipment and information processing to perform activities that had been performed by people and facilitating electronic communication between people. Over the last few decades, automation has improved HRM efficiency by reducing the number of people needed to perform routine tasks. Using automation can free HRM experts to concentrate on ways to determine how human resource management can help the organization meet its goals so technology also can make this function more valuable.[30] For example, information technology provides ways to build and improve systems for knowledge generation and sharing, as part of a learning organization. Among the applications are databases or networking sites where employees can store and share their knowledge, online directories of employee skills and experiences, and online libraries of learning resources, such as technical manuals and employees' reports from seminars and training programs.

Transaction Processing
Computations and calculations involved in reviewing and documenting HRM decisions and practices.

Decision Support Systems
Computer software systems designed to help managers solve problems by showing how results vary when the manager alters assumptions or data.

Expert Systems
Computer systems that support decision making by incorporating the decision rules used by people who are considered to have expertise in a certain area.

HRM Applications

As computers become ever more powerful, new technologies continue to be introduced. These range from software for individual tasks performed on a mobile device to complex systems that enable the analysis of HR data gathered from a multinational workforce. At any scale, the systems typically take the form of transaction processing, decision support systems, and expert systems.[31]

Transaction processing refers to computations and calculations involved in reviewing and documenting HRM decisions and practices. It includes documenting decisions and actions associated with employee relocation, training expenses, and enrollments in courses and benefit plans. Transaction processing also includes the activities required to meet government reporting requirements, such as filling out EEO-1 reports, on which employers report information about employees' race and gender by job category. Computers enable companies to perform these tasks more efficiently. Employers can fill out computerized forms and store HRM information in databases (data stored electronically in user-specified categories), so that it is easier to find, sort, and report.

Decision support systems are computer software systems designed to help managers solve problems. They usually include a "what if?" feature that managers can use to enter different assumptions or data and see how the likely outcomes will change. By applying internal data or research results, this type of system can help managers make decisions for human resource planning. The manager can, for example, try out different assumptions about turnover rates to see how those assumptions affect the number of new employees needed. Or the manager can test a range of assumptions about the availability of a certain skill in the labor market, looking at the impact of the assumptions on the success of different recruiting plans. Possible applications for a decision support system include forecasting (discussed in Chapter 5) and succession planning (discussed in Chapter 8).

Expert systems can help with complicated business decisions such as scheduling the optimal number of employees for slow and busy work periods.
Grigvovan/Shutterstock

Expert systems are computer systems that incorporate the decision rules used by people who are considered to have expertise in a certain area. The systems help users make decisions by recommending actions based on the decision rules and the information provided by the users. An expert system is designed to recommend the same actions that a human expert would in a similar situation. For example, an expert system could guide an interviewer during the selection process. Some organizations use expert systems to help employees decide how to allocate their money for benefits (when the company offers a set of choices) and help managers schedule the labor needed to complete projects. Expert systems can deliver both high quality and lower costs. By using the decision processes of experts, an expert system helps many people to arrive at decisions that reflect the expert's knowledge. An expert system helps avoid the errors that can result from fatigue and decision-making biases, such as biases in appraising employee performance. An expert system can increase efficiency by enabling fewer or less-skilled employees to do work that otherwise would require many highly skilled employees.

In today's HR departments, transaction processing, decision support systems, and expert systems may incorporate artificial intelligence (AI) to automate processes, as described in Chapter 2. Furthermore, these systems often are part of a broader human resource information system, which can provide computing power for insightful analysis. Typically, these technologies are linked to employees through a network such as an intranet. Information systems and networks have been evolving rapidly; the following descriptions provide a basic introduction.

Human Resource Information Systems

A standard feature of a modern HRIS is the use of *relational databases,* which store data in separate files that can be linked by common elements. These common elements are fields identifying the type of data. Commonly used fields for an HR database include name, Social Security number, job status (full- or part-time), hiring date, position, title, rate of pay, citizenship status, job history, job location, mailing address, birth date, and emergency contacts. A relational database lets a user sort the data by any of the fields. For example, depending on how the database is set up, the user might be able to look up tables listing employees by location, rates of pay for various jobs, or employees who have completed certain training courses. This system is far more sophisticated than the old-fashioned method of filing employee data by name, with one file per employee.

The ability to locate and combine many categories of data has a multitude of uses in human resource management. Databases have been developed to track employee benefit costs, training courses, and compensation. The system can meet the needs of line managers as well as the HR department. On an oil rig, for example, management might look up data listing employee names along with safety equipment issued and appropriate skill certification. HR managers at headquarters might look up data on the same employees to gather information about wage rates or training programs needed. Another popular use of an HRIS is applicant tracking, or maintaining and retrieving records of job applicants. This is much faster and easier than trying to sort through stacks of résumés. With relational databases, HR staff can retrieve information about specific applicants or obtain lists of applicants with specific skills, career goals, work history, and employment background. Such information is useful for HR planning, recruitment, succession planning, and career development. Taking the process a step further, the system could store information related to hiring and terminations. By analyzing such data, the HR department could measure the long-term success of its recruiting and selection processes.

HR Dashboard
A display of a series of HR measures, showing the measure and progress toward meeting it.

One of the most creative developments in HRIS technology is the **HR dashboard,** a display of a series of HR-related indicators, or measures, showing human resource goals and objectives and the progress toward meeting them. Managers with access to the HRIS can look at the HR dashboard for an easy-to-scan review of HR performance. One Asian telecommunications company has a system of dashboards reporting data in real time.

The company's 1,000 business teams can view data about customer satisfaction, employee satisfaction, profitability, and more. This ensures that managers are accountable for results and able to act quickly when conditions change.[32]

The power of an HRIS to process so much data is making analytical skills a key part of human resource management. Organizations are increasingly seeking out HR professionals who can make data-driven decisions. At its most useful, this involves *predictive analytics*–using data about past and present conditions and the relationships between factors to forecast what will happen in the future if a particular decision is made. It might be tempting to turn over predictive analytics to the computer's artificial intelligence, directing the software, for instance, to find any factors in common among top-selling salespeople or engineers who stay for five years or more. With enough data points, the analysis will find some factors are most common–but they may be purely coincidental or unintentionally biased.[33] Useful data-driven HR begins with a knowledge of the business and of the ways that human resource management affects performance.[34]

Decision makers need to apply that knowledge and some creative thinking to make predictions that can be tested and refined. For example, to learn why many start-up companies fail, Alistair Shepherd learned about team dynamics and gathered data on relationship quality. He found that shared values play a key role, so he tested surveys of values from online dating websites to see if he could predict successful teams based on team members' values. The initial tests worked well enough that he formed a people analytics consulting firm to help others apply the ideas.[35]

HR Analytics & Decision Making

How can predictive analytics help solve real company problems? No firm wants to lose valued high-performing employees, but often employers do not know the employees are thinking about leaving until it is too late. A recent study by Gardner, Van Iddekinge, and Hom found that employees often show behaviors predictive of quitting. The extensive validation study across a number of different employee groups identified the following behaviors as signs that an employee may be thinking about leaving the organization:

1. Their work productivity has decreased more than usual.
2. They have acted less like a team player than usual.
3. They have been doing the minimum amount of work more frequently.
4. They have been less interested in pleasing their manager than usual.
5. They have been less willing to commit to long-term timelines than usual.
6. They have exhibited a negative change in attitude.
7. They have exhibited less effort and work motivation than usual.
8. They have exhibited less focus on job-related matters than usual.
9. They have expressed dissatisfaction with their current job more frequently than usual.
10. They have expressed dissatisfaction with their supervisor more frequently than usual.
11. They have left early from work more frequently than usual.
12. They have lost enthusiasm for the mission of the organization.
13. They have shown less interest in working with customers than usual.

Questions

1. How could a company measure the behaviors listed? Note any problems you see with measuring some or all of these variables.

2. Suppose that a company has been gathering this kind of information about its employees. How might information technology help the company act on this information?

Source: T. M. Garder, C. H. Van Iddekinge, & P. W. Hom, "If You've Got Leavin' on Your Mind: The Identification and Validation of Pre-quitting Behaviors," *Journal of Management.* Published online August 29, 2016.

Human Resource Management Online: E-HRM

As we discussed in Chapter 2, more and more organizations are engaging in e-HRM, providing HR-related information over the Internet. Because much human resource information is confidential, organizations may do this with an intranet, which uses Internet technology but allows access only to authorized users (such as the organization's employees). For HR professionals, Internet access also offers a way to research new developments, post job openings, trade ideas with colleagues in other organizations, and obtain government documents. In this way, e-HRM combines company-specific information on a secure intranet with links to the resources on the broader Internet.

As Internet use has increasingly taken the form of social-media applications, e-HRM has moved in this direction as well. Generally speaking, social media bring networks of people together to collaborate on projects, solve problems, or socialize. Social-media applications for human resource management include YouTube access to instructional videos, Facebook-style networking sites where employees can share project updates and ideas for improvement, web pages where employees can praise peers' accomplishments and deliver rewards, and crowdsourcing tools for performance appraisals. In terms of job design, social media can promote teamwork by providing an easy means of collaboration, and for recruiting over great distances social media allow virtual job fairs and/or selection interviews. As the use of social media continues to expand, creative minds will devise many other applications that forward-thinking HR professionals can introduce as ways to get employees more fully engaged with the organization and one another.

A benefit of e-HRM is that employees can help themselves to the information they need when they need it, instead of contacting an HR staff person. For example, employees can go online to enroll in or select benefits, submit insurance claims, or fill out employee satisfaction surveys. This can be more convenient for the employees, as well as more economical for the HR department. Employees also appreciate the convenience of getting their training online, at the time and place of their choosing, preferably in short chunks as needed. Salespeople, for example, can watch online training videos between sales calls. Or suppose an organization wants to improve performance management by having managers give more frequent feedback. Instead of sending them to a class about feedback, e-HRM can offer tools that make it easier for managers to record examples of their employees' performance and walk the managers through the process of using these records to communicate the feedback constructively.

Many companies use social-media applications as part of their e-HRM strategies to coach and train employees.
FG Trade/Getty Images

Companies Should Listen as Well as Talk on Social Media

Several job-related websites with social-media functions, including Glassdoor, Indeed, Job Crowd, and Vault, let employees post anonymous reviews of their employers. When employees are happy, these comments make recruiting easier. But when employees dislike their jobs, social media begins to look like a problem for employers.

The creators of these services say employers should see an opportunity even in the negative comments. Consciously or not, employees are providing employers with a constantly updated source of data about their culture and their employees' state of mind. Furthermore, with HRISs and artificial intelligence, employers can monitor the content of employees' posts to find patterns in the comments. For example, complaints about stress might be coming from a particular department, or complaints about a lack of vision might be coming from a particular location. This kind of information suggests not only which elements of the work system need attention, but also whether problems are organization wide or limited to particular areas.

These sites generally provide a way for employers to post comments and respond. This is an opportunity to express appreciation for insights and, when comments are critical, demonstrate concern for the situation.

Of course, actions are what matter most. Suppose employees have a pattern of indicating that management does not value their contributions. Managers who seek a high-performance organization will appreciate the opportunity to correct the problem before the damage to employee engagement gets worse. When leadership improves and employees begin to see evidence that their managers do in fact value their contributions, this change should begin to show up in the comments. At that point, not only does the organization look better to people reading the website, it really is performing better. That means employees are more engaged, which should lead to better performance in terms of business measures such as sales and profits.

Questions

1. Suppose you work in the HR department of a manufacturing company. Your team analyzes social-media data and learns that employees are complaining they don't see opportunities for career growth. Would you define this as a social-media problem or an HR problem? Why?
2. Continuing with your role in question 1, suppose an employee writes online that your company has no real training program, when in fact it has an online learning program, including recommended lessons for employees at every level and in every department. You have been asked to post a reply to this comment. Write a brief reply that you think would present honest information, a positive image of the company, and a professional tone.

Sources: "How to Keep Complaints from Spreading: Limiting the Fallout from Negative Social Media Posts," *Harvard Business Review,* May-June 2020, pp. 19–22; Nathan Resnick, "Why Social Media Is Key to Keeping Employees Engaged at Work," *The Next Web,* July 11, 2019, https://thenextweb.com; Marca Clark, "What Is Employee Engagement and Why Does It Matter?" *Glassdoor blog,* January 17, 2018, https://www.glassdoor.com; Roy Mauer, "Looking through the Glassdoor," *HR Magazine,* February 2017, pp. 24–25.

Most administrative and information-gathering activities in human resource management can be part of e-HRM. For example, online recruiting has become a significant part of the total recruiting effort, as candidates submit applications online and consult social media to learn about potential employers (see "HRM Social"). For selection decisions, candidates may take tests and record interview responses online. Aspects of job design–for example, schedules, delivery routes, and production layouts–may be done using online software systems that share the information with the relevant people. Online appraisal or talent management systems provide data that can help managers spot high performers to reward or types of skills where additional training is a priority. Many types of training can be conducted online, as we discussed earlier in this chapter and in Chapter 7. Online surveys of employee satisfaction can be quick and easy to fill out. Besides providing a way to administer the survey, an intranet is an effective vehicle for communicating the results of the survey and management's planned response.

Not only does e-HRM provide efficient ways to carry out human resource functions, it also poses new challenges to employees and new issues for HR managers to address. The Internet's ability to link people anytime, anywhere has accelerated such trends as globalization, the importance of knowledge sharing, the need for flexibility, and cloud computing. Cloud computing is another recent advance in technology that has several implications for HR practices. **Cloud computing** involves using a network of remote servers hosted on the Internet to store, manage, and process data. These services are offered by data centers around the world (and not within an organization's offices) and are collectively called "the cloud." These services offer the ability to access information that's delivered on demand from any device, anywhere, at any time. In the wake of the COVID-19 global pandemic, many companies slashed their in-house IT spending and increased expenditures on cloud services, which gave them a certain amount of agility to deal with HR challenges and other business interruptions.[36]

Cloud Computing
The practice of using a network of remote servers hosted on the Internet to store, manage, and process data.

These trends change the work environment for employees. For example, employees in the Internet age are expected to be highly committed but flexible, able to move from job to job. Employees also may be connected to the organization 24/7. In the car, on vacation, in airports, and even in the bathroom, employees with handheld computers can be interrupted by work demands. Organizations depend on their human resource departments to help prepare employees for this changing work world through such activities as training, career development, performance management, and benefits packages that meet the need for flexibility and help employees manage stress.

LO 9-6 Summarize ways to measure the effectiveness of human resource management.

Effectiveness of Human Resource Management

In recent years, human resource management at some organizations has responded to the quest for total quality management by taking a customer-oriented approach. For an organization's human resource division, "customers" are the organization as a whole and its other divisions. They are customers of HRM because they depend on HRM to provide a variety of services that result in a supply of talented, motivated employees. Taking this customer-oriented approach, human resource management defines its customer groups, customer needs, and the activities required to meet those needs, as shown in Table 9.2. These definitions give an organization a basis for defining goals and measures of success.

Depending on the situation, a number of techniques are available for measuring HRM's effectiveness in meeting its customers' needs. These techniques include reviewing a set of key indicators, measuring the outcomes of specific HRM activity, and measuring the economic value of HRM programs.

HRM Audit
A formal review of the outcomes of HRM functions, based on identifying key HRM functions and measures of business performance.

Human Resource Management Audits

An **HRM audit** is a formal review of the outcomes of HRM functions. To conduct the audit, the HR department identifies key functions and the key measures of business performance and customer satisfaction that would indicate each function is succeeding. Table 9.3 lists examples of these measures for a variety of HRM functions: staffing, compensation, benefits,

TABLE 9.2
Customer-Oriented Perspective of Human Resource Management

WHO ARE OUR CUSTOMERS?	WHAT DO OUR CUSTOMERS NEED?	HOW DO WE MEET CUSTOMER NEEDS?
Line managers	Committed employees	Qualified staffing
Strategic planners	Competent employees	Performance management
Employees		Rewards Training and development

training, appraisal and development, and overall effectiveness. The audit may also look at any other measure associated with successful management of human resources—for instance, compliance with equal employment opportunity laws, succession planning, maintaining a safe workplace, and positive labor relations. An HRM audit using customer satisfaction measures supports the customer-oriented approach to human resource management.

After identifying performance measures for the HRM audit, the staff carries out the audit by gathering information. The information for the key business indicators is usually available in the organization's documents. Sometimes the HR department has to create new documents for gathering specific types of data. The usual way to measure customer satisfaction is to conduct surveys. Employee attitude surveys, which we will discuss further in Chapter 11, provide information about the satisfaction of these internal customers. Many

TABLE 9.3

Key Measures of Success for an HRM Audit

BUSINESS INDICATORS	CUSTOMER SATISFACTION MEASURES
Staffing	
Average days taken to fill open requisitions Ratio of acceptances to offers made Ratio of minority/women applicants to representation in local labor market Per capita requirement costs Average years of experience/education of hires per job family	Anticipation of personnel needs Timeliness of referring qualified workers to line supervisors Treatment of applicants Skill in handling terminations Adaptability to changing labor market conditions
Compensation	
Per capita (average) merit increases Ratio of recommendations for reclassification to number of employees Percentage of overtime hours to straight time Ratio of average salary offers to average salary in community	Fairness of existing job evaluation system in assigning grades and salaries Competitiveness in local labor market Relationship between pay and performance Employee satisfaction with pay
Benefits	
Average unemployment compensation payment (UCP) Average workers' compensation payment (WCP) Benefit cost per payroll dollar Percentage of sick leave to total pay	Promptness in handling claims Fairness and consistency in the application of benefit policies Communication of benefits to employees Assistance provided to line managers in reducing potential for unnecessary claims
Training	
Percentage of employees participating in training programs per job family Percentage of employees receiving tuition refunds Training dollars per employee	Extent to which training programs meet the needs of employees and the company Communication to employees about available training opportunities Quality of introduction/orientation programs
Employee appraisal and development	
Distribution of performance appraisal ratings Appropriate psychometric properties of appraisal forms	Assistance in identifying management potential Organizational development activities provided by HRM department
Overall effectiveness	
Ratio of personnel staff to employee population Turnover rate Absenteeism rate Ratio of per capita revenues to per capita cost Net income per employee	Accuracy and clarity of information provided to managers and employees Competence and expertise of staff Working relationship between organizations and HRM department

Sources: Society for Human Resource Management, "Conducting Human Resource Audits," June 16, 2016, https://www.shrm.org; Anne S. Tsui and Luis R. Gomez-Mejia, "Evaluating Human Resource Effectiveness," in *Human Resource Management: Evolving Roles & Responsibilities* (New York: Wiley, 1988), Chapter 15.

organizations conduct surveys of top line executives to get a better view of how HRM practices affect the organization's business success. To benefit from the HR profession's best practices, companies also may invite external auditing teams to audit specific HR functions. In New Hampshire, Claremont Savings Bank hired an outside specialist to conduct a comprehensive audit of its HRM practices, focusing on payroll. The auditor showed the bank's HR department how to ensure that its payroll contractor was submitting all the required taxes, and it verified that the correct amounts were being deducted for the benefits each employee had signed up for. Based on this positive experience, Claremont now conducts an external audit every three years, as well as yearly internal audits.[37]

Analyzing the Effect of HRM Programs

HR Analytics
Type of assessment of HRM effectiveness that involves determining the impact of, or the financial cost and benefits of, a program or practice.

Another way to measure HRM effectiveness is the use of **HR analytics.** This process involves measuring a program's success in terms of whether it achieved its objectives and whether it delivered value in an economic sense. For example, if the organization sets up a training program, it should set up goals for that program, such as the training's effects on learning, behavior, and performance improvement (results). The analysis would then measure whether the training program achieved the preset goals. To learn how KinderCare has used data analytics to turn a struggling organization into a high performer, see "Best Practices."

The analysis can take an economic approach that measures the dollar value of the program's costs and benefits. Successful programs should deliver value that is greater than the programs' costs. Costs include employees' compensation as well as the costs to administer HRM programs such as training, employee development, or satisfaction surveys. Benefits could include a reduction in the costs associated with employee absenteeism and turnover, as well as improved productivity associated with better selection and training programs.

In general, HR departments should be able to improve their performance through some combination of greater efficiency and greater effectiveness. Greater efficiency means the HR department uses fewer and less-costly resources to perform its functions. Greater effectiveness means that what the HR department does–for example, selecting employees or setting up a performance management system–has a more beneficial effect on employees' and the organization's performance. The computing power available to today's organizations, coupled with people who have skills in HR analytics, enables companies to find more ways than ever to identify practices associated with greater efficiency and effectiveness. For example, global information and measurement company Nielsen discovered that for every 1% decrease in employee attrition, the company could avoid nearly $5 million in business costs. Data analysis revealed that employee mobility within the organization was a key driver of retention. As a result, the company created an HR program to promote internal mobility, which enabled Nielsen to save more than $10 million in the first year of the program.[38]

A promising technique for HR analytics is *organizational network analysis,* which measures communication networks–that is, who is communicating with whom, and how often.[39] Patterns of communication can indicate, for example, which roles need to collaborate to complete projects, which is useful information for HR planning. The patterns also can show who seems to be a hub for a lot of the communication within or between work groups. These patterns might suggest needs for better knowledge-sharing systems or training. Or a person who is in many networks may be someone to consider for leadership development. If some employees or teams seem to be missing from most communication networks, the organization may need to investigate whether it needs to improve in areas such as onboarding, job design, or diversity and inclusion, among other possibilities. To carry out organizational network analysis, organizations collect data on the paths e-mail and instant messages follow, as well as posts on message boards or social-media sites. They may conduct surveys

Data Helps KinderCare Build Success

Every week, 170,000 families take their young children to a KinderCare facility for day care and education. The demand for these services is intense, but for several years, KinderCare was in a state of decline and posting losses. Rumors circulated that the company would declare bankruptcy. Someone needed to teach KinderCare's management how to perform better, and that person was Wei-Li Chong, hired in 2012 to be the executive vice president of people and operations—that is, the HR function—at the Portland, Oregon, headquarters.

Chong quickly began applying his HR experience in the retailing industry to the problems of building a high-performance child care organization. Every step of the way, he was guided by analytics and an appreciation of the key role played by the organization's teachers.

Chong hypothesized that success would be impossible unless KinderCare hired teachers who would deliver a high-quality experience to children and their families. He partnered with Gallup to interview hundreds of teachers and identify the qualities of the most effective ones. This process defined a set of characteristics, which became the basis of a new selection questionnaire. Not everyone was open minded about this direction from HR, so the department worked first with centers where administrators were interested, and soon those centers began showing an impact from better hiring decisions. Eventually the others came onboard.

KinderCare, under Chong and his successor (following Chong's promotion to president), extended the data-driven management to employee engagement. The company asked teachers and other employees what would make their jobs better. It implemented ideas such as a relaxed dress code, employee benefits including a program to make purchases at a discount, and improvements to the phone system teachers use to get support from headquarters. In addition, reflecting the higher quality of employees being hired, KinderCare increased the budget for compensation. Finally, it equipped the teachers with better resources—in particular, a revised curriculum based on research in early-childhood education. KinderCare evaluated the success of the new curriculum by measuring the progress of its kindergarten students relative to their peers in other educational settings.

KinderCare measured the impact on employees, the children and families served, and the organization's business performance. The percentage of engaged employees more than doubled, and employee turnover among teachers dropped. The kindergarten students outperformed their peers elsewhere. And for business measures, the company that had been declining saw growth higher than it ever had been, along with a return to profitability.

Questions

1. Based on the information given, list the outcomes KinderCare was trying to achieve.
2. What kinds of data did KinderCare use to set goals and measure performance?

Sources: "KinderCare Education Named 2019 Gallup Great Workplace for Third Consecutive Year," April 23, 2019, https://www.kc-education.com; Deborah Stadtler, "Case Study: Data Drives Bottom-Line Results," *HR People + Strategy,* May 1, 2018, https://blog.hrps.org; John Chandler, "HR Leadership Winner, Large Company Category: Kelsey Troy, KinderCare Education," *Portland (OR) Business Journal,* August 18, 2017, pp. 1, 22; Anna Marum, "KinderCare Uses Big Data to Turn Company Profitable," *Oregon Business News,* August 12, 2017, http://www.oregonlive.com.

asking employees whom they talk with to get various kinds of information and support. In some cases, they may use tracking devices to see who is near whom. For all of these sources of data, the investigation collects the paths of the messages, not their content, in order to protect employees' privacy.

HRM's potential to affect employees' well-being and the organization's performance makes human resource management an exciting field. As we have shown throughout the book, every HRM function calls for decisions that have the potential to help individuals and organizations achieve their goals. For HR managers to fulfill that potential, they must ensure that their decisions are well grounded. The field of human resource management provides tremendous opportunity to future researchers and managers who want to make a difference in many people's lives.

THINKING ETHICALLY

IS ANALYZING EMPLOYEE SENTIMENT AN INVASION OF PRIVACY?

As scientists and information technology experts develop more ways to gather data, questions arise about whether limits should define the kinds of data that are appropriate to gather and analyze. When it comes to employees' feelings, for example, is there an ethical limit to what organizations should know about them individually or as a group? Many people feel comfortable answering an anonymous survey, but what about collecting "data" in the form of the words people write to each other in e-mails, text messages, social-media posts, and online collaboration systems (which enable document sharing and group comments)?

Take the case of employee anxiety and depression, or even everyday stress at work. These conditions have obvious interest for employers, since an overly anxious or stressed-out employee could be more likely to have impaired judgment, take more time off, and run into problems getting along with customers or team members. If these conditions occur more often in certain parts of the company, management might want to investigate whether poor leadership or new work design is to blame. An organization could apply software that uses artificial intelligence to analyze workers' communications, first learning which patterns of words tend to be associated with conditions such as high stress and then identifying where these patterns are occurring.

Another issue involves the limitations of artificial intelligence. It can analyze straightforward messages, but so far, it does not always perform well at recognizing sarcasm. This would raise issues if the organization is trying to find sources of unhappiness, which might be when people tend to be more sarcastic.

The use of AI will continue to advance, and quite possibly, employees' attitudes toward sentiment analysis will depend on the culture of the organization. If employees view managers as ethical—trustworthy and fair—they are more likely to believe that the organization will keep its promises to protect privacy and use only anonymous data. They also might be more forgiving if the software misinterprets some kinds of messages. In a culture where managers have a reputation for punishing employees they dislike, trust will be low overall, and employees are likelier to see the data collection as an intrusion.

Questions

1. Suppose you work for an organization that is considering the use of software to analyze employee sentiment as the company rolls out a new set of work processes. How could the organization protect employees' right of free consent?
2. How could the organization address employees' right of privacy?

Sources: Samantha McLaren, "What Is Employee Sentiment Analysis and Why Does It Matter?" *People Doc,* October 10, 2019, https://www.people-doc.com; Roy Maurer, "Employee Sentiment Analysis Shows HR All the Feels," *Society for Human Resource Management,* August 20, 2019, https://www.shrm.org; Falon Fatemi, "How AI Can Drive Employee Engagement?" *Forbes,* July 5, 2019, https://www.forbes.com; Carolyn Axtell, "Big Data Could Bring about Workplace Utopia or the Office from Hell," *The Conversation,* January 4, 2018, https://theconversation.com.

SUMMARY

LO 9-1 Define high-performance work systems, and identify the elements of such a system.

- A high-performance work system is the right combination of people, technology, and organizational structure that makes full use of the organization's resources and opportunities in achieving its goals.
- The elements of a high-performance work system are organizational structure, task design, people, reward systems, and information systems. These elements must work together in a smoothly functioning whole.

LO 9-2 Summarize the outcomes of a high-performance work system.

- A high-performance work system achieves the organization's goals, typically including growth, productivity, profitability, and a strong reputation.
- On the way to achieving these overall goals, the high-performance work system meets such intermediate goals as high quality, innovation, customer satisfaction, job satisfaction, and reduced absenteeism and turnover.

LO 9-3 Describe the conditions that create a high-performance work system.

- Many conditions contribute to high-performance work systems by giving employees skills, incentives, knowledge, autonomy, and employee satisfaction.
- Teamwork and empowerment can make work more satisfying and provide a means for employees to improve quality and productivity.
- Organizations can improve performance by creating a learning organization in which people constantly

learn and share knowledge so that they continually expand their capacity to achieve the results they desire.
- In a high-performance organization, employees experience job satisfaction or even "occupational intimacy."
- For long-run high performance, organizations and employees must be ethical as well.

LO 9-4 Explain how human resource management can contribute to high performance.

- Jobs should be designed to foster teamwork and employee empowerment.
- Recruitment and selection should focus on obtaining employees who have the qualities necessary for teamwork, empowerment, and knowledge sharing.
- When the organization selects for teamwork and decision-making skills, it may have to provide training in specific job tasks. Training also is important because of its role in creating a learning organization.
- The performance management system should be related to the organization's goals, with a focus on meeting internal and external customers' needs.
- Compensation should include links to performance, and employees should be included in decisions about compensation.
- Research suggests that it is more effective to improve HRM practices as a whole than to focus on one or two isolated practices.

LO 9-5 Discuss the role of HRM technology in high-performance work systems.

- Technology can improve the efficiency of the human resource management functions and support knowledge sharing.
- HRM applications involve transaction processing, decision support systems, and expert systems.
- These often are part of a human resource information system using relational databases, which can improve the efficiency of routine tasks and the quality of decisions.
- With Internet technology such as cloud computing, organizations can use e-HRM to let all the organization's employees help themselves to the HR information they need whenever they need it.

LO 9-6 Summarize ways to measure the effectiveness of human resource management.

- Taking a customer-oriented approach, HRM can improve quality by defining the internal customers who use its services and determining whether it is meeting those customers' needs.
- One way to do this is with an HRM audit, a formal review of the outcomes of HRM functions. The audit may look at any measure associated with successful management of human resources. Audit information may come from the organization's documents and surveys of customer satisfaction.
- Another way to measure HRM effectiveness is to analyze specific programs or activities. HR analytics can measure success in terms of whether a program met its objectives and whether it delivered value in an economic sense, such as by leading to productivity improvements.
- Another promising technique for HR analytics is organizational network analysis, which measures communication networks—who is communicating with whom and how often. Patterns of communication can indicate, for example, which roles need to collaborate on projects or who seems to be the center of communication within and between work groups.

KEY TERMS

REVIEW AND DISCUSSION QUESTIONS

1. What is a high-performance work system? What are its elements? Which of these elements involve human resource management? *(LO 9-1)*
2. As it has become clear that HRM can help create and maintain high-performance work systems, it appears that organizations will need two kinds of human resource professionals. One kind focuses on identifying how HRM can contribute to high performance. The other kind develops expertise in particular HRM functions, such as how to administer a benefits program

that complies with legal requirements. Which aspect of HRM is more interesting to you? Why? *(LO 9-2)*

3. How can teamwork, empowerment, knowledge sharing, and job satisfaction contribute to high performance? *(LO 9-3)*
4. If an organization can win customers, employees, or investors through deception, why would ethical behavior contribute to high performance? *(LO 9-3)*
5. How can an organization promote ethical behavior among its employees? *(LO 9-3)*
6. Summarize how each of the following HR functions can contribute to high performance. *(LO 9-4)*
   a. Job design
   b. Recruitment and selection
   c. Training and development
   d. Performance management
   e. Compensation
7. How can HRM technology make a human resource department more productive? How can technology improve the quality of HRM decisions? *(LO 9-5)*
8. Why should human resource departments measure their effectiveness? What are some ways they can go about measuring effectiveness? *(LO 9-6)*

SELF-ASSESSMENT EXERCISE

How Ethical Are You?

Read each of the following descriptions. For each, circle whether you believe the behavior described is ethical or unethical.

1. A company president found that a competitor had made an important scientific discovery that would sharply reduce the profits of his own company. The president hired a key employee of the competitor in an attempt to learn the details of the discovery. — Ethical / Unethical
2. To increase profits, a general manager used a production process that exceeded legal limits for environmental pollution. — Ethical / Unethical
3. Because of pressure from her brokerage firm, a stockbroker recommended a type of bond that she did not consider to be a good investment. — Ethical / Unethical
4. A small business received one-fourth of its revenues in the form of cash. On the company's income tax forms, the owner reported only one-half of the cash receipts. — Ethical / Unethical
5. A corporate executive promoted a loyal friend and competent manager to the position of divisional vice president in preference to a better qualified manager with whom she had no close ties. — Ethical / Unethical
6. An employer received applications for a supervisor's position from two equally qualified applicants. The employer hired the male applicant because he thought some employees might resent being supervised by a female. — Ethical / Unethical
7. An engineer discovered what he perceived to be a product design flaw that constituted a safety hazard. His company declined to correct the flaw. The engineer decided to keep quiet, rather than taking his complaint outside the company. — Ethical / Unethical
8. A comptroller selected a legal method of financial reporting that concealed some embarrassing financial facts. Otherwise, those facts would have been public knowledge. — Ethical / Unethical
9. A company paid a $350,000 "consulting" fee to an official of a foreign country. In return, the official promised to help the company obtain a contract that should produce a $10 million profit for the company. — Ethical / Unethical
10. A member of a corporation's board of directors learned that her company intended to announce a stock split and increase its dividend. On the basis of this favorable information, the director bought additional shares of the company's stock. Following the announcement of the information, she sold the stock at a gain. — Ethical / Unethical

Now score your results. How many actions did you judge to be unethical?

All of these actions are unethical. The more of the actions you judged to be unethical, the better your understanding of ethical business behavior.

Source: Based on S. Morris et al., "A Test of Environmental, Situational, and Personal Influences on the Ethical Intentions of CEOs." *Business and Society* 34 (1995), pp. 119–147.

TAKING RESPONSIBILITY

Empowered Employees Achieve Excellence at Johnson Controls

Organizations as diverse as hospitals, schools, and factories turn to Johnson Controls to make their facilities safe and comfortable. Johnson Controls sells products and related technology and services to provide heating and cooling, humidity control, ventilation, and security in all kinds of buildings. To help customers meet their needs for energy consumption and cost control, the company's 105,000 employees must be constantly innovating and improving quality.

At the heart of Johnson Controls' success is its reliance on teamwork in manufacturing. The company's Norman, Oklahoma, facility is a case in point. At this location, 700 manufacturing employees produce equipment for heating, ventilation, and air conditioning (HVAC). They are assigned to 20-member high-performance teams, which meet once a week to evaluate and solve problems they have identified. For example, when a team noticed that coils in its products were being damaged, the team investigated the process and traced the problem to removing and replacing a screw on a panel. The simple solution was for the workers at an earlier manufacturing station to leave the screw loose, which ended up saving the company thousands of dollars. The high-performance teams also address safety issues. The company credits the continuous-improvement process in the Norman plant for a 25% increase in productivity, cost savings of $5 million, zero accidents, and a decline in product defects.

The factory in Norman also provides examples of knowledge sharing and information technology. The team meetings provide an ideal setting for ensuring that workers understand the company's values and performance. The company's information technology includes a manufacturing execution system, which provides up-to-the-minute data about inputs needed from inventory and progress against the schedule for whatever is production. Operators use scanners to track the movement of components and get information about what items will be made next.

While the systems in the Norman plant provide efficiency, other activities illustrate the level of agility possible when employees are empowered. When management observed the impact of the coronavirus epidemic on its plant in Wuhan, China, it began preparing for the impact on its U.S. operations, keeping in mind that one of its key customer groups is hospitals. The company appointed sales executive Lisa Roy to lead the response, and she set up projects to meet hospitals' needs for safe temporary environments to handle the surge in highly infectious patients. For example, the Army Corps of Engineers was building a hospital on Long Island, and Johnson Controls took on setting up its video surveillance system, nurse call system, fire alarms, and wireless network–a six-month project that would have to be completed in 20 days.

While the goal of saving lives is an obvious motivator, workers in Norman have their own sense of purpose, contributing to team goals and serving the company's mission to transform its customers' environments. Turnover during the move to teamwork has fallen, reaching less than 5% in a recent year–one more measure of Johnson Controls' high performance.

Questions

1. What elements of a high-performance work system are described here?
2. In what way does the use of teamwork contribute to high performance at Johnson Controls? How does the use of technology support teamwork?

Sources: Corporate website, "About Us" and "Careers," https://www.johnsoncontrols.com, accessed April 24, 2020; Bob Tita, "To Fight Coronavirus, a Johnson Controls Executive Urges Agility," *The Wall Street Journal,* April 13, 2020, https://www.wsj.com; John Hitch, "2018 IW Best Plants Winner: Johnson Controls Gives the OK to Empower Workers," *Industry Week,* March 12, 2019, https://www.industryweek.com.

MANAGING TALENT

How Adobe's People and Rewards Contribute to High Performance

Adobe Systems is probably best known as the company behind the software for creating and reading PDF documents. What users don't see when filling in a PDF form are the ingredients a company needs to succeed in the competitive, fast-changing software industry. And Adobe *is* succeeding, as measured by one-year revenue growth of 25% and profit growth of 45%.

One ingredient of that success is that Adobe designs and rewards work in ways that promote innovation. Adobe's vice president of innovation, Mark Randall, wanted to create "a whole culture of experimenting," so he equipped employees with a set of software tools called Kickbox, as well as the opportunity to participate in workshops on how to use it. Kickbox leads the user step by step through the process of creating and developing an idea. Any employee may use Kickbox on company time, so the company is in effect supporting projects without the bureaucracy of an approval process. Randall acknowledges that this means it is paying for some failed ideas, but he insists that failure "teaches people how to respond to what customers need or want." And as they learn, successes follow. An example of an innovation that emerged through this process is DeepFont, pattern recognition software that helps designers select the perfect type font for a project by analyzing photos of ideas.

Another ingredient is a set of practices for bringing loyal employees onboard, despite the demands of business growth (adding 4,000 employees per year) and the talent poaching that is rampant in the industry. Jeff Vijungco, Adobe's vice president of global talent, has a background in recruiting coupled with a passion for employee development. He combines the two perspectives to ensure that new employees quickly embark on a path to job success and career growth. Vijungco directed recruiters to check in with new employees periodically during their first few months and to work with the talent development team to ensure that talent needs are being filled and employees have the resources they need to meet their responsibilities. This coupling of recruitment and development supports Adobe's goal of creating a culture of learning.

As with recruiting and developing, Adobe crosses traditional boundaries to couple employee experience and customer experience. The executive team includes an executive vice president of customer and employee experience, Donna Morris. She not only measures both groups' engagement with the company, she identifies how highly engaged employees create highly engaged customers. This makes HR professionals focus on the business payoff of their work. Thus, they have identified performance measures for each employee that tie the employee's success to measures of customer satisfaction. And the company has set up the technology for employees to be able to listen directly to customers using the products the employees are involved with.

Questions

1. Would you consider Adobe a high-performance organization? Why or why not?
2. How do the practices described in this case relate to the principles of empowerment, knowledge sharing, and employee engagement?

Sources: Todd Kunsman, "The Brand Ambassador Role: How Adobe Maximizes Employee Advocacy," *Everyone Social,* December 17, 2019, https://everyone-social.com; Will Bunch, "Melding the Employee/Customer Experiences at Adobe," *Human Resource Executive,* July 30, 2018, https://www.hrexecutive.com; Denise Lee Yohn, "Fuse Customer Experience and Employee Experience to Drive Your Growth," *Forbes,* March 6, 2018, https://www.forbes.com; Sarah Fister Gale, "Creating a Recruitment Process That Sticks," *Chief Learning Officer,* May 2016, pp. 48–49; Anne Fisher, "How Adobe Sparks Innovation by Paying People to Fail," *Fortune,* April 5, 2016, http://fortune.com.

HR IN SMALL BUSINESS

Auto Dealers Sold on Employee Satisfaction

Auto dealerships have in recent years had difficulty maintaining a workforce of talented, engaged employees. Turnover rates at some dealerships are as high as 60% or more for salespeople and 50% for service staff. This is especially critical for these companies because people who can build satisfying relationships are central to the success of selling and servicing vehicles. People will not return to buy another car or have their car serviced if they don't trust the people they dealt with in the past. Intensifying the problem is competition from online car-shopping services. Successful dealerships are able to overcome the hurdles by building engagement through valuable, meaningful work.

High-performance dealerships look for ways to ensure that employees are empowered. At the Penske Automotive Group, executive vice president John Cragg realized that he was delegating assignments without actually empowering his people; that is, they had plenty of work to do but not necessarily the means to make a significant contribution. He began to work more closely with the HR department to identify how to give his employees developmental opportunities. Their satisfaction improved, and employee turnover declined. Mercedes-Benz of Raleigh, North Carolina, adds a weekly dose of empathetic leadership it calls Affirmation Friday. The employees start the day standing in a circle and make a positive statement of their own choosing; often, this includes expressions of appreciation for co-workers. Employees come to understand one another better, and they welcome the positive feedback they receive. The dealership's general manager, Bonnie Gramling, says employee retention rates are at an all-time high since the company instituted the program.

Empowerment works only insofar as employees have the skills needed to succeed. Therefore, dealers are increasingly considering the need for training. Audi Warwick in Rhode Island set up a "feeder system" akin to baseball's minor leagues. Entry-level employees get started doing routine tasks while they learn on the job from more experienced co-workers. As they gain skills, they move into their role in sales or service at higher pay. This process builds positive working relationships along with knowledge of sales and service. It also has lowered turnover to an industry-beating 20%.

Technology plays an essential role in improving performance at auto dealerships. For employees to compete with online competition, they need to have access to the technology their customers are using. Top-performing dealerships provide their employees with both the software and the training necessary to keep up in this area. For many employees, access to high-tech tools and the chance to stay on the leading edge of what's new is not only helpful but also makes work more interesting.

Questions

1. How does low employee turnover enable high performance at an auto dealership?
2. Briefly describe another way, besides the ones given, that human resource management could help make a dealership a high-performance organization. For ideas, you might consider the organizational conditions that contribute to high performance.

Sources: Sarah Kominek, "Affirmations Boost Morale and Retention," *Automotive News,* December 16, 2019, https://www.autonews.com; Jackie Charniga, "Feeder System Helps Dealership Grow Talent," *Automotive News,* December 9, 2019, https://www.autonews.com; Bradd Craver, Ethan Forchette, Christopher De Santis, and Ryan Robinson, *Changing Lanes on Talent in the Auto Retail Sector: Evolving from Customer to Human Experience,* Deloitte, July 31, 2019, https://www2.deloitte.com; Cox Automotive, "Younger Generations Could Provide Answer to Dealership Turnover Issue," news release, *PRNewswire,* July 23, 2019, https://www.prnewswire.com.

NOTES

1. ADP, "About Us," accessed April 21, 2020, https://www.adp.com; "Companies: ADP," Comparably, accessed April 21, 2020, https://www.comparably.com; "Fortune 500: ADP," *Fortune,* 2019, https://fortune.com; "How AI Can Help Redesign the Employee Experience," *Forbes,* November 29, 2018, https://www.forbes.com; Chip Cutter, "The Best-Managed Companies of 2019–and How They Got That Way," *The Wall Street Journal,* November 22, 2019, https://www.wsj.com.
2. S. Snell and J. Dean, "Integrated Manufacturing and Human Resource Management: A Human Capital Perspective," *Academy of Management "Journal* 35 (1992), pp. 467–504.
3. J. Zhang, M. N. Akhtar, P. M. Bal, Y. Zhang, and U. Talat, "How Do High-Performance Work Systems Affect Individual Outcomes: A Multilevel Perspective," *Frontiers in Psychology,* April 2018, https://frontiersin.org; J. Combs, Y. Liu, A. Hall, and D. Ketchen, "How Much Do High-Performance Work Practices Matter? A Meta-Analysis of Their Effects on Organizational Performance," *Personnel Psychology* 59 (2006), pp. 501–528.
4. C. Atiyeh and R. Blackwell, "Massive Takata Airbag Recall: Everything You Need to Know, Including Full List of Affected Vehicles," *Car and Driver,* February 21, 2020, https://www.caranddriver.com.
5. A. Gale and S. McLain, "Companies Everywhere Copied Japanese Manufacturing; Now the Model Is Cracking," *The Wall Street Journal,* February 4, 2018, https://www.wsj.com.
6. A. Camp, H. de la Boutetière, and G. Vadnai-Tolub, "Linking Employee Engagement to Customer Satisfaction at Starwood," *McKinsey & Company,* April 15, 2019, https://www.mckinsey.com; J. Cava and C. Fernandez, "Case Study: Starwood Hotels," *People + Strategy,* Fall 2017, pp. 32–36.
7. "Leading the Social Enterprise: Reinvent with a Human Focus," *2019 Deloitte Global Human Capital Trends,* https://www2.deloitte.com, accessed April 22, 2020; M. Schneider, "The 8 Keys to High-Performing Office Culture: The Best Employees Take Cues from Great Managers," *Inc.,* October 9, 2017, https://www.inc.com; M. Buckingham, "Leadership and Navigation: It's All About Teams," *HR Magazine,* December 2015, https://www.shrm.org.
8. "A People-Centric Approach to Widespread Success," *Fortune,* March 2020, p. 84.
9. D. Senge, "The Learning Organization Made Plain and Simple," *Training and Development Journal,* October 1991, pp. 37–44.
10. D. Grebow and S. J. Gill, "Engaging Managers to Support Continual Learning," *TD,* September 2017, pp. 76–77; M. Feffer, "Eight Tips for Creating a Learning Culture," *HR Magazine,* August 2017, pp. 51–54; M. A. Gephart, V. J. Marsick, M. E. Van Buren, and M. S. Spiro, "Learning Organizations Come Alive," *Training and Development* 50 (1996), pp. 34–45.
11. H. Burkett, "10 Characteristics of a Sustainable Learning Organization," *TD,* https://www.td.org, accessed April 22, 2020; D. Grebow and S. J. Gill, "Engaging Managers to Support Continual Learning," *TD,* September 2017, pp. 7677; M. Feffer, "Eight Tips for Creating a Learning Culture," *HR Magazine,* August 2017, pp. 51–54.
12. S. S. Janus, "Becoming a Knowledge-Sharing Organization," *World Bank Group,* https://openknowledge.worldbank.org, accessed April 22, 2020; T. T. Baldwin, C. Danielson, and W. Wiggenhorn, "The Evolution of Learning Strategies in Organizations: From Employee Development to Business Redefinition," *Academy of Management Executive* 11 (1997), pp. 47–58; J. J. Martocchio and T. T. Baldwin, "The Evolution of Strategic Organizational Training," in *Research in Personnel and Human Resource Management* 15, ed. G. R. Ferris (Greenwich, CT: JAI Press, 1997), pp. 1–46.
13. D. Belkin, "How to Prepare College Graduates for an AI World," *The Wall Street Journal,* February 19, 2018, https://www.wsj.com.
14. T. A. Judge, C. J. Thoresen, J. E. Bono, and G. K. Patton, "The Job Satisfaction-Job Performance Relationship: A Qualitative and Quantitative Review," *Psychological Bulletin* 127 (2001), pp. 376–407; R. A. Katzell, D. E. Thompson, and R. A. Guzzo, "How Job Satisfaction and Job Performance Are and Are Not Linked," in *Job Satisfaction,* eds. C. J. Cranny, P. C. Smith, and E. F. Stone (New York: Lexington Books, 1992), pp. 195–217.
15. J. Harter, "4 Factors Driving Record-High Employee Engagement in U.S.," *Gallup,* February 4, 2020, https://www.gallup.com.

16. Kincentric, "2019 Trends in Global Employment Engagement," https://www.kincentric.com, accessed April 22, 2020.
17. Forbes HR Council, "15 Effective Ways HR Can Help Create a Sustainable Company Culture," *Forbes,* https://www.forbes.com, accessed April 22, 2020; J. Faragher, "Why Do So Few Staff Feel Their Employer Lives Up to Its Brand?" *Personnel Today,* March 19, 2018, https://www.personneltoday.com; T. Maylett, "How Amazon Aligns Employee Experience and Business Results," *Entrepreneur,* April 14, 2017, https://www.entrepreneur.com.
18. P. E. Boverie and M. Kroth, *Transforming Work: The Five Keys to Achieving Trust, Commitment, and Passion in the Workplace* (Cambridge, MA: Perseus, 2001), pp. 71–72, 79.
19. R. P. Gephart Jr., "Introduction to the Brave New Workplace: Organizational Behavior in the Electronic Age," *Journal of Organizational Behavior* 23 (2002), pp. 327–344.
20. C. L. Hart, "Lies in the Workplace: The Effects of Honesty and Dishonesty on the Job," *Psychology Today,* July 29, 2019, https://www.psychologytoday.com; J. Levy, "Science Has Confirmed That Honest Really Is the Best Policy in the Workplace," *Entrepreneur,* April 13, 2018, https://www.entrepreneur.com.
21. Costco Wholesale Corporation, "Code of Ethics and Mission Statement," https://www.costco.com, accessed April 22, 2020; M. L. Stallard, "Whole Connections," *TD,* November 2017, pp. 52–56.
22. N. Epley and A. Kumar, "How to Design an Ethical Organization," *Harvard Business Review,* https://hbr.org, accessed April 22, 2020.
23. Baylor University, "Feelings of Ethical Superiority Can Lead to Workplace Ostracism, Social Undermining, Baylor Study Says," news release, April 24, 2018, https://www.baylor.edu.
24. R. Lawrence, "HR's Role in High-Performing Companies," *American Management Association,* January 24, 2019, https://www.amanet.org; G. Markova, "Can Human Resource Management Make a Big Difference in a Small Company?" *International Journal of Strategic Management* 9, no. 2 (2009), pp. 73–80.
25. B. Becker and M. A. Huselid, "High-Performance Work Systems and Firm Performance: A Synthesis of Research and Managerial Implications," in *Research in Personnel and Human Resource Management* 16, ed. G. R. Ferris (Stamford, CT: JAI Press, 1998), pp. 53–101.
26. B. Becker and B. Gerhart, "The Impact of Human Resource Management on Organizational Performance: Progress and Prospects," *Academy of Management Journal* 39 (1996), pp. 779–801.
27. M. Holleran, "Internet of Things Is Here: Are Your Field Workers Equipped with the Right Technology?" *Utility Products,* October 2017, https://www.utilityproducts.com.
28. H. J. Bernardin, C. M. Hagan, J. S. Kane, and P. Villanova, "Effective Performance Management: A Focus on Precision, Customers, and Situational Constraints," in *Performance Appraisal: State of the Art in Practice,* ed. J. W. Smither (San Francisco: Jossey-Bass, 1998), p. 56.
29. A. Gallo, "How to Discuss Pay with Your Employees," *Harvard Business Review,* https://hbr.org, accessed April 22, 2020; D. Wesley, "How Salary Transparency Empowers Employees–and When Not to Use It," *Entrepreneur,* November 9, 2016, https://www.entrepreneur.com.
30. J. Starkman, "HR Technology Trends That Can Empower Your Employees–and Your Business," *Business Journals,* May 10, 2019, https://www.bizjournals.com.
31. "You Can't Fit HR into One Product: Revisiting the 'Best of Breed' Debate," *Workforce,* August 2015, http://www.workforce.com; R. Broderick and J. W. Boudreau, "Human Resource Management, Information Technology, and the Competitive Edge," *Academy of Management Executive* 6 (1992), pp. 7–17.
32. J. Bersin, T. McDowell, A. Rahnema, and Y. van Durme, "The Organization of the Future: Arriving Now," in *Rewriting the Rules for the Digital Age: 2017 Deloitte Global Human Capital Trends* (Deloitte University Press, 2017), p. 23.
33. B. Marr, "Future of People Analytics: What Lies Ahead for Data-Driven HR?" *Forbes,* February 14, 2020, https://www.forbes.com; B. Petti, "Four Keys to Becoming a Data-Driven HR Leader," *Gallup Business Journal,* May 3, 2018, https://news.gallup.com.
34. J. Meister, "Ten HR Trends in the Age of Artificial Intelligence," *Forbes,* January 8, 2019, https://www.forbes.com; T. Bell, "Viewpoint: AI Says I Have a 12% Chance of Succeeding at My Job," *Society for Human Resource Management,* February 20, 2018, https://www.shrm.org; D. Zielinski, "Get Intelligent on AI," *HR Magazine,* November 2017, pp. 60–61.
35. "About Saberr," https://www.saberr.com, accessed April 24, 2020.
36. A. Loten, "Companies Devote Shrinking Tech Budgets to Cloud, AI," *The Wall Street Journal,* April 23, 2020, https://www.wsj.com.
37. E. Krell, "Auditing Your HR Department," *HR Magazine,* September 2011, https://www.shrm.org.
38. L. Schmidt and D. Green, "This Is Why Data Is Now More Essential Than Ever in HR," *Fast Company,* May 31, 2019, https://www.fastcompany.com.
39. "Organizational Network Analysis," https://www2.deloitte.com, accessed April 24, 2020; D. Green, "The Role of Organisational Network Analysis in People Analytics," *LinkedIn,* May 23, 2018, https://www.linkedin.com.

Managing Employees' Performance

10

Asking employees to provide insight about their supervisor's performance has helped Kronos provide managers with feedback to develop their leadership skills.

Juice Flair/Shutterstock

What Do I Need to Know?

After reading this chapter, you should be able to:

LO 10-1 Identify the activities involved in performance management.

LO 10-2 Discuss the purposes of performance management systems.

LO 10-3 Define five criteria for measuring the effectiveness of a performance management system.

LO 10-4 Compare the major methods for measuring performance.

LO 10-5 Describe major sources of performance information in terms of their advantages and disadvantages.

LO 10-6 Define types of rating errors, and explain how to minimize them.

LO 10-7 Explain how to provide performance feedback effectively.

LO 10-8 Summarize ways to produce improvement in unsatisfactory performance.

LO 10-9 Discuss legal and ethical issues that affect performance management.

Introduction

As a leading provider of workforce management software, Kronos is in a strong position to apply data analytics to its own employees and business performance. For years the company had been tracking employee engagement and found that its performance in that area had leveled off, with departments consistently performing far above or far below the company average. To see if it could improve, the HR team decided to focus on managers' leadership skills. They investigated the behaviors of managers in the highest- and lowest-performing areas of the company and compared these with management practices at highly admired companies. From this investigation, they came up with four measures of successful managers at Kronos: open and honest communication, encouragement of employee development, empowerment of employees, and holistic support of employees.

Next, the Kronos HR team wrote questions asking how well managers communicate, develop, empower, and support employees. They added these to the employee engagement survey, asking each employee to answer them with regard to his or her direct supervisor. Even the CEO was the subject of these questions. Communication about this upward feedback emphasized that the data would be used to help managers develop their leadership skills, not to reward or punish anyone.

Many managers found the results helpful. For example, a director in his first management position was surprised to learn that his employees did not find him available to talk. With guidance from HR, he addressed the concerns and dramatically improved his scores in the first year. Kronos CEO Chris Todd received ratings that his team wasn't having developmental discussions with him—something he hadn't considered that senior executives would even desire. Todd held one-on-one discussions and was surprised by how much he hadn't known about his direct reports. Overall, the company is reporting higher management engagement, better employee retention, and a decline in employee turnover since gathering this upward feedback.[1]

Performance Management
The process through which managers ensure that employees' activities and outputs contribute to the organization's goals.

Identifying desired behaviors and targets, and then measuring how well employees are carrying out the behaviors and hitting the targets are elements of performance management. **Performance management** is the process through which managers ensure that employees' activities and outputs contribute to the organization's goals. This process requires knowing what activities and outputs are desired, observing whether they occur, and providing feedback to help employees meet expectations. In the course of providing feedback, managers and employees may identify performance problems and establish ways to resolve those problems.

In this chapter we examine a variety of approaches to performance management. We begin by describing the activities involved in managing performance, then discuss the purpose of carrying out this process. Next, we discuss specific approaches to performance management, including the strengths and weaknesses of each approach. We also look at various sources of performance information. The next section explores the kinds of errors that commonly occur during the assessment of performance, as well as ways to reduce those errors. Then we describe ways of giving performance feedback effectively and intervening when performance must improve. Finally, we summarize legal and ethical issues affecting performance management.

LO 10-1 Identify the activities involved in performance management.

The Process of Performance Management

Many employees dread the annual performance appraisal meeting at which a boss picks apart the employee's behaviors from the past year. However, as we discussed in Chapter 9, performance management can potentially deliver many benefits—to individual employees as well as to the organization as a whole. Effective performance management can tell top performers they are valued, encourage communication between managers and their employees, establish consistent standards for evaluating employees, and help the organization identify its strongest and weakest employees. To meet these objectives, companies must think of effective performance management as a process, not an event.

Figure 10.1 shows the six steps in the performance management process. As shown in the model, feedback and formal performance evaluation are important parts of the process; however, they are not the only critical components. An effective performance management process contributes to the company's overall competitive advantage and must be given visible support by the CEO and other senior managers. This support ensures that the process is consistently used across the company, appraisals are completed on time, and giving and receiving ongoing performance feedback is recognized as an accepted part of the company's culture.

The first two steps of the process involve identifying what the company is trying to accomplish (its goals or objectives) and developing employee goals and actions to achieve these outcomes. Typically the outcomes benefit customers, the employee's peers or team members, and the organization itself. The goals, behaviors, and activities should be measurable and become part of the employee's job description.

Step 3 in the process—organizational support—involves providing employees with training, necessary resources and tools, and ongoing feedback between the employee and manager, which focuses on accomplishments as well as issues and challenges that influence performance. For effective performance management, both the manager and the employee have to value feedback and exchange it on a regular basis—not just once or twice a year. Also, the manager needs to make time to provide ongoing feedback to the employee and learn how to give and receive it.

FIGURE 10.1
Steps in the Performance Management Process

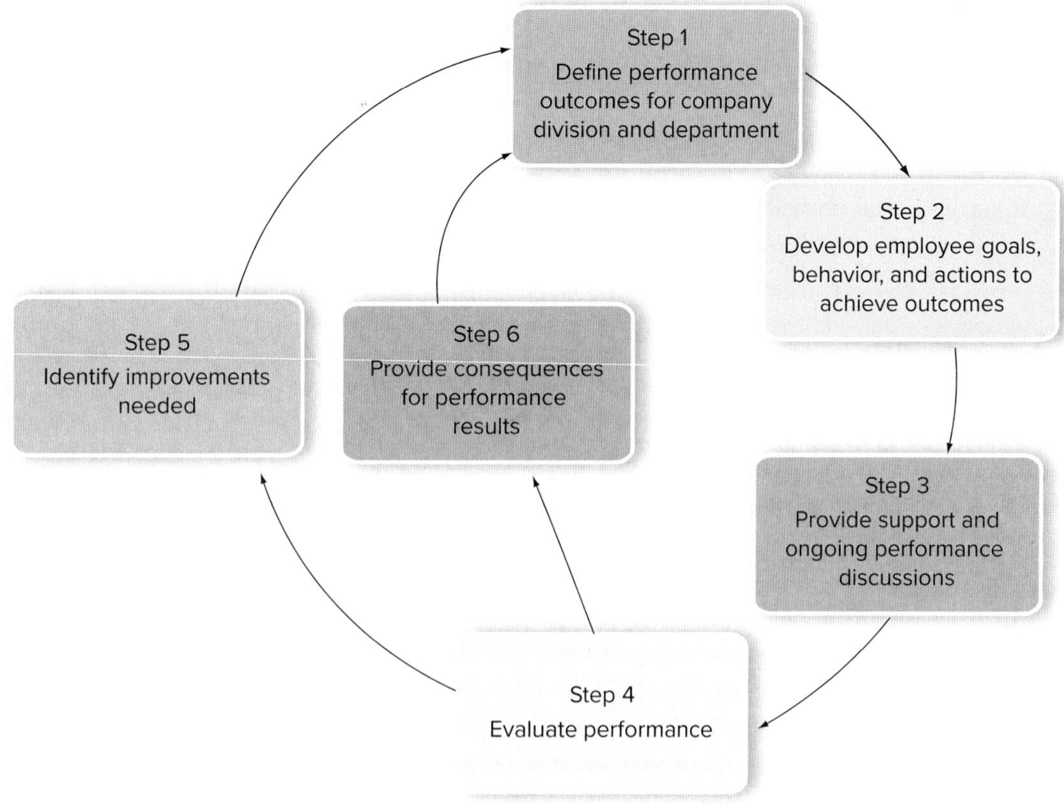

Sources: Based on E. Pulakos, *Performance Management* (Oxford: Wiley-Blackwell, 2009); H. Aguinis, "An Expanded View of Performance Management," in *Performance Management*, eds. J. W. Smith and M. London (San Francisco: Jossey-Bass, 2009), pp. 1–43; J. Russell and L. Russell, "Talk Me Through It: The Next Level of Performance Management," *T + D*, April 2010, pp. 42–48.

Step 4 involves evaluating performance: the manager and employee discuss and compare targeted goals and supporting behavior with actual results. This step includes the annual formal performance review.

The final steps of the performance management process involve both the employee and the manager identifying what the employee can do to capitalize on performance strengths and address weaknesses (step 5) and providing consequences for achieving (or failing to achieve) performance outcomes (such as pay increases, bonuses, or action plans) (step 6). This includes identifying training needs; adjusting the type or frequency of feedback the manager provides to the employee; clarifying, adjusting, or modifying performance outcomes; and discussing behaviors or activities that need improvement.

To be effective, the entire performance management process should be reviewed each year to ensure that what is being measured at the employee level aligns strategically with company, division, and departmental goals and objectives.[2]

Purposes of Performance Management

LO 10-2 Discuss the purposes of performance management systems.

Organizations establish performance management systems to meet three broad purposes: strategic, administrative, and developmental. As you read examples in the rest of this chapter

Best Practices

Real-Time Performance Management at Goldman Sachs

In the past, employees at Goldman Sachs, one of the world's leading investment and banking firms, could expect to be rated each year on a scale of 1 to 9. Perhaps it felt great to be a "9," but the number did not help them do much to improve their contribution to the organization or guide their career development. A low rating was just demoralizing—and typically a sign that one would be asked to leave. Making matters worse, the rating process involved closed-door discussions among managers, which could create a feeling that the scores were mysterious, even unfair. Furthermore, the company surveyed employees and learned that many wished they did not have to wait as long to learn how well they were doing. So a few years ago, Goldman set out to make its performance management more relevant to its strategy and its employees' ambitions.

The first change was to replace the scoring system with more specific feedback on what employees can do to improve their performance. In addition, the annual reviews, based on data from the employee's manager and several co-workers, were expanded to more frequent meetings between employees and their managers. The goal was for employees to improve their performance throughout the year, rather than waiting for an end-of-year grade.

Over the following months, Goldman made it easier to provide even more frequent feedback. It rolled out an in-house mobile app called Ongoing Feedback 360+, which lets an employee's manager and colleagues deliver informal feedback at any time. The idea is that when an employee completes a big transaction, presentation, or product launch, others can praise wins or offer ideas for doing better next time. The employee can view a summary of the year's feedback on a dashboard display.

Goldman's HR team sees the changes as a way to empower employees and create a high-performance work system where they will want to stay. The Ongoing Feedback app is intended to support this goal by promoting teamwork and a commitment to excellence.

Questions

1. How would it support the organization's strategy to give employees specific guidance in how to improve?
2. Which of the changes described here contribute to the developmental purpose of Goldman's performance management system?

Sources: Goldman Sachs, "Ongoing Feedback 360+: How It Works," https://www.goldmansachs.com, accessed April 24, 2020; "A New Era for Goldman Sachs and Performance Appraisals," *Impraise blog,* https://blog.impraise.com, accessed April 24, 2020; Julie Cook Ramirez, "The Future of Feedback," *Human Resource Executive,* March 15, 2018, https://hrexecutive.com; Liz Hoffman, "Goldman Goes beyond Annual Review with Real-Time Employee Feedback," *The Wall Street Journal,* April 21, 2017, https://www.wsj.com.

and in the "Best Practices" box, think about which purposes of performance management the companies and managers are or should be meeting.

The *strategic purpose* of effective performance management is to help the organization achieve its business objectives. It does this by helping to link employees' behavior with the organization's goals. Performance management starts with defining what the organization expects from each employee. It measures each employee's performance to identify where those expectations are and are not being met. This enables the organization to take corrective action, such as training, incentives, or discipline. Performance management can achieve its strategic purpose only when measurements are truly linked to the organization's goals and when the goals and feedback about performance are communicated to employees. A Scandinavian insurance company addressed productivity problems by improving how its performance management system served its strategy. The company brought together managers at all levels to define what improvements were needed and set performance measures for making those improvements. It obtained employee feedback on whether the performance measures were relevant, and it established weekly meetings with team leaders to ensure the targets continue to be appropriate for business conditions. With these changes, the company saw a substantial improvement in productivity.[3]

The *administrative purpose* of a performance management system refers to the ways in which organizations use the system to provide information for day-to-day decisions about salary, benefits, and recognition programs. Performance management can also support decision making related to employee retention, termination for poor behavior, and hiring or layoffs. Because performance management supports these administrative decisions, the information in a performance appraisal can have a great impact on the future of individual employees. Managers recognize this, which is the reason they may feel uncomfortable conducting performance appraisals when the appraisal information is negative and, therefore, likely to lead to a layoff, disappointing pay increase, or other negative outcome.

Finally, performance management has a *developmental purpose:* it serves as a basis for developing employees' knowledge and skills. Even employees who are meeting expectations can become more valuable when they hear and discuss performance feedback. Effective performance feedback makes employees aware of their strengths and of the areas in which they can improve. GE, which once was known for performance management systems that emphasized sorting the high from the low achievers, has been placing more emphasis on the developmental purpose of performance management. Employees seek input from their customers and use it to set goals. Managers are charged with inspiring and empowering their people, rather than simply rating them.[4]

Criteria for Effective Performance Management

LO 10-3 Define five criteria for measuring the effectiveness of a performance management system.

In Chapter 6 we saw that there are many ways to predict performance of a job candidate. Similarly, there are many ways to measure the performance of an employee. For performance management to achieve its goals, its methods for measuring performance must be good. Selecting these measures is a critical part of planning a performance management system. Several criteria determine the effectiveness of performance measures:

- *Fit with strategy*–A performance management system should aim at achieving employee behavior and attitudes that support the organization's strategy, goals, and culture. If a company emphasizes customer service, then its performance management system should define the kinds of behavior that contribute to good customer service. Performance appraisals should measure whether employees are engaging in those behaviors. Feedback should help employees improve in those areas. When an organization's strategy changes, human resource personnel should help managers assess how the performance management system should change to serve the new strategy.
- *Validity*–As we discussed in Chapter 6, *validity* is the extent to which a measurement tool actually measures what it is intended to measure. In the case of performance appraisal, validity refers to whether the appraisal measures all the relevant aspects of performance and omits irrelevant aspects of performance. Figure 10.2 shows two sets of information. The circle on the left represents all the information in a performance appraisal; the circle on the right represents all relevant measures of job performance. The overlap of the circles contains the valid information. Information that is gathered but irrelevant is "contamination." Comparing salespeople based on how many calls they make to customers could be a contaminated measure. Making a lot of calls does not necessarily improve sales or customer satisfaction, unless every salesperson makes only well-planned calls. Information that is not gathered but is relevant represents a deficiency of the performance measure. For example, suppose a company measures whether employees have good attendance records but not whether they work efficiently. This limited performance appraisal is unlikely to provide a full picture of employees' contribution to the company. Performance measures should minimize both contamination and deficiency.

FIGURE 10.2
Contamination and Deficiency of a Job Performance Measure

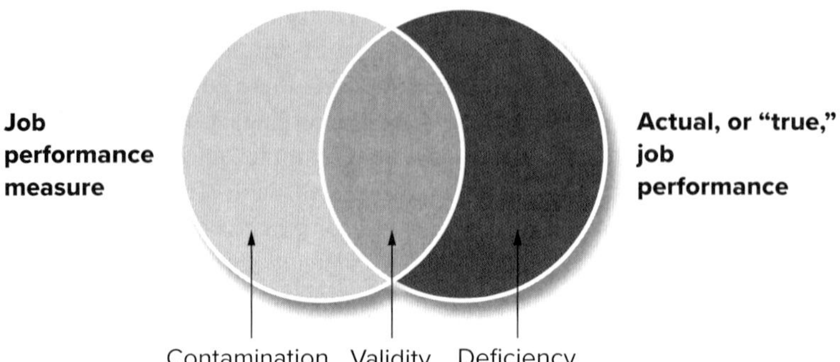

- *Reliability*—With regard to a performance measure, reliability describes the consistency of the results that the performance measure will deliver. *Interrater reliability* is consistency of results when more than one person measures performance. Simply asking a supervisor to rate an employee's performance on a scale of 1 to 5 would likely have low interrater reliability; the rating will differ depending on who is scoring the employees. *Test-retest reliability* refers to consistency of results over time. If a performance measure lacks test-retest reliability, determining whether an employee's performance has truly changed over time will be impossible.
- *Acceptability*—Whether or not a measure is valid and reliable, it must meet the practical standard of being acceptable to the people who use it. The users include the employee's supervisor and anyone else who measures the employee's performance. They also include the employee being evaluated. For example, the people who use a performance measure must believe that it is not too time consuming. Likewise, if employees being evaluated believe the measure is unfair, they will not use the feedback as a basis for improving their performance. In general, employees are likelier to see feedback as fair, and therefore acceptable, if it compares their recent performance with their earlier performance, rather than ratings that compare the performance of co-workers. When employees are compared with co-workers, they tend to doubt that the ratings take full account of the specifics of their performance.[5]
- *Specific feedback*—A performance measure should specifically tell employees what is expected of them and how they can meet those expectations. Being specific helps performance management meet the goals of supporting strategy and developing employees. If a measure does not specify what an employee must do to help the organization achieve its goals, it does not support the strategy. If the measure fails to point out employees' performance problems, they will not know how to improve.

In recent years, managers have expressed increasing frustration with performance management systems not meeting these criteria. They have complained that measurements don't help them distinguish between high and low performers or help them improve performance. Some even call the systems abusive or counterproductive. Some talk about "blowing up" the system. However, it is important to keep in mind that eliminating performance reviews altogether is associated with lower-quality feedback and declining employee engagement. Furthermore, companies that say they are "blowing up" performance appraisal actually tend to be modifying the system, not eliminating it. The "Did You Know?" feature describes some common modifications. The ideal response is to learn what methods of performance management are effective and to apply those lessons.[6]

Did You Know?

Reviews Are Getting Shorter and More Frequent

In an OfficeTeam survey of more than 300 HR managers in the United States, about half said they had updated their performance appraisal process in the past two years. Over one-third said they had shortened the process or increased the frequency of giving feedback to employees. In the survey, 40% of respondents said they conduct formal appraisals once a year, but almost as many (38%) do so two to four times per year. In contrast, a similar survey conducted four years earlier found that barely a quarter (27%) held performance appraisals more than once a year.

These changes are in keeping with the idea of ensuring that employees get feedback in a timely fashion, so they can improve their performance. If employees wait a year for feedback, they more often will be surprised with what they hear. When appraisal sessions bring surprises, employees are less likely to feel that the process is fair, and the organization has to wait longer to see improvement.

Question

Which interview process would you expect to be more effective—a lengthy review once a year or four brief reviews spread three months apart? Why?

Sources: Elizabeth Uviebinene, "Annual Performance Reviews Do a Disservice to Workers and Firms," *Financial Times,* November 28, 2019, https://www.ft.com; Eliza Blanchard, "Reevaluating Employee Evaluations," *TD,* March 2019, https://www.td.org; Cynthia Kong, "Time to Review the Performance Review?" *Robert Half,* December 12, 2018, https://www.roberthalf.com.

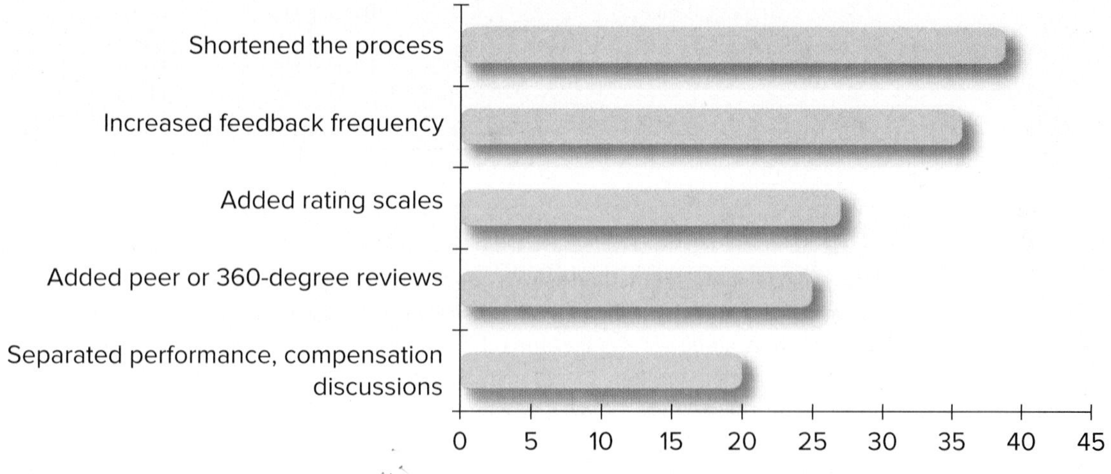

Methods for Measuring Performance

LO 10-4 Compare the major methods for measuring performance.

Organizations have developed a wide variety of methods for measuring performance. Some methods rank each employee to compare employees' performance. Other methods break down the evaluation into ratings of individual attributes, behaviors, or results. Many organizations use a measurement system that includes a variety of the preceding measures, as in the case of applying total quality management to performance management. Table 10.1 compares these methods in terms of our criteria for effective performance management.

TABLE 10.1

Basic Approaches to Performance Measurement

	CRITERIA				
APPROACH	FIT WITH STRATEGY	VALIDITY	RELIABILITY	ACCEPTABILITY	FEEDBACK SPECIFICITY
Comparative	Poor, unless manager takes time to make link	Can be high if ratings are done carefully	Depends on rater, but usually no measure of agreement used	Moderate; easy to develop and use but resistant to normative standard	Very low
Attribute	Usually low; requires manager to make link	Usually low; can be fine if developed carefully	Usually low; can be improved by specific definitions of attributes	High; easy to develop and use	Very low
Behavioral	Can be quite high	Usually high; minimizes contamination and deficiency	Usually high	Moderate; difficult to develop, but accepted well for use	Very high
Results	Very high	Usually high; can be both contaminated and deficient	High; main problem can be test–retest—depends on timing of measure	High; usually developed with input from those to be evaluated	High regarding results, but low regarding behaviors necessary to achieve them
Quality	Very high	High, but can be both contaminated and deficient	High	High; usually developed with input from those to be evaluated	High regarding results, but low regarding behaviors necessary to achieve them

Making Comparisons

The performance appraisal method may require the rater to compare one individual's performance with that of others. This method involves some form of ranking, in which some employees are best, some are average, and others are worst. The usual techniques for making comparisons are simple ranking, forced distribution, and paired comparison.

Simple Ranking
Method of performance measurement that requires managers to rank employees in their group from the highest performer to the poorest performer.

Simple ranking requires managers to rank employees in their group from the highest performer to the poorest performer. In a variation of this approach, *alternation ranking,* the manager works from a list of employees. First, the manager decides which employee is best and crosses that person's name off the list. From the remaining names, the manager selects the worst employee and crosses off that name. The process continues with the manager selecting the second best, second worst, third best, and so on, until all the employees have been ranked. The major downside of ranking involves validity. To state a performance measure as broadly as "best" or "worst" doesn't define what exactly is good or bad about the person's contribution to the organization. Ranking therefore raises questions about fairness.

Forced-Distribution Method
Method of performance measurement that assigns a certain percentage of employees to each category in a set of categories.

Another way to compare employees' performance is with the **forced-distribution method.** This type of performance measurement assigns a certain percentage of employees to each category in a set of categories. For example, the organization might establish the following percentages and categories:

- Exceptional–5%
- Exceeds standards–25%

- Meets standards–55%
- Room for improvement–10%
- Not acceptable–5%

The manager completing the performance appraisal would rate 5% of his or her employees as exceptional, 25% as exceeding standards, and so on. A forced-distribution approach works best if the members of a group really do vary this much in terms of their performance. It overcomes the temptation to rate everyone high in order to avoid conflict. Research simulating some features of forced rankings found that they improved performance when combined with goals and rewards, especially in the first few years, when the system eliminated the poorest performers.[7] However, a manager who does very well at selecting, motivating, and training employees will have a group of high performers. This manager would have difficulty assigning employees to the bottom categories. In that situation, saying that some employees require improvement or are "not acceptable" not only will be inaccurate, but will hurt morale.

Another variation on rankings is the **paired-comparison method.** This approach involves comparing each employee with each other employee to establish rankings. Suppose a manager has five employees, Allen, Barbara, Caitlin, David, and Edgar. The manager compares Allen's performance to Barbara's and assigns one point to whichever employee is the higher performer. Then the manager compares Allen's performance to Caitlin's, then to David's, and finally to Edgar's. The manager repeats this process with Barbara, comparing her performance to Caitlin's, David's, and Edgar's. When the manager has compared every pair of employees, the manager counts the number of points for each employee. The employee with the most points is considered the top-ranked employee. Clearly, this method is time consuming if a group has more than a handful of employees. For a group of 15, the manager must make 105 comparisons.

Paired-Comparison Method
Method of performance measurement that compares each employee with each other employee to establish rankings.

In spite of the drawbacks, ranking employees offers some benefits. It counteracts the tendency to avoid controversy by rating everyone favorably or near the center of the scale. Also, if some managers tend to evaluate behavior more strictly (or more leniently) than others, a ranking system can erase that tendency from performance scores. Therefore, ranking systems can be useful for supporting decisions about how to distribute pay raises or layoffs. Some ranking systems are easy to use, which makes them acceptable to the managers who use them. A major drawback of rankings is that they often are not linked to the organization's goals. Also, a simple ranking system leaves the basis for the ranking open to interpretation. In that case, the rankings are not helpful for employee development and may hurt morale or result in legal challenges.

Rating Individuals

Instead of focusing on arranging a group of employees from best to worst, performance measurement can look at each employee's performance relative to a uniform set of standards. The measurement may evaluate employees in terms of attributes (characteristics or traits) believed desirable. Or the measurements may identify whether employees have *behaved* in desirable ways, such as closing sales or completing assignments. For both approaches, the performance management system must identify the desired attributes or behaviors, then provide a form on which the manager can rate the employee in terms of those attributes or behaviors. Typically, the form includes a rating scale, such as a scale from 1 to 5, where 1 is the worst performance and 5 is the best.

Graphic Rating Scale
Method of performance measurement that lists traits and provides a rating scale for each trait; the employer uses the scale to indicate the extent to which an employee displays each trait.

Rating Attributes

The most widely used method for rating attributes is the **graphic rating scale.** This method lists traits and provides a rating scale for each trait. The employer uses the scale to indicate the extent to which the employee being rated displays the traits.

Mc Graw Hill connect

Visit your instructor's Connect® course and access your eBook to view this video.

"Overwhelmingly, our people said, 'We want ratings. We don't want you to eliminate ratings [in performance assessments], we think it's important to know where we stand.'"

—Mirian M. Graddick-Weir
Executive Vice President, Human Resources, Merck

Source: Video Produced for the Center for Executive Succession in the Darla Moore School of Business at the University of South Carolina by Coal Powered Filmworks

The rating scale may provide points to circle (as on a scale going from 1 for poor to 5 for excellent), or it may provide a line representing a range of scores, with the manager marking a place along the line. Figure 10.3 shows an example of a graphic rating scale that uses a set of ratings from 1 to 5. A drawback of this approach is that it leaves to the particular manager the decisions about what is "excellent knowledge" or "commendable judgment" or "poor interpersonal skills." The result is low reliability because managers are likely to arrive at different judgments.

To get around this problem, some organizations use **mixed-standard scales,** which use several statements describing each trait to produce a final score for that trait. The manager scores the employee in terms of how the employee compares to each statement. Consider the sample mixed-standard scale in Figure 10.4. To create this scale, the organization determined that the relevant traits are initiative, intelligence, and relations with others. For each trait, sentences were written to describe a person having a high level of that trait, a medium level, and a low level. The sentences for the traits were rearranged so that the nine statements about the three traits are mixed together. The manager who uses this scale reads each sentence, then indicates whether the employee performs above (+), at (0), or below (−) the level described. The key in the middle section of Figure 10.4 tells how to use the pluses, zeros, and minuses to score performance. Someone who excels at every level of performance (pluses for high, medium, and low performance) receives a score of 7 for that trait. Someone who fails to live up to every description of performance (minuses for high, medium, and low) receives a score of 1 for that trait. The bottom of Figure 10.4 calculates the scores for the ratings used in this example.

Mixed-Standard Scales
Method of performance measurement that uses several statements describing each trait to produce a final score for that trait.

FIGURE 10.3
Example of a Graphic Rating Scale

The following areas of performance are significant to most positions. Indicate your assessment of performance on each dimension by circling the appropriate rating.

PERFORMANCE DIMENSION	RATING				
	DISTINGUISHED	EXCELLENT	COMMENDABLE	ADEQUATE	POOR
Knowledge	5	4	3	2	1
Communication	5	4	3	2	1
Judgment	5	4	3	2	1
Managerial skill	5	4	3	2	1
Quality performance	5	4	3	2	1
Teamwork	5	4	3	2	1
Interpersonal skills	5	4	3	2	1
Initiative	5	4	3	2	1
Creativity	5	4	3	2	1
Problem solving	5	4	3	2	1

FIGURE 10.4
Example of a Mixed-Standard Scale

Three traits being assessed:	**Levels of performance in statements:**
Initiative (INTV)	High (H)
Intelligence (INTG)	Medium (M)
Relations with others (RWO)	Low (L)

Instructions: Please indicate next to each statement whether the employee's performance is above (+), equal to (0), or below (−) the statement.

INTV	H	1. This employee is a real self-starter. The employee always takes the initiative and his/her superior never has to prod this individual.	+
INTG	M	2. While perhaps this employee is not a genius, s/he is a lot more intelligent than many people I know.	+
RWO	L	3. This employee has a tendency to get into unnecessary conflicts with other people.	0
INTV	M	4. While generally this employee shows initiative, occasionally his/her superior must prod him/her to complete work.	+
INTG	L	5. Although this employee is slower than some in understanding things, and may take a bit longer in learning new things, s/he is of average intelligence.	+
RWO	H	6. This employee is on good terms with everyone. S/he can get along with people even when s/he does not agree with them.	−
INTV	L	7. This employee has a bit of a tendency to sit around and wait for directions.	+
INTG	H	8. This employee is extremely intelligent, and s/he learns very rapidly.	−
RWO	M	9. This employee gets along with most people. Only very occasionally does s/he have conflicts with others on the job, and these are likely to be minor.	−

Scoring Key:

	STATEMENTS			SCORE
	HIGH	MEDIUM	LOW	
	+	+	+	7
	0	+	+	6
	−	+	+	5
	−	0	+	4
	−	−	+	3
	−	−	0	2
	−	−	−	1

Example score from preceding ratings:

	STATEMENTS			SCORE
	HIGH	MEDIUM	LOW	
Initiative	+	+	+	7
Intelligence	0	+	+	6
Relations with others	−	−	0	2

Rating attributes is the most popular way to measure performance in organizations. In general, attribute-based performance methods are easy to develop and can be applied to a wide variety of jobs and organizations. If the organization is careful to identify which attributes are associated with high performance, and to define them carefully on the appraisal form, these methods can be reliable and valid. However, appraisal forms often fail to meet this standard. In addition, measurement of attributes is rarely linked to the organization's strategy. Furthermore, employees tend, perhaps rightly, to be defensive about receiving a mere numerical rating on some attribute. How would you feel if you were told you scored 2 on a 5-point scale of initiative or communication skill? The number might seem arbitrary, and it doesn't tell you how to improve.

Rating Behaviors One way to overcome the drawbacks of rating attributes is to measure employees' behavior. To rate behaviors, the organization begins by defining which behaviors are associated with success on the job. Which kinds of employee behavior help the organization achieve its goals? The appraisal form asks the manager to rate an employee in terms of each of the identified behaviors.

Critical-Incident Method
Method of performance measurement based on managers' records of specific examples of the employee acting in ways that are either effective or ineffective.

One way to rate behaviors is with the **critical-incident method.** This approach requires managers to keep a record of specific examples of the employee acting in ways that are either effective or ineffective. Here's an example of a critical incident in the performance evaluation of an appliance repair person:

> A customer called in about a refrigerator that was not cooling and was making a clicking noise every few minutes. The technician prediagnosed the cause of the problem and checked his truck for the necessary parts. When he found he did not have them, he checked the parts out from inventory so that the customer's refrigerator would be repaired on his first visit and the customer would be satisfied promptly.

This incident provides evidence of the employee's knowledge of refrigerator repair and concern for efficiency and customer satisfaction. Evaluating performance in this specific way gives employees feedback about what they do well and what they do poorly. The manager can also relate the incidents to how the employee is helping the company achieve its goals. Keeping a daily or weekly log of critical incidents requires significant effort, however, and managers may resist this requirement. Also, critical incidents may be unique, so they may not support comparisons among employees.

Behaviorally Anchored Rating Scale (BARS)
Method of performance measurement that rates behavior in terms of a scale showing specific statements of behavior that describe different levels of performance.

A **behaviorally anchored rating scale (BARS)** builds on the critical-incidents approach. The BARS method is intended to define performance dimensions specifically using statements of behavior that describe different levels of performance.[8] (The statements are "anchors" of the performance levels.) For example, consider the various levels of behavior associated with a patrol officer preparing for duty. The highest rating on the 7-point scale could include the following behaviors: early to work; gathers all necessary equipment needed for work; and previews previous shift's activities and any news/updates before roll call. The lowest statement on the scale (rating 1) describes behavior associated with poor performance (e.g., late for roll call; does not check equipment; and not prepared for shift activities). These statements are based on data about past performance. The organization gathers many critical incidents representing effective and ineffective performance, then classifies them from most to least effective. When experts about the job agree the statements clearly represent levels of performance, they are used as anchors to guide the rater. Although BARS can improve interrater reliability, this method can bias the manager's memory. The statements used as anchors can help managers remember similar behaviors, at the expense of other critical incidents.[9]

Behavioral Observation Scale (BOS)
A variation of a BARS which uses all behaviors necessary for effective performance to rate performance at a task.

A **behavioral observation scale (BOS)** is a variation of a BARS. Like a BARS, a BOS is developed from critical incidents.[10] However, whereas a BARS discards many examples in creating the rating scale, a BOS uses many of them to define all behaviors necessary for effective performance (or behaviors that signal ineffective performance). As a result, a BOS may use 15 behaviors to define levels of performance. Also, a BOS asks the manager to rate the frequency with which the employee has exhibited the behavior during the rating period. These ratings are averaged to compute an overall performance rating. Figure 10.5 provides a simplified example of a BOS for measuring the behavior "overcoming resistance to change."

FIGURE 10.5

Example of a Behavioral Observation Scale

Overcoming Resistance to Change

Directions: Rate the frequency of each behavior from 1 (Almost Never) to 5 (Almost Always).

	Almost Never				Almost Always
1. Describes the details of the change to employees.	1	2	3	4	5
2. Explains why the change is necessary.	1	2	3	4	5
3. Discusses how the change will affect the employee.	1	2	3	4	5
4. Listens to the employee's concerns.	1	2	3	4	5
5. Asks the employee for help in making the change work.	1	2	3	4	5
6. If necessary, specifies the date for a follow-up meeting to respond to the employee's concerns.	1	2	3	4	5

Score: Total number of points = ____________________

Performance

Points	*Performance Rating*
6–10	Below adequate
11–15	Adequate
16–20	Full
21–25	Excellent
26–30	Superior

Scores are set by management.

A major drawback of this method is the amount of information required. A BOS can have 80 or more behaviors, and the manager must remember how often the employee exhibited each behavior in a 6- to 12-month rating period. This is taxing enough for one employee, but managers often must rate 10 or more employees. Even so, compared to BARS and graphic rating scales, managers and employees have said they prefer BOS for ease of use, providing feedback, maintaining objectivity, and suggesting training needs.[11]

Another approach to assessment builds directly on a branch of psychology called *behaviorism,* which holds that individuals' future behavior is determined by their past experiences—specifically, the ways in which past behaviors have been reinforced. People tend to repeat behaviors that have been rewarded in the past. Providing feedback and reinforcement can therefore modify individuals' future behavior. Applied to behavior in organizations, **organizational behavior modification (OBM)** is a plan for managing the behavior of employees through a formal system of feedback and reinforcement. Specific OBM techniques vary, but most have four components:[12]

Organizational Behavior Modification (OBM)
A plan for managing the behavior of employees through a formal system of feedback and reinforcement.

1. Define a set of key behaviors necessary for job performance.
2. Use a measurement system to assess whether the employee exhibits the key behaviors.
3. Inform employees of the key behaviors, perhaps in terms of goals for how often to exhibit the behaviors.
4. Provide feedback and reinforcement based on employees' behavior.

OBM techniques have been used in a variety of settings. For example, a community mental health agency used OBM to increase the rates and timeliness of critical job behaviors by showing employees the connection between job behaviors and the agency's accomplishments.[13] This process identified job behaviors related to administration, record keeping, and service provided to clients. Feedback and reinforcement improved staff performance. OBM also increased the frequency of safety behaviors in a processing plant.[14]

Behavioral approaches such as organizational behavior modification and rating scales can be very effective. These methods can link the company's goals to the specific behavior required to achieve those goals. Behavioral methods also can generate specific feedback, along with guidance in areas requiring improvements. As a result, these methods tend to be valid. The people to be measured often help in developing the measures, so acceptance tends to be high as well. When raters are well trained, reliability also tends to be high. However, behavioral methods do not work as well for complex jobs in which it is difficult to see a link between behavior and results or there is more than one good way to achieve success. For example, women studied in high-tech and professional-services firms tended to get feedback emphasizing how they communicate. This could be relevant in light of research where peers (male and female) judged women harshly when they spoke forcefully.[15] But focusing on communication style overlooks the value of the communicator's messages. Does the problem behavior in communication breakdowns lie with the speaker, the hearers, or both?

Measuring Results

Performance measurement can focus on managing the objective, measurable results of a job or work group. Results might include sales, costs, or productivity (output per worker or per dollar spent on production), among many possible measures. Two of the most popular methods for measuring results are measurement of productivity and management by objectives.

Productivity is an important measure of success because getting more done with a smaller amount of resources (money or people) increases the company's profits. Productivity usually refers to the output of production workers, but it can be used more generally as a performance measure. To do this, the organization identifies the products–set of activities or objectives–it expects a group or individual to accomplish. At a repair shop, for instance, a product might be something like "quality of repair." The next step is to define how to measure production of these products. For quality of repair, the repair shop could track the percentage of items returned because they still do not work after a repair and the percentage of quality-control inspections passed. For each measure, the organization decides what level of performance is desired. Finally, the organization sets up a system for tracking these measures and giving employees feedback about their performance in terms of these measures. This type of performance measurement can be time consuming to set up, but research suggests it can improve productivity.[16]

Management by Objectives (MBO)
A system in which people at each level of the organization set goals in a process that flows from top to bottom, so employees at all levels are contributing to the organization's overall goals; these goals become the standards for evaluating each employee's performance.

Management by objectives (MBO) is a system in which people at each level of the organization set goals in a process that flows from top to bottom, so employees at all levels are contributing to the organization's overall goals. These goals become the standards for evaluating each employee's performance. An MBO system has three components:[17]

1. Goals are specific, difficult, and objective. The goals listed in the second column of Table 10.2 provide two examples for a bank.
2. Managers and their employees work together to set the goals.
3. The manager gives objective feedback through the rating period to monitor progress toward the goals. The two right-hand columns in Table 10.2 are examples of feedback given after one year.

TABLE 10.2

Management by Objectives: Two Objectives for a Bank

KEY RESULT AREA	OBJECTIVE	% COMPLETE	ACTUAL PERFORMANCE
Loan portfolio management	Increase portfolio value by 10% over the next 12 months	90	Increased portfolio value by 9% over the past 12 months
Sales	Generate fee income of $30,000 over the next 12 months	150	Generated fee income of $45,000 over the past 12 months

MBO can have a very positive effect on an organization's performance. In 70 studies of MBO's performance, 68 showed that productivity improved.[18] The productivity gains tended to be greatest when top management was highly committed to MBO. Also, because staff members are involved in setting goals, it is likely that MBO systems effectively link individual employees' performance with the organization's overall goals.

In general, evaluation of results can be less subjective than other kinds of performance measurement. This makes measuring results highly acceptable to employees and managers alike. Results-oriented performance measurement is also relatively easy to link to the organization's goals. However, measuring results has problems with validity because results may be affected by circumstances beyond each employee's performance. Also, if the organization measures only final results, it may fail to measure significant aspects of performance that are not directly related to those results. If individuals focus only on aspects of performance that are measured, they may neglect significant skills or behaviors. For example, one company measured how well employees in the purchasing department kept costs down and how efficiently people in the manufacturing department made its products. When the purchasing department kept its costs under control by ordering cheap materials, production slowed down, making overall costs higher–but the purchasing manager earned a bonus for high performance.[19] A final limitation of evaluation based on results is that these measures do not provide guidance on how to improve.

Total Quality Management

The principles of *total quality management,* introduced in Chapter 2, provide methods for performance measurement and management. Total quality management (TQM) differs from traditional performance measurement in that it assesses both individual performance and the system within which the individual works. This assessment is a process through which employees and their customers work together to set standards and measure performance, with the overall goal being to improve customer satisfaction. In this sense, an employee's customers may be inside or outside the organization; a "customer" is whoever uses the goods or services produced by the employee. The feedback aims at helping employees continuously improve the satisfaction of their customers. The focus on continuously improving customer satisfaction is intended to avoid the pitfall of rating individuals on outcomes, such as sales or profits, over which they do not have complete control.

With TQM, performance measurement essentially combines measurements of attributes and results. The feedback in TQM is of two kinds: (1) subjective feedback from managers, peers, and customers about the employee's personal qualities such as cooperation and initiative; and (2) objective feedback based on the work process. The second kind of feedback comes from a variety of methods called *statistical quality control.* These methods use charts to detail causes of problems, measures of performance, or relationships between work-related variables. Employees are responsible for tracking these measures to identify areas

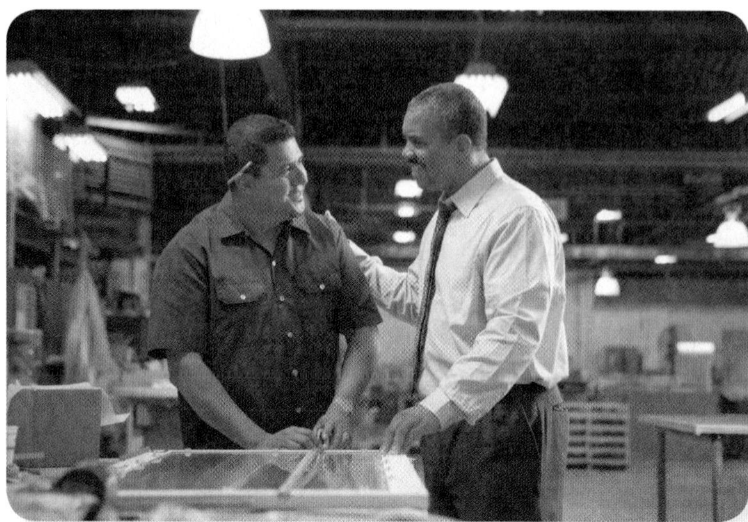

A TQM approach to performance measurement includes subjective feedback from managers, peers, and customers as well as objective feedback based on the work process.
John Fedele/Blend Images LLC

where they can avoid or correct problems. Because of the focus on systems, this feedback may result in changes to a work process, rather than assuming that a performance problem is the fault of an employee. The TQM system's focus has practical benefits, but it does not serve as well to support decisions about work assignments, training, or compensation.

LO 10-5 Describe major sources of performance information in terms of their advantages and disadvantages.

Sources of Performance Information

All the methods of performance measurement require decisions about who will collect and analyze the performance information. To qualify for this task, a person should have an understanding of the job requirements and the opportunity to see the employee doing the job. The traditional approach is for managers to gather information about their employees' performances and arrive at performance ratings. However, many sources are possible. Possibilities of information sources include managers, peers, subordinates, self, and customers.

Using just one person as a source of information poses certain problems. People tend to like some people more than others, and those feelings can bias how an employee's efforts are perceived. Also, one person is likely to see an employee in a limited number of situations. A supervisor, for example, cannot see how an employee behaves when the supervisor is not watching—for example, when a service technician is at the customer's facility. To get as complete an assessment as possible, some organizations combine information from most or all of the possible sources, in what is called a **360-degree performance appraisal.**

360-Degree Performance Appraisal Performance measurement that combines information from the employee's managers, peers, subordinates, self, and customers.

Managers

The most-used source of performance information is the employee's manager. It is usually safe for organizations to assume that supervisors have extensive knowledge of the job requirements and that they have enough opportunity to observe their employees. In other words, managers possess the basic qualifications for this responsibility. Another advantage of using managers to evaluate performance is that they have an incentive to provide accurate and helpful feedback because their own success depends so much on their employees' performance.[20] Finally, when managers try to observe employee behavior or discuss performance issues in the feedback session, their feedback can improve performance, and employees tend to perceive the appraisal as accurate.[21]

Still, in some situations, problems can occur with using supervisors as the source of performance information. For employees in some jobs, the supervisor does not have enough opportunity to observe the employee performing job duties. A sales manager with many outside salespeople cannot be with the salespeople on many visits to customers. Even if the sales manager does make a point of traveling with salespeople for a few days, they are likely to be on their best behavior while the manager is there. The manager cannot observe how they perform at other times.

Peers

Another source of performance information is the employee's peers or co-workers. Peers are an excellent source of information about performance in a job where the supervisor does not often observe the employee. Examples include law enforcement and sales. For these and other jobs, peers may have the most opportunity to observe the employee in day-to-day activities. Peers have expert knowledge of job requirements. They also bring a different perspective to the evaluation and can provide extremely valid assessments of performance.[22] Peer reviews also are in keeping with today's experience of social media, in which people are used to rating their experiences and one another's messages (see "HRM Social").

Peer evaluations obviously have some potential disadvantages. Friendships (or rivalries) have the potential to bias ratings. Research, however, has provided little evidence that this is a problem.[23] Another disadvantage is that when the evaluations are done to support administrative decisions, peers are uncomfortable with rating employees for decisions that may affect themselves. Generally, peers are more favorable toward participating in reviews to be used for employee development, as when organizations use them to strengthen teamwork.[24]

Subordinates

For evaluating the performance of managers, subordinates are an especially valuable source of information. Subordinates–the people reporting to the manager–often have the best chance to see how well a manager treats employees. Adobe Systems uses data from regular employee engagement surveys as a source of subordinate information. Managers who score low in behaviors such as delivering feedback and coaching employees receive training in how to improve.[25]

Subordinate evaluations have some potential problems because of the power relationships involved. Subordinates are reluctant to say negative things about the person to whom they report; they prefer to provide feedback anonymously. Managers, however, have a more positive reaction to this type of feedback when the subordinates are identified. When feedback forms require that the subordinates identify themselves, they tend to give the manager higher ratings.[26] Another problem is that when managers receive ratings from their subordinates, the employees have more power, so managers tend to emphasize employee satisfaction, even at the expense of productivity. This issue arises primarily when the evaluations are used for administrative decisions. Therefore, as with peer evaluations, subordinate evaluations are most appropriate for developmental purposes. To protect employees, the process should be anonymous and use at least three employees to rate each manager.

Using Apps for Real-Time Feedback

People who participate in social media—and that especially but not exclusively includes younger workers—are used to quickly responding when they see an idea or image that appeals to them. Further, for those making posts, getting a response such as a thumbs-up icon, thanks, retweet, or thoughtful comment becomes a valued affirmation. Social-media users become accustomed to receiving those jolts of encouragement every day, so waiting weeks or months for performance feedback feels like a long vacuum of uncertainty and even invisibility.

To fill that void, software companies are offering apps to speed the delivery of workplace feedback from peers as well as supervisors. At companies equipping employees with apps like Impraise, Reflektive, and Engagedly, someone who sees a colleague score a win or appreciates assistance from a co-worker can immediately send out a public or private message to reinforce the behavior. Some apps also provide dashboards that display progress toward goals. Apps also may tabulate response data for use in preparing formal performance appraisals.

Messages visible throughout the organization are appropriate for highlighting behavior that supports the organization's strategy and values. Receiving public praise for great customer service or a big sale is a reward for the employee. It also helps the rest of the organization by pointing out behaviors that are valued and perhaps sparking some friendly rivalry to see who will do best at delighting others.

Apps that enable private messaging and note taking provide avenues for feedback about how to improve. For example, a manager might notice that an employee struggles to remain calm when customers are upset. The manager can immediately record a note to schedule a meeting and initiate a coaching process, so the employee can learn to address this situation. Or for a simpler matter, a private message might be enough. For example, during a meeting, the manager might notice that an employee needs to know more about a topic. The manager texts the employee, "Martha, who was sitting across from you at this afternoon's meeting, knows a lot about the design of the PGX module. See if she has time to meet with you tomorrow, to bring you up to speed." These kinds of interventions can bring immediate performance improvements.

The biggest concern about these apps is that users might think they substitute for face-to-face, in-depth conversations. It's easy to click a heart icon and almost as easy to send a two-sentence message. Greater insight requires a deeper level of coaching. Ideally, managers will combine the real-time feedback of the apps with continued use of performance reviews.

Questions

1. Would you expect co-workers' feedback on an app to be mostly helpful or unhelpful? Why?
2. Would you expect managers' feedback to be mostly helpful or unhelpful? Why?

Sources: Engagedly website, https://engagedly.com, accessed April 24, 2020; ADP, "Performance Management and Employee Engagement," https://app.adp.com, accessed April 24, 2020; Caroline Hroncich, "An App That Takes the Annual Employee Review Mobile," *Employee Benefit News,* September 10, 2018, https://www.benefitnews.com; Elizabeth Dunn, "Can the Annual Review Be Replaced by an App?" *Entrepreneur,* May 2, 2018, https://www.entrepreneur.com.

HR Analytics and Decision Making

Research into behavior at a Korean health-food company found that the direction of feedback is related to its impact on performance–specifically, on creativity as rated by supervisors. Managers became more creative (a 9% increase) after receiving negative ratings from employees. However, negative downward and peer reviews were associated with a decrease in creativity. The pattern held regardless of the age and sex of the manager, and an experiment in which U.S. college students role-played organizational performance found that the pattern was consistent across cultures.

The researchers interpreted this to mean that downward and peer reviews feel threatening, so they make employees more cautious and less creative. In contrast, because upward reviews are less associated with risk, managers can apply what they learn to improve their performance. However, a later study at another company found that managers who received criticism in upward feedback later took a variety of retaliatory actions against their critics, such as unfavorable reviews and social exclusion.

Questions

1. How can this type of analysis help a company provide effective employee development?
2. How can a company reduce the likelihood of retaliation against employees who criticize their managers?

Source: Yeun Joon Kim, "A Subordinate's Criticism Makes You More Creative," *Harvard Business Review,* March–April 2020, pp. 30–31.

Self

No one has a greater chance to observe the employee's behavior on the job than does the employee himself or herself. Self-ratings are rarely used alone, but they can contribute valuable information. A common approach is to have employees evaluate their own performance before the feedback session. This activity gets employees thinking about their performance. Areas of disagreement between the self-appraisal and other evaluations can be fruitful topics for the feedback session. At the Australia-based software company Atlassian, self appraisals are part of weekly performance feedback. Employees use an online app that displays performance-related questions, such as "How often have you stretched yourself?" and lets employees move a dot along a scale with a range of possible answers. The responses then serve as a catalyst for discussion in meetings between each employee and his or her supervisor.[27]

The obvious problem with self-ratings is that individuals have a tendency to inflate assessments of their performance. Especially if the ratings will be used for administrative decisions, exaggerating one's contributions has practical benefits. Also, social psychologists have found that, in general, people tend to blame outside circumstances for their failures while taking a large part of the credit for their successes. Supervisors can soften this tendency by providing frequent feedback, but because people tend to perceive situations this way, self appraisals are not appropriate as the basis for administrative decisions.[28]

Customers

Services are often produced and consumed on the spot, so the customer is often the only person who directly observes the service performance and may be the best source of performance information. Many companies in service industries have introduced customer evaluations of employee performance. For example, local branches of the U.S. Post Office include a link to a customer survey on their transaction receipts. Businesses that make service calls to residences often follow up with an invitation to complete a survey of service quality via e-mail or text.

Customer feedback is one source of information used in performance appraisals. Other sources include managers, peers, subordinates, and employees themselves.
Ronnie Kaufman/Getty Images

Using customer evaluations of employee performance is appropriate in two situations.[29] The first is when an employee's job requires direct service to the customer or linking the customer to other services within the organization. Second, customer evaluations are appropriate when the organization is interested in gathering information to determine what products and services the customer wants. That is, customer evaluations contribute to the organization's goals by enabling HRM to support the organization's marketing activities. In this regard, customer evaluations are useful both for evaluating an employee's performance and for helping to determine whether the organization can improve customer service by making changes in HRM activities such as training or compensation.

The weakness of customer surveys for performance measurement is their expense. The expenses of a traditional survey can add up to hundreds of dollars to evaluate one individual. Many organizations therefore limit the information gathering to short periods once a year.

LO 10-6 Define types of rating errors, and explain how to minimize them.

Errors in Performance Measurement

As we noted in the previous section, one reason for gathering information from several sources is that performance measurements are not completely objective and errors can occur. People observe behavior, and they have no practical way of knowing all the circumstances, intentions, and outcomes related to that behavior, so they interpret what they see. In doing so, observers make a number of judgment calls and in some situations may even distort information on purpose. Therefore, fairness in rating performance and interpreting performance appraisals requires that managers understand the kinds of distortions that commonly occur.

Types of Rating Errors

Several kinds of errors and biases commonly influence performance measurements (see Figure 10.6):

- People often tend to give a higher evaluation to people they consider similar to themselves. Most of us think of ourselves as effective, so if others are like us, they must be effective, too. Research has demonstrated that this effect is strong. Unfortunately, it is sometimes wrong, and when similarity is based on characteristics such as race or sex, the decisions may be discriminatory.[30]
- If the rater compares an individual, not against an objective standard, but against other employees, *contrast errors* occur. A competent performer who works with exceptional people may be rated lower than competent simply because of the contrast.
- Raters make *distributional errors* when they tend to use only one part of a rating scale. The error is called *leniency* when the reviewer rates everyone near the top, *strictness* when the rater favors lower rankings, and *central tendency* when the rater puts everyone near the middle of the scale. Distributional errors make it difficult to compare employees rated by the same person. Also, if different raters make different kinds of distributional errors, scores by these raters cannot be compared.
- Raters often let their opinion of one quality color their opinion of others. For example, someone who speaks well might be seen as helpful or talented in other areas simply because of the overall good impression created by this one quality. Or someone who is occasionally tardy might be seen as lacking in motivation. When the bias is in a favorable direction, this is called the *halo error.* When it involves negative ratings, it is called the *horns error.* Halo error can mistakenly tell employees they don't need to improve in any area, while horns error can cause employees to feel frustrated and defensive.

Ways to Reduce Errors

Usually people make these errors unintentionally, especially when the criteria for measuring performance are not very specific. Raters can be trained to avoid rating errors.[31] Prospective raters watch videos whose scripts or storylines are designed to lead them to make specific

FIGURE 10.6
Possible Ratings Errors in Performance Measurement

Similar-to-Me Error
Overrating people who seem similar

Contrast Error
Underrating people who seem different

Errors in Distribution
Overusing part of a rating scale

Leniency

10
8
6
4
2
0

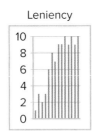

Strictness

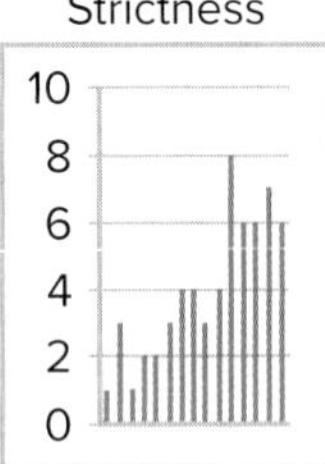

Central Tendency

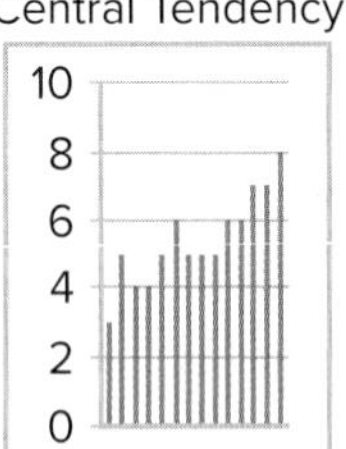

Halo Error
Overrating based on one good quality

Horns Error
Underrating based on one poor quality

rating errors. After rating the fictional employees in the videos, raters discuss their rating decisions and how such errors affected their rating decisions. Training programs offer tips for avoiding the errors in the future.

Another training method for raters focuses on the complex nature of employee performance.[32] Raters learn to look at many aspects of performance that deserve their attention. Actual examples of performance are studied to bring out various performance dimensions and the standards for those dimensions. This training aims to help raters evaluate employees' performance more thoroughly and accurately.

Besides training raters, a growing number of organizations are bringing data analytics into the rating process. While computers and wearable devices can track employees' activities, analytic software can find patterns in what employees do, as well as in the messages they post within the organization's computer network and beyond. For example, when revising its performance management review system, IBM asked employees to post their ideas on the company's internal social network platform. Receiving thousands of comments, IBM used text analysis software and discovered the majority of employees did not like their performances being graded on a curve. Thanks to data analytics, the company modified the performance management system taking into account the employees' sentiments.[33]

Political Behavior in Performance Appraisals

Unintentional errors are not the only cause of inaccurate performance measurement. Sometimes the people rating performance distort an evaluation on purpose to advance their personal goals. The motivation may even be as simple as wanting to avoid the discomfort of delivering unfavorable news (see "HR Oops!"). This kind of appraisal politics is unhealthy especially because the resulting feedback does not focus on helping employees contribute to

"Sugarcoating" Employee Feedback Doesn't Help

Evidence suggests that managers describe their employees' performance in favorable tones, even if that means they don't get the point across clearly. Surveys of managers and employees about recent performance appraisals found that employees thought the reviews were favorable even when the managers intended to indicate a need for improvement. Further investigation supported the researchers' hypothesis that managers hoped vague comments would be interpreted correctly.

Avoiding criticism and expressing the appraisal in "nice" language may sound like the kind way to treat employees, but it leaves them operating with incorrect assumptions about how well they are contributing. Furthermore, it creates a written performance record that is inaccurate. Not only do employees fail to correct problems they don't realize exist, but planning for future training and development is then based on false assumptions. Further, if the employee needs to be disciplined in the future, the company cannot justify these actions based on inaccurate written documentation.

For employees seeking accurate feedback, it may be helpful to state a request for an accurate assessment. Managers can help by giving brief feedback frequently (at least once a week), which tends to be more accurate because it is less uncomfortable to deliver. In addition, employers should take measures to create systems that favor accurate feedback. One way is to use assessments that involve specific questions about behavior, requesting examples. Such assessments help managers provide information not just about problems but also about a path to do better in the future. In addition, the HR department can make itself available to devise accurate, constructive feedback in difficult situations.

Questions

1. Why do you think it feels uncomfortable to deliver feedback about performance areas requiring improvement? Why is it important for managers to deliver this feedback anyway?
2. Suppose your manager gives you performance feedback that includes criticism. What way of receiving it would most benefit your career?

Sources: Cheyna Brower and Nate Dvorak, "Why Employees Are Fed Up with Feedback," *Gallup,* October 11, 2019, https://www.gallup.com; Michael Schaerer and Roderick Swaab, "Are You Sugarcoating Your Feedback without Realizing It?" *Harvard Business Review,* October 8, 2019, https://hbr.org; Paul Falcone, "Don't Sugarcoat Performance Reviews," *Society for Human Resource Management,* August 22, 2019, https://www.shrm.org.

the organization's goals. High-performing employees who are rated unfairly will become frustrated, and low-performing employees who are overrated will be rewarded rather than encouraged to improve. Therefore, organizations try to identify and discourage appraisal politics.

Several characteristics of appraisal systems and company culture tend to encourage appraisal politics. Appraisal politics are most likely to occur when raters are accountable to the employee being rated, the goals of rating are not compatible with one another, performance appraisal is directly linked to highly desirable rewards, top executives tolerate or ignore distorted ratings, and senior employees tell newcomers company "folklore" that includes stories about distorted ratings.

Despite its problems, political behavior occurs in every organization. Organizations can minimize appraisal politics by establishing an appraisal system that is fair. One technique is to hold a **calibration meeting,** a gathering at which managers discuss employee performance ratings and provide evidence supporting their ratings with the goal of eliminating the influence of rating errors. As they discuss ratings and the ways they arrive at ratings, managers may identify undervalued employees, notice whether they are much harsher or more lenient than other managers, and help each other focus on how well ratings are associated with relevant performance outcomes. Surveys have found a majority of organizations holding calibration meetings, with changes to evaluations being a common result. Information systems also can provide data analytics for managers to use in calibrating their

Calibration Meeting
Meeting at which managers discuss employee performance ratings and provide evidence supporting their ratings with the goal of eliminating the influence of rating errors.

ratings.[34] The organization can also help managers give accurate and fair appraisals by training them to use the appraisal process, encouraging them to recognize accomplishments that the employees themselves have not identified, and fostering a climate of openness in which employees feel they can be honest about their weaknesses.[35]

Giving Performance Feedback

LO 10-7 Explain how to provide performance feedback effectively.

Once the manager and others have measured an employee's performance, this information must be given to the employee. Only after the employee has received feedback can he or she begin to plan how to correct any shortcomings. Although the feedback stage of performance management is essential, it is uncomfortable for managers and employees. Delivering feedback feels to the manager as if he or she is standing in judgment of others–a role few people enjoy. Receiving criticism feels even worse. Fortunately, managers can do much to smooth the feedback process and make it effective.

Scheduling Performance Feedback

Performance feedback should be a regular, expected management activity. The custom or policy at many organizations is to give formal performance feedback once a year. But annual feedback is not enough. One reason is that managers are responsible for correcting performance deficiencies as soon as they occur. If the manager notices a problem with an employee's behavior in June, but the annual appraisal is scheduled for November, the employee will miss months of opportunities for improvement.

Another reason for frequent performance feedback is that feedback is most effective when the information does not surprise the employee. If an employee has to wait for up to a year to learn what the manager thinks of his work, the employee will wonder whether he is meeting expectations. Employees should instead receive feedback so often that they know what the manager will say during their annual performance review.

Finally, employees have indicated that they are motivated and directed by regular feedback; they want to know if they are on the right track. In this way, frequent feedback supports employee engagement. Vapotherm, a medical-device manufacturer based in New Hampshire, met this demand by shifting from annual reviews by supervisors to quarterly reviews in which employees summarize their performance and then discuss the summary with their supervisor.[36]

Preparing for a Feedback Session

Managers should be well prepared for each formal feedback session. The manager should create the right context for the meeting. The location should be neutral. If the manager's office is the site of unpleasant conversations, a conference room may be more appropriate. In announcing the meeting to an employee, the manager should describe it as a chance to discuss the role of the employee, the role of the manager, and the relationship between them. Managers should also say (and believe) that they would like the meeting to be an open dialogue. The content of the feedback session and the type of language used can determine the success of this meeting.

Managers should also enable the employee to be well prepared. The manager should ask the employee to complete a self-assessment ahead of time. The self-assessment requires employees to think about their performance over the past rating period and to be aware of their strengths and weaknesses so they can participate more fully in the discussion. Even though employees may tend to overstate their accomplishments, the self-assessment can help the manager and employee identify areas for discussion. When the purpose of the assessment is to define areas for development, employees may actually understate their performance. Also, differences between the manager's and the employee's rating may be fruitful areas for discussion.

When giving performance feedback, do it in an appropriate meeting place that is neutral and free of distractions. What other factors are important for a feedback session? Ryan McVay/Getty Images

Conducting the Feedback Session

During the feedback session, managers can take any of three approaches. In the "tell-and-sell" approach, managers tell the employees their ratings and then justify those ratings. In the "tell-and-listen" approach, managers tell employees their ratings and then let the employees explain their side of the story. In the "problem-solving" approach, managers and employees work together to solve performance problems in an atmosphere of respect and encouragement. Problem solving thus focuses as much on the future as on the past. Not surprisingly, research demonstrates that the problem-solving approach is superior. Perhaps surprisingly, most managers rely on the tell-and-sell approach.[37]

Managers can improve employee satisfaction with the feedback process by letting employees voice their opinions and discuss performance goals.[38] This requires careful listening as well as clear speaking. Open-ended questions that seek the employee's view can help get a two-way conversation off the ground. The following questions are some examples:[39]

- What have you learned?
- What skills would you like to develop?
- What do you think the next steps should be?

The content of the feedback should be specific, emphasizing behavior, not personalities. For example, "You did not meet the deadline" can open a conversation about what needs to change, but "You're not motivated" may make the employee feel defensive and angry. The feedback session should end with goal setting and a decision about when to follow up.

Many managers assume that feedback should focus on problem areas. After all, fixing a problem should lead to better performance. However, researchers are learning that the most impact comes from focusing on the employee's areas of strength and building on those.[40] Evidence suggests that employees then tend to see their manager as more supportive and trustworthy, so they are more open to receiving both praise and constructive criticism. In contrast, criticism often has the unintended consequence of motivating people to get feedback from more positive sources, avoiding the sources of criticism. Although managers may feel more uncomfortable giving critical feedback, many fall back on criticism. One possible reason is that they may not know how to give positive feedback. The "HR How To" box provides some guidelines.

The feedback session should conclude by starting another round of the performance management process–specifically, setting or revising goals for the coming period, including timelines for progress reviews and goal attainment. Goal setting is essential, because it is one of the most effective motivators of high performance. It results in increased satisfaction, motivation to improve, and performance improvement.[41]

LO 10-8 Summarize ways to produce improvement in unsatisfactory performance.

Finding Solutions to Performance Problems

When performance evaluation indicates that an employee's performance is below standard, the feedback process should launch an effort to correct the problem. Even when the employee is meeting current standards, the feedback session may identify areas in which the employee can improve in order to contribute more to the organization in a current or future

Delivering Positive Feedback

The feedback with the best track record of contributing to performance improvement is positive—that is, praise for and reinforcement of an employee's strengths and successes. Here are some guidelines for delivering effective positive feedback:

- Build a constructive environment by cultivating a positive attitude toward employees and colleagues. Consider that you and they are able to improve, and express a genuine interest in others' well being. This carries over into performance-related conversations and ensures they are authentic, not marred by fake enthusiasm.
- Focus on goals and a vision for the employee, work group, and organization. Putting feedback into this context has the potential to get employees excited about improving and contributing more. It also helps with aligning performance and strategy.
- Look for positive results and behaviors, and give specific feedback about them. That is, name details of the situation, behavior, and impact you observed.
- Separate feedback messages from promises (or threats). So, for example, if an employee delivered a compelling presentation, give feedback about what the employee did to make the presentation so effective, as well as how it affected the audience. Save thoughts about pay increases, promotions, or other rewards for another time.

Questions

1. When you receive feedback (at work, in school, or in your personal life), is it easier for you to accept praise or criticism? Do you think you learn equally well from both?
2. Think about an example of praiseworthy behavior you have observed recently, at work or anywhere else. Imagine you have an opportunity to give this person positive feedback. Applying the list of guidelines, write a brief statement of positive feedback for the person. (If you have the chance, give the feedback, and observe the person's reaction.)

Sources: A. Davis, "Positive Feedback? Negative Feedback? 11 Ways to Productively Share Feedback," *Inc.*, February 25, 2019, https://www.inc.com; Jhana Team, "How to Give More Powerful Positive Feedback," *Glassdoor*, https://www.glassdoor.com, January 6, 2019; Joseph Folkman, "Why Is It So Difficult for Leaders to Give Positive Feedback?" *Forbes*, October 20, 2017, https://www.forbes.com; Patty Gaul, "Tell Them What's on Your Mind," *TD*, August 2017, p. 18; Gordon Tredgold, "Six Keys to Giving Positive Feedback That Drives Better Results," *Inc.*, January 25, 2017.

job. In sum, the final feedback stage of performance management involves identifying areas for improvement and ways to improve performance in those areas.

The most effective way to improve performance varies according to the employee's ability and motivation. In general, when employees have high levels of ability and motivation, they perform at or above standards. But when they lack ability, motivation, or both, corrective action is needed. The type of action called for depends on what the employee lacks:

- *Lack of ability*–When a motivated employee lacks knowledge, skills, or abilities in some area, the manager may offer coaching, training, and more detailed feedback. Sometimes it is appropriate to restructure the job so the employee can handle it.
- *Lack of motivation*–Managers with an unmotivated employee can explore ways to demonstrate that the employee is being treated fairly and rewarded adequately. The solution may be as simple as more positive feedback (praise). Employees may need a referral for counseling or help with stress management.
- *Lack of both*–Performance may improve if the manager directs the employee's attention to the significance of the problem by withholding rewards or providing specific feedback. If the employee does not respond, the manager may have to demote or terminate the employee.
- *Lack of neither*–As a rule, employees who combine high ability with high motivation are solid performers. However, the manager should by no means ignore these employees. They are likely to want opportunities for development and may be able to contribute

FIGURE 10.7
Questions for Diagnosing Remedies to Performance Problems

Inputs
• Does the employee know what he or she is supposed to do?
• Are procedures clear and logical?
• Do employees have adequate resources (supplies, tools, time, etc.)?
• Do other work demands conflict with performance?
Feedback
• Does the employee get frequent performance feedback?
• Is feedback timely, accurate, and understandable?
Goals/Objectives
• Are goals specified?
• Does the employee know the goals?
• Does the employee believe the goals are achievable and fair?
Rewards/ Consequences
• Are there rewards for superior performance?
• Are the rewards valued?
• Are the rewards timely?
• Are there rewards (such as co-worker approval) for falling short?

Sources: Based on G. Rummler, "In Search of the Holy Performance Grail," *Training and Development,* April 1996, pp. 26–31; C. Reinhart, "How to Leap over Barriers to Performance," *Training and Development,* January 2000, pp. 20–24; F. Wilmouth, C. Prigmore, and M. Brya, "HPT Models: An Overview of the Major Models in the Field," *Performance Improvement* 41 (2002), pp. 14–21.

even more than they already are. Furthermore, such valuable employees are apt to leave if they see no potential for growth. To maintain high motivation levels, the manager should use rewards, direct feedback, and growth opportunities.

Of course, some performance problems cannot be pinned simply on the employee's characteristics. Managers also should consider whether the organization can address the problem with better resources, systems, and management. Figure 10.7 identifies some questions for managers to ask when identifying other possible remedies.

LO 10-9 Discuss legal and ethical issues that affect performance management.

Legal and Ethical Issues in Performance Management

In developing and using performance management systems, human resource professionals need to ensure that these systems meet legal requirements, such as the avoidance of discrimination. In addition, performance management systems should meet ethical standards, such as protection of employees' privacy.

Legal Requirements for Performance Management

Because performance measures play a central role in decisions about pay, promotions, and discipline, employment-related lawsuits often challenge an organization's performance management system. Lawsuits related to performance management usually involve charges of discrimination or unjust dismissal.

Discrimination claims often allege that the performance management system discriminated against employees on the basis of their race or sex. Many performance measures are subjective, and measurement errors, such as those described earlier in the chapter, can easily occur. The U.S. Supreme Court has held that the selection guidelines in the federal government's *Uniform Guidelines on Employee Selection Procedures* also apply to performance measurement.[42] In general, these guidelines (discussed in Chapters 3 and 6) require that organizations avoid using criteria such as race and age as a basis for employment decisions. This requires overcoming widespread rating errors. A substantial body of evidence has shown that white and Black raters tend to give higher ratings to members of their own racial group, even after rater training—especially when one group is only a small percentage of the total work group.[43] In addition, stereotypes play a role in how raters score a person on measures of traits such as leadership. In the absence of more specific criteria, raters tend to score a man who behaves assertively as having a strong leadership style, but a woman typically receives a lower score: "pushy" if she has an assertive style or "weak" if she leads in less visible ways.[44]

With regard to lawsuits filed on the grounds of unjust dismissal, the usual claim is that the person was dismissed for reasons besides the ones that the employer states. Suppose an employee who works for a defense contractor discloses that the company defrauded the government. If the company fires the employee, the employee might argue that the firing was a way to punish the employee for blowing the whistle. In this type of situation, courts generally focus on the employer's performance management system, looking to see whether the firing could have been based on poor performance. To defend itself, the employer would need a performance management system that provides evidence to support its employment decisions.

To protect against both kinds of lawsuits, it is important to have a legally defensible performance management system.[45] Such a system would be based on valid job analyses, as described in Chapter 4, with the requirements for job success clearly communicated to employees. Performance measurement should evaluate behaviors or results rather than traits. For example, managers' evaluations look at their teams' results, not at whether the managers have "leadership." The organization should use multiple raters (including self-appraisals) and train raters in how to use the system. The organization should provide for a review of all performance ratings by upper-level managers and set up a system for employees to appeal when they believe they were evaluated unfairly. Along with feedback, the system should include a process for coaching or training employees to help them improve, rather than simply dismissing poor performers.

Electronic Monitoring and Employee Privacy

Computer technology now supports many performance management systems. Organizations often store records of employees' performance ratings, disciplinary actions, and work-rule violations in electronic databases. Many companies use computers, sensors, and mobile devices to monitor productivity and other performance measures electronically. GE, for example, has increased the flow of performance-related data throughout the company, on the assumption that this gives its people more information, enabling better decisions about how to improve performance.[46]

Although electronic monitoring can improve productivity, it also generates privacy concerns. Critics point out that an employer should not monitor employees when it has no reason to believe anything is wrong. They complain that monitoring systems threaten to make the workplace an electronic sweatshop in which employees are treated as robots, robbing them of dignity. Some note that employees' performances should be measured by accomplishments, not just time spent at desks or workbenches. Electronic systems should not be a substitute for careful management. When monitoring is necessary, managers should communicate the reasons for using it. Monitoring may be used more positively to gather information for coaching employees and helping them develop their skills. Finally, organizations must protect the privacy of performance measurements, as they must do with other employee records.

THINKING ETHICALLY

WHAT ARE THE ETHICAL BOUNDARIES OF TRACKING EMPLOYEE ACTIVITIES?

Mobile and wearable devices are making it easier than ever to track what employees do at work. True, measuring physical motions of workers goes back to the industrial age. But motion-sensing devices (think Fitbit fitness trackers or Apple watches for the workplace) make data collection precise and affordable. Add to this the ease of data entry via smartphones and tablets, as well as computers positioned on workstations, and there are almost no limits to what employers can know about employees' activities.

Examples of how employers are using the technology include the measurement of computer keystrokes, employee traffic patterns as they walk, and driving patterns of employees who travel or make deliveries in company vehicles. At Florida Hospital Celebration Health, nurses and patient care technicians wear badges in which sensors detect where they are throughout each shift. Analysis of data can identify sources of inefficiency affecting performance–for example, that nearby supply stations are improperly stocked. An ad agency has employees sign in each day by posting selfies on a designated social-media service; it says the advantage is that it can easily keep attendance when employees are working off-site.

Along with the ability to gather data come questions about whether some kinds of data are or should be off limits. In the United States, federal law gives employers latitude to observe employees on the job, but the monitoring has to be in working areas during work hours. Also, employers should be careful to use monitoring consistently and not in a way that targets groups protected by fair-employment laws. While complying with the law, employers also need to consider ethical boundaries such as fairness, consent, and mutual respect.

One relevant consideration is that data can empower employees as well as management. In one situation, an employee juggling home and work responsibilities asked to start work at 10 a.m. The company was reluctant, but when it measured her performance, it found that this employee was significantly more productive on the days she started later. Armed with the data, the employee made the case for a flexible work arrangement.

Questions

1. How can high-tech collection of performance data be done consistently with the basic human rights upheld by the U.S. Constitution, such as the rights of free speech and due process?
2. Imagine you work for a hospital that wants to track the travel patterns of its nurses to ensure they work efficiently and that each patient is visited a certain number of times each day. What measures would you recommend to promote fairness in the way the system is implemented?

Sources: Peter Holley, "Wearable Technology Started by Tracking Steps. Soon It May Allow Your Boss to Track Your Performance," *The Washington Post,* June 28, 2019, https://www.washingtonpost.com; Jan Guardian, "What Are the Ethical and Technical Issues in Tracking Your Employees?" *HR Technologist,* April 18, 2019, https://www.hrtechnologist.com; Josh Bersin, Joe Mariani, Kelly Monahan, and Brad Winn, "Will Employees Be the Next Cloud-Connected 'Thing' in the New Era of IoT?" *People + Strategy,* Summer 2017, pp. 60–64; "The Future of Wearables in the Workplace," *Management Today,* December 2015/January 2016, pp. 52–55; Chitra Narayanan, "Roll Call on Twitter," *Business Today,* July 19, 2015, pp. 34–35; Lee Michael Katz, "Big Employer Is Watching," *HR Magazine,* June 2015, pp. 67–74.

SUMMARY

LO 10-1 Identify the activities involved in performance management.

- Performance management is the process through which managers ensure that employees' activities and outputs contribute to the organization's goals.
- First, the organization specifies which aspects of performance are relevant to the organization.
- Next, the organization measures the relevant aspects of performance through performance appraisal.
- Finally, in performance feedback sessions, managers provide employees with information about their performance so they can adjust their behavior to meet the organization's goals. Feedback includes efforts to identify and solve problems.

LO 10-2 Discuss the purposes of performance management systems.

- Organizations establish performance management systems to meet three broad purposes.
- The *strategic purpose* is aimed at meeting business objectives. The system does this by helping to link employees' behavior with the organization's goals.
- The *administrative purpose* of performance management is to provide information for day-to-day decisions about salary, benefits, recognition, and retention or termination.
- The *developmental purpose* of performance management is using the system as a basis for developing employees' knowledge and skills.

LO 10-3 Define five criteria for measuring the effectiveness of a performance management system.

- Performance measures should be *strategic*—fitting with the organization's strategy by supporting its goals and culture.
- Performance measures should be *valid,* so they measure all the relevant aspects of performance and do not measure irrelevant aspects of performance.
- These measures should also provide interrater and test-retest *reliability,* so that appraisals are consistent among raters and over time.
- Performance measurement systems should be *acceptable* to the people who use them or receive feedback from them.
- A performance measure should be *specific,* telling employees what is expected of them and how they can meet those expectations.

LO 10-4 Compare the major methods for measuring performance.

- Performance measurement may use *ranking* systems such as simple ranking, forced distribution, or paired comparisons to compare one individual's performance with that of other employees.
- These methods may be time consuming, and they will be seen as unfair if actual performance is not distributed in the same way as the ranking system requires.
- However, ranking counteracts some forms of rater bias and helps distinguish employees for administrative decisions.
- Other approaches involve *rating* employees' attributes, behaviors, or outcomes.
- Rating attributes is relatively simple but not always valid, unless attributes are specifically defined.
- Rating behaviors requires a great deal of information, but these methods can be very effective. They can link behaviors to goals, and ratings by trained raters may be highly reliable. Rating results, such as productivity or achievement of objectives, tends to be less subjective than other kinds of rating, making this approach highly acceptable.
- Validity may be a problem because of factors outside the employee's control. This method also tends not to provide much basis for determining how to improve.
- Focusing on quality can provide practical benefits, but is not as useful for administrative and developmental decisions.

LO 10-5 Describe major sources of performance information in terms of their advantages and disadvantages.

- Performance information may come from an employee's self-appraisal and from appraisals by the employee's supervisor, employees, peers, and customers.
- Using only one source makes the appraisal more subjective. Organizations may combine many sources into a 360-degree performance appraisal.
- Gathering information from each employee's manager may produce accurate information, unless the supervisor has little opportunity to observe the employee.
- Peers are an excellent source of information about performance in a job where the supervisor does not often observe the employee. Disadvantages are that friendships (or rivalries) may bias ratings and peers may be uncomfortable with the role of rating a friend.
- Subordinates often have the best chance to see how a manager treats employees. Employees may be reluctant to contribute honest opinions about a supervisor unless they can provide information anonymously.
- Self-appraisals may be biased, but they do come from the person with the most knowledge of the

employee's behavior on the job, and they provide a basis for discussion in feedback sessions, opening up fruitful comparisons and areas of disagreement between the self-appraisal and other appraisals.
- Customers may be an excellent source of performance information, although obtaining customer feedback tends to be expensive.

LO 10-6 Define types of rating errors, and explain how to minimize them.

- People observe behavior often without a practical way of knowing all the relevant circumstances and outcomes, so they necessarily interpret what they see.
- A common tendency is to give higher evaluations to people we consider similar to ourselves.
- Other errors involve using only part of the rating scale: Giving all employees ratings at the high end of the scale is called leniency error. Rating everyone at the low end of the scale is called strictness error. Rating all employees at or near the middle is called central tendency.
- The halo error refers to rating employees positively in all areas because of strong performance observed in one area.
- The horns error is rating employees negatively in all areas because of weak performance observed in one area.
- Ways to reduce rater error are training raters to be aware of their tendencies to make rating errors and training them to be sensitive to the complex nature of employee performance so they will consider many aspects of performance in greater depth.
- Politics also may influence ratings. Organizations can minimize appraisal politics by establishing a fair appraisal system and bringing managers together to discuss ratings in calibration meetings.

LO 10-7 Explain how to provide performance feedback effectively.

- Performance feedback should be a regular, scheduled management activity so that employees can correct problems as soon as they occur.
- Managers should prepare by establishing a neutral location, emphasizing that the feedback session will be a chance for discussion, and asking the employee to prepare a self-assessment.
- During the feedback session, managers should strive for a problem-solving approach and encourage employees to voice their opinions and discuss performance goals.
- The manager should look for opportunities to praise and should limit criticism.
- The discussion should focus on behavior and results rather than on personalities.

LO 10-8 Summarize ways to produce improvement in unsatisfactory performance.

- For an employee who is motivated but lacks ability, the manager should provide coaching and training, give detailed feedback about performance, and consider restructuring the job.
- For an employee who has ability but lacks motivation, the manager should investigate whether outside problems are a distraction and, if so, refer the employee for help. If the problem has to do with the employee's not feeling appreciated or rewarded, the manager should try to deliver more praise and evaluate whether additional pay and other rewards are appropriate.
- For an employee lacking both ability and motivation, the manager should consider whether the employee is a good fit for the position. Specific feedback or withholding rewards may spur improvement, or the employee may have to be demoted or terminated.
- Solid employees who are high in ability and motivation will continue so and may be able to contribute even more if the manager provides appropriate direct feedback, rewards, and opportunities for development.

LO 10-9 Discuss legal and ethical issues that affect performance management.

- Lawsuits related to performance management usually involve charges of discrimination or unjust dismissal. Managers must make sure that performance management systems and decisions treat employees equally, without regard to their race, sex, or other protected status.
- Organizations can do this by establishing and using valid performance measures and by training raters to evaluate performance accurately. A system is more likely to be legally defensible if it is based on behaviors and results, rather than on traits, and if multiple raters evaluate each person's performance.
- The system should include a process for coaching or training employees to help them improve, rather than simply dismissing poor performers.
- An ethical issue of performance management is the use of electronic monitoring. This type of performance measurement provides detailed, accurate information, but employees may find it demoralizing, degrading, and stressful.
- Employees are more likely to accept electronic monitoring if the organization explains its purpose, links it to help in improving performance, and keeps the performance data private.

KEY TERMS

performance management, 300
simple ranking, 306
forced-distribution method, 306
paired-comparison method, 307
graphic rating scale, 307
mixed-standard scales, 308
critical-incident method, 310
behaviorally anchored rating scale (BARS), 310
behavioral observation scale (BOS), 310
organizational behavior modification (OBM), 311
management by objectives (MBO), 312
360-degree performance appraisal, 314
calibration meeting, 320

REVIEW AND DISCUSSION QUESTIONS

1. How does a complete performance management system differ from the use of annual performance appraisals? *(LO 10-1)*
2. Give two examples of an administrative decision that would be based on performance management information. Give two examples of developmental decisions based on this type of information. *(LO 10-2)*
3. How can involving employees in the creation of performance standards improve the effectiveness of a performance management system? (Consider the criteria for effectiveness listed in this chapter.) *(LO 10-3)*
4. Consider how you might rate the performance of three instructors from whom you are currently taking a course. (If you are currently taking only one or two courses, consider this course and two you recently completed.) *(LO 10-4)*
   a. Would it be harder to *rate* the instructors' performance or to *rank* their performance? Why?
   b. Write three items to use in rating the instructors—one each to rate them in terms of an attribute, a behavior, and an outcome.
   c. Which measure in (*b*) do you think is most valid? Most reliable? Why?
   d. Many colleges use questionnaires to gather data from students about their instructors' performance. Would it be appropriate to use the data for administrative decisions? Developmental decisions? Other decisions? Why or why not?
5. Imagine that a pet supply store is establishing a new performance management system to help employees provide better customer service. Management needs to decide who should participate in measuring the performance of each of the store's salespeople. From what sources should the store gather information? Why? *(LO 10-5)*
6. Would the same sources be appropriate if the store in Question 5 used the performance appraisals to support decisions about which employees to promote? Explain. *(LO 10-6)*
7. Suppose you were recently promoted to a supervisory job in a company where you have worked for two years. You genuinely like almost all your co-workers, who now report to you. The only exception is one employee, who dresses more formally than the others and frequently tells jokes that embarrass you and the other workers. Given your preexisting feelings for the employees, how can you measure their performance fairly and effectively? *(LO 10-7)*
8. Continuing the example in Question 7, imagine that you are preparing for your first performance feedback session. You want the feedback to be effective—that is, you want the feedback to result in improved performance. List five or six steps you can take to achieve your goal. *(LO 10-7)*
9. Besides giving employees feedback, what steps can a manager take to improve employees' performance? *(LO 10-8)*
10. Suppose you are a human resource professional helping to improve the performance management system of a company that sells and services office equipment. The company operates a call center that takes calls from customers who are having problems with their equipment. Call center employees are supposed to verify that the problem is not one the customer can easily handle (for example, equipment that will not operate because it has come unplugged). Then, if the problem is not resolved over the phone, the employees arrange for service technicians to visit the customer. The company can charge the customer only if a service technician visits, so performance management of the call center employees focuses on productivity—how quickly they can complete a call and move on to the next caller. To measure this performance efficiently and accurately, the company uses electronic monitoring. *(LO 10-9)*
    a. How would you expect the employees to react to the electronic monitoring? How might the organization address the employees' concerns?
    b. Besides productivity in terms of number of calls, what other performance measures should the performance management system include?
    c. How should the organization gather information about the other performance measures?

SELF-ASSESSMENT EXERCISE

Mc Graw Hill connect

Do You Like Receiving Feedback?

To test your attitudes toward feedback, take the following quiz. Read each statement, and write A next to each statement you agree with. If you disagree with the statement, write D.

_____ 1. I like being told how well I am doing on a project.

_____ 2. Even though I may think I have done a good job, I feel a lot more confident when someone else tells me so.

_____ 3. Even when I think I could have done something better, I feel good when other people think well of me for what I have done.

_____ 4. It is important for me to know what people think of my work.

_____ 5. I think my instructor would think worse of me if I asked him or her for feedback.

_____ 6. I would be nervous about asking my instructor how she or he evaluates my behavior in class.

_____ 7. It is not a good idea to ask my fellow students for feedback; they might think I am incompetent.

_____ 8. It is embarrassing to ask other students for their impression of how I am doing in class.

_____ 9. It would bother me to ask the instructor for feedback.

_____ 10. It is not a good idea to ask the instructor for feedback because he or she might think I am incompetent.

_____ 11. It is embarrassing to ask the instructor for feedback.

_____ 12. It is better to try to figure out how I am doing on my own, rather than to ask other students for feedback.

For statements 1–4, add the total number of As: _____
For statements 5–12, add the total number of As: _____
For statements 1–4, the greater the number of As, the greater your preference for and trust in feedback from others. For statements 5–12, the greater the number of As, the greater the risk you believe there is in asking for feedback.

How might this information be useful in understanding how you react to feedback in school or on the job?

Sources: Based on D. B. Fedor. R. B. Rensvold. and S. M. Adams, "An Investigation of Factors Expected to Affect Feedback Seeking: A Longitudinal Field Study," *Personnel Psychology* 45 (1992), pp. 779–805; S. J. Asford, "Feedback Seeking in Individual Adaptation: A Resource Perspective," *Academy of Management Journal* 29 (1986), pp. 465–487.

TAKING RESPONSIBILITY

Asana's Performance Management Aligns with Its Values

Dustin Moskovitz and Justin Rosenstein founded their software company, Asana, because they had not only an idea for a product, but also a vision for how to operate. The product, also called Asana (the Sanskrit word for a pose in yoga), is software for enabling teamwork. The vision is to apply Eastern wisdom traditions to create a culture of clarity, authenticity, and mindfulness. That vision provides the defining criteria for performance management, and the result is a workplace in which key stakeholders—employees in Silicon Valley's highly competitive market for high-tech workers—feel valued and empowered.

Asana offers a means of operating in which everyone has clear goals and responsibilities, coupled with a high degree of authority. This exists within an environment of constant observation, learning, and improvement. In this context, performance management is not so much about checking up on employees to find out what they have been doing; Asana's own teamwork software takes care of that. Rather, performance management is about enabling employees to continue improving along with the entire company.

Goal setting applies the principle of clarity. Asana presents the company's purpose as a pyramid. At the top is the mission, to "help humanity thrive by enabling all teams to work together effortlessly." Below that is an easily understood three-part strategy of making a product that enables effortless teamwork, getting the product to all teams, and making Asana the company that does both of these better than any other. To carry out the strategy, the company sets roughly a dozen business, product, and internal objectives for the year. Every team has key results to achieve some of these objectives, and every employee works at projects aimed at the key results. Cross-functional teams define the higher-level goals in twice-yearly meetings to review the previous six months' performance. And once a year, each employee defines personal goals that align with the objectives in the pyramid.

The degree of empowerment is a striking feature of work at Asana. The planning process identifies every task and piece of work, with a deadline for each. Each one is called an area of responsibility (AOR), and each is assigned to one person, the AOR holder, based on the person's expertise. AOR holders are encouraged to discuss issues with their colleagues, but they have the full authority to make decisions within their area. To enable wise use of this authority, all employees receive leadership training that includes listening, giving and receiving feedback nondefensively, and "holding beliefs lightly," that is, being open to new ideas.

This degree of empowerment would make it difficult for a manager to offer performance feedback in the form of directions to improve. Rather, the emphasis is on mentoring and coaching. Employees complete annual self-reviews, and regular peer reviews provide another source of performance data. Managers meet frequently one-on-one with their direct reports. Because the Asana software is already telling managers what their people have accomplished and whether they are on track toward goals, the meetings focus on employees' needs and goals. When problems arise at any level of the organization–including when an employee leaves–the response is to conduct an analysis of the underlying reasons so that processes can be improved.

So far, this approach is delivering exceptional performance, including high sales growth and employee satisfaction. Maintaining a culture in a fast-growing company is difficult, but the founders point out that change is built into Asana's method of operating. If the culture stops working, the owners hold their beliefs lightly and will move the company into a new pose.

Questions

1. How well do you think Asana's approach to performance management meets the (a) strategic, (b) administrative, and (c) strategic purposes of performance management? Use evidence from the case to support your opinions.
2. Like other high-tech companies, Asana is struggling to build a more diverse workforce. Identify two ways the company is or could be ensuring that its performance management system does not discriminate.

Sources: Corporate website, "Our Company," https://asana.com, accessed April 24, 2020; Anne Binder, "How We've Designed a Culture That Fuels Our Business Results," *Asana blog,* November 7, 2019, https://blog.asana.com; Jeff Bercovici, "Two Facebook Alums Seek a New Corporate Zen," *Inc.,* June 2018, pp. 76–78; Sarah Lewis-Kulin, "The Secret to Asana's Company Culture," *Fortune,* March 1, 2018, http://fortune.com; John Courtney, "How Does Asana Do Performance Management," *PerformYard Talent Management Blog,* November 21, 2017, http://blog.performyard.com; Rachel Zurer, "How Asana Designs Its Successful, Authentic Company Culture," *Conscious Company,* November 1, 2017, https://consciouscompanymedia.com; David Ongchoco, "Asana's Head of People Ops Shares What Goes into One of Tech's Best Company Cultures," *Huffington Post,* July 17, 2017, https://www.huffingtonpost.com.

MANAGING TALENT

Performance Management Boosted Service at Genpact

Genpact is a global business consulting firm. Its more than 90,000 employees help the world's large corporations improve their business processes. The firm, which started as a division of General Electric, applies data analytics to a wide variety of business problems. To explore its performance in satisfying customers, Genpact brought in a leader in the field, Peter Gloor, a research scientist at MIT who also runs a consulting firm called Galaxy Advisors, which specializes in the field of network analysis, or the study of communications patterns.

Gloor observed that Genpact's client communications contained data that Galaxy's Condor system could gather and analyze to identify relevant performance measures. At Genpact, 176 teams of up to several hundred members worked with key accounts. Galaxy would assign 26 teams to its analysis, and the other 150 would be a control group, continuing with its normal practices. Condor would not read the contents of Genpact's messages to clients but would collect information *about* the e-mail between team members and clients: the frequency of the Genpact employee responding without checking with a supervisor, the simplicity of language in the subject line, the speed of responding, and the extent to which the client dealt with only one employee. The data would become performance feedback that teams could use to identify areas for improvement.

Over a two-year period, Condor analyzed more than 4.5 million messages. Twice a year, Genpact conducted a customer satisfaction survey in which clients indicated their likelihood to recommend Genpact. The early results confirmed Gloor's prediction that teams whose communications were direct (no supervisor needed), simple, and speedy and that continued with the same Genpact employee would be associated with greater customer satisfaction. Each month during this period, team leaders met to learn their team's performance on the four measures, and they took this information back to their teams, so all the participating employees could see which measures needed improvement.

The employees received performance feedback–data on communication patterns–once each quarter. Initially, results were provided at the level of the individual team member, in order to contribute to individual improvement. However, this raised concerns that lower-performing employees could feel punished for participating in the project. So the feedback shifted to a team-level focus. Even without the individual feedback, Genpact employees could see what needed to improve, and they shifted their communication behaviors to ones associated with client satisfaction. By the end of the test program, client satisfaction scores in the group using the Condor data rose 5%, while they fell by 12% for teams in the control group, resulting in a 17-percentage-point gap in favor of the teams getting the feedback on their communication behavior.

Questions

1. How well do you think Genpact's network analysis approach to performance management met the criteria for effectiveness? Explain.
2. If you were in Genpact's human resource department, would you recommend that the company roll out the same kind of performance feedback to the remaining teams? Why or why not?

Sources: Genpact website, https://www.genpact.com, accessed April 24, 2020; Galaxy Advisors website, http://www.galaxyadvisors.com, accessed April 24, 2020; "A Novel Way to Boost Client Satisfaction," *Harvard Business Review*, March–April 2019, pp. 17–21; Edmund Tadros, "Companies Track Staff Emails to Monitor Dissent and Predict Unrest," *Financial Review*, April 23, 2019, https://www.afr.com.

HR IN SMALL BUSINESS

A New Foundation for Performance Management at RiverRock

RiverRock Real Estate Group provides property management services to owners of office, industrial, and retail properties in California and Arizona. It also offers construction management and accounting services. RiverRock, which calls its employees "RockStars," was founded in 2003 and nearly doubled in size within its first two decades. Its strategy is to provide superior customer service at a fair price. In support of its customer-centric approach, the firm recently hired as chief strategy officer David Pogue, who has a background in implementing socially responsible strategies.

The firm has taken a flexible approach to performance management. According to Kathy Valentine, RiverRock's vice president of human resources, RiverRock at one point shifted away from a rigid system of annual performance reviews. Instead, the company would expect managers to provide "constant feedback." Valentine said most employees were happy with the informal approach, but after a while, some employees began requesting a more structured process. Valentine observed that the requests came mainly from employees in the millennial generation, and she interpreted this as a sign that employees in the early part of their career are seeking more guidance or are less confident to ask for informal feedback. In her experience, the long-tenured employees feel they get enough feedback from informal conversations.

RiverRock's next approach was intended to balance informal communication and a structured system. Managers are expected to meet with employees in what the firm calls "RAP [review, analyze, plan] sessions." A RAP session is a meeting to discuss performance relative to goals set in the previous session, followed by a discussion of goals for the next period. The discussion is supposed to be based on answers to several open-ended questions on a one-page document. The goal of these sessions is to provide coaching and career planning; their content is unconnected to compensation decisions.

Valentine says the more structured process has improved communication overall at RiverRock. Some supervisors mentioned to her that they were surprised at what they learned from employees about their career goals–information that has become useful for succession planning. RiverRock's founder and principal, John Combs, agrees that the RAP session format is an improvement and a way to ensure feedback in support of high performance.

Questions

1. Imagine that Kathy Valentine hired you to consult on RiverRock's approach to performance management. What would you tell her are the strengths and weaknesses of the firm's current methods?
2. As a small, people-oriented business, RiverRock might not have the capabilities for a sophisticated, data-driven approach to performance management. Even so, suggest a few steps the firm could take to improve this process.

Sources: RiverRock Real Estate Group website, "About Us," https://www.riverrockreg.com, accessed April 24, 2020; "RiverRock Embarks on Company-Wide Strategic Business Plan Adding Chief Strategy Officer David Pogue," news release, https://www.riverrockreg.com, accessed April 24, 2020; Kelsi Maree Borland, "RiverRock Launches New Business Model," *GlobeSt*, January 31, 2020, https://www.globest.com; Nancye J. Kirk, "Under Review," *JPM*, March/April 2019, pp. 20–23.

NOTES

1. David Almeda and Kim Nugent, "The Case for Measuring Managers at Kronos," *HR People + Strategy*, Winter 2019, https://www.hrps.org.
2. Discussion based on E. Pulakos, *Performance Management* (Oxford: Wiley-Blackwell, 2009); H. Aguinis, "An Expanded View of Performance Management," in *Performance Management*, eds. J. W. Smith and M. London (San Francisco: Jossey-Bass, 2009), pp. 1–43; J. Russell and L. Russell, "Talk Me Through It: The Next Level of Performance Management," *T + D*, April 2010, pp. 42–48.

3. B. Hancock, E. Hioe, and B. Schaninger, "The Fairness Factor in Performance Management," *McKinsey Quarterly,* April 2018, https://www.mckinsey.com.
4. "How GE Renews Performance Management: From Stack Ranking to Continuous," *Impraise blog,* https://www.impraise.com, accessed April 24, 2020; Max Nisen, "How Millennials Forced GE to Scrap Performance Reviews," *The Atlantic,* August 18, 2015, https://www.theatlantic.com.
5. J. Chun, J. Brockner, and D. De Cremer, "People Don't Want to Be Compared with Others in Performance Reviews: They Want to Be Compared with Themselves," *Harvard Business Review,* March 22, 2018, https://hbr.org.
6. Ibid.; J. Gifford, P. Urwin, and A. Cerqua, *Strength-Based Performance Conversations: An Organisational Field Trial,* Chartered Institute of Personnel and Development, November 2017, https://www.cebglobal.com; P. Cappelli and A. Tavis, "The Performance Management Evolution," *Harvard Business Review,* October 2016, pp. 58–67; A. Fox, "Curing What Ails Performance Reviews," *HR Magazine,* January 2009, pp. 52–57.
7. S. Scullen, P. Bergey, and L. Aiman-Smith, "Forced Choice Distribution Systems and the Improvement of Workforce Potential: A Baseline Simulation," *Personnel Psychology* 58 (2005), pp. 1–32.
8. H. J. Kell, M. P. Martin-Raugh, L. M. Carney, P. A. Inglese, L. Chen, and G. Feng, "Exploring Methods for Developing Behaviorally Anchored Rating Scales for Evaluating Structured Interview Performance," *ETS Research Report Series,* January 2018, pp. 1–11; P. Smith and L. Kendall, "Retranslation of Expectations: An Approach to the Construction of Unambiguous Anchors for Rating Scales," *Journal of Applied Psychology* 47 (1963), pp. 149–155.
9. K. Murphy and J. Constans, "Behavioral Anchors as a Source of Bias in Rating," *Journal of Applied Psychology* 72 (1987), pp. 573–577; M. Piotrowski, J. Barnes-Farrel, and F. Estig, "Behaviorally Anchored Bias: A Replication and Extension of Murphy and Constans," *Journal of Applied Psychology* 74 (1989), pp. 823–826; R. Harvey, "Job Analysis," in *Handbook of Industrial and Organizational Psychology,* 2nd ed. (Palo Alto, CA: Consulting Psychologists Press, 1991).
10. G. Latham and K. Wexley, *Increasing Productivity through Performance Appraisal* (Boston: Addison-Wesley, 1981).
11. U. Wiersma and G. Latham, "The Practicality of Behavioral Observation Scales, Behavioral Expectation Scales, and Trait Scales," *Personnel Psychology* 39 (1986), pp. 619–628.
12. D. C. Anderson, C. Crowell, J. Sucec, K. Gilligan, and M. Wikoff, "Behavior Management of Client Contacts in a Real Estate Brokerage: Getting Agents to Sell More," *Journal of Organizational Behavior Management* 4 (2001), pp. 580–590; F. Luthans and R. Kreitner, *Organizational Behavior Modification and Beyond* (Glenview, IL: Scott-Foresman, 1975).
13. K. L. Langeland, C. M. Jones, and T. C. Mawhinney, "Improving Staff Performance in a Community Mental Health Setting: Job Analysis, Training, Goal Setting, Feedback, and Years of Data," *Journal of Organizational Behavior Management* 18 (1998), pp. 21–43.
14. J. Komaki, R. Collins, and P. Penn, "The Role of Performance Antecedents and Consequences in Work Motivation," *Journal of Applied Psychology* 67 (1982), pp. 334–340.
15. S. Correll and C. Simard, "Research: Vague Feedback Is Holding Women Back," *Harvard Business Review,* April 29, 2016, https://hbr.org; J. Grenny and D. Maxfield, "Emotional Inequality at Work," *Training,* November/December 2015, pp. 46–48; S. Snell, "Control Theory in Strategic Human Resource Management: The Mediating Effect of Administrative Information," *Academy of Management Journal* 35 (1992), pp. 292–327.
16. R. Pritchard, S. Jones, P. Roth, K. Stuebing, and S. Ekeberg, "The Evaluation of an Integrated Approach to Measuring Organizational Productivity," *Personnel Psychology* 42 (1989), pp. 69–115.
17. G. Odiorne, *MOBII: A System of Managerial Leadership for the 80s* (Belmont, CA: Pitman, 1986).
18. R. Rodgers and J. Hunter, "Impact of Management by Objectives on Organizational Productivity," *Journal of Applied Psychology* 76 (1991), pp. 322–326.
19. P. Wright, J. George, S. Farnsworth, and G. McMahan, "Productivity and Extra-role Behavior: The Effects of Goals and Incentives on Spontaneous Helping," *Journal of Applied Psychology* 78, no. 3 (1993), pp. 374–381; M. Ledyard and J. Tillman, "Do Your Metrics Measure Up?" *Material Handling and Logistics,* December 2013, pp. 27–29.
20. R. Heneman, K. Wexley, and M. Moore, "Performance Rating Accuracy: A Critical Review," *Journal of Business Research* 15 (1987), pp. 431–448.
21. T. Becker and R. Klimoski, "A Field Study of the Relationship between the Organizational Feedback Environment and Performance," *Personnel Psychology* 42 (1989), pp. 343–358; H. M. Findley, W. F. Giles, and K. W. Mossholder, "Performance Appraisal and Systems Facets: Relationships with Contextual Performance," *Journal of Applied Psychology* 85 (2000), pp. 634–640.
22. K. Wexley and R. Klimoski, "Performance Appraisal: An Update," in *Research in Personnel and Human Resource Management,* vol. 2, eds. K. Rowland and G. Ferris (Greenwich, CT: JAI Press, 1984).
23. S. Pollock, "4 Ways to Get the Most Out of Peer Assessments," *ClearCompany blog,* December 27, 2019, https://blog.clearcompany.com; F. Landy and J. Farr, *The Measurement of Work Performance: Methods, Theory, and Applications* (New York: Academic Press, 1983).
24. M. Derven, "What about Teams?" *TD,* November 2017, pp. 40–45; M. B. Mehta, "Peer Evaluations Hit the Factory Floor," *ISE Magazine,* January 2017, pp. 45–48; G. McEvoy and P. Buller, "User Acceptance of Peer Appraisals in an Industrial Setting," *Personnel Psychology* 40 (1987), pp. 785–797.
25. D. Morris, "Death to the Performance Review: How Adobe Reinvented Performance Management and Transformed Its Business," *WorldatWork Journal,* https://www.adobe.com, accessed April 24, 2020.
26. D. Antonioni, "The Effects of Feedback Accountability on Upward Appraisal Ratings," *Personnel Psychology* 47 (1994), pp. 349–356.
27. C. Kehayas, "Do These Things to Prepare for a Performance Review," *Fast Company,* December 13, 2018, https://www.fastcompany.com; R. E. Silverman, "Performance Reviews Lose Steam," *The Wall Street Journal,* December 19, 2011, https://www.wsj.com.
28. H. Heidemeier and K. Moser, "Self-Other Agreement in Job Performance Rating: A Meta-Analytic Test of a Process Model," *Journal of Applied Psychology* 94 (2008), pp. 353–370.
29. J. Bernardin, C. Hagan, J. Kane, and P. Villanova, "Effective Performance Management: A Focus on Precision, Customers, and Situational Constraints," in *Performance Appraisal: State of*

the Art in Practice, ed. J. W. Smither (San Francisco: Jossey-Bass, 1998), pp. 3–48.

30. K. Wexley and W. Nemeroff, "Effects of Racial Prejudice, Race of Applicant, and Biographical Similarity on Interviewer Evaluations of Job Applicants," *Journal of Social and Behavioral Sciences* 20 (1974), pp. 66–78.
31. D. Smith, "Training Programs for Performance Appraisal: A Review," *Academy of Management Review* 11 (1986), pp. 22–40; G. Latham, K. Wexley, and E. Pursell, "Training Managers to Minimize Rating Errors in the Observation of Behavior," *Journal of Applied Psychology* 60 (1975), pp. 550–555.
32. E. Pulakos, "A Comparison of Rater Training Programs: Error Training and Accuracy Training," *Journal of Applied Psychology* 69 (1984), pp. 581–588.
33. B. Marr, "5 Inspiring Ways Organizations Are Using HR Data," *Forbes,* https://www.forbes.com, accessed April 24, 2020.
34. Derven, "What about Teams?"; A. P. Tenbrink and M. G. Schwendeman, "Let's Talk It Out: The Effects of Calibration Meetings on Performance Ratings," *Journal of Human Performance* 32 (2019), pp. 107–128.
35. S. W. J. Kozlowski, G. T. Chao, and R. F. Morrison, "Games Raters Play: Politics, Strategies, and Impression Management in Performance Appraisal," in *Performance Appraisal: State of the Art in Practice,* pp. 163–205; C. Rosen, P. Levy, and R. Hall, "Placing Perceptions of Politics in the Context of the Feedback Environment, Employee Attitudes, and Job Performance," *Journal of Applied Psychology* 91 (2006), pp. 211–220.
36. N. Sloan, D. Agarwal, S. S. Garr, and K. Pastakia, "Performance Management: Play a Winning Hand," in *Rewriting the Rules for the Digital Age: 2017 Deloitte Global Human Capital Trends* (Deloitte University Press, 2017), p. 66; S. Murphy and M. J. Mowry, "How Am I Doing?" *Business NH,* September 2017, pp. 70–72; M. Weinstein, "Annual Review under Review," *Training,* July/August 2016, pp. 22–29.
37. M. V. Rafter, "Upon Further Review: Ellyn Shook," *Workforce,* January 2017, http://www.workforce.com; K. Wexley, V. Singh, and G. Yukl, "Subordinate Participation in Three Types of Appraisal Interviews," *Journal of Applied Psychology* 58 (1973), pp. 54–57; K. Wexley, "Appraisal Interview," in *Performance Assessment,* ed. R. A. Berk (Baltimore: Johns Hopkins University Press, 1986), pp. 167–185; B. D. Cawley, L. M. Keeping, and P. E. Levy, "Participation in the Performance Appraisal Process and Employee Reactions: A Meta-analytic Review of Field Investigations," *Journal of Applied Psychology* 83, no. 3 (1998), pp. 615–663; H. Aguinis, *Performance Management* (Upper Saddle River, NJ: Pearson Prentice-Hall, 2007).
38. R. Hanson and E. Pulakos, *Putting the "Performance" Back in Performance Management* (Alexandria, VA: Society for Human Resource Management, 2015); B. D. Cawley, L. M. Keeping, and P. E. Levy, "Participation in the Performance Appraisal Process and Employee Reactions: A Meta-analytic Review of Field Investigations," *Journal of Applied Psychology* 83, no. 3 (1998), pp. 615–663; W. Giles and K. Mossholder, "Employee Reactions to Contextual and Session Components of Performance Appraisal," *Journal of Applied Psychology* 75 (1990), pp. 371–377.
39. M. Buckingham, "Out with the Old, in with . . .," *TD,* August 2016, pp. 44–48; "Goodyear Performance Management Optimization Case Study," presented to MHR 4328 Performance Management Class, The Ohio State University, September 6, 2016.
40. Gifford et al., *Strengths-Based Performance Conversations;* Scott Berinato, "Negative Feedback Rarely Leads to Improvement: Mr. Green, Defend Your Research," *Harvard Business Review,* January–February 2018, pp. 32–33; Joseph Folkman, "Why Is It So Difficult for Leaders to Give Positive Feedback?" *Forbes,* October 20, 2017, https://www.forbes.com.
41. S. Chowdhury, E. Hioe, and B. Schaninger, "Harnessing the Power of Performance Management," McKinsey & Company, April 2018, https://www.mckinsey.com; C. Crossley, C. Cooper, and T. Wernsing, "Making Things Happen through Challenging Goals: Leader Proactivity, Trust, and Business-Unit Performance," *Journal of Applied Psychology* 98 (2013), pp. 540–549; E. Locke and G. Latham, *A Theory of Goal Setting and Task Performance* (Englewood Cliffs, NJ: Prentice Hall, 1990); H. Klein, S. Snell, and K. Wexley, "A Systems Model of the Performance Appraisal Interview Process," *Industrial Relations* 26 (1987), pp. 267–280.
42. *Brito v. Zia Co.,* 478 F.2d 1200 (10th Cir. 1973).
43. K. Kraiger and J. Ford, "A Meta-Analysis of Ratee Race Effects in Performance Rating," *Journal of Applied Psychology* 70 (1985), pp. 56–65; P. Sackett, C. DuBois, and A. Noe, "Tokenism in Performance Evaluation: The Effects of Work Group Representation on Male-Female and White-Black Differences in Performance Ratings," *Journal of Applied Psychology* 76 (1991), pp. 263–267.
44. C. Kostoula, "How to Design Performance Reviews That Don't Fail Women," *Fast Company,* January 22, 2018, https://www.fastcompany.com.
45. G. Barrett and M. Kernan, "Performance Appraisal and Terminations: A Review of Court Decisions since *Brito v. Zia* with Implications for Personnel Practices," *Personnel Psychology* 40 (1987), pp. 489–503; H. Feild and W. Holley, "The Relationship of Performance Appraisal System Characteristics to Verdicts in Selected Employment Discrimination Cases," *Academy of Management Journal* 25 (1982), pp. 392–406; J. M. Werner and M. C. Bolino, "Explaining U.S. Courts of Appeals Decisions Involving Performance Appraisal: Accuracy, Fairness, and Validation," *Personnel Psychology* 50 (1997), pp. 1–24; J. Segal, "Performance Management Blunders," *HR Magazine,* November 2010, pp. 75–77.
46. Sloan et al., "Performance Management"; J. Bersin, "Transformative Tech: A Disruptive Year Ahead," *HR Magazine,* February 2017, pp. 29–36.

Separating and Retaining Employees

11

Aflac's low employee turnover rate can be attributed in part to the HR team coaching employees on updating their résumés and refreshing their skills when interviewing for new jobs within the company.

PIXDUCE/Alamy Stock Photo

What Do I Need to Know?

After reading this chapter, you should be able to:

LO 11-1 Distinguish between involuntary and voluntary turnover, and describe their effects on an organization.

LO 11-2 Discuss how employees determine whether the organization treats them fairly.

LO 11-3 Identify legal requirements for employee discipline.

LO 11-4 Summarize ways in which organizations can discipline employees fairly.

LO 11-5 Explain how job dissatisfaction affects employee behavior.

LO 11-6 Describe how organizations contribute to employees' job satisfaction and retain key employees.

Introduction

Among insurance companies, the employee turnover rate is 10.8%, meaning that more than one in ten employees quits in a given year. Some companies are doing better, of course. Aflac is one of those companies. On average, its employees stay for almost 18 years.

Aflac's chief human resources officer, Matthew Owenby, credits what he describes as creating individual relationships with employees. That is, each employee takes ownership of his or her career, and the company supports that effort. Aflac has a Career Success Center, and employees meet as often as they want to with someone in the center to craft a career plan that identifies specific skills needed and a path to acquiring those skills.

Aflac also asks its employees about their career experiences. The HR team learned several years ago that employees found it difficult to obtain promotions and developmental job changes. They learned that because employees stay with the company for a relatively long time, they don't get much practice in applying for a new position. Their skills of résumé writing and interviewing get rusty. This situation placed internal candidates at a disadvantage to external candidates seeking positions at Aflac. So the HR department began to provide coaching on updating résumés and training in effective participation in job interviews. The company now tracks its success in employees obtaining promotions.

Aflac also encourages employees to stay by offering benefits such as on-site child care that are aimed at enabling workers to continue working through major life changes. It affirms commitment to the organization by giving employees awards for length of service.[1]

Like Aflac, every organization must meet the challenges of retaining good employees. Research provides evidence that retaining employees helps retain customers and increase sales.[2] Organizations with low turnover and satisfied employees tend

Visit your instructor's Connect® course and access your eBook to view this video.

"But you know you have a successful organization when the people who work for you and work with you will openly and with a great deal of comfort say, 'I'm looking for another job.'"

—Jerrold Williams, Chief HR Officer
Daymon Worldwide

Source: Video Produced for the Center for Executive Succession in the Darla Moore School of Business at the University of South Carolina by Coal Powered Filmworks

to perform better.[3] On the other side of the coin, organizations have to act when an employee's performance consistently falls short. Sometimes terminating a poor performer is the only way to show fairness, ensure quality, and maintain customer satisfaction.

This chapter explores the dual challenges of separating and retaining employees (see Table 11.1). We begin by distinguishing involuntary and voluntary turnover, describing how each affects the organization. Next we explore the separation process, including ways to manage this process fairly. Finally, we discuss measures the organization can take to encourage employees to stay. These topics provide a transition between Parts 3 and 4 of this book. The previous chapters considered how to assess and improve performance, and this chapter describes measures to take depending on whether performance is high or low. Part 4 discusses pay and benefits, both of which play an important role in employee retention.

LO 11-1 Distinguish between involuntary and voluntary turnover, and describe their effects on an organization.

Involuntary Turnover Turnover initiated by an employer (often with employees who would prefer to stay).

Voluntary Turnover Turnover initiated by employees (often when the organization would prefer to keep them).

Managing Voluntary and Involuntary Turnover

Organizations must try to ensure that good performers want to stay with the organization and that employees whose performance is chronically low are encouraged–or forced–to leave. Both of these challenges involve *employee turnover,* that is, employees leaving the organization. When the organization initiates the turnover (often with employees who would prefer to stay), the result is **involuntary turnover.** Examples include terminating an employee for drug use or laying off employees during an economic downturn, such as the one caused globally by the COVID-19 pandemic. Most organizations use the word *termination* to refer only to a discharge related to a discipline problem, but some organizations call any involuntary turnover a termination. When the employees initiate the turnover (often when the organization would prefer to keep them), it is **voluntary turnover.** Employees may leave to retire or to take a job with a different organization. Typically, the employees who leave voluntarily are either the organization's worst performers, who quit before they are fired, or its best performers, who can most easily find attractive new opportunities.[4]

In general, organizations try to avoid the need for involuntary turnover and to minimize voluntary turnover, especially among top performers. Both kinds of turnover are

TABLE 11.1
HR Practices That Support Effective Separation and Retention

SEPARATING EMPLOYEES	RETAINING EMPLOYEES
(Managing Involuntary Turnover)	***(Minimizing Voluntary Turnover)***
Establishing fair and legally defensible processes for discipline (including, if necessary, termination)	Providing management training and employee benefits that enable discipline to drive performance improvement
Establishing fair and legally defensible processes for layoffs	Promoting employee engagement Preventing job withdrawal Promoting job satisfaction

TABLE 11.2
Costs Associated with Turnover

INVOLUNTARY TURNOVER	VOLUNTARY TURNOVER
Recruiting, selecting, and training replacements	Recruiting, selecting, and training replacements
Lost productivity	Lost productivity
Lawsuits	Loss of talented employees
Workplace violence	

costly, as summarized in Table 11.2. Replacing workers is expensive, and the economic growth since the 2008–2009 recession made open positions increasingly difficult to fill, especially at small companies. Even when employers find people to hire, new employees need time to learn their jobs and build teamwork skills.[5] Employees who leave out of anger and frustration may not be shy about generating unfavorable publicity or even suing a former employer.

For a number of reasons, discharging employees can be very difficult. First, the decision has legal aspects that can affect the organization. Historically, if the organization and employee do not have a specific employment contract, the employer or employee may end the employment relationship at any time. This is the *employment-at-will doctrine,* described in Chapter 5. This doctrine has eroded significantly, however. Employees who have been terminated sometimes sue their employers for wrongful discharge. Some judges have considered that employment at will is limited where managers make statements that amount to an implied contract; a discharge also can be found illegal if it violates a law (such as antidiscrimination laws) or public policy (for example, firing an employee for refusing to do something illegal).[6] In a typical lawsuit for wrongful discharge, the former employee tries to establish that the discharge violated either an implied agreement or public policy. Although these claims are often settled out of court, the costs to defend them and negotiate a settlement can be significant.

Along with the financial risks of dismissing an employee, there are issues of personal safety. Distressing as it is that some former employees go to the courts, far worse are the employees who react to a termination decision with violence. Violence in the workplace has become a major organizational problem. Although any number of organizational actions or decisions may incite violence among employees, the "nothing else to lose" aspect of an employee's dismissal makes the situation dangerous. Companies report more than 25,000 workplace injuries a year at the hands of employees who claim their stress levels pushed them over the edge.[7] An engineer who worked for the city of Virginia Beach for more than a decade sent a resignation letter to his supervisor and then inexplicably shot 12 of his colleagues, including his boss, before he was fatally wounded in a tragic workplace incident in 2019. Independent investigators say they have no clear motive for the shooting, although they confirm the shooter had endured several personal struggles in recent years, including a divorce, which may have contributed to his stress. According to reports, the shooter also complained about feeling "singled out" for unsatisfactory performance at work.[8]

Competition for qualified, motivated workers in the STEM (scientific, technology, engineering, and medical) fields is intense. Retaining these employees is especially critical to an organization's overall success.
Klaus Tiedge/Blend Images LLC

Retaining talent is not always easy either, and recent trends have made this more difficult than ever. Today's psychological contract, in which workers feel responsibility for their own careers rather than loyalty to a particular employer, makes voluntary turnover more likely.

The low unemployment rate associated with years of economic expansion has improved employees' odds of finding better pay or a more interesting job if they quit. In fact, recent research by global staffing firm Robert Half suggests that nearly 43% of workers plan on looking for a new job within the next year.[9] Also, competing organizations are constantly looking at each other's top performers. For high-demand positions, such as software engineers, "poaching talent" from other companies has become the norm.

Despite these difficulties, effective human resource management can help the organization achieve its goals for both kinds of turnover. This generally means a fair and legal separation (involuntary turnover) when necessary for high performance, as well as a low rate of voluntary turnover.

Employee Separation

Personnel selection, training, and compensation are intended to provide the organization with high-performing employees, but in practice, some employees fail to meet requirements or violate company policies. When this happens, separation is not inevitable, but organizations need to respond with a discipline program. Discipline is essential, because ignoring performance problems would create a negative environment for everyone else, as described in "HR How To." The discipline program needs to provide for the possibility that an employee will not improve and will have to be dismissed.

Given the problems outlined in the previous section, it is easy to see why organizations must develop a standardized, systematic approach to discipline and discharge. These decisions should not be left solely to the discretion of individual managers or supervisors. Policies that can lead to employee separation should be based on principles of justice and law, and they should allow for various ways to intervene.

LO 11-2 Discuss how employees determine whether the organization treats them fairly.

Principles of Justice

The sensitivity of a system for disciplining and possibly terminating employees is obvious, and it is critical that the system be seen as fair. Employees form conclusions about the system's fairness based on the system's outcomes and procedures and the way managers treat employees when carrying out those procedures. Figure 11.1 summarizes these principles as outcome fairness, procedural justice, and interactional justice. Outcome fairness involves the ends of a discipline process, while procedural and interactional justice focus on the means to those ends. Not only is behavior ethical that is in accord with these principles, but research has also linked the last two categories of justice with employee satisfaction and productivity.[10] In considering these principles, however, keep in mind that individuals differ in how strongly they react to perceived injustice.[11]

Outcome Fairness
A judgment that the consequences given to employees are just.

People's perception of **outcome fairness** depends on their judgment that the consequences of a decision to employees are just. As shown in Figure 11.1, one employee's consequences should be consistent with other employees' consequences. Suppose several employees went out to lunch, returned drunk, and were reprimanded. A few weeks later, another employee was fired for being drunk at work. Employees might well conclude that outcomes are not fair because they are inconsistent. Another basis for outcome fairness is that everyone should know what to expect. Organizations promote outcome fairness when they clearly communicate policies regarding the consequences of inappropriate behavior. Finally, the outcome should be proportionate to the behavior. Terminating an employee for being late to work, especially if this is the first time the employee is late, would seem out of proportion to the offense in most situations. Employees' sense of outcome fairness usually would reserve loss of a job for the most serious offenses.

Dealing with Rude Behavior at Work

Rude behavior from co-workers, such as ignoring someone or making sarcastic remarks, might seem like an ordinary situation that employees should learn to handle. But there is evidence that rudeness is more than a minor annoyance. It has been associated with damage to productivity and employees' commitment to the organization, as well as employee turnover. An experiment involving teams of hospital workers found that when teams were overseen by a person who made rude remarks, the teams made more errors because they communicated and collaborated less. Besides the performance issues, this behavior can cross a line into harassment or abuse that triggers a lawsuit related to discrimination, workplace safety, or employer negligence.

Given that rudeness affects performance and places the organization at risk, managers need to be aware of this conduct and intervene. An important starting point is to establish mutual respect as a standard of behavior for work teams and the organization as a whole. Especially if there are questions about what civil behavior looks like, the organization should provide training in what it expects from its people. Teamwork training can provide practice in the interpersonal skills needed for respectful, productive behavior. Training of managers should also address reasons why it is important to respond when rude behavior occurs.

In addition, the organization's discipline process should define the kinds of rude and bullying behavior that will trigger discipline. Examples could include gossiping about coworkers' personal lives, making insults or slurs, angry shouting and acts of violence such as throwing objects at people, and intimidating or humiliating treatment of others.

If it seems possible that the rude employee's behavior might veer into intimidating or violent actions, prepare safety measures before engaging with him or her. Measures might include meeting in a private but visible location and having a witness present. The organization's security team could be a resource for preparing such measures. Also, the manager and HR staff member should keep the discussion focused on standards and behavior, rather than getting caught up in any emotions and name calling.

Questions

1. Suppose a shift leader in a warehouse shouts angrily at employees and calls them names when he is displeased with performance. Occasionally, he throws a box or tape dispenser. What would be the likely consequences of management ignoring this behavior? What would be the likely consequences of management carrying out a discipline process?
2. Suppose you are the HR manager at the company where this shift leader works. Would you advise management to launch disciplinary action? Why or why not?

Sources: "Managing Difficult Employees and Disruptive Behaviors," *Society for Human Resource Management,* https://www.shrm.org, accessed April 29, 2020; Shannon G. Taylor, Donald H. Kluemper, W. Matthew Bowler, and Jonathan R. B. Halbesleben, "Why People Get Away with Being Rude at Work," *Harvard Business Review,* July 10, 2019, https://hbr.org; Jathan Janove, "Mistakes Managers Make," *HR Magazine,* June/July 2017, pp. 53–59; Gurpreet Dhaliwal, "How Rudeness between Health-Care Workers Can Cost Lives," *The Wall Street Journal,* February 27, 2017, https://blogs.wsj.com.

People's perception of **procedural justice** is their judgment that fair methods were used to determine the consequences an employee receives. Figure 11.1 shows six principles that determine whether people perceive procedures as fair. The procedures should be consistent from one person to another, and the manager using them should suppress any personal biases. The procedures should be based on accurate information, not rumors or falsehoods. The procedures should also be correctable, meaning the system includes safeguards, such as channels for appealing a decision or correcting errors. The procedures should take into account the concerns of all the groups affected—for example, by gathering information from employees, customers, and managers. Finally, the procedures should be consistent with prevailing ethical standards, such as concerns for privacy and honesty.

Procedural Justice
A judgment that fair methods were used to determine the consequences an employee receives.

A perception of **interactional justice** is a judgment that the organization carried out its actions in a way that took the employee's feelings into account. It is a judgment about the ways in which managers interact with their employees. A disciplinary action meets the

Interactional Justice
A judgment that the organization carried out its actions in a way that took the employee's feelings into account.

FIGURE 11.1
Principles of Justice

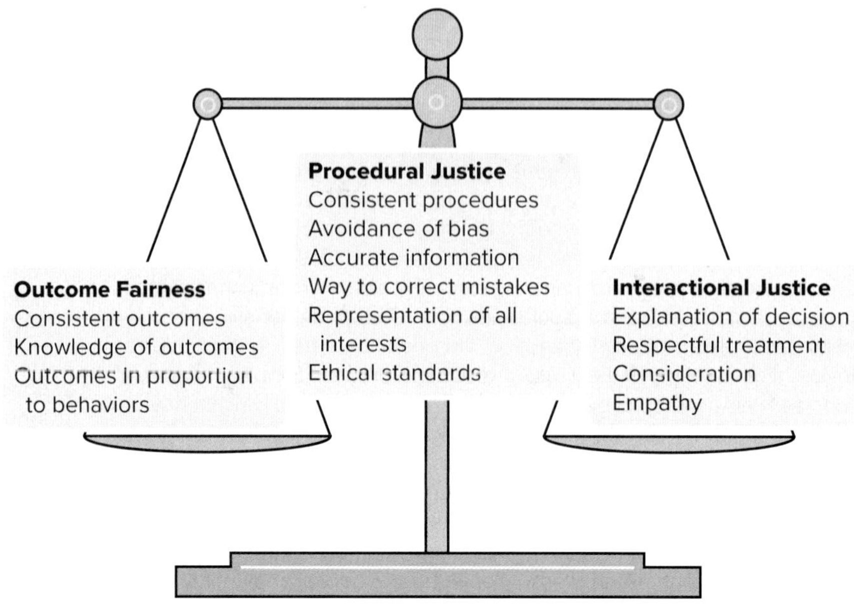

standards of interactional justice if the manager explains to the employee how the action is procedurally just. The manager should listen to the employee. The manager should also treat the employee with dignity and respect and should empathize with the employee's feelings. Even when a manager discharges an employee for doing something wrong, the manager can speak politely and state the reasons for the action. These efforts to achieve interactional justice are especially important when managing an employee who has a high level of hostility and is at greater risk of responding with violence.[12]

LO 11-3 Identify legal requirements for employee discipline.

Legal Requirements

The law gives employers wide latitude in hiring and firing, but employers must meet certain requirements. They must avoid wrongful discharge and illegal discrimination. They also must meet standards related to employees' privacy and adequate notice of layoffs.

Wrongful Discharge As we noted earlier in the chapter, discipline practices must avoid the charge of wrongful discharge. First, this means the discharge may not violate an implied agreement. Terminating an employee might violate an implied agreement if the employer had promised the employee job security or if the action is inconsistent with company policies. An example might be that an organization has stated that an employee with an unexcused absence will receive a warning for the first violation, but an angry supervisor fires an employee for being absent on the day of an important meeting.

Another reason a discharge may be considered wrongful is that it violates public policy. Violations of public policy include terminating the employee for refusing to do something illegal, unethical, or unsafe. Suppose an employee refuses to dump chemicals into the sewer system; firing that employee could be a violation of public policy. It is also a violation of public policy to terminate an employee for doing what the law requires–for example, cooperating with a government investigation, reporting illegal behavior by the employer, or reporting for jury duty.

HR professionals can help organizations avoid (and defend against) charges of wrongful discharge by establishing and communicating policies for handling misbehavior. They should define unacceptable behaviors and identify how the organization will respond to them. Managers should follow these procedures consistently and document precisely the reasons for disciplinary action. In addition, the organization should train managers to avoid making promises that imply job security (for example, "As long as you keep up that level of performance, you'll have a job with us"). Finally, in writing and reviewing employee handbooks, HR professionals should avoid any statements that could be interpreted as employment contracts. When there is any doubt about a statement, the organization should seek legal advice. The "HRM Social" box describes how these principles apply to an issue currently causing problems for employers: employees using social media in ways that waste time or hurt the company's public image.

Discrimination Another benefit of a formal discipline policy is that it helps the organization comply with equal employment opportunity requirements. As in other employment matters, employers must make decisions without regard to individuals' age, sex, race, or other protected status. If two employees steal from the employer but one is disciplined more harshly than the other, the employee who receives the harsher punishment could look for the cause in his or her being of a particular race, country of origin, or some other group. Evenhanded, carefully documented discipline can avoid such claims.

Employees' Privacy The courts also have long protected individuals' privacy in many situations. At the same time, employers have legitimate reasons for learning about some personal matters, especially when behavior outside the workplace can affect productivity, workplace safety, and employee morale. Employers therefore need to ensure that the information they gather and use is relevant to these matters. For example, safety and security make it legitimate to require drug testing of all employees holding jobs such as police officer, firefighter, and airline flight crew.[13] Governments at the federal, state, and local levels have many laws affecting drug-testing programs, so it is wise to get legal advice before planning such tests. Legal advice could be especially helpful in the case of marijuana, given that some states permit it for medical use only, other states allow its recreational use, while still other states and the federal government have maintained its illegal status.[14]

Privacy issues also surface when employers wish to search or monitor employees on the job. An employer that suspects theft, drug use, or other misdeeds on the job may wish to search employees for evidence. In general, random searches of areas such as desks, lockers, toolboxes, and communications such as e-mails are permissible, so long as the employer can establish that there is probable cause for the search and the organization has work rules that provide for searches.[15] Employers can act fairly and minimize the likelihood of a lawsuit by publicizing the search policy, applying it consistently, asking for the employee's consent before the search begins, and conducting the search discreetly. Also, when a search is a random check, it is important to clarify that no one has been accused of misdeeds.[16]

No matter how sensitively the organization gathers information leading to disciplinary actions, it should also consider privacy issues when deciding who will see the information.[17] In general, it is advisable to share the information only with people who have a business need to see it–for example, the employee's supervisor, union officials, and in some cases, coworkers. Letting outsiders know the reasons for terminating an employee can embarrass the employee, who might file a defamation lawsuit. HR professionals can help organizations avoid such lawsuits by working with managers to determine fact-based explanations and to decide who needs to see these explanations. Another approach is to analyze and share data about groups, such as departments or business units, and to share data about individuals only when the analysis uncovers possibly illegal or risky behavior that the company needs to investigate.

Table 11.3 summarizes these measures for protecting employees' privacy.

Firing an Employee for Social-Media Use

Intentionally and unintentionally, social-media users find themselves in trouble with their employers. An employee handling social media for Marriott clicked "like" on a Twitter post for a group promoting nationhood for Tibet, triggering a complaint from the Chinese government (which views Tibet as part of China). A university health system employee used her personal Twitter account identifying herself as a nurse to tweet an offensively worded post about the dangers of young white men. And a Google employee used internal communication channels to complain about efforts to promote diversity, in particular questioning whether females' biology made them less apt to succeed there. None of these employees still work for those organizations.

Employees are often surprised to discover that "freedom of speech" does not mean they can post anything on social media and keep their job. That constitutional right protects them from being prosecuted for their speech, not from firing. Young employees who by habit choose sharing over privacy also may be surprised to find that their employers are more concerned about protecting their brand from bad publicity.

Nasty or controversial posts by employees, especially at the workplace and when associated with the employer's accounts, can hurt employers by angering stakeholders, including customers and employees. Beyond this, employees who spend work time on personal social-media accounts are in effect loafing—being paid for time they are not working. Therefore, employers are reasonable to require that employees use social media responsibly.

As with other kinds of harmful behavior, discipline policies need to spell out what social-media use will be considered cause for disciplinary action. For example, the policy might say that any posts using the organization's brand or identifying the employee with the organization must be consistent with the organization's mission and values. Messages that create a hostile work environment should be banned to prevent charges of harassment. To combat loafing, the policy might ban all personal use during work hours. However, some employers are more lenient because they see short social-media breaks as a way for employees to recharge and experience better work-life balance, or because social-media tools are part of the way employees connect and learn. Whatever the standards, the response to violations should be consistently used in accordance with them.

Questions

1. Suppose a company's employee handbook says, "We welcome the free flow of ideas, no matter how controversial. Our employees express themselves freely on our employee networking site." Then an employee posts an angry, racist rant. What problem could this company encounter if it fires the angry employee and the employee claims a wrongful discharge?
2. How much social-media use at work would you define as "too much"? Why?

Sources: June D. Bell, "Firing for Online Behavior," *Society for Human Resource Management,* https://www.shrm.org, accessed April 29, 2020; Wayne Ma, "Marriott Employee Roy Jones Hit 'Like,' then China Got Mad," *The Wall Street Journal,* March 3, 2018, https://www.wsj.com; Genevieve Douglas, "HR Misconduct Went Viral; Now What?" *Bloomberg News,* February 7, 2018, https://www.bna.com; Rob Burgess, "In Legal Gray Area, Social Media Use May Impact Work Life," *Indiana Lawyer,* November 29, 2017, https://www.theindianalawyer.com; Emma Kate Fittes, James Briggs, and Domenica Bongiovanni, "IU Health Says Nurse 'No Longer an Employee' Following Controversial Tweet," *IndyStar,* November 26, 2017, https://www.indystar.com; Yoree Koh and Kelsey Gee, "Google Uproar Highlights Questions over What You Can or Cannot Say at Work," *The Wall Street Journal,* August 8, 2017, https://www.wsj.com; Donald H. Kluemper, Arjun Mitra, and Siting Wang, "Social Media Use in HRM," *Research in Personnel and Human Resources Management* 34 (2016), pp. 153–207.

TABLE 11.3

Measures for Protecting Employees' Privacy

Measures
Ensure that information is relevant.
Publicize information-gathering policies and consequences.
Request consent before gathering information.
Treat employees consistently.
Conduct searches discreetly.
Share information only with those who need it.

Notification of Layoffs Sometimes terminations are necessary, not because of individuals' misdeeds, but because the organization determines that for economic reasons it must close a facility. An organization that plans such broad-scale layoffs may be subject to the Workers' Adjustment Retraining and Notification Act (WARN). This federal law requires that organizations with more than 100 employees give 60 days' notice before any closing or layoff that will affect at least 50 full-time employees. If employers covered by this law do not give notice to the employees (and their union, if applicable), they may have to provide back pay and fringe benefits and pay penalties as well. Several states and cities have similar laws, and the federal law contains a number of exemptions. Therefore, it is important to seek legal advice before implementing a plant closing.

The unprecedented closing of U.S. work facilities and related layoffs caused by COVID-19 may be considered exceptions to the WARN legislation regarding 60-day notice requirements. According to legal professionals, the pandemic would be considered an "unforeseen business circumstance" that was not reasonably anticipated at the time the 60-day notice would have been required to be given to employees.[18]

Progressive Discipline

LO 11-4 Summarize ways in which organizations can discipline employees fairly.

Organizations look for methods of handling problem behavior that are fair, legal, and effective. A popular principle for responding effectively is the **hot-stove rule.** According to this principle, discipline should be like a hot stove: The glowing or burning stove gives warning not to touch. Anyone who ignores the warning will be burned. The stove has no feelings to influence which people it burns, and it delivers the same burn to any touch. Finally, the burn is immediate. Like the hot stove, an organization's discipline should give warning and have consequences that are consistent, objective, and immediate.

Hot-Stove Rule
Principle of discipline that says discipline should be like a hot stove, giving clear warning and following up with consistent, objective, immediate consequences.

The principles of justice suggest that the organization prepare for problems by establishing a formal discipline process in which the consequences become more serious if the employee repeats the offense. Such a system is called **progressive discipline.** A typical progressive discipline system identifies and communicates unacceptable behaviors and responds to a series of offenses with the actions shown in Figure 11.2–spoken and then written warnings, temporary suspension, and finally, termination. This process fulfills the purpose of discipline by teaching employees what is expected of them and creating a situation in which employees must try to do what is expected. It seeks to prevent misbehavior (by publishing rules) and to correct, rather than merely punish, misbehavior.

Progressive Discipline
A formal discipline process in which the consequences become more serious if the employee repeats the offense.

Such procedures may seem exasperatingly slow, especially when the employee's misdeeds hurt the team's performance. In the end, however, if an employee must be discharged, careful use of the procedure increases other employees' belief that the organization is fair and reduces the likelihood that the problem employee will sue (or at least that the employee will win in court). For situations in which misbehavior is dangerous, the organization may establish a stricter policy, even terminating an employee for the first offense. In that case, it

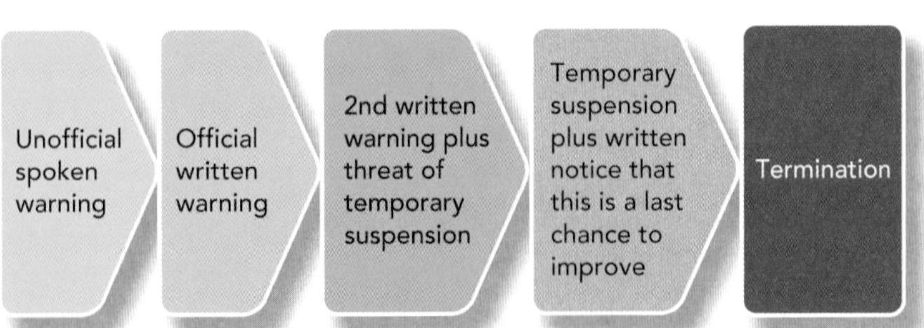

FIGURE 11.2
Progressive Discipline Responses

is especially important to communicate the procedure–not only to ensure fairness but also to prevent the dangerous misbehavior.

Creating a formal discipline process is a primary responsibility of the human resource department. The HR professional should consult with supervisors and managers to identify unacceptable behaviors and establish rules and consequences for violating the rules. The rules should cover disciplinary problems such as the following behaviors encountered in many organizations:

- Tardiness
- Absenteeism
- Unsafe work practices
- Poor quantity or quality of work
- Sexual harassment of co-workers
- Coming to work impaired by alcohol or drugs
- Theft of company property
- Cyberslacking (conducting personal business online during work hours)

For each infraction, the HR professional would identify a series of responses, such as those in Figure 11.2. In addition, the organization must communicate these rules and consequences in writing to every employee. Ways of publishing rules include presenting them in an employee handbook, posting them on the company's intranet, and displaying them on a bulletin board. Supervisors should be familiar with the rules, so that they can discuss them with employees and apply them consistently.

Along with rules and a progression of consequences for violating the rules, a progressive discipline system should have requirements for documenting the rules, offenses, and responses. For issuing an unofficial warning about a less-serious offense, it may be enough to have a witness present. Even then, a written record would be helpful in case the employee repeats the offense in the future. The organization should provide a document for managers to file, recording the nature and date of the offense, the specific improvement expected, and the consequences of the offense. It is also helpful to indicate how the offense affects the performance of the individual employee, others in the group, or the organization as a whole. These documents are important for demonstrating to a problem employee why he or she has been suspended or terminated. They also back up the organization's actions if it should have to defend a lawsuit. Following the hot-stove rule, the supervisor should complete and discuss the documentation immediately after becoming aware of the offense. A copy of the records should be placed in the employee's personnel file. The organization may have a policy of removing records of warnings after a period such as six months, on the grounds that the employee has learned from the experience.

As we noted in the earlier discussion of procedural justice, the discipline system should provide an opportunity to hear every point of view and to correct errors, following a procedure that is consistent for all employees.[19] Discipline should never come as a shock or leave employees unclear about what they did wrong. As soon as possible and before discussing and filing records of misbehavior, it is important for the supervisor to investigate the incident. The employee should be made aware of what he or she is said to have done wrong and should have an opportunity to present his or her version of events. Anyone who witnessed the alleged misdeed also should have an opportunity to present his or her version of what happened. All the statements should be recorded in writing, signed, and dated. In general, employees who belong to a union have a right to the presence of a union representative during a formal investigation interview if they request representation. Finally, employers can support the discipline system's fairness by using a performance management system that gathers objective performance data.

Besides developing these policies, HR professionals have a role in carrying out progressive discipline.[20] In meetings to announce disciplinary actions, it is wise to include two representatives of the organization. Usually the employee's supervisor presents the information, and a representative from the HR department acts as a witness. This person can help the meeting stay on track and, if necessary, can later confirm what happened during the meeting. Especially at the termination stage of the process, the employee may be angry, so it is helpful to be straightforward but polite. The supervisor should state the reason for the meeting, the nature of the problem behavior, and the consequences. When an employee is suspended or terminated, the organization should designate a person to escort the employee from the building to protect the organization's people and property.

Alternative Dispute Resolution

Sometimes problems are easier to solve when an impartial person helps create the solution. Therefore, at various points in the discipline process, the employee or organization might want to bring in someone to help with problem solving. Rather than turning to the courts every time an outsider is desired, more and more organizations are using **alternative dispute resolution (ADR).** A variety of ADR techniques show promise for resolving disputes in a timely, constructive, cost-effective manner (see Figure 11.3):

Alternative Dispute Resolution (ADR)
Methods of solving a problem by bringing in an impartial outsider but not using the court system.

Open-Door Policy
An organization's policy of making managers available to hear complaints.

Peer Review
Process for resolving disputes by taking them to a panel composed of representatives from the organization at the same levels as the people in the dispute.

Mediation
Conflict resolution procedure in which a mediator hears the views of both sides and facilitates the negotiation process but has no formal authority to dictate a resolution.

Arbitration
Conflict resolution procedure in which an arbitrator or arbitration board determines a binding settlement.

1. **Open-door policy**—Based on the expectation that two people in conflict should first try to arrive at a settlement together, the organization has a policy of making managers available to hear complaints. Typically, the first "open door" is that of the employee's immediate supervisor, and if the employee does not get a resolution from that person, the employee may appeal to managers at higher levels. This policy works only to the degree that employees trust management and managers who hear complaints listen and are able to act.
2. **Peer review**—The people in conflict take their conflict to a panel composed of representatives from the organization at the same levels as the people in the dispute. The panel hears the case and tries to help the parties arrive at a settlement. To set up a panel to hear disputes as they arise, the organization may assign managers to positions on the panel and have employees elect nonmanagement panel members.
3. **Mediation**—A neutral party from outside the organization hears the case and tries to help the people in conflict arrive at a settlement. The process is not binding, meaning the mediator cannot force a solution.
4. **Arbitration**—A professional arbitrator from outside the organization hears the case and resolves it by making a decision. Most arbitrators are experienced employment lawyers or retired judges. The employee and employer both have to accept this person's decision.

Typically, an organization's ADR process begins with an open-door policy, which is the simplest, most direct, and least expensive way to settle a dispute. When the parties to a dispute cannot resolve it themselves, the organization can move the dispute to peer review,

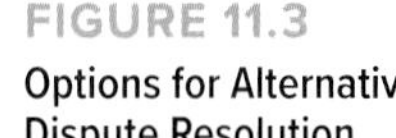
FIGURE 11.3
Options for Alternative Dispute Resolution

mediation, or arbitration. At some organizations, if mediation fails, the process moves to arbitration as a third and final option. Although arbitration is a formal process involving an outsider, it tends to be much faster, simpler, and more private than a lawsuit.[21]

Employee Assistance Programs

While ADR is effective in dealing with problems related to performance and disputes between people at work, many of the problems that lead an organization to want to terminate an employee involve drug or alcohol abuse. In these cases, the organization's discipline program should also incorporate an **employee assistance program (EAP).** An EAP is a referral service that employees can use to seek professional treatment for emotional problems or substance abuse. EAPs began in the 1950s with a focus on treating alcoholism, and in the 1980s they expanded into drug treatment. Today, many are now fully integrated into employers' overall health benefits plans, where they refer employees to covered mental health services. As described in the "Did You Know?" box, today's crisis of opioid abuse may make EAPs a particularly valuable resources for employers and employees alike.

Employee Assistance Program (EAP)
A referral service that employees can use to seek professional treatment for emotional problems or substance abuse.

EAPs vary widely, but most share some basic elements. First, the programs are usually identified in official documents published by the employer, such as employee handbooks. Supervisors (and union representatives when workers belong to a union) are trained to use the referral service for employees whom they suspect of having health-related problems. The organization also trains employees to use the system to refer themselves when necessary. The organization regularly evaluates the costs and benefits of the program, usually once a year.

Outplacement Counseling

An employee who has been discharged is likely to feel angry and confused about what to do next. If the person feels there is nothing to lose and nowhere else to turn, the potential for violence or a lawsuit is greater than most organizations are willing to tolerate. This concern is one reason many organizations provide **outplacement counseling,** which tries to help dismissed employees manage the transition from one job to another. Organizations also may address ongoing poor performance with discussion about whether the employee is a good fit for the current job. Rather than simply firing the poor performer, the supervisor may encourage this person to think about leaving. In this situation, the availability of outplacement counseling may help the employee decide to look for another job. This approach may protect the dignity of the employee who leaves and promote a sense of fairness.

Outplacement Counseling
A service in which professionals try to help dismissed employees manage the transition from one job to another.

Some organizations have their own staff for conducting outplacement counseling. Other organizations have contracts with outside providers to help with individual cases. Either way, the goals for outplacement programs are to help the former employee address the psychological issues associated with losing a job—grief, depression, and fear—while at the same time helping the person find a new job.

The use of outplacement firms has become far more common since John Challenger witnessed IBM's first-ever round of major layoffs in 1993. Challenger's father, James, started the first outplacement firm in the United States, when downsizing was not yet a part of the business vocabulary. Today firms such as Challenger, Gray & Christmas and Lee Hecht Harrison regularly dispatch counselors to help laid-off people recover from the shock of joblessness, polish their résumés, conduct job searches, and practice interviewing.

Whatever the reason for downsizing, asking employees to leave is a setback for the employee and for the company. Retaining people who can contribute knowledge and talent is essential to business success. Therefore, the remainder of this chapter explores issues related to retaining employees.

Did You Know?

Opioid Abuse Is a Problem for Workers and Employers

The overuse of opioids is causing a crisis in communities, including at work. A recent study found that more than 11 million Americans misused an opioid painkiller within a one-year period. These medications are associated with a high rate of addiction, making the overuse persistent and difficult to overcome.

The impact on the workplace—including absenteeism, health care costs, and injuries caused by persons under the influence—has been felt by more than two-thirds of employers. One-third of employers are aware of a worker dealing with a family member affected by opioid overuse, and one-tenth know of an employee who overdosed.

Furthermore, opioid use seems to be shrinking the labor force. Labor force participation rates (people working or looking for work) have fallen in recent years, and declines are sharpest where opioid prescribing is greatest.

Employers need to be cautious about dismissing employees who misuse opioids, because when such behavior reaches the level of opioid use disorder, it is considered the symptom of an illness. Consequently, the Americans with Disabilities Act may require accommodations. An employee assistance program may be a way for employers to address the problem by connecting a user with treatment resources.

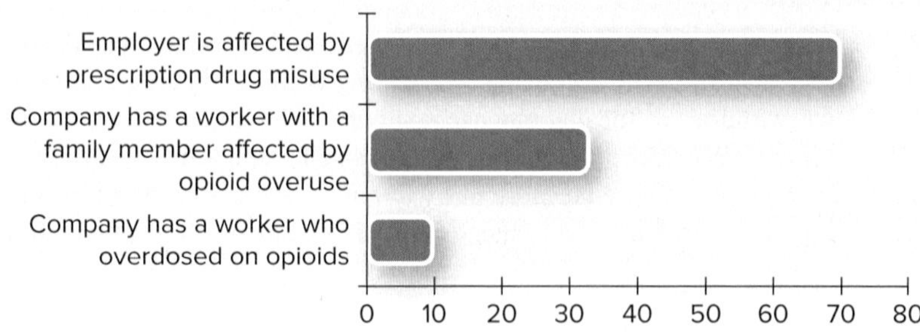

Question

A manager suspects that an employee who returns to work following back surgery has become addicted to painkillers. How would the Americans with Disabilities Act apply to the way the manager should handle this situation? (If you need a review of ADA guidelines, see Chapter 3.)

Sources: "Poll: 75% of Employers Say Their Workplace Impacted by Opioid Use," *National Safety Council,* March 17, 2019, https://www.nsc.org; Angela N. Johnson, "Opioid Crisis: Keeping the Workplace Drug-Free and ADA Compliant," *HR Daily Advisor,* May 31, 2018, https://hrdailyadvisor.blr.com; Deborah Happ, "The Opioid Crisis and the Workplace," *BusinesssWest,* January 22, 2018, p. 12; National Safety Council, *Prescription Nation 2018: Facing America's Opioid Epidemic,* 2018, https://www.nsc.org.

Employee Engagement

Although employee separation is necessary when an organization needs fewer people or has an employee who cannot or will not correct a performance problem, HR professionals say their biggest challenge today is employee *retention,* or reducing voluntary turnover.[22] Ideally, of course, HR's goal in promoting retention is not merely to prevent employees from quitting. Rather, retention efforts also address employee engagement, defined in Chapter 9 as the degree to which employees are fully involved in their work and the strength of their commitment to their job and company. Highly involved and committed employees give their companies a clear competitive advantage, including greater productivity, better customer service, and lower turnover.[23] Thus, promoting employee engagement is a way to improve retention along with other performance measures.

One organization that is attuned to the importance of employee engagement is the global consulting and professional-services firm EY (formerly Ernst & Young). When the firm saw an uptick in employee turnover in one region of the United States, it investigated data such as interviews with departing employees and surveys of employee engagement. From this analysis, it identified several areas in which it could improve. The company worked with managers to improve their supervision, such as delivering better performance feedback. The HR team also is more actively working with employees to define career paths and opportunities within the firm. The effort soon began to show improvements in employee engagement scores, along with the return of some employees who had left.[24]

Job Withdrawal

Job Withdrawal
A set of behaviors with which employees try to avoid the work situation physically, mentally, or emotionally.

A basic but important step on the path toward an engaged workforce is to prevent a broad negative condition called **job withdrawal**—or a set of behaviors with which employees try to avoid the work situation physically, mentally, or emotionally. Job withdrawal results when circumstances such as the nature of the job, supervisors and co-workers, pay levels, or the employee's own disposition cause the employee to become dissatisfied with the job. This job dissatisfaction produces job withdrawal (see Figure 11.4). Job withdrawal may take the form of behavior change, physical job withdrawal, or psychological withdrawal. Some researchers believe employees engage in the three forms of withdrawal behavior in that order, while others think they select from these behaviors to address the particular sources of job dissatisfaction they experience.[25] Although the specifics of these models vary, the consensus is that withdrawal behaviors are related to one another and are at least partially caused by job dissatisfaction.[26]

LO 11-5 Explain how job dissatisfaction affects employee behavior.

Job Dissatisfaction

Many aspects of people and organizations can cause job dissatisfaction, and managers and HR professionals need to be aware of them because correcting them can increase job satisfaction and prevent job withdrawal. Ideally, managers should catch and correct job dissatisfaction early because there is evidence linking changes in satisfaction levels to turnover: when satisfaction is falling, employees are far more likely to quit.[27] The causes of job dissatisfaction identified in Figure 11.4 fall into four categories: personal dispositions, tasks and roles, supervisors and co-workers, and pay and benefits.

Personal Dispositions Job dissatisfaction is a feeling experienced by individuals, so it is not surprising that many researchers have studied individual personality differences to see if some kinds of people are more disposed to be dissatisfied with their jobs. In general, job turnover (and presumably dissatisfaction leading up to it) is higher among employees who are low in emotional stability, conscientiousness, and agreeableness.[28] In addition, two other personal qualities associated with job satisfaction are negative affectivity and negative self-evaluations.

FIGURE 11.4
Job Withdrawal Process

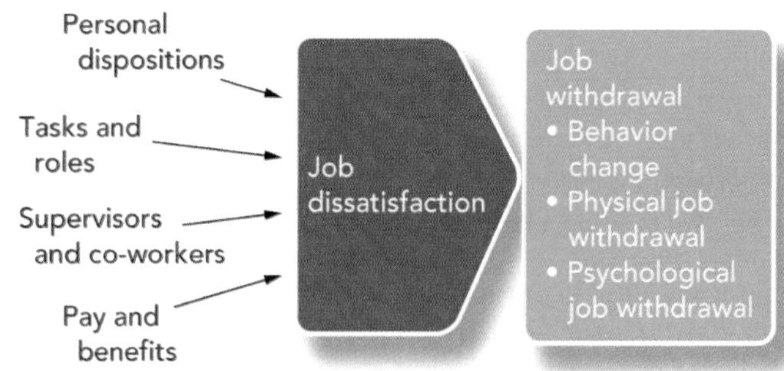

Negative affectivity means pervasive low levels of satisfaction with all aspects of life, compared with other people's feelings. People with negative affectivity experience feelings such as anger, contempt, disgust, guilt, fear, and nervousness more than other people do, at work and away. They tend to focus on the negative aspects of themselves and others.[29] Not surprisingly, people with negative affectivity tend to be dissatisfied with their jobs, even after changing employers or occupations.[30]

Core self-evaluations are bottom-line opinions individuals have of themselves and may be positive or negative. People with a positive core self-evaluation have high self-esteem, believe in their ability to accomplish their goals, and are emotionally stable. They also tend to experience job satisfaction.[31] Part of the reason for their satisfaction is that they tend to seek out and obtain jobs with desirable characteristics, and when they are in a situation they dislike, they are more likely to seek change in socially acceptable ways.[32] In contrast, people with negative core self-evaluations tend to blame other people for their problems, including their dissatisfying jobs. They are less likely to work toward change; they either do nothing or act aggressively toward the people they blame.[33]

Tasks and Roles As a predictor of job dissatisfaction, nothing surpasses the nature of the task itself.[34] Many aspects of a task have been linked to dissatisfaction. Of particular significance are the complexity of the task, the degree of physical strain and exertion required, and the value the employee places on the task.[35] In general, employees (especially women) are bored and dissatisfied with simple, repetitive jobs.[36] People also are more dissatisfied with jobs requiring a great deal of physical strain and exertion. Because automation has removed much of the physical strain associated with jobs, employers often overlook this consideration. Still, many jobs remain physically demanding. Finally, employees feel dissatisfied if their work is not related to something they value.

Employees not only perform specific tasks but also have roles within the organization.[37] A person's **role** consists of the set of behaviors that people expect of a person in that job. These expected behaviors include the formally defined duties of the job but also much more. Sometimes things get complicated or confusing. Co-workers, supervisors, and customers have expectations for how the employee should behave, often going far beyond a formal job description and having a large impact on the employee's work satisfaction. Several role-related sources of dissatisfaction are the following:

Role
The set of behaviors that people expect of a person in a particular job.

- **Role ambiguity** is uncertainty about what the organization and others expect from the employee in terms of what to do or how to do it. Employees suffer when they are unclear about work methods, scheduling, and performance criteria, perhaps because others hold different ideas about these. Employees particularly want to know how the organization will evaluate their performance. When they aren't sure, they become dissatisfied.[38]
- **Role conflict** is an employee's recognition that demands of the job are incompatible or contradictory; a person cannot meet all the demands. For example, a company might bring together employees from different functions to work on a team to develop a new product. Team members feel role conflict when they realize that their team leader and functional manager have conflicting expectations of them. Also, many employees may feel conflict between work roles and family roles. A role conflict may be triggered by an organization's request that an employee take an assignment overseas. Foreign assignments can be highly disruptive to family members, and the resulting role conflict is the top reason that people quit overseas assignments.[39]
- **Role overload** results when too many expectations or demands are placed on a person. (The opposite situation is *role underload.*) After an organization downsizes, for example, it may expect so much of the remaining employees that they experience role overload.

Role Ambiguity
Uncertainty about what the organization expects from the employee in terms of what to do or how to do it.

Role Conflict
An employee's recognition that demands of the job are incompatible or contradictory.

Role Overload
A state in which too many expectations or demands are placed on a person.

HR Oops!

Employers Don't See the Toll of Overwork

Today many companies are concerned that as employees move up within the organizational hierarchy, the share of women falls, with few women in the upper ranks. Managers typically conclude that at some point, the pressure of balancing work and family makes it impossible for women to compete for top-level jobs. However, recent research suggests that this conclusion is based more on assumptions than on employees' real experiences. Worse, the usual reasoning has become a substitute for correcting the underlying role overload afflicting both men and women.

The researchers—a professor at Harvard Business School and a professor at Florida State University—responded to a large consulting firm's request for insight into creating opportunities for women. Since the firm had already been analyzing workforce data, the researchers dug deeper, interviewing 33 female consultants and 74 male consultants plus four executives in the firm's HR department. Men and women alike described difficulty balancing work and family roles, because the company valued providing clients with a massive amount of information in short time frames, with availability around the clock. They suggested that much of what they delivered didn't meet client needs as much as it met company values. At first, men and women would speak as if this were harder for female employees, but as the researchers probed for details, men also admitted feeling frustrated and unhappy but were more likely to joke about it or change the subject. Furthermore, the usual opinions about women in the workforce were contradicted by data showing that men advanced faster than even women without children.

At the organization under study, the heavy workload is a given, so the company offers alternative work arrangements such as part-time work for employees who need more family time. However, encouragement to use these arrangements has been directed mainly at female employees, and those who take the accommodations fall off the fast track for development opportunities. Men distressed by the role overload could not imagine themselves seeking accommodations they thought of as being for women, but many left the firm for better working conditions. In sum, the firm was losing management talent (men and women) from its pipeline as it used exhausted and stressed-out workers to deliver clients more information than most could absorb.

The professors advised the firm to set realistic work requirements. Top management's response was to double down on describing role overload as an inevitable hardship of being a woman in the workforce.

Questions

1. How would you expect role overload to affect a company's performance?
2. If the firm described here comes to see that role overload is interfering with high performance, what changes could it make to reduce the role overload?

Sources: Robin J. Ely and Irene Padavic, "What's Really Holding Women Back?" *Harvard Business Review,* March–April 2020, pp. 58–67; Sarah Green Carmichael, "Men Need to Join the Battle against Overwork," *Bloomberg,* February 21, 2020, https://www.bloomberg.com; Danielle Kost, "Women Pay a Higher Career Price in Today's Always-On Work Culture," *Working Knowledge* (Harvard Business School), April 20, 2019, https://hbswk.hbs.edu.

Military reservists who are sent overseas often experience role conflict among *three* roles: soldier, family member, and civilian employee. Overseas assignments often intensify role conflicts.
Ariel Skelley/Getty Images

The "HR Oops!" box discusses the impact of role overload on women and men.

Supervisors and Co-workers Negative behavior by managers and peers in the workplace can produce tremendous dissatisfaction. Often much of the responsibility for positive relationships is placed on direct supervisors. For example, employees want their supervisors to define expectations clearly, measure progress fairly and accurately, and acknowledge their accomplishments.[40] Employees want supervisors to see them as individuals and help create the conditions in which they can succeed—for example, giving assignments suitable for their skills and providing access to the necessary resources. Employees want some evidence that the company's leaders respect and care about them, so they are more likely to be dissatisfied if management is distant and unresponsive.

In other cases, conflicts between employees left unaddressed by management may cause job dissatisfaction severe enough to lead to withdrawal or departure. Research suggests that turnover is higher when employees do not feel that their values and beliefs fit with their work group's values and beliefs.[41] Furthermore uncivil behavior by co-workers generates unhappiness that manifests in a variety of ways, such as decreased commitment, effort, and performance.[42]

Pay and Benefits For all the concern with positive relationships and interesting work, it is important to keep in mind that employees definitely care about their earnings. A job is the primary source of income and financial security for most people. Pay also is an indicator of status within the organization and in society at large, so it contributes to some people's self-worth. For all these reasons, satisfaction with pay is significant for retaining employees. Decisions about pay and benefits are so important and complex that the chapters of Part 4 are devoted to this topic.

With regard to job satisfaction, the pay level–that is, the amount of income associated with each job–is especially important. Employers seeking to lure away another organization's employees often do so by offering higher pay. Benefits, such as insurance and vacation time, are also important, but employees often have difficulty measuring their worth. Therefore, although benefits influence job satisfaction, employees may not always consider them as much as pay itself.

Behavior Change

A reasonable expectation is that an employee's first response to dissatisfaction would be to try to change the conditions that generate the dissatisfaction. As the employee tries to bring about changes in policy or personnel, the efforts may involve confrontation and conflict with the employee's supervisor. In an organization where employees are represented by a union, as we will discuss in Chapter 15, more grievances might be filed.

From the manager's point of view, the complaints, confrontations, and grievances may feel threatening. On closer inspection, however, this is an opportunity for the manager to learn about and solve a potentially important problem. When a secure and supportive manager properly channels employees' expressions of dissatisfaction, the results can include greater employee engagement, lower turnover, and substantial improvements in the organization's performance.[43]

When employees cannot work with management to make changes, they may look for help from outside the organization. Some employees may engage in *whistle-blowing,* taking their charges to the media in the hope that if the public learns about the situation, the organization will be forced to change. From the organization's point of view, whistle-blowing is harmful because of the negative publicity.[44]

Another way employees may go outside the organization for help is to file a lawsuit. This way to force change is available if the employee is disputing policies on the grounds that they violate state and federal laws, such as those forbidding employment discrimination or requiring safe working conditions. Defending a lawsuit is costly, both financially and in terms of the employer's image, whether the organization wins or loses. Most employers would prefer to avoid lawsuits and whistle-blowing. Keeping employees satisfied is one way to do this.

Physical Job Withdrawal

If behavior change has failed or seems impossible, a dissatisfied worker may physically withdraw from the job. Options for physically leaving a job range from arriving late to calling in sick, requesting a transfer, or leaving the organization altogether. Even while they are on the job, employees may withdraw by not actually working. All these options are costly to the employer.

Finding a new job is rarely easy and can take months, so employees often are cautious about quitting. Employees who would like to quit may be late for work. Tardiness is costly because late employees are not contributing for part of the day. Especially when work is done by teams, the tardiness creates difficulties that spill over and affect the entire team's ability to work. Absenteeism is even more of a problem. Research by the CDC Foundation found that absenteeism reduced productivity by an amount equivalent to more than $1,600 per employee.[45]

An employee who is dissatisfied because of circumstances related to the specific job–for example, an unpleasant workplace or unfair supervisor–may be able to resolve that problem with a job transfer. If the source of the dissatisfaction is organizational policies or practices, such as low pay scales, the employee may leave the organization altogether. These forms of physical job withdrawal contribute to high turnover rates. As a result, the organization faces the costs of replacing the employees (often thousands of dollars per employee), as well as lost productivity and sometimes lost sales until replacement employees learn the jobs. Adding to the challenge, employees are more likely to quit when they see a good chance to find another job–which suggests that quitting is greatest for the hardest-to-fill positions during times when the competition for labor is stiff.[46]

Organizations need to be concerned with their overall turnover rates as well as the nature of the turnover in terms of who is staying and who is leaving. For example, young workers tend to change jobs more often than workers who are 35 and older. This difference had led some people to speculate that millennial workers (born between 1981 and 1998) are job hoppers compared with the next-older cohort, called Generation X. But more recent data from the Labor Department show millennial workers staying with their employers longer as they become older. The rate of leaving a job is about the same for millennials and Gen Xers until they turn 35. After that, the likelihood of staying with the employer longer is slightly *greater* for millennials. This is consistent with the fact that millennials are likelier than older generations to hold a college degree; greater education is associated with a lower rate of job change.[47]

Psychological Withdrawal

Employees need not leave the company in order to withdraw from their jobs. Especially if they have been unable to find another job, they may psychologically remove themselves. They are physically at work, but their minds are elsewhere.

Job Involvement
The degree to which people identify themselves with their jobs.

Psychological withdrawal can take several forms. An employee who is primarily dissatisfied with the job itself may display a very low level of job involvement. **Job involvement** is the degree to which people identify themselves with their jobs. People with a high level of job involvement consider their work an important part of their life. Doing well at work contributes to their sense of who they are (their *self-concept*). For a dissatisfied employee with low job involvement, performing well or poorly does not affect the person's self-concept.

Organizational Commitment
The degree to which an employee identifies with the organization and is willing to put forth effort on its behalf.

When an employee is dissatisfied with the organization as a whole, the person's organizational commitment may be low. **Organizational commitment** is the degree to which an employee identifies with the organization and is willing to put forth effort on its behalf.[48] To understand "identifying with" an organization, think about students who are enthusiastic about school. They wear clothing with logos, sign up for extra activities, and use "we" or team names to refer to themselves as part of the student body. In a business context, a study analyzed newly hired employees' language in their e-mails. The study found that some of the employees quickly began using language that resembled the patterns of veteran employees, while others' language patterns remained unchanged. The employees who adopted the prevailing language of their company were likelier to stay and thrive; the others were likely to leave, voluntarily or involuntarily.[49] Consistent with this study's results, employees with high organizational commitment will stretch themselves to help the organization through difficult times, such as the front-line health care and grocery store workers who became global heroes during the COVID-19 pandemic. Employees with low organizational commitment are likely to leave at the first opportunity for a better job. They have a strong intention to leave, so like employees with low job involvement, they are hard to motivate.

Job Satisfaction

LO 11-6 Describe how organizations contribute to employees' job satisfaction and retain key employees.

Clearly, organizations want to prevent withdrawal behaviors. As we saw in Figure 11.4, the driving force behind job withdrawal is dissatisfaction. To prevent job withdrawal, organizations therefore need to promote **job satisfaction,** a pleasant feeling resulting from the perception that one's job fulfills or allows for the fulfillment of one's important job values.[50] This definition has three components:

Job Satisfaction
A pleasant feeling resulting from the perception that one's job fulfills or allows for the fulfillment of one's important job values.

- Job satisfaction is related to a person's *values,* defined as "what a person consciously or unconsciously desires to obtain."
- Different employees have different views of which values are *important,* so the same circumstances can produce different levels of job satisfaction.
- Job satisfaction is based on *perception,* not always on an objective and complete measurement of the situation. Each person compares the job situation to his or her values, and people are likely to differ in what they perceive.

In sum, people will be satisfied with their jobs as long as they perceive that their jobs meet their important values. As shown in Figure 11.5, organizations can contribute to job satisfaction by addressing the four sources of job dissatisfaction we identified earlier: personal dispositions, job tasks and roles, supervisors and co-workers, and pay and benefits.

FIGURE 11.5
Increasing Job Satisfaction

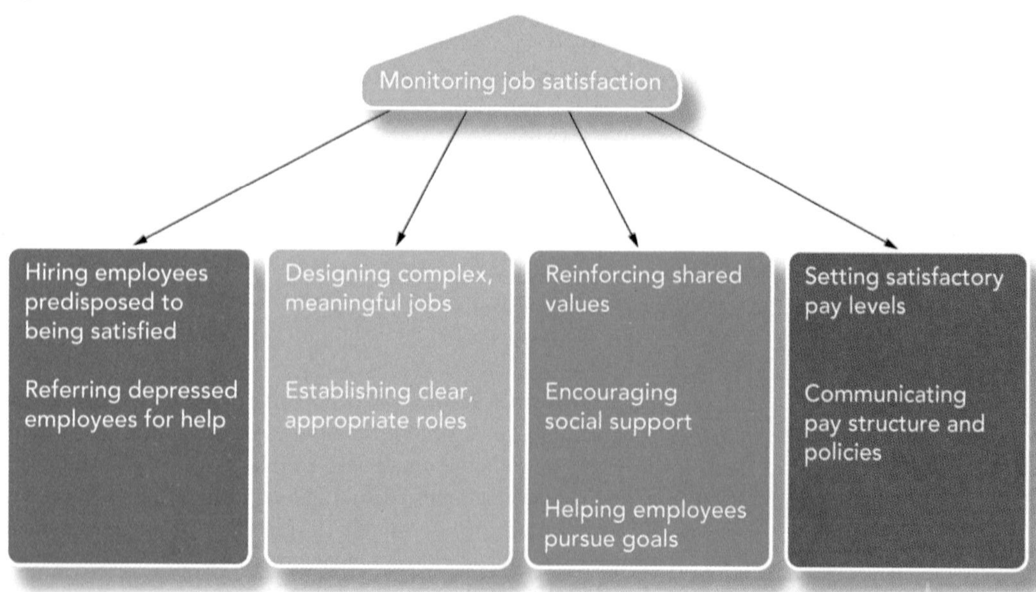

Personal Dispositions

In our discussion of job withdrawal, we noted that sometimes personal qualities of the employee, such as negative affectivity and negative core self-evaluation, are associated with job dissatisfaction. This linkage suggests that employee selection in the first instance plays a role in raising overall levels of employee satisfaction. People making the selection decisions should look for evidence of whether employees are predisposed to being satisfied.[51] Interviews should explore employees' satisfaction with past jobs. If an applicant says he was dissatisfied with his past six jobs, what makes the employer think the person won't be dissatisfied with the organization's vacant position?

Psychologists have explored which personal qualities are associated with having a positive attitude about work.[52] One finding is that such people keep their failures in perspective by thinking of their career in terms of the big picture, not dwelling too much on one victory or disappointment. Also, their commitment to the purpose of their work overrides fear of failure, so they are determined to act, even in the face of uncertainty. They also express their interest in their work by sharing knowledge and developing less-experienced employees.

Tasks and Roles

Organizations can improve job satisfaction by making jobs more complex and meaningful, as we discussed in Chapter 4. Some of the methods available for this approach to job design are job enrichment and job rotation. Organizations also can increase satisfaction by developing clear and appropriate job roles.

Job Complexity Gallup's research into employee engagement found that a majority of employees consider it "very important" for their job to give them a chance to "do what they do best." In fact, this is the most-cited job attribute that employees say they consider in deciding whether to leave the company to take a job somewhere else.[53] Jobs that call upon employees' best are likely to involve some degree of complexity.

Appropriate tasks and roles include safety precautions, especially when work could involve risks to workers' health and safety. Kim Steele/Getty Images

Not only can job design add to enriching complexity, but employees themselves sometimes take measures to make their work more interesting. Some employees bring personal music players with headsets to work so they can listen to music or radio shows while they are working. Many supervisors disapprove, worrying that the headsets will interfere with the employees' ability to provide good customer service. However, in simple jobs with minimal customer contact (like processing paperwork or entering data into computers), research suggests that personal headsets can improve performance. One study examined the use of stereo headsets by workers in 32 jobs at a large retailing company. The stereo-using group outperformed the no-stereo group on simple jobs (like invoice processor), but performed worse than the stereo-free group on complex jobs (such as accountant).[54]

Meaningful Work When it comes to generating satisfaction, the most important aspect of work is the degree to which it is meaningfully related to workers' core values. Alex Parren, digital marketing and content manager of Sundried, told an interviewer that she "love[s] working for Sundried because the ethics resonate with my own." Sundried is an eco-friendly clothing company that uses fabric manufactured from coffee grounds. Parren takes pride in informing others about how her company reuses a waste product to make high-quality activewear. Similarly, MGM Resorts built employee satisfaction when it repositioned itself to be less focused on simply operating casinos and more on delivering entertainment to guests. Along with the easily remembered tagline "We are the show," the company taught employees at all levels how they could bring the idea to life by greeting guests, hearing their needs, and taking action to create exceptional experiences. Employees became enthusiastic about this chance to make an impact, and MGM's business results improved along with employees' job satisfaction.[55]

Clear and Appropriate Roles Organizations can do much to avoid role-related sources of dissatisfaction. They can define roles, clearly spelling out work methods, schedules, and performance measures. They can be realistic about the number of hours required to complete job requirements. When jobs require overtime hours, the employer must be prepared to comply with laws requiring overtime pay, as well as to help employees manage the conflict between work and family roles.

Role Analysis Technique
A process of formally identifying expectations associated with a role.

To help employees manage role conflict, employers have turned to policies that increase the flexibility of work arrangements. These may include employee benefits that ease the burden of child care and elder care, along with policies that allow for flexible schedules and telecommuting. Employees, especially women, place high value on policies that promote work-life balance and employee well-being. Employees also say they are looking for jobs that allow for flexible hours and working off-site.[56] Organizations with these "family-friendly" policies also have enjoyed improvements in performance, especially at companies that employ a large percentage of women.[57] Chapter 14 discusses such benefits in greater detail.

Because role problems rank just behind job problems in creating job dissatisfaction, some interventions aim directly at role elements. One of these is the **role analysis technique,** a process of formally identifying expectations associated with a role. The technique follows the steps shown in Figure 11.6. The *role occupant* (the person who fills a role) and each member of the person's *role set* (people who directly interact with this employee) each write down their expectations for the role. They meet to discuss their expectations and develop a preliminary list of the role's duties and behaviors, trying to resolve any conflicts among expectations. Next, the role occupant lists what he or she expects of others in the set, and the group meets again to reach a consensus on these expectations. Finally, the group modifies its preliminary list and reaches a consensus on the occupant's role. This process may uncover instances of overload and underload, and the group tries to trade off requirements to develop more balanced roles.

FIGURE 11.6
Steps in the Role Analysis Technique

Members of role set write expectations for role

Members of role set discuss expectations

Preliminary list of role's duties and behaviors

Role occupant lists expectations for others in role set

Members of role set discuss expectations and reach consensus on occupant's role

Modified list of role's duties and behaviors

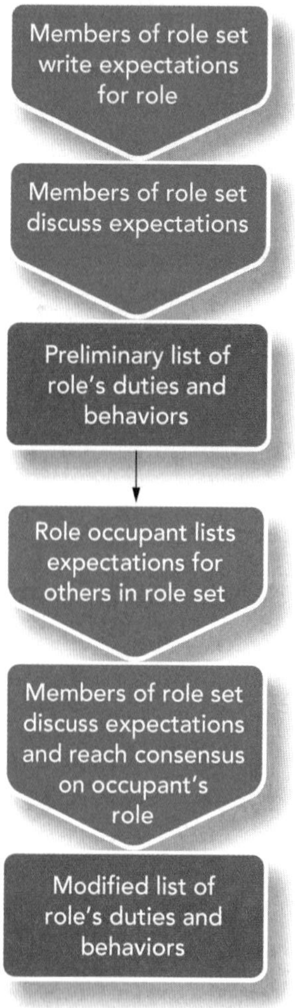

Supervisors and Co-Workers

The two primary sets of people in an organization who affect job satisfaction are co-workers and supervisors. A person may be satisfied with these people for one of three reasons:

1. The people share the same values, attitudes, and philosophies. Most individuals find this very important, and many organizations try to foster a culture of shared values. Even when this does not occur across the whole organization, values shared between workers and their supervisor can increase satisfaction.[58]
2. The co-workers and supervisor may provide social support, meaning they are sympathetic and caring. Social support greatly increases job satisfaction, whether the support comes from supervisors or co-workers.[59] Turnover is also lower among employees who experience support from other members of the organization.[60]

Employees Are the Most Valuable Asset at Quicken Loans

A lending company based in Detroit might not sound like a great place to work, but Quicken Loans, headquartered in the Motor City, keeps landing on *Fortune*'s list of the Best Companies to Work For and *Computerworld*'s list of Best Places to Work in IT (information technology). Both honors say something good is happening with job satisfaction, because employee surveys play a large part in determining which companies earn the recognition.

One of the main sources of satisfaction at Quicken Loans is the supportive work relationships and the culture that promotes them. Dan Jones recalls starting at Quicken as a software/data engineer and finding a complex problem involving several systems. He went to the team leader, assuming the problem would be assigned to a more experienced person. But the team leader encouraged Jones to tackle the problem and he learned from the experience. Inspired by what he calls a "culture of empowerment," Jones went on to become the company's vice president of business intelligence.

Another major source of satisfaction at Quicken Loans is designing jobs and feedback so employees can see the importance of what they do. Employees see importance in the company's work to help customers buy a home, and they take pride in its commitment to help rebuild the troubled city where it is located. Nishant Gupta, a software solutions architect, gained a sense of purpose when he participated in a development program that gave him first-hand experience of how customers apply for a mortgage. That customer's-eye view helped him determine ways to improve the process and make home buying easier.

Vice chairman and former CEO Bill Emerson sums up the company's practices by saying, "We win when our team members [employees] feel connected to the company." He contributes to that feeling by holding regular meetings with employees to talk about whatever they believe can improve the company. His efforts have paid off in a high level of commitment; in a survey by the Great Place to Work Institute, more than 90% of Quicken Loan employees say they feel good about the ways the company contributes to the community; the way new employees are made to feel welcome; and the way management fosters a good working environment for all.

Questions

1. What qualities of job relationships do Quicken Loans' employees value? How does the company promote such relationships?
2. How do tasks and roles contribute to job satisfaction at Quicken Loans?

Sources: Great Place to Work, "Quicken Loans," https://www.greatplacetowork.com, accessed April 29, 2020; "100 Best Companies to Work For: Quicken Loans," *Fortune,* https://fortune.com, accessed April 29, 2020; "Rocket Mortgage by Quicken Loans: Our Awards," https://www.myrocketcareer.com, accessed April 29, 2020; J. Purcell, "Quicken Loans: Committed to Employee Well-Being and Strong Communities," *Forbes,* December 10, 2019, https://www.forbes.com; Julia King, "Best Places to Work in IT, No. 1 (Large): Quicken Loans," *Computerworld,* June–July 2017, pp. 8–13.

3. The co-workers or supervisor may help the person attain some valued outcome. For example, they can help a new employee figure out what goals to pursue and how to achieve them.[61]

For an example of an organization where these kinds of relationships contribute to satisfaction, see "Best Practices."

Because a supportive environment reduces dissatisfaction, many organizations foster team building both on and off the job (such as with softball or bowling leagues). The idea is that playing together as a team will strengthen ties among group members and develop relationships in which individuals feel supported by one another. Of course, team efforts can be built around business goals, too. Some employers teach employees about financial performance measures, so they see how their efforts contribute to business performance and rewards. At WP Engine, an Austin company that hosts clients' websites, every newly hired employee learns what the company's performance measures mean and how his or her job connects to them. The effort has created a culture in which employees look out for one another when problems arise.[62] Organizations also create a supportive environment by developing their managers' mentoring skills and helping to set up these beneficial relationships.[63] (Mentoring was described in Chapter 8.)

Employees' own job satisfaction also interacts with the job satisfaction of co-workers. In a study of more than 5,000 employees in 150 businesses, employees with declining job satisfaction were more likely to stay on the job if co-workers' satisfaction was rising. Employees who experienced rising satisfaction were more likely to quit if their co-workers were growing less satisfied. In effect, when employees were out of step with their co-workers, their likelihood of quitting was influenced by the co-workers' job satisfaction.[64]

Pay and Benefits

Organizations recognize the importance of pay in their negotiations with job candidates. HR professionals can support their organizations in this area by repeatedly monitoring pay levels in their industry and for the professions or trades they employ. As we noted in Chapter 5 and will discuss further in Chapter 12, organizations make decisions about whether to match or exceed the industry averages. Also, HR professionals can increase job satisfaction by communicating to employees the value of their benefits.

Two other aspects of pay satisfaction influence job satisfaction. One is satisfaction with pay structure–the way the organization assigns different pay levels to different levels and job categories. A manager of a sales force, for example, might be satisfied with her pay level until she discovers that some of the sales representatives she supervises are earning more than she is. The other important aspect of pay satisfaction is pay raises. People generally expect that their pay will increase over time. They will be satisfied if their expectations are met or dissatisfied if raises fall short of expectations. HR professionals can contribute to these sources of job satisfaction by helping to communicate the reasoning behind the organization's pay structure and pay raises. For example, sometimes economic conditions force an organization to limit pay raises. If employees understand the circumstances (and recognize that the same conditions are likely to be affecting other employers), they may feel less dissatisfied.

Monitoring Job Satisfaction

Employers can better retain employees if they are aware of satisfaction levels, so they can make changes if employees are dissatisfied. The usual way to measure job satisfaction is with some kind of survey. A systematic, ongoing program of employee surveys should be part of the organization's human resource strategy. This program allows the organization to monitor trends and prevent voluntary turnover. For monitoring and responding to trends, companies are increasingly using frequent (weekly or even daily) one-question "pulse surveys" to deliver a stream of data in support of agile decision making. More in-depth one-time surveys can be helpful around the time of an organizational change such as a merger that could have important consequences for job satisfaction. In addition, ongoing surveys give the organization a way to measure whether policies adopted to improve job satisfaction and employee retention are working.

Organizations can also compare results from different departments to identify groups with successful practices that may apply elsewhere in the organization. Another benefit is that some scales provide data that organizations can use to compare themselves to others in the same industry. This information will be valuable for creating and reviewing human resource policies that enable organizations to attract and retain employees in a competitive job market. Finally, conducting surveys gives employees a chance to be heard, so the practice itself can contribute to employee satisfaction.

To obtain a survey instrument, an excellent place to begin is with one of the many established scales. The validity and reliability of many satisfaction scales have been tested, so it is

FIGURE 11.7
Example of Job Descriptive Index (JDI)

Instructions: Think of your present work. What is it like most of the time? In the blank beside each word given below, write

__Y__ for "Yes" if it describes your work
__N__ for "No" if it does NOT describe your work
__?__ if you cannot decide

Work Itself	**Pay**	**Promotion Opportunities**
____ Routine	____ Less than I deserve	____ Dead-end job
____ Satisfying	____ Highly paid	____ Unfair policies
____ Good	____ Insecure	____ Based on ablility

Supervision	**Co-workers**
____ Impolite	____ Intelligent
____ Praises good work	____ Responsible
____ Doesn't supervise enough	____ Boring

Source: W. K. Balzar, D. C. Smith, D. E. Kravitz, S. E. Lovell, K. B. Paul, B. A. Reilly, and C. E. Reilly, *User's Manual for the Job Descriptive Index (JDI)* (Bowling Green, OH: Bowling Green State University, 1990).

possible to compare the survey instruments. The main reason for the organization to create its own scale would be that it wants to measure satisfaction with aspects of work that are specific to the organization (such as satisfaction with a particular health plan).

A widely used measure of job satisfaction is the Job Descriptive Index (JDI). The JDI emphasizes specific aspects of satisfaction—pay, the work itself, supervision, co-workers, and promotions. Figure 11.7 shows several items from the JDI scale. Other scales measure general satisfaction, using broad questions such as "All in all, how satisfied are you with your job?"[65] Some scales avoid language altogether, relying on pictures. The faces scale in Figure 11.8 is an example of this type of measure. Other scales exist for measuring more specific aspects of satisfaction. For example, the Pay Satisfaction Questionnaire (PSQ) measures satisfaction with specific aspects of pay, such as pay levels, structure, and raises.[66]

Along with administering surveys, more organizations are analyzing basic HR data to look for patterns that could be related to employee separation and/or retention. The results may confirm expectations or generate surprises that merit further investigation. Either way, they can help HR departments and managers determine which efforts deliver the best return. The HR team at a financial-services company used analytics to rescue a difficult growth strategy that was at risk of failure. The strategy involved departments using data and information systems to innovate quickly even as resources were shrinking. In some departments, however, employees were getting worn out and discouraged—a setup for job dissatisfaction and disengagement. The HR department set up a performance dashboard that top executives could use to monitor the weekly number of hours worked by employees on each team, including a team average and a breakdown of hours per employee. Executives then could identify teams

FIGURE 11.8
Example of a Simplified, Nonverbal Measure of Job Satisfaction

Job Satisfaction from the Faces Scale
Consider all aspects of your job. Circle the face that best describes your feelings about your job in general.

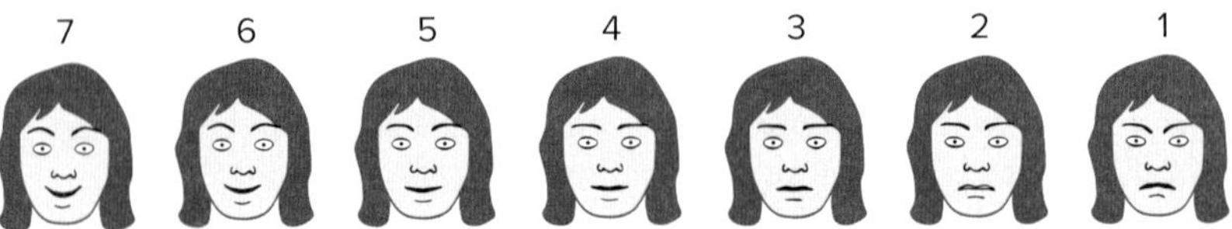

Source: Based on R. B. Dunham and J. B. Herman, *Journal of Applied Psychology* 60 (1975), pp. 629–631.

where everyone was overextended and teams that might be better positioned to take on the next new project.[67] By using the dashboard to make decisions about assignments, they could prevent such retention-related problems as role conflict and role overload.

HR Analytics & Decision Making

Almost half of U.S. school principals leave their posts within three years on the job, and almost one in five leaves each year. Some retire; others move to another position in the same or another school district. The turnover is costly because districts must prepare and recruit replacements. Also, students' performance often suffers during a change in school leadership.

Researchers analyzing data about principals in elementary through high schools in Texas found that female principals were likelier to stay on the job and male principals were likelier to be promoted. Promotions were also likelier for principals at middle and high schools than for those at elementary schools. Turnover was higher at urban than at rural schools.

Separately, the Texas Elementary Principals and Supervisors Association asks members about their careers. In a recent survey, 31% of respondents said they envisioned advancing their career in another position. Among these respondents, top reasons for changing jobs were the current job's demands, a lack of support, and desire for better pay and working conditions.

Questions

1. Suppose you work in a school district's HR department and want to advise on the selection of principals. Based on the data given, suggest one question to investigate by gathering data about your school district.
2. Suggest one way a district could address the sources of job dissatisfaction among principals.

Source: Denisa R. Superville, "Principal Turnover Is a Problem. New Data Could Help Districts Combat It," *Education Week,* December 19, 2019, https://www.edweek.org.

In spite of surveys and other efforts to retain employees, some employees inevitably will leave the organization. This presents another opportunity to gather information for retaining employees: the **exit interview**—a meeting of the departing employee with the employee's supervisor and/or a human resource specialist to discuss the employee's reasons for leaving. A well-conducted exit interview can uncover reasons why employees leave and perhaps set the stage for some of them to return. HR professionals can help make exit interviews more successful by arranging for the employee to talk to someone from the HR department (rather than the departing employee's supervisor) in a neutral location or over the phone.[68] Questions should start out open-ended and general, giving the employee a chance to name the source of the dissatisfaction or explain why leaving is attractive.

Exit Interview
A meeting of a departing employee with the employee's supervisor and/or a human resource specialist to discuss the employee's reasons for leaving.

A recruiter armed with information about what caused a specific person to leave may be able to negotiate a return when the situation changes. And when several exiting employees give similar reasons for leaving, management should consider whether this indicates a need for change. At Penske Automotive Group, for example, asking each departing employee why he or she was leaving provided the dealership group with useful data. Management learned that its employee selection process was not yielding high-quality employees, so it tightened up the process and quickly improved employee retention.[69] In the war for talent, the best way to manage retention is to engage in a battle for every valued employee, even when it looks as if the battle has been lost.

THINKING ETHICALLY

HOW CAN FIRING BE DONE ETHICALLY FROM A DISTANCE?

When the COVID-19 pandemic prompted social distancing, many employers began to practice physical distancing, arranging for employees to do their work at home when possible. However, stay-at-home requirements quickly brought about an economic slowdown, including layoffs wherever sales dried up. Employers who could not keep their employees working had to find a way to get out the word without calling together employees for an in-person meeting.

Remote termination has a huge pitfall: how to keep the news from leaking and spreading through the grapevine at lightning speed. At the same time, companies need to protect individuals' privacy and secure their own systems from vandalism by upset former employees while offering as much of a human touch as is possible when people must remain at a distance. If managers make individual phone calls, for example, the first few people contacted might want to call or text their soon-to-be-former colleagues and share the news of the layoff. And employees who are logged into the company's internal network or who have company-owned devices might be tempted to grab some data while they can.

Balancing these concerns is difficult in any situation. It became impossible for some companies conducting layoffs at a time when millions were losing their jobs and only workers in essential industries were allowed to be at workplaces. A scooter-sharing company tried to conduct a layoff during a videoconference described as being an update about COVID-19. Attendees quickly noticed that they were attending a view-only presentation, not a discussion, and that the uncomfortable-sounding voice behind the screen-shared message was describing a layoff. As the message ended, their computers automatically rebooted, locking them out. Managers later followed up with individual phone calls, but the CEO agreed that the process was awkward.

At a software company, rattled employees were told to expect either an e-mail confirming continued employment or a Zoom invitation to a conference to discuss severance pay. At least one employee understood only after she logged in that it was to be about a layoff, and distressed, she muted her audio and shut down the video camera, so she could maintain her dignity while listening. Conversely, an employee at a marketing firm wishes that the phone call he received from his CEO had been scheduled on Skype, so he could have read the facial expressions of his former boss.

Questions

1. How well does employment termination by video conference meet the principles of justice described in this chapter?
2. How well does it respect the basic human rights described in Chapter 1?

Sources: Kathryn Dill, "First People Were Sent Home to Work; Now They're Getting Laid Off Remotely," *The Wall Street Journal,* April 2, 2020, https://www.wsj.com; Matthew Parsons, "TripActions CEO Defends Controversial Layoffs Strategy," *Skift,* March 27, 2020, https://skift.com; Ben Bergman, "'It Felt Like a Black Mirror Episode': The Inside Account of How Bird Laid Off 406 People in Two Minutes via a Zoom Webinar," *dot.la,* April 1, 2020, https://dot.la; Sam Shead, "Coronavirus: Start-Ups Use Zoom App to Lay Off Staff," *BBC,* March 30, 2020, https://www.bbc.com.

SUMMARY

LO 11-1 Distinguish between involuntary and voluntary turnover, and describe their effects on an organization.

- Involuntary turnover occurs when the organization requires employees to leave, often when they would prefer to stay.
- Voluntary turnover occurs when employees initiate the turnover, often when the organization would prefer to keep them.
- Both are costly because of the need to recruit, hire, and train replacements. Involuntary turnover can also result in lawsuits and even violence.

LO 11-2 Discuss how employees determine whether the organization treats them fairly.

- Employees draw conclusions based on the outcomes of decisions regarding them, the procedures applied, and the way managers treat employees when carrying out those procedures.
- Outcome fairness is a judgment that the consequences are just. The consequences should be consistent, expected, and in proportion to the significance of the behavior.
- Procedural justice is a judgment that fair methods were used to determine the consequences. The procedures should be consistent, unbiased, based on accurate information, and correctable. They should take into account the viewpoints of everyone involved, and they should be consistent with prevailing ethical standards.
- Interactional justice is a judgment that the organization carried out its actions in a way that took the employee's feelings into account—for example, by listening to the employee and treating the employee with dignity.

LO 11-3 Identify legal requirements for employee discipline.

- Employee discipline should not result in wrongful discharge, such as a termination that violates an implied contract or public policy.
- Discipline should be administered evenhandedly, without discrimination.
- Discipline should respect individual employees' privacy. Searches and surveillance should be for a legitimate business purpose, and employees should know about and consent to them. Reasons behind disciplinary actions should be shared only with those who need to know them.
- When termination is part of a plant closing, employees should receive the legally required notice, if applicable.

LO 11-4 Summarize ways in which organizations can discipline employees fairly.

- Discipline should follow the principles of the hot-stove rule, meaning discipline should give warning and have consequences that are consistent, objective, and immediate.
- A system that can meet these requirements is called progressive discipline, in which rules are established and communicated, and increasingly severe consequences follow each violation of the rules. Usually, consequences range from a spoken warning through written warnings, suspension, and termination. These actions should be documented in writing.
- Organizations also may resolve problems through alternative dispute resolution, including an open-door policy, peer review, mediation, and arbitration.
- When performance problems seem to result from substance abuse or mental illness, the manager may refer the employee to an employee assistance program.
- When a manager terminates an employee or encourages an employee to leave, outplacement counseling may smooth the process.

LO 11-5 Explain how job dissatisfaction affects employee behavior.

- Circumstances involving the nature of a job, supervisors and co-workers, pay levels, or the employee's own disposition may produce job dissatisfaction.
- When employees become dissatisfied, they may engage in job withdrawal: behavior change, physical job withdrawal, or psychological job withdrawal.
- Behavior change means employees try to bring about changes in policy and personnel through inside action or through whistle-blowing or lawsuits.
- Physical job withdrawal may range from tardiness and absenteeism to job transfer or leaving the organization altogether.
- Psychological withdrawal involves displaying low levels of job involvement and organizational commitment. It is especially likely when employees cannot find another job.

LO 11-6 Describe how organizations contribute to employees' job satisfaction and retain key employees.

- Organizations can try to identify and select employees who have personal dispositions associated with job satisfaction.
- They can make jobs more complex and meaningful—for example, through job enrichment and job rotation.
- They can use methods such as the role analysis technique to make roles clear and appropriate.
- They can reinforce shared values and encourage social support among employees.
- They can try to establish satisfactory pay levels and communicate with employees about pay structure and pay raises.
- Monitoring job satisfaction helps organizations identify which of these actions are likely to be most beneficial.

KEY TERMS

involuntary turnover, 336
voluntary turnover, 336
outcome fairness, 338
procedural justice, 339
interactional justice, 339
hot-stove rule, 343
progressive discipline, 343
alternative dispute resolution (ADR), 345
open-door policy, 345
peer review, 345
mediation, 345
arbitration, 345
employee assistance program (EAP), 346
outplacement counseling, 346
job withdrawal, 348
role, 349
role ambiguity, 349
role conflict, 349
role overload, 349
job involvement, 352
organizational commitment, 352
job satisfaction, 353
role analysis technique, 355
exit interview, 359

REVIEW AND DISCUSSION QUESTIONS

1. Give an example of voluntary turnover and an example of involuntary turnover. Why should organizations try to reduce both kinds of turnover? *(LO 11-1)*
2. A member of a restaurant's serving staff is chronically late to work. From the organization's point of view, what fairness issues are involved in deciding how to handle this situation? In what ways might the employee's and other servers' ideas of fairness be different? *(LO 11-2)*
3. For the situation in Question 2, how would a formal discipline policy help the organization address issues of fairness? *(LO 11-2)*
4. In what type of situation would an employer have a legitimate reason for learning about an employee's personal matters outside the workplace? *(LO 11-3)*
5. The progressive discipline process described in this chapter is meant to be fair and understandable, but it tends to be slow. Try to think of two or three offenses that should result in immediate discharge, rather than follow all the steps of progressive discipline. Explain why you selected these offenses. If the dismissed employee sued, do you think the organization would be able to defend its action in court? *(LO 11-4)*
6. A risk of disciplining employees is that some employees retaliate. To avoid that risk, what organizational policies might encourage low-performing employees to leave while encouraging high-performing employees to stay? (Consider the sources of employee satisfaction and dissatisfaction discussed in this chapter.) *(LO 11-5)*
7. List forms of behavior that can signal job withdrawal. Choose one of the behaviors you listed, and describe how you would respond if an otherwise valuable employee whom you supervised engaged in this kind of behavior. *(LO 11-5)*
8. What are the four factors that influence an employee's job dissatisfaction (or satisfaction)? Which of these do you think an employer can most easily change? Which would be the most expensive to change? *(LO 11-5)*
9. Consider your current job or a job you recently held. Overall, were you satisfied or dissatisfied with that job? How did your level of satisfaction or dissatisfaction affect your behavior on the job? Is your own experience consistent with this chapter's models of job withdrawal and job satisfaction? *(LO 11-5)*
10. Suppose you are an HR professional who convinced your company's management to conduct a survey of employee satisfaction. Your budget was limited, and you could not afford a test that went into great detail. Rather, you investigated overall job satisfaction and learned that it is low, especially among employees in three departments. You know that management is concerned about spending a lot for HR programs because sales are in a slump, but you want to address the issue of low job satisfaction. Suggest some ways you might begin to make a difference, even with a small budget. How will you convince management to try your ideas? *(LO 11-6)*
11. Why are exit interviews important? Should an organization care about the opinions of people who are leaving? How are those opinions relevant to employee separation and retention? *(LO 11-6)*

SELF-ASSESSMENT EXERCISE

Mc Graw Hill connect

Which Job Characteristics Are Important to You?

The characteristics of your job influence your overall satisfaction with the job. One way to be satisfied at work is to find a job with the characteristics that you find desirable. The following assessment is a look at what kind of job is likely to satisfy you.

The following phrases describe different job characteristics. Read each phrase, then circle a number to indicate how much of the job characteristic you would like. Use the following scale: 1 = very little; 2 = little; 3 = a moderate amount; 4 = much; 5 = very much.

1. The opportunity to perform a number of different activities each day	1 2 3 4 5
2. Contributing something significant to the company	1 2 3 4 5
3. The freedom to determine how to do my job	1 2 3 4 5
4. The ability to see projects or jobs through to completion, rather than performing only one piece of the job	1 2 3 4 5
5. Seeing the results of my work, so I can get an idea of how well I am doing the job	1 2 3 4 5
6. A feeling that the quality of my work is important to others in the company	1 2 3 4 5
7. The need to use a variety of complex skills	1 2 3 4 5
8. Responsibility to act and make decisions independently of managers or supervisors	1 2 3 4 5
9. Time and resources to do an entire piece of work from beginning to end	1 2 3 4 5
10. Getting feedback about my performance from the work itself	1 2 3 4 5

Skill Variety: The degree to which a job requires you to use a variety of skills.

Item 1: _____ + Item 7: _____ = _____

Task Identity: The degree to which a job requires completion of a whole and identifiable piece of work.

Item 4: _____ + Item 9: _____ = _____

Task Significance: The degree to which a job has an impact on the lives or work of others.

Item 2: _____ + Item 6: _____ = _____

Autonomy: The degree to which a job provides freedom, empowerment, and discretion in scheduling the work and determining processes and procedures for completing the work.

Item 3; _____ + Item 8: _____ = _____

Feedback: The degree to which carrying out job-related tasks and activities provides you with direct and clear information about your effectiveness.

Item 5 _____ + Item 10: _____ = _____

Add the scores for the pairs of items that measure each job characteristic. A higher score for a characteristic means that characteristic is more important to you.

Source: Adapted from R. Daft and R. Noe, *Organizational Behavior* (New York: Harcourt, 2001).

TAKING RESPONSIBILITY

When Making Lysol Became a Mission

The Somerset, New Jersey, factory that makes Lysol disinfectant spray faced a dramatic challenge in March 2020, when its demand tripled in response to the spread of the novel coronavirus in the United States. Near the major outbreak in New York, many American workers wanted or needed to stay home, but Lysol was one of the products identified by the Centers for Disease Control and Prevention (CDC) as effective in killing the virus. Store shelves were quickly emptied of the existing supply. Somehow, the company needed to replenish stocks while operating safely at peak capacity. Could it do so and still retain its workforce?

The answer is yes, and the key was the company's sense of mission. Workers who had previously thought of Lysol as an ordinary cleaning product realized they were helping to fight the virus. At one point, Saad Islam, head of the factory's operations, held meetings at the end of each shift to show employees the spread of the virus and the empty shelves in grocery stores. He and other managers impressed on the employees that the round-the-clock work was a serious matter. Employees also heard their family and neighbors describe the product as something they depended on to stay safe.

The Somerset workers stepped up to the challenge. For example, Gabe Scuderi began staying to work into the shift after his, logging 12-hour days and working six days a week. Another worker, Steve Esock, has been with the company for over 30 years and says this situation was harder than others he has seen, but when the product was needed so badly, "the plant comes together, and we get it done." And maintenance mechanic Omar Ortiz said, "Everybody is counting on us to do our part."

The spirit at the Somerset facility was consistent with the values of its parent company, Britain-based Reckitt Benckiser Group. Its mission is "the relentless pursuit of a cleaner, healthier world," and its aim is to meet that mission with good products, information, and education. Lysol is a particularly important brand for this strategy, because as the company notes, personal hygiene "is the foundation of health." During the pandemic, the company ramped up production worldwide without raising its suggested retail prices. It did this despite adding worker protections such as staggering shifts and installing barriers to shield workers from one another.

Reckitt Benckiser's CEO, Laxman Narasimhan, had joined the company just months before the coronavirus outbreak. In the summer of 2019, his goal was to restart flagging sales; suddenly he was trying to meet soaring demand. Because of the global nature of the pandemic, he had some practice by the time it reached the United States and the New Jersey plant. In China, the company set up testing and physical distancing of employees, arranged for more buses to take workers to factories so they could sit farther apart, and rented hotel rooms for those who could not travel. As the virus spread in Europe and the United States, the company shrank its product mix so it could operate more efficiently and increase quantities.

Questions

1. What might be some employee retention challenges when a company suddenly has to start operating as fast as possible in an emergency?
2. Besides the sense of mission, how else could Reckitt Benckiser and its New Jersey facility retain employees during a stressful period such as the COVID-19 pandemic?

Sources: Reckitt Benckiser, "About Us" and "Our Commitment to Customers and Consumers in Response to COVID-19," https://www.rb.com, accessed April 29, 2020; Michael M. Phillips, "The Workers at a Lysol Plant Have a Mission Now," *The Wall Street Journal,* April 21, 2020, https://www.wsj.com; Saabira Chaudhuri, "Lysol Maker's Boss on Condom Sales and Living with Mom during the Pandemic," *The Wall Street Journal,* April 6, 2020, https://www.wsj.com; Jessica Guynn, "Looking for Lysol Spray and Clorox Wipes? COVID-19 Wiped Out Disinfectants, But Here's When You Can Buy Again," *USA Today,* April 9, 2020, https://www.usatoday.com.

MANAGING TALENT

Walmart Refocuses Its Employee Retention Strategies

For Walmart, the competitive environment keeps getting tougher. The company, which operates 5,000 stores and employs more than 1.5 million people in the United States, is trying to stay ahead of the trend toward online shopping. Meanwhile, continually falling unemployment rates have been making employee retention difficult. Somehow the company needs to keep getting more efficient (which means spending less) while maintaining employee engagement.

Competing with online retailers, especially Amazon, requires low prices, because price comparisons are easy online. It also replaces some demand for store employees and need for workers in warehouses and other parts of the distribution system. Walmart has addressed these challenges by restructuring work and closing some lower-performing stores, including more than five dozen Sam's Club stores. The cuts free up money for offering more generous pay and benefits and for directing more resources to online retailing. Some of the Sam's Club stores that closed were to be converted to distribution centers.

The restructuring decisions include a revised approach to store management, with fewer assistant managers. Walmart also cut department managers in certain departments such as mobile phones, where it could bring in representatives from the phone service providers. In addition, store closures helped to set the stage for several rounds of layoffs: the downsizing of store payrolls by 16,000 and elimination of 7,000 back-office jobs in stores in 2016, layoffs of 1,000 corporate positions in 2017, and the elimination of another 10,000 store jobs and 1,000 headquarters employees in 2018. Automation has enabled a 15% reduction in the number of workers per square foot in stores. But many of the laid-off employees, according to Walmart, were able to move to different positions within the company. At the same time, Walmart is placing more workers in warehouse jobs and store positions that fill online orders.

At the same time, the company cannot just be a job cutter and maintain its strength in the labor market. Even as it closes stores, Walmart has announced pay increases from \$9 an hour starting pay in 2015 to \$10 in 2017, and \$12 starting pay in 2020 at more than 500 U.S. stores. Early in 2018, in what it said was a response to cuts in the federal income tax rate, Walmart announced that it would spend about \$400 million to give employees wage increases (raising starting pay to \$11 per hour) and one-time bonuses of up to \$1,000. The new hourly pay rate matched wages paid by Target and came closer to the \$13 paid by Costco.

Walmart's management appreciates that pay alone will not be enough to create employee engagement, especially for relatively low-paying retail jobs. So the company has announced other initiatives aimed at making the company a preferred employer. Along with the 2018 pay raises and bonuses, Walmart announced it would extend to store employees the paid family leave benefits previously available only to office workers. At the same time, the company promised to spend some of its savings from lower taxes on training. Months later, Walmart announced it would pay college tuition for employees who pursue degrees in business or supply chain management at three schools selected by Walmart for the program. And in a bid to make work more comfortable, Walmart announced it would relax its blue-shirt-and-khakis dress code to allow a variety of solid-color clothing.

Questions

1. What circumstances described in this case make employee retention challenging for Walmart?
2. What sources of job satisfaction is Walmart providing, according to the information given? Name two other sources of job satisfaction that you think could improve job satisfaction and employee retention in Walmart stores.

Sources: "How Walmart Manages the Country's Largest Hourly Workforce," *Workstream*, https://www.workstream.us, accessed April 29, 2020; Anne D'Innocenzio, "Walmart Is Raising Starting Hourly Wage to \$12 at 500 Stores to Lure Workers, Aid Service," *USA Today*, January 24, 2020, https://www.usatoday.com; Sarah Nassauer, "Walmart to Pay Certain College Costs for U.S. Store Workers," *The Wall Street Journal*, May 30, 2018, https://www.wsj.com; Natasha Bach, "Walmart Employees Rejoice, You Soon May Be Able to Burn Those Khakis," *Fortune*, April 20, 2018, http://fortune.com; Sarah Nassauer, "Walmart to Trim Store Management Ranks," *The Wall Street Journal*, February 13, 2018, https://www.wsj.com; Sarah Nassauer, "Wal-Mart Plans to Cut More than 1,000 Corporate Jobs," *The Wall Street Journal*, January 12, 2018, https://www.wsj.com; Joseph Pisani and Alexandra Olson, "Walmart Boosts Employees' Starting Pay, while Some Sam's Club Workers Lose Their Jobs," *Chicago Tribune*, January 12, 2018, http://www.chicagotribune.com.

HR IN SMALL BUSINESS

Why Employees Stay at Holiday Inn Mart Plaza

The Holiday Inn Chicago Mart Plaza River North is a great place to visit, located near the Chicago River and downtown shopping, but is it also a great place to work? The 521-room hotel's 200-plus employees think so; their votes helped make it the first-place small employer on the *Chicago Tribune*'s list of Top Workplaces.

Employees who described the hotel for the *Tribune* focused especially on personal relationships. Tina Beverly, the hotel's HR director, describes the workplace as a "family environment" stressing teamwork. Francine Johnson, a room service employee, gives specifics, saying employees all "treat each other with respect" and learn from one another. She enjoys learning to fill in for other roles, including cashier, hostess, and bar worker. Karolina Diamond, who manages the front office, sees employees as a unified team. She says that when problems arise, "we work together to figure out how to fix them."

Johnson also credits the work environment. She told the *Tribune* that she loves going to work because "there's always something interesting going on." Diamond shares that attitude. She admitted that she had planned to stay at the hotel for two years or less but likes the work environment so much that she is still there six years later.

The hotel also keeps employees engaged through shared goals and regular communication with management. As Johnson puts it, "the main goal is to keep the guests happy." Employees are invited to participate in community outreach programs, such as serving meals to residents of the nearby Ronald McDonald House and partnering with a local elementary school. These projects build positive relationships among the participants. Communication includes daily departmental meetings to get an overview of activities and quarterly town hall meetings where executives announce plans to all the employees. The HR leaders meet monthly with small groups of employees, so they can field questions and ideas. And a phone app makes it easy for staff members to stay connected. Beverly, the HR director, also takes a daily walk through the hotel to visit the employees where they work. These efforts are consistent with the strategy of the hotel's parent organization, InterContinental Hotels Group, which aims to create "an environment where our people are happy and love coming to work." (Hotel owners purchase individual hotels from IHG under a variety of brands, including Holiday Inn.)

Holiday Inn Mart Plaza's efforts to create an engaging work environment have contributed to its success. While the average employee turnover in the hotel industry is approximately two years, one-third of the hotel's employees have worked there for at least twenty years. In addition, the hotel has enjoyed favorable revenue growth.

Questions

1. Of the factors that can contribute to employees' job satisfaction, which are present at Holiday Inn Mart Plaza, according to the information given?
2. Suggest one other action the hotel's management could take that would contribute to employee retention.

Sources: Suzanne Cosgrove, "No. 1: At Holiday Inn Mart Plaza There's an App to Aid Communication, But the Hotel's Family Spirit Is the Real Key," *Chicago Tribune,* November 8, 2019, https://www.chicagotribune.com; "Top Workplaces: Holiday Inn Chicago Mart Plaza River North," *Chicago Tribune,* https://top-workplaces.com, accessed April 29, 2020; InterContinental Hotels Group home page and careers page, https://www.ihgplc.com and https://www.careers.ihg.com, accessed April 29, 2020.

NOTES

1. K. Smith, "Retention Plan," *Best's Review,* February 2019, pp. 46–49.
2. J. D. Shaw, M. K. Duffy, J. L. Johnson, and D. E. Lockhart, "Turnover, Social Capital Losses, and Performance," *Academy of Management Journal* 48 (2005), pp. 594–606; R. Batt, "Managing Customer Services: Human Resource Practices, Quit Rates, and Sales Growth," *Academy of Management Journal* 45 (2002), pp. 587–597.
3. A. Chamberlain and D. Zhao, "The Key to Happy Customers? Happy Employees," *Harvard Business Review,* August 19, 2019, https://hbr.org; T. Y. Park and J. D. Shaw, "Turnover Rates and Organizational Performance: A Meta-Analysis," *Journal of Applied Psychology* 98 (2013), pp. 268–309.
4. W. J. Becker and R. Cropanzano, "Dynamic Aspects of Voluntary Turnover: An Integrated Approach to Curvilinearity in the Performance-Turnover Relationship," *Journal of Applied Psychology* 96 (2011), pp. 233–246.
5. M. Tabaka, "Training a New Employee Is Time-Consuming. 6 Ways to Get New Recruits Up to Speed—Fast," *Inc.,* February 4, 2019, https://www.inc.com; A. Morelix, "They Are the Companies That Are (and Aren't) Hiring Right Now," *Inc.,* March-April 2018, https://www.inc.com; S. Payne, "The Proven Links between Retention and Employee Experience," *Workforce,* May 2017, https://www.workforce.com.
6. The Lorrie Willey, "The Public Policy Exception to Employment at Will: Balancing Employer's Right and the Public Interest," *Journal of Legal, Ethical and Regulatory Issues* 12, no. 1 (2009), pp. 55–72; Mitch Baker, "Commentary: 'At Will' Firing Shouldn't Lack a Reason," *Daily Journal of Commerce, Portland,* January 17, 2008, Business & Company Resource Center, http://galenet.galegroup.com.
7. Occupational Safety and Health Administration, "Workplace Violence," https://www.osha.gov, accessed April 29, 2020; National Safety Council, "Assaults Fourth Leading Cause of Workplace Deaths," https://www.nsc.org, accessed April 29, 2020.
8. S. McCammon, "Independent Probe of Virginia Beach Shooting Leaves Many Unanswered Questions," *NPR,* November 13, 2019, https://www.npr.org; M. Holcombe, H. Yan, and M. Morales, "New Details Emerge in the Virginia Beach Mass Shooting That Left 12 People Dead," *CNN,* June 3, 2019, https://www.cnn.com.
9. S. McClear, "43% of Workers to Look for a New Job in the Next 12 Months," *The Ladders,* August 14, 2019, https://www.theladders.com.

10. B. J. Tepper, "Relationship among Supervisors' and Subordinates' Procedural Justice Perceptions and Organizational Citizenship Behaviors," *Academy of Management Journal* 46 (2003), pp. 97–105; T. Simons and Q. Roberson, "Why Managers Should Care about Fairness: The Effects of Aggregate Justice Perception on Organizational Outcomes," *Journal of Applied Psychology* 88 (2003), pp. 432–443; C. M. Holmvall and D. R. Bobocel, "What Fair Procedures Say about Me: Self-Construals and Reactions to Procedural Fairness," *Organizational Behavior and Human Decision Processes* 105 (2008), pp. 147–168.
11. E. C. Bianchi and J. Brockner, "In the Eyes of the Beholder: The Role of Dispositional Trust in Judgments of Procedural and Interactional Justice," *Organizational Behavior and Human Decision Processes* 118 (2012), pp. 46–59.
12. T. A. Judge, B. A. Scott, and R. Ilies, "Hostility, Job Attitudes and Workplace Deviance: A Test of a Multilevel Model," *Journal of Applied Psychology* 91 (2006), pp. 126–138.
13. *Harmon v. Thornburgh,* CA, DC No. 88-5265 (July 30, 1989); *Treasury Employees Union v. Von Raab,* U.S. Sup. Ct. No. 86-18796 (March 21, 1989); *City of Annapolis v. United Food & Commercial Workers Local 400,* Md. Ct. App. No. 38 (November 6, 1989); *Skinner v. Railway Labor Executives Association,* U.S. Sup. Ct. No. 87-1555 (March 21, 1989); *Bluestein v. Skinner,* 908 F 451, 9th Cir. (1990).
14. L. Schencker, "Using Marijuana Is Legal—But It Can Still Get You Fired. 'Human Resource Professionals in Illinois Will Have Their Hands Full,'" *Chicago Tribune,* January 10, 2020, https://www.chicagotribune.com; A. Martinez, "Marijuana Accommodations in the Workplace: Your Employees Are Smoking Pot—Now What?" *Forbes,* October 1, 2019, https://www.forbes.com; T. Lytle, "Marijuana and the Workplace: It's Complicated," *HR Magazine,* August 28, 2019, https://shrm.org.
15. "Workplace Searches and Interrogations," *FindLaw,* https://employment.findlaw.com, accessed April 29, 2020; "Workplace Searches: Dos and Don'ts," *Nolo,* https://www.nolo.com, accessed April 29, 2020; D. J. Hoekstra, "Workplace Searches: A Legal Overview," *Labor Law Journal* 47, no. 2 (February 1996), pp. 127–138.
16. G. Henshaw and K. Youmans, "Employee Privacy in the Workplace and an Employer's Right to Conduct Workplace Searches and Surveillance," *SHRM Legal Report,* Spring 1990, pp. 1–5; B. K. Repa, *Your Rights in the Workplace* (Berkeley, CA: Nolo Press, 1997).
17. K. Cavanaugh, "Announcement of Employee Termination—What to Tell Staff," *Insperity Blog,* https://www.insperity.com, accessed April 29, 2020; "Your Rights in the Workplace: Privacy Rights," *Nolo,* https://www.nolo.com, accessed April 29, 2020; R. S. Soderstrom and J. R. Murray, "Defamation in Employment: Suits by At-Will Employees," *FICC Quarterly,* Summer 1992, pp. 395–426.
18. D. M. Busch and E. Follansbee, "The WARN Act and COVID-19: What Are Employers Obligated to Do?" https://mintz.com, accessed April 29, 2020; D. Gallagher and P. Kirkland, "Meat Processing Plants across the US Are Closing Due to the Pandemic. Will Consumers Feel the Impact?" *CNN Business,* April 27, 2020, https://www.cnn.com.
19. C. Cutter, "The Debate in HR: What's the Best Way to Fire Someone?" *The Wall Street Journal,* April 10, 2019, https://www.wsj.com; "Does Inconsistency Always Kill the Cat?" *National Law Review,* August 5, 2019, https://www.natlawreview.com.
20. "Progressive Discipline Policy—Single Disciplinary Process," *Society for Human Resource Management,* https://www.shrm.org, accessed April 29, 2020; S. Bingham, "Why Progressive Discipline Doesn't Work (and What to Do Instead)," *Fast Company,* October 30, 2019, https://www.fastcompany.com.
21. Resolution Systems Institute, "Why Do Courts Use ADR?" https://www.aboutrsi.org, accessed April 29, 2020; D. Shontz, F. Kipperman, and V. Soma, *Business-to-Business Arbitration in the United States: Perceptions of Corporate Counsel* (Rand Institute for Civil Justice, 2011), https://www.rand.org.
22. "Managing for Employee Retention," *Society for Human Resource Management,* https://www.shrm.org, accessed April 29, 2020; S. Florentine, "Employee Retention: 8 Strategies for Retaining Top Talent," *CIO,* February 27, 2019, https://www.cio.com.
23. J. Boitnott, "5 Ways Employee Engagement Makes Your Company More Competitive," *Entrepreneur,* https://www.entrepreneur.com, accessed April 29, 2020; C. Richardson, "Employee Engagement Isn't Just a Buzzword—It's a Competitive Advantage," *The Globe and Mail,* January 2, 2019, https://www.theglobeandmail.com.
24. B. Crowell, "Elevating the Employee Experience," *TD,* January 2017, pp. 52–56.
25. D. W. Baruch, "Why They Terminate," *Journal of Consulting Psychology* 8 (1944), pp. 35–46; J. G. Rosse, "Relations among Lateness, Absence and Turnover: Is There a Progression of Withdrawal?" *Human Relations* 41 (1988), pp. 517–531; C. Hulin, "Adaptation, Persistence and Commitment in Organizations," in *Handbook of Industrial & Organizational Psychology,* 2nd ed., eds. M. D. Dunnette and L. M. Hough (Palo Alto, CA: Consulting Psychologists Press, 1991), pp. 443–450; E. R. Burris, J. R. Detert, and D. S. Chiaburu, "Quitting before Leaving: The Mediating Effects of Psychological Attachment and Detachment on Voice," *Journal of Applied Psychology* 93 (2008), pp. 912–922.
26. D. A. Harrison, D. A. Newman, and P. L. Roth, "How Important Are Job Attitudes? Meta-analytic Comparisons of Integrative Behavioral Outcomes and Time Sequences," *Academy of Management Journal* 49 (2006), pp. 305–325.
27. G. Chen, R. E. Ployhart, H. C. Thomas, N. Anderson, and P. D. Bliese, "The Power of Momentum: A New Model of Dynamic Relationships between Job Satisfaction Change and Turnover Intentions," *Academy of Management Journal,* 54 (2011), pp. 159–181.
28. R. D. Zimmerman, "Understanding the Impact of Personality Traits on Individuals' Turnover Decisions: A Meta-analysis," *Personnel Psychology* 61 (2008), pp. 309–348.
29. T. A. Judge, E. A. Locke, C. C. Durham, and A. N. Kluger, "Dispositional Effects on Job and Life Satisfaction: The Role of Core Evaluations," *Journal of Applied Psychology* 83 (1998), pp. 17–34.
30. B. M. Staw, N. E. Bell, and J. A. Clausen, "The Dispositional Approach to Job Attitudes: A Lifetime Longitudinal Test," *Administrative Science Quarterly* 31 (1986), pp. 56–78; B. M. Staw and J. Ross, "Stability in the Midst of Change: A Dispositional Approach to Job Attitudes," *Journal of Applied Psychology* 70 (1985), pp. 469–480; R. P. Steel and J. R. Rentsch, "The Dispositional Model of Job Attitudes Revisited: Findings of a 10-Year Study," *Journal of Applied Psychology* 82 (1997), pp. 873–879.
31. T. A. Judge and J. E. Bono, "Relationship of Core Self-Evaluation Traits—Self-Esteem, Generalized Self-Efficacy, Locus of Control, and Emotional Stability—with Job Satisfaction and Job

Performance: A Meta-Analysis," *Journal of Applied Psychology* 86 (2001), pp. 80–92.

32. T. A. Judge, J. E. Bono, and E. A. Locke, "Personality and Job Satisfaction: The Mediating Role of Job Characteristics," *Journal of Applied Psychology* 85 (2000), pp. 237–249.
33. S. C. Douglas and M. J. Martinko, "Exploring the Role of Individual Differences in the Prediction of Workplace Aggression," *Journal of Applied Psychology* 86 (2001), pp. 547–559.
34. B. A. Gerhart, "How Important Are Dispositional Factors as Determinants of Job Satisfaction? Implications for Job Design and Other Personnel Programs," *Journal of Applied Psychology* 72 (1987), pp. 493–502.
35. E. F. Stone and H. G. Gueutal, "An Empirical Derivation of the Dimensions along Which Characteristics of Jobs Are Perceived," *Academy of Management Journal* 28 (1985), pp. 376–396.
36. L. W. Porter and R. M. Steers, "Organizational Work and Personal Factors in Employee Absenteeism and Turnover," *Psychological Bulletin* 80 (1973), pp. 151–176; S. Melamed, I. Ben-Avi, J. Luz, and M. S. Green, "Objective and Subjective Work Monotony: Effects on Job Satisfaction, Psychological Distress, and Absenteeism in Blue Collar Workers," *Journal of Applied Psychology* 80 (1995), pp. 29–42.
37. D. R. Ilgen and J. R. Hollenbeck, "The Structure of Work: Job Design and Roles," in M. D. Dunnette and L. M. Hough (eds.), *Handbook of Industrial and Organizational Psychology,* 2nd ed. (Palo Alto, CA: Consulting Psychologists Press, 1991), pp. 165–207.
38. J. A. Breaugh and J. P. Colihan, "Measuring Facets of Job Ambiguity: Construct Validity Evidence," *Journal of Applied Psychology* 79 (1994), pp. 191–201.
39. M. A. Shaffer and D. A. Harrison, "Expatriates' Psychological Withdrawal from Interpersonal Assignments: Work, Nonwork, and Family Influences," *Personnel Psychology* 51 (1998), pp. 87–118.
40. "5 Traits Employees Want in a Boss," *Business News Daily,* March 13, 2020, https://www.businessnewsdaily.com; E. N. Sherf, V. Venkataramani, and R. S. Gajendran, "Too Busy to Be Fair? The Effect of Workload and Rewards on Managers' Justice Rule Adherence," *Academy of Management Journal,* April 18, 2019, https://journals.aom.org.
41. J. M. Sacco and N. Schmitt, "A Dynamic Multilevel Model of Demographic Diversity and Misfit Effects," *Journal of Applied Psychology* 90 (2005), pp. 203–231; R. E. Ployhart, J. A. Weekley, and K. Baughman, "The Structure and Function of Human Capital Emergence: A Multilevel Examination of the Attraction–Selection–Attrition Model," *Academy of Management Journal* 49 (2006), pp. 661–677.
42. S. Lim, L. M. Cortina, and V. J. Magley, "Personal and Work-Group Incivility: Impact on Work and Health Outcomes," *Journal of Applied Psychology* 93 (2008), pp. 95–107.
43. E. J. McClean, E. R. Burris, and J. R. Detert, "When Does Voice Lead to Exit? It Depends on Leadership," *Academy of Management Review* 56 (2013), pp. 525–548.
44. "The Whistleblower's Dilemma: Do the Risks Outweigh the Benefits?" *Knowledge@Wharton,* November 5, 2019, https://knowledge.wharton.upenn.edu.
45. S. Horvath, "How Employers Can Fight Absenteeism, Presenteeism with Benefits," *Employee Benefit News,* March 15, 2018, https://www.benefitnews.com.
46. J. Cox, "It's Never Been This Hard for Companies to Find Qualified Workers," *CNBC,* February 19, 2020, https://www.cnbc.com; E. Cole, "Low Unemployment, High Job Growth Create Hiring Problems for Businesses," *News Tribune,* July 21, 2019, https://www.newstribune.com.
47. R. Fry, "Millennials Aren't Job-Hopping Any Faster than Generation X Did," Pew Research Center, April 19, 2017, http://www.pewresearch.org.
48. R. T. Mowday, R. M. Steers, and L. W. Porter, "The Measurement of Organizational Commitment," *Journal of Vocational Behavior* 14 (1979), pp. 224–247.
49. J. S. Lublin, "The Telltale Sign a New Hire Isn't Fitting In," *The Wall Street Journal,* June 10, 2017, https://www.wsj.com.
50. E. A. Locke, "The Nature and Causes of Job Dissatisfaction," in *The Handbook of Industrial & Organizational Psychology,* ed. M. D. Dunnette (Chicago: Rand McNally, 1976), pp. 901–969.
51. N. A. Bowling, T. A. Beehr, S. H. Wagner, and T. M. Libkuman, "Adaptation-Level Theory, Opponent Process Theory, and Dispositions: An Integrated Approach to the Stability of Job Satisfaction," *Journal of Applied Psychology* 90 (2005), pp. 1044–1053.
52. For these and other examples, see David DiSalvo, "10 Reasons Why Some People Love What They Do," *Psychology Today,* May/June 2013, pp. 48–50.
53. Gallup, *State of the American Workplace,* https://www.gallup.com, accessed April 29, 2020.
54. G. R. Oldham, A. Cummings, L. J. Mischel, J. M. Schmidtke, and J. Zhou, "Listen While You Work? Quasi-experimental Relations between Personal-Stereo Headset Use and Employee Work Responses," *Journal of Applied Psychology* 80 (1995), pp. 547–564.
55. D. L. Yohn, "Engaging Employees Starts with Remembering What Your Company Stands For," *Harvard Business Review,* March 13, 2018, https://hbr.org; A. Miller, "Q&A: Alex Parren," *Wearables,* October 2017, p. 26.
56. Gallup, *State of the American Workplace,* pp. 25–30, 149; D. Teten, "A Family-Friendly Work Environment Is a Powerful Recruiting and Retention Tool," *Entrepreneur,* January 3, 2019, https://www.entrepreneur.com.
57. J. E. Perry-Smith, "Work Family Human Resource Bundles and Perceived Organizational Performance," *Academy of Management Journal* 43 (2000), pp. 801–815; M. M. Arthur, "Share Price Reactions to Work-Family Initiatives: An Institutional Perspective," *Academy of Management Journal* 46 (2003), pp. 497–505.
58. B. M. Meglino, E. C. Ravlin, and C. L. Adkins, "A Work Values Approach to Corporate Culture: A Field Test of the Value Congruence Process and Its Relationship to Individual Outcomes," *Journal of Applied Psychology* 74 (1989), pp. 424–433.
59. G. C. Ganster, M. R. Fusilier, and B. T. Mayes, "Role of Social Support in the Experience of Stress at Work," *Journal of Applied Psychology* 71 (1986), pp. 102–111.
60. R. Eisenberger, F. Stinghamber, C. Vandenberghe, I. L. Sucharski, and L. Rhoades, "Perceived Supervisor Support: Contributions to Perceived Organizational Support and Employee Retention," *Journal of Applied Psychology* 87 (2002), pp. 565–573.
61. R. T. Keller, "A Test of the Path-Goal Theory of Leadership with Need for Clarity as a Moderator in Research and Development Organizations," *Journal of Applied Psychology* 74 (1989), pp. 208–212.

62. Kate Rockwood, "P&L to the People!" *Inc.,* February 2017, pp. 56–57.
63. S. C. Payne and A. H. Huffman, "A Longitudinal Examination of the Influence of Mentoring on Organizational Commitment and Turnover," *Academy of Management Journal* 48 (2005), pp. 158–168.
64. D. Liu, T. R. Mitchell, T. W. Lee, B. C. Holtom, and T. R. Hinken, "When Employees Are Out of Step with Co-workers: How Job Satisfaction Trajectory and Dispersion Influence Individual and Unit-Level Voluntary Turnover," *Academy of Management Journal* 55 (2012), pp. 1360–1380.
65. D. Cronquist, "How to Measure Employee Satisfaction," *BambooHR blog,* August 8, 2019, https://www.bamboohr.com; R. P. Quinn and G. L. Staines, *The 1977 Quality of Employment Survey* (Ann Arbor, MI: Survey Research Center, Institute for Social Research, University of Michigan, 1979).
66. T. Judge and T. Welbourne, "A Confirmatory Investigation of the Dimensionality of the Pay Satisfaction Questionnaire," *Journal of Applied Psychology* 79 (1994), pp. 461–466.
67. Chantrelle Nielsen and Natalie McCullough, "How People Analytics Can Help You Change Process, Culture, and Strategy," *Harvard Business Review,* May 17, 2018, https://hbr.org.
68. M. Levin, "3 Reasons Why Good Exit Interviews Are Important to Your Culture, and How to Do Them Right," *Inc.,* https://www.inc.com, accessed April 29, 2020; E. Spain and B. Groysberg, "Making Exit Interviews Count," *Harvard Business Review,* https://hbr.org, accessed April 29, 2020.
69. Jamie LaReau, "Tweaks Trim Turnover," *Automotive News,* October 16, 2017, https://www.autonews.com.

Compensating Human Resources

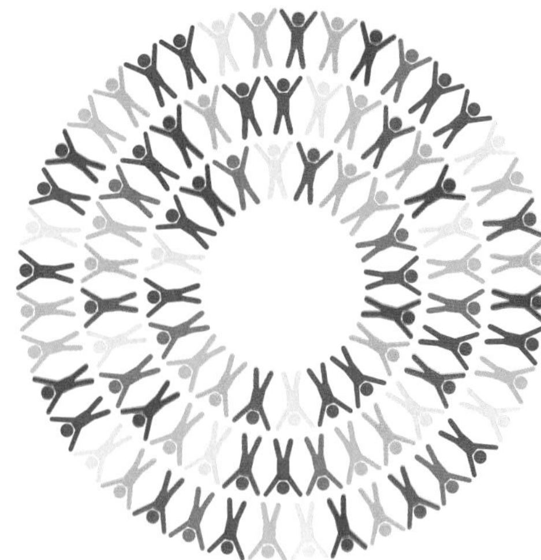

freesoulproduction/Shutterstock

PART FOUR

12 Establishing a Pay Structure

Introduction

Dan Schulman, the CEO of PayPal, was raised by parents who advocated for civil rights, and they passed along to him their attitude of caring for others. Schulman started out in sales for AT&T but eventually became disillusioned with the model of selling customers a set number of minutes per month, whether they actually used that level of service or not. He moved into a management position with Virgin Mobile, which was bringing to the United States its alternative model of a prepaid plan with no fees, so customers with limited budgets could buy only what they needed. Virgin founder Richard Branson became a mentor in thinking about how a company could be socially responsible, and Schulman later brought that vision to PayPal.

Schulman sees PayPal's mission as democratizing financial services, so more people can participate in the economy. He extends that thinking to the company's relationship with its employees. The company conducts surveys of employee experience, and in one survey, Schulman learned that 60% of employees working in call centers or other hourly positions at PayPal had difficulty covering their expenses. Like other businesses, PayPal had been committed to paying them what many consider a living wage, around $15 an hour. But especially in some cities, that amount was not enough to put employees on a solid financial footing. Schulman took a look at their pay in an uncommon way: for each company location, he obtained an estimate of essential living expenses. Then so pay was no lower than these estimates, he raised the wage rate of one-third of PayPal's employees. He also slashed by an average of 58% what employees pay for their health insurance. And PayPal issued grants of PayPal stock shares to employees who did not already have a stake in the company. Finally, so employees could truly benefit from these changes, he provided them with a "financial wellness" training program.

PayPal CEO Dan Schulman insists that employees be paid a living wage that puts them on a solid financial footing for success.

ZUMA Press, Inc./Alamy Stock Photo

What Do I Need to Know?

After reading this chapter, you should be able to:

LO 12-1 Identify the kinds of decisions involved in establishing a pay structure.

LO 12-2 Summarize legal requirements for pay policies.

LO 12-3 Discuss how economic forces influence decisions about pay.

LO 12-4 Describe how employees evaluate the fairness of a pay structure.

LO 12-5 Explain how organizations design pay structures related to jobs.

LO 12-6 Describe alternatives to job-based pay.

LO 12-7 Summarize how to ensure that pay is actually in line with the pay structure.

LO 12-8 Discuss issues related to paying employees serving in the military and paying executives.

While the cost of these compensation changes totaled tens of millions of dollars, Schulman defends the move as being both patriotic and practical. He insists that PayPal's long-term success requires employees passionate about the company and its mission. After Schulman joined PayPal and the compensation overhaul, PayPal's stock price almost doubled, and the number of customers it serves also has doubled.[1]

From the employer's point of view, pay is a powerful tool for meeting the organization's goals. Pay has a large impact on employee attitudes and behaviors. It influences which kinds of employees are attracted to (and remain with) the organization. By rewarding certain behaviors, it can align employees' interests with the organization's goals. Employees care about policies affecting earnings because the policies affect the employees' income and standard of living. Besides the level of pay, employees care about the fairness of pay compared with what others earn. Also, employees consider pay a sign of status and success. They attach great importance to pay decisions when they evaluate their relationship with their employer. For these reasons, organizations must carefully manage and communicate decisions about pay.

At the same time, pay is a major cost. Depending on the organization's industry, the cost might range from an amount equivalent to 5% of revenues up to almost 40%. Keeping these costs reasonable is therefore important for achieving profit goals. In recent years, even as a strengthening economy increases the demand for labor, stiff global competition is pushing companies to keep a lid on pay rates. Employers consider options such as linking pay to performance or hiring less-experienced workers, even if they require more training.[2]

This chapter explores how companies compensate employees with pay and benefits. It describes how managers weigh the importance and costs of pay to arrive at a structure for compensation and levels of pay for different jobs. We first define the basic decisions in terms of pay structure and pay level. Next, we look at several considerations that influence these decisions: legal requirements related to pay, economic forces, the nature of the organization's jobs, and employees' judgments about the fairness of pay levels. We describe methods for evaluating jobs and market data to arrive at a pay structure. We then summarize alternatives to the usual focus on jobs. The chapter closes with a look at two issues of current importance–pay for employees on leave to serve in the military and pay for executives.

Mc Graw Hill connect

Visit your instructor's Connect® course and access your eBook to view this video.

"My job, and the one that I keep in the forefront, is always make sure that you're representing the associate who's not in the room."
—Tim Hourigan
Executive Vice President, Human Resources, The Home Depot

Video Produced for the Center for Executive Succession in the Darla Moore School of Business at the University of South Carolina by Coal Powered Filmworks.

Decisions about Pay

LO 12-1 Identify the kinds of decisions involved in establishing a pay structure.

Because pay is important both in its effect on employees and on account of its cost, organizations need to plan what they will pay employees in each job. An unplanned approach, in which each employee's pay is independently negotiated, will likely result in unfairness, dissatisfaction, and rates that are either overly expensive or so low that positions are hard to fill. Organizations therefore make decisions about two aspects of pay structure: job structure and pay level. **Job structure** consists of the relative pay for different jobs within the

Job Structure
The relative pay for different jobs within the organization.

FIGURE 12.1
Issues in Developing a Pay Structure

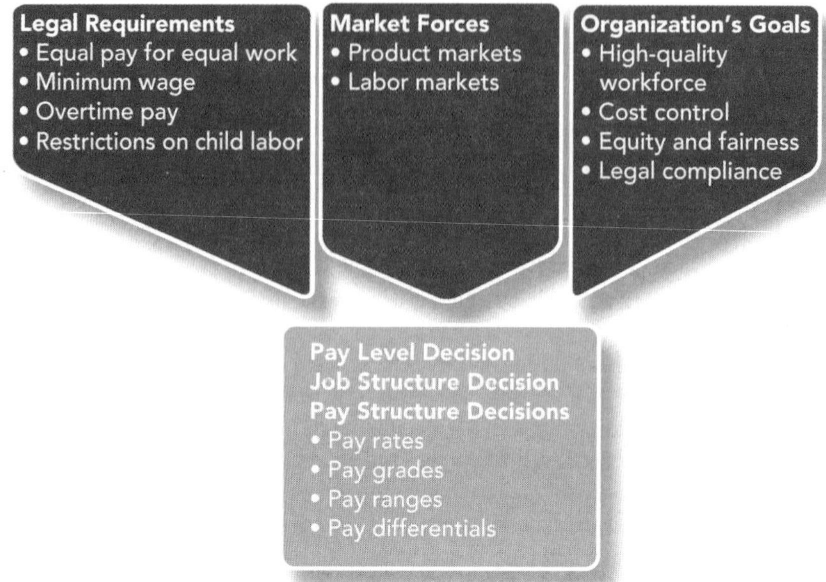

organization. It establishes relative pay among different functions and different levels of responsibility. For example, job structure defines the difference in pay between an entry-level accountant and an entry-level assembler, as well as the difference between an entry-level accountant, the accounting department manager, and the organization's comptroller. **Pay level** is the average amount (including wages, salaries, and bonuses) the organization pays for a particular job. Together, job structure and pay levels establish a **pay structure** that helps the organization achieve goals related to employee motivation, cost control, and the ability to attract and retain talented human resources.

Pay Level
The average amount (including wages, salaries, and bonuses) the organization pays for a particular job.

Pay Structure
The pay policy resulting from job structure and pay level decisions.

The organization's job structure and pay levels are policies of the organization rather than the amount a particular employee earns. For example, an organization's pay structure could include the range of pay that a person may earn in the job of entry-level accountant. An individual accountant could be earning an amount anywhere within that range. Typically, the amount a person earns depends on the individual's qualifications, accomplishments, and experience. The individual's pay may also depend partly on how well the organization performs. This chapter focuses on the organization's decisions about pay structure, and the next chapter will explore decisions that affect the amount of pay an individual earns.

Especially in an organization with hundreds or thousands of employees, it would be impractical for managers and the human resource department to make an entirely unique decision about each employee's pay. The decision would have to weigh so many factors that this approach would be expensive, difficult, and often unsatisfactory. Establishing a pay structure simplifies the process of making decisions about individual employees' pay by grouping together employees with similar jobs. As shown in Figure 12.1, human resource professionals develop this pay structure based on legal requirements, market forces, and the organization's goals, such as attracting a high-quality workforce and meeting principles of fairness.

LO 12-2 Summarize legal requirements for pay policies.

Legal Requirements for Pay

Pay policies and practices in the United States are subject to government laws and regulations. For example, just as competing businesses may not conspire to set prices, they may not conspire to set wage rates. In addition, government regulation affects pay structure in the areas of equal employment opportunity, minimum wages, pay for overtime, and

Closing the Pay Gap

In recent years, accusations against high-profile individuals drew attention to the problem of workplace harassment, especially as experienced by women. The #TimesUp hashtag on social media signaled that women and men were determined to see change. And along with respectful treatment, women indicated that they expected equal pay. Here are some actions that companies can take to close the pay gap between male and female workers:

- Review pay structures and payroll data to find any pay gaps that exist. Good intentions alone do not ensure that pay is equal. If the HR department is unaware of pay disparities and employees discover them, the situation is awkward, because the employees might suspect that they have been treated unfairly or that the company discriminates.
- If there are pay gaps, investigate the reasons. Gaps related to differences in education, experience, job duties, and so on may explain a legitimate pay gap. Managers should understand and be prepared to explain such gaps. They also should ensure they are doing enough to give employees proper encouragement to participate in development activities. In this way, employees become eligible for higher pay because of their growing skills.
- Be more transparent about pay decisions. Most companies are hesitant to disclose what each employee earns. For those reluctant about full disclosure, an intermediate step would be to disclose the range of pay for each type of job.
- During employee recruiting and selection, avoid asking candidates about their pay history. These questions, which some states have outlawed, can have the effect of locking in past discrimination by building job offers on existing pay levels, rather than the new hire's value to the organization. An alternative is to disclose the organization's pay ranges and the criteria for placing an individual within the range, so that the candidate can consider whether the pay is acceptable.

Questions

1. Suppose a company investigates its pay structure and finds that female managers earn less than male managers because they have not spent much time managing sales and production functions. Which of the ideas listed here would you recommend as a way to address this pay gap?
2. Suppose a company investigates its pay structure and finds that female engineers earn less than male engineers with the same qualifications because the men request higher salaries when they apply for jobs. Which of the ideas listed here would you recommend?

Sources: Abigail Hess, "8 Steps Economists Say Could Help Close the Gender Pay Gap," *CNBC,* May 9, 2019, https://www.cnbc.com; Shelley Zalis, "Equal Pay Day 2019: How to Close the Wage Gap for Good," *Forbes,* April 2, 2019, https://www.forbes.com; Kelsey Gee, "Why Asking about Current Pay Is the New Taboo for Prospective Employers," *The Wall Street Journal,* April 18, 2018, https://www.wsj.com; Challenger, Gray & Christmas, "Nearly Half of Companies Reviewing Pay Structures in Light of #TimesUp," news release, February 28, 2018, https://www.challengergray.com.

prevailing wages for federal contractors. All of an organization's decisions about pay should comply with the applicable laws.

Equal Employment Opportunity

Under the laws governing equal employment opportunity, described in Chapter 3, employers may not base differences in pay on an employee's age, sex, race, or other protected status. Any differences in pay must instead be tied to such business-related considerations as job responsibilities or performance. The goal is for employers to provide *equal pay for equal work.* Job descriptions, job structures, and pay structures can help organizations demonstrate that they are upholding these laws. Recent public outcries over the treatment of women in the workplace have renewed attention to the issue of equal pay; the "HR How To" box provides some additional guidance on addressing this issue.

The equal opportunity laws do not guarantee equal pay for men and women, whites and minorities, or any other groups, because so many legitimate factors, from education to

Two employees who do the same job cannot be paid different wages because of race, sex, or age. Only if there are differences in their experience, skills, seniority, or job performance are there legal reasons why their pay might be different.
Robert Kneschke/Shutterstock

choice of occupation, affect a person's earnings. In fact, numbers show that women and racial minorities in the United States tend to earn less than white men. Among full-time workers in the first few months of 2020, women on average earned 81 cents for every dollar earned by men. Among male employees, Black workers earned 75 cents for every dollar earned by white workers, and Hispanic workers earned 70 cents. A racial gap among Black and Hispanic female employees also exists, at 85 and 78 cents per dollar, respectively.[3] (These numbers do not reflect the impact of the COVID-19 on U.S. wages and unemployment.) Even when these figures are adjusted to take into account education, experience, and occupation, the earnings gap does not completely close.[4] Among executives, one cause of lower pay for women appears to be that less of their pay is tied to performance (for example, bonuses and stock, described in the next chapter).[5]

One explanation for historically lower pay for women has been that employers have undervalued work performed by women–in particular, placing a lower value on occupations traditionally dominated by women. Some policy makers have proposed a remedy for this called equal pay for *comparable worth.* This policy uses job evaluation (described later in the chapter) to establish the worth of an organization's jobs in terms of such criteria as their difficulty and their importance to the organization. The employer then compares the evaluation points awarded to each job with the pay for each job. If jobs have the same number of evaluation points, they should be paid equally. If they are not, pay of the lower-paid job is raised to meet the goal of comparable worth.

Comparable-worth policies are controversial. From an economic standpoint, the obvious drawback of such a policy is that raising pay for some jobs places the employer at an economic disadvantage relative to employers that pay the market rate. In addition, a free-market economy assumes that people will take differences in pay into account when they choose a career. The courts allow organizations to defend themselves against claims of discrimination by showing that they pay the going market rate.[6] Businesses are reluctant to place themselves at an economic disadvantage, but many state governments adjust pay to achieve equal pay for comparable worth. Also, at both private and government organizations, policies designed to shatter the "glass ceiling" (discussed in Chapter 8) can help to address the problem of unequal pay. For an example of a company that has navigated the pitfalls, see the "Best Practices" box.

Employers considering how to address equal employment opportunity should bear in mind that the consequences of pay discrimination can be far reaching. The Lilly Ledbetter Fair Pay Act of 2009, described in Chapter 3, allows employees claiming discrimination to treat each receipt of a paycheck as an instance of discrimination for purposes of determining their eligibility to file a complaint.

Minimum Wage
The lowest amount that employers may pay under federal or state law, stated as an amount of pay per hour.

Fair Labor Standards Act (FLSA)
Federal law that establishes a minimum wage and requirements for overtime pay and child labor.

Minimum Wage

In the United States, employers must pay at least the **minimum wage** established by law. (A *wage* is the rate of pay per hour.) At the federal level, the 1938 **Fair Labor Standards Act (FLSA)** establishes a minimum wage that is now $7.25 per hour. The FLSA also permits a lower "training wage," which employers may pay to workers under the age of 20 for a period of up to 90 days. This subminimum wage is approximately 85% of the minimum wage. Some states have laws specifying minimum wages; in these states, employers must pay whichever rate is higher.

Best Practices

Intel Boosts Women's Pay to Close the Gender Gap

For years, companies in the high-tech industry have struggled to acquire and keep enough talent. Although tech companies insist that they are recruiting widely, seeking a diverse workforce, they also acknowledge that women and people of color tend to be underrepresented.

One company that is doing something about it is microchip maker Intel. Despite the complexity of having over 100,000 employees in more than 50 countries, Intel brought together its HR and legal departments, with the assistance of a vendor of statistical modeling techniques, to analyze its pay structure, including salaries, bonuses, and grants of stock to employees. Specifically, the company wanted to know if employees doing comparable work were being paid comparably, taking into account variables such as job performance and number of years with Intel. The analysis found a gender pay gap of 2.6% on average globally, including a gap of 0.7% in the United States.

Intel was determined to close the gap. It began giving raises to underpaid female workers, and at the beginning of 2019, it announced that the gap had been bridged; on average, female employees were making as much as males in comparable positions. The raises added to Intel's expenses, but it is a sound investment, according to HR vice president Julie Ann Overcash. Overcash notes that gender equity is an essential part of achieving an inclusive culture, which is associated with high performance. She also reported that employee turnover has fallen since Intel began reporting on its progress in achieving comparable pay for comparable work.

Intel has continued to hold itself accountable for fair treatment. It not only reports pay and other employment data to the Equal Employment Opportunity Commission, but also makes the data public. Intel recently reported that women are underrepresented in high management levels in some countries where it operates. It also publicly stated its commitment to do better. Besides increasing opportunities for women in countries where they are underrepresented, Intel aims to close the gap in pay between employees of color and white employees in comparable positions.

Questions

1. Why do you think Intel would decide to make its diversity and pay data public? How would you expect this to affect hiring and employee retention?
2. Would you want to work for a company that has set and achieved comparable-pay goals for employees, as measured by gender and racial/ethnic group? Why or why not?

Sources: Steven Musli, "Intel Offers Detailed Look into Employee Pay Disparities," *CNET*, December 10, 2019, https://www.cnet.com; Tamara Lytle, "A Question of Fairness," *HR Magazine*, Summer 2019, pp. 41–45; Abrar Al-Heeti, "Intel Says It Closed Its Pay Gap Globally," *CNET*, January 22, 2019, https://www.cnet.com.

From the standpoint of social policy, an issue related to the minimum wage is that it tends to be lower than the earnings required for a full-time worker to rise above the poverty level. A number of cities have therefore passed laws requiring a so-called *living wage*, essentially a minimum wage based on the cost of living in a particular region.

Overtime Pay

Another requirement of the FLSA is that employers must pay higher wages for overtime, defined as hours worked beyond 40 hours per week. The overtime rate under the FLSA is one and a half times the employee's usual hourly rate, including any bonuses and piece-rate payments (amounts paid per item produced). The overtime rate applies to the hours worked beyond 40 in one week. Time worked includes not only hours spent on production or sales but also time on such activities as attending required classes, cleaning up the work site, or traveling between work sites. Figure 12.2 shows how this applies to an employee who works 50 hours to earn a base rate of $12 per hour plus a weekly bonus of $40. The overtime pay is based on the base pay ($480) plus the bonus ($40), for a rate of $13.00 per hour. For each

FIGURE 12.2
Computing Overtime Pay

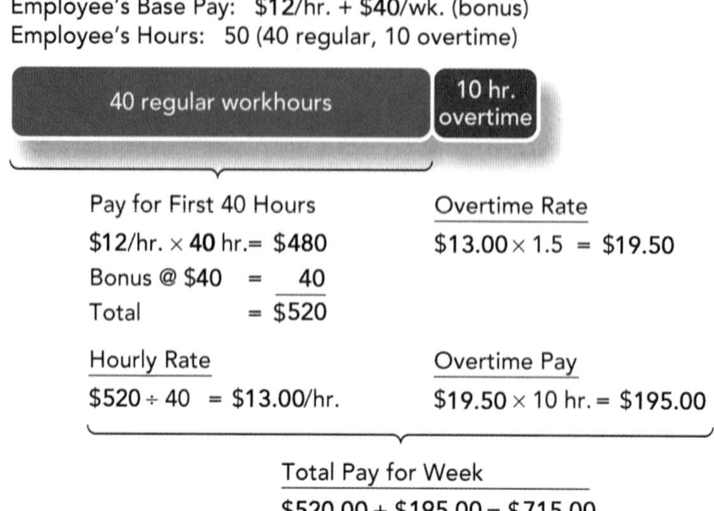

of the 10 hours of overtime, the employee would earn $19.50, so the overtime pay is $195.00 ($19.50 times 10). When employees are paid per unit produced or when they receive a monthly or quarterly bonus, those payments must be converted into wages per hour, so that the employer can include these amounts when figuring the correct overtime rate.

Overtime pay is required, whether or not the employer specifically asked or expected the employee to work more than 40 hours. In other words, if the employer knows the employee is working overtime but does not pay time and a half, the employer may be violating the FLSA.

Exempt Employees Managers, outside salespeople, and any other employees not covered by the FLSA requirement for overtime pay.

Not everyone is eligible for overtime pay. Under the FLSA, executive, professional, administrative, and highly compensated white-collar employees are considered **exempt employees,** meaning employers need not pay them one and a half times their regular pay for working more than 40 hours per week. Exempt status depends on the employee's job responsibilities, salary level, and "salary basis," meaning that the employee is paid a given amount regardless of the number of hours worked or quality of the work. Paying an employee on a salary basis means the organization expects that this person can manage his or her own time to get the work done, so the employer may deduct from the employee's pay only in certain limited circumstances, such as disciplinary action or for unpaid leave for personal reasons. Additional exceptions apply to certain occupations, including outside salespersons, teachers, and certain computer professionals. Thus, the standards are fairly complicated. In 2020, the Department of Labor increased the earnings thresholds necessary to exempt executive, administrative, and professional employees from FLSA's minimum wage and overtime pay requirements. For more details about the final rule, refer to the Labor Department's Wage and Hour Division website page at https://www.dol.gov/agencies/whd.[7]

Nonexempt Employees Employees covered by the FLSA requirements for overtime pay.

Any employee who is not in one of the exempt categories is called a **nonexempt employee.** Most workers paid on an hourly basis are nonexempt and therefore subject to the laws governing overtime pay. However, paying a salary does not necessarily mean a job is exempt.

Child Labor

In the early years of the Industrial Revolution, employers could pay low wages by hiring children. The FLSA now sharply restricts the use of child labor, with the aim of protecting children's health, safety, and educational opportunities. The restrictions apply to children younger than 18. Under the FLSA, children aged 16 and 17 may not be employed in hazardous occupations defined by the Department of Labor, such as mining, meatpacking, and certain kinds of manufacturing using heavy machinery. Children aged 14 and 15 may work only outside school hours in jobs defined as nonhazardous and for limited time periods. A child under age 14 may not be employed in any work associated with interstate commerce, except work performed in a nonhazardous job for a business entirely owned by the child's parent or guardian. A few additional exemptions from this ban include acting, babysitting, and delivering newspapers to consumers.

Besides the FLSA, state laws also restrict the use of child labor. Many states have laws requiring working papers or work permits for minors, and many states restrict the number of hours or times of day that minors aged 16 and older may work. Before hiring any workers under the age of 18, employers must ensure they are complying with the child labor laws of their state, as well as the FLSA requirements for their industry.

Prevailing Wages

Two additional federal laws, the Davis-Bacon Act of 1931 and the Walsh-Healy Public Contracts Act of 1936, govern pay policies of federal contractors. Under these laws, federal contractors must pay their employees at rates at least equal to the prevailing wages in the area. The calculation of prevailing rates must be based on 30% of the local labor force. Typically, the rates are based on relevant union contracts. Pay earned by union members tends to be higher than the pay of nonunion workers in similar jobs, so the effect of these laws is to raise the lower limit of pay an employer can offer.

These laws do not cover all companies. Davis-Bacon covers construction contractors that receive more than $2,000 in federal money. Walsh-Healy covers all government contractors receiving $10,000 or more in federal funds.

Pay Ratio Reporting

Along with laws governing pay policies and practice, the Dodd-Frank Wall Street Reform and Consumer Protection Act of 2010 adds a requirement related to communicating one outcome of pay structure: the ratio of CEO pay to the pay of a typical worker.[8] Under Dodd-Frank, public companies in the United States are required to include this ratio in their annual financial statements. The ratio compares the CEO's compensation to that of the company's median employee, meaning the one whose earnings are at the median for employees' pay. The ratio would be very high in an organization where the CEO's compensation is high but employees typically hold low-paying positions. It would be lower in an organization with highly paid employees, such as doctors or information technology workers. Determination of the median employee excludes contract workers, and it includes employees outside the United States, unless they represent a very small share of the organization's workforce.

The required reporting is intended to increase transparency and make social responsibility a more vital part of pay policies. With a brighter light shining on this aspect of pay decisions, organizations more than ever need to be able to communicate their HR policies clearly. At the same time, anyone reviewing the ratios needs to understand which workers are included in each organization's calculation of its pay. For example, Amazon, usually considered a tech company, recently reported its median worker's pay as just $32,015. That amount would be low for a tech worker, but in fact, it shows that a large share of Amazon workers have warehouse jobs.[9] Thus, it would be difficult to compare Amazon's ratio with the pay ratios of other tech companies with mostly software-related jobs. Later in this chapter, we will apply these ratios to ethical questions related to pay.

LO 12-3 Discuss how economic forces influence decisions about pay.

Economic Influences on Pay

An organization cannot make spending decisions independent of the economy. Organizations must keep costs low enough that they can sell their products profitably, yet they must be able to attract workers in a competitive labor market. Decisions about how to respond to the economic forces of product markets and labor markets limit an organization's choices about pay structure.

Product Markets

The organization's *product market* includes organizations that offer competing goods and services. In other words, the organizations in a product market are competing to serve the same customers. To succeed in their product markets, organizations must be able to sell their goods and services at a quantity and price that will bring them a sufficient profit. They may try to win customers by being superior in a number of areas, including quality, customer service, and price. An important influence on price is the cost to produce the goods and services for sale. As we mentioned earlier, the cost of labor is a significant part of an organization's costs.

If an organization's labor costs are higher than those of its competitors, it will be under pressure to charge more than competitors charge for similar products. If one company spends $50 in labor costs to make a product and its competitor spends only $35, the second company will be more profitable unless the first company can justify a higher price to customers. This is a major reason behind the shift of so many manufacturing facilities from the United States to other countries with lower overall labor costs—for example, to Mexico and China. However, labor costs in those other countries rise with the growth in demand for workers. At the same time, organizations use technology and other methods to improve productivity, meaning each employee produces more. Thus, while China once had a huge advantage in labor costs, a recent study by Oxford Economics found that the advantage had shrunk to just 4% because wages have risen in China (outpacing productivity gains) while productivity has risen strongly in the United States even as employers continue to hold the line on pay increases.[10]

Product markets place an upper limit on the pay an organization will offer. This upper limit is most important when labor costs are a large part of an organization's total costs and when the organization's customers place great importance on price. Organizations that want to lure top-quality employees by offering generous salaries therefore have to find ways to automate routine activities (so that labor is a smaller part of total costs) or to persuade customers that high quality is worth a premium price. Organizations under pressure to cut labor costs may respond by reducing staff levels, freezing pay levels, postponing hiring decisions, or requiring employees to bear more of the cost of benefits such as insurance premiums.

Labor Markets

Besides competing to sell their products, organizations must compete to obtain human resources in *labor markets*. In general, workers prefer higher-paying jobs and avoid employers that offer less money for the same type of job. Some workers—though not a majority—will make an effort to negotiate higher pay when applying for a job (see "Did You Know?"). Through these efforts and preferences, competition for labor establishes the minimum an organization must pay to hire an employee for a particular job. If an organization pays less than the minimum, employees will look for jobs with other organizations.

An organization's competitors in labor markets typically include companies with similar products and companies in other industries that hire similar employees. For example, a truck transportation firm would want to know the pay earned by truck drivers at competing firms as well as truck drivers for manufacturers that do their own shipping, drivers for

Did You Know?

A Majority of Workers Are Willing to Negotiate Pay

With a strong economy and a low national unemployment rate over the last few years (before the pandemic), some workers recognized their bargaining power and began to negotiate pay. According to a recent survey by the Robert Half staffing firm, more than half of people receiving a job offer engaged in negotiations for higher pay. Nearly seven in ten men tried to negotiate, but only four in ten women did. Younger workers were likelier to negotiate than older ones.

The instinct to hold back makes sense at least some of the time, according to Suzy Welch, writer and former editor-in-chief of *Harvard Business Review.* Welch recommends accepting an offer that is within 10% or 15% of the desired pay, in order to get off to a positive start at the new organization. A person who excels on the job can then negotiate a raise from a position of greater strength.

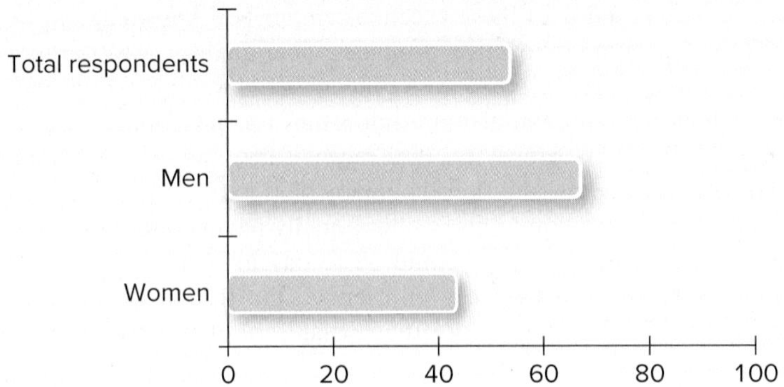

Question

Have you ever tried negotiating for higher pay? If so, what did you learn from the experience? If not, what do you think you might gain or lose from trying?

Sources: Robert Half, "Survey: 55 Percent of Workers Negotiated Pay with Last Job Offer," http://rh-us.mediaroom.com, accessed May 1, 2020; Robin Madell, "The Exact Words to Use When Negotiating Salary in a Job Offer," *US News & World Report,* March 4, 2020, https://money.usnews.com; Betsy Mikel, "Don't Make This Mistake When Negotiating Your Salary," *Inc.,* February 9, 2018, https://www.inc.com.

moving and storage companies, and drivers for stores that provide delivery services. In setting pay levels for its bookkeepers and administrative assistants, the company would probably define its labor market differently because bookkeepers and administrative assistants work for most kinds of businesses. The company would likely look for data on the earnings of bookkeepers and administrative assistants in the region. For all these jobs, the company wants to know what others are paying so that it will pay enough to attract and keep qualified employees.

Another influence on labor markets is the *cost of living*–the cost of a household's typical expenses, such as house payments, groceries, medical care, and gasoline. In some parts of the country, the cost of living is higher than in others, so the local labor markets there will likely demand higher pay. Also, over time, the cost of living tends to rise. When the cost of living is rising rapidly, labor markets demand pay increases. The federal government tracks trends in the nation's cost of living with a measure called the Consumer Price Index (CPI). Following and studying changes in the CPI can help employers prepare for changes in the demands of the labor market.

Pay Level: Deciding What to Pay

Although labor and product markets limit organizations' choices about pay levels, there is a range within which organizations can make decisions.[11] The size of this range

There is a strong demand for nurses in the labor market. What this means for hospitals is that they have to pay competitive wages and other perks to attract and retain staff. How does this differ from the retail industry's current labor market? Tom Grill/Getty Images

depends on the details of the organization's competitive environment. If many workers are competing for a few jobs, employers will have more choice. Similarly, employers can be more flexible about pay policies if they use technology and work design to get better results from employees than their competitors do.

When organizations have a broad range in which to make decisions about pay, they can choose to pay at, above, or below the rate set by market forces. Economic theory holds that the most profitable level, all things being equal, would be at the market rate. Often, however, all things are not equal from one employer to another. For instance, an organization may gain an advantage by paying above the market rate if it uses the higher pay as one means to attract top talent and then uses these excellent employees' knowledge to be more innovative, produce higher quality, or work more efficiently. This strategy is widely used for software engineers and developers, considering that these jobs are in high demand and also are important for developing cutting-edge products and improving business processes. In a recent survey about employers' pay practices, about half of respondents said their company pays extra to get and keep high-demand talent. A popular way of doing this is intentionally paying above the market rate. For example, an organization's policy could be to pay its workers overall at the 50th percentile (that is, matching market pay on average) but to aim for the 75th percentile for high-demand workers (paying more than what 75% of workers earn in comparable jobs).[12]

This approach is based on the view of employees as resources. Higher pay may be an investment in superior human resources. Having higher labor costs than your competitors is not necessarily bad if you also have the best and most effective workforce, which produces more products of better quality. Pay policies are one of the most important human resource tools for encouraging desired employee behaviors and discouraging undesired behaviors. Therefore, organizations must evaluate pay as more than a cost–it is an investment that can generate returns in attracting, retaining, and motivating a high-quality workforce. For this reason, paying above the going rate may be advantageous for an organization that empowers employees or that cannot closely watch employees (as with repair technicians who travel to customers). Those employers might use high pay to attract and retain top candidates and to motivate them to do their best because they want to keep their high-paying jobs.[13]

HR Analytics & Decision Making

Over the past few years, the wage rates and business performance of Walmart and Costco have provided interesting data for comparing the success of different pricing strategies. Walmart competes primarily on product cost, whereas Costco charges slightly more, and customer service plays a larger role in attracting customers. In recent years, Walmart has paid an entry-level wage of $11 per hour, while at the same time, Costco's lowest wage was $14. The founder of Costco has said his company aims to pay the "highest wages in all of retail."

The higher wages at Costco seem to matter, as that company has experienced much lower employee turnover. It was recently pegged at 7%, compared with the 60 to 70% experienced by other retailers. Costco also has earned higher scores on the American Customer Satisfaction Index. Presumably, as long as Walmart can continue to offer the lowest prices, each company is following a compensation strategy consistent with its business goals.

Questions

1. What advantages and disadvantages do you see in Walmart's compensation strategy and in Costco's?
2. What other data would you want to have when comparing the success of these two compensation strategies?

Sources: H. Weisbaum, "There Are America's Favorite Online and Brick-and-Mortar Stores. Is Yours on the List?" *NBC News*, March 6, 2020, https://www.nbc.com; S. Nassauer, "Costco to Raise Starting Wage to $14 an Hour," *The Wall Street Journal*, January 11, 2019, https://www.wsj.com; J. Calfas, "This Company Has the Best Pay and Benefits, According to Employees," *Money*, February 27, 2018, http://time.com/money; T. Relihan, "How Costco's Obsession with Culture Drove Success," *Ideas Made to Matter*, MIT Management Sloan School, May 11, 2018, https://mitsloan.mit.edu.

Gathering Information about Market Pay

To compete for talent, organizations use **benchmarking,** a procedure in which an organization compares its own practices against those of successful competitors. In terms of compensation, benchmarking involves the use of pay surveys. These provide information about the going rates of pay at competitors in the organization's product and labor markets. An organization can conduct its own surveys, but the federal government and other organizations make a great deal of data available already. In addition, as described in "HRM Social," employers and individuals can find crowdsourced data online, some of it at no charge.

Benchmarking
A procedure in which an organization compares its own practices against those of successful competitors.

Pay surveys are available for many kinds of industries (product markets) and jobs (labor markets). The primary collector of this kind of data in the United States is the Bureau of Labor Statistics, which conducts an ongoing National Compensation Survey measuring wages, salaries, and benefits paid to the nation's employees. Employers might compare free data such as the government publishes with purchased data from professional organizations, including the Society for Human Resource Management, and consulting groups, including Aon Hewitt, Mercer, PayScale, Willis Towers Watson, and WorldatWork.[14] Consulting firms charge for the service but can tailor data to their clients' needs. Employers also should investigate what compensation surveys are available from any industry or trade groups their company belongs to. For any source, they should investigate the quality of the data, including the sample size, collection dates, and relevance to the employer's location and industry.

Human resource professionals need to determine whether to gather data focusing on particular industries or on job categories. Industry-specific data are especially relevant for jobs with skills that are specific to the type of product. For jobs with skills that can be transferred to companies in other industries, surveys of job classifications will be more relevant.

Crowdsourcing Pay Data

The idea of "crowdsourcing" information became well known with Wikipedia. Social-media tools have enabled many other ongoing group projects for gathering, editing, and sharing information. Not surprisingly, considering the importance of earning money, some crowdsourcing projects focus on gathering data about employees' pay.

Jobs websites such as Glassdoor and PayScale offer crowdsourced pay data, and Indeed includes employee-supplied salary data as one of its information sources. The primary advantages for users are easy access to the data at a low cost. Popular websites can collect a large volume of responses inexpensively and make the results available conveniently at little or no cost to the user.

Ensuring the quality of crowdsourced data is difficult, however. If the numbers come from a self-selecting group of employees, responses may reflect a subset of the population—say, employees who are relatively young, come from regions with the most access to computers, or have strong feelings about their earnings. Perhaps responses will come from employees at just one or two companies in an industry. Data users might not know how old the data are or whether data for a job title take into account other measures such as years of experience or level of competency. A well-done survey by a professional service could address these concerns.

Despite the drawbacks, the use of crowdsourced data is changing the role of pay data in the labor market. Workers are informing themselves with pay data, so they do not read job offers or evaluate their current pay in a vacuum. Furthermore, the very existence of crowdsourced data creates a climate of greater transparency. Employers need to recognize that workers, especially in younger generations, expect at least some transparency from employers. Employers not only need to inform themselves about pay levels in the labor market (including the levels job seekers are reading on crowdsourced websites), but also need to establish pay policies and be able to explain how they use the policies and data to arrive at decisions about pay. These employer communication skills also are important for addressing salary-related comments on social-media sites: if candidate or employee comments about the company include misinformation, the company may be able to post corrections and clarifications and even flag inaccurate content for review by the website.

Questions

1. Suggest one or two reasons why an employer might want to look up crowdsourced pay data.
2. Suppose a customer service supervisor contacts the HR office because he looked up pay data for that job and learned he is paid $10,000 less than the average. His own manager didn't have an answer and referred him to HR. How should HR professionals prepare for this kind of situation?

Sources: "How to Crowdsource Employee Data to Promote Salary Transparency," *Medium,* September 6, 2019, https://medium.com; Sambhav Rakyan and Jasbir Singh, "A Fresh Perspective on Crowdsourced Pay Data," Willis Towers Watson, September 15, 2017, https://www.towerswatson.com; Roy Maurer, "Looking through the Glassdoor," interview with Robert Hohman, *HR Magazine,* February 2017, pp. 24–25; John Sumser, "Differences between HR-Reported and Crowd-Sourced Compensation Data," *Salary.com,* 2017, http://www2.salary.com.

LO 12-4 Describe how employees evaluate the fairness of a pay structure.

Employee Judgments about Pay Fairness

In developing a pay structure, it is important to keep in mind employees' opinions about fairness. After all, one of the purposes of pay is to motivate employees, and they will not be motivated by pay if they think it is unfair.

Judging Fairness (Equity)

Employees evaluate their pay relative to the pay of other employees. Social scientists have studied this kind of comparison and developed *equity theory* to describe how people make judgments about fairness.[15] According to equity theory, people measure outcomes such as pay in terms of their inputs. For example, an employee might think of her pay in terms of her master's degree, her 12 years of experience, and her 60-hour workweeks. To decide whether a level of pay is equitable, the person compares her ratio of outcomes and inputs with other people's outcome/input ratios, as shown in Figure 12.3. The person might notice that an employee with less education or experience is earning more than she is (unfair) or that an employee who works 80 hours a week is earning more (fair). In general, employees compare their pay and contributions against their peers inside and outside the organization:

- *External equity* describes fairness of one's pay relative to what employees in other organizations earn for doing the same job.
- *Internal equity* describes fairness of one's pay relative to other employees in the same organization. Employees make these comparisons relative to co-workers doing the same job, as well as employees at higher and lower levels.

Employees' conclusions about equity depend on what they choose as a standard of comparison. The results can be surprising. For example, some organizations have set up two-tier wage systems as a way to cut labor costs without cutting employees' existing salaries. Typically, employers announce these programs as a way to avoid moving jobs out of the country or closing down altogether. In a two-tier wage system, existing employees continue on at their current (upper-tier) pay rate while new employees sign on for less pay (the lower tier). One might expect reaction among employees in the lower tier that the pay structure is unfair. But a study of these employees found that they were *more* satisfied than the top-tier employees.[16] The lower-tier employees were comparing their pay not with that of the upper-tier employees but with the other alternatives they saw for themselves: lower-paying jobs or unemployment.

The ways employees respond to their impressions about equity can have a great impact on the organization. Typically, if employees see their pay as equitable, their attitudes and behavior continue unchanged. If employees see themselves as receiving an advantage, they usually rethink the situation to see it as merely equitable. But if employees conclude that they are underrewarded, they are likely to make up the difference in one of three ways. They might put forth less effort (reducing their inputs), find a way to increase their outcomes (for example, stealing), or withdraw by leaving the organization or refusing to cooperate. Employees' beliefs about fairness also influence their willingness to accept transfers or promotions. For example, if a job change involves more work, employees will expect higher pay.

Equity: Pay Seems Fair

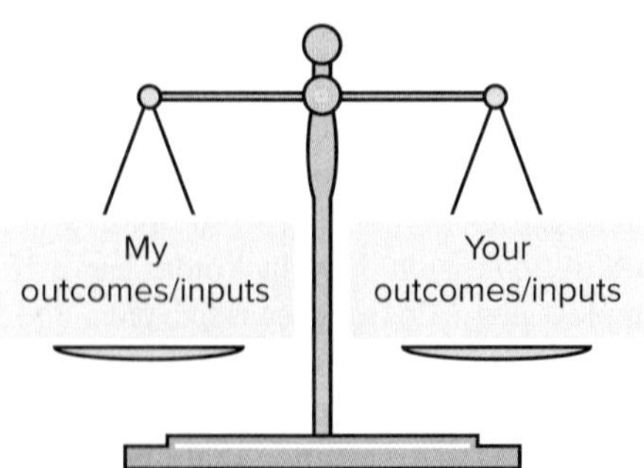

Inequity: Pay Seems Unfair

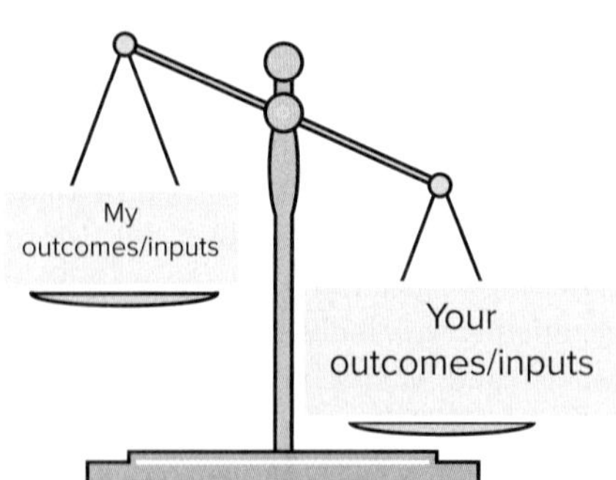

FIGURE 12.3
Opinions about Fairness: Pay Equity

Employees Doubt Their Pay Is Fair

A recent survey by PayScale asked more than 500,000 employees about their experiences, and the results painted a dim picture of their compensation-related perceptions. The survey asked about their pay and perceptions and also compared those responses with the company's data on market pay. According to the responses, only about one-fifth (19%) believe they are paid fairly. One year later, a smaller survey uncovered similar results.

This attitude, however, may be driven more by perception than by reality. Of the respondents who said they are paid less than the market rate, only 11% reported pay below the market rate in PayScale's database for that job. And job satisfaction was related more to employees' perceptions of fairness than to the level of pay they reported. Salary.com has seen a similar pattern, in which many employees incorrectly believe they are underpaid. Often, a reason is that their job titles are inflated relative to work responsibilities, so they are comparing themselves with the wrong set of employees.

Employers are not helpless in this situation. The PayScale survey further reported that only about one-fourth of employees (23%) see a transparent process for setting pay rates in their organization. This suggests that employers can increase the perception of fairness by ensuring that fair practices are in place and then communicating about pay more effectively. Employers also can address equity concerns more broadly, alongside other sources of employee satisfaction. For example, they can provide clear career paths, recognition for accomplishments, positive relationships with managers, and interesting, meaningful work.

Questions

1. Based on the evidence given, what seem to be likely reasons why most employees doubt they are paid fairly?
2. Suggest one or two ways that better communication could address the issues you identified in question 1.

Sources: PayScale, *The Great Divide: How a Lack of Trust Is Driving HR and Managers Apart,* 2018 Best Practices Report, https://www.payscale.com, accessed May 1, 2020; "Employees Are Always Looking for a New Job," *Salary.com*, https://www.salary.com, accessed May 1, 2020; Jingcong Zhao, "Why Your Employees Feel Like They Are Not Fairly Paid," February 26, 2019, https://www.payscale.com; Stephen Miller, "Pay Fairness Perception Beats Higher Pay for Improving Employee Engagement," *Society for Human Resource Management*, November 8, 2017, https://www.shrm.org.

Communicating Fairness

Equity theory tells organizations that employees care about their pay relative to what others are earning and that these feelings are based on what the employees *perceive* (what they notice and form judgments about). An organization can do much to contribute to what employees know and, as a result, what they perceive. If the organization researches salary levels and concludes that it is paying its employees generously, it should communicate this. If the employees do not know what the organization learned from its research, they may reach an entirely different conclusion about their pay. Those conclusions can reduce job satisfaction and can even spread beyond the workplace to job seekers and customers. Some evidence suggests that when customers have unfavorable impressions of CEO/employee pay ratios and pay gaps between men and women, their impressions can translate into intentions not to buy.[17] For more implications of employee perceptions, see the "HR Oops!" box.

Employers must also recognize that employees know much more about what other employers pay now than they did before the Internet became popular. In the past, when gathering wage and salary data was expensive and difficult, employers had more leeway in negotiating with individual employees. Today's employees can go to websites like Glassdoor, Indeed, and Salary.com to find hundreds of links to wage and salary data. For a fee, executive search firms such as Korn Ferry provide data. Resources like these give employees information about what other workers are earning, along with the expectation that information will be shared. This means employers will face increased pressure to clearly explain their pay policies. A recent survey found that employers are gradually sharing more information, moving from facts about a worker's own paycheck to complete openness about pay structure:[18]

- *Paycheck:* Details about the individual employee's pay.
- *Market data:* Description of the data used for decision making.
- *Pay planning:* Data about pay ranges and potential for future earnings.
- *Pay strategy:* Explanation of how pay decisions relate to the organization's objectives.
- *Open salary:* Full disclosure of the organization's pay ranges and salaries paid.

Most companies are at the "paycheck" level of disclosure for current pay. Many, however, have reached the third and fourth levels of disclosure in discussions of employees' potential to earn more.

Managers play the most significant role in communication because they interact with their employees each day. The HR department should prepare them to explain why the organization's pay structure is designed as it is and to judge whether employee concerns about the structure indicate a need for change. A common issue is whether to reclassify a job because its content has changed. If an employee takes on more responsibility, the employee will often ask the manager for help in seeking more pay for the job.

Job Structure: Relative Value of Jobs

LO 12-5 Explain how organizations design pay structures related to jobs.

Along with market forces and principles of fairness, organizations consider the relative contribution each job should make to the organization's overall performance. In general, an organization's top executives have a great impact on the organization's performance, so they tend to be paid much more than entry-level workers. Executives at the same level of the organization—for example, the vice president of marketing and the vice president of information systems—tend to be paid similar amounts. Creation of a pay structure requires that the organization develop an internal structure showing the relative contribution of its various jobs.

One typical way of doing this is with a **job evaluation,** an administrative procedure for measuring the relative worth of the organization's jobs. Usually, the organization does this by assembling and training a job evaluation committee, consisting of people familiar with the jobs to be evaluated. The committee often includes a human resource specialist and, if its budget permits, may hire an outside consultant.

Job Evaluation
An administrative procedure for measuring the relative internal worth of the organization's jobs.

To conduct a job evaluation, the committee identifies each job's *compensable factors,* meaning the characteristics of a job that the organization values and chooses to pay for. As shown in Table 12.1, an organization might value the experience and education of people performing computer-related jobs, as well as the complexity of those jobs. Other compensable factors might include working conditions and responsibility. Based on the job attributes defined by job analysis (discussed in Chapter 4), the jobs are rated for each factor. The rater assigns each factor a certain number of points, giving more points to factors when they are considered more important and when the job requires a high level of that factor. Often the number of points comes from one of the *point manuals* published by trade groups and

TABLE 12.1
Job Evaluation of Three Jobs with Three Factors

	COMPENSABLE FACTORS			
JOB TITLE	EXPERIENCE	EDUCATION	COMPLEXITY	TOTAL
Computer operator	40	30	40	110
Computer programmer	40	50	65	155
Systems analyst	65	60	85	210

management consultants. If necessary, the organization can adapt the scores in the point manual to the organization's situation or even develop its own point manual. As in the example in Table 12.1, the scores for each factor are totaled to arrive at an overall evaluation for each job.

Job evaluations provide the basis for decisions about relative internal worth. According to the sample assessments in Table 12.1, the job of systems analyst is worth almost twice as much to this organization as the job of computer operator. Therefore, the organization would be willing to pay almost twice as much for the work of a systems analyst as it would for the work of a computer operator.

The organization may limit its pay survey to jobs evaluated as *key jobs.* These are jobs that have relatively stable content and are common among many organizations, so it is possible to obtain survey data about what people earn in these jobs. Organizations can make the process of creating a pay structure more practical by defining key jobs. Research for creating the pay structure is limited to the key jobs that play a significant role in the organization. Pay for the key jobs can be based on survey data, and pay for the organization's other jobs can be based on the organization's job structure. A job with a higher evaluation score than a particular key job would receive higher pay than that key job.

Hourly Wage
Rate of pay per hour worked.

Piecework Rate
Rate of pay per unit produced.

Salary
Rate of pay per week, month, or year worked.

Pay Structure: Putting It All Together

As we described in the first section of this chapter, the pay structure reflects decisions about how much to pay (pay level) and the relative value of each job (job structure). The organization's pay structure should reflect what the organization knows about market forces, as well as its own unique goals and the relative contribution of each job to achieving the goals. By balancing this external and internal information, the organization's goal is to set levels of pay that employees will consider equitable and motivating.

Organizations typically apply the information by establishing some combination of pay rates, pay grades, and pay ranges. Within this structure, they may state the pay in terms of a rate per hour, commonly called an **hourly wage;** a rate of pay for each unit produced, known as a **piecework rate;** or a rate of pay per month or year, called a **salary.**

Popular actors, such as Dwayne Johnson, are evaluated by their impact on box office receipts and other revenues and then compensated based on these evaluations. Samir Hussein/Getty Images

Pay Rates

If the organization's main concern is to match what people are earning in comparable jobs, the organization can base pay directly on market research of as many of its key jobs as possible. To do this, the organization looks for survey data for each job title. If it finds data from more than one survey, it must weigh the results based on their quality and relevance. The final number represents what the competition pays. In light of that knowledge, the organization decides what it will pay for the job.

The next step is to determine salaries for the nonkey jobs, for which the organization has no survey data. Instead, the person developing the pay structure creates a graph like the one in Figure 12.4. The vertical axis shows a range of possible pay rates, and the horizontal axis measures the points from the job evaluation. The analyst plots points according to the job evaluation and pay rate for each key job. Finally, the analyst fits a line, called a

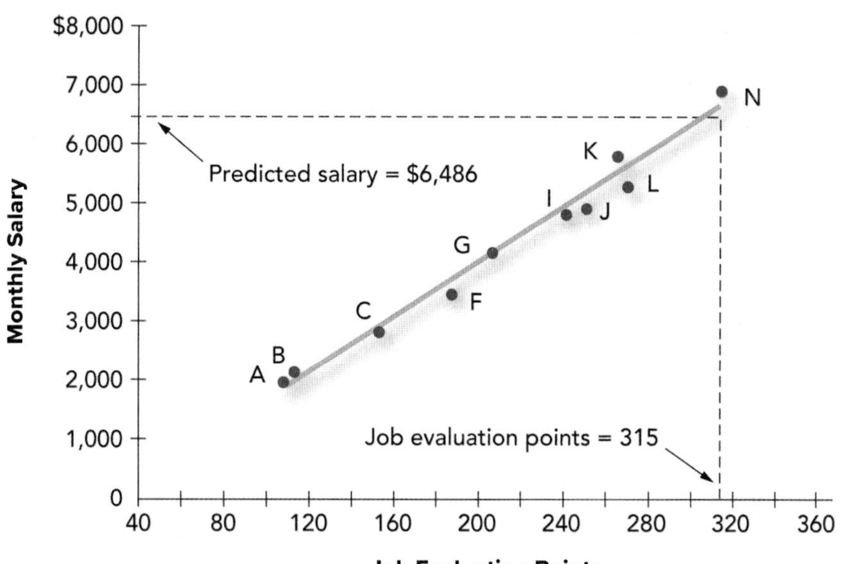

FIGURE 12.4
Pay Policy Lines

pay policy line, to the points plotted. (This can be done statistically on a computer, using a procedure called regression analysis.) Mathematically, this line shows the relationship between job evaluation and rate of pay. Thus, the line slopes upward from left to right, and if higher-level jobs are especially valuable to the organization, the line may curve upward to indicate even greater pay for high-level jobs. Using this line, the analyst can estimate the market pay level for a given job evaluation. Looking at the graph will give approximate numbers, or the regression analysis will provide an equation for calculating the rate of pay. For example, using the pay policy line in Figure 12.4, a job with 315 evaluation points would have a predicted salary of $6,486 per month.

Pay Policy Line
A graphed line showing the mathematical relationship between job evaluation points and pay rate.

The pay policy line reflects the pay structure in the market, which does not always match rates in the organization (see key job F in Figure 12.4). Survey data may show that people in certain jobs are actually earning significantly more or less than the amount shown on the pay policy line. For example, some kinds of expertise are in short supply. People with that expertise can command higher salaries because they can easily leave one employer to get higher pay somewhere else. Suppose, in contrast, that local businesses have laid off many warehouse employees. Because so many of these workers are looking for jobs, organizations may be able to pay them less than the rate that job evaluation points would suggest.

When job structure and market data conflict in these ways, organizations have to decide on a way to resolve the two. One approach is to stick to the job evaluations and pay according to the employees' worth to the organization. Organizations that do so will be paying more or less than they have to, so they will likely have more difficulty competing for customers or employees. A way to moderate this approach is to consider the importance of each position to the organization's goals.[19] If a position is critical for meeting the organization's goals, paying more than competitors pay may be worthwhile.

At the other extreme, the organization could base pay entirely on market forces. However, this approach also has some practical drawbacks. One is that employees may conclude that pay rates are unfair. Two vice presidents or two supervisors will expect to receive similar pay because their responsibilities are similar. If the differences between their pay are large, because of different market rates, the lower-paid employee will likely be dissatisfied.

Also, if the organization's development plans include rotating managers through different assignments, the managers will be reluctant to participate if managers in some departments receive lower pay. Organizations therefore must weigh all the objectives of their pay structure to arrive at suitable rates. The trend in today's increasingly competitive labor market has been a shift in favor of external market-based comparisons.[20]

Pay Grades

Pay Grades
Sets of jobs having similar worth or content, grouped together to establish rates of pay.

A large organization could have hundreds or even thousands of different jobs. Setting a pay rate for each job would be extremely complex. Therefore, many organizations group jobs into **pay grades**—sets of jobs having similar worth or content, grouped together to establish rates of pay. For example, the organization could establish five pay grades, with the same pay available to employees holding any job within the same grade.

A drawback of pay grades is that grouping jobs will result in rates of pay for individual jobs that do not precisely match the levels specified by the market and the organization's job structure. Suppose, for example, that the organization groups together its senior accountants (with a job evaluation of 255 points) and its senior systems analysts (with a job evaluation of 270 points). Surveys might show that the market rate of pay for systems analysts is higher than that for accountants. In addition, the job evaluations give more points to systems analysts. Even so, for simplicity's sake, the organization pays the same rate for the two jobs because they are in the same pay grade. The organization would have to pay more than the market requires for accountants or pay less than the market rate for systems analysts (so it would probably have difficulty recruiting and retaining them).

Pay Ranges

Pay Range
A set of possible pay rates defined by a minimum, maximum, and midpoint of pay for employees holding a particular job or a job within a particular pay grade.

Usually organizations want some flexibility in setting pay for individual jobs. They want to be able to pay the most valuable employees the highest amounts and to give rewards for performance, as described in the next chapter. Flexibility also helps the organization balance conflicting information from market surveys and job evaluations. Therefore, pay structure usually includes a **pay range** for each job or pay grade. In other words, the organization establishes a minimum, maximum, and midpoint of pay for employees holding a particular job or a job within a particular pay grade. Employees holding the same job may receive somewhat different pay, depending on where their pay falls within the range.

A typical approach is to use the market rate or the pay policy line as the midpoint of a range for the job or pay grade. The minimum and maximum values for the range may also be based on market surveys of those amounts. Pay ranges are most common for white-collar jobs and for jobs that are not covered by union contracts. Figure 12.5 shows an example of pay ranges based on the pay policy line in Figure 12.4. Notice that the jobs are grouped into five pay grades, each with its own pay range. In this example, the range is widest for employees who are at higher levels in terms of their job evaluation points. That is because the performance of these higher-level employees will likely have more effect on the organization's performance, so the organization needs more latitude to reward them. For instance, as discussed earlier, the organization may want to select a higher point in the range to attract an employee who is more critical to achieving the organization's goals.

Usually pay ranges overlap somewhat, so that the highest pay in one grade is somewhat higher than the lowest pay in the next grade. Overlapping ranges gives the organization more flexibility in transferring employees among jobs, because transfers need not always involve a change in pay. On the other hand, the less overlap, the more important it is to earn promotions in order to keep getting raises. Assuming the organization wants to motivate

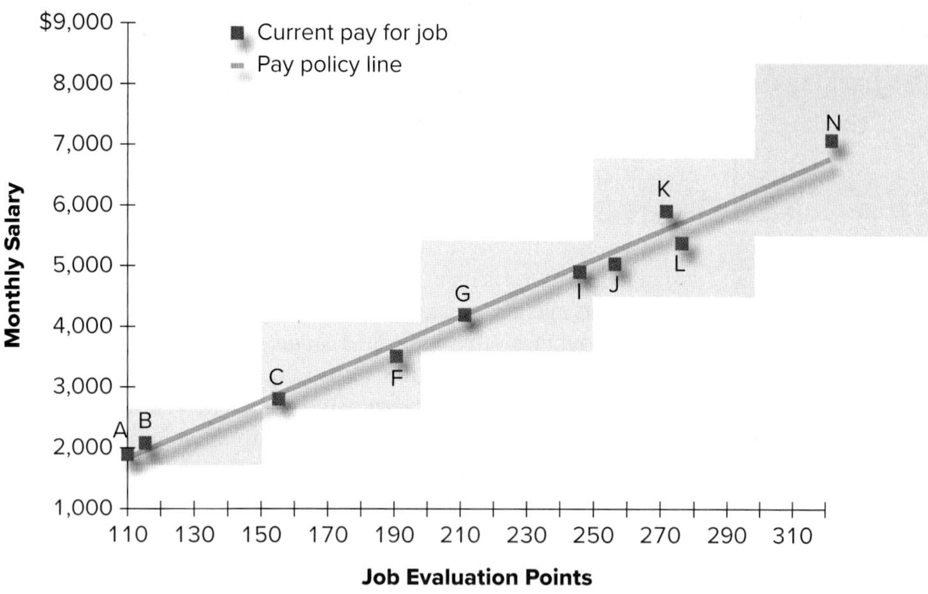

FIGURE 12.5
Sample Pay Grade Structure

employees through promotions (and assuming enough opportunities for promotion are available), the organization will want to limit the overlap from one level to the next.

Pay Differentials

In some situations organizations adjust pay to reflect differences in working conditions or labor markets. For example, an organization may pay extra to employees who work the night shift because night hours are less desirable for most workers. Similarly, organizations may pay extra to employees in locations where living expenses are higher or the competition for talent more intense. These adjustments are called **pay differentials.**

Pay Differential
Adjustment to a pay rate to reflect differences in working conditions or labor markets.

A survey of businesses in the United States found that almost three-quarters have a policy of providing pay differentials based on geographic location.[21] These differentials are intended as a way to treat employees fairly without regard to where they work. The most common approach is to move an employee higher in the pay structure to compensate for higher living costs. For instance, according to the Bureau of Labor Statistics, the average human resource manager earns $116,720 in Huntsville, Alabama, and $140,565 in the San Francisco area. One reason could be a higher cost of living in San Francisco. This pay policy can become expensive for organizations that must operate in tight labor markets or high-cost locations. Also, organizations need to handle the delicate issue of how to pay employees transferred to areas where pay rates tend to be lower.

Alternatives to Job-Based Pay

LO 12-6 Describe alternatives to job-based pay.

The traditional and most widely used approach to developing a pay structure focuses on setting pay for jobs or groups of jobs.[22] This emphasis on jobs has some limitations. The precise definition of a job's responsibilities can contribute to an attitude that some activities "are not in my job description," at the expense of flexibility, innovation, quality, and customer service. Also, the job structure's focus on higher pay for higher status can work against an effort at empowerment. Organizations may avoid change because it requires repeating the time-consuming process of creating job descriptions and related paperwork. Another change-related problem is that when the organization needs a new set of knowledge, skills,

Night hours are less desirable for most workers. Therefore, some companies pay a differential for night work to compensate them. Peter Cavanagh/Alamy Stock Photo

and abilities, the existing pay structure may be rewarding the wrong behaviors. Finally, a pay structure that rewards employees for winning promotions may discourage them from gaining valuable experience through lateral career moves.

Organizations have responded to these problems with a number of alternatives to job-based pay structures. Some organizations have found greater flexibility through **delayering,** or reducing the number of levels in the organization's job structure. By combining more assignments into a single layer, organizations give managers more flexibility in making assignments and awarding pay increases. These broader groupings often are called *broad bands.* In the 1990s, IBM changed from a pay structure with 5,000 job titles and 24 salary grades to one with 1,200 jobs and 10 bands. When IBM began using broad bands, it replaced its point-factor job evaluation system with an approach based on matching jobs to descriptions. Job descriptions are assigned to the band whose characteristics best match those in the job description. Broad bands reduce the opportunities for promoting employees, so organizations that eliminate layers in their job descriptions must find other ways to reward employees.

Delayering
Reducing the number of levels in the organization's job structure.

Another way organizations have responded to the limitations of job-based pay has been to move away from the link to jobs and toward pay structures that reward employees based on their knowledge and skills.[23] **Skill-based pay systems** are pay structures that set pay according to the employees' level of skill or knowledge and what they are capable of doing. Paying for skills makes sense at organizations where changing technology requires employees to continually widen and deepen their knowledge. For example, modern machinery often requires that operators know how to program and monitor computers to perform a variety of tasks. Skill-based pay also supports efforts to empower employees and enrich jobs because it encourages employees to add to their knowledge so they can make decisions in many areas. In this way, skill-based pay helps organizations become more flexible and innovative. More generally, skill-based pay can encourage a climate of learning and adaptability and give employees a broader view of how the organization functions. These changes should help employees use their knowledge and ideas more productively. A field study of a manufacturing plant found that changing to a skill-based pay structure led to better quality and lower labor costs.[24]

Skill-Based Pay Systems
Pay structures that set pay according to the employees' levels of skill or knowledge and what they are capable of doing.

Of course, skill-based pay has its own disadvantages.[25] It rewards employees for acquiring skills but does not provide a way to ensure that employees can use their new skills. The result may be that the organization is paying employees more for learning skills that the employer is not benefiting from. The challenge for HRM is to design work so that the work design and pay structure support each other. Also, if employees learn skills very quickly, they may reach the maximum pay level so quickly that it will become difficult to reward them appropriately. Skill-based pay does not necessarily provide an alternative to the bureaucracy and paperwork of traditional pay structures because it requires records related to skills, training, and knowledge acquired. Finally, gathering market data about skill-based pay is difficult because most wage and salary surveys are job-based.

LO 12-7 Summarize how to ensure that pay is actually in line with the pay structure.

Pay Structure and Actual Pay

Usually the human resource department is responsible for establishing the organization's pay structure. But building a structure is not the end of the organization's decisions about pay structure. The structure represents the organization's policy, but what the organization actually does may be different. As part of its management responsibility, the HR department therefore should compare actual pay to the pay structure, making sure that policies and practices match.

Pay Grade: 1
Midpoint of Range: $2,175 per month

Salaries of Employees in Pay Grade	
Employee 1	$2,306
Employee 2	$2,066
Employee 3	$2,523
Employee 4	$2,414

Compa-Ratio

$$\frac{\text{Average}}{\text{Midpoint}} = \frac{\$2{,}327.25}{\$2{,}175.00} = 1.07$$

Average Salary of Employees

$2,306 + $2,066 + $2,523 + $2,414 = $9,309

$9,309 ÷ 4 = $2,327.25

FIGURE 12.6
Finding a Compa-Ratio

A common way to do this is to measure a *compa-ratio,* the ratio of average pay to the midpoint of the pay range. Figure 12.6 shows an example. Assuming the organization has pay grades, the organization would find a compa-ratio for each pay grade: the average paid to all employees in the pay grade divided by the midpoint for the pay grade. If the average equals the midpoint, the compa-ratio is 1. More often, the compa-ratio is somewhat above 1 (meaning the average pay is above the midpoint for the pay grade) or below 1 (meaning the average pay is below the midpoint).

Assuming that the pay structure is well planned to support the organization's goals, the compa-ratios should be close to 1. A compa-ratio greater than 1 suggests that the organization is paying more than planned for human resources and may have difficulty keeping costs under control. A compa-ratio less than 1 suggests that the organization is underpaying for human resources relative to its target and may have difficulty attracting and keeping qualified employees. When compa-ratios are more or less than 1, the numbers signal a need for the HR department to work with managers to identify whether to adjust the pay structure or the organization's pay practices. The compa-ratios may indicate that the pay structure no longer reflects market rates of pay. Or maybe performance appraisals need to be more accurate, as discussed in Chapter 10.

Current Issues Involving Pay Structure

LO 12-8 Discuss issues related to paying employees serving in the military and paying executives.

An organization's policies regarding pay structure greatly influence employees' and even the general public's opinions about the organization. Issues affecting pay structure therefore can hurt or help the organization's reputation and ability to recruit, motivate, and keep employees. Recent issues related to pay structure include decisions about paying employees on active military duty and decisions about how much to pay the organization's top executives.

Pay during Military Duty

As we noted in Chapter 3, the Uniformed Services Employment and Reemployment Rights Act (USERRA) requires employers to make jobs available to their workers when they return after fulfilling military duties for up to five years. During the time these employees are performing their military service, the employer faces decisions related to paying these people. The armed services pay service members during their time of duty, but military pay often falls short of what they would earn in their civilian jobs. Some employers have chosen to support their employees by paying the difference between their military and civilian earnings for extended periods. Starbucks pays employees for the time they take off to meet service obligations for the armed forces or National Guard, up to 80 hours per year. Employees can use the benefit to cover time for traveling and for making transitions between work and military service.[26]

Policies to make up the difference between military pay and civilian pay are costly. The employer is paying employees while they are not working for the organization, and it may have to hire temporary employees as well. This challenge has posed a significant hardship on some employers since 2002, as hundreds of thousands of Reservists and National Guard members have been mobilized. Even so, as the nation copes with this challenge, hundreds of employers have decided that maintaining positive relations with employees–and the goodwill of the American public–makes the expense worthwhile.

Pay for Executives

The media have drawn public attention to the issue of executive pay. The issue attracts notice because of the very high pay that the top executives of major U.S. companies have received in recent years. For example, recent reviews of executive compensation at the largest publicly owned companies in the United States found that median compensation of chief executive offices has surpassed $17 million. However, most CEOs do not run a Fortune 500 or S&P 500 company, and broader studies have found more modest–though still high–executive pay. A study by Chief Executive Group found that CEOs at private companies received median compensation of $350,622.[27] Notice also that as shown in Figure 12.7, only a small share of the average compensation paid to CEOs is in the form of a salary. Most CEO compensation takes the form of performance-related pay, such as bonuses and stock. This variable pay, discussed in the next chapter, causes the pay of executives to vary much more widely than other employees' earnings.

Although these high amounts apply to only a small proportion of the total workforce, the issue of executive pay is relevant to pay structure in terms of equity theory. As we discussed earlier in the chapter, employees draw conclusions about the fairness of pay by making comparisons among employees' inputs and outcomes. By many comparisons, U.S. CEOs' pay is high. The Economic Policy Institute's analysis of CEO pay at the 350 largest U.S. companies found that the ratio of CEO pay relative to the average annual pay of the company's workers rose rapidly during the 1990s and currently exceeds 270-to-1. Neither that research nor *The Wall Street Journal*'s analysis of CEO pay at the top 500 companies found a relationship between the amount of pay a CEO earned and the company's performance.[28] To assess the fairness of this ratio, equity theory would consider not only the size of executive pay relative to pay for other employees but also the amount the CEOs contribute. An organization's executives potentially have a much greater effect on the organization's performance than its lowest-paid employees have. But if they do not seem to contribute 270 times more, employees will see the compensation as unfair.

FIGURE 12.7
Average CEO Pay at 300 Largest U.S. Companies

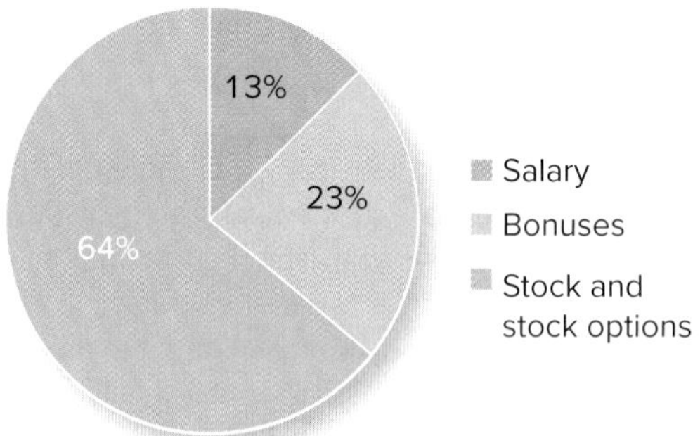

Note: Stock and stock options category includes restricted stock and performance rewards (stock and cash).

Source: David F. Larcker and Brian Tayan, *CEO Compensation: Data Spotlight*, Stanford Graduate School of Business Corporate Governance Research Initiative, https://www.gsb.stanford.edu, accessed May 1, 2020.

Top executives help to set the tone or culture of the organization, and employees at all levels are affected by behavior at the top. As a result, the equity of executive pay can affect more employees than, say, equity among warehouse workers or salesclerks. Recognizing this issue, Warren Buffett takes home a modest salary—for example, total compensation of less than $500,000 to run a company valued in the hundreds of billions of dollars. During the COVID-19 pandemic, some CEOs reduced their salaries or stopped taking them altogether. For example, Yum Brands CEO David Gibbs stopped taking a salary for most of 2020, using the money in part to pay one-time bonuses to managers of its KFC, Pizza Hut, and Taco Bell chains.[29] These executives are hardly poor, of course; most of their wealth comes from their stock holdings.

One study that investigated this issue compared the pay of rank-and-file employees and executives in various business units.[30] In business units where the difference in pay was greater, customer satisfaction was lower. The researchers speculated that employees thought pay was inequitable and adjusted their behavior to provide lower inputs by putting forth less effort to satisfy customers. To avoid this type of situation, organizations need to plan not only *how much* to pay managers and executives, but also *how* to pay them. In the next chapter, we will explore many of the options available.

THINKING ETHICALLY

WHAT CONDITIONS SHAPE PERCEPTIONS OF PAY FAIRNESS?

Especially for positions requiring a college degree, jobs in nonprofit organizations tend to pay less than jobs at for-profit companies. For example, a salary survey of California workers found HR employees at nonprofits earning an average of $10,000 less per year than their counterparts in the for-profit sector. The work may be as complex, but these organizations tend to pay less because they have difficulty allocating more funds to payroll. One reason is that decisions to support nonprofits often measure organizations' performance based on their overhead—that is, the percentage of spending that goes to salaries and other expenses to keep the organization running, relative to spending that goes to providing services. In such an analysis, spending for long-term planning or workforce development seems "wasted." Measuring performance by other measures, such as achievement of an organization's mission, is more difficult and less common.

The people who take jobs at a nonprofit generally do so because they share the organization's values and care about its mission. They may accept low pay because they want the organization to spend as much as it can to carry out its work. However, surveys show these workers have difficulty making ends meet, and consequently, many of them leave for better-paying work. Furthermore, nonprofit organizations struggle to build a diverse workforce. Workers can better afford to stay in low-paying jobs if they receive support from a higher-earning spouse or earned college degrees without borrowing—situations that are less common among people of color.

Employers might say it is fair to pay employees less than they could earn at a different kind of organization as long as the employees are satisfied. Some recent research into pay at more than 750 businesses indicates that employees do take into account their organization's situation in assessing the fairness of their pay. That study asked about job satisfaction and compensation, among other measures, and ranked companies according to the responses to each measure. Not surprisingly, at the highest-paying companies, employees were more likely than average to be satisfied with their pay. But at the lowest-paying companies, satisfaction depended on financial performance. If the companies had poor financial performance, employees were relatively satisfied; evidently, they assumed their pay was what the company could afford. If the company was doing well financially, however, employees were very dissatisfied with low pay.

Questions

1. Why do you think employees at high-performing companies were more dissatisfied with low pay? How might justice be an issue?
2. How do you evaluate the ethics of paying employees less to work for a nonprofit than a comparable employee would earn in another industry?

Sources: Jim Rendon, "Low Pay Is Driving Workers Away," *Chronicle of Philanthropy* 31, no. 11 (September 2019), pp. 8–17; Rick Wartzman and Lawrence Crosby, "The Link between Pay and Job Satisfaction Comes with a Twist," *The Wall Street Journal,* August 12, 2019, https://www.wsj.com; Michelle Cheng, "The Surprising Salary Comparisons for Jobs in the For-Profit vs. Nonprofit Sectors," *Quartz,* May 30, 2019, https://qz.com.

SUMMARY

LO 12-1 Identify the kinds of decisions involved in establishing a pay structure.

- A job structure establishes relative pay for different jobs within the organization.
- Organizations establish relative pay for different functions and different levels of responsibility for each function.
- They also must establish pay levels, or the average paid for the different jobs.
- These decisions are based on the organization's goals, market data, legal requirements, and principles of fairness.
- Together, job structure and pay level establish a pay structure policy.

LO 12-2 Summarize legal requirements for pay policies.

- To meet the standard of equal employment opportunity, employers must provide equal pay for equal work, regardless of an employee's age, race, sex, or other protected status. Differences in pay must relate to factors such as a person's qualifications or market levels of pay.
- Under the Fair Labor Standards Act (FLSA), the employer must pay at least the minimum wage established by law. Some state and local governments have established higher minimum wages.
- The FLSA also requires overtime pay—at one and a half times the employee's regular pay rate, including bonuses—for hours worked beyond 40 in each week. Managers, professionals, and outside salespersons are exempt from the overtime pay requirement.
- Employers must meet FLSA requirements concerning child labor.
- Federal contractors also must meet requirements to pay at least the prevailing wage in the area where their employees work.

LO 12-3 Discuss how economic forces influence decisions about pay.

- To remain competitive, employers must meet the demands of product and labor markets.
- Product markets seek to buy at the lowest price, so organizations must limit their costs as much as possible. In this way, product markets place an upper limit on the pay an employer can afford to offer.
- Labor markets consist of workers who want to earn as much as possible. To attract and keep workers, employers must pay at least the going rate in their labor markets.
- Organizations make decisions about whether to pay at, above, or below the pay rate set by these market forces.
- Paying above the market rate may make the organization less competitive in product markets but give it an advantage in labor markets. The organization benefits only if it can attract the best candidates and provide the systems that motivate and enable them to do their best work.
- Organizations that pay below the market rate need creative practices for recruiting and training workers so that they can find and keep enough qualified people.

LO 12-4 Describe how employees evaluate the fairness of a pay structure.

- According to equity theory, employees think of their pay relative to their inputs, such as training, experience, and effort. To decide whether their pay is equitable, they compare their outcome (pay)/input ratio with other people's outcome/input ratios.
- Employees make these comparisons with people doing the same job in other organizations and with people doing the same or different jobs in the same organization.
- If employees conclude that their outcome/input ratio is less than the comparison person's, they conclude that their pay is unfair and may engage in behaviors to create a situation they think is fair.

LO 12-5 Explain how organizations design pay structures related to jobs.

- Organizations typically begin with a job evaluation to measure the relative worth of their jobs. A job evaluation committee identifies each job's compensable factors and rates each factor.
- The committee may use a point manual to assign an appropriate number of points to each job.
- The committee can research market pay levels for key jobs and then identify appropriate rates of pay for other jobs based on their number of points relative to the key jobs. The organization can do this with a pay policy line, which plots a salary for each job.
- The organization can combine jobs into several groups, called pay grades.
- For each pay grade or job, the organization typically establishes a pay range, using the market rate or pay policy line as the midpoint.
- Differences in working conditions or labor markets sometimes call for the use of pay differentials to adjust pay levels.

LO 12-6 Describe alternatives to job-based pay.

- To obtain more flexibility, organizations may use delayering. They reduce the levels in the organization's job structure, creating broad bands of jobs with a pay range for each.

- Organizations may use skill-based pay. They reward employees according to their knowledge and skills by establishing skill-based pay systems. These are structures that set pay according to the employees' level of knowledge and capabilities.
- Skill-based pay encourages employees to be more flexible and adapt to changing technology. However, if the organization does not also provide systems in which employees can apply new skills, it may be paying them for skills they do not actually use.

LO 12-7 Summarize how to ensure that pay is actually in line with the pay structure.

- The human resource department should routinely compare actual pay with the pay structure to see that policies and practices match.
- A common way to do this is to measure a compa-ratio for each job or pay grade. The compa-ratio is the ratio of average pay to the midpoint of the pay range.
- Assuming the pay structure supports the organization's goals, the compa-ratios should be close to 1.
- When compa-ratios are more or less than 1, the HR department should work with managers to identify whether to adjust the pay structure or the organization's pay practices.

LO 12-8 Discuss issues related to paying employees serving in the military and paying executives.

- The Uniformed Services Employment and Reemployment Rights Act requires employers to make jobs available to any of their employees who leave to fulfill military duties for up to five years.
- While these employees are performing their military service, many are earning far less. To demonstrate their commitment to these employees and to earn the public's goodwill, many companies pay the difference between their military and civilian earnings, even though this policy is costly.
- Executive pay has drawn public scrutiny because top executive pay is much higher than average workers' pay.
- The great difference is an issue in terms of equity theory. Chief executive officers have an extremely large impact on the organization's performance, but critics complain that when performance falters, executive pay does not decline as fast as the organization's profits or stock price.
- Top executives help set the organization's tone or culture, and employees at all levels are affected by the behavior of the people at the top. Therefore, employees' opinions about the equity of executive pay can have a large effect on the organization's performance.

KEY TERMS

job structure, 371
pay level, 372
pay structure, 372
minimum wage, 374
Fair Labor Standards Act (FLSA), 374
exempt employees, 376
nonexempt employees, 376
benchmarking, 381
job evaluation, 385
hourly wage, 386
piecework rate, 386
salary, 386
pay policy line, 387
pay grades, 388
pay range, 388
pay differential, 389
delayering, 390
skill-based pay systems, 390

REVIEW AND DISCUSSION QUESTIONS

1. In setting up a pay structure, what legal requirements must an organization meet? Which of these do you think would be most challenging for a small start-up business? Why? *(LO 12-1)*
2. In gathering data for its pay policies, what product markets would a city's hospital want to use as a basis for comparison? What labor markets would be relevant? How might the labor markets for surgeons be different from the labor markets for nursing aides? *(LO 12-1)*
3. Why might an organization choose to pay employees more than the market rate? Why might it choose to pay less? What are the consequences of paying more or less than the market rate? *(LO 12-3)*
4. Suppose you work in the HR department of a manufacturing company that is planning to enrich jobs by having production workers work in teams and rotate through various jobs. The pay structure will have to be adjusted to fit this new work design. How would you

expect the employees to evaluate the fairness of their pay in their redesigned jobs? In terms of equity theory, what comparisons would they be likely to make? *(LO 12-4)*
5. Summarize the way organizations use information about jobs as a basis for a pay structure. *(LO 12-5)*
6. Imagine that you manage human resources for a small business. You have recently prepared a report on the market rate of pay for salespeople, and the company's owner says the market rate is too high. The company cannot afford this level of pay, and furthermore, paying that much would cause salespeople to earn more than most of the company's managers. Suggest three possible measures the company might take to help resolve this conflict. *(LO 12-5)*
7. What are the advantages of establishing pay ranges, rather than specific pay levels, for each job? What are the drawbacks of this approach? (LO 12-5)
8. Suppose the company in Question 1 wants to establish a skills-based pay structure. What would be some advantages of this approach? List the issues the company should be prepared to address in setting up this system. *Consider the kinds of information you will need and the ways employees may react to the new pay structure. (LO 12-6)*
9. Why do some employers subsidize the pay of military reserve members called up to active duty? If the military instead paid these people the wage they command in the civilian market (that is, the salary they earn at their regular jobs), who would bear the cost? When neither the reserve members' employers nor the military pays reserve members their civilian wage, reserve members and their families bear the cost. In your opinion, who *should* bear this cost—employers, taxpayers, or service members (or someone else)? *(LO 12-8)*
10. Do you think U.S. companies pay their chief executives too much? Why or why not? *(LO 12-8)*

SELF-ASSESSMENT EXERCISE

How Do You Rank on the Four Dimensions of Pay Satisfaction?

Consider your current job or a job you had in the past. For each of the following pay characteristics, indicate your level of satisfaction by using the following scale: 1 = very dissatisfied; 2 = somewhat dissatisfied: 3 = neither satisfied nor dissatisfied; 4 = somewhat satisfied; 5 = very satisfied.

_____ 1. My take-home pay
_____ 2. My current pay
_____ 3. My overall level of pay
_____ 4. Size of my current salary
_____ 5, My benefits package
_____ 6. Amount the company pays toward my benefits
_____ 7. The value of my benefits
_____ 8. The number of benefits I receive
_____ 9. My most recent raise
_____ 10. Influence my manager has over my pay
_____ 11. The raises I have typically received in the past
_____ 12. The company's pay structure
_____ 13. Information the company gives about pay issues of concern to me
_____ 14. Pay of other jobs in the company
_____ 15. Consistency of the company's pay policies
_____ 16. How my raises are determined
_____ 17. Differences in pay among jobs in the company
_____ 18. The way the company administers pay

These 18 items measure four dimensions of pay satisfaction. Find your total score for each set of item numbers to measure your satisfaction with each dimension.

Pay Level
Total of items 1, 2, 3, 4, 9: _____
Benefits
Total of items 5, 6, 7, 8: _____
Pay Structure and Administration
Total of items 12, 13, 14, 15, 17, 18: _____
Pay Raises
Total of items 10, 11, 16: _____

Considering the principles discussed in this chapter, how could your company improve (or how could it have improved) your satisfaction on each dimension?

Source: Based on H. G. Heneman III and D. P. Schwab, "Pay Satisfaction: Its Multidimensional Nature and Measurement," *International Journal of Psychology* 20 (1985), pp. 129–41.

TAKING RESPONSIBILITY

IKEA Tries to Provide a Living Wage for Workers

Along with a legal requirement to pay at least the minimum wage, some employers also see a social responsibility requirement to pay workers at least a living wage—that is, enough to provide themselves and their families with the basics of daily life. Paying a living wage is one way to treat employees with dignity.

Sweden-based furniture and home furnishings retailer IKEA is among the companies that have committed to paying a living wage. IKEA in 2014 announced that in the United States it would raise the lowest hourly wage it pays, going from $9.17 per hour to a nationwide average of $10.76. The change affects about half of the employees in its 38 existing stores and will apply to those hired at new locations.

The $10.76 figure was not a set amount that would apply nationwide, but an average across facilities. IKEA calculates a minimum for each store based on the local cost of living. It uses the MIT Living Wage Calculator, which factors in the costs of food, housing, taxes, and transportation. IKEA's wages are based on the amounts calculated for a single person without children. In Pittsburgh and West Chester, Ohio, the minimum was set at $8.69; at the other extreme, workers in Woodbridge, Virginia, received wages starting at $13.22 per hour. Thus, wages are influenced by employee needs, not solely based on market rates. IKEA also said it would review wages every year. Although the company did not commit to raising rates every time the calculator shows a higher cost of living, it did raise wages again in 2016, setting the new minimum at $11.87 per hour.

Before the wage increase, IKEA already exceeded the federal minimum wage of $7.25. IKEA also is generous relative to competitors. In the same year IKEA announced its first increase, Gap, whose stores include Old Navy and Banana Republic, announced it would phase in an increase to $9 in 2014 and then to $10 in 2015. Following IKEA's announcement of the $10.76 minimum wage, Walmart's Twitter account sent a tweet saying its "average hourly wage for full and part time associates is $11.81." However, Walmart did not draw a comparison with its hourly minimum.

IKEA sees the establishment of a living wage as supporting its mission of creating a better everyday life for people—in this case, its employees. Rob Olson, IKEA's chief financial officer, indicated that the company did not intend to raise prices to make up for the added expense of higher wages. Rather, management hoped that because the company "invests in" its employees, they in turn will invest more of themselves in the stores and their customers.

Questions

1. What are some risks and challenges that IKEA is likely to face as a result of basing its minimum pay on the living-wage formula, rather than just legal requirements and the market rate?
2. Given that IKEA's management considers the living wage to be consistent with the company's mission, what advice would you give the company for implementing it successfully?

Sources: IKEA, "Working Here," https://seeacareerwithus.com, accessed May 1, 2020; PayScale, "Average Hourly Rate for IKEA Employees," https://www.payscale.com, accessed May 1, 2020; Beth Kowitt, "At IKEA: No Ranks, No Rancor," *Fortune,* March 15, 2016, https://fortune.com; Anna Prior, "IKEA to Raise Minimum Wage at U.S. Stores," *The Wall Street Journal,* June 26, 2014, https://www.wsj.com; Steven Greenhouse, "Ikea to Increase Minimum Hourly Pay," *The New York Times,* June 26, 2014, https://www.nytimes.com; Jena McGregor, "Ikea to Raise Workers' Pay to a 'Living Wage,'" *The Washington Post,* June 26, 2014, https://www.washingtonpost.com; Mark Lennihan, "IKEA Gets Flexible with Minimum Worker Pay," *Christian Science Monitor,* June 26, 2014, https://www.csmonitor.com.

MANAGING TALENT

TSA Tries to Improve Its Pay Structure

As a U.S. government agency, the Transportation Security Administration (TSA) has a pay structure set within limits imposed by Congress and administered by the executive branch. So far, that structure has been less than ideal. TSA security officers are paid under an agency-specific structure, which includes eight pay levels. The bottom level sets starting pay in a range of about $28,000 to $41,000, from which they move up to a higher band of $33,000 to $47,000. Within each band, agents are paid more or less based on pay rates in the regions where they work. Part-time employees, who account for a majority of the workforce, are paid less. In some locations, TSA officers earn 30% less than the average income per person and less than they could be earning as security officers working for private companies.

The pay structure has contributed to making the TSA one of the least satisfied departments of the federal government. Employee turnover has been about 17% overall and 27% among part-time agents. Turnover is especially high at airports where private security firms offer higher pay. In two recent years, the TSA hired more than 19,300 agents while losing 15,500 even as air travel was increasing. An investigation sponsored by the agency found that pay was the main reason agents quit. In the Best Places to Work survey, the TSA ranks 315 out of 415 federal agencies participating. Along with limited opportunities for career advancement, low pay is one of the top reasons employees give for expressing dissatisfaction.

Some employees and union officials favor taking the pay decisions out of TSA's hands by moving employees on to the General Schedule pay structure that covers three-quarters of federal employees. The GS structure would set agents' pay at amounts between $990 and $9,700 more per year, and it would build in periodic salary increases. In the spring of 2020, the U.S. House of Representatives passed a bill that would put TSA employees on the GS system; however, the bill was not expected to pass the Senate or be signed by the president that year.

Meanwhile, the TSA's leadership has been investigating ways to improve the pay structure more strategically. Switching to the GS pay structure would narrow the pay increases available in the higher-pay regions, and it would limit opportunities to reward high performance. The TSA's approach would be to target raises where turnover has been the greatest problem, under the expectation that reducing the cost to replace lost workers would free up funds to pay additional raises. The agency's leaders also intend to create clearer performance standards, and these could be used to identify "model officers" who could receive larger raises.

Questions

1. Describe the economic forces affecting pay at the Transportation Security Administration.
2. Suppose you are advising the TSA as it plans to improve the pay structure as described in the last paragraph. Offer some advice to the agency on how to communicate these changes.

Sources: "House Passes Bill to Move TSA under the GS System; Would Mean Big Raise for Some," *Fedweek,* March 10, 2020, https://www.fedweek.com; David Thornton, "TSA Examining Pay, Retention Options as Part of Workforce Reforms," Federal News Network, August 7, 2019, https://federalnewsnetwork.com; Joe Davidson, "TSA Staffing and Morale Both Suffering from Agency's Persistently Low Salaries," *The Washington Post,* June 13, 2019, https://www.washingtonpost.com; Nicole Ogrysko, "Low Pay Biggest Driver of Turnover among TSA Frontline Workers, Panel Finds," *Federal News Network,* May 22, 2019, https://federalnewsnetwork.com.

HR IN SMALL BUSINESS

The Riveter Builds Empowering Pay Practices

Amy Nelson began to think about salary structure in a new way after an employee of her start-up, The Riveter, asked for a raise. The employee had been on the job for just a few months, which suggested the employee was reconsidering whether the pay The Riveter had offered was adequate. The manager who brought the request to Nelson said this employee had discussed salary with a co-worker and learned that the co-worker was being paid more for a similar position.

Until then, Nelson had not thought about paying her roughly 100 employees in a methodical way. Her own background was as a corporate lawyer in a professional firm where the culture assumed that everyone qualified to work there would be skilled at negotiation. In that environment, it felt rude to ask others about their pay. Now Nelson was running her own company, which offers co-working space, targeting female remote and independent workers. She had left her career in the law because she had experienced being denied opportunities when she became a mother. Unlike other companies offering space to workers, The Riveter also includes services to build a support network for members, with the intention they will help one another gain opportunities to succeed. Nelson realized she didn't have to fall back on her previous experience of another company's values and practices.

Nelson considered that her mission was to empower the women who use her workspaces, as well as the fact that her mostly young staff had grown up in an era of information sharing. She concluded that her organization's culture would require more openness, and this in turn required some structure that could be communicated to the employees. So under Nelson's leadership, The Riveter established pay bands for each position in the organization, and it made these public. Although Nelson recognized that individual employees might not be pleased with how they were paid relative to the others, she was determined to stick to the idea of empowering her employees by giving them access to information.

Questions

1. Besides the considerations described here, what are several other issues The Riveter should consider in developing its pay structure?
2. How should Amy Nelson expect her employees to judge the equity of their pay?

Sources: "Amy Nelson, The Riveter," My Founder Story, https://www.myfounderstory.com, accessed May 1, 2020; Susan Dominus, "Breaking the Salary Sharing Taboo," *The New York Times,* February 19, 2020, https://www.nytimes.com; Taylor Soper, "Women-Focused Co-working Startup The Riveter Cuts Five Positions as It Aims to Grow Digital Arm," *GeekWire,* January 17, 2020, https://www.geekwire.com; Anna Hecht, "Why This Former Lawyer Wants to Transform Workplaces 'Built by and for Men,'" *CNBC,* September 3, 2019, https://www.cnbc.com.

NOTES

1. A. Harris, "Ahead of the Pack," *Fast Company,* May/June 2020, pp. 64–88; H. J. Cordes, "PayPal Wants 'Passionate Employees': So the Company Boosted Pay, Slashed Health Insurance Costs," *Omaha World-Herald,* December 14, 2019, https://www.omaha.com.
2. Bureau of National Affairs, "Survey Finds Emphasis on Comp Cost Containment," *Report on Salary Surveys,* February 2016, pp. 14–15; Bureau of National Affairs, "Studies Examine Wage Growth in 2016," *Report on Salary Surveys,* October 2015, pp. 6–7, 10.

3. Bureau of Labor Statistics, "Usual Weekly Earnings of Wage and Salary Workers, First Quarter 2020," news release, April 15, 2020, https://www.bls.gov.
4. B. Gerhart, "Gender Differences in Current and Starting Salaries: The Role of Performance, College Major, and Job Title," *Industrial and Labor Relations Review* 43 (1990), pp. 418–433; G. G. Cain, "The Economic Analysis of Labor Market Discrimination: A Survey," in *Handbook of Labor Economics,* eds. O. Ashenfelter and R. Layard (New York: North-Holland, 1986), pp. 694–785; F. D. Blau and L. M. Kahn, "The Gender Pay Gap: Have Women Gone as Far as They Can?" *Academy of Management Perspectives,* February 2007, pp. 7–23.
5. C. Kulich, G. Trojanowski, M. K. Ryan, S. A. Haslam, and L. R. R. Renneboog, "Who Gets the Carrot and Who Gets the Stick? Evidence of Gender Disparities in Executive Remuneration," *Strategic Management Journal* 32 (2011), pp. 301–321; F. Muñoz-Bullón, "Gender-Level Differences among High-Level Executives," *Industrial Relations* 49 (2010), pp. 346–370.
6. B. Gerhart and J. Newman, *Compensation,* 13th ed. (New York: McGraw-Hill, 2020); S. L. Rynes and G. T. Milkovich, "Wage Surveys: Dispelling Some Myths about the 'Market Wage,'" *Personnel Psychology* 39 (1986), pp. 71–90.
7. Department of Labor, "Final Rule: Overtime Update," https://www.dol.gov, accessed May 1, 2020; M. Kappel, "Giddy-Up, Employers! The New Overtime Rule Is Comin' in 2020," *Forbes,* December 26, 2019, https://www.forbes.com.
8. E. Wolff-Mann, "The 19 Companies with CEOs Paid over 1,000x More Than the Median Employee," *Yahoo Finance,* February 12, 2020; S. Miller, "New Guidance Eases–But Won't Delay–CEO Pay Ratio Reporting," *Society for Human Resource Management,* September 28, 2017, https://www.shrm.org.
9. ZipRecruiter, "Amazon Warehouse Salary," https://www.ziprecruiter.com, accessed May 1, 2020.
10. Reuters, "US Productivity Rebounds in Fourth Quarter as Labor Costs Growth Slows," *CNBC,* February 6, 2020, https://www.cnbc.com; S. Yan, "'Made in China' Labor Is Not Actually That Cheap," *CNN Money,* March 17, 2016, http://money.cnn.com.
11. B. Gerhart and G. T. Milkovich, "Organizational Differences in Managerial Compensation and Financial Performance," *Academy of Management Journal* 33 (1990), pp. 663–691; E. L. Groshen, "Why Do Wages Vary among Employers?" *Economic Review* 24 (1988), pp. 19–38.
12. *The Great Divide: How a Lack of Trust Is Driving HR and Managers Apart,* 2018 Compensation Best Practices Report, *PayScale,* https://www.payscale.com.
13. G. A. Akerlof, "Gift Exchange and Efficiency-Wage Theory: Four Views," *American Economic Review* 74 (1984), pp. 79–83; J. L. Yellen, "Efficiency Wage Models of Unemployment," *American Economic Review* 74 (1984), pp. 200–205; B. Klaas and J. A. McClendon, "To Lead, Lag, or Match: Estimating the Financial Impact of Pay Level Policies," *Personnel Psychology* 49 (1996), pp. 121–141; S. C. Currall, A. J. Towler, T. A. Judge, and L. Kohn, "Pay Satisfaction and Organizational Outcomes," *Personnel Psychology* 58 (2005), pp. 613–640; A. L. Heavey, J. A. Holwerda, and J. P. Hausknecht, "Causes and Consequences of Collective Turnover: A Meta-analytic Review," *Journal of Applied Psychology* 98 (2013), pp. 412–453.
14. PayScale, *The Great Divide; The Business Imperative to Modernize Compensation,* "Three Ways to Modernize Your Compensation Strategy," *Compensation Today* (PayScale), February 5, 2018, https://www.payscale.com.
15. J. D. Shaw, "Pay Levels and Pay Changes," in *Handbook of Industrial, Work and Organizational Psychology,* eds. N. Anderson, D. S. Ones, H. K. Sinangil, and C. Viswesvaran (Thousand Oaks, CA: Sage, 2015), pp. 169–195; E. Della Torre, M. Pelagatti, and L. Solari, "Internal and External Equity in Compensation Systems, Organizational Absenteeism, and the Role of the Explained Inequalities," *Human Relations* 68 (2015), pp. 409–440; D. Card, M. Alexandre, E. Moretti, and E. Saez, "Inequality at Work: The Effect of Peer Salaries on Job Satisfaction," *American Economic Review* 102 (2012), pp. 2981–3003; J. S. Adams, "Inequity in Social Exchange," in *Advances in Experimental Social Psychology,* ed. L. Berkowitz (New York: Academic Press, 1965); P. S. Goodman, "An Examination of Referents Used in the Evaluation of Pay," *Organizational Behavior and Human Performance* 12 (1974), pp. 170–195; C. O. Trevor and D. L. Wazeter, "A Contingent View of Reactions to Objective Pay Conditions: Interdependence among Pay Structure Characteristics and Pay Relative to Internal and External Referents," *Journal of Applied Psychology* 91 (2006), pp. 1260–1275; M. M. Harris, F. Anseel, and F. Lievens, "Keeping Up with the Joneses: A Field Study of the Relationships among Upward, Lateral, and Downward Comparisons and Pay Level Satisfaction," *Journal of Applied Psychology* 93, no. 3 (May 2008), pp. 665–673; Gordon D. A. Brown, Jonathan Gardner, Andrew J. Oswald, and Jing Qian, "Does Wage Rank Affect Employees' Well-Being?" *Industrial Relations* 47, no. 3 (July 2008), p. 355.
16. P. Capelli and P. D. Sherer, "Assessing Worker Attitudes under a Two-Tier Wage Plan," *Industrial and Labor Relations Review* 43 (1990), pp. 225–244.
17. B. Mohan and M. I. Norton, "Consumers Care about CEO-Employees Pay Ratios," *The Wall Street Journal,* May 20, 2018, https://www.wsj.com.
18. PayScale, *The Great Divide,* pp. 25–26.
19. J. P. Pfeffer and A. Davis-Blake, "Understanding Organizational Wage Structures: A Resource Dependence Approach," *Academy of Management Journal* 30 (1987), pp. 437–455.
20. Gerhart and Newman, *Compensation;* M. Bidwell, F. Briscoe, I. Fernandez-Mateo, and A. Sterling, "The Employment Relationship and Inequality: How and Why Changes in Employment Practices Are Reshaping Rewards in Organizations," *Academy of Management Annals* 7, no. 1 (2013), pp. 61–121; G. E. Ledford, "The Changing Landscape of Employee Rewards: Observations and Prescriptions," *Organizational Dynamics* 43, no. 3 (2014), pp. 168–79.
21. Mercer, "US Geographic Salary Differential Tool," https://www.imercer.com, accessed May 1, 2020; L. Higgins, "Different Locations, Different Pay: Getting Pay Differentials Right," *HR Daily Advisor,* March 14, 2017, https://hrdailyadvisor.blr.com.
22. This section draws freely on B. Gerhart and R. D. Bretz, "Employee Compensation," in *Organization and Management of Advanced Manufacturing,* ed. W. Karwowski and G. Salvendy (New York: Wiley, 1994), pp. 81–101.
23. E. E. Lawler III, *Strategic Pay* (San Francisco: Jossey-Bass, 1990); G. E. Ledford, "Paying for the Skills, Knowledge, Competencies of Knowledge Workers," *Compensation and Benefits Review,* July–August 1995, p. 55; G. Ledford, "Factors Affecting the Long-Term Success of Skill-Based Pay," *WorldatWork Journal,* First Quarter 2008, pp. 6–18; E. C. Dierdorff and E. A. Surface, "If You Pay for Skills, Will They Learn? Skill Change

and Maintenance under a Skill-Based Pay System," *Journal of Management* 34 (2008), pp. 721–743.

24. B. C. Murray and B. Gerhart, "An Empirical Analysis of a Skill-Based Pay Program and Plant Performance Outcomes," *Academy of Management Journal* 41, no. 1 (1998), pp. 68–78.
25. Ibid.; N. Gupta, D. Jenkins, and W. Curington, "Paying for Knowledge: Myths and Realities," *National Productivity Review*, Spring 1986, pp. 107–123; J. D. Shaw, N. Gupta, A. Mitra, and G. E. Ledford, "Success and Survival of Skill-Based Pay Plans," *Journal of Management* 31 (2005), pp. 28–49.
26. "Starbucks Military Commitment," https://www.starbucks.com, accessed May 1, 2020.
27. W. Cooper, "CEO and Senior Executive Compensation in Private Companies 2018–19," *Chief Executive*, April 24, 2019, https://chiefexecutive.net.
28. L. Mishel and J. Wolfe, "CEO Compensation Has Grown 940% Since 1978," *Economic Policy Institute*, August 14, 2019, https://www.epi.org; V. Furhmans, "CEO Pay and Performance Often Don't March Up," *The Wall Street Journal*, May 14, 2018, https://www.wsj.com.
29. J. Eaglesham and I. Pacheco, "Coronavirus Crimps Some CEO Salaries But Not All," *The Wall Street Journal*, April 24, 2020, https://www.wsj.com; T. Francis and J. Zhang, "How Much DO CEOs Make?" *The Wall Street Journal*, May 9, 2018, https://www.wsj.com.
30. D. M. Cowherd and D. I. Levine, "Product Quality and Pay Equity between Lower-Level Employees and Top Management: An Investigation of Distributive Justice Theory," *Administrative Science Quarterly* 37 (1992), pp. 302–320.

Recognizing Employee Contributions with Pay

13

To promote retention, Waste Pro pays employees an annual bonus based on years of service as well as bonuses tied to exceptional performance.

JOE BURBANK/KRT/Newscom

What Do I Need to Know?

After reading this chapter, you should be able to:

LO 13-1 Discuss the connection between incentive pay and employee performance.

LO 13-2 Describe how organizations recognize individual performance.

LO 13-3 Identify ways to recognize group performance.

LO 13-4 Explain how organizations link pay to their overall performance.

LO 13-5 Describe how organizations combine incentive plans in a "balanced scorecard."

LO 13-6 Summarize processes that can contribute to the success of incentive programs.

LO 13-7 Discuss issues related to performance-based pay for executives.

Introduction

Waste Pro, a waste collection service with 75 locations in nine states in the southeastern United States, was founded with the strategy of competing on excellent service, not just low prices. But collecting garbage is hard work with relatively low pay, and the company needed a way to retain and motivate its workforce. It seized on the idea of paying bonuses in addition to hourly or daily wages. To promote retention, workers get an annual bonus of $250 for each year of service.

Waste Pro also pays bonuses tied to exceptional performance. Drivers can earn a $10,000 Safety Award, and helpers (the employees who toss waste into the back of a truck) recently became eligible to earn a $5,000 Helper Safety Performance Bonus. Employees know in advance what the conditions are for earning these bonuses. To earn a Safety Award, a driver must have a three-year record of no accidents, injuries, or property damage; a positive attitude and attendance record; excellent customer service; and a well-kept truck. To earn the award for helpers, an employee must be a full-time employee who over three years has had no unscheduled absences, customer complaints, property or vehicle damage, or rule violations. Helpers also must keep trucks clean to be eligible.

In the first 15 years of this program, Waste Pro has paid Safety Award bonuses to more than 300 drivers. In 2019, it announced the first two recipients of its Helper Safety Performance Bonus. The pay is granted along with public acknowledgment of the workers' contributions.[1]

Waste Pro became, according to its website, the only privately held U.S. company to pay drivers a $10,000 safety bonus in order to stand out as an excellent employer and service provider. Its bonuses reward employees for staying with the company and behaving in ways that support the company's goals. In this chapter we focus on using pay to recognize and reward employees' contributions to the organization's success. Employees' pay does not depend solely on the jobs they hold. Instead, organizations vary the amount paid according to differences in performance of the individual, group, or whole organization, as well as differences in employee qualities such as seniority and skills.[2]

Incentive Pay
Forms of pay linked to an employee's performance as an individual, group member, or organization member.

In contrast to decisions about pay structure, organizations have wide discretion in setting performance-related pay, called **incentive pay.** Organizations can tie incentive pay to individual performance, profits, or many other measures of success. They select incentives based on their costs, expected influence on performance, and fit with the organization's broader HR and company policies and goals. These decisions are significant. A study of 150 organizations found that the way organizations paid employees was strongly associated with their level of profitability.[3]

This chapter explores the choices available to organizations with regard to incentive pay. First the chapter describes the link between pay and employee performance. Next we discuss ways organizations provide a variety of pay incentives to individuals. The next two sections describe pay related to group and organizational performance. We then explore the organization's processes that can support the use of incentive pay. Finally, we discuss incentive pay for the organization's executives.

LO 13-1 Discuss the connection between incentive pay and employee performance.

Incentive Pay

Along with wages and salaries, many organizations offer *incentive pay*—that is, pay specifically designed to energize, direct, or maintain employees' behavior. Incentive pay is influential because the amount paid is linked to certain predefined behaviors or outcomes. For example, as we will see in this chapter, an organization can pay a salesperson a *commission* for closing a sale, or the members of a production department can earn a *bonus* for meeting a monthly production goal. Usually these payments are in addition to wages and salaries. Knowing they can earn extra money for closing sales or meeting departmental goals, the employees often try harder or get more creative than they might without the incentive pay. In addition, the policy of offering higher pay for higher performance can make an organization attractive to high performers when it is trying to recruit and retain these valuable employees.[4] For reasons such as these, companies are devoting a growing share of payroll budgets to incentive pay. A recent survey found that more than 75% of companies use variable pay as part of their total compensation to employees, as annual merit raises have remained flat over the past few years.[5] The variable pay rates are even higher in certain industries, including finance, insurance, and retailing.

Visit your instructor's Connect® course and access your eBook to view this video.

"People want to know that their hard work and their results are going to be rewarded appropriately, and that ultimately we don't want to pay our lower performers the same as we pay our higher performers."
—Timothy J. Richmond, Senior Vice President, Human Resources, AbbVie

Video produced for the Center for Executive Succession in the Darla Moore School of Business at the University of South Carolina by Coal Powered Filmworks.

For incentive pay to motivate employees to contribute to the organization's success, the pay plans must be well designed. In particular, effective plans meet the following requirements:

- Performance measures are linked to the organization's goals.
- Employees believe they can meet performance standards.
- The organization gives employees the resources they need to meet their goals.
- Employees value the rewards given.
- Employees believe the reward system is fair.
- The pay plan takes it into account that employees might ignore any goals that are not rewarded.

Because incentive pay is linked to particular outcomes or behaviors, the organization is encouraging employees to demonstrate those chosen outcomes and behaviors. As obvious as that may sound, the implications are more complicated. If incentive pay is extremely rewarding, employees might focus only on the performance measures rewarded under the plan and ignore measures that are not rewarded. Suppose an organization pays managers a bonus when employees are satisfied; this policy might interfere with other management goals. A manager who doesn't quite know how to inspire employees to do their best might be tempted to fall back on overly positive performance appraisals, letting work slide to keep everyone happy. Similarly, many call centers pay employees based on how many calls they handle, as an incentive to work quickly and efficiently. However, speedy call handling does not necessarily foster good customer relationships. As we will see in this chapter, organizations may combine a number of incentives so employees do not focus on one measure to the exclusion of others.

Although many call centers pay employees based on how many calls they handle, this incentive doesn't necessarily foster good customer relationships. leaf/123RF

Attitudes that influence the success of incentive pay include whether employees value the rewards and think the pay plan is fair. The stronger the intensity of the incentive, the stronger the motivation, even if the motivation is not the one the organization intended.[6] For example, if teachers earn a bonus if their students perform well on standardized tests, they will likely try harder to prepare students for testing. But if the bonus is very large, some teachers might be so eager for the high test scores that they consider unethical ways to improve the test results. Similarly, if a bank pays loan officers an incentive related to the number of mortgage loans they issue, a large incentive might motivate some loan officers to grant loans that are too risky, thereby earning the rewards but possibly placing the bank at risk.

Although most, if not all, employees value pay, it is important to remember that earning money is not the only reason people try to do a good job. The "HR Oops!" feature describes some pitfalls of focusing purely on money as a motivator. As we discuss in other chapters (see Chapters 4, 10, and 14), people also want interesting work, appreciation for their efforts, flexibility, and a sense of belonging to the work group–not to mention the inner satisfaction of work well done. Therefore, a complete plan for motivating and compensating employees has many components, from pay to work design to developing managers so they can exercise positive leadership.

With regard to the fairness of incentive pay, the preceding chapter described equity theory, which explains how employees form judgments about the fairness of a pay structure. The same process applies to judgments about incentive pay. In general, employees compare their efforts and rewards with those of other employees, considering a plan to be fair when the rewards are distributed according to what the employees contribute.

The remainder of this chapter identifies elements of incentive pay systems. We consider each option's strengths and limitations with regard to these principles. The many kinds of incentive pay fall into three broad categories: incentives linked to individual, group, or organizational performance. Choices from these categories should consider not only their strengths and weaknesses, but also their fit with the organization's goals. The choice of incentive pay may affect not only the level of motivation but also the kinds of employees who are attracted to and stay with the organization. For example, there is some evidence that organizations with team-based rewards will tend to attract employees who are more team-oriented, whereas rewards tied to individual performance make an organization more

Incentivizing Stress

Pay for performance is intended to give people an incentive to aim high and achieve the employer's goals. But some recent research suggests that performance-based pay can have a different result: it can generate mental-health problems, which in turn can interfere with high performance.

In this study, researchers at Washington University in Saint Louis and at Denmark's Aarhus University gathered two kinds of data about more than 300,000 workers in 1,309 companies: the company's use of performance-based pay and the number of employees filling prescriptions for medications used to treat anxiety and depression. Analyzing data by company, not by individual employee, they found that at companies adopting pay for performance, the use of anxiety and depression medications increased by 5.7%. In their analysis, the researchers assumed that more employees felt depressed or anxious than went so far as to seek treatment and fill prescriptions, and further that some people might have sought help and pursued treatments other than medication. The researchers noted that in the companies with greater employee use of medications for anxiety and depression, employee turnover was higher. The impact on mental health was greatest among older workers, and the impact on turnover was greatest among female employees.

Other research offers some clues about what might be happening and how to reduce the negative impact of incentive pay on mental health. A survey by the Canadian Payroll Association found that stress about personal finances is a significant distraction at work, with about seven in ten respondents saying they spend about 30 minutes of a typical workday addressing such issues. The uncertainty of performance-based pay could make such problems more complex and therefore more distracting. And a study looking at performance incentives at auto dealerships found that employees performed worse when the dealers had a program of paying out incentives in advance and taking them back if targets weren't met, rather than paying only incentives earned, suggesting that fear of loss was affecting job performance. The bottom line is that HR departments can contribute to higher performance with pay plans and other practices that evoke confidence and competence rather than uncertainty and fear.

Questions

1. Do the mental-health issues associated with pay for performance indicate that a company should avoid incentive pay? Explain your reasoning.
2. Suppose you work in the HR department of a company that provides incentive pay for meeting customer satisfaction targets. What HR practices could help the company ensure that the incentive pay is motivational rather than a source of anxiety and depression?

Sources: Lamar Pierce, Alex Rees-Jones, and Charlotte Blank, "The Negative Consequences of Loss-Framed Performance Incentives," NBER working paper 26619, January 2020, http://www.nber.org; "Financial Stress Is Impacting Work Performance, Survey Finds," *Advisor's Edge,* September 4, 2019, https://www.advisor.ca; "Performance-Based Pay Linked to Employee Mental-Health Problems, Study Shows," *The Source* (Washington University in St. Louis), March 20, 2019, https://source.wustl.edu.

attractive to those who think and act independently, as individuals.[7] Given the potential impact, organizations not only should weigh the strengths and weaknesses in selecting types of incentive pay but also should measure the results of these programs.

LO 13-2 Describe how organizations recognize individual performance.

Pay for Individual Performance

Organizations may reward individual performance with a variety of incentives:

- Piecework rates
- Standard hour plans
- Merit pay
- Individual bonuses
- Sales commissions

Piecework Rates

As an incentive to work efficiently, some organizations pay production workers a **piecework rate,** a wage based on the amount they produce. The amount paid per unit is set at a level that rewards employees for above-average production volume. For example, suppose that, on average, assemblers can finish 10 components in an hour. If the organization wants to pay its average assemblers $8 per hour, it can pay a piecework rate of $8/hour divided by 10 components/hour, or $.80 per component. An assembler who produces the average of 10 components per hour earns an amount equal to $8 per hour. An assembler who produces 12 components in an hour would earn $.80 × 12, or $9.60 per hour. This is an example of a **straight piecework plan** because the employer pays the same rate per piece no matter how much the worker produces.

Piecework Rate
Rate of pay per unit produced.

Straight Piecework Plan
Incentive pay in which the employer pays the same rate per piece, no matter how much the worker produces.

A variation on straight piecework is **differential piece rates** (also called *rising* and *falling differentials*), in which the piece rate depends on the amount produced. If the worker produces more than the standard output, the piece rate is higher. If the worker produces at or below the standard, the amount paid per piece is lower. In the preceding example, the differential piece rate could be $1 per component for components exceeding 12 per hour and $.80 per component for up to 12 components per hour.

Differential Piece Rates
Incentive pay in which the piece rate is higher when a greater amount is produced.

In one study, the use of piece rates increased production output by 30%—more than any other motivational device evaluated.[8] An obvious advantage of piece rates is the direct link between how much work the employee does and the amount the employee earns. This type of pay is easy to understand and seems fair to many people, if they think the production standard is reasonable. In spite of their advantages, piece rates are relatively rare, for several reasons.[9] Most jobs, including those of managers, have no physical output, so it is hard to develop an appropriate performance measure. This type of incentive is most suited for very routine, standardized jobs with output that is easy to measure. For complex jobs or jobs with outputs that are hard to measure, piecework plans do not apply very well. Also, unless a plan is well designed to include performance standards, it might not reward employees for focusing on quality or customer satisfaction if doing so interferes with the day's output. A bonus based on number of faucets produced gives production workers no incentive to stop a manufacturing line to correct a quality-control problem. Production-oriented goals may do nothing to encourage employees to learn new skills or cooperate with others. Therefore, individual incentives such as these may be a poor incentive in an organization that wants to encourage teamwork. They may not be helpful in an organization with complex jobs, employee empowerment, and team-based problem solving.

Standard Hour Plan
An incentive plan that pays workers extra for work done in less than a preset "standard time."

Standard Hour Plans

Another quantity-oriented incentive for production workers is the **standard hour plan,** an incentive plan that pays workers extra for work done in less than a preset "standard time." The organization determines a standard time to complete a task, such as tuning up a car engine. If the mechanic completes the work in less than the standard time, the mechanic receives an amount of pay equal to the wage for the full standard time. Suppose the standard time for tuning up an engine is 2 hours. If the mechanic finishes a tune-up in 1½ hours, the mechanic earns 2 hours' worth of pay in 1½ hours. Working that fast over the course of a week could add significantly to the mechanic's pay.

In terms of their pros and cons, standard hour plans are much like piecework plans. They encourage employees to work as fast as they can, but not necessarily to care about quality or customer service. Also, they succeed only if employees want the extra money more than they want to work at a pace that feels comfortable.

Piece-rate pay plans typically are suited for routine, standardized jobs with output that is easy to measure.
ImagineChina/AP Images

Merit Pay

Merit Pay
A system of linking pay increases to ratings on performance appraisals.

Almost all organizations have established some program of **merit pay**—a system of linking pay increases to ratings on performance appraisals. (Chapter 10 described the content and use of performance appraisals.) To make the merit increases consistent, so they will be seen as fair, many merit pay programs use a *merit increase grid,* such as the sample in Table 13.1. As the table shows, the decisions about merit pay are based on two factors: the individual's performance rating and the individual's compa-ratio (pay relative to average pay, as defined in Chapter 12). This system gives the biggest pay increases to the best performers and to those whose pay is relatively low for their job. At the highest extreme, an exceptional employee earning 80% of the average pay for his job could receive a 7% merit raise. An employee rated as "below expectations" would receive a raise only if that employee was earning relatively low pay for the job (compa-ratio of 90% or less).

Organizations establish and revise merit increase grids in light of changing economic conditions. When organizations revise pay ranges, employees have new compa-ratios. A higher pay range would result in lower compa-ratios, causing employees to become eligible for bigger merit increases. An advantage of merit pay is therefore that it makes the reward more valuable by relating it to economic conditions.

A drawback is that conditions can shrink the available range of increases. During recent years, budgets for pay increases were about 2% to 4% of pay, so average performers could receive a 3% raise and top performers perhaps as much as 5%. (These percentages do not take into account the impact of COVID-19 on the U.S. economy in 2020.) The 2-percentage-point difference, after taxes and other deductions, would amount to only a few dollars per week on a salary of $40,000 per year. Over an entire career, the bigger increases for top performers can grow into a major change, but viewed on a year-by-year basis, they may not deliver much of an incentive to excel.[10] As Figure 13.1 shows, a typical spread of pay raises across all employees is just a few percentage points. However, experts advise making pay increases far greater for top performers than for average employees—and not rewarding the poor performers with a raise at all.[11] Imagine if the raises given to the bottom two categories in Figure 13.1 instead went toward 7% or greater raises for the one-quarter of employees who are high performers. This type of decision signals that excellence is rewarded. As the unemployment rate continues to fall, upward pressure on wages may increase the possible range for merit increases. If average pay rises by 4% or more, there are more dollars to distribute among high- and middle-performing employees.

Another advantage of merit pay is that it provides a method for rewarding performance in all of the dimensions measured in the organization's performance management system. If that system is appropriately designed to measure all the important job behaviors, then the merit pay is linked to the behaviors the organization desires. Some evidence suggests that high performers have an outsize impact on the company's value, so this kind of motivation is both strategic and equitable. When employees see the rewards as fair, that perception influences their behavior.[12]

A drawback of merit pay, from the employer's standpoint, is that it can quickly become expensive. In the not uncommon situation of managers rating most employees' performance

TABLE 13.1
Sample Merit Increase Grid: Recommended Salary Increase

	COMPA-RATIO[a]		
PERFORMANCE RATING	80%–90%	91%–110%	111%–120%
Exceeds expectations	7%	5%	3%
Meets expectations	4%	3%	2%
Below expectations	2%	—	—

[a]Compa-ratio is the employee's salary divided by the midpoint of his or her salary range.

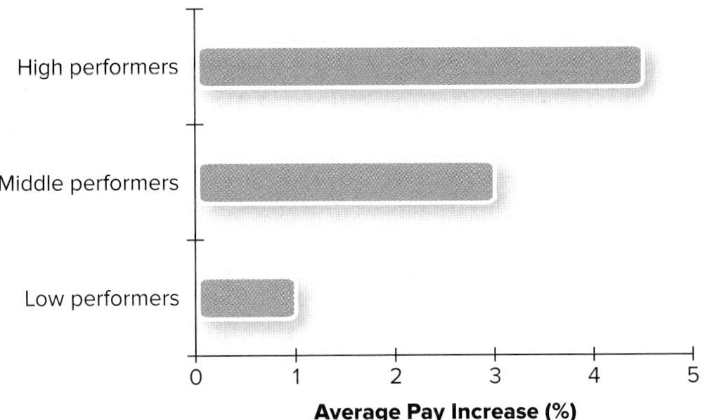

FIGURE 13.1
Ratings and Raises: Under-Rewarding the Best

Sources: "BLR's 2018–2019 Pay Budget and Salary Data Survey," *HR Daily Advisor,* https://hrdailyadvisor.blr.com, accessed May 5, 2020; Mercer, "Key Findings: Mercer's 2019/2020 US Compensation Planning Survey," August 12, 2019, https://www.mercer.us.

in the top two categories (out of four or five), many employees are eligible for the biggest merit increases, and their pay rises rapidly. This cost is one reason some organizations have established guidelines about the percentage of employees that may receive the top rating, as discussed in Chapter 10. Another correction might be to use 360-degree performance feedback (discussed in Chapter 8), but so far, organizations have not used multisource data for pay decisions.[13]

Another drawback of merit pay is that it makes assumptions that can be misleading. Rewarding employees for superior performance ratings assumes that those ratings depend on employees' ability and motivation. But performance may actually depend on forces outside the employee's control, such as managers' rating biases, the level of cooperation from co-workers, or the degree to which the organization gives employees the authority, training, and resources they need. Under these conditions, employees will likely conclude that the merit pay system is unfair.

Quality guru W. Edwards Deming also criticizes merit pay for discouraging teamwork. For example, if employees in the purchasing department are evaluated based on the number or cost of contracts they negotiate, they may have little interest in the quality of the materials they buy, even when the manufacturing department is having quality problems. Group incentives are one response to this concern. However, recent evidence suggests that well-designed merit pay actually promotes success at the group or team level. The effectiveness of these approaches for rewarding teamwork depends on the level of cooperation desired and the choice of performance measures.[14]

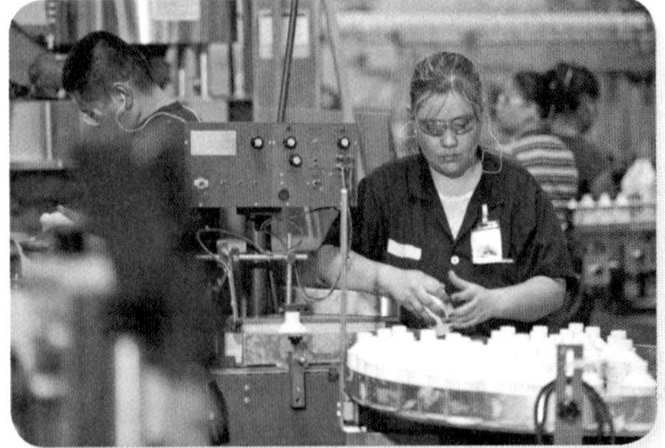
Performance bonuses for production workers are not rolled into base pay. The bonuses could be tied to various measures, including the quantity of products shipped in a specific time period.
DreamPictures/Shannon Faulk/Blend Images LLC

Performance Bonuses

Like merit pay, performance bonuses reward individual performance, but bonuses are not rolled into base pay. The employee must re-earn them during each performance period. In some cases the bonus is a one-time reward. Bonuses may also be linked to objective performance measures, rather than subjective ratings. As described in "Did You Know?" most companies are tying bonuses to a combination of performance measures.

Did You Know?

Bonuses Typically Are Based on Multiple Metrics

Many companies pay bonuses; a recent survey of midsize and large employers found that these companies were devoting about 13% of their payroll spending to this type of compensation. Less than one-fourth of respondents tied bonuses purely to individual performance, however. This may be because such bonuses are at the manager's discretion and therefore are harder to administer in a way that employees see as fair. The most popular way to determine a bonus was by measuring performance on multiple levels, such as individual, team, and company performance measures.

A separate study found that about three-quarters of companies offer year-end bonuses. In that study, 52% of workers said they expected such a bonus. This can set expectations for managers who are evaluating employees' performance. And in a survey of organizations with tech workers, about one-third of respondents said they use discretionary bonuses as a way to retain top talent, well behind the use of merit pay (60%), which has a longer-term impact on employees who stick around.

Question

Thinking of yourself as an employee (in a current job or one you would like to have), would you rather receive a $500 bonus for something special you did or $500 at the end of the year if your whole department meets its goals? Explain your reasoning.

Sources: Sheryl Estrada, "High-Performing Tech Workers See Pay Increases While Average Wages Stagnate," *HR Dive,* March 11, 2020, https://www.hrdive.com; Carol Patton, "Here Are the Latest Trends in Employee Bonuses," *HR Executive,* December 31, 2019, https://hrexecutive.com; "Are Year-End Bonuses in the Works?" *Robert Half* (blog), December 3, 2019, https://www.roberthalf.com.

% of Companies Using Incentive Pay

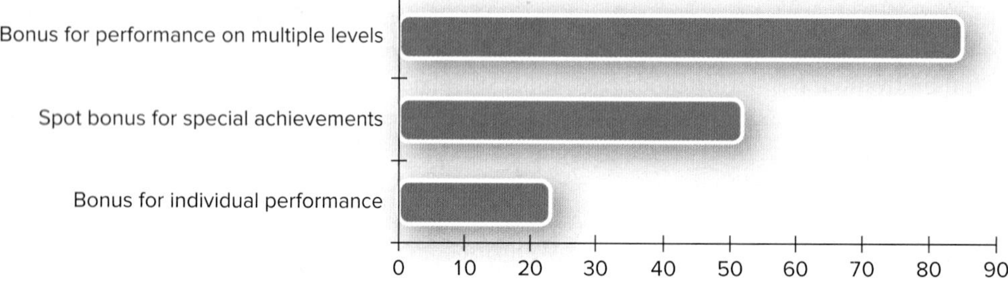

In a recent survey, the most common size of bonuses for technical and clerical workers was in the range of $1,000 to $5,000; bonuses paid to managers tended to be larger.[15]

Bonuses for individual performance can be extremely effective and give the organization great flexibility in deciding what kinds of behavior to reward. In many cases, employees receive bonuses for meeting such routine targets as sales or production numbers. Airlines can reward good customer service with bonuses for meeting goals for on-time performance, and trucking firms can reward safe practices with bonuses for accident-free driving. Companies can award bonuses for learning, innovation, or any other behavior they associate with success.

All this flexibility makes it essential to be sure bonuses are tied to behavior that makes a difference to the organization's overall performance. Also, employees have to have some control over whether they can meet the bonus requirements. For example, not all employees can control an organization's sales. A recent study considered the experience of using a monthly incentive with health care providers. Their performance was better if management made an occasional exception to prevent the providers' income from dropping as much as the formula would require during months when revenues were low.[16]

Adding to the flexibility of annual or more frequent bonuses, organizations also may motivate employees with one-time bonuses. For example, when one organization acquires another, it usually wants to retain certain valuable employees in the organization it is buying. Therefore, it is common for organizations involved in an acquisition to pay *retention bonuses*—one-time incentives paid in exchange for remaining with the company—to top managers, engineers, top-performing salespeople, and information technology specialists. A global survey of large companies that had completed a merger or acquisition found that most companies retained at least 80% of the employees who signed retention agreements offering them a bonus to stay. The most successful companies focused on key skills or leadership roles in order to identify who would be offered a bonus.[17]

Sales Commissions

A variation on piece rates and bonuses is the payment of **commissions,** or pay calculated as a percentage of sales. For instance, a furniture salesperson might earn commissions equaling 6% times the price of the furniture the person sells during the period. Selling a $2,000 couch would add $120 to the salesperson's commissions for the period. Commission rates vary tremendously from one industry and company to another. Examples reported include an average rate between 5.0% and 6.0% for real estate, and 5% to 20% of the annual premium for car insurance (paid to an independent insurance agent).[18]

Commissions
Incentive pay calculated as a percentage of sales.

Some salespeople earn a commission in addition to a base salary; others earn only commissions—a pay arrangement called a *straight commission plan.* Straight commissions are common for insurance and real estate agents and car salespeople. Other salespeople earn no commissions at all, but a straight salary. Paying most or all of a salesperson's compensation in the form of salary frees the salesperson to focus on developing customer goodwill. Paying most or all of a salesperson's compensation in the form of commissions encourages the salesperson to focus on closing sales. In this way, differences in salespeople's compensation directly influence how they spend their time, how they treat customers, and how much the organization sells. DCH Montclair Acura met this challenge by paying its managers commissions based partly on the dealership's overall performance, not just the performance of their department. This way, the sales and service managers see their teams' work as contributing to meeting customers' overall needs. Previously, a sales manager might have seen used-car repairs cutting into profits, or the service manager might not have cared about fast turnaround contributing to sales.[19]

The nature of salespeople's compensation also affects the kinds of people who will want to take and keep sales jobs with the organization (see "Best Practices" for a case in point). Hard-driving, ambitious, risk-taking salespeople might enjoy the potential rewards of a straight commission plan. An organization that wants salespeople to concentrate on listening to customers and building relationships might want to attract a different kind of salesperson by offering more of the pay in the form of a salary. Basing part or all of a salesperson's pay on commissions assumes that the organization wants to attract people with some willingness to take risks. That assumption could apply to many good salespeople, but risk taking is not a primary job requirement of every employer.

Pay for Group Performance

LO 13-3 Identify ways to recognize group performance.

Employers may address the drawbacks of individual incentives by including group incentives in the organization's compensation plan. To win group incentives, employees must

Best Practices

AutoNation Offers a Choice of Commissions

Like most car dealerships, AutoNation has relied on commission-based pay packages for its salespeople. However, as the company reviewed its goals for employee retention, it realized one hurdle was that few young workers find this arrangement attractive. Across the industry, turnover among salespeople is about 67%. Although AutoNation says it does better than the industry average, management realized employee retention was an area with room for improvement. AutoNation is the largest car retailer in the United States, selling more than 600,000 vehicles a year, so its demand for labor is particularly great.

AutoNation decided to take a flexible approach to commissions. It began offering its sales staff an option it calls Pay Plan Plus, which pays a base salary plus bonuses. Salespeople who prefer to earn commissions can keep the old pay plan. Following the launch of Pay Plan Plus, 70% of the sales force made the change.

Especially with such promising early results, Marc Cannon, chief marketing officer, expressed hope that the option of working for a salary would do more than reduce employee turnover. He also hopes that it will attract more workers thinking of a new career but reluctant to take on the risks of commission-based selling.

Questions

1. What kind of workers do you think would choose each of AutoNation's pay structures? Which kind would you rather buy a car from?
2. Why do you think most workers chose the new pay plan? Which plan is more attractive to you?

Sources: AutoNation, "Corporate Profile," https://investors.autonation.com, accessed May 5, 2020; Dave Druzynski, "Your Pay Plan Is Driving Talent Away," *F&I Showroom,* January 17, 2019, https://www.fi-magazine.com; Phil Villegas, "Wards Auto Megadealer 100 Numbers Go Up and Up," *Wards Auto,* June 7, 2018, https://www.wardsauto.com; Hannah Lutz, "70% of AutoNation Sales Staffers Opt for New Pay Plan," *Automotive News,* May 8, 2017, https://www.autonews.com.

cooperate and share knowledge so that the entire group can meet its performance targets. Common group incentives include gainsharing, bonuses, and team awards.

Gainsharing

Gainsharing
Group incentive program that measures improvements in productivity and effectiveness objectives and distributes a portion of each gain to employees.

Organizations that want employees to focus on efficiency may adopt a **gainsharing** program, which measures increases in productivity and effectiveness and distributes a portion of each gain to employees. For example, if a factory enjoys a productivity gain worth $30,000, half the gain might be the company's share. The other $15,000 would be distributed among the employees in the factory. Knowing that they can enjoy a financial benefit from helping the company be more productive, employees supposedly will look for ways to work more efficiently and improve the way the factory operates.

Gainsharing addresses the challenge of identifying appropriate performance measures for complex jobs. For example, how would a hospital measure the production of its nurses—in terms of satisfying patients, keeping costs down, or completing a number of tasks? Each of these measures oversimplifies the complex responsibilities involved in nursing care. Even for simpler jobs, setting acceptable standards and measuring performance can be complicated. Gainsharing frees employees to determine how to improve their own and their group's performance. It also broadens employees' focus beyond their individual interests. But in contrast to profit sharing, discussed later, it keeps the performance measures within a range of activity that most employees believe they can influence. Organizations can enhance the likelihood of a gain by providing a means for employees to share knowledge and make suggestions, as we will discuss in the last section of this chapter.

Gainsharing is most likely to succeed when organizations provide the right conditions. Among the conditions identified, the following are among the most common:[20]

- Management commitment
- Need for change or strong commitment to continuous improvement
- Management acceptance and encouragement of employee input
- High levels of cooperation and interaction
- Employment security
- Information sharing on productivity and costs
- Goal setting
- Commitment of all involved parties to the process of change and improvement
- Performance standard and calculation that employees understand and consider fair and that is closely related to managerial objectives
- Employees who value working in groups

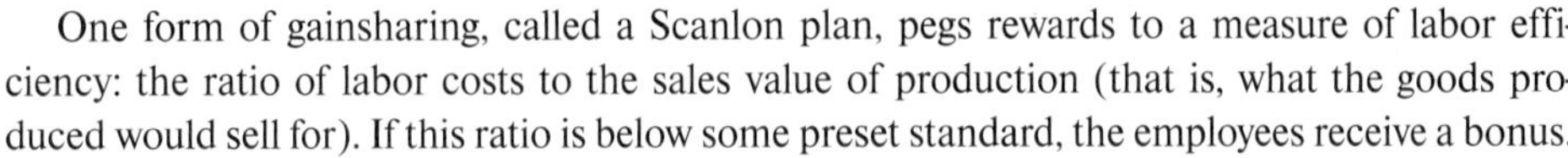

Group members who meet a sales goal or a product development team that successfully launches a new product may be rewarded with a bonus for group performance. What are some advantages and disadvantages of group bonuses?
Nattakorn Maneerat/Getty Images

One form of gainsharing, called a Scanlon plan, pegs rewards to a measure of labor efficiency: the ratio of labor costs to the sales value of production (that is, what the goods produced would sell for). If this ratio is below some preset standard, the employees receive a bonus.

Group Bonuses and Team Awards

In contrast to gainsharing plans, which typically reward the performance of all employees at a facility, bonuses for group performance tend to be for smaller work groups.[21] These bonuses reward the members of a group for attaining a specific goal, usually measured in terms of physical output. Team awards are similar to group bonuses, but they are more likely to use a broad range of performance measures, such as cost savings, successful completion of a project, or even meeting deadlines.

Both types of incentives have the advantage that they encourage group or team members to cooperate so that they can achieve their goal. However, depending on the reward system, competition among individuals may be replaced by competition among groups. Competition may be healthy in some situations, as when groups try to outdo one another in satisfying customers. On the downside, competition can also prevent necessary cooperation among groups. To avoid this, the organization should carefully set the performance goals for these incentives so that concern for costs or sales does not obscure other objectives, such as quality, customer service, and ethical behavior.

Selmax Corporation, which makes plastic products, uses group bonuses to support its focus on continuous improvement in quality and productivity. The production team has daily goals for measures such as machine run time and reject rates, and every employee earns points for meeting those goals. Points are subtracted for any safety incidents and customer complaints. At the end of each quarter, employees receive bonuses tied to the number of points earned.[22]

Pay for Organizational Performance

LO 13-4 Explain how organizations link pay to their overall performance.

Two important ways organizations measure their performance are in terms of their profits and their stock price. In a competitive marketplace, profits result when an organization is efficiently providing products that customers want at a price they are willing to pay. Stock is the owners' investment in a corporation; when the stock price is rising, the value of that investment is growing. Rather than trying to figure out what performance measures will motivate employees to do the things that generate high profits and a rising stock price, many organizations offer incentive pay tied to those organizational performance measures. The expectation is that employees will focus on what is best for the organization.

These organization-level incentives can motivate employees to align their activities with the organization's goals. At the same time, linking incentives to the organization's profits or stock price exposes employees to a high degree of risk. Profits and stock price can soar very high very fast, but they can also fall. The result is a great deal of uncertainty about the amount of incentive pay each employee will receive in each period. Therefore, these kinds of incentive pay are likely to be most effective in organizations that emphasize growth and innovation, which tend to need employees who thrive in a risk-taking environment.[23]

Profit Sharing

Profit Sharing
Incentive pay in which payments are a percentage of the organization's profits and do not become part of the employees' base salary.

Under **profit sharing,** payments are a percentage of the organization's profits and do not become part of the employees' base salary. For example, General Motors provides for profit sharing in its contract with its workers' union, the United Auto Workers. Depending on how large GM's profits are in relation to its total sales for the year, a percentage of the company's profits are divided among the workers according to how many hours they worked during the year. For example, for 2019, each eligible GM worker received a check for $8,000.[24] The formula for computing and dividing the profit-sharing bonus is included in the union contract.

There are several reasons an organization might use profit sharing. It may encourage employees to think more like owners, taking a broad view of what they need to do in order to make the organization more effective. They are more likely to cooperate and less likely to focus on narrow self-interest. Also, profit sharing has the practical advantage of costing less when the organization is experiencing financial difficulties. If the organization has little or no profit, this incentive pay is small or nonexistent, so employers may not need to rely as much on layoffs to reduce costs.[25]

Does profit sharing help organizations perform better? The evidence is not yet clear. Although research supports a link between profit-sharing payments and profits, researchers have questioned which of these causes the other.[26] For example, Ford, Chrysler, and GM have similar profit-sharing plans in their contracts with the United Auto Workers, but the payouts are not always the same. In 2019, the average worker received $8,000 from GM, $7,280 from Ford, and $6,600 from Fiat Chrysler. Because the plans are similar, something other than profit sharing must have made GM and Fiat Chrysler more profitable than Ford.

Differences in payouts, as in the preceding example, raise questions not only about the effectiveness of the plans but about equity. Assuming that workers at Ford, Chrysler, and GM have similar jobs, they would expect to receive similar profit-sharing checks. In the year of this example, Fiat Chrysler workers might have seen their incentive pay as being inequitable unless Fiat Chrysler could show that GM workers did more to earn their big checks. Employees also may feel that small profit-sharing checks are unfair because they have little control over profits. If profit sharing is offered to all employees but most employees think only management decisions about products, price, and marketing have much impact on profits, they will conclude that there is little connection between their actions and their rewards. In that case, profit-sharing plans will have little impact on employee behavior. This problem is even greater when employees have to wait for months before profits are distributed. The time lag between high-performance behavior and financial rewards is simply too long to be motivating.

Given the limitations of profit-sharing plans, one strategy is to use them as a component of a pay system that includes other kinds of pay more directly linked to individual behavior. This increases employees' commitment to organizational goals while addressing concerns about fairness.

Stock Ownership

While profit-sharing plans are intended to encourage employees to "think like owners," a stock ownership plan actually makes employees part owners of the organization. Like profit sharing, employee ownership is intended as a way to encourage employees to focus on the success of the organization as a whole. The drawbacks of stock ownership as a form of incentive pay are similar to those of profit sharing. Specifically, it may not have a strong effect on individuals' motivation.[27] Employees might not see a strong link between their actions and the company's stock price, especially in larger organizations. The link between pay and performance is even harder to appreciate because the financial benefits mostly come when the stock is sold–typically when the employee leaves the organization.

Ownership programs usually take the form of *stock options* or *employee stock ownership plans.* These are illustrated in Figure 13.2.

Stock Options One way to distribute stock to employees is to grant them **stock options**–the right to buy a certain number of shares of stock at a specified price. (Purchasing the stock is called *exercising* the option.) Suppose that in 2020 a company's employees received options to purchase the company's stock at $10 per share. The employees will benefit if the stock price rises above $10 per share because they can pay $10 for something (a share of stock) that is worth more than $10. If in 2025 the stock is worth $30, they can exercise their options and buy stock for $10 a share. If they want to, they can sell their stock for the market price of $30, receiving a gain of $20 for each share of stock. Of course, stock prices can also fall. If the 2025 stock price is only $8, the employees would not bother to exercise the options.

Stock Options
Rights to buy a certain number of shares of stock at a specified price.

Traditionally, organizations have granted stock options to their executives. During the 1990s, many organizations pushed eligibility for options further down in the organization's structure. Walmart and PepsiCo are among the large companies that have granted stock options to employees at all levels. Stock values were rising so fast during the 1990s that options were extremely rewarding for a time.

Some studies suggest that organizations perform better when a large percentage of top and middle managers are eligible for long-term incentives such as stock options. This evidence is consistent with the idea of encouraging employees to think like owners.[28] It is not clear whether these findings would hold up for lower-level employees. They may see much less opportunity to influence the company's performance in the stock market.

Employee Stock Ownership Plans Although stock options are most often used with top management, a broader arrangement is the **employee stock ownership plan (ESOP).** In an ESOP, the organization distributes shares of stock to its employees by placing the stock into a trust managed on the employees' behalf. Employees receive regular reports on the value of their stock, and when they leave the organization, they may sell the stock to the organization or (if it is a publicly traded company) on the open market.

Employee Stock Ownership Plan (ESOP)
An arrangement in which the organization distributes shares of stock to all its employees by placing it in a trust.

FIGURE 13.2
Types of Pay for Organizational Performance

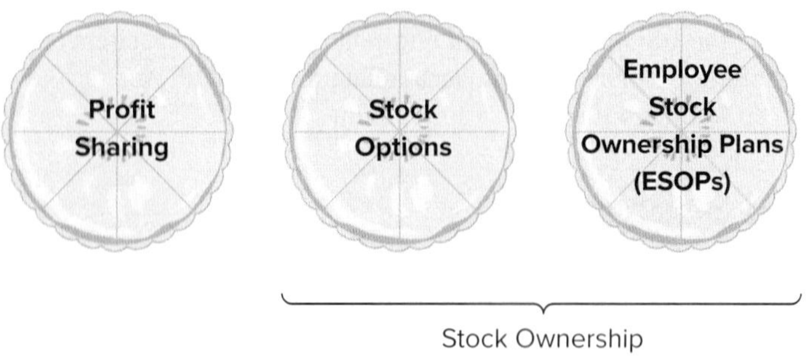

FIGURE 13.3
Number of Companies with ESOPs

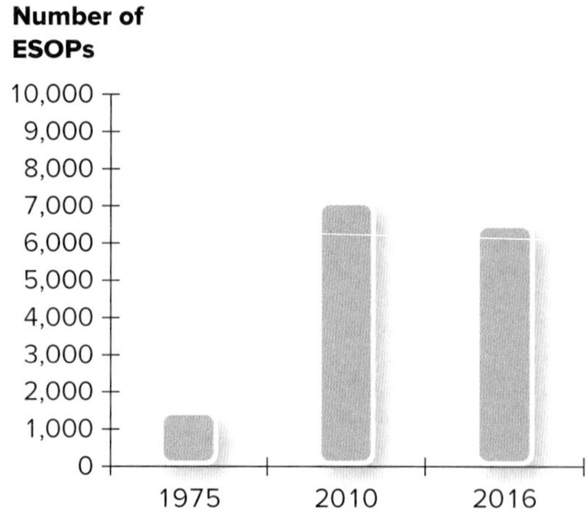

Source: National Center for Employee Ownership, "Employee Ownership by the Numbers," https://www.nceo.org, accessed August 23, 2020.

ESOPs are the most common form of employee ownership. The number of employees in such plans increased from approximately 250,000 in 1975 to more than 10.6 million active participants (those who are currently employed and earning benefits) in 2016, the most recent year for which data are available.[29] The number of participants has grown even while the number of companies offering ESOPs has shrunk somewhat, as shown in Figure 13.3.

ESOPs raise a number of issues. On the negative side, they carry a significant risk for employees. By law, an ESOP must invest at least 51% of its assets in the company's own stock (in contrast to other kinds of stock funds that hold a wide diversity of companies). Problems with the company's performance therefore can take away significant value from the ESOP. Many companies set up ESOPs to hold retirement funds, so these risks directly affect employees' retirement income. Adding to the risk, funds in an ESOP are not guaranteed by the Pension Benefit Guarantee Corporation (described in Chapter 14). Sometimes employees use an ESOP to buy their company when it is experiencing financial problems; this is a highly risky investment.

Still, ESOPs can be attractive to employers. Along with tax and financing advantages, ESOPs give employers a way to build pride in and commitment to the organization. Employees have a right to participate in votes by shareholders (if the stock is registered on a national exchange, such as the New York Stock Exchange).[30] This means that employees participate somewhat in corporate-level decision making. Still, the overall level of participation in decisions appears to vary significantly among organizations with ESOPs. Some research suggests that the benefits of ESOPs are greatest when employee participation is high. At EOC, a heavy-equipment manufacturer in Texas, all employees participate in the company's ESOP, and the CEO considers the employees to be highly engaged and focused on the company's success. In addition, the ESOP helps attract and retain talent. Offer letters to job candidates include the amount of money they can accumulate in an ESOP over various time periods, which helps keep voluntary turnover to a minimum.[31]

LO 13-5 Describe how organizations combine incentive plans in a "balanced scorecard."

Balanced Scorecard

As the preceding descriptions indicate, any form of incentive pay has advantages and disadvantages. For example, relying exclusively on merit pay or other individual incentives may produce a workforce that cares greatly about meeting those objectives but competes to achieve them at the expense of cooperating to achieve organizational goals. Relying heavily on profit sharing or stock ownership may increase cooperation but do little to motivate day-to-day effort or to attract and retain top individual performers. Because of this, many organizations design a mix of pay programs. The aim is to balance the disadvantages of one type of incentive pay with the advantages of another type.

One way to accomplish this goal is to design a **balanced scorecard**–a combination of performance measures directed toward the company's long- and short-term goals and used as the basis for awarding incentive pay. A corporation would have financial goals to satisfy its stockholders (owners), quality- and price-related goals to satisfy its customers, efficiency goals to ensure better operations, and goals related to acquiring skills and knowledge for the future to fully tap into employees' potential. Different jobs would contribute to those goals in different ways. For example, an engineer could develop products that better meet customer needs and can be produced more efficiently. The engineer could also develop knowledge of new technologies in order to contribute more to the organization in the future. A salesperson's goals would include measures related to sales volume, customer service, and learning about product markets and customer needs. Organizations customize their balanced scorecards according to their markets, products, and objectives. The scorecards of a company that is emphasizing low costs and prices would be different from the scorecards of a company emphasizing innovative use of new technology. Table 13.2 shows the kinds of information that go into a balanced scorecard. The "HRM Social" box explores another kind of information that could be added to balanced scorecards in the digital age.

Balanced Scorecard
A combination of performance measures directed toward the company's long- and short-term goals and used as the basis for awarding incentive pay.

Not only does the balanced scorecard combine the advantages of different incentive-pay plans, it helps employees understand the organization's goals. By communicating the balanced scorecard to employees, the organization shows employees information about what its goals are and what it expects employees to accomplish. Examples might include measures for revenues, costs, resource use, and worker health and safety. For the example

TABLE 13.2

Sample Balanced Scorecard for an Electric Cooperative

		GOALS		
PERFORMANCE CATEGORY	CRITICAL SUCCESS FACTORS	BASE (2%)	TARGET (3%)	STRETCH (5%)
Member service (40% of incentive pay)	Reliability (average interruption duration)	140 min.	130 min.	120 min.
	Customer satisfaction (index from quarterly survey)	9.0	9.1	9.2
Financial performance (25% of incentive pay)	Total operating expenses (¢/kilowatt-hour)	4.03¢	3.99¢	3.95¢
	Cash flow (% of investment)	75%	80%	85%
Internal processes (20% of incentive pay)	Safety (safety index based on injury rate and severity)	4.6	3.6	2.6
Innovation and learning (15% of incentive pay)	Member value (revenue/kWh sold)	Budget	−10% state median	−13% state median
	Efficiency and effectiveness (total margins/no. employees)	$534,400	$37,200	$40,000

Sources: Tim Sullivan, Tony Thomas, and Henry Cano, "Managing What You Measure: Lessons from the Balanced Scorecard," *Tech Advantage*, February 24, 2015, http://www.techadvantage.org; Tim Sullivan and Henry Cano, "Introducing a Balanced Scorecard for Electric Cooperatives: A Tool for Measuring and Improving Results," *Management Quarterly*, Winter 2009, Business & Company Resource Center, http://galenet.galegroup.com.

Social-Media Measures for a Balanced Scorecard

Vacationers and business travelers love to swap recommendations and cautionary tales. Not only is the storytelling fun, but it generates ideas for future trips. Hotels, restaurants, and other travel and entertainment organizations have the potential to join the conversation by participating in social media. But consider the situation of a major hotel chain that gets high marks for comfort and its loyalty program and yet has a negative reputation for the booking process only because the main social-media story is one online conversation that went wrong and went viral.

Clearly, better performance on social media could help this organization, and other social-media laggards. One way to improve performance is to reward it. So far, however, social-media participation is a new enough activity that organizations are still learning what to measure and reward.

The fundamental starting point in adopting social-media measures is business goals, not social-media services or metrics. Managers must identify the organization's goals for sales and for customer acquisition and retention. Then they consider how social media could support these goals by building and strengthening customer relationships. In the hotel industry, for example, managers would consider that Instagram is now a primary place where people share images (and therefore stories) about their travels. A company familiar with Facebook therefore would not set a performance measure to increase Facebook likes just because it is already on Facebook. Rather, it would set objectives to get a certain number and kind of responses associated with satisfaction and sales, and then managers would be responsible for determining where to post and what to say.

Another area in which organizations have room for improvement is in responding to messages. People tagging an organization's name in a post are often looking for a response. They might be highly satisfied and eager to spread the word, or they might be upset and looking for assistance. Organizations, however, are responding to these posts at very low rates. Here, too, a better approach is to set metrics for responsiveness and satisfaction, charging decision makers with determining how to find relevant posts and respond. A variety of analytics tools are available for analyzing social-media content to gauge emotions and to flag trending topics and relevant posts. Then the organization needs people who are able to respond effectively—and rewards them for their successes.

Questions

1. Suppose a hotel decided to add social-media responsiveness to a balanced scorecard for its marketing and customer-service managers. What percentage of the total pay do you think should be based on this score? Why?
2. Many marketers have not yet shown results from use of social media. Do you think linking rewards to social-media results would correct this problem? Why or why not?

Sources: DJ Vallauri, "Your Hotel's Social Media Reputation Is More Important Than Ever," *Hospitality Net,* March 16, 2020, https://www.hospitalitynet.org; Melonie Dodaro, "The ROI of Social Media: Measuring What Matters," *Social Media Today,* April 10, 2019, https://www.socialmediatoday.com; Alicia Hoisington, "Hotels Need to Pay Better Attention to Social Media to Drive Revenue," *Hotel Management,* March 6, 2018, https://www.hotelmanagement.net; Lisa Montenegro, "Social Media: Measuring the ROI," *Forbes,* January 30, 2018, https://www.forbes.com; Keith A. Quesenberry, "The Basic Social Media Mistakes Companies Still Make," *Harvard Business Review,* January 2, 2018, https://hbr.org.

in Table 13.2, the organization indicates not only that the manager should meet the four performance objectives but also that it is especially concerned with effective service to co-op members, because almost half the incentive is based on this one target.

LO 13-6 Summarize processes that can contribute to the success of incentive programs.

Processes That Make Incentives Work

As we explained in Chapter 12, communication and employee participation can contribute to a belief that the organization's pay structure is fair. In the same way, the process by which the organization creates and administers incentive pay can help it use incentives to achieve the goal of motivating employees. The monetary rewards of gainsharing, for example, can substantially improve productivity,[32] but the organization can set up the process to be even more effective. In a study of an automotive parts plant, productivity rose when the gainsharing plan added employee participation in the form of monthly meetings with managers to discuss the gainsharing plan and ways to increase productivity. A related study asked employees what motivated them to participate actively in the plan (for example, by making suggestions for improvement). According to employees, other factors besides the pay itself were important–especially the ability to influence and control the way their work was done.[33] Considerations such as these are especially important during economic slowdowns, when compensation budgets tend to be limited.

HR Analytics & Decision Making

Data on employee preferences, coupled with the recent emphasis on establishing favorable "employee experiences," is leading more organizations to tailor not just how much employees earn but also how and when they get paid. While direct deposit has replaced a paper paycheck for most employees, some–especially newer and lower-paid workers–lack bank accounts. These employees might prefer to have their pay credited to a debit card, PayPal account, or digital wallet accessible through a smartphone app. Some employees might want to receive their pay biweekly or monthly, while others might need earnings ahead of payday, especially around holidays. A global survey of employees found that 36% of workers–and almost half of workers in Generation Z–would turn down an offer from a company that didn't provide options for receiving pay.

These options make managing payroll far more complex. Whereas printing a check for each employee puts everyone on the same schedule and requires only the employer's bank account information, flexible-pay systems involve different account types and numbers, as well as different pay schedules. Furthermore, each state and many cities have their own rules governing payroll. Multiplied by thousands of employees, the variations are countless. At the same time, employers have to ensure they have enough cash on hand to pay on variable schedules, including higher amounts around major holidays or other occasions that lead employees to request pay early. Thus, offering flexible pay requires that employers invest in information technology to process all the data.

Questions

1. Would you expect that offering variable pay would add to an employer's costs? Explain.
2. If you were advising an organization that was considering variable pay, what kinds of data would you suggest the organization gather to evaluate the initiative's success?

Sources: "ADP on Prepaid Cards, Digital Wallets' Role in the Future of Payroll," *PYMNTS*, February 28, 2020, https://www.pymnts.com; Gwen Moran, "Should You Be Able to Pick When You Get Paid?" *Fast Company*, January 24, 2020, https://www.fastcompany.com.

Participation in Decisions

Employee participation in pay-related decisions can be part of a general move toward employee empowerment. If employees are involved in decisions about incentive pay plans and employees' eligibility for incentives, the process of creating and administering these plans can be more complex.[34] There is also a risk that employees will make decisions that are in their interests at the expense of the organization's interests. However, employees have hands-on knowledge about the kinds of behavior that can help the organization perform well, and they can see whether individuals are displaying that behavior.[35] Therefore, in spite of the potential risks, employee participation can contribute to the success of an incentive plan. This is especially true when monetary incentives encourage the monitoring of performance and when the organization fosters a spirit of trust and cooperation.

These conditions are in place at Batesville Products, an Indiana manufacturer that has a strategy of continuous improvement. Management shares scheduling and quality goals and results with its manufacturing employees. The employees are eligible for a modified form of profit sharing, measured as revenues minus categories of costs over which the employees have influence. That way, employees can see a connection between their efforts and results, and between results and the profit-sharing benefits.[36]

Communication

Along with empowerment, communicating with employees is important. It demonstrates to employees that the pay plan is fair. Also, when employees understand the requirements of the incentive pay plan, the plan is more likely to influence their behavior as desired. Organizations do this by providing statements showing each employee his or her total compensation (see "HR How To"). Employees also turn to their managers for information about their pay. This places a responsibility on HR departments to ensure that managers are well trained in how to explain the organization's policies and pay decisions. Evidence suggests that only a small share of organizations provide this training; the ones that do have an edge in improving employee satisfaction and retention.[37]

It is particularly important to communicate with employees when changing the plan. Employees tend to feel concerned about changes. Pay is a frequent topic of rumors and assumptions based on incomplete information, partly because of pay's importance to employees.

LO 13-7 Discuss issues related to performance-based pay for executives.

Incentive Pay for Executives

Because executives have a much stronger influence over the organization's performance than other employees do, incentive pay for executives warrants special attention. Assuming that incentives influence performance, decisions about incentives for executives should have a great impact on how well the executives and the organization perform. Along with overall pay levels for executives (discussed in Chapter 12), organizations need to create incentive plans for this small but important group of employees.

To encourage executives to develop a commitment to the organization's long-term success, executive compensation often combines short-term and long-term incentives. *Short-term incentives* include bonuses based on the year's profits, return on investment, or other measures related to the organization's goals. Sometimes, to gain tax advantages, the actual payment of the bonus is deferred (for example, by making it part of a retirement plan). *Long-term incentives* include stock options and stock purchase plans. The rationale for these long-term incentives is that executives will want to do what is best for the organization because that will cause the value of their stock to grow.

Researchers have tried in vain to find a link between the size of CEOs' incentive pay and companies' performance in terms of profits or other financial measures.[38] In an analysis of CEO pay at 400 U.S.-traded companies, only 2 of the 10 top-paid CEOs returned positive shareholder value in a recent year. And in a study that compared historical CEO pay with the companies' performance over the following three years, CEOs who earned in the top 10% saw their companies do increasingly *worse* than others over the three years that followed. Of course, incentive pay is generally tied to one's past accomplishments, not (formally) to expectations. However, the highly paid executives in the study took more risks that did not pay off, so if the incentives made them overconfident, this type of pay was not meeting long-range objectives.

HR How To

Making Incentive Pay Part of a Total-Rewards Package

As organizations become increasingly strategic about their compensation plans, they consider incentive pay part of a total package of rewards, along with salary, career paths, and more. Furthermore, they consider the total rewards part of their methods for recruiting and retaining talent. Of course, the value of total rewards is greatest when employees understand what they are getting—and that requires effective communication. Here are some guidelines for a total-rewards approach to compensation:

- Learn about employees and their concerns. At some organizations, many employees might struggle to manage finances or family responsibilities. At others, the most common challenge might be seeing a connection between efforts and rewards. As much as possible, align incentives with the concerns facing employees—and make that alignment part of the organization's messages about compensation.
- Craft total-rewards statements that deliver personal information to each employee about the pay and other rewards he or she is eligible to receive. Recruiters also can prepare these statements to accompany job offers. Along with pay, the statements should include the value of benefits, training opportunities, and other rewards for working at the organization.
- Use graphics as well as text in messages about rewards. Graphs and other visual information can help employees take in the value of rewards and the ways to earn and use them.
- Measure the effectiveness of communication. Conduct frequent short surveys to see if employees understand incentives, including their monetary value and how to earn them. Check whether they understand what their managers are telling them about pay. Respond to the results by improving the organization's messages and training managers to talk about compensation.

Questions

1. Suppose you work for a company that pays profit-related bonuses to its employees and wants to communicate the value of this part of its total rewards. What kind of message about the bonuses would give you, as an employee, a positive feeling about your total rewards?
2. Suppose you work in the HR department of the company in question 1. You learn that nonmanagement employees are most concerned about financing living expenses, like homes and cars, while managers are most concerned about saving for retirement. How would you adjust your company's messages about the bonuses to appeal to these two different groups?

Sources: Paycor, "How to Drive Employee Engagement with Total Compensation Statements," December 24, 2019, https://www.paycor.com; "Total Compensation: 3 Tips for Better Employee Communication," January 3, 2019, https://www.compa.as; Stephen Miller, "How Total Rewards Can Drive Performance Management Success," *Society for Human Resource Management,* May 31, 2018, https://www.shrm.org; Gregg Apirian, "Eight Tips for Building an Effective Total Rewards Communication Strategy," *Forbes,* May 15, 2017, https://www.forbes.com.

A corporation's shareholders–its owners–want the corporation to encourage managers to act in the owners' best interests. They want managers to care about the company's profits and stock price, and incentive pay can encourage this interest. One study has found that relying on such long-term incentives is associated with greater profitability.[39]

Performance Measures for Executives

The balanced-scorecard approach is useful in designing executive pay. Some companies use a balanced scorecard that combines measures of whether the organization is delivering value to shareholders, customers, and employees. Rewarding achievement of a variety of goals in a balanced scorecard reduces the temptation to win bonuses by manipulating financial data.

Regulators and shareholders have pressured companies to do a better job of linking executive pay and performance. The Securities and Exchange Commission (SEC) has required companies to more clearly report executive compensation levels and the company's performance relative to that of competitors. These reporting requirements shine a light on situations where executives of poorly performing companies receive high pay, so companies feel more pressure to link pay to performance. The Dodd-Frank Wall Street Reform and Consumer Protection Act, passed in 2010, requires that public companies report the ratio of median compensation of all its employees to the CEO's total compensation. Dodd-Frank also gives shareholders a "say on pay," meaning shareholders may vote to indicate their approval or disapproval of the company's executive pay plans.

Ethical Issues

Incentive pay for executives lays the groundwork for significant ethical issues. When an organization links pay to its stock performance, executives need the ethical backbone to be honest about their company's performance even when dishonesty or clever shading of the truth offers the tempting potential for large earnings. Scandals show that the results can be disastrous when unethical behavior comes to light. Investigations of Wells Fargo, for example, revealed that ambitious performance goals once thought to have been behind the bank's successful growth were instead driving employees and executives to engage in misdeeds to hit their targets. Employees earning bonuses linked to revenues were overcharging clients–even when those clients were other Wells Fargo departments–relative to agreed-upon fees. Others were opening fictitious bank accounts for customers without their knowledge. When the behavior came to light, the board of directors took the unusual step of awarding executives no bonuses and requesting they return part of their compensation that had been paid as stock. Several years later, a group of these former Wells Fargo execs still face more than $59 million in fines and bans from the U.S. banking industry over their roles in the scandal.[40]

Among these issues is one we have already touched on in this chapter: the difficulty of setting performance measures that encourage precisely the behavior desired. In the case of incentives tied to stock performance, executives may be tempted to inflate the stock price in order to enjoy bonuses and valuable stock options. The intent is for the executive to boost stock value through efficient operations, technological innovation, effective leadership, and so on. Unfortunately, individuals at some companies determined that they could obtain faster results through accounting practices that stretched the norms in order to present the company's performance in the best light. When such practices are discovered to be misleading, stock prices plunge and the company's reputation is damaged, sometimes beyond repair.

A related issue when executive pay includes stock or stock options is insider trading. When executives are stockholders, they have a dual role as owners and managers. This places them at an advantage over others who want to invest in the company. An individual, a pension fund, or other investors have less information about the company than its managers do–for example, whether product development is proceeding on schedule, whether a financing deal is in the works, and so on. An executive who knows about these activities could therefore reap a windfall in the stock market by buying or selling stock based on knowledge about the company's future. The SEC places strict limits on this "insider trading," but some executives have violated these limits. In the worst cases executives have sold stock, secretly knowing their company was failing, before the stock price collapsed. The losers are the employees, retirees, and other investors who hold the now-worthless stock.

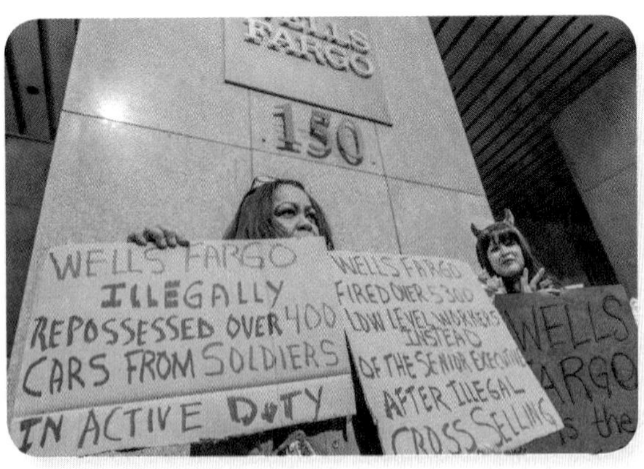

When Wells Fargo managers and employees opened fictitious accounts for existing customers to meet aggressive sales goals, the company's board took the unusual step of not awarding bonuses to executives.
Erik McGregor/Pacific Press/LightRocket/Getty Images

As recent news stories have reminded us, linking pay to stock price can reward unethical behavior, at least in the short term and at least in the minds of a handful of executives. Yet, given the motivational power of incentive pay, organizations cannot afford to abandon incentives for their executives. These temptations are among the reasons that executive positions demand individuals who maintain the highest ethical standards.

THINKING ETHICALLY

SHOULD WORKERS GET HAZARD PAY IN A PANDEMIC?

While variable pay generally involves compensating employees according to what they accomplish, employers also can adjust pay to recognize workers for taking on significant challenges. Hazard pay is pay above the agreed-on wage or salary to compensate employees for carrying out hazardous duties or doing work that causes extreme physical comfort and distress that can't be eased with the use of protective devices. During the COVID-19 pandemic, some employees sought and some employers offered hazard pay for working in conditions where employees might have to be exposed to the novel coronavirus. For nurses, paramedics, police officers, grocery clerks, and others, working even while wearing protective equipment could pose a hazard of infection.

Hazard pay is not required by law, but federal government employees are eligible for 25% hazard pay if exposed to "virulent biologicals," when protective devices do not completely protect them. Amazon and various supermarket chains announced $2-an-hour temporary pay increases for employees who work with the public. Kroger called the additional pay a "Hero Bonus," and Albertsons termed it "Appreciation Pay." Other companies, including Walmart, Walgreens, and CVS have paid workers one-time bonuses between $150 and $500. This additional pay added to companies' expenses at a time when the economy overall had dramatically slowed, but it did provide an incentive for workers to stay on the job.

Advocates of paying hazard pay during the pandemic noted that many of these jobs already are at the low end of U.S. earnings, and households that depend on wages from a worker who is cleaning hospital rooms, driving a bus, or delivering groceries have little to fall back on if that worker becomes ill. Furthermore, especially in the early months of the pandemic, companies had difficulty obtaining enough personal protective equipment for their workers. From this perspective, it is a matter of basic human rights that people who are risking their health to serve society's needs should be compensated.

A major objection to hazard pay is that employers might use it as a substitute for creating safe working conditions. Another concern is the cost of raising wages, which employees might come to expect will continue at the higher level after the risk subsides. Companies might have to lay off some workers or even go out of business if they cannot earn profits while compensating employees at a higher pay level.

Questions

1. Review the list of employee rights in the ethics section of Chapter 1. Which, if any, of those rights apply to the question of whether to offer hazard pay during a pandemic? Explain.
2. During a pandemic, how can a company address the issue of hazard pay in a way that results in the greatest good for the largest number of people?

Sources: Te-Ping Chen and Katherine Sayre, "Call It Hero Pay or Hazard Pay, Essential Workers Want More of It," *The Wall Street Journal,* May 4, 2020, https://www.wsj.com; "Hazard Pay," U.S. Department of Labor, https://www.dol.gov, accessed May 4, 2020; Paige Smith and Fatima Hussein, "Hazard Pay Plans Poised to Outlast Virus with Bipartisan Push," *Daily Labor Report,* April 13, 2020, https://news.bloomberglaw.com; Molly Kinder, "COVID-19's Essential Workers Deserve Hazard Pay; Here's Why–and How It Should Work," *Brookings,* April 10, 2020, https://www.brookings.edu; Catherine Thorbecke, "What to Know about Hazard Pay If You're Working during Coronavirus Crisis," *ABC News,* April 3, 2020, https://abcnews.go.com.

SUMMARY

LO 13-1 Discuss the connection between incentive pay and employee performance.

- Incentive pay is pay tied to individual performance, profits, or other measures of success.
- Organizations select forms of incentive pay to energize, direct, or control employees' behavior.
- It is influential because the amount paid is linked to predefined behaviors or outcomes.

- To be effective, incentive pay should encourage the kinds of behavior that are most needed, and employees must believe they have the ability to meet the performance standards. Employees must value the rewards, have the resources they need to meet the standards, and believe the pay plan is fair.

LO 13-2 Describe how organizations recognize individual performance.

- Organizations may recognize individual performance through such incentives as piecework rates, standard hour plans, merit pay, sales commissions, and bonuses for meeting individual performance objectives.
- Piecework rates pay employees according to the amount they produce.
- Standard hour plans pay workers extra for work done in less than a preset "standard time."
- Merit pay links increases in wages or salaries to ratings on performance appraisals.
- Bonuses are similar to merit pay, because they are paid for meeting individual goals, but they are not rolled into base pay, and they usually are based on achieving a specific output rather than subjective performance ratings.
- A sales commission is incentive pay calculated as a percentage of sales closed by a salesperson.

LO 13-3 Identify ways to recognize group performance.

- Common group incentives include gainsharing, bonuses, and team awards.
- Gainsharing programs measure increases in productivity and distribute a portion of each gain to employees.
- Group bonuses reward the members of a group for attaining a specific goal, usually measured in terms of physical output.
- Team awards are more likely to use a broad range of performance measures, such as cost savings, successful completion of a project, or meeting a deadline.

LO 13-4 Explain how organizations link pay to their overall performance.

- Incentives for meeting organizational objectives include profit sharing and stock ownership.
- Profit-sharing plans pay workers a percentage of the organization's profits; these payments do not become part of the employees' base salary.
- Stock ownership incentives may take the form of stock options or employee stock ownership plans.
- A stock option is the right to buy a certain number of shares at a specified price. The employee benefits by exercising the option at a price lower than the market price, so the employee benefits when the company's stock price rises.
- An employee stock ownership plan (ESOP) is an arrangement in which the organization distributes shares of its stock to employees by placing the stock in a trust managed on the employees' behalf. When employees leave the organization, they may sell their shares of the stock.

LO 13-5 Describe how organizations combine incentive plans in a "balanced scorecard."

- A balanced scorecard is a combination of performance measures directed toward the company's long- and short-term goals and used as the basis for awarding incentive pay.
- Typically, it includes financial goals to satisfy stockholders, quality- and price-related goals for customer satisfaction, efficiency goals for improved operations, and goals related to acquiring skills and knowledge for the future.
- The mix of pay programs is intended to balance the disadvantages of one type of incentive with the advantages of another type.
- The balanced scorecard also helps employees to understand and care about the organization's goals.

LO 13-6 Summarize processes that can contribute to the success of incentive programs.

- Communication and participation in decisions can contribute to employees' feeling that the organization's incentive pay plans are fair.
- Employee participation in pay-related decisions can be part of a general move toward employee empowerment. Employees may put their own interests first in developing the plan, but they also have firsthand insight into the kinds of behavior that can contribute to organizational goals.
- Communicating with employees is important because it demonstrates that the pay plan is fair and helps them understand what is expected of them. Communication is especially important when the organization is changing its pay plan.

LO 13-7 Discuss issues related to performance-based pay for executives.

- Because executives have such a strong influence over the organization's performance, incentive pay for them receives special attention.
- Executive pay usually combines long-term and short-term incentives. By motivating executives, these incentives can significantly affect the organization's performance.
- The size of incentives should be motivating but also meet standards for equity.
- Performance measures should encourage behavior that is in the organization's best interests, including ethical behavior. Executives need ethical standards that keep them from insider trading or deceptive practices designed to manipulate the organization's stock price.

KEY TERMS

incentive pay, 402
piecework rate, 405
straight piecework plan, 405
differential piece rates, 405
standard hour plan, 405
merit pay, 406
commissions, 409
gainsharing, 410
profit sharing, 412
stock options, 413
employee stock ownership plan (ESOP), 413
balanced scoreboard, 415

REVIEW AND DISCUSSION QUESTIONS

1. With some organizations and jobs, pay is primarily wages or salaries, and with others, incentive pay is more important. For each of the following jobs, state whether you think the pay should emphasize base pay (wages and salaries) or incentive pay (bonuses, profit sharing, and so on). Give a reason for each. *(LO 13-1)*
   a. An accountant at a manufacturing company.
   b. A salesperson for a software company.
   c. A chief executive officer.
   d. A physician in a health clinic.
2. Consider your current job or a job that you have recently held. Would you be most motivated in response to incentives based on your individual performance, your group's performance, or the organization's overall performance (profits or stock price)? Why? *(LO 13-2)*
3. What are the pros and cons of linking incentive pay to individual performance? How can organizations address the negatives? *(LO 13-2)*
4. Suppose you are a human resource professional at a company that is setting up work teams for production and sales. What group incentives would you recommend to support this new work arrangement? *(LO 13-3)*
5. Why do some organizations link incentive pay to the organization's overall performance? Is it appropriate to use stock performance as an incentive for employees at all levels? Why or why not? *(LO 13-4)*
6. Stock options have been called the pay program that "built Silicon Valley" because of their key role as incentive pay for employees in high-tech companies. They were popular during the 1990s, when the stock market was rising rapidly. Since then, the stock market has experienced some sharp declines as well as recoveries. *(LO 13-4)*
   a. How would you expect this change to affect employees' attitudes toward stock options as incentive pay?
   b. How would you expect this change to affect the effectiveness of stock options as an incentive?
7. Based on the balanced scorecard in Table 13.2, find the incentive pay for an employee earning a salary of $4,000 a month in each of the following situations. *(LO 13-5)*
   a. The company met all of its target goals for the year. (Multiply the percentage at the top of the table by the employee's salary.)
   b. The company met only its target goals for financial performance (25% of the total incentive pay) but none of the other goals.
   c. The company met its stretch goals for financial performance and its base goals in the other areas. (For each category of goals, multiply the percentages by the employee's salary, and then add the amounts together.)
8. Why might a balanced scorecard like the one in Question 7 be more effective than simply using merit pay for a manager? *(LO 13-5)*
9. How can the way an organization creates and carries out its incentive plan improve the effectiveness of that plan? *(LO 13-6)*
10. In a typical large corporation, the majority of the chief executive's pay is tied to the company's stock price. What are some benefits of this pay strategy? Some risks? How can organizations address the risks? *(LO 13-7)*

SELF-ASSESSMENT EXERCISE

What Motivates You at Work?

Pay is only one type of incentive that can motivate you to perform well and contribute to your satisfaction at work. This survey will help you understand what motivates you at work. Consider each aspect of work and rate its importance to you, using the following scale: 5 = very important, 4 = somewhat important, 3 = neutral, 2 = somewhat unimportant, 1 = very unimportant.

Salary or wages	1	2	3	4	5
Cash bonuses	1	2	3	4	5
Boss's management style	1	2	3	4	5
Location of workplace	1	2	3	4	5
Commute	1	2	3	4	5
Job security	1	2	3	4	5

Opportunity for advancement	1	2	3	4	5
Work environment	1	2	3	4	5
Level of independence in job	1	2	3	4	5
Level of teamwork required for job	1	2	3	4	5
Other (enter your own):					
______________________	1	2	3	4	5
______________________	1	2	3	4	5
______________________	1	2	3	4	5

Which aspects of work received a score of 5? A score of 4? These are the ones you believe motivate you to perform well and make you happy in your job. Which aspects of work received a score of 1 or 2? These are least likely to motivate you. Is pay the only way to motivate you?

Source: Based on the "Job Assessor" found at www.salarymonster.com, accessed August 2002.

TAKING RESPONSIBILITY

BNY Mellon Shares the Wealth with Employees

When Congress passed a corporate tax cut that took effect in 2018, employees and economists alike speculated about where the increase to companies' bottom lines would be directed. Would more wealth flow to employees in the form of pay increases or to investors in the form of dividends paid out or investments aimed at increasing companies' value? And would any money directed to employees go mainly to executives or be shared with employees at all levels?

Bank of New York Mellon Corporation chose a path that demonstrated concern for multiple stakeholders. The bank–which focuses on serving large banks, mutual funds, and other big investors–announced that the tax reduction would add more than $400 million to income of $1.13 billion. Most of the additional after-tax income would be split between increasing corporate value and paying employees more. CEO Charles Scharf, in a memo to employees, described the decision in terms of social responsibility: "We strongly believe in our responsibility to our employees to share the tax benefit from a lower tax rate, as well as to invest as much as we intelligently can to build the company for the future so we can serve our clients, communities and shareholders for the long term."

On the corporate-value side, BNY Mellon said it would add more to its planned investments in technology projects aimed at improving the company's future performance. Investors who had hoped the company would provide them with a more immediate benefit such as bigger dividends were disappointed, as evidenced by a dip in the bank's stock price. Other banks, including Bank of America and U.S. Bancorp, had announced they would use most of their additional income to improve returns for stockholders. However, as BNY Mellon moved into the next year with a strong financial performance, stock prices recovered and rose.

BNY Mellon's additional spending on employees took the form of an increase in entry-level pay to $15 per hour. The increase mainly affected about 1,000 employees in the operations unit out of 52,500 employees overall. The plan was in noticeable contrast to many employers' decisions to pay one-time bonuses rather than raising pay levels.

BNY Mellon also indicated that it would continue with plans made before the tax cut. These included cost-saving efforts that would reduce the size of the workforce and consolidate it in a smaller headquarters. The company also had planned to pay dividends and buy back stock, transferring some of its value to investors.

Questions

1. BNY Mellon used its additional profits to increase entry-level pay levels rather than offering incentive pay such as merit increases or bonuses. What advantages of incentive pay was the bank forgoing?
2. What HR-related goal might the bank meet by raising entry-level pay instead of paying a one-time bonus?

Sources: BNY Mellon, "Annual Report 2019," https://www.bnymellon.com, accessed May 5, 2020; Matt Egan, "The Surprise Winners of the Bank Regulation Roll-Back," *CNN Money,* May 23, 2018, http://money.cnn.com; "BNY Mellon Profit Beats on Strong Growth across Businesses," Reuters, April 19, 2018, https://www.reuters.com; Justin Baer and Keiko Morris, "Bank of New York Mellon Plans to Move Its Corporate Headquarters in Lower Manhattan," *The Wall Street Journal,* January 31, 2018, https://www.wsj.com; Justin Baer, "BNY Mellon to Raise Wages for 1,000 Employees Following Tax Overhaul," *The Wall Street Journal,* January 18, 2018, https://www.wsj.com.

MANAGING TALENT

Employees Are Getting a Bite of Apple's Stock

For the past several years, Apple has awarded restricted shares of stock to hourly as well as salaried workers. Apple had been giving this type of incentive pay to managers and selected employees in product groups, which is common in the computer industry, but the new plan made just about all employees eligible. This was unusual because it covered Apple's retail workers (who represent about half of its total workforce) and call center employees.

Under Apple's earlier incentive program, product managers could recommend employees for stock grants. Each recommendation then went to the board of directors for approval. This process made it impractical for stock to be given to very many of Apple's tens of thousands of full-time employees. Employees also had been eligible to buy Apple stock at a discount through an employee stock purchase plan.

Apple did not publicly disclose the conditions for receiving stock or the size of the awards, but reports said the value would start at $1,000 to $2,000. The incentives would increase based on length of service and other criteria. The stock units are restricted, so they vest (become eligible for the employee to collect at the preset fair-market price) over a given period of time. More recently, following a major corporate tax cut, Apple announced bonuses in the form of restricted stock grants worth $2,500. These would go to full- and part-time employees below senior management in all departments worldwide.

Despite the wider access to stock grants, the really big payouts go to the top executives. Most recently, Apple paid CEO Tim Cook about $11.6 million, including a salary of $3 million and cash bonus of $7.7 million. But most of his wealth comes from grants of Apple stock, including vested shares valued at $113.5 million and unvested shares worth nearly $400 million.

The massive value of Cook's unvested shares gives him a strong reason to stay at Apple. But what about other employees? Reporters from *Yahoo Finance* talked to some tech workers and found that many of them sell their shares in order to invest the money in a more diverse portfolio of stocks. Some, though, are enthusiastic enough about their employer's future that they hold on to the shares they receive.

Questions

1. How can Apple's HR department promote the success of its program of stock grants?
2. If you worked in Apple's HR department, what kind(s) of individual incentives would you use? Would these be in addition to the stock incentives or in place of the stock rewards? Explain.

Sources: Mark Gurman and Bloomberg, "Here's How Much Apple CEO Tim Cook Made Last Year," *Fortune*, January 3, 2020, https://fortune.com; Mark Gurman, "Apple Gives Employees $2,500 Bonuses after New Tax Law," *Bloomberg News*, January 17, 2018, https://www.bloomberg.com; Seung Lee, "Apple CEO Tim Cook Gets a Big Bump in Pay, Use of Private Aircraft," *San Jose Mercury News*, December 28, 2017, https://www.mercurynews.com; J. P. Mangalindan and Krystal Hu, "What Silicon Valley Employees Are Doing with Their Red-Hot Stock Grants," *Yahoo Finance*, July 26, 2017, https://finance.yahoo.com; Jena McGregor, "Apple Opens Up Stock Awards to All Employees—Even Hourly Retail Workers," *Washington Post*, October 15, 2015, https://www.washingtonpost.com; Jordan Golson, "Apple Expands Executive Stock Award Programs to All Apple Employees," *Tech Republic*, October 15, 2015, http://www.techrepublic.com; Jack Nicas, "Apple Expands Stock Program to All Employees, Including Those in Retail Stores," *Wall Street Journal*, October 14, 2015, http://www.wsj.com.

HR IN SMALL BUSINESS

A Sweet Incentive at Mr. Holmes Bakehouse

The high costs of operating in California have been the undoing of many small businesses there. For companies employing minimum-wage workers, the problem recently intensified when the state launched a series of $1 increases in that wage from 2020 through 2023. Unlike business owners who threw up their hands, Aaron Caddel decided to see if he could figure out a way for his bakery, Mr. Holmes Bakehouse, to pay employees more and remain profitable.

Caddel and his management team arrived at a version of merit pay based on the quantity and quality of output. For two years, they studied what work needed to be done in their California kitchens. For each position, they identified three core procedures and three performance levels for each procedure. They also established pay levels corresponding to the performance levels.

Each employee starts at level one. When employees can get high-quality work done faster, they can move up by passing a test that shows they can work at the higher level. Those who pass get the higher pay tied to the higher level. Most rise to the challenge; those who don't can choose to move back to a lower level if they want to remain at Mr. Holmes Bakehouse. Every six months, employees are invited to see if they can pass the test for the next level.

Initially, some employees resisted a pay structure in which new employees sometimes surpass longer-term workers. But most were inspired by the potential for improved pay. After a little more than a year, more than two-thirds of the employees had reached level three for their position and were earning at least $20 per hour—more than the minimum wage and more than other bakeries in town were paying. For Caddel, the bottom-line impact was positive because the level-three employees had become 50% more productive than they had been. The increased efficiency exceeded the increased payroll expense, so profit margins actually rose along with employees' pay.

With these changes, employee turnover fell to 13% in an industry with an average turnover close to 75%. Furthermore, as word got around about the $20-an-hour positions at Mr. Holmes Bakehouse, the difficulties of filling minimum-wage jobs in pricey San Francisco evaporated. Caddel concludes that he achieved his goal of a win-win solution to the talent problem: higher earnings for his employees and higher profits for his business.

Questions

1. What conditions do you think made incentive pay successful at Mr. Holmes Bakehouse? (Consider, for example, the requirements for effective incentive plans listed on page 402.)
2. How could employee participation and communication with employees contribute to the effectiveness of performance pay at Mr. Holmes Bakehouse?

Sources: Joanna Fantozzi, "Making the (Pay) Grade," *Restaurant Hospitality,* March 2020, pp. 16–17; Brian Amick, "Can Pay-for-Performance Systems Work?" *Bake,* February 10, 2020, https://www.bakemag.com; Chloe Sorvino, "Has Mr. Holmes Bakehouse Unlocked the Key to the Restaurant Industry's Labor Crisis?" *Forbes,* January 3, 2020, https://www.forbes.com.

NOTES

1. Corporate website, "Careers," https://www.wasteprousa.com, accessed May 5, 2020; "Employees Receive Waste Pro's First $5,000 Helper Bonus," *Waste 360,* February 5, 2019, https://www.waste360.com.
2. This chapter draws freely on several literature reviews: B. Gerhart and G. T. Milkovich, "Employee Compensation: Research and Practice," in *Handbook of Industrial and Organizational Psychology,* 2nd ed., eds. M. D. Dunnette and L. M. Hough (Palo Alto, CA: Consulting Psychologists Press, 1992), vol. 3; B. Gerhart and S. L. Rynes, *Compensation: Theory, Evidence, and Strategic Implications* (Thousand Oaks, CA: Sage, 2003); B. Gerhart, "Compensation Strategy and Organization Performance," in *Compensation in Organizations: Current Research and Practice,* eds. S. L. Rynes and B. Gerhart (San Francisco: Jossey-Bass, 2000), pp. 151–194; B. Gerhart, S. L. Rynes, and I. S. Fulmer, "Compensation," *Academy of Management Annals* 3 (2009); Barry Gerhart and Meiyu Fang, "Pay for (Individual) Performance: Issues, Claims, Evidence and the Role of Sorting Effects," *Human Resource Management Review* 24 (2014), pp. 41–52.
3. B. Gerhart and G. T. Milkovich, "Organizational Differences in Managerial Compensation and Financial Performance," *Academy of Management Journal* 33 (1990), pp. 663–691.
4. S. Carnahan, R. Agarwal, and B. A. Campbell, "Heterogeneity in Turnover: The Effect of Relative Compensation Dispersion of Firms on the Mobility and Entrepreneurship of Extreme Performers," *Strategic Management Journal* 33 (2012), pp. 1411–1430; J. D. Shaw, "Pay Dispersion, Storing, and Organizational Performance," *Academy of Management Discoveries* 1 (2015), pp. 165–179; G. T. Milkovich and A. K. Wigdor, *Pay for Performance* (Washington, DC: National Academy Press, 1991); Gerhart and Milkovich, "Employee Compensation"; Gerhart and Rynes, *Compensation;* A. Nyberg, "Retaining Your High Performers: Moderators of the Performance-Job Satisfaction–Voluntary Turnover Relationship," *Journal of Applied Psychology* 95, no. 3 (2010), pp. 440–453; C. O. Trevor, G. Reilly, and B. Gerhart, "Reconsidering Pay Dispersion's Effect on the Performance of Interdependent Work: Reconciling Sorting and Pay Inequality," *Academy of Management Journal* 55 (2012), pp. 585–610.
5. C. Harrison, "77% of Organizations Offering Variable Pay Plans," *Salary.com,* January 8, 2019, https://www.salary.com; Payscale, *Variable Pay Playbook,* 2018, https://www.payscale.com.
6. B. Gerhart, "Incentives and Pay for Performance in the Workplace," *Advances in Motivation Science* 4 (2017), pp. 91–140; B. Gerhart and M. Fang, "Competence and Pay for Performance," in *Handbook of Competence and Motivation,* 2nd ed., eds. A. J. Elliot, C. S. Dweck, and D. S. Yeager (New York: Guilford, 2017); D. Pohler and J. A. Schmidt, "Does Pay-for-Performance Strain the Employment Relationship? The Effect of Manager Bonus Eligibility on Nonmanagement Employee Turnover," *Personnel Psychology* 69 (2015), pp. 395–429.
7. R. D. Bretz, R. A. Ash, and G. F. Dreher, "Do People Make the Place? An Examination of the Attraction-Selection-Attrition Hypothesis," Personnel Psychology 42 (1989), pp. 561–581; T. A. Judge and R. D. Bretz, "Effect of Values on Job Choice Decisions," *Journal of Applied Psychology* 77 (1992), pp. 261–271; D. M. Cable and T. A. Judge, "Pay Performance and Job Search Decisions: A Person-Organization Fit Perspective," *Personnel Psychology* 47 (1994), pp. 317–348.
8. E. A. Locke, D. B. Feren, V. M. McCaleb, K. N. Shaw, and A. T. Denny, "The Relative Effectiveness of Four Methods of Motivating Employee Performance," in *Changes in Working Life,* eds. K. D. Duncan, M. M. Gruenberg, and D. Wallis (New York: Wiley, 1980), pp. 363–388.
9. Gerhart and Milkovich, "Employee Compensation."
10. S. Miller, "Address Pay Compression or Risk Employee Flight," Society for Human Resource Management, June 1, 2018, https://www.shrm.org; *The Great Divide: How a Lack of Trust Is Driving HR and Managers Apart,* 2018 Compensation Best Practices Report, PayScale, http://www.payscale.com; WorldatWork, "WorldatWork Report: U.S. Salary Budget Increases Come in at 3 Percent," news release, August 1, 2017, https://www.worldatwork.org; F. Giancola, "Are High-Performing Employees Being Adequately Rewarded under Merit Pay Plans?" *Employee Benefit Plan Review,* November 2015, pp. 13–16; E. E. Lawler III, "Pay for Performance: A Strategic Analysis," in *Compensation and Benefits,* ed. L. R. Gomez-Mejia (Washington, DC: Bureau of National Affairs, 1989).
11. L. Leritz, "Principles of Merit Pay," Economic Research Institute, 2012, http://www.erieri.com; J. Dahm and P. Sanborn, "Addressing Talent and Rewards in 'The New Normal,'" Aon Hewitt, 2010, http://aonhewitt.com; S. Miller, "Pay for Performance: Make It More than a Catchphrase," *SHRM Online* Compensation Discipline, May 30, 2011, http://www.shrm.org.
12. B. Gerhart and J. M. Newman, *Compensation,* 13th ed. (New York: McGraw-Hill, 2020); K. Abosch and B. Gerhart, "The Case for Differentiated Pay for Performance," WorldatWork Total Rewards Conference and Exhibition, 2013; H. Aguinis and E. O'Boyle, "Star Performers in Twenty-First Century Organizations," *Personnel Psychology* 67, no. 2 (2014), pp. 313–350; J. D. Shaw, "Pay Dispersion," *Annual Review of Organizational Psychology and Organizational Behavior* 1, no. 1 (2014), pp. 521–544; P. E. Downes and D. Choi, "Employee Reactions to Pay Dispersion: A Typology of Existing Research," *Human Resource Management*

Review, 24, no. 1 (2014), pp. 53–66; A. Bucciol, N. J. Foss, and M. Piovesan, "Pay Dispersion and Performance in Teams," *PloS ONE* 9, no. 11 (2014), e112631; C. O. Trevor, G. Reilly, and B. Gerhart, "Reconsidering Pay Dispersion's Effect on the Performance of Interdependent Work: Reconciling Sorting and Pay Inequality," *Academy of Management Journal* 55 (2012), pp. 585–610.

13. A. J. Nyberg, J. R. Pieper, and C. O. Trevor, "Pay-for-Performance's Effect on Future Employee Performance: Integrating Psychological and Economic Principles toward a Contingency Perspective," *Journal of Management* 42, no. 7 (2016).
14. Gerhart and Fang, "Pay for (Individual) Performance"; Shaw, "Pay Dispersion"; W. He, L. R. Long, and B. Kuras, "Workgroup Salary Dispersion and Turnover Intention in China: A Contingent Examination of Individual Differences and the Dual Deprivation Path Explanation," *Human Resource Management* 55 (2015), pp. 301–320; S. A. Conroy and N. Gupta, "Team Pay-for-Performance: The Devil Is in the Details," *Group and Organization Management* 41, no. 1 (2016), pp. 32–65.
15. *Bonus Programs and Practices,* WorldatWork, July 2016, https://www.worldatwork.org.
16. M. A. Maltarich, A. J. Nyberg, G. Reilly, Dhuha Abdulsalam, and M. Martin, "Pay-for-Performance, Sometimes: An Interdisciplinary Approach to Integrating Economic Rationality with Psychological Emotion to Predict Individual Performance," *Academy of Management Journal* 60, no. 6 (2017), pp. 2155–2174.
17. D. McCann, "M&A Retention Bonuses Pay Off," *CFO,* December 2017, p. 19.
18. N. McLachlan and L. Walker, "How Much Do Insurance Agents Make?" *US Insurance Agents,* March 19, 2020, https://usinsuranceagents.com; D. Bortz, "The Real Estate Commission: A Guide to Who Pays, How Much, and More," *Realtor.com,* April 15, 2019, https://www.realtor.com.
19. J. Charniga, "Pay Plan Keeps Peace between Sales, Service," *Automotive News,* April 10, 2017, http://www.autonews.com.
20. T. L. Ross and R. A. Ross, "Gainsharing: Sharing Improved Performance," in *The Compensation Handbook,* 3rd ed., eds. M. L. Rock and L. A. Berger (New York: McGraw-Hill, 1991).
21. T. M. Welbourne and L. R. Gomez-Mejia, "Team Incentives in the Workplace," in *The Compensation Handbook,* 3rd ed.
22. T. Deligio, "Meet Plastics' Preeminent Processors," *Plastics Technology,* March 2017, pp. 32–36.
23. L. Mosca, "The Motivating Power of 'Pay for Performance,'" *Forbes,* March 22, 2018, https://www.forbes.com.
24. K. Hall, "GM Will Pay Profit-Sharing Checks of $8,000," *The Detroit News,* February 5, 2020, https://www.detroitnews.com.
25. This idea has been referred to as the "share economy." See M. L. Weitzman, "The Simple Macroeconomics of Profit Sharing," *American Economic Review* 75 (1985), pp. 937–953. For supportive research, see the following studies: J. Chelius and R. S. Smith, "Profit Sharing and Employment Stability," *Industrial and Labor Relations Review* 43 (1990), pp. 256S–273S; B. Gerhart and L. O. Trevor, "Employment Stability under Different Managerial Compensation Systems," working paper (Cornell University Center for Advanced Human Resource Studies, 1995); D. L. Kruse, "Profit Sharing and Employment Variability: Microeconomic Evidence on the Weitzman Theory," *Industrial and Labor Relations Review* 44 (1991), pp. 437–453.
26. Gerhart and Milkovich, "Employee Compensation"; M. L. Weitzman and D. L. Kruse, "Profit Sharing and Productivity," in *Paying for Productivity,* ed. A. S. Blinder (Washington, DC: Brookings Institution, 1990); D. L. Kruse, *Profit Sharing: Does It Make a Difference?* (Kalamazoo, MI: Upjohn Institute, 1993); M. Magnan and S. St.-Onge, "The Impact of Profit Sharing on the Performance of Financial Services Firms," *Journal of Management Studies* 42 (2005), pp. 761–791.
27. E. H. O'Boyle, P. C. Patel, and E. Gonzalez-Mulé, "Employee Ownership and Firm Performance: A Meta-analysis," *Human Resource Management Journal* 26, no. 4 (2016), pp. 425–448.
28. Gerhart and Milkovich, "Organizational Differences in Managerial Compensation."
29. National Center for Employee Ownership, "Employee Ownership by the Numbers," September 2019, https://www.nceo.org.
30. M. A. Conte and J. Svejnar, "The Performance Effects of Employee Ownership Plans," in *Paying for Productivity,* pp. 245–294.
31. Ibid.; S. Caminiti, "A Wealth-Building Tool Often More Coveted than a 401(k) Plan by Employees," *CNBC,* December 4, 2018, https://www.cnbc.com; T. H. Hammer, "New Developments in Profit Sharing, Gainsharing, and Employee Ownership," in *Productivity in Organizations,* eds. J. P. Campbell, R. J. Campbell, et al. (San Francisco: Jossey-Bass, 1988); K. J. Klein, "Employee Stock Ownership and Employee Attitudes: A Test of Three Models," *Journal of Applied Psychology* 72 (1987), pp. 319–332.
32. R. T. Kaufman, "The Effects of Improshare on Productivity," *Industrial and Labor Relations Review* 45 (1992), pp. 311–322; M. H. Schuster, "The Scanlon Plan: A Longitudinal Analysis," *Journal of Applied Behavioral Science* 20 (1984), pp. 23–28; J. A. Wagner III, P. Rubin, and T. J. Callahan, "Incentive Payment and Nonmanagerial Productivity: An Interrupted Time Series Analysis of Magnitude and Trend," *Organizational Behavior and Human Decision Processes* 42 (1988), pp. 47–74.
33. C. R. Gowen III and S. A. Jennings, "The Effects of Changes in Participation and Group Size on Gainsharing Success: A Case Study," *Journal of Organizational Behavior Management* 11 (1991), pp. 147–169.
34. D. I. Levine and L. D. Tyson, "Participation, Productivity, and the Firm's Environment," in *Paying for Productivity.*
35. T. Welbourne, D. Balkin, and L. Gomez-Mejia, "Gainsharing and Mutual Monitoring: A Combined Agency-Organizational Justice Interpretation," *Academy of Management Journal* 38 (1995), pp. 881–899.
36. S. Wetzel, "Batesville Products Inc. Measures Up," *Modern Casting,* September 2017, pp. 18–22.
37. PayScale, *The Great Divide,* pp. 23–32.
38. T. Francis and V. Furhmans, "Big Companies Pay CEOs for Good Performance—and Bad," *The Wall Street Journal,* May 17, 2019, https://www.wsj.com; M. J. Cooper, H. Gulen, and P. R. Rau, "Performance for Pay? The Relation Between CEO Incentive Compensation and Future Stock Price Performance," November 1, 2016, available at Social Science Research Network, https://papers.ssrn.com.
39. Gerhart and Milkovich, "Organizational Differences in Managerial Compensation;" B. Gerhart, S. L. Rynes, and I. S. Fulmer, "Pay and Performance: Individuals, Groups, and "Executives," *Academy of Management Annals* 3 (2009), pp. 251–315.
40. Bloomberg News, "Frozen Wells Fargo Bonuses Show a Peril for Bankers after Crisis," *Investment News,* February 6, 2020, https://www.investmentnews.com; Bloomberg News, "Ex-Wells Fargo Leaders Face $59 Million in Fines over Scandals," *Investment News,* January 13, 2020, https://www.investmentnews.com; E. Glazer and A. Hufford, "Wells Fargo: Top Executives Won't Get Cash Bonus for 2016," *The Wall Street Journal,* March 1, 2017, https://www.wsj.com.

14 Providing Employee Benefits

Introduction

Even in the best of times, serving the public in a coffee shop can be a stressful job. Add in the challenges of balancing work and family life, and it gets harder. Workers at Starbucks who are dealing with stress and other mental-health concerns now have some help from their employer, thanks to the company's decision to add mental-health benefits to its compensation package. Starbucks will pay for up to 20 in-person or online therapy sessions per year for all workers, including part-timers, as well as members of their immediate families. The company also pays for subscriptions to various self-care apps to help employees enjoy healthy lives. These benefits followed a trial of offering a meditation app, which more than 60,000 employees downloaded.

Besides being on the leading edge of offering mental-health benefits, Starbucks has a total compensation package that includes many more familiar offerings. Employees can choose from various plans for medical, dental, and vision care, as well as life and disability insurance. Starbucks also will match employee contributions to a company-sponsored retirement savings plan. Employees earn paid time off for vacation and sick leave, and salaried workers also are eligible for two personal days off with pay. The company also has paid holidays; store employees who work on a holiday earn one and a half times their regular pay. Some employees are eligible for additional benefits, including paid parental leave, tuition reimbursement, and purchase of transit passes with pretax earnings.

Starbucks' benefits package is a way for the company to make working there rewarding even in difficult times. When restaurants were affected by the COVID-19 epidemic in 2020, the company boosted pay by $3 per hour but also allowed employees to stay home and be paid "catastrophe pay" at their regular pay level.[1]

Starbucks recently added mental-health benefits to its employee compensation package, as well as "catastrophe pay" for those working during the COVID-19 pandemic.

Michele Eve Sandberg/Shutterstock

What Do I Need to Know?

After reading this chapter, you should be able to:

LO 14-1 Discuss the importance of benefits as a part of employee compensation.

LO 14-2 Summarize the types of employee benefits required by law.

LO 14-3 Describe the most common forms of paid leave.

LO 14-4 Identify the kinds of insurance benefits offered by employers.

LO 14-5 Define the types of retirement plans offered by employers.

LO 14-6 Describe how organizations use other benefits to match employees' wants and needs.

LO 14-7 Explain how to choose the contents of an employee benefits package.

LO 14-8 Summarize the regulations affecting how employers design and administer benefits programs.

LO 14-9 Discuss the importance of effectively communicating the nature and value of benefits to employees.

Establishing programs for workers' comfort and self-care goes beyond pay for work done. From an HR standpoint, they are a part of employees' total rewards. In general, a total compensation package includes some combination of wages or salary, incentive pay, and benefits. The term for compensation in forms other than cash is **employee benefits.** More widely used examples of benefits include employer-paid health insurance, retirement savings plans, and paid vacations, among a wide range of possibilities.

Employee Benefits Compensation in forms other than cash.

This chapter describes the contents of an employee benefits package and the way organizations administer employee benefits. We begin by discussing the important role of benefits as a part of employee compensation. The following sections define major types of employee benefits: benefits required by law, paid leave, insurance policies, retirement plans, and other benefits. We then discuss how to choose which of these alternatives to include in an employee benefits package so that it contributes to meeting the organization's goals. The next section summarizes the regulations affecting how employers design and administer benefits programs. Finally, we explain why and how organizations should effectively communicate with employees about their benefits.

The Role of Employee Benefits

LO 14-1 Discuss the importance of benefits as a part of employee compensation.

As a part of the total compensation paid to employees, benefits serve functions similar to pay. Benefits contribute to attracting, retaining, and motivating employees. The variety of possible benefits also helps employers tailor their compensation to the kinds of employees they need. Different employees look for different types of benefits. Employers need to examine their benefits package regularly to see whether they meet the needs of today. At the same time, benefits packages are more complex than pay structures, so benefits are harder for employees to understand and appreciate. Even if employers spend large sums on benefits, if employees do not understand how to use them or why they are valuable, the cost of the benefits will be largely wasted.[2] Employers need to communicate effectively so that the benefits succeed in motivating employees.

Employees have come to expect that benefits will help them maintain economic security. Social Security contributions, pensions, and retirement savings plans help employees prepare for their retirement. Insurance plans help to protect employees from unexpected costs such as hospital bills. This important role of benefits is one reason benefits are subject to government regulation. Some benefits, such as Social Security, are required by law. Other regulations establish requirements that benefits must meet to obtain the most favorable tax treatment. Later in this chapter we will describe some of the most significant regulations affecting benefits.

Even though many kinds of benefits are not required by law, they have become so common that today's employees expect them. Many employers find that attracting qualified workers requires them to provide medical and retirement benefits of some sort. A large employer without such benefits would be highly unusual and would have difficulty competing in the labor market. Still, the nature of the benefits package changes over time, as we will discuss at various points throughout the chapter.

Like other forms of compensation, benefits impose significant costs. On average, out of every dollar spent on compensation, nearly 30 cents goes to benefits. As Figure 14.1 shows, this

Visit your instructor's Connect® course and access your eBook to view this video.

"We see the HTA triggering a marketplace of competition where buyers of health care challenge providers of health care to compete with each other in a better way."
—Robert Andrews, CEO
Health Transformation Alliance

Video produced for the Center for Executive Succession in the Darla Moore School of Business at the University of South Carolina by Coal Powered Filmworks.

FIGURE 14.1
Benefits as a Percentage of Total Compensation

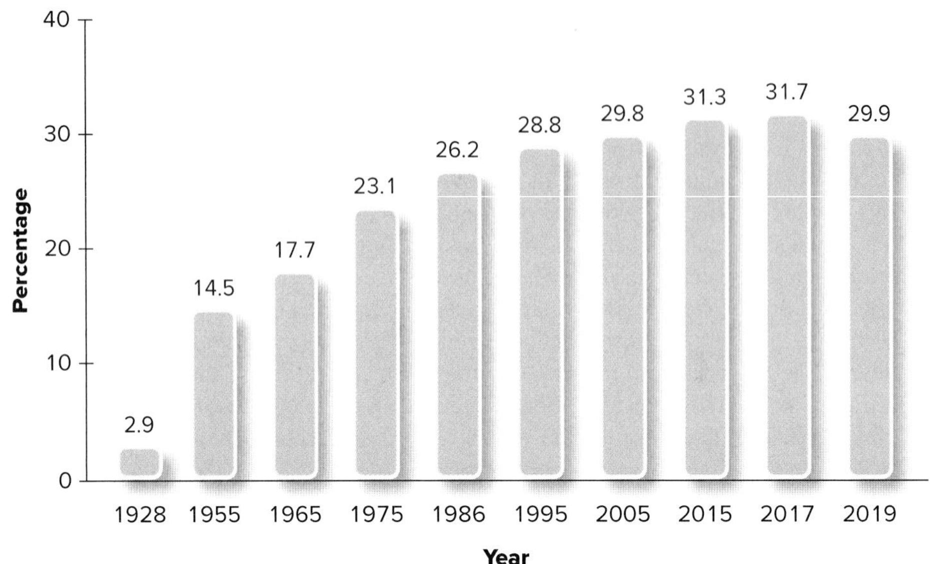

Source: Bureau of Labor Statistics, "Employer Costs for Employee Compensation," http://data.bls.gov, accessed May 7, 2020.

share has grown over the past decades, despite the dip experienced in 2019. As a result of the COVID-19 pandemic in 2020, it is likely health care costs will push benefit costs higher over the next several years. Regardless of current economic challenges, these numbers indicate that an organization managing its labor costs must pay careful attention to the cost of its employee benefits.

Why do organizations pay a growing share of compensation in the form of benefits? It would be simpler to pay all compensation in cash and let employees buy their own insurance and contribute to their own savings plans. That arrangement would also give employees greater control over what their compensation buys. However, several forces have made benefits a significant part of compensation packages. One is that laws require employers to provide certain benefits, such as contributions to Social Security and unemployment insurance. Also, tax laws can make benefits favorable to employees. For example, employees do not pay income taxes on most benefits they receive, but they pay income taxes on cash compensation. Therefore, an employee who receives a $1,000 raise "takes home" less than the full $1,000, but an employee who receives an additional $1,000 worth of benefits receives the full benefits. Another cost advantage of paying benefits is that employers, especially large ones, often can get a better deal on insurance or other programs than employees can obtain on their own. Finally, some employers assemble creative benefits packages that set them apart in the competition for talent. When tax cuts passed in 2017 increased AutoNation's earnings, it seized the opportunity to raise total compensation in an attention-getting way, purchasing cancer insurance to cover a disease that can be financially as well as physically devastating. Similarly, the Recovery Project, a provider of physical and occupational therapy, is a small business with limited means. Instead of competing in the labor market with wages alone, it shares profits in fun ways such as giving employees electronics or tickets to sporting events.[3]

LO 14-2 Summarize the types of employee benefits required by law.

Benefits Required by Law

The federal and state governments require various forms of social insurance to protect workers from the financial hardships of being out of work. In general, Social Security provides support for retired workers, unemployment insurance assists laid-off workers, and

TABLE 14.1
Benefits Required by Law

BENEFIT	EMPLOYER REQUIREMENT
Social Security	Flat payroll tax on employees and employers
Unemployment insurance	Payroll tax on employers that depends on state requirements and experience rating
Workers' compensation insurance	Provide coverage according to state requirements. Premiums depend on experience rating
Family and medical leave	Up to 12 weeks of unpaid leave for childbirth, adoption, or serious illness
Health care	For employers with at least 50 employees, payment of a penalty to the federal government if the employer does not meet conditions for providing health insurance benefits

workers' compensation insurance provides benefits and services to workers injured on the job. Employers must also provide unpaid leave for certain family and medical needs. Because these benefits are required by law, employers cannot gain an advantage in the labor market by offering them, nor can they design the nature of these benefits. Rather, the emphasis must be on complying with the details of the law. Table 14.1 summarizes legally required benefits.

Social Security

In 1935 the federal Social Security Act established old-age insurance and unemployment insurance. Congress later amended the act to add survivor's insurance (1939), disability insurance (1956), hospital insurance (Medicare Part A, 1965), and medical insurance (Medicare Part B, 1965) for older individuals. Together, the law and its amendments created what is now the Old Age, Survivors, Disability, and Health Insurance (OASDHI) program, informally known as **Social Security.** This program covers over 90% of U.S. employees. The main exceptions are railroad and federal, state, and local government employees, who often have their own plans.

Social Security
The federal Old Age, Survivors, Disability, and Health Insurance (OASDHI) program, which combines old age (retirement) insurance, survivor's insurance, disability insurance, hospital insurance (Medicare Part A), and medical insurance (Medicare Part B) for older individuals.

Workers who meet eligibility requirements receive the retirement benefits according to their age and earnings history. If they elect to begin receiving benefits at full retirement age, they can receive full benefits, or if they elect to begin receiving benefits at age 62, they receive benefits at a permanently reduced level. The full retirement age rises with birth year: a person born in 1940 reaches full retirement age at 65 years and 6 months, and a person born in 1960 or later reaches full retirement age at 67. The benefit amount rises with the person's past earnings, but the level goes up very little after a certain level. In 2020 the maximum benefit for a worker who retires at full retirement age was $3,011 per month and $3,790 for a worker who delays retirement until age 70. The government increases the payments each year according to the growth in the consumer price index. Also, spouses of covered earners receive benefits, even if they have no covered earnings. They receive either the benefit associated with their own earnings or one-half of the amount received by the covered earner, whichever is greater.

Benefits may be reduced if the worker is still earning wages above a maximum, called the *exempt amount.* In 2020 the exempt amount was $18,240 for beneficiaries under the full retirement age. A beneficiary in that age range who earns more than the exempt amount sees a reduction in his or her benefit. The amount of the reduction is $1 for every $2 the person earns above the exempt amount. For example, a 63-year-old who earned $20,240 would have earned $2,000 above the exempt amount, so the person's Social Security benefits would be reduced by $1,000. During the year a worker reaches full retirement age, the maximum untaxed earnings are $48,600 (in 2020), and benefits are reduced $1 for every $3 in earnings. Beginning in the month they reach full retirement age, workers face no reduction in benefits for earning above the exempt amount. For workers below that age, the penalty increases the incentive to retire or at least reduce the number of hours worked. Adding to this incentive, Social Security benefits are free from federal income taxes and free from state taxes in about one-third of the states.

Employers and employees share the cost of Social Security through a payroll tax. The percentage is set by law and has changed from time to time. In 2020, employers and employees each paid a tax of 6.2%, or 12.4% total, on the first $137,700 of the employee's earnings. Of that, the majority goes to OASDI, and 2.9% of earnings go to Medicare (Part A). For earnings above $137,700, only the 2.9% for Medicare is assessed, with half paid by the employer and half paid by the employee. For earnings above $200,000, the employer must withhold an additional Medicare tax of 0.9% from the employee's pay.

Unemployment Insurance

Unemployment Insurance
A federally mandated program to minimize the hardships of unemployment through payments to unemployed workers, help in finding new jobs, and incentives to stabilize employment.

Along with OASDHI, the Social Security Act of 1935 established a program of **unemployment insurance.** This program has four objectives related to minimizing the hardships of unemployment. It provides payments to offset lost income during involuntary unemployment, and it helps unemployed workers find new jobs. The payment of unemployment insurance taxes gives employers an incentive to stabilize employment. And providing workers with income during short-term layoffs preserves investments in worker skills because workers can afford to wait to return to their employer, rather than start over with another organization. Technically, the federal government left it to each state's discretion to establish an unemployment insurance program. At the same time, the Social Security Act created a tax incentive structure that quickly led every state to establish the program.

Most of the funding for unemployment insurance comes from federal and state taxes on employers. Employers who pay their state taxes currently pay a federal tax that after tax credits generally equals 0.6% of the first $7,000 of each employee's wages. The state tax rate varies from less than 1% to more than 18%, and the taxable wage base ranges from $7,000 to $47,300, so the amount paid depends a great deal on where the company is located.[4] Also, some states charge new employers whatever rate is the average for their industry, so the amount of tax paid in those states also depends on the type of business. In the recession of 2008–2009, layoffs were so widespread that unemployment insurance funds were drained and many states dramatically hiked premiums for unemployment insurance. In the COVID-19 pandemic of 2020, more than 30 million people lost their jobs and filed for unemployment benefits—a number that dwarfed the unemployment claims filed a little more than a decade before. Even with extensive intervention by the federal government to subsidize and shore up state unemployment funds, as of this writing it's unclear what toll the pandemic will take on the unemployment insurance funds of the states hardest hit by the outbreak.[5]

Experience Rating
The number of employees a company has laid off in the past and the cost of providing them with unemployment benefits.

No state imposes the same tax rate on every employer in the state. The size of the unemployment insurance tax imposed on each employer depends on the employer's **experience rating**—the number of employees the company laid off in the past and the cost of providing them with unemployment benefits. Employers with a history of laying off a large share of their workforce pay higher taxes than those with few layoffs. In some states, an employer with very few layoffs may pay no state tax. In contrast, an employer with a poor experience rating could pay a tax as high as 5.4% to 15.4%, depending on the state. The use of experience ratings gives employers some control over the cost of unemployment insurance. Careful human resource planning can minimize layoffs and keep their experience rating favorable. For a look at some challenges of doing this, see "HR How To."

To receive benefits, workers must meet four conditions:

1. They meet requirements demonstrating they had been employed (often 52 weeks or four quarters of work at a minimum level of pay).
2. They are available for work.

Opting for Furloughs

A company facing an unplanned-for drop in demand might decide to reduce its workforce by laying off workers. The layoff generally ends the obligation to pay wages or salaries and to continue benefits, except for already-earned benefits such as paid time off. Then if business improves, the company must bear the expense of recruiting and selecting new workers. Employers might wish to avoid the hiring process, especially if they expect the downturn to last only a few months. This was the case for many employers during the onset of the COVID-19 pandemic. Many considered a furlough instead of layoffs.

Furloughs resemble layoffs, but some legal requirements for pay and benefits differ. Managers should consider the general issues raised here, focused on U.S. law, while keeping in mind that each state and many localities have stricter requirements and that laws may change. Also, employers may be parties to contracts limiting what they may do.

A furlough differs from a layoff in how it redefines the company's relationship with the employee. In a layoff, the employee goes off the payroll, and the employment relationship ends. In a furlough, the company is saying it temporarily will not use the employee's services or temporarily will reduce the employee's hours. Whether the furloughed employee receives pay depends on whether the employee is "exempt" as described in Chapter 12. An exempt employee is not paid by hours worked, so a furloughed exempt employee must be paid in full for any week in which the employee works at all, although in many cases, the company can lower that salary.

Some employers continue paying for health insurance. If they do not, the workers likely have a right to continue paying for coverage under the company's plan for some period of time. If the employee is participating in a retirement plan under an agreement that calls for employer contributions, these would continue, unless the employer formally amends the plan. Also, an employer may ask furloughed workers to use vacation or other paid time off; this can be required or optional.

Furloughed employees, even those working reduced hours, may qualify for unemployment compensation when not being paid for time off. This means the company's experience rating may rise, causing an increase in taxes. (In the case of furloughs and layoffs associated with COVID-19, some state legislatures eased this impact.) Given that furloughs, like layoffs, involve costs, employers might prefer to consider other ways to reduce expenses, such as reducing bonuses, travel expenses, and optional employee benefits.

Questions

1. From the employer's perspective, how do furloughs affect employee benefits?
2. Suppose you had worked in the HR department of a five-store clothing retailer during the start of the COVID-19 pandemic. Would you have recommended layoffs, furloughs, or neither? Explain your reasoning.

Sources: Doug Holmes and David Baffa, "Unemployment Insurance and Furlough Q&As," *Society for Human Resource Management,* April 16, 2020, https://www.shrm.org; Patrick W. Spangler, "Conducting Layoffs and Furloughs Resulting from COVID-19 Business Impact," *National Law Review,* April 16, 2020, https://www.natlawreview.com; Isaac Mamaysky, "Furloughs: Weighing the Unemployment Costs and Benefits," *Law360,* April 6, 2020, https://www.law360.com; Fatima Hussein, "Covid-19 Forces Employers to Weigh Layoffs versus Furloughs," *Daily Labor Report,* March 25, 2020, https://news.bloomberglaw.com.

3. They are actively seeking work. This requirement includes registering at the local unemployment office.
4. They were not discharged for cause (such as willful misconduct), did not quit voluntarily, and are not out of work because of a labor dispute (such as a union member on strike).

Workers who meet these conditions receive benefits at the level set by the state—typically about half the person's previous earnings—for a period of 26 weeks. States with a sustained unemployment rate above a particular threshold or significantly above recent levels also offer extended benefits for up to 13 weeks. Sometimes Congress funds emergency extended benefits, which happened during the COVID-19 pandemic. All states have minimum and maximum weekly benefit levels.

Workers' Compensation

Workers' Compensation
State programs that provide benefits to workers who suffer work-related injuries or illnesses, or to their survivors.

Decades ago, workers who suffered work-related injury or illness had to bear the cost unless they won a lawsuit against their employer. Those who sued often lost the case because of the defenses available to employers. Today, the states have passed **workers' compensation** laws, which help workers with the expenses resulting from job-related accidents and illnesses.[6] These laws operate under a principle of *no-fault liability,* meaning that an employee does not need to show that the employer was grossly negligent in order to receive compensation, and the employer is protected from lawsuits. The employer loses this protection if it intentionally contributes to a dangerous workplace. Employees are not eligible if their injuries are self-inflicted or if they result from intoxication or "willful disregard of safety rules."[7]

About 9 out of 10 U.S. workers are covered by state workers' compensation laws, with the level of coverage varying from state to state. The benefits fall into four major categories: (1) disability income, (2) medical care, (3) death benefits, and (4) rehabilitative services. The amount of income varies from state to state but is typically two-thirds of the worker's earnings before the disability. The benefits are tax free.

The states differ in terms of how they fund workers' compensation insurance. Some states have a single state fund. Most states allow employers to purchase coverage from private insurance companies. Most also permit self-funding by employers. The cost of the workers' compensation insurance depends on the kinds of occupations involved, the state where the company is located, and the employer's experience rating. Premiums for low-risk occupations may be less than 1% of payroll. For some of the most hazardous occupations, the cost may be as high as 100% of payroll. Costs also vary from state to state, so that one state's program requires higher premiums than another state's program. As with unemployment insurance, unfavorable experience ratings lead to higher premiums. Organizations can minimize the cost of this benefit by keeping workplaces safe and making employees and their managers conscious of safety issues, as discussed in Chapter 3.

Unpaid Family and Medical Leave

Family and Medical Leave Act (FMLA)
Federal law requiring organizations with 50 or more employees to provide up to 12 weeks of unpaid leave after childbirth or adoption; to care for a seriously ill family member or for an employee's own serious illness; or to take care of urgent needs that arise when a spouse, child, or parent in the National Guard or Reserve is called to active duty.

In the United States, unpaid leave is required by law for certain family needs. Specifically, the **Family and Medical Leave Act (FMLA)** of 1993 requires organizations with 50 or more employees within a 75-mile radius to provide as much as 12 weeks of unpaid leave after childbirth or adoption; to care for a seriously ill child, spouse, or parent, for an employee's own serious illness; or to take care of urgent needs that arise when a spouse, child, or parent in the National Guard or Reserve is called to active duty. In addition, if a family member (child, spouse, parent, or next of kin) is injured while serving on active military duty, the employee may take up to 26 weeks of unpaid leave under FMLA. Employers must also guarantee these employees the same or a comparable job when they return to work. The law does not cover employees who have less than one year of service, work fewer than 25 hours per week, or are among the organization's 10% highest paid. The 12 weeks of unpaid leave amount to a smaller benefit than is typical of Japan and most countries in Western Europe. Japan and West European nations typically require paid family leave. In a recent survey of 41 countries conducted by the Organisation for Economic Co-Operation and Development (OECD), the United States ranked *last* in government-mandated paid leave for new parents. But some progress is being made. Several states now require companies to give employees paid leave, and President Trump recently signed legislation that would provide federal workers, both women and men, with 12 weeks of paid leave to care for a newborn or adopted child.[8]

Experience with the Family and Medical Leave Act suggests that many employees take unpaid leave (as much as 10% of the workforce at a time), but few employees take the full 12 weeks. About a third of them take days intermittently, and the average length of a leave is 14.2 days. The most common reason for taking a leave was to care for one's own health conditions, especially following a surgery or related to a pregnancy. An obvious reason for not taking the full 12 weeks is that not everyone can afford three months without pay, especially when responsible for the expenses that accompany childbirth, adoption, or serious illness. Nevertheless, employers do need to keep track of leave requests to prevent abuse of the policy.

When employees experience pregnancy and childbirth, employers must also comply with the Pregnancy Discrimination Act, described in Chapter 3. If an employee is temporarily unable to perform her job due to pregnancy, the employer must treat her in the same way as any other temporarily disabled employee. For example, the employer may provide modified tasks, alternative assignments, disability leave, or leave without pay.

The Family and Medical Leave Act requires companies with 50 or more employees to provide up to 12 weeks of unpaid leave after childbirth or adoption.
Ingram Publishing/SuperStock

HR Analytics & Decision Making

Some organizations that have added or expanded paid family leave have reported that these changes in benefits are associated with improved employee retention. Several years ago, for example, Google expanded its paid parental leave from 12 to 18 weeks, after which the retention rate of mothers following the arrival of a new child increased by 50%. Best Buy reported a 14-percentage-point decline in turnover (falling from 46% to 32% over four years) following its introduction of a paid-leave program.

Organizations also have measured other benefits, including improved recruiting and better health among employees and their family members. In a survey by Deloitte, 77% of employees said paid parental leave affected their choice of an employer. In addition, half of respondents said they would prefer more parental leave over a pay increase. And after Nestlé put in place a policy expanding 26 weeks of parental leave (14 of them paid), parents participating in the program took their children to the doctor for sick visits less often, and health care costs for these employees' infants were 12% lower.

These results do not prove that paid leave causes lower turnover and health care expenses, because the companies did not set up control groups of employees not receiving the benefits. Nevertheless, the companies assert the logic that employees who can take time for their children's needs will be more satisfied with their jobs and therefore likelier to stay with the company.

Questions

1. What could these companies have learned if, before rolling out new benefits to the whole workforce, they had set up a test of their paid leave in which some employees were in a control group not receiving the benefits? Why do you think none of the companies did this?
2. What could these companies learn if they also had data on the costs they bore to offer paid family or parental leave?

Sources: Alex Van Abbema, "How Best Buy Cut Its Staff Turnover More than 30 Percent in Four Years," *Minneapolis/St. Paul Business Journal*, December 6, 2018, https://www.bizjournals.com/twincities; Kathryn Mayer, "Major Employers Join Forces to Move the Needle on Paid Leave," *Employee Benefit News*, November 15, 2018, http://www.benefitnews.com; "Paid Family and Medical Leave: Good for Business," National Partnership for Women & Families, September 2018, http://www.nationalpartnership.org; Terri L. Rhodes, "Paid Family Leave Is Increasing Employee Retention Rates," *Risk & Insurance*, July 18, 2018, https://riskandinsurance.com.

Health Care Benefits

Patient Protection and Affordable Care Act Health care reform law passed in 2010 that includes incentives and penalties for employers providing health insurance as a benefit.

In 2010, Congress passed the **Patient Protection and Affordable Care Act,** a complex package of changes in how health care is to be paid for, including requirements for insurance companies, incentives and penalties for employers providing health insurance as a benefit, expansion of public funding, and creation of health insurance exchanges as an option for the sale of health insurance. The law does not require companies to offer health insurance benefits, but it does require medium-sized and large companies to choose between offering health insurance that meets its standards or paying a penalty. It also includes requirements for providing information to employees.

Whether an organization must make the choice to cover employees or pay a penalty depends on the number of full-time employees. In general, to avoid a penalty, an organization with at least 50 full-time employees (or full- and part-time employees equivalent to 50 or more) must offer affordable health care coverage of at least minimum value. They must provide this coverage to at least 95% of full-time employees. Organizations with at least 50 employees that do not meet these requirements must pay an Employer Shared Responsibility Penalty. The amount is adjusted for inflation each year; in 2020, it was $2,570 times the number of full-time employees after the first 30.

Employers with fewer than 50 employees are not subject to the Employer Shared Responsibility Penalty. However, the Affordable Care Act tries to encourage these small employers to offer health coverage. They may buy health insurance from the Small Business Health Options Program (SHOP), available through brokers who registered with SHOP. In addition, organizations with fewer than 25 employees may qualify for tax credits. If they buy insurance through the SHOP Marketplace, they may be eligible for a credit of up to 50% of the insurance premiums.

Employers that provide health coverage to at least 250 employees must also meet reporting requirements. On the W-2 forms that report employees' earnings, they must indicate the value of the health benefits in terms of the cost paid by employer and employee. Organizations with fewer employees also may report this information–and may want to, as a way to show employees the value of the benefits they receive.

Because the law is complex, HR professionals must continue to educate themselves about the requirements and communicate often with employees, many of whom may be worried about how the law affects their health care benefits. A useful source of information continues to be the government's website at www.healthcare.gov.

Optional Benefits Programs

Other types of benefits are optional. These include various kinds of insurance, retirement plans, and paid leave. Figure 14.2 shows the percentage of full-time workers having access to the most common employee benefits. (Part-time workers often have access to and receive fewer benefits.) The most widely offered benefits are paid leave for vacations and holidays, life and medical insurance, and retirement plans. In general, benefits packages at smaller companies tend to be more limited than at larger companies.

Benefits such as health insurance often extend to employees' dependents. Traditionally these benefits have covered employees, their spouses, and dependent children. Today many employers also cover *domestic partners,* as defined either by local law or by the companies themselves. Typically a domestic partner is an adult nonrelative who lives with the employee in a relationship defined as permanent and financially interdependent. Benefits provided to domestic partners do not have the same tax advantages as benefits provided to spouses. The partner's benefits are taxed as wages of the employee receiving the benefits. Despite this

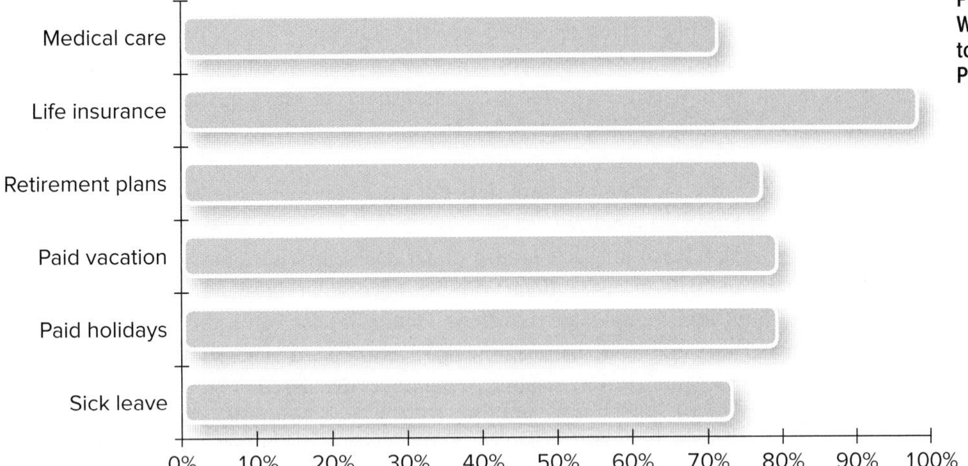

FIGURE 14.2
Percentage of Full-Time Workers with Access to Selected Benefit Programs

Source: Bureau of Labor Statistics, "Employee Benefits in the United States, March 2019," news release, September 19, 2019, https://www.bls.gov.

difference in tax treatment, offering domestic-partner benefits has let employers provide employees in a same-sex relationship with benefit packages comparable to those for employees married to someone of the opposite sex. In 2015, however, the Supreme Court removed legal barriers to same-sex marriage nationwide. Since then, the trend has been a shift away from benefits for domestic partners and toward benefits for spouses regardless of gender. The latter approach is simpler to administer because it spares the employer from figuring out different procedures according to the laws of each state.[9]

Paid Leave

LO 14-3 Describe the most common forms of paid leave.

The major categories of paid leave are vacations, holidays, and sick leave. Employers also should establish policies for other situations that may require time off. Many organizations provide paid leave for jury duty, funerals of family members, and military duty. Some organizations provide for other paid leave, such as time off to vote or to donate blood. Establishing policies communicates the organization's values, clarifies what employees can expect, and prevents situations in which unequal treatment leads to claims of unfairness.

Paid time off is a way for employees to enjoy time with their families and to refresh their bodies and spirits. Is paid time off an important factor for you when accepting a position?
moorboard/SuperStock

At first blush, paid vacation, holidays, sick leave, and other paid leave may not seem to make economic sense. The employer pays the employee for time spent not working, so the employer receives nothing in return for the pay. Some employers may see little direct advantage. This may be the reason Western European countries require a minimum number of paid vacation days, with new employees receiving 25 or 30 days off in many countries. The United States, in contrast, has no such legal requirement. According to the National Compensation Survey Conducted by the U.S. Bureau of Labor Statistics four times a year, U.S. workers average 10 days of paid vacation annually after one year of service and 15 days of paid vacation after five years.[10] It is up to

U.S. employers to decide whether offering paid leave to workers provides a competitive advantage in recruiting and retaining employees.

Paid holidays are time off on specified days in addition to vacation time. In Western Europe and the United States, employees typically have about 10 paid holidays each year, regardless of length of service. The most common paid holidays in the United States are New Year's Day, Memorial Day, Independence Day, Labor Day, Thanksgiving Day, and Christmas Day.

Sick-leave programs pay employees for days not worked because of illness. The amount of sick leave is often based on length of service, so that it accumulates over time—for example, one day added to sick leave for each month of service. Employers must decide how many sick days to grant and whether to let them continue accumulating year after year. If sick days accumulate without limit, employees can "save" them in case of disability. If an employee becomes disabled, the employee can use up the accumulated sick days, receiving full pay rather than smaller payments from disability insurance, discussed later. Some employers let sick days accumulate for only a year, and unused sick days "disappear" at year's end. This may provide an unintended incentive to use up sick days. Some healthy employees may call in sick near the end of the year so that they can obtain the benefit of the paid leave before it disappears. Employers might counter this tendency by paying employees for some or all of their unused sick days at the end of the year or when the employees retire or resign.

An organization's policies for time off may include other forms of paid and unpaid leave. For a workforce that values flexibility, the organization may offer paid *personal days,* days off that employees may schedule according to their personal needs, with the supervisor's approval. Typically organizations offer a few personal days in addition to sick leave. *Floating holidays* are paid holidays that vary from year to year. The organization may schedule floating holidays so that they extend a Tuesday or Thursday holiday into a long weekend. Organizations may also give employees discretion over the scheduling of floating holidays.

The most flexible approach to time off is to grant each employee a bank of *paid time off,* in which the employer pools personal days, sick days, and vacation days for employees to use as they choose. This flexibility is especially attractive to younger workers, who tend to rate work/life balance as one of the most important sources of job satisfaction. For the employer, paid time off (PTO) removes the need to keep records of why employees are absent—sick, on vacation, or on personal business. This also avoids awkwardness for employees who don't feel well or have urgent personal matters but have used up their time off for such needs. With these advantages in mind, one-third to more than half of employers have reported offering PTO benefits.[11]

Employers should also establish policies for leaves without pay—for example, leaves of absence to pursue nonwork goals or to meet family needs. Unpaid leave is an employee benefit because the employee usually retains seniority and benefits during the leave.

LO 14-4 Identify the kinds of insurance benefits offered by employers.

Group Insurance

As we noted earlier, rates for group insurance are typically lower than for individual policies. Also, unlike wages and salaries, insurance benefits are not subject to income tax. When employees receive insurance as a benefit, rather than higher pay so they can buy their own insurance, employees can get more for their money. Because of this, most employees value group insurance. The most common types of insurance offered as employee benefits are medical, life, and disability insurance. As noted in the earlier discussion of benefits required under law, in 2014 it became a federal requirement that medium-sized and large businesses offer health insurance to their employees or pay a penalty. For smaller businesses, medical insurance is an optional benefit, and businesses continue to have many choices in the types of coverage they offer.

Medical Insurance Although few employees fully appreciate what health insurance costs the employer, most value this benefit and look for it when they are contemplating a job offer.[12] As Figure 14.2 shows, more than 70% of full-time employees receive medical benefits. The policies typically cover three basic types of medical expenses: hospital expenses, surgical expenses, and visits to physicians. Some employers offer additional coverage, such as dental care, vision care, birthing centers, and prescription drug programs. Under the Mental Health Parity and Addiction Equity Act of 2008, if health insurance plans for employees include coverage for mental health care, that care must include the same scope of financial and treatment coverage as treatment for other illnesses. This means that deductibles, copayments, coinsurance, and the number of covered days for hospitalization must be the same for treating mental illness as for other illnesses. This law exempts companies with fewer than 50 employees. Companies in states with stricter requirements must also meet the state requirements. While the law does not require health insurance to include coverage of mental health care, most insurance plans sold to large groups already included such coverage when the law took effect.[13]

Employers that offer medical insurance must meet the requirements of the **Consolidated Omnibus Budget Reconciliation Act (COBRA)** of 1985. This federal law requires employers to permit employees to extend their health insurance coverage at group rates for up to 36 months following a "qualifying event." Qualifying events include termination (except for gross misconduct), a reduction in hours that leads to loss of health insurance, and the employee's death (in which case the surviving spouse or dependent child would extend the coverage). To extend the coverage, the employee or the surviving spouse or dependent must pay for the insurance, but the payments are at the group rate. These employees and their families must have access to the same services as those who did not lose their health insurance.

Consolidated Omnibus Budget Reconciliation Act (COBRA)
Federal law that requires employers to permit employees or their dependents to extend their health insurance coverage at group rates for up to 36 months following a qualifying event, such as a layoff, reduction in hours, or the employee's death.

As we will discuss later in this chapter, health insurance is a significant share of benefits costs at U.S. organizations. Until the past few years, the cost of employee health benefits was rising faster—at times much faster—than other compensation, including wages and salaries.[14] Figure 14.3 shows that the United States spends much more of its total wealth on health care than other countries do. Most Western European countries have nationalized health systems, but the majority of Americans with coverage for health care expenses get it through their own or a family member's employer. The increase in the number of employees who lacked insurance because their employers could not afford this benefit was a major reason cited for passage of the Patient Protection and Affordable Care Act.

Employers have looked for ways to control the cost of health care coverage while keeping this valuable benefit. They have used variations of managed care, employee-driven savings, and promotion of employee wellness:

- With *managed care,* the insurer plays a role in decisions about health care, aimed at avoiding unnecessary procedures. The insurer may conduct claims review, studying claims to determine whether procedures are effective for the type of illness or injury. Patients may be required to obtain approval before hospital admissions, and the insurer may require alternatives to hospital stays—for example, outpatient surgery or home health care.
- A **health maintenance organization (HMO)** is a health care plan that requires patients to receive their medical care from the HMO's health care professionals, many of whom are paid a flat salary, and provides all services on a prepaid basis. In other words, the premiums paid for the HMO cover all the patient's visits and procedures, without an additional payment from the patient. By paying physicians a salary, rather than a fee for each service, the HMO hopes to remove any incentive to provide more services than the patients really need. HMO coverage tends to cost less than traditional health insurance.

Health Maintenance Organization (HMO)
A health care plan that requires patients to receive their medical care from the HMO's health care professionals, who are often paid a flat salary, and provides all services on a prepaid basis.

FIGURE 14.3
Health Care Costs in Various Countries

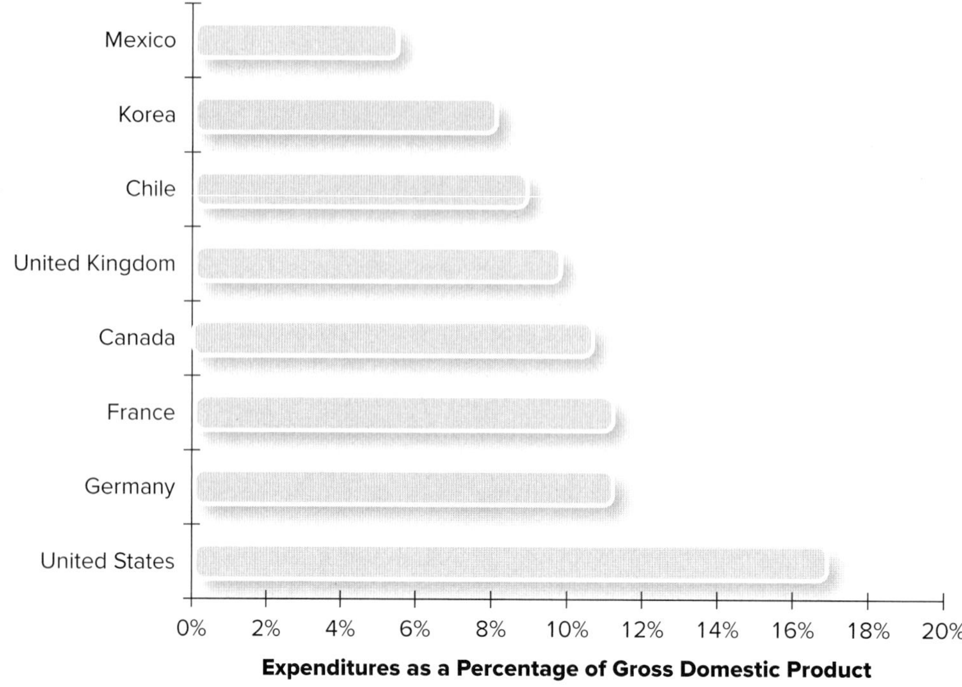

Source: Organisation for Economic Co-operation and Development, "Health Spending," OECD Data, https://data.oecd.org, accessed May 7, 2020.

The downside is that employees sometimes complain that cost-control incentives work so well that they are denied access to services they actually need.

Preferred Provider Organization (PPO)
A health care plan that contracts with health care professionals to provide services at a reduced fee and gives patients financial incentives to use network providers.

Flexible Spending Account
Employee-controlled pretax earnings set aside to pay for certain eligible expenses, such as health care expenses, during the same year.

High-deductible Health Plans (HDHPs)
Health care plans that provide incentives for employees to make decisions that help lower health care costs.

- A **preferred provider organization (PPO)** is a health care plan that contracts with health care professionals to provide services at a reduced fee. Often, the PPO does not require employees to use providers in the network, but it pays a larger share of the cost of services from PPO providers. For example, the employee might pay 10% of the cost of a test by an in-network provider and 20% if the employee goes out of the PPO network. PPOs are the most widely used health plan among U.S. employers. A recent survey by the Kaiser Family Foundation found that 44% of workers with health insurance were enrolled in PPOs, compared with 19% in HMOs.[15]
- With a **flexible spending account,** employees set aside a portion of pretax earnings to pay for eligible expenses. In particular, a *medical savings account* lets employees use their pretax savings to pay for qualified health care expenses (for example, payment of premiums). To avoid taxation, the money in the account must meet IRS requirements. Contributions to this account may not exceed a specified limit ($2,750 in 2020) and must be designated in advance. The money in the account may be spent on health care expenses of the employee and employee's dependents during the plan year. At the end of the year, remaining funds in the account—with limited exceptions—revert to the employer. The major advantage of flexible spending accounts is that the money in the account is not taxed, so employees will have more take-home pay. But if they do not use all the money in the flexible spending account, they lose the amount they do not spend. Therefore, employees are most likely to benefit from a flexible spending account if they have predictable health care expenses, such as insurance premiums.
- **High-deductible health plans (HDHPs)** are intended to provide health coverage in a way that gets employees involved as consumers making decisions to lower costs. An HDHP

typically brings together insurance with a high deductible and a medical savings account with a specified limit ($2,700 in 2020) that the employee contributes to as a payroll deduction. The difference between a flexible spending account and a savings account linked to an HDHP is that the employee may carry over the dollar amount in the HDHP savings account rather than lose the savings balance at the end of the year. The potential to reduce the cost of providing health insurance has made HDHPs an attractive option for employers, especially large companies. The share of employees enrolled in HDHPs has been rising, reaching 30% in 2019.[16]

- Seeing that small percentages of employees opt for cost-saving HMOs and HDHPs, employers have sought better ways to pay for health care than fees for services. A few are turning to new models that the Affordable Care Act supported as part of Medicare reforms: *accountable care organizations (ACOs)*. Rather than a type of insurance, an ACO is a network of health care providers that practice value-based care; they agree to be paid based on results. Providers might spend more time talking with patients and following up on healthy behaviors, thereby promoting better health at a lower cost than drugs and surgery. UnitedHealthcare has seen lower costs and higher quality result from its willingness to reimburse for this type of care.[17] As more employers learn about ACOs, these may become an attractive alternative to offering cost-focused health benefits.
- An **employee wellness program (EWP)** is a set of communications, activities, and facilities designed to change health-related behaviors in ways that reduce health risks. Typically an EWP aims at specific health risks, such as high blood pressure, high cholesterol levels, smoking, and obesity, by encouraging preventive measures such as exercise and good nutrition. *Passive* programs provide information and services, but no formal support or motivation to use the program. Examples include health education (such as lunchtime courses) and fitness facilities. *Active* wellness programs assume that behavior change requires support and reinforcement along with awareness and opportunity. Such a program may include counselors who tailor programs to individual employees' needs, take baseline measurements (for example, blood pressure and weight), and take follow-up measures for comparison to the baseline. In general, passive health education programs cost less than fitness facilities and active wellness programs.[18] Active methods, however, have shown more impact in promoting healthy behaviors. In recent surveys, employees mostly doubted that they had adopted healthier habits as a result of a wellness program.

Employee Wellness Program (EWP)
A set of communications, activities, and facilities designed to change health-related behaviors in ways that reduce health risks.

Short-Term Disability Insurance
Insurance that pays a percentage of a disabled employee's salary as benefits to the employee for six months or less.

Life Insurance Employers may provide life insurance to employees or offer the opportunity to buy coverage at low group rates. With a *term life insurance* policy, if the employee dies during the term of the policy, the employee's beneficiaries receive a payment called the death benefit. In policies purchased as an employee benefit, the usual death benefit is twice the employee's yearly pay. The policies may provide additional benefits for accidental death and dismemberment (loss of a body part such as a hand or foot). Along with a basic policy, the employer may give employees the option of purchasing additional coverage, usually at a nominal cost.

Many companies offer wellness programs such as yoga classes to encourage employees to reduce their health risks as insurance costs climb for both workers and employers. Wavebreakmedia Ltd/Getty Images

Disability Insurance Employees risk losing their incomes if a disability makes them unable to work. Disability insurance provides protection against this loss of income. Typically, **short-term disability insurance** provides benefits for six months or less.

Long-Term Disability Insurance
Insurance that pays a percentage of a disabled employee's salary after an initial period and potentially for the rest of the employee's life.

Long-term disability insurance provides benefits after that initial period, potentially for the rest of the disabled employee's life. Disability payments are a percentage of the employee's salary—typically 50% to 70%. Payments under short-term plans may be higher. Often the policy sets a maximum amount that may be paid each month. Because its limits make it more affordable, short-term disability coverage is offered by more employers. Fewer than half of employers offer long-term plans.

In planning an employee benefits package, the organization should keep in mind that Social Security includes some long-term disability benefits. To manage benefits costs, the employer should ensure that the disability insurance is coordinated with Social Security and any other programs that help workers who become disabled.

Contributory Plan
Retirement plan funded by contributions from the employer and employee.

Long-Term Care Insurance The cost of long-term care, such as care in a nursing home, can be devastating. Today, with more people living to an advanced age, many people are concerned about affording long-term care. Some employers address this concern by offering long-term care insurance. These policies provide benefits toward the cost of long-term care and related medical expenses.

LO 14-5 Define the types of retirement plans offered by employers.

Retirement Plans

Noncontributory Plan
Retirement plan funded entirely by contributions from the employer.

Defined-Benefit Plan
Pension plan that guarantees a specified level of retirement income.

Despite the image of retired people living on their Social Security checks, Figure 14.4 shows that those checks amount to less than half of a retired person's income. Among persons over age 65, pensions and retirement savings provided a significant share of income in recent years. Employers have no obligation to offer retirement plans beyond the protection of Social Security, but most offer some form of pension or retirement savings plan. About half of employees working for private businesses (that is, nongovernment jobs) have employer-sponsored retirement plans. These plans are most common for higher-earning employees. Among employees earning the top one-fourth of incomes, 90% participate in a retirement plan, and less than half of the employees in the bottom one-fourth have such plans.[19] Retirement plans may be **contributory plans,** meaning they are funded by contributions from the employer and employee, or **noncontributory plans,** meaning all the contributions come from the employer.

Employee Retirement Income Security Act (ERISA)
Federal law that increased the responsibility of pension plan trustees to protect retirees, established certain rights related to vesting and portability, and created the Pension Benefit Guarantee Corporation.

Pension Benefit Guarantee Corporation (PBGC)
Federal agency that insures retirement benefits and guarantees retirees a basic benefit if the employer experiences financial difficulties.

Defined-Benefit Plans Employers have a choice of using retirement plans that define the amount to be paid out after retirement or plans that define the amount the employer will invest each year. A **defined-benefit plan** guarantees a specified level of retirement income. Usually the amount of this defined benefit is calculated for each employee based on the employee's years of service, age, and earnings level (for example, the average of the employee's five highest-earnings years). Using years of service as part of the basis for calculating benefits gives employees an incentive to stay with the organization as long as they can, so it can help to reduce voluntary turnover.

Defined-benefit plans must meet the funding requirements of the **Employee Retirement Income Security Act (ERISA)** of 1974. This law increased the responsibility of pension plan trustees to protect retirees, established certain rights related to vesting (earning a right to receive the pension) and *portability* (being able to move retirement savings when changing employers), and created the **Pension Benefit Guarantee Corporation (PBGC).** The PBGC is the federal agency that insures retirement benefits and guarantees retirees a basic benefit if the employer experiences financial difficulties. To fund the PBGC, employers must make annual contributions at a flat rate per fund participant ($30 for multi-employer plans in 2020). Plans that are *underfunded*—meaning the employer does not contribute enough to the plan each year to meet future obligations—must pay an additional premium tied to the amount by which the plan is underfunded.[20]

With a defined-benefit plan, the employer sets up a pension fund to invest the contributions. As required by ERISA, the employer must contribute enough for the plan to cover all the benefits to be paid out to retirees. If the pension fund earns less than expected, the employer makes up the difference from other sources. If the employer experiences financial difficulties so that it must end or reduce employee pension benefits, the PBGC provides a basic benefit, which does not necessarily cover the full amount promised by the employer's pension plan.

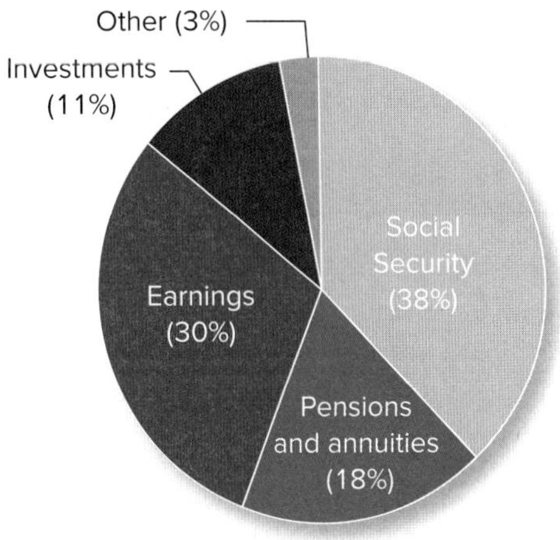

FIGURE 14.4
Sources of Income for Persons 65 and Older

Source: EBRI Databook on Employee Benefits, Chapter 3 (Employee Benefit Research Institute, July 2014), https://www.ebri.org.

Defined-Contribution Plans An alternative to defined benefits is a **defined-contribution plan,** which sets up an individual account for each employee and specifies the size of the investment into that account, rather than the amount to be paid out upon retirement.

The amount the retiree receives will depend on the account's performance. Many kinds of defined-contribution plans are available, including the following:

- *Money purchase plan*—The employer specifies a level of annual contributions (for example, 10% of salary). The contributions are invested, and when the employee retires, he or she is entitled to receive the amount of the contributions plus the investment earnings. ("Money purchase" refers to the fact that when employees retire, they often buy an annuity with the money, rather than taking it as a lump sum.)
- *Profit-sharing and employee stock ownership plans*—As we saw in Chapter 13, incentive pay may take the form of profit sharing and employee stock ownership plans (ESOPs). These payments may be set up so that the money goes into retirement plans. By defining its contributions in terms of stock or a share of profits, the organization has more flexibility to contribute less dollar value in lean years and more in good years.
- *Section 401(k) plans*—Employees contribute a percentage of their earnings, and employers may make matching contributions. The amount employees contribute is not taxed as part of their income until they receive it from the plan. The federal government limits the amount that may be contributed each year. The limit is $19,500 in 2020 and is subject to cost-of-living increases in years after 2018. The contribution limits are higher for persons 50 and older.[21]

Defined-Contribution Plan
Retirement plan in which the employer sets up an individual account for each employee and specifies the size of the investment into that account.

These plans free employers from the risks that investments will not perform as well as expected. They put the responsibility for wise investing squarely on the shoulders of each employee. A defined-contribution plan is also easier to administer. The employer need not calculate payments based on age and service, and payments to the PBGC are not required. Considering the advantages to employers, it is not surprising that a growing share of retirement plans are defined-contribution plans. Since the 1980s, the share of employees participating in defined-benefit plans has been steadily falling, and the share participating in defined-contribution plans has risen. By 2019, just 13% of employees participated in a defined-benefit plan, compared with 45% participating in defined-contribution plans (62% had access to such a plan, versus 17% with access to a defined-benefit plan).[22]

When retirement plans make individual employees responsible for investment decisions, the employees need information about retirement planning (and often help with motivation, too, as described in "HR Oops!"). Retirement savings plans often give employees much control over decisions about when and how much to invest. Many employees do not appreciate

Underused Retirement Benefits

While defined-contribution plans are popular with employers, many employees don't participate or save enough. Worse, the shortfall hits lower-income workers particularly hard. In a survey of retirees by Transamerica, only about one-third had worked for a company that offered retirement benefits, and many retired before the age at which they can receive the maximum Social Security benefits. In a study for Boston College's Center for Retirement Research, roughly 90% of workers in the top one-fifth by income had retirement accounts, while the share was close to 10% for the bottom one-fifth. Furthermore, the balances in these accounts were only about one-third of what they would have been if employees had consistently invested in them.

Reasons for low participation and underfunding include the fact that these plans were introduced recently enough that they didn't exist throughout the careers of older workers. However, other issues are within employers' control. Many employers do not offer the plans, and those that do may not help employees understand the potential of investing even small amounts. And as a practical matter, low-wage employees might need all of their earnings to cover their existing expenses, so they don't see participation as possible.

Concerned employers have many ways to respond. Employers without retirement plans can investigate lower-cost arrangements such as a simplified employee pension plan. Companies can ensure that total compensation packages include benefits that build financial security—for example, adequate insurance. They can provide training or access to educational resources about budgeting, saving, investing, and retirement planning. Research by Charles Schwab found that if employees used an online retirement-planning tool, many were motivated to prepare better. Almost half said they increased contributions to their 401(k). Three in ten said they changed their spending habits, and the same share said they sought additional advice. Employers also can develop employment practices that better retain older workers, perhaps by letting them transition from full-time to part-time work or from fast-paced to less stressful positions.

A new way to help employees prepare is to help them pay down student loans so they can save more. Unum lets employees take cash in exchange for some of their 28 paid days off and use it for student loan repayment, and Hulu pays a fixed amount toward student loans. Fidelity pays up to $2,000 per year per employee with at least six months on the job. The company says turnover among participants in the program is 75% below the level before the program.

Questions

1. For a small business that wants to boost participation in its 401(k) plan, which idea would you recommend that it try first? Why?
2. How can it benefit an employer to ensure that employees fund their retirement plans?

Sources: Michael Hiltzik, "Two Rival Experts Agree—401(k) Plans Haven't Helped You Save Enough for Retirement," *Los Angeles Times,* November 5, 2019, https://www.latimes.com; Catherine Collinson, "Retiree Reflections: Seven Ways Employers Can Do More to Help Workers Prepare for Retirement," *Benefits Quarterly,* third quarter 2019, pp. 8–15; Anne Tergesen, "Employers Try a New Perk: Matching Student Loan Payments with 401(k) Contributions," *The Wall Street Journal,* October 10, 2019, https://www.wsj.com; Nick Otto, "Employees Have Big Retirement Goals: Simple Tools May Help Them Reach Them," *Employee Benefit News,* June 24, 2019, https://www.benefitnews.com.

the importance of beginning to save early in their careers. As Figure 14.5 shows, an employee who invests $3,000 a year ($250 a month) between the ages of 21 and 29 will have far more at age 65 than an employee who invests the same amount between ages 31 and 39. Another important lesson is to diversify investments. Based on investment performance between 1928 and 2016, stocks earned an average of close to 10% per year, bonds earned about 4%, and low-risk (cash) investments earned less than 4%. But in any given year, one of these types of investments might outperform the other. And within the categories of stocks and bonds, it is important to invest in a wide variety of companies. If one company performs poorly, the investments in other companies might perform better. However, studies of investment decisions by employees have found that few employees have followed basic guidelines for diversifying investments among stocks, bonds, and savings accounts according to their age and investment needs.[23] To help employees handle such risks, some organizations provide financial planning as a separate benefit, offer an option to have a professional invest the funds in a 401(k) plan, or direct funds into default investments called target date funds (TDFs), which are geared toward the needs of employees at different life stages.

Also, under the Pension Protection Act of 2006, defined-contribution plans that hold publicly traded securities must give employees the option to sell stock in the company they work for and must offer them at least three investment options other than the company's own stock. The law also allows employers to promote retirement saving by enrolling workers automatically and having their contributions automatically increase along with wages (employees can opt out). Since the law was enacted, automatic enrollment has become widespread.

In spite of these challenges, defined-contribution plans also offer an advantage to employees in today's highly mobile workforce. They do not penalize employees for changing jobs. With these plans, retirement earnings are less related to the number of years an employee stays with a company.

FIGURE 14.5
Value of Retirement Savings Invested at Different Ages

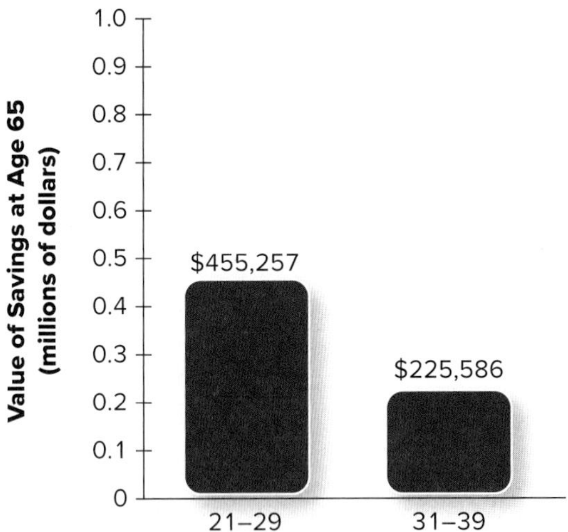

Note: Investment portfolio consists of 60% stocks, 30% bonds, and 10% cash (e.g., money-market funds, bank savings accounts), assuming average rates of return based on historical rates from 1928 to 2016.

Sources: Data from Aswath Damodaran, "Annual Returns on Stocks, T. Bonds and T. Bills: 1928–Current," http://people.stern.nyu.edu/adamodar/New_Home_Page/datafile/histretSP.html.

Cash Balance Plans An increasingly popular way to combine the advantages of defined-benefit plans and defined-contribution plans is to use a **cash balance plan.** This type of retirement plan consists of individual accounts, as in a 401(k) plan. But in contrast to a 401(k), all the contributions come from the employer. Usually, the employer contributes a percentage of the employee's salary, say, 4% or 5%. The money in the cash balance plan earns interest according to a predetermined rate, such as the rate paid on U.S. Treasury bills. Employers guarantee this rate as in a defined-benefit plan. This arrangement helps employers plan their contributions and helps employees predict their retirement benefits. If employees change jobs, they generally can roll over the balance into an individual retirement account.

Cash Balance Plan
Retirement plan in which the employer sets up an individual account for each employee and contributes a percentage of the employee's salary; the account earns interest at a predefined rate.

A switch from traditional defined-benefit plans to cash balance plans, like any major change, requires employers to consider the effects on employees as well as on the organization's bottom line. Defined-benefit plans are most generous to older employees with many years of service, and cash balance plans are most generous to young employees who will have many years ahead in which to earn interest. For an organization with many experienced employees, switching from a defined-benefit plan can produce great savings in pension benefits. In that case, the older workers are the greatest losers, unless the organization adjusts the program to retain their benefits. After IBM switched to a cash-benefit plan, a group of employees filed an age discrimination lawsuit. IBM won the lawsuit on appeal, and the Pension Protection Act of 2006 seeks to clarify the legal requirements of such plans. As a result, some companies may renew their interest in cash balance plans, but IBM has decided to focus on its 401(k) plan.

Government Requirements for Vesting and Communication Along with requirements for funding defined-benefit plans, ERISA specifies a number of requirements related to eligibility for benefits and communication with employees. ERISA guarantees

Vesting Rights
Guarantee that when employees become participants in a pension plan and work a specified number of years, they will receive a pension at retirement age, regardless of whether they remained with the employer.

employees that when they become participants in a pension plan and work a specified number of years, they earn a right to a pension upon retirement. These rights are called **vesting rights.** Employees whose contributions are *vested* have met the requirements (enrolling and length of service) to receive a pension at retirement age, regardless of whether they remained with the employer until that time. Employees' own contributions to their pension plans are always completely vested. In most cases, the vesting of employer-funded pension benefits must take place under one of two schedules selected by the employer:

1. The employer may vest employees after five years and may provide zero vesting until that time.
2. The employer may vest employees over a three- to seven-year period, with at least 20% vesting in the third year and at least an additional 20% in each year after the third year.

These two schedules represent minimum requirements. Employers may vest employees more quickly if they wish. Two less common situations have different vesting requirements. One is a "top-heavy" pension plan, meaning pension benefits for *key employees* (such as highly paid top managers) exceed a government-specified share of total pension benefits. A top-heavy plan requires faster vesting for nonkey employees. Another exception from the usual schedule involves multiemployer pension plans. These plans need not provide vesting until after 10 years of employment.

The intent of vesting requirements is to protect employees by preventing employers from terminating them before they meet retirement age in order to avoid paying pension benefits. In addition, it is illegal for employers to transfer or lay off employees as a way to avoid pension obligations, even if these changes are motivated partly by business need.[24] One way employers may legally try to minimize pension costs is in choosing a vesting schedule. For example, if many employees leave after three or four years of employment, the five-year vesting schedule would minimize pension costs.

Summary Plan Description
Report that describes a pension plan's funding, eligibility requirements, risks, and other details.

ERISA's reporting and disclosure requirements involve the Internal Revenue Service, the Department of Labor, and employees.[25] Within 90 days after employees enter a plan, they must receive a **summary plan description (SPD),** a report that describes the plan's funding, eligibility requirements, risks, and other details. If the employee requests one, the employer must also make available an individual benefit statement, which describes the employee's vested and unvested benefits. Many employers provide such information regularly, without waiting for employee requests. This type of communication helps employees understand and value their retirement benefits.

LO 14-6 Describe how organizations use other benefits to match employees' wants and needs.

"Family-Friendly" Benefits

As employers have recognized the significance of employees' need to manage conflicts between their work and family roles, many have added "family-friendly" benefits to their employee benefits.[26] These benefits include family leave policies and child care. The programs discussed here apply directly to the subset of employees with family responsibilities. However, family-friendly benefits often have spillover effects in the form of loyalty because employees see the benefits as evidence that the organization cares about its people.[27] The following types of benefits are typical:

- *Family leave*—Family or parental leave grants employees time off to care for children and other dependents. As discussed earlier in the chapter, federal law requires 12 weeks of unpaid leave. Companies may choose to offer more generous leave policies, and eight states (California, Connecticut, Massachusetts, New Jersey, New York, Oregon, Rhode Island, Washington) and the District of Columbia have requirements for paid family leave. Recent data from the Census Bureau show only 14% of workers having paid family leave, so employees wanting paid time off to care for a child most often have to make do with paid vacation or sick days. In contrast, most industrialized nations provide paid maternal leave and often paternal leave as well. Tech companies, which compete in a tight labor market, are among the leaders in offering paid maternity and paternity leave. For example, Netflix offers a full year of paid leave for new parents following the birth or adoption of their child; Microsoft offers up to 22 weeks, and Facebook offers four months of paid leave. Facebook also recently announced it is offering employees up to a month of paid leave to care for family members affected by COVID-19.[28]

- *Child care*–Child care benefits may take several forms, requiring different levels of organizational involvement. The lowest level of involvement is for the organization to supply and help employees collect information about the cost and quality of available child care. At the next level, organizations provide vouchers or discounts for employees to use at existing child care facilities. At the highest level of involvement, the employer provides child care at or near the work site. Staffing a child care facility is costly and involves important liability concerns. At the same time, the results of this type of benefit, in terms of reducing absenteeism and enhancing productivity, have been mixed.[29] In a recent survey of employers by the Families and Work Institute, the most common form of child-care benefits (offered by 61%) was a dependent care assistance plan, which lets employees set aside pretax income to pay for child care. A resource and referral program was the second most common benefit, offered by 37%.[30]
- *College savings*–As workers' children grow up, their needs shift from maternity leave and child care to college tuition. Some organizations have supported this concern by sponsoring tax-favored *529 savings plans.* These plans, named after the section of the Internal Revenue Code that regulates them, let parents and other family members defer taxes on the earnings of their deposits into the 529 account. Some states also provide a (limited) tax deduction for these contributions. As an employee benefit, organizations can arrange with a broker to offer direct deposit of a portion of employees' paychecks into their accounts. Besides offering the convenience of direct deposit, employers can negotiate lower management fees. At Johns Hopkins Bayview Medical Center, all employees are eligible to participate in a college savings plan that deducts contributions from employees' paychecks. This benefit is part of a compensation package designed to promote employees' personal and professional growth; related benefits include tuition reimbursement for employees (up to full tuition) and their dependent children (up to 50% reimbursement).[31] Consider also the potential for the ideas in the "HRM Social" box to further enhance the value of college savings plans.
- *Elder care*–As the population of the nation's elderly grows, so do the demands on adult children to care for elderly parents, aunts, and uncles. When these people become ill or disabled, they rely on family or professional caregivers. Responsibilities such as providing assistance, paying for professional caregivers, and locating services can be expensive, time consuming, and exhausting, often distracting employees from their work roles. In response, many employers have added elder care benefits. These programs often started by offering employees information and referrals; today these resources are often made available online. More recent enhancements of elder care benefits include referrals to decision support from experts in geriatric care, insurance, and the law, as well as flexible hours and paid time off. Employees at Johnson & Johnson have free use of a service that assesses elderly relatives' needs, helps the employee plan and coordinate services, reviews care facilities, helps employees select caregivers, assists with paperwork, and provides referrals to community services.[32] Even companies that cannot afford to offer counseling or referral services can use intranets to provide links to helpful websites such as the National Alliance for Caregiving (www.caregiving.org) and the National Council on Aging (www.benefitscheckup.org).

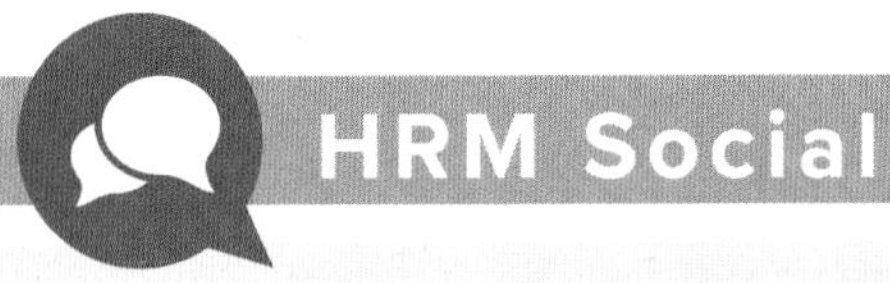

Crowdfunding for College Savings Plans

Some fortunate young people have parents who were able to set up a 529 savings plan, perhaps nudged into it as an employee benefit. That resource could be getting even bigger if there are grandparents or others who want to provide a brighter future by donating to the plan. And imagine how the savings would grow if the plan were open to contributions from anyone who might want to give a gift—say, at occasions like high school graduation. The value of this employee benefit grows along with the savings plan's deposits.

Franklin Templeton, which offers various investment products, saw this potential and decided to make it happen through a crowdfunding system. Crowdfunding combines the social aspects of online media with the desire to fund projects through gifts, business investments, or charitable contributions. A few examples are GoFundMe, Indiegogo, and Kickstarter.

Franklin Templeton created a system it calls Sprying (pronounced "spring"). An account holder uses Sprying to set up a profile with information about the savings plan's goals. Sprying provides the account holder with a secure URL for the profile page, which the person can share with family and friends through e-mail or social media. Visitors to the profile page can select an amount between $10 and $2,500 to contribute to the savings plan. (They don't see the details of what is in the account.) In the first year of the plan, thousands of account holders signed up for the service.

A survey of parents by the College Savings Foundation found that they want to help their children pay for college. Nine out of ten said it would help to have options to receive gifts online. The responses suggest that especially for employees with children, a 529 plan as an employee benefit would be welcome, and even more so with an option like Sprying.

Questions

1. How does a system such as Sprying affect the value of 529 plans as an employee benefit?
2. What kinds of employees would you expect to welcome the employee benefit of a 529 savings plan with a crowdfunding feature?

Sources: Franklin Templeton, "Sprying," https://www.franklintempleton.com, accessed May 8, 2020; John Manganaro, "An Experiment in Crowd Funded 529 College Savings," *PlanAdviser,* June 12, 2018, https://www.planadviser.com; Roger Michaud, "Sprying into Saving for College," *Beyond Bulls and Bears (Franklin Templeton blog),* May 22, 2017, http://us.beyondbullsandbears.com.

Other Benefits

The scope of possible employee benefits is limited only by the imagination of the organization's decision makers. Organizations have developed a wide variety of benefits to meet the needs of employees and to attract and keep the kinds of workers who will be of value to the organization. Traditional extras include subsidized cafeterias, on-site health care for minor injuries or illnesses, and moving expenses for newly hired or relocating employees. Stores and manufacturers may offer employee discounts on their products.

To encourage learning and attract the kinds of employees who wish to develop their knowledge and skills, many organizations offer *tuition reimbursement* programs. A typical program covers tuition and related expenses for courses that are relevant to the employee's current job or future career at the organization. Employees are reimbursed for these expenses after they demonstrate they have completed an approved course.

Especially for demanding, high-stress jobs, organizations may look for benefits that help employees put in the necessary long hours and alleviate stress. Recreational activities such as on-site basketball courts or company-sponsored softball teams provide for social interaction as well as physical activity. Employers may reward hard-working groups or individuals with a trip for a weekend, a meal, or any activity employees are likely to enjoy. Ruby Receptionists offers its clients phone-answering services handled by staff at its Portland, Oregon, offices or other remote locations. To keep skilled workers engaged in what is often considered an entry-level job, Ruby offers five-week paid sabbaticals after every five years, themed office parties, onsite fitness classes, and 24-hour access to the office space (which includes a deck, barbecue, and Xbox) for those who want a place to hang out together or host a party.[33]

In order to provide a relaxed environment for their employees, some companies allow employees to bring their pets to work. What other unique benefits do companies offer their employees?
Stuart O'Sullivan/Getty Images

Selecting Employee Benefits

Although the government requires certain benefits, employers have wide latitude in creating the total benefits package they offer employees.[34] Decisions about which benefits to include should take into account the organization's goals, its budget, and the expectations of the organization's current employees and those it wishes to recruit in the future. Employees have come to expect certain things from employers. An organization that does not offer the expected benefits will have more difficulty attracting and keeping talented workers. Also, if employees believe their employer feels no commitment to their welfare, they are less likely to feel committed to their employer.

The Organization's Objectives

A logical place to begin selecting employee benefits is to establish objectives for the benefits package. This helps an organization select the most effective benefits and monitor whether the benefits are doing what they should. Table 14.2 is an example of one organization's benefits objectives. Unfortunately, research suggests that most organizations do not have written benefits objectives.

LO 14-7 Explain how to choose the contents of an employee benefits package.

Among companies that do set goals, common objectives include controlling the cost of health care benefits and retaining employees.[35] The first goal explains the growing use of wellness programs and consumer-directed health plans. For the second goal, employees do say that valued benefits keep them from walking away, but employers need to learn what employees care about. A study of truck drivers found that companies offering defined-contribution retirement plans had better safety records. The researchers speculated that this employee benefit drew more job applicants and improved retention among older drivers, who tend to drive more safely. And in a study that investigated the value employees place on flexible work arrangements, those earning above the median pay and those age 57 or older said they would give up the most base pay to obtain flexibility.[36]

Employees' Expectations and Values

Employees expect to receive benefits that are legally required and widely available, and they value benefits they are likely to use. To meet employee expectations about benefits, it can be helpful to see what other organizations offer. Employers can purchase survey information about benefits packages from private consultants. In addition, the Bureau of Labor Statistics gathers benefits data. The BLS website (www.bls.gov) is therefore a good place to check for free information about employee benefits in the United States. With regard to value, medical insurance is a high-value benefit because employees usually realize that surgery or a major illness can be financially devastating. In contrast, HR professionals responding to a survey by the Society for Human Resource Management saw a lesser role for wellness programs and disability insurance benefits in attracting and keeping talent.[37]

TABLE 14.2
An Organization's Benefits Objectives

- To establish and maintain an employee benefit program that is based primarily on the employees' needs for leisure time and on protection against the risks of old age, loss of health, and loss of life.
- To establish and maintain an employee benefit program that complements the efforts of employees on their own behalf.
- To evaluate the employee benefit plan annually for its effect on employee morale and productivity, giving consideration to turnover, unfilled positions, attendance, employees' complaints, and employees' opinions.
- To compare the employee benefit plan annually with that of other leading companies in the same field and to maintain a benefit plan with an overall level of benefits based on cost per employee that falls within the second quintile of these companies.
- To maintain a level of benefits for nonunion employees that represents the same level of expenditures per employee as for union employees.
- To determine annually the costs of new, changed, and existing programs as percentages of salaries and wages and to maintain these percentages as much as possible.
- To self-fund benefits to the extent that a long-run cost savings can be expected for the firm and catastrophic losses can be avoided.
- To coordinate all benefits with social insurance programs to which the company makes payments.
- To provide benefits on a noncontributory basis except for dependent coverage, for which employees should pay a portion of the cost.
- To maintain continual communications with all employees concerning benefit programs.

Source: B.T. Beam Jr. and J.J. McFadden, *Employee Benefits*, 3rd ed. Dearborn Financial Publishing, Inc. 1992.

Employers should also consider that the value employees place on various benefits is likely to differ from one employee to another. At a broad level, basic demographic factors such as age and sex can influence the kinds of benefits employees want. An older workforce is more likely to be concerned about (and use) medical coverage, life insurance, and pensions. A workforce with a high percentage of women of childbearing age may care more about disability or family leave. Young, unmarried men and women often place more value on pay than on benefits. However, these are only general observations; organizations should check which considerations apply to their own employees and identify more specific needs and differences. One approach is to use surveys to ask employees about the kinds of benefits they value. The survey should be carefully worded so as not to raise employees' expectations by seeming to promise all the benefits asked about at no cost to the employee.

The choice of benefits may influence current employees' satisfaction and may also affect the organization's recruiting, in terms of both the ease of recruiting and the kinds of employees attracted to the organization. For example, a benefits package that has strong medical benefits and pensions may be particularly attractive to older people or to those with many dependents. Such benefits may attract people with extensive experience and those who wish to make a long-term commitment to the organization. This strategy may be especially beneficial when turnover costs are very high. On the other hand, offering generous health care benefits may attract and retain people with high health care costs. Thus, organizations need to consider the signals sent by their benefits package as they set goals for benefits and select benefits to offer.

Cafeteria-Style Plan
A benefits plan that offers employees a set of alternatives from which they can choose the types and amounts of benefits they want.

Organizations can address differences in employees' needs and empower their employees by offering flexible benefits plans in place of a single benefits package for all employees. These plans, often called **cafeteria-style plans,** offer employees a set of alternatives from which they can choose the types and amounts of benefits they want. The plans vary. Some impose minimum levels for certain benefits, such as health care coverage; some allow better employees to receive money in exchange for choosing a "light" package; and some let employees pay extra for the privilege of receiving more benefits. For example, some plans let employees give up vacation days for more pay or to purchase extra vacation days in exchange for a reduction in pay.

Cafeteria-style plans have a number of advantages.[38] The selection process can make employees more aware of the value of the benefits, particularly when the plan assigns each employee a sum of money to allocate to benefits. Also, the individual choice in a cafeteria plan enables each employee to match his or her needs to the company's benefits, increasing the plan's actual value to the employee. And because employees would not select benefits they don't want, the company avoids the cost of providing employees with benefits they don't value. Another way to control costs is to give employees incentives to choose lower-cost options. For example, the employee's deductible on a higher-cost health plan could be larger than on a relatively low-cost HMO.

A drawback of cafeteria-style plans is that they have a higher administrative cost, especially in the design and start-up stages. Organizations can avoid some of the higher cost, however, by using software packages and standardized plans that have been developed for employers wishing to offer cafeteria-style benefits. Another possible drawback is that employee selection of benefits will increase rather than decrease costs because employees will select the kinds of benefits they expect to need the most. For example, an employee expecting to need a lot of dental work is more likely to sign up for a dental plan. The heavy use of the dental coverage would then drive up the employer's premiums for that coverage. Costs can also be difficult to estimate when employees select their benefits.

Benefits' Costs

Employers also need to consider benefits costs. One place to start is with general information about the average costs of various benefits types. Widely used sources of cost data include the Bureau of Labor Statistics (BLS), Employee Benefit Research Institute, and U.S. Chamber of Commerce. Annual surveys by the Chamber of Commerce state the cost of benefits as a percentage of total payroll costs and in dollar terms. In addition, the ability to process "big data" is enabling more employers to identify specific areas where they can rein in benefits costs without reducing the value of their compensation packages to employees.

Employers can use data about costs to help them select the kinds of benefits to offer. But in balancing these decisions against organizational goals and employee benefits, the organization may decide to offer certain high-cost benefits while also looking for ways to control the cost of those benefits. The highest-cost items tend to offer the most room for savings, but only if the items permit choice or negotiation. Also, as we noted earlier, organizations can control certain costs such as workers' compensation by improving their experience ratings. Finally, it is important to identify whether spending on benefits also delivers some kind of return to the company; in that case, benefits spending is a kind of "investment" that may make a higher cost worthwhile. For an example of a company doing so with regard to mental-health benefits, see "Best Practices."

In recent years, benefits related to health care have attracted particular attention because these costs have risen very rapidly and because employers have a number of options. Concern over costs has prompted many employers to shift from traditional health insurance to PPOs and HDHPs. Some employers shift more of the cost to employees. They may lower the employer's payments by increasing the amounts employees pay for deductibles and coinsurance (the employee's share of the payment for services). Or they may require employees to pay some or all of the difference in cost between traditional insurance and a lower-cost plan. Excluding or limiting coverage for certain types of claims also can slow the increase in health insurance costs. Shifting costs to employees offers short-term savings (HDHPs, for example, can save at least 10% of the cost of a PPO). Evidence suggests, however, that employees with high deductibles are avoiding preventive health care, putting them at risk to need pricier care

Best Practices

Bell Canada's Mental-Health Initiative

Bell Canada has come out ahead in its four-pronged initiative to promote workplace mental health. The telecommunications company's effort, called "Bell Let's Talk," combines messages to combat the stigma of mental health, improved access to care, support for research, and efforts to build a healthy workplace. The combination of activities is intended to prevent mental illness, promote recovery, and support employees who are recovering from or living with mental illnesses. The program launched in 2010, with its performance tracked using more than 90 measures. Initially, Let's Talk cost Bell money, but after a few years, the program began to show a positive return on investment.

Bell's initiative included an expansion of benefits for psychological care, but it is about much more than just insurance. The company regularly conducts campaigns to raise awareness and encourage employees with concerns to seek help. Employees have access to an EAP and apps to help them locate counseling. By a recent count, more than one-third take advantage of the EAP—almost double the usage rate before Let's Talk and more than double the rate typical of the telecom industry and Canadian workplaces overall. Getting support pays off in lower use of short-term disability benefits. In addition, Bell gives managers a return-to-work checklist and mandatory training so they can help employees who do take disability leave make a smooth transition back to work with accommodations if needed. This has helped the company reduce the rate of disability relapse and claim recurrence by more than 50%.

Bell has more than 52,000 employees, and its mental-health initiative was the largest such program in Canada. But in a study by Deloitte looking at the experience of ten Canadian companies, its outcome was not out of the ordinary. At the seven companies that shared performance data with the researcher, the median return on investment (in Canadian dollars) was $1.62 for every dollar spent, and at companies with a program in place for at least three years, the median return was higher, at $2.18. Companies in the United States also are getting onboard and seeing results from a variety of mental-health initiatives, such as expanded insurance coverage, stipends, open communication to reduce stigma, and online tools for locating therapists.

Questions

1. What are some ways to measure the cost of mental-health benefits?
2. What are some ways to measure the benefits?

Sources: "Workplace Mental Health at Bell Canada," *MQ*, https://www.mqmentalhealth.org, accessed May 8, 2020; Sarah Chapman, Ariel Kangasniemi, Laura Maxwell, and Marie Sereneo, *The ROI in Workplace Mental Health Programs: Good for People, Good for Business*, Deloitte, November 4, 2019, https://www2.deloitte.com; Sophie Downes, "Today's Top Workplaces Are Prioritizing Mental Health: Here Are the Five Ways They're Doing It," *Inc.*, May 16, 2019, https://www.inc.com.

in the future for the consequences of untreated conditions. Looking for a more creative solution, Amazon, Berkshire Hathaway, and JPMorgan Chase have formed a not-for-profit partnership called Haven Healthcare, which provides employees with health care that meets high standards for quality and cost. The companies have been testing the new health-care venture and have started to roll out program offerings to some employees in a handful of states. As of this writing, details about this new approach to health care have been preliminary.[39]

LO 14-8 Summarize the regulations affecting how employers design and administer benefits programs.

Legal Requirements for Employee Benefits

As we discussed earlier in this chapter, some benefits are required by law. This requirement adds to the cost of compensating employees. Organizations looking for ways to control staffing costs may look for ways to structure the workforce so as to minimize the expense of benefits. They may require overtime rather than adding new employees, hire part-time rather than full-time workers (because part-time employees generally receive much smaller benefits packages), and use independent contractors rather than hire employees. Some of these choices are limited by legal requirements, however. For example, the Fair Labor Standards

Act requires overtime pay for nonexempt workers, as discussed in Chapter 12. Also, the Internal Revenue Service strictly limits the definition of "independent contractors," so that employers cannot avoid legal obligations by classifying workers as self-employed when the organization receives the benefits of a permanent employee. Other legal requirements involve tax treatment of benefits, antidiscrimination laws, and accounting for benefits.

Tax Treatment of Benefits

The IRS provides more favorable tax treatment of benefits classified as *qualified plans.* The details vary from one type of benefit to another. In the case of retirement plans, the advantages include the ability for employees to immediately take a tax deduction for the funds they contribute to the plans, no immediate tax on employees for the amount the employer contributes, and tax-free earnings on the money in the retirement fund.[40]

To obtain status as a qualified plan, a benefit plan must meet certain requirements.[41] In the case of pensions, these involve vesting and nondiscrimination rules. The nondiscrimination rules provide tax benefits to plans that do not discriminate in favor of the organization's "highly compensated employees." To receive the benefits, the organization cannot set up a retirement plan that provides benefits exclusively to the organization's owners and top managers. The requirements encourage employers to provide important benefits such as pensions to a broad spectrum of employees. Before offering pension plans and other benefits, organizations should have them reviewed by an expert who can advise on whether the benefits are qualified plans.

Antidiscrimination Laws

As we discussed in Chapter 3, a number of laws are intended to provide equal employment opportunity without regard to race, sex, age, disability, and several other protected categories. Some of these laws apply to the organization's benefits policies.

Legal treatment of men and women includes equal access to benefits, so the organization may not use the employee's gender as the basis for providing more limited benefits. That is the rationale for the Pregnancy Discrimination Act, which requires that employers treat pregnancy as it treats any disability. If an employee needs time off for conditions related to pregnancy or childbirth, the employee would receive whatever disability benefits the organization offers to employees who take disability leave for other reasons. Another area of concern in the treatment of male and female employees is pension benefits. On average, women live longer than men, so on average, pension benefits for female employees are more expensive (because the organization pays the pension longer), other things being equal. Some organizations have used this difference as a basis for requiring that female employees contribute more than male employees to defined benefit plans. The Supreme Court in 1978 determined that such a requirement is illegal.[42] According to the Supreme Court, the law is intended to protect individuals, and when women are considered on an individual basis (not as averages), not every woman outlives every man. Equal treatment based on sex applies similarly to spousal benefits, as when the Labor Department determined that the FMLA provisions granting time off to care for a spouse apply whether that spouse is of the same or the opposite sex.[43]

Age discrimination is also relevant to benefits policies. Two major issues have received attention under the Age Discrimination in Employment Act (ADEA) and amendments. First, employers must take care not to discriminate against workers over age 40 in providing pay or benefits. For example, employers may not set an age at which retirement benefits stop growing as a way to pressure older workers to retire.[44] Also, early-retirement incentive programs need to meet certain standards. The programs may not coerce employees to retire, they must provide accurate information about the options available, and they must give employees enough time to make a decision. In effect, employees must really have a choice about whether they retire.

When employers offer early retirement, they often ask employees to sign waivers saying they will not pursue claims under the ADEA. The Older Workers Benefit Protection Act of 1990 set guidelines for using these waivers. The waivers must be voluntary and understandable to the employee and employer, and they must spell out the employee's rights under the ADEA. Also, in exchange for signing the waiver, the employee must receive "compensation," that is, greater benefits than he or she would otherwise receive upon retirement. The employer must inform employees that they may consult a lawyer before signing, and employees must have time to make a decision about signing–21 days before signing plus 7 days afterward in which they can revoke the agreement.

The Americans with Disabilities Act imposes requirements related to health insurance. Under the ADA, employees with disabilities must have "equal access to whatever health insurance coverage the employer provides other employees." Even so, the terms and conditions of health insurance may be based on risk factors–as long as the employer does not use this basis as a way to escape offering health insurance to someone with a disability. From the standpoint of avoiding legal challenges, an employer who has risk-based insurance and then hires an employee with a disability is in a stronger position than an employer who switches to a risk-based policy after hiring a disabled employee.[45]

Accounting Requirements

Companies' financial statements must meet the many requirements of the Financial Accounting Standards Board (FASB). These accounting requirements are intended to ensure that financial statements are a true picture of the company's financial status and that outsiders, including potential lenders and investors, can understand and compare financial statements. Under FASB standards, employers must set aside the funds they expect to need for benefits to be paid after retirement, rather than funding those benefits on a pay-as-you-go basis. On financial statements, those funds must appear as future cost obligations. For companies with substantial retirement benefits, reporting those benefits as future cost obligations greatly lowers income each year. Along with rising benefits costs, this reporting requirement has encouraged many companies to scale back benefits to retirees.

LO 14-9 Discuss the importance of effectively communicating the nature and value of benefits to employees.

Communicating Benefits to Employees

Organizations must communicate benefits information to employees so that they will appreciate the value of their benefits. This is essential so that benefits can achieve their objective of attracting, motivating, and retaining employees. Employees are interested in their benefits, and they need a great deal of detailed information to take advantage of benefits such as health insurance and 401(k) plans. It follows that electronic technology such as the Internet and supporting databases can play a significant role in modern benefit systems.

In practice, it is difficult for employees and job applicants to understand the value of their benefits (see "Did You Know?"). This is especially true for the complexities of health insurance and the nuances of getting the most out of retirement benefits. The edge in the labor market goes to employers that help them understand. These employers figure out how to use plain language, and they spread messages through multiple channels, online and offline. Mark Johnson, CEO of Creative Benefits Solutions, suggests breaking up messages into digestible chunks, such as theme-related messages sent out four times a year, not all at once when it is time to enroll in plans. Johnson also notes that an internal blog can combine information with a convenient way to ask questions. And Kevin McNamara, senior enrollment strategist with The Standard, an insurance company, applies decision support

Did You Know?

Many Employees Need Help to Understand Their Benefits

Only about half of employees express confidence that they understand their benefits. A survey by the Employee Benefit Research Institute found that just over half say they understand their health benefits very or extremely well, and less than half say the same about their other benefits.

Consistent with this, in a survey by MetLife, only half of employees said the communications they receive about employee benefits are easy to understand. The same number said those communications succeeded in educating them to select the benefits that would best meet their needs.

This is particularly an issue for benefits that give employees responsibility for managing the value of their benefits. For example, Fidelity Investments found that employees whose health plans include health savings accounts often don't realize they could be investing unused funds. A majority of participants with Fidelity accounts who could be investing unused funds don't do so.

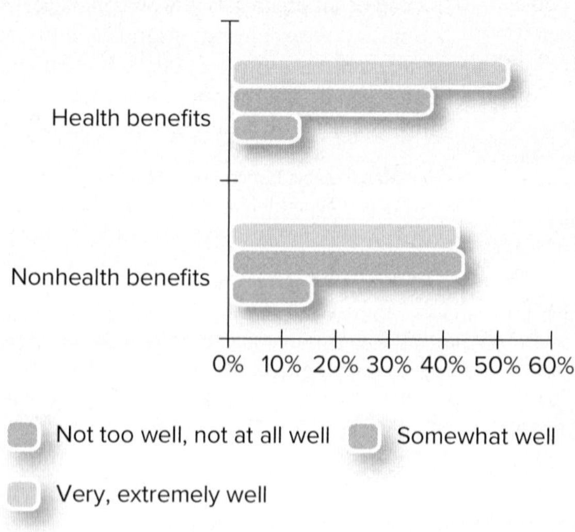

Question

Why should it matter to employers if employees don't understand the benefits they receive?

Sources: MetLife, "Thriving in the New Work-Life World: MetLife's 17th Annual U.S. Employee Benefit Trends Study 2019," https://www.metlife.com, accessed May 8, 2020; Paula Aven Gladych, "More Employers Adopt HAS Programs but Questions Remain," *Employee Benefit News,* June 15, 2018, https://www.benefitnews.com; Paul Fronstin and Lisa Greenwald, "The State of Employee Benefits: Findings from the 2017 Health and Workplace Benefits Survey," *Issue Brief* (Employee Benefit Research Institute), no. 448, April 10, 2018, https://www.ebri.org.

software. The company analyzed how employees learn and make decisions, and then used the data to create profiles of four basic learning styles. Employees receiving benefit communications determine which profile matches them, and then they receive messages tailored to appeal to their style.[46] Besides simply delivering information about benefits' value, some companies, including Danone North America, also offer tools that help employees select and use benefits. An example is software that uses data about an employee's demographics and health status to recommend the health insurance option that best fits the employee's needs.[47]

Employers have many options for communicating information about benefits. To increase the likelihood that employees will receive and understand the messages, employers can combine several media, such as brochures, question-and-answer meetings, intranet pages, text messages, and e-mail. Some other possible media include paycheck inserts, retirement or health coaching, training programs, and benefits fairs. An investment of creativity in communications to employees can reap great returns in the form of committed, satisfied employees.

THINKING ETHICALLY

IS IT FAIR PART-TIMERS RARELY GET BENEFITS?

Today, roughly one in five employees holds a part-time job (and no full-time job), either because they seek flexibility or they have not been able to get work with a full-time schedule. These employees typically receive fewer benefits than full-time workers. One study found that 25% of part-time employees receive health insurance benefits, and 32% have retirement plans. Part-time jobs also may pay strictly based on hours worked, with no paid time off.

Some employees view part-time jobs as employers' way to keep costs down by not offering the benefits packages that workers today have come to expect for full-time work. This cost-saving tactic especially drew attention in recent years when the Affordable Care Act began imposing penalties on employers that decline to offer health insurance to full-time workers. Shifting workers to part-time status was identified as a cost-saving response to the penalties.

Stories that reinforce a dim view of this approach include white-collar workers being hired for part-time salaried work and then being expected to put in extra hours to meet their goals. If the situation results in working full-time or nearly full-time without benefits alongside workers in full-time positions with full benefits (who may work much longer hours), the supposedly part-time workers may see an injustice.

Some employers are addressing negative perceptions of part-time jobs by offering more benefits to their part-timers. A survey by Mercer found that about half of large employers offer health insurance to part-timers. UPS, for example, offers benefits to part-time workers as a way to improve the quality of its job applicants. Employers need to check with benefits providers to make sure insurance policies and other plans are available to cover part-time workers. Sometimes these employees must work a minimum number of hours—say, for example, 20 hours per week.

Questions

1. If an employer offers health insurance and paid vacation to full-time but not part-time employees, who is helped? Who is harmed? Weighing the help against the harm, would you consider this policy ethical?
2. Imagine an organization where managers work full-time and receive health insurance, retirement plans, and paid time off, while the staff members work part-time and do not receive these benefits. How would you evaluate the justice of this situation?

Sources: Margie Zable Fisher, "Why More Employers Are Offering Benefits to Part-Timers," *MarketWatch,* February 11, 2020, https://www.marketwatch.org; Lin Grensing-Pophal, "When Gig Workers Want Benefits, Should You Offer Them?" *Society for Human Resource Management,* July 25, 2019, https://www.shrm.org; Yasemin Sim Esmen, "The Gig Economy Grows but Employees' Benefits Lag," *Employee Benefit Adviser,* June 15, 2018, https://www.employeebenefitadviser.com; Liz Ryan, "No—I Won't Work Full-Time for Part-Time Pay," *Forbes,* January 12, 2018, https://www.forbes.com; "Five Things about Offering Part-Time Employee Benefits," Paychex, March 21, 2018, https://www.paychex.com.

SUMMARY

LO 14-1 Discuss the importance of benefits as a part of employee compensation.

- Compensation includes wages and salaries, incentive pay, and benefits.
- Like other forms of compensation, benefits help employers attract, retain, and motivate employees.
- The variety of possible benefits helps employers tailor compensation packages to attract the right kinds of employees.
- Employees expect at least a minimum level of benefits, and providing more than the minimum helps an organization compete in the labor market.
- Benefits are also a significant expense.
- Employers provide benefits because employees value them, and many benefits are required by law.

LO 14-2 Summarize the types of employee benefits required by law.

- Employers must contribute to the Old Age, Survivors, Disability, and Health Insurance program known as Social Security through a payroll tax shared by employers and employees.
- Employers must pay federal and state taxes for unemployment insurance, based on each employer's experience rating, or percentage of employees a company has laid off in the past.
- State laws require that employers purchase workers' compensation insurance.
- Under the Family and Medical Leave Act, employees who need to care for a baby following birth or adoption or for an ill family member must be granted unpaid leave of up to 12 weeks.

- Under the Patient Protection and Affordable Care Act, organizations with 50 or more employees must choose between providing employees with health insurance or paying an Employer Shared Responsibility Penalty.

LO 14-3 Describe the most common forms of paid leave.

- The major categories of paid leave are vacations, holidays, and sick leave.
- At large U.S. companies, paid vacation is typically less than is common in Western Europe.
- The typical number of paid holidays is 10 in both Western Europe and the United States.
- Sick leave programs often provide full salary replacement for a limited period of time, with the amount of sick leave usually based on length of service. Policies are needed to determine how the organization will handle unused sick days at the end of each year. Some organizations let employees roll over some or all of the unused sick days into the next year, and others let unused days expire at the end of the year.
- Other forms of paid leave include personal days and floating holidays.

LO 14-4 Identify the kinds of insurance benefits offered by employers.

- Medical insurance is one of the most valued employee benefits. Such policies typically cover hospital expenses, surgical expenses, and visits to physicians. Some employers offer additional coverage, such as dental care, vision care, birthing centers, and prescription drug programs.
- Under the Consolidated Omnibus Budget Reconciliation Act of 1985, employees must be permitted to extend their health insurance coverage at group rates for up to 36 months after they leave the organization.
- To manage the costs of health insurance, most organizations offer coverage through a health maintenance organization, or preferred provider organization, or they may offer flexible spending accounts, perhaps in conjunction with a consumer-driven health plan. Some encourage healthy behaviors through an employee wellness program.
- Life insurance usually takes the form of group term life insurance, with the usual benefit being two times the employee's yearly pay.
- Employers may also offer short-term and/or long-term disability insurance, with disability payments being a percentage of the employee's salary.
- Some employers provide long-term care insurance to pay the costs associated with long-term care such as nursing home care.

LO 14-5 Define the types of retirement plans offered by employers.

- Retirement plans may be contributory, meaning funded by contributions from employer and employee, or noncontributory, meaning funded only by the employer.
- These plans may be defined-benefit plans or defined-contribution plans.
- Defined-benefit plans guarantee a specified level of retirement income, usually based on the employee's years of service, age, and earnings level. Benefits under these plans are protected by the Pension Benefit Guarantee Corporation.
- In a defined-contribution plan, such as a 401(k) plan, the employer sets up an individual account for each employee and guarantees the size of the investment into that account, rather than the amount to be paid out on retirement. Because employees have control over investment decisions, the organization may also offer financial planning services as an employee benefit.
- A cash balance plan combines some advantages of defined-benefit plans and defined-contribution plans. The employer sets up individual accounts and contributes a percentage of each employee's salary. The account earns interest at a predetermined rate, so the contributions and benefits are easier to predict.

LO 14-6 Describe how organizations use other benefits to match employees' wants and needs.

- Employers have responded to work-family role conflicts by offering family-friendly benefits, including paid family leave, child care services or referrals, college savings plans, and elder care information and support.
- Other employee benefits have traditionally included subsidized cafeterias, on-site health clinics, and reimbursement of moving expenses.
- Stores and manufacturers may offer discounts on their products.
- Tuition reimbursement encourages employees to continue learning.
- Recreational services and employee outings provide social interaction as well as stress relief.

LO 14-7 Explain how to choose the contents of an employee benefits package.

- A logical place to begin is to establish organizational objectives and select benefits that support those objectives.
- Organizations should also consider employees' expectations and values. At a minimum, organizations offer the benefits employees have come to view as basic;

some organizations go so far as to match extra benefits to individual employees' needs and interests.

- Cafeteria-style plans are an intermediate step that gives employees control over the benefits they receive.
- Employers must also weigh the costs of benefits, which are significant.

LO 14-8 Summarize the regulations affecting how employers design and administer benefits programs.

- Employers must provide the benefits that are required by law, and they may not improperly classify employees as "independent contractors" to avoid paying benefits.
- Tax treatment of qualified plans is favorable, so organizations need to learn the requirements for setting up benefits as qualified plans—for example, ensuring that pension plans do not discriminate in favor of the organization's highly compensated employees.
- Employers may not use employees' gender as the basis for discriminating against anyone, as in pension benefits on the basis that women as a group may live longer. Nor may employers discriminate against workers over age 40 in providing pay or benefits, such as pressuring older workers to retire by limiting retirement benefits.
- When employers offer early retirement, they must meet the requirements of the Older Workers Benefit Protection Act of 1990.
- Under the Americans with Disabilities Act, employers must give disabled employees equal access to health insurance.
- To meet the requirements of the Financial Accounting Standards Board, employers must set aside the funds they expect to need for retirement benefits ahead of time, rather than funding the benefits on a pay-as-you-go basis.

LO 14-9 Discuss the importance of effectively communicating the nature and value of benefits to employees.

- Communicating information about benefits is important so that employees will appreciate the value of their benefits.
- Communicating their value is the main way benefits attract, motivate, and retain employees.
- Employers have many options for communicating information about benefits, such as brochures, meetings, intranets, text messages, and e-mail. Using a combination of such methods increases employees' understanding.

KEY TERMS

employee benefits, 429
Social Security, 431
unemployment insurance, 432
experience rating, 432
workers' compensation, 434
Family and Medical Leave Act (FMLA), 434
Patient Protection and Affordable Care Act, 436
Consolidated Omnibus Budget Reconciliation Act (COBRA), 439
health maintenance organization (HMO), 439
preferred provider organization (PPO), 440
flexible spending account, 440
high-deductible health plans (HDHPs), 440
employee wellness program (EWP), 441
short-term disability insurance, 441
long-term disability insurance, 442
contributory plan, 442
noncontributory plan, 442
defined-benefit plan, 442
Employee Retirement Income Security Act (ERISA), 442
Pension Benefit Guarantee Corporation (PBGC), 442
defined-contribution plan, 443
cash balance plan, 445
vesting rights, 446
summary plan description (SPD), 446
cafeteria-style plan, 450

REVIEW AND DISCUSSION QUESTIONS

1. Why do employers provide employee benefits, rather than providing all compensation in the form of pay and letting employees buy the services they want? *(LO 14-1)*
2. Of the benefits discussed in this chapter, list the ones you consider essential—that is, the benefits you would require in any job offer. Why are these benefits important to you? *(LO 14-1)*
3. Define the types of benefits required by law. How can organizations minimize the cost of these benefits while complying with the relevant laws? *(LO 14-2)*
4. What are some advantages of offering a generous package of insurance benefits? What are some drawbacks of generous insurance benefits? *(LO 14-3)*

5. Imagine that you are the human resource manager of a small architectural firm. You learn that the monthly premiums for the company's existing health insurance policy will rise by 15% next year. What can you suggest to help your company manage this rising cost? *(LO 14-4)*
6. In principle, health insurance would be most attractive to employees with large medical expenses, and retirement benefits would be most attractive to older employees. What else might a company include in its benefits package to appeal to young, healthy employees? How might the company structure its benefits so these employees can take advantage of the benefits they care about most? *(LO 14-6)*
7. What issues should an organization consider in selecting a package of employee benefits? How should an employer manage the trade-offs among these considerations? *(LO 14-7)*
8. How do tax laws and accounting regulations affect benefits packages? *(LO 14-8)*
9. What legal requirements might apply to a family leave policy? Suggest how this type of policy should be set up to meet those requirements. *(LO 14-8)*
10. Why is it important to communicate information about employee benefits? Suppose you work in the HR department of a company that has decided to add new benefits—dental and vision insurance plus an additional two days of paid time off for "personal days." How would you recommend communicating this change? What information should your messages include? *(LO 14-9)*

SELF-ASSESSMENT EXERCISE

Which Benefits Are Important to You?

One way companies determine which types of benefits to provide is to use a survey asking employees which types of benefits are important to them. Read the following list of employee benefits. For each benefit, mark an X in the column that indicates whether it is important to you or not.

Benefit	Important to Have	Not Important to Have	% Employers Offering
Dependent-care flexible spending account	_____	_____	70%
Flextime	_____	_____	64
Ability to bring child to work in case of emergency	_____	_____	30
Elder-care referral services	_____	_____	21
Adoption assistance	_____	_____	21
On-site child care center	_____	_____	6
Gym subsidy	_____	_____	28
Vaccinations on site (e.g., flu shots)	_____	_____	61
On-site fitness center	_____	_____	26
Casual dress days (every day)	_____	_____	53
Organization-sponsored sports teams	_____	_____	39
Food services/subsidized cafeteria	_____	_____	29
Travel-planning services	_____	_____	27
Dry-cleaning services	_____	_____	15
Massage therapy services at work	_____	_____	12
Self-defense training	_____	_____	6
Concierge services	_____	_____	4

Compare your importance ratings for each benefit to the corresponding number in the right-hand column that indicates the percentage of employers that offer the benefit. Are you likely to find jobs that provide the benefits you want? Explain.

Source: Based on Figure 2. "Percent of Employers Offering Work/Life Benefits (by Year)," in *Workplace Visions* 4 (2002), p. 3, published by the Society for Human Resource Management.

TAKING RESPONSIBILITY

Kronos Trusts Employees Enough to Give Unlimited PTO

Kronos recently joined the small subset of employers who give their employees unlimited paid time off. The Massachusetts-based provider of software and services for workplace management has 5,000 employees globally, including almost 1,500 at its headquarters. Because some countries have legal requirements for vacation time, Kronos's unlimited-vacation policy applies only in the United States and Canada.

Kronos launched the policy because it was struggling to fill positions at its headquarters. The company hires mostly technology experts, and the job market for college graduates is very tight in Massachusetts. At one point, 300 positions were unfilled. When recruiters asked candidates what was holding them back from accepting an offer, one issue that repeatedly surfaced was vacation. Most companies, including Kronos, gave new workers about two weeks' vacation, adding to the days as the workers stayed on. Experienced job candidates balked at the offer to start at Kronos with two weeks' vacation when they had earned their way to three or four weeks at their current job.

Kronos's CEO, Aron Ain, and Chief People Officer Dave Almeda considered the situation. They took into account that the jobs at Kronos attract the kind of people who take responsibility for their work and may be finishing tasks at home or on the road, even during days they have designated as time off. If they were working when they were not clocked in, the executives concluded, they could certainly be trusted to get the job done.

Some managers and employees resisted the new policy. A few managers worried that employees would abuse the policy and that the process of approving time off would be difficult. For these managers, Kronos provided support, training, and nudges to align with the corporate culture. Some longtime employees complained because they had been using their vacation time as a kind of savings plan. Instead of taking the days off, they saved them up in order to get paid for them when they eventually left the company. Kronos's leaders reminded them that this was not the purpose of a vacation policy. Furthermore, to address concerns of fairness, it took the savings of not having these future payments and used the funds to pay for additional employee benefits, including greater contributions to retirement plans.

Predictions that employees would abuse the policy did not come true. Kronos continued to keep track of employees' use of time off. The average number of days taken rose slightly, from 14 days to 16.6, well within the range the policy had in mind. Employee engagement scores rose slightly, and employee turnover dropped significantly.

Questions

1. What business benefits is Kronos seeking from providing an unlimited-vacation benefit?
2. Imagine you worked in Kronos's HR department when it launched this benefit. What would you say in messages explaining the new benefit to employees?

Sources: "Kronos Case Study: Implementing Unlimited Vacation," Workforce Institute, https://workforceinstitute.org, accessed May 8, 2020; John Boitnott, "The Pros and Cons of an Unlimited Vacation Policy (and How It Affects Your Employees)," *Inc.*, January 30, 2018, https://www.inc.com; Aron Ain, "The CEO of Kronos on Launching an Unlimited Vacation Policy," *Harvard Business Review*, November-December 2017, pp. 38–42; Scott Mautz, "This CEO Launched an Unlimited Vacation Policy: Here's How It Worked Out," *Inc.*, November 14, 2017, https://www.inc.com.

MANAGING TALENT

Investing in Young Workers at Credit Suisse

Financial services might seem like another world from the high-tech businesses that are transforming how we make purchases and gather information, but both industries are in a talent competition for people with quantitative and computer skills. As many workers see more appeal in Silicon Valley than Wall Street, multinational financial services giants like Credit Suisse are sweetening employee benefits in an effort to lure and keep the best talent.

Credit Suisse recently aimed to make itself more attractive to young workers by creating generous benefits for parents. The firm raised its 12 weeks of paid parental leave to 20 weeks—a change that not only far exceeds the requirements of the Family and Medical Leave Act but is more generous that the paid leave offered by other financial services companies. The policy covers hourly as well as salaried employees who work at least 20 hours a week. It applies to both mothers and fathers, as long as they are the baby's primary caregiver. They may take the leave at any time during the first 12 months after the baby is born. Parents who are not the primary caregiver are eligible for a week of paid leave plus 19 weeks of unpaid leave.

The difference from its competitors' benefits was deliberate, according to Elizabeth Donnelly, Credit Suisse's head of benefits for the Americas, who says the company routinely monitors what competing firms and high-tech companies are offering. Donnelly and her team also monitor employees' opinions and behavior to identify what benefits are valuable. New employees rate family-friendly benefits as particularly important, and Credit Suisse has found that employee turnover is notably higher among those who recently completed a maternity leave. The firm continues to monitor the data following the implementation of the new policy, to see whether it has an impact on hiring and retention.

Along with the change in parental leave, Credit Suisse added some other benefits to help parents balance work and family needs. It will provide employees who are new parents, and their managers, with coaching in how to prepare for time off and make the transition back to work. For those who need to travel in the first year of their baby's life, Credit Suisse will cover the cost of a nanny to accompany the employee and care for the baby.

Of course, having a baby is not the only milestone that brings challenges in balancing one's life. Another way in which Credit Suisse has tried to assist with work/life balance is with a policy it calls "Protecting Friday Night," announced for employees in Europe, the Middle East, and Africa. The policy directs employees to leave by 7 p.m. on Fridays and not return until at least midday Saturday–unless they are completing a major deal.

Questions

1. How do Credit Suisse's actions to offer family-friendly benefits relate to its business objectives?
2. How are employees who are not expecting to become new parents likely to react to the decisions described here? What should Credit Suisse do for these other employees?

Sources: Credit Suisse, "At Work," https://www.credit-suisse.com/careers, accessed May 8, 2020; Freya Berry, "Credit Suisse Seeks to Make Friday Nights Special for Staff," *Reuters,* June 2, 2016, http://www.reuters.com; Marianne Calnan, "Credit Suisse Acts for Parental Support," *Employee Benefits,* January 2016, p. 5; Rachel Emma Silverman, "Family Leave Gaining Momentum in the Workplace," *Wall Street Journal,* January 5, 2016, http://www.wsj.com; Rachel Emma Silverman, "Credit Suisse Is Raising the Stakes in Wall Street's Parental-Leave Arms Race," *Wall Street Journal,* November 30, 2015, http://blogs.wsj.com.

HR IN SMALL BUSINESS

Bombas Makes Socks Well and Treats People Better

Before founding Bombas with Randy Goldberg, David Heath had already started three other companies. What got him going on this fourth project was learning that the top clothing donation requested by homeless shelters is socks. Heath was aware of how Toms and Warby Parker had succeeded at making donations part of their business strategies (for shoes and glasses), and he wanted to do the same with socks. He and Goldberg set out to develop socks that would be so comfortable and appealing that they could make a viable business out of donating a pair of socks for every pair sold. After two years in product development, they began selling Bombas socks online.

The founders were as committed to treating employees well as they were to helping the homeless. They were determined to build an organization in which people feel welcome and included. This would require open communication to build an atmosphere of respect and trust. Trust also is expressed in employee benefits that include unlimited vacation, unlimited sick leave, and unlimited remote work. Along with this, employees receive fully paid health insurance, a company match on its 401(k) plan, bonuses, and pay at above the average for comparable jobs in the region. Along with this, the company spends about $10,000 to $20,000 a year to help employees with difficult situations. The company also takes all its employees to twice-yearly nonworking retreats, as a way to build relationships in a fun setting such as an Arizona dude ranch.

According to the Great Place to Work survey, 98% of employees say Bombas has "special and unique benefits," and as many describe management as "honest and ethical." Almost all (99%) say they "feel good about the ways we contribute to the community."

In its first six years, Bombas grew to more than 140 employees and revenues surpassing $100 million, and it had donated more than 30 million socks to organizations serving the homeless. In that time, only seven people left the company, a remarkably low turnover rate.

Questions

1. Of the employee benefits mentioned in this case, which do you think are most important for keeping the workforce engaged at Bombas?
2. If you were responsible for human resource management at Bombas, how would you suggest the company measure the success of its benefits package?

Sources: "Bombas," Certified Companies, Great Place to Work, https://www.greatplacetowork.com, accessed May 8, 2020; Kathy Caprino, "Bombas: How This Mission-Driven Organization Remains Profitable and Impactful, Even in Crisis Times," *Forbes,* March 30, 2020, https://www.forbes.com; Kimberly Weisul, "Bombas: Charitable at the Start, Profitable by Year Three, and Only Three Employees Have Ever Quit," *Inc.,* June 2019, https://www.inc.com.

NOTES

1. P. Thomas, "Starbucks to Offer Free Therapy to All Workers," *The Wall Street Journal,* March 16, 2020, https://www.wsj.com; Starbucks careers page, https://www.starbucks.com, accessed April 30, 2020; J. La Roche, "Starbucks Extends Pay for All Workers Whether They Show Up or Not until May," *Yahoo Finance,* April 1, 2020, https://finance.yahoo.com.
2. B. Gerhart and G. T. Milkovich, "Employee Compensation: Research and Practice," in *Handbook of Industrial and Organizational Psychology,* 2nd ed., eds. M. D. Dunnette and L. M. Hough (Palo Alto, CA: Consulting Psychologists Press, 1992), vol. 3; J. Swist, "Benefits Communications: Measuring Impact and Values," *Employee Benefit Plan Review,* September 2002, pp. 24–26.
3. K. Mayer, "AutoNation Adds Cancer Benefit, Boosts 401(k) Match," *Employee Benefit News,* January 18, 2018, https://www.benefitnews.com; R. Damico, "Giving Back to Employees When Business Is Good," *Crain's Detroit Business,* May 8, 2017, http://www.crainsdetroit.com.
4. U.S. Department of Labor, Employment and Training Administration, "Comparison of State Unemployment Laws," chapter 2, https://oui.doleta.gov, last updated January 1, 2019.
5. C. Jones, "Jobless Claims Climb to 33M in Seven Weeks as Nation Braces for Historic Unemployment Rate," *USA Today,* May 7, 2020, https://www.usatoday.com.
6. J. V. Nackley, *Primer on Workers' Compensation* (Washington, DC: Bureau of National Affairs, 1989); T. Thomason, T. P. Schmidle, and J. F. Burton, *Workers' Compensation* (Kalamazoo, MI: Upjohn Institute, 2001).
7. B. T. Beam Jr. and J. J. McFadden, *Employee Benefits,* 6th ed. (Chicago: Dearborn Financial Publishing, 2000).
8. N. Ogrysko, "New Federal Paid Parental Leave Benefits Will Be Ready without Delay, OPM Says," *Federal News Network,* March 10, 2020, https://federalnewsnetwork.com; G. Livingston and D. Thomas, "Among 41 Countries, Only U.S. Lacks Paid Parental Leave," *Pew Research,* December 16, 2019, https://www.pewresearch.org.
9. S. Miller, "Same-Sex Domestic Partner Benefits Waning," *HR Magazine,* October 2017, p. 16.
10. U.S. Bureau of Labor Statistics, "National Compensation Survey: Table 37. Paid Vacations: Number of Annual Days by Service Requirement, Civilian Workers," March 2019, https://www.bls.gov.
11. Paycor, "The Difference Between Vacation and Paid Time Off," January 13, 2020, https://www.paycor.com; D. Braff, "Reimagining Time Off," *HR Magazine,* April 2018, pp. 46–53.
12. S. McLaren, "These Companies Are Reinventing Their Health Benefits—and Creating a Major Competitive Advantage," *LinkedIn Talent Blog,* April 27, 2019, https://business.linkedin.com.
13. American Psychological Association, "Does Your Insurance Cover Mental Health Services?" https://www.apa.org, accessed May 7, 2020; G. Dangor, "'Mental Health Parity' Is Still an Elusive Goal in U.S. Insurance Coverage," *NPR,* June 7, 2019, https://www.npr.org.
14. Bureau of Labor Statistics, "Employment Cost Index—March 2020," https://www.bls.gov, accessed May 7, 2020.
15. Kaiser Family Foundation, "Employer Health Benefits: 2019 Summary of Findings," http://files.kff.org, accessed May 7, 2020.
16. Ibid., pp. 2–3.
17. Centers for Medicare & Medicaid Services, "Accountable Care Organizations (ACOs): General Information," https://innovation.cms.gov, accessed May 7, 2020; T. Beaton, "UnitedHealthcare Finds Value-Based Care Closed 50M Gaps in Care," *HealthPayer Intelligence,* March 2, 2018, https://healthpayerintelligence.com.
18. "Employers Overestimate Impact of Wellness Programs and Incentives on Employees' Health Behavior," *Compensation Management News,* March 2, 2018, https://compensation.blr.com; J. C. Erfurt, A. Foote, and M. A. Heirich, "The Cost-Effectiveness of Worksite Wellness Programs for Hypertension Control, Weight Loss, Smoking Cessation and Exercise," *Personnel Psychology* 45 (1992), pp. 5–27.
19. Bureau of Labor Statistics, "Employee Benefits in the United States—March 2019," https://www.bls.gov, accessed May 7, 2020.
20. Pension Benefit Guaranty Corporation, "Premium Rates," https://www.pbgc.gov, accessed May 7, 2020.
21. Internal Revenue Service, "401(k) Contribution Limit Increases to $19,500 for 2020; Catch-up Limit Rises to $6,500," November 6, 2019, https://www.irs.gov.
22. Bureau of Labor Statistics, "Union Workers More Likely Than Nonunion Workers to Have Retirement Benefits in 2019," TED: The Economics Daily, October 25, 2019, https://www.bls.gov.
23. A. Damodaran, "Annual Returns on Stocks, T. Bonds, and T. Bills: 1928–Current," January 5, 2019, https://pages.stern.nyu.edu; Burton G. Malkiel, "Investing for 2016 in an Expensive Market," *The Wall Street Journal,* December 30, 2015, http://www.wsj.com.
24. "Supreme Court Lets Stand Third Circuit Ruling That Pension Avoidance Scheme Is ERISA Violation," *Daily Labor Report,* no. 234 (December 8, 1987), p. A-14, summarizing *Continental Can Company v. Gavalik.*
25. Beam and McFadden, *Employee Benefits.*
26. G. M. Spreitzer, L. Cameron, and L. Garrett, "Alternative Work Arrangements: Two Images of the New World of Work," *Annual Review of Organizational Psychology and Organizational Behavior* 4 (2017), pp. 473–499; J. H. Wayne, M. M. Butts, W. J. Casper, and T. D. Allen, "In Search of Balance: A Conceptual and Empirical Integration of Multiple Meanings of Work-Family Balance," *Personnel Psychology* 70 (2016), pp. 167–210; A. Mandeville, J. Halbesleben, and M. Whitman, "Misalignment and Misperception in Preferences to Utilize Family-Friendly Benefits: Implications for Benefit Utilization and Work-Family Conflict," *Personnel Psychology* 69 (2016), pp. 895–929; T. D. Allen, R. C. Johnson, K. M. Kiburz, and K. M. Shockley, "Work-Family Conflict and Flexible Work Arrangements: Deconstructing Flexibility," *Personnel Psychology* 66 (2013), pp. 345–376.
27. S. L. Grover and K. J. Crooker, "Who Appreciates Family Responsive Human Resource Policies: The Impact of Family-Friendly Policies on the Organizational Attachment of Parents and Non-parents," *Personnel Psychology* 48 (1995), pp. 271–288; M. A. Arthur, "Share Price Reactions to Work-Family Initiatives: An Institutional Perspective," *Academy of Management Journal* 46 (2003), p. 497; J. E. Perry-Smith and T. Blum, "Work-Family Human Resource Bundles and Perceived Organizational Performance," *Academy of Management Journal* 43 (2000), pp. 1107–1117.

28. S. Rodriguez, "Facebook Is Offering Employees Up to a Month of Paid Leave to Care for Sick Family Members," *CNBC*, March 23, 2020, https://www.cnbc.com; R. Blakely-Gray, "What Are the States with Paid Family Leave?" *Patriot Software,* June 17, 2019, https://www.patriotsoftware.com; R. Molla, "Netflix Parents Get a Paid Year Off and Amazon Pays for Spouses' Parental Leave," *Recode,* January 31, 2018, https://www.recode.net.
29. E. E. Kossek, "Diversity in Child Care Assistance Needs: Employee Problems, Preferences, and Work-Related Outcomes," *Personnel Psychology* 43 (1990), pp. 769-791.
30. Kenneth Matos and Ellen Galinsky, "2014 National Study of Employers," Families and Work Institute, 2014, http://www.familiesandwork.org.
31. Johns Hopkins Medicine, "Employee Benefits: Tuition Reimbursement/College Savings Plan," Bayview Jobs, http://www.bayviewjobs.org, accessed April 27, 2012.
32. National Alliance for Caregiving, *Best Practices in Workplace Eldercare,* March 2012, http://www.caregiving.org.
33. Great Place to Work, "Ruby Receptionists," June 17, 2015, http://reviews.greatplacetowork.com.
34. R. Broderick and B. Gerhart, "Nonwage Compensation," in *The Human Resource Management Handbook,* eds. D. Lewin, D. J. B. Mitchell, and M. A. Zadi (San Francisco: JAI Press, 1996).
35. MetLife, "Thriving in the New Work-Life World: MetLife's 17th Annual U.S. Employee Benefit Trends Study 2019," https://www.metlife.com, accessed May 8, 2020.
36. S. Werner, C. S. Kuiate, T. R. Noland, and A. J. Francia, "Benefits and Strategic Outcomes: Are Supplemental Retirement Plans and Safer Driving Related in the US Trucking Industry?" *Human Resource Management* 55 (2015), pp. 885-900; T. Eriksson and N. Kristensen, "Wages or Fringes? Some Evidence on Trade-Offs and Sorting," *Journal of Labor Economics* 32, no. 4 (2014), pp. 899-928.
37. S. Miller, "Employers Boost Benefits to Win and Keep Top Talent," *Society for Human Resource Management,* June 25, 2019, https://www.shrm.org.
38. Beam and McFadden, *Employee Benefits;* A. Caza, M. W. McCarter, and G. B. Northcraft, "Performance Benefits of Reward Choice: A Procedural Justice Perspective," *Human Resource Management Journal* 25 (2015), pp. 184-199.
39. L. Dyrda, "Haven Has Been Quiet for the Past 2 Years–What Does That Mean for Healthcare?" *Becker's Hospital Review,* February 3, 2020, https://www.beckershospitalreview.com; M. F. Davis, C. Koons, and M. Day, "JPMorgan Tests Its Amazon-Berkshire Health Venture on Bank Employees," *Bloomberg,* November 1, 2019, https://www.bloomberg.com.
40. Beam and McFadden, *Employee Benefits,* p. 359.
41. For a description of these rules, see M. M. Sarli, "Nondiscrimination Rules for Qualified Plans: The General Test," *Compensation and Benefits Review* 23, no. 5 (September-October 1991), pp. 56-67.
42. *Los Angeles Department of Water & Power v. Manhart,* 435 U.S. S. Ct. 702 (1978), 16 E.P.D. 8250.
43. "FMLA for Same-Sex Couples Is Nationwide," *Payroll Manager's Letter,* April 7, 2015, p. 1.
44. S. K. Hoffman, "Discrimination Litigation Relating to Employee Benefits," *Labor Law Journal,* June 1992, pp. 362-381.
45. Ibid., p. 375.
46. A. Burjek, "Workday, Interrupted," *Workforce,* January 2018, http://www.workforce.com.
47. S. Livingston, "Savvy Tools to Help Pick and Choose," *Business Insurance,* September 14, 2015, Business Insights: Global, http://bi.galegroup.com.

Meeting Other HR Goals

freesoulproduction/Shutterstock

15 Collective Bargaining and Labor Relations

Introduction

At the federal prison in Elkton, Ohio, a correctional officer named Gregory Darven realized he had come into contact with someone infected with the novel strain of coronavirus causing a pandemic at the time. He reported this to the prison's medical staff. They sent him home, where he contacted his own doctor, who followed the guidelines of the Centers for Disease Control and Prevention, directing Darven to stay home for two weeks. He then submitted a request for a 14-day emergency administrative leave, but the prison administration told him to use his personal sick leave instead or else return to work.

From Darven's perspective, the requirement to use his sick leave was unfair, because he didn't feel sick or able to have prevented his exposure to the virus in the workplace. However, he had an avenue to protest the decision: He and other prison workers are represented by the Council of Prison Locals of the American Federal of Government Employees (AFGE). He filed a complaint with the local council, whose president agreed that it was unfair for him to use personal leave when the prison had "put us in harm's way." The AFGE, which had received similar complaints from other employees, filed an imminent-danger report with the Occupational Safety and Health Administration on behalf of all its members in this situation.

Prison management viewed the situation differently. An official stated that the Bureau of Prisons was taking "aggressive steps" to protect workers, including limitations on visitors and on the movement of inmates, as well as screening and quarantining of new inmates. It also had recently begun issuing surgical masks to inmates and staff. Around the time of the complaint, 253 federal inmates and 84 employees (out of 145,613 total inmates and 36,530 total employees) had tested positive for COVID-19; eight inmates and no employees had died.[1]

Union representation can provide some benefit to workers in potentially dangerous occupations, such as corrections officer.

Jim West/imageBROKER/Shutterstock

What Do I Need to Know?

After reading this chapter, you should be able to:

- **LO 15-1** Define unions and labor relations and their role in organizations.
- **LO 15-2** Identify the labor relations goals of management, labor unions, and society.
- **LO 15-3** Summarize laws and regulations that affect labor relations.
- **LO 15-4** Describe the union organizing process.
- **LO 15-5** Explain how management and unions negotiate contracts.
- **LO 15-6** Summarize the practice of contract administration.
- **LO 15-7** Describe new approaches to labor-management relations.

The differing opinions about whether employees were adequately protected to avoid catching and spreading COVID-19 illustrate how employees and management often find themselves at odds. When workers perceive that their perspective on matters of safety or justice is being ignored, they might try to present a unified voice to management, seeking strength in numbers. Some workers have pursued this strategy by forming unions. Then the situation becomes more complex. Employees may or may not continue to see the union representatives as speaking for them. Ultimately, then, managers and unions each have an opportunity to build constructive relationships with workers.

When unions become a presence in an organization, human resource management must direct more attention to the interests of employees as a group. In general, employees and employers share the same interests. They both benefit when the organization is strong and growing, providing employees with jobs and employers with profits. Although the interests of employers and employees overlap, they obviously are not identical. In the case of pay, workers benefit from higher pay, but high pay cuts into the organization's profits, unless pay increases are associated with higher productivity or better customer service. Workers may negotiate differences with their employers individually, or they may form unions to negotiate on their behalf. This chapter explores human resource activities in organizations where employees belong to unions or where employees are seeking to organize unions.

We begin by formally defining unions and labor relations, and then describe the scope and impact of union activity. We next summarize government laws and regulations affecting unions and labor relations. The following three sections detail types of activities involving unions: union organizing, contract negotiation, and contract administration. Finally, we identify ways in which unions and management are working together in arrangements that are more cooperative than the traditional labor-management relationship.

Role of Unions and Labor Relations

LO 15-1 Define unions and labor relations and their role in organizations.

In the United States today, most workers act as individuals to select jobs that are acceptable to them and to negotiate pay, benefits, flexible hours, and other work conditions. Especially when there is stiff competition for labor and employees have hard-to-replace skills, this arrangement produces satisfactory results for most employees. At times, however, workers have believed that their needs and interests do not receive enough consideration from management. One response by workers is to act collectively by forming and joining labor **unions,** organizations formed for the purpose of representing their members' interests and resolving conflicts with employers.

Unions
Organizations formed for the purpose of representing their members' interests in dealing with employers.

Unions have a role because some degree of conflict is inevitable between workers and management.[2] As we noted earlier, for example, managers can increase profits by lowering workers' pay, but workers benefit in the short term if lower profits result because their pay is higher. Still, this type of conflict is more complex than a simple trade-off, such as wages versus profits. Rising profits can help employees by driving up profit sharing or other benefits, and falling profits can result in layoffs and a lack of investment. Although employers can use programs like profit sharing to help align employee interests with their own, some remaining divergence of interests is inevitable. Newspaper employees, for example, have felt their trust in management and confidence in the future erode as changing technology has brought wave after wave of layoffs and cutbacks. Employees at several papers, including the *Orlando Sentinel* and the *Los Angeles Times,* have reacted by forming unions.[3] Labor unions represent worker interests, and the collective bargaining process provides a way to manage the conflict. In other words, through systems for hearing complaints and negotiating labor contracts, unions and managers resolve conflicts between employers and employees.

The largest union in the United States is the National Education Association with 3 million members.
Tim Pannell/SuperStock

As unionization of workers became more common, universities developed training in how to manage union-management interactions. This specialty, called **labor relations,** emphasizes skills that managers and union leaders can use to foster effective labor-management cooperation, minimize costly forms of conflict (such as strikes), and seek win-win solutions to disagreements. Labor relations involves three levels of decisions:[4]

1. *Labor relations strategy*—For management, the decision involves whether the organization will work with unions or develop (or maintain) nonunion operations. This decision is influenced by outside forces such as public opinion and competition. For unions, the decision involves whether to fight changes in how unions relate to the organization or accept new kinds of labor-management relationships.
2. *Negotiating contracts*—As we will describe later in this chapter, contract negotiations in a union setting involve decisions about pay structure, job security, work rules, workplace safety, and many other issues. These decisions affect workers' and the employer's situation for the term of the contract.
3. *Administering contracts*—These decisions involve day-to-day activities in which union members and the organization's managers may have disagreements. Issues include complaints of work rules being violated or workers being treated unfairly in particular situations. A formal grievance procedure is typically used to resolve these issues.

Labor Relations
Field that emphasizes skills that managers and union leaders can use to minimize costly forms of conflict (such as strikes) and seek win-win solutions to disagreements.

Later sections in this chapter describe how managers and unions carry out the activities connected with these levels of decisions, as well as the goals and legal constraints affecting these activities.

National and International Unions

Most union members belong to a national or international union. In the United States, the largest unions are the National Education Association (NEA), which has 3 million members, and the Service Employees International Union (SEIU), with 1.9 million members. In the number three spot is the American Federation of Teachers (AFT) with 1.7 million members.[5]

Craft Union
Labor union whose members all have a particular skill or occupation.

Labor unions may be either craft or industrial unions. The members of a **craft union** all have a particular skill or occupation. Examples include the International Brotherhood of Electrical Workers for electricians and the National Education Association for teachers. Craft unions are often responsible for training their members through apprenticeships and for supplying craft workers to employers. For example, an employer would send requests for carpenters to the union hiring hall, which would decide which carpenters to send out. In this way, craft workers may work for many employers over time but have a constant link to the union. A craft union's bargaining power depends greatly on its control over the supply of its workers.

Industrial Union
Labor union whose members are linked by their work in a particular industry.

In contrast, **industrial unions** consist of members who are linked by their work in a particular industry. Examples include the Communication Workers of America and the American Federation of State, County, and Municipal Employees. Typically, an industrial union represents many different occupations. Membership in the union is the result of working for a particular employer in the industry. Changing employers is less common than it is among craft workers, and employees who change employers remain members of the same union only if they happen to move to other employers covered by that union. Another difference is that whereas a craft union may restrict the number of skilled craftsmen—say, carpenters—to maintain higher wages, industrial unions try to organize as many employees in as wide a range of skills as possible.

Most national unions in the United States are affiliated with the **American Federation of Labor and Congress of Industrial Organizations (AFL-CIO).** The AFL-CIO is not a labor union but an association that seeks to advance the shared interests of its member unions at the national level, much as the Chamber of Commerce and the National Association of Manufacturers do for their member employers. Approximately 55 national and international unions are affiliated with the AFL-CIO. An important responsibility of the AFL-CIO is to represent labor's interests in public policy issues, such as labor law, economic policy, and occupational safety and health. The organization also provides information and analysis that member unions can use in their activities. In 2005, several unions broke away from the AFL-CIO to form an alliance called Change to Win, which is focused on innovative organizing campaigns. This group includes four unions representing a membership of more than 4.5 million workers.

American Federation of Labor and Congress of Industrial Organizations (AFL-CIO)
An association that seeks to advance the shared interests of its member unions at the national level.

Local Unions

Most national unions consist of multiple local units. Even when a national union plays the most critical role in negotiating the terms of a collective bargaining contract, negotiation occurs at the local level for work rules and other issues that are locally determined. In addition, administration of the contract largely takes place at the local union level. As a result, most day-to-day interaction between labor and management involves the local union.

Membership in the local union depends on the type of union. For an industrial union, the local may correspond to a single large facility or to a number of small facilities. In a craft union, the local may cover a city or a region.

Typically, the local union elects officers, such as president, vice president, and treasurer. The officers may be responsible for contract negotiation, or the local may form a bargaining committee for that purpose. When the union is engaged in bargaining, the national union provides help, including background data about other settlements, technical advice, and the leadership of a representative from the national office.

Individual members participate in local unions in various ways. At meetings of the local union, they elect officials and vote on resolutions to strike. Most of workers' contact is with the **union steward,** an employee elected by union members to represent them in ensuring that the terms of the contract are enforced. The union steward helps investigate complaints and represents employees to supervisors and other managers when employees file grievances alleging contract violations. When the union deals with several employers, as in the case of a craft union, a *business representative* performs some of the same functions as a union steward. Because of union stewards' and business representatives' close involvement with employees, it is to management's advantage to cultivate positive working relationships with them.

Union Steward
An employee elected by union members to represent them in ensuring that the terms of the labor contract are enforced.

Trends in Union Membership

Union membership in the United States peaked in the 1950s, reaching over one-third of employees. Since then, the share of employees who belong to unions has fallen. It now stands at 10.3% overall and 6.2% of private-sector employment.[6] As Figure 15.1 indicates, union membership has fallen steadily since the 1980s. The decline has been driven by falling union membership in the private sector, while the share of government workers in unions has mostly held steady.

FIGURE 15.1
Union Membership Density among U.S. Wage and Salary Workers, 1979–2019[a]

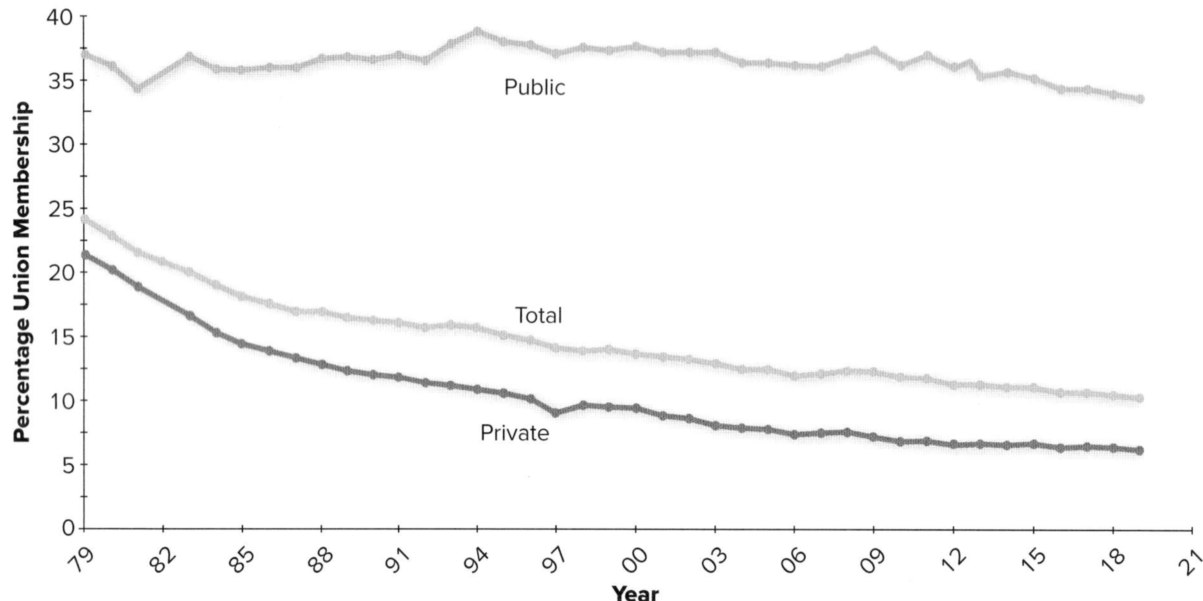

[a]Percentage of total, private-sector, and public-sector wage and salary workers who are union members. Beginning in 1977, workers belonging to "an employee association similar to a union" are included as members.

Source: Data for 1973–2001 from B. T. Hirsch and D. A. MacPherson, *Union Membership and Earnings Data Book 2001* (Washington, DC: Bureau of National Affairs, 2002), using data from U.S. Current Population Surveys. Data for 2002 through 2019 from Bureau of Labor Statistics, Current Population Survey, https://data.bls.gov, extracted May 13, 2020.

The decline in union membership has been attributed to several factors:[7]

- *Change in the structure of the economy*–Much recent job growth has occurred in the service sector of the economy, while union strength has traditionally been among urban blue-collar workers. Services industries such as finance, insurance, and real estate have lower union representation than manufacturing. Also, much business growth has been in the South, where workers are less likely to join unions.
- *Management efforts to control costs*–On average, unionized workers receive higher pay than their nonunionized counterparts, and the pressure is greater because of international competition. In the past, union membership across an industry such as automobiles or steel resulted in similar wages and work requirements for all competitors. Today, U.S. producers must compete with companies that have entirely different pay scales and work rules, often placing the U.S. companies at a disadvantage.
- *Human resource practices*–Competition for scarce human resources can lead employers to offer much of what employees traditionally sought through union membership.
- *Government regulation*–Stricter regulation in such areas as workplace safety and equal employment opportunity leaves fewer areas in which unions can show an advantage over what employers must already offer.

As Figure 15.2 indicates, the percentage of U.S. workers who belong to unions is lower than in many other countries. More dramatic is the difference in "coverage"–the percentage of employees whose terms and conditions of employment are governed by a union contract, whether or not the employees are technically union members. In Western Europe, it is common to have coverage rates of 80% to 90%, so the influence of labor unions far outstrips

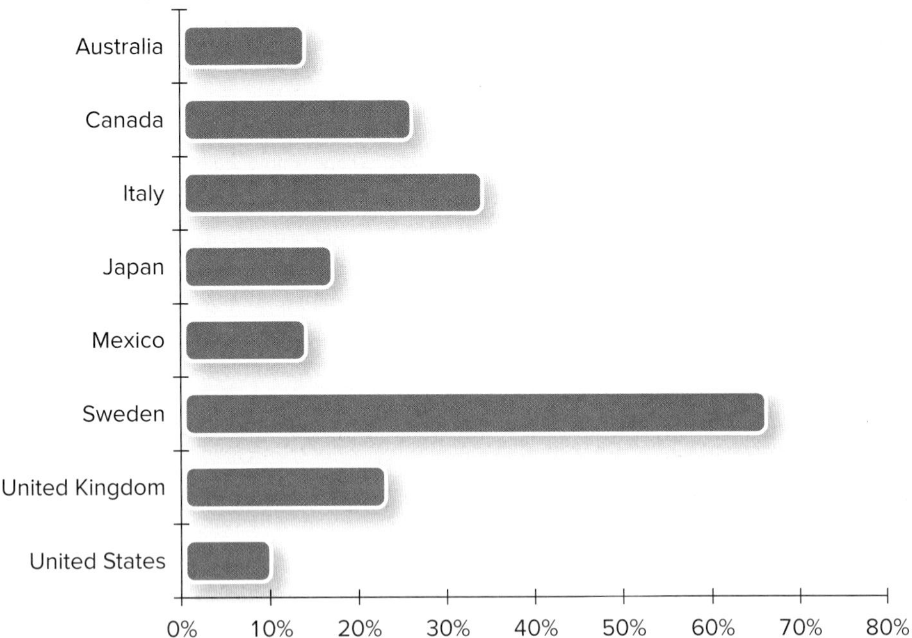

FIGURE 15.2
Union Membership Rates in Selected Countries

Note: Latest year available (2017 or 2018).

Source: Organisation for Economic Co-operation and Development, OECD.Stat, https://stats.oecd.org, accessed May 13, 2020.

what membership levels would imply.[8] Also, employees in Western Europe tend to have a larger formal role in decision making than in the United States. This role, including worker representatives on boards of directors, is often mandated by the government. But as markets become more and more global, pressure to cut labor costs and increase productivity is likely to be stronger in every country. Unless unions can help companies improve productivity or organize new production facilities opened in lower-wage countries, union influence may decline in countries where it is now strong.

Although union members are a smaller share of the U.S. workforce, they are a significant part of many industries' labor markets. Along with strength in numbers, large unions have strength in dollars. Union retirement funds, taken together, are huge. Unions try to use their investment decisions in ways that influence businesses. The "Did You Know?" box presents some statistics on union members.

Unions in Government

Unlike union membership for workers in businesses, union membership among government workers has remained strong. Union membership in the public sector grew during the 1960s and 1970s and has remained steady ever since. Over one-third of government employees are union members, and a larger share are covered by collective bargaining agreements. Among them are nurses, park rangers, school librarians, corrections officers, and many workers in clerical and other white-collar occupations. One reason for this strength is that government regulations and laws support the right of government workers to organize. In 1962 Executive Order 10988 established collective bargaining rights for federal employees. By the end of the 1960s, most states had passed similar laws.

Labor relations with government workers are different in some respects, such as regarding the right to strike. Strikes are illegal for federal workers and for state workers in most states.

Did You Know?

Profile of a Typical Union Worker

In the United States today, a worker 55 or older is far more likely to be a union member than a young worker is. Men are slightly more likely than women to be union members. Workers in education and protective services jobs—that is, teachers, police officers, and firefighters—are most likely to be in a union. In contrast, only 2.8% of salespeople are members of unions.

Question

What trend shown in Figure 15.1 helps to explain why jobs in education and protective services have the highest rates of unionization?

Sources: Bureau of Labor Statistics, "Labor Force Statistics from the Current Population Survey," https://www.bls.gov, accessed May 12, 2020; Bureau of Labor Statistics, "Union Members, 2019," news release, January 22, 2020, https://www.bls.gov.

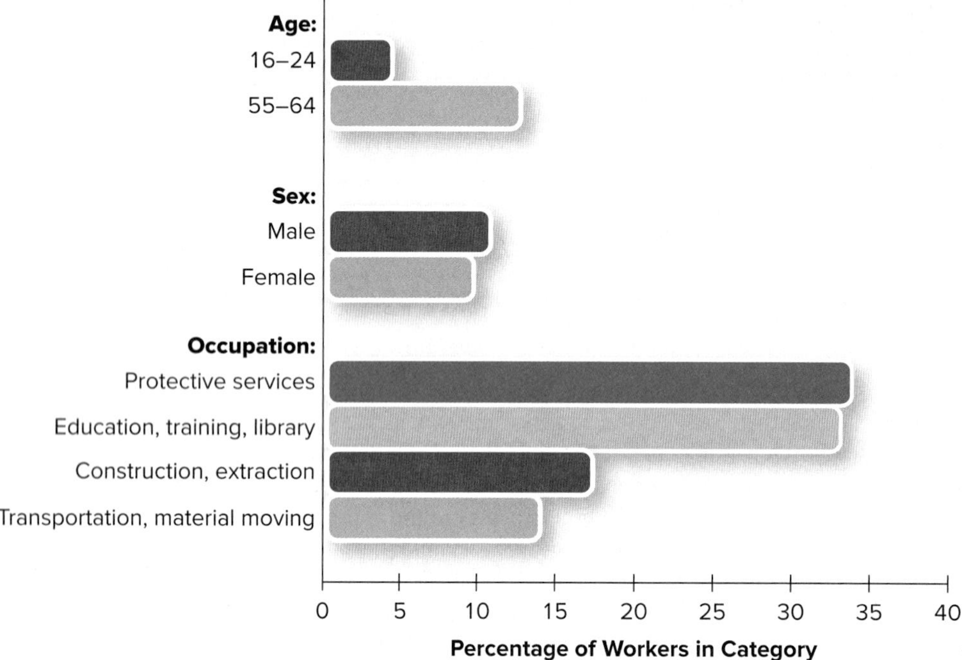

At the local level, all states prohibit strikes by police (Hawaii being a partial exception) and firefighters (Idaho being the exception). Teachers and state employees are somewhat more likely to have the right to strike, depending on the state.

Impact of Unions on Company Performance

Organizations are concerned about whether union organizing and bargaining will hurt their performance, in particular, unions' impact on productivity, profits, and stock performance. Researchers have studied the general relationship between unionization and these performance measures. Through skillful labor relations, organizations can positively influence outcomes.

There has been much debate regarding the effects of unions on productivity.[9] One view is that unions decrease productivity because of work rules and limits on workloads set by union contracts and production lost to such union actions as strikes and work slowdowns.

At the same time, unions can have positive effects on productivity.[10] They can reduce turnover by giving employees a route for resolving problems.[11] Unions emphasize pay systems based on seniority, which remove incentives for employees to compete rather than cooperate. The introduction of a union also may force an employer to improve its management practices and pay greater attention to employee ideas.

Despite their sometimes contentious relationship, Boeing and the International Association of Machinists and Aerospace Workers continue to work together to create an equitable work environment for both the company and its employees. Monty Rakusen/Getty Images

Although there is evidence that unions have both positive and negative effects on productivity, most studies have found that union workers are more productive than nonunion workers. Still, questions remain. Are highly productive workers more likely to form unions, or does a union make workers more productive? The answer is unclear. In theory, if unions caused greater productivity, we would expect union membership to be rising, not falling as it has been.[12]

Even if unions do raise productivity, a company's profits and stock performance may still suffer if unions raise wage and benefits costs more than the productivity gain. On average, union members receive higher wages and more generous benefits than nonunion workers, and evidence shows that unions have a large negative effect on profits. Also, union coverage tends to decline faster in companies with a lower return to shareholders.[13] In summary, companies wishing to become more competitive must continually monitor their labor relations strategy.

The studies tend to look at the average effects of unions, not at individual companies or innovative labor relations. Some organizations excel at labor relations, and some have worked with unions to meet business needs. For example, manufacturers have reported that it is difficult to find enough skilled labor. Many companies depend on unions to recruit and train new workers through apprenticeship programs.

Goals of Management, Labor Unions, and Society

LO 15-2 Identify the labor relations goals of management, labor unions, and society.

Resolving conflicts in a positive way is usually easiest when the parties involved understand each other's goals.[14] Although individual cases vary, we can draw some general conclusions about the goals of labor unions and management. Society, too, has goals for labor and business, given form in the laws regulating labor relations.

Management Goals

Management goals are to increase the organization's profits. Managers tend to prefer options that lower costs and raise output. When deciding whether to discourage employees from forming a union, a concern is that a union will create higher costs in wages and benefits, as well as raise the risk of work stoppages. Managers may also fear that a union will make managers and workers into adversaries or limit management's discretion in making business and employment decisions. This outlook is one reason management may embrace policies and practices that lead to high job satisfaction, in hopes that satisfied employees will not be inclined to form unions.

When an employer has recognized a union, management's goals continue to emphasize restraining costs and improving output. Managers continue to prefer to keep the organization's operations flexible, so they can adjust activities to meet competitive challenges and customer demands. Therefore, in their labor relations, managers prefer to limit increases in wages and benefits and to retain as much control as they can over work rules and schedules.

Best Practices

UAW Helps Spirit AeroSystems Reduce Benefits Costs

A big challenge facing manufacturers like Spirit AeroSystems in the United States is how to keep a lid on payroll costs when wages elsewhere in the world are often much lower. Spirit, based in Wichita, Kansas, makes large aircraft components, including fuselages and wings. In addition to Wichita, it has two facilities in Oklahoma, one in North Carolina, and others in France, Malaysia, and Scotland. Management recently considered moving jobs in Oklahoma to an overseas location to cut costs.

The workers in Oklahoma are represented by the United Auto Workers, and that union sprang into action with a way to address total compensation: control spending on the most expensive employee benefit, health insurance. The UAW was involved in developing a program called SolidaritUS, a new approach to managing the cost of health care. Union-owned SolidaritUS sets up clinics to provide primary care. The clinics are staffed with providers paid a salary, rather than a fee for each service, plus bonuses for meeting targets for health outcomes and patient satisfaction. Because the owners' intention is to serve members rather than earn a profit, their expectation is that they will have less incentive than other health care providers to raise prices.

The UAW proposed setting up SolidaritUS clinics for the workers at Spirit AeroSystems. They would have the option to visit other doctors for primary care, but clinic visits would involve no out-of-pocket costs, while patients would pay a deductible elsewhere. Management agreed to try this approach, and SolidaritUS set up four clinics, staffed to offer same-day appointments and 24-hour access by phone. Although many employees were concerned whether the clinic quality would be adequate, surveys soon showed that employees were more than satisfied. As employees enjoyed the convenience of clinic visits, the company noted a drop-off in more expensive visits to emergency departments and urgent-care facilities. Insurance premiums, which had been rising at 6% or more per year, were flat. Spirit kept the Oklahoma jobs in Oklahoma.

Questions

1. What were the goals of management in this example?
2. What were the goals of the UAW in this example?

Sources: Spirit AeroSystems, "About Us, and "Careers," https://www.spiritaero.com, accessed May 13, 2020; Shelby Livingston, "Labor Unions Strike Back at Rising Health Costs," *Modern Healthcare,* July 22, 2019, https://www:modernhealthcare.com; Shelby Livingston, "Union-Owned Provider Says It Focuses on Care, Not Profits," *Modern Healthcare,* July 22, 2019, https://www.modernhealthcare.com.

The "Best Practices" feature describes how one union addressed this preference in a way that resulted in a win-win negotiation.

Labor Union Goals

In general, labor unions have the goals of obtaining pay and working conditions that satisfy their members and of giving members a voice in decisions that affect them. Traditionally, they obtain these goals by gaining power in numbers. The more workers who belong to a union, the greater the union's power. More members translates into greater ability to halt or disrupt production. Larger unions also have greater financial resources for continuing a strike; the union can help to make up for the wages the workers lose during a strike. The threat of a long strike–stated or implied–can make an employer more willing to meet the union's demands. Thus, with these advantages in mind, unions look for ways to increase their numbers. For example, companies in certain industries hire many independent contractors, who are ineligible to form a union, so unions have run campaigns challenging the independent-contractor status of groups of workers.[15] Such efforts, of course, are most effective if the independent contractors are unhappy with their treatment or compensation packages. Happy contractors more often prefer their independence.

As we noted earlier, union membership is indeed linked to better compensation. In 2019, unionized workers received, on average, wages 20% higher than nonunion workers.[16] Benefits packages also tend to be more generous for union members. However, union goals related to compensation have become more complex since globalization's downward pressure on wages. Especially in manufacturing, some unions have accepted two-tier wage systems in which existing workers' wage rates are protected while new workers are hired at a lower tier. Unions accepted the arrangements when employers were struggling through a severe recession a decade ago. But as the demand for labor has tightened, unions are negotiating contracts that include provisions for moving up the bottom tier to close the gap.[17]

As in the case of two-tier wage structures, unions typically want to influence the *way* pay and promotions are determined. Unlike management, which tries to consider employees as individuals so that pay and promotion decisions relate to performance differences, unions try to build group solidarity and avoid possible arbitrary treatment of employees. To do so, unions focus on equal pay for equal work. They try to have any pay differences based on seniority, on the grounds that this measure is more objective than performance evaluations. As a result, where workers are represented by a union, it is common for all employees in a particular job classification to be paid at the same rate.

Along with compensation, union members often are concerned about working conditions. For example, unsafe conditions are one motivation to form a union. Unions may conduct safety training for their members. They may partner with management to identify ways of getting work done more efficiently as well as more safely.

The survival and security of a union depend on its ability to ensure a regular flow of new members and member dues to support the services it provides. Therefore, unions typically place high priority on negotiating two types of contract provisions with an employer that are critical to a union's security and viability: checkoff provisions and provisions relating to union membership or contribution.

Under a **checkoff provision,** the employer, on behalf of the union, automatically deducts union dues from employees' paychecks. Security provisions related to union membership are *closed shop, union shop, agency shop,* and *maintenance of membership.*

The strongest union security arrangement is a **closed shop,** under which a person must be a union member before being hired. Under the National Labor Relations Act, discussed later in this chapter, closed shops are illegal. A legal membership arrangement that supports the goals of labor unions is the **union shop,** an arrangement that requires an employee to join the union within a certain time (30 days) after beginning employment. A similar alternative is the **agency shop,** which requires the payment of union dues but not union membership. **Maintenance of membership** rules do not require union membership but do require that employees who join the union remain members for a certain period of time, such as the length of the contract. As we will discuss later in the chapter, some states forbid union shops, agency shops, and maintenance of membership.

All these provisions are ways to address unions' concern about "free riders"—employees who benefit from union activities without belonging to a union. By law, all members of a bargaining unit, whether union members or not, must be represented by the union. If the union must offer services to all bargaining unit members but some of them are not dues-paying union members, the union may not have enough financial resources to operate successfully.

Societal Goals

The activities of unions and management take place within the context of society, with society's values driving the laws and regulations that affect labor relations. An issue that has received much attention recently is whether unions infringe on individual rights when they require membership and/or dues. In 2018, the Supreme Court limited public unions' power

Checkoff Provision
Contract provision under which the employer, on behalf of the union, automatically deducts union dues from employees' paychecks.

Closed Shop
Union security arrangement under which a person must be a union member before being hired; illegal for those covered by the National Labor Relations Act.

Union Shop
Union security arrangement that requires employees to join the union within a certain amount of time (30 days) after beginning employment.

Agency Shop
Union security arrangement that requires the payment of union dues but not union membership.

Maintenance of Membership
Union security rules not requiring union membership but requiring that employees who join the union remain members for a certain period of time.

in this regard with respect to government employees in a case in which the plaintiff, Mark Janus, an Illinois state government worker, had objected to a monthly payroll deduction of $45 for his local AFSCME union.[18] In a 5-to-4 decision, the court held that public-employee unions may not require workers to pay dues, because the unions' activities, such as bargaining with a government body, may be considered inherently political and have the effect of being speech protected by the First Amendment. Therefore, declining to support those actions (by not paying union fees) is a First Amendment right of public-union members. The court's ruling did not address private-sector unions.

As long ago as the late 1800s and early 1900s, industrial relations scholars saw unions as a way to make up for individual employees' limited bargaining power.[19] At that time, clashes between workers and management could be violent, and many people hoped that unions would replace the violence with negotiation. Since then, observers have expressed concern that unions in certain industries have become too strong, achieving their goals at the expense of employers' ability to compete or meet other objectives. But even former Senator Orrin Hatch, described by *BusinessWeek* as "labor's archrival on Capitol Hill," has spoken of a need for unions:

> There are always going to be people who take advantage of workers. Unions even that out, to their credit. We need them to level the field between labor and management. If you didn't have unions, it would be very difficult for even enlightened employers not to take advantage of workers on wages and working conditions, because of [competition from less-enlightened] rivals. I'm among the first to say I believe in unions.[20]

Senator Hatch's statement implies that society's goal for unions is to ensure that workers have a voice in how they are treated by their employers. As we will see in the next section, this view has produced a set of laws and regulations intended to give workers the right to join unions if they so wish.

LO 15-3 Summarize laws and regulations that affect labor relations.

Laws and Regulations Affecting Labor Relations

The laws and regulations pertaining to labor relations affect unions' size and bargaining power, so they significantly affect the degree to which unions, management, and society achieve their varied goals. These laws and regulations set limits on union structure and administration and the ways in which unions and management interact.

National Labor Relations Act (NLRA)

National Labor Relations Act (NLRA) Federal law that supports collective bargaining and sets out the rights of employees to form unions.

Perhaps the most dramatic example of labor laws' influence is the 1935 passage of the Wagner Act, also known as the **National Labor Relations Act (NLRA),** which actively supported collective bargaining. After Congress passed the NLRA, union membership in the United States nearly tripled, from 3 million in 1933 to 8.8 million (19.2% of employment) in 1939.[21]

Before the 1930s, the U.S. legal system was generally hostile to unions. The courts tended to view unions as coercive organizations that hindered free trade. Unions' focus on collective voice and collective action (such as strikes and boycotts) did not fit well with the U.S. emphasis on capitalism, individualism, freedom of contract, and property rights.[22] Then the Great Depression of the 1930s shifted public attitudes toward business and the free-enterprise system. Unemployment rates as high as 25% and a steep fall in production between 1929 and 1933 focused attention on employee rights and the shortcomings of the economic system of the time. The nation was in crisis, and President Franklin Roosevelt responded dramatically with the New Deal. On the labor front, the 1935 NLRA ushered in an era of public policy for labor unions, enshrining collective bargaining as the preferred way to settle labor-management disputes.

Employee Rights in the Social-Media Era

Under the National Labor Relations Act, employees may choose to take part in union organizing or other activities on behalf of a union. That includes talking to one another on social media about organizing.

When employees post comments about working conditions or wages, this subject matter falls within the area protected by the NLRA. Furthermore, when employees react to co-workers' comments with a "like," this is also protected activity. This is true whether or not the workers are represented by a union.

Employers have not always realized they need to consider this when disciplining employees for online conduct that creates a bad impression of the company. For example, when an employee at an ambulance company posted Facebook messages about disciplinary actions taken against her, some colleagues posted suggestions on how to respond to the company about her eventual termination. The company then learned that firing the employee violated the NLRA because the employee was engaged in social-media conversations with co-workers, which is considered a protected activity.

This standard certainly does *not* mean that employees can say whatever they want without any consequences. For example, the NLRA does not address political, religious, or other personal comments by employees. Nor did it protect the auto dealership employee who embarrassed the dealership (and a customer) when the employee posted photos of a Land Rover driven into a pond during a test drive.

This area of the law is developing as arbitrators and courts begin to handle an increasing number of complaints. HR professionals should keep up-to-date with the news on this topic as rulings continue to define the boundaries of allowable and forbidden behavior.

Questions

1. What is the difference between the way the NLRA treats an organization wanting to discipline (a) a group of workers complaining about their work schedules on Facebook and (b) an employee who posts hateful political remarks in a comment on her LinkedIn page, where she is identified as an employee?
2. Suppose you are reading employee reviews on the Glassdoor page for a company where you are considering applying for a job. You see one comment saying the supervisors don't care about employees, and you see ten favorable comments about the company's supervisors. As a job seeker, how would you weigh those comments? From the perspective of the employer, what ideas does this give you for how to minimize the negative impact of speech that is protected under NLRA but could hurt the company's reputation?

Sources: Lisa Nagele-Piazza, "NLRB Memo Clarifies Rules for Workplace Social Media Policies," *Society for Human Resource Management,* August 28, 2019, https://www.shrm.org; Lisa Nagele-Piazza, "Can Employees Be Fired for Off-Duty Conduct?" *Society for Human Resource Management,* October 24, 2017, https://www.shrm.org; Mark Theodore, "Two Employees, Social Media, an Unlawful Policy . . . What Could Possibly Go Wrong?" *National Law Review,* August 4, 2017, https://www.natlawreview.com.

Section 7 of the NLRA sets out the rights of employees, including the "right to self-organization, to form, join, or assist labor organizations, to bargain collectively through representatives of their own choosing, and to engage in other concerted activities for the purpose of collective bargaining."[23] Employees also have the right to refrain from these activities, unless union membership is a condition of employment. The following activities are among those protected under the NLRA:

- Union organizing.
- Joining a union, whether recognized by the employer or not.
- Going out on strike to secure better working conditions.
- Refraining from activity on behalf of the union.

As discussed in "HRM Social," these rights apply not only to individual and face-to-face actions, but also to activities that take place online.

Most employees in the private sector are covered by the NLRA. However, workers employed under the following conditions are not covered:[24]

- Employed as a supervisor.
- Employed by a parent or spouse.
- Employed as an independent contractor.
- Employed in the domestic service of any person or family in a home.
- Employed as agricultural laborers.
- Employed by an employer subject to the Railway Labor Act.
- Employed by a federal, state, or local government.
- Employed by any other person who is not an employer as defined in the NLRA.

State or local laws may provide additional coverage. For example, California's 1975 Agricultural Labor Relations Act covers agricultural workers in that state.

In Section 8(a), the NLRA prohibits certain activities by employers as unfair labor practices. In general, employers may not interfere with, restrain, or coerce employees in exercising their rights to join or assist a labor organization or to refrain from such activities. Employers may not dominate or interfere with the formation or activities of a labor union. They may not discriminate in any aspect of employment that attempts to encourage or discourage union activity, nor may they discriminate against employees for providing testimony related to enforcement of the NLRA. Finally, employers may not refuse to bargain collectively with a labor organization that has standing under the act. For more guidance in complying with the NLRA, see the examples in Table 15.1.

When employers or unions violate the NLRA, remedies typically include ordering that unfair labor practices stop. Employers may be required to rehire workers, with or without back pay. The NLRA is not a criminal law, and violators may not be assigned punitive damages (fines to punish rather than merely make up for the harm done).

TABLE 15.1

Unfair Labor Practices: Examples

EMPLOYERS SHOULD NOT . . .
Threaten employees with loss of their jobs or benefits if they join or vote for a union
Threaten to close down a plant if it is organized by a union
Question employees about their union membership or activities in a way that restrains or coerces them
Take an active part in organizing a union or committee to represent employees
Discharge employees for urging other employees to join a union
Promise benefits (e.g., a holiday or better working conditions) to employees if they don't support a union
Ask employees or job applicants about union-organizing activities they might have engaged in
Prevent employees from promoting a union (e.g., distributing literature) during breaks and other nonworking hours
Discourage employees from conversations or other activities aimed at improving working conditions
Spy on employee activities to determine workers' views about a union
EMPLOYERS SHOULD . . .
Allow employees to wear union logos on shirts or jackets
Bargain about the effects of a decision to close one of the employer's facilities

Sources: National Labor Relations Board, "Employer/Union Rights and Obligations," https://www.nlrb.gov, accessed May 13, 2020; "Dos and Don'ts for Supervisors During a Union Organizing Campaign," *MRA*, https://www.mranet.org, accessed May 13, 2020; Gary S. Fealk, "NLRA Covers Nonunion Employers, Too," *HR Hero*, December 4, 2013, https://www.hrhero.com.

Laws Amending the NLRA

Originally the NLRA did not list any unfair labor practices by unions. In later amendments to the NLRA—the Taft-Hartley Act of 1947 and the Landrum-Griffin Act of 1959—Congress established some restrictions on union practices deemed unfair to employers and union members.

Under the Taft-Hartley Act, unions may not restrain employers through actions such as the following:[25]

- Mass picketing in such numbers that nonstriking employees physically cannot enter the workplace.
- Engaging in violent acts in connection with a strike.
- Threatening employees with physical injury or job loss if they do not support union activities.
- During contract negotiations, insisting on illegal provisions, provisions that the employer may hire only workers who are union members or "satisfactory" to the union, or working conditions to be determined by a group to which the employer does not belong.
- Terminating an existing contract and striking for a new one without notifying the employer, the Federal Mediation and Conciliation Service, and the state mediation service (where one exists).

The Taft-Hartley Act also allows the states to pass so-called **right-to-work laws,** which make union shops, maintenance of membership, and agency shops illegal. The idea behind such laws is that requiring union membership or the payment of union dues restricts the employees' right to freedom of association. In other words, employees should be free to choose whether they join a union or other group. Of course, unions have a different point of view. The union perspective—which may legally be applied only to private-sector workers—is that unions provide services to all members of a bargaining unit (such as all of a company's workers), and all members who receive the benefits of a union should pay union dues. Figure 15.3 indicates which states currently have right-to-work laws.

Right-to-Work Laws
State laws that make union shops, maintenance of membership, and agency shops illegal.

The Landrum-Griffin Act regulates unions' actions with regard to their members, including financial disclosure and the conduct of elections. This law establishes and protects rights

FIGURE 15.3
States with Right-to-Work Laws

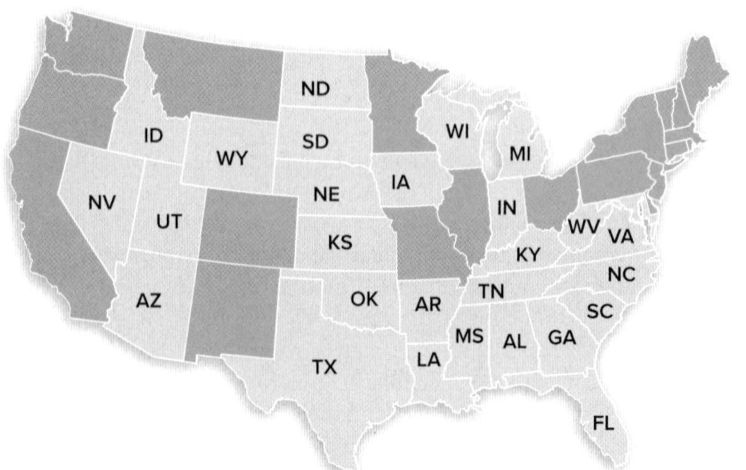

Sources: National Conference of State Legislatures, "Right to Work Resources," https://www.ncsl.org, accessed May 13, 2020; E. Watkins, "Unions Notch Win in Deep-Red Missouri with Rejection of Right-to-Work Law," *CNN*, https://www.cnn.com, accessed May 13, 2020.

of union members. These include the right to nominate candidates for union office, participate in union meetings and secret-ballot elections, and examine unions' financial records.

National Labor Relations Board (NLRB)

National Labor Relations Board (NLRB) Federal government agency that enforces the NLRA by conducting and certifying representation elections and investigating unfair labor practices.

Enforcement of the NLRA rests with the **National Labor Relations Board (NLRB).** This federal government agency consists of a five-member board, the general counsel, and 52 regional and other field offices. Because the NLRB is a federal agency, its enforcement actions are limited to companies that have an impact on interstate commerce, but as a practical matter, this extends to all but purely local businesses. For federal government workers under the Civil Service Reform Act of 1978, Title VII, the Federal Labor Relations Authority has a role similar to that of the NLRB. Many states have similar agencies to administer their laws governing state and local government workers.

The NLRB has two major functions: to conduct and certify representation elections and to prevent unfair labor practices. It does not initiate either of these actions but responds to requests for action.

Representation Elections The NLRB is responsible for ensuring that the organizing process follows certain steps, described in the next section. Depending on the response to organizing efforts, the NLRB conducts elections. When a majority of workers vote in favor of a union, the NLRB certifies it as the exclusive representative of a group of employees. The NLRB also conducts elections to decertify unions, following the same process as for representation elections.

The NLRB is also responsible for determining the appropriate bargaining unit and the employees who are eligible to participate in organizing activities. As we stated earlier, bargaining units may not include certain types of employees, such as agricultural laborers, independent contractors, supervisors, and managers. Beyond this, the NLRB attempts to group together employees who have a community of interest in their wages, hours, and working conditions. A unit may cover employees in one facility or multiple facilities within a single employer, or the unit may cover multiple employers. In general, employees on the payroll just before the ordering of an election are eligible to vote, although this rule is modified in some cases, for example, when employment in the industry is irregular. Most employees who are on strike and who have been replaced by other employees are eligible to vote in an election (such as a decertification election) that occurs within 12 months of the onset of the strike.

Prevention of Unfair Labor Practices The NLRB prevents unfair labor practices by educating employers and employees about their rights and responsibilities under the National Labor Relations Act and by responding to complaints. It does this by publishing guidance, laying out its rules. The "HR How To" provides an example describing NLRB guidance related to employee handbooks.

The handling of complaints regarding unfair labor practices begins when someone files a charge. The deadline for filing a charge is six months after the alleged unfair practice. All parties must be served with a copy of the charge. (Registered mail is recommended.) The charge is investigated by a regional office. If, after investigating, the NLRB finds the charge has merit and issues a complaint, two actions are possible. The NLRB may defer to a grievance procedure agreed on by the employer and the union; grievances are discussed later in this chapter. Or a hearing may be held before an administrative law judge. The judge makes a recommendation, which either party may appeal.

The NLRB has the authority to issue cease-and-desist orders to halt unfair labor practices. It also can order the employer to reinstate workers, with or without back pay. The NLRB can set aside the results of an election if it believes either the union or the employer

HR How To

Writing an Employee Handbook That Follows NLRB Guidance

During the past few years, rulings by the National Labor Relations Board strictly enforced employee rights with regard to policies in companies' employee handbooks. If a handbook set limits so broadly that employees might perceive a limitation of their rights under the National Labor Relations Act, the NLRB would declare such policies to be invalid.

This opened up so much room for employees to embarrass employers that the NLRB saw a need for better information. In June 2018, the board issued new guidance, sorting rules into those that are generally lawful, those requiring evaluation on a case-by-case basis, and those that are unlawful on their face. Here are some ways that employers can meet the new requirements.

- Distinguish between criticism of working conditions and nasty comments about individuals. Policies may forbid behavior—including comments and photo sharing—that involves rude, uncivil, and unbusiness-like messages about individuals.
- Focus on behavior that interferes with work. Policies may forbid insubordination and failure to cooperate, as well as behavior that creates a disturbance or puts the employee in competition with the company.
- Protect the company's intellectual property (nontangible assets like logos, copyrights, and trade secrets). Require that employees obtain written approval before taking pictures or making recordings at work, as well as before using logos or other company-owned property. Restrictions on using the company's name fall into the gray area requiring closer scrutiny. However, employers can prohibit statements that amount to defamation (statements that are false and damaging to the reputation of the company) or misrepresentation (statements that are false and affect someone's decision to enter into a contract with the company).
- Expect NLRB scrutiny of policies that limit employees' conduct outside of work or forbid statements that are false (but not necessarily defamation or misrepresentation in the legal sense).
- Avoid policies that limit behaviors specifically protected under the NLRA, including rules against discussing compensation or working conditions and rules that prohibit joining outside organizations.

Questions

1. Based on the information given, rewrite the following handbook statement to make it better follow the NLRB's guidance: "Employees may not say negative things about the company on social media."
2. As in question 1, rewrite the following handbook statement: "Employees may not post photos of co-workers on social media."

Sources: Jon Hyman, "NLRB Offers Significant Guidance on Its New(ish) Employee Handbook Rules," *Workforce,* July 9, 2019, https://www.workforce.com; Poyner Spruill LLP, "Fresh NLRB Guidance Eases Workplace Policy Restrictions," *JD Supra,* June 21, 2018, https://www.jdsupra.com; Erin Mulvaney, "Whole Foods Can't Erase NLRB Ruling against Workplace Recording Policy," *National Law Journal,* May 2, 2018, https://www.law.com; William Welkowitz, "NLRB Shifts Standard for Deciding if Employee Handbook Rules Are Lawful," *Labor and Employment Blog,* March 8, 2018, https://www.bna.com.

has created "an atmosphere of confusion or fear of reprisals."[26] If an employer or union refuses to comply with an NLRB order, the board has the authority to petition the U.S. Court of Appeals. The court may enforce the order, recommend it to the NLRB for modification, change the order itself, or set it aside altogether. For an example of an issue that has been the subject of petitions to the court of appeals, see the "HR Oops!" feature.

Union Organizing

LO 15-4 Describe the union organizing process.

Unions begin their involvement with an organization's employees by conducting an organizing campaign. To meet its objectives, a union needs to convince a majority of workers that they should receive better pay or other employment conditions and that the union will help them do so. The employer's objectives will depend on its strategy–whether it seeks to work with a union or convince employees that they are better off without union representation.

When Offensive Speech Is Protected

Many organizations try to create a civil workplace in which co-workers are respectful and diversity is valued. The opposite condition—a workplace in which some employees feel harassed—is prohibited by laws protecting equal employment opportunity. But an individual's speech, which can contribute to either kind of situation, is protected by the National Labor Relations Act when it pertains to working conditions and wages. Some companies, including most famously Google, have been surprised to discover that when they tried to enforce rules about civility, the NLRB found that they engaged in unfair labor practices.

In the case involving Google, an employee used the company's internal social-networking site to complain about the company's diversity policies, in particular its treatment of employees who express views the employee considered "conservative." The employee's language, even in the NLRB's review of the complaint, included comments that were "somewhat insensitive towards women and minorities in light of the conversation's context." Google fired the employee for violating employee policies, including downloading company documents on a personal device, but the NLRB held that the employee's comments did not rise to the level of harassment and that Google's policies were too broad to be clear.

However, in an earlier, similar case involving Google, the NLRB had allowed the termination of an employee whose complaints about diversity policies did reach the level of harassment.

Google settled the case in which the NLRB found it overreached, and the company provided employees with a detailed statement about their rights to speak about workplace conditions. However, other companies caught in similar situations have asked the appeals court to intervene, given the potential for free speech to involve harassment. Past NLRB rulings have protected workers using racial epithets while on strike or in meetings about company policy, and these employers have brought their concerns about harassment to the appeals court. Judges have requested greater clarity from the NLRB. A few years ago, the NLRB began working with the Equal Employment Opportunity Commission to develop joint guidance for employers, but the agencies discontinued the effort before finishing. This leaves employers waiting for guidance today. At least one attorney has noted that employers might cautiously consider that the penalties for violating equal employment laws can be significantly costlier than for violating NLRB requirements, but no one wants to advise employers to ignore either law.

Questions

1. What is the NLRB's role in ensuring companies follow the law when employees use offensive language to talk about wages and working conditions?
2. What would you advise a company to do if it has an employee who uses racist or sexist language to complain about work policies?

Sources: Rachel Adams Ladeau, "NLRB Poised to Trim Protections for Offensive Comments," *New England In-House,* February 27, 2020, https://newengland-inhouse.com; Jennifer Carsen, "Google Engineer's Complaint about Diversity Was Protected, NLRB Says," *HR Dive,* February 19, 2020, https://www.hrdive.com; Jennifer Elias, "Google Will Now Post This List of Employee 'Rights' at HQ as Part of Legal Settlement," *CNBC,* September 13, 2019, https://www.cnbc.com.

The Process of Organizing

The organizing process begins when union representatives make contact with employees, present their message about the union, and invite them to sign an authorization card. For the organization process to continue, at least 30% of the employees must sign an authorization card.

If over half the employees sign an authorization card, the union may request that the employer voluntarily recognize the union. If the employer agrees, the NLRB certifies the union as the exclusive representative of employees. If the employer refuses, or if only 30% to 50% of employees signed cards, the NLRB conducts a secret-ballot election. The arrangements are made in one of two ways:

1. For a *consent election,* the employer and the union seeking representation arrive at an agreement stating the time and place of the election, the choices included on the ballot, and a way to determine who is eligible to vote.
2. For a *stipulation election,* the parties cannot agree on all of these terms, so the NLRB dictates the time and place, ballot choices, and method of determining eligibility.

On the ballot, workers vote for or against union representation, and they may also have a choice from among more than one union. If the union (or one of the unions on the ballot) wins a majority of votes, the NLRB certifies the union. If the ballot includes more than one union and neither gains a simple majority, the NLRB holds a runoff election.

As noted earlier, if the NLRB finds the election was not conducted fairly, it may set aside the results and call for a new election. Conduct that may lead to an election result's being set aside includes the following examples:[27]

- Threats of loss of jobs or benefits by an employer or union to influence votes or organizing activities.
- A grant of benefits or a promise of benefits as a means of influencing votes or organizing activities.
- Campaign speeches by management or union representatives to assembled groups of employees on company time less than 24 hours before an election.
- The actual use or threat of physical force or violence to influence votes or organizing activities.

After certification, there are limits on future elections. Once the NLRB has certified a union as the exclusive representative of a group of employees, it will not permit additional elections for one year. Also, after the union and employer have finished negotiating a contract, an election cannot be held for the time of the contract period or for three years, whichever comes first. The parties to the contract may agree not to hold an election for longer than three years, but an outside party (another union) cannot be barred for more than three years. Note that both union certifications and union elections can be conducted online.

Management Strategies

Sometimes an employer will recognize a union after a majority of employees have signed authorization cards. More often, there is a hotly contested election campaign. During the campaign, unions try to persuade employees that their wages, benefits, treatment by employers, and chances to influence workplace decisions are too poor or small and that the union will be able to obtain improvements in these areas. Management typically responds with its own messages providing an opposite point of view. Management messages say the organization has provided a valuable package of wages and benefits and has treated employees well. Management also argues that the union will not be able to keep its promises but will instead create costs for employees, such as union dues and lost income during strikes.

Employers use a variety of methods to oppose unions in organizing campaigns.[28] Their efforts range from hiring consultants to distributing leaflets and letters to presenting the company's viewpoint at meetings of employees. Some management efforts go beyond what the law permits, especially in the eyes of union organizers. Why would employers break the law? One explanation is that the consequences, such as reinstating workers with back pay, are small compared to the benefits.[29] If coercing workers away from joining a union saves the company the higher wages, benefits, and other costs of a unionized workforce, management may feel an incentive to accept costs like back pay.

Supervisors have the most direct contact with employees. Thus, as Table 15.2 indicates, it is critical that they establish good relationships with employees even before there is any attempt at union organizing. Supervisors also must know what *not* to do if a union drive takes place. They should be trained in the legal principles discussed earlier in this chapter.

Union Strategies

The traditional union organizing strategy has been for organizers to call or visit employees at home, when possible, to talk about issues like pay and job security. They also may reach out through e-mail and keep employees informed on social media.

Associate Union Membership
Alternative form of union membership in which members receive discounts on insurance and credit cards rather than representation in collective bargaining.

Beyond encouraging workers to sign authorization cards and vote for the union, organizers use some creative alternatives to traditional organizing activities. They sometimes offer workers **associate union membership,** which is not linked to an employee's workplace and does not provide representation in collective bargaining. Rather, an associate member receives other services, such as discounts on health and life insurance or credit cards.[30] In return for these benefits, the union receives membership dues and a broader base of support for its activities. Associate membership may be attractive to employees who wish to join a union but cannot because their workplace is not organized by a union.

Corporate Campaigns
Bringing public, financial, or political pressure on employers during union organization and contract negotiation.

Another alternative to traditional organizing is to conduct **corporate campaigns**—bringing public, financial, or political pressure on employers during union organization and contract negotiation.[31] The Amalgamated Clothing and Textile Workers Union (ACTWU) corporate campaign against textile maker J. P. Stevens during the late 1970s was one of the first successful corporate campaigns and served as a model for those that followed. The ACTWU organized a boycott of J. P. Stevens products and threatened to withdraw its

TABLE 15.2
What Supervisors Should and Should Not Do to Discourage Unions

WHAT TO DO:
Report any direct or indirect signs of union activity to a core management group.
Deal with employees by carefully stating the company's response to pro-union arguments. These responses should be coordinated by the company to maintain consistency and to avoid threats or promises. Take away union issues by following effective management practices all the time:
Deliver recognition and appreciation.
Solve employee problems.
Protect employees from harassment or humiliation.
Provide business-related information.
Be consistent in treatment of different employees.
Accommodate special circumstances where appropriate.
Ensure due process in performance management.
Treat all employees with dignity and respect.
WHAT TO AVOID:
Threatening employees with harsher terms and conditions of employment or employment loss if they engage in union activity.
Interrogating employees about pro-union or anti-union sentiments that they or others may have or reviewing union authorization cards or pro-union petitions.
Promising employees that they will receive favorable terms or conditions of employment if they forgo union activity.
Spying on employees known to be, or suspected of being, engaged in pro-union activities.

Source: J. A. Segal, "Unshackle Your Supervisors to Stay Union Free," *HR Magazine,* June 1998.

pension funds from financial institutions where J. P. Stevens officers acted as directors. The company eventually agreed to a contract with ACTWU.[32]

Another winning union organizing strategy is to negotiate employer neutrality and card-check provisions into a contract. Under a *neutrality provision,* the employer pledges not to oppose organizing attempts elsewhere in the company. A *card-check provision* is an agreement that if a certain percentage–by law, at least a majority–of employees sign an authorization card, the employer will recognize their union representation. An impartial outside agency, such as the American Arbitration Association, counts the cards. Evidence suggests that this strategy can be very effective for unions.[33]

Decertifying a Union

The Taft-Hartley Act expanded union members' right to be represented by leaders of their own choosing to include the right to vote out an existing union. This action is called *decertifying* the union. Decertification follows the same process as a representation election. An election to decertify a union may not take place when a contract is in effect.

The number of decertification elections has increased from about 5% of all elections in the 1950s and 1960s to more than double that rate in recent years. In fiscal year 2018, the NLRB reported that nearly 9% of elections were decertification elections.[34]

Collective Bargaining

LO 15-5 Explain how management and unions negotiate contracts.

When the NLRB has certified a union, that union represents employees during contract negotiations. In **collective bargaining,** a union negotiates on behalf of its members with management representatives to arrive at a contract defining conditions of employment for the term of the contract and to resolve differences in the way they interpret the contract. Typical contracts include provisions for pay, benefits, work rules, and resolution of workers' grievances. Table 15.3 shows typical provisions negotiated in collective bargaining contracts.

Collective Bargaining Negotiation between union representatives and management representatives to arrive at a contract defining conditions of employment for the term of the contract and to administer that contract.

Collective bargaining differs from one situation to another in terms of *bargaining structure*–that is, the range of employees and employers covered by the contract. A contract may involve a narrow group of employees in a craft union or a broad group in an industrial union. Contracts may cover one or several facilities of the same employer, or the bargaining structure may involve several employers. Many more interests must be considered in collective bargaining for an industrial union with a bargaining structure that includes several employers than in collective bargaining for a craft union in a single facility.

The majority of contract negotiations take place between unions and employers that have been through the process before. In the typical situation, management has come to accept the union as an organization it must work with. The situation can be very different when a union has just been certified and is negotiating its first contract. In over one-fourth of negotiations for a first contract, the parties are unable to reach an agreement.[35]

Bargaining over New Contracts

Clearly, the outcome of contract negotiations can have important consequences for labor costs, productivity, and the organization's ability to compete. Therefore, unions and management need to prepare carefully for collective bargaining. Preparation includes establishing objectives for the contract, reviewing the old contract, gathering data (such as compensation paid by competitors and the company's ability to survive a strike), predicting the likely demands to be made, and establishing the cost of meeting the demands.[36] This preparation can help negotiators develop a plan for how to negotiate.

TABLE 15.3

Typical Provisions in Collective Bargaining Contracts

Establishment and administration of the agreement	Contract duration and reopening and renegotiation provisions Grievance procedures Arbitration and mediation Strikes and lockouts Contract enforcement
Functions, rights, and responsibilities	Management rights clauses Subcontracting Union activities on company time and premises Union–management cooperation Regulation of technological change Advance notice and consultation
Wage determination and administration	Rate structure and wage differentials Incentive systems and production bonus plans Production standards and time studies Job classification and job evaluation Wage adjustments—individual and general
Job or income security	Hiring and transfer arrangements Employment and income guarantees Supplemental unemployment benefit plans Regulation of overtime, shift work, etc. Reduction of hours to forestall layoffs Layoff procedures; seniority; recall Promotion practices Training and retraining Relocation allowances Severance pay and layoff benefit plans
Plant operations	Work and shop rules Rest periods and other in-plant time allowances Safety and health Hours of work and premium pay practices Shift operations Hazardous work Discipline and discharge
Paid and unpaid leave	Vacations, holidays, sick leave Funeral and personal leave Military leave and jury duty
Employee benefit plans	Health and insurance plans Pension plans Profit-sharing, stock purchase, and thrift plans Bonus plans
Special groups	Apprentices and learners Workers with disabilities Veterans Union representatives

Source: Adapted from T. A. Kochan, *Collective Bargaining and Industrial Relations* (Homewood, IL: Richard D. Irwin, 1980), p. 29. Original data from J. W. Bloch, "Union Contracts—A New Series of Studies," *Monthly Labor Review 87* (October 1964), pp. 1184–85.

Negotiations go through various stages.[37] In the earliest stages, many more people are often present than in later stages. On the union side, this may give all the various internal interest groups a chance to participate and voice their goals. Their input helps communicate to management what will satisfy union members and may help the union achieve greater solidarity. At this stage, union negotiators often present a long list of proposals, partly to satisfy members and partly to introduce enough issues that they will have flexibility later in the process. Management may or may not present proposals of its own. Sometimes management prefers to react to the union's proposals.

During the middle stages of the process, each side must make a series of decisions, even though the outcome is uncertain. How important is each issue to the other side? How likely is it that disagreement on particular issues will result in a strike? When and to what extent should one side signal its willingness to compromise?

In the final stage of negotiations, pressure for an agreement increases. Public negotiations may be only part of the process. Negotiators from each side may hold one-on-one meetings or small-group meetings where they escape some public relations pressures. A neutral third party may act as a go-between or facilitator. In some cases, bargaining breaks down as the two sides find they cannot reach a mutually acceptable agreement. The outcome depends partly on the relative bargaining power of each party. That power, in turn, depends on each party's ability to withstand a strike, which costs the workers their pay during the strike and costs the employer lost production and possibly lost customers.

When Bargaining Breaks Down

The intended outcome of collective bargaining is a contract with terms acceptable to both parties. If one or both sides determine that negotiation alone will not produce such an agreement, bargaining breaks down. To bring this impasse to an end, work may stop, or the parties may bring in outside help to resolve their differences.

Work Stoppages

In the past, a breakdown in bargaining often led union members to stop working, a practice called a strike. Management also can initiate a type of work stoppage known as a lockout. However, the number of work stoppages (strikes and lockouts) has plunged since the 1950s, although 2018 and 2019 saw significant increases in work stoppages compared to previous years in the last decade (Figure 15.4).

Strike
A collective decision by union members not to work until certain demands or conditions are met.

A **strike** is a collective decision of the union members not to work until certain demands or conditions are met. The union members vote, and if the majority favors a strike, they all go on strike at that time or when union leaders believe the time is right. Strikes are typically accompanied by *picketing*—the union stations members near the worksite with signs indicating the union is on strike. During the strike, the union members do not receive pay from their employer, but the union may be able to make up for some of the lost pay. The employer loses production unless it can hire replacement workers, and even then, productivity may be reduced. Often, other unions support striking workers by refusing to cross their picket line—for example, refusing to make deliveries to a company during a strike.

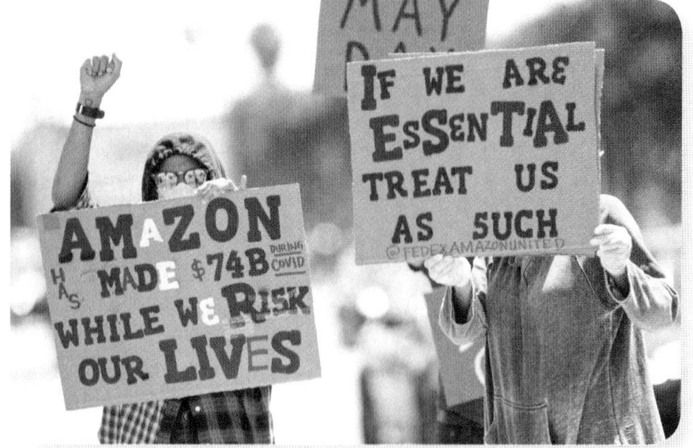

On May Day 2020, Amazon workers, including those at Whole Foods, called for a walkout/sickout in protest over inadequate workplace protections during the COVID-19 pandemic. VALERIE MACON/AFP/Getty Images

A primary reason strikes are rare is that a strike is seldom in the best interests of either party. Not only do workers lose wages and

FIGURE 15.4
Work Stoppages Involving 1,000 or More Workers

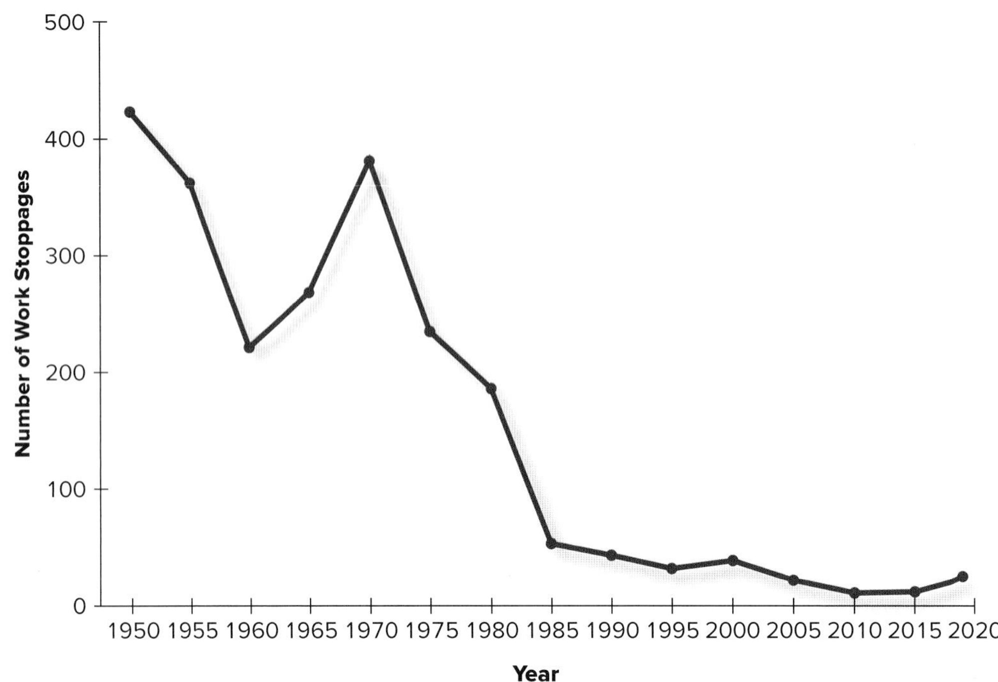

Note: Because strikes are most likely in large bargaining units, these numbers represent most lost working time in the United States.

Source: Bureau of Labor Statistics, Work Stoppage Data, http://data.bls.gov, accessed May 13, 2020.

employers lose production, but the negative experience of a strike can make future interactions more difficult. When strikes do occur, the conduct of each party during the strike can do lasting harm to labor-management relations. Violence by either side or threats of job loss or actual job loss because jobs went to replacement workers can make future relations difficult. Finally, many government employees do not have a right to strike, and their percentage among unionized employees overall has risen in recent decades, as we discussed earlier.

Lockout
An employer's exclusion of workers from a workplace until they meet certain conditions.

In a **lockout,** the employer excludes workers from the workplace until they meet certain conditions. During the 1990s and 2000s, lockouts accounted for less than 5% of work stoppages, but they have become a larger share, mainly because unions are much more reluctant to strike. In other words, the rate of lockouts has been falling, but the rate of strikes has been falling faster.[38] Some of the most widely noticed lockouts are those involving sports leagues, including the National Hockey League and National Football League. During a lockout, an employer may hire replacement workers, which makes the tactic powerful in bargaining with a union.

Mediation
Conflict resolution procedure in which a mediator hears the views of both sides and facilitates the negotiation process but has no formal authority to dictate a resolution.

Alternatives to Work Stoppages Because work stoppages are so costly and risky, unions and employers generally prefer other methods for resolving conflicts. Three common alternatives rely on a neutral third party, usually provided by the Federal Mediation and Conciliation Service (FMCS):

- **Mediation** is the least formal and most widely used of these procedures. A mediator hears the views of both sides and facilitates the negotiation process. The mediator has no formal authority to dictate a resolution, so a strike remains a possibility. In a survey studying negotiations between unions and large businesses, mediation was used in almost 4 out of 10 negotiation efforts.[39]

- A **fact finder,** most often used for negotiations with governmental bodies, typically reports on the reasons for the dispute, the views and arguments of both sides, and (sometimes) a recommended settlement, which the parties may decline. The public nature of these recommendations may pressure the parties to settle. Even if they do not accept the fact finder's recommended settlement, the fact finder may identify or frame issues in a way that makes agreement easier.
- Under **arbitration,** the most formal type of outside intervention, an arbitrator or arbitration board determines a settlement that is *binding,* meaning the parties have to accept it. In conventional arbitration, the arbitrator fashions the solution. In "final-offer arbitration," the arbitrator must choose either management's or the union's final offer for each issue or for the contract as a whole. "Rights arbitration" focuses on enforcing or interpreting contract terms. Arbitration in the writing of contracts or setting of contract terms has traditionally been reserved for special circumstances such as negotiations between unions and government agencies, where strikes may be illegal or especially costly.

Fact Finder
Third party to collective bargaining who reports the reasons for a dispute, the views and arguments of both sides, and possibly a recommended settlement, which the parties may decline.

Arbitration
Conflict resolution procedure in which an arbitrator or arbitration board determines a binding settlement.

Contract Administration

LO 15-6 Summarize the practice of contract administration.

Although the process of negotiating a labor agreement (including the occasional strike) receives the most publicity, other union-management activities occur far more often. Bargaining over a new contract typically occurs only about every three years, but administering labor contracts goes on day after day, year after year. The two activities are linked, of course. Vague or inconsistent language in the contract can make administering the contract more difficult. The difficulties can create conflict that spills over into the next round of negotiations.[40] Events during negotiations–strikes, the use of replacement workers, or violence by either side–also can lead to difficulties in working successfully under a conflict.

Contract administration includes carrying out the terms of the agreement and resolving conflicts over interpretation or violation of the agreement. Under a labor contract, the process for resolving these conflicts is called a **grievance procedure.** This procedure has a key influence on success in contract administration. A grievance procedure may be started by an employee or discharged employee who believes the employer violated the contract or by a union representative on behalf of a group of workers or union representatives.

Grievance Procedure
The process for resolving union-management conflicts over interpretation or violation of a collective bargaining agreement.

For grievances launched by an employee, a typical grievance procedure follows the steps shown in Figure 15.5. The grievance may be settled during any of the four steps. In the first step, the employee talks to his or her supervisor about the problem. If this conversation is unsatisfactory, the employee may involve the union steward in further discussion. The union steward and employee decide whether the problem has been resolved and, if not, whether it is a contract violation. If the problem was not resolved and does seem to be a contract violation, the union moves to step 2, putting the grievance in writing and submitting it to a line manager. The union steward meets with a management representative to try to resolve the problem. Management consults with the industrial relations staff and puts its response in writing too at this second stage. If step 2 fails to resolve the problem, the union appeals the grievance to top line management and representatives of the industrial relations staff. The union may involve more local or international officers in discussions at this stage (see step 3 in Figure 15.5). The decision resulting from the appeal is put into writing. If the grievance is still not resolved, the union may decide (step 4) to appeal the grievance to an arbitrator. If

FIGURE 15.5

Steps in an Employee-Initiated Grievance Procedure

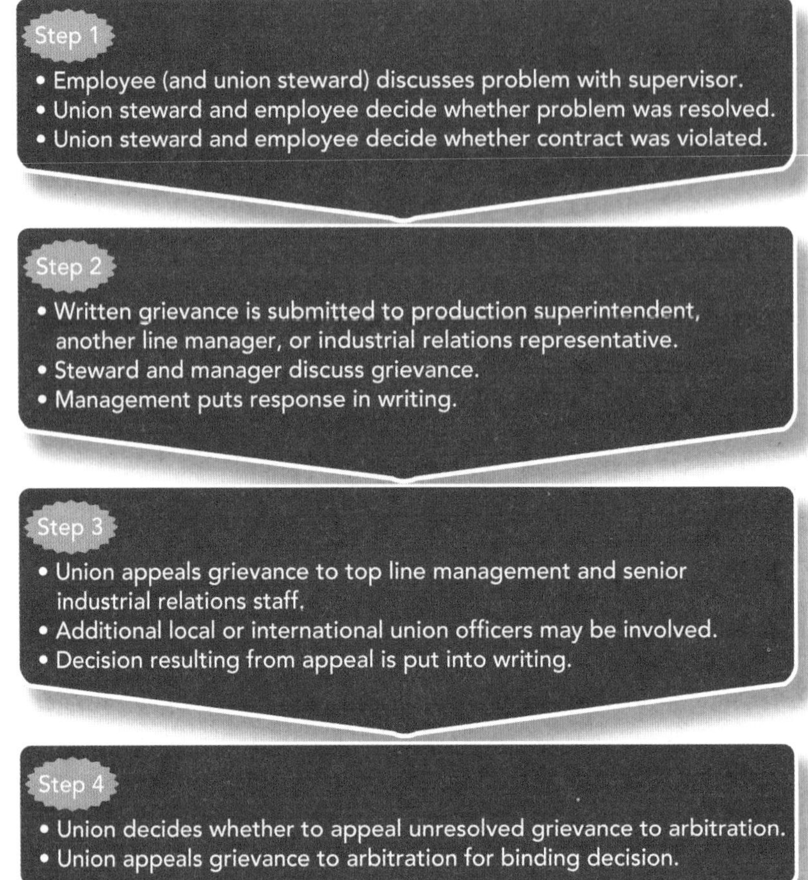

Step 1
• Employee (and union steward) discusses problem with supervisor.
• Union steward and employee decide whether problem was resolved.
• Union steward and employee decide whether contract was violated.
Step 2
• Written grievance is submitted to production superintendent, another line manager, or industrial relations representative.
• Steward and manager discuss grievance.
• Management puts response in writing.
Step 3
• Union appeals grievance to top line management and senior industrial relations staff.
• Additional local or international union officers may be involved.
• Decision resulting from appeal is put into writing.
Step 4
• Union decides whether to appeal unresolved grievance to arbitration.
• Union appeals grievance to arbitration for binding decision.

Sources: J. W. Budd, *Labor Relations,* 6th ed. (New York: McGraw-Hill, 2020); J. A. Fossum, *Labor Relations* (Boston: McGraw-Hill/Irwin, 2002), pp. 448–452; T. Kochan, *Collective Bargaining and Industrial Relations* (Homewood, IL: Richard D. Irwin, 1980), p. 395.

the grievance involves a discharged employee, the process may begin at step 2 or 3, however, and the time limits between steps may be shorter. Grievances filed by the union on behalf of a group may begin at step 1 or step 2.

The majority of grievances are settled during the earlier steps of the process. This reduces delays and avoids the costs of arbitration. If a grievance does reach arbitration, the arbitrator makes the final ruling in the matter. Based on a series of Supreme Court decisions, courts generally avoid reviewing arbitrators' decisions and focus only on whether the grievance involved an issue that is subject to arbitration under the contract.[41]

Employers can judge a grievance procedure in terms of various criteria.[42] One consideration is effectiveness: how well the procedure resolves day-to-day contract questions. A second basic consideration is efficiency: whether it resolves issues at a reasonable cost and without major delays. The company also should consider how well the grievance procedure adapts to changing circumstances. For example, if sales drop off and the company needs to cut costs, how clear are the provisions related to layoffs and subcontracting of work? In the case of contracts covering multiple business units, the procedure should allow for resolving local contract issues, such as work rules at a particular facility. Companies also should consider whether the grievance procedure is fair—whether it treats employees equitably and gives them a voice in the process.

From the point of view of employees, the grievance procedure is an important means of getting fair treatment in the workplace. Its success depends on whether it provides for all the kinds of problems that are likely to arise (such as how to handle a business slowdown), whether employees feel they can file a grievance without being punished for it, and whether employees believe their union representatives will follow through. Under the National Labor Relations Act, the union has a *duty of fair representation,* which means the union must give equal representation to all members of the bargaining unit, whether or not they actually belong to the union.

New Approaches to Labor Relations

LO 15-7 Describe new approaches to labor-management relations.

The growing role of employee empowerment and the shrinking size of union membership have helped to establish new approaches to labor relations. Among these developments are an emphasis on cooperation between unions and management and the use of nonunion systems for employee representation.

Labor–Management Cooperation

The traditional understanding of union-management relations is that the two parties are adversaries, meaning each side is competing to win at the expense of the other. There have always been exceptions to this approach. And since at least the 1980s, there seems to be wider acceptance of the view that greater cooperation can increase employee commitment and motivation while making the workplace more flexible.[43] Also, evidence suggests that employees who worked under traditional labor relations systems and then under the new, more cooperative systems prefer the cooperative approach.[44]

Cooperation between labor and management may feature employee involvement in decision making, self-managing employee teams, labor-management problem-solving teams, broadly defined jobs, and sharing of financial gains and business information with employees.[45] The search for a win-win solution requires that unions and their members understand the limits on what an employer can afford in a competitive marketplace.

Without the union's support, efforts at employee empowerment are less likely to survive and less likely to be effective if they do survive.[46] Unions have often resisted employee empowerment programs, precisely because the programs try to change workplace relations and the role that unions play. Union leaders have feared that such programs will weaken unions' role as independent representatives of employee interests. Indeed, the National Labor Relations Act makes it an unfair labor practice for an employer to "dominate or interfere with the formation or administration of any labor organization or contribute financial or other support to it."

When unions and management face off in contract negotiations, both sides try to work toward a win–win outcome for both the company and its workers. Here GM CEO Mary Barra shakes hands with UAW President Gary Jones as they begin contract talks. Bill Pugliano/Getty Images

Although employers must be careful to meet legal requirements, the NLRB has clearly supported employee involvement in work teams and decision making. For example, in a 2001 ruling, the NLRB found that employee participation committees at Crown Cork & Seal's aluminum-can factory did not violate federal labor law.[47] Those committees make and carry out decisions regarding a wide range of issues, including production, quality, training, safety, and certain types of discipline. The NLRB determined that the committees were not employer dominated. Instead of "dealing with" management, where employees make proposals for management to accept or reject, the committees exercise authority within boundaries set by management, similar to the authority of a first-line supervisor. In spite of the legal concerns, cooperative approaches to labor relations likely contribute to an organization's success.[48]

Nonunion Representation Systems

Given that only a little more than 10% of workers are now represented by unions, what recourse do the other 89% have if they want someone to represent their interests to management? Employees want some form of representation, which often involves "substitutes" for unions. A recent survey of hundreds of U.S. workers found that 17% were covered by a collective bargaining agreement, and another 28% said they had some form of management-established system to represent them.[49] The management-established system involved representatives of the employees meeting with management to discuss working conditions including wages and benefits. Both groups of workers were equally likely to say the employee representatives could be "counted on to stand up for workers." It is important to note that these "substitutes" may violate the NLRA. However, they exist because the legal guidelines covering these systems are ambiguous. It is difficult for unions to make the case that a company illegally organizes its employees into "company unions" unless the union has previously tried to organize the employees. Moreover, the punishments that companies can receive from the NLRB for these types of violations are limited.

Another nonunion approach is the *worker center,* a nonprofit organization offering its members services such as training, legal advice, lobbying, and worker advocacy.[50] Examples include the National Domestic Workers Alliance, the Restaurant Opportunities Center, the National Day Laborers Organizing Network, and the Farmworker Association of Florida. These organizations receive funds from labor unions and private foundations. Their activities include helping to organize union campaigns, filing claims for unpaid wages, and training low-income and immigrant workers about their rights. Sometimes they negotiate with management of the companies that contract for workers, such as retailers that contract for janitorial services. In Minnesota, a worker center obtained an agreement from Target to contract only with janitorial services meeting certain employment standards. The agreement created conditions more favorable for janitors in the area to form unions at the companies employing them. Employer organizations, including the U.S. Chamber of Commerce, are concerned that worker centers cross a line into union activities, which should make them subject to the laws governing labor organizations. The Labor Department under the Obama administration investigated the issue but did not take action. The Labor Department under the Trump Administration, however, says it has reason to believe that the Minneapolis worker center is a labor organization and has asked for additional information before issuing a ruling. As of this writing, the Labor Department has not taken additional action; however, worker centers around the country are on high alert and according to officials, "prepared to push back" in the courts.[51]

THINKING ETHICALLY

FREE RIDE OR FREE SPEECH?

As this chapter explains, union goals include security provisions, such as agency shops, to ensure a regular flow of union dues. Right-to-work states forbid these provisions, but in Illinois (which is not a right-to-work state), personal care assistants providing services through the state-run programs serving people with disabilities or in rehabilitation were required to pay union dues, whether or not they wanted to join the union. A majority of the personal care assistants had voted to make the Service Employees International Union (SEIU) their representative in 2003. The collective bargaining agreement included a "fair share" provision that required nonmembers of the union to pay not the full amount of dues, but a proportionate share of union costs for collective bargaining and contract administration.

Several of the personal care assistants sued the state government, saying the "fair share" provision violated their rights to freedom of speech and freedom of association. They lost the case in district court and in the appellate court, but the U.S. Supreme Court disagreed in a 5–4 vote. According to the majority, the concern that workers should not get a free ride does not override concern for workers' First Amendment rights. Their ruling applied to the particular case of "quasi-public" workers who are paid by but not directly supervised by the government. When a person's employer is a government entity, the union's stance in bargaining with that government could conflict with a worker's political views. The court saw the requirement to support the union by paying dues as potentially forcing people to support the union's political message over the workers' own views. The dissenting view emphasized the fairness and protection provided by a system in which a single body representing workers' interests bargains with the government entity and no workers can take advantage of the resulting benefits for free.

Early expectations were that the SEIU would lose up to one-third of the revenue from workers who were not union members. However, representatives of the union say that the Supreme Court motivated the SEIU to work harder at reaching out to workers, resulting in a surge of interest. Another union representing a similar group of workers, the Domestic Workers of America, reported that it signed up more than 30,000 new members, doubling its membership. Other unions' leaders reported that the case made workers more attuned to issues of equity and power. At one local of the American Federation of State, County and Municipal Employees, 150 of 200 payers of fair-share fees converted to full dues-paying status. The Supreme Court in 2018 bolstered the state's position with its ruling that public employees do not have to pay unions a fee to bargain for them, but the California example suggests there is still a future for public-sector unions.

Questions

1. What issues of fairness and equity come into play in this case?
2. How well does the outcome of this case represent respect for basic human rights? How well does it do the greatest good for the greatest number?

Sources: Rebecca Rainey and Ian Kullgren, "1 Year after Janus, Unions Are Flush," *Politico,* May 17, 2019, https://www.politico.com; Robert Holly, "How Home Care Paved the Way for SCOTUS' Janus Ruling," *Home Health Care News,* June 28, 2018, https://homehealthcarenews.com; Margot Roosevelt, "Will the Supreme Court's Janus Decision Sink California Unions?" *Orange County Register,* June 27, 2018, https://www.ocregister.com; Oyez Project, *"Harris v. Quinn,"* IIT Chicago-Kent College of Law, July 19, 2014, https://www.oyez.org; Cynthia Estlund and William E. Forbath, "The War on Workers," *New York Times,* July 2, 2014, http://www.nytimes.com; Lydia DePillis, "Why *Harris v. Quinn* Isn't as Bad for Workers as It Sounds," *Washington Post,* July 1, 2014, http://www.-washingtonpost.com; Daniel Fisher, "Public-Sector Unions Survive Supreme Court Review, Barely," *Forbes,* June 30, 2014, http://www.forbes.com.

SUMMARY

LO 15-1 Define unions and labor relations and their role in organizations.

- A union is an organization formed for the purpose of representing its members in resolving conflicts with employers.
- Labor relations is the management specialty emphasizing skills that managers and union leaders can use to minimize costly forms of conflict and to seek win-win solutions to disagreements.
- Unions—often locals belonging to national and international organizations—engage in organizing, collective bargaining, and contract administration with businesses and government organizations.
- In the United States, union membership has been declining among businesses but has held steady with government employees.
- Unionization is associated with more generous compensation and higher productivity but lower profits. Unions may reduce a business's flexibility and economic performance, but some companies rely on union expertise—for example, to train skilled workers.

LO 15-2 Identify the labor relations goals of management, labor unions, and society.

- Management goals are to increase the organization's profits. Managers generally expect that unions will make these goals harder to achieve.
- Labor unions have the goal of obtaining pay and working conditions that satisfy their members. They obtain these results by gaining power in numbers.
- Society's values have included the hope that the existence of unions will replace conflict or violence between workers and employers with fruitful negotiation.

LO 15-3 Summarize laws and regulations that affect labor relations.

- The National Labor Relations Act supports the use of collective bargaining and sets out the rights of employees, including the right to organize, join a union, and go on strike. The NLRA prohibits unfair labor practices by employers, including interference with efforts to form a labor union and discrimination against employees who engage in union activities.
- The Taft-Hartley Act and Landrum-Griffin Act establish restrictions on union practices that restrain workers, such as their preventing employees from working during a strike or determining whom an employer may hire.
- The Taft-Hartley Act also permits state right-to-work laws.

LO 15-4 Describe the union organizing process.

- Organizing begins when union representatives contact employees and invite them to sign an authorization card.
- If over half the employees sign a card, the union may request that the employer voluntarily recognize the union.
- If the employer refuses or if 30% to 50% of employees signed authorization cards, the NLRB conducts a secret-ballot election.
- If the union wins, the NLRB certifies the union.
- If the union loses but the NLRB finds that the election was not conducted fairly, it may set aside the results and call a new election.

LO 15-5 Explain how management and unions negotiate contracts.

- Negotiations take place between representatives of the union and the management bargaining unit. The majority of negotiations involve parties that have been through the process before.
- The process begins with preparation, including research into the other side's strengths and demands. In the early stages of negotiation, many more people are present than at later stages.
- The union presents its demands, and management sometimes presents demands as well.
- Then the sides evaluate the demands and the likelihood of a strike.
- In the final stages, pressure for an agreement increases and a neutral third party may be called on to help reach a resolution.
- If bargaining breaks down, the impasse may be broken with a strike, lockout, mediation, fact finder, or arbitration.

LO 15-6 Summarize the practice of contract administration.

- Contract administration is a daily activity under the labor agreement. It includes carrying out the terms of the agreement and resolving conflicts over interpretation or violation of the contract.
- Conflicts are resolved through a grievance procedure. Typically, the grievance procedure begins with an employee talking to his or her supervisor about the problem and possibly involving the union steward in the discussion.
- If this does not resolve the conflict, the union files a written grievance with a line manager, and union and management representatives meet to discuss the problem.
- If this effort fails, the union appeals the grievance to top line management and the industrial relations staff.
- If the appeal fails, the union may appeal the grievance to an arbitrator.

LO 15-7 Describe new approaches to labor–management relations.

- The growing role of employee empowerment and the shrinking size of union membership have helped to propel new approaches to labor relations, including an emphasis on cooperation between unions and management and the use of nonunion systems for employee representation.
- In contrast to the traditional view that labor and management are adversaries, some organizations and unions work more cooperatively. Cooperation may feature employee involvement in decision making, self-managing employee teams, labor-management problem-solving teams, broadly defined jobs, and sharing of financial gains and business information with employees.
- If such cooperation is tainted by attempts of the employer to dominate or interfere with labor organizations, however, such as by dealing with wages, grievances, or working conditions, it may be illegal under the NLRA.

- In spite of such legal concerns, cooperative labor relations seem to contribute to an organization's success.
- In some organizations without a union, there is a management-established system to represent workers.
- Another nonunion approach is the worker center, a nonprofit organization offering its members services such as training, legal advice, lobbying, and worker advocacy.
- Most worker centers are not part of unions, so they are not constrained by some of the requirements on unions. Instead of negotiating contracts with management, worker centers pressure employers through publicity campaigns, and they lobby legislators to pass laws favorable to their members.

KEY TERMS

unions, 467
labor relations, 468
craft union, 468
industrial union, 468
American Federation of Labor and Congress of Industrial Organizations (AFL-CIO), 469
union steward, 469
checkoff provision, 475
closed shop, 475
union shop, 475
agency shop, 475
maintenance of membership, 475
National Labor Relations Act (NLRA), 476
right-to-work laws, 479
National Labor Relations Board (NLRB), 480
associate union membership, 484
corporate campaigns, 484
collective bargaining, 485
strike, 487
lockout, 488
mediation, 488
fact finder, 489
arbitration, 489
grievance procedure, 489

REVIEW AND DISCUSSION QUESTIONS

1. Why do employees join labor unions? Did you ever belong to a labor union? If you did, do you think union membership benefited you? If you did not, do you think a union would have benefited you? Why or why not? *(LO 15-1)*
2. Why do managers at most companies prefer that unions not represent their employees? Can unions provide benefits to an employer? Explain. *(LO 15-2)*
3. How has union membership in the United States changed over the past few decades? How does union membership in the United States compare with union membership in other countries? How might these patterns in union membership affect the HR decisions of an international company? *(LO 15-2)*
4. What legal responsibilities do employers have regarding unions? What are the legal requirements affecting unions? *(LO 15-3)*
5. Suppose you are the HR manager for a chain of clothing stores. You learn that union representatives have been encouraging the stores' employees to sign authorization cards. What events can follow in this process of organizing? Suggest some ways that you might respond in your role as HR manager. *(LO 15-4)*
6. If the parties negotiating a labor contract are unable to reach an agreement, what actions can resolve the situation? *(LO 15-5)*
7. Why are strikes uncommon? Under what conditions might management choose to accept a strike? *(LO 15-5)*
8. What are the usual steps in a grievance procedure? What are the advantages of resolving a grievance in the first step? What skills would a supervisor need so grievances can be resolved in the first step? *(LO 15-6)*
9. What can a company gain from union-management cooperation? What can workers gain? *(LO 15-7)*
10. What are the legal restrictions on labor-management cooperation? *(LO 15-7)*

SELF-ASSESSMENT EXERCISE

Would You Join a Union?

Would you join a union? Each of the following phrases expresses an opinion about the effects of a union on employees' jobs. For each phrase, circle a number on the scale to indicate whether you agree that a union would affect your job as described by the phrase.

Having a union would result in . . .	Strongly Disagree				Strongly Agree
1. Increased wages	1	2	3	4	5
2. Improved benefits	1	2	3	4	5
3. Protection from being fired	1	2	3	4	5
4. More promotions	1	2	3	4	5
5. Better work hours	1	2	3	4	5
6. Improved productivity	1	2	3	4	5
7. Better working conditions	1	2	3	4	5
8. Fewer accidents at work	1	2	3	4	5
9. More interesting work	1	2	3	4	5
10. Easier handling of employee problems	1	2	3	4	5
11. Increased work disruptions	5	4	3	2	1
12. More disagreements between employees and management	5	4	3	2	1
13. Work stoppages	5	4	3	2	1

Add up your total score. The highest score possible is 65; the lowest, 13. The higher your score, the more you see value in unions, and the more likely you would be to join a union.

Source: Based on S. A. Youngblood, A. S. DeNisi. J. L. Molleston, and W. H. Mobley, "The Impact of Work Environment, Instrumentality Beliefs, Perceived Union Image, and Subjective Norms on Union Voting Intentions," *Academy of Management Journal* 27 (1984), pp. 576–590.

TAKING RESPONSIBILITY

Teamsters and UPS Strike a Deal for the 21st Century

The Internet is changing everything for UPS, especially if it can get the union on board. The company originally grew by making local deliveries of packages to retailers and other business customers. For decades, its brown trucks have been departing from a network of warehouses on a Monday-through-Friday schedule. But nowadays, with most consumers doing some of their shopping online, half its deliveries go to consumers at their residences. Delivering one package at a time from house to house is less efficient and therefore less profitable. The problem is compounded by UPS's old warehouses, only a fraction of which are automated. This puts UPS at a disadvantage relative to FedEx and Amazon, which entered the market late enough to build more modern facilities, geared toward the needs of online shoppers.

In this environment, UPS needed to negotiate a new contract with its employees' union, the Teamsters. The previous five-year contract would be ending in mid-2018, so early in the year, Teamsters representatives made their opening offer. They focused on the changing landscape of work. Their initial demands focused on working conditions. They wanted an earlier end to late-night deliveries, the addition of new drivers to handle the increased demand, and no use of drones or driverless vehicles to make deliveries. For its part, UPS was more focused on how to move ahead technologically. Its business plans called for catching up to the competition in efficiency by automating its facilities–a change that has the potential to lower the number of employees needed. However, the company has said that the union has not slowed automation.

Another area of discussion was work hours. The Teamsters were concerned about overworked drivers and wanted UPS to avoid adding Sunday deliveries. UPS wanted to keep open the possibility of Sunday deliveries and to address the overtime issue of high pay for weekend work. Drivers working Saturdays were earning double-time pay, at rates exceeding $70 an hour. The company and Teamsters settled on the creation of a new position: a "hybrid driver," who would work Tuesday through Saturday or Sunday through Thursday, with starting pay at $15 per hour and no overtime for the weekend day worked. In contrast, the existing contract had a "hybrid" position, which differed in that it involved working more than one part-time shift at a little more than the part-time wage.

After several months of negotiation, the parties indicated that they had reached an agreement in principle. It included pay raises, with starting pay rising annually, beginning at $13 in the first year and reaching $15.50 in 2022. Employees would pay a larger contribution toward their benefits, and the pension plan would increase. Also included in the contract was the hybrid driver position.

As it neared the expiration of the contract, union members voted for a strike authorization. This did not necessarily signal a strike, but it was a tactic to indicate to management that the union was serious about getting a favorable contract. Two weeks later, the parties announced they had reached an agreement for the workers to vote on. The process averted what would have been a significant strike, as the Teamsters union represents about 260,000 UPS workers.

Questions

1. Based on the information given, which of the terms in the new contract are favorable for workers? Which terms are favorable for UPS?

2. What effects, if any, do you think the employment contract will have on UPS's ability to meet its goals for serving customers and improving efficiency?

Sources: UPS, "UPS Labor Contract Update: May 2019," https://www.investors.ups.com, accessed May 14, 2020; Carolyn Tribble Greer, "UPS, Teamsters Agree in Principle on National Labor Pact," *Louisville Business First,* June 22, 2018, https://www.bizjournals.com; Paul Ziobro, "UPS, Teamsters Reach Handshake Deal on New Contract," *The Wall Street Journal,* June 21, 2018, https://www.wsj.com; Paul Ziobro, "UPS's $20 Billion Problem: Operations Stuck in the 20th Century," *The Wall Street Journal,* June 15, 2018, https://www.wsj.com; Bloomberg, "UPS Has 260,000 Union Workers and They've Just Authorized a Strike," *Fortune,* June 6, 2018, http://fortune.com; Paul Ziobro, "UPS and Teamsters Discuss Two-Tier Wages, Sunday Deliveries," *The Wall Street Journal,* May 9, 2018, https://www.wsj.com; Paul Ziobro, "Teamsters Tell UPS: No Drones or Driverless Trucks," *The Wall Street Journal,* January 24, 2018, https://www.wsj.com.

MANAGING TALENT

Ford and UAW Ride a U-Turn in Demand

In less than six months, the challenges of labor relations at Ford Motor Company took a radical change in direction. In the fall of 2019, the company was negotiating a new labor contract during the world's longest economic expansion following the global recession of more than a decade before. But by the spring of 2020, a global pandemic had spread to the United States, and the question became how to weather the risks, both economic and financial.

The contract negotiations took place after the United Auto Workers had signed a deal with General Motors. The UAW normally negotiates with one of the major automakers first, then tries to seek similar deals with the others. The path to a contract with GM had included a 40-day strike in an economy that was near full employment, and that agreement included pay increases and kept workers' share of health insurance premiums at 3%. The UAW sought similar wages and benefits for Ford's 56,000 unionized factory workers. Ford was in the process of restructuring in an effort to improve profits, which were weak compared with its competitors.

In December 2019, Ford and the UAW signed a four-year contract. It included plans to add or retain 8,500 jobs at a cost of $6 billion to retool factories and expand production in the United States. New production would include electric pickup trucks and assembly of batteries. Ford viewed the effort as a way to build on its strengths in building trucks and SUVs, as well as to prepare for an expected shift toward electric vehicles.

Then the coronavirus began to take a toll on world economies. Factories began closing in Europe as the disease spread there from China, and Ford began to prepare for a downturn in demand. As cases began to tick upward during March 2020, union officials began to publicly express the concerns they were hearing from their members. Many employees were afraid to work in factories where a thousand or more people touch a single product and workers normally wear gloves but no facial protection. In Dearborn, Michigan, UAW Local 600 filed a grievance against Ford, requesting more protection against the spread of the virus, including a two-week work stoppage and frequent cleaning of shared facilities. Leaders of other union locals joined in.

Initially, Ford and other companies responded to the concern by adjusting work schedules and figuring out how to limit physical contact between workers. But within days of the grievances, as demand tumbled and a worker at the Dearborn Ford plant tested positive for the virus, Ford and others decided to close plants. During the shutdown, some workers would be eligible for sick pay. The company said UAW workers with at least one year of service would earn 75% of their regular pay from a combination of unemployment benefits and supplemental payments from Ford.

Then, in yet another twist, Ford reacted to rising complaints that the United States did not have enough ventilators to treat COVID patients. The company called on its engineers to apply their expertise at highly efficient production to making these completely different products. Ventilators are normally made in relatively small lots under little time pressure, but Ford's engineers studied models and determined how to speed up the production process. Ford trained hundreds of employees how to assemble this vital equipment while maintaining safe distances from one another. The company's goal was to assemble 50,000 ventilators by early July, and the assembly workers who would do this were drawn from about 500 who volunteered for the assignment. At the same time, Ford reported a loss for the first quarter 2020 and announced in April that it hoped to phase in a restart of vehicle production by the end of June.

Questions

1. In this account, what goals of management and what goals of unions can you identify?
2. How would you have recommended that Ford react to the grievances filed about worker health during the coronavirus outbreak in North America? Explain your reasoning.

Sources: Mike Colias, "Ford Looks to Conserve Cash amid $600 Million Preliminary Loss," *The Wall Street Journal,* April 13, 2020, https://www.wsj.com; Mike Colias, "Auto Giants Trade Drills for Tweezers in Bid to Rush

Coronavirus Ventilators," *The Wall Street Journal,* April 12, 2020, https://www.wsj.com; Neal E. Boudette, "Automakers to Close Factories in North America," *The New York Times,* March 18, 2020, https://www.nytimes.com; Breana Noble, "Autoworkers Disgruntled as U.S. Production Continues amid Virus Outbreak," *Detroit News,* March 16, 2020, https://www.detroitnews.com; Mike Colias, "Ford to Create 3,000 Factory Jobs in Michigan as Part of New UAW Contract," *The Wall Street Journal,* December 17, 2019, https://www.wsj.com; Nora Naughton, "United Auto Workers Strikes Tentative Labor Deal with Ford," *The Wall Street Journal,* October 30, 2019, https://www.wsj.com.

HR IN SMALL BUSINESS

Kickstarter Employees Vote to Unionize

Brooklyn-based Kickstarter was founded to fund opportunities for creative people. People with ideas post them on Kickstarter's website, along with a request for donations. If the donations meet the goals set by the creator, the creators can keep the money; otherwise, Kickstarter voids the donations. In its first decade Kickstarter reported it had grown to more than 150 employees and had helped creators raise more than $4.5 billion to fund 170,000 projects.

About that time, it ran into a public relations problem that became a labor relations problem. One of the projects on the site was a comic book called *Always Punch Nazis.* While some people saw it as a satire opposing racism, others saw it as a work advocating violence. Some of Kickstarter's employees held strong views on the issue but began to feel they had little control in the decision making about whether to leave the project on the company's website. Calling for greater transparency from management, these workers began to advocate for forming a union.

The employees who engaged in organizing said they had the backing of a majority of the workers and asked Kickstarter to recognize a union. The company refused, saying it wanted the employees to vote in a secret-ballot election conducted by the National Labor Relations Board (NLRB). While this was playing out, semiannual performance appraisals were completed, and two of the employees who had been organizing were terminated. Both former employees said they had been fired in retaliation for organizing, but management said they were dismissed for performance problems documented in the review process.

The organizing effort moved forward, with management saying a union would not be in the best interests of employees and the company. CEO Aziz Hasan said the "inherently adversarial" approach of union-management negotiations was inconsistent with Kickstarter's problem-solving culture. Nevertheless, in a 46-to-37 vote, the employees approved representation by the Office and Professional Employees International Union (OPEIU). The union announced that it planned to begin negotiating a contract with Kickstarter as soon as possible, focusing on equal pay and inclusive hiring practices. It also filed charges with the NLRB related to the earlier firing of the two employees involved in organizing.

Just two months after the vote, Kickstarter was struggling to stay alive during a significant economic downturn. The number of projects on the site had fallen by 35%, with no sign of a turnaround, and the prior year's profits had already been reinvested in the business. Management explored cost-cutting efforts, including pay cuts for management, but would have to conduct layoffs. Now with the OPEIU representing employees, managers negotiated with union representatives about layoffs. Union members would be offered voluntary buyouts, and terms for any additional layoffs included four months of severance pay and continued health insurance for up to six months.

Questions

1. According to the information given, how well did Kickstarter comply with National Labor Relations Act requirements? Note any areas where you believe they could have done better.
2. If bargaining ever breaks down between Kickstarter management and the OPEIU, what option would you recommend the parties try first to resolve differences?

Sources: Kim Lyons, "Kickstarter Union Reaches Agreement with Management for Laid-Off Workers," *The Verge,* May 2, 2020, https://www.theverge.com; Ashley Carman, "Kickstarter Plans Layoffs after New Projects on the Site Drop Off by 35 Percent," *The Verge,* April 20, 2020, https://www.theverge.com; Kate Conger and Noam Scheiber, "Kickstarter Employees Vote to Unionize in a Big Step for Tech," *The New York Times,* February 18, 2020, https://www.nytimes.com; Michael Gold, "Kickstarter Calls Itself Progressive, but about That Union," *The New York Times,* October 15, 2019, https://www.nytimes.com; Russell Brandom, "Kickstarter Faces Union Backlash after Firing Two Organizers," *The Verge,* September 12, 2019, https://www.theverge.com.

NOTES

1. J. Davidson, "Unions for Prison, VA Workers File 'Imminent Danger' Reports about Coronavirus Conditions," *The Washington Post,* April 9, 2020, https:/www.washingtonpost.com.
2. J. T. Dunlop, *Industrial Relations Systems* (New York: Holt, 1958); C. Kerr, "Industrial Conflict and Its Mediation," *American Journal of Sociology* 60 (1954), pp. 230–245.

3. D. Plotkin, "Journalists at Orlando Sentinel Unionize to Battle New 'Vulture Capitalist' Owners," *Orlando Weekly,* February 25, 2020, https://www.orlandoweekly.com; S. Knolle, "Safety Net," *Editor & Publisher,* May 2018, pp. 33–37.
4. T. A. Kochan, *Collective Bargaining and Industrial Relations* (Homewood, IL: Richard D. Irwin, 1980), p. 25; H. C. Katz and T. A. Kochan, *An Introduction to Collective Bargaining and Industrial Relations,* 3rd ed. (New York: McGraw-Hill, 2004).
5. J. Anderson, "30 Most Powerful Unions in America," *Yahoo Finance,* April 7, 2020, https://finance.yahoo.com.
6. Bureau of Labor Statistics, "Union Members–2019," news release, January 22, 2020, https://www.bls.gov.
7. Katz and Kochan, *An Introduction to Collective Bargaining,* building on J. Fiorito and C. L. Maranto, "The Contemporary Decline of Union Strength," *Contemporary Policy Issues* 3 (1987), pp. 12–27; G. N. Chaison and J. Rose, "The Macrodeterminants of Union Growth and Decline," in *The State of the Unions,* eds. G. Strauss et al. (Madison, WI: Industrial Relations Research Association, 1991).
8. C. Brewster, "Levels of Analysis in Strategic HRM: Questions Raised by Comparative Research," Conference on Research and Theory in HRM, Cornell University, October 1997.
9. J. T. Addison and B. T. Hirsch, "Union Effects on Productivity, Profits, and Growth: Has the Long Run Arrived?" *Journal of Labor Economics* 7 (1989), pp. 72–105; R. B. Freeman and J. L. Medoff, "The Two Faces of Unionism," *Public Interest* 57 (Fall 1979), pp. 69–93.
10. L. Mishel and P. Voos, *Unions and Economic Competitiveness* (Armonk, NY: M. E. Sharpe, 1991); Freeman and Medoff, "Two Faces"; S. Slichter, J. Healy, and E. R. Livernash, *The Impact of Collective Bargaining on Management* (Washington, DC: Brookings Institution, 1960).
11. A. O. Hirschman, *Exit, Voice, and Loyalty* (Cambridge, MA: Harvard University Press, 1970); R. Batt, A. J. S. Colvin, and J. Keefe, "Employee Voice, Human Resource Practices, and Quit Rates: Evidence from the Telecommunications Industry," *Industrial and Labor Relations Review* 55 (1970), pp. 573–594.
12. R. B. Freeman and J. L. Medoff, *What Do Unions Do?* (New York: Basic Books, 1984); Addison and Hirsch, "Union Effects on Productivity"; M. Ash and J. A. Seago, "The Effect of Registered Nurses Unions on Heart-Attack Mortality," *Industrial and Labor Relations Review* 57 (2004), p. 422; C. Doucouliagos and P. Laroche, "What Do Unions Do to Productivity? A Meta-Analysis," *Industrial Relations* 42 (2003), pp. 650–691.
13. D. S. Lee and A. Mas, "Long-Run Impacts of Unions on Firms: New Evidence from Financial Markets, 1961–1999," *Quarterly Journal of Economics* 172 (2012), pp. 333–378; B. E. Becker and C. A. Olson, "Unions and Firm Profits," *Industrial Relations* 31, no. 3 (1992), pp. 395–415; B. T. Hirsch and B. A. Morgan, "Shareholder Risks and Returns in Union and Nonunion Firms," *Industrial and Labor Relations Review* 47, no. 2 (1994), pp. 302–318; Hristos Doucouliagos and Patrice Laroche, "Unions and Profits: A Meta-Regression Analysis," *Industrial Relations* 48, no. 1 (January 2008), p. 146.
14. H. Doucouliagos, R. B. Freeman, and P. Laroche, *The Economics of Trade Unions: A Study of a Research Field and Its Findings* (London: Routledge, 2017).
15. D. Sparkman, "Unions Step Up Attacks on Independent Contractor Status," *Material Handling & Logistics,* April 2017, p. 13.
16. Bureau of Labor Statistics, "Union Members–2019."
17. S. Horsley, "2-Tiered Wages under Fire: Workers Challenge Unequal Pay for Equal Work," *NPR,* May 21, 2019, https://www.npr.org.
18. *Janus v. American Federation of State, County, and Municipal Employees, Council 31,* docket no. 16-1466, argued February 26, 2018, decided June 27, 2018; see also Jess Bravin, "Supreme Court Deals Blow to Public-Sector Unions," *The Wall Street Journal,* June 27, 2018, https://www.wsj.com.
19. S. Webb and B. Webb, *Industrial Democracy* (London: Longmans, Green, 1897); J. R. Commons, *Institutional Economics* (New York: Macmillan, 1934).
20. "Why America Needs Unions, but Not the Kind It Has Now," *Bloomberg Businessweek,* May 23, 1994, p. 70.
21. E. E. Herman, J. L. Schwatz, and A. Kuhn, *Collective Bargaining and Labor Relations* (Englewood Cliffs, NJ: Prentice Hall, 1992).
22. Kochan, *Collective Bargaining and Industrial Relations,* p. 61.
23. National Labor Relations Board, *Basic Guide to the National Labor Relations Act* (Washington, DC: U.S. Government Printing Office, 1997).
24. National Labor Relations Board, "Employee Rights," http://www.nlrb.gov, accessed May 13, 2020.
25. National Labor Relations Board, *Basic Guide.*
26. Ibid.
27. National Labor Relations Board, "Election-Related Content," http://www.nlrb.gov, accessed May 13, 2020; NLRB, "Employer/Union Rights and Obligations," https://www.nlrb.gov, accessed May 13, 2020.
28. R. B. Freeman and M. M. Kleiner, "Employer Behavior in the Face of Union Organizing Drives," *Industrial and Labor Relations Review* 43, no. 4 (April 1990), pp. 351–365.
29. J. A. Fossum, *Labor Relations,* 8th ed. (New York: McGraw-Hill, 2002), p. 149.
30. Herman et al., *Collective Bargaining;* P. Jarley and J. Fiorito, "Associate Membership: Unionism or Consumerism?" *Industrial and Labor Relations Review* 43 (1990), pp. 209–224.
31. Katz and Kochan, *An Introduction to Collective Bargaining.*
32. Ibid.
33. A. E. Eaton and J. Kriesky, "Union Organizing under Neutrality and Card Check Agreements," *Industrial and Labor Relations Review* 55 (2001), pp. 42–59.
34. R. Combs, "Analysis: Five Metrics That Explain the State of the Unions," *Bloomberg Law,* April 24, 2019, https://news.bloomberglaw.com.
35. Chaison and Rose, "The Macrodeterminants of Union Growth and Decline."
36. Fossum, *Labor Relations,* p. 262.
37. C. M. Steven, *Strategy and Collective Bargaining Negotiations* (New York: McGraw-Hill, 1963); Katz and Kochan, *An Introduction to Collective Bargaining.*
38. Kochan, *Collective Bargaining and Industrial Relations,* p. 272.
39. Robert Combs, "Labor Stats and Facts: Lockout Rates Continue to Surge," *Bloomberg BNA,* October 17, 2012, http://www.bna.com.
40. Katz and Kochan, *An Introduction to Collective Bargaining.*
41. *United Steelworkers v. American Manufacturing Company,* 363 U.S. 564 (1960); *United Steelworkers v. Warrior Gulf and Navigation Company,* 363 U.S. 574 (1960); *United Steelworkers v. Enterprise Wheel and Car Corporation,* 363 U.S. 593 (1960).
42. Kochan, *Collective Bargaining and Industrial Relations,* p. 386; John W. Budd and Alexander J. S. Colvin, "Improved Metrics for

Workplace Dispute Resolution Procedures: Efficiency, Equity, and Voice," *Industrial Relations* 47, no. 3 (July 2008), p. 460.

43. T. A. Kochan, H. C. Katz, and R. B. McKersie, *The Transformation of American Industrial Relations* (New York: Basic Books, 1986), chap. 6; E. Appelbaum, T. Bailey, and P. Berg, *Manufacturing Advantage: Why High-Performance Work Systems Pay Off* (Ithaca, NY: Cornell University Press, 2000).
44. L. W. Hunter, J. P. MacDuffie, and L. Doucet, "What Makes Teams Take? Employee Reactions to Work Reforms," *Industrial and Labor Relations Review* 55 (2002), pp. 448–472.
45. J. B. Arthur, "The Link between Business Strategy and Industrial Relations Systems in American Steel Minimills," *Industrial and Labor Relations Review* 45 (1992), pp. 488–506; M. Schuster, "Union Management Cooperation," in *Employee and Labor Relations,* ed. J. A. Fossum (Washington, DC: Bureau of National Affairs, 1990); E. Cohen-Rosenthal and C. Burton, *Mutual Gains: A Guide to Union-Management Cooperation,* 2nd ed. (Ithaca, NY: ILR Press, 1993); T. A. Kochan and P. Osterman, *The Mutual Gains Enterprise* (Boston: Harvard Business School Press, 1994); E. Applebaum and R. Batt, *The New American Workplace* (Ithaca, NY: ILR Press, 1994).
46. A. E. Eaton, "Factors Contributing to the Survival of Employee Participation Programs in Unionized Settings," *Industrial and Labor Relations Review* 47, no. 3 (1994), pp. 371–389.
47. "NLRB 4-0 Approves Crown Cork & Seal's Use of Seven Employee Participation Committees," *HR News,* September 3, 2001.
48. Kochan and Osterman, *The Mutual Gains Enterprise;* W. N. Cooke, "Employee Participation Programs, Group-Based Incentives, and Company Performance: A Union-Nonunion Comparison," *Industrial and Labor Relations Review* 47, no. 4 (1994), pp. 594–609; C. Doucouliagos, "Worker Participation and Productivity in Labor-Managed and Participatory Capitalist Firms: A Meta-Analysis," *Industrial and Labor Relations Review* 49, no. 1 (1995), pp. 58–77; S. J. Deery and R. D. Iverson, "Labor-Management Cooperation: Antecedents and Impact on Organizational Performance," *Industrial and Labor Relations Review* 58 (2005), pp. 588–609; James Combs, Yongmei Liu, Angela Hall, and David Ketchen, "How Much Do High–Performance Work Practices Matter? A Meta-analysis of Their Effects on Organizational Performance," *Personnel Psychology* 59, no. 3 (2006), pp. 501–528; Robert D. Mohr and Cindy Zoghi, "High-Involvement Work Design and Job Satisfaction," *Industrial and Labor Relations Review* 61, no. 3 (April 2008), pp. 275–296; T. Rabl, M. Jayasinghe, B. Gerhart, and T. M. Köhlmann, "How Much Does Country Matter? A Meta-analysis of the HPWP Systems–Business Performance Relationship," *Academy of Management Annual Meeting Proceedings,* August 2011.
49. J. Godard and C. Frege, "Labor Unions, Alternative Forms of Representation, and the Exercise of Authority Relations in U.S. Workplaces," *Industrial and Labor Relations Review* 6 (2013), pp. 142–168.
50. B. Penn and J. Lee, "'Worker Center or Union' Probe May Be Sign of Things to Come," *Bloomberg News,* March 15, 2018, https://www.bna.com; S. P. Redmond, "The Emerging Role of Worker Centers: An Update," U.S. Chamber of Commerce, December 6, 2017, https://www.uschamber.com.
51. B. Penn, "Worker Centers Primed to Test We're-Not-Unions Stance in Court," *Bloomberg Law,* January 17, 2020, https://news.bloomberglaw.com.

Managing Human Resources Globally

Depending on the country, some companies operating globally may need to provide employees the ability to work remotely from a different location based on government rules and local culture.

OJO Images Ltd/Alamy Stock Photo

What Do I Need to Know?

After reading this chapter, you should be able to:

LO 16-1 Summarize how the growth in international business activity affects human resource management.

LO 16-2 Identify the factors that most strongly influence HRM in international markets.

LO 16-3 Discuss how differences among countries affect HR planning at organizations with international operations.

LO 16-4 Describe how companies select and train human resources in a global labor market.

LO 16-5 Discuss challenges related to managing performance and compensating employees from other countries.

LO 16-6 Explain how employers prepare managers for international assignments and for their return home.

Introduction

When Miika Härkönen's wife started months of parental leave after the birth of their baby, he was ready for a change, too. Härkönen, a senior team manager for Helsinki-based Ambientia, asked for permission to work from Spain for six months. He listed his essential tasks (including supervision of the 20 employees on his team) and how he would complete them from a home office. His boss approved the plan, and Härkönen worked from an apartment in Malaga, Spain, keeping connected through video conferences, messaging via Slack, and traveling occasionally to Ambientia's facilities in Finland. He adjusted his hours to be available during meetings in Helsinki, one hour ahead, and to enjoy the warmer climate and his family. When Härkönen returned to working in Helsinki, he felt the time away had refreshed his outlook and improved his productivity.

While Härkönen's request to relocate for half a year would be disconcerting to managers in many locations, companies operating in Finland are very flexible. One reason is Finland's Working Hours Act, which gives the majority of full-time employees significant rights to adjust their working hours and locations. Workers might put in some of their 40 hours per week at a summer cottage or work longer some weeks in order to get short workweeks when they want to travel. This flexibility is appealing in Finland, where people trust one another to a high degree. Finnish culture also values equality, financial, security, and decision making that aims for a consensus—values consistent with the idea of employees collaborating with their employers to arrange schedules that meet the needs of all.[1]

Employers with facilities in Finland need to comply with the Working Hours Act at those facilities, whether or not the culture is the same at their headquarters. With Helsinki being a technology hub, the impact—and the culture—of flexibility could spread to many workplaces.

The laws and culture of each country shape the way organizations operate in each place. Therefore, at organizations with facilities in more than one country, human resource management takes place on an international scale. This chapter discusses the HR issues that organizations must address in a world of global competition. We begin by describing how the global nature of business is affecting human resource management in modern organizations. Next, we identify how global differences among countries affect an organization's decisions about human resources. In the following sections we explore HR planning, selection, training, and compensation practices in international settings. Finally, we examine guidelines for managing employees sent on international assignments.

LO 16-1 Summarize how the growth in international business activity affects human resource management.

HRM in a Global Environment

The environment in which organizations operate is rapidly becoming a global one. More and more companies are entering international markets by exporting their products, building facilities in other countries, and entering into alliances with foreign companies. At the same time, companies based in other countries are investing and setting up operations in the United States. Indeed, most organizations now function in the global economy, and a growing number of HR departments are serving an international workforce. Even small companies are touched by these trends, as described in "Best Practices."

What is behind the trend toward expansion into global markets? Foreign countries can provide a business with new markets in which there are millions or billions of new customers; developing countries often provide such markets, but developed countries do so as well. In addition, companies set up operations overseas because they can operate with lower labor costs. Finally, thanks to advances in telecommunications and information technology, companies can more easily spread work around the globe, wherever they find the right mix of labor costs and abilities. Teams with members in different time zones can keep projects moving around the clock, or projects can be assigned according to regions with particular areas of expertise. Together, this mix of advantages can cause the location of business activities to flow from one country to another. For example, low-cost labor brought manufacturing of many products to China. But as a result of COVID-19 and its spread in that country, many companies, including Google, Microsoft, and Apple are looking to move production of hardware components to other places in Asia, such as Vietnam and Thailand.[2]

Global activities are simplified and encouraged by trade agreements among nations. For example, most countries in Western Europe belong to the European Union and share a common currency, the euro. Canada, Mexico, and the United States have encouraged trade among themselves with the USMCA trade pact, a revised version of the NAFTA trade agreement. The World Trade Organization (WTO) resolves trade disputes among more than 100 participating nations. Conversely, international trade becomes more complex when organizations pull back from trade agreements or otherwise restrict the free movement of goods and labor. This may raise costs, but the response may be to shift, rather than slow, patterns of global activity. For example, Guadalajara, Mexico, is emerging as a tech hub as the U.S. government focuses more on limiting immigration. Because Guadalajara has a growing pool of young workers who were educated in the United States but lacked the documents to remain, the city offers U.S. businesses a way to fill high-tech jobs with workers who speak English fluently, setting them up in facilities much closer to the States than alternative labor markets such as India.[3]

As these trends and arrangements encourage international trade, they increase and change the demands on human resource management. Organizations with customers or suppliers in other countries need employees who understand those customers or suppliers. Organizations that operate facilities in foreign countries need to understand the laws and customs that apply to employees in those countries. They may have to prepare managers and other personnel to take international assignments. They have to adapt their human resource plans and policies

Best Practices

Chobani's Global Outlook Was in Place Right from the Start

The history of yogurt maker Chobani is one of the iconic stories of immigrants living the American dream. Its founder, Hamdi Ulukaya, is a Kurd who grew up in a cheese-making family in Turkey. As a student, he attracted threats from the Turkish police when he became interested in Kurdish rights. Seeking safety, he left the country to attend college in New York, working two jobs to cover his expenses. A few years later, a brother joined him in New York, and they used money from family members to set up a small business making feta cheese.

A decade later, Ulukaya had built up the resources to act when he saw an old factory for sale in the town of South Edmeston, New York. It was a shuttered Kraft facility that had been used to produce Breyers yogurt; the price was just $700,000, including equipment. Ulukaya saw a chance to make and sell the kind of yogurt he grew up with, now known in the U.S. as "Greek yogurt." He obtained a loan from the Small Business Administration and hired several of the laid-off Kraft employees to produce a trial run. With high-quality products and some smart marketing decisions, the product was soon selling fast.

As the company has grown, Ulukaya has balanced shrewd competitiveness with a compassion developed during his difficult years as an endangered resident of Turkey and a vulnerable immigrant to America with very limited English skills. He channeled that compassion into a vision of building the company of the future, one that sees its people as the creators of its value. He was pleased to offer jobs to the experienced yogurt makers who had been laid off by Kraft. When he needed still more workers, he turned to a local center aiding refugees. Today at the original plant and the company's more recently opened facility in Idaho, Chobani's workforce is almost one-third immigrants; roughly one-fifth of the employees are refugees. Their appreciation for an opportunity in the United States has made them extremely loyal and hardworking employees. Furthermore, the resulting corporate culture is one with a strong sense of community and a sense of purpose.

Under Ulukaya's leadership, the privately held company has been a success by many measures. Competing against industry giants Danone and General Mills, the company has a 19% share of yogurt sales and 36% of Greek yogurt sales. It is rapidly launching new product lines and expanding internationally, including sales to Australia, Mexico, and New Zealand. The company also excels in treatment of its employees, landing a spot on the list of Great Places to Work. It has a policy of six weeks of paid parental leave following birth or adoption. Ulukaya recently announced a program aimed at sharing equity (ownership of stock) with workers. Giving equity and ownership stakes to his employees should help Chobani maintain the founder's vision for years to come.

Questions

1. What signs of a "global" business environment can you identify in this description of Chobani?
2. Thinking about the HR activities you have studied in the previous chapters, identify some activities that you expect would be affected by Ulukaya's decision to hire refugees and other immigrants.

Sources: "Chobani Appoints Peter McGuiness as President amidst Strong Business Performance," *Markets Insider,* August 28, 2019, https://markets.businessinsider.com; Jim Vinoski, "Chobani's Hamdi Ulukaya Throws Down the Gauntlet with His "Anti-CEO Playbook," *Forbes,* June 29, 2019, https://www.forbes.com; Christine Lagorio-Chafkin, "Hamdi Ulukaya on Bringing Humanity to Leadership," *Inc.,* June 2018, pp. 37–38; "Chobani, LLC," Great Place to Work, http://reviews.greatplacetowork.com, accessed July 3, 2018; David Gelles, "Chobani, the Greek Yogurt Maker, Reclaims Control of Its Finances," *New York Times,* June 28, 2018, https://www.nytimes.com.

to different settings. Even if some practices are the same worldwide, the company now has to communicate them to its international workforce. A variety of international activities require managers to understand HRM principles and practices prevalent in global markets.

Employees in an International Workforce

Organizations that operate globally are very likely to employ citizens of more than one country. Employees may come from the employer's parent country, a host country, or a third country. The **parent country** is the country in which the organization's headquarters is located. For example, the United States is the parent country of General Motors, because GM's headquarters is in Michigan. A GM employee who was born in the United States and

Parent Country
The country in which an organization's headquarters is located.

As companies in the United States and Europe outsource jobs in order to keep costs low, countries such as India continue to see employment rates hold steady or even rise.
Terry Vine/Getty Images

works at GM's headquarters or one of its U.S. factories is therefore a *parent-country national.*

A **host country** is a country (other than the parent country) in which an organization operates a facility. Mexico is a host country of Ford Motor Company because Ford has operations there. Any Mexican workers hired to work at Ford's Mexican facilities would be *host-country nationals,* that is, employees who are citizens of the host country.

A **third country** refers to a country that is neither the parent country nor the host country. (The organization may or may not have a facility in the third country.) In the example of Ford's operations in Mexico, the company could hire an Australian manager to work there. The Australian manager would be a *third-country national* because the manager is neither from the parent country (the United States) nor from the host country (Mexico).

When organizations operate overseas, they must decide whether to hire parent-country nationals, host-country nationals, or third-country nationals for the overseas operations. Usually they hire a combination of these. In general, employees assigned to work in another country are called **expatriates** ("expats" for short). In the Ford example, the U.S. and Australian managers working in Mexico would be expatriates during those assignments.

The extent to which organizations use parent-country, host-country, or third-country nationals varies. For BioMotiv, a drug development company based in Cleveland, hiring third-country nationals is a practical necessity. The company's CEO, Baiju Shah, says a large proportion of scientists with advanced degrees in the United States are people who came here to pursue their education. Filling research positions with top talent is easier when hiring immigrants. Other organizations operate in dozens of countries. Among them are consulting firm EY and food service company Sodexo, both of which make a point of recruiting globally in order to attract talent with deep knowledge of the customers and locations where they operate.[4]

Host Country
A country (other than the parent country) in which an organization operates a facility.

Third Country
A country that is neither the parent country nor the host country of an employer.

Expatriates
Employees assigned to work in another country.

Employers in the Global Marketplace

Just as there are different ways for employees to participate in international business–as parent-country, host-country, or third-county nationals–there are also different ways for employers to do business globally, ranging from simply shipping products to customers in other countries to transforming the organization into a truly global one, with operations, employees, and customers in many countries. Figure 16.1 shows the major levels of global participation.

Most organizations begin by serving customers and clients within a domestic marketplace. Typically, a company's founder has an idea for serving a local, regional, or national market. The business must recruit, hire, train, and compensate employees to produce the product, and these people usually come from the business owner's local labor market. Selection and training focus on employees' technical abilities and, to some extent, interpersonal skills. Pay levels reflect local labor conditions. If the product succeeds, the company might expand operations to other domestic locations, and HRM decisions become more complex as the organization draws from a larger labor market and needs systems for training and motivating employees in several locations. As the employer's workforce grows, it is also

FIGURE 16.1
Levels of Global Participation

likely to become more diverse. Even in small domestic organizations, a significant share of workers may be immigrants. In this way, even domestic companies are affected by issues related to the global economy.

As organizations grow, they often begin to meet demand from customers in other countries. The usual way for a company to start entering foreign markets is by *exporting,* or shipping domestically produced items to other countries to be sold there. Eventually it may become economically desirable to set up operations in one or more foreign countries. An organization that does so becomes an **international organization.** The decision to participate in international activities raises a host of HR issues, including the basic question of whether a particular location provides an environment where the organization can successfully acquire and manage human resources.

International Organization
An organization that sets up one or a few facilities in one or a few foreign countries.

Whereas international companies build one or a few facilities in another country, **multinational companies** go overseas on a broader scale. They build facilities in a number of different countries as a way to reduce production and distribution costs. In general, when organizations become multinationals, they move production facilities from relatively high-cost locations to lower-cost locations. The lower-cost locations may have lower average wage rates, or they may reduce distribution costs by being nearer to customers. The HRM challenges faced by a multinational company are similar to but larger than those of an international organization because more countries are involved. More than ever, the organization needs to hire managers who can function in a variety of settings, give them necessary training, and provide flexible compensation systems that take into account the different pay rates, tax systems, and costs of living from one country to another.

Multinational Company
An organization that builds facilities in a number of different countries in an effort to minimize production and distribution costs.

At the highest level of involvement in the global marketplace are **global organizations.** These flexible organizations compete by offering top products tailored to segments of the market while keeping costs as low as possible. A global organization locates each facility based on the ability to effectively, efficiently, and flexibly produce a product or service, using cultural differences as an advantage. Rather than treating differences in other countries as a challenge to overcome, a global organization treats different cultures as equals. It may have multiple headquarters spread across the globe, so decisions are more decentralized. Sometimes a global organization is "born global," meaning its founders conceived of and implemented a global strategy from the start.[5] Being born global is relatively more common among technology businesses, such as Spotify and Skype, because they meet a need that exists around the world, often selling to customers that have international activities and

Global Organization
An organization that chooses to locate a facility based on the ability to effectively, efficiently, and flexibly produce a product or service, using cultural differences as an advantage.

selling a product that is not expensive to transport. A born-global company has a chance to grow faster than a similar company that starts by focusing only on its domestic market.

A global organization needs HRM practices that encourage flexibility and are based on an in-depth knowledge of differences among countries. Global organizations must be able to recruit, develop, retain, and use managers who can get results across national boundaries. Thus, a global organization needs a **transnational HRM system** that features decision making from a global perspective, managers from many countries, and ideas contributed by people from a variety of cultures.[6] Decisions that are the outcome of a transnational HRM system balance uniformity (for fairness) with flexibility (to account for cultural and legal differences). This balance and the variety of perspectives should work together to improve the quality of decision making. The participants from various countries and cultures contribute ideas from a position of equality, rather than the parent country's culture dominating. When these practices become embedded not only in an organization's human resource management but also in its overall culture and strategy, the organization is sometimes referred to as a *transnational organization.* In practice, a "transnational" organization may not differ much from a high-performance global organization.

Transnational HRM System
Type of HRM system that makes decisions from a global perspective, includes managers from many countries, and is based on ideas contributed by people representing a variety of cultures.

Factors Affecting HRM in International Markets

LO 16-2 Identify the factors that most strongly influence HRM in international markets.

Whatever their level of global participation, organizations that operate in more than one country must recognize that the countries are not identical and differ in terms of many factors. To simplify this discussion, we focus on four major factors:

- Culture
- Education
- Economic systems
- Political-legal systems

Visit your instructor's Connect® course and access your eBook to view this video.

"Getting that first hire right, we've found, is the key differentiator for how well an operation will evolve over time in a region or not" —Christine M. Pambianchi, Senior Vice President of Human Resources, Corning

Video produced for the Center for Executive Succession in the Darla Moore School of Business at the University of South Carolina by Coal Powered Filmworks.

Culture

By far the most important influence on international HRM is the culture of the country in which a facility is located. *Culture* is a community's set of shared assumptions about how the world works and what ideals are worth striving for.[7] Cultural influences may be expressed through customs, languages, religions, and so on.

Culture is important to HRM for two reasons. First, it often determines the other three international influences. Culture can greatly affect a country's laws because laws often are based on the culture's definitions of right and wrong. Culture also influences what people value, so it affects people's economic systems and efforts to invest in education.

Even more important for understanding human resource management, culture often determines the effectiveness of various HRM practices. Practices that are effective in the United States, for example, may fail or even backfire in a country with different beliefs and values. Consider the six dimensions of culture that Geert Hofstede identified in his classic study of culture:[8]

1. *Individualism/collectivism* describes the strength of the relation between an individual and other individuals in the society. In cultures that are high in individualism, such as

the United States, Great Britain, and the Netherlands, people tend to think and act as individuals rather than as members of a group. People in these countries are expected to stand on their own two feet, rather than be protected by the group. In cultures that are high in collectivism, such as Colombia, Pakistan, and Taiwan, people think of themselves mainly as group members. They are expected to devote themselves to the interests of the community, and the community is expected to protect them when they are in trouble.

2. *Power distance* concerns the way the culture deals with unequal distribution of power and defines the amount of inequality that is normal. In countries with large power distances, including India and the Philippines, the culture defines it as normal to maintain large differences in power. In countries with small power distances, such as Denmark and Israel, people try to eliminate inequalities. One way to see differences in power distance is in the way people talk to one another. In the high-power-distance countries of Mexico and Japan, people address one another with titles (Señor Smith, Smith-san). At the other extreme, in the United States, in most situations people use one another's first names—behavior that would be disrespectful in other cultures.
3. *Uncertainty avoidance* describes how cultures handle the fact that the future is unpredictable. High uncertainty avoidance refers to a strong cultural preference for structured situations. In countries such as Greece and Portugal, people tend to rely heavily on religion, law, and technology to give them a degree of security and clear rules about how to behave. In countries with low uncertainty avoidance, including Singapore and Jamaica, people seem to take each day as it comes.
4. *Masculinity/femininity* is the emphasis a culture places on practices or qualities that have traditionally been considered masculine or feminine. A "masculine" culture is a culture that values achievement, money making, assertiveness, and competition. A "feminine" culture is one that places a high value on relationships, service, care for the weak, and preserving the environment. In this model, Germany and Japan are examples of masculine cultures, and Sweden and Norway are examples of feminine cultures.
5. *Long-term/short-term orientation* suggests whether the focus of cultural values is on the future (long term) or the past and present (short term). Cultures with a long-term orientation value saving and persistence, which tend to pay off in the future. Many Asian countries, including Japan and China, have a long-term orientation. Short-term orientations, as in the cultures of the United States, Russia, and West Africa, promote respect for past tradition and for fulfilling social obligations in the present.
6. *Indulgence/restraint* describes the extent to which a culture controls the desire to pursue enjoyment and fun. An indulgent culture allows relative freedom to seek pleasure, and its values place relatively great importance on leisure and freedom of speech. Such cultures, which include Mexico, the United States, and Canada, tend to have more people who describe themselves as happy and perceive they have personal control over their life. A restrained culture tends to control the impulse to gratify personal needs, and it imposes strict social norms. Examples include Russia and China.

In Taiwan, a country that is high in collectivism, co-workers consider themselves more as group members instead of individuals.
Imagemore Co., Ltd./Corbis

Such cultural characteristics as these influence the ways members of an organization behave toward one another, as well as their attitudes toward various HRM practices.

For instance, cultures differ strongly in their opinions about how managers should lead, how decisions should be handled, and what motivates employees. In Germany, managers achieve their status by demonstrating technical skills, and employees look to managers to assign tasks and resolve technical problems. In the Netherlands, managers focus on seeking agreement, exchanging views, and balancing the interests of the people affected by a decision.[9] Clearly, differences like these would affect how an organization selects and trains its managers and measures their performance.

Cultures strongly influence the appropriateness of HRM practices. For example, the extent to which a culture is individualist or collectivist will affect the success of a compensation program. Compensation tied to individual performance may be seen as fairer and more motivating by members of an individualist culture; a culture favoring individualism will be more accepting of great differences in pay between the organization's highest- and lowest-paid employees. Collectivist cultures tend to have much flatter pay structures.

HR Analytics & Decision Making

Although national culture is important, research suggests that its importance may be overstated. Researchers reexamining Hofstede's original work found that, in addition to differences across nations, significant cultural differences also existed within nations. They further found that the differences in cultures across organizations within countries was larger than the differences across countries. Their results imply that although one cannot ignore national culture, one must not think that certain HR practices may not be effective simply based on a regard for national culture. People of varying cultural backgrounds within a nation will be drawn to organizations whose cultures better match their individual, as opposed to national, value systems.

In addition, many observers have suggested that the effectiveness of high-performance work systems (HPWS) depends on the cultural or institutional constraints, such that they may be ineffective in cultures that exhibit high power distance or high collectivism. However, a meta-analysis revealed that the effects of HPWS on firm performance were positive in all cultures, and contrary to expectations, if anything, higher in the cultures where the cultural hypothesis suggested they would be lower.

Questions

1. A company has prospered with a string of innovations stimulated by an organizational culture promoting competition, goal achievement, and assertiveness, values associated with Hofstede's concept of a "masculine" culture. Could the company succeed with these same practices in Norway, where the culture tends to be "feminine"? Why or why not?
2. A company has become a high-performance work system in the United States through employee empowerment and continuous improvement. If the company wants to expand into other countries, should it plan to abandon this approach in countries with high power distance? Why or why not?

Sources: T. Rable, M. Jayasinghe, B. Gerhart, and T. Kuhlmann, "A Meta-Analysis of Country Differences in the High-Performance Work System–Business Performance Relationship: The Roles of National Culture and Managerial Discretion." *Journal of Applied Psychology* 99, no. 6 (2014), pp. 1011–1041; B. Gerhart and M. Fang, "National Culture and Human Resource Management Assumptions and Evidence," *International Journal of Human Resource Management* 16, no. 6 (June 2005), pp. 971–986.

The success of HRM decisions related to job design, benefits, performance management, and other systems related to employee motivation also will be shaped by culture. In an interesting study comparing call center workers in India (a collectivist culture) and the United States (an individualistic culture), researchers found that in the United States, employee turnover depended more on person–job fit than on person–organization fit. In the United States, employees were less likely to quit if they felt that they had the right skills, resources, and personality to succeed on the job. In India, what mattered more was for employees to feel they fit in well with the organization and were well connected to the organization and the community.[10]

Finally, cultural differences can affect how people communicate and how they coordinate their activities. In collectivist cultures, people tend to value group decision making, as in the previous example. When a person raised in an individualistic culture must work closely with people from a collectivist culture, communication problems and conflicts often occur. People from the collectivist culture tend to collaborate heavily and may evaluate the individualistic person as unwilling to cooperate and share information with them. Cultural differences in communication affected the way a North American agricultural company embarked on employee empowerment at its facilities in the United States and Brazil.[11] Empowerment requires information sharing, but in Brazil, high power distance leads employees to expect managers to make decisions, so they do not desire information that is appropriately held by managers. Empowering the Brazilian employees required involving managers directly in giving and sharing information to show that this practice was in keeping with the traditional chain of command. Also, because uncertainty avoidance is another aspect of Brazilian culture, managers explained that greater information sharing would reduce uncertainty about their work. At the same time, greater collectivism in Brazil made employees comfortable with the day-to-day communication of teamwork. The individualistic U.S. employees needed to be sold more on this aspect of empowerment.

Because of these challenges, organizations must prepare managers to recognize and handle cultural differences. They may recruit managers with knowledge of other cultures or provide training, as described later in the chapter. For expatriate assignments, organizations may need to conduct an extensive selection process to identify individuals who can adapt to new environments. At the same time, it is important to be wary of stereotypes and avoid exaggerating the importance of cultural differences. Recent research that examined Hofstede's model of cultural differences found that differences among organizations within a particular culture were sometimes larger than differences from country to country.[12] This finding suggests that it is important for an organization to match its HR practices to its values; individuals who share those values are likely to be interested in working for the organization. China's Haier Group, the world's largest appliance maker, established a goal of creating an entrepreneur-style culture, in which employees are motivated to innovate in service of customer needs. The HR department has supported employee training and knowledge sharing, along with the restructuring of work into networks and "microenterprises" in which employees are responsible for starting up new internal businesses. In the resulting climate, employees place a high value on innovation and independence; they have earned patents and launched profitable new products.[13]

Education and Skill Levels

Countries also differ in the degree to which their labor markets include people with education and skills of value to employers. As discussed in Chapter 1, the United States suffers from a shortage of skilled workers in many occupations, and the problem is expected to increase. For example, the need for knowledge workers (engineers, teachers, scientists, health care workers) is expected to grow almost twice as fast as the overall rate of job growth in the United States.[14] On the other hand, the labor markets in many countries are very attractive because they offer high skill levels and low wages.

Educational opportunities also vary from one country to another. In general, spending on education is greater per pupil in high-income countries than in poorer countries. Poverty, diseases such as AIDS, and political turmoil keep children away from school in some areas. Globally, top spenders on education include Luxembourg, Austria, the United States, and Norway. Spending rates differ at the primary, secondary, and post-secondary levels. The United States ranks fourth in spending after high school and third in spending on primary education.[15]

Companies with foreign operations locate in countries where they can find suitable employees. The education and skill levels of a country's labor force affect how and the extent to which companies want to operate there. In countries with a poorly educated population, companies will limit their activities to low-skill, low-wage jobs. In contrast, India's large pool of well-trained technical workers is one reason that the country has become a popular location for outsourcing computer programming jobs.

Economic System

A country's economic system, whether capitalist or socialist, as well as the government's involvement in the economy through taxes or compensation, price controls, and other activities, influences human resource management practices in a number of ways.

As with all aspects of a region's or country's life, the economic system and culture are likely to be closely tied, providing many of the incentives or disincentives for developing the value of the labor force. Socialist economic systems provide ample opportunities for educational development because the education system is free to students. At the same time, socialism may not provide economic rewards (higher pay) for increasing one's education. In capitalist systems, students bear more of the cost of their education, but employers reward those who invest in education.

The health of an economic system affects human resource management. In developed countries with great wealth, labor costs are relatively high. Such differences show up in compensation systems and in recruiting and selection decisions. As China's economy has developed and costs have risen, businesspeople have increasingly gone to other countries to seek growth opportunities. More and more wind up in Africa, where gains in education and employment are fueling rapid expansion in demand in several countries. One such entrepreneur is Sun Jian, who researched types of goods that would be expensive to ship, thereby settling on ceramic tile as an ideal product to make and sell in Nigeria. Of course, local residents also see—and seize—business opportunities. Some observers think African entrepreneurship is being slowed by a cultural focus on one's place in the community over one's potential as an individual, along with avoidance of admitting weaknesses or errors. However, as African entrepreneurs build networks where they can support and learn from one another, African-owned enterprises like iRoko (online movies) and Volatia (translation services) may become the world's next famous start-ups.[16]

Students at the University of Warsaw in Poland are provided with a government-supported education. In general, former Soviet bloc countries tend to be generous in funding education, so they tend to have highly educated and skilled labor forces. Capitalist countries such as the United States generally leave higher education up to individual students to pay for, but the labor market rewards students who earn a college degree.
ArtMediaFactory/Shutterstock

In general, socialist systems take a higher percentage of each worker's income as the worker's income increases. Capitalist systems tend to let workers keep more of their earnings. In this way, socialism redistributes wealth from high earners to the poor, whereas capitalism apparently rewards individual accomplishments. In any case, because the amount of take-home pay a worker receives after taxes may thus differ from country to country, in an organization that pays two managers in two countries $100,000 each, the manager in one country might take home more than the manager in the other country. Such differences make pay structures more complicated when they cross national boundaries, and they can affect recruiting of candidates from more than one country.

Political-Legal System

A country's political-legal system–its government, laws, and regulations–strongly impinges on human resource management. The country's laws often dictate the requirements for certain HRM practices, such as training, compensation, hiring, firing, and layoffs. For example, dissatisfaction with the European Union's principle of free movement of labor across member countries, which led to high immigration rates in the United Kingdom, was undoubtedly an important consideration by UK voters in their support of a 2016 referendum to leave the EU. From employers' perspective, leaving the EU–informally called "Brexit"–has already reduced the pool of available workers now that UK officials have announced a points-based immigration system to be introduced in January 2021. The goal of the new system is twofold: (1) allow skilled talent from outside the UK access to the UK job market and (2) end free movement of labor (which is encouraged among EU nations), thus giving the country more control over its borders. Industry leaders warned the new plan will "spell absolute disaster" for business sectors that pay lower wages, including health care, manufacturing, and hospitality (hotels and restaurants).[17]

As we noted in the discussion of culture, the political-legal system arises to a large degree from the culture in which it exists, so laws and regulations reflect cultural values. For example, the United States has led the world in eliminating discrimination in the workplace. Because this value is important in U.S. culture, the nation has legal safeguards such as the equal employment opportunity laws discussed in Chapter 3, which affect hiring and other HRM decisions. As a society, the United States also has strong beliefs regarding the fairness of pay systems. Thus, the Fair Labor Standards Act (discussed in Chapter 12), among other laws and regulations, sets a minimum wage for a variety of jobs. Other laws and regulations dictate much of the process of negotiation between unions and management. All these are examples of laws and regulations that affect the practice of HRM in the United States.

Similarly, laws and regulations in other countries reflect the norms of their cultures. For several decades, Malaysia addressed the economic disparity between ethnic Malays and the more prosperous ethnic Chinese with affirmative-action programs that included quotas for Malays in college admissions and hiring. Over that time, many ethnic Chinese emigrated from Malaysia, and an ethnic Malay middle class developed, paving the way for the government to plan a rollback of the policy.[18] In Western Europe, where many countries have had strong socialist parties, some laws have been aimed at protecting the rights and benefits of workers. The European Union has agreed that employers in member nations must respect certain rights of workers, including workplace health and safety; equal opportunities for men and women; protection against discrimination based on sex, race, religion, age, disability, and sexual orientation; and labor laws that set standards for work hours and other conditions of work.

Recently, national governments have affected employers by imposing tariffs, or taxes on goods originating from particular countries. For companies that depend heavily on sales in the countries imposing tariffs, these actions shape decisions about where to locate production facilities. And those decisions, in turn, give rise to the need for planning to hire and/or relocate employees. The decisions are particularly complex in today's manufacturing environment, where many products involve closely managed supply chains, with components sourced based on areas' manufacturing strengths and their ability to fill orders quickly. For example, U.S. automakers must consider where they buy components, and the suppliers of those components must consider where they buy steel, aluminum, and any other materials subject to tariffs. Similarly, microchips designed in the United States typically begin the manufacturing process here and then are shipped to China for final assembly and packaging. Tariffs imposed by the U.S. government treat the chips as Chinese imports subject to tariffs when sold in the United States. An option would be to build manufacturing facilities in the United States–an option that would require significant HR planning, given that China is where the assembly expertise has developed.[19]

An organization that expands internationally must gain expertise in the host country's legal requirements and ways of dealing with its legal system, often leading organizations to hire one or more host-country nationals to help in the process. Some countries have laws requiring that a certain percentage of the employees of any foreign-owned subsidiary be host-country nationals, and in the context of our discussion here, this legal challenge to an organization's HRM may hold an advantage if handled creatively.

LO 16-3 Discuss how differences among countries affect HR planning at organizations with international operations.

Human Resource Planning in a Global Economy

As economic and technological change creates a global environment for organizations, human resource planning is involved in decisions about participating as an exporter or as an international, multinational, or global company. Even purely domestic companies may draw talent from the international labor market. As organizations consider decisions about their level of international activity, HR professionals should provide information about the relevant human resource issues, such as local market pay rates and labor laws. When organizations decide to operate internationally or globally, human resource planning involves decisions about where and how many employees are needed for each international facility.

Decisions about where to locate include HR considerations such as the cost and availability of qualified workers. In addition, HR specialists must work with other members of the organization to weigh these considerations against financial and operational requirements. Increasingly, advances in technology are making automation a viable low-cost option for getting work done. Furthermore, other factors are in play. Many people assume that lower labor costs are the main or even the only reason why U.S. auto companies build factories in Mexico. Indeed, the labor cost to assemble a vehicle in Mexico is as much as $700 less than in the United States. But the total advantages differ according to other factors, including where vehicles are sold. For a vehicle sold in the United States, parts as well as labor cost less in Mexico, but the cost to transport the vehicle to dealers is higher, resulting in a net cost advantage of $1,200. For a car sold in Europe, the advantage of Mexico over the United States rises to $4,300, mainly because Mexico has negotiated an exemption from the tariffs imposed on vehicles by the European Union. The Mexican government has further contributed to its desirability as a manufacturing location by investing in technical training and upgrading its ports.[20]

Other location decisions involve outsourcing, described in Chapter 2, and job design, described in Chapter 4. Many companies have boosted efficiency by arranging to have specific functions performed by outside contractors. Many–but not all–of these arrangements involve workers outside the United States in lower-wage countries. Countries also vary in the extent to which organizations can and do set up work-from-home arrangements (see "Did You Know?").

In Chapter 5 we saw that human resource planning includes decisions to hire and lay off workers to prepare for the organization's expected needs. Compared with other countries, the United States allows employers wide latitude in reducing their workforce, giving U.S.

Did You Know?

Work-at-Home Options Most Common in Developed West

While the COVID-19 pandemic forced some organizations to allow employees to work from home, a majority of workers want to continue having that option. However, not all occupations are suited for at-home work.

An analysis of the potential for work-at-home arrangements looked at particular occupations to see which could be done from home and their share of countries' total jobs. According to that analysis, fewer than one in five workers are in occupations that could be performed at home. However, in developed nations, the share rises to 23%. Regional variations are even greater, with about 30% of workers in North America and Western Europe having jobs that could be done at home, compared with 8% of South Asian workers and 6% of workers in sub-Saharan Africa.

Often, the differences have to do with the availability of information technology and telecommunications. High-tech work can be especially flexible; in some cases, organizations are breaking down projects into specific tasks that can be assigned to qualified workers anywhere the organization operates. However, home-based workers, especially in less-developed areas, could be in occupations such as sewing or farm work.

Question

Suppose you work in the HR department of an accounting firm that is considering opening several offices in Asia. Would you recommend that the decision makers assess the potential for work-at-home options when comparing different locations? Why or why not?

Sources: Janine Berg, Florence Bonnet, and Sergei Soares, "Working from Home: Estimating the Worldwide Potential," *Vox,* May 11, 2020, https://voxeu.org; Neil Franklin, "Three Quarters of Workers Want the Choice to Work from Home after Lockdown," *Workplace Insight,* May 5, 2020, https://workplaceinsight.net; Ravin Jesuthasan, Tracey Malcolm, and Susan Cantrell, "How the Coronavirus Crisis Is Redefining Jobs," *Harvard Business Review,* April 22, 2020, https://hbr.org.

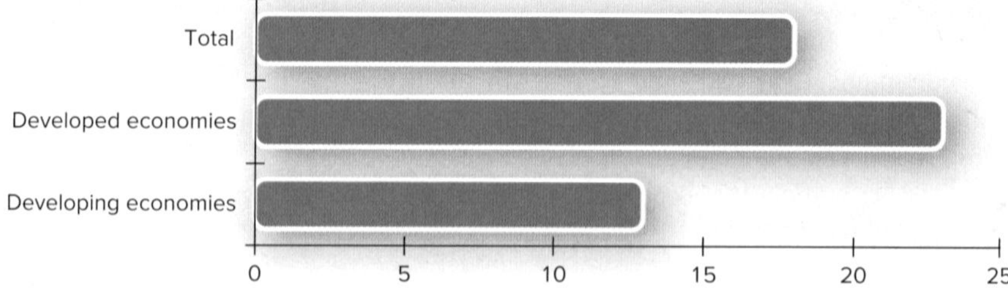

employers the option of hiring for peak needs, then laying off employees if needs decline. Other governments place more emphasis on protecting workers' jobs. European countries, and France in particular, tend to be very strict in this regard.

Selecting Employees in a Global Labor Market

LO 16-4 Describe how companies select and train human resources in a global labor market.

Many companies, such as Microsoft, have headquarters in the United States plus facilities in locations around the world. To be effective, employees in the Microsoft Mexico operations in Mexico City must understand that region's business and social culture. Organizations often meet this need by hiring host-country nationals to fill most of their foreign positions. A key reason is that a host-country national can more easily understand the values and customs of the local workforce than someone from another part of the world can. Also, training for and transporting families to foreign assignments is more expensive than

Qualities associated with success in foreign assignments are the ability to communicate in the foreign country, flexibility, enjoying a challenging situation, and support from family members. What would persuade you to take a foreign assignment?
Rob Brimson/The Image Bank/Getty Images

hiring people in the foreign country. Employees may be reluctant to take a foreign assignment because of the difficulty of moving overseas. Sometimes the move requires the employee's spouse to quit a job, and some countries will not allow the employee's spouse to seek work, even if jobs might be available.

Even so, organizations fill many key foreign positions with parent-country or third-country nationals. Sometimes a person's technical and human relations skills outweigh the advantages of hiring locally. In other situations, the local labor market simply does not offer enough qualified people. For example, employers whose jobs involve a high degree of physical labor report difficulty recruiting U.S.-born workers, so they turn to immigrant labor to fill positions.[21] Employers in Saudi Arabia have faced a similar situation. For years, oil wealth made it possible for the government to spare citizens from having to work physically demanding jobs and instead put them on the government payroll in well-paid positions with low demands. Jobs in retailing, construction, and hospitality were filled by third-party nationals from India and the Philippines. However, the Saudi government imposes quotas for Saudi employees, and recently it raised the quotas, restricting foreigners from working in certain sectors of the economy. The result of this change in policy has been a massive exodus of foreigners from the Saudi labor force.[22]

Whether the organization is hiring immigrants or selecting parent-country or third-country nationals for foreign assignments, some basic principles of selection apply. Selection of employees for foreign assignments should reflect criteria that have been associated with success in working overseas:

- Competency in the employee's area of expertise.
- Ability to communicate verbally and nonverbally in the foreign country.
- Flexibility, tolerance of ambiguity, and sensitivity to cultural differences.
- Motivation to succeed and enjoyment of challenges.
- Willingness to learn about the foreign country's culture, language, and customs.
- Support from family members.[23]

In research conducted a number of years ago, the factor most strongly influencing whether an employee completed a foreign assignment was the comfort of the employee's spouse and family.[24] Personality may also be important. Research has found that the employees who are most likely to successfully complete their overseas assignments are those who are extroverted (outgoing), agreeable (cooperative and tolerant), and conscientious (dependable and achievement oriented).[25]

Qualities of flexibility, motivation, agreeableness, and conscientiousness are so important because of the challenges involved in entering another culture. The emotions that accompany an overseas assignment tend to follow stages like those in Figure 16.2.[26] For a month or so after arriving, the foreign worker enjoys a "honeymoon" of fascination and euphoria as the employee enjoys the novelty of the new culture and compares its interesting similarities to or differences from the employee's own culture. Before long, the employee's mood declines as he or she notices more unpleasant differences and experiences feelings of isolation, criticism, stereotyping, and even hostility. As the mood reaches bottom, the employee is experiencing **culture shock,** the disillusionment and discomfort that occur during the process of adjusting to a new culture and its norms, values, and perspectives. Eventually, if employees persist and continue learning about their host country's

Culture Shock
Disillusionment and discomfort that occur during the process of adjusting to a new culture.

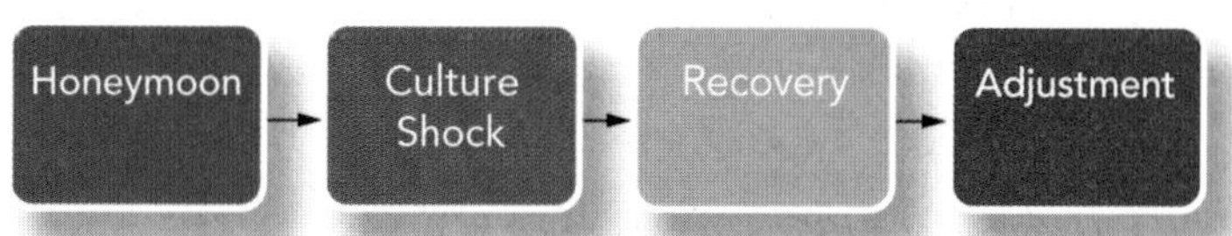

FIGURE 16.2
Emotional Stages Associated with a Foreign Assignment

Sources: Debra Bruno, "Repatriation Blues: Expats Struggle with the Dark Side of Coming Home," *The Wall Street Journal,* April 15, 2015, http://blogs.wsj.com; Delia Flanja, "Culture Shock in Intercultural Communication," *Studia Europaea* (October 2009), Business & Company Resource Center, http://galenet.galegroup.com.

culture, they begin to recover from culture shock as they develop a greater understanding and a support network. As the employee's language skills and comfort increase, the employee's mood should improve as well. Eventually, the employee reaches a stage of adjustment in which he or she accepts and enjoys the host country's culture.

Training and Developing a Global Workforce

In an organization whose employees come from more than one country, some special challenges arise with regard to training and development: (1) Training and development programs should be effective for all participating employees, regardless of their country of origin. (2) When organizations hire employees to work in a foreign country or transfer them to another country, the employer needs to provide the employees with training in how to handle the challenges associated with working in the foreign country.

Training Programs for an International Workforce

Developers of effective training programs for an international workforce must ask certain questions.[27] The first is to establish the objectives for the training and its content. Decisions about the training should support those objectives. The developers should next ask what training techniques, strategies, and media to use. Some will be more effective than others, depending on the learners' language and culture, as well as the content of the training. For example, in preparation U.S. employees might expect to discuss and ask questions about the training content, whereas employees from other cultures might consider this level of participation to be disrespectful, so for them some additional support might be called for. Language differences will require translations and perhaps a translator at training activities. Next, the developers should identify any other interventions and conditions that must be in place for the training to meet its objectives. For example, training is more likely to meet its objectives if it is linked to performance management and has the full support of management. Finally, the developers of a training program should identify who in the organization should be involved in reviewing and approving the training program.

The plan for the training program must consider international differences among trainees. For example, economic and educational differences might influence employees' access to and ability to use web-based training. Cultural differences may influence whether they will consider it appropriate to ask questions and whether they expect the trainer to spend time becoming acquainted with employees or to get down to business immediately. Table 16.1 provides examples of how cultural characteristics can affect training design.

Cross-Cultural Preparation

When an organization selects an employee for a position in a foreign country, it must prepare the employee for the foreign assignment. This kind of training is called **cross-cultural preparation,** preparing employees to work across national and cultural boundaries, and it

Cross-Cultural Preparation
Training to prepare employees and their family members for an assignment in a foreign country.

TABLE 16.1

Effects of Culture on Training Design

CULTURAL DIMENSION	IMPACT ON TRAINING
Individualism	Culture high in individualism expects participation in exercises and questioning to be determined by status in the company or culture.
Uncertainty avoidance	Culture high in uncertainty avoidance expects formal instructional environments. There is less tolerance for impromptu style.
Masculinity	Culture low in masculinity values relationships with fellow trainees. Female trainers are less likely to be resisted in low-masculinity cultures.
Power distance	Culture high in power distance expects trainers to be experts. Trainers are expected to be authoritarian and controlling of session.
Time orientation	Culture with a long-term orientation will have trainees who are likely to accept development plans and assignments.

Source: Based on B. Filipczak, "Think Locally, Act Globally," *Training*, January 1997, pp. 41–48.

often includes family members who will accompany the employee on the assignment. The training is necessary for all three phases of an international assignment:

1. Preparation for *departure*—language instruction and an orientation to the foreign country's culture.
2. The *assignment* itself—some combination of a formal program and mentoring relationship to provide ongoing further information about the foreign country's culture.
3. Preparation for the *return* home—providing information about the employee's community and home-country workplace (from company newsletters, local newspapers, and so on).

Methods for providing this training may range from lectures for employees and their families to visits to culturally diverse communities.[28] Employees and their families may also spend time visiting a local family from the country where they will be working. In the later section on managing expatriates, we provide more detail about cross-cultural preparation.

Cross-cultural preparation is important. Research links it to lower turnover among expatriates, greater willingness to accept another overseas assignment, and greater perceived contribution to business outcomes.[29] When a data company sent Paul Bailey from his home country, Britain, to manage an office in the United States, he discovered the importance of preparation. He had expected U.S. business culture to resemble that in Britain, but before long, he discovered that his employees had unexpected ideas about leadership and other norms. Six months into his assignment, he took a course in cultural differences, which helped him understand his co-workers' behavior.

It is important for employers to remember that returning home is also a challenge when employees have been away for months or years. They typically need time—at least a few days—to readjust to the culture they left behind. Furthermore, for the employees and their organizations to get maximum value from the overseas assignment, the returning employees should have opportunities to share what they learned. The company might set up meetings for returning employees and their colleagues, make returning expats available for panel discussions, invite them to blog about their experience during and after the assignment, and include data about international assignments in online databases used for promotions, employee development, and knowledge sharing.[30]

Global Employee Development

At global organizations, international assignments are a part of many career paths. The organization benefits most if it applies the principles of employee development in deciding which employees should be offered jobs in other countries. Career development helps expatriate and inpatriate employees make the transitions to and from their assignments and helps the organization apply the knowledge the employees obtain from these assignments.

Performance Management across National Boundaries

LO 16-5 Discuss challenges related to managing performance and compensating employees from other countries.

The general principles of performance management may apply in most countries, but the specific methods that work in one country may fail in another. Therefore, organizations have to consider legal requirements, local business practices, and national cultures when they establish performance management methods in other countries. Differences may include which behaviors are rated, how and the extent to which performance is measured, who performs the rating, and how feedback is provided.[31]

For example, National Rental Car uses a behaviorally based rating scale for customer service representatives. To measure the extent to which customer service representatives' behaviors contribute to the company's goal of improving customer service, the scale measures behaviors such as smiling, making eye contact, greeting customers, and solving customer problems. Depending on the country, different behaviors may be appropriate. In Japan, culturally defined standards for polite behavior include the angle of bowing as well as proper back alignment and eye contact. In Ghana and many other African nations, appropriate measures would include behaviors that reflect loyalty and repaying of obligations as well as behaviors related to following regulations and procedures.

The extent to which managers measure performance may also vary from one country to another. In rapidly changing regions, such as Southeast Asia, the organization may have to update its performance plans more often than once a year.

Feedback is another area in which differences can occur. Employees around the world appreciate positive feedback, but U.S. employees are much more used to direct feedback than are employees in other countries. In Mexico managers are expected to provide positive feedback before focusing the discussion on behaviors the employee needs to improve.[32] At the Thai office of Singapore Airlines, managers resisted giving negative feedback to employees because they feared this would cause them to have bad karma, contributing to their reincarnation at a lower level in their next life.[33] The airlines therefore allowed the managers to adapt their feedback process to fit local cultures.

Compensating an International Workforce

The chapters in Part 4 explained that compensation includes decisions about pay structure, incentive pay, and employee benefits. All these decisions become more complex when an organization has an international workforce. Looking at CEO pay, for example, Bloomberg's analysis of the large companies trading in the major stock indexes of 22 nations found wide variations. The average pay of the CEO of a U.S.-based company was four times the global average of $3.55 million. The closest follower-ups were CEOs in Switzerland and the Netherlands, at two and a half times the global average. And looking at the ratio of the CEO's pay to that of the average worker, the United States again tops the list at 265 times, followed by India at 229 times—but with much lower pay for the average employee. An organization with offices in multiple countries would need to recognize that pay considered fair at its headquarters might look much different to employees and investors in other locations.[34]

FIGURE 16.3
Earnings in Selected Occupation Groups in Three Countries

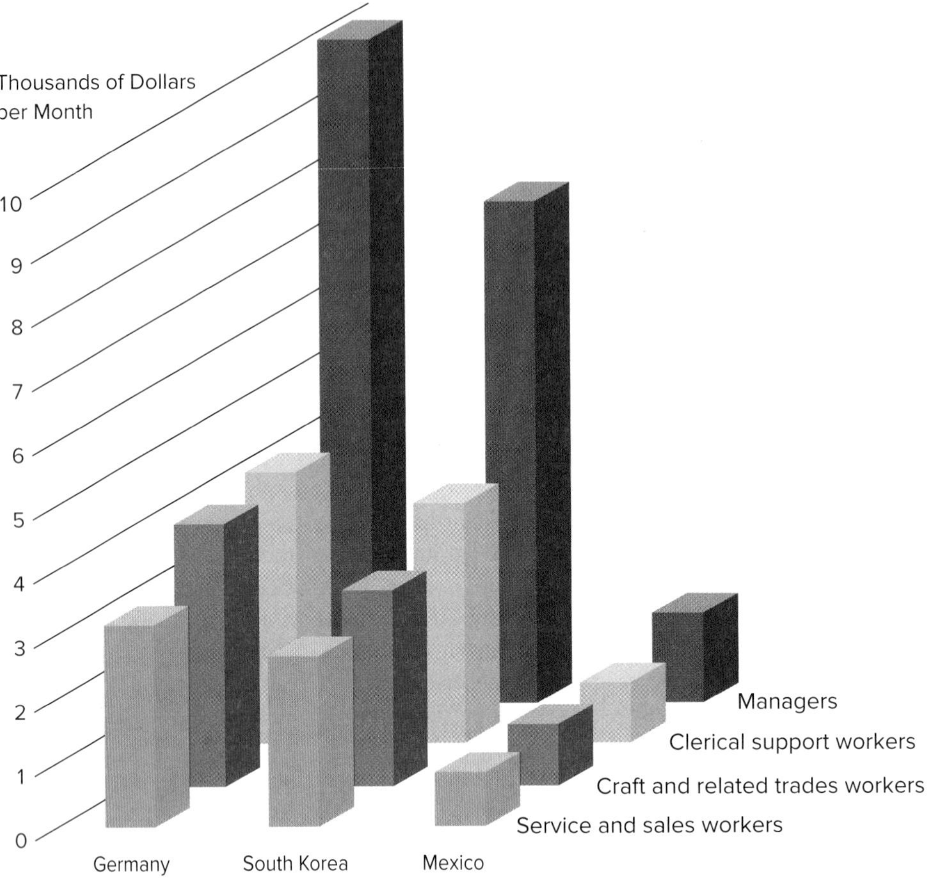

Source: Wage and hour data from International Labour Organization, ILOSTAT, Multi Country Reports, http://www.ilo.org, accessed July 2, 2018.

Pay Structure

As Figure 16.3 shows, market pay structures can differ substantially across countries in terms of both pay level and the relative worth of jobs. For example, compared with the labor market in Germany, the market in Mexico provides much lower pay levels overall. And in South Korea relative to the other two countries, clerical workers enjoy a larger pay advantage relative to craft and trade workers. Or consider the starting pay for engineers: a survey of engineering students found most experience different expectations around the world. At one extreme, students in Switzerland expected, on average, annual pay of $79,243, and students in the United States expected $62,948. In contrast, students in Egypt expected $7,458, and students in Vietnam expected to earn just $6,397.[35]

Differences such as these create a dilemma for global companies: Should pay levels and differences reflect what workers are used to in their own countries? Or should they reflect the earnings of colleagues in the country of the facility, or earnings at the company headquarters? For example, should a German engineer posted to Mumbai be paid according to the standard in Frankfurt or the standard in Mumbai? If the standard is Frankfurt, the engineers in Mumbai will likely see the German engineer's pay as unfair. If the standard is Mumbai, the company will likely find it impossible to persuade a German engineer to take an assignment in Mumbai. Dilemmas such as these make a global compensation strategy important as a way to show employees that the pay structure is designed to be fair and related to the value that employees bring to the organization.

These decisions affect a company's costs and ability to compete. The average hourly labor costs in industrialized countries such as Switzerland, Norway, and the United States are far higher than these costs in newly industrialized countries such as Turkey, Mexico, and the Philippines.[36] As a result, we often hear that U.S. labor costs are too high to allow U.S. companies to compete effectively unless the companies shift operations to low-cost foreign subsidiaries. That conclusion oversimplifies the situation for many companies. Merely comparing wages ignores differences in education, skills, and productivity.[37] If an organization gets more or higher-quality output from a higher-wage workforce, the higher wages may be worth the cost. Besides this, if the organization has many positions requiring highly skilled workers, it may need to operate in (or hire immigrants from) a country with a strong educational system, regardless of labor costs. In addition, labor costs may be outweighed by other factors, such as transportation costs or access to resources or customers. Finally, increasing automation of processes is reducing the demand for labor and the significance of differences in labor costs.

Cultural and legal differences also can affect pay structure. An example of a cultural impact on pay would be a culture's widespread practice of paying holiday bonuses. An example of a legal matter affecting pay would be taxation of earnings. The United States requires that American workers file tax returns, regardless of location, and may have to pay taxes if their earnings pass a threshold ($107,600 as of this writing).[38] For American managers or other high earners sent overseas, the employer would have to decide whether to adjust pay levels to account for the U.S. taxation.

Incentive Pay

Besides setting a pay structure, the organization must make decisions with regard to incentive pay, such as bonuses and stock options. Although stock options became a common form of incentive pay in the United States during the 1990s, European businesses did not begin to embrace this type of compensation until the end of that decade.

However, the United States and Europe differ in the way they award stock options. European companies usually link the options to specific performance goals, such as the increase in a company's share price compared with that of its competitors.

Employee Benefits

As in the United States, compensation packages in other countries include benefits. Decisions about benefits must take into account the laws of each country involved, as well as employees' expectations and values in those countries. Some countries require paid maternity leave, and some countries have nationalized health care systems, which would affect the value of private health insurance in a compensation package. Pension plans are more widespread in parts of Western Europe than in the United States and Japan. Over 90% of workers in Switzerland have pension plans, as do all workers in France. Among workers with pension plans, U.S. workers are significantly less likely to have defined benefit plans than workers in Japan or Germany.

Paid vacation, discussed in Chapter 14, tends to be more generous in Western Europe than in the United States. Figure 16.4 compares the number of hours the average employee works in various countries. Of these countries, only in Mexico, Chile, and South Korea do workers put in more hours than U.S. workers. In the other countries, the norm is to work fewer hours than a U.S. worker over the course of a year.

FIGURE 16.4
Average Hours Worked in Selected Countries

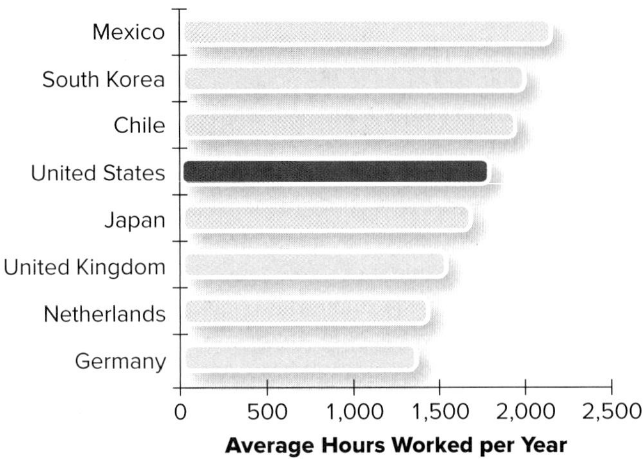

Source: Organisation for Economic Co-operation and Development, "Average Annual Hours Actually Worked per Worker," OECD.Stat, https://stats.oecd.org, accessed May 15, 2020.

International Labor Relations

Companies that operate across national boundaries often need to work with unions in more than one country. Organizations establish policies and goals for labor relations, for overseeing labor agreements, and for monitoring labor performance (for example, output and productivity).[39] The day-to-day decisions about labor relations are usually handled by each foreign subsidiary. The reason is that labor relations on an international scale involve differences in laws, attitudes, and economic systems, as well as differences in negotiation styles.

At least in comparison with European organizations, U.S. organizations exert more centralized control over labor relations in the various countries where they operate.[40] U.S. management therefore must recognize differences in how various countries understand and regulate labor relations. For example, in the United States, collective bargaining usually involves negotiations between a union local and an organization's management, but in Sweden and Germany, collective bargaining generally involves negotiations between an employer's organization and a union representing an entire industry's employees.[41]

Legal differences range from who may form a union to how much latitude an organization is allowed in laying off workers. In some situations, governments get involved to protect workers. After an eight-story factory collapsed in Dhaka, Bangladesh, killing more than 1,100 people, the government of Bangladesh relaxed rules that had made it difficult for the country's workers to unionize. Until then, workers had to obtain permission from factory owners before forming trade unions.[42]

International labor relations must also take into account that negotiations between labor and management take place in a different social context, not just different economic and legal contexts. Cultural differences that affect other interactions come into play in labor negotiations as well. Negotiators will approach the process differently depending on whether the culture views the process as primarily cooperative or competitive and whether it is local practice to negotiate a deal by starting with the specifics or agreeing on overall principles.[43] Working with host-country nationals can help organizations navigate such differences in negotiation style.

HR How To

Making the Most of an Expat Assignment

When well-managed, expatriate assignments can be a tremendous career opportunity. They are a chance to see more of the markets served by the organization and get a deeper perspective on the challenges and opportunities facing the company. Seeing new parts of the world can be exciting in of itself. Furthermore, employees with overseas experience and foreign-language skills tend to be more valuable in the labor market.

While the employer has a responsibility to plan for the HR challenges, the expatriate employee plays the key role in making the experience a success. Here are some suggestions for filling that role:

- Learn as much as possible about the culture of the host country. In particular, learn to speak and write the language.
- Accept invitations and opportunities to spend time with co-workers from the host country's culture. Listen carefully, and pay attention to how people interact and navigate through situations. This increases cultural knowledge and opens a chance to build friendships, which can make the time on the assignment both more productive and more pleasant.
- Participate in social networks for expatriates. Get to know those who are having positive experiences, and learn from them how to make the most of this opportunity.
- Engage in some self-assessment and discussion with management to identify the strengths you bring to the assignment. In some cultures, employees will expect authority to be based at least partly on length of service or position in the community. An expatriate will need to respect what the employees bring to the table but also may need to assert reasons why he or she needs to participate in discussions or exercise authority.
- Make sure any family members included in the move are open to the change. Identify the impact on each person, as well as the options for making the most of the experience. Try to find some wins for each person, such as a great school or a social network. Engage family members in lessons about the culture and language.
- Adopt a flexible outlook. When efforts do not yield the expect results, stop and assess the situation. Perhaps you or the others are making assumptions that do not work in the specific context.

Questions

1. What aspects of an expatriate assignment described here sound most appealing to you?
2. What aspects sound most difficult? How could an HR department assist with these?

Sources: Sue Bryant, "10 Tips for Managing Successful International Assignments," *Country Navigator,* August 20, 2019, https://www.countrynavigator.com; Randy Steinlauf, "Learn from My Experience: 3 Ways to Ensure Expat Success," *CEO World,* January 24, 2019, https://ceoworld.biz; Aideen O'Byrne, "Nurture Connections to Enhance Expatriate Success," *TD,* May 2018, pp. 38–42; Ryan McMunn, "Taking a Job Overseas Is Challenging, but So Rewarding," *Entrepreneur,* March 11, 2017, https://www.entrepreneur.com; Katia Viachos, "Making Your Expat Assignment Easier on Your Family," *Harvard Business Review,* March 10, 2017, https://hbr.org.

Managing Expatriates

At some point, most international and global organizations assign managers to foreign posts. (See "HR How To" for the expatriate's view of these assignments.) These assignments give rise to significant human resource challenges, from selecting managers for these assignments to preparing them, compensating them, and helping them adjust to a return home. The same kinds of HRM principles that apply to domestic positions can help organizations avoid mistakes in managing expatriates: planning and goal setting, selection aimed at achieving the HR goals, and performance management that includes evaluation of whether the overseas assignment delivered value relative to the costs involved.[44] Employers also can increase the likelihood of a successful assignment by ensuring that employees and their families have the resources they need.

Selecting Expatriate Managers

The challenge of managing expatriate managers begins with determining which individuals in the organization are most capable of handling an assignment in another country. Expatriate managers need technical competence in the area of operations, in part to help them earn the respect of subordinates. Of course, many other skills are also necessary for success in any management job, especially one that involves working overseas. Depending on the nature of the assignment and the culture where it is located, the organization should consider each candidate's skills, learning style, and approach to problem solving. Each of these should be related to achievement of the organization's goals, such as solving a particular problem, transferring knowledge to host-country employees, or developing future leaders for the organization.[45]

A successful expatriate manager must be sensitive to the host country's cultural norms, flexible enough to adapt to those norms, and strong enough to survive the culture shock of living in another culture. In addition, if the manager has a family, the family members must be able to adapt to a new culture. Adaptation requires three kinds of skills:[46]

1. Ability to maintain a positive self-image and feeling of well-being.
2. Ability to foster relationships with the host-country nationals.
3. Ability to perceive and evaluate the host country's environment accurately.

Some of the most important factors for expatriate adjustment, according to research, are the overseas work environment (including employees and culture), ability to communicate in the host country's language, job characteristics (freedom, autonomy, and variety), opportunities for leisure activities, urban environment (pollution, traffic, beauty), work–life balance, living quarters, family life, local friendships, and contact with those in the country left behind.[47] To assess candidates' ability to adapt to a new environment, interviews should address topics such as the ones listed in Table 16.2. The interviewer should be certain to give candidates a clear and complete preview of the assignment and the host-country culture. This helps the candidate evaluate the assignment and consider it in terms of his or her family situation, so the employer does not violate the employee's privacy.[48] These principles apply whether the candidates for international assignments are host-country or third-country nationals.

LO 16-6 Explain how employers prepare managers for international assignments and for their return home.

Preparing Expatriates

Once the organization has selected a manager for an overseas assignment, it is necessary to prepare that person through training and development. Because expatriate success depends so much on the entire family's adjustment, the employee's spouse should be included in the preparation activities. Employees selected for expatriate assignments already have job-related skills, so preparation for expatriate assignments often focuses on cross-cultural training—that is, training in what to expect from the host country's culture. The general purpose of cross-cultural training is to create an appreciation of the host country's culture so expatriates can behave appropriately.[49] Paradoxically, this requires developing a greater awareness of one's own culture so that the expatriate manager can recognize differences and similarities between the cultures and, perhaps, home-culture biases. Consider, for example, the statements in Figure 16.5, which are comments made by visitors to the United States. Do you think these observations accurately describe U.S. culture?

On a more specific level, cross-cultural training for foreign assignments includes the details of how to behave in business settings in another country—the ways people behave in meetings, how employees expect managers to treat them, and so on. As an example, Germans value promptness for meetings to a much greater extent than do Latin Americans—and

TABLE 16.2

Selected Topics for Assessing Candidates for Overseas Assignments

Motivation

- What are the candidate's reasons and degree of interest in wanting an overseas assignment?
- Does the candidate have a realistic understanding of what is required in working and living overseas?
- What is the spouse's attitude toward an overseas assignment?

Health

- Are there any health issues with the candidate or family members that might impact the success of the overseas assignment?

Language ability

- Does the candidate have the potential to learn a new language?
- Does the candidate's spouse have the ability to learn a new language?

Family considerations

- How many moves has the family made among different cities or parts of the United States? What problems were encountered?
- What is the spouse's goal in this move overseas?
- How many children are in the family and what are their ages? Will all the children move as part of the overseas assignment?
- Has divorce or its potential, or the death of a family member had a negative effect on the family's cohesiveness?
- Are there any adjustment problems the candidate would expect should the family move overseas?

Resourcefulness and initiative

- Is the candidate independent and capable of standing by his or her decisions?
- Is the candidate able to meet objectives and produce positive results with whatever human resources and facilities are available regardless of challenges that might arise in a foreign business environment?
- Can the candidate operate without a clear definition of responsibility and authority?
- Will the candidate be able to explain the goals of the company and its mission to local managers and workers?
- Does the candidate possess sufficient self-discipline and self-confidence to handle complex problems?
- Can the candidate operate effectively in a foreign country without normal communications and supporting services?

Adaptability

- Is the candidate cooperative, open to the opinions of others, and able to compromise?
- How does the candidate react to new situations and efforts to understand and appreciate cultural differences?
- How does the candidate react to criticism, constructive or otherwise?
- Will the candidate be able to make and develop contacts with peers in a foreign country?
- Does the candidate demonstrate patience when dealing with problems? Is he or she resilient and able to move forward after setbacks?

Career planning

- Does the candidate consider the assignment more than a temporary overseas trip?
- Is the overseas assignment consistent with the candidate's career development and one that was planned by the company?
- What is the candidate's overall attitude toward the company?
- Is there any history or indication of interpersonal problems with this candidate?

Financial

- Are there any current financial and/or legal considerations that might affect the assignment (e.g., house or car purchase, college expenses)?
- Will undue financial pressures be put upon the candidate and his or her family as a result of an overseas assignment?

Sources: P. Caligiuri, *Cultural Agility: Building a Pipeline of Successful Global Professionals* (San Francisco: Jossey-Bass, 2012); P. Caligiuri, D. Lepak, and J. Bonache, *Managing the Global Workforce* (West Sussex, United Kingdom: John Wiley & Sons, 2010); M. Shaffer, D. Harrison, H. Gregersen, S. Black, and L. Ferzandi, "You Can Take It with You: Individual Differences and Expatriate Effectiveness," *Journal of Applied Psychology* 91 (2006), pp. 109–125; P. Caligiuri, "Developing Global Leaders," *Human Resource Management Review* 16 (2006), pp. 219–228; P. Caligiuri, M. Hyland, A. Joshi, and A. Bross, "Testing a Theoretical Model for Examining the Relationship between Family Adjustment and Expatriates' Work Adjustment," *Journal of Applied Psychology* 83 (1998), pp. 598–614; David M. Noer, *Multinational People Management: A Guide for Organizations and Employees* (Arlington, VA: Bureau of National Affairs, 1975).

so on. How should one behave when first meeting one's business counterparts in another culture? The "outgoing" personality style so valued in the United States may seem quite rude in other parts of the world.[50] Ideally, the company also provides training for an expatriate manager's team in the host country.

FIGURE 16.5
Impressions of Americans: Comments by Visitors to the United States

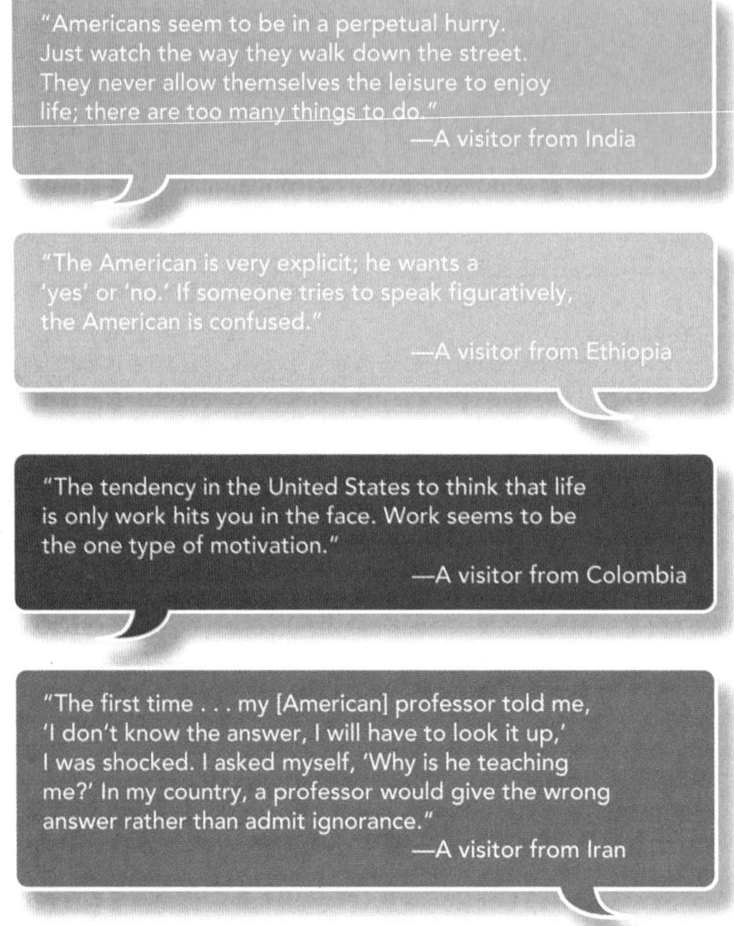

"Americans seem to be in a perpetual hurry. Just watch the way they walk down the street. They never allow themselves the leisure to enjoy life; there are too many things to do."
—A visitor from India
"The American is very explicit; he wants a 'yes' or 'no.' If someone tries to speak figuratively, the American is confused."
—A visitor from Ethiopia
"The tendency in the United States to think that life is only work hits you in the face. Work seems to be the one type of motivation."
—A visitor from Colombia
"The first time . . . my [American] professor told me, 'I don't know the answer, I will have to look it up,' I was shocked. I asked myself, 'Why is he teaching me?' In my country, a professor would give the wrong answer rather than admit ignorance."
—A visitor from Iran

Source: J. Feig and G. Blair, *There Is a Difference,* 2nd ed. (Washington, DC: Meridian House International, 1980), cited in N. Adler, *International Dimensions of Organizational Behavior,* 2nd ed. (Boston: PWS-Kent, 1991).

Employees preparing for a foreign assignment also need information about such practical matters as housing, schools, recreation, shopping, and health care facilities in the country where they will be living. Especially for employees being posted to developing economies, the employer should address concerns about safety and security. Related to these issues, some high-growth destinations, such as China and India, have had major problems with air pollution. Employers can help employees cope with this health hazard–for example, by providing air purifiers and extra time off to visit cleaner locales for fresh air.[51]

Communication in another country often requires a determined attempt to learn a new language. Some employers try to select managers who speak the language of the host country, and a few provide language training. Most companies assume that employees in the host country will be able to speak the host country's language. Even if this is true, host country nationals are not likely to be fluent in the home country's language, so language barriers remain.

Along with cross-cultural training, preparation of the expatriate should include career development activities. Before leaving for a foreign assignment, expatriates should discuss

HRM Social

Social-Media Usage Keeps Expats in the Loop

Organizations send employees to positions overseas in order to develop their capabilities or place talent where it can contribute most to the organization. The value of these assignments is greatest when the expatriate employees are able to fully engage with the host country co-workers and context, as well as stay connected with headquarters and colleagues in their home country. In this way, knowledge is flowing throughout the entire international organization. Maintaining all these ties is complex, but tools such as social media can help.

Social media can help employees stay connected to their home base. On a basic level, maintaining co-worker and family relationships contributes to the expatriate's mental health. It also maintains channels for employees to share what they are learning and stay in view when managers back home are considering new assignments and promotions. Social media are particularly effective channels for these purposes because they can include photos, videos, voice, and immediate back-and-forth to enrich these messages.

Social media also can help employees deepen ties to their host country and co-workers at the overseas assignment. Employees can join social-media groups of people who work at the facility, share common interests, or love the host-country location. They can get to know their local colleagues more fully, invite help navigating new situations, and find enjoyable things to do in the host country. This not only makes the overseas assignment more pleasant, it also equips the expat employee to communicate and work more effectively with colleagues and customers in the host culture.

Given the potential for social media to strengthen ties in the home and host countries, it is important for expatriate employees to balance communication in each direction. Using free time solely to communicate with family, friends, and co-workers back home will make the transition to the new country more difficult. Using social media only with people in the host location could isolate the employee from important contacts and relationships back home, making return more difficult. Training for employees can cover how to balance technology use and how to use the various kinds of social media available in the host country and at the company's facilities there.

Questions

1. Why is it important for an employee on an overseas assignment to stay in touch with co-workers and family back home? Why is it important for the employee to communicate with people in the host country?
2. Imagine you handle a construction firm's training program. The company wants to send a manager to Japan to open a new office. What training would you recommend providing about social-media use?

Sources: "Login Credentials: Social Media Use for International Assignment," *MSI blog*, October 26, 2019, https://msigts.com; Tom Coughlan, David Fogarty, and Sara Fogarty, "Virtual Proximity to Promote Expatriate Cultural Adjustment, Innovation, and the Reduction of Stress Levels," *International Journal of Applied Management and Technology* 18, no. 1 (2019), pp. 33–47; "Repatriation: Can Social Media Make a Difference?" *Relocate*, April 12, 2019, https://www.relocatemagazine.com.

with their managers how the foreign assignment fits into their career plans and what types of positions they can expect upon their return. This prepares the expatriate to develop valuable skills during the overseas assignment and eases the return home when the assignment is complete. Coaching during the assignment also can improve the likelihood that the expatriate will succeed.

When the employee leaves for the assignment, the preparation process should continue. Expatriate colleagues, coaches, and mentors can help the employee learn to navigate challenges as they arise (see "HRM Social"). For example, workers in a new culture sometimes experience internal conflict when the culture where they are working expects them to behave in a way that conflicts with values they learned from their own culture. For example, an Italian manager had difficulty motivating an Indian workforce because the employees were used to authoritarian leadership, and the manager felt as if that style was harsh and disempowering. By talking over the problem with experienced expatriates, the manager came to understand why the situation was so awkward and frustrating. He identified specific ways in which he could be more assertive without losing his temper, so that his Indian employees would better understand what was expected of them. Practicing a new style of leadership became more satisfying as the manager realized that the employees valued his style and that he was becoming a more capable cross-cultural leader.[52]

Managing Expatriates' Performance

Performance management of expatriates requires clear goals for the overseas assignment and frequent evaluation of whether the expatriate employee is on track to meet those goals. Communication technology including e-mail and teleconferencing provides a variety of ways for expats' managers to keep in touch with these employees to discuss and diagnose issues before they can interfere with performance. In addition, before employees leave for an overseas assignment, HR should work with managers to develop criteria measuring the success of the assignment.[53] Measures such as productivity should take into account any local factors that could make expected performance different in the host country than in the company's home country. For example, a country's labor laws or the reliability of the electrical supply could affect the facility's output and efficiency.

Compensating Expatriates

One of the greatest challenges of managing expatriates is determining the compensation package. Most organizations use a *balance sheet approach* to determine the total amount of the package. This approach adjusts the manager's compensation so that it gives the manager the same standard of living as in the home country plus extra pay for the inconvenience of locating overseas. As shown in Figure 16.6, the balance sheet approach begins by determining the purchasing power of compensation for the same type of job in the manager's own country—that is, how much a person can buy, after taxes, in terms of housing, goods and services, and a reserve for savings. Next, this amount is compared with the cost (in dollars, for a U.S. company) of these same expenses in the foreign country. In Figure 16.6, the greater size of the second column means the costs for a similar standard of living in the foreign country are much higher in every category except the reserve amount. For the expatriate in this situation, the employer would pay the additional costs, as shown by the third column. Finally, the expatriate receives additional purchasing power from premiums and incentives. Because of these added incentives, the expatriate's purchasing power is more than what the manager could buy at home with the salary for an equivalent job. (Compare the fourth column with the first.) These compensation practices can make expatriate assignments very expensive. Some companies are trying to hold down costs by forgoing the move and asking employees to be "commuters" or "globally mobile" employees who work in the host country for a few months, returning home as often as every weekend.[54] This may appeal to employees reluctant to commit to a move, but the exhaustion of jet lag and the price of staying in hotels can override any relocation-related expenses.

After setting the total pay, the organization divides this amount into the four components of a total pay package:

1. *Base salary*—Determining the base salary is complex because different countries use different currencies (dollars, yen, euros, and so on). The exchange rate—the rate at which one currency may be exchanged for another—constantly shifts in response to a host of economic forces, so the real value of a salary in terms of dollars is constantly changing. Also, as discussed earlier, the base salary may be comparable to the pay of other managers at headquarters or comparable to other managers at the foreign subsidiary.

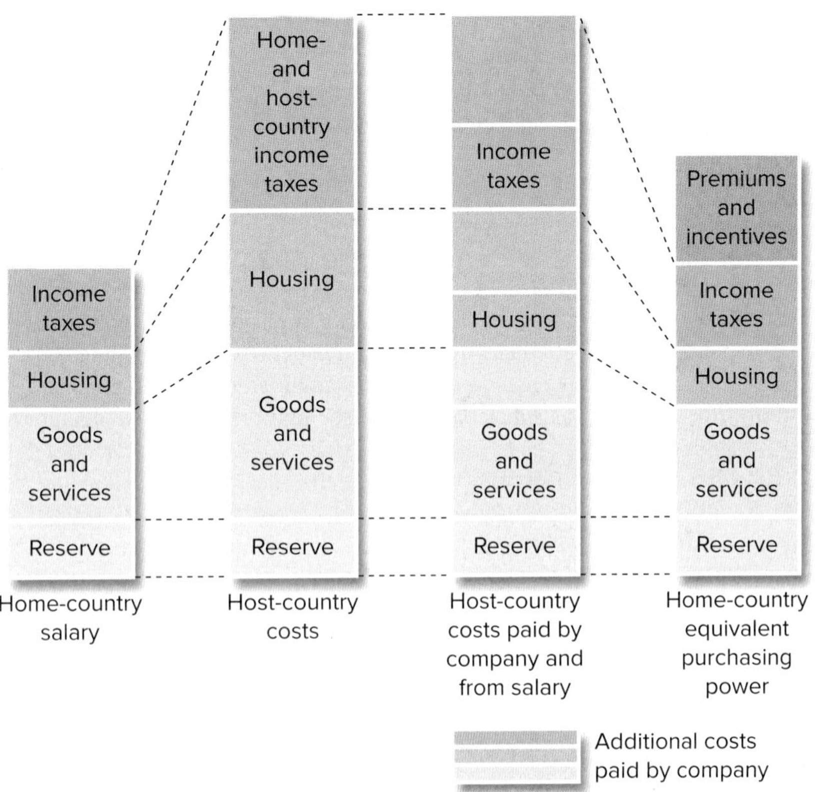

FIGURE 16.6
The Balance Sheet for Determining Expatriate Compensation

Source: From C. Reynolds, "Compensation of Overseas Personnel," in *Handbook of Human Resource Administration*, 2nd ed., ed. by J. J. Famularo, McGraw-Hill, 1986, p. 51. Reprinted with permission of The McGraw-Hill Companies, Inc.

Because many organizations pay a salary premium as an incentive to accept an overseas assignment, expatriates' salaries are often higher than pay for staying at headquarters.

2. *Tax equalization allowance*–Companies have different systems for taxing income, and in many countries, tax rates are much higher than in the United States. Usually, the employer of an expatriate withholds the amount of tax to be paid in the parent country, then pays all of the taxes due in the country where the expatriate is working.
3. *Benefits*–Most benefits issues have to do with whether an employee can use the same benefits in the foreign country. For example, if an expatriate has been contributing to a pension plan in the United States, does this person have a new pension in the foreign country? Or can the expatriate continue to contribute to the U.S. pension plan? Similarly, health benefits may involve receiving care at certain health facilities. While the person is abroad, does the same health plan cover services received in the foreign country? In one case, flying a manager back to the United States for certain procedures actually would have cost less than having the procedures done in the country where the person was working. But the company's health plans did not permit this alternative. An employer may offer expatriates additional benefits to address the problem of uprooting the spouse when assigning an employee overseas.
4. *Allowances to make a foreign assignment more attractive*–Cost-of-living allowances make up the differences in expenses for day-to-day needs. Housing allowances ensure that the expatriate can maintain the same standard of living as in the United States. Education

allowances reimburse expatriates who pay tuition for their children to attend private English-speaking schools. Relocation allowances cover the expenses of making the move to the foreign country, including transportation, shipping or storage of possessions, and expenses for temporary housing until the employee can rent or purchase a home.

Figure 16.7 is an example of a summary sheet for an expatriate manager's compensation package, showing a variety of allowances.

Helping Expatriates Return Home

Repatriation
The process of preparing expatriates to return home from a foreign assignment.

As the expatriate's assignment nears its end, the human resource department faces a final challenge: helping the expatriate make the transition back to his or her home country. The process of preparing expatriates to return home from a foreign assignment is called **repatriation.** Reentry is not as simple as it might sound (see "HR Oops!"). Culture shock

FIGURE 16.7
Sample of an International Assignment Allowance Form

John H. Doe
Name

1 October 2021
Effective date

Singapore
Location of assignment

Manager, SLS./Serv. AP/ME
Title

Houston, Texas	1234	202	202
Home base	**Emp. no.**	**LCA code**	**Tax code**

Reason for Change: International Assignment

	Old	**New**
Monthly base salary		$ 8,000.00
Living cost allowance		$ 2,363.00
Foreign service premium		$ 900.00
Area allowance		-0-
Gross monthly salary		$11,263.00
Housing deduction		$ 700.00
Hypothetical tax		$ 780.00
Other		
Net monthly salary		$ 9,783.00

Prepared by **Date**

Vice President, Human Resources **Date**

Expats Often Become Ex-Employees

By some accounts, more than half of employees sent on international assignments end up quitting within the first two years of returning to the home country. In one company studied, 100% left within one year. Considering that companies spend as much as three times an employee's annual salary for an overseas assignment, this failure to reintegrate expats is an expensive one indeed.

Returning home and experiencing culture shock in reverse is already difficult but does not explain leaving one's employer. The high turnover likely has more to do with the employer's failure to show that it values what the employee learned overseas and has planned a way to apply it across the organization. A corporation in Korea had a process of asking returning expats to spend a few weeks preparing reports about what they learned, but the reports were never used. Another company sent a marketing executive on a five-year assignment in Germany, where she learned the language and developed a set of new leaders. When she returned home, full of new ideas, the company placed her in a position with less responsibility and said her ideas "will not work here." She left for a job at another company, which benefited from the first company's investment in her development.

Companies can avoid these costly mistakes with plans for repatriation that respect the value of the expat's experiences. A company can begin the effort while the employee is still on the assignment. For example, the company can assign a manager in the home office to mentor the expat and speak about that person's accomplishments to colleagues, so that the person is not forgotten while away. Periodic return visits also may help to keep the employee connected and the information flowing. Performance management should include measurement of the kinds of skills a person learns from cross-cultural assignments—for example, better leadership and negotiation skills from learning to see a situation from several perspectives.

Such efforts matter. The research showing 50% turnover among expatriates also shows that the rate falls to 25% in companies that provide repatriation training and to 10% if the training starts before the employee's return.

Questions

1. What changes would you expect to observe in an employee who completes an overseas assignment? What value could these bring to the employer?
2. Suppose you work in the HR department of a company that sends high-potential employees on two-year overseas assignments. The company handles repatriation with a briefing and training program when the employee returns, and it has a 25% turnover rate. How would you suggest the company improve the turnover rate?

Sources: Marie-Therese Claes, "Learning Other Cultures," *BizEd,* March/April 2020, pp. 47–50; Neal R. Goodman, "Expat Exodus," *TD,* November 2019, pp. 50–55; Allen Smith, "Dealing with Culture Shock," *HR Magazine,* Summer 2019, pp. 22–23.

takes place in reverse. The experience has changed the expatriate, and the company's and expatriate's home cultures have changed as well. Also, because of differences in economies and compensation levels, a returning expatriate may experience a decline in living standards. The standard of living for an expatriate in many countries includes maid service, a limousine, private schools, and clubs.

Companies are increasingly making efforts to help expatriates through this transition. Two activities help the process along: communication and validation.[55] Communication refers to the expatriate receiving information and recognizing changes while abroad. The more the organization keeps in contact with the expatriate, the more effective and satisfied the person will be upon return. The expatriate plays a role in this process as well. Expatriates should work at maintaining important contacts in the company and industry. Communication related to career development before and during the overseas assignment also should help the employee return to a position that is challenging and interesting. Validation means giving the expatriate recognition for the overseas service when this person returns home. Expatriates who receive praise and recognition from colleagues and top managers for their overseas service and future contribution have fewer troubles with reentry than those whose contributions are disregarded. Validation should also include planning for how the returning employee will contribute to the organization. What skills will this person bring back? What position will he or she fill?

L'Oréal addresses the challenges of repatriation. When U.S. employees return to the cosmetics company's office, they repeat the orientation program for new employees. Jacob Bonk, a human resource executive at L'Oréal, was no exception when he returned to the United States after working in China for four years. His U.S. supervisor also encouraged him to spend time rebuilding his professional network at the company, especially during his first month back.[56]

THINKING ETHICALLY

WHAT DO EMPLOYERS OWE LGBT EMPLOYEES IN EXPAT ASSIGNMENTS?

When lesbian, gay, bisexual, or transgender (LGBT) employees are offered an assignment in another country, they face some considerations that aren't likely to affect their straight colleagues: how their sexual orientation will be treated in the new country. While some countries have relaxed attitudes, dozens frown on or even criminalize same-sex relationships and other behavior that doesn't conform to their gender norms. An assignment in one of those countries could be uncomfortable at best and dangerous at worst. In countries that outlaw same-sex relations, punishments include prison and, in a few cases, even the death penalty. Even where the laws aren't enforced, they contribute to a climate in which people don't report violence against or blackmail of LGBT persons. With this in mind, gay managers acknowledge turning down foreign assignments in order to protect themselves.

LGBT employees who accept these assignments can expect some extra surprises or challenges. One challenge—easier for single and childless employees—is a need to hide their identity. An employee of a British company, while working in Nigeria, asked her British HR department not to share with her local colleagues that her next of kin was her wife, because she expected problems could result. On the positive side, some employees find gay subcultures that warmly welcome them and help them navigate the new culture where they are posted. And some find that being an expat already marks them as "different" in the eyes of locals, so the sexual orientation doesn't matter much.

Given that LGBT employees often are treated differently in foreign assignments, employers have to determine what their role will be in offering the assignments. First, they need to consider that some employees may not have disclosed their status. Making assumptions about employees' family ties may cause a company to neglect accommodations such as travel allowances for someone whose partner remains in the home country. Employers that know the expat's LGBT status might offer overseas assignments only in countries where they believe the employee can travel and live safely. Or they might ensure that their cross-cultural training touches on these issues, regardless of any assumptions about employees' sexual orientation, so that all employees can make informed decisions. Some companies with a commitment to equal opportunity go further and try to influence change in the countries where they operate—for example by pointing out that anti-LGBT laws make the countries less attractive to multinational businesses.

Questions

1. How would you apply the principle of justice or fairness to employers' decisions about whether and how to offer foreign assignments to LGBT employees?
2. What would be the most ethical way for employers to address the safety risks of asking a gay employee to work in a country such as Dubai, Russia, or Uganda, where laws are hostile to homosexuality?

Sources: "LGBT Expats and Their Partners," *InterNations,* https://www.internations.org, accessed May 15, 2020; Bruce Einhorn, "Multinationals Seeking Top Expat Talent Battle Anti-LGBT Laws," *Bloomberg Businessweek,* June 18, 2019, https://www.bloomberg.com; Emma Jacobs, "LGBT Employees Face Hurdles at Home and Abroad," *Financial Times,* May 6, 2018, https://www.ft.com; Ronald Alsop, "Is This the Most Dangerous Expat Assignment?" *BBC,* March 31, 2016, https://www.bbc.com; Debra Bruno, "When the Closet Travels with You: For Gay Expats, Life Abroad Brings Challenges," *The Wall Street Journal,* October 11, 2015, https://blogs.wsj.com.

SUMMARY

LO 16-1 Summarize how the growth in international business activity affects human resource management.

- More and more companies are entering international markets by exporting and operating foreign facilities.
- Organizations therefore need employees who understand customers and suppliers in other countries. They need to understand local laws and customs and be able to adapt their plans to local situations.
- Organizations may hire a combination of parent-country, host-country, and third-country nationals.
- They may operate on the scale of an exporter or an international, global, or multinational organization.
- A global organization needs a transnational HRM system, which makes decisions from a global perspective, includes managers from many countries, and is based on ideas contributed by people representing a variety of cultures.

LO 16-2 Identify the factors that most strongly influence HRM in international markets.

- Culture is by far the most important influence. Each market's culture is its set of shared assumptions about how the world works and what ideals are worth striving for.
- A culture has the dimensions of individualism/collectivism, high or low power distance, high or low uncertainty avoidance, masculinity/femininity, and long-term or short-term orientation.
- Education is a second influence. Countries differ in the degree to which their labor markets include people with education and skills of value to employers.
- Another influence is the foreign country's political-legal system—its government, laws, and regulations.
- A final influence is a country's economic system. The system may be capitalist or socialist. The government's involvement in the country's economy, such as through taxes and price controls, is a strong factor determining HRM practices.

LO 16-3 Discuss how differences among countries affect HR planning at organizations with international operations.

- As organizations consider decisions about their level of international activity, HR professionals should provide information about the relevant human resource issues.
- When organizations decide to operate internationally or globally, HR planning involves decisions about where and how many employees are needed for each international facility.
- Some countries limit employers' ability to lay off workers, so organizations would be less likely to staff for peak periods. Other countries allow employers more flexibility in meeting human resource needs. HRM professionals need to be conversant with such differences.

LO 16-4 Describe how companies select and train human resources in a global labor market.

- Many organizations with foreign operations fill most positions with host-country nationals. These employees can more easily understand the values and customs of the local workforce, and hiring locally tends to be less expensive than moving employees to new locations.
- Organizations also fill foreign positions with parent-country and third-country nationals who have human relations skills associated with success in foreign assignments.
- When sending employees on foreign assignments, organizations prepare the employees (and often their families) through cross-cultural training.
- Before the assignment, the training provides instruction in the foreign country's language and culture.
- During the assignment, there is communication with the home country and mentoring.
- For the return home, the employer provides further training and development to aid retention.

LO 16-5 Discuss challenges related to managing performance and compensating employees from other countries.

- Pay structures can differ substantially among countries in terms of pay level and the relative worth of jobs.
- Organizations must decide whether to set pay levels and differences in terms of what workers are used to in their own countries or in terms of what employees' colleagues earn at headquarters. Typically, companies have resolved this dilemma by linking pay and benefits more closely to those of the employee's country, but this practice may be weakening so that it depends more on the nature and length of the foreign assignment.
- These decisions affect the organization's costs and ability to compete, so organizations consider local labor costs in their location decisions.
- Along with the basic pay structure, organizations must make decisions regarding incentive pay, such as bonuses and stock options.
- Laws may dictate differences in benefit packages, and the value of benefits will differ if a country requires them or makes them a government service.

LO 16-6 Explain how employers prepare managers for international assignments and for their return home.

- When an organization has selected a manager for an overseas assignment, it must prepare the person for the experience. In cross-cultural training, the soon-to-be expatriate learns about the foreign culture he or she is heading to, and studies her or his own home-country culture as well for insight. The trainee is given a detailed briefing on how to behave in business settings in the new country.
- Along with cross-cultural training, preparation of the expatriate should include career development activities to help the individual acquire valuable career skills during the foreign assignment and at the end of the assignment to handle repatriation successfully.
- Communication of changes at home and validation of a job well done abroad help the expatriate through the repatriation process.

KEY TERMS

parent country, 503
host country, 504
third country, 504
expatriates, 504
international organization, 505
multinational company, 505
global organization, 505
transnational HRM system, 506
culture shock, 514
cross-cultural preparation, 515
repatriation, 528

REVIEW AND DISCUSSION QUESTIONS

1. Identify the parent country, host country(ies), and third country(ies) in the following example: A global soft-drink company called Cold Cola has headquarters in Atlanta, Georgia. It operates production facilities in Athens, Greece, and in Jakarta, Indonesia. The company has assigned a manager from Boston to head the Athens facility and a manager from Hong Kong to manage the Jakarta facility. *(LO 16-1)*
2. What are some HRM challenges that arise when a U.S. company expands from domestic markets by exporting? When it changes from simply exporting to operating as an international company? When an international company becomes a global company? *(LO 16-2)*
3. In recent years, many U.S. companies have invested in Russia and sent U.S. managers there in an attempt to transplant U.S.-style management. According to Hofstede, U.S. culture has low power distance, uncertainty avoidance, and long-term orientation and high individuality and masculinity. Russia's culture has high power distance and uncertainty avoidance, low masculinity and long-term orientation, and moderate individuality. In light of what you know about cultural differences, how well do you think U.S. managers can succeed in each of the following U.S.-style HRM practices? (Explain your reasons.) *(LO 16-2)*
   a. Selection decisions based on extensive assessment of individual abilities.
   b. Appraisals based on individual performance.
   c. Systems for gathering suggestions from workers.
   d. Self-managing work teams.
4. Besides cultural differences, what other factors affect human resource management in an organization with international operations? *(LO 16-2)*
5. Suppose you work in the HR department of a company that is expanding into a country where the law and culture make it difficult to lay off employees. How should your knowledge of that difficulty affect human resource planning for the overseas operations? *(LO 16-3)*
6. Why do multinational organizations hire host-country nationals to fill most of their foreign positions, rather than sending expatriates for most jobs? *(LO 16-4)*
7. Suppose an organization decides to improve collaboration and knowledge sharing by developing an intranet to link its global workforce. It needs to train employees in several different countries to use this system. List the possible cultural issues you can think of that the training program should take into account. *(LO 16-4)*
8. For an organization with operations in three different countries, what are some advantages and disadvantages of setting compensation according to the labor markets in the countries where the employees live and work? What are some advantages and disadvantages of setting compensation according to the labor market in the company's headquarters? Would the best arrangement be different for the company's top executives and its production workers? Explain. *(LO 16-5)*
9. What abilities make a candidate more likely to succeed in an assignment as an expatriate? Which of these abilities do you have? How might a person acquire these abilities? *(LO 16-6)*
10. In the past, a large share of expatriate managers from the United States have returned home before successfully completing their foreign assignments. Suggest some possible reasons for the high failure rate. What can HR departments do to increase the success of expatriates? *(LO 16-6)*

SELF-ASSESSMENT EXERCISE

How Likely Are You to Succeed in an Expatriate Assignment?

The following list includes a number of qualities that have been identified as being associated with success in an expatriate assignment. Rate the degree to which you possess each quality, using the following scale:

1 = very low
2 = low
3 = moderate
4 = high
5 = very high

_____ Resourcefulness/resilience
_____ Adaptability/flexibility
_____ Emotional stability
_____ Ability to deal with ambiguity/uncertainty/differences
_____ Desire to work with people who are different
_____ Cultural empathy/sensitivity
_____ Tolerance of others' views, especially when they differ from your own
_____ Sensitivity to feelings and attitudes of others
_____ Good health and wellness

Add up your total score for the items. The higher your score, the greater your likelihood of success. Qualities that you rated low would be considered weaknesses for an expatriate assignment. Keep in mind that you will also need to be technically competent for the assignment, and your spouse and family (if applicable) must be adaptable and willing to live abroad.

Source: Based on "Rating Scale on Successful Expatriate Qualities." from P. R. Harris and R. T. Moran. *Managing Cultural Differences,* 3rd ed. (Houston: Gulf, 1991), p. 569.

TAKING RESPONSIBILITY

Automation Changes Bangladesh Garment Industry

Clothing was once made near customers, but as managers began to see the potential of using low-cost labor overseas, production in the United States and Europe began shifting to lower-wage countries in Asia—first to Taiwan and South Korea, then to Thailand and China, and later to other countries including Bangladesh. Every time production moved, it provided poor people a means of earning an income, sending their children to school, and inching out of poverty. But as countries develop, wages rise, and suppliers seek to open in new locations.

As Bangladesh moved into the number-two spot in global exports of apparel, the garment industry meant development in Bangladesh. More and more of the work in Bangladesh has been in this industry, which now represents more than 80% of the country's exports. For this development to continue, as the labor force expands, Bangladesh needs about 2 million jobs a year. However, the number of garment-making jobs created each year has been shrinking, even as output continues to rise.

In 2013, the industry came under fire when an eight-story factory building called Rana Plaza collapsed. The facility, which housed five different factories making clothes for several major brands, was improperly constructed, and cracks were showing, but the owner insisted it was sound, and employers insisted employees come to work or be fired. On the day it crumbled, more than 1,100 garment workers died, and thousands more were injured. The Bangladeshi government, labor organizations, and the factories' customers all began insisting on better safety for workers. Workers felt empowered to press for better conditions, and one strike shut down more than 50 factories for a week. The government also raised the minimum monthly salary to about $64 (or about 32 cents an hour), up more than 75% from the previous minimum pay. And as these consequences were unfolding, new low-cost competition was developing in East African nations.

At the same time as workers were demanding improved conditions, technology began making real strides in automating the process of making garments. Computer-programmed machines that knit and stitch items can replace hundreds of workers in each factory. The few dozen who are left mainly keep an eye on the machines and occasionally clean them. For apparel makers, this vastly reduces labor costs and improves speed to market while making safety concerns easier to manage.

The adoption of technology has delivered garment manufacturers advantages beyond low expenses for labor. Consumers want to make frequent inexpensive purchases, and automation makes it profitable to sell a pair of jeans to the retailer for as little as $5. Automation also reduces the problem of labor disputes by giving the employers a strong hand in negotiations. Those who dare to strike are more often dismissed.

Automation also opens up options for manufacturers who want to locate nearer their American and European buyers. A Chinese apparel company has opened an automated sewing factory in Arkansas, and Adidas announced it would open automated shoe factories in Germany and Atlanta, Georgia.

Questions

1. Based on the information given, and from the perspective of a clothing company's management, what social, economic, and legal forces make Bangladesh an attractive labor market for producing apparel? What forces make it a difficult labor market?
2. Looking at the information in this case in terms of social responsibility, would you recommend that clothing brands operate or buy from Bangladeshi factories or that they go elsewhere? Which stakeholders are you considering in your answer (for example, mainly customers, employees, investors, or communities)?

Sources: "Bangladesh Garment Workers Return to Work amid Lockdown," *Aljazeera,* April 27, 2020, https://www.alijazeera.com; Andre Tartar, "China Sets the Pace in Race to Build the Factory of the Future," *Bloomberg,* June 12, 2019, https://www.bloomberg.com; Jon Emont, "The Robots Are Coming for Garment Workers; That's Good for the U.S., Bad for Poor Countries," *The Wall Street Journal,* February 16, 2018, https://www.wsj.com; Peter Coy, "Five Years after Collapse in Bangladesh, Safety Programs Are Expiring," *Bloomberg Businessweek,* April 17, 2018, http://www.bloomberg.com/businessweek; International Labour Organization, "Bangladesh: Improving Safety in the Garment Industry," news release, January 17, 2018, http://www.ilo.org; Kiran Stacey, "Bangladesh Garment-Making Success Prompts Fears for Wider Economy," *Financial Times,* January 5, 2017, https://www.ft.com.

MANAGING TALENT

Geely Goes Global with Volvo (and Others)

If you haven't heard of Geely yet, you will soon if CEO Li Shufu attains his goal to head the first Chinese automaker to operate on a global scale. The project started when Geely was a modest maker of motorcycles, and Li turned over his Mercedes to his employees as a model to study. They took it apart but couldn't reassemble it. By 1996, however, they had built their first auto model, the Geely No. 1, which launched a decade of operations as a small domestic business selling economy cars. In 2006, Geely entered models in the Detroit Auto Show, only to garner reviews that the cars were out of date. Still, Li learned from every setback and persevered.

Geely's next move was to bring in expertise through acquisitions. In 2007, Li returned to the Detroit show and stopped in Ford's booth with an offer to buy Volvo, the Swedish brand then owned by Ford. The Ford executives turned him down, but financial crisis swiftly hit the economy, and Ford needed cash to stay afloat. They ended up selling Volvo to Geely after all—at a price below what they had paid to acquire it.

Volvo managers and employees in Europe were nervous about their unfamiliar owners. However, Li convinced them that his goal was to finance their operations and learn from their expertise. With freedom in decision making and enough cash to invest in new products, Volvo soon began enjoying increased profits from sales of more up-to-date models (including innovations Ford had been unable to fund). Geely, in turn, brought in Peter Horbury, the former head of design for Volvo, from Britain to advise on the design of Geely's new models. The more professionally designed Geely cars became a hit in China. Furthermore, Volvo opened its first U.S. assembly plant in South Carolina in 2018. The company has ambitious plans for growth there, but tariffs imposed by the United States, European Union, and China clouded the future at the time of the plant's opening, since the plan was to import engines and batteries and to sell half of its sedans and SUVs in Europe and China.

Other acquisitions by Geely include Volvo Group, which makes trucks; Lotus, a British maker of sports cars and race cars; and London Electric Vehicle Company, which makes electric-powered taxis. The company also has a stake in Daimler, maker of the Mercedes Benz. In an echo of the company's start, Li's desire is not to influence Daimler's operations, but to learn from its expertise in technology and design.

Being based in China presents opportunities and challenges. On the opportunity side, the government is trying to deal with major air pollution by providing consumers with incentives to buy electric cars. Geely is using that incentive to focus on developing electric and hybrid vehicles—technology that can be applied also to Volvo's line, positioning the European subsidiary to meet the demand for fuel efficiency in the West. Further, the Chinese-owned company was able to negotiate with government regulators approval for a subsidiary to make Korean-model batteries in China, despite the Chinese regulation requiring that vehicle batteries be made by Chinese companies. Competitors from other countries complained that as foreigners, they could not negotiate such favorable treatment; they were forming joint ventures with Chinese companies to gain access to Chinese technology.

With all of these plans in the works, Li intends for Geely to become the next big global vehicle manufacturer, comparable to General Motors, Ford, and Toyota. So far, Geely has become the best-selling Chinese brand in China—no small feat in the world's largest market for cars.

Questions

1. Would you categorize Geely as an international, multinational, or global organization? Why?
2. Suppose you are a Geely HR executive, and Li asks you to consider the idea of sending expatriate managers

from China to run its various subsidiaries, rather than letting the units operate independently and share technical knowledge. Summarize some pros and cons of this approach to managing the subsidiaries.

Sources: Chris Isidore, "Proposed Volvo-Geely Merger Could Create China's First Global Auto Powerhouse," *CNN Business,* February 11, 2020, https://www.cnn.com; Glenn Brooks, "Could Geely Become as Big as Volkswagen AG?" *Just Auto,* June 28, 2018, https://www.just-auto.com; Chu Charleston, "The New US Car Factory Exposing the Contradictions and Perils of Trump's Kamikaze Trade War," *Independent,* June 26, 2018, https://www.independent.co.uk; Shuji Nakayama and Kosei Fukao, "Volvo Cars Opens First Plant in US as Auto Tariffs Loom," *Nikkei Asia,* June 21, 2018, https://asia.nikkei.com; "China's Geely Completes Deal to Buy AB Volvo Stake," *Reuters,* June 18, 2018, https://www.reuters.com; Fred Lambert, "Geely's Volvo Electric Vehicles Are Using Korean Batteries Made in China and the Competition Isn't Happy," *Electrek,* May 17, 2018, https://electrek.co.

HR IN SMALL BUSINESS

RM International Builds a Cultural Bridge for Tech Innovators

Ricardo Mora is a descendant of entrepreneurs and a serial entrepreneur. One of his grandfathers started the first customs brokerage in Ciudad Juárez, Mexico. His father, besides working in manufacturing management, earned money as a translator, and his mother ran a business bottling salsa. Mora's own businesses have included mobile-phone stores, restaurants, investing, and start-up assistance for other entrepreneurs. His enterprises are incorporated as RM International.

All of Mora's businesses have reflected the context in which he lives: a border community where the people from two countries interact so much that they function as neighbors. Mora, born in El Paso, Texas, is a U.S. citizen who grew up in Juárez. As a child, he crossed the border daily to attend school in Texas. Now he lives in El Paso, works mainly in Juárez, and owns businesses on both sides of the border. Mora notes that the distance between El Paso and the next-closest U.S. town is much farther than the distance between El Paso and Juárez. Likewise, Juárez is much nearer to El Paso than to the closest Mexican city. Thus, residents of the two cities—a population of more than 2.5 million—find it more natural to cross the border than to make the longer drive on their own side.

Mora launched his first business while attending college in El Paso in the early 1990s. He sold cell phones while that was a new and attractive product in Mexico. He opened a store to sell the phones in Juárez, and as sales grew, he expanded to 32 stores in Mexico and 6 in the United States. He later sold the U.S. stores and moved into the restaurant businesses, opening U.S. franchises of a Mexican chain called El Taco Tote.

As he built his wealth and looked for investment opportunities, he observed that the more than 300 Juárez *maquiladoras,* or factories serving large U.S.-based companies, were meeting strong demand for basic manufacturing but could see much greater opportunities if they could apply modern technology. So Mora created a business incubator called Juárez Technology Hub (T-Hub), backed by investments from several large corporations. The incubator provides space for members to work on business plans and puts on workshops; as of 2018, it counted 100 companies renting space and 300 tech jobs created. In partnership with a similar El Paso incubator, T-Hub runs workshops for six Mexican companies and six U.S. companies at a time, meeting on both sides of the border. The initiative, called Bridge Accelerator, has been creating investment and jobs on both sides of the border. Bridge Accelerator helps participants develop successful businesses at the same time as they are learning how to work across the cultural differences of the two countries.

Questions

1. Would you describe RM International as a "born-global" company? Why or why not?
2. What are three or four HR challenges that RM International faces as a consequence of operating in two different countries?

Sources: Ricardo Mora, "How I Built Businesses on Both Sides of the Border—and Why We Shouldn't Have It Any Other Way," *Inc.,* July/August 2019, pp. 44–47; Julian Resendiz, "Border Cities Team Up to Help Businesses Cash in on Global Trade," *KXAN,* October 25, 2019, https://www.kxan.com; Brendan O'Boyle, "AQ Top Five Urban Visionaries: Ricardo Mora," *Americas Quarterly,* October 10, 2018, https://www.americasquarterly.org.

NOTES

1. M. Savage, "Why Finland Leads the World in Flexible Work," *BBC,* August 8, 2019, https://www.bbc.com.
2. R. Bromby, "China Faces Economic Hit as Countries Seek to Bring Factories Back Home," *Small Caps,* May 7, 2020, https://smallcaps.com; A. Kharpal, "Apple, Microsoft, Google Look to Move Production Away from China. That's Not Going to Be Easy," *CNBC,* March 4, 2020, https://www.cnbc.com.

3. D. Bonello, "Silicon Valley Is Going to Mexico . . . for Talent," *OZY,* August 18, 2019, https://www.ozy.com; D. Luhnow, "Pushed from the U.S. They Find Hope in Mexico's Silicon Valley," *The Wall Street Journal,* March 1, 2018, https://www.wsj.com.
4. D. W. Brin, "Recruit Globally," *HR Magazine,* June-August 2018, pp. 40–45; D. J. Guth, "Northeast Ohio Embraces Immigrants in New Economy," *Crain's Cleveland Business,* April 21, 2018, https://www.crainscleveland.com.
5. P. M. García, "Born Global Companies Take Center Stage," *Beyond Borders* (Inter-American Development Bank blog), October 15, 2019, https://blogs.iadb.org; L.Taylor, "Explaining the Rise of Born-Global Firms: A New Generation of Entrepreneur Set on Global Development," *The Sociable,* August 31, 2017, https://sociable.co; S. Tanev, "Global from the Start: The Characteristics of Born-Global Firms in the Technology Sector," *Technology Innovation Management Review,* March 2012, pp. 5–8.
6. V. Sathe, *Culture and Related Corporate Realities* (Homewood, IL: Richard D. Irwin, 1985); M. Rokeach, *Beliefs, Attitudes, and Values* (San Francisco: Jossey-Bass, 1968).
7. N. Adler, *International Dimensions of Organizational Behavior,* 2nd ed. (Boston: PWS-Kent, 1991).
8. G. Hofstede, "Dimensions of National Cultures in Fifty Countries and Three Regions," in *Expectations in Cross-Cultural Psychology,* eds. J. Deregowski, S. Dziurawiec, and R. C. Annis (Lisse, Netherlands: Swets and Zeitlinger, 1983); G. Hofstede, "Dimensionalizing Cultures: The Hofstede Model in Context," in *Online Readings in Psychology and Culture* 2, no. 1 (2011), https://doi.org/10.9707/2307-0919.1014; G. Hofstede, G. J. Hofstede, and M. Minkov, *Cultures and Organizations: Software of the Mind,* 3rd ed. (New York: McGraw-Hill Professional, 2010).
9. G. Hofstede, "Cultural Constraints in Management Theories," *Academy of Management Executive* 7 (1993), pp. 81–90.
10. A Ramesh and M. Gelfland, "Will They Stay or Will They Go? The Role of Job Embeddedness in Predicting Turnover in Individualistic and Collectivistic Cultures," *Journal of Applied Psychology* 95, no. 5 (2010), pp. 807–823.
11. W. A. Randolph and M. Sashkin, "Can Organizational Empowerment Work in Multinational Settings?" *Academy of Management Executive* 16, no. 1 (2002), pp. 102–115.
12. B. Gerhart and M. Fang, "National Culture and Human Resource Management: Assumptions and Evidence," *International Journal of Human Resource Management* 16, no. 6 (June 2005), pp. 971–986.
13. Z. Sun, "Where Every Employee Is an Entrepreneur," *TD,* February 2018, pp. 47–50.
14. J. Radford, "Key Findings about U.S. Immigrants," *Pew Research Center,* June 17, 2019, https://www.pewresearch.org; L. A. West Jr. and W. A. Bogumil Jr., "Foreign Knowledge Workers as a Strategic Staffing Option," *Academy of Management Executive* 14, no. 4 (2000), pp. 71–83.
15. Organisation for Economic Co-operation and Development (OECD), "Education Spending," OECD Data, https://data.oecd.org, accessed May 15, 2020.
16. I. Y. Sun, "The World's Next Great Manufacturing Center," *Harvard Business Review,* May–June 2017, pp. 124–129; Idil Abshir, "The Greatness of Failure," *Entrepreneur,* May 2017, pp. 53–58.
17. L. O'Carroll, P. Walker, and L. Brooks, "UK to Close Door to Non-English Speakers and Unskilled Workers," *The Guardian,* February 18, 2020, https://www.theguardian.com.
18. J. Hookway, "Affirmative Action Drove Many Chinese Malaysians Abroad; Now They're Thinking about Coming Home," *The Wall Street Journal,* May 17, 2018, https://www.wsj.com.
19. G. Ip, "That Noise You Hear Is the Sound of Globalization Going into Reverse," *The Wall Street Journal,* June 27, 2018, https://www.wsj.com; J. Greene, "Chip Makers: We'll End Up Paying Tariffs on Our Own Goods," *The Wall Street Journal,* June 15, 2018, https://www.wsj.com; J. D. Stoll, "In Auto Tariffs, a High-Stakes Game of Chicken," *The Wall Street Journal,* May 25, 2018, https://www.wsj.com.
20. "The Move to Assemble Vehicles in Mexico Is about More than Low Wages," Center for Automotive Research, January 17, 2017, https://www.cargroup.org; *The Growing Role of Mexico in the North American Automotive Industry: Trends, Drivers and Forecasts,* Center for Automotive Research, July 2016, https://www.cargroup.org.
21. L. Meckler, "Businesses Beg for More Low-Skill Visas, Putting White House in a Bind," *The Wall Street Journal,* March 30, 2018, https://www.wsj.com.
22. K. Fahim, "Saudi Arabia Encouraged Foreign Workers to Leave–and Is Struggling after So Many Did," *The Washington Post,* February 2, 2019, https://www.washingtonpost.com; M. Stancati and D. Abdulaziz, "Saudi Arabia's Economic Revamp Means More Jobs for Saudis–if Only They Wanted Them," *The Wall Street Journal,* June 19, 2018, https://www.wsj.com.
23. W. A. Arthur Jr. and W. Bennett Jr., "The International Assignee: The Relative Importance of Factors Perceived to Contribute to Success," *Personnel Psychology* 48 (1995), pp. 99–114; G. M. Spreitzer, M. W. McCall Jr., and J. D. Mahoney, "Early Identification of International Executive Potential," *Journal of Applied Psychology* 82 (1997), pp. 6–29.
24. J. S. Black and J. K. Stephens, "The Influence of the Spouse on American Expatriate Adjustment and Intent to Stay in Pacific Rim Overseas Assignments," *Journal of Management* 15 (1989), pp. 529–544.
25. P. Caligiuri, "The Big Five Personality Characteristics as Predictors of Expatriates' Desire to Terminate the Assignment and Supervisor-Rated Performance," *Personnel Psychology* 53 (2000), pp. 67–88.
26. D. Flanja, "Culture Shock in Intercultural Communication," *Studia Europaea* (October 2009), Business & Company Resource Center, http://galenet.galegroup.com.
27. D. M. Gayeski, C. Sanchirico, and J. Anderson, "Designing Training for Global Environments: Knowing What Questions to Ask," *Performance Improvement Quarterly* 15, no. 2 (2002), pp. 15–31.
28. S. Bryant, "10 Tips for Managing Successful International Assignments," *Country Navigator,* August 20, 2019, https://countrynavigator.com; J. S. Black and M. Mendenhall, "A Practical but Theory-Based Framework for Selecting Cross-Cultural Training Methods," in *Readings and Cases in International Human Resource Management,* eds. M. Mendenhall and G. Oddou (Boston: PWS-Kent, 1991), pp. 177–204.
29. J. Simms, "People Don't Seem So Keen to Move to Our US Offices All of a Sudden . . . ," *People Management,* March 2017, pp. 46–48; A. N. Kassar, Amal Rouhana, and Sophie Lythreatis, "Cross-Cultural Training: Its Effects on the Satisfaction and Turnover of Expatriate Employees," *SAM Advanced Management Journal* (Autumn 2015), pp. 4–18.
30. G. Wilson, "How to Prepare Employees for International Assignment Success," *ECA International,* February 23, 2017, https://

www.eca-international.com; A. Molinsky and M. Hahn, "Five Types for Managing Successful Overseas Assignments," *Harvard Business Review,* March 16, 2016, https://hbr.org.

31. D. D. Davis, "International Performance Measurement and Management," in *Performance Appraisal: State of the Art in Practice,* ed. J. W. Smither (San Francisco: Jossey-Bass, 1998), pp. 95–131.
32. M. Gowan, S. Ibarreche, and C. Lackey, "Doing the Right Things in Mexico," *Academy of Management Executive* 10 (1996), pp. 74–81.
33. L. S. Chee, "Singapore Airlines: Strategic Human Resource Initiatives," in *International Human Resource Management: Think Globally, Act Locally,* ed. D. Torrington (Upper Saddle River, NJ: Prentice Hall, 1994), pp. 143–159.
34. E. Duffin, "Pay Gap between CEOs and Average Workers, by Country 2018," *Statista,* March 20, 2020, https://www.statista.com; A. Melin and W. Lu, "CEOs in U.S., India Earn the Most Compared with Average Workers," *Bloomberg News,* December 28, 2017, https://www.bloomberg.com.
35. "The Cost of Talent," *HR Magazine,* March 2017, p. 13.
36. "International Comparisons of Hourly Compensation Costs in Manufacturing, 2016: Summary Tables," The Conference Board, April 19, 2018, https://www.conference-board.org.
37. "International Comparisons of Manufacturing Productivity and Unit Labor Costs Trends, 2016," The Conference Board, May 17, 2017, https://www.conference-board.org; D. Acemoglu and M. Dell, "Productivity Differences between and within Countries," *American Economic Journal: Macroeconomics 2010* 2, no. 1 (2010), pp. 169–188; Levinson, "U.S. Manufacturing in International Perspective."
38. Internal Revenue Service, "Foreign Earned Income Exclusion," https://www.irs.gov, accessed May 14, 2020.
39. D. Matthews, "Europe Could Have the Secret to Saving America's Unions," *Vox,* https://www.vox.com, accessed May 15, 2020; S. Wertheim and M. Chakrabarti, "What the Future Holds for Labor Unions," *WBUR,* August 14, 2019, https://www.wbur.org.
40. J. La Palombara and S. Blank, *Multinational Corporations and National Elites: A Study of Tensions* (New York: Conference Board, 1976); A. B. Sim, "Decentralized Management of Subsidiaries and Their Performance: A Comparative Study of American, British and Japanese Subsidiaries in Malaysia," *Management International Review* 17, no. 2 (1977), pp. 45–51; Y. K. Shetty, "Managing the Multinational Corporation: European and American Styles," *Management International Review* 19, no. 3 (1979), pp. 39–48; J. Hamill, "Labor Relations Decision-Making within Multinational Corporations," *Industrial Relations Journal* 15, no. 2 (1984), pp. 30–34.
41. Matthews, "Europe Could Have the Secret to Saving America's Unions."
42. T. Connell, "Bangladesh Garment Workers: New Blocks to Form Unions," *Solidarity Center,* February 10, 2020, https://www.solidaritycenter.org; R. Paul and S. Quadir, "Bangladesh Garment Unions Say New Factory Oversight Deal Risks Worker Safety," *Reuters,* May 21, 2019, https://www.reuters.com.
43. J. K. Sebenius, "The Hidden Challenge of Cross-Border Negotiations," *Harvard Business Review,* March 2002, pp. 76–85.
44. R. Pal, "Beyond the Numbers, What Is HR's Role in International Assignments?" *People Matters,* May 25, 2018, https://www.peoplematters.in; K. Gurchiek, "HR Best Practices Can Lead to a Better Expat Experience," *Society for Human Resource Management,* March 22, 2016, https://www.shrm.org.
45. M. Harvey and M. M. Novicevic, "Selecting Expatriates for Increasingly Complex Global Assignments," *Career Development International* 6, no. 2 (2001), pp. 69–86.
46. M. Mendenhall and G. Oddou, "The Dimensions of Expatriate Acculturation," *Academy of Management Review* 10 (1985), pp. 39–47.
47. T. Hippler, P. Caligiuri, J. Johnson, and N. Baytalskaya, "The Development and Validation of a Theory-Based Expatriate Adjustment Scale," *International Journal of Human Resource Management* 25, no. 14 (2014), pp. 1938–1959.
48. J. I. Sanchez, P. E. Spector, and C. L. Cooper, "Adapting to a Boundaryless World: A Developmental Expatriate Model," *Academy of Management Executive* 14, no. 2 (2000), pp. 96–106.
49. P. J. Dowling, D. E. Welch, and R. S. Schuler, *International Human Resource Management,* 3rd ed. (Cincinnati: South-Western, 1999), pp. 335–336.
50. Sanchez, Spector, and Cooper, "Adapting to a Boundaryless World."
51. D. Douiyssi, "Navigating Challenging Markets When Relocating Employees," *Benefits,* January 2017, pp. 14–19.
52. A. L. Molinsky, "Code Switching between Cultures," *Harvard Business Review,* January–February 2012, pp. 140–141.
53. J. S. Lublin, "Going Overseas for a Job? Coming Home Is the Hard Part," *The Wall Street Journal,* September 5, 2017, https://www.wsj.com.
54. Simms, "People Don't Seem So Keen"; J. Mutter, "Supporting Your Globally-Mobile Employees and Their Families," *Management,* May 2018, pp. M4–M5.
55. A. Molinsky and M. Hahn, "How to Return Home After an Assignment Abroad," *Harvard Business Review,* October 24, 2017, https://hbr.org.
56. Lublin, "Going Overseas for a Job?"

Glossary

360-Degree Performance Appraisal Performance measurement that combines information from the employee's managers, peers, subordinates, self, and customers.

Achievement Tests Tests that measure a person's existing knowledge and skills.

Action Learning Training in which teams get an actual problem, work on solving it and commit to an action plan, and are accountable for carrying it out.

Adventure Learning A teamwork and leadership training program based on the use of challenging, structured outdoor activities.

Affirmative Action An organization's active effort to find opportunities to hire or promote people in a particular group.

Agency Shop Union security arrangement that requires the payment of union dues but not union membership.

Alternative Dispute Resolution (ADR) Methods of solving a problem by bringing in an impartial outsider but not using the court system.

Alternative Work Arrangements Methods of staffing other than the traditional hiring of full-time employees (for example, use of independent contractors, on-call workers, temporary workers, and contract workers).

American Federation of Labor and Congress of Industrial Organizations (AFL-CIO) An association that seeks to advance the shared interests of its member unions at the national level.

Applicant-Tracking System Automated approach to selection process that reviews electronically submitted résumés, matches them against company selection criteria, and allows hiring managers to track job candidate information and hiring outcomes.

Apprenticeship A work-study training method that teaches job skills through a combination of on-the-job training and classroom training.

Aptitude Tests Tests that assess how well a person can learn or acquire skills and abilities.

Arbitration Conflict resolution procedure in which an arbitrator or arbitration board determines a binding settlement.

Artificial Intelligence (AI) Technology that simulates human thinking, applying experience to deliver better results over time.

Assessment Collecting information and providing feedback to employees about their behavior, communication style, or skills.

Assessment Center A wide variety of specific selection programs that use multiple selection methods to rate applicants or job incumbents on their management potential.

Associate Union Membership Alternative form of union membership in which members receive discounts on insurance and credit cards rather than representation in collective bargaining.

Avatars Computer depictions of trainees, which the trainees manipulate in an online role-play.

Balanced Scorecard A combination of performance measures directed toward the company's long- and short-term goals and used as the basis for awarding incentive pay.

Behavior Description Interview (BDI) A structured interview in which the interviewer asks the candidate to describe how he or she handled a type of situation in the past.

Behavioral Observation Scale (BOS) A variation of a BARS which uses all behaviors necessary for effective performance to rate performance at a task.

Behaviorally Anchored Rating Scale (BARS) Method of performance measurement that rates behavior in terms of a scale showing specific statements of behavior that describe different levels of performance.

Benchmarking A procedure in which an organization compares its own practices against those of successful competitors.

Bona Fide Occupational Qualification (BFOQ) A necessary (not merely preferred) qualification for performing a job.

Brand Alignment The process of ensuring that HR policies, practices, and programs support or are congruent with an organization's overall culture (or brand), products, and services.

Cafeteria-Style Plan A benefits plan that offers employees a set of alternatives from which they can choose the types and amounts of benefits they want.

Calibration Meeting Meeting at which managers discuss employee performance ratings and provide evidence supporting their ratings with the goal of eliminating the influence of rating errors.

Cash Balance Plan Retirement plan in which the employer sets up an individual account for each employee and contributes a percentage of the employee's salary; the account earns interest at a predefined rate.

Checkoff Provision Contract provision under which the employer, on behalf of the union, automatically deducts union dues from employees' paychecks.

Closed Shop Union security arrangement under which a person must be a union member before being hired; illegal for those covered by the National Labor Relations Act.

Cloud Computing The practice of using a network of remote servers hosted on the Internet to store, manage, and process data.

Coach A peer or manager who works with an employee to motivate the employee, help him or her develop skills, and provide reinforcement and feedback.

Cognitive Ability Tests Tests designed to measure such mental abilities as verbal skills, quantitative skills, and reasoning ability.

Collective Bargaining Negotiation between union representatives and management representatives to arrive at a contract defining conditions of employment for the term of the contract and to administer that contract.

Commissions Incentive pay calculated as a percentage of sales.

Communities of Practice Groups of employees who work together, learn from each other, and develop a common understanding of how to get work accomplished.

Compensatory Model Process of arriving at a selection decision in which a very high score on one type of assessment can make up for a low score on another.

Competency An area of personal capability that enables employees to perform their work successfully.

Concurrent Validation Research that consists of administering a test to people who currently hold a job, then comparing their scores to existing measures of job performance.

Consolidated Omnibus Budget Reconciliation Act (COBRA) Federal law that requires employers to permit employees or their dependents to extend their health insurance coverage at group rates for up to 36 months following a qualifying event, such as a layoff, reduction in hours, or the employee's death.

Construct Validity Consistency between a high score on a test and high level of a construct such as intelligence or leadership ability, as well as between mastery of this construct and successful performance of the job.

Content Validity Consistency between the test items or problems and the kinds of situations or problems that occur on the job.

Continuous Learning Each employee's and each group's ongoing efforts to gather information and apply the information to their decisions in a learning organization.

Contributory Plan Retirement plan funded by contributions from the employer and employee.

Coordination Training Team training that teaches the team how to share information and make decisions to obtain the best team performance.

Core Competency A set of knowledges and skills that make the organization superior to competitors and create value for customers.

Corporate Campaigns Bringing public, financial, or political pressure on employers during union organization and contract negotiation.

Cost per Hire The total amount of money spent to fill a vacancy. The number is computed by finding the cost of using a particular recruitment source and dividing that cost by the number of people hired to fill that type of vacancy.

Craft Union Labor union whose members all have a particular skill or occupation.

Criterion-Related Validity A measure of validity based on showing a substantial correlation between test scores and job performance scores.

Critical-Incident Method Method of performance measurement based on managers' records of specific examples of the employee acting in ways that are either effective or ineffective.

Cross-Cultural Preparation Training to prepare employees and their family members for an assignment in a foreign country.

Cross-Training Team training in which team members understand and practice each other's skills so that they are prepared to step in and take another member's place.

Culture Shock Disillusionment and discomfort that occur during the process of adjusting to a new culture.

Decision Support Systems Computer software systems designed to help managers solve problems by showing how results vary when the manager alters assumptions or data.

Defined-Benefit Plan Pension plan that guarantees a specified level of retirement income.

Defined-Contribution Plan Retirement plan in which the employer sets up an individual account for each employee and specifies the size of the investment into that account.

Delayering Reducing the number of levels in the organization's job structure.

Development The acquisition of knowledge, skills, and behaviors that improve an employee's ability to meet changes in job requirements and in customer demands.

Differential Piece Rates Incentive pay in which the piece rate is higher when a greater amount is produced.

Direct Applicants People who apply for a vacancy without prompting from the organization.

Disability Under the Americans with Disabilities Act, a physical or mental impairment that substantially limits one or more major life activities, a record of having such an impairment, or being regarded as having such an impairment.

DiSC Brand of assessment tool that identifies individuals' behavioral patterns in terms of dominance, influence, steadiness, and conscientiousness.

Disparate Impact A condition in which employment practices are seemingly neutral yet disproportionately exclude a protected group from employment opportunities.

Disparate Treatment Differing treatment of individuals, where the differences are based on the individuals' race, color, religion, sex, national origin, age, or disability status.

Diversity The characteristics of individuals that make them unique.

Diversity Training Training designed to change employee attitudes about diversity and/or develop skills needed to work with a diverse workforce.

Downsizing The planned elimination of large numbers of personnel with the goal of enhancing the organization's competitiveness.

Downward Move Assignment of an employee to a position with less responsibility and authority.

Due-Process Policies Policies that formally lay out the steps an employee may take to appeal the employer's decision to terminate that employee.

E-Learning Receiving training via the Internet or the organization's intranet.

EEO-1 Report The EEOC's Employer Information Report, which details the number of women and minorities employed in nine different job categories.

Electronic Performance Support System (EPSS) Computer application that provides access to skills training, information, and expert advice as needed.

Employee Assistance Program (EAP) A referral service that employees can use to seek professional treatment for emotional problems or substance abuse.

Employee Benefits Compensation in forms other than cash.

Employee Development The combination of formal education, job experiences, relationships, and assessment of personality and abilities to help employees prepare for the future of their careers.

Employee Empowerment Giving employees responsibility and authority to make decisions regarding all aspects of product development or customer service.

Employee Engagement The degree to which employees are fully involved in their work and the strength of their job and company commitment.

Employee Retirement Income Security Act (ERISA) Federal law that increased the responsibility of pension plan trustees to protect retirees, established certain rights related to vesting and portability, and created the Pension Benefit Guarantee Corporation.

Employee Stock Ownership Plan (ESOP) An arrangement in which the organization distributes shares of stock to all its employees by placing them in a trust.

Employee Wellness Program (EWP) A set of communications, activities, and facilities designed to change health-related behaviors in ways that reduce health risks.

Employment at Will Employment principle that if there is no specific employment contract saying otherwise, the employer or employee may end an employment relationship at any time, regardless of cause.

Equal Employment Opportunity (EEO) The condition in which all individuals have an equal chance for employment, regardless of their race, color, religion, sex, age, disability, or national origin.

Equal Employment Opportunity Commission (EEOC) Agency of the Department of Justice charged with enforcing Title VII of the Civil Rights Act of 1964 and other antidiscrimination laws.

Ergonomics The study of the interface between individuals' physiology and the characteristics of the physical work environment.

Ethics The fundamental principles of right and wrong.

Evidence-Based HR Collecting and using data to show that human resource practices have a positive influence on the company's bottom line or key stakeholders.

Exempt Employees Managers, outside salespeople, and any other employees not covered by the FLSA requirement for overtime pay.

Exit Interview A meeting of a departing employee with the employee's supervisor and/or a human resource specialist to discuss the employee's reasons for leaving.

Expatriates Employees assigned to work in another country.

Experience Rating The number of employees a company has laid off in the past and the cost of providing them with unemployment benefits.

Experiential Programs Training programs in which participants learn concepts and apply them by simulating behaviors involved and analyzing the activity, connecting it with real-life situations.

Expert Systems Computer systems that support decision making by incorporating the decision rules used by people who are considered to have expertise in a certain area.

External Labor Market Individuals who are actively seeking employment.

Externship Employee development through a full-time temporary position at another organization.

Fact Finder Third party to collective bargaining who reports the reasons for a dispute, the views and arguments of both sides, and possibly a recommended settlement, which the parties may decline.

Fair Labor Standards Act (FLSA) Federal law that establishes a minimum wage and requirements for overtime pay and child labor.

Family and Medical Leave Act (FMLA) Federal law requiring organizations with 50 or more employees to provide up to 12 weeks of unpaid leave after childbirth or adoption; to care for a seriously ill family member or for an employee's own serious illness; or to take care of urgent needs that arise when a spouse, child, or parent in the National Guard or Reserve is called to active duty.

Feedback Information employers give employees about their skills and knowledge and where these assets fit into the organization's plans.

Fleishman Job Analysis System Job analysis technique that asks subject-matter experts to evaluate a job in terms of the abilities required to perform the job.

Flexible Spending Account Employee-controlled pretax earnings set aside to pay for certain eligible expenses, such as health care expenses, during the same year.

Flextime A scheduling policy in which full-time employees may choose starting and ending times within guidelines specified by the organization.

Forced-Distribution Method Method of performance measurement that assigns a certain percentage of employees to each category in a set of categories.

Forecasting The attempts to determine the supply of and demand for various types of human resources to predict areas within the organization where there will be labor shortages or surpluses.

Four-Fifths Rule Rule of thumb that provides (or shows) evidence of potential discrimination if an organization's hiring rate for a minority group is less than four-fifths the hiring rate for the majority group.

Gainsharing Group incentive program that measures improvements in productivity and effectiveness objectives and distributes a portion of each gain to employees.

Generalizable Valid in other contexts beyond the context in which the selection method was developed.

Gig Economy Situation in which companies rely primarily on alternative work arrangements to meet service and product demands.

Glass Ceiling Circumstances resembling an invisible barrier that keep most women and minorities from attaining the top jobs in organizations.

Global Organization An organization that chooses to locate a facility based on the ability to effectively, efficiently, and flexibly produce a product or service, using cultural differences as an advantage.

Graphic Rating Scale Method of performance measurement that lists traits and provides a rating scale for each trait; the employer uses the scale to indicate the extent to which an employee displays each trait.

Grievance Procedure The process for resolving union-management conflicts over interpretation or violation of a collective bargaining agreement.

Health Maintenance Organization (HMO) A health care plan that requires patients to receive their medical care from the HMO's health care professionals, who are often paid a flat salary, and provides all services on a prepaid basis.

High-deductible Health Plans (HDHPs) Health care plans that provide incentives for employees to make decisions that help lower health care costs.

High-Performance Work System An organization in which technology, organizational structure, people, and processes work together seamlessly to give an organization an advantage in the competitive environment.

Host Country A country (other than the parent country) in which an organization operates a facility.

Hot-Stove Rule Principle of discipline that says discipline should be like a hot stove, giving clear warning and following up with consistent, objective, immediate consequences.

Hourly Wage Rate of pay per hour worked.

HR Analytics Type of assessment of HRM effectiveness that involves determining the impact of, or the financial cost and benefits of, a program or practice.

HR Dashboard A display of a series of HR measures, showing the measure and progress toward meeting it.

HRM Audit A formal review of the outcomes of HRM functions, based on identifying key HRM functions and measures of business performance.

Human Capital An organization's employees, described in terms of their training, experience, judgment, intelligence, relationships, and insight.

Human Resource Information System (HRIS) A computer system used to acquire, store, manipulate, analyze, retrieve, and distribute information related to an organization's human resources.

Human Resource Management (HRM) The policies, practices, and systems that influence employees' behavior, attitudes, and performance.

Human Resource Planning Identifying the numbers and types of employees the organization will require in order to meet its objectives.

Immigration Reform and Control Act of 1986 Federal law requiring employers to verify and maintain records on applicants' legal rights to work in the United States.

Incentive Pay Forms of pay linked to an employee's performance as an individual, group member, or organization member.

Inclusion Creating a work environment in which individuals are treated fairly and with mutual respect and have equal access to opportunities and resources so that they can contribute fully to the organization's success.

Industrial Engineering The study of jobs to find the simplest way to structure work in order to maximize efficiency.

Industrial Union Labor union whose members are linked by their work in a particular industry.

Instructional Design A process of systematically developing training to meet specified needs.

Interactional Justice A judgment that the organization carried out its actions in a way that took the employee's feelings into account.

Internal Labor Force An organization's workers (its employees and the people who have contracts to work at the organization).

International Organization An organization that sets up one or a few facilities in one or a few foreign countries.

Internship On-the-job learning sponsored by an educational institution as a component of an academic program.

Involuntary Turnover Turnover initiated by an employer (often with employees who would prefer to stay).

Job A set of related duties.

Job Analysis The process of getting detailed information about jobs.

Job Description A list of the tasks, duties, and responsibilities (TDRs) that a particular job entails.

Job Design The process of defining how work will be performed and what tasks will be required in a given job.

Job Enlargement Broadening the types of tasks performed in a job.

Job Enrichment Empowering workers by adding more decision-making authority to jobs.

Job Evaluation An administrative procedure for measuring the relative internal worth of the organization's jobs.

Job Experiences The combination of relationships, problems, demands, tasks, and other features of an employee's job.

Job Extension Enlarging jobs by combining several relatively simple jobs to form a job with a wider range of tasks.

Job Hazard Analysis Technique Safety promotion technique that involves breaking down a job into basic elements, then rating each element for its potential for harm or injury.

Job Involvement The degree to which people identify themselves with their jobs.

Job Posting The process of communicating information about a job vacancy on company bulletin boards, in employee publications, on corporate intranets, and anywhere else the organization communicates with employees.

Job Rotation Enlarging jobs by moving employees among several different jobs.

Job Satisfaction A pleasant feeling resulting from the perception that one's job fulfills or allows for the fulfillment of one's important job values.

Job Sharing A work option in which two part-time employees carry out the tasks associated with a single job.

Job Specification A list of the knowledge, skills, abilities, and other characteristics (KSAOs) that an individual must have to perform a particular job.

Job Structure The relative pay for different jobs within the organization.

Job Withdrawal A set of behaviors with which employees try to avoid the work situation physically, mentally, or emotionally.

Knowledge Workers Employees whose main contribution to the organization is specialized knowledge, such as knowledge of customers, a process, or a profession.

Labor Relations Field that emphasizes skills that managers and union leaders can use to minimize costly forms of conflict (such as strikes) and seek win-win solutions to disagreements.

Leaderless Group Discussion An assessment center exercise in which a team of five to seven employees is assigned a problem and must work together to solve it within a certain time period.

Leading Indicators Objective measures that accurately predict future labor demand.

Learning Management System (LMS) A computer application that automates the administration, development, and delivery of training programs.

Learning Organization An organization that supports lifelong learning by enabling all employees to acquire and share knowledge.

Lockout An employer's exclusion of workers from a workplace until they meet certain conditions.

Long-Term Disability Insurance Insurance that pays a percentage of a disabled employee's salary after an initial period and potentially for the rest of the employee's life.

Maintenance of Membership Union security rules not requiring union membership but requiring that employees who join the union remain members for a certain period of time.

Management by Objectives (MBO) A system in which people at each level of the organization set goals in a process that flows from top to bottom, so employees at all levels are contributing to the organization's overall goals; these goals become the standards for evaluating each employee's performance.

Mediation Conflict resolution procedure in which a mediator hears the views of both sides and facilitates the negotiation process but has no formal authority to dictate a resolution.

Mentor An experienced, productive senior employee who helps develop a less experienced employee (a protégé).

Merit Pay A system of linking pay increases to ratings on performance appraisals.

Minimum Wage The lowest amount that employers may pay under federal or state law, stated as an amount of pay per hour.

Mixed-Standard Scales Method of performance measurement that uses several statements describing each trait to produce a final score for that trait.

Multinational Company An organization that builds facilities in a number of different countries in an effort to minimize production and distribution costs.

Multiple-Hurdle Model Process of arriving at a selection decision by eliminating some candidates at each stage of the selection process.

Myers-Briggs Type Indicator (MBTI) Psychological inventory that identifies individuals' preferences for source of energy, means of information gathering, way of decision making, and lifestyle, providing information for team building and leadership development.

National Labor Relations Act (NLRA) Federal law that supports collective bargaining and sets out the rights of employees to form unions.

National Labor Relations Board (NLRB) Federal government agency that enforces the NLRA by conducting and certifying representation elections and investigating unfair labor practices.

Needs Assessment The process of evaluating the organization, individual employees, and employees' tasks to determine what kinds of training, if any, are necessary.

Nepotism The practice of hiring relatives.

Noncontributory Plan Retirement plan funded entirely by contributions from the employer.

Nondirective Interview A selection interview in which the interviewer has great discretion in choosing questions to ask each candidate.

Nonexempt Employees Employees covered by the FLSA requirements for overtime pay.

Occupational Safety and Health Act U.S. law authorizing the federal government to establish and enforce occupational safety and health standards for all places of employment engaging in interstate commerce.

Occupational Safety and Health Administration (OSHA) Labor Department agency responsible for inspecting employers, applying safety and health standards, and levying fines for violation.

Office of Federal Contract Compliance Programs (OFCCP) The agency responsible for enforcing the executive orders that cover companies doing business with the federal government.

Offshoring Moving operations from the country where a company is headquartered to a country where pay rates are lower but the necessary skills are available.

On-the-Job Training (OJT) Training methods in which a person with job experience and skill guides trainees in practicing job skills at the workplace.

Onboarding Ongoing process that aims to prepare new employees for full participation in the organization.

Open-Door Policy An organization's policy of making managers available to hear complaints.

Organization Analysis A process for determining the appropriateness of training by evaluating the characteristics of the organization.

Organizational Behavior Modification (OBM) A plan for managing the behavior of employees through a formal system of feedback and reinforcement.

Organizational Commitment The degree to which an employee identifies with the organization and is willing to put forth effort on its behalf.

Orientation Training designed to prepare employees to perform their jobs effectively, learn about their organization, and establish work relationships.

Outcome Fairness A judgment that the consequences given to employees are just.

Outplacement Counseling A service in which professionals try to help dismissed employees manage the transition from one job to another.

Outsourcing Contracting with another organization (vendor, third-party provider, or consultant) to provide services.

Paired-Comparison Method Method of performance measurement that compares each employee with each other employee to establish rankings.

Panel Interview Selection interview in which several members of the organization meet to interview each candidate.

Parent Country The country in which an organization's headquarters is located.

Patient Protection and Affordable Care Act Health care reform law passed in 2010 that includes incentives and penalties for employers providing health insurance as a benefit.

Pay Differential Adjustment to a pay rate to reflect differences in working conditions or labor markets.

Pay Grades Sets of jobs having similar worth or content, grouped together to establish rates of pay.

Pay Level The average amount (including wages, salaries, and bonuses) the organization pays for a particular job.

Pay Policy Line A graphed line showing the mathematical relationship between job evaluation points and pay rate.

Pay Range A set of possible pay rates defined by a minimum, maximum, and midpoint of pay for employees holding a particular job or a job within a particular pay grade.

Pay Structure The pay policy resulting from job structure and pay level decisions.

Peer Review Process for resolving disputes by taking them to a panel composed of representatives from the organization at the same levels as the people in the dispute.

Pension Benefit Guarantee Corporation (PBGC) Federal agency that insures retirement benefits and guarantees retirees a basic benefit if the employer experiences financial difficulties.

Performance Management The process through which managers ensure that employees' activities and outputs contribute to the organization's goals.

Person Analysis A process for determining individuals' needs and readiness for training.

Personnel Selection The process through which organizations make decisions about who will or will not be invited to join the organization.

Piecework Rate Rate of pay per unit produced.

Position The set of duties (job) performed by a particular person.

Position Analysis Questionnaire (PAQ) A standardized job analysis questionnaire containing 194 questions about work behaviors, work conditions, and job characteristics that apply to a wide variety of jobs.

Predictive Validation Research that uses the test scores of all applicants and looks for a relationship between the scores and the future performance of the applicants who were hired.

Preferred Provider Organization (PPO) A health care plan that contracts with health care professionals to provide services at a reduced fee and gives patients financial incentives to use network providers.

Procedural Justice A judgment that fair methods were used to determine the consequences an employee receives.

Profit Sharing Incentive pay in which payments are a percentage of the organization's profits and do not become part of the employees' base salary.

Progressive Discipline A formal discipline process in which the consequences become more serious if the employee repeats the offense.

Promotion Assignment of an employee to a position with greater challenges, more responsibility, and more authority than in the previous job, usually accompanied by a pay increase.

Protean Career A career that frequently changes based on changes in the person's interests, abilities, and values and in the work environment.

Psychological Contract A description of what an employee expects to contribute in an employment relationship and what the employer will provide the employee in exchange for those contributions.

Readability The difficulty level of written materials.

Readiness for Training A combination of employee characteristics and positive work environment that permit training.

Realistic Job Preview Background information about a job's positive and negative qualities.

Reasonable Accommodation An employer's obligation to do something to enable an otherwise qualified person to perform a job.

Recruiting Any activity carried on by the organization with the primary purpose of identifying and attracting potential employees.

Recruitment The process through which the organization seeks applicants for potential employment.

Reengineering A complete review of the organization's critical work processes to make them more efficient and able to deliver higher quality.

Referrals People who apply for a vacancy because someone in the organization prompted them to do so.

Reliability The extent to which a measurement is from random error.

Repatriation The process of preparing expatriates to return home from a foreign assignment.

Reshoring Reestablishing operations back in the country where a company is headquartered due to quality and flexibility concerns.

Right-to-Work Laws State laws that make union shops, maintenance of membership, and agency shops illegal.

Role The set of behaviors that people expect of a person in a particular job.

Role Ambiguity Uncertainty about what the organization expects from the employee in terms of what to do or how to do it.

Role Analysis Technique A process of formally identifying expectations associated with a role.

Role Conflict An employee's recognition that demands of the job are incompatible or contradictory.

Role Overload A state in which too many expectations or demands are placed on a person.

Sabbatical A leave of absence from an organization to renew or develop skills.

Salary Rate of pay per week, month, or year worked.

Selection The process by which the organization attempts to identify applicants with the necessary knowledge, skills, abilities, and other characteristics that will help the organization achieve its goals.

Self-Assessment The use of information by employees to determine their career interests, values, aptitudes, and behavioral tendencies.

Self-Service System in which employees have online access to information about HR issues and go online to enroll themselves in programs and provide feedback through surveys.

Sexual Harassment Unwelcome sexual advances as defined by the EEOC.

Short-Term Disability Insurance Insurance that pays a percentage of a disabled employee's salary as benefits to the employee for six months or less.

Simple Ranking Method of performance measurement that requires managers to rank employees in their group from the highest performer to the poorest performer.

Simulation A training method that represents a real-life situation, with trainees making decisions resulting in outcomes that mirror what would happen on the job.

Situational Interview A structured interview in which the interviewer describes a situation likely to arise on the job, then asks the candidate what he or she would do in that situation.

Skill-Based Pay Systems Pay structures that set pay according to the employees' levels of skill or knowledge and what they are capable of doing.

Social Security The federal Old Age, Survivors, Disability, and Health Insurance (OASDHI) program, which combines old age (retirement) insurance, survivor's insurance, disability insurance, hospital insurance (Medicare Part A), and medical insurance (Medicare Part B) for older individuals.

Stakeholders The parties with an interest in the company's success (typically, shareholders, the community, customers, and employees).

Standard Hour Plan An incentive plan that pays workers extra for work done in less than a preset "standard time."

Stock Options Rights to buy a certain number of shares of stock at a specified price.

Straight Piecework Plan Incentive pay in which the employer pays the same rate per piece, no matter how much the worker produces.

Strike A collective decision by union members not to work until certain demands or conditions are met.

Structured Interview A selection interview that consists of a predetermined set of questions for the interviewer to ask.

Succession Planning The process of identifying and tracking high-potential employees who will be able to fill top management positions when they become vacant.

Summary Plan Description Report that describes a pension plan's funding, eligibility requirements, risks, and other details.

Sustainability An organization's ability to profit without depleting its resources, including employees, natural resources, and the support of the surrounding community.

Talent Management A systematic, planned effort to attract, retain, develop, and motivate highly skilled employees and managers.

Task Analysis The process of identifying the tasks, knowledge, skills, and behaviors that training should emphasize.

Team Leader Training Training in the skills necessary for effectively leading the organization's teams.

Teamwork The assignment of work to groups of employees with various skills who interact to assemble a product or provide a service.

Third Country A country that is neither the parent country nor the host country of an employer.

Total Quality Management (TQM) A companywide effort to continuously improve the ways people, machines, and systems accomplish work.

Training An organization's planned efforts to help employees acquire job-related knowledge, skills, abilities, and behaviors, with the goal of applying these on the job.

Transaction Processing Computations and calculations involved in reviewing and documenting HRM decisions and practices.

Transfer Assignment of an employee to a position in a different area of the company, usually in a lateral move.

Transfer of Training On-the-job use of knowledge, skills, and behaviors learned in training.

Transitional Matrix A chart that lists job categories held in one period and shows the proportion of employees in each of those job categories in a future period.

Transnational HRM System Type of HRM system that makes decisions from a global perspective, includes managers from many countries, and is based on ideas contributed by people representing a variety of cultures.

Trend Analysis Constructing and applying statistical models that predict labor demand for the next year, given relatively objective statistics from the previous year.

Unemployment Insurance A federally mandated program to minimize the hardships of unemployment through payments to unemployed workers, help in finding new jobs, and incentives to stabilize employment.

Uniform Guidelines on Employee Selection Procedures Guidelines issued by the EEOC and other agencies to identify how an organization should develop and administer its system for selecting employees so as not to violate anti-discrimination laws.

Union Shop Union security arrangement that requires employees to join the union within a certain amount of time (30 days) after beginning employment.

Union Steward An employee elected by union members to represent them in ensuring that the terms of the labor contract are enforced.

Unions Organizations formed for the purpose of representing their members' interests in dealing with employers.

Utility The extent to which something provides economic value greater than its cost.

Validity The extent to which performance on a measure (such as a test score) is related to what the measure is designed to assess (such as job performance).

Vesting Rights Guarantee that when employees become participants in a pension plan and work a specified number of years, they will receive a pension at retirement age, regardless of whether they remained with the employer.

Virtual Reality A computer-based technology that provides an interactive, three-dimensional learning experience.

Voluntary Turnover Turnover initiated by employees (often when the organization would prefer to keep them).

Work Flow Design The process of analyzing the tasks necessary for the production of a product or service.

Workers' Compensation State programs that provide benefits to workers who suffer work-related injuries or illnesses, or to their survivors.

Workforce Analytics The use of quantitative tools and scientific methods to analyze data from human resource databases and other sources to make evidence-based decisions that support business goals.

Workforce Utilization Review A comparison of the proportion of employees in protected groups with the proportion that each group represents in the relevant labor market.

Yield Ratio A ratio that expresses the percentage of applicants who successfully move from one stage of the recruitment and selection process to the next.

Name Index

Subject Index